Twentieth Century History of Clearfield County, Pennsylvania, and Representative Citizens

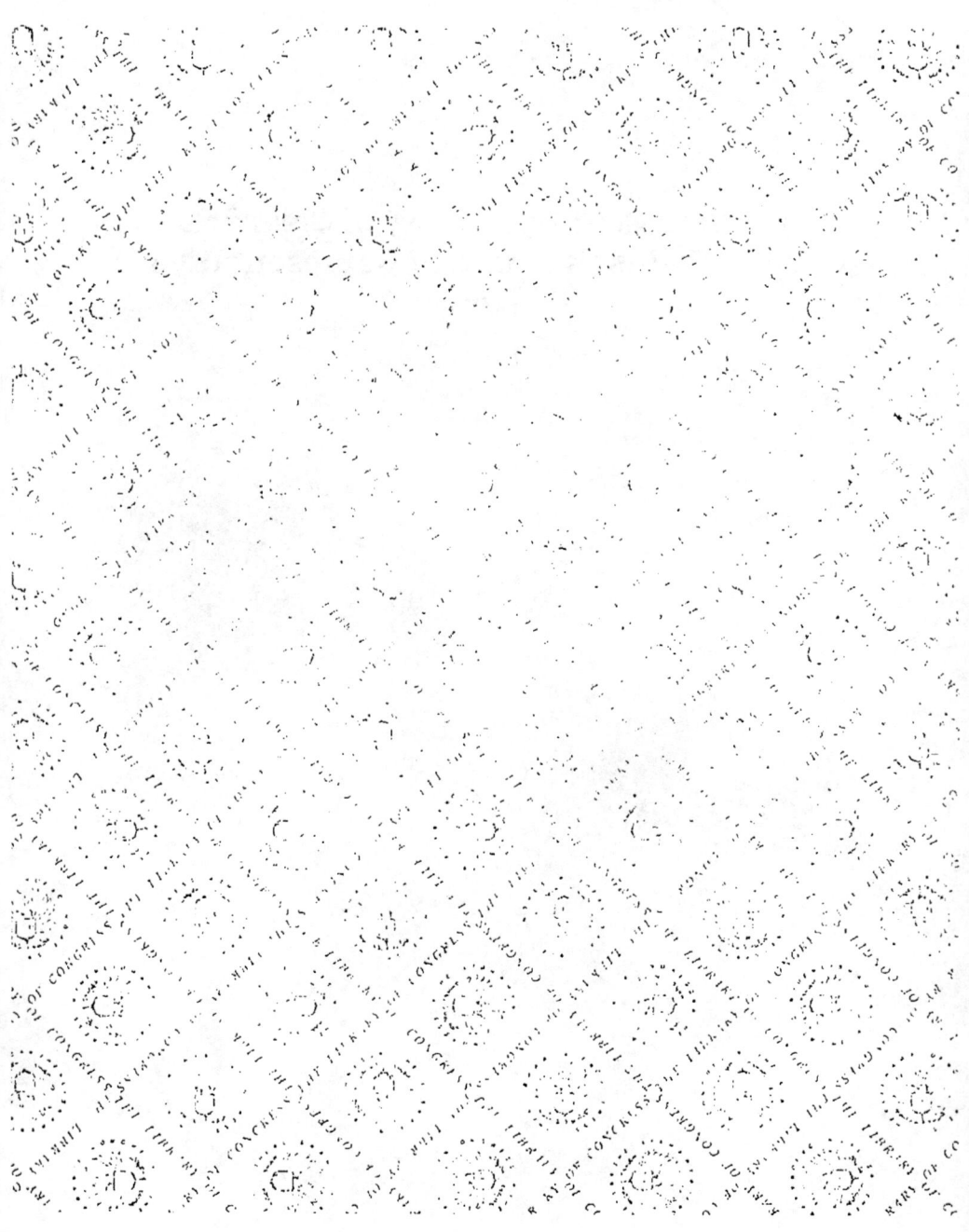

TWENTIETH CENTURY HISTORY

OF

CLEARFIELD COUNTY

PENNSYLVANIA

AND

REPRESENTATIVE CITIZENS

BY

ROLAND D. SWOOPE, Jr.

" Study History, for it is Philosophy Teaching by Example "

PUBLISHED BY

RICHMOND-ARNOLD PUBLISHING CO.

F J Richmond, *President*   C R Arnold, *Secretary and Treasurer*

CHICAGO, ILL

PREFACE

Only those who have undertaken similar work can appreciate the amount of labor involved in preparing a history of a great county like Clearfield, particularly when, as in this instance, so much of the early history of the county is dependent upon local tradition and practically all of the early settlers have passed away

While great care has been taken to avoid mistakes, it is but natural that in a work of such an extensive scope errors will occur and for such as may be found in the book, the editor asks the indulgence of the reader

Whatever be its merits or imperfections, the work of preparation has been one of great interest and instruction to the editor

To the many persons who have so kindly aided us by giving information and data, we desire to take this method of returning our sincere thanks

ROLAND D SWOOPE, JR

CURWENSVILLE, PA,
June, 1911

NOTE.—Sketches unrevised by subscribers are distinguished by a small asterisk (*)

CONTENTS

CHAPTER I

PAGE

GEOGRAPHY, TOPOGRAPHY AND GEOLOGY . 19
Dimensions and Acreage of the County—Its Situation and Boundaries
—Hills and Valleys—Streams—Character of the Soil—Geological Strata
—Coal Measures—Conglomerate—Mahoning Sandstone—The Three
Great Coal Basins—Fire-clay—Limestone-Oil and Gas-Iron Ore, Etc.

CHAPTER II

INDIAN OCCUPATION 22
The Andastes—Their Conflict with the Iroquois and Partial Destruction—Brule's Expedition—His Capture and Escape—The Lennia-Lenapes
or Delawares—The Monceys—Their Subjection by the Iroquois—The
Shawnees and Tuscaroras—Retreat of the Indians

CHAPTER III

LAND TITLES . . 24
Charles the Second's Grant to William Penn—Penn's Lease from Gov-
ernor Dongan—Indian Deed Confirming the Purchase—Indian Deed to
Penn's Heirs—The Articles of Consideration—Penn's Will—His Sale to the
Crown—Thomas Penn Assumes Charge of the Province—First Surveys
—Early Land Owners—Litigation over Titles

CHAPTER IV

THE EARLY SETTLERS . . 27
Character of Clearfield County's Early Population—Former Political
Divisions—The First White Settler—The Leading Pioneers of the County
and the Credit Due Them

CHAPTER V

ORGANIZATION OF THE COUNTY 30
Penn's Division of Pennsylvania into Three Counties—Thirty-six
Counties Formed in 1803—Additions in 1804, Including Clearfield County
—The Act in Regard to Same—Annexation of Clearfield to Centre County
—Settlement of Jurisdiction—Appointment of Commissioners to Select
Seat of Justice—The Site Selected and Named Clearfield—Population of
the County in 1806—Election Laws—Organization of the Townships and
Boroughs

5

CHAPTER VI

COUNTY AND OTHER OFFICIALS   38
    A List of the Principal State and County Officials—United States Sen-
ators—Representatives in Congress—U S District Attorney—U S
Marshall—Clerk of House of Representatives—State Officers—Senators,
Representatives—President Judges—Associate Judges—Deputy Attorneys
—General and District Attorneys—Sheriffs—Registers and Recorders—
Treasurers—Prothonotaries—County Superintendents—County Commis-
sioners and Clerks

CHAPTER VII

MILITARY HISTORY AND THE COUNTY MILITIA—THE CIVIL WAR .   . . 44
    Loyalty of Clearfield County's Sons—Military Organizations Before
the War—Thirty-fourth Regiment, Fifth Reserves—Its General and Individual Record, Officers and Men—Forty-second Regiment, "Bucktails"—
The Fifty-first Regiment—Fifty-ninth Regiment, Second Cavalry—Eighty-
fourth Regiment

CHAPTER VIII

MILITARY HISTORY—THE CIVIL WAR—CONTINUED   74
    History of the One Hundred and Fifth Regiment—Roster of Officers
and Men—History of the One Hundred and Forty-ninth Regiment, with
Roster—In Other Commands—Independent Battalion

CHAPTER IX

THE SPANISH-AMERICAN WAR 115
    History of the Fifth Regiment Pennsylvania Volunteer Infantry, with
Roster and Individual Records

CHAPTER X

THE PRESS   174
    A Sketch of Journalism in Clearfield County—The First County Paper
—A Home-made Press—The "Banner"—Clearfield Republican—Clearfield
Whig—Raftsman's Journal—Clearfield Citizen—The Times-Monitor—
Evening Herald—Clearfield County Times—Curwensville Herald—County
Review—The Mountaineer—DuBois Morning Courier—DuBois Express—
The Enterprise—DuBois Morning Journal—Houtzdale Citizen—Osceola
Reveille—The Leader-Courier—Coalport Standard—The Hustler, and
Other Newspapers

CHAPTER XI

THE BENCH OF CLEARFIELD COUNTY 178
Clearfield County's Judicial Connection with Centre County Previous
to 1822—The Act of 1822 Providing for the Holding of Courts in Clear-
field County—Population at That Time—Provision for Keeping Prisoners
—Sketches of Hon Charles Huston, Hon Thomas Burnside, Hon George
W Woodward, Hon Robert C White, Hon John G Knox, Hon James
T Hale—The Twenty-fifth District Formed—Hon James Burnside, Hon
James Gamble, Judge Linn, Hon Joseph B McEnally, Hon Charles A
Mayer—Act of 1874 Providing for an Addition Law Judge—Hon John
H Orvis Appointed—Clearfield County Created a Separate Judicial Dis-
trict—Hon David L Krebs, Hon Cyrus Gordon—Hon. Allison O Smith

CHAPTER XII

THE BAR OF CLEARFIELD COUNTY—FORMER MEMBERS.... 184
Character of the Clearfield County Bar—First Resident Member of the
Bar—Sketches of Leading Members of the Bar in Former Days

CHAPTER XIII

CLEARFIELD COUNTY BAR—PRESENT MEMBERS 193
Brief Biographical Notices of the Present Members of the Clearfield
County Bar

CHAPTER XIV

THE MEDICAL PROFESSION 199
Early Physicians of the County—Registration Law of 1881—Alphabet-
ical List of Physicians who have Registered in the County from 1881 to the
Present Time, with Biographical Mention

CHAPTER XV

PUBLIC INSTITUTIONS 214
The Clearfield Hospital—The DuBois Hospital—The Clearfield County
Home

CHAPTER XVI

EDUCATION 220
A History of the Schools from 1834 to the Present Time—School Law
of 1834—Compulsary School Law—Early Schools and Schoolhouses—
Schools and Academies of Clearfield, Curwensville, DuBois and Other
Towns

CHAPTER XVII

TRANSPORTATION FACILITIES 224
    Turnpike Days—Water Transportation—The Tyrone and Clearfield
Railroad—The Pennsylvania & Northern—The Buffalo, Rochester & Pitts-
burg R R —The Karthaus R R —The Beech Creek R R —The Cresson,
Clearfield County & New York Short Route R R —The Philipsburg R R
—The Clearfield Southern R R —The West Branch R R —The Curwens-
ville & Bower R R —The Buffalo & Susquehanna R R —The Franklin
& Clearfield R R —The DuBois Street Railway—The Philipsburg Street
Railway Co

CHAPTER XVIII

MANUFACTURERS 227
    The Lumber Industry—Method of Operating—Rafting—Log Drivers
and Lumber Arks—Conflict with "Square Timber" Men—Marking the
Logs—Erection of Saw-mills—Decline of the Business—The Fire Brick
Industry—Firms and Companies Engaged in the Business—The Tanning
Industry.

CHAPTER XIX

FINANCIAL INSTITUTIONS 233
    Banking in the Early History of the County—Private and State Banks
—Special Act of the Legislature Necessary to Incorporation Before 1860—
The Act of 1860—Unreliability of the State Banks—Passage of the
National Banking Law—Banks of Clearfield County with their Officers and
Directors

CHAPTER XX

AGRICULTURE 239
    The Patrons of Husbandry, "The Grange"—Object of the Society—
When Founded—The First Grange Founded in Clearfield County—Other
Branches of the Society—The Clearfield County Agricultural Society

CHAPTER XXI

COAL PRODUCTION AND DEVELOPMENT 242
    Early Coal Shipments—Early Coal Mines and Railroads—The Mos-
hannon Branch of the T & C R R —Coal Companies and Proprietors—
Description of the Mines, with Character of the Product, Quantity Mined
and Shipped, etc

CHAPTER XXII

RELIGIOUS DEVELOPMENT   .   .   251
        Pioneer Clergy of the County—First Services of the Different De-
nominations—Early Churches and Meeting-houses—Growth of the Various
Churches—Y M C A

CHAPTER XXIII

THE TOWNSHIPS   258
        Sketches of the Different Townships—When Erected—Boundaries—
Population and Principal Occupations of the Inhabitants, etc

CHAPTER XXIV

THE BOROUGHS 318
        Historical Sketches of the Boroughs of Brisbin, Burnside, Chester Hill,
Clearfield, Coalport, Curwensville, DuBois, Glen Hope, Grampian, Houtz-
dale, Irvona, Lumber City, Mahaffey, Newburg, New Washington, Osceola
Mills, Ramey, Troutville, Wallaceton and Westover

CHAPTER XXV

STATISTICS   333
        Increase in Population Shown by Census Returns by Townships—
Wealth of the County—Summary of Assessments for 1910

REPRESENTATIVE CITIZENS   337

INDEX

Adamson, James	812
Addleman, Charles C	675
Addleman, G Lloyd	801
Ake, Dr N F K	374
Alexander, Hon Joseph	760
Ardary, James M	539
Ardary, John R	539
Arnold, Samuel	779
Aughenbaugh, Austin H	826
Bailey, Charles C	462
Bailey, J D	689
Bailey, Joseph	462
Bailey, Lewis E	791
Ball, John	943
Barnett, D H	752
Barrett, Prof H J	580
Baummer, George J	751
Beatty, Austin	721
Beauseigneur, Joseph	745
Beauseigneur, Peter	370
Beuseigneur, Q E	670
Beish, Isaac	573
Bell, Arthur A	766
Bell, Mrs Eliza C	699
Bell, Emory W	921
Bell, John W	699
Bell, Singleton	196
Bellis, Enoch	617
Bensinger, Joe	507
Betts, Frederick G	981
Betts, William I	981
Betts, Hon William W	973
Beyer, Lewis W	458
Bickford, S M	567
Bigler, George R	197
Bigler, Hon William	337
Bigler, William D	181

Bilger, George M	475
Billotte, E D	456
Bird, E T	475
Blakeslee, Austin	464
Blandy, E C	498
Bloom, Conrad	657
Bloom, Harvey	655
Bloom, John I	548
Bloom, John J	602
Bloom, John W	896
Bloom, Mrs Luella	726
Bloom, T Jeff	485
Bloom, W Sloss	726
Bloom Zachariah M	679
Boag, John	436
Boal, Caleb T	546
Boal, James	546
Bonsall, Amos	511
Boone, Charles	598
Boose, Earl G	198
Borst, Joseph J	781
Bouch, George W	349
Boulton Hon Harry	443
Bowman, H L	423
Bowman, Jonathan	423
Bowman, Stacy	899
Boyce, Murray L	909
Boyce, William M	759
Boyer, Louis E	198
Boyle, J J	966
Bressler, David	725
Breth, Adam	776
Briel J S	837
Brothers, Charles F	848
Brown, Albert S	960
Brown David	600
Brown, Charles	580
Brown Perry	600

11

Brown, Peter   451
Brown, William H   580
Bryan, Dr Wallace S   474
Buterbaugh, Jesse   937
Byers, Harry   197
Byers, James W   860
Byers, John M   868

Caldwell, James R   748
Caldwell, Reuben   834
Calkins W L   198
Campbell, Frank M   915
Campman, Frederick   904
Carr, C P   644
Carr, W S   897
Casey, T F   977
Cathcart, Grant   569
Cathcart, James   570
Cathcart, William M   574
Cathcart, W W   653
Chapman, Joseph H   938
Chase, A R   197
Chase, Benj F   197
Chase, John M   367
Chase, Rev John M   367
Chase, Wm A   195
Chick, William   653
Clary, H B   953
Cole, Arthur L   195
Coleman, Henry M   918
Collins, Dr Howard A   971
Conley, Frank G   626
Conner Harry C   667
Conner, John B   979
Conner, John C   667
Cooker, Frank R   884
Copelin, George S   553
Cornely, Charles L   591
Cornely, Dr J M   729
Corp, Jacob W   577
Coudriet, Lawrence M   910
Cowder, A W   465
Cowen, I W   566
Cox, Michael J   404
Craig, Frank   418
Craig Michael   362
Croyl, James H   401
Curry, G B   594

Dale, John A   400
Dale, Joseph L   668
Dale, Roland E   814

Darr, Lucius L.   846
Davidson, Archer   734
Davidson, Mack   731
Davis, Elisha M   341
Davis, Joseph   721
Davis, J T   908
Davis, Thomas R   485
Davison, James   833
DeHaas, William T   505
Denling, W A   655
Densham, William H   962
Derminer, Jules   839
Derrick, W E   445
Dewalt, William A   474
Diehl, Blair W   829
Diehl Harry E   973
Diehl, John C   733
Diem, Henry J   735
Dietz, Frank R   735
Doherty, John   514
Doll, Joseph A   641
Dotts, John   489
Dotts, Philip   489
Draucker, Arthur M   935
Draucker, Perry W   678
DuBois, John   631
DuBois, John E   630
Dunlap, David T   661
Dunlap, John R   760
Dyer, Fred J   681

Echard, Samuel B   357
Edlund, John F   823
Edwards, Leno W   197
Eisenman, Samuel A   713
Elliott, Dr C B   358
Erhard, C E   652
Estricher, Frank W   426
Evans, Frank W   833

Fargo, Waldo R   906
Fawcett, John E   591
Fennell William   742
Ferguson, Edward W   773
Fielding, Frank   193
Finsthwait, Franklin   765
First National Bank of Osceola   498
Flegal, Dr I S   865
Flegal, William T.   533
Forsyth, John C   197
Foulke, John T   404
Fowler, Edward   561

Fowler, Samuel E	931	Hartshorn, Benjamin	818
Frendberg, Andrew	856	Hartswick, Howard B	196
Frendberg, Charles	867	Hay, Isaac D	619
Fry, Howard M	851	Hay, William T	619
Fulford, George M	380	Heberling, John	665
Fulford, John H	380	Hegarty, David	330
Fulton, David	842	Hegarty, Jerry	342
		Hegarty, Reuben	506
Gafley, Thomas	502	Helper, William	858
Gallagher, Patrick	810	Helsel, William	700
Gallaher, John F	483	Henderson, David R	639
Gallaher, George W	424	Henderson, Elwood S	652
Gatehouse, James	381	Henderson, Dr J L	457
Gearhart, J E	343	Henderson, Robert	639
George, Richard H	954	Henderson, Samuel T	717
Gill, Charles G	488	Henderson, William A	639
Gill, Josiah	488	Henderson, William H	747
Gilliland, Joseph	889	Henry, Edgar T	787
Gilliland, Dr W S	824	Hensal, David C	771
Gilmartin, M J	565	Hepburn, Samuel T	834
Gingery, Dorsey J	383	Herron, Hon David S	552
Ginter, George	443	Hertlein, Christian M	816
Ginter, Henry E	443	Hess, E W	425
Gleason, James A	198	Hess, C H	782
Glenn, Asher G G	372	Hibner, Delos E	527
Goff, Manley B	458	Hibner, John E	527
Gordon, Hon Cyrus	717	Hickman, Henry	638
Gorman, Anthony M	547	Higgins, Joseph G	517
Goss, G O	755	Hile, Allen W	590
Gould, William A	558	Hile, Anthony	402
Graham, John A	681	Hile, Anthony	427
Grattan, Patrick	454	Hile, C A	590
Green, John A	425	Hile, James H	402
Griffith, S Dorsey	978	Hile, Lewis L	803
Groff, John F	630	Hileman, Clark	340
Grove, Harvey B	467	Hiller, Frederick J	372
Guinzburg, Frank	722	Hiller, Philip Ernest	372
		Hiller's Sons, Isaac	371
Haag, Adam J	628	Hilliard, Henry	836
Haag, Amos G	862	Hilling, William	394
Haag, Christian B	357	Holden, John S	744
Hagerty, William A	972	Holt, John	477
Hahne, Frank	544	Holt, Reuben	477
Halfpenney, George Y	857	Hoover, Daniel W	565
Harber, Alfred J	945	Hoover, Henry	844
Harder, Hon John E	968	Horning, John H	892
Harper, Dr Francis W	749	Horton, J K	197
Harris, Hon Frank G	374	Hosler, Rush N	949
Harris, Frank G	194	Houst, Rev Anthony	896
Harris, Hon George A	634	Howe, C Cyrenius	803
Harris, John	514	Howe, Frank A	905
Harrison, Frederick J	802	Hoyt, Charles E	611

14 INDEX

Name	Page	Name	Page
Hoyt, Hiram M	590	Kisten, Herman C	835
Hoyt, Isaac	590	Keen, Thomas E	692
Hoyt, James S	420	Kelley, James H	511
Hoyt, Margaret	694	Kelly, M J	365
Hoyt, T C	639	Kephart, Simon	541
Hughes, Edward L	528	Kester, I M	504
Hullihen, Balsar	718	Kester, Isaac M	504
Humphreys, Thomas	662	King, Dr H O.	904
Hunter, A J	414	King, Samuel M	629
Hunter, Alfred R	413	Kinney, John M	800
Hunter, John H	414	Kinports, Porter	624
Hunter, Robert E	470	Kirk, A M & Son	654
Hurd, John W	955	Kirk, Dr George B	893
Hurd, Melvin J	531	Kirk George C	433
Hurd, Dr Michael	343	Kirk Henry P	654
Hutchinson, Adam S	742	Kirk James E	976
Hutton, Frank	195	Klare Andrew J	871
		Klingman R F	581
Ifert, Uriah J	599	Kline, J F	400
Imhof, Fred C	616	Knarr, Hon George A	567
Impson, Lewis M	827	Knarr George L	568
Ireland, Thaddeus	512	Knarr, Hon Henry S	608
Irwin, Alexander H	904	Knepp, Isaac	356
Irwin, Ellis	413	Knepp, Matthew	417
Irwin, John F	415	Kohler, Fred	682
		Kopp, William J	854
Jackson, Dr Robert	976	Krach William F	732
Jacobson, Gilbert	951	Kramer Aaron G	194
Johnson, A J	915	Kratzer, Capt J Elliott	763
Johnson Charles A	847	Kresge, Harry F	584
Johnson, Edgar A	851	Kujawa, Joseph A	793
Johnson, Elah	678	Kuntz, Jacob L	637
Johnson, Gust A	814	Kyler Leonard	442
Johnson, Guy L	900		
Johnson, John A	664	Laing Hon James W	966
Johnson, Joseph	362	Lamont Reynold	853
Johnson Matthew W	821	Langsford, William C	934
Johnson, Walfrid	878	Lansberry, Archie B	832
Johnston, David W	528	Larock Joseph	889
Johnston, Geo W	720	Leafgren, Andrew	810
Johnston, John C	627	Leavy, Fred B	898
Johnston Robert M	828	Lee, Ash B	711
Johnston, Watson L	720	Lee, John	592
Jones, Harry L	863	Lee Rev Samuel	743
Jones, Robert K	607	Leib, J Lewis	770
Jones, Samuel M	579	Leipold Dr Bert E	488
Jones, William J	478	Leonard Alvin U	396
Jury Isaiah	769	Leonard, James O	646
		Lewis, Marshall H	894
Kantz, Edwin F	864	Liddle Andrew	556
Kantz, George D	912	Liddle W H	556
Kantz, Reuben B	887	Lightner, John L	389

Lightner, John L	389	McMurray, Charles D	449
Little Wesley D	935	McMurray, G R	355
Liveright, Alfred M	453	McQuillen, John T	463
Linfield, Henry	594	McQuown, J A	787
Long, W O	940	McQuown, J S	638
Lott, Hon Fred	793	McQuown, Martin L	196
Loughhead, David P	377	McQuown, William W	503
Lowell, Horace H	605	MacMinn, Herman S	924
Lowell, Thomas J	605	Magee, John A	879
Lukehart, Geo A	198	Mahaffey, E B	361
Lumadue, William F	428	Mahaffey, James	737
Luther, James B	455	Mahaffey John C	785
Luther, J G	455	Mahaffey, William T	755
Luzier, T S	664	Mahaffey, William T	785
Lyons, William H	689	Maines, Alonzo Bigler	918
Lytle, J B	404	Mapes, M V	737
		Mattern, Charles O	553
McCamley, James J	441	Matthews, Ira E	839
McCardell, Abner B	417	Maurer, R S	867
McCardell, David A	524	Maxwell, Charles B	964
McCardell, Elmer B	382	Means, Prof Herbert G	508
McClelland, John A	864	Meas, James I	326
McClure, John R	677	Meckley, Samuel T	523
McClure, Wilson	677	Menzie, William	626
McCracken, Edward M	921	Merris, John E	538
McCracken, Fred S	914	Merritt, Berten	875
McCracken, John W	197	Merritt, George	876
McCracken, Joseph N	775	Merritt, Howard M	876
McCracken, Lewis	916	Merritt, John	876
McCreery, John S	870	Miller, Jacob H	969
McCrossin James	618	Miller, Lewis P	942
McCrossin, John H	466	Miller, Dr S J	370
McCully, Alfred D	903	Miller, Wm C	196
McCully, Solomon	348	Miller, W H	593
McCurdy, Daniel W	191	Mills, John	520
McDermott, Peter	885	Milsom Daniel	930
McDonald, Charles A	623	Minns, George Jr	360
McDonald, Mrs Mary C	518	Mitchell, David	832
McDowell, James E	922	Mitchell, James	429
McEnally, Hon Joseph B	487	Mitchell, James T	772
McEnally, Wright	487	Mitchell, Oscar	194
McFarlane James F	498	Mitchell, William	429
McGarvey, John J	734	Moore, Charles W	359
McGarvey, Robert H	691	Montgomery, Andrew J	970
McGee James W	571	Moore, Herbert A	198
McGonigal, James L	950	Moore, James S	468
McGrath John B	531	Moore, N R	450
McIntosh, David	557	Moore, Samuel R	897
McKeage, George A	869	Moore, William S	625
McKeehen, H D	620	Morrow, Mathew T	604
McLarren, John	498	Moshannon Coal Company, The	965
McMullen, George F	453	Mossop, Frederick	423

Mossop, Richard	423	Patrick, Dallas	729
Mott, Nelson F	841	Patton, Charles E	963
Moulthrop, Hon Alonzo S	587	Penepacker, Charles F	961
Mountz Mrs Ella	782	Pentz, W C	195
Moyer, Daniel	932	Peters, A G	428
Moyer, Daniel A	958	Peterson, Andrew J	828
Moyer, Peter	958	Peterson, Anton	825
Muirhead, Robert S	869	Phillips, Zachary T	917
Murray, Aaron	389	Pifer, Charles E	438
Murray, Alexander	772	Pifer, George W	438
Murray, Hazard A	197	Pifer, James H	438
Murray, Thomas H	772	Pilkington, Fred	723
		Piper, Dr W S	391
Neeper, Leonard R	797	Planten George H	582
Neff, Gideon D	612	Pollum, Dr James I	831
Neff, Isaiah	912	Porter, Miles R	578
Neff, J B	612	Porter, Robert	578
Nelson, S A	483	Potter, Hon Johnson W, M D	405
Newcomb, Mitchell	379	Potter, William B	944
Newcomer, Josiah R	770	Powell, A J	463
Norris, Blake W	891	Powell, George	391
Norris, James R	794	Powell, William J	391
Norris, Capt John H	749	Pritchard, Lewis A	956
Norris, Ord L	788	Purnell, Dr. Howard G	581
Notter, Charles H	473		
Nowry, John	620	Radebaugh, John S	606
Nowry, Robert	620	Radebaugh, William H	606
		Rafferty, James L	623
Oaks, George W	362	Rafferty, John Y	623
O'Connor, John	881	Rauch, J Wilson	861
O'Laughlin, James P	197	Rea, James A	908
Olson, Emil	871	Read, David R	707
Owens, Emory E	877	Read, Dr. F B	932
Owens, Harry M	713	Read, George W	874
Owens, Henry	712	Read, J Perry	707
Owens, James C.	948	Read, S C	685
		Reams, William A	642
Park, Dr Milo E	798	Redding, James	484
Passmore, Eli L	696	Reed, A H	930
Passmore, George C	670	Reed, Frank B	402
Patchin, Aaron	656	Reese, George W	857
Patchin, Aaron W	392	Reese, James W	813
Patchin, Carl E	736	Reidy, Michael	384
Patchin Family	656	Reiley, Dr W Edgar	850
Patchin, John	656	Reiter, John W	830
Patchin, Hon John H	501	Renaud, Ernest	395
Patchin, Ray C	392	Ribling Hon Henry	804
Patchin, William E	469	Richards, Daniel	368
Paterson, Alexander	824	Richards, James	368
Patterson, Alex	196	Richards, Josiah S	436
Patterson, Wm H	193	Richner, Hon Jesse	937
Patrick, Hon Charles B	645	Robacker, Charles E	891

Robbins, Lewis C   880
Robison, Cyrus   433
Robison, Samuel   433
Roessner, Joseph W   672
Ross, Frank   869
Ross, George C   886
Rousey, Henry   969
Rowles, C P   738
Rowles, Dr John F   934
Rowles, Joseph H   525
Rowles, Dr Lewis C   769
Rowles, L William   525
Rudolph, Phineas W   774
Rumberger, Amos H   413
Rusnak, Martin   938

Sancroft, Jacob   859
Sankey, Mrs Laura N   386
Sceurman, Jacob W   393
Schmitt, F W   401
Schnars, E   534
Schryver, William T   777
Schultz, William   846
Schwer, Matthias   817
Scofield, Fred R   198
Scollins, John J   974
Seyler, Joseph   650
Shadeck, Matthew   849
Shafer, Albert   419
Shafer, Jonathan   671
Shafer, Samuel   419
Shaffer, Emanuel S   961
Shaffer, John R   706
Shaw, A B   339
Shaw, Joseph   394
Shaw, Richard   399
Shaw, William M   355
Shepherd, Nathaniel H   946
Shimel, H M   539
Shimel, M F   569
Shoff, Abram C   452
Shoff, C C   497
Shoff, Harry J   719
Shoff, Robert M   844
Shugart, George B   373
Slaughenhoupt, J A   516
Sloppy, George H   725
Sloppy, K A   683
Smail, T D   902
Smathers, Dr Wilson J   738
Smeal, Daniel J   888
Smith, Allison O   353

Smith, Elmer B   884
Smith, Frank   572
Smith, Frank S   601
Smith, George W   684
Smith, Harvey T   384
Smith, H W   194
Smith, James B   666
Smith James L   597
Smith John N   941
Smyers, George W   440
Sneddon, J S   597
Snyder, John F   195
Snyder, Thomas G   533
Snyder, T Lansing   526
Sommerville, James L.   919
Soulsby, James E   782
Spackman, James   416
Spackman, Dr James P   803
Spackman, William   416
Spencer, H W   476
Spencer, L W   476
Stagner, Henry   724
Stanley, G M   907
Stauffer, James B   675
Steinkerchner, Joseph C.   952
Steinkerchner, William B   951
Stephens, A P   520
Stevens, Blair   711
Stevens, Lloyd C   560
Stevenson, John   503
Stewart, Leslie   842
Stone, John   385
Stott, Peter   933
Straw, Enoch I   515
Straw, Harrison   441
Straw, Isaac   515
Straw, John T   704
Straw, Perry C   634
Straw, Uriah H   .. 616
Strickland, J C   703
Strickland, William H   559
Sullivan, Dr John C   961
Sullivan, Patrick T   466
Sunderland, Thomas J   822
Sweeney, Harrison H   . 506
Swoope, Henry B   686
Swoope, J B   .   547
Swoope, Roland D   365
Swoope, Roland D , Jr   396
Swoope, Wm I   196

Tate, Ira F   561

2

Telford, Mrs Lavina	695	Watson, James	. 792
Thompson, Edward A	872	Way, David	. .. 613
Thompson, Roll B	377	Way, Thomas L	. .. 613
Thompson, R William	414	Weaver, Charles C	 980
Thomson, William H	554	Weaver, James L.	... 651
Thorp, C A	883	Weaver, John H	. . 790
Tobias, William L	903	Weber, George J	.. 923
Todd H W	498	Webster, Edward W.	909
Tonkin, Robert D	901	Welch, Walter	. 197
Torrence, Charles L	479	Welty, S B	. 714
Towns, George E	598	Wilkinson, John H.	649
Tozer, Salmon	874	Williams, A C	... 588
Tozer, William F	378	Williams, David	. 699
Turner, E K	545	Williams, Luther H	. . . 345
Turner, James K, Esq	537	Wilson, Dr Robert V.	461
Turley, Edgar W	369	Wilson, Smith V V	. . . 194
Turley, George W	369	Wilson, Dr Ward O	. 435
Tyler, David	658	Wingert, William	... 406
		Wink, William T	.. . 583
Urey, John M	197	Wise, S J	 746
		Wise, William L	. 646
Van Tassel, A R	519	Womer George D	. . 820
Veeser John	513	Wood, Dr George W	382
Viebahn, Edward A	584	Woods, Franklin M	800
Viebahn, Julius	479	Woodside, Dr H A	449
		Woodward, A H	 196
Wachob, George B	697	Woodward, Walter H	. 347
Wagner, Harry E	640	Woolridge Edward H	504
Walker, E J	391	Work, Aaron N	. 570
Walker, George W	514	Work John N	708
Wall, Isaiah	350	Wrye, Charles	. 957
Wall, James D	430	Wynn, D Ross	. 601
Wall, Miles	809		
Wall Thomas	430	Yeaney Dr Gillespie B	. 371
Wall, W I	350	Yingling, Isaac J	877
Wallace, Harry F	194	Yingling William Irwin	801
Wallace, Robert	510	Young Augustus J	832
Wallace, William A	490	Young, David S	709
Wallace William L	497	Young, John W.	. 691
Walls, Harvey	710	Young, Newton B	. 811
Ward Prof Harry E	967		
Waring, De Lancey H	939	Zeigler, George W	196
Waterworth, Dr S J	519		

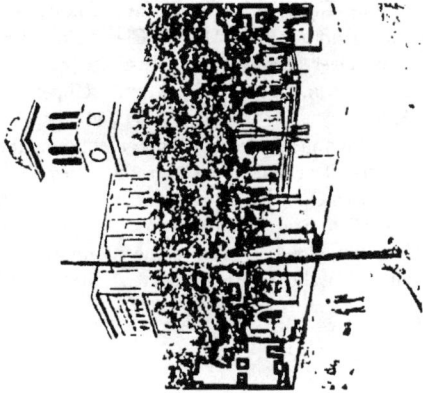

Dimeling Hotel, Clearfield

Clearfield County Jail, Clearfield

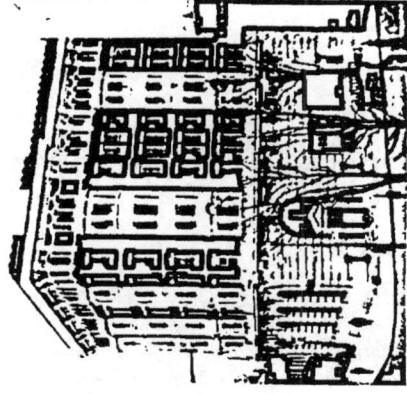

Clearfield County Court House, Clearfield

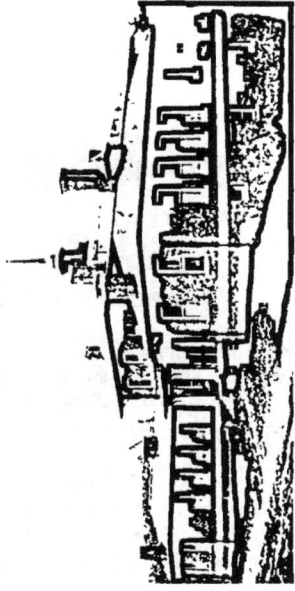

Clearfield Hospital, Clearfield

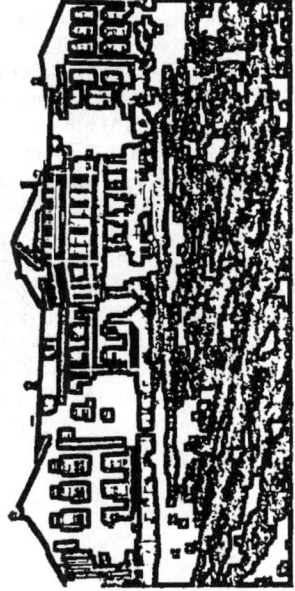

Clearfield County Home, Clearfield

History of Clearfield County .

CHAPTER I

GEOGRAPHY, TOPOGRAPHY AND GEOLOGY

Dimensions and Acreage of the County—Its Situation and Boundaries—Hills and Valleys—Streams—Character of the Soil—Geological Strata—Coal Measures—Conglomerate—Mahoning Sandstone—The Three Great Coal Basins—Fire-Clay—Limestone—Oil and Gas—Iron Ore, Etc

Geography—Clearfield County is one of the largest in Pennsylvania, covering a territory of thirty-six and seventeen-twentieth miles from north to south, and about forty and one-half miles from east to west It has an area of eleven hundred and thirty square miles, or seven hundred and twenty-three thousand two hundred acres

It lies a little to the west of the center of the State on parallel 41°, 4' north latitude, and longitude 1°, 30' west from Washington, D C It is bounded on the north by Elk and Cameron, on the east by Centre and Clinton, on the south by Cambria and on the west by Jefferson and Indiana counties

Topography—Clearfield County is situated in the western foothills of the Allegheny Mountains, lying between the main ridge and the great secondary formation known as the "Stony Mountains" Although at some points these hills reach an altitude of from sixteen to twenty-two hundred feet, they form no distinct chains, but are interspersed with table-lands and valleys

The county is traversed by a number of streams, the most important of which is the West branch of the Susquehanna river, which has its source in Cambria county and enters Clearfield County at its southwestern boundary It flows in a northeasterly direction through the county in a winding course of nearly one hundred miles, entering Clinton County at its western boundary Finally it unites with the North Branch at Sunbury, Northumberland County, forming the broad Susquehanna which empties its waters into Chesapeake Bay The most important tributaries to the West Branch within Clearfield County are Chest, Anderson, Montgomery, Moose, Clearfield, Moshannon, Deer, Sandy and Musquito creeks, and Lick Run, Trout Run and Upper Three Run

Moshannon Creek forms the boundary between Clearfield and Centre counties

Clearfield Creek has two tributaries—Little Clearfield and Muddy Run

Chest Creek traverses the mountainous territory in the Southern part of the county

19

Anderson Creek has its source in the northeastern part of the county, and unites with the West Branch at Curwensville. It has several tributaries, the most important of which is Little Anderson Creek.

These various streams furnish splendid natural drainage to all sections of the county, and in the valleys traversed by them, large areas of very fertile land, suitable for agricultural purposes, are to be found.

The highlands are well watered by smaller streams, and the soil is especially adapted for farming land. Although it is only since the exhaustion of the timber supply in the county, in the last fifteen years, that attention has been turned to agriculture, today some of the finest and most profitable farms in the state lie within the boundaries of Clearfield County.

Geology—Geology is the science which treats of the history of the earth and its life, especially as recorded in the rocks.

The principal authorities on the science of geology have agreed upon the following classification of the different periods of time indicated by the rock formation.

AGES	AEONS	ORGANIC REIGNS
Caenozoic	Quaternary Tertiary	Man Mammals
Mesozoic	Cretaceous Jurassic Triassic	Reptiles and Birds
Palaeozoic	Upper Carboniferous Lower Carboniferous Devonian Silurian Cambrian	Amphibians and Land Animals Fishes Marine Invertebrates
Eozoic	Huronian Laurentian	Protozoans

The principal geological measures appearing in the formations within Clearfield County are the lower carboniferous measures of the Paleozoic formation. It is by reason of the existence of these measures that the county is so rich in mineral wealth. What is known as the Pottsville or Seral conglomerate is the foundation of all the great coal fields and no productive coal measures have ever been found beneath this rock.

The conglomerate is a coarse sand rock, containing large, white flint-like pebbles, and is a species of silicious quartz. Wherever it is found, it is considered as a sure indication of the presence of coal in the hills covering this rock. The out-crop of this conglomerate is usually found in the beds of streams, where the water has washed away the soil and exposed the surface of the rock.

Clearfield County contains seven veins of bituminous coal that are thick enough to be profitably mined. These veins are designated by letters, the bottom vein being generally known as "A" and the top, or cap vein, as "G." Between veins "B" and "C" is an intermediate vein, usually found at a distance of thirty feet above "B." Between "C" and "D" are also found intermediate veins at about the same distance.

Above the "G" or cap vein is found the Mahoning sandstone, the presence of which indicates the top of the coal measures. Still above this are found the rocks composing what are known as the barren measures, such as are found near Ramey and capping the summits of the Bloomington Ridge south of Curwensville.

There are three great coal basins which pass through the county in a general southwest and northeast direction. These are known as the first, second and third coal basins, and are separated by two anticlinals known as the first and second axis The third basin is separated by the Boon's mountain anticlinal from the basin of Jefferson and Elk counties, known as the fourth coal basin

The first basin covers the coal territory of Gulich, Bigler, Beccaria, Woodward and Morris townships, which include the Coalport, Madera, Houtzdale, Osceola, Philipsburg and Morrisdale coal developments

The second basin includes the Ansonville Gazzam, Boardman and Karthaus sub-basins and the Penn township sub-basin

The third basin contains the Brady, Sandy, and Huston townships, and the DuBois coal territory

A more detailed account of the various coal measures and their operation may be found in the chapter relating to the history of the coal interests of the county

Another geological formation of great importance to the county is the fire-clay, which is found at the bottom of the lower coal measures in all three of the coal basins that pass through the county. It is found in veins, ranging from four to twelve feet in thickness, and is usually in three layers It is of superior quality and has been developed by manufacturing the various kinds of brick, which now forms one of the principal industries of the county

In many places in the county are found extensive deposits of sandstone, which have been quarried on a large scale, the stone, on account of its peculiar qualities, and extreme purity and whiteness, is specially adapted for building purposes and bridge work

Three beds of limestone have been found about two hundred feet above the river in Greenwood township Various experiments have been made in burning this limestone, but it has been found to be too impure to make good lime

Several test wells were drilled for oil and gas, but were abandoned before reaching the proper strata, although all the geological formations along Anderson Creek indicate that oil and gas will be found when wells are drilled to sufficient depth

Small deposits of iron ore have been found at various points in the county Attempts have been made to utilize this ore, the principal one by Peter A Karthaus at the old furnace on Moshannon Creek, but this enterprise did not prove successful

CHAPTER II

INDIAN OCCUPATION

The Andastes—Their Conflict with the Iroquois and Partial Destruction—Brule's Expedition —His Capture and Escape—The Lenni-Lenapes or Delawares—The Monceys—Their Subjection by the Iroquois—The Shawnees and Tuscaroras—Retreat of the Indians

A great tribe of Indians known as the Andastes occupied the country now called western Pennsylvania as early as the sixteenth century This tribe belonged to the Algonquin family and were bitter enemies of the Iroquois, with whom they carried on continual war, until only a remnant of the Andastes remained These survivors finally settled near the mouth of the river now known as the Susquehanna, and were called Susquehannocks or Conestoga Indians

In Champlain's narrative of his voyage of 1618, which is the earliest account we have of the West Branch valley, it is recorded that he sent a Frenchman, named Etienne Brule, with a small party of Indians to endeavor to secure the assistance of the Andastes in his attack on the Iroquois towns Brule succeeded in this design, and marched with a large party of Andastes to join Champlain, but was unable to reach him, because prior to his arrival Champlain had been forced to retreat Brule returned with the Andastes to their camp, and spent the balance of the year with them From there he attempted, with guides furnished by the Andastes, to reach Quebec, but was captured by the Iroquois Finally he escaped, and after many perils rejoined Champlain

After the Andastes left the West Branch valley, it was inhabited by the Lenni-Lenapes or Delaware tribe, who were also of the Algonquin family The term "Lenni-Lenape" meant "Original People," and they were divided into various tribes

The Moncey, or Wolf tribe, the most active and warlike of them all, occupied the mountainous country between the Blue Mountains and the sources of the Susquehanna river

After the Iroquois had succeeded in driving out the Andastes, they made war upon the Lenni-Lenapes, whom they soon conquered Terms of peace were made, by which the Delawares gave up their lands to the Iroquois, and thereafter held them as tenants of that powerful tribe

The Shawnee and Tuscarora tribes, by permission of the Iroquois, moved from the Carolinas northward and occupied, with the Lenni-Lenapes, the country along the West Branch valley These Indians occupied this territory until about 1750, when they were driven out by the encroachments of the white men, and moved west of the Ohio river.

22

There is no reliable data upon which to found a history of any greater length than we have given in this brief resume of the territory which is now Clearfield county, at the time it was occupied by the Indians There are many legends and traditions which have been handed down from the time the first white men followed the Indian paths through the West Branch Valley, but all of these are so intermingled with the Indian history of other sections of the State that to properly tell it would require more space than we have at our command

Suffice it to say that in this region, as in all others where the white man met the red man in the inevitable conflict of the superior against the inferior race, the Indians were forced back, and ever backward, toward the setting sun, from whence tradition told them they had come The war-whoop was heard no longer, and the last Indian was driven from his beloved hunting grounds along the river "Otzinachson"

CHAPTER III .

LAND TITLES

Charles the Second's Grant to William Penn—Penn's Lease from Governor Dongan—Indian Deed Confirming the Purchase—Indian Deed to Penn's Heirs—The Articles of Consideration—Penn's Will—His Sale to the Crown—Thomas Penn Assumes Charge of the Province—First Surveys—Early Land Owners—Litigation Over Titles

The lands in the province of Pennsylvania were granted to William Penn by King Charles II of Great Britain by Royal Charter, dated the fourth day of March, A. D 1681, in payment of a claim which Penn's father, Admiral William Penn, had at the time of his death against the English Government, amounting to £16,000.

Under this charter Penn and his descendants claimed title to all the lands in the province, but in order to avoid trouble with the Indians, Penn's representatives, on coming into possession, negotiated with the various tribes for a release of their claim to the lands

In Vol 1, of Pennsylvania Archives, pages 121 and 122, may be found a copy of the curious instrument, dated January 12, 1696, by which William Penn leased from Thomas Dongan, late governor of New York, for one thousand years, at the annual rental of a "pepper corn," the lands of which Clearfield County is a part

Governor Dongan had acquired from the Iroquois, either by purchase or gift, the title which they claimed to said lands by right of conquest On January 13, 1696, Dongan made a deed to William Penn for the same lands for a consideration of £100, and on September 13, 1700, the Indian chiefs occupying these lands confirmed the purchase by William Penn by a deed which may be found recorded in the Recorder's office at Philadelphia, in Deed book F, Vol VIII, page 242

By an article of agreement, dated April 23, 1701, recorded at Philadelphia in Deed book F, Vol VIII, page 243, the chiefs of the Susquehanna Indians confirmed the deed of Governor Dongan.

Thirty-five years later, October 11, 1736, at a great council called at Philadelphia a large number of chiefs, representing the different tribes, executed a deed forever releasing to John, Thomas and Richard Penn all titles and claims to the Susquehanna lands This deed is also recorded in Philadelphia, in Deed book G, Vol V, page 277 This deed describes the property conveyed as follows:

"They, the said Kakiskerowand, Tayenhunty, Caxhaayn, Kuchdachary Saweegateeos, Sachems or Chiefs of the Nations of ye Onondagoe-Kanickhungo, TagachskahoIoo, Sagoayaton-dackquas, Ashcoalaax, Hetquantagech-

24

ta, Sachems or Chiefs of the Senekaes, Sayueh-sanyunt, Sunaratchy, Kanawatoe, Tecochtsee gherochgoo, Sachems of Chiefs of the Cayoo-goes, Saliscaquoh, Shecalamy, Tahashwanga-roras, Sachems or Chiefs of the Oneydoes, and Sawantga and Tyeros, Sachems or Chiefs of the Tuskaroros, for themselves and on behalf of all the five nations aforesaid, and every of them, have given, granted, bargained, sold, Released and Confirmed, and by these presents Do, and every one of them doth give, grant, Bargain, sell, release and Confirm unto the said proprietaries, John Penn, Thomas Penn and Richard Penn, their Heirs, Successors and Assigns, all the said River Susquehannah, with the lands lying on both sides thereof, to Extend Eastward as far as the heads of the Branches or Springs which run into the said Susquehannah And all the lands lying on the West side of the said River to the setting of the Sun, and to extend from the mouth of the said River Northward, up the same to the Hills or mountains called in the language of the said Nations, the Tyannuntasacta, or Endless hills, and by the Delaware Indians, the Kekkachtananin Hills, together, also, with all the islands in the said River, Ways, Waters, Watercourses, Woods, Underwoods, Timber and Trees, Mountains, Hills, Mines, Valleys, Minerals, Quarries, Rights, Liberties, Privileges, Advantages, Hereditaments and Appurtenances thereunto belonging, or in any wise appertaining"

Among the articles mentioned as the consideration of this curious document, and particularly interesting on account of the well-known peace-loving qualities of the Penns are 500 lbs of powder, 600 lbs of lead, 45 guns and 25 gallons of rum, besides 200 lbs of tobacco, and 1,000 pipes

William Penn died in 1713, and by his will, his property in the province was devised to his wife, Hannah, in trust to sell so much of his estate as was necessary to pay his indebtedness, and then to convey to his son by a former wife 40,000 acres of land, and all the residue of his lands in the province to his children by his second wife—John, Thomas and Richard

After Penn made this will, he agreed to sell his Pennsylvania property to the Crown for £12,000 and received part of the purchase money This agreement of sale was never consummated, but it caused litigation between the widow and children which was, however, finally compromised

In 1732 Thomas Penn came to this country to take charge of the province for himself and brothers, in whom the title of William Penn was then vested

In 1779 the Commonwealth of Pennsylvania purchased the title of the Penns for the sum of £130,000 sterling, by virtue of an act of assembly, approved June 28th, 1779, known as the Devesting Act

The first surveys of the land in the territory now composing Clearfield County were made as early as 1769

Among the earliest surveyors were Judge Smith, James Harris, Canan, Samuel Brady, the Indian fighter, and Daniel Turner

After the lands were opened to purchase, they were rapidly taken up and surveyed, and patents issued to the purchasers, most of whom were non-residents

Among the largest land-holders were the Holland Land Company, Nicklin and Griffith, James Hopkins, McConnell and Reynolds, James Yard, Cramer and Bates, the Keatings, Charles Mead, Thomas Kitland, William Parker, James Wilson, Samuel M Fox, Henry

Drinker, George Roberts, Joseph P Morris, Robert Morris, John Hallowell, Walter Stewart, Archibald McCall, Richard Peters, Rawle and Morgan, Phillips and Company, James C Fisher and William Scott These men owned many thousand acres of land in what is now Clearfield County.

For many years after the organization of the county there was tedious and expensive litigation over land titles, most of which was caused by the difficulties encountered by the early surveyors, but these disputes were finally settled by the Supreme Court.

CHAPTER IV

THE EARLY SETTLERS

Character of Clearfield County's Early Population—Former Political Divisions—The First White Settler—The Leading Pioneers of the County and the Credit Due Them

The future character of the population of a country is largely dependent upon the type of men and women who were the first to locate in it, and the people of Clearfield County are fortunate in the fact that those who originally settled here, who cut out roads through its forests, cleared its first farms and made themselves homes, were of that strong and sturdy stock that produces men able to cope with great difficulties and overcome them These were the kind of men who were the early pioneers in opening up the territory now Clearfield County and battling with the forces of nature

Prior to the year 1804, what is now the great and rich County of Clearfield was a part of Lycoming and Huntington Counties These counties were divided by the West Branch of the Susquehanna, those living on its Northern or Western bank being located in Lycoming county, while those who settled on its Southern or Eastern bank became citizens of Huntingdon county

It has long been a disputed question as to who was the first resident in the territory now comprising Clearfield County Undoubtedly the first white *settler* was a man known as Captain Edward Rickerts, mentioned in the journal of James Harris, who surveyed along Clearfield Creek in the autumn of 1784 But it is argued that Captain Rickerts did not remain long enough in this section of the country to be counted as a resident So it is generally conceded that James Woodside, who settled in the vicinity now known as Brady township in 1785, was the first white resident of what is now Clearfield county A monument to his memory was erected in Luthersburg cemetery in 1886, and a year previous the centennial of his birth was celebrated in the town of Luthersburg

Some old residents of the central part of the county still insist that Daniel Ogden, who settled on the site of the present town of Clearfield in 1797, has a right to this honor However, it is entirely possible that Mr Woodside lived on the western side of the great forests for many years, without ever coming in contact with Mr Ogden This theory peacefully settles the discussion and so we shall adopt it here

The next pioneer to come "up the river" was Arthur Bell, who arrived soon after Daniel Ogden He settled in the locality now known as Bell township His son, Grier, is said to have been the first white child born in this county Next came Casper Hockenberry

27

and James McCracken, who were related by marriage to Arthur Bell, and settled near him In 1799 Thomas McClure, better known as "Squire" McClure, came to this vicinity from Cumberland

About this time a widow by the name of Lewis, but called "Granny Leathers" came to Clearfield and started a distillery When the War of 1812 broke out, Granny disappeared, but her son, David, remained He, with several other men, made a good living by holding up and robbing the wagons of Bellefonte merchants Finally they were captured by several Center county citizens, and David was shot, and died Settlement became more rapid after 1800, and we shall not attempt to make more than a mention of the numerous families who came to this section of the country from 1800 until the year Clearfield county was organized Longer accounts of some of these men may be found in the histories of the various townships and boroughs

Martin Hoover, who came from York county, settled in 1801, in what afterwards became Lawrence township, and Alexander Read, (who became the first postmaster in the county) settled in the vicinity the following year Frederick Hennich, or Haney, built a home near Hoover about this time, and in 1803 Abraham Hess same from York county and located on Clearfield creek Paul Clover, the first resident on the site of Curwensville made a settlement in 1801 at the junction of Anderson creek and the Susquehanna river Robert Askey settled just below this place at about the same time David Litz made a clearing at the place afterwards known as Litz's bridge He is said to have floated the first log raft down the river Joseph Leonard occupied the cabin built by Captain Rickerts on Clearfield creek

Abraham Leonard settled on the Showshoe and Packersville turnpike in 1801. John Owens and Robert Graham settled on the opposite side of the creek about this time Abraham Passmore, Henry Irwin, Thomas Mapes and Daniel Turner located along the river in 1802

Settlements were being made farther east at the same time, in 1801 Jacob Wise, Robert Anderson and a man named Potter made homes along Moshannon Creek In 1802 John Kline settled near Montgomery creek, and Hugh Frazier built a cabin on Wolf Run John Carothers built a house a few miles farther down the river the same year

William Bloom made a clearing along the Susquehanna in 1801 on the land now called the Irvin Farm A few years ago Colonel E A Irvin of Curwensville had the site of this settlement marked by a sign bearing a suitable inscription

Others who settled along the river about this time were Robert Creswell, Benjamin Jordon, George and John Welch, John Ferguson, Peter Young, Samuel Ewing, Nicholas Straw, Samuel Fulton (the first prothonotary) and Leonard Kyler, for whose family Kylertown is named After the organization of Clearfield county in 1804, the population of this territory increased rapidly

Of the many who came then, we mention the following Thomas Forcey, Joseph Patterson (a maker of spinning-wheels), John Moore, William Tate, Robert Maxwell, William Kersey, James and Samuel Ardery, Benjamin Hartshorn (who built the first tannery in this county), John Bennett, Nun England, William Hepburn, Joseph Spencer, Francis Stephens, Samuel Cochran (an escaped slave), James Gallagher, Hugh Carson, James Moore (at whose home the first public religious services were held), the Johnsons, David Wall, Caleb Davis, Gideon Widemire, Jonathan Wain, Dr Coleman (who named our Grampian Hills), Joseph Boone, Abraham Goos, Nicholas and Henry Kephart, Valentine and David Flegal, Absalom Pierce, John Gearhart, Benjamin and Nicholas Smeal, James Rhea, James McNeil, the McKees, Dunlaps, Cathcarts, Ames, Feltwells, Thompsons, Currys, Williamses and Swans; Robert Collins, Jacob Spencer, William Alexander, Robert and Samuel Hagerty, Ignatius Thompson, Moses Norris, John Rowles, Archibald and Robert Shaw, David Hanna, the Smileys, Dillons and Goons

From this time on, the country opened up by these courageous and industrious pioneers became more thickly populated year by year Large and productive farms were made, good roads built, towns and villages sprang up, until today it is hard for us to realize that all this country was once a vast forest It is harder still for us with our latter day comforts and luxuries to understand the privations and hardships which these first citizens endured But as we read these names, which have come to stand for so much in our country, state and nation, we are moved to a deeper respect and appreciation of these men who made our country, our prosperity—and even *ourselves,* possible!

CHAPTER V

ORGANIZATION OF THE COUNTY

*Penn's Division of Pennsylvania into Three Counties—Thirty-six Counties Formed in 1803—
Additions in 1804, Including Clearfield County—The Act in Regard to Same—Annexation of Clearfield to Centre County—Settlement of Jurisdiction—Appointment of Commissioners to Select Seat of Justice—The Site Selected and Named Clearfield—Population
of the County—Election Laws—Organization of the Townships and Boroughs—Historical Society—Clearfield—The County Seat* ·

In 1682 William Penn divided the original
territory of Pennsylvania into three counties—
Philadelphia, Bucks and Chester No other
division was made for nearly 50 years, when
Lancaster was formed from part of Chester
in 1729

Other counties were created in quick succession until, in 1803, Pennsylvania was divided
into thirty-six counties as follows· Philadelphia, Bucks, Chester, Lancaster, York, Cumberland, Berks Northampton, Bedford, Northumberland, Westmoreland, Washington Fayette, Franklin, Montgomery, Dauphin, Luzerne, Huntingdon, Allegheny, Delaware,
Mifflin, Somerset, Lycoming Greene, Wayne,
Armstrong, Adams, Butler, Beaver, Centre,
Crawford, Erie, Mercer, Venango, Warren
and Indiana

On the twenty-sixth of March, 1804, by an
Act of Legislature, six new counties were
added to these They were Jefferson, Mc-
Kean Potter Tioga, Cambria and Clearfield

The following is that part of the Act refer-
ring to the boundaries and erection of Clearfield county

"Section III And be it further enacted by
the authority aforesaid, That so much of the
county of Lycoming included in the following
boundaries, to wit Beginning where the line
dividing Cannon's and Brodhead's district
strikes the west branch of the Susquehanna
River, thence north along the said district
line until a due west course from thence will
strike the southeast corner of McKean county,
thence west along the southern boundary of
McKean county to the line of Jefferson county, thence southwesterly along the line of Jefferson county to where Hunter's district line
crosses Sandy Lick Creek, thence south along
the district line to the Canoe Place on Susquehanna River, thence an easterly course to the
southwesterly corner of Centre county on the
heads of Muchanon Creek; thence down the
Muchanon Creek, the several courses thereof to
its mouth, thence down the west branch of the
Susquehanna River to the place of beginning,
be, and the same is hereby erected into a separate county to be henceforth called Clearfield
county, and the place of holding the courts of
justice in and for said the county, shall be fixed

by the Legislature at any place which may be most beneficial and convenient for the said county "

It will be noticed that no mention is made of Huntingdon county, although at that time the lands lying between Moshannon creek and the West branch were a part of Huntingdon county, so that Clearfield was formed from parts of both Huntingdon and Lycoming counties

Section VII provided for the appointment of three commissioners to mark the boundaries of the county

The next section provided "That as soon as it shall appear by an enumeration of the taxable inhabitants within the counties thus created, that any of them according to the rates which shall then be established for apportioning the representation among the several counties of the Commonwealth, shall be entitled to a separate representation, provision shall be made by law for apportioning the said representation, and enabling such county to be represented separately, and to hold the courts of justice at such place in said county as is, or hereafter may be, fixed for holding the same by the Legislature, and to choose their county officers in like manner as the other counties of this Commonwealth "

Section IX required the governor to appoint three trustees "who shall receive proposals in writing for the grant or conveyance of any lands within the county, or the transfer of any other property, or the payment of any money for the use of said county, for fixing the place of holding courts of justice in the county "

And further, in Section XI it is provided "That for the present convenience of the inhabitants of said counties of Clearfield and McKean and until an enumeration of the taxable inhabitants of the said counties shall be made.

and it shall be otherwise directed by law, the said counties of Clearfield and McKean shall be and the same are hereby annexed to the county of Centre, and the jurisdiction of the several courts of the county of Centre, and the authority of the judges thereof shall extend over, and shall operate and be effectual within said counties of Clearfield and McKean "

This annexation of Clearfield to Centre in the early days of our county's history has given rise to the mistaken idea that Clearfield was once a part of Centre county We hope that the above quotation will correct this impression

It is not strange that a question soon arose as to just how great an extent the officers of Centre county had power in Clearfield county

This question was settled in 1805 by an Act which announced that the jurisdiction of Centre county justices of the peace did not extend over this county in cases of debts or demands, but provided that the authority of the commissioners and other officers of Centre county should extend over and be full and effectual in this county Also, that the inhabitants of this county were entitled to exercise and enjoy the same rights and privileges, and to be subject to the same regulations as if this were a part of Centre county, and further, that the Centre county officers should keep separate books of the affairs of this county

By Section IV it is provided "That the county of Clearfield shall be an election district, and the electors thereof shall hold their general elections at the house of Benjamin Jordon, in the said district. and shall be entitled to vote for members of the Federal and State Legislatures, sheriffs, commissioners, and other county officers for Centre county "

The above named district was known as

"Chencleclamousche," and it comprised the entire county

In the year 1803, the governor issued the following order.

"Pennsylvania, ss
Thomas McKean

(Place of the Great Seal) In the name and by the authority of the Commonwealth of Pennsylvania Thomas McKean, Governor of the said Commonwealth

"To Roland Curtin of the County of Centre, John Fleming, of the county of Lycoming, and James Smith of the county of

"Gentlemen —

"Sends Greeting

"Whereas, In and by an Act of the General Assembly of this Commonwealth, dated the fourth day of April, instant, it is amongst other things provided, that the governor shall be authorized and empowered to appoint three disinterested commissioners, who do not reside or own any land in the County of Clearfield, which Commissioners, or a majority of them, shall meet at the house of Benjamin Patton in the town of Bellefonte, on the twentieth day of May next, and from thence proceed to view and determine on the most eligible and proper situation for the seat of justice and public buildings for the county of Clearfield

"Now Know Ye, That having full confidence in your integrity, judgment and abilities, I have appointed, and by these presents I do appoint you the said Roland Curtin, John Fleming and James Smith, Commissioners for the purpose aforesaid Hereby requiring you and each of you, with all convenient dispatch to proceed in the execution of the trust in you reposed as aforesaid, and to make a full and accurate report in writing, into the office of the Secretary of the Commonwealth, on or before the first Monday of December next

"Given under my Hand and the Great Seal of the State at Lancaster, this sixth day of April, Anno Domini, 1805, and of the Commonwealth the twenty-ninth

"By the Governor,

"T M THOMPSON,
"Secretary of the Commonwealth"

These commissioners met as directed on the twentieth of May, at the house of Benjamin Patton in Bellefonte

Several proposals were made to them and they visited the county in order to examine these localities They considered the lands of Paul Clover, at the mouth of Anderson creek, those at the junction of Clearfield creek and the Susquehanna, and also the farm of Martin Hoover, about half way between Chencleclamousche and Curwensville

Finally they decided upon the lands of Abraham Witmer as a site for the county seat, upon which the Indian town of Chencleclamousche had stood

Abraham Witmer, who was a resident of Lancaster, gave a town lot for the court-house, another for the jail, one for a market, and three for an academy

Besides all this land, he contributed three thousand dollars, half of which was to be used in erecting the public buildings and the other half for the use of an academy or public school

The Commissioners made the following report to the Governor as soon as the location was decided upon

"SIR —By virtue of an act of the General Assembly of the Commonwealth of Pennsylvania, entitled, 'An act authorizing the appointment of Commissioners to fix upon a proper site, for the seat of justice in Clearfield county'

"We, the subscribers, appointed by his excellency, the governor, agreeable to the provisions of the above mentioned act. passed on the tenth day of April in the year of our Lord one thousand eight hundred and five —Report, That agreeable to the provisions of the above mentioned act, we met in the house of Benjamin Patton, in the town of Bellefonte, on the twentieth day of May, one thousand eight hundred and five, and after receiving the different proposals made by several persons, proceeded to view and determine on the most eligible and proper situation for the seat of justice and public buildings for the said county of Clearfield, and do find that the old town of Chincleclamouse in the said county (the property of Abraham Witmer of the township of Lancaster in the county of Lancaster and Commonwealth of Pennsylvania) situated on the south side of the west branch of the Susquehanna river in the county aforesaid, is the most eligible and proper situation for the seat of justice and public buildings in the said county, and that we have laid out the said town, and we also further report that we have received from the said Abraham Witmer, his bond, which is hereto annexed for the conveyance of certain lots and the payment of certain sums of money at the time and for the purpose therein mentioned

"We are with respect your humble servants,

"ROLAND CURTIN,
"JNO FLEMING,
'JAS SMITH "

"To Thomas McKean
"Thompson, Esq, Secy "

The proceedings of the General Assembly, following and relating to the report of the Commissioners, confirmed their report as follows. "The commissioners appointed by this act fixed the place of holding the courts, etc, on lands of Abraham Witmer, at Chingleglamouch, old town, on the west branch of Susquehanna, and the new county town is now laid out and called Clearfield "

The elections of the district of "Chencleclamousche" (which embraced the entire county) were appointed to be held at the house of Benjamin Jordon, the counties of Lycoming, Centre, Clearfield, McKean, Tioga, and Potter, having an aggregate of four thousand five hundred taxables, were entitled to have one member in the State Senate, while Centre, Clearfield and McKean counties were entitled by number of taxables to one member of the House of Representatives

Clearfield County itself, by the enumeration of taxable inhabitants in 1806, was found to have a total of 104, sixteen of whom were single

The township of Chincleclamousche was divided in 1807, and two new townships, Beccaria and Bradford, were formed

The next enumeration of taxables, in 1808, showed Chincleclamousche to have 111, Bradford 36 and Beccaria 28—a total of 175, which proved that the county taxables had increased in two years by just 71 !

In 1812 the General Assembly passed a law providing that the electors of the county be authorized to choose Commissioners at the next election, in October, and "that the powers and authority of the Commissioners of Centre county over Clearfield county cease and determine, except the provision relating to the selection of jurors, in which case the Commissioners of Centre county shall retain jurisdiction in the county "

Finally, the limited organization of the county was made complete by the Act approved January 29th, 1822, by which Clearfield county became entitled to all the rights and privileges of other counties of the State It also authorized that courts should be held in the county, the Courts of Common Pleas, Quarter Sessions, and "such other courts as by law are authorized " The first term of court was appointed to be held the following October, and all suits already commenced by citizens of the county, and then pending, were transferred from Centre to Clearfield county, but all county prisoners were left in the Bellefonte jail until one could be erected in Clearfield

In the 106 years which have elapsed since the organization of our county, it has grown from a poorly organized, sparsely populated group of three townships, having in all a taxable population of 175, to the splendid organization comprising 30 rich townships and 20 prosperous boroughs, with a total population of nearly 100,000 which we know today as Clearfield county !

3

ORGANIZATION OF TOWNSHIPS AND BOROUGHS

From the time of its organization until the year 1807, Clearfield County had but one township, known by the Indian name of "Chincleclamousche." This township comprised the entire territory of the county, and had a taxable population of 104

This arrangement was found to be very inconvenient, for often citizens, in order to vote, had to travel a distance of from fifteen to thirty miles to the place of holding elections— a distance which was most difficult to cover in those days of few and almost impassable roads

So, in 1807 two divisions were made of old Chincleclamousche, and the townships Bradford and Beccaria were formed from the part south and east of the West Branch

This was better than before, but soon the voters grew tired of the unnecessary inconvenience arising because of the large territory included in each township So again Chincleclamousche was divided and in 1813 Pike and Lawrence townships were made

For the same reasons of greater convenience Covington and Gibson townships were formed in 1817 from that part of Chincleclamousche lying north of the West Branch

Gibson township had a brief life, for in 1843 part of it was taken in forming Elk county, and the rest was added to the township adjoining it

Sinnamahoning township (afterwards named Fox) was also short-lived Erected in 1821, part of it was, in 1868, added to Synder township, Jefferson county, part to Horton township, Elk county, and part to Huston township of this county.

From this time on new divisions of the original township of Chincleclamousche were made, until that name was dropped altogether.

Following is a list of the present townships in order of their formation Bradford and Beccaria, 1807, Pike and Lawrence, 1813; Covington, 1817; Brady and Chest, 1826; Decatur, 1828, Girard, 1832, Penn and Jordan, 1834, Bell and Burnside, 1835, Morris, 1836; Boggs, 1838; Ferguson, Huston and Karthaus, 1839; Goshen, 1845, Woodward, 1846, Union, 1848, Knox, 1854, Graham, 1856, Gulich, 1858, Bloom, 1860, Pine, 1873, Greenwood, 1875, Sandy, 1878, Bigler, 1882, Cooper, 1884

Boroughs—The first town to become independent of its township and to be incorporated was the old town of Chincleclamousche, better known then as "Old Town"

In the year 1840 this village became a borough under the name of Clearfield

The town of Curwensville, laid out by John Curwen in 1798, was the next to become a borough It was incorporated as such in 1851, and for seven years Clearfield and Curwensville shared the distinction of being the only boroughs in the county

But in 1858 the hamlet of Lumberville became a borough under the name of Lumber City, and in 1859 New Washington and in 1864 Osceola were incorporated

No other boroughs were added to this list for eight years, when, in 1872, the village of Houtzdale was incorporated From that year on the number of boroughs increased rapidly and in the following order Wallaceton, 1873, Burnside, 1874, Newburgh, 1875; DuBois and Glen Hope, 1881; Chester, Hill, Coalport, Brisbin and West Clearfield 1883; Grampian, 1885, Mahaffey, 1889, Trautville and Irvona, 1890, Ramey, 1893; Westover, 1895.

South First Street, Clearfield

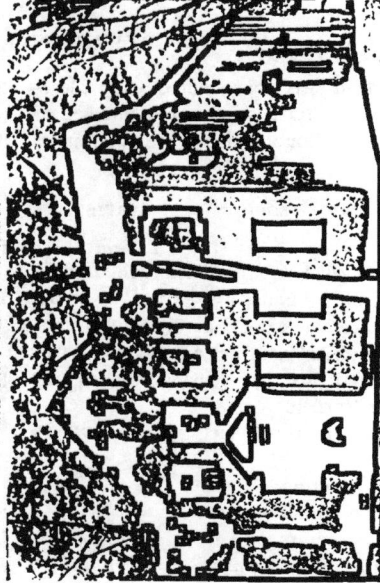

Y. M. C. A. Building, Clearfield

Second and Market Streets, Clearfield

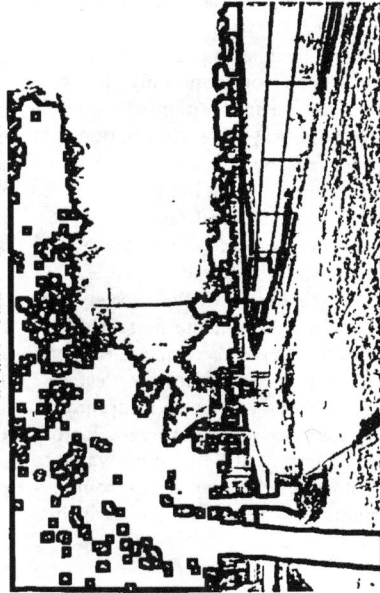

South Second Street, Clearfield

West Clearfield was consolidated with Clearfield in the year 1901, so that the number of boroughs in the County at the present time is twenty

THE HISTORICAL SOCIETY OF CLEARFIELD COUNTY

The Historical Society of Clearfield County was incorporated August 15th, 1910 The object of the Society is the collection and preservation of historical data pertaining to the natural, civil and literary development of the County of Clearfield

Membership in the Society is divided into three classes

1st Contributing members
2nd Corresponding members
3rd Honorary members

The Contributing membership is limited to thirty persons, residing in Clearfield County, elected by ballot, and who each pay annual dues not less than $5 00

Corresponding membership consists of persons residing in the County and duly elected to membership, who in consideration of their services or contributions to the Association, are not required to pay dues

Honorary membership is limited to fifteen persons, not residing in the County of Clearfield, who shall contribute to the Society or the cause of historical research

Four stated meetings of the Society are held each year, to wit On the first Mondays of March, June, September and December At the June meeting, the officers are elected

This society which has been incorporated, during the preparation of the present history of Clearfield County, will be of great value to the future historian, who may desire some reliable information in regard to the early history of the County, and by reference to the records of this society, will be able to ascertain the facts without the great difficulty and delay experienced by the editor of the present history

The present officers of the Society are as follows·

Thomas H Murray, President, W C. Pentz, Vice President, Alexander Paterson, Treasurer, L C Norris, Secretary

Trustees—Thomas H Murray, Roland D. Swoope, A B Reed, Singleton Bell, John P. Short, A M Liveright

CLEARFIELD—THE COUNTY SEAT

Long before the history of the white man in this region began, there had been an Indian village on the present site of Clearfield This group of native huts was called in the Indian tongue "Acht-schingi-clamme," the English of which is, "It almost joins " This referred to the bend in the river at this point Another interpretation of Acht-schingi-clamme is given in the journal of Bishop Ettwein, who will be mentioned later He says it signifies "No one tarries here willingly," and has reference to an old Indian legend of an eccentric brave, who hid in the rocks along the river bank and terrified his tribesmen by "appearing in frightful shapes "

The few early chroniclers who mentioned Acht-schingi-clamme in their writings, spelled the word as it sounded to them, and so we have the following wide diversity of spelling from which to choose "Chincleclamoose," "Chinklacamoose," "Shinglemuce," "Shinglaclamush," "Chinglecamouche" and "Cluncleclamousche " The last of these is the one most generally used

The first recorded history of this ancient

town begins with the French and Indian war, at which time the French started to build a fort at this point They were attacked by the English, and the Indians, themselves, burned their village rather than have it taken by the enemy

The same year (1758) Frederick Post, a Moravian, passed through the remains of this village on his way to the Ohio to confer with the Indians there Of the fourteen years which intervened from this time until the flight of the Moravians to Ohio, we have no history

In 1772 this band of 151 souls set forth on their long journey from the banks of the North Branch to the Ohio

They were divided into two companies, one of which was in the charge of Bishop John Ettwein The latter kept a careful journal of daily events, from which we quote the following "Tuesday, July 14th—Reached Clearfield Creek, where the buffalos formerly cleared large tracts of undergrowth so as to give them the appearance of cleared fields Hence the Indians called the creek "Clearfield " This repudiates the theory that the Indians, themselves, cleared fields here, as is generally understood Here again recorded history ceases, and for twenty-five years we have no facts concerning this spot

In 1797, Daniel Ogden and his son, Matthew, came "up the river" and settled near the ruins of old "Chincleclamousche " Here other settlers came in the next few years, and a little settlement called "Old Town," sprang up This name referred, of course, to the ancient Indian village

After the organization of Clearfield County in 1804, the next step was to decide upon the location for a county seat It was quite natural that the site of "Old Town," located at almost the exact centre of the county and having

long been recognized as a favorable place for dwellings, should be selected for this purpose Most of the land belonged to Abraham Witmer, of Lancaster county, who donated several lots and three thousand dollars for the erection of public buildings The town now received the name of Clearfield and was laid out in the following way Market street, the main street running east and west, was laid on the old Milesburg road, and the northern and southern limits of the town lay two squares on each side of this street Walnut and Locust lay parallel to Market on the North, and Cherry and Pine on the South The river formed the western boundary and streets ran north and south as follows Water street, Front or First street, Second street, Third street and Fourth street, which formed the eastern boundary

The first jail was built on Second street, near Cherry It was a very rude structure of logs, but it was used until the erection of a new jail, on the site of the present Opera house block This was used until 1870, when the jail now in use was erected

The first courthouse was built in 1814, on the corner of Second and Market streets, and was in use for forty-six years In 1860, a new building was started, and the present courthouse was completed in 1862

The academy was built on First street, near Cherry, and for many years was the only source of education (beyond the rude country schools) in the county. Many pupils came from miles around to receive their education here The old building was torn down a few years ago to make room for the fine new High School building The old academy was the last of the original public buildings to be destroyed, and the hundreds of men and women throughout the county who had, at some time in their lives, been pupils there, marked with deep regret the passing of this last monument to the early days of the county seat.

In this chapter we have attempted to give a brief history of the historic site of the county seat, from the beginning of its history to its incorporation as a borough in 1840 Its further history may be found under the title "Borough of Clearfield"

CHAPTER VI

COUNTY AND OTHER OFFICIALS

A List of the Principal State and County Officials—United States Senators—Representatives in Congress—U S District Attorney—U S Marshal—Clerk of House of Representatives—State Officers—Senators, Representatives—Present Judges—Associate Judges—Deputy Attorneys—General and District Attorneys—Sheriffs—Registers and Recorders—Treasurers — Prothonotaries — County Superintendents — County Commissioners and Clerks

UNITED STATES OFFICERS

United States Senators
William Bigler—1855-61
William A Wallace—1875-81
Representatives in Congress
Alexander Irvin—30th Congress 1847-49
John Patton—38th and 50th Congresses—1861-63, 1887-89.
James Kerr—51st Congress 1889-1891
William C Arnold—54th and 55th Congress 1895-99
United States District Attorney
H Bucher Swoope—1869-74
United States Marshal
Alexander Irvin
Clerk of House of Representatives
James Kerr—1891-1895

STATE OFFICERS

Governor
William Bigler—1852-5
State Treasurer
Frank G Harris—1902-04
State Senators:

William Bigler, 1842
Alexander Irvin, 1847
William A Wallace, 1863-75
Thomas J Boyer, 1876.
William W Betts, 1887-94
M L McQuown, 1895-1898
William C Heinle, 1899-1902.
Alexander E Patton, 1903-04
Edward A Irvin, 1904-06
George M Dimeling, 1907.
Members of the House of Representatives in the State Legislature.
Martin Hoover, first (date unknown)
Greenwood Bell, second (date unknown)
John Irvin, third (date unknown).
1837-38—James Ferguson.
1839-40—James H Lafferty
1841-42—G R Barrett
1844-45—Lewis W. Smith
1846-47—Charles S Worrell
1848-49—George Walters
1850-51—William J Hemphill
1853-54—A. Caldwell
1858-62-3-4—T. J Boyer.

38

1867-68—Thomas J McCullough
1872-73—John Lawshe
1874—Johnson W Potter
1875-76—W R Hartshorne
1877-78—Aaron C Tate
1879-80—A D Bennett
1881-82—James Flynn
1883-84—J P Taylor
1885-86—J H Norris
1887-88—Aaron G Kramer
1889-92—John F Farrell, P S Weber
1893-94—John K Gorman, Charles S King
1895-96—John H Patchin, C D Ames
1897-1902—Frank G Harris, Joseph Alexander
1903-06—Harry Boulton, F R. Scofield
1907-08—Jonathan Currier, A. S Moulthrop, Peter Gearhart
1909-10—Jonathan Currier, A S Moulthrop, S R Hamilton

President Judges
1822-6—Charles Huston
1826-41—Thomas Burnside
1841-51—George W Woodward
1851-52—R G White
1852-3—John C Knox
1853—James T Hale
1853-59—James Burnside
1859—James Gamble
1859-68—Samuel Linn
1868—Joseph B McEnally
1868-84—Charles A Mayer
1875-84—John H Orvis (addl law judge)
1884-94—David L Krebs
1894-1904—Cyrus Gordon
1904—Allison O Smith

Associate Judges
1822-6—Francis W Rawle, Moses Boggs
1826-40—Moses Boggs, Hugh Jordon

1840-41—Moses Boggs, James Ferguson
1841-6—James Ferguson, John Patton
1846-51—Abram K Wright, James T Leonard
1851-6—Richard Shaw, John P Hoyt
1856-61—William L. Moore, Benjamin Bonsall
1861-6—James Bloom, John D Thompson
1866-71—Samuel Cloyd, Jacob Wilhelm
1871-6—William C Foley, John J Read
1876-81—Vincent Holt, Abram Ogden
1881-6—John L Cuttle, John Hockenberry

Deputy Attorneys-General and District Attorneys
Samuel M Green
Josiah W Smith
Samuel H Tyson
George R Barrett
Lewis W Smith
John F Weaver
D Rush Petrikin
George W Hecker
J B McEnally
Joseph S Frantz
Thomas J McCullough
Robert J Wallace
Israel Test
William M McCullough
A W Walters
Frank Fielding
William McCullough
Joseph F McKenrick
Smith V Wilson
Singleton Bell
Americus H Woodward
William I Swoope
James H Kelley

Sheriffs
1822—Greenwood Bell

1823-6—Greenwood Bell
1826-9—William Bloom
1829-32—Lebbus Luther
1832-5—Robert Ross
1835-8—James Ferguson
1838-41—Abram K Wright
1841-4—George Leech
1844-7—Ellis Irwin
1847-50—John Stites
1850-3—Alexander Caldwell
1853-6—William Powell
1856-9—Josiah R Read
1859-62—Frederick G Miller
1862-5—Edwin Perks
1865-8—Jacob A Faust.
1868-71—Cyrenius Howe.
1871-4—Justin J Pie
1874-7—William R McPherson
1877-80—Andrew Pentz, Jr
1880-3—James Mahaffey
1883-6—R Newton Shaw
1886-89—Jesse E Dale
1889-92—Edgar L McCloskey
1892-95—Fred M Cardon
1895-98—Frank Smith
1898-1901—David D Gingery.
1901-04—Hugh McCullough
1904-07—James P Staver
1907-10—Cornelius Allen
1910—E H Woolridge

Registers and Recorders
1856-62—James Wrigley
1862-68—I G Barger
1868-75—Asbury W Lee
1875-81—L J Morgan
1881-87—George Ferguson
1887-93—D R Fullerton
1893-99—Bine Koozer
1899-1905—E E Jimeson
1905—W T DeHaas

Treasurers
Arthur Bell
Samuel Coleman
Samuel Fulton
Alexander B Reed
James Ferguson
Alexander Irvin
G Philip Geulich
Martin Hoover
James T Leonard
Christopher Kratzer
D W Moore
Robert Wallace
J W Wright
Isaac Bloom.
Arthur Bell
John McPherson
Eli Bloom
John McPherson
George B Goodlander.
Joseph Shaw
Christopher Kratzer.
D W Moore
William K Wrigley.
Lever Flegal
Samuel P Wilson
David W Wise
David McGaughey
Philip Botts
John W Wrigley
John M Troxell.
James Mitchell
James McLaughlin
W C Goss
Leslie Stewart
William Boyce

Prothonotaries
1822—Samuel Fulton
1825—Reuben Winslow
1827—Joseph Boone

1836—Ellis Irwin
1839—James T Leonard
1842—Alexander Irwin
1846—William C Welch, Ellis Irwin (by appointment)
1851—William Porter
1857—George Walters, James T Leonard (by appointment)
1860—John L Cuttle
1863—D F Etzweiler
1869—Aaron C Tate
1875—Eli Bloom
1881—James Kerr
1887—Alfred M Bloom
1893—Dorsey J Gingery
1899—Grant H Thompson
1905—Roll B Thompson
County Superintendents
1854-7—A T Schryver
1857-60—L L Still
1860-3—J. Broomall
1863-6—C B Stanford
1866-72—G W Snyder
1872-8—J A Gregory
1878-84—M L McQuown
1884-90—Matthew Savage
1890-95—G W Weaver
1895-1902—E C Shields
1902—Wm E Tobias
County Commissioners and Clerks
1812-13—Hugh Jordon, Samuel Fulton, Robert Maxwell, Clerk, Joseph Boone
1814-15—Hugh Jordon, William Tate, Robert Maxwell, Clerk, Joseph Boone
1817-18—Thomas McClure, David Ferguson, Robert Ross, Clerk, Joseph Boone
1819—David Ferguson, Robert Ross, William Ogden, Clerk, Joseph Boone
1820—William Ogden, Greenwood Bell, Alexander Read, Jr, Clerk, Joseph Boone

1821—Alexander Read, Jr, Matthew Ogden, Greenwood Bell, Clerk, David Ferguson
1822—Alexander Read, George Welch, Abraham Leonard, Clerk, David Ferguson
1823—George Welch, Elisha Schofield, Martin Nichols, Clerk, James Reed
1824—Martin Nichols, Elisha Schofield, George Welch, Clerk, James Reed
1825—Schofield, Nichols, Job England, Clerk James Reed
1826—England, Nichols, George Wilson, Clerk, James Reed
1827—England, Wilson, Joseph Hoover, Clerk, James Reed
1828—Joseph Hoover, George Ross, Robert Wilson, Clerk, James Reed
1829—Hoover, Ross, A Caldwell, Clerk, Lewis W Smith
1830—Ross, Caldwell, J Schnarrs, Clerk, Jas T Leonard
1831—Caldwell, Schnarrs, George Leech, Clerk, Jas T Leonard
1832—Schnarrs, Leech, Ignatius Thompson, Clerk, Jas T Leonard
1833—Leech, Thompson, I H Warwick, Clerk, Jas T Leonard
1834—Warwick, Thompson, Matthew Ogden, Clerk, L W Smith
1835—Warwick, Ogden, Smith Mead; Clerk, L W Smith
1836—Ogden, Mead, William Dunlap, Clerk, L W Smith
1837—Mead, Dunlap, James B Graham; Clerk L W Smith
1838—Dunlap, Graham, Isaac Goodfellow, Clerk, James Reed
1839—Graham, Goodfellow, John Stites, Clerk, James Reed
1840—Goodfellow, Stites, John McMurray, Clerk, G R Barrett

1841—McMurray, Stites. James B Caldwell, Clerk, H B Beissel

1842—McMurray, Caldwell, George C Passmore, Clerk, H B Beissel

1843—Caldwell, Passmore, John Carlisle, Clerk, H B Beissel

1844—Passmore, Carlisle, Grier Bell, Clerk, H B Beissel

1845—Carlisle, Bell, Samuel Johnson, Clerk. H B Beissel

1846—Johnson, Bell, Abram Kyler, Clerk, H P Thompson

1847—Johnson, Kyler, James A Reed, Clerk, H P Thompson

1848—Kyler, Reed, James Elder, Clerk, H P Thompson

1849—Reed, Elder, Benjamin Bonsall, Clerk, W. A Wallace

1850—Elder, Bonsall, S Way, Clerk, H B Beissel

1851—Bonsall, Way, William Alexander, Clerk, Jno F Irwin

1852—Way, Alexander, Philip Hevener, Clerk, G. B Goodlander

1853—Alexander, Hevener, Samuel Shoff; Clerk, G B Goodlander

1854—Hevener, Shoff, R Mahaffey: Clerk, G B Goodlander

1855—Shoff, Mahaffey, David Ross, Clerk, R J Wallace

1856—Mahaffey, Ross, J Wilhelm; Clerk, R J Wallace

1857—Ross, Wilhelm, John Irvin, Clerk, R J Wallace

1858—Wilhelm, Irvin, George Erhard, Clerk, R J Wallace

1859—Irvin, Erhard, William McCracken; Clerk, William Bradley

1860—Erhard, McCracken, William Merrill; Clerk, William Bradley

1861—McCracken, Merrill, S C. Thompson; Clerk, William Bradley

1862—Merrill, Thompson, Jacob Kuntz, Clerk, William Bradley

1863—Thompson, Kuntz, Thomas Dougherty, Clerk, William Bradley

1864—Kuntz, Dougherty, Amos Read, Clerk, William Bradley

1865—Dougherty, Read. Conrad Baker; Clerk, William Bradley.

1866—Read, Baker, Charles S Worrel, Clerk, William Bradley.

1867—Baker, Worrel, Henry Stone; Clerk, William Bradley.

1868—Worrel, Stone, Othello Smead, Clerk, William Bradley

1869—Stone, Smead, S H Shaffner, Clerk, G B Goodlander.

1870—Smead, Shaffner, Samuel H Hindman, Clerk, G B Goodlander

1871—Shaffner, Hindman, David Buck, Clerk, G B Goodlander.

1872—Hindman, F F. Conteret, Gilbert Tozer, Clerk, G B Goodlander

1873—Conteret, John D. Thompson, Gilbert Tozer; Clerk, G B Goodlander

1874—Same

1875—Conrad W Kyler, Thompson, Clark Brown, Clerk, G B. Goodlander

1876-7-8—Brown, Thomas A McGee, Harris Hoover; Clerk, John W Howe

1879-80-1—Conrad W. Kyler, Elah Johnson, John Norris; Clerk, Jacob A. Foss

1882-3-4—C K McDonald, John T Straw, John Picard, Clerk, R A Campbell

1885-6-7—James Savage, C K McDonald, Clark Brown, Clerk, R A Campbell

1888—James Savage, George I Thompson, Jacob Mock; Clerk, W V Wright

1891—George I Thompson, E. G. Gearhart, John McGaughey; Clerk, Geo E Owens

1894—W T Ross, James S Read, A E Woolridge, Clerk, Harry E Rowles

1897—A E Woolridge, W C. Davis, D H Waring, Clerk, P T Davis

1900—W C Davis, C H Cole, H J. Diem, Clerk, P T Davis

1903—C P Rowles, S R Hamilton, B F Wilhelm, Clerk, A K. Staver

1906—Same

1909—J S Richards, W C Langsford, D J Gingery, Clerk, L C Norris

CHAPTER VII

MILITARY HISTORY AND THE COUNTY MILITIA—THE CIVIL WAR

Loyalty of Clearfield County's Sons—Military Organizations Before the War—Thirty-fourth Regiment, Fifth Reserves—Its General and Individual Record, Officers and Men—Forty-second Regiment, "Bucktails"—The Fifty-first Regiment—Fifty-ninth Regiment, Second Cavalry—Eighty-fourth Regiment

In all the great army which struggled for the preservation of the Union during the stirring days of the Civil war, there were no braver men nor truer patriots than the sons of Clearfield county By the deeds they did and the hardships they endured, they shared in making possible the glorious Union of today.

But these men were not alone in this loyalty to their country, for when, thirty-three years later, the clouds of war again gathered on the horizon of our national life, the sons of those veterans who fought in that other war, also struggled to uphold the righteous principles of freedom which our nation had adopted It is with pride that we record the names and deeds of Clearfield county's brave sons, and we trust that new loyalty and patriotism may be inspired in the hearts of those who read the pages of this brief military history

Before the days of our Civil war, a volunteer battalion was organized under the State law This organization was made in 1840, with George R Barrett in command By 1841 the battalion had increased in numbers until it was possible to form a regiment of

about six companies of sixty men each Major Barrett was now made colonel, and E W. Wise became major The regiment annually attended the State encampment—journeys not easily accomplished in those days of no railroads, for it was often necessary to march forty or fifty miles to the camp This organization existed for about seven years

A section of the State militia, of which Hon William Bigler was colonel, was in existence about the same time It was here that Hon John Patton received his title of "General" Hon William A Wallace was captain of another organization known as the "Guards" These three comprised the only military organizations existing in the county before the war days Although of brief duration, these military companies helped to keep alive the spirit of patriotism in the hearts of the citizens, for nothing is more inspiring than the tramp of many feet, marching in unison, the sight of gay uniforms, and the sound of fife and drum

So, although the militia of the early days of our county had no opportunity to engage in actual warfare, who shall say how great

44

was its influence in arousing and strengthening the loyalty and patriotism of the citizens of Clearfield county?

THIRTY-FOURTH REGIMENT—FIFTH RESERVES

This regiment was organized at Camp Curtin June 20, 1861, and together with the "Bucktails" was sent to the relief of Colonel Lew Wallace, at Cumberland, Md On July 13th they were stationed at Bridge 21, on the Baltimore & Ohio Railroad which had been burned by the rebels From that point they moved to New Creek July 22d they were sent to Piedmont to protect the Unionists After the battle of Bull Run July 21st, they were ordered to Washington and from there to Harrisburg On August 8th they were ordered back to Washington and went into camp at Tennallytown On the 14th of September they were reviewed by Governor Curtin, President Lincoln, General McClellan and others On December 20th, the regiment was ordered to Dranesville and on the 9th of April, 1862, they occupied Manassas On May 7th they arrived at Falmouth and on May 25th crossed the Rappahannock June 9th they were ordered to Mechanicsville and composed part of the right wing of McClellan's army, five miles from Richmond, where they engaged in what is known as the "Seven Days' Battle," in which the Confederate forces were routed They were then ordered to Acquia Creek and from there to Washington where they participated in the Second Battle of Bull Run They also took part in the battles of Antietam and Fredericksburg In February, 1863, they were again ordered to Washington and encamped at Miner's Hill The regiment took part in the battle of Gettysburg, did guard duty along the Orange and Alexandria

railroad, and in February, 1864, had a battle with guerrillas near Brentzville, where Major Larimer was killed May 4, 1864, under Grant, they crossed the Rapidan and engaged in the battle of the Wilderness The regiment participated in the engagements which followed until May 31, 1864, when their term of service expired and they were mustered out at Harrisburg, Pa, on the 11th of June, 1864

Field and Staff

Colonels —Seneca G Simmons, June 21, 1861, killed at Charles City Cross Roads, June 30, 1862

Joseph W Fisher, May 15, 1861, promoted from lieutenant-colonel August 1, 1862, brevet brigadier-general November 4, 1865, mustered out with regiment June 11, 1864

Lieutenant-Colonels —George Dare, June 21, 1861, promoted from major August 1, 1862, killed at Wilderness May 6, 1864

Alfred M Smith, May 15, 1861, promoted from captain Company C to major February 22, 1864, to lieutenant-colonel May 7, 1864, to brevet colonel March 13, 1865, mustered out with regiment June 11, 1864

Majors —Frank Zentmyer, June 21, 1861, promoted from captain Company I, August 1, 1862, killed at Fredericksburg December 13, 1862, burial record, died at Richmond, Va, December 31, 1862

J Harvey Larimer, May 15, 1861, promoted from captain Company E ,May 1, 1863, killed at Bristow Station, February 14, 1864

James A McPherran, June 16, 1861, promoted from captain Company F, May 7, 1864, to brevet lieutenant-colonel March 13, 1865, mustered out with regiment June 11, 1864

Adjutants —A G Mason, June 21, 1861, discharged March 27, 1863, to accept appointment on General Meade's staff, brevet major

August 1, 1864, brevet lieutenant-colonel March 13, 1865

John L Wright, May 15, 1861, mustered out with regiment June 11, 1864, brevet captain March 13, 1865

Quartermaster —Samuel Evans, June 21, 1861, commissioned captain May 7, 1864, not mustered, brevet captain March 13, 1865, mustered out with regiment June 11, 1864

Surgeons —John T. Carpenter, June 21, 1861, promoted and transferred to Western army as brigade surgeon

Samuel G Sane, September 16, 1861, promoted surgeon of enrollment board, 16th district, Pa , March 10, 1864, to assist surgeon-general, Pa , to brevet lieutenant-colonel March 13, 1865

Henry A Grim, April 16, 1862, promoted from assistant surgeon 12th regiment P V R C , mustered out with regiment June 11, 1864

Assistant Surgeons —N. P Marsh, June 21, 1861, promoted surgeon 4th regiment Pa Cavalry, 64th regiment P V

E Donnelly, June 21, 1861, promoted to surgeon 31st regiment P. V , April 28, 1862

W H Davis, June 27, 1862, promoted to surgeon 33d regiment P V , December 20, 1862

J M Groff, August 2, 1862, discharged on surgeon's certificate July 21, 1863

O C Johnson, March 9, 1863, discharged on surgeon's certificate September 28, 1863

H T Whitman, September 16, 1863, wounded at Bethesda Church May 30, 1864, mustered out with regiment June 11, 1864, brevet major March 13, 1865

Chaplain —S L M. Consor; mustered out by special order of war department November 1, 1862

Sergeant-Majors —E L Reber, June 21, 1861; transferred to 191st P V ; veteran

R. M Smith, June 21, 1861, promoted to second lieutenant August 8, 1862, transferred to Company G

G P Swoope, June 21, 1861, promoted to first lieutenant March 4, 1863; transferred to Company I.

Quartermaster-Sergeant — Harry Mullen, June 21, 1861, transferred to 191st P. V ; veteran

Commissary-Sergeant —J W. Harris, June 21, 1861, transferred to 191st P V , veteran

Hospital Steward —John H. Johnson, July 21, 1861, transferred to 191st P V , veteran

Principal Musicians —E. L. Scott, June 21, 1861, mustered out with regiment June 11, 1864

W L Smeadley, June 21, 1861, transferred to 191st P V , veteran

COMPANY C

Recruited in Clearfield County

Captains —J Oscar Loraine, June 21, 1861, resigned November 7, 1861

Alfred M Smith, May 15, 1861, promoted from sergeant to first lieutenant July 25, 1861; to captain November 15, 1861, to major February 22, 1864

David McGaughey, June 21, 1861, promoted from sergeant to first lieutenant November 16, 1861, to captain March 22, 1864, brevet major March 13, 1865; wounded at Wilderness May 9, 1864; mustered out with company June 11, 1864

First Lieutenants —J Harvey Larrimer, May 15, 1861; promoted to captain Company F July 12, 1861.

John E Potter, June 21, 1861; promoted from corporal to second lieutenant August 15,

1862, to first lieutenant March 22, 1864, mustered out with company June 11, 1864

Second Lieutenant —John W Bigler, June 21, 1861, resigned June 22, 1862

First Sergeant —Wm A Ogden, June 21, 1861, commissioned captain June 4, 1864, not mustered, mustered out with company June 11, 1864

Sergeants —Thos H Wilson, June 21, 1861, mustered out with company June 11, 1864

James C Miller, June 21, 1861, mustered out with company June 11, 1864

James L. McPherson, June 21, 1861, mustered out with company June 11, 1864

George B Hancock, June 21, 1861, mustered out with company June 11, 1864

John Huidekoper, June 21, 1861, promoted to second lieutenant Company 3, 150th regiment P V, October 30, 1862

Martin Mullen, June 21, 1861, killed at Fredericksburg December 13. 1862

Corporals —Wm C McGonagle, June 21, 1861, mustered out with company June 11, 1864

Oliver Conklin, June 21, 1861, absent, wounded, at muster out

Smith B Williams, June 21, 1861, mustered out with company June 11, 1864

Jos W Folmer, June 21, 1861, mustered out with company June 11, 1864

Edward Blingler, June 21, 1861, mustered out with company June 11 1864

Richard S Carr, June 21, 1861; discharged October 24, 1863, for wounds received in action

Bolivar T. Bilger, June 21, 1861; killed at Fredericksburg December 13, 1862

John W. Hoy, June 21, 1861; killed in action June 30, 1862

James Leonard, June 21, 1861, killed in action June 30, 1862

George W Young, June 21, 1861, killed at Bristow Station October 14

E S Woolstencroft, June 21, 1861, deserted May 4, 1862

Musicians —David McR Betto, June 21, 1861, promoted to second lieutenant Company E March 5, 1863

Lyman McC Shaw, August 8, 1861, deserted July 5, 1862

Privates —Wm B Beamer, June 21, 1861; mustered out with company June 11, 1864

Wm M Bahans, June 21, 1861, discharged November 9: 1861

Wm Baughman, June 21, 1861, discharged on surgeon's certificate October 23, 1862

Samuel I Burge, July 21, 1861, discharged on surgeon's certificate May 4, 1863

Solomon M Bailey, April 7, 1864, transferred to 191st P V June 6, 1864

Math J Caldwell, July 21, 1861, mustered out with company June 11, 1864

Robert E Carson, June 21, 1861, transferred to V R C, mustered out with company June 11, 1864

Daniel Curley, June 21, 1861, mustered out with company June 11, 1864

John M Caldwell, July 21, 1861, discharged on surgeon's certificate September 25, 1861

John A Coyle, June 21, 1861, discharged May 15, 1863, for wounds received in action

Alexander Carr, June 21, 1861; killed at Fredericksburg December 13, 1862; burial record, died at Richmond, Va, December 31, 1862

J H DeHass, June 21, 1861, mustered out with company June 11, 1864

John Dolan, August 30, 1862, discharged July 31, 1863, for wounds received in action.

Benj F Derrick, June 21, 1861, killed at Bristow Station October 14, 1863

Wm Evans, April 8, 1864, transferred to 191st P V June 6, 1864.

Henry J Fisher, June 21, 1861, mustered out with company June 11, 1864

Hiram France, June 21, 1861, discharged November 12, 1862, for wounds received in action

Miles Ford, June 21, 1861, killed in action June 30, 1862

Henry J Fitchner, July 22, 1861, deserted August 12, 1862

John A Green, July 21, 1861, mustered out with company June 11, 1864

Henry Garver, June 21, 1861, transferred from V R C; mustered out with company June 11, 1864

Loren Goodfellow, November 1, 1861, transferred to 191st P. V June 6, 1864

Claudius Girard, December 23, 1863, transferred to 191st P V June 6, 1864

Wm A Haight, June 21, 1861; mustered out with company July 11, 1864

Henry A Harlan, June 21, 1861, mustered out with company July 11, 1864

Wm R Hemphill, June 21, 1861, discharged on surgeon's certificate December 20, 1862

David B Horn, April 7, 1864, transferred to 191st P V June 6, 1864

Philo B Harris, June 21, 1861; killed at Fredericksburg, December 13, 1862

David W Horn, March 30, 1864, killed at Wilderness May 9, 1864

Joseph Jackson, June 21, 1861, discharged on surgeon's certificate September 13, 1862

Wm Jones, June 21, 1861, deserted September 16, 1862

John T. Kirk, June 21, 1861, mustered out with company July 11, 1864

Douglas N Koons, June 21, 1861, discharged, date unknown

Geo W. Lingle, June 21, 1861; mustered out with company July 11, 1864

James I Leightley, June 21, 1861; mustered out with company June 11, 1864

Robert C Larrimer, June 21, 1861; mustered out with company June 11, 1864

Joseph Lines, June 21, 1861; transferred from V R C, mustered out with company June 11, 1864

James Lingle, June 21, 1861; mustered out with company June 11, 1864

Geo W. Livergood, June 21, 1861; discharged on surgeon's certificate November 24, 1862

Sampson B Lingle, June 21, 1861, discharged April 4, 1863, for wounds received in action

Rob Livingston, July 15, 1861; died at Camp Tenally, Md, September 13, 1861

Stephen D Logan, June 21, 1861; died at Harrison's Landing, Va, August 5, 1862.

Martin Livergood, July 15, 1861, died at Annapolis, Md, September 24, 1862

Chas W. Mitchell, June 21, 1861; transferred from V R C; mustered out with company June 11, 1864

Patrick Malone, June 21, 1861; mustered out with company June 11, 1864

Wesley B Miller, June 21, 1861; mustered out with company June 11, 1864.

Lorine Merrell, June 21, 1861, discharged on surgeon's certificate, date unknown

Henry S Merrell, June 21, 1861; died at Philadelphia August 14, 1862

John Maughamer, June 21, 1861, deserted April 4, 1863

Martin McCallister, June 21, 1861, absent, wounded, at muster out

Archibald McDonald, June 21, 1861, discharged on surgeon's certificate January 11, 1863

W L McGaughey, June 21, 1861, killed at Fredericksburg December 13, 1862

Michael O'Leary, June 21, 1861, mustered out with company June 11, 1864

H F. Passmore, June 21, 1861, discharged January 11, 1863, for wounds received in action

David Payne, June 21, 1861, killed in action June 30, 1862

Thos W Potter, June 21, 1861, killed at Fredericksburg December 13, 1862.

Wm. Robinson, June 21, 1861; died at Washington, D C, March 26, 1863, buried in Military Asylum Cemetery

Geo. H. Sweet, June 21, 1861, mustered out with company June 11, 1864

Oliver St. George, June 21, 1861, transferred to western gunboat service February 17, 1862.

David Smay, February 26, 1864, transferred to 191st P V. June 6, 1864

Christian Smay, February 26, 1864, transferred to 191st P. V. June 6, 1864

H B Spachman, June 21, 1861, died at Camp Curtin, Harrisburg, August 9, 1861

Philip G Shaffner, June 21, 1861, killed in action June 30, 1862

Henry B Smith, June 21, 1861, killed in action June 30, 1862

Peter F Stout, June 21, 1861, killed at Gaines's Mill, June 27, 1862

Martin Stone, June 21, 1861, killed at Gaines's Mill, June 27, 1862

Geo W Soule, June 21, 1861, killed at Bull Run, August 30, 1862

David R P Shirey, June 21, 1861, deserted June 9, 1862

John Verner, June 21, 1861, deserted September 14, 1862

Harrison Welton, June 21, 1861, deserted January 22, 1862

Nicholas Zeigler, April 7, 1864, transferred to 191st P V June 6, 1864

FORTY-SECOND REGIMENT—"BUCKTAILS"

This regiment was one of the most noted ones in the Army of the Potomac On the 24th of April, 1861, one hundred men had assembled at a rafting-place on the Sinnamahoning, where they constructed transports The only uniform was a red shirt, black pants, and a bucktail in the cap Two days later, three hundred and fifteen strong, they embarked on three rafts, and with a green hickory pole, surmounted by a bucktail, for a flag staff, the stars and stripes flying, and fife and drum rousing the echoes of the mountain sides. onward down the West Branch sailed the patriotic flotilla

Authority had been given to muster them in as the Seventeenth (three months) Regiment An organization was commenced with Thomas L Kane as colonel, but as a Seventeenth Regiment had been mustered in at Philadelphia, the organization was not consummated, and Colonel Kane, declining a commission, was mustered in as a private May 13, 1861

Other companies were recruited—one in Warren county, one in Chester, one in Perry, one in Clearfield, one in Carbon, and two in Tioga, and the material had been assembled for a first-class regiment On the 13th day of

June a regimental election was held, which resulted in the selection of Thomas L Kane as colonel, but, with that patriotism which always marked the career of an unselfish soldier, he resigned, that Lieutenant-Colonel Biddle, who had served in Mexico, might be placed in command The name of the organization was changed from the "Rifle Regiment," to "Kane Rifle Regiment of Pennsylvania Reserve Corps," and started into service as the Forty-second of the line, although it was universally known as the "Bucktail Regiment "

June 21st, with the Fifth, Colonel Simmons, and Barr's Battery, the Forty-second was ordered to the support of Colonel Wallace, at Cumberland, Md , but before reaching that place Colonel Wallace, in accordance with orders, had moved to Martinsburg

July 12th, Lieutenant-Colonel Kane, with a scouting party of sixty men, crossed into Virginia, and at New Creek village were surrounded by McDonald's cavalry A stubborn engagement took place, in which the Confederates were worsted Colonel Biddle, with his command, moved to the relief of Kane, and dispatched the latter with two hundred men to follow the enemy He came upon them at Ridgeville, nine miles from New Creek, and after a skirmish, took possession Colonel Biddle arrived, and the next morning the force fell back to New Creek and Piedmont, which position they held until July 27th, when ordered to Harrisburg, where they were reviewed by Governor Curtin August 1st On the 6th of August they were ordered to report to General Banks, at Harper's Ferry October 1st the command moved to Tennallytown and joined the Reserves December 12th, Colonel Biddle resigned to go to Congress, having been elected from Philadelphia

December 20th, the Forty-second, under Lieutenant-Colonel Kane, marched with Orr's Brigade to Dranesville, where the enemy was in force It was here that Colonel Kane was shot in the face, the ball crashing through the roof of his mouth, inflicting a painful wound Bandaging his face, he continued to advance with his men and amid the smoke of the contest, fought with Spartan determination

On the 10th of March, 1862, the Bucktails moved to Alexandria The Reserves were then assigned to the First Corps, and the Bucktails ordered to Falmouth The middle of May found them within six miles of Hanover Court-house It was at this time that Colonel Kane, with four companies, was ordered to join Fremont In the pursuit of Jackson up the Shenandoah valley, the Bucktails were in the extreme advance Colonel Kane with his scouts—one hundred men—had a stubborn fight with General Ashby at Harrisonburg; the latter had with him Stuart's brigade Bravely the "Bucktails" held their ground, waiting reinforcements, but in this they were disappointed In the fight Colonel Kane was wounded and taken prisoner Captain Taylor, admiring the brave commander, dashed through the fire and smoke to rescue him, and was also captured The Confederates were so strongly impressed by such an exhibition of self-sacrifice and bravery, that they offered to parole him, but he and Colonel Kane refused. The loss of the "Bucktails" in killed, wounded, and prisoners, was fifty-two—half the number engaged.

The other six companies—four hundred strong—went into camp at Dispatch Station June 13th they participated in a skirmish with Stuart's Cavalry at White House, the Federal base of supplies. June 27th they were ordered to Gaines's Mills, and participated in that memorable engagement, pronounced by military men as one of the most desperate conflicts of the first two years of the rebellion On the evening of the 28th they commenced to march through White Oak Swamp, and on the night of the 29th performed picket duty on the Richmond road leading to Charles City, and took part in the battle of Charles City Cross Roads fought June 30th

From the Peninsula the regiment proceeded to Warrenton and participated in the second battle of Bull Run

Returning to the four companies remaining with Fremont's Corps (now Sigel's), after the battle of Cross Keys, we find them engaged at Cedar Mountain On the 19th of August they encamped at Brandy Station, on the Orange and Alexandria railroad, where Lieutenant-Colonel Kane joined them, he having been held a prisoner of war since the fight at Harrisonburg August 22d they marched back to Catlett's Station Then occurred another of General J E B Stuart's wild rides for the purpose of capturing General Pope and his headquarters' train Colonel Kane with a few men, met some of Stuart's horsemen at Cedar Run bridge, and with a single volley drove them in confusion Moving into Maryland they took part in the battle of South Mountain September 14th, and the next day at 3 P M reached the battle field of Antietam In the two days the regiment lost in killed and wounded one hundred and ten officers and men The next fight was at Fredericksburg December 12th the Reserves crossed to the right bank of the Rappahannock

February 6, 1863, they were ordered to the defenses of Washington, and established camp at Fairfax, June 25th, were ordered to join

the Fifth Corps, then marching into Pennsylvania, and were participants in the battle of Gettysburg The remaining months of 1863 they were constantly on the skirmish line, and at the close of the campaign went into winter quarters at Bristow Station, where they remained until the last of April, 1864, April 29th, broke camp and reached Culpepper on the 30th, May 4th, crossed the Rapidan and took part in the battle of the Wilderness They distinguished themselves at Spottsylvania, at Mountain Run they made two assaults on the enemy's works, but they were unsuccessful May 11th occurred the assault by the entire army On the 12th the "Bucktails" were employed picking off Confederate artillery men

The last fight of the "Bucktails" was on the Mechanicsville road, May 30th, their term of enlistment expiring that day The regiment was mustered out at Harrisburg June 11, 1864

On the Fourth of July, 1866, the bunting which floated over the rafts in 1861, and which they had carried in their campaigns amid the blaze of artillery and the leaden storm of infantry, was borne in procession in Philadelphia by the veterans, and delivered to the governor of the State amid the cheers of assembled thousands

Company K of this regiment was recruited at Curwensville, with Edward A Irvin, captain

Field and Staff

Colonels —Thomas L Kane, May 12, 1861, mustered as private May 13, 1861, promoted to colonel June 12, 1861, resigned and elected lieutenant-colonel June 13 1861, wounded at Dranesville December 28, 1861, and at Harrisburg June 6, 1862, promoted to brigadier-general September 7, 1862, to brevet major-general March 13, 1865, resigned November 7, 1863

Chas J. Biddle, May 29, 1861, resigned February 1, 1862

Hugh W. McNeil, May 20, 1861; promoted from captain Company D January 22, 1862, killed at Antietam September 16, 1862

Charles F Taylor, May 28, 1861, promoted from captain Company H March 1, 1863; killed at Gettysburg July 2, 1863

Lieutenant-Colonel — Alanson E Niles, May 31, 1861, promoted from captain Company E to major March 1, 1863, to lieutenant-colonel May 15, 1863, resigned March 28, 1864

Majors —Roy Stone, May 29, 1861, promoted to major June 13, 1861, to colonel of 149th P V August 29, 1862

W R Hartshorn, May 29, 1861, promoted to adjutant February, 1862, to major May 22, 1863, mustered out with regiment June 11, 1864

Adjutants —John T. A. Jewett, May 29, 1861, promoted to captain Company D February 5, 1862

Roger Sherman, May 28, 1861, promoted from sergeant-major to adjutant May 23, 1862; resigned March 21, 1864

Quartermasters:—Henry D Patton, May 29, 1861; promoted to captain and A Q M. U. S. V December 1, 1862.

Lucius Truman, May 29, 1861, transferred to 190th P V May 31, 1864

Surgeons.—S. D Freeman, May 29, 1861, resigned October 1, 1862

John J Comfort, December 17, 1862, transferred to 190th P V May 31, 1864; brevet lieutenant-colonel March 13, 1865

Assistant Surgeons —W T Humphrey,

June 21, 1861, promoted to surgeon 149th P. V September 5, 1862

W B Jones, August 2, 1862, resigned November 1, 1862

Daniel O Crouch, December 1, 1862, resigned June 10, 1863

Lafayette Butler, September 30, 1863; transferred to 190th P. V. May 30, 1864

Chaplain —W. H D. Patton, August 3, 1861, resigned November 11, 1862

Sergeant-Major —Wm. Baker, August 15, 1862, transferred to 190th P. V May 31, 1864.

Quartermaster-Sergeant —Wm C Hunter, May 21, 1861, transferred to 190th P V May 31, 1864; veteran

Commissary-Sergeant —John Semon, May 29, 1861, promoted from corporal Company K January 1, 1863; mustered out with company June 11, 1864

Hospital Stewards —R Fenton Ward, May 29, 1861; promoted to second lieutenant Company I July 1, 1862

Jeremiah J Starr, May 28, 1861, transferred to 190th P. V. May 31, 1864; veteran

Principal Musician —Henry Zundel, May 29, 1861, promoted from private to company F September, 1863; mustered out with company June 11, 1864

COMPANY K

Recruited in Curwensville, Clearfield County

Captains —Edward A. Irvin, May 29, 1861; commissioned lieutenant-colonel September 10, 1862, not mustered; discharged May 1, 1863, for wounds received in action

James M. Welch, May 29, 1861, promoted from second lieutenant March 21, 1863, transferred to V R C September 12, 1863.

First Lieutenants.—W. R Hartshorn, May

29, 1861, promoted to adjutant February, 1862

John P. Bard, May 29, 1861, promoted from sergeant to second lieutenant March 17, 1863, to brevet captain March 13, 1865, mustered out with company June 11, 1864

Second Lieutenants —Daniel C Dale, May 29, 1861, promoted from sergeant March 23, 1862, died February 17, 1863

John E Kratzer, May 29, 1861, promoted from sergeant February 17, 1863, transferred to V R C May 31, 1864

First Sergeants—Thos J Thompson, May 29, 1861, transferred to 190th P V May 31, 1864, veteran

Lewis Hoover, May 29, 1861, mustered out with company June 11, 1864

Daniel Blett, May 29, 1861, promoted to second lieutenant Company F July 1, 1863

John H Norris, May 29, 1861, transferred to 190th P V May 31, 1864, veteran

James F Ross, May 29, 1861, transferred to 109th P V. May 31, 1864, veteran

Wm G Addleman, May 29, 1861, discharged May 24, 1864, for wounds received in action, date unknown

James G Hill, May 29, 1861, discharged on surgeon's certificate May 8, 1862

Corporals —Edmund M. Curry, May 29, 1861, mustered out with company June 11, 1864

Wm F Wilson, May 29, 1861, mustered out with company June 11, 1864

Robert G McCracken, May 29, 1861, mustered out with company June 11, 1864

Alex Robertson, May 29, 1861, mustered out with company June 11, 1864

David M Glenn, May 29, 1861, mustered out with company June 11, 1864

Cortes Bloom, May 29, 1861, discharged November 28, 1862, for wounds received in action, date unknown

Abraham Carson, May 29, 1861, discharged March 6, 1863, for wounds received in action, date unknown

Samuel Reed, May 29, 1861, discharged April 23, 1863, for wounds received in action, date unknown

Amos Swift, July 31, 1861, transferred to 190th P V. May 31, 1864, veteran

John Lemon, May 29, 1861, promoted to sergeant January 1, 1863

John H Wilson, May 29, 1861, died December 9, 1861

Privates —John M Addleman, October 3, 1861, transferred to 190th P V May 31, 1864

Isaiah Bloom, May 29, 1861, mustered out with company June 11, 1864

Enos Bloom, May 29, 1861, mustered out with company June 11, 1864

Zachariah Bailey, May 29, 1861, mustered out with company June 11, 1864

Richard J Bard, May 29, 1861, discharged on surgeon's certificate November 20, 1861

James L Barr, March 21, 1862, discharged on surgeon's certificate December 3, 1862

John F Barnes, July 1, 1861, transferred to 190th P V May 31, 1864, veteran

Arnold Bloom, October 3, 1861; transferred to 190th P V May 31, 1864

James C Billis, May 28, 1861; transferred to Company H, November 1, 1861

John B Brink, February 29, 1864, transferred to 190th P V. May 31, 1864

Joseph P Broomall, October 3, 1861, killed at South Mountain September 14, 1862

Andrew J Cupples, May 29, 1861, wounded at Wilderness May 7, 1864; absent at muster out

Henry Cogley, May 31, 1861, mustered out with company June 11, 1864

John H Coulter, May 29, 1861, mustered out with company June 11, 1864

Thos Conklin, May 29, 1861, mustered out with company June 11, 1864

Chas M Clark, May 29, 1861, discharged on surgeon's certificate August 10, 1861

Arthur Conner, May 29, 1861, discharged on surgeon's certificate November 1, 1862

D R P Chatham, May 29, 1861, transferred to U S Sig Corps August 29, 1862

Jacob Connelly, February 29, 1864, transferred to 190th P V May 31, 1864

Wm S Cummings, May 29, 1861, killed at Antietam September 17, 1862

Frank Chase, July 1, 1861, deserted April 13, 1862

Mamming S Dunn, May 29, 1861, mustered out with company June 11, 1864

G P Dougham, October 3, 1861, discharged on surgeon's certificate December 11, 1862

Wm G Denick, March 28, 1864, transferred to 190th P V May 31, 1864

Levi Ennis, May 29, 1861, mustered out with company June 11, 1864

James Flanigan, July 31, 1861, discharged on surgeon's certificate November 21, 1861

Frank A Fleming, October 3, 1861, discharged on surgeon's certificate, date unknown

Isaac Fruze, May 29, 1861, discharged on surgeon's certificate May 30, 1863

James Frantz, October 3, 1861, discharged on surgeon's certificate March 10, 1863

Robt R Fleming, February 29, 1864, transferred to 190th P V May 31, 1864

Adam Fogle, February 9, 1864, transferred to 190th P V May 31, 1864

A Harrison Frantz, May 29, 1861, captured, died at Belle Isle, Va, July 15, 1862

Martin F Frantz, October 3, 1861, deserted December 1, 1862

James Glenn, November 18, 1861, wounded in action, date unknown, discharged on surgeon's certificate May 16, 1862

Charles M Goff, March 28, 1864, transferred to 190th P V May 31, 1864

Samuel Gunsalus, March 28, 1864, transferred to 190th P. V. May 31, 1864

Burton Granger, May 29, 1861, died October 2, 1862, of wounds received in action

Ellis J Hall, May 29, 1861, mustered out with company June 11, 1864

Lorenzo D Hile, May 29, 1861, mustered out with company June 11, 1864

John Henry, October 3, 1861, transferred to 190th P V May 31, 1864, veteran

John W Haslet, May 29, 1861; transferred to 190th P V May 31, 1864, veteran

Henry J Hall, July 31, 1861, transferred to 109th P V May 31, 1864, veteran

Joseph K Henry, May 29, 1861, discharged on surgeon's certificate July 20, 1861.

C Hockenburg, October 3, 1861; discharged on surgeon's certificate April 19, 1862

Thomas Homitter, May 29, 1861, discharged on surgeon's certificate June 26, 1862

William Hosford, July 1, 1861, discharged on surgeon's certificate December 1, 1862

Thos Humphrey, October 3, 1861; wounded in action, date unknown, discharged on surgeon's certificate December 1, 1862

W M Humphrey, July 1, 1861, discharged on surgeon's certificate April 20, 1863.

Edward Halcomb, May 29, 1861; transferred to Company D, October 12, 1861

James Henry, May 29, 1861, killed at Bull Run August 29, 1862

Charles Hall, July 31, 1861, killed at Antietam September 17, 1862

William Hinnigh, May 29, 1861, killed in action May 7, 1864

Austin Irvin, July 1, 1861, died March 6, 1863

Peter Jaggers, July 31, 1861, transferred to Company D, November 1, 1861

Samuel Kingston, July 31, 1861, discharged January 20, 1862, for wounds received in action, date unknown

John Kratzer, May 29, 1861, killed at Bull Run August 30, 1862

George W Knapp, July 1, 1861, died September 23, 1862, on board transport from Richmond

Frost Littlefield, May 29, 1861, mustered out with company June 11, 1864

Cyrus B Lower, October 27, 1863, transferred to 190th P V May 31, 1864

Ephraim Morrow, May 29, 1861, transferred to Signal Corps August, 1861

Isaiah McDonald, May 29, 1861, mustered out with company June 11, 1864

Peter C McKee, May 29, 1861, mustered out with company June 11, 1864

Charles R McCrum, May 29, 1861, discharged on surgeon's certificate April 11, 1862

Geo W McDonald, May 29, 1861, transferred to 190th P V May 31, 1864, veteran

Alexander McDonald, October 3, 1861, transferred to 190th P V. May 31, 1864, veteran

John Moyer, May 29, 1861, discharged on surgeon's certificate January 1, 1862

Casper P Mason, May 29, 1861, discharged on surgeon's certificate April 10, 1863

Samuel Mortimer, May 29, 1861, died September 10, 1863, from wounds received in action, date unknown

Hiram McClenahan May 29, 1861, transferred to 44th P V November 1, 1861

Francis C Morrow, July 1, 1861, transferred to 190th P V May 31, 1864

Nath A McCloskey, May 29, 1861, died November 28, 1861

And'n J Montonz, May 29, 1861, died May, 1864, of wounds received in action

David McCullough, May 29, 1861, deserted December 8, 1862

George O'Leary, July 1, 1861, discharged on surgeon's certificate November 20, 1861

Peter Piper, May 29, 1861, discharged on surgeon's certificate July 30, 1862

Robert B Pettingill, May 28, 1861, transferred to Company H, October 12, 1861

John Rish, May 29, 1861, died June 11, 1864, of wound received at Bethesda Church May 30, 1864, buried in National Cemetery, Arlington

Thomas Riley, May 29, 1861, killed at South Mountain September 14, 1862

Reuben Rex, May 29, 1861, discharged on surgeon's certificate June 11, 1862

Robert W Ross, October 3, 1861, died January 7, 1863, of wounds received in action

Edward D Stock, May 29, 1861, mustered out with company June 11, 1864

Joseph G Spencer, May 29, 1861, discharged on surgeon's certificate September 22, 1861

James Spence, October 3, 1861, discharged on surgeon's certificate September 1, 1862

Abel Sonders, July 21, 1863; discharged on surgeon's certificate November 19, 1862

Joseph Shirk, May 29, 1861, discharged on surgeon's certificate December 22, 1862

Philander Smith, May 29, 1861, discharged on surgeon's certificate, date unknown

George B Scott, May 29, 1861, discharged February 9, 1863, for wounds received in action, date unknown

Daniel Shaver, May 29, 1861, discharged April 20, 1863, for wounds received in action, date unknown

Peter Spargo, May 29, 1861, transferred to United States Signal Corps August 23, 1863

Jesse E Shaver, March 28, 1864, transferred to 190th P V. May 31, 1864

Porter Smith, May 29, 1861; killed at Fredericksburg December 13, 1862

Wm H Spence, May 29, 1861; deserted August 7, 1861

Dwight Seaman, May 29, 1861, deserted, date unknown

George W Taylor, May 29, 1861, discharged May 25, 1863, for wounds received in action, date unknown

Daniel F. Williams, May 29, 1861; discharged on surgeon's certificate December 22, 1862

Joseph Williams, October 3, 1861, transferred to 190th P. V May 31, 1864, veteran

James M Williams, February 27, 1864, died May, 1864, of wounds received in action

THE FIFTY-FIRST REGIMENT

The portion of this regiment that was recruited in Clearfield county was exceedingly small, only comprising a contingent of sixteen men, enlisted by Peter A Gaulin, who afterwards was promoted to captain of Company G A major portion of these were enlisted in October, 1861, for the regular three years' service, but some slight accessions were made in 1864

The greater portion of the regiment was raised in the counties of Montgomery, Union, Snyder, Centre, and Northampton. The field officers were John F. Hartranft, colonel; Thomas S Bell, lieutenant-colonel; Edwin Schall, major.

Those of the regiment from Clearfield county were recruited mainly from the northern part. The muster-roll of that part of Company G shows the name, rank, date of muster, and disposition of each man

Captain —Peter A Gaulin, October 17, 1861; promoted from second to first lieutenant February 12, 1862, to captain January 11, 1863, resigned March 16, 1864.

First Sergeant —Wm. Heichel, October 17, 1861; promoted from sergeant to first sergeant February 13, 1865; mustered out with company July 27, 1865

Sergeants —George Dumont, October 17, 1861, promoted from corporal to sergeant February 13, 1865; mustered out with company, veteran

Lewis Cartuyvel, October 17, 1861; promoted to quartermaster-sergeant March 9, 1865, veteran

Corporals —Serdon Rolley, February 28, 1864; mustered out with company July 27, 1865

Charles Heichel, February 29, 1864; promoted to corporal April 6, 1865; mustered out July 27, 1865

Wm Maurer, October 17, 1861; mustered out October 16, 1864—expiration of term

Privates —Philip Cayot, October 17, 1861; absent, sick, when mustered out; veteran

Cornelius Conway, October 17, 1861, discharged on surgeon's certificate, date unknown

Huston Heickel, October 17, 1861; transferred to Veteran Reserve Corps, date unknown

Wm Mackey, October 17, 1861, died in Kentucky, date unknown

Jno McGonegal, September 27, 1864, drafted, discharged by general order June 1, 1865

August Rolley, October 17, 1861, captured, died at Andersonville, Ga, May 29, 1864, grave 1454

Nicholas Rolley, October 17, 1861, discharged on surgeon's certificate June 6, 1865, veteran

Christian Simons, October 17, 1861, discharged on surgeon's certificate, date unknown

Wallis Wiggins, October 17, 1861, killed at Antietam September 17, 1862

FIFTY-NINTH REGIMENT—SECOND CAVALRY

The proportion of this regiment that was recruited in Clearfield county was exceedingly small, less than fifty men, and they were attached to Company F These men were recruited in the eastern part of the county by Thomas G Snyder, who was made first lieutenant, and who died of wounds received at Occoquan, Va, on December 28, 1862 The regiment was raised in the fall of 1861, in various sections of the State, and rendezvoused at Camp Patterson, six miles from Philadelphia The field officers were as follows· Richard Price Butler, colonel, Joseph P Brinton, lieutenant-colonel, Charles F Taggard and J Archambault, majors

At Baltimore the regiment was reviewed by General Dix At Cloud's Mills it was assigned to the brigade commanded by General Cooke, First Reserve Army Crops, General Sturgis, but in August was transferred to General Buford's brigade Its first engagement took place near Culpepper, and afterwards participated in the Bull Run fight, where it lost heavily On September 10, Buford was appointed to McClellan's staff, and Colonel Price succeeded to the command of the brigade On October 1 the regiment was transferred to General Bayard's command, and assigned to the First Brigade They were constantly scouting until late in December, when. on the 28th they fell into an ambuscade at Occoquan and suffered a great loss Lieutenant Thomas G Snyder was mortally wounded and captured here. He died in the enemy's hands In killed, wounded and missing it lost over one hundred men The regiment wintered at Accotink

In April, 1863, at Fairfax Court-house, it was assigned to the Second Brigade of General Stahel's Division In June it participated in the Gettysburg campaign, conducted twenty-five hundred prisoners to Westminster, and on the 7th rejoined the army at Middletown It started in pursuit of Lee's army and went as far as Warrenton, and afterwards did guard duty at Meade's headquarters It was then assigned to the Second Brigade Its subsequent history is told by the engagement at Beverly's Ford, on the heights around Rappahannock Station, the raid on Luray, after which it again went into winter quarters The next year it moved with the Army of the Potomac and went with Sheridan on his memorable raid, and rejoined the army on the 25th In Sheridan's second raid it also engaged Its subsequent career was identified with the Army of the Potomac, at Wyatt's Farm, Boydton Plank Road, McDowell's Hill, and Five Forks, and was present at Lee's surrender at Appomattox The regiment was mustered out of service at Cloud's Mills, July 13, 1865, after which "the boys" returned home, all but the dead, whose bones are bleaching from the Potomac to the Blackwater

EIGHTY-FOURTH PENNSYLVANIA VOLUNTEER INFANTRY

This regiment was organized under a special order from the war department, issued by General Cameron, then secretary of war, to General J Y James, of Warren county, William G Murray, of Blair county, as colonel, Thomas C McDowell, of Dauphin county, as lieutenant-colonel, Walter Barrett, of Clearfield county, as major, Thomas H Craig, of Blair county, as adjutant, Dr G F Hoop, of Clearfield county, as surgeon, C A W Redlick, of Allegheny county, as assistant surgeon, Alexander McLeod, of Clearfield, as chaplain, and J Miles Kephart, of Centre county, as quartermaster

The point of rendezvous was Camp Crossman, three miles from Huntingdon Late in the fall of 1861 the regiment moved to Camp Curtis, at Harrisburg In December of the same year the regiment was ordered to Hancock, Md, to protect that point from a threatened invasion by the command of General Jackson There the regiment received their arms in the afternoon, and the next morning, before daylight, was ordered to march to the town of Bath to assist in bringing away a battery of artillery Before they reached that point they were informed of the near approach of Jackson's army They succeeded in securing the artillery, but one-half of the regiment was compelled to wade the Potomac River to escape capture

From there, under command of General Lander, they marched to Cumberland, Md,

from whence, in a few days, they went into camp at a point on the Paw Paw River, where General Lander formed his division They remained at this point until the early spring of 1862 General Lander having died during the winter, General James Shields was appointed to command

As soon as the season permitted, the camp was broken up and the division moved to Martinsburg, Va At this time Clearfield county was represented by Company G, captain, Merrick Howsler, of Cameron county, Company H, captain, William M Behan, Company I, captain, Joseph L Kirby, first lieutenant, Clarence L Barrett, second lieutenant, John B Ferguson, Company K, captain, Matthew Ogden, and second lieutenant, John S Jury, also from Clearfield county were Fred Barrett and Richard H Shaw, hospital stewards At the point last above referred to, the Eighty-fourth was brigaded with the One Hundred and Tenth Pennsylvania, the Fourteenth Indiana, and the Thirteenth Indiana Upon the arrival of the division in Martinsburg, immediate preparation was made to attack General Jackson at Winchester, Va In less than a week the whole force was marching to that point. When the division arrived at Winchester, it was found that Jackson had retired down the Shenandoah valley.

Early on the morning of March 22 the pickets were driven in, and by ten o'clock the battle of Kernstown was commanded It raged fiercely until in the afternoon Here Colonel Murray was killed, evidently by a sharpshooter The figure "84" in his cap was driven into his brain by the force of the bullet; also Captain Patrick Gallagher, of Company E, and Lieutenant Charles Reem, of Company A Nearly one-half of the regiment were killed or wounded The regiment was made the subject of a special complimentary order from the commanding general for gallantry upon this occasion

Following under the various commanders, from the second battle of Bull Run, it participated in all the battles until it was finally merged, January 13, 1865, with the Fifty-seventh Pennsylvania Infantry, and ceased to hold its place in the Pennsylvania line

Field and Staff

Colonels —William G Murray, December 23, 1861, killed at Winchester, March 23, 1862

Samuel M Bowman, June 21, 1862, promoted to brevet brigadier-general March 13, 1865, discharged May 15, 1865

Lieutenant-Colonels —T C McDowell, December 18, 1861, resigned July, 1862

Walter Barrett, December 23, 1861, promoted from major, resigned September 10, 1862

Thomas H Craig, December 24, 1861, promoted from adjutant to major July 31, 1862, to lieutenant-colonel October 1, 1862, resigned December 21, 1862

Milton Opp, October 1, 1861, promoted from captain Company F to major October 1, 1862, to lieutenant-colonel December 23, 1862, died May 9 of wounds received at Wilderness, Va, May 6, 1864

George Zinn, October 1, 1861, promoted from captain Company D to major December 23, 1862, to lieutenant-colonel August 1, 1864, wounded in action October 1, 1864, promoted to colonel 57th P V March 19, 1865

Adjutants —Joseph J Vaughan, June 21, 1862, promoted to adjutant June 21, 1863, discharged January 17, 1865

Edmund Mather, September 21, 1861, promoted from first lieutenant Company B, January 18, 1863; transferred to V R C November 26, 1863, discharged December 16, 1863

Charles W Forrester, October 1, 1862, promoted from second lieutenant Company F, January 1, 1864, to captain Company G, 57th P V, January 13, 1865

Quartermaster —J Miles Kephart, December 20, 1861, mustered out December 31, 1864—expiration of term

Surgeons —Gibboney F Hoop, December 18, 1861, resigned September 12, 1863

John S Waggoner, February 2, 1863, wounded at Chancellorsville, Va, May 3, 1863, promoted from assistant surgeon October 24, 1863, resigned April 15, 1864

S B Sturdevant, August 19, 1864, mustered out January 13, 1865

John P Norman, June 1, 1863, promoted from assistant surgeon April 25, 1864, resigned July 3, 1864

Assistant Surgeons —C A W Redlick, December 18, 1861, promoted to surgeon 136th P V September 2, 1862

G W Thompson, August 1, 1862, resigned August 31, 1862

James D McClure, September 13, 1862, promoted to surgeon 147th P V May 14, 1863

William Jack, June 7, 1864, transferred to 57th P V January 13, 1865

Chaplains —Alexander McLeod, December 28, 1861, discharged October 6, 1862

John Thomas, February 27, 1864, discharged January 13, 1865

Sergeant-Majors —William M Gwinn, December 5, 1861, promoted to second lieutenant Company C, April 23, 1862

John W Kissel, December 9, 1861, promoted from private Company F, to second lieutenant Company D, December 23, 1862

John S Jury, 1861, promoted to second lieutenant Company K, October 3, 1864

Quartermaster - Sergeants. — Harvey S Wells, October 24, 1861, promoted to first lieutenant company F, February 19, 1864

Gabriel H Ramey, December 23, 1861, promoted from private Company F, discharged December 13, 1864—expiration of term

Commissary-Sergeant —J Russell Wingate, December 24, 1861, promoted from private Company D to second lieutenant Company G, October 15, 1862

Principal Musicians —Foster Wighennan, December 24, 1861, promoted from private Company D, not accounted for; veteran

Thaddeus Albert, December 5, 1861, promoted from private Company F, not accounted for

Hospital Stewards —Frederick Barrett, December 24, 1861, promoted from private Company D

Richard H Shaw, 1861, promoted from private Company K

COMPANY II

Recruited in Clearfield and Dauphin Counties

Captains —Wm Bahan, September 24, 1862, discharged June 8, 1863

Clarence G Jackson, August 2, 1862, promoted from second to first lieutenant January 18, 1863, to captain July 1, 1863; wounded and captured at Chancellorsville, Va, May 3, 1863, transferred to Company H, 57th P V January 13, 1865.

First Lieutenants —Alexander R Nininger, August 6, 1862, promoted from second lieutenant, discharged January 17, 1863

James S Mitchell, March 17, 1862; promoted from first sergeant to second lieutenant January 18, 1863, to first lieutenant July 1, 1863, transferred to Company H, 57th P V January 13, 1865

Second Lieutenant —William A Wilson, May 28, 1862, wounded at Chancellorsville, Va, May 3, 1863, promoted from private July 1, 1863, transferred to Company H, 57th P V January 13, 1865

Sergeants —Arthur C Gilbert, June 5, 1862, promoted to first lieutenant Company I, October 1, 1862

William F Fox, June 5, 1862; wounded at Chancellorsville, Va, May 3, 1863; not accounted for

Andrew D Seely, August 6, 1862, transferred to Company H, 57th P V. January 13, 1865

Privates —James Burk, June 5, 1862, died October 24, 1864, buried in National Cemetery, Arlington, Va

James Bassett, June 5, 1862, transferred to Company H, 57th P V January 13, 1865

C Frank Barton, August 6, 1862, captured at Chancellorsville, Va, May 3, 1863.

William Beach, September 13, 1862; not accounted for

James J. Briner, September 23, 1862, not accounted for.

David M Bryan, September 15, 1862, not accounted for

Charles E Crawford, June 5, 1862, transferred to Company H, 57th P V, January 13, 1865

James Curry, July 7, 1862, not accounted for

Martin Cosgrove, July 18, 1862; not accounted for.

John Campbell, July 31, 1862; captured at

Chancellorsville, Va , May 3, 1863, transferred to Company H, 57th P V January 13, 1865

Frank Cook, August 13, 1862, not accounted for

James Chamberlain, August 25, 1862, transferred to Company H, 57th P V, January 13, 1865

Isaac Chase, September 13, 1862, not accounted for

Frederick Conklin, September 11, 1862, captured, died at Salisbury, N C, November 8, 1864

James Dunlap, July 5, 1862, not accounted for

Washington Dibert, May 20, 1864, transferred to Company H, 57th P V, January 13, 1865

Wm L Dewalt, June 5, 1862, captured at Chancellorsville, Va , May 3, 1863

Felix Despies', July 7, 1862, not accounted for

Wm J Duryea, August 8, 1862, transferred to Company H, 57th P V , January 13, 1865

Thomas Dailey, August 11, 1862, transferred to Company H, 57th P V , January 13, 1865

Nicholas Eisman, July 31, 1862, transferred to Company H, 57th P V , January 13, 1865

David Estep, September 23, 1862, transferred to Company E

Uriah M Edgar, September 23, 1863, not accounted for

Frederick Fink, July 31, 1862, not accounted for

Charles H Frees, August 25, 1862, wounded and captured at Chancellorsville, Va , May 3, 1863

Samuel S Fowler, August 25, 1862, not accounted for

Nelson Green, June 5, 1862, not accounted for

Joseph Glasgow, June 5, 1862, not accounted for

John Garrigan, June 5, 1862, not accounted for

Joseph Griffith, July 7, 1862, transferred to Company H, 57th P V , January 13, 1865

Willett C Gearhart, August 6, 1862, not accounted for

Edward Gillnett, September 13, 1862, not accounted for

Joseph L Hughes, July 7, 1862, not accounted for

Benj F Hughes, July 7, 1862, not accounted for

John Harrington, August 6, 1862, wounded and captured at Chancellorsville, Va , May 3, 1863

George Hiney, killed at Chancellorsville, Va , May 3, 1863

James M Jordon, September 10, 1862, not accounted for

Salisbury H James, not accounted for

George A Kline, August 6, 1862, captured at Chancellorsville, Va , May 3, 1863, transferred to Company H, 57th P V , January 13, 1865

Frank Lewis, June 5, 1862, transferred to Company H, 57th P V , January 13, 1865

Joseph Lindemuth, June 5, 1862, not accounted for

James M Lewis, May 17, 1862, transferred to Company K

Thomas B Lou, August 21, 1862, transferred to V R C , died at Washington, D C , March 8, 1864

William H Lane, September 5, 1862;

transferred to Company H, 57th P V, January 13, 1865

Francis A Leas, September 13, 1862, not accounted for

George Maguire, June 5, 1862, not accounted for

Thomas E Merchant, June 25, 1862, transferred to Company F

Oscar B Millard, August 6, 1862, not accounted for

Thomas B Miller, August 21, 1862, not accounted for

Henry Manes, September 1, 1862, captured at Chancellorsville, Va, May 3, 1863, transferred to company H, 57th P V, January 13, 1865

Wm H McE   , June 5, 1862, not accounted for

James McGowan, August 5, 1862, not accounted for

Garrett Nolan, June 5, 1862, not accounted for

Jacob Nevil, October 3, 1862, transferred to company H, 57th P V, January 13, 1865

Daniel Oberly, September 17, 1862 transferred to company I, 57th P V, January 13, 1865

Levi Ostrander, September 30, 1862, transferred to company I, 57th P V, January 13, 1865

Herman Perry, June 5, 1862, not accounted for

John Pea, August 6, 1862; transferred to company H, 57th P V, January 13, 1865

Augustus B Pearce, September 13. 1862, not accounted for

Benjamin F Peterman, September 17, 1862, not accounted for

Daniel Quick, August 6, 1862, transferred to company H, 57th P V, January 13, 1865

George Rehr, June 5, 1862, not accounted for

William H Ruch, August 6, 1862; transferred to company H, 57th P. V, January 13, 1865

James J Ruch, August 6, 1862, transferred to company H, 57th P V, January 13, 1865

Allen B Reams, August 30, 1862, transferred to company K, 57th P V, January 13, 1865

William H Shaffer, June 5, 1862, not accounted for.

John Schneiber, July 7, 1862, transferred to V R C, September 26, 1863, discharged July 6, 1865

John Stifer, August 6, 1862, not accounted for

Jacob Stoner, September 5, 1862; not accounted for

Joshua P Sherman, August 6, 1862; not accounted for

Alonzo Solt, August 21, 1862; not accounted for

Andrew J. Sollery, September 12, 1862; transferred to company H, 57th P V, January 13. 1865

George Thompson, June 5, 1862, not accounted for

Timothy Torsey, July 18, 1862, not accounted for

Thomas Wright, June 5, 1862, not accounted for

Amos Whitnight, August 6, 1862; not accounted for

Abner Welsh, August 6, 1862; wounded at Chancellorsville, Va, May 3, 1863, not accounted for

Joseph P. Warren, August 21, 1862; not accounted for

Daniel Wilhelm. August 11, 1862, not accounted for

William Young, August 5, 1862, not accounted for

Rudolph L Young, August 30, 1862, transferred to company K, 57th P V. January 13, 1865

COMPANY I

Recruited in Clearfield and Blair Counties

Captains—Joseph L Curby, September 25, 1861, resigned September 10, 1862

John H Comfort, November 17, 1862, resigned November 28, 1862

Arthur C Gilbert, June 5, 1862, promoted from sergeant company H, to first lieutenant October 1, 1862, to captain, resigned April 15, 1863

John R Ross, November 15, 1862, promoted from first lieutenant May 1, 1863, wounded at Chancellorsville, Va, May 3, 1863, promoted to brevet major April 9, 1865, transferred to company I, 57th P V, January 13, 1865

First Lieutenants—Isaac Hooper, September 16, 1861, resigned February 14, 1862

Clarence L Barett, February 1, 1862, promoted from second lieutenant February 15, 1862, resigned August 2, 1862

John B Ferguson, 1861, promoted from first sergeant to second lieutenant February 15, 1862, to first lieutenant, resigned November 15, 1862

George S Good November 17, 1862, promoted from second lieutenant May 1, 1863, wounded and captured at Chancellorsville, Va, May 3, 1863, captured at Mine Run November 30, 1863, discharged December 31, 1864

Second Lieutenants—John W Paulley,

September 25, 1861, resigned January 31, 1862

Alban H Nixon, October 24, 1861, promoted from sergeant to second lieutenant March 3, 1862, to first lieutenant company K, January 18, 1863

First Sergeant—Hiram F Willis September 20, 1862, promoted to first sergeant, commissioned second lieutenant May 1, 1863, not mustered, wounded at Chancellorsville, Va, May 3, 1863, discharged to accept commission in V R C

Sergeants—Thomas Gouldsberry, 1861, transferred to company K, 1862

A G Jamison, 1861, not accounted for

William Clouser, 1861, not accounted for

William W Alsbach, 1861, transferred to company K, 1862

Corporals—Johnson Cassidy, 1861, transferred to company K, 1862

James Gorman, 1861, transferred to company K, 1862

Ellis Hart, 1861, discharged, date unknown

Robert Jamison, 1861, transferred to company K, 1862

Isaac Manes, 1861, transferred to company K, 1862

Alexander Reed, 1861, transferred to company K, 1862

Joseph Repetto, 1861, not accounted for

Charles White, 1861, transferred to company K, 1862

Musician—Simon C Whitmer, 1861, not accounted for

Privates—Thomas Adams 1861, transferred to company K, 1862

Howard D Avery, September 30, 1862, transferred to company I, 57th P V, January 13, 1865

Joseph Apt, 1861, transferred to company K, 1862.

John Brady, 1861, discharged May 10, 1862

Henry C Bowers, 1861, transferred to company K, 1862

Joseph Bennett, 1861; not accounted for

Houser Baltzer, 1861, discharged, date unknown

Jacob N Brigham, September 30, 1862; captured at Chancellorsville, Va, May 5, 1863, died August 2, 1864; buried at Cyprus Hill Cemetery, L I

Daniel L Brown, 1861, died at Annapolis, Md, June 15, of wounds received at Chancellorsville, Va, May 3, 1863

Eliphalet W Bruch, 1861, transferred to company I, 57th P V, January 13, 1865

Truman Brigham, 1861, not accounted for

William Bone, October 29, 1862, transferred to company I, 57th P V, January 13, 1865

Demetrius Barnhart, November 4, 1862; transferred to company I, 57th P V, January 13, 1865

Jacob Bastain, September 27, 1862; transferred to company B

James Burk, September 29, 1862, not accounted for

Samuel H Boyer, October 6, 1862; not accounted for

Daniel C Boyer, October 6, 1862, died June 12, 1864, buried in National Cemetery, Arlington, Va

Nelson Bliss, 1861, transferred to company K, 1862   •

Newton Bailey, 1861, transferred to company K, 1862

Samuel Bailey, 1861, transferred to company K, 1862

William Booze, 1861, transferred to company K, 1862

Gemmil Baker, 1861, transferred to company K, 1862

Anson N Bidwell, March 31, 1864; transferred to company I, 57th P. V, January 13, 1865

Walter Barrett, March 31, 1864, not accounted for

John B Campbell, 1861, transferred to company K, 1862

Samuel Curry, 1861; discharged, date unknown

Geo W. Colmer, 1861, transferred to company K, 1862

John Cramer, 1861, not accounted for

John Cunningham, 1861; not accounted for.

Wayne Campbell, October 29, 1862, wounded at Chancellorsville, Va, May 3, 1863; transferred to company I, 57th P. V, January 13, 1865

Zartis Campbell, October 29, 1862, transferred to company I, 57th P. V, January 13, 1865

John Clements, November 6, 1862, not accounted for.

Valentine Culp, 1861, not accounted for.

Christopher Cassidy, 1861; transferred to company K, 1862

John J Charles, March 31, 1864; transferred to company I, 57th P V, January 13, 1865

John H Davis, 1861; discharged, date unknown

Elias Dexter, September 30, 1862, not accounted for

Judson Davy, September 30, 1862; transferred to company I, 57th P V, January 13, 1865

James A Davis, September 30, 1862, trans-

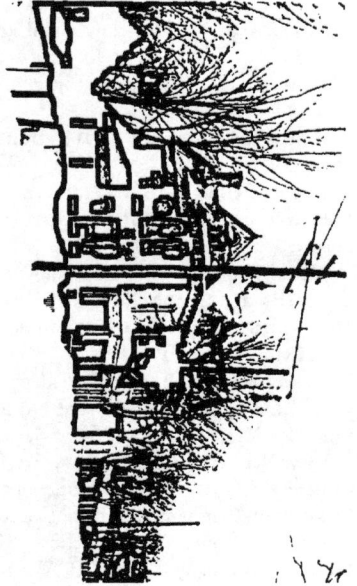

H S Knan Property

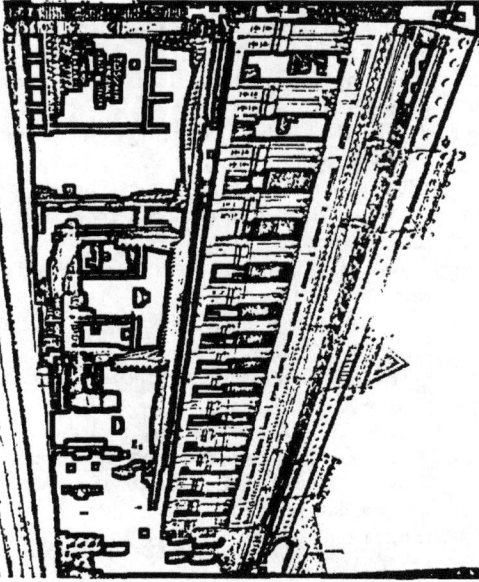

H S Knan Block, Dallas, Pa

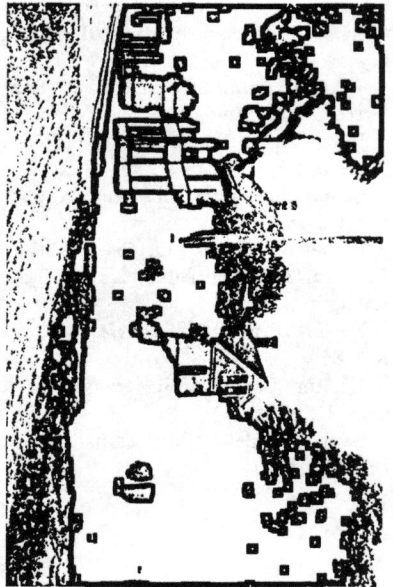

H S Knar Property

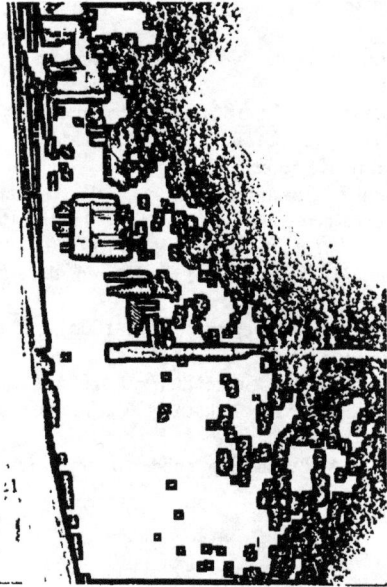

H S Knan Property

ferred to company I, 57th P V, January 13, 1865

Frank Duaenhaffer, November 4, 1862, captured at Chancellorsville, Va, May 3, 1863, transferred to company I, 57th P V, January 13, 1865

John Dash, 1861, deserted, date unknown

Daniel Elmore, October 25, 1862, not accounted for

John Evans, 1861, not accounted for

Henry Evans, 1861, deserted, date unknown

Alexander Funk, 1861, died, date unknown

Sidney Farley, 1861, not accounted for

John H Ferguson, 1861, wounded at Port Republic, June 9, 1862, transferred to company K, 1862

James H Ferguson, 1861, transferred to Company K, 1862

William Frampton, September 30, 1862, not accounted for

John W Frampton, September 30, 1862, not accounted for

Isaac Frampton, March 31, 1864, not accounted for

John Green, 1861, transferred to Company K, 1862

Abraham Glunt, 1861, died, date unknown

Joseph M Gavitt, September 30, 1862, not accounted for

John G Guthrie, November 4, 1862, not accounted for

Edward Gibson, September 15, 1862, not accounted for

Charles Gearhart, November 6, 1862, not accounted for

Theo J Garretson, 1861, transferred to Company K, 1862

Jacob Gilnett, 1861, transferred to Company K. 1862

John R Gaston, March 31, 1864, not accounted for

John Hoggencamp, September 30, 1862, not accounted for

William Hoffman, September 30, 1862, captured. died at Alexandria, Va, February 8, 1865, grave 2993

James Haas, October 6, 1862, transferred to company G, 57th P V, January 13, 1865

Jonathan Haas, September 15, 1862, transferred to company G, 57th P V, January 13, 1865

George W Harp, October 6, 1862, not accounted for

Samuel Hughes, 1861, not accounted for.

Peter S Hart, 1861, wounded on picket June 19, 1864. transferred to company K, 57th P V. January 13, 1865, veteran

George Hoffman, 1861, transferred to company K, 1862

William Hagerty, 1861, transferred to Company K, 1862

Uriah Haneigh, 1861, transferred to Company K, 1862

James Hepburn, 1861, transferred to Company K, 1862

Jno Heitzenrether, 1861, not accounted for

Robert Harbridge, 1861, transferred to Company K, 1862

Joel Hofford, 1861, transferred to Company K, 1862

James A Haines, 1861, not accounted for

Samuel Hare, 1861, transferred to company K, 1862

William A Hallowell, 1861, not accounted for

Ephraim Hanes, March 3, 1864, not accounted for

Patrick Hagerty, March 30, 1864, not accounted for

Samuel H Hulse, March 31, 1864, not accounted for

Samuel Johnson, 1861; transferred to company K, 1862

Chester T Jackson, September 30, 1862, not accounted for

James Jefferson, September 29, 1862, not accounted for

Jacob Kessler, September 30, 1862, captured at Chancellorsville, Va, May 3, 1863

Levi Kessler, September 30, 1862, transferred to company I, 57th P. V, January 13, 1865

Orlando Krigbaum, October 6, 1862, transferred to company G, 57th P V, January 13, 1865

William Kratzer, 1861, transferred to company K, 1862

Robert L Lydic, 1861, transferred to company K, 1862

Joseph L Lydic, 1861, transferred to company K, 1862

Justice Lukins, September 30, 1862, not accounted for

David Luke, September 30, 1862, not accounted for

George Lloyd, September 15, 1862, not accounted for

A B Lawrence, September 15, 1862, transferred to company B

H K Lawrence, September 15, 1862, transferred to company B

James M Lewis, May 17, 1862, transferred to company H

Ellis Manes, 1861; deserted, date unknown

Isaac Miller, 1861, deserted, date unknown

Orange J Michaels, 1861; transferred to company K, 1862

John Miles, 1861, discharged, date unknown

John Mark, 1861, transferred to company K, 1862

James Mosher, September 30, 1862; not accounted for.

George W Marks, September 30, 1862; transferred to V R. C, discharged July 5, 1865

Andrew J Mosher, September 30, 1862, wounded at Chancellorsville, Va, May 3, 1863, transferred to company I, 57th P. V, January 13, 1865

John L Markles, September 30, 1862; wounded at Chancellorsville, Va, May 3, 1863, not accounted for

John Mosher, September 30, 1862; not accounted for

John P Myers, September 30, 1862, wounded at Chancellorsville, Va, May 3, 1863, not accounted for.

Amos J Mitchell, September 30, 1862; not accounted for

Virgil B Mitchell, October 29, 1862; wounded at Chancellorsville, Va, May 3, 1863, not accounted for

Andrew J Marks, September 30, 1862, captured at Chancellorsville, Va, May 3, 1863; transferred to company I, 57th P V, January 13, 1865

Jacob S Miller, December 21, 1861, transferred to company K, 1862.

Dennis Maghar, March 30, 1864, not accounted for.

Daniel McGowan, September 30, 1862, not accounted for

John McAleer, 1861, not accounted for

F McCracken, 1861, not accounted for

Philip McCracken, 1861, transferred to company K, 1862

William McAfoose, 1861; transferred to company K, 1862

Edwin North, September 30, 1862, wounded at Chancellorsville, Va, May 3, 1863, transferred to company I, 57th P V, January 13, 1865

Samuel Olinger, 1861, died at Alexandria, Va, July 1862

William Oliver, September 30, 1862, not accounted for

Levi Ostrander, September 30, 1862, transferred to company I, 57th P V, January 13, 1865

George C Parsons, September 30, 1862, not accounted for

John Poudler, 1861, deserted, date unknown

Theodore Pardee, 1861, drowned at Hancock, Md, date unknown

Jackson Potter, 1861, died at Alexandria, Va, date unknown

Jacob Rup, 1861, transferred to company K, 1862

James Reed, 1861, not accounted for

Robert L Rodkey, 1861, transferred to company K 1862

George W Rogers, September 30, 1862; transferred to company K, 57th P V, January 13, 1865

Arthur Robbins, September 15, 1862, transferred to company B

Jacob Ramard, November 6, 1862, not accounted for

James Rue, March 31, 1864, transferred to company I, 57th P V, January 13, 1865

James G Robinson, March 31, 1864, transferred to company K, 57th P V, January 13, 1865

David L Sutliff, September 30, 1862, died August 1, 1864, buried in National Cemetery, Antietam, Md, section 26, lot D, grave 409

Joseph G Sutliff, September 30, 1862, died May 19, 1864, buried in National Cemetery, Arlington, Va

Jerome Skinner, September 30, 1862, not accounted for

Bradley Sherwood, September 30, 1862, transferred to company I, 57th P V, January 13, 1865

Jesse Scott, October 29, 1862, not accounted for

H E Schemerhorn, October 29, 1862, not accounted for

John Shister, September 15, 1862, not accounted for

Cyrus Stebbins, November 14, 1862, not accounted for

William Scott, September 15, 1862, not accounted for

John W Simonton, 1861, captured, died at Richmond, Va, March 27, 1864

Henry Sell, 1861, discharged, date unknown

Henry Stugart, 1861, transferred to company K, 1862

John B Shankle, 1861, transferred to Company K, 1862

D F Stanberger, 1861, deserted, date unknown

Robert Sayers, March 31, 1864, not accounted for

George Taylor, September 30, 1862, not accounted for.

Hamlet H Taylor, March 31, 1864, transferred to company H, 57th P V, January 13, 1865

Adam Ulrich, September 15, 1862, transferred to company B

John Varner, 1861, not accounted for

Thomas Wisner, 1861, not accounted for

Franklin Weaver, 1861, transferred to company K, 1862

John Woodward, 1861, not accounted for.

Samuel C White, September 30, 1862, not accounted for

Osmer White, September 30, 1862, not accounted for

James Wright, September 30, 1862, not accounted for

Samuel Williams, September 30, 1862, not accounted for

George W Welton, September 30, 1862, not accounted for

Moses Wood, September 30, 1862, transferred to company I, 57th P V, January 13, 1865

Henry D Wood, September 30, 1862, transferred to company I, 57th P V, January 13, 1865

Richard Williams, September 30, 1862, not accounted for

Abraham Whipple, September 15, 1862, not accounted for

And Wadsworth, September 27, 1862, not accounted for

COMPANY K

Recruited in Clearfield County

Captains —Matthew Ogden, September 13, 1861, resigned November 20, 1862

Jacob Peterman, November 20, 1862, killed at Chancellorsville, Va, May 3, 1863

Albert H Nixon, October 24, 1861, captured at Bull Run August, 1862, promoted from second lieutenant company I to first lieutenant January 18, 1863, to captain July 28, 1863, captured at Chancellorsville May 3, 1863, wounded at Mine Run November 27, 1863, and at Cold Harbor, Va, with loss of arm, June 1, 1864, promoted to brevet major and lieutenant-colonel March 13, 1865

First Lieutenants —Charles H Volk, September 23, 1861, resigned July 8, 1862

Luther B Sampson, October 3, 1861, promoted to sergeant October 23, 1861, to second lieutenant June 21, 1862; to first lieutenant May 1, 1863, to captain company F, September 3, 1864

Second Lieutenants —John S Jury, 1861, promoted from sergeant-major to second lieutenant October 3, 1864, to first lieutenant December 14, 1864, transferred to company K, 57th P V, January 13, 1865

John W Taylor, September 14, 1861, resigned June 21, 1862.

James B Davidson, December 5, 1861, promoted from first sergeant July 1, 1863, discharged April 30, 1864

James M Lewis, May 17, 1862, promoted to second lieutenant November 17, 1864, transferred to company I, 57th P V, January 13, 1865

First Sergeant —Isaac Manes, December 7, 1861, promoted from sergeant May 3, 1863, transferred to company K, 57th P V, January 13, 1865, veteran

Sergeants —Peter A Young, 1861, discharged November 24, 1862

Martin V Pearce, 1861, deserted January 14, 1862

Daniel Graham, 1861, wounded and captured at Port Republic, Va, June 9, 1862; captured at Chancellorsville, Va, May 3, 1863

George W Ogden, 1861, discharged February 7, 1863

Wm K Armagast, 1861, died November 13, 1862

Charles Hall, 1861, killed at Deep Bottom, Va, August 16, 1864

William W Alsbach, 1861; discharged February 7, 1863

Charles White, 1861, promoted from private, wounded and captured at Chancellorsville, Va, May 3, 1863

James H Ferguson, 1861, captured at Chancellorsville, Va, May 3, 1863

Robert H Jamison, December 5, 1861, promoted from private, captured at Chancellorsville, Va, May 3, 1863, transferred to company K, 57th P V, January 13, 1865, veteran

Corporals —William A Nelson, October 24, 1861, captured at Chancellorsville, Va, May 3, 1863, wounded October 18, 1864, transferred to company K, 57th P V, January 13, 1865, veteran

Richard J Conklin, 1861, deserted, date unknown

Simon Hamlin, 1861, died at Cumberland, Md, May 30, 1862

John B Miller, 1861, deserted February 7, 1862

Cornelius Wilson, 1861, died May 31, 1863

Joseph H Barger, December 5, 1861, captured at Chancellorsville, Va, May 3, 1863, wounded at Pleasant Hill June 1, 1864, transferred to company K, 57th P V, January 13, 1865, veteran

George S Kyler, 1861, discharged October 14, 1863

R J Shaffner, October 24, 1861, captured at Chancellorsville, Va, May 3, 1863, transferred to company K, 57th P V, January 13, 1865, veteran

Matthew O Tate, 1861, wounded and captured at Chancellorsville, Va, May 3, 1863

Wm B Hemphill, August 16, 1861, transferred to company K, 57th P V, January 13, 1865

Robert Harbridge, December 7, 1861, transferred to company K, 57th P V, January 13, 1865, veteran

Musicians —Frederick H Jordan, October 24, 1861, transferred to company K, 57th P V, January 13, 1865, veteran

William Taylor, October 24, 1861, discharged July 7, 1862

Privates —Robert Archy, 1861, discharged 1862

John W Antes, 1861, deserted, date unknown

Elijah Ashenfelter, 1861, died February 8, 1863

Perry Addleman, August 16, 1862, captured at Chancellorsville, Va, May 3, 1863, transferred to company K, 57th P V, January 13, 1865

Thomas Adams, 1861, died at Alexandria, Va, January 7, 1863, of wounds received at Port Republic June 9, 1863, grave 667

Joseph Apt, 1861, not accounted for

Victor L Abbott, April 7, 1864, wounded at Deep Bottom, Va, August 15, 1864, transferred to company K, 57th P V, January 13, 1865

Otto C Buck, 1861, died November 20, 1864, buried in National Cemetery, Arlington, Va

George Baughman, 1861, not accounted for

David Buck, 1861, discharged October 30, for wounds received at Bull Run, Va August 30, 1862

Henry Bigham, 1861, wounded at Port Republic, Va, June 9, 1862

William Booze, 1861, not accounted for

Samuel Bailey, 1861, discharged January 9, 1863

Newton Bailey, 1861, not accounted for

Nelson Bliss, 1861, not accounted for

John Brimmer, 1861, discharged December 3, 1861

Henry C Bowers, December 7, 1861,

transferred to company K, 57th P V, January 13, 1865, veteran

Gemmil Baker, 1861, discharged March 3, 1863

George Baines, March 31, 1864; not accounted for

John R Carr, 1861, discharged December 23 for wounds received at Winchester, Va, March 23, 1862

Solomon Cupler, 1861, died at Harrisburg, Pa, January 5, 1862

Peter Curley, 1861, discharged, date unknown

Samuel Cross, 1861, discharged February 8, 1863

Michael Culp, 1861, transferred to V R C, date unknown

William Clouser, 1861; not acounted for

Valentine Culp, 1861, not accounted for

John B Campbell, 1861, not accounted for

George W Comer, December 7, 1861, wounded at Chancellorsville, Va, May 3, 1863, transferred to company K, 57th P V, January 13, 1865

Christopher Cassidy, 1861, wounded at Chancellorsville, Va, May 3, 1863, transferred to company K, 57th P V, January 13, 1865

Johnson Cassidy, 1861, not accounted for

Solomon Cassidy, December 7, 1861, captured at Chancellorsville, Va, May 3, 1863, transferred to company K, 57th P V, January 13, 1865; veteran

John Dash, 1861; transferred to company I.

Levi Drocker, 1861, deserted, date unknown

Samuel B Devore, October 24, 1861, captured at Chancellorsville, Va, May 3, 1863; transferred to company K, 57th P V, January 13, 1865

Roland Dixon, 1861, deserted October 14, 1861

Levi H Derrick, March 4, 1864; wounded at Pleasant Hill, Va, June 1, 1864, transferred to company K, 57th P V, January 13, 1865

Robert Dane, March 4, 1864, wounded at Wilderness May 5, 1864, not accounted for

Alfred Everhart, April 7, 1864, wounded at Wilderness May 5, 1864, transferred to company K, 57th P. V, January 13, 1865

John Fontenroy, 1861, captured at Chancellorsville, Va, May 3, 1863

Sidney Farley, 1861, not accounted for

John H Ferguson, 1861, not accounted for

James Gomlic, 1861, not accounted for

Robert Graham, October 24, 1861; captured at Chancellorsville, Va, May 3, 1863, transferred to company K, 57th P V, January 13, 1865; veteran

James L Graham, 1861, killed at Winchester, Va, March 23, 1862

John Grady, 1861, not accounted for

Jacob Gilnett, December 7, 1861, killed at Pleasant Hill, Va, June 1, 1864; veteran

Edward Gilnett, 1861, wounded at Fredericksburg, Va, December 13, 1862, not accounted for

James Garley; discharged, date unknown

Theo J Garretson, 1861, not accounted for

John Green, 1861; killed at Mine Run, Va, November 27, 1863

Thos Gouldsberry, 1861; not accounted for

James Gorman, 1861, wounded and captured at Chancellorsville, Va, May 3, 1863

Harvey H Hite, 1861, not accounted for

Henry C Heise, 1861; captured at Chancellorsville, Va, May 3, 1863.

Samuel Hare, December 7, 1861; wounded at Chancellorsville, Va, May 3, 1863, and

Wilderness May 4, 1864, transferred to company K, 57th P V, January 13, 1865, veteran

Joel Hufford, 1861, wounded and captured at Chancellorsville, Va, May 3, 1863, discharged September 25, 1863

Samuel Hamlin, died, date unknown

George Hoffman, 1861, wounded and captured at Chancellorsville, Va, May 3, 1863, not accounted for

Uriah Haneigh, 1861, not accounted for

James Hepburn, December 7, 1861, wounded at Wilderness, Va, May 3, 1864, transferred to company K, 57th P V, January 13, 1865, veteran

William Hagerty, 1861, not accounted for

Thomas H Irvine, 1861, deserted, date unknown

Gratz M Johnson, 1861, wounded at Cedar Mountain August 9, 1862, Bull Run August 30, 1862, and Chancellorsville, Va, May 3, 1863, not accounted for

Samuel Johnson, December 7, 1861, not accounted for

Ellis Kyler, 1861, discharged December 9 for wounds received at Port Republic, Va, June 9, 1862

Peter A Kyler, 1861, died at Winchester, Va, June 7, 1862, burial in National Cemetery, lot 10

John Kennedy, 1861, discharged July 10, 1862

John Krise, 1861, deserted June 5, 1862

Joseph Kretzer, November 2, 1861, discharged November 18, 1864—expiration of term

William Kretzer, 1861, killed at Chancellorsville, Va, May 3, 1863

John Kesigle, 1861, wounded and captured at Chancellorsville, Va, May 3, 1863

William Luzier, 1861, wounded at Winchester, Va, March 23, 1862, not accounted for

Henry Lightner, 1861, not acounted for

John Luzier, October 24, 1861, captured at Chancellorsville, Va, May 3, 1863, exchanged, not accounted for, veteran

John Lytle, 1861, wounded and captured at Chancellorsville, Va, May 3, 1863

Isaac Lyons, 1861, discharged February 11, 1863

Henry Lubold, December 5, 1861, wounded at Cedar Mountain August 9, 1862, Bull Run August 30, 1862, Chancellorsville May 3, 1863, and Wilderness May 6, 1864, transferred to company K, 57th P V, January 13, 1865, veteran

Mervin Ludlow, 1861, deserted June 16, 1862

Joseph Larrion, killed June 19, 1864

Joseph L Lydic, 1861, wounded at Chancellorsville, Va, May 3, 1863, veteran

Robert L Lydic, December 7, 1861, transferred to company K, 57th P V, January 13, 1865

James A Meade, October 24, 1861, captured at Chancellorsville, Va, May 3, 1863, transferred to company K, 57th P V, January 13, 1865, veteran

Adam Miller, 1861, deserted February 7, 1862

James Maguire, 1861, not accounted for

Miles Miller, 1861, not accounted for

George Morkret, December 5, 1861, transferred to company K, 58th P V, January 13, 1865, veteran

Jacob S Miller, December 21, 1861, transferred to company I, 57th P V, January 13, 1865

William Moley, killed at Wilderness, Va, May 6, 1864

Orange J Michaels, 1861, not accounted for

John Mark, December 5, 1861, captured at Chancellorsville, Va, May 3, 1863, transferred to company K, 57th P V, January 13, 1865, veteran

Philip McCracken, December 7, 1861, wounded at Cedar Mountain August 9, 1862, and Wilderness May 6, 1864, transferred to company K, 57th P V, January 13, 1865, veteran

William McAfoose, 1861, discharged January 9, 1863

Samuel McLaughlin, 1861, discharged March 9, 1863

John Nesemer, 1861, transferred to V R C, date unknown

Christopher Netzel, October 2, 1862, wounded at Chancellorsville, Va, May 3, 1863, transferred to company K, 57th P V, January 13, 1865

William S Ogden, 1861, discharged November 24, 1863

James W Owens, 1861, not accounted for

Henry C Owens, 1861, wounded at Port Republic, Va, June 9, 1862, not accounted for

Jonas L Pownall, October 24, 1861, captured at Chancellorsville, Va, May 3, 1863, transferred to company K, 57th P V, January 13, 1865, veteran

Andrew Peters, 1861, discharged July 4, 1862

James C Reams, 1861, discharged February 11, 1863

Michael Reep, 1861, killed at Spottsylvania C H, May 12, 1864

Isaac Robinson, 1861, died, date unknown.

John Riddle, 1861, not accounted for

Bretlan A Reams, August 30, 1862; wounded at Chancellorsville, Va, May 3, 1863, transferred to company K, 57th P V, January 13, 1865

George W Rowles, 1861, deserted October 14, 1861

John F Rote, 1861, deserted September 25, 1861

Alexander Reed, 1861, wounded at Thoroughfare Gap, Va, August 28, 1862, killed at Spottsylvania C H, May 12, 1864

Jacob Reep, December 7, 1861, transferred to company K, 57th P V, January 13, 1865

Robert L Rodkey, December 7, 1861; wounded and captured at Chancellorsville, Va, May 3, 1863, transferred to company K, 57th P V, January 13, 1865, veteran

Samuel J Rodkey, February 22, 1864; transferred to company K, 57th P V, January 13, 1865

Daniel G Smith, 1861; killed at Winchester, Va, March 23, 1862, buried in National Cemetery, lot 10

A C Spanogle, 1861, discharged, date unknown

John H Shimel, October 24, 1861, transferred to company K, 57th P V, January 13, 1865, veteran

Richard H Shaw, 1861, promoted to hospital steward, date unknown

Samuel Snoddy, 1861, wounded at Wilderness, Va, May 6, 1864; not accounted for

Michael Stejbig, 1861, not accounted for

John Solomons, December 5, 1861, captured at Chancellorsville, Va, May 3, 1863; wounded at Spottsylvania C H May 12, 1864, transferred to company K, 57th P V., January 13, 1865, veteran

Jacob Schooly, 1861, not accounted for.

Nicholas Simpson, 1861, discharged February 21, 1863

Joseph F Stouffer, August 11, 1862, transferred to company K, 57th P V, January 13, 1865

John B Shankle, December 7, 1861; wounded at Wilderness, Va, May 5, 1864, and Deep Bottom, August 15, 1864, transferred to company K, 57th P V, January 13, 1865, veteran

Henry Stugart, 1861, discharged March 9, 1863

Charles Snyder, October 24, 1861, transferred to company K, 57th P V, January 13, 1865, veteran

John A Shankle, March 31, 1864, transferred to company K, 57th P V, January 13, 1865

John Thompson, October 24, 1861 transferred to company K, 57th P V, January 13, 1865, veteran

Nathan B Trude, March 31, 1864, wounded at Pleasant Hill, Va, June 1, 1864, transferred to company K, 57th P V, January 13, 1865

Jacob Wainright, 1861, killed at Winchester, Va, March 23, 1862, buried in National Cemetery, lot 9

Daniel K Weld, 1861, discharged December 6, 1862

G Waldenmyer, 1861, discharged, date unknown

Edward Welsh, 1861, discharged February 8, 1862

Franklin Weaver, 1861, wounded and captured at Chancellorsville, Va, May 3, 1863

John F Weaver, March 31, 1864, not accounted for

Rudolph L Young, August 30, 1862, wounded October 27, 1864, transferred to company H

CHAPTER VIII

MILITARY HISTORY—THE CIVIL WAR—CONTINUED

History of the One Hundred and Fifth Regiment—Roster of Officers and Men—History of the One Hundred and Forty-ninth Regiment, with Roster—In Other Commands—Independent Battalion

ONE HUNDRED AND FIFTH REGIMENT

Early in the month of August, 1861, Amor A McKnight, who had seen service as one of the three months' men, was authorized to raise a regiment for the three years' service The men enlisted were mainly from what was at that time known as the "Wild Cat" district, being the congressional district of which this county then formed a part The sturdy residents responded quickly and nobly to the call, an organization was completed, and field officers elected as follows Amor A Mc-Knight, colonel, W W Corbett, lieutenant-colonel, M M Dick, major The regiment rendezvoused at Pittsburgh, but were not long permitted to remain there, as, early in October, the command was ordered to the front, and in pursuance thereof went to Washington and encamped for a brief time, and then moved to a point about one mile south of Alexandria, known as Camp Jameson, where they went into winter quarters Here it was assigned to Jameson's Brigade, which was made up in the main of Pennsylvania troops In March following, 1862, they broke camp and were transported to Fortress Monroe, and immediately participated in the siege of Yorktown, doing guard duty and suffering only from sickness caused by the unhealthful locality in which they were placed Upon the evacuation of the place by the enemy, they joined in pursuit, and after a hard march through rain and mud reached Williamsburg The next day, May 4, they were advanced as skirmishers, and planted the colors on the principal fort of the enemy It was next engaged at Fair Oaks, where it got into exceedingly close quarters, but through the coolness and efficiency of the officers in command, and the bravery and determined fighting done by the men, it was eventually victorious and escaped annihilation and capture, but not without serious loss and injury to officers and men The result of this battle to the regiment was forty-one killed, one hundred and fifty wounded, and seventeen missing Headley, in mentioning the part taken by the One Hundred and Fifth during the battle of Fair Oaks, says "Napoleon's veterans never stood firmer during a devastating fire " On the 26th and 27th of June following the regiment was again engaged at the battles of Mechanicsville and Gaines's Mill, but met with no serious loss

After this the army fell back and began a retreat to the James River, and Jameson's Brigade was placed under command of General Robinson During this retreat, in which the Federal forces were hard pressed by the Confederates, the regiment was constantly under orders and frequently exposed to the enemy's fire On the 30th, at Charles City Cross Roads, it had a sharp engagement with the rebels in repelling an attempt on the part of the latter to capture a battery, in which the regiment lost fifty men in killed and wounded At Malvern Hill, the next day, it was under a heavy artillery fire, but not closely engaged At the close of the campaign on the Peninsula, the regiment was assigned to duty in guarding the railroad between Manasas and Warrentown Junction At the Second Bull Run it was again hotly engaged and its ranks fearfully decimated by being in an open position and exposed to the deadly fire of the enemy, but nevertheless held firmly to its place in support of a battery At sundown it was relieved and placed on picket duty until nearly midnight, and then moved to Centreville, where it lay until the 31st General Kearney, in his report of the Second Bull Run fight, says "The One Hundred and Fifth Pennsylvania Volunteers were not wanting They are Pennsylvanians—mountain men—again have they been fearfully decimated The desperate charge of these regiments sustains the past history of this division "

The regiment was, at the close of Pope's campaign, ordered into the defenses of Washington, and remained there until after the battle of Antietam On the 28th of October following it moved to White's Ford, crossed the Potomac and proceeded to the Ball's Bluff battle ground, where for several days it was engaged in scouting expeditions in the vicinity of Leesburg and Millville With the main army it then advanced to the Rappahannock, and on the 24th of November reached Falmouth On the 13th of December it crossed the river, and at a double quick went to the relief of the Pennsylvania Reserves, who were hotly engaged and hard pressed, and took a position in the rear of Randolph's battery At dusk it advanced and lay upon their arms in front of the battery for a space of thirty-six hours, within the reach of, but concealed from the rebel sharpshooters, but was then relieved and returned to camp across the river From this time until the latter part of January, 1863, the regiment remained in camp, and were then ordered to move, but owing to the impassable condition of the roads, were compelled to return

The troops were reviewed by Governor Curtin on the 26th day of March, and on the 10th of April following were visited by President Lincoln and General Hooker, the latter having now been advanced to the chief command On the 28th of April the brigade to which the regiment was attached, started on the Chancellorsville campaign and occupied a prominent position in the engagements that followed, charging here and there in the thickest of the fight, constantly under the terrible fire of artillery and infantry, suffering every hardship known to modern warfare, until on the 5th of May it was ordered across the river to Falmouth In killed, wounded, and missing the regiment lost in this battle an aggregate of seventy-seven men out of three hundred and forty-seven that entered, among the killed being the gallant Colonel McKnight Then commenced the move to the northward, and the regiment reached the scene of Gettysburg on the night of July 1, and on the day following Companies A, C, D, F, and I were deployed as skirmishers in support of the Sixty-third regiment, where they remained until afternoon when they were called in, and with the regiment, took a position on the right of the brigade when battle commenced During the terrible battle that ensued the regiment behaved nobly, and fought as brave men can fight, first advancing and then retiring, officers and men alike being cut down under the merciless artillery and infantry fire, until at night, they took a position on the road connecting Cemetery Ridge with Round Top Of two hundred and forty-seven men who went into this fight, the regiment lost in killed, wounded and missing, one hundred and sixty-eight, more than half of its numerical strength

Gettysburg over, after a series of movements, and a sharp brush at Auburn, the regiment brought up at Fairfax Station, where for a brief time it was assigned to provost duty, but again advanced, and in the latter part of November took part in the battle of Locust Grove At the close of the Mine Run campaign it went into winter quarters at Brandy Station

On the 28th of December two hundred and forty men, nearly the entire strength of the regiment, re-enlisted, and were given a veteran furlough While away about fifty recruits were obtained

Early in May of the succeeding year preparations for the spring campaign were completed, and refreshed and recruited the regiment moved with the army to participate in the memorable seven-days battle of the Wilderness Next came Petersburg, in which it took part, and after that the raid on the Weldon Railroad, July 26 the regiment participated in the

movement across the James River, and returned in time to be of good service during the events that followed, but suffered severe losses. Colonel Craig was mortally wounded and died a day later In the various attacks on the Weldon Railroad that followed during the fall and early winter, it took a lively part, after which it again went into winter quarters

The next spring, 1865, the regiment engaged at Hatcher's Run and Sailor's Creek, and upon the surrender of General Lee marched, by way of Richmond, to Bailey's Cross Roads, where it encamped On June 23 it marched in the grand review at Washington, and on the 11th of July was finally mustered out of service

Field and Staff

Colonels —Amor A McKnight, October 12, 1861, wounded at Fair Oaks May 31, 1862, resigned July 28, 1862, recommissioned September 20, 1862, killed at Chancellorsville, Va, May 3, 1863

Calvin A Craig, August 28, 1861; promoted from captain company C to lieutenant-colonel April 20, 1863, to colonel May 4, 1863; wounded at Gettysburg July 2, 1863, at Wilderness May 5, 1864, and at Petersburg June 1864, died August 17th of wounds received at Deep Bottom, August 16, 1864

James Miller, October 23, 1861, promoted from captain company K to major January 14, 1865, to colonel May 15, 1865, mustered out with regiment July 11, 1865, veteran

Lieutenant-Colonels —William W Corbet, October 12, 1861, commissioned colonel July 29, 1862, not mustered, resigned September 10, 1862

J W Greenawalt, September 4, 1861, promoted from captain company E to major November 29, 1862, to lieutenant-colonel May 4,

1863, died May 17th of wounds received at Wilderness May 5, 1864

Oliver C Reddic, September 1, 1861, promoted from captain company I, May 15, 1865, mustered out with regiment July 11, 1865, veteran

Majors —Mungo M Dick, September 4, 1861, promoted from captain company E, September 20, 1861, resigned August 9, 1862

Levi Bird Duff, May 1, 1861, promoted from captain company D May 4, 1863, commissioned lieutenant-colonel May 18, 1864, not mustered, discharged October 25th for wounds, with loss of leg, received at Petersburg June 18, 1864

Adjutants —Orlando Gray August 29, 1861, promoted from first lieutenant company H, September 15, 1861, resigned August 26, 1862

John H Woodward, September 4, 1861, promoted from private company E to principal musician October 1, 1861 to sergeant-major, to adjutant August 27, 1862, to first lieutenant company G November 27, 1862

Hillis McKown, October 24, 1861, promoted from private company C to sergeant-major February 10, 1863, to adjutant September 28, 1864, mustered out with regiment July 11, 1865, veteran

Quartermasters — Robert J Nicholson, September 9, 1861, promoted from first lieutenant company B, October 1, 1861, resigned October 16, 1862

Harrison M Coon, October 25, 1861, promoted from private company G to quartermaster-sergeant October 26, 1861, to quartermaster November 27, 1862, discharged on surgeon's certificate August 8, 1864

Joseph G Craig, September 15, 1861, promoted from first lieutenant, company C to ad-

jutant March 28, 1863, to quartermaster September 28, 1864, mustered out with regiment July 11, 1865

Surgeons —Alexander P Heichhold, October 23, 1861, resigned September 12, 1862

William Watson, September 16, 1862, discharged by general order May 27, 1865

Adam Wenger, November 7, 1862, promoted from assistant surgeon June 2, 1865, mustered out with regiment July 11, 1865

Assistant Surgeons —William F Smith, October 15, 1861, resigned September 12, 1862

George W Ewing, August 4, 1862, promoted to surgeon 115th P V April 7, 1863

Aaron C Vaughn, May 15, 1863, discharged on surgeon's certificate September 3, 1864

Joseph Taylor, June 7, 1865, mustered out with regiment July 11, 1865

Chaplains —Darius S Steadman, October 12, 1861, resigned June 23, 1862

John C Truesdale, June 1, 1864, mustered out with regiment July 11, 1865

Sergeant-Majors —W H McLaughlin, October 23, 1861, transferred to Company H, July 1, 1862

George Van Vliet, October 23, 1861, promoted from first sergeant, Company I, to sergeant-major June 5, 1862, to first lieutenant Company H, July 11, 1862

Robert J Boyington, October 5, 1861, promoted from sergeant Company I, to second lieutenant Company I, February 6, 1863

Tilton Reynolds, September 1, 1861, promoted from private Company H, September 28, 1864 to captain Company H, November 24, 1864, veteran

Ivester H Dean, February 29, 1864, promoted from corporal Company K, November

24, 1864, mustered out with regiment July 11, 1865, veteran

Quartermaster Sergeants — Fleming Y Caldwell, September 9, 1861, promoted from private Company A to commissary sergeant September 20, 1861, to quartermaster-sergeant January 7, 1865, mustered out with regiment July 11, 1865, veteran

Benj M Stauffer, October 25, 1861, promoted from private Company G, November 1, 1862, mustered out with regiment July 11, 1865, veteran

Hospital Steward —Charles D Shrieves, December 16, 1861, mustered out with regiment July 11, 1865, veteran

Commissary Sergeants —John Coon, October 25, 1861, promoted from private Company G, January 7, 1865, mustered out with regiment July 11, 1865, veteran

D R Crawford, October 23, 1861, discharged September 25, 1864, veteran

Principal Musicians —Andrew McKown, August 28, 1861, promoted from corporal Company D, August 28, 1863, mustered out, expiration of term

Eli B Clemson, August 28, 1861, promoted from private Company D, September 1, 1864, mustered out with regiment July 11, 1865, veteran

Joseph Lichtenberger, August 1, 1861, mustered out with regiment July 11, 1865, veteran

James H. Craig, October 24, 1861, promoted from sergeant Company C, August 28, 1864, discharged September 25, 1864, veteran

COMPANY C

Recruited in Clearfield and Clarion Counties

Captains —Calvin A Craig, August 28,

1861, wounded at Bull Run August 29, 1862, promoted to lieutenant-colonel April 20, 1863

Charles E Patton, August 28, 1861, promoted from first lieutenant April 20, 1863, killed at Boydton Plank Road October 27, 1864

Joseph B Brown, October 21, 1861; promoted to corporal December 1, 1861, to sergeant, January 1, 1862, to first sergeant October 3, 1863, to first lieutenant March 1, 1864, to captain November 7, 1864, mustered out with company July 11, 1865

First Lieutenants —Joseph Craig, September 15, 1861, promoted to first lieutenant July 29, 1862, to adjutant March 28, 1863

William H Hewitt, August 31, 1861, promoted to first lieutenant May 14, 1863, discharged by general order May 19, 1865

Richard G Warden, August 26, 1861, promoted from sergeant to first sergeant November 1, 1864, to first lieutenant June 8, 1865; mustered out with company July 11, 1865, veteran

Second Lieutenants —Isaac A Dunston, October 25, 1861, promoted from first sergeant July 29, 1862, to second lieutenant May 1, 1863, died August 2d, of wounds received at Gettysburg July 2, 1863

Henry H Michaels, October 25, 1861; promoted to corporal April 1, 1864, to sergeant November 1, 1864; to second lieutenant June 8, 1865, mustered out with company July 11, 1865, veteran

First Sergeants —John R Osborn, January 4, 1864, promoted to corporal January 1, 1865, to first sergeant June 8, 1865, mustered out with company July 11, 1865; veteran

Addison Lau, September 12, 1861, died June 17th of wounds received at North Anna River May 23, 1864, veteran

George Laing, December 24, 1863, promoted from sergeant September 15, 1864, commissioned second lieutenant October 22, 1864, not mustered, discharged by general order May 17, 1865, veteran

David H McCauley, December 24, 1863, promoted from sergeant March 1, 1864, discharged February 22, 1865, veteran

Sergeants —Charles C. Weaver, October 25, 1861, promoted to corporal April 1, 1864, to sergeant August 28, 1864, mustered out with company July 11, 1865, veteran

Samuel H Mays, October 25, 1861, promoted to corporal August 28, 1864, to sergeant May 17, 1865, mustered out with company July 11, 1865, veteran

James E Lafferty, October 25, 1861, promoted to corporal August 28, 1864, to sergeant May 29, 1865, mustered out with company July 11, 1865, veteran

Horace H Ferman, December 24, 1863, promoted from corporal June 1, 1864, discharged February 22, 1865, veteran

Charles Rodgers, September 9, 1863, drafted, promoted to corporal January 1, 1865, to sergeant June 8. 1865, mustered out with company July 11, 1865

Samuel Lattimore, December 24, 1863, wounded at Petersburg June 21, 1864, discharged February 22, 1865, veteran

John H Piersall, December 24, 1863, promoted from private June 1, 1864, discharged February 22, 1865, veteran

William D Lyttle, December 24, 1863, promoted from private January 24, 1864, discharged February 22, 1865, veteran

Stewart Orr, October 25, 1861, promoted to corporal April 1, 1864; to sergeant August 28, 1864, discharged by general order May 29, 1865, veteran.

William McNutt, October 24, 1861, discharged on surgeon's certificate February 4, 1863

John Clary, August 28, 1861, promoted from corporal April 1, 1862, discharged August 28, 1864—expiration of term

Andrew A Harley, August 28, 1861, promoted to corporal April 1, 1863, to sergeant May 1, 1863, discharged August 28, 1864— expiration of term

James H Craig, October 24, 1861, promoted to principal musician August 28, 1864, veteran

William P Lowry, October 24, 1861, transferred to V R C December 1, 1864, veteran

Corporals —Isaac G Miller, October 21, 1861, promoted to corporal June, 1864, mustered out with company July 11, 1865, veteran

John Ashbaugh, July 17, 1863, drafted, promoted to corporal January 1, 1865, mustered out with company July 11, 1865

Eli H Chilson, October 21, 1861, promoted to corporal June 1, 1864, mustered out with company June 11, 1865, veteran

Isaac Lytle, October 16, 1861, promoted to corporal May 29, 1865, mustered out with company July 11, 1865, veteran

Aaron Young. February 12, 1864, promoted to corporal June 8, 1865, mustered out with company July 11, 1865

James W Watkins, February 18, 1864, promoted to corporal June 8, 1865; mustered out with company July 11, 1865

John H Hager, July 16, 1863, drafted, promoted to corporal June 8, 1865, mustered out with company July 11, 1865

James B Allison, October 21, 1861; died at White Oak Swamp June 28, 1862

Richard M Rockey, October 24, 1861, discharged on surgeon's certificate June 16, 1862

Samuel James, October 24, 1861; discharged on surgeon's certificate August 7, 1862

Edward Keefer, October 24, 1861, discharged on surgeon's certificate September 26, 1862

James W Spears, October 24, 1861, discharged on surgeon's certificate September 1, 1862

Andrew G Sager, October 23, 1861, promoted to corporal August 28, 1864, discharged by general order June 6, 1865, veteran

George Warden, January 4, 1864, transferred to V R C December 28, 1864, veteran

William Whipple, August 28, 1861, not on muster-out roll

Musicians —Andrew Stedham, December 25, 1863, mustered out with company July 11, 1865, veteran

Charles F Cross, December 25, 1863, mustered out with company July 11, 1865, veteran

Privates —Robert Allen, April 22, 1864, mustered out with company July 11, 1865

T T Armagost, October 24, 1861, died at Savage Station July 1, 1862

James A Ardery, October 24, 1861, deserted December 15, 1862

William Allshouse, August 28, 1861, discharged August 27, 1864—expiration of term

David Allison, October 24, 1861; discharged on surgeon's certificate August 13, 1862

Levi Allshouse, July 17, 1863, mustered out with company July 11, 1865

Robert E Alexander, February 29, 1864; absent, sick, at muster out

F M Bookwalter, February 15, 1864; mustered out with company July 11, 1865

George A. Brown, July 16, 1863; drafted, mustered out with company July 11, 1865

Levi Bush, September 7, 1863, drafted, mustered out with company July 11, 1865

James Biggins, March 31, 1864, wounded in action June 16, 1864—expiration of term

George W Bennett, December 31, 1861, died at Chester, Pa, August 5th, of wounds received at Charles City Cross Roads, Va, June 30, 1862

John Burton, July 30, 1864, drafted, missing in action near Hatcher's Run March 29, 1865

Wm H Bookwalter, April 8, 1862, discharged on surgeon's certificate December 20, 1862

F O Bookwalter, April 8, 1862, discharged on surgeon's certificate January 6, 1863

Wm Bunnel, October 24, 1861; discharged on surgeon's certificate March 28, 1863.

Charles L Brooks, September 9, 1863, drafted, discharged January 21, 1865, for wounds received in action September 4, 1864

Hezekiah Bowser, February 11, 1864, discharged by general order June 5, 1865.

Benn Bannister, September 5, 1861; deserted, returned, discharged by general order May 17, 1865

Wm J Crick, October 25, 1861: deserted, returned, mustered out with company July 11, 1865

Simon Crandall, March 29, 1864, mustered out with company July 11, 1865

E P Cochran, February 22, 1864, mustered out with company July 11, 1865

· Craig Carnery, July 13, 1863, drafted, mustered out with company July 11, 1865

John C Church, July 11, 1863, drafted, mustered out with company July 11, 1865

Benj F Coursin, July 18, 1863, drafted, discharged by general order July 27, 1865

A J Cyphert, April 12, 1861, discharged on surgeon's certificate November 25, 1862

Jesse R Craig, October 24, 1861, discharged on surgeon's certificate January 29, 1863

George Clinger, April 8, 1862, discharged on surgeon's certificate March 28, 1863

David Cyphert April 8, 1862, discharged on surgeon's certificate August 17, 1863

George G Cyphert, October 24, 1861, discharged May 27, 1864, for wounds received at Chancellorsville, May 2, 1863

James K Cyphert, April 12, 1862, discharged April 18, 1865—expiration of term

George Camp, July 10, 1864, drafted, discharged by general order June 13, 1865

M G DeVallance, April 9, 1864, wounded in action June 16, 1864, mustered out with company July 11, 1865

George Dugan, October 25, 1861, mustered out with company July 11, 1865, veteran

John Divinne, June 14, 1864, drafted, mustered out with company July 11, 1865

Geo W Davis, October 24, 1861, died at Camp Franklin, Va, December 5, 1861

James Day, September 8, 1863, drafted, deserted May 3, 1864

John Divine, April 14, 1864, discharged by general order May 29, 1865

David Dugan, August 28, 1861, discharged March 1, 1865, for wounds received at Deep Bottom August 16, 1864, veteran

James Devanny, July 16, 1863; drafted, transferred to Company D, February 26, 1864

6

Andrew Dougan, February 29, 1864, not on muster-out roll

William O Easton, March 1, 1864, mustered out with company July 11, 1865

Andrew Eicher, July 16, 1864, drafted, transferred to Company D, February 26, 1864

Edward Floyd, April 13, 1864, wounded at Opequan August 16, 1864, mustered out with company July 11, 1865

Alanson R Felt, April 9, 1864, mustered out with company July 11, 1865, veteran

William George, July 18, 1863, drafted, mustered out with company July 11, 1865

Archibald George, October 25, 1861, absent on furlough at muster-out, veteran

E A Gooderham, October 24, 1861, killed at Malvern Hill, July 1, 1862

John Goodman, October 24, 1861, discharged on surgeon's certificate February 11, 1863

John Gould, June 17, 1864, drafted, discharged on surgeon's certificate March 18, 1865

Albert Gordon, July 28, 1864, discharged by general order May 22, 1865

Richard Holland, July 29, 1864, substitute, mustered out with company July 11, 1865

Lee Hileman, September 16, 1863, drafted, mustered out with company July 11, 1864

Samuel Harrison, Sr, July 10, 1863, mustered out with company July 11, 1865

Miles Haden, February 24, 1864, mustered out with company July 11, 1865

Lebanah H Hetrick, July, 1863, drafted, mustered out with company July 11, 1865

James A Harley, October 25, 1861, deserted, returned, mustered out with company July 11, 1865

Charles Hammond, June 10, 1864, substitute, absent, sick, at muster out

George Hilbert, October 25, 1861, wounded at Wilderness May 5, 1864, absent at muster out; veteran

Henry Hamma, January 4, 1864, wounded at Boydton Plank Road October 27, 1864, absent at muster out, veteran

Edward Harrison, October 24, 1861, died at Philadelphia December 12, 1862

Joseph L Harley, August 28, 1861, discharged August 28, 1864—expiration of term

J W. T Hollopiter, August 28, 1861, discharged August 28, 1864—expiration of term

David Hettick, April 18, 1862, discharged April 8, 1865—expiration of term

Ann Hager, July, 1863, drafted, discharged by general order May 29, 1865

William Hamma, October, 1861, transferred to Company D, February 26, 1864, veteran

Robert Hunter, August 1, 1861, transferred to Company D, February 26, 1864

John Isaman, July 18, 1863, drafted, mustered out with company July 11, 1865

John Ingham, March 10, 1864, wounded at Wilderness May 5, 1864, absent at muster out

John C Johnson, April 9, 1864, wounded at Wilderness May 6, 1864, absent at muster out

Jesse Kearnigham, March 29, 1864, mustered out with company July 11, 1865

David Kidder, July 11, 1863, drafted, mustered out with company July 11, 1865

Samuel Keifer, October 25, 1861, absent on furlough at muster out, veteran

M S Kirkpatrick, April 8, 1862 discharged on surgeon's certificate February 11, 1863

Patrick Long, March 4, 1864, mustered out with company July 11, 1865

Thomas B Lines, March 16, 1864; missing in action at Wilderness May 6, 1864

John Mott, October 16, 1861, mustered out with company July 11, 1865, veteran.

Robert Moore, March 24, 1864, mustered out with company July 11, 1865

William Mattis, March 20, 1865, substitute, mustered out with company July 11, 1865

John Mays, October 24, 1861, died September 8th of wounds received at Bull Run August 29, 1862

David Michael, October 24, 1861, discharged on surgeon's certificate August 10, 1862

John Mills, February 26, 1864, discharged by general order May 29, 1865

Obediah Mills, October 24, 1861, discharged on surgeon's certificate January 19, 1862

Thomas M Mitchell, August 28, 1861; discharged August 28, 1864—expiration of term

David Mitchell, October 24, 1861; discharged on surgeon's certificate April 11, 1863

Edwin Marquis, July 24, 1863; drafted, transferred to Company D, February 26, 1864

Allen Morrison, October 24, 1861, discharged on surgeon's certificate January 11, 1863

James Maloy, October 24, 1861, discharged October 24th for wounds received at Charles City Cross Roads June 30, 1862.

John W McCormick, October 24, 1861; killed at Spottsylvania Court House May 12, 1864

Henry McCormick, October 24, 1861; died of wounds received at Bull Run August 29, 1862

Geo D Funkhouser, January 4, 1864, mustered out with company July 11, 1865, veteran

Wm H Fetter, February 27, 1864, mustered out with company July 11, 1865

Jacob Fry, October 24, 1861, killed at Gettysburg July 3, 1863, buried in National Cemetery, section C, grave 90

John M Fry, October 24, 1861, died at Alexandria December 18, 1861, burial record, died at Alexandria, Va, December 11, 1863, grave 1164

David Fleck, October 24, 1861, died at Camp Jameson, Va, January 18, 1862, burial record, died at Alexandria, Va, December 9, 1864, grave 1139

Perry C Fox, April 9, 1864, missing in action near Petersburg June 22, 1864

David Girts, February 4, 1864, mustered out with company July 11, 1865, veteran

George McGlaughlin, October 24, 1861, died July 11th of wounds received at Fair Oaks May 31, 1862

Ab'm McGlaughlin, October 24, 1861, died at Philadelphia June 25, 1862, burial record, September 28, 1862

Robert McFadden, October 24, 1861, discharged on surgeon's certificate October 4, 1862

David McKown, July 17, 1863, drafted, discharged by general order May 29, 1865

Ross McCoy, October 24, 1861, discharged on surgeon's certificate November 8, 1862

Hillis McKown, October 24, 1861, promoted to sergeant-major February 10, 1863

Isaac McCullough, September 9, 1861, not on muster-out roll

David P Nall, October 24, 1861, killed at Auburn, Va, October 13, 1863

Adam Nuff, April 18, 1862, discharged on surgeon's certificate October 22, 1862

Wm J Newgant, September 9, 1861, not on muster-out roll

Jacob S Oburn, July 29, 1864, substitute, mustered out with company July 11, 1865

Joseph R Ogden, February 26, 1864, absent, sick, at muster out

Robert Owens, October 24, 1861, discharged on surgeon's certificate January 20, 1865, veteran

George W Peck, March 20, 1864, mustered out with company July 11, 1865

Michael Phillips, March 29, 1864, mustered out with company July 11, 1865

Coleman E Parris, April 9, 1864, mustered out with company July 11, 1865

William Pike, April 29, 1864, wounded at Petersburg June 15, 1864, absent at muster out

Frederick Peters, December 24, 1863, killed at Hatcher's Run March 25, 1865

Jonathan Pierce, October 24, 1861, died June 23d of wounds received at Wilderness May 5, 1864, veteran

Oliver N Powell, October 24, 1861, discharged on surgeon's certificate August 6, 1862

Jacob F Phillips, October 24, 1861, discharged on surgeon's certificate February 20, 1863

John Palmer, September 9, 1863, drafted, transferred to Company D, February 26, 1863

F Rumbarger, July 29, 1864, substitute, discharged by general order May 29, 1865

Abraham J Riggles, December 27, 1863, deserted, returned, mustered out with company July 11, 1865

Edgar E Riddell, September 30th,

wounded at Wilderness May 6, 1864, absent at muster out

David Richards, March 10, 1864, wounded at Spottsylvania C H May 10, 1864, absent at muster out

George Reich, April 18, 1862, wounded at Mine Run November 27, 1863, discharged April 10, 1865

Jeremiah Rhodes, October 24, 1861, died July 16th, of wounds received at Gettysburg July 3, 1863; buried in National Cemetery, section A, grave 67

William Rockey, August 28, 1861, discharged August 27, 1864—expiration of term

Isaac N Rainey, October 24, 1861, discharged on surgeon's certificate January 24, 1863

John S Rockey, October 24, 1861, discharged on surgeon's certificate August 20, 1863

David P Reich, October 24, 1861, discharged on surgeon's certificate November 3, 1862

Joseph Kinsel, March 23, 1864, transferred to Company D, February 26, 1865

John Scott, October 25, 1861, mustered out with company July 11, 1865, veteran

Emery E Stitt, July 17, 1863, drafted, mustered out with company July 11, 1865

William C Smith, July 17, 1863, drafted, mustered out with company July 11, 1865

George W Saunders, September 30, 1861, mustered out with company July 11, 1865; veteran

Michael Shanhan, September 30. 1861; mustered out with company July 11. 1865, veteran

David R Shannon, February 13, 1864, wounded at Wilderness May 6, 1864, absent at muster out

David Shagel, July 18, 1863, drafted, wounded at Wilderness May 6, 1864, discharged by general order July 19, 1865

Ann Sibley, April 7, 1864, wounded at Wilderness May 5, 1864, absent at muster out

Barnard Smith, March 10, 1864; wounded at Wilderness May 5, 1864, absent at muster out

Philip Smith, October 24, 1861, killed at Wilderness May 5, 1864, veteran

Templeton Sayers, October 24, 1861, died at Camp Jameson, Va, November 30, 1861

James Sallinger, October 24, 1861, died at Harrison's Landing July 8, 1862

James Schofield, October 24, 1861, died near Alexandria October 7, 1862

Jacob Sealor, October 24, 1861; died at Point Lookout August 16, 1862

John Shields, April 27, 1864, missing in action near Petersburg June 22, 1864

James Stephenson, July 2, 1863, drafted, deserted January 10, 1865

William Speady, August 28, 1861, discharged August 27, 1864—expiration of term

Daniel Sarver, August 22, 1862, discharged by general order May 29, 1865

Francis Snyder, July 16, 1863, drafted, discharged January 2, 1865, for wounds received at Wilderness May 6, 1864

Francis Smith, April 8, 1862, discharged on surgeon's certificate August 7, 1862

George Settlemoyer, December 31, 1861, discharged on surgeon's certificate August 7, 1862

John Sollinger, October 24, 1861, discharged on surgeon's certificate December 18, 1862

Palmer J Stephens, October 24, 1861; discharged on surgeon's certificate January 15. 1863

Jackson Spears, October 24, 1861, discharged on surgeon's certificate May 29, 1863

H Schreckengost, October 24, 1861, discharged December 22d for wounds received at Chancellorsville May 3, 1863

George Stokes, February 29, 1864, transferred to Company D, February 26, 1864, veteran

John Smith, July 11, 1863, drafted, transferred to Company D, February 26, 1864

John Stedham, August 1, 1861, transferred to Company D, February 26, 1864

Peter L Smith, September 9, 1861, not on muster-out roll

Thomas M Tantlinger, September 9, 1861, substitute, died at Washington April 4, 1865, burial record, March 27, 1865, buried in National Cemetery, Arlington, Va

John H Twining, March 26, 1864, missing in action at Wilderness May 6, 1864

Isaac Turner, June 7, 1864, substitute, transferred to V R C September 25, 1864

Wm W Vaneps, March 11, 1864, mustered out with company July 11, 1865

Philip W Welch, June 22, 1864, substitute, mustered out with company July 11, 1865

Alexander Walker, September 9, 1863, drafted, mustered out with company July 11, 1865

Samuel F Williams, September 30, 1861, mustered out with company July 11, 1865, veteran

William C Wilson, June 30, 1864, substitute, killed at Deep Bottom August 16, 1864, burial record, died at Philadelphia September 16, 1864

John A L Wilson, March 25, 1864, died at City Point January 24, 1865

James Woods, October 24, 1861, discharged on surgeon's certificate September 26, 1862

Samuel Walker, October 24, 1861, discharged on surgeon's certificate April 14, 1862

William Westover, October 24, 1861, discharged on surgeon's certificate February 17, 1863

John Withrow, August 28, 1861, discharged August 27, 1864—expiration of term

Thomas F Wilson, February 29, 1864, transferred to Company D, February 26, 1865

Abraham Young, August 28, 1861, discharged August 27, 1864—expiration of term

COMPANY D

Recruited in Allegheny and Clearfield Counties

Captains—John Rose, August 28, 1861, resigned January 27, 1862

Levi Bird Duff, May 1, 1861, wounded at Fair Oaks May 31, 1862, promoted from corporal Company A, 38th P V February 8, 1862, to major May 4, 1863

Isaac L Platt, August 28, 1861, promoted from sergeant to first sergeant January 28, 1862, to first lieutenant July 1, 1862, to captain April 21, 1864, discharged October 8, 1864—expiration of term

William Kelly, August 28, 1861, promoted to corporal February 28, 1862, to sergeant July 1, 1862, to first sergeant July 1, 1863, to captain November 26, 1864, mustered out with company July 11, 1865, veteran

First Lieutenants—Wm W Worrell, August 28, 1861, resigned January 27, 1862

J P. R Cummisky, February 6 1862, killed at Fair Oaks May 31, 1862

Joseph L Evans, September 12, 1861, promoted to second lieutenant December 15, 1864, to first lieutenant May 15. 1865, mustered out with company July 11, 1865, veteran

Horace Warner, December 1, 1864, promoted from 2d U S Sharpshooters February 18, 1865, discharged March 15, 1865

Second Lieutenants —Charles C Wilson, August 28, 1861, resigned January 27, 1862

George Gibson, August 1, 1861, promoted from first sergeant December 1, 1864; to second lieutenant May 15, 1865; mustered out with company July 11, 1865, veteran

Charles H. Powers, August 28, 1861, promoted to first sergeant August 31, 1861, to second lieutenant January 28, 1862, killed at Chancellorsville May 3, 1863

James Silvis, August 28, 1861, promoted from sergeant to first sergeant November 1, 1862, to second lieutenant July 1, 1863; discharged on surgeon's certificate August 6, 1864

First Sergeants —J K P McCullough, August 1, 1861, promoted to sergeant November 26, 1864, to first sergeant May 15, 1865, mustered out with company July 11, 1865, veteran

Sergeants —John McKindig, August 1, 1861, promoted to sergeant November 26, 1864; mustered out with company July 11, 1865; veteran

George O Riggs, August 28, 1861, promoted to corporal December 31, 1864, to sergeant May 15, 1865, mustered out with company July 11, 1865, veteran

Wm C McGarvey, August 28, 1861, promoted to corporal December 1, 1862, to sergeant May 15, 1865; mustered out with company July 11, 1865, veteran

Milton Craven, August 28, 1861, promoted to corporal April 30, 1863; to sergeant March 1, 1864, wounded, with loss of arm, at Wilderness May 6, 1864; absent in hospital at muster out, veteran

Ebenezer Bullers, August 28, 1861; promoted to corporal July, 1862, to sergeant April 1, 1863, discharged August 28, 1864—expiration of term

John C Johnson, August 28, 1861, promoted to sergeant July 1, 1862, discharged on surgeon's certificate February 1, 1863

Mahlon B Loux, August 28, 1861, promoted to corporal March 1, 1862, to sergeant June 30, 1863, discharged August 28, 1864—expiration of term

Isaac M Temple, August 28, 1861, discharged on surgeon's certificate December 30, 1862

Corporals —Joseph F Wolford, August 1, 1861, promoted to corporal December 31, 1864, mustered out with company July 11, 1865, veteran

John R Shaffer, August 28, 1861, promoted to corporal December 31, 1864; mustered out with company July 11, 1865; veteran

Robert Scott, February 10, 1864, promoted to corporal December 31, 1864, mustered out with company July 11, 1865, veteran

James Hare, August 1, 1861, promoted to corporal March 1, 1865; mustered out with company July 11, 1865, veteran

Osborn Hod, February 28, 1864; promoted to corporal May 15, 1865, mustered out with company July 11, 1865.

Edward Kline, August 28, 1861; promoted to corporal May 15, 1865, mustered out with company July 11, 1865, veteran

Daniel R Snyder, August 28, 1861, died June 1st of wounds received at Wilderness May 6, 1864, veteran

James H. Green, August 28, 1861, discharged August 2, 1862.

Gilbraith Patterson, August 28, 1861; died December 6, 1864

Charles E Hoel, August 28, 1861; promoted to corporal April 30, 1863, wounded at Wilderness May 6th, and with loss of arm at Spottsylvania C H May 10, 1864, discharged August 28, 1864—expiration of term

John B Horning, August 28, 1861, discharged on surgeon's certificate January 8, 1863

Darius Vastbinder, August 28, 1861, promoted to corporal March 1, 1865, discharged by general order May 29, 1865

D H Paulhamus, August 28, 1861, discharged December 10th, for wounds received at Gettysburg July 2, 1863

Andrew McKown, August 28, 1861, promoted to principal musician August 28, 1863

Jerome B Taylor, August 28, 1861, transferred to V R C October 2, 1863

Privates—Milton J Adams, March 21, 1864, wounded at Spottsylvania C H May 12, 1864, absent at hospital at muster-out, veteran

Benjamin F Alexander, April 18, 1864, discharged by general order June 24, 1865

Amos Ashkettle, August 28, 1861, discharged on surgeon's certificate April 4, 1862

Ebenezer O Bartlett, August 28, 1861, mustered out with company July 11, 1865; veteran

John Berchtold, June 13, 1864, substitute, mustered out with company July 11, 1865

John Bickerton, July 16, 1863, drafted, mustered out with company July 11, 1865

Philip Black, March 31, 1864, mustered out with company July 11, 1865

Daniel Bowers, March 31, 1864, mustered out with company July 11, 1865

John Boyle, August 1, 1861; mustered out with company July 11, 1865, veteran

John Becker, September 7, 1863, drafted,

wounded at Wilderness May 6, 1864, absent in hospital at muster out

David Bell, August 28, 1861, died June 23d —burial record, June 26th—of wounds received at Fair Oaks May 31, 1862, buried in Cypress Hill Cemetery, L I

Richard Bedell, August 28, 1861, discharged August 28, 1864—expiration of term.

Silas Bouse, August 28, 1861, transferred to V R C November 1, 1863, returned June 25, 1864, discharged August 28, 1864—expiration of term

Oliver P Boyd, July 11, 1863, drafted, discharged by general order June 6, 1865

John Bulgar, February 26, 1864, discharged September 21, 1864

Asa Bowdish, August 28, 1861, discharged October 29, 1861

Byron Bryant, August 28, 1861, discharged August 28, 1864—expiration of term

Wm Cameron, July 25, 1864, substitute, mustered out with company July 11, 1865

Christopher Chadderton, July 20, 1864, substitute, mustered out with company July 11, 1865

John S Christie, August 28, 1861, mustered out with company July 11, 1865, veteran

George Colston, August 1, 1861, mustered out with company July 11, 1865, veteran.

Isaiah Corbett, December 26, 1863, mustered out with company July 11, 1865

James R Corbett, August 28, 1861, mustered out with company July 11, 1861, veteran

Samuel Criswell, August 28, 1861, killed at Charles City Cross Roads June 30, 1862

Andrew Christie, August 28, 1861, died June 17th of wounds received at Petersburg, June 16, 1864, buried in National Cemetery,

City Point, section E, division 1, grave 135, veteran

Edward Cox, March 18, 1865, substitute, deserted June 24, 1865

Anson L Curry, August 28, 1861, deserted November, 1862

Joel Clark, August 28, 1861; discharged August 28, 1864—expiration of term

Vincent Crabtree, March 16, 1865, substitute, discharged by general order May 29, 1865

James M Cree, August 28, 1861, discharged on surgeon's certificate January 8, 1863

Eli B Clemson, August 28, 1861, promoted to principal musician September 1, 1864, veteran

Francis Davis, February 22, 1864, drafted, mustered out with company July 11, 1865

William Dunn, August 25, 1861, mustered out with company July 11, 1865, veteran

Thomas Davis, February 22, 1864, drafted, died December 31, 1864, buried in National Cemetery, Arlington, Va

James Devanny, July 16, 1863, drafted, captured June 22, 1864

Matthew Eagleson, July 11, 1863, drafted, died February 19, 1865, buried in Poplar Grove National Cemetery, Petersburg, Va, section D, division C, grave 33

Andrew Eicher, July 16, 1863, drafted, missing in action at Boydton Plank Road, Va, October 27, 1864

James Fair, August 1, 1861, mustered out with company July 11, 1865, veteran

Samuel Free, February 27, 1864, drafted; mustered out with company July 11, 1865

Calvin Fryer, March 18, 1865, substitute, mustered out with company July 11, 1865

John Fleming, July 10, 1863, drafted,

wounded October 2, 1864, absent in hospital at muster out.

Jacob Frickie, June 30, 1864, substitute, absent, sick, at muster out

C Fischer, June 29, 1864, substitute, deserted July 29, 1864

Charles M Frazier, March 22, 1862; discharged March 22, 1865—expiration of term

Ransom Freeman, August 28, 1861, discharged on surgeon's certificate March 18, 1862

Simon Fulton, August 28, 1861; discharged on surgeon's certificate February 9, 1863

Charles Frick, March 23, 1865, discharged by general order May 29, 1865.

Charles Graham, August 28, 1861 mustered out with company July 11, 1865, veteran

William Griffith, February 15, 1865, mustered out with company July 11, 1865

James K Grimley, March 23, 1865, substitute, mustered out with company July 11, 1865

Samuel Gross, March 23, 1865, substitute, mustered out with company July 11, 1865

James Gracey, July 11, 1863, drafted, discharged by general order May 29, 1865

Andrew Henderson, July 18, 1863, drafted, mustered out with company July 11, 1865

Alexander D Hoel, October 25, 1861; mustered out with company July 11, 1865; veteran

Henry Houser, March 18, 1865, substitute; mustered out with company July 11, 1865

Josiah M. Hays, July 16, 1863, drafted; absent, sick, at muster out

Samuel S Hays, February 22, 1864, drafted, died at Beverly, N. J, October 9, 1864

John Hilliard, August 28, 1861, died De-

Cherry Tree (West End)

William Penn Monument Cherry Tree

First National Bank, Cherry Tree

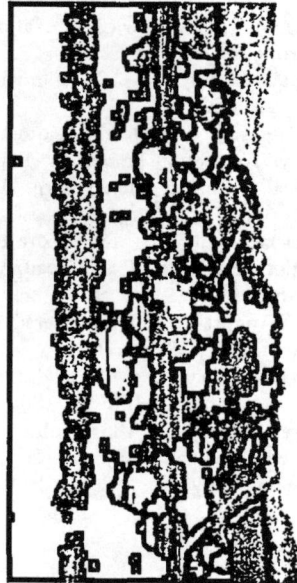

Panoramic View of Cherry Tree

cember 15, 1862, buried at Point Lookout, Md

Sebastian Hogan, August 28, 1861, died October 6, 1861

Robert Hunter, August 1, 1861, missing in action at Spottsylvania C H May 12, 1863.

Isaiah Haines, August 25, 1861, discharged on surgeon's certificate April 4, 1862

William Hamma, October 9, 1861, discharged by general order May 29, 1865, veteran

Nathaniel B Hipple, August 28, 1861, discharged on surgeon's certificate April 4, 1862

William B Hoel, August 28, 1861, discharged on surgeon's certificate January 8, 1863

George Hollenbeck, September 30, 1862, discharged by general order May 29, 1865

Lyman Hegley, August 28, 1861, transferred to V R C November 6, 1863

John Hennessy, March 2, 1865, not on muster-out roll

Eli Ice, July 29, 1864, substitute, discharged on surgeon's certificate June, 1865

Wilder Jackson, September 2, 1863, drafted, mustered out with company July 11, 1865

Jonathan Jamison, August 1, 1861, mustered out with company July 11, 1865, veteran

James Kelly, February 7, 1865, mustered out with company July 11, 1865

John Knoll, February 7, 1865, mustered out with company July 11, 1865

Gottfried Kammur, March 16, 1865, substitute, deserted March 27, 1865

Henry Keys, August 28, 1861, discharged on surgeon's certificate March 27, 1862

Joseph F Kirby, August 28, 1861; discharged on surgeon's certificate December 27, 1862

John Klinger, August 28, 1861, discharged September 3rd for wounds received at Glendale, Va, June 30, 1862

Edward Knapp, August 28, 1861, discharged August 28, 1864—expiration of term

Frank Livingston, August 28, 1861, deserted June 27, 1863

William Lightner, August 28, 1861, discharged on surgeon's certificate March 25, 1862

John Mayberry, July 29, 1864, substitute, mustered out with company July 11, 1865

David Mulholland, October 25, 1861, mustered out with company July 11, 1865, veteran

James Murphy, August 7, 1862, wounded at Chancellorsville, May 3, 1863, absent in hospital at muster out

Edwin Marquis, July 24, 1863, drafted, missing in action September 13, 1864

James Mack, March 16, 1865, substitute, deserted April 28, 1865

Thomas J Morrison, March 17, 1865, substitute, deserted June 25, 1865

Malvin Munger, October 25, 1861, transferred to 33rd N Y V August 31, 1862

Archibald F Mason, October 28, 1861 discharged on surgeon's certificate February 27, 1863

Henry Marquett, September 4, 1863, drafted, prisoner from October 27, 1864, to March 4, 1865, discharged by general order June 17, 1865

James McAtee, August 1, 1861, mustered out with company July 11, 1865, veteran

Charles A McCosh, August 1, 1861, mustered out with company July 11, 1865, veteran

Samuel McFadden, August 28, 1861, mustered out with company July 11, 1865, veteran

William McKelvy, August 1, 1861, mustered out with company July 11, 1865, veteran

Alexander P McArdle, August 28, 1861, discharged on surgeon's certificate August 4, 1862

David McCardle, August 28, 1861, discharged August 28, 1864—expiration of term

Reed McFadden, August 28, 1861, discharged on surgeon's certificate November 6, 1861.

Sam McLaughlin, August 28, 1861; discharged on surgeon's certificate November 28, 1863

John McLaughlin, August 28, 1861, transferred to V R C September 12, 1863

Irwin McCutcheon, August 1, 1861, transferred to V R C August 1, 1864, veteran

Nathan Noble, August 28, 1861, captured at Gaines's Mills, June 27, 1862, died July 20, 1862

· Benjamin Newcomb, August 28, 1861, discharged on surgeon's certificate August 10, 1862

James O'Nell, September 4, 1863, substitute, deserted September 23, 1863

Casper Pitcher, June 13, 1864, substitute; mustered out with company July 11, 1865

William Pennington, August 28, 1861; killed at Fairoaks May 31, 1862

George Plotner, August 28, 1861, killed at Fairoaks, May 31, 1862

Joseph Pete, March 18, 1865; deserted June 25, 1865

Josiah Y Reppeard, March 31, 1864; killed at Wilderness May 5, 1864

William Riddle, August 28, 1861, killed at Fairoaks May 31, 1862.

George L Riley, March 31, 1864, killed at Wilderness May 5, 1864

Charles B. Ross, August 28, 1861, killed at Fairoaks May 31, 1862

Joseph Riensel, March 23, 1864, captured at Boydton Plank Road October 27, 1864; died at Annapolis, Md, March 16, 1865

John Robinson, March 18, 1865, deserted June 5, 1865.

Isaac L Rearick, July 18, 1863, drafted, discharged on surgeon's certificate February 5, 1865

Solomon B Riggs, August 28, 1861; discharged April 20, 1865, for wounds received at Petersburg June 22, 1864.

John Rorabaugh, August 28, 1861, transferred to V R C November 6, 1863

William M Riggs, August 28, 1861, transferred to V R C December 20, 1863

Samuel K Shipley, September 4, 1863, substitute, deserted; returned, out with company July 11, 1865

Andrew Sites, August 28, 1861, mustered out with company July 11, 1865; veteran

George Smith, August 1, 1861, mustered out with company July 11, 1865, veteran

Herman Sneer, September 4, 1863; drafted, mustered out with company July 11, 1865.

George Staum, June 13, 1864, substitute, mustered out with company July 11, 1865

George J Stiles, September 4, 1863; drafted, mustered out with company July 11, 1865

Gershom Saxton, August 28, 1861; killed at Wilderness May 5, 1864

William Shaffer, August 28, 1861; killed at Deep Bottom August 16, 1864, veteran

William Smith, August 28, 1861, captured June 22, 1862, died in Richmond July 2, 1862

Henry Shaffner, August 28, 1861, died July 2nd of wounds received at Fairoaks May 31, 1862

George Stokes, February 28, 1864, captured, died at Salisbury, N C, January 23, 1865, veteran

John Smith, July 11, 1863, drafted, missing in action at Boydton Plank Road October 27, 1864

Samuel Sharp, September 1, 1863, substitute, deserted June 25, 1865

Richard Smith, March 16, 1865, substitute, deserted April 1, 1865

Isaac Solly, August 28, 1861, discharged on surgeon's certificate October 4, 1862

William H Saxton, August 28, 1861, transferred to 10th U S Infantry December 20, 1862

Robert Shull, August 19, 1862, discharged by general order May 29, 1865

Perry Smith, August 28, 1861, discharged on surgeon's certificate December 31, 1862

Almon Spencer, March 22, 1862, discharged March 22, 1864—expiration of term

John Stedham, April 1, 1861, captured, discharged May 19, 1865—expiration of term

Harvey D Thompson, July 15, 1863, drafted, discharged by general order June 24, 1865

James Thompson, February 14, 1865, wounded at Sailor's Creek, Va, April 6, 1865, absent in hospital at muster out

William Todd, March 16, 1865, substitute, deserted June 25, 1865

Robert Tozer, August 28, 1861, discharged on surgeon's certificate April 4, 1862

Solomon Tozer, August 28, 1861, dis-charged on surgeon's certificate February 11, 1863

Charles Truck, March 25, 1865, substitute, discharged by general order May 29, 1865

Boswell C Thorn, August 28, 1861, transferred to V R C December 15, 1863

Gabriel Vastbinder, August 28, 1861, discharged on surgeon s certificate November 11, 1862

Anthony Williams, August 1, 1864, substitute, mustered out with company July 11, 1865

William Wilson, February 12, 1864, mustered out with company July 11, 1865

William Woodward, March 31, 1864, mustered out with company July 11, 1865

Henry C Wykoff, March 22, 1862, mustered out with company July 11, 1865, veteran

John Wilson, August 28, 1861, killed at Fair Oaks, May 31, 1862

George Wood, August 28, 1861, killed at Fair Oaks, May 31, 1862

William Williams, July 27, 1864, substitute, deserted February 4, 1865

Charles D Warner, September 8, 1863, drafted, discharged by general order June 23, 1865

John Williams, August 28, 1861, discharged on surgeon's certificate June 27, 1862

Ellis Wilson, August 28, 1861, discharged on surgeon's certificate February 2, 1863

George Wilson, August 28, 1861, discharged on surgeon's certificate December 13, 1862

Thomas F Wilson, February 29, 1864, prisoner from September 10, 1864, to March 12, 1865, discharged by general order June 6, 1865

Henry B White, July 11, 1863, drafted, transferred to V R C January 5, 1865

George Yingling, February 25, 1864, wounded at Boydton Plank Road October 28, 1864, absent in hospital at muster out

John Yingling, August 28, 1861, killed at Petersburg June 16, 1864, buried in National Cemetery, City Point, section D, division 1, grave 78, veteran

Company F

Recruited in Clearfield, Indiana and Venango Counties

Captains —Robert Kirk, September 9, 1861, wounded at Fair Oaks May 31, 1862, and at Bull Run August 29, 1862, killed at Chancellorsville May 3, 1863

John Daugherty, September 9, 1861, promoted to first sergeant January 2, 1862, to second lieutenant September 29, 1862, to first lieutenant November 26, 1862, to captain August 19, 1863, mustered out October 7, 1864 —expiration of term

William Kemper, September 17, 1861, promoted from corporal to sergeant January 2, 1862, to first sergeant September 29 1862, to second lieutenant January 1, 1863, to captain November 24, 1864, mustered out with company July 11, 1865

First Lieutenants —James B Greggir, September 9, 1861, wounded at Fair Oaks, May 31, 1862, resigned October 24, 1862

Henry P McKillip, September 9 1861, promoted to corporal January 1, 1863, to sergeant July 1, 1863, to first sergeant April 1, 1864 to first lieutenant November 26, 1864, mustered out with company July 11, 1865, veteran

Second Lieutenants —David Ratchft, October 25, 1861, resigned December 2, 1861

Ezra B Baird, September 9, 1861, promoted from first sergeant to second lieutenant January 2, 1862, wounded at Fair Oaks May 31, 1862, resigned October 24, 1862

Ogg Neil, February 19, 1862, promoted to corporal August 28, 1863, to sergeant July 1, 1864, to first sergeant December 17, 1864, to second lieutenant June 8, 1865, mustered out with company July 11, 1865, veteran

First Sergeants —William T Stewart, September 17, 1861, promoted to corporal, August 27, 1863, to sergeant July 1, 1864, to first sergeant June 9, 1865, mustered out with company July 11, 1865, veteran

Jacob S Smith, September 9, 1861, promoted from sergeant January 1, 1863, killed at Chancellorsville May 3, 1863

Sergeants —Lewis Findley, August 28, 1861, promoted to corporal July 1, 1864, to sergeant September 1, 1864, mustered out with company July 11, 1865, veteran

Wm W Hazelett, September 17, 1861, promoted to corporal September 1, 1864, to sergeant December 17, 1864, mustered out with company July 11, 1865, veteran

John M Brewer, February 28, 1864, promoted to corporal September 1, 1864, to sergeant December 17, 1864, mustered out with company July 11, 1865

Samuel H Pound, February 17, 1862, promoted to corporal December 17, 1864, to sergeant June 9, 1865, mustered out with company July 11, 1865, veteran

Robert Doty, September 9, 1861, promoted from corporal to sergeant September 9, 1862, killed at Gettysburg July 2, 1863, buried in National Cemetery, section E, grave 9

John W Smith, September 9, 1861, promoted to corporal August 28, 1863, to sergeant

April 1, 1864, killed at Petersburg June 18, 1864, veteran

Samuel Adamson, September 9, 1861, died May 20, 1863, of wounds received in action, burial in Military Asylum Cemetery, D C

John Hendricks, October 25, 1861, discharged October 25, 1864—expiration of term

Elijah Pantall, October 25, 1861, transferred to V R C March 4, 1864

Jonathan Brindle, October 25, 1861, transferred to V R C June 18, 1864

Corporals —Luke Loomis, Jr, July 8, 1864; drafted, promoted to corporal December 17, 1864, mustered out with company July 11, 1865

Joshua Pearce, September 9, 1861, promoted to corporal June 9, 1865, mustered out with company July 11, 1865, veteran

Joseph Taylor, September 9, 1861, promoted to corporal June 9, 1865 mustered out with company July 11, 1865, veteran

Wm H Hazelett, September 17, 1861, promoted to corporal June 9, 1865, mustered out with company July 11, 1865, veteran

Charles B Gill, August 28, 1861, promoted to corporal September 1, 1864, absent, wounded, at muster out, veteran

John W Lynn, July 16, 1863, drafted, discharged by general order June 24, 1865

John N Means, February 28, 1864, promoted to corporal June 9, 1865

Lewis D Ensinger, September 9, 1861, promoted to corporal January 1, 1862, killed at Charles City Cross Roads June 30, 1862

Ira F Mott, September 3, 1861, promoted to corporal August 28, 1863, killed at Wilderness May 5, 1864, veteran

George B Hall, September 17, 1861, discharged on surgeon's certificate October 12, 1864, veteran

George W McFadden, August 28, 1861, prisoner from October 27, 1864, to March 2, 1865, discharged by general order June 5, 1865, veteran

Thomas Niel, October 19, 1861, discharged on surgeon's certificate March 4, 1865, veteran

Irwin B Nicodemus, May 7, 1862, discharged May 19, 1864—expiration of term

James Randolph, September 9, 1861, discharged on surgeon's certificate June 30, 1863

George W Randolph, September 9, 1861, discharged October 25, 1862, for wounds received in action

John N Vanhorn, October 25, 1861, discharged on surgeon's certificate February 6, 1863

Peter Wheelan, November 2, 1861, discharged November 1, 1864—expiration of term

George W Campbell, September 9, 1861, discharged February 25, 1863, for wounds received in action

Privates —Wm H H Anthony, September 17, 1861, missing in action at Spottsylvania C H May 12, 1864, veteran

Jonathan Ayers, February 25, 1864, missing in action at Boydton Plank Road October 27, 1864

James D Anthony, October 25, 1861, discharged on surgeon's certificate October 14, 1862

Thos S Anderson, September 9, 1861, discharged February 6, 1863, for wounds received in action

James Aul, October 25, 1861, transferred to V R C July 1, 1864

William W Brillhart, February 10, 1864, mustered out with company July 11, 1865

John W Bryant, August 2, 1864, mustered out with company July 11, 1865

Jacob L Bee, February 11, 1864, absent, sick, at muster out

John W Brooks, September 9, 1861, discharged on surgeon's certificate March 25, 1863

Charles Berry, October 25, 1861, discharged on surgeon's certificate February 18, 1863

James Buher, July 7, 1864, substitute; prisoner from August 16, 1864, to March 13, 1865, discharged by general order June 29, 1865

John H Bush, February 28, 1864, absent, wounded, at muster out

James Crock, September 9, 1861, killed at Fair Oaks May 31, 1863

James Crawford, March 16, 1865, substitute, deserted June 23, 1865

John Carr, March 18, 1865, substitute, deserted April 27, 1865

Samuel Cochran, September 9, 1861, deserted June 30, 1863, returned, discharged May 25, 1865, to date expiration of term

John Cupler, September 9, 1863, discharged February 15, 1863, for wounds received in action

Wm A Chambers, April 30, 1862 transferred to V R C October 1, 1863

Perry C Cupler, September 9, 1861, transferred to V R C September 1, 1863

Michael Dolan, March 18, 1865, substitute: absent, sick, at muster out

William W Dixon, February 14, 1864, absent on furlough at muster out

Peter Depp, September 9, 1861, killed at Chancellorsville May 3, 1863

Henry H Depp, September 9, 1861, died at New Haven, Conn, July 6, 1862, of wounds received in action

Peter Dalton, March 18, 1865; substitute, deserted July 1, 1865

Thomas Daily, March 10, 1865, substitute; deserted June 26, 1865

Patrick Delaney, March 17, 1865, substitute, deserted May 15, 1865

Philip B Depp, September 9, 1861, discharged on surgeon's certificate November 12, 1861

John P Drum, October 25, 1861; discharged on surgeon's certificate January 1, 1863

James Drum, September 9, 1861, discharged July 23, 1863, for wounds received in action

Jonathan Doty, September 9, 1861, mustered out September 30, 1864—expiration of term

Samuel Edwards, September 17, 1861, discharged on surgeon's certificate November 12, 1861

Chauncey A Ellis, October 25, 1861, mustered out September 9, 1864—expiration of term

John M Fleming, September 17, 1861, mustered out with company July 11, 1864, veteran

Alfred Foltz, March 5, 1865, substitute, absent, sick, at muster out

Wm Fitzgerald, March 17, 1865, substitute, deserted April 4, 1865

Samuel Fry, October 26, 1861, discharged January 2, 1863, for wounds received in action

John F Fulmer, September 9, 1861; discharged September 8, 1864—expiration of term

Samuel D Fulmer, September 9, 1861, discharged August 24, 1864, for wounds received in action

Thomas S Guiles, March 15, 1865, substitute, deserted June 23, 1865

Stephen Gleeson, March 16, 1865, substitute, mustered out with company July 11, 1865

George Gossor, March 3, 1865, substitute, mustered out with company July 11, 1865

James Gallagher, March 13, 1865, drafted, mustered out with company July 11, 1865

Joseph Graham, February 23, 1865, drafted, mustered out with company July 11, 1865

Anthony A Gallagher, July 15, 1864, drafted, absent, sick, at muster out

Henry A L Girts, September 9, 1862, transferred to V R C October 1, 1863, discharged by general order June 29, 1865

Jonathan Himes, September 3, 1861, mustered out with company July 11, 1865, veteran

Wm S Hendricks, September 17, 1861, mustered out with company July 11, 1865, veteran

Isaac Hendricks, February 28, 1864, mustered out with company July 11, 1865

Joseph Hill, September 9, 1861, killed at Fair Oaks May 31, 1862

Alonzo Hemstreat, September 9, 1861, killed at Gettysburg July 2, 1863

George W Hoover, October 25, 1861, died at Fortress Monroe June 4, 1862, of wounds received in action

Benjamin B Hall, February 29, 1864, captured, died at Andersonville, Ga, July 17, 1864, grave, 3474

John Hare, March 17, 1865, substitute, deserted April 27, 1865

James Hopkins, September 9, 1862, deserted October, 1863

Thomas Hombs, January 30, 1864, deserted May 6, 1864

H H Hollowell, October 26, 1861, deserted October, 1863

Simon D Hugus, September 9, 1861, discharged on surgeon's certificate March 14, 1862

John C Hollowell, October 26, 1861, discharged on surgeon's certificate November 1, 1862

Thomas M Hauck, October 25, 1861; discharged on surgeon's certificate December 24, 1862

Edward Hogan, March 17, 1865, substitute, discharged on surgeon's certificate June 11, 1865

Geo W Hollowell, September 9, 1861, discharged January 13, 1863, for wounds received in action

Samuel Hannah, September 9, 1861, transferred to 1st U S Cavalry January 17, 1863

George K Hoover, October 26, 1861, transferred to V R C October 7, 1863

Daniel Johnston, October 25, 1861, killed at Bull Run August 29, 1862

John D Jewell, September 3, 1861, mustered out with company July 11, 1865, veteran

Jackson Jones, July 11, 1863, drafted, mustered out with company July 11, 1865

James A Johnston, June 9, 1864, substitute, killed near Weldon Railroad, Va, October 2, 1864

Robert J Jewett, February 17, 1862, died at Washington, D C, June 4, 1864, of wounds received in action, buried in National Cemetery, Arlington, Va, veteran

James Jenkins, July 27, 1864, drafted,

missing in action at Deep Bottom, Va , October 2, 1864

Amos S Knauer, March 11, 1865, drafted, mustered out with company July 11, 1865

Harrison Keltz, September 9, 1861, deserted June 25, 1863, returned April 25, 1865, mustered out with company July 11, 1865

Charles Kleffer, October 25, 1861, died at Camp Jameson, Va , January 28, 1862

John Kelly, March 16, 1865, substitute, deserted April 2, 1865

John Kelly, June 27, 1862, captured, died at Salisbury, N C, Dec 15, 1864

Jacob Kurtz, March 16, 1865, substitute, deserted April 2, 1865

Thomas Kennan, March 17, 1865, substitute, deserted June 29, 1865

Robert S Laughry, February 24, 1864, mustered out with company July 11, 1865

Levi S Lust, March 18, 1865, substitute, mustered out with company July 11, 1865

Nicholas Lutcher, March 17, 1865, substitute, mustered out with company July 11, 1865

Charles Lyle, January 29, 1864, killed at Wilderness, Va , May 5, 1864, buried in Wilderness burial grounds

John Myer, March 16, 1865, substitute; mustered out with company July 11, 1865

Edward Mingus, March 18, 1865, substitute, deserted, returned June 29, 1865, mustered out with company July 11, 1865

George R Moyer, March 16, 1865, substitute, mustered out with company July 11, 1865

Garret P Mattis, March 17, 1865, substitute, mustered out with company July 11, 1865

Peter Morgan, March 22, 1865, substitute, discharged by general order July 12, 1865

Wm Mann, January 16, 1863; killed at Sailor's Creek, Va , April 6, 1865

Scott Mitchell, June 4, 1864, substitute; died November 6, 1864

Wm C Martin, September 17, 1861, died January 6, 1865, veteran

Geo W Maynard, September 9, 1861, missing in action at Wilderness, Va , May 5, 1864

George Moore, March 15, 1865; substitute; deserted May 20, 1865

John Miller, September 9, 1861, discharged on surgeon's certificate January 29, 1863

Jas A Minish, September 9, 1861, discharged September 8, 1864—expiration of term

James McCarty, March 17, 1865; substitute, absent, wounded, at muster out

Rob McMannes, October 26, 1861, died at Harrison's Landing, Va , July 20, 1862

Michael McDannell, March 16, 1865, substitute, deserted April 27, 1865

Thomas McFadden, March 17, 1865, substitute, deserted April 1, 1865

John McKean, September 9, 1861, discharged on surgeon's certificate January 11, 1863

Sam A McGhee, September 9, 1861; discharged September 8, 1864—expiration of term

Wm T Niel, May 7, 1862, discharged on surgeon's certificate August 6, 1862.

Thomas Orr, September 9, 1861, killed at Bull Run, Va , August 29, 1862

Wm O'Brian, March 16, 1865, substitute, deserted April 4, 1865

Matthew O'Donnell, March 17, 1865, substitute, deserted April 1, 1865

Chas W O'Niel, March 18, 1865, substitute, deserted June 24, 1865

James O'Bran, September 9, 1861, discharged September 10, 1862, for wounds received in action

Thomas O'Brichel, September 9, 1861, discharged September 8, 1864—expiration of term

Charles Parry, March 18, 1865, substitute; discharged by general order June 12, 1865

David R Porter, January 11, 1864, died at Philadelphia, Pa, February 13, 1865

Jas R Pounds, October 25, 1861, missing in action at Gettysburg, Pa, July 2, 1863

Jackson Piper, October 25, 1861, discharged on surgeon's certificate December 11, 1862

Adam Ritz, March 18, 1865, substitute, mustered out with company July 11, 1865

Enos Ratzel, March 18, 1865, drafted, mustered out with company July 11, 1865

Amos Redky, March 24, 1865, drafted, mustered out with company July 11, 1865

John Riley, March 16, 1865, substitute, deserted April 5, 1865

Jacob Reel, March 21, 1865, drafted, mustered out with company July 11, 1865

Peter Rourke, March 16, 1865, substitute, deserted July 1, 1865

Irwin Robinson, February 15, 1864, discharged on surgeon's certificate April 20, 1865

Jas W Shaffer, March 19, 1862, mustered out with company July 11, 1865, veteran

Isaac Smith, July 16, 1863, drafted, mustered out with company July 11, 1865

Geo Shields, September 8, 1862, deserted June 30, 1863, returned November 14, 1864, mustered out with company July 11, 1865

John Schmidt, March 17, 1865, substitute, mustered out with company July 11, 1865

Asher A Sellers, February 24, 1865, drafted, mustered out with company July 11, 1865

John Service, August 28, 1861, absent, wounded, at muster out, veteran

David Simpson, February 14, 1864, discharged by general order June 27, 1865

Chas Smouse, September 9, 1861, killed at Fredericksburg, Va, December 13, 1864

David S Simpson, September 9, 1861, killed at Chancellorsville, Va, May 3, 1863

Samuel Stevenson, July 1, 1864, substitute, captured, died at Salisbury, N C, December 27, 1864

Lewis Stern, June 13, 1864, substitute, missing in action at Boydton Plank Road, Va, October 27, 1864

James S Smith, February 28, 1864, substitute, missing in action at Boydton Plank Road, Va, October 27, 1864

Dan Sullivan, March 16, 1865, substitute, deserted April 5, 1865

Andrew J Smith, September 8, 1862, deserted October, 1863

Henry Shaffer, October 25, 1861, discharged on surgeon's certificate September 15, 1862

Peter C Spencer, October 25, 1861, discharged on surgeon's certificate December 31, 1862

John Stewart, October 25, 1861, discharged on surgeon's certificate January 30, 1863

David C Simpson, February 14, 1864, discharged by general order June 2, 1865

Daniel Tallman, September 9, 1861, deserted May 10, 1862

Sterling M Thomas, September 9, 1861, deserted April 1, 1862

Peter Vanoligan, March 18, 1865, substitute, mustered out with company July 11, 1865

John Vorece, March 10, 1865, substitute, deserted May 2, 1865

Sam W Walker, February 18, 1864, mustered out with company July 11, 1865

Isaac Wray, February 18, 1864, mustered out with company July 11, 1865

Newton Wilson, July 16, 1863, drafted, mustered out with company July 11, 1865

Moses White, March 17, 1865, substitute, mustered out with company July 11, 1865

Conrad Wolf, March 15, 1865, substitute, mustered out with company July 11, 1865

Henry Wimmer, March 17, 1865, substitute, mustered out with company July 11, 1865

John Williams, March 16, 1865, substitute, absent, sick, at muster out

Wm H Wilson, September 9, 1861, killed at Fair Oaks, Va, May 31, 1862

Albert C Wheeler, September 9, 1861, killed at Charles City Cross Roads June 30, 1862

David Willard, September 3, 1861, killed at Wilderness, Va, May 5, 1864, veteran

John P Williamson, October 26 1861, captured, died 1862

Joseph White, October 25, 1861, captured, died date unknown

Ferdinand Wagner, March 17, 1865, substitute, deserted April 1, 1865

David K Williams, October 26, 1862, transferred to Company F, 18th Regiment, Veteran Reserve Corps, January 20, 1865

George W Young, October 26, 1861, died at New Haven, Conn, June 28, 1862

THE ONE HUNDRED AND FORTY-NINTH REGIMENT—BUCKTAILS

Organized July, 1862

The successes achieved and the gallant services rendered by the original famous "Bucktails" induced the war department to organize and equip other similar regiments In less than twenty days the One Hundred and Forty-ninth and the One Hundred and Fiftieth regiments were formed and ready to receive their equipments for the field These two were suddenly called to the defense of the nation's capitol, as the hosts of the Confederacy had invaded Maryland and seriously threatened the whole region around Washington

Clearfield county was represented in the One Hundred and Forty-ninth, either in whole or in part, in the formation of Companies B and E Upon the complete organization of the regiment the following were the field officers: Roy Stone, colonel; Walton Dright, lieutenant-colonel, George W Speer, major For the remaining part of the year 1862, and until the middle of February of the succeeding year, the regiment remained on duty in the vicinity of Washington, after which they were ordered to the front, and proceeded to Belle Plain, Va, where with the One Hundred and Forty-third Pennsylvania they formed the Second Brigade of the First Army Corps, and Colonel Stone was placed in command

They were first under fire from the enemy on the Rappahannock, a short distance from Pollock's Mills, and held firmly to their position Early the next morning, May 2, it marched to join the main army in the fierce battle at Chancellorsville and arrived there before daylight on the morning of the 3d, and at once began the construction of rifle-pits For several days and nights following the regiments were engaged, reconnoitering and skirmishing here and there, attacking the enemy's pickets and capturing several prisoners, and generally rendering commendable service, bravely facing danger with the fearlessness of veterans

Following close upon the heels of Chancellorsville came the Gettysburg campaign, General Lee, commanding the Confederate forces, having moved northward early in June During the first and second days the regiment was actively engaged, occupying prominent and important positions, and exposed to an almost constant fire from the enemy's battery or sharpshooters During the third day it was held in reserve and was marching to meet Pickett's division when the Confederate forces withdrew In this long and bloody fight the regiment certainly established the fact that the name by which they were known, "Bucktails," was worthily applied, but the command fared badly at Gettysburg Colonel Stone, the gallant commander, was severely wounded, as was Lieutenant Colonel Dwight, Captain John Irvin, of Company B, and Lieutenant Mitchell, of Company E In his official report of the Gettysburg fight General Doubleday says "I relied greatly on Stone's Brigade to hold the post assigned it (between the brigades of Cutler and Meredith), as I soon saw that I should be obliged to change front with a portion of my line, to face the northwest, and his brigade held the pivot of the movement My confidence in this noble body of men was not misplaced They repulsed the repeated attacks of vastly superior numbers, and maintained their position until the final retreat of the whole line" After the battle the regiment lay encamped for a day or two on the field, and started with the army in pursuit of Lee and his retreating forces The events that followed during the fall campaign were unimportant, and early in December, they went into winter quarters near Culpeper

Early in May of the year 1864, the brigade was prepared for the spring campaign and moved from their winter camp to a point near the old Wilderness Tavern, but remaining there but a single night, again moved forward out on the Log road, where a line of battle was formed, then pushing forward met the enemy in a fierce and almost hand to hand conflict, but having an inferior position for successful battle, was slowly forced back to the Lacy House, where they re-formed and were held in reserve for the rest of the day In this encounter the regiment suffered severely at the hands of the rebels, being taken at a great disadvantage and somewhat by surprise Early in the evening, however, the regiment retrieved its loss, having been moved to the right of the Second Corps, led the charge and drove the enemy from his position, and with but slight loss to its own force On the morning of the 6th the battle was renewed with all its vigor, with success at first, but later the whole line was compelled to fall back leaving the brave commander, Wadsworth, dying on the field In the afternoon the brigade was ordered to a charge against Longstreet's forces in the hope of recovering a lost position, and nobly was the order executed, after which the regiment was relieved and retired to the rear for rest and recuperation In this two days' contest the regiment lost in killed, fifteen, in wounded, ninety-nine, and in prisoners taken, ninety-two—about one-fourth of its entire number

On the morning of the 18th, after an all night march, the regiment reached Laurel Hill, and immediately went to the relief of the cavalry Although very much fatigued from its long march, and being in an exposed position, it held firmly to its ground during the day, and

at evening threw up breast works   After a day
in reserve it again went to the front attacking
the enemy and driving them into their works
On the 12th they again charged, but were repulsed with some loss   The men then went
to support the Sixth Corps, and took a position at the front where they were exposed to
the merciless fire of the rebel sharpshooters
They then moved again, and during the night
of the 13th to a position one mile east of
Spottsylvania Court-house   With the First
Division the regiment moved on to Petersburg,
and both in the siege and assault upon the enemy's works its was actively engaged   It was
then under command of Colonel John Irvin,
he having been promoted to that rank April
22, 1864   From the time of the opening of
the campaign in May, until the close of the
month of July, the One Hundred and Forty-
ninth Regiment, according to the report of
Colonel Irvin, lost two commissioned officers,
and thirty-two men killed, six commissioned
officers, and two hundred and forty-three men
wounded, and one hundred and twenty-one
missing, an aggregate of four hundred and
four

On the 18th of August, 1864, the regiment
joined in the first assault on the Weldon Railroad   Although at close quarters, and in a severe struggle, on account of an admirable position, its loss was very light, while that of
the beaten enemy was quite severe   On the
11th of September, they were relieved from
duty at the front and went into reserve, and
so continued until the 7th of December, when
it joined in the grand raid upon the Weldon
Railroad, and on the return therefrom acted as
rear guard, in which position they were con-
tinually harassed by the Confederate cavalry

In the early part of February, 1865, it
joined the movement to Dabney's Mills, and
participated in the engagement at that point,
the last conflict at arms in which the gallant
regiment took an active part   It was then detached from the Army of the Potomac and
sent to Elmira, N Y, where, with the One
Hundred and Fiftieth, it was on guard duty
at the camp for rebel prisoners   Here it remained until the close of its term of service,
and was mustered out on the 24th of June, and
proceeding to Harrisburg was paid off, and
finally disbanded

Field and Staff

Colonels —Roy Stone, August 30, 1862,
wounded at Gettysburg, July 1, 1863, bre-
vetted brigadier-general September 7, 1864,
discharged by special order January 27,
1865

John Irvin, August 26, 1862, promoted
from captain company B, to major February 10, 1864, to lieutenant-colonel April 22,
1864, to colonel February 21, 1865, discharged by special order August 4, 1865

Lieutenant - Colonels — Walton Dwight,
August 27, 1862, promoted from captain
company K, August 29, 1862, wounded at
Gettysburg, Pa, July 1, 1863, discharged
by special order March 31, 1864

James Glenn, August 23, 1862, promoted
from captain company D, to major April 22,
1864, to lieutenant-colonel February 21,
1865, discharged by special order August 4,
1865

Majors —George W Speer, August 26,
1862; promoted from captain Company I,
August 29, 1862, discharged by special order March 23, 1865

Edwin S Osborne, August 30, 1862, promoted from captain Company F, February

25, 1865, discharged by special order July 21, 1865

Adjutants —John E Parsons, August 30, 1862, promoted to captain and assistant adjutant-general U S Vols June 30, 1864, resigned January 30, 1865

John F Irwin, August 26, 1862, promoted from first lieutenant company B. September 5, 1864, mustered out with regiment June 24, 1865

Quartermasters — John M Chase August 26, 1862, promoted from first lieutenant Company B, August 29. 1862, discharged by special order May 10, 1863

Darius F Ellsworth, August 26, 1862, promoted from private Company K, to quarter-master sergeant February 21, 1863, to quartermaster November 22. 1863, to captain and A Q M U S Vols June 30, 1864, mustered out September 20, 1865

George W Turner, August 22, 1862, promoted from sergeant Company F, to quartermaster-sergeant November 22, 1863, to quartermaster October 18, 1864, mustered out with regiment June 24, 1865

Surgeons —W T Humphrey. September 12, 1862, discharged by special order January 17, 1865

Ab'm Harshberger, November 22, 1863, promoted from assistant surgeon February 4, 1865, mustered out with regiment June 24, 1865

Assistant Surgeons —W R D Blackwood. September 12, 1862, promoted to surgeon 40th Regiment P V, April 28, 1863

White G Hunter, September 12, 1862, promoted to surgeon 211th Regiment P V, September 22, 1864

William H King, March 23, 1863, pro-

moted to surgeon 182d Regiment P V, July 27, 1863

David W Riggs, February 15, 1865, mustered out with regiment June 24, 1866

John Graham, April 17, 1865, mustered out with regiment June 24, 1865

Chaplain —James F Calkins, June 3, 1863, mustered out with regiment June 24. 1865

Sergeant - Majors — David Allen, August 26, 1862, promoted from private Company H, September 21, 1862, transferred to Company H, June 18, 1865

William T Easton, August 23. 1862, promoted from sergeant Company D, January 1, 1864, to first sergeant 32d Regiment U S C T March 28, 1864, and to captain 103d Regiment U S C T March 18, 1865, discharged May 5, 1866

Henry Landrus, August 30, 1862, promoted from sergeant Company G, April 3, 1864, wounded and captured at Wilderness, Va, May 5, 1864, discharged by general order May 31, 1865

W M Berkstresser, August 12, 1863, drafted, promoted from private company G, June 1, 1865, mustered out with regiment June 24, 1865

Hospital Steward —Adelbert J Higgle, August 26, 1862, promoted from private company K, September 12, 1862, mustered out with regiment June 24, 1865

Quartermaster - Sergeant — Samuel L Miles, August 26, 1862, promoted from private company B, to commissary-sergeant September 12, 1862, to quartermaster-sergeant October 18, 1864, mustered out with regiment June 24, 1865

Commissary-Sergeant — Charles A Davidson, August 26, 1862, promoted from private company F, October 18, 1864, mustered out with regiment June 24, 1865

Principal Musician —Henry Moyer, August 19, 1862, promoted from musician Company C, March 1, 1864, mustered out with regiment June 24, 1865

Company B

Captains —John Irvin, August 26 1862, wounded at Gettysburg, Pa, July 1, 1863, promoted to major February 10, 1864

William Holden, August 26, 1862, promoted from second to first Lieutenant May 16, 1863, to captain February 11, 1864, discharged December 21, 1864

John L Rex, August 26, 1862, promoted from sergeant to first sergeant February 12, 1863, to second lieutenant February 20, 1864, to first lieutenant September 5, 1864, to captain January 30, 1865, mustered out with company June 24, 1865

First-Lieutenants —John M Chase, August 26, 1862; promoted to quartermaster August 29, 1862

John F Irvin, August 26, 1862, promoted from sergeant to second lieutenant September 30, 1862, to first lieutenant February 20, 1864, to adjutant September 5, 1864

Albert B Cole, August 26, 1862, promoted from sergeant to first sergeant, to second lieutenant September 5, 1864, to first lieutenant January 30, 1865, killed at Hatcher's Run, Va, February 6, 1865

Milton McClure, August 29, 1862, promoted to corporal February 14, 1863, to sergeant September 5, 1864, to first lieutenant March 27, 1865, mustered out with company June 24, 1865

Second Lieutenant —Newton Read, August 26, 1862, promoted from corporal to sergeant August 31, 1864, to second lieutenant June 7, 1865, mustered out with company June 24, 1865

First Sergeant —Oscar B Welch, August 26, 1862, wounded at Laurel, Va, May 8, 1864, promoted from corporal to sergeant, to first sergeant September 5, 1864, absent in hospital at muster out

Sergeants —William I Bard, August 26, 1862, wounded at Spottsylvania C H, May 10, 1864, promoted from corporal February 20, 1864, mustered out with company June 24, 1865

John Henry, August 26, 1862, wounded at Wilderness, Va, May 6, 1864, promoted to corporal February 27, 1863, to sergeant June 6, 1865, mustered out with company June 24, 1865

Edward Livingston, August 26, 1862, wounded at Wilderness, Va, May 5, 1864, promoted to corporal September 1, 1863, to sergeant June 6, 1865, mustered out with company June 24, 1865

Charles W. Needler, August 29, 1862, promoted to corporal February 14, 1863, to sergeant February 20, 1864, missing in action at Wilderness, Va, May 5, 1864

Robert Fleming, August 26, 1862, discharged on surgeon's certificate June 26, 1865

Daniel Shunkweiler, August 26, 1862, wounded at Gettysburg, Pa, July 1, 1863, transferred to Veteran Reserve Corps, date unknown

Corporals —Andrew S Wall, August 26, 1862, promoted to corporal February 20, 1864, mustered out with company June 24, 1865

Joseph Baish, August 26, 1862, wounded at Laurel Hill, Va, May 8, 1864; promoted to corporal February 20, 1864, mustered out with company June 24, 1865

John H Smith, August 26, 1862, promoted to corporal September 5, 1864, mustered out with company June 24, 1865

Daniel W Sloppy, August 26, 1862, promoted to corporal September 5, 1864, mustered out with company June 24, 1865

Marion Sharp, August 26, 1862, wounded at Petersburg, Va, June 18, 1864, promoted to corporal June 6, 1865, mustered out with company June 24, 1865

Charles P McMasters, August 26, 1862, wounded at North Anna River, Va, May 23, 1864, promoted to corporal June 6, 1865, mustered out with company June 24, 1865

Horace N Toby, August 19, 1863, drafted, promoted to corporal June 6, 1865, mustered out with company June 24, 1865

George Hagen, August 26, 1862, promoted to corporal February 12, 1863, missing in action at Wilderness, Va, May 6, 1864

William Curry, August 26, 1862, died at Washington, D C, October 7, 1862

Ellis Lewis, August 26, 1862, promoted to corporal, killed at Gettysburg, Pa, July 1, 1863

John P Spencer, August 26, 1862, promoted to corporal, killed at Wilderness, Va, May 6, 1864

Thomas Adams, August 26, 1862, deserted February 8, 1863

William Sloppy, August 26, 1862, deserted July 1, 1863

Musicians —George L Way, August 26, 1862, mustered out with company June 24, 1865.

David A Wilson, August 26, 1862, mustered out with company June 24, 1865

Privates —Joseph Alexander, August 26, 1862, wounded at Gettysburg, Pa, July 1, 1863, transferred to Veteran Reserve Corps January 10, 1865, discharged by general order June 27, 1865

Bernard Adams, August 26, 1862, killed at Gettysburg, Pa, July 1, 1863

John Blair, August 26, 1862, mustered out with company June 24, 1865

Abraham T Bloom, August 26, 1862, wounded at Wilderness, Va, May 5, 1864, absent in hospital at muster out

David Bloom, August 26, 1862, missing in action at Wilderness, Va, May 5, 1864

Calvin Becannan, August 13, 1863, drafted, missing in action at Wilderness, Va, May 5, 1864

John W Bowers, March 6, 1865 mustered out with company June 24, 1865

Jacob Burtner, August 13, 1863, drafted, mustered out with company June 24 1865

Benj F Brant, August 26, 1863, drafted, wounded at Wilderness, Va, May 5, 1864, absent in hospital at muster out

John B Bott, September 19, 1863, substitute, absent in hospital at muster out

Andrew J Brant, September 23, 1863, substitute, wounded at Wilderness, Va, May 5, 1864, absent in hospital at muster out

Willis G Button, October 16, 1863, substitute, wounded at Petersburg, Va, June 18, 1864, discharged by general order May 31, 1865

Simon B Benson, October 16, 1863, substitute, mustered out with company June 24, 1865

Henry M Bloom, August 26, 1862, discharged by special order January 31, 1863

Jas M Boal, August 26, 1862, discharged by surgeon's certificate April 14, 1863

Reuben K Barnhart, August 19, 1863, drafted, discharged by general order May 24, 1865

Conrad Barrett, August 26, 1862, wounded at North Anna River, Va, May 22, 1864, transferred to Veteran Reserve Corps, discharged by general order July 29, 1865

Jacob D Birsh, August 26, 1862, deserted, returned, discharged by special order July 8, 1865

Chas D Button, October 19, 1863, substitute, killed at Laurel Hill, Va, May 5, 1864

John H Curry, August 26, 1862, wounded at Wilderness, Va, May 5, 1864, mustered out with company June 24, 1865

Jas L Clark, August 26, 1862, mustered out with company June 24, 1865

Wm H Connell, August 26, 1862, wounded at Wilderness, Va, May 5. 1864, mustered out with company June 24, 1865

Geo W Curry, August 26, 1862, discharged on surgeon's certificate, February 11, 1863

David C Cady, August 19, 1863, drafted, transferred to United States Navy April 22, 1864

Samuel Connor, August 13, 1864, transferred to Company A, 49th Regiment P V, date unknown

James Cree, September 5, 1863, substitute, died at Culpeper, Va, December 28, 1864

John Crance, August 19, 1863, drafted; wounded at Wilderness, Va, May 5, 1864, died at Alexandria, Va, May 16, 1864

Richard A Curry, August 26, 1862, killed at Gettysburg, July 1, 1863

Joseph D Dale, August 26, 1862, mustered out with company June 24, 1865

Wm Delancy, March 5, 1865, mustered out with company June 24, 1865

John P Doan, August 19, 1863, drafted, discharged on surgeon's certificate March 24, 1864

Daniel R Davis, August 26, 1862; wounded at Gettysburg, Pa, July 1, 1863, discharged by general order June 29, 1865

Wm P Dixon, August 26, 1862; transferred to Veteran Reserve Corps, date unknown

Rob P Dixon, August 26, 1862, died at Andersonville, Ga, July 26, 1864; grave 4087

Eli Erhart, August 26, 1862, discharged on surgeon's certificate February 27, 1863

Michael Fulermer, August 13, 1863, drafted, mustered out with company June 24, 1864

Cornelius Fitzgerald, August 24. 1863; drafted. absent in hospital at muster out

Luther Fisler, August 16, 1863, substitute, missing in action at Wilderness, Va, May 5, 1864

David Fink, August 26, 1862, missing in action at Wilderness, Va, May 5, 1864

Mortimer Farley, March 31, 1864; mustered out with company June 24, 1865

Henry Farley, November 7, 1863, captured at Wilderness, Va, May 5, 1864, discharged by special order April 8, 1865

Morris Farley, August 26, 1862, wounded at Weldon Railroad, Va, Aug 21, 1864; transferred to Veteran Reserve Corps, date unknown

Wm Fleming, August 26, 1862, killed at Gettysburg, Pa, July 1, 1863

Wm C Gibbs, October 13, 1864, mustered out with company June 24, 1865

Samuel Gafford, August 18, 1863, drafted; captured at Wilderness, Va, May 5, 1864, discharged by general order June 8, 1865

Samuel George, August 26, 1862; transferred to Veteran Reserve Corps, date unknown

Benjamin F George, August 26, 1862, killed at Gettysburg, Pa, July 1, 1863

David C Heiges, August 26, 1862, absent in hospital at muster out

Andrew Heiges, August 26, 1862, missing in action at Wilderness, Va, May 5, 1864

George W Hardinger, August 26, 1863, drafted, missing in action at Wilderness, Va, May 5, 1864

Wm Hardegan, August 26, 1863, drafted, wounded at Wilderness, Va, May 5, 1864, absent in hospital at muster out

James K Hancock, August 26, 1862, mustered out with company June 24, 1865

Charles Hawk, September 16, 1863, substitute, discharged by special order March 25, 1864

James W Henry, August 26, 1862, discharged by general order May 19, 1865

Wm H Harding, November 7, 1863, captured at Wilderness, Va, May 5, 1864, discharged by general order June 12, 1865

Miles H Hang, August 26, 1862, transferred to Veteran Reserve Corps, discharged by general order July 12, 1865

Bailey Heiges, September 24, 1863, substitute, died at Washington, D C, December 20, 1863, buried in Military Asylum Cemetery

Alexander Haney, August 26, 1862, died at Washington, D C, February 5, 1864

Andrew T. Jackson, August 26, 1862, deserted, returned, discharged by special order July 8, 1865.

Barnard Kemper, September 12, 1868; drafted; mustered out with company June 24, 1865

Levi Kegg, September 23, 1863, substitute, wounded at Wilderness, Va, May 5, 1864, absent in hospital at muster out

Darius Knapp, August 19, 1863, drafted; died at Culpeper C H Va, December 28, 1865

George W Leech, November 8, 1863, mustered out with company June 24, 1865

Andrew Lembie, September 26, 1863, substitute, mustered out with company June 24, 1865

David W Lee, August 26, 1862, drafted, mustered out with company June 24, 1865

Jacob T Leins, August 26, 1862, wounded at Gettysburg, Pa, July 1, 1863, discharged on surgeon's certificate April 2, 1864

John Lininger, August 26, 1862, wounded at Gettysburg, Pa, July 1, 1863, transferred to Veteran Reserve Corps, date unknown

Wm Lewis, August 26, 1862, deserted July 1, 1863

James B Martin, March 7, 1865, mustered out with company June 24, 1865

John H Mock, October 2, 1863, substitute, mustered out with company June 24, 1865

Luke S Munn, August 26, 1862, discharged on surgeon's certificate April 1, 1864

Wm A Moore, March 7, 1865, mustered out with company June 24, 1865

Samuel L Miles, August 26, 1862, promoted to commissary-sergeant September 12, 1862

John A Murphy, August 26, 1862, died at Philadelphia, Pa, July 11, 1865, buried in Military Asylum Cemetery, Washington, D C

James L McCullough, August 26, 1862, absent in hospital at muster out

James M McDowell, August 26, 1862, wounded at Gettysburg, Pa, July 1, 1863, discharged on surgeon's certificate April 23, 1864

George McDowel, August 26, 1862, discharged by special order October 14, 1862

Harvey McCracken, August 26. 1862, wounded at Gettysburg, Pa, July 1, 1863, transferred to Veteran Reserve Corps, discharged by general order July 17, 1865

William H McKee, August 26, 1862, died at Washington, D C, November 21, 1862

Thomas McKenzie, August 17, 1863, drafted, killed at Wilderness, Va, May 6, 1864

Samuel McClure, August 26, 1862, killed at Gettysburg, Pa, July 1, 1863

James M McKee, August 26, 1862, deserted February 8, 1863

William H McDonald, August 26, 1862, deserted February 12, 1863

Shadrik H Phillips, August 26, 1862, died August 22, 1863, buried in Cypress Hill Cemetery, L I, grave 815

Joseph G Russell, March 8, 1865, mustered out with company June 24, 1865

Philip Rigard, September 15, 1863, drafted wounded at Wilderness, Va, May 5, 1864, mustered out with company June 24, 1865

Henry Runyan, August 13, 1863, drafted; discharged by special order July 18, 1865

Richard Rowls, August 26, 1862, deserted June 14, 1865

Harvey F Smith, March 8, 1865, mustered out with company June 24, 1865

Daniel Smith, August 26, 1862, missing in action at Wilderness, Va, May 5, 1865

Samuel Stine, August 14, 1863, drafted, mustered out with company June 24, 1865

Rob H Slocum, April 23, 1864, mustered out with company June 24, 1865

Wm H Stage, August 26, 1862, discharged by special order September 2, 1863

Jacob Seigler, August 14, 1863, drafted: wounded at Cold Harbor, Va, June 2. 1864, discharged by general order May 17, 1865

Benjamin F Shave, August 19, 1863, drafted, wounded at Hatcher's Run, Va, February 6. 1865, discharged by general order May 16, 1865

Daniel Shumber, September 15, 1863, substitute, deserted, returned, discharged by special order July 8, 1865

William Smith, August 26, 1862, deserted February 12, 1863, returned, discharged by special order July 8, 1865

Columbus Smith, Aug 26, 1862, deserted; returned, discharged by special order July 8, 1865

Franklin Smith, August 26, 1862, deserted, returned, discharged by special order July 8, 1865

Sylvanus Snyder, August 26, 1862, wounded at Gettysburg, Va., July 1, 1863; transferred to Veteran Reserve Corps, date unknown

W Stambaugh, August 26, 1862, died at Orange Court House, Va, of wounds received at Wilderness, Va, May 5, 1864

Andrew J Sawer, August 19, 1863, substitute, killed at Laurel Hill, Va, May 8, 1865

William Slocum, August 19, 1863; drafted, died at Washington, D C, December 19, 1864; buried in National Cemetery, Arlington, Va

Samuel Starr, August 26, 1862; killed at Gettysburg, Pa, July 1, 1863

Willis Taylor, March 8, 1865; mustered out with company June 24, 1865

Thomas Templeton, February 25, 1865, deserted June 14. 1865

Martin Van Buren, March 10, 1865, mustered out with company June 24, 1865

Amos Wall, March 1, 1865, mustered out with company June 24, 1865

Jos G Williams, August 26, 1862, wounded at Wilderness, Va, May 5, 1864, mustered out with company June 24, 1865

Henry Wynn, Jr, September 15, 1863, drafted, wounded at Spottsylvania Court House, May 16, 1864, mustered out with company June 24, 1865

Ira C Wood, August 19, 1863, drafted, mustered out with company June 24, 1865

Wm S Ward, August 16, 1863, drafted, mustered out with company June 24, 1865

Alex J Wolford, September 23, 1863, substitute, wounded at Weldon Railroad, Va, September 20, 1864

Francis Ward, September 14, 1863, substitute, missing in action at Wilderness, Va, May 5, 1864

John Waterson, August 26, 1862, missing in action at Wilderness, Va, May 5, 1864

James A Wilson, August 26, 1862, discharged on surgeon's certificate December 12, 1862

John Wimer, August 26, 1862, discharged on surgeon's certificate March 12, 1863

John Wolf, September 19, 1865, substitute, captured at Wilderness, Va, May 5, 1864, discharged by general order June 12, 1865

John Whitfield, August 26, 1862; drafted, discharged September 7, 1863

Joseph Whitman, August 26, 1862, transferred to Veteran Reserve Corps, discharged by general order November 18, 1865

Jacob Zerr, September 23, 1863, drafted, absent in hospital at muster out

Company E

Captains —Zara C McCullough, August 30, 1862, discharged on surgeon's certificate December 12, 1863

Amos Row, August 30, 1862, promoted from first lieutenant January 30, 1864, wounded at Hatcher's Run, Va, February 6, 1865, mustered out with company June 24, 1865

First Lieutenant —Thomas Liddell, August 23, 1862, promoted from first sergeant to second lieutenant February 3, 1864, to first lieutenant April 22, 1864, wounded at Wilderness, Va, May 5, 1864, mustered out with company June 24, 1865

Second Lieutenants —Meredith L Jones, August 30, 1862, commissioned first lieutenant December 11, 1863, not mustered, discharged on surgeon's certificate March 18, 1864

Robert A Mitchell, August 23 1862, wounded at Gettysburg, Pa, July 1, 1863, and at Petersburg, Va, June 18, 1864, promoted from sergeant to first sergeant February 3, 1864, to second lieutenant April 22, 1864, mustered out with company June 24, 1865

First Sergeant —James W Irwin, August 23, 1862, wounded at Gettysburg, Pa, July 1, 1863, and at Wilderness, Va, May 5, 1864, promoted from sergeant April 26, 1864, mustered out with company June 24, 1865

Sergeants —Wesley H Shirey, August 29, 1862, promoted to corporal November 1, 1862, to sergeant May 1, 1865, mustered out with company June 24, 1865

Hiram H Hawk, August 26, 1862, promoted to corporal January 1, 1863, to sergeant January 1, 1864, wounded at Petersburg, Va,

May 8, 1864, mustered out with company June 24, 1865

Abednego Crane, August 23, 1862, promoted to corporal September 1, 1863, to sergeant April 26, 1864, wounded at Laurel Hill, Va, May 8, 1864, mustered out with company June 24, 1865

Milton S Lawhead, August 23, 1862, promoted to corporal September 1, 1863, to sergeant September 26, 1864, mustered out with company June 24, 1865

Cornelius Owens, August 23, 1862, wounded at Gettysburg, Pa, July 1, 1863, promoted to second lieutenant 41st Regiment U S C T September 26, 1864, discharged September 30, 1865

William L Antes, August 23, 1862, wounded at Gettysburg, Pa, July 1, 1863, transferred to Veteran Reserve Corps March 15, 1864

George W Miller, August 23, 1862, promoted from corporal April 26, 1864, killed at Wilderness, Va, May 5, 1864

Corporals —Michael B Cramer, August 23, 1862, wounded at Gettysburg, Pa, July 1, 1863, promoted to corporal November 1, 1863, captured at Wilderness, Va, May 5, 1864, died at Florence, S C, or Salisbury, N C, January 10, 1865

George W Luzere, August 29, 1862, promoted to corporal November 1, 1863; mustered out with company June 24, 1865

John M McCumber, August 23, 1862, promoted to corporal January 1, 1864, mustered out with company June 24, 1865.

John W Dehess, August 23, 1862, wounded at Wilderness, Va, May 5, 1864, promoted to corporal April 26, 1864, discharged by general order July 6, 1865

William F Krise, August 23, 1862, promoted to corporal April 26, 1864, mustered out with company June 24, 1865

William L Taylor, August 23, 1862, wounded at Gettysburg, Pa, July 1, 1863, and at Wilderness, Va, May 5, 1864, promoted to corporal April 26, 1864, mustered out with company June 24, 1865

Jason Kirk, Jr, August 23, 1862, discharged by general order May 13, 1865

John H. Mason, August 23, 1862, discharged January 28, 1864, for wounds received at Gettysburg, Pa, July 1, 1863

William Pierce, August 24, 1862, discharged January 7, 1864, for wounds received at Gettysburg, Pa, July 1, 1863

Stephen Brundage, August 29, 1862, promoted to corporal, died at Washington, D C, October 30, 1862

James A Birchfield, August 23, 1862, promoted to corporal, died at Clearfield, Pa, August 18, 1863.

Abram B Davis, August 23, 1862, died at Washington, D C, September 29, 1862

Benj B McPherson, August 23, 1862, promoted to corporal, killed at Gettysburg, Pa, July 1, 1863

Musicians —James H West, August 23, 1862, mustered out with company June 24, 1865

Hiram G Blair, August 29, 1862, mustered out with company June 24, 1865

Privates —Henry C Alleman, September 19, 1863, drafted, wounded at Wilderness, Va, May 5, 1864, mustered out with company June 24, 1865

John Allen, September 14, 1863; drafted, discharged by special order December 18, 1863

Joshua Armstrong, August 23, 1862, discharged on surgeon's certificate December 5, 1863

John W Alworth, August 29, 1862, discharged on surgeon's certificate December 10, 1863

George W Ardry, August 23, 1862, died at Bealton Station, Va, September 9, 1863

Robert J Alexander, September 22, 1863, drafted, died at Alexandria, Va, December 20, 1863, burial record, December 22, 1863, grave 1219

John R Ball, August 23, 1862, wounded at Wilderness, Va, May 5, 1864, mustered out with company June 24, 1865

Daniel Baker, August 27, 1863, drafted, discharged by general order June 2, 1865

John A Bobst, August 15, 1863, drafted, wounded at Laurel Hill, Va, May 8, 1864, mustered out with company June 24, 1865

Frederick Beesecker, August 27, 1863, drafted, mustered out with company June 24, 1865

George Baight, August 24, 1863, drafted, mustered out with company June 24, 1865

Thomas Boyden, August 15, 1863, drafted, mustered out with company June 24, 1865

David Bowman, October 14, 1863, drafted, wounded at Wilderness, Va, May 5, 1864, and at Hatcher's Run, February 6, 1865, mustered out with company June 24, 1865

James Baine, August 15, 1863, drafted, mustered out with company June 24, 1865

John F Bowman, October 14, 1863, drafted, wounded at Laurel Hill, Va, May 8, 1864, transferred to V R C, discharged by general order July 31, 1865

James S Bradley, August 23, 1862, dis-

charged on surgeon's certificate March 25, 1863

James H Bush, August 25, 1862, wounded at Wilderness, Va, May 5, 1864, and at Hatcher's Run, February 6, 1865, discharged by general order May 17, 1865

Perry A Bush, August 14, 1863, drafted, captured at Wilderness, Va, May 5, 1864, discharged by general order June 12, 1865

Michael Baine, September 12, 1863, drafted, discharged by special order September 13, 1864

David B Bernard, August 23, 1862, transferred to Veteran Reserve Corps March 30, 1864, discharged August 23, 1865—expiration of term

James R Brewer, August 25, 1863, drafted, died at Alexandria, Va, June 6th, of wounds received at Laurel Hill, May 8, 1864

George W Bowman, October 14, 1863, drafted, died at Andersonville, Ga, October 18th of wounds received at Wilderness, May 5, 1864, grave 11087

Calvin Bowman, October 14, 1863, drafted, died at Washington, D C, May 18, 1864, buried in National Cemetery, Arlington, Va

'William Carr, August 23, 1862, missing in action at Wilderness, Va, May 5, 1864

Jos P Catherman, August 23, 1862, mustered out with company June 24, 1865

Benj F Carr, August 23, 1862, captured at Wilderness, Va, May 6, 1864, died at Annapolis, Md, March 11, 1865

Joseph M Cook, August 15, 1863 drafted, mustered out with company June 24, 1865

Francis Culloton, August 15, 1863.

drafted, mustered out with company June 24, 1865

Justice Carey, September 11, 1863, drafted, wounded at Wilderness, Va, May 5, 1864, discharged by general order June 24, 1865

John M Caldwell, August 23, 1862, discharged on surgeon's certificate November 26, 1862

Peter Curley, August 23, 1862, wounded at Gettysburg, Pa, July 1, 1863, transferred to Veteran Reserve Corps December 15, 1863

David Cramer, August 23, 1862, wounded at Laurel Hill, Va, May 8, 1864, died at Washington, D C, June 3rd—burial record June 6th—of wounds received at Spottsylvania C H, Va, May 12, 1864, buried in Cypress Hill Cemetery, L I

John L Cavender, September 15, 1863, drafted, captured at Wilderness, Va, May 5th, died at Andersonville, Ga, September 14, 1864, grave 8700

Patrick Culloton, August 29, 1862, deserted January 29, 1863

Valentine Dice, February 26, 1864, wounded at Wilderness, Va, May 5 1864, absent at muster out

David Dulberger, August 15, 1863, drafted, mustered out with company June 24, 1865

Edwin R Dailey, August 29, 1862, discharged on surgeon's certificate April 1, 1863

Jas H Daugherty, August 29, 1862, discharged on surgeon's certificate April 1, 1863

Wm Davis, August 15, 1863, drafted, died at Washington, D C, January 2, 1864

John Darcy, August 29, 1862, died at Belle Plaine, Va, March 11, 1863

Tobias Edward, August 15, 1863, drafted, captured at Weldon Railroad, Va, August 21, 1864, discharged by general order June 12, 1865

John Funk, August 15, 1862, drafted; wounded at Petersburg, Pa, June 18, 1864, mustered out with company June 24, 1865

James M Fox, August 23, 1862, discharged on surgeon's certificate March 21, 1864

Frank Freel, August 23, 1862, wounded at Gettysburg, Pa, July 1, 1863, transferred to Veteran Reserve Corps February 15, 1864

Charles Fry, August 15, 1862, drafted, died December 27, 1863—burial record December 28th—at Alexandria, Va, grave 1236

James W Goss, August 23, 1862, wounded at Gettysburg, Pa, July 1, 1863, absent in hospital at muster out

Edward Goss, August 23, 1862, wounded at Gettysburg, Pa, July 1, 1863, mustered out with company June 24, 1865

Charles H Garrison, August 29, 1862, wounded at Wilderness, Va, May 5, 1864, mustered out with company June 24, 1865

Frederick Gamp, October 16, 1863, drafted, discharged by general order, June, 1865

Samuel C Gephart, August 24, 1863, drafted, wounded at Laurel Hill, Va, May 8, 1864, mustered out with company June 24, 1865

Jas W Guthery, September 22, 1863, drafted, mustered out with company June 24, 1865

Augustus Grey, February 7, 1865, discharged by general order June 2, 1865

Wm Grey, February 24, 1865, mustered out with company June 24, 1865

Henry P Hummel, August 29, 1862, wounded at Gettysburg, Pa, July 1, 1863, mustered out with company June 24, 1865

Wm Gready, August 29, 1863, deserted January 29, 1863

Nathan Haring, August 29, 1863, missing in action at Gettysburg, Pa, July 1, 1863

Andrew Hamaker, August 14, 1863, drafted, wounded at Wilderness, Va, May 5, 1864, mustered out with company June 24, 1865

Wm Hoover, August 23, 1862, discharged on surgeon's certificate March 20, 1863

Michael Hinkle, August 15, 1863, drafted, wounded at Wilderness, Va, May 5, 1864, discharged by general order May 17, 1865

Elias Heddings, October 15, 1863, drafted, died at Washington, D C, May 19th of wounds received at Spottsylvania C H, Va, May 12, 1864, buried in National Cemetery, Arlington

Martin Hashuishall, August 17 1863, drafted, wounded and captured at Wilderness, Va, May 5, 1864, died at Andersonville, Ga, September 27, 1864, grave 9843

Wm H Ike, August 25 1862, captured at Wilderness, Va, May 5, 1864, died at Wilmington, N C, March 26, 1865 buried in National Cemetery grave 1002

John C Johnson, August 23, 1862, absent in hospital at muster out

James T Jones, August 23, 1862, died at Washington, D C, November 20, 1862

Oliver H P Krise, August 23, 1862, wounded at Wilderness, Va, May 5, 1864, mustered out with company June 24, 1865

Daniel S Kephart, August 23, 1862, missing in action at Gettysburg, Pa, July 1, 1863

John Kivlan, August 29, 1862, discharged on surgeon's certificate December 28, 1862

Andrew Krise, August 23, 1862, deserted, dishonorably discharged June 18, 1864

Christian Lanich, August 23, 1862, mustered out with company June 24, 1865

James Lucas, August 29, 1862, wounded and missing in action at Gettysburg, Pa, July 1, 1863

Joseph Linard, August 17, 1863, drafted wounded at Wilderness, Va, May 5, 1864, mustered out with company June 24, 1865

Chas Larimer, August 23, 1863, wounded at Gettysburg, Pa, July 1, 1863, discharged by general order June 12, 1865

Harvey Lloyd, August 23, 1862, transferred to Veteran Reserve Corps December 15, 1861

William Mays, August 30, 1862, mustered out with company June 24, 1865

John Miller, September 14, 1863, drafted, mustered out with company June 24 1865

David S Maxwell, August 17, 1863, drafted, mustered out with company June 24, 1865

James D Maffit, August 23, 1862, discharged on surgeon's certificate January 12, 1863

Alonzo J W Merrell, August 23, 1862, discharged on surgeon's certificate February 11, 1863

Thomas E Miller, August 23, 1862, discharged on surgeon's certificate April 1, 1863

William L Mackey, August 23, 1862, died at Washington, D C, January 12, 1863, buried in Military Asylum Cemetery

William H Miller, August 25, 1862, deserted February 16, 1863

George McCanns, August 17, 1863, drafted, mustered out with company June 24, 1865

James D McMullin, February 7, 1865, mustered out with company June 24, 1865

Patrick McCall, August 29, 1862, deserted January 29, 1863

Levi F Noss, August 14, 1863, drafted, mustered out with company June 24, 1865

John H Ogden, August 23, 1862, mustered out with company June 24, 1865

William H Phillips, August 23, 1862, missing in action at Gettysburg, Pa, July 1, 1863

Henry W Peters, August 23, 1862, mustered out with company June 24, 1865

Benjamin F Peterson, August 27, 1862, drafted, mustered out with company June 24, 1865

Peter Pfeffer, August 23, 1862, discharged on surgeon's certificate April 1, 1863

James Rinehart, August 23, 1862, wounded at Gettysburg, Pa, July 1, 1863, absent, sick, at muster out

Henry Rose, August 14, 1863, drafted, discharged by special order June 29, 1865

Lazarus A Riggle, August 15 1863, drafted, wounded at Wilderness, Va, May 5, 1864, mustered out with company June 14, 1865

Cortes Reams, August 23, 1862, transferred to Veteran Reserve Corps December 15, 1863

William S Renshaw, October 16, 1863, drafted captured at Weldon Railroad, Va, August 21, 1864, died at Salisbury, N C, December 26, 1864

J C W Reynolds, August 23, 1862, deserted November 26, 1862

Elias Schoepp, August 23, 1862, mustered out with company June 24, 1865

Henry B Snyder, September 14, 1863; drafted, missing in action at Wilderness, Va, May 5, 1864

Henry A Snyder, August 14, 1863; drafted; mustered out with company June 24, 1865

James Steele, August 28, 1863, drafted, mustered out with company June 24, 1865

James C Sutton, February 7, 1865; mustered out with company June 24, 1865

Oliver Smith, August 29, 1862, died at Washington, D C, June 18, 1863, buried in Military Asylum Cemetery

Henry Shaffer, August 13, 1863, drafted, died at Warrentown Junction, Va, November 9, 1863

William F Snyder, September 14, 1863, drafted, died at Warrentown Junction, Va, November 12, 1863

William O Snyder, August 27, 1863, drafted, died at Paoli Mills, Va, December 18, 1863, buried in National Cemetery, Culpeper C H, block 1, section A, row 9, grave 302

Samuel Smith, August 23, 1862, deserted February 3, 1863

Levi L Tate, August 23, 1862, absent on detached service at muster out

John Titus, August 29, 1862, killed at Wilderness, Va, May 5, 1864

Edward Tinsdale, October 6, 1863, drafted, captured May 21, 1864, died at Andersonville, Ga, July 28, 1864, grave 4160

Joseph R Weasner, August 23, 1862, mustered out with company June 24, 1865.

John Woleslagle, August 29, 1862, discharged on surgeon's certificate October 2, 1864

Chester O Wells, August 23, 1862, dis-

H. S. KNARR STORE

H. S. KNARR BARN

H. S. KNARR STOCK FARM

charged on surgeon's certificate January 30, 1863

Phil M. Woleslagle, August 29, 1862, transferred to Veteran Reserve Corps December 1, 1863

Edward Williamson, October 16, 1863, drafted, wounded and captured at North Anna River, Va, May 23, 1864, died at Richmond June 6, 1864

Samuel Yocum, August 14, 1863, drafted, wounded at Wilderness, Va, May 5, 59th Regiment, 2d Cavalry, 1864, mustered out with company June 24, 1865

Company F

Recruited in Clearfield and Centre Counties

Captains —P Benner Wilson, August 18, 1861, promoted to major October 28, 1862

W W Anderson, September 14, 1861, promoted from 1st lieutenant, company E, to captain, February 2, 1863, to major 181st Regiment P V, February 18, 1864

Clement R See, November 10, 1861, promoted from 2d to 1st lieutenant October 2, 1862, to captain April 23, 1864, wounded at St Mary's Church, Va, June 24, 1864, discharged September 6, 1864

William H Sheller, October 10, 1861, promoted from 1st sergeant to 2d lieutenant May 2, 1864, to captain December 25, 1864, transferred to company F, 1st Cavalry, June 17, 1865, veteran

IN OTHER COMMANDS

From the upper part of the county a contingent of some fifteen men were enlisted, which formed a part of Company H, of the Sixty-Fourth Regiment—the Fourth Cavalry They were enlisted mainly in Burnside and the surrounding townships, but the

military record gives this county no credit for any part of that or any other company of the Sixty-Fourth The regiment entered the service in October, 1861, and was mustered out in July, 1865

Clearfield county was also represented in Battery A, First Regiment of artillery—Campbell's Battery, the Forty-Third in the line The contingent was small, comprising less than ten recruits

INDEPENDENT BATTALION

Mustered in July 3-28, 1863—Discharged August 8, 1863

Field and Staff

Lieutenant Colonel —John M'Keage

Major —Richard J Crozier

Adjutant —Edmund Bedell

Quartermaster —John H Keatley

Surgeon.—John Feay

Assistant Surgeon —Joseph F Wilson

Sergeant Major —Thomas J Moore

Quartermaster Sergeant —H Lloyd Irvine

Commissary Sergeant —Orlando L Swope

Hospital Steward —Jacob L Bralher

Company C

Captain —Henry B Swoope

First Lieutenant —Richard S Carr

Second Lieutenant —Thomas C Geary

First Sergeant—Charles Hemphill

Sergeants —George Newson, Isaiah Hancock, Allen M Hunter, George A Boal

Corporals —John Hoover, Scott Flegal, Alexander Speadey, Isaiah Warrick. Aaron Cramer. William A Derby, Jordan Fox, William Lawhead

8

Musicians —James McCullough, Matthias Shea

Privates —Samuel Ardy, Edward Bowers, Jacob L Brallier (pr to Hos Stew, July 11, 1863), John Carnes, Edward Carter, Frederick Cardon, John Carter, Samuel Caldwell, Hiram Caldwell, William Carnes, John L Conklin, James L Davis, Sidney W Fox, Newton Fulton, Peter Feaster, William Fauver, Martin L Gulick, Samuel Gillong, Samuel Gill, Samuel Huston, John A Hoffman, William L Irvin, John Jordan, Harry L Kessler, Albert Logan, James Lyman, Samuel S Moore, Robert Michaels, Daniel M'Mullin, Samuel M'Cleary, John M'Intyre, Frederick S Nevling, Greenbury B Nevling, Westley Nevling, Isaac Norris, Milton A J Ogden, Robert S Ross, George B. Reninger, Ira Shaffer, James W Stewart, Edward L Stoughton, David L. Siby, Joseph Shirk, Joseph H. Smith, John L Shaffner, Henry C Shaffner, Hardman H Stephens, James Sybert, George Shimmel, Andrew Snyder, Harvey Smith, Robert Tozer, Ernest Wilson, Samuel Watson, William Wollslagle.

CHAPTER IX

THE SPANISH-AMERICAN WAR

History of the Fifth Regiment Pennsylvania Volunteer Infantry, with Roster and Individual Records

FIFTH REGIMENT PENNSYLVANIA VOLUNTEER INFANTRY

Pursuant to General Orders No 7, A G O, dated April 25, 1898, the Fifth Regiment Infantry, N G P, on April 27, 1898, left their respective home stations, and proceeded by rail to Mt Gretna, Pa, where they arrived early on the morning of April 28th, being the first infantry organization in the division to reach the point of mobilization The total strength of the regiment when it reported for duty was 37 officers and 483 enlisted men, a total of 520 men

On May 11, 1898, the regiment was mustered into service of the United States by Major W A Thompson, U S Army, and comprised thirty-seven officers and six hundred and four enlisted men Pursuant to telegraphic orders from the War Department, the regiment broke camp at Mt Gretna on the morning of May 17, 1898, and at 12 30 P M started by rail for Chickamauga, Georgia The regiment arrived at Battlefield Station, Chickamauga Park, Georgia, on the afternoon of May 19th, at 5 P M, bivouacked for the night on Snodgrass Hill, and on the morning of May 20th marched three miles and went into camp along Alexander Bridge road The regiment was assigned to the First Brigade, Third Division, First Army Corps On June 20th, Majors John P Kennedy and Robert C McNamara were detailed to recruit the companies of their respective battalions to one hundred and six men, the full complement being readily secured and all the recruits having reported by July 4, 1898

Orders were received on June 29, 1898, to recruit a third battalion of four companies of one hundred and six men each The work of recruiting and mustering the additional battalion was placed in charge of Captain Hugh S Taylor, Company B Within three weeks all the companies had been mustered in, and had reported for duty at Camp George H Thomas Company I was recruited at Somerset, Company K, at Wellsboro, Company L, at Clearfield, and Company M, at Gettysburg Lieutenant Colonel Rufus C Elder was placed in command of the First Battalion Major John P Kennedy, formerly of the First Battalion, was assigned to the command of the Second Battalion, and Major Robert C McNamara, formerly of the Second Battalion, to command of the Third August 12, 1898, the regiment moved about one-half mile nearer Battlefield Station, and encamped along the Brotherton road Here there was good drainage and higher ground On the afternoon of the 22d, the regiment left Ross-ville and traveled by rail to Camp Hamilton, near Lexington, Ky, a distance of two hundred and fifty miles, the first battalion reaching its destination on the 23d of August, and the other battalion on the 24th The camp at Lexington was all that could be desired for health or beautiful surroundings

On September 17, 1898, the regiment was granted a thirty days' furlough and each company was directed to proceed to its home station The headquarters of the regiment were established at Altoona, Pa After the expiration of the furlough, ten days were given for muster out, and this time was afterwards increased an additional twenty days to give the regiment an opportunity to participate in the Peace Jubilee at Philadelphia, on October 27, 1898 The regiment was finally mustered out, November 7, 1898

ROSTER

Abernathy, Frederick C, Priv Co K, Res Charleston, Pa, Enrd July 11, 1898, M I July 14, 1898, M O with Co Nov 7, 1898

Abernathy, Joseph W, Priv Co K, Res Mardin, Pa, Enrd July 12, 1898, M I July 14, 1898, Prom Corp July 23, 1898, G O 8 c s Regt, M O with Co Nov 7, 1898

Adams, Reuben A, Priv Co H, Res Johnston, Pa (N G P), enrd April 27, 1898, M I May 11, 1898, Prom Corp Sept 10, 1898, M O with Co Nov 7, 1898

Adams, Zenas B, Priv Co D; Res Blairs-ville, Pa, (N G P), Enrd April 27, 1898, M I May 11, 1898, M O with Co Nov 7, 1898

Agan, Thomas, Priv Co L, Res Philipsburg, Pa, Enrd July 13, 1898, M I July 14, 1898, M O with Co. Nov 7, 1898

Agey, Frank S, Priv. Co F, Res Indiana, Pa, Enrd June 22, 1898, M I June 22, 1898; M O with Co. Nov. 7, 1898

Ahlborn, George C, Priv Co H, Res Johnstown, Pa (N G P), Enrd April 27, 1898, M. I May 11, 1898; M. O. with Co Nov 7, 1898

Aikens, Howard W, Sgt. Co G; Res Lewistown, Pa (N G P.), Enrd April 27, 1898, M I May 11, 1898, M O with Co Nov. 7, 1898

Akins, Oliver C, Priv Co D, Res Saltsburg, Pa, Enrd June 24, 1898, M I June 24, 1898, M O with Co Nov. 7, 1898

Albert, Leon H, Priv Co E, Res Woodland, Pa, Enrd June 20, 1898; M I June 20, 1898, M O with Co Nov 7, 1898

Alexander, James W., Sgt Co B, Res Bellefonte, Pa (N G P), Enrd April 27, 1898, M I May 11, 1898, M O with Co Nov 7, 1898

Allen, John T, Priv. Co G; Res Lewistown, Pa, Enrd May 10, 1898, M I May 11, 1898; M O with Co Nov 7, 1898

Allen, William H, Priv. Co B; Res Bellefonte, Pa, Enrd May 7, 1898, M I May 11, 1898, M O with Co Nov 7, 1898.

Amberson, William S, Priv Co M; Res Waynesboro, Pa, Enrd July 20, 1898, M I July 20, 1898, M O with Co Nov 7, 1898

Anderson, Blake W, Priv Co C, Res Hollidaysburg, Pa, Enrd June 21, 1898, M I June 21, 1898, M O with Co Nov 7, 1898

Anderson, Charles E, Priv Co L, Res Clearfield, Pa , Enrd July 14, 1898, M I July 14, 1898, died from wounds self-inflicted Aug 20, 1898

Anderson, Samuel, Priv Co L, Res Du-Bois, Pa , Enrd July 13, 1898, M I July 14, 1898, M O with Co Nov 7, 1898

Anderson, Telford M , Priv Co F, Res Indiana, Pa (N G P), Enrd April 27, 1898, M I May 11, 1898, M O with Co Nov 7, 1898

Andrews, Samuel A, Corp Co C, Res Duncansville, Pa (N G P), Enrd April 27, 1898, M I May 11, 1898, M O with Co Nov 7, 1898

Apker, Alba M, Priv Co L, Res DuBois, Pa , Enrd July 13, 1898, M I July 14, 1898, M O with Co as Corp Nov 7, 1898

Archey, John O, Priv Co G, Res Belleville, Pa , Enrd June 29, 1898, M I June 29, 1898, M O with Co Nov 7, 1898

Ardary, Charles B , Priv Co E Res Clearfield, Pa (N G P), Enrd April 27, 1898, M I May 11, 1898, M I with Co Nov 7, 1898

Ardary, Oscar B , Priv Co L, Res Curwensville, Pa , Enrd July 14, 1898, M I July 14, 1898, M O with Co Nov 7, 1898

Armour, Frank, Priv Co D, Res West Fairfield, Pa , Enrd May 9, 1898, M I May 11, 1898, Prom Corp June 28, 1898, Prom Sgt July 31, 1898, M O with Co Nov 7, 1898

Armstrong, James E , Priv Co H, Res Johnstown, Pa , Enrd May 9, 1898, M I May 11, 1898, M O with Co Nov 7, 1898

Arnold Ellsworth J, Priv Co G, Res Lewistown, Pa , Enrd June 29, 1898, M I June 29, 1898, M O with Co Nov 7, 1898

Ashcom, Dick, Priv Co F, Res Ligonier, Pa , Enrd May 9, 1898, M I May 11, 1898, M O with Co Nov 7, 1898

Ault, John S , Priv Co A, Res Cornpropst Mills, Pa , Enrd June 23, 1898, M I June 23, 1898, M O with Co Nov 7, 1898

Ault, William C, Priv Co K, Res. Liberty, Pa , Enrd July 14, 1898, M I July 14, 1898, M O with Co Nov 7, 1898

Aurand, Clyde, Priv Co G, Res Lewistown, Pa (N G P), Enrd April 27, 1898, M I May 11, 1898, M O with Co Nov 7, 1898

Aurand, James F, Priv Co G, Res Lewistown, Pa (N G P), Enrd April 27, 1898, M I May 11, 1898, M O with Co Nov 7, 1898

Ayers, Frank S, Priv Co I, Res McAlevy's Fort, Pa , Enrd July 5, 1898, M I July 8, 1898, M O with Co Nov 7, 1898

Ayers, Harry E, Priv Co C, Res Olivia, Pa ; Enrd April 28, 1898, M I May 11, 1898, M O with Co Nov 7, 1898

Ayers, Hays S, Priv Co I, Res Listie, Pa , Enrd July 6, 1898, M I July 8, 1898, M O with Co Nov 7, 1898

Ayers, Walter H, Priv Co F, Res Rochester Mills, Pa (M G P), Enrd April 27, 1898, M I May 11, 1898, Prom Corp June 28, 1898, M O with Co Nov 7, 1898

Bailey, Arthur L, 1st Sgt Co K, Res Wellsboro, Pa , Enrd July 12, 1898, M I July 14, 1898, Apptd 1st Sgt July 23, 1898, per G O 8 c s Regt , M O with Co Nov 7, 1898

Bailey, Joseph O W, Priv Co K Res Mansfield, Pa , Enrd July 12, 1898, M I July 14, 1898, M O with Co Nov 7, 1898

Bailey, Ralph J, Priv Co K, Res Mansfield, Pa , Enrd July 12, 1898, M I July

14, 1898, Prom Sgt July 23, 1898, G O 8 c s Regt, M O with Co Nov 7, 1898

Baker, James R, Priv Co D, Res Blacklick, Pa (N G P), Enrd April 27, 1898, M I May 11, 1898, Apptd Artf June 3, 1898, M O with Co Nov 7, 1898

Baker, Merrill, Priv Co H, Res Johnstown, Pa, Enrd June 27, 1898, M I June 27, 1898, M O with Co Nov 7, 1898

Baldridge, Joseph G, Priv Co H, Res Greensburg, Pa, Enrd July 14, 1898, M I July 14, 1898, M O with Co Nov 7, 1898

Baldwin, Charles W, Priv Co I, Res Somerset, Pa, Enrd July 8, 1898, M. I July 8, 1898, M O with Co Nov. 7, 1898.

Bane, John A, Priv Co I, Res Meyersdale, Pa, Enrd July 6, 1898, M I July 8, 1898, M O with Co Nov 7, 1898

Banker, William L, Priv Co K, Res Tioga, Pa, Enrd July 12, 1898, M I July 14, 1898, M O with Co Nov 7, 1898

Bannon, George C, Priv Co G, Res Lewistown, Pa, Enrd May 10, 1898, M I May 11, 1898, M O with Co Nov 7, 1898

Bare, John S, Capt Co A, Res Huntingdon, Pa (N G P), Enrd April 27, 1898, M I May 11, 1898, M O with Co Nov 7, 1898

Barger, Orval E, Priv Co G, Res Reedsville, Pa, Enrd June 29, 1898, M I. June 29, 1898, M O with Co Nov 7, 1898

Barnes, William F, Priv Co. B; Res Bellefonte, Pa (N G P), Enrd April 27, 1898, M I May 11, 1898, Prom Corp June 30, 1898, M O with Co Nov 7, 1898

Barnett, Edmond B, Priv Co I, Res Somerset, Pa, Enrd July 7, 1898, M I July 8, 1898, Prom Corp July 16, 1898, M O. with Co Nov 7, 1898

Barnett, George W, Priv Co F, Res Johnstown, Pa., Enrd May 9, 1898; M I May 11, 1898, M O with Co Nov 7, 1898

Barnhart, Charles W, Priv Co M, Res. York, Pa, Enrd July 20, 1898, M I July 20, 1898, M O with Co Nov. 7, 1898

Barr, David S, 1st Lieut Co C, Res Altoona, Pa (N G. P), Enrd April 27, 1898, M I May 11, 1898, M O with Co Nov 7, 1898

Barr, James C, Corp Co A, Res Huntingdon, Pa (N G P); Enrd April 27, 1898, M I May 11, 1898, M O with Co Nov 7, 1898

Barratt, Fred F, Priv Co E, Res Clearfield, Pa, Enrd May 3, 1898, M I May 11, 1898. Apptd Wag June 27, 1898, Transfd to 3d Div Amb. Corps, per S O 29, 1st A C Hdq, dated July 19, 1898

Barrett, Harry M, Priv Co F, Res Loop, Pa, Enrd June 23, 1898, M I June 23, 1898; M O with Co Nov 7, 1898

Bartley, James P, Priv Co C, Res Altoona, Pa, Enrd June 21, 1898, M I June 21, 1898, M O with Co Nov 7, 1898

Barto, Benjamin R, Priv Co D, Res. Blairsville, Pa, Enrd June 24, 1898, M I June 24, 1898; M O with Co Nov 7. 1898

Bathurst, Charles W, Q M, Res Huntingdon, Pa (N G P.), Enrd April 27, 1898, M I May 5, 1898, M O with Regt. Nov 7, 1898

Bathurst, Samuel P, Priv Co B, Res Roland, Pa, Enrd May 7, 1898; M I May 11, 1898, M O with Co Nov. 7, 1898

Bathurst, Zebulum, Priv. Co L, Res Chester Hill, Pa, Enrd July 13, 1898, M I July 14, 1898, M O with Co as cook, Nov 7, 1898

Baumer, William J, Priv Co H, Res.

Johnstown, Pa ; Enrd June 28, 1898, M I June 28, 1898, M O with Co Nov 7, 1898

Bayard, Roger T, Priv Co B, Res Bellefonte, Pa (N G P), Enrd April 27, 1898, M I May 11, 1898, M O with Co Nov 7, 1898

Beachtel, William L, Priv Co M, Res Wentz, Md, Enrd July 18, 1898, M I July 20, 1898, M O with Co Nov 7, 1898

Beard, Charles C, Priv Co C, Res Altoona, Pa (N G P), Enrd April 27, 1898, M I May 11, 1898, M O with Co Nov 7, 1898

Beaver, Charles J, Priv Co G, Res Lewistown, Pa, Enrd May 10, 1898, M I May 11, 1898, M O with Co Nov 7, 1898

Beitler, Frank A, Priv Co M, Res Gettysburg, Pa, Enrd July 18, 1898, M I July 20, 1898, M O with Co Nov 7, 1898

Bell, Jesse S, Priv Co F, Res Marion Centre, Pa (N G P), Enrd April 27, 1898, M I May 11, 1898, Prom Corp June 28, 1898, M O with Co Nov 7, 1898

Bellinger, Floyd, Priv Co K, Res Charleston, Pa, Enrd July 11, 1898, M I July 14, 1898, M O with Co Nov 7, 1898

Benford, Bernard H, Priv Co I, Res Somerset, Pa, Enrd July 4, 1898, M I July 8, 1898, M O with Co Nov 7, 1898

Benford, Harry C, Priv Co I, Res Somerset, Pa, Enrd July 6, 1898, M I July 8, 1898, M O with Co Nov. 7, 1898

Bennett, Marion A, Priv Co M, Res Seven Stars, Pa, Enrd July 19, 1898, M I July 20, 1898, M O with Co Nov 7, 1898

Benson, Edward, Priv Co L, Res Curwensville, Pa ; Enrd July 14, 1898, M I July 14, 1898; M O with Co Nov 7, 1898

Best, Irvin W, Priv Co E, Res Clearfield, Pa (N G P), Enrd April 27, 1898, M. I May 11, 1898, M O with Co Nov 7, 1898

Biesecker, Charles, Priv Co I, Res Somerset, Pa, Enrd July 5, 1898, M I July 8, 1898, M O with Co Nov 7, 1898

Bird, Cyrus M, Priv Co I, Res Meyersdale, Pa, Enrd July 6, 1898, M I July 8, 1898, M O with Co Nov 7, 1898

Bittner, Edward A, Priv Co I, Res Garrett, Pa, Enrd July 5, 1898, M I July 8, 1898, M O with Co Nov 7, 1898

Bixby, Walter S, Priv Co K, Res Middlebury, Pa, Enrd July 12, 1898, M I July 14, 1898; M O with Co Nov 7, 1898

Black, Victor H, Priv Co A, Res Huntingdon, Pa ; Enrd June 23, 1898, M I June 23, 1898, M O with Co Nov 7, 1898

Blake, George, Priv Co I, Res Boynton, Pa, Enrd July 6, 1898, M I July 8, 1898; M O with Co Nov 7, 1898

Blake, Roland G, Priv Co C, Res Martinsburg, Pa, Enrd May 10, 1898, M I May 11, 1898, M O with Co Nov 7, 1898

Blakeley, Joseph A, Corp Co F, Res Indiana, Pa (N G P), Enrd April 27, 1898, M I May 11, 1898, died at Sternberg Hosp Camp Thomas, Ga, Aug 25, 1898

Bliss, Willard D, Priv Co K, Res Wellsboro, Pa, Enrd July 12, 1898, M I. July 14, 1898, M O. with Co Nov 7, 1898

Bloom, Thomas M, Priv Co E, Res Curwensville, Pa, Enrd May 9, 1898, M I May 11, 1898, M O with Co Nov 7, 1898

Bloom, Zane C, Priv Co E, Res Clearfield, Pa, Enrd June 21, 1898, M I June 21, 1898, M O with Co Nov 7, 1898

Blough, Nathaniel, Sgt Co H, Res Johnstown, Pa (N G P), Enrd April 27,

1898, M I May 11, 1898, M O with Co Nov 7, 1898

Boger, Allen E, Priv Co I, Res Hays Mills, Pa , Enrd July 6, 1898, M I July 8, 1898, M O with Co Nov 7, 1898

Bookhamer, David G, Priv Co C, Res Altoona, Pa , Enrd May 7, 1898, M I May 11, 1898, M O with Co Nov 7, 1898

Bookhamer, Isaac L, Priv Co A, Res Huntingdon, Pa (N G P), Enrd April 27, 1898, M I May 11, 1898, Prom Corp. June 28, 1898, M O with Co Nov 7, 1898

Bottorf, Charles W, Priv Co G, Res. Lewistown, Pa , Enrd May 10, 1898, M I May 11, 1898, died Sept 13, 1898

Bowen, Charles R, Corp Co H, Res Johnstown, Pa (N G P), Enrd April 27, 1898, M I May 11, 1898, M O with Co Nov 7, 1898

Bowen, John R, Priv Co K, Res Wellsboro, Pa , Enrd July 12, 1898, M I July 14, 1898, M O with Co Nov 7, 1898

Bower, H Harris, Priv Co L, Res Lewisburg, Pa , Enrd July 13, 1898, M I July 14, 1898, M O with Co as Sgt Nov 7, 1898

Bowman, Albert J, Priv Co A, Res Huntingdon, Pa (N G P), Enrd April 27, 1898, M I May 11, 1898, M O with Co Nov 7, 1898

Bowman, Oscar F, Priv Co H, Res Johnstown, Pa (N. G P.), Enrd April 27, 1898, M I May 11, 1898, Prom Corp Sept 10, 1898, M O with Co Nov 7, 1898

Boyer, Emanuel D, Corp Co A, Res Huntingdon, Pa (N G P), Enrd April 27, 1898, M I May 11, 1898, M O with Co Nov 7, 1898

Bradley, William S, Priv Co B; Res Axeman, Pa , Enrd May 7, 1898, M I May 11, 1898, M O with Co Nov 7, 1898

Brady, Charles A, Priv. Co F, Res. Chambersville, Pa ; Enrd June 22, 1898; M I June 22, 1898, M O with Co Nov. 7, 1898

Brady, Myrl W, Priv. Co F, Res Covode, Pa , Enrd June 23, 1898, M I June 23, 1898, M O with Co Nov. 7, 1898

Brallier, John K, Priv Co D, Res Indiana, Pa , Enrd May 9, 1898, M I May 11, 1898, M O with Co Nov 7, 1898

Brant, Henry C, Priv Co M; Res York, Pa , Enrd July 20, 1898, M. I July 20, 1898, Prom Corp Aug 1, 1898, M O with Co Nov 7, 1898

Brant, Thomas C, Priv Co C, Res. Huntingdon, Pa , Enrd May 10, 1898, M I May 11, 1898, M O with Co Nov 7, 1898

Brechbiel, George A, Mus Co D, Res Altoona, Pa (N G P), Enrd April 27, 1898, M I May 11, 1898; M. O with Co. Nov 7, 1898

Brecher, Henry, Jr, Priv Co K, Res Marshfield, Pa., Enrd July 12, 1898, M I July 14, 1898, M O with Co Nov 7, 1898

Brehman, Frank, Corp Co C, Res Altoona, Pa (N G P), Enrd April 27, 1898; M I May 11, 1898; Prom Q M Sgt Aug 31, 1898, M O with Co Nov 7, 1898

Brenneman, John R, Priv Co A; Res Huntingdon, Pa , Enrd May 7, 1898; M I May 11, 1898, M O with Co Nov 7, 1898

Bridge, Edward G, Priv Co D, Res Blairsville, Pa ; Enrd June 24, 1898, M I. June 24, 1898, M O with Co Nov 7, 1898

Britten, William H, Priv Co L, Res Osceola Mills, Pa , Enrd July 14, 1898, M I July 14, 1898, M O with Co Nov 7, 1898

Brosius, Raymond S, Priv Co H, Res Johnstown, Pa , Enrd June 27, 1898, M. I

June 27, 1898, Transfd. to 3d Div Hosp corps, July 20, 1898

Brosius, Roy B., Priv Co E, Res Clearfield, Pa (N G P), Enrd April 27, 1898, M I May 11, 1898, M O with Co Nov 7, 1898

Brown, Burt A., Priv Co F, Res Indiana Pa., Enrd June 22, 1898, M I June 22, 1898, M O with Co Nov 7, 1898

Brown, Charles A., Priv Co K. Res Olmsville, Pa., Enrd July 12 1898, M I July 14, 1898, M O with Co Nov 7, 1898

Brown, Henry E., Priv Co C, Res Duncansville, Pa (N G P), Enrd April 27, 1898, M I May 11, 1898, M O with Co Nov 7, 1898

Brown, James, Priv Co E. Res Clearfield, Pa (N G P), Enrd April 27, 1898, M I May 11, 1898, M O with Co Nov 7, 1898

Brown, John, Priv Co B Res Milesburg, Pa., Enrd June 27, 1898, M I June 27, 1898, M O with Co Nov 7, 1898

Brown, John, Priv Co K, Res Wellsboro, Pa., Enrd July 12, 1898, M I July 14, 1898, M O with Co Nov 7, 1898

Brown, Robert D., Priv Co D, Res Saltsburg, Pa., Enrd May 9, 1898, M I May 11, 1898, M O with Co Nov 7, 1898

Brown, Robert K., Priv Co E, Res DuBois, Pa., Enrd June 20, 1898. M I June 20, 1898, M O with Co Nov 7, 1898

Buchanan, Joseph B., Priv Co F, Res Homer City, Pa (N G P), Enrd April 27, 1898, M I May 11, 1898, M O with Co Nov 7, 1898

Bunn, Herbert H., Priv Co A, Res Huntingdon, Pa (N G P), Enrd April 27, 1898, M I May 11, 1898, M O with Co Nov 7, 1898

Bunnell, John M., Priv Co L. Res Gram-

pian, Pa., Enrd July 14, 1898, M I July 14, 1898, M O with Co Nov 7, 1898

Burchfield, Herbert E., Q M Sgt., Res Altoona, Pa (N G P), Enrd April 27, 1898, M I May 11, 1898, Prom to 2d Lient Co K, Aug 14, 1898, Comsd Aug 10, 1898, M I Aug 14, 1898, joined for duty same day, M O with Co Nov 7, 1898

Burchfield, Theodore, Col., Res Altoona, Pa (N G P), Enrd April 27, 1898, M I May 11, 1898, M O with Regt Nov 7, 1898

Burk, Calvin, Priv Co I, Res Queen, Pa., Enrd July 4, 1898, M I July 8, 1898, M O with Co Nov 7, 1898

Burk, John W., Artf Co H, Res Conemaugh, Pa (N G P), Enrd April 27, 1898, M I May 11, 1898, M O with Co Nov 7, 1898

Burnhimer, Andrew H., Priv Co F, Res Tanoma, Pa., Enrd June 23, 1898, M I June 22, 1898. M O with Co Nov 7, 1898.

Bush, Benjamin W., Priv Co K, Res Williamsport, Pa., Enrd July 13, 1898, M I July 14, 1898, M O with Co as Artf, Nov 7, 1898

Bushman, Samuel M., Priv Co M, Res. Gettysburg, Pa., Enrd July 15, 1898, M I July 20, 1898, M O with Co Nov 7, 1898

Buskey, John E., Priv Co I, Res Meyersdale, Pa., Enrd July 6, 1898, M I July 8, 1898, M O with Co Nov 7, 1898

Butler, Joseph H., Sgt Maj., Res Altoona, Pa (N G P), Enrd April 27 1898, M I May 11, 1898, Dischd Aug 12, 1898, per S O 186 A G O

Butt, Harry J., Priv Co M, Res Gettysburg, Pa., Enrd July 18, 1898, M I July 20, 1898, M O with Co Nov 7, 1898

Burford, Joseph, Priv Co F, Res Indiana, Pa , Enrd May 9, 1898, M I May 11, 1898, M O with Co Nov 7, 1898

Byerly, Paul R , Priv Co E, Res Millersville, Pa , Enrd May 2, 1898, M I May 11, 1898, Prom. Corp June 27, 1898, M O with Co Nov. 7, 1898

Byers, Harry, 1st Sgt Co E, Res Clearfield, Pa (N G P), Enrd April 27, 1898, M I May 1, 1898, M O with Co Nov 7, 1898

Cadwalader, George W , Priv Co B, Res Philipsburg, Pa , Enrd May 7, 1898, M I May 11, 1898, M O with Co Nov 7, 1898

Cairns, James, Priv Co K , Res Blossburg, Pa , Enrd July 11, 1898, M I July 14, 1898, M. O with Co Nov 7, 1898

Caldwell, David, Priv Co C, Res Hollidaysburg, Pa , Enrd May 10, 1898, M I May 11, 1898, M O with Co Nov 7, 1898

Caldwell, David M , Battn Adj , Res Indiana, Pa (N G P), Enrd April 27, 1898, M I May 11, 1898, M O with Regt Nov 7, 1898

Calhoun, Austin J , Priv Co G, Res Mifflintown, Pa , Enrd May 10, 1898, M I. May 11, 1898; M O with Co Nov 7, 1898

Callahan, Harry E , Priv Co K , Res Slate Run, Pa , Enrd July 12, 1898, M I. July 14, 1898, M O with Co Nov 7, 1898.

Calvin, Samuel, Priv Co C, Res Hollidaysburg, Pa , Enrd June 21, 1898, M. I. June 21, 1898, M O with Co Nov 7, 1898

Cameron, Thomas B , Priv Co D, Res Bolivar, Pa , Enrd June 25, 1898, M I June 25, 1898, M O with Co Nov 7, 1898

Cameron, William H , Priv Co L, Res. Clearfield, Pa , Enrd July 14, 1898, M I July 14, 1898, M O with Co Nov 7, 1898

Campbell, Daniel, Priv Co K, Res

Wellsboro, Pa , Enrd. July 12, 1898, M I July 14, 1898, M. O with Co Nov 7, 1898

Campbell, David M , Priv. Co F; Res. Blairville, Pa , Enrd June 22, 1898; M I June 22, 1898, M O with Co Nov. 7, 1898

Campbell, Edward S , Priv Co C, Res Altoona, Pa , Enrd June 20, 1898, M I June 20, 1898, M O with Co Nov 7, 1898

Campbell, George W , Priv Co D, Res Blacklick, Pa (N G P), Enrd April 27, 1898, M I May 11, 1898, M O with Co Nov 7, 1898

Campbell, Lee, Priv. Co F; Res Rochester Mills, Pa , Enrd May 9, 1898, M I May 11, 1898, M O with Co Nov 7, 1898

Canedy, Albert, Priv. Co K, Res Tioga, Pa , Enrd July 12, 1898, M I July 14, 1898, M O with Co Nov 7, 1898

Carey, Thomas D , Priv Co I, Res Sligo, Pa , Enrd July 5, 1898, M I July 8, 1898. Prom Corp July 16, 1898, M. O with Co Nov 7, 1898

Carey, William J , Priv Co L, Res Philipsburg, Pa , Enrd July 13, 1898, M I July 14, 1898, M O with Co Nov 7, 1898.

Carlson, Gust , Priv. Co. K, Res Knapp, Pa , Enrd. July 13, 1898; M I July 14, 1898, M O. with Co Nov 7, 1898

Carly, W J , Priv. Co L; Res Chester Hill, Pa , Enrd July 13, 1898, M I. July 14, 1898, M O with Co Nov. 7, 1898

Carmon, Oliver, Priv Co A, Res Huntingdon, Pa (N. G P); Enrd April 27, 1898, M. I May 11, 1898; M. O with Co Nov 7, 1898

Carothers, Joseph A , Priv. Co G, Res Lewistown, Pa (N G. P); Enrd April 27, 1898, M I May 11, 1898, Prom Corp Aug. 16, 1898, M O with Co Nov 7, 1898

Carpenter, George B , Q M. Sgt Co H:

Res Johnstown, Pa (N G P), Enrd April 27, 1898, M I May 11, 1898, M O with Co Nov 7, 1898

Carson, Charles, Priv Co G, Res Reedsville, Pa , Enrd June 29, 1898, M I June 29, 1898, M O with Co Nov 7, 1898

Carson, Oscar W , Priv Co M, Res Bendersville, Pa , Enrd July 15, 1898, M. I July 20, 1898, M O with Co Nov 7, 1898

Cartwright, Orville B , Mus Co R, Res Altoona, Pa (N G P), Enrd April 27, 1898, M I May 11, 1898, M O with Co Nov 7, 1898

Cass, Edwin A , Priv Co K, Res Farmington Centre, Pa , Enrd July 12, 1898, M I July 14, 1898, M O with Co Nov 7, 1898

Cass, Eugene L , Priv Co K, Res Farmington Centre, Pa , Enrd July 12, 1898, M I July 14, 1898, M O with Co Nov 7, 1898

Cassidy, David, Priv Co C, Res Altoona, Pa , Enrd May 10, 1898, M I May 11, 1898, M O with Co Nov 7, 1898

Cathcart, James A , Corp Co F, Res. Chambersville, Pa (N G P); Enrd April 27, 1898, M I May 11, 1898, M O with Co Nov 7, 1898

Catlin, Edson J , 2d Lt Co K, Res Wellsboro, Pa , Enrd July 12, 1898, M. I July 14, 1898, Comsd 1st Lieut Aug 10, 1898, M I. 1st Lieut Aug 14, 1898, M O with Co Nov 7, 1898

Chambers, Archibald C , Priv Co L, Res Houtzdale, Pa , Enrd July 14, 1898, M I July 14, 1898, M O with Co Nov 7, 1898

Chambers, John, Jr , Priv Co E, Res DuBois, Pa , Enrd June 20, 1898, M I June 20, 1898, M. O with Co Nov 7, 1898

Charles, Harry, Priv Co B, Res Milesburg, Pa , Enrd June 28, 1898, M I June 28, 1898, M O with Co Nov 7, 1898

Chase, John W , Priv Co E, Res Clearfield, Pa (N G P), Enrd April 27, 1898, M I May 11, 1898, Prom Corp May 11, 1898, M O with Co Nov 7, 1898

Chase, Thomas M , Priv Co E, Res Clearfield, Pa (N G P), Enrd April 27, 1898, M I May 11, 1898, M O with Co Nov 7, 1898

Chase, William C , Priv Co E, Res Clearfield, Pa , Enrd May 9, 1898, M I May 11, 1898, M O with Co Nov 7, 1898

Chorpenning, Roy A , Priv Co E, Res Clearfield, Pa (N G P), Enrd April 27, 1898, M I May 11, 1898, M O with Co Nov 7, 1898

Christner, Francis, Priv Co I, Res Garrett, Pa , Enrd July 5, 1898, M I July 8, 1898, M O with Co Nov 7, 1898

Christy, James H , Priv. Co C, Res Hollidaysburg, Pa , Enrd May 10, 1898; M I May 11, 1898, M O with Co Nov 7, 1898

Clark, Benjamin F , Priv Co K, Res Mansfield, Pa , Enrd July 12, 1898, M I July 14, 1898, M O with Co Nov 7, 1898

Clark, C B , Priv Co L, Res DuBois, Pa , Enrd July 13, 1898, M I July 14, 1898, M O with Co as Sgt Nov 7, 1898

Clark, Frank E , Priv Co H, Res Johnstown, Pa , Enrd June 27, 1898, M I June 27, 1898, M O with Co Nov 7, 1898

Clark, Frank S , Sgt Co H, Res Johnstown, Pa (N G P), Enrd April 27, 1898, M I May 11, 1898 M O with Co Nov 7, 1898

Clarke, Harry L , Priv Co G, Res Lewistown, Pa , Enrd May 10 1898, M I May 11, 1898, M O with Co Nov 7, 1898

Clary, Harry B , Priv Co L, Res Grampian, Pa ; Enrd July 14, 1898, M I July 14,

1898, Prom Corp Sept 1, 1898, M O with Co Nov 7, 1898

Clawson, Ellis R, Priv Co D, Res Branch, Pa, Enrd June 24, 1898, M I June 24, 1898, M O with Co Nov 7, 1898

Clawson, Harry S, Priv Co F, Res Smathers, Pa (N G P), Enrd April 27, 1898, M I May 11, 1898, M O with Co Nov 7, 1898

Clayson, Berton, Priv Co K, Res Slate Run, Pa, Enrd July 12, 1898, M I July 14, 1898, M O with Co Nov 7, 1898

Cleaver, Albert W, Priv Co L, Res Clearfield, Pa, Enrd July 13, 1898, M. I July 14, 1898, M. O with Co Nov 7, 1898

Clinger, John W, Priv Co H, Res Johnstown, Pa (N G P), Enrd April 27, 1898 M. I May 11, 1898, M O with Co Nov 7, 1898

Cochrane, Charles F, Priv Co I, Res Elk Pa, Enrd July 8, 1898; M I July 8, 1898, M O with Co Nov 7, 1898

Cochrane, Charles F, Priv Co I, Res Elk Lick Pa, Enrd July 6, 1898, M I July 8, 1898, M O with Co Nov 7, 1898

Cole, Frank W, Priv Co B, Res Bellefonte, Pa, Enrd June 28, 1898, M I June 28, 1898, M O with Co Nov 7, 1898

Cole, Thomas H, Priv Co L, Res Philipsburg, Pa, Enrd July 14, 1898, M I July 14, 1898, M O with Co Nov 7, 1898

Coleman, Paul, Priv Co F, Res Clarksburg, Pa, Enrd June 22, 1898, M I June 22, 1898, M O with Co Nov 7, 1898

Coleman, William E, Private Co F, Res Indiana, Pa (N G P), Enrd April 27, 1898; M I May 11, 1898, M O with Co Nov 7, 1898

Coleman William S, Priv Co F, Res Clarksburg, Pa, Enrd June 22, 1898, M I June 22, 1898, M O with Co Nov 7, 1898

Collar, Jacob, Priv Co L, Res. Munson, Pa, Enrd July 13, 1898, M I July 14, 1898, M O with Co Nov 7, 1898

Colony, George H, Priv Co K, Res Mansfield, Pa, Enrd July 11, 1898, M I July 14, 1898, M O with Co Nov 7, 1898

Confer, Miles, Priv Co E, Res Woodland, Pa, Enrd May 9, 1898, M I May 11, 1898; M O with Co Nov 7, 1898

Conklin, Roscoe, Priv Co E, Res Clearfield, Pa, Enrd June 20, 1898, M. I June 20, 1898, M O with Co Nov 7, 1898

Conklin, William G, Priv Co E; Res Clearfield, Pa (N G P), Enrd April 27, 1898, M I May 11, 1898, Prom Corp May 11, 1898, M O with Co Nov 7, 1898

Conlan, Frank, Priv Co L, Res DuBois, Pa, Enrd July 14, 1898, M I July 14, 1898; M O with Co Nov 7, 1898

Conley, James T, Priv. Co I; Res Elk Lick, Pa, Enrd July 6 1898, M I. July 8, 1898, M O with Co Nov 7, 1898

Connolly, Francis P, Priv Co M, Res York, Pa, Enrd July 20, 1898, M I July 20, 1898, M. O with Co Nov 7, 1898

Conrad, George S, Priv Co A, Res Huntingdon, Pa, Enrd May 7, 1898, M I May 11, 1898, M O with Co Nov 7, 1898

Conrad, Winfield F, Priv Co A, Res Orbisonia, Pa, Enrd May 7, 1898, M I May 11, 1898, M O with Co Nov 7, 1898

Cooney, Henry B, Priv Co H, Res Johnstown, Pa, Enrd May 9, 1898, M. I May 11, 1898; M O with Co Nov 7, 1898

Coonsie, Reuben H, Priv Co E; Res DuBois, Pa; Enrd June 20, 1898; M. I June 20, 1898; M O with Co Nov 7, 1898

Cope, John B, Priv Co M, Res Gettysburg, Pa , Enrd July 15, 1898, M I July 20, 1898, Prom Corp Aug 1, 1898, M O with Co Nov 7, 1898

Copenhaver, Courtland G , Priv Co E, Res Ramey, Pa , Enrd June 20, 1898, M I June 20, 1898, M O with Co Nov 7, 1898

Corbin, George B , Corp Co A, Res Huntingdon, Pa (N G P), Enrd April 27, 1898, M I May 11, 1898, M O with Co Nov 7, 1898

Corbin, Frank M , Priv Co A, Res Huntingdon, Pa , Enrd May 7, 1898, M I May 11, 1898, M O with Co Nov 7, 1898

Cornelius, Leslie A , Priv Co A, Res Huntingdon, Pa (N G P), Enrd April 27, 1898, M I May 11, 1898, M O with Co Nov 7, 1898

Corwell, James A , Priv Co M, Res Fairfield, Pa , Enrd July 16, 1898, M I July 20 1898, M O with Co Nov 7, 1898

Coulter, Charles A , Priv Co A, Res Huntingdon, Pa , Enrd May 7, 1898, M I May 11, 1898, M O with Co Nov 7, 1898

Coulter, Thomas J , Priv Co A, Res Huntingdon, Pa , Enrd June 24, 1898, M I June 24, 1898, M O with Co Nov 7, 1898

Countryman, George F , Priv Co I, Res Lavansville, Pa , Enrd July 6, 1898, M I July 8, 1898, M O with Co Nov 7, 1898

Cover, William T , Priv Co C Res Altoona, Pa , Enrd May 10, 1898, M I May 11, 1898, M O with Co Nov 7, 1898

Cowen, George, Priv Co L, Res Philipsburg, Pa , Enrd July 13, 1898, M I July 14, 1898, M O with Co Nov 7, 1898

Cox, Clyde R , Priv Co B, Res Roland Pa , Enrd May 7, 1898, M I May 11, 1898, M O with Co Nov 7, 1898

Crain, John H , Priv Co B Res Port Matilda, Pa (N G P), Enrd April 27, 1898

M I May 11, 1898, M O with Co Nov 7, 1898

Cramer, Louis L , Priv Co F, Res Creekside, Pa (N G P), Enrd April 27, 1898, M I May 11, 1898, M O with Co Nov 7, 1898

Crawford, John E , Priv Co L, Res Osceola Mills, Pa , Enrd July 14, 1898, M I July 14, 1898, M O with Co Nov 7, 1898

Cree, Nathan A , Priv Co A, Res Huntingdon, Pa , Enrd June 23, 1898, M I June 23, 1898, M O with Co Nov 7, 1898

Cresswell, George E , Priv Co G, Res Lewistown, Pa , Enrd May 11, 1898, M I May 11, 1898, M O with Co Nov 7, 1898

Crissman, George H , Priv Co G, Res Lewistown, Pa (N G P), Enrd April 27, 1898, M I May 11, 1898, Prom Corp June 28, 1898, M O with Co Nov 7, 1898

Cronmiller, John H , Priv Co E, Res Curwensville, Pa (N G P), Enrd April 27, 1898; M I May 11, 1898, M O with Co Nov 7, 1898

Crossley, Charles R , Priv Co K, Res Mansfield, Pa , Enrd July 11, 1898, M I July 14, 1898, Prom Corp July 23, 1898, G O 8 cs Regt , M O with Co Nov 7, 1898

Crotty, Walter J , Priv Co G, Res Lewistown, Pa , Enrd May 10, 1898, M I May 11, 1898, M O with Co Nov 7, 1898

Crum, Ira A , Priv Co C, Res Altoona, Pa , Enrd June 20, 1898, M I June 20, 1898, M O with Co Nov 7, 1898

Cullison, Asa C , Priv Co M, Res Gettysburg, Pa , Enrd July 18, 1898, M I July 20, 1898, M O with Co Nov 7, 1898

Cummings, Oscar F Priv Co D, Res Blairsville, Pa (N G P), Enrd April 27,

1898, M I May 11, 1898, M O. with Co Nov 7, 1898

Cummins, Robert D, Priv Co I, Res Somerset, Pa, Enrd July 4, 1898, M I July 8, 1898, M O with Co Nov 7, 1898

Cunningham, Harry C, Priv Co C, Res Altoona, Pa, Enrd May 10, 1898, M I May 11, 1898, M O with Co Nov 7, 1898

Currens, John E, Priv Co M, Res Gettysburg, Pa, Enrd July 15, 1898, M I July 20, 1898, M O with Co Nov 7, 1898

Curry, Jesse S, Priv Co D, Res Blairsville, Pa (N G P), Enrd April 27, 1898, M I May 11, 1898, M O with Co Nov 7, 1898

Curtin, J Latimer, Priv Co B, Res Roland, Pa (N G P), Enrd April 27, 1898, M I May 11, 1898, M O with Co Nov 7, 1898

Custer, Irvin B, Priv Co H, Res Vinco, Pa, Enrd June 28, 1898, M I June 28, 1898, M O with Co Nov 7, 1898

Dale, David, Priv Co H, Res Lemont. Pa, Enrd April 29, 1898, M I May 11, 1898, M O with Co Nov 7, 1898

Daley, R Clarence, Priv Co R, Res Romola, Pa (N G P), Enrd April 27, 1898, M I May 11, 1898, Prom Corp June 30, 1898, M O with Co Nov 7, 1898

Dally, William P, Priv Co M, Res Gettysburg, Pa, Enrd July 15, 1898, M I July 20, 1898, M O with Co Nov 7, 1898

Daly, Sheridan J, Priv Co L, Res DuBois, Pa, Enrd July 14, 1898, M I July 14, 1898, Prom Q M Sgt Sept 1, 1898, G O 31 Regt Hdq ; M O with Co Nov 7, 1898

Darby, Arthur, Mus Co D, Res Altoona, Pa (N G P), Enrd April 27, 1898, M I May 11, 1898, M O with Co Nov 7, 1898

Daugherty, David N, Priv Co F; Res Indiana, Pa ; Enrd May 9, 1898; M I. May 11, 1898, M O with Co Nov 7, 1898

Davis, Edward, Priv. Co B, Res Philipsburg, Pa, Enrd May 7, 1898, M I May 11, 1898, M O with Co Nov 7, 1898

Davis, Ivan, Priv Co I, Res Elk Lick, Pa ; Enrd July 6, 1898, M I. July 8, 1898, M O with Co Nov 7, 1898

Davis, James F, Priv. Co I, Res Listie, Pa, Enrd July 5, 1898, M I July 8, 1898; M O with Co Nov 7, 1898

Davis, Oscar M, Priv Co H, Res Conemaugh, Pa, Enrd June 28, 1898, M I June 28, 1898, M O with Co Nov 7, 1898

Davis, Perry, Priv Co I, Res Listonburg, Pa, Enrd July 7, 1898, M I July 8, 1898, M O with Co Nov. 7, 1898

Davis, Thomas H, Priv Co I; Res Listonburg, Pa, Enrd July 7, 1898, M I July 8, 1898, M O with Co Nov 7, 1898

Deane, Alan B, Priv Co K, Res Wellsboro, Pa, Enrd July 12, 1898; M I July 14, 1898, M O with Co Nov 7, 1898

Deats, George W, Priv Co K, Res Keeneyville, Pa, Enrd July 12, 1898, M I July 14, 1898, M O with Co Nov 7, 1898

Decker, James E, Priv Co H, Res Johnstown, Pa, Enrd May 9, 1898, M I May 11, 1898, Prom Corp June 28, 1898 M O with Co Nov 7, 1898

DeForrest, Jesse F, Priv Co A, Res Huntingdon, Pa (N G P), Enrd April 27, 1898, M I May 11, 1898; M O with Co Nov 7, 1898

De Hass, Charles J, Priv Co E, Res Kerrmoor, Pa, Enrd June 21, 1898; M I June 21, 1898, M O with Co Nov 7, 1898

De Hass, David W, Priv Co E, Res Kerrmoor, Pa, Enrd June 21, 1898, M I June 21, 1898, M O with Co Nov 7, 1898

De Huff, Edward F, Priv Co A, Res Huntingdon, Pa, Enrd June 23, 1898, M. I June 23, 1898, M O with Co Nov 7, 1898

Deitz, George K, Priv Co I, Res Listie, Pa, Enrd July 6. 1898, M I July 8, 1898, M O with Co Nov 7, 1898

Delozier, Frederick, Priv Co C, Res Altoona, Pa, Enrd May 10. 1898. M I May 11, 1898, Apptd Ms Sept 1. 1898, M O with Co Nov. 7, 1898

Delozier, Joseph, Priv Co C, Res Hollidaysburg, Pa (N G P) Enrd April 27, 1898, M I May 11, 1898, M O with Co Nov 7, 1898

Denning, Oden R, Priv Co E, Res Clearfield, Pa (N G P). Enrd April 27, 1898, M I May 11, 1898, M O with Co Nov 7, 1898

De Turk, Benjamin H, Mus Co A, Res Altoona, Pa (N G P), Enrd April 27, 1898, M I May 11, 1898, M O with Co Nov 7, 1898

Detwiler, Calvin, Priv Co C, Res Yellow Springs, Pa, Enrd May 10 1898. M I May 11, 1898, M O with Co Nov 7, 1898

Dibble, Amos W, Priv Co K Res Wellsboro, Pa, Enrd July 12, 1898 M I July 14, 1898, M O with Co Nov 7. 1898

Dibble, John C. Priv Co K, Res Draper, Pa, Enrd July 12, 1898, M I July 14, 1898, M O with Co Nov 7, 1898

Dibble, William G, Priv Co K, Res Olmsville, Pa, Enrd July 12 1898 M I July 14, 1898. died at Sternberg Hosp, Chicamauga, Ga, Aug 31. 1898

Diehl, James F. Priv Co M, Res Gettysburg, Pa, Enrd July 15. 1898, M I July 20, 1898. M O with Co Nov 7, 1898

Dipple. Charles P. Priv Co G, Res Lewistown, Pa, Enrd May 10, 1898, M I May 11, 1898, detached Aug 12, S O 23, as mounted orderly for the Comdg officer, M O with Co Nov 7. 1898

Ditzer, Joseph, Priv Co C. Res Hollidaysburg, Pa Enrd April 28, 1898, M I May 11, 1898. M O with Co Nov 7, 1898

Dixon, Edward E, Priv Co D. Res Blacklick, Pa, Enrd June 24, 1898, M I June 24, 1898, M O with Co Nov 7, 1898

Dodson, Lewis M. Priv Co M, Res York, Pa, Enrd July 19, 1898. M I July 20, 1898, Prom Corp Sept 1, 1898. M O with Co Nov 7, 1898

Doty, James H, Priv Co E, Res DuBois, Pa, Enrd June 20, 1898, M I June 20, 1898, M O with Co Nov 7, 1898

Doud, Claud R, Priv Co K. Res Blossburg, Pa, Enrd July 11. 1898, M I July 14, 1898, M O with Co Nov 7, 1898

Douds, Robert S. Priv Co D, Res Saltsburg, Pa, Enrd May 9. 1898, M I May 11, 1898, M O with Co Nov 7, 1898

Dougherty, John F, Priv Co L, Res Clearfield, Pa, Enrd July 13, 1898, M I July 14, 1898, M O with Co Nov 7, 1898

Dougherty, Thomas M, Priv Co L, Res Houtzdale, Pa, Enrd July 14, 1898, M I. July 14, 1898. M O with Co Nov 7, 1898

Downs, Milton H, Priv Co L, Res Philipsburg, Pa, Enrd July 14, 1898, M I July 14, 1898, M O with Co Nov 7, 1898

Dressler, Herbert A, Priv Co E, Res Reedsville, Pa, Enrd May 9. 1898. M I May 11, 1898, M O with Co Nov 7, 1898

Dunkle, John C, 1st Lieut Co A, Res Huntingdon, Pa (N G P), Enrd April 27, 1898, M I. May 11, 1898, M O with Co Nov 7, 1898

Dunlap, Edwin D, Priv Co D, Res Blairsville, Pa (N G P), Enrd April 27,

1898, M I May 11, 1898, M O with Co Nov 7, 1898

Dunn, Milton, Priv Co L, Res DuBois, Pa , Enrd July 14, 1898, M I July 14, 1898, M O with Co Nov 7, 1898

Dunn, Samuel F , Priv Co K, Res Wellsboro, Pa , Enrd July 14, 1898, M I July 14, 1898, M O with Co Nov 7, 1898

Dupont, Frederick O , Priv Co I, Res Rockwood, Pa , Enrd July 8, 1898, M I July 8, 1898, M O with Co Nov 7, 1898

Dwyer, Frank, Priv Co E, Res DuBois, Pa , Enrd June 20, 1898, M I June 20, 1898, M O with Co Nov. 7, 1898

Dye, Robert, Priv Co I, Res Somerset, Pa , Enrd July 4, 1898, M I July 8, 1898, M O with Co Nov 7, 1898

Earhart, Harry W , Priv Co F, Res Indiana, Pa, Enrd May 9, 1898, M I May 11, 1898, M O with Co Nov 7, 1898

Eberhart, George A , Corp Co D, Res Bellefonte, Pa (N G P), Enrd April 27, 1898, M I May 11, 1898, M O with Co Nov 7, 1898

Eboch, Edward T , Priv Co B, Res Philipsburg, Pa ; Enrd May 7, 1898, M I May 11, 1898, M O with Co Nov 7, 1898

Eboch, Theodore H , Priv Co B, Res Philipsburg, Pa , Enrd June 27, 1898, M I June 27, 1898, M O with Co Nov 7, 1898

Ebright, Josiah M , Mus Co H, Res Altoona, Pa (N G P), Enrd April 27, 1898, M I May 11, 1898, M O with Co Nov 7, 1898

Eck, Emanuel E , 2d Lieut Co A, Res Huntingdon, Pa (N G P), Enrd April 27, 1898, M I May 11, 1898, M O as 2d Lieut Co A, 5th P V I , July 14, 1898, to accept Apptmt as 1st Lieut M I as 1st Lieut Co I, 5th P V I , July 15, 1898, M O. with Co Nov 7, 1898

Eckley, Don Pedro, Priv Co L, Res Wallaceton, Pa , Enrd July 14, 1898, M. I. July 14, 1898, M O. with Co Nov. 7, 1898

Eddington, Alex , Priv. Co L, Res Philipsburg, Pa , Enrd. July 13, 1898, M I July 14, 1898, M O with Co Nov 7, 1898.

Edwards, Paul J , Sgt Co K, Res Westfield, Pa , Enrd July 11, 1898, M I July 14, 1898, Apptd Sgt July 23, 1898, G O. 8, c s Regt , M O with Co Nov 7, 1898.

Eichinger, Harper, Priv Co G, Res Johnstown, Pa , Enrd June 29, 1898, M. I. June 29, 1898, M O with Co Nov 7, 1898

Elder, Rufus C , Lieut Col , Res Lewistown, Pa (N G P), Enrd April 27, 1898, M I May 11, 1898, M O with Co Nov 7, 1898

Eline, John A , Priv Co M, Res. York, Pa , Enrd July 19, 1898, M I July 20, 1898, M O with Co Nov. 7, 1898

Elkin, William F , 2d Lieut Co F, Res Indiana, Pa (N G P), Enrd April 27, 1898, M I May 11, 1898, M O with Co Nov 7, 1898

Elkin, William F , Jr , Priv. Co F, Res. Jeannette, Pa , Enrd May 9, 1898, M I May 11, 1898, M O with Co Nov 7, 1898

Ellis, Frank S , Priv Co G, Res Lewistown, Pa (N G P); Enrd April 27, 1898, M I May 11, 1898, M O with Co Nov 7, 1898

Ellis, William A , Priv Co G, Res Mifflintown, Pa , Enrd May 10, 1898, M I May 11, 1898, M O with Co Nov 7, 1898

Ellis, William V , Sgt Co A, Res Huntingdon, Pa (N G P), Enrd April 27, 1898, M I May 11, 1898, M O with Co Nov 7, 1898

Eminhizer, Abraham H, Priv Co B, Res Bellefonte, Pa (N G P), Enrd April 27, 1898, M I May 11, 1898, Apptd Wag May 23, 1898, M O with Co Nov 7, 1898

Endres, William, Priv Co E, Res Clearfield, Pa, Enrd May 9, 1898, M I May 11, 1898, M O with Co Nov 7, 1898

Engelbach, George K, Corp Co H, Res Johnstown, Pa (N G P), Enrd April 27, 1898, M I. May 11, 1898, M O with Co Nov 7, 1898

Engle, Calvin U, Priv Co I, Res Elk Lick, Pa, Enrd July 4, 1898, M I July 8, 1898, M O with Co Nov 7, 1898

Engle, Irwin J, Priv Co I, Res Elk Lick, Pa, Enrd July 4, 1898, M I July 8, 1898, Prom Corp July 16, 1898, M O with Co Nov 7, 1898

English, Roscoe H, Priv Co K, Res Wellsboro, Pa, Enrd July 12, 1898, M I July 14, 1898; Apptd Corp July 23, 1898, M O with Co Nov 7, 1898

English, Thomas W, Corp Co H, Res Johnstown, Pa (N G P), Enrd April 27, 1898, M I May 1, 1898, Prom Sgt Sept 10, 1898, M O with Co Nov 7, 1898

Ennish, Henry N, Priv Co G, Res Yeagertown, Pa, Enrd June 29, 1898, M I June 29, 1898, M O with Co Nov 7, 1898

Enos, Wilson G, Priv Co I, Res Elk Lick, Pa, Enrd July 5, 1898, M I July 8, 1898, died at Mercy Hosp Pittsburg, Pa, Sept 18, 1898

Erb, Andrew B, Corp Co D, Res Blairsville, Pa (N G P), Enrd April 27, 1898, M I May 11, 1898, M O with Co Nov 7, 1898

Erb, John E, Priv Co B, Res Philips-burg, Pa, Enrd May 7, 1898, M. I May 11, 1898, M O with Co Nov 7, 1898

Ergler, Joseph F, Priv. Co A, Res Huntingdon, Pa, Enrd April 27, 1898, M I. May 11, 1898, M O with Co Nov 7, 1898

Ertel, William G, Priv Co B, Res Howard, Pa, Enrd. May 7, 1898, M I May 11, 1898, M O. with Co Nov 7, 1898

Estricher, Charles C, Priv Co E, Res New Washington, Pa, Enrd June 21, 1898, M I June 21, 1898, M O with Co Nov 7, 1898

Everhart, Daniel W, Priv Co M, Res York, Pa, Enrd July 20, 1898. M I July 20, 1898, M O with Co Nov 7, 1898

Everitt, Charles F, Corp Co K, Res Westfield, Pa., Enrd July 12, 1898, M I. July 14, 1898, Apptd Corp July 23, 1898, G O 8 c s Regt, M O with Co Nov 7, 1898

Ewing, Charles, Priv Co I, Res Everett, Pa, Enrd July 5, 1898, M I July 8, 1898; transfd as Corp to 3d Div Hosp Corps July 20, 1898, per S O 29

Fagan, Hubert E, Priv Co C, Res. Huntingdon. Pa, Enrd May 10, 1898, M I May 11, 1898, M O with Co Nov 7, 1898

Fails, Harvey, Priv Co D. Res Blacklick, Pa (N G P), Enrd April 27, 1898, M I May 11, 1898, M O with Co Nov 7, 1898

Fair, Ira H, Priv Co A, Res Huntingdon, Pa, Enrd May 7, 1898, M I May 11, 1898, M O with Co Nov 7, 1898

Fair, John S, Adj, Res Altoona, Pa (N G P), Enrd April 27, 1898, M I May 5, 1898, M O with Regt Nov 7, 1898

Fair, Philip W, Priv Co C, Res Altoona, Pa (N G P), Enrd April 27, 1898, M I May 11, 1898, M O with Co Nov 7, 1898

Farley, John T , Priv. Co E , Res Clearfield, Pa , Enrd June 20, 1898, M. I June 20, 1898, M O with Co Nov 7, 1898

Faust, Edward H , Priv Co L , Res. Houtzdale, Pa , Enrd July 14, 1898, M I July 14, 1898, M O with Co Nov 7, 1898

Fauver, James F , Priv Co E , Res Clearfield, Pa. (N G P), Enrd April 27, 1898, M I May 11, 1898, M O with Co Nov 7, 1898

Fee, Harry W , Sgt Co F , Res Indiana, Pa (N G P), Enrd. as Corp April 27, 1898, M I as Sgt May 11, 1898, M O with Co Nov 7, 1898.

Feidt, G A , Priv Co E. Res, Indiana, Pa , Enrd June 21, 1898, M I June 21, 1898, M O with Co Nov 7, 1898

Feigler, Franklin D , Priv Co M, Res Winterstown, Pa , Enrd July 10, 1898, M I July 20, 1898, M O with Co Nov 7, 1898

Feit, George J , Priv Co F , Res Indiana, Pa (N G P), Enrd April 27, 1898; M I May 11, 1898, Prom Sgt June 28, 1898, M O with Co Nov 7, 1898

Felding, William H , Priv Co B , Res Lindenhall, Pa , Enrd June 27, 1898, M I June 27, 1898, M O with Co Nov 7, 1898

Fennell, William H , Priv Co D , Res Saltsburg, Pa , Enrd May 9, 1898, M I May 11, 1898, M O with Co Nov 7, 1898

Fenstermacher, William L , Priv Co M , Res Gettysburg, Pa , Enrd July 15, 1898, M I July 20, 1898, M O with Co Nov 7, 1898

Ferell, Charles, Priv Co I , Res Addison, Pa , Enrd July 5, 1898, M I July 8, 1898; M O with Co Nov 7, 1898

Fickes, George, Priv Co M , Res York, Pa , Enrd July 19, 1898, M I July 20, 1898; M O with Co Nov 7, 1898

Field, Harry B , Priv Co K , Res. Wellsboro, Pa , Enrd July 11, 1898, M I July 14, 1898, Apptd Q M. Sgt July 23, 1898, G O c s Regt ; M. O with Co Nov 7, 1898

Filler, Harry K , Priv. Co. I , Res Rainsburg, Pa , Enrd. July 5, 1898, M I July 8, 1898, M. O with Co Nov 7, 1898

Finn, Daniel J , Priv Co. C , Res Hollidaysburg, Pa. (N. G P.); Enrd April 27, 1898, M I May 11, 1898, M. O with Co. Nov 7, 1898.

Fisher, Arthur P , Priv Co A , Res Huntingdon, Pa , Enrd May 7, 1898, M I May 11, 1898; M O with Co Nov. 7, 1898

Fisher, Harry W , Priv Co E , Res Huntingdon, Pa , Enrd April 27, 1898, M. I May 11, 1898, M O with Co Nov. 7, 1898

Fisher, Oliver S , Priv Co D , Res Blairsville, Pa , Enrd June 24, 1898, M. I. June 24, 1898, M O with Co Nov. 7, 1898

Fissel, Frank, Priv Co C ; Res Duncansville, Pa., Enrd May 10, 1898, M I May 11, 1898, M O with Co Nov 7, 1898

Fister, Harry A , Priv Co E , Res Clearfield, Pa , Enrd May 9, 1898, M I May 11, 1898, M O with Co Nov 7, 1898

Fite, Charles J , Priv Co H , Res Pittsburgh, Pa , Enrd April 29, 1898, M I May 11, 1898, Prom Corp June 28, 1898, M. O with Co Nov 7, 1898

Fix, David D , Sgt Co H ; Res Johnstown, Pa (N G P), Enrd April 27, 1898; M I May 11, 1898, Dischd Aug 10, 1898; par 16 S O 187 A G. O

Fleck, Cecil W., Priv Co E , Res Clearfield, Pa (N. G P.), Enrd April 27, 1898; M I May 11, 1898, M O with Co Nov 7, 1898

Fleitz, Joseph P , Priv Co K, Res Hills Creek, Pa , Enrd July 12, 1898, M I July 14, 1898, M O with Co Nov 7, 1898

Fleming, Giles, Priv Co K, Res Tioga, Pa , Enrd July 12, 1898, M I July 14, 1898, M O with Co Nov 7, 1898

Fleming, James A , Priv Co F, Res Crete, Pa (N G P), Enrd April 27, 1898, M I May 11, 1898, M O with Co Nov 7, 1898

Flinn, Frank, Priv Co H, Res Johnstown, Pa , Enrd June 27, 1898, M I June 27, 1898, M O with Co Nov 7, 1898

Flynn, Michael, Priv Co D, Res Cokeville, Pa , Enrd June 25, 1898, M I June 25, 1898, M O with Co Nov 7, 1898

Fogle, Warren E , Priv Co I, Res Berlin, Pa , Enrd July 5, 1898, M I July 8, 1898, M O with Co Nov 7, 1898

Folk, Elmer E , Priv Co I Res Elk Lick, Pa , Enrd July 7, 1898, M I July 8, 1898, M O with Co Nov 7, 1898

Fonner, Joseph, Priv Co C Res Williamsburg, Pa , Enrd May 10, 1898, M I May 11, 1898; M O with Co Nov 7, 1898

Force, Fred, Priv Co L Res Curwensville, Pa , Enrd July 13, 1898, M I July 14, 1898, reduced from rank of Corp at his own request Aug 1, 1908, detailed as Mus Sept 1, 1898, M O with Co Nov 7, 1898

Ford, Henry H , Priv Co D, Res West Fairfield, Pa; Enrd June 24, 1898, M I June 24, 1898, Apptd Co cook July 31, 1898; M O with Co Nov 7, 1898

Forquer, James, Priv Co I, Res Ursina, Pa ; Enrd July 6, 1898, M I July 8, 1898, M. O with Co Nov 7, 1898

Forsha, Addison, Sgt Co D, Res Knights, Pa (N G P); Enrd April 27, 1898, M. I May 11, 1898, M O with Co Nov. 7, 1898

Fort, Clarence W , Priv Co L, Res Curwensville, Pa , Enrd July 14, 1898, M I July 14, 1898, M O with Co Nov 7, 1898

Fosselman, John J, Priv Co F, Res Donnelly Mills, Pa , Enrd May 9, 1898, M I May 11, 1898, M O with Co Nov 7, 1898

Foster, John V , Priv Co G, Res Lewistown, Pa (N G P), Enrd April 27, 1898, M I May 11, 1898, M O with Co Nov 7, 1898

Foster, Richard, Priv Co H, Res Johnstown, Pa , Enrd May 9, 1898, M I May 11, 1898, M O with Co Nov 7, 1898

France, Edgar W , Priv Co D, Res Knights, Pa (N G P), Enrd April 27, 1898, M I May 11, 1898, M O with Co Nov 7, 1898

Francis, Bert , Priv Co K, Res Delmar, Pa , Enrd July 12, 1898, M I July 14, 1898, M O with Co as Corp Nov 7, 1898

Frank, Frederick, Priv Co B; Res Penn Hall, Pa , Enrd May 7, 1898, M I May 11, 1898, M O with Co Nov 7, 1898

Frankhouser, Harry A , Priv Co G, Res Lewistown, Pa , Enrd June 29, 1898, M I June 29, 1898, M O with Co Nov 7, 1898

Frankhouser, Ralph, Priv Co L, Res Curwensville, Pa , Enrd July 14, 1898, M I July 14, 1898, M O with Co Nov 7, 1898

Franks, John L , Priv Co B, Res Milesburg, Pa ; Enrd May 7, 1898, M I May 11, 1898, M O with Co Nov 7, 1898

Franson, Gust W , Priv Co L, Res DuBois, Pa ; Enrd July 14, 1898, M I July 14, 1898, M O with Co Nov 7, 1898

Frazier, Harry D , Priv Co C, Res Hollidaysburg, Pa (N G P), Enrd April 27,

1898, M I May 11, 1898, M O with Co Nov. 7, 1898

Freeman, Ralph, Priv Co L, Res Grampian, Pa, Enrd July 14, 1898, M I July 14, 1898, M O with Co Nov 7, 1898

French, David B, Priv Co K, Res Farmington, Pa, Enrd July 11, 1898, M I. July 14, 1898, M O with Co Nov 7, 1898

Fritz, Jacob L, Priv Co D, Res. Blairsville, Pa, Enrd June 24, 1898, M I June 24, 1898, M O with Co Nov 7, 1898

Frybarger, Andrew, Priv Co G, Res Lewistown, Pa, Enrd May 10, 1898, M I May 11, 1898, Apptd Wag July 1, 1898, M O with Co Nov 7, 1898

Fulton, J D, Priv Co H, Res Johnstown, Pa. Enrd June 27, 1898, M I June 27, 1898, M O with Co Nov 7, 1898

Gallagher, Ira H, Priv Co I, Res Trent, Pa, Enrd July 6, 1898, M I July 8, 1898, deserted Aug 12, 1898, at Chickamauga Park, Georgia

Gambell, Ralph E, 1st Lieut Co K, Res Wellsboro, Pa, Enrd July 12, 1898, M I July 14, 1898, Comsd Capt Aug 10, 1898, M I as Capt Aug 14, 1898, M O with Co Nov 7, 1898

Gamble, Gibson, Priv Co K, Res Cedar Run, Pa; Enrd July 13, 1898, M I July 14, 1898; M O with Co Nov 7, 1898

Gantz, Samuel S, Priv. Co E, Res Lewistown, Pa, Enrd May 9, 1898, M I May 11, 1898; M O with Co Nov 7, 1898

Garbrick, Philip F, 1st Sgt Co B, Res Bellefonte, Pa (N G P), Enrd April 27, 1898, M I May 11, 1898, M O with Co Nov 7, 1898

Gardner, Benjamin K, Priv Co G, Res Lewistown, Pa (N G P), Enrd April 27,

1898; M. I. May 11, 1898, M. O with Co. Nov 7, 1898.

Gardner, Harry A., Priv Co B, Res. Philipsburg, Pa., Enrd June 27, 1898; M. I. June 27, 1898, M O with Co Nov 7, 1898

Garis, Charles, Sgt Co B, Res. Bellefonte, Pa (N G P), Enrd. April 27, 1898; M I May 11, 1898, died at Div Hosp Aug 28, 1898.

Garland, George W, Priv. Co. C, Res. Duncansville, Pa, Enrd May 10, 1898; M I May 11, 1898, M O with Co Nov 7, 1898

Garland, William L, Mus Co C, Res Philadelphia, Pa. (N G P), Enrd April 27, 1898, as Mus in Co E, Tranfd to Co C May 7, 1898, M. I Co C, May 11, 1898; Prom to Prin Mus Sept 1, 1898, per Regtl. G. O 29, M O with Regt Nov 7, 1898

Garman, Daniel E, Priv Co H, Res Johnstown, Pa., Enrd May 9, 1898, M I May 11, 1898, M. O. with Co Nov. 7, 1898

Garman, Thomas W., Priv Co H, Res. Scalp Level, Pa, Enrd June 27, 1898, M I. June 27, 1898, M. O with Co. Nov. 7, 1898

Garner, Jacob E T., Priv. Co A; Res. Huntingdon, Pa (N. G P.), Enrd April 27, 1898, M I May 11, 1898, M. O. with Co Nov 7, 1898

Garrett, Oliver P., Corp Co G; Res Lewistown, Pa (N G P), Enrd. April 27, 1898, M I May 11, 1898, M. O. with Co. Nov. 7, 1898

Gasteiger, Justus A, Priv. Co I, Res Somerset, Pa, Enrd July 5, 1898, M. I. July 8, 1898, M O with Co Nov 7, 1898

Gasteiger, Louis D, Priv Co I, Res. Somerset, Pa, Enrd July 5, 1898, M I July 8, 1898; Prom Sgt July 16, 1898, M O with Co Nov 7, 1898

Gaulin, Peter J S, Priv Co E, Res

Clearfield, Pa (N G P), Enrd April 27, 1898, M I May 11, 1898, Prom Corp May 11, 1898, Prom Sgt June 27, 1898, M O with Co Nov 7, 1898

Gearhart, Ralph, Priv Co L, Res Blue Ball, Pa , Enrd July 14, 1898, M I July 14, 1898, M O with Co Nov 7, 1898

Geesey, Charles II , Jr , Priv Co D Res Altoona, Pa , Enrd April 27, 1898, M I May 11, 1898, Transfd to 3d Div Amb Corps 1st Corps June 27, 1898

Geiselman, John W , Priv Co M, Res Fairplay, Pa , Enrd July 15, 1898, M I July 20, 1898, M O with Co Nov 7, 1898

Geissinger, Andrew B , Priv Co A, Res Huntingdon, Pa , Enrd June 23, 1898, M I June 23, 1898, M O with Co Nov 7, 1898

Geissinger, Michael L , Priv Co A Res Mill Creek, Pa , Enrd June 24 1898, M I June 24, 1898, M O with Co Nov 7, 1898

George, David H , Priv Co F Res Blairsville, Pa (N G P), Enrd April 27, 1898, M I May 11, 1898, M O with Co Nov 7, 1898

George, France M , Priv Co D, Res Knights, Pa (N G P) Enrd April 27, 1898, M I May 11, 1898, M O with Co Nov 7, 1898

George, Herbert C , Priv Co D Res Knights, Po (N G P), Enrd April 27, 1898, M I May 11, 1898, M O with Co Nov 7, 1898

George, James H , Corp Co D, Res Blairsville, Pa (N G P), Enrd April 27, 1898, M I May 11, 1898 Prom Sgt June 3, 1898, M O with Co Nov 7, 1898

Gephart, Adam, Priv Co II, Res Johnstown, Pa , Enrd May 9, 1898, M I May 11, 1898, M O with Co Nov 7 1898

Gerhard, Calvin S , Priv Co D, Res Blacklick, Pa , Enrd May 9, 1898, M I May 11, 1898, Prom Corp July 31, 1898, M O with Co Nov 7, 1898

Gettig, Samuel D , Sgt Co B , Res Bellefonte, Pa (N G P), Enrd April 27, 1898, M I May 11, 1898, M O with Co Nov 7, 1898

Getty, Clarence H , Priv Co H, Res Johnstown, Pa , Enrd June 27, 1898, M I June 27, 1898, M O with Co Nov 7, 1898

Ghuer, John E , Priv Co E, Res Benore, Pa , Enrd May 7, 1898, M I May 11, 1898, M O with Co Nov 7, 1898

Gibboney, James, Priv Co G, Res Lewistown, Pa , Enrd May 10, 1898, M I May 11, 1898, M O with Co Nov 7, 1898

Gibbons, Walker G , Priv Co C, Res Altoona, Pa , Enrd June 21, 1898, M I June 21, 1898, M O with Co Nov 7, 1898

Gilbert, Frederick J , Priv Co A, Res Huntingdon, Pa (N G P), Enrd April 27, 1898, M I May 11, 1898, M O with Co Nov 7, 1898

Gillaspie, John A , Priv Co C, Res Altoona, Pa (N G P), Enrd April 27, 1898, M I May 11, 1898, Prom Corp June 28, 1898, M O with Co Nov 7, 1898

Gillin, James, Priv Co H Res Vinco, Pa , Enrd June 27, 1898, M I June 27, 1898 M O with Co Nov 7, 1898

Gladhill, James L , Priv Co M, Res Fairfield, Pa , Enrd July 15 1898, M I July 20 1898, M O with Co Nov 7, 1898

Glazier, Herbert S , Priv Co A Res Philadelphia, Pa , Enrd June 23, 1898 M I June 23, 1898, M O with Co Nov 7, 1898

Glazier, John H , Priv Co A, Res Huntingdon, Pa , Enrd May 7 1898, M I May 11, 1898, M O with Co Nov 7, 1898

Glessner, Charles W, Priv Co M, Res York, Pa, Enrd July 19. 1898, M I July 20, 1898, M O with Co Nov 7, 1898

Glover, Samuel P, Asst Surg, Res Altoona, Pa. Enrd May 10, 1898, M I May 11, 1898, M O with Regt Nov 7, 1898

Godard, Edgar E, Priv Co A, Res Huntingdon, Pa, Enrd June 23, 1898, M I June 23, 1898, M O with Co Nov 7, 1898

Goddard, John S, Priv Co H, Res Johnstown, Pa, Enrd June 27, 1898 M I June 27, 1898, M O with Co Nov 7, 1898

Godel, Peter, Priv Co L, Res Gearhartbille, Pa, Enrd July 13, 1898, M I July 14, 1898, M O with Co as Corp Nov 7, 1898

Gohn, Philip S, Priv Co I, Res Somerset, Pa, Enrd July 5, 1898, M I July 8, 1898, M O with Co Nov 7, 1898

Gonder, George A, Priv Co H, Res Johnstown, Pa (N G P), Enrd April 27, 1898, M I May 11, 1898, M O with Co Nov 7, 1898

Good, Irvin H, Priv Co I, Res Trent, Pa, Enrd July 5, 1898, M I July 8, 1898, M O. with Co Nov 7, 1898

Goodman, Harry J, 1st Sergt Co A, Res Huntingdon, Pa. (N G P.), Enrd April 27, 1898; M I May 11, 1898, Dischd July 14, 1898, to accept appointment as 2d Lieut of same Co, Apptd 2d Lieut July 15, 1898; M. O with Co Nov. 7, 1898

Goodman, Wesley L, Priv Co C, Res Altoona, Pa, Enrd June 20, 1898, M I June 20, 1898, M. O. with Co Nov 7, 1898

Goodwin, Temple E, Priv Co K, Charleston, Pa, Enrd July 11, 1898, M I July 14, 1898, M O with Co Nov 7, 1898

Gorman, John W, Priv Co F, Res Horton, Pa (N. G P), Enrd. April 27, 1898,

M I May 11, 1898, M O with Co Nov 7, 1898

Goshorn, Ulysses S, Priv Co B, Res Philipsburg, Pa, Enrd May 7, 1898, M, I May 11, 1898, M O with Co Nov 7, 1898

Goss, Herbert N, Priv Co G, Res Cross Grove. Pa, Enrd June 29, 1898, M I June 29, 1898, M O with Co Nov 7, 1898

Goss, James H, Priv Co G, Res Lewistown, Pa, Enrd June 29, 1898, M I June 29, 1898, M O with Co Nov 7, 1898

Grabbe, William A, Priv Co G, Res Lewistown, Pa, Enrd May 10, 1898, M I May 11, 1898, M O with Co Nov 7, 1898

Graham, H C, Priv Co L, Res Clearfield, Pa; Enrd July 14, 1898, M I July 14, 1898, M. O with Co Nov 7, 1898

Graham, Lloyd, Priv Co L, Res Clearfield, Pa, Enrd July 13, 1898, M I July 14, 1898, M. O with Co Nov 7, 1898

Graham, Samuel M, Priv Co B, Res Philipsburg, Pa, Enrd April 28, 1898, M I May 11, 1898, Prom Corp May 26, 1898, M O. with Co. Nov 7, 1898

Gratz, Simon, Priv. Co G; Res Orbisonia, Pa; Enrd. May 10, 1898, M I. May 11, 1898; M O with Co. Nov. 7, 1898

Gray, Victor, Q M. Sgt Co L, Res Philipsburg, Pa; Enrd July 13, 1898, M I. July 14, 1898, Reduced to ranks at his own request August 31, 1898, M O with Co Nov 7, 1898

Graybill, John H, Priv Co M, Res East York, Pa, Enrd July 20, 1898, M I July 20, 1898; M O with Co Nov 7, 1898

Grazier, Durbin H, Priv Co H, Res. Fishertown, Pa; Enrd May 9, 1898, M I. May 11, 1898; M O with Co Nov 7, 1898

Green, Vern S, Priv. Co K, Res Brownlee, Pa , Enrd July 11, 1898, M I July 14, 1898, M O with Co Nov 7, 1898

Greene, William A , Priv Co C, Res Tipton, Pa , Enrd June 20, 1898, M I June 20, 1898, M O with Co Nov 7, 1898

Greenwood, Charles T , Priv Co D, Res Scottdale, Pa (N G P). Enrd April 27, 1898, M I May 11, 1898, M O with Co Nov 7, 1898

Grenoble, Cline J. Priv Co B, Res Pleasant Gap, Pa (N G P). Enrd April 27, 1898, M I May 11, 1898, M O with Co Nov 7, 1898

Grew, Adam, Priv Co I, Res Summit Mills, Pa , Enrd July 7, 1898, M I July 8, 1898, M O with Co Nov 7. 1898

Griesemer, Jack M , Priv Co L, Res Du-Bois, Pa , Enrd July 14, 1898, M I July 14, 1898, M O with Co as 1st Sgt Nov 7, 1898

Griesemer, John E , Priv Co L, Res Du-Bois, Pa , Enrd July 13, 1898, M I July 14, 1898, M O with Co as Corp Nov 9, 1898

Griest, Harry R , Priv Co B, Res Fleming, Pa (N G P), Enrd April 27, 1898, M I May 11, 1898, Prom Corp June 30, 1898, M. O with Co Nov 7, 1898

Griffith, Charles K , Priv Co F, Res Scottdale, Pa , Enrd June 23, 1898, M I June 23, 1898, M O with Co Nov 7, 1898

Griffith, William C , Priv Co H, Res Johnstown, Pa , Enrd May 9, 1898, M I May 11, 1898, Transfd to 3d Div Amb Corps July 2, 1898, per S O 10

Groff, John, Priv Co I, Res Berlin, Pa , Enrd July 5, 1898, M I July 8, 1898, Prom Corp July 16, 1898, M O with Co Nov 7 1898

Groom, Henry, Priv Co G, Res Balston

Spa, N Y , Enrd May 10, 1898, M I May 11, 1898, M O with Co Nov 7, 1898

Grove, Albert, Priv Co A , Res Huntingdon, Pa (N G P), Enrd April 27, 1898; M I May 11, 1898, M O with Co Nov 7, 1898

Growden, Thomas J , Priv Co E, Res Cumberland Valley, Pa , Enrd May 2, 1898, M I May 11, 1898, M O with Co Nov 7, 1898

Gushard, William I , Priv Co G, Res Patterson, Pa , Enrd June 29, 1898, M I June 29, 1898, M O with Co Nov 7, 1898

Haddie, Edgar M , Priv Co H; Res Johnstown, Pa (N G P), Enrd April 27, 1898, M I May 11, 1898, M O with Co Nov. 7, 1898

Hagarman, Basil E , Priv Co M, Res Centennial, Pa , Enrd July 18, 1898, M I July 20, 1898, M O with Co Nov 7, 1898

Hainsey, Harry, Sgt Co H, Res Johnstown, Pa (N G P), Enrd April 27, 1898, M I May 11, 1898, Dischd July 7, 1898, per S O 155 A G O

Halferty, Clarence A , Priv Co D, Res New Florence, Pa , Enrd June 25, 1898; M I June 25, 1898, M O with Co Nov 7, 1898

Halferty, Harry M , Priv Co D, Res New Florence, Pa , Enrd June 24, 1898, M I June 24, 1898, M O with Co Nov 7, 1898

Hall, Silas J , Priv Co A , Res Mill Creek, Pa , Enrd June 25, 1898, M I June 25, 1898, M O with Co Nov 7, 1898

Hamilton, Joseph, Priv Co C, Res Hollidaysburg, Pa , Enrd May 10, 1898, M I May 11, 1898, M O with Co Nov 7, 1898

Hammaker, Samuel H , Priv Co C, Res

Altoona, Pa , Enrd June 20, 1898, M I. June 20, 1898, M O with Co Nov 7, 1898

Hamme, Charles L , Priv Co M, Res. Hanover, Pa , Enrd July 15, 1898, M I July 20, 1898, M O with Co Nov 7, 1898

Hammer, George H , Priv Co F, Res Conner, Pa (N G P), Enrd April 27, 1898, M I May 11, 1898, M O with Co Nov 7, 1898.

Hammers, James S , Priv Co F, Res Indiana, Pa (N G P), Enrd April 27, 1898, M I May 11, 1898. Prom Corp June 28, 1898, M O with Co Nov 7, 1898

Hammond, Fred , Priv Co K, Res Elkland, Pa . Enrd July 11, 1898, M I. July 14, 1898, M O with Co Nov 7, 1898

Hampton, Harry E , Priv Co L, Res Curwensville, Pa , Enrd July 14, 1898, M I July 14, 1898, M O with Co Nov 7, 1898

Hanawalt, Reuben E , Priv Co G, Res Lewistown, Pa , Enrd May 10, 1898, M I. May 11, 1898, M O with Co Nov 7, 1898

Hancock, Edward, Priv Co L, Res Philipsburg, Pa . Enrd July 13, 1898, M I July 14, 1898, M O with Co Nov 7, 1898

Hanley, William E , Priv Co C, Res Duncansville, Pa (N G P), Enrd April 27, 1898, M I May 11, 1898, M O with Co Nov 7, 1898

Hannel, Blair, Priv Co C, Res Duncansville, Pa , Enrd May 10, 1898, M I May 11, 1898, M O with Co Nov 7, 1898

Hanson, C E , Priv Co L, Res Jamestown, N Y , Enrd July 12, 1898, M I July 14, 1898, M O with Co Nov 7, 1898

Harder, John E , Capt Co L, Res Clearfield, Pa , Enrd July 14, 1898, M I July 14, 1898, M O with Co Nov 7, 1898

Hakcom Harry, Priv Co D, Res Blairsville, Pa (N G P), Enrd April 27, 1898,

M I May 11, 1898; M. O. with Co Nov. 7, 1898

Harmon, Zenas E., Priv Co F, Res Indiana, Pa (N G P.); Enrd April 27, 1898; M I May 11, 1898; M O with Co Nov 7, 1898

Harper, Horace M , Priv Co B, Res Fleming, Pa (N G P); Enrd April 27, 1898, M I May 11, 1898, M O with Co Nov 7, 1898

Harrier, Orin, Priv Co E, Res. Shiloh, Pa , Enrd June 20, 1898; M I. June 20, 1898, M O with Co Nov 7, 1898

Harris, Alexander S , Priv Co B, Res Bellefonte, Pa , Enrd June 27, 1898, M I June 27, 1898, M O with Co Nov 7, 1898

Harris, John V , Priv Co G, Res Lewistown, Pa (N G P), Enrd April 27, 1898; M, I May 11, 1898, M O with Co Nov 7, 1898

Harrison, William N , Priv Co K; Res Wellsboro, Pa , Enrd July 12, 1898, M I. July 14, 1898, M O with Co Nov 7, 1898

Harshbarger, James, Priv Co G, Res. Newton Hamilton, Pa , Enrd May 10, 1898, M I May 11, 1898, M O with Co Nov 7, 1898

Hartman, George P , Priv Co L; Res. DuBois, Pa , Enrd July 13, 1898; M I July 14, 1898, M O with Co Nov 7, 1898

Hartman, Joseph F , Chaplain , Res Altoona, Pa (N G P), Enrd April 27, 1898; M I May 11, 1898. Resigned July 25, 1898.

Hartzell, Charles Z , Priv Co C , Res. Newport, Pa., Enrd June 20, 1898, M I June 20, 1898, M O with Co. Nov 7, 1898

Harwick, Edgar G , Priv Co E; Res Clearfield, Pa (N G P): Enrd April 27, 1898, M I May 11, 1898, M O with Co. Nov 7, 1898

Harvey, Charles D , Priv Co K , Res Covington, Pa , Enrd July 12, 1898, M I July 14, 1898. M O with Co Nov 7, 1898

Harvey, John S , Priv Co G , Res Lewistown, Pa , Enrd May 10, 1898. M I May 11, 1898, M O with Co Nov 7, 1898

Hatfield, William H , Priv Co A , Res Pittsburg, Pa , Enrd May 7, 1898, M I May 11, 1898, M O with Co Nov 7, 1898

Hathaway, George M , Priv Co K , Res Wellsboro, Pa , Enrd July 12. 1898, M I July 14, 1898, M O with Co Nov. 7, 1898

Hauck, E K , Priv Co L , Res DuBois, Pa . Enrd July 13, 1898, M I July 14, 1898. M O with Co Nov 7, 1898

Hauser, Harry, Priv Co C , Res Altoona, Pa , Enrd May 10, 1898, M I May 11, 1898, M O with Co Nov 7, 1898

Hawn, Robert M , Corp Co A , Res Huntingdon, Pa (N G P), Enrd April 27. 1898, M I May 11, 1898, Prom Sgt June 28, 1898, M O with Co Nov 7, 1898

Hay, George B . Priv Co L , Res DuBois, Pa . Enrd July 14, 1898. M I July 14, 1898, M O. with Co Nov 7. 1898

Hayes, Robert G , Asst Surg . Res Bellefonte, Pa (N G P). Enrd April 27, 1898, M I May 5, 1898. M O with Regt Nov 7, 1898

Hazel, D Oliver. Priv Co B Res Bellefonte, Pa (N G P) , Enrd April 27. 1898. M I May 11, 1898, M O with Co Nov 7, 1898

Hazel, John M , Priv Co B. Res Axeman, Pa (N G P) , Enrd April 27, 1898, M I May 11, 1898, M O with Co Nov 7, 1898

Hazlett, Ernest M . Priv Co K , Res Nelson, Pa , Enrd July 12, 1898; M I July 14, 1898, died Aug 30, 1898, at 3d Div Hosp , Chickamauga, Ga

Hazlett, Roy S , Priv Co F , Res Kent, Pa , Enrd June 23, 1898, M I June 23, 1898, M O with Co Nov 7, 1898

Heath, Joseph H , Priv Co I , Res Lull, Pa , Enrd July 5, 1898, M I July 8, 1898, M O with Co Nov 7, 1898

Heaton, Harry A , Priv Co B , Res Bellefonte, Pa , Enrd June 27, 1898, M I June 27, 1898, M O with Co Nov 7, 1898

Heichel, Jack A , Priv Co K , Res Blanchard, Pa , Enrd July 12, 1898, M I July 14, 1898, M O with Co Nov 7, 1898

Heiges, Colvin, Priv Co M , Res Franklintown, Pa , Enrd July 19, 1898, M I July 20, 1898, M O with Co Nov 7, 1898

Heller, George J , Priv Co G , Res Lewistown, Pa , Enrd May 10, 1898, M I May 11, 1898, M. O with Co Nov 7, 1898

Hemphill, Charles P , Priv Co E , Res Clearfield, Pa (N G P), Enrd April 27, 1898, M I May 11, 1898, M O with Co Nov 7, 1898

Hemphill, Samuel J , Priv Co A , Res Huntingdon, Pa (N G P), Enrd April 27, 1898, M I May 11, 1898, Prom to Corp July 28, 1898, M O with Co Nov 7, 1898

Henderson, Alexander, Priv Co D , Res Bolivar, Pa , Enrd June 24, 1898, M I June 24, 1898, M O with Co Nov 7, 1898

Henderson, Clark C , Priv Co D , Res Bolivar, Pa , Enrd May 9, 1898, M I May 11, 1898, M O with Co Nov 7, 1898

Henderson, Ross, Priv Co D , Res Bolivar, Pa (N G P), Enrd April 27, 1898; M I May 11, 1898. M O with Co Nov 7, 1898

Hengst, Allison, Priv Co C , Res Hollidaysburg, Pa (N G P), Enrd April 27, 1898; M I May 11, 1898, Prom to Corp June 28, 1898, M O with Co Nov 7, 1898

Herald, William B, Priv Co H, Res Conemaugh, Pa (N G P), Enrd April 27, 1898, M I May 11, 1898, M O with Co Nov 7, 1898

Herb, George C, Priv Co I, Res Somerset, Pa, Enrd July 4, 1898, M I July 8, 1898, M O with Co Nov 7, 1898

Herbst, Harry H, Priv Co M; Res North Hopeville, Pa, Enrd July 19, 1898, M I July 20, 1898, M O with Co Nov 7, 1898

Hering, George A, Priv Co D, Res Altoona, Pa, Enrd June 20, 1898, M I June 20, 1898, M O with Co Nov 7, 1898

Hershey, Harry B, Priv Co H, Res Johnstown, Pa, Enrd May 9, 1898, M I May 11, 1898, M O with Co Nov 7, 1898

Heslop, Wesley J, Priv Co H, Res Johnstown, Pa, Enrd May 9, 1898, M I May 11, 1898, M O with Co Nov 7, 1898

Hess, Harry H, Priv Co L, Res Houtzdale, Pa, Enrd July 14, 1898, M I July 14, 1898, M O with Co as Corp Nov 7, 1898

Hess, William M, Priv Co B, Res Philipsburg, Pa, Enrd April 28, 1898, M I May 11, 1898, M O with Co Nov 7, 1898

Hickok, Ross, 1st Lieut Co M, Res Harrisburg, Pa, Enrd Aug 8, 1898, M I Aug 8, 1898, Enlisted as Priv in Baty A, Pa Arty, at Camp Hastings, May 5, 1898, Dischd at Newport News, Va, July 28, 1898, to accept commission, Apptd 1st Lieut Co M July 28, 1898, M I as 1st Lieut Camp Thomas, Chickamauga Park, Ga, Aug 8, 1898, M O with Co Nov 7, 1898

Hicks, Howard, Priv Co A, Res Huntingdon, Pa, Enrd June 23, 1898, M I June 23, 1898, M O with Co Nov 7, 1898

Hill Charles, Priv Co M, Res York, Pa; Enrd July 20, 1898, M I July 20, 1898, M O with Co Nov 7, 1898

Hill, Don J, Q M. Sgt Co F, Res Indiana, Pa (N G P.), Enrd April 27, 1898; M I May 11, 1898, M O with Co Nov 7, 1898

Hill, Edgar W, Priv Co C, Res Hollidaysburg, Pa (N G P.), Enrd April 27, 1898, M I May 11, 1898, Prom Corp June 28, 1868, M O with Co Nov 7, 1898

Hill, John M, Priv Co G, Res Northumberland, Pa, Enrd June 29, 1898, M I June 28, 1898, M O with Co Nov 7, 1898

Hill, Joseph, Priv Co D, Res Cokeville, Pa, Enrd May 9, 1898, M I May 11, 1898, M O with Co Nov 7, 1898

Hill, Joseph A, Priv Co D, Res Saltsburg, Pa, Enrd May 9, 1898, M I May 11, 1898, M O with Co Nov 7, 1898

Hills, Frank D, Priv Co K, Res Farmington, Pa, Enrd July 11, 1898, M I May 11, 1898, M O with Co Nov 7, 1898

Hobbs, James F, Priv Co H, Res Johnstown, Pa, Enrd May 9, 1898, M I May 11, 1898, M O with Co Nov 7, 1898

Hoblitzell, Frank W, Priv Co I, Res Meyersdale, Pa, Enrd July 5, 1898; M I July 8, 1898, Apptd 2d Lieut July 14, 1898; Comsd July 12, 1898; M I. July 15, 1898; M O with Co Nov 7, 1898, as 2d Lieut

Hoecht, James C, Priv Co M, Res Franklintown, Pa, Enrd July 18, 1898; M I July 20, 1898, M O with Co Nov. 7, 1898

Hoff, R C, Priv Co C, Res Altoona, Pa, Enrd June 20, 1898, M. I June 20, 1898, M O with Co Nov 7, 1898

Hoffman, Burkett W, Priv. Co A, Res Huntingdon, Pa (N G P), Enrd April 27, 1898, M I May 11, 1898, M O with Co Nov 7, 1898

Hoffman, David H, Priv Co G; Res Lewistown, Pa (N G P), Enrd April 27, 1898;

M I May 11, 1898, M O with Co Nov 7, 1898

Hoffman, Fred W Priv Co H, Res Johnstown, Pa , Enrd June 27, 1898, M I June 27, 1898, M O with Co Nov 7, 1898

Hoffman, James, Priv Co A, Res Huntingdon, Pa , Enrd June 23, 1898, M I June 23, 1898, M O with Co Nov 7, 1898

Hoffman, William H , Priv Co G, Res Lewiston, Pa (N G P). Enrd April 30 1898, M I May 11, 1898, M O with Co Nov 7, 1898

Hollen, Ira A , Priv Co C, Res Juniata, Pa , Enrd June 20, 1898 M I June 20 1898, M O with Co Nov 7, 1898

Hollopetor, Cyrel B , Priv Co L, Res Rockton, Pa , Enrd July 14, 1898, M I July 14, 1898, M O with Co Nov 7, 1898

Homan, George W Priv Co H, Res Hollidaysburg, Pa , Enrd April 27, 1898, M I May 11, 1898, died June 27, 1898, at 3d Div Hosp of typhoid fever

Homan, William L , Priv Co M, Res Gettysburg, Pa , Enrd July 16, 1898, M I July 20, 1898, Apptd Cook July 22, 1898, M O with Co Nov 7, 1898

Hoover, Charles S , Priv Co K, Res Cross Fork, Pa , Enrd July 12, 1898, M I July 14, 1898, M O with Co Nov 7, 1898

Hoover, Edwin B , Priv Co K Res Olean, N Y , Enrd July 12, 1898, M I July 14, 1898, M O with Co Nov 7, 1898

Hoover, George P , Priv Co B, Res Fleming, Pa , Enrd June 28, 1898, M I June 28, 1898, M O with Co Nov 7, 1898

Hoover, Hayes, Priv Co H, Res Springhope, Pa , Enrd June 27, 1898, M I June 27, 1898, M O with Co Nov 7, 1898

Hopkins, Miles C , Priv Co C, Res Altoona, Pa , Enrd June 20, 1898, M I June 20, 1898, M O with Co Nov 7, 1898

Hornick, Leander G , Priv Co H, Res Johnstown, Pa , Enrd June 27, 1898, M I June 27, 1898, M O with Co Nov 7, 1898

Hospelhorn, James L , Priv Co M Res Fairplay, Pa , Enrd July 15, 1898, M I July 20, 1898, M O with Co Nov 7, 1898

Hostetler, Braden F , Priv Co I, Res Trent, Pa , Enrd July 6, 1898, M I July 8, 1898 M O with Co Nov 7, 1898

Householder, Eugene B , Priv Co A, Res Hopewell, Pa , Enrd June 23, 1898, M I June 23, 1898, M O with Co Nov 7, 1898

Householder, Robert E , Priv Co D, Res Ligonier, Pa , Enrd May 9 1898 M I May 11, 1898, M O with Co Nov 7, 1898

Howard, Dwight L , Priv Co M, Res Bendersville, Pa , Enrd July 18, 1898, M I July 20, 1898, M O with Co Nov 7, 1898

Hoy, Harry M , Priv Co B, Res Milheim, Pa , Enrd May 7, 1898, M I May 11, 1898, M O with Co Nov 7, 1898

Huey, Charles E , Priv Co F, Res Indiana, Pa (N G P), Enrd April 27, 1898, M I May 11, 1898, M O with Co Nov 7, 1898

Huey, Frank E Priv Co B, Res Fillmore, Pa , Enrd June 27, 1898, M I June 27, 1898, M O with Co Nov 7, 1898

Hugg, Toner A , Priv Co B, Res Milesburg, Pa , Enrd June 28, 1898, M I June 28, 1898, M O with Co Nov 7, 1898

Hughes, Samuel H , 1st Lieut Co F, Res Indiana, Pa (N G P), Enrd April 27, 1898, M I May 11, 1898, M O with Co Nov 7, 1898

Hulslander, Frederick L , Priv Co K, Res Slate Run, Pa , Enrd July 11, 1898, M I July 14, 1898, M O with Co Nov 7, 1898

Hurst, William P, Priv Co I, Res Somerset, Pa , Enrd July 4, 1898, M I July 8, 1898, Prom Corp July 16, 1898, M O with Co Nov 7, 1898

Huston, Augustus E, Priv Co D, Res Black Lick, Pa , Enrd June 24, 1898, M I June 24, 1898, M O with Co Nov 7, 1898

Huston, George T, 1st Lieut Co H, Res Johnstown, Pa (N G P), Enrd April 27, 1898, M I May 11, 1898, M O with Co Nov 7, 1898

Huston, Joseph N, Priv Co F, Res Blairsville, Pa , Enrd June 23, 1898, M I June 23, 1898, M O with Co Nov 7, 1898

Hutchison, Chester F, Priv Co E, Res Philipsburg, Pa , Enrd May 2, 1898, M I May 11, 1898, M O with Co Nov 7, 1898

Inscho, Frederick E, Priv Co K, Res Westfield, Pa , Enrd July 13, 1898 M I July 14, 1898, M O with Co Nov 7, 1898

Irvin, John E, Priv Co A, Res Huntingdon, Pa , Enrd May 7, 1898, M I May 11, 1898, M O with Co Nov 7, 1898

Irwin, Elbridge B, Priv Co E, Res Clearfield, Pa (N G P), Enrd April 27, 1898, M I May 11, 1898, M O with Co Nov 7, 1898

Irwin, George C, Priv Co C, Res Hollidaysburg, Pa (, G P), Enrd April 27, 1898, M I May 11, 1898 Prom Corp June 28 1898, M O with Co Nov 7, 1898

Iseman, John W, Priv Co D, Res Blairsville, Pa (N G P), Enrd April 27, 1898, M I May 11, 1898, Prom Corp June 28, 1898, M O with Co Nov 7, 1898

Isenberg, Edmund R, Priv Co A, Res Huntingdon, Pa (N G P), Enrd April 27, 1898, M I May 11, 1898, M O with Co Nov 7, 1898

Isenberg, James H, Priv Co A, Res Huntingdon, Pa (N G P.); Enrd April 27, 1898, M I May 11, 1898; M. O with Co Nov 7, 1898

Isett, James H, Priv Co A, Res Huntingdon, Pa (N G P), Enrd April 27, 1898, M I May 11, 1898, Prom Corp June 28, 1898. M O with Co Nov 7, 1898

Isett, Samuel E, Priv Co C, Res. Williamsburg, Pa , Enrd June 21, 1908, M I June 21, 1898, M O with Co No 7, 1898

Ivison, John J, Priv Co C, Res Altoona, Pa , Enrd June 20, 1898, M I June 20, 1898. M O with Co Nov 7, 1898

Jack, James P, Priv Co F, Res Kent, Pa , Enrd June 23, 1898; M I June 23, 1898, M O with Co No 7, 1898

Jackson, Chauncey T, Priv Co D, Res Blairsville, Pa (N G P), Enrd April 27, 1898, M I May 11, 1898, Prom Corp June 28, 1898, M O with Co Nov 7, 1898

Jackson, George L, 1st Lieut Co B, Res. Bellefonte, Pa (N G P), Enrd April 27, 1898, M I May 11, 1898, M O with Co. Nov 7, 1898

Jackson, Harry A, Priv Co B, Res Bellefonte, Pa ; Enrd June 27, 1898, M I June 23, 1898, M O with Co Nov 7, 1898

Jacobs, Edward W, Priv Co E, Res Clearfield, Pa (N G P), Enrd April 27, 1898, M I May 11, 1898, M O with Co. Nov 7, 1898

Jacoby, Emory A, Priv Co M, Res Centennial, Pa , Enrd July 18, 1898; M I July 20, 1898, M O with Co Nov 7, 1898

Jamison, William F, Priv Co F; Res Indiana, Pa , Enrd May 9, 1898, M I May 11 1898, M O with Co Nov 7, 1898

Jenkins, J Arthur, Priv Co D, Res Salisburg, Pa , Enrd June 24, 1898, M I June 24, 1898, M O with Co Nov 7, 1898

Jenkins, Richard, Priv Co D, Res Blairsville, Pa , Enrd June 25, 1898, M I June 25, 1898, M O with Co Nov 7, 1898

Jobe, Marion E, Priv Co M, Res York Springs, Pa , Enrd July 15, 1898, M I July 20, 1898, Prom Corp Aug 1, 1898, Sgt Sept 1, 1898, M O with Co Nov 7, 1898

Johnson, Albert S, Mus Co F, Res Altoona, Pa (N G P), Enrd April 27, 1898, M I May 11, 1898, M O with Co Nov 7, 1898

Johnson, Charles, Priv Co L, Res Winburne, Pa , Enrd July 14, 1898, M I July 14, 1898, M O with Co Nov 7, 1898

Johnson, John E, Priv Co L, Res DuBois, Pa , Enrd July 13, 1898, M I July 14, 1898, M O with Co Nov 7, 1898

Johnson, Joseph M, Mus Co G, Res Altoona, Pa (N G P), Enrd April 27, 1898, M I May 11, 1898, M O with Co Nov 7, 1898

Johnson, Swan, Priv Co L, Res Winburne, Pa , Enrd July 14, 1898, M I July 14, 1898, M O with Co Nov 7, 1898

Johnston, Harry L, Q M Sgt Co C, Res Altoona, Pa (N. G P), Enrd May 10, 1898, M I May 11, 1898, Prom Sgt Maj Aug 13, 1898 by Regtl G O 19 (on F & S Roll enrolled April 27, 1898); M O with Regt Nov 7, 1898

Johnston, John P, Priv Co B, Res Philipsburg, Pa , Enrd May 7, 1898, M I May 11, 1898, M O with Co Nov 7, 1898

Johnston, William W, Priv Co F, Res Pittsburg, Pa , Enrd May 9, 1898, M I May 11, 1898, M O with Co Nov 7, 1898

Jones, Charles S, Corp Co G, Res Lewistown, Pa (N G P), Enrd April 27, 1898, M I May 11, 1898, M O with Co Nov 7, 1898

Jones, Edwin T, Priv Co D, Res Blairsville, Pa , Enrd May 9, 1898, M I May 11, 1898, M O with Co Nov 7, 1898

Jones, George H, Priv Co H, Res Johnstown, Pa , Enrd May 9, 1898, M I May 11, 1898, M O with Co Nov 7, 1898

Johnstonbaugh, John L, Priv Co B, Res State College, Pa , Enrd May 7, 1898, M I May 11, 1898, Apptd Mus Aug 11, 1898, M O with Co Nov 7, 1898

Jordan, William, Priv Co E, Res Clearfield, Pa (N G P), Enrd April 27, 1898, M I May 11, 1898, M O with Co Nov 7, 1898

Judy, George C, Priv Co H, Res Johnstown, Pa , Enrd June 27, 1898, M I June 27, 1898, M O with Co Nov 7, 1898

Kalbach, W D, Priv Co D, Res Blairsville, Pa , Enrd June 24, 1898, M I June 24, 1898, M O with Co Nov 7, 1898

Kamerly, James C, Priv Co C, Res Hollidaysburg, Pa (N G P), Enrd April 27, 1898, M I May 11, 1898, M O with Co Nov 7, 1898

Kann, Charles R, Priv Co I, Res Berlin, Pa , Enrd July 5, 1898, M I July 8, 1898, M O with Co Nov 7, 1898

Kantner, Asberry, Priv Co C Res Duncansville, Pa (N G P), Enrd April 27, 1898, M I May 11 1898, M O with Co Nov 7, 1898

Kappes, Frederick W, Priv Co M, Res Gettysburg, Pa , Enrd July 15, 1898, M I July 20, 1898, M O with Co Nov 7, 1898

Kase, Charles H, Priv Co B Res Bellefonte Pa (N G P), Enrd April 27, 1898, M I May 11, 1898, Tranfd to 3d Div 1st A C Hosp June 9, 1898

Kauffman, James S, Sgt Co. F Res Homer City, Pa (N G P), Enrd April 27,

1898, M. I May 11, 1898, M O with Co Nov 7, 1898

Kautz, William H , Priv Co I , Res Jenners, Pa , Enrd July 5, 1898, M I July 8, 1898, Prom Corp July 16, 1898, M O with Co Nov 7, 1898

Keeney, Clarence A , Priv Co K, Res. Hammond, Pa , Enrd July 11, 1898, M I July 14, 1898, Prom Corp July 23, 1898, G O 8 C s Regt , M. O with Co Nov 7, 1898

Keesey, Adam, Priv Co M, Res York, Pa , Enrd July 20, 1898, M I July 20, 1898, M O with Co Nov 7, 1898

Keime, Urban, Priv Co M, Res Gettysburg, Pa , Enrd July 20, 1898, M. I July 20, 1898, M O with Co Nov 7, 1898

Keith, John deK , Priv Co H , Res Gettysburg, Pa , Enrd April 29, 1898, M I May 11, 1898; M O with Co Nov 7, 1898

Keller, John O , Corp Co B , Res Bellefonte, Pa (N G P), Enrd April 27, 1898, M I May 11, 1898, M. O with Co Nov 7, 1898

Keller, William W , Priv Co B , Res Pine Grove Mills, Pa , Enrd June 27, 1898, M I June 27, 1898, M O with Co Nov 7, 1898

Kellerman, Hickman J , Priv Co B , Res Bellefonte. Pa (N G P), Enrd April 27, 1898, M I May 11, 1898, M O with Co Nov 7, 1898

Kelley, William P , 1st Lieut Co E , Res Clearfield, Pa (N G P), Enrd April 27, 1898, M I May 11, 1898, M O with Co Nov 7, 1898

Kelly, Aaron B , Priv Co L; Res Wigton, Pa . Enrd July 13, 1898, M I July 14, 1898, M O with Co Nov 7, 1898

Kelly, Harry J , Priv Co D, Res Blairsville, Pa (N. G P), Enrd. April 27, 1898, M I May 11, 1898, M. O with Co. Nov 7, 1898

Kemery, Victor M , Priv Co H , Res Medix Run, Pa , Enrd June 27, 1898; M I June 27, 1898, M O with Co Nov. 7, 1898

Kempfer, John J , Priv Co F , Res Selinsgrove, Pa , Enrd June 23, 1898, M I June 23, 1898, M O Nov 7, 1898.

Kennedy, Jesse F , Priv. Co A, Res Huntingdon, Pa (N G P), Enrd April 27, 1898, M I May 11, 1898, M O with Co Nov 7, 1898

Kennedy, John P , Maj , Res Blairsville, Pa (N G P), Enrd April 27, 1898, M I. May 11, 1898, M O with Regt Nov 7, 1898.

Kennedy, Rodney C , Priv Co K , Res Wellsboro, Pa , Enrd July 12, 1898, M I July 14, 1898, M O with Co Nov 7, 1898

Kennedy, Thomas S , Priv Co G , Res Lewistown, Pa (N G P), Enrd April 27, 1898, M I May 11, 1898, M O with Co as Corp Nov 7, 1898

Kennedy, William A , Priv Co A , Res Mill Creek, Pa , Enrd June 23, 1898, M I June 23, 1898, M O with Co Nov 7, 1898

Kephart, Charles B , Priv Co H; Res. Taneytown, Md , Enrd April 29, 1898, M I May 11, 1898, M O with Co Nov 7, 1898

Kephart, John A , Priv Co E , Res Clearfield, Pa (N G P), Enrd April 27, 1898; M I May 11, 1898, M O with Co Nov 7, 1898

Kerr, James B , Priv Co E , Res Newtonburg, Pa , Enrd June 21, 1898; M I. June 21, 1898, M O with Co Nov 7, 1898.

Kerr, John M , Priv Co F , Res Shelocta, Pa (N. G P); Enrd April 27, 1898; M. I. May 11, 1898, M O with Co Nov 7, 1898

Kerr, Steele H , Priv Co F , Res Indiana, Pa (N G P), Enrd April 27, 1898, M I May 11, 1898, M O with Co Nov 7, 1898

Kerrigan, William B , Priv Co I , Res Sand Patch, Pa , Enrd July 6, 1898, M I July 8, 1898, M O with Co Nov 7, 1898

Kerstetter, Stover L , Priv Co G , Res Milheim, Pa ; Enrd June 29, 1898, M I June 29, 1898, M O with Co Nov 7, 1898

Kiebler, Paul E , Priv Co D , Res Saltsburg, Pa , Enrd April 27, 1898, M I May 11, 1898, M O with Co Nov 7, 1898

Kieferle, Harry C , Priv Co G , Res Mt Union, Pa , Enrd June 29, 1898, M I June 29, 1898, M O with Co Nov 7, 1898

Kilbourne, Louis H , Sgt Co K , Res Wellsboro, Pa , Enrd July 11, 1898, M I July 14, 1898, Prom Sgt July 23, 1898, G O 8 c s Regt , M O with Co Nov 7, 1898

Killinger, Claude C , Priv Co C , Res Altoona, Pa , Enrd June 20, 1898, M I June 20, 1898, M O with Co Nov 7, 1898

Kime, George E , Priv Co M , Res Gettysburg, Pa , Enrd July 15, 1898, M I July 20, 1898, M O with Co Nov 7, 1898

Kine, Charles F , Priv Co I , Res Kingwood, Pa ; Enrd July 5, 1898, M I July 8, 1898, Prom Sgt July 16, 1898, M O with Co Nov 7, 1898

King, Curtis W , Priv Co M , Res Gettysburg, Pa , Enrd July 15, 1898, M I July 20, 1898, M O with Co Nov 7, 1898

King, Harry S , Priv Co D , Res Saltsburg, Pa ; Enrd May 9, 1898, M I May 11, 1898, M O with Co Nov 7, 1898

Kinley, William C , Priv Co G , Res Lewistown, Pa , Enrd May 10, 1898, M I May 11, 1898, Prom Corp June 28, 1898, M O with Co Nov 7, 1898

Kinneman, Charles L , Priv Co M ; Res Abbottstown, Pa , Enrd July 15 1898, M I July 20, 1898, M O with Co Nov 7, 1898

Kipp, William A , Priv Co D , Res Leechburg, Pa , Enrd June 24, 1898, M I June 24, 1898, M O with Co Nov 7, 1898

Kirkwood, Robert C , Priv Co H , Res Johnstown, Pa (N G P), Enrd April 27, 1898, M I May 11, 1898, M O with Co Nov 7, 1898

Kissinger, Ambrose L , Priv Co M , Res York, Pa , Enrd July 20, 1898, M I July 20, 1898, M O with Co Nov 7, 1898

Klinefelter, Daniel W , Priv Co H , Res Conemaugh, Pa (N G P), Enrd April 27, 1898, M I May 11, 1898, Dischd as Wag Oct 14, 1898, per telegram from W Dept

Knepp, Cloyd B , Priv Co G , Res Lewistown, Pa (N G P), Enrd April 27, 1898, M I May 11, 1898, Prom Corp June 28, 1898, M O with Co Nov 7, 1898

Knipple, Delinger C , Priv Co I , Res Queen, Pa , Enrd July 4, 1898, M I July 8, 1898, M O with Co Nov 7, 1898

Knisely, Calvin, Priv Co I , Res Alum Bank, Pa , Enrd July 4, 1898, M I July 8, 1898, M O with Co Nov 7, 1898

Koch, Daniel J , Priv Co B , Res Fair brook, Pa , Enrd June 27, 1898, M I June 27, 1898, M O with Co Nov 7, 1898

Koch, William J , Priv Co M , Res Gettysburg, Pa , Enrd July 15, 1898, M I July 20, 1898, M O with Co Nov 7, 1898

Kolher, Anthony M , Priv Co H , Res Johnstown, Pa (N G P), Enrd April 27, 1898, M I May 11, 1898, M O with Co Nov 7, 1898

Koontz, Arthur B , Priv Co H , Res Johnstown, Pa , Enrd May 9, 1898, M I. May 11, 1898, M O with Co Nov. 7, 1898

Kooser, Ernest O , Capt Co I ; Res.

Somerset, Pa , Enrd July 6, 1898, M I July 8, 1898, M O Nov 7, 1898

Krape, Frank F , Priv Co E , Res Spring Mills, Pa (N G P), Enrd April 27, 1898, M I May 11, 1898, M O with Co Nov 7, 1898

Krebs, William M , Priv Co G, Res Shindle, Pa , Enrd June 29, 1898, M I June 29, 1898, M O with Co Nov 7, 1898

Kreider, Oscar B , Priv Co M, Res Gettysburg, Pa , Enrd July 15, 1898, M I July 20, 1898, M O with Co as Mus Nov 7, 1898

Kreiger, Harry C , Priv Co H , Res Johnstown, Pa , Enrd May 9, 1898, M I May 11, 1898, M O with Co Nov 7, 1898

Kunkle, Charles L , Priv Co F, Res Creekside, Pa (N G P), Enrd April 27, 1898, M I May 11, 1898, M O with Co Nov 7, 1898

Kunkle, Frank P , Priv Co D, Res Saltsburg, Pa (N G P), Enrd April 27, 1898, M I May 11, 1898, M O with Co Nov 7, 1898

Kurtz, Nathan E , Priv Co G, Res Lewistown, Pa ; Enrd May 10, 1898, M I May 11, 1898, M O with Co Nov 7, 1898

Kvainstrom, Gust , Priv Co K, Res Slate Run, Pa , Enrd July 12, 1898, M I July 14, 1898, M O with Co Nov 7, 1898

Lamb, Benjamin, Jr , Priv Co L, Res Gearhartsville, Pa , Enrd July 13, 1898, M I July 14, 1898, M O with Co Nov 7, 1898

Lambing, Benjamin W , Priv Co F, Res Nolo, Pa , Enrd June 22, 1898, M I June 22, 1898, M O with Co Nov 7, 1898

Landerkin, Lewis E , Priv Co D, Res Blairsville, Pa (N G P), Enrd April 27,

1898, M I May 11, 1898, M O with Co Nov 7, 1898

Landis, Bert F , Priv. Co I, Res Somerset, Pa , Enrd July 5, 1898, M I. July 8, 1898, M O with Co Nov 7, 1898

Landis, Norman B , Priv Co I, Res Meyersdale, Pa , Enrd July 8, 1898, M I July 8, 1898, M O with Co Nov. 7, 1898.

Langham, Harl B , Priv Co F. Res Indiana, Pa (N G P), Enrd April 27, 1898, M I May 11, 1898, M O. with Co Nov 7, 1908

Langham, Robert M , Priv Co F, Res Indiana, Pa , Enrd May 9, 1898, M I May 11. 1898. M O with Co Nov 7, 1898

Lardin, Lewis E , Priv Co H; Res Johnstown, Pa , Enrd June 28, 1898, M I June 28, 1898, M O with Co Nov 7, 1898

Large, William W , Priv Co D, Res Livermore, Pa , Enrd June 24, 1898, M I June 24, 1898, M O with Co Nov. 7, 1898.

Lasher, Edward, Priv Co C, Res Hollidaysburg, Pa (N G P), Enrd April 27, 1898, M I May 11, 1898, M O with Co Nov 7, 1898

Lathers, Thomas P , Priv Co C, Res. Altoona, Pa , Enrd June 21, 1898, M I June 21, 1898; M O with Co Nov 7, 1898

Lathers, William J , Priv Co L, Res. Gearhartsville, Pa , Enrd July 13, 1898; M I July 14, 1898, M O with Co Nov. 7, 1898

Lawhead, Edward M , Priv Co D, Res. Leechburg, Pa , Enrd June 25, 1898, M I. June 25, 1898, M O with Co Nov 7, 1898

Lawhead, Fred R , Priv. Co. L; Res. Clearfield, Pa , Enrd July 14, 1898, M I. July 14, 1898. M O with Co Nov 7. 1898

Lawrence, John I , Priv Co M Res McSherrytown, Pa , Enrd July 15, 1898, M I

July 20, 1898, Prom Corp Aug 1, 1898, M O with Co Nov 7, 1898

Lay, William G, Priv Co K, Res Sullivan, Pa, Enrd July 12, 1898, M I July 14, 1898, M O with Co Nov 7, 1898

Leabhart, Archie E, Priv Co A, Res Huntingdon, Pa, Enrd June 23, 1898, M I June 23, 1898, M O with Co Nov 7, 1898

Leamer, William C, Priv Co C, Res Altoona, Pa (N G P), Enrd April 27, 1898, M I May 11, 1898, M O with Co Nov 7, 1898

Leathers, George H, Priv Co B, Res Howard, Pa, Enrd May 7, 1898, M I May 11, 1898, M O with Co Nov 7, 1898

Lefever, Curtis A, Priv Co M, Res Littlestown, Pa, Enrd July 15, 1898, M I July 20, 1898, M O with Co Nov 7, 1898

Leffard, William D, Priv Co A, Res Huntingdon, Pa (N G P), Enrd April 27, 1898, M I May 11, 1898, M O with Co Nov 7, 1898

Legore, Harry F, Priv Co M, Res Silver Run, Md, Enrd July 15, 1898, M I July 20, 1898, Apptd Wag Aug 1, 1898, M O with Co Nov 7, 1898

Leighow, Oscar M, Priv Co E, Res Woodland, Pa, Enrd June 20, 1898, M I June 20, 1898, M O with Co Nov 7, 1898

Leipold, Frank D, Priv Co E, Res Clearfield, Pa (N G P), Enrd April 27, 1898, M I May 11, 1898, Transfd to N C Staff June 21, 1898, as Prin Mus by G O 7, Hdqt 5th Regt P V, M O with Regt Nov 7, 1898

Letterman, Frank H, Sgt Co A, Res Huntingdon, Pa (N G P), Enrd April 27, 1898, M I May 11, 1898, Prom 1st Sgt July 28, 1898, M O with Co Nov 7, 1898

Lewis, Iddo M, Priv Co F, Res Locust Lane, Pa (N G P), Enrd April 27, 1898, M I May 11, 1898, M O with Co Nov 7, 1898

Liddick, Thurston, Priv Co G, Res Lewistown, Pa, Enrd May 10, 1898, M I May 11, 1898, M O with Co Nov 7, 1898

Lightfoot, Charles C, Mus Co G, Res Altoona, Pa (N G P), Enrd April 27, 1898, M I May 11, 1898, M O with Co Nov 7, 1898

Lightner, Blake, Priv Co E, Res Irvona, Pa, Enrd May 9, 1898, M I May 11, 1898, M O with Co Nov 7, 1898

Likens, Homer B, Priv Co A, Res Huntingdon, Pa, Enrd May 7, 1898, M I May 11, 1898, M O with Co Nov 7, 1898

Lindsay, Charles B, Priv Co F, Res Indiana, Pa (N G P), Enrd April 27, 1898, M I May 11, 1898, M O with Co Nov 7, 1898

Lindsey, Harry R, Priv Co L, Res Troutville, Pa, Enrd July 14, 1898, M I July 14, 1898, M O with Co Nov 7, 1898

Linton, Reuben M, Priv Co I, Res Somerset, Pa, Enrd July 5, 1898, M I July 8, 1898, Prom 1st Sgt July 16, 1898, M O. with Co Nov 7, 1898

Lippart, Edward, Priv Co E, Res Clearfield, Pa (N G P), Enrd April 27, 1898, M I May 11, 1898, M O with Co Nov 7, 1898

Lippart, Jacob, Priv Co E, Res Clearfield, Pa (N G P), Enrd April 27, 1898, M I May 11, 1898, M O with Co Nov 7, 1898

Little, Edward S, Priv Co M, Res York, Pa, Enrd July 20, 1898, M I July 20, 1898; M O with Co Nov 7, 1898

Little, Frank, Priv Co A, Res Huntingdon, Pa (N. G P), Enrd April 27, 1898, M I May 11, 1898, Prom Corp June 28, 1898, M O with Co Nov 7, 1898

Litzinger, David W, Priv Co H, Res Johnstown, Pa (N G P), Enrd April 27, 1898, M I May 11, 1898, M O with Co Nov 7, 1898

Livengood, Harry, Priv Co I, Res Elk Lick, Pa, Enrd July 5, 1898. M I July 8, 1898, M O with Co Nov 7, 1898

Livingston, Charles F, Priv Co D, Res Blairsville, Pa (N G P), Enrd April 27, 1898, M I May 11, 1898, M. O with Co Nov 7, 1898

Lloyd William, Priv Co L, Res Philipsburg, Pa, Enrd July 13, 1898, M I July 14, 1898, M O with Co Nov 7, 1898

Logan, George, Priv Co E. Res Clearfield, Pa (N G, P), Enrd April 27, 1898, M I May 11, 1898, Prom Corp June 27, 1898, M O with Co Nov 7, 1898

Logan, Ward, Q M Sgt Co E, Res Clearfield, Pa (N G P), Enrd April 27, 1898, M I May 11, 1898, M O with Co Nov 7, 1898

Lohr, Frank C, Priv Co F, Res Indiana, Pa (N G P), Enrd April 27, 1898, M I May 11, 1898, Prom Corp Aug 30, 1898, M O with Co Nov 7, 1898

Long, Clyde Z, Priv Co B, Res Howard, Pa (N G P), Enrd April 27, 1898, M I May 11, 1898, M O with Co Nov 7, 1898

Long, Henry W, Priv Co I, Res Somerset, Pa, Enrd July 4, 1898, M I July 8, 1898, M O with Co Nov 7 1898

Long, William, Priv Co C, Res Hollidaysburg, Pa (N G P), Enrd April 27, 1898; M I May 11, 1898, M O with Co Nov 7, 1898

Lose, John W, Corp Co B, Res Belle-fonte, Pa (N G P), Enrd April 27, 1898; M I May 11, 1898, Prom Q M. Sgt. by Regtl G O 4, May 11, 1898, M O with Co. Nov 7, 1898

Lott, Henry G, Priv Co M, Res Gettysburg, Pa, Enrd July 15, 1898. M I July 20, 1898, M O with Co Nov 7, 1898

Lotz, Edward M, Priv Co C, Res Duncansville, Pa, Enrd May 10, 1898, M. I May 11, 1898, M O with Co Nov 7, 1898

Louther, Valentine C, Priv Co H, Res. Johnstown, Pa (N G P), Enrd April 27, 1898, M I May 11, 1898, M O with Co Nov 7, 1898

Low, Andrew L, Priv Co M, Res Fairfield, Pa, Enrd July 16, 1898, M I July 20, 1898, M O with Co Nov 7, 1898

Loyd, Robert P, Priv Co E, Res Philipsburg, Pa, Enrd May 7, 1898, M I May 11, 1898, M O with Co Nov 7, 1898

Lucas, Benjamin W, Priv Co B, Res Howard, Pa, Enrd May 7, 1898, M I May 11, 1898 M O with Co Nov 7, 1898

Lucas, D Cameron, Priv Co L, Res Wigton, Pa, Enrd July 14, 1898, M I July 14, 1898, M O with Co as Sgt Nov 7, 1898

Lucas, Samuel L, Priv Co B, Res Fleming, Pa (N G P); Enrd April 27, 1898, M I May 11, 1898, M O with Co Nov 7, 1898

Ludwig, Albert L, Priv Co I, Res Friendsville, Md, Enrd July 6, 1898, M I July 8, 1898, M O with Co Nov 7, 1898

Lumadue, George M, Priv Co E; Res Woodland, Pa, Enrd May 9, 1898, M I May 11, 1898, M O with Co Nov 7, 1898

Luther, Edgar A, Priv. Co H, Res Johnstown, Pa (N G P.); Enrd April 27, 1898; M I May 11, 1898, Dischd by S O from Sect War Sept 23, 1898

Luther, William J , Priv Co H, Res Johnstown, Pa (N G P), Enrd April 27, 1898, M I May 11, 1898, M O with Co Nov 7, 1898

Lutz, Simon M , Priv Co H, Res Bedford, Pa , Enrd April 29, 1898, M I May 11, 1898, Tranfd to Reserve Amb Corps June 27, 1898, per S O 5

Lynn, Nelson, Sgt Co C, Res Hollidaysburg, Pa (N G P), Enrd April 27, 1898, M I May 11, 1898, M O with Co Nov 7, 1898

Lyons, Robert B , Priv Co A, Res Birmingham, Pa , Enrd June 23, 1898, M I June 23, 1898, M O with Co Nov 7, 1898

Lytel, Oram C , Priv Co F, Res Glen Richey, Pa , Enrd May 9, 1898, M I May 11, 1898, Tranfd to Reserve Amb Corps July 3, 1898, per S O 5

Maginnis, George M , Priv Co L, Res DuBois, Pa , Enrd July 14, 1898, M I July 14, 1898, M O with Co Nov 7, 1898

Mahaffey, James G , Priv Co E, Res Clearfield, Pa (N G P), Enrd April 27 1898, M I May 11, 1898, Prom Corp June 27, 1898, M O with Co Nov 7, 1898

Mahaffey, James T , Priv Co E, Res McGees Mills, Pa , Enrd May 9, 1898, M I May 11, 1898, died at St Joseph Hosp , Lexington, Ky , Sept 10, 1898

Mahaffey, Paul R , Priv Co E, Res Clearfield, Pa , Enrd May 9, 1898, M I May 11, 1898, M O with Co Nov 7, 1898

Mahan, William M , Capt Co F, Res Indiana, Pa (N G P), Enrd April 27, 1898, M I May 11, 1898, M O with Co Nov 7, 1898

Mallory, Thomas C , Priv Co B, Res Bellefonte, Pa (N G P), Enrd April 27,

1898, M I May 11, 1898, M O with Co Nov 7, 1898

Malone, James, Priv Co C, Res Hollidaysburg, Pa , Enrd May 10, 1898, M I May 11, 1898, M O with Co Nov 7, 1898

Marietta, George W , Priv Co D, Res Livermore, Pa (N G P), Enrd April 27, 1898, M I May 11, 1898, M O with Co Nov 7, 1898

Markle, George N , Priv Co L, Res Clearfield, Pa , Enrd July 13, 1898, M I July 14, 1898, Prom Corp Sept 1, 1898, M O with Co Nov 7, 1898

Markle, Lee, Priv Co E, Res DuBois Pa , Enrd June 21, 1898, M I June 21, 1898, M O with Co Nov 7, 1898

Markley, Milton C , Priv Co C, Res Altoona, Pa , Enrd May 10 1898, M I May 11, 1898, M O with Co Nov 7, 1898

Marsh, Benjamin O , Priv Co F, Res Indiana, Pa , Enrd June 22, 1898, M I June 22, 1898, M O with Co Nov 7, 1898

Marsh, James A , Priv Co H, Res Johnstown, Pa , Enrd June 27, 1898, M I June 27, 1898, M O with Co Nov 7, 1898

Marshall, George M , Priv Co F, Res Indiana, Pa , Enrd May 9, 1898, M I May 11, 1898, M O with Co Nov 7, 1898

Marshall, John R , Priv Co F, Res Indiana, Pa (N G P), Enrd April 27, 1898; M I May 11, 1898, M O with Co Nov 7, 1898

Martin, George A , Priv Co M, Res Gettysburg, Pa , Enrd July 15, 1898, M I July 20, 1898, M O with Co Nov 7, 1898

Martin, George W , Priv Co A, Res Huntingdon, Pa , Enrd April 27, 1898, M I May 11, 1898, M O with Co Nov 7, 1898

Martin, Harry, Priv Co C, Res Duncansville, Pa (N G P), Enrd April 27, 1898,

M I May 11, 1898, Prom Corp June 28, 1898, M O with Co Nov 7, 1898

Martin, Howard W, Priv Co A, Res Huntingdon, Pa Enrd June 23, 1898, M I June 23, 1898, M O with Co Nov 7, 1898

Martin, John C, Priv Co A, Res Huntingdon, Pa (N G P), Enrd April 27, 1898. M I May 11, 1898, M O with Co Nov 7, 1898

Martin, Lemon, Priv Co C, Res Duncansville, Pa (N G P), Enrd April 27, 1898, M I May 11, 1898, M O with Co Nov 7, 1898

Martz, Harry A, Priv Co C, Res Lewistown, Pa (N G P), Enrd April 27, 1898, M I May 11, 1898, M O with Co Nov 7, 1898

Martz, John D, Priv Co F, Res Congruity, Pa , Enrd May 9, 1898, M I May 11, 1898, M O with Co Nov 7, 1898

Mateer, Nelson, Priv Co C, Res Hollidaysburg, Pa (N G P), Enrd April 27, 1898, M I May 11, 1898, M O with Co Nov 7, 1898

Mathews, Bert I, Priv Co D, Res Ligonier, Pa , Enrd May 9, 1898, M I May 11, 1898, M O with Co Nov 7, 1898

Matlack, Lewis H , 2d Lieut Co L, Res Philadelphia, Pa (N G P), Enrd in Co F, 1st Regt , as Corp, April 28, 1898, M I May 11, 1898; Apptd 2d Lieut Co L, 5th Regt , July 20, 1898, M I July 31, 1898, M O with Co L Nov 7, 1898

Matthews, Charles, Priv Co C, Res Altoona, Pa , Enrd June 20, 1898, M I June 20 1898, M O with Co Nov 7, 1898

Matthews, Edward B , Priv Co G, Res Lewistown, Pa , Enrd June 29, 1898, M I June 29, 1898, M O with Co Nov 7, 1898

May, James E , Priv Co H, Res Johnstown, Pa (N G P), Enrd April 27, 1898. M I May 11, 1898, M O with Co Nov. 7, 1898

May, Leroy, Priv Co H, Res Johnstown. Pa (N G P), Enrd April 27, 1898, M I May 11, 1898, M O with Co Nov 7 1898

May, Samuel M, Priv Co I, Res Meyersdale, Pa , Enrd July 5, 1898, M I July 8, 1898, M O with Co Nov 7, 1898

Mays, Frank E, Priv Co E, Res Osceola Mills, Pa , Enrd April 27, 1898, M. I. May 11, 1898, Prom to Artf June 27, 1898, taken sick at his home in Osceola Mills, failed to report Oct , 1898, died Tuesday, Nov 8, 1898

McCafferty, Dorsey G, Sgt Co G, Res Lewistown, Pa (N G P), Enrd. April 27, 1898. M I May 11, 1898, M O with Co Nov 7, 1898

McCall, Hugh C, Priv Co M, Res York, Pa , Enrd July 20, 1898, M I July 20, 1898; M O with Co Nov 7, 1898

McCall, Jacob A, Priv Co B, Res Philipsburg, Pa , Enrd May 7, 1898, M I May 11, 1898, M O with Co Nov 7, 1898

McCamant, Thomas M, Priv Co A, Res Huntingdon, Pa , Enrd May 7, 1898; M I May 11, 1898, M O with Co Nov 7, 1898

McCann, James M, Priv Co L, Res Osceola Mills, Pa , Enrd July 14, 1898, M I. July 14, 1898, M O with Co as Corp Nov 7, 1898

McCaulay, Harry, Priv Co G; Res Bellefonte, Pa , Enrd May 10, 1898, M I May 11, 1898, M O with Co Nov. 7, 1898

McCausland, William H, Priv Co B, Res Philipsburg, Pa , Enrd June 27, 1898; M I June 27, 1898, M O with Co Nov 7, 1898

McClaran, Rome V, Priv Co D, Res Saltsburg, Pa , Enrd April 27, 1898, M I May 11, 1898, M O with Co Nov 7, 1898

McClean, Robert B, Priv Co M, Res Gettysburg, Pa, Enrd July 15, 1898, M I July 20, 1898, Prom Q M Sgt Aug 1, 1898, M O with Co Nov 7, 1898

McClellan, Burl, Priv Co E Res Clearfield, Pa, Enrd June 20 1898, M I June 20, 1898, M O with Co Nov 7, 1898

McClellan, George B, Priv Co E, Res Clearfield, Pa (N G P), Enrd April 27, 1898, M I May 11, 1898, M O with Co Nov 7, 1898

McClellan, Harley, Priv Co G, Res Mifflintown, Pa, Enrd May 10, 1898, M I May 11, 1898, M O with Co Nov 7, 1898

McCloskey, George A, Mus Co F, Res Altoona, Pa (N G P), Enrd April 27, 1898, M I May 11 1898, M O with Co Nov 7, 1898

McComish, Charles D, Priv Co F, Res Indiana Pa (N G P), Enrd April 27, 1898, M I May 11, 1898, M O with Co Nov 7, 1898

McComish, Ralph C, Priv Co F, Res Indiana, Pa, Enrd May 9, 1898, M I May 11, 1898, M O with Co Nov 7, 1898

McCoy, Robert M, Priv Co F, Res Cookport, Pa, Enrd June 2, 1898, M I June 22, 1898, M O with Co Nov 7, 1898

McCrady, Manuel, Priv Co F, Res Glen Campbell, Pa (N G P), Enrd April 27, 1898, M I May 11, 1898, Prom Corp June 28, 1898, M O with Co Nov 7, 1898

McCreary, George S, Sgt Co G, Res Lewistown, Pa (N G P), Enrd April 27, 1898, M I May 11, 1898, M O with Co Nov 7, 1898

McCrossin, Edward G, Priv Co E, Res Clearfield, Pa (N G P), Enrd April 27, 1898, M I May 11, 1898, M O with Co Nov 7, 1898

McCrossin, James G, Priv Co E, Res Osceola Mills, Pa, Enrd June 21, 1898, M I June 21, 1898, M O with Co Nov 7, 1898

McCullough, A, Priv Co L, Res DuBois, Pa, Enrd July 13, 1898, M I July 14, 1898, M O with Co Nov 7, 1898

McCullough, Charles H, Priv Co C, Res Altoona, Pa, Enrd May 10, 1898, M I May 11, 1898, M O with Co Nov 7, 1898

McCullough, Frederick E, Priv Co K, Res Farmington, Pa, Enrd July 12, 1898, M I July 14, 1898, M O with Co Nov 7, 1898

McCune, Edward N, Priv Co H, Res. Johnstown, Pa, Enrd June 27, 1898, M I June 27, 1898, M O with Co Nov 7, 1898

McCune, Philip, Priv Co D, Res Cokeville, Pa; Enrd May 9, 1898, M I May 11, 1898, M O with Co Nov 7, 1898

McDonnell, James W, Priv Co M, Res. Gettysburg, Pa, Enrd July 15, 1898, M I July 20, 1898, M O with Co Nov 7, 1898

McElcarr, William G, Priv Co H, Res Johnstown, Pa (N G P), Enrd April 27, 1898, M I May 11, 1898, M O with Co Nov 7, 1898

McElrath, Charles F, Priv Co G, Res Beaver Springs, Pa, Enrd June 29, 1898, M I June 28, 1898, M O with Co Nov 7, 1898

McElwee, Wilson H, Priv Co A, Res. Huntingdon, Pa (N G P) Enrd April 27, 1898, M I May 11, 1898, M O with Co Nov 7, 1898

McEntire, Lindsey W, Priv Co M, Res Clarion, Pa, Enrd July 15, 1898, M I June 20, 1898, M O with Co as Mus Nov 7, 1898

McFadden, John, Priv Co C Res Hollidaysburg, Pa (N G P), Enrd April 27,

1898, M. I May 11, 1898, M O with Co. Nov 7, 1898

McFeaters, William, Priv Co D, Res Blacklick, Pa , Enrd May 9, 1898, M I May 11, 1898, M O with Co Nov. 7, 1898

McGarey, John, Priv Co E, Res Clearfield, Pa (N G P), Enrd April 27, 1898, M I May 11, 1898, M O with Co Nov 7, 1898

McGhee, W E , Priv Co. E, Res DuBois, Pa , Enrd June 20, 1898, M I June 20, 1898, M O with Co Nov 7, 1898

McGunigal, Samuel A , Priv Co H, Res Johnstown, Pa (N G P), Enrd April 27, 1898, M I May 11, 1898, M O with Co Nov 7, 1898

McHenry, David, Priv Co F, Res Indiana, Pa , Enrd May 9, 1898, M I May 11, 1898, M O with Co Nov 7, 1898

McIlhenny, James G , Priv Co M, Res Gettysburg. Pa , Enrd July 15, 1898, M I July 20, 1898, Prom Corp Aug 1, 1898, M O with Co Nov 7, 1898

McIlroy, James T , Priv Co A; Res Huntingdon, Pa , Enrd. June 23, 1898, M. I June 23, 1898, M O with Co Nov 7, 1898

McIntyre, J C , Priv Co L, Res Wigont, Pa , Enrd July 14, 1898, M I. July 14, 1898, M O with Co as Artf Nov. 7, 1898

McJunkin, William P , Priv Co D; Res. Ebenezer, Pa (N G P). Enrd April 27, 1898, M I May 11, 1898, M O. with Co. Nov 7, 1898

McKee, Harry D , Priv Co C, Res Roaring Spring, Pa , Enrd June 21, 1898, M I June 21, 1898, M O with Co Nov. 7, 1898

McKee, William C , Sgt Co D, Res Blairsville, Pa (N G P), Enrd April 28, 1898, M I May 11, 1898, Dischd July 31, 1898, to accept commission as 2d Lieut ,

Prom to 2d Lieut. July 31, 1898, M. O. with Co. Nov 7, 1898

McKown, George W., Priv. Co M; Res. Tunkhannock, Pa , Enrd. July 20, 1898; M. I July 20, 1898, M O with Co Nov 7, 1898.

McLain, James, Priv. Co B, Res. Johnstown, Pa , Enrd May 9, 1898, M. I May 11, 1898, M. O with Co Nov 7, 1898.

McLaughlin, Frank W., Priv. Co. F, Res. Davis, Pa (N. G P.), Enrd April 27, 1898; M I May 11, 1898, M O. with Co Nov. 7, 1898

McLaughlin, John A , Corp Co. F, Res. Davis, Pa (N. G P), Enrd April 27, 1898, M I May 11, 1898, Prom. Corp May 11, 1898, M. O. with Co Nov. 7, 1898.

McManaway, Harry F., Priv. Co B, Res Penn Hall, Pa , Enrd. May 7, 1898; M I May 11, 1898, M. O. with Co Nov 7, 1898

McMichael, George W , Priv Co A; Res. Huntingdon, Pa., Enrd. June 23, 1898 M I June 23, 1898, M. O. with Co. Nov. 7, 1898

McNamara, Robert C , Maj , Res. Bedford, Pa (N. G P), Enrd April 27, 1898; M. I May 11, 1898, M O. with Regt. Nov. 7, 1898

McPherran, Alton, Priv. Co G; Res Yeagertown, Pa., Enrd. May 10, 1898; M I. May 11, 1898, M. O. with Co. Nov. 7, 1898

Meese, William B , Priv. Co G; Res Bellefonte, Pa , Enrd. June 28, 1898; M. I June 28, 1898, M. O with Co Nov 7, 1898.

Meise, J. H., Priv. Co. L, Res Clearfield, Pa , Enrd July 14, 1898; M I July 14, 1898; M O with Co Nov 7, 1898

Meller, Harry B , Priv Co C; Res Altoona, Pa (N G P); Enrd April 27, 1898;

H. S. KNARR PROPERTY

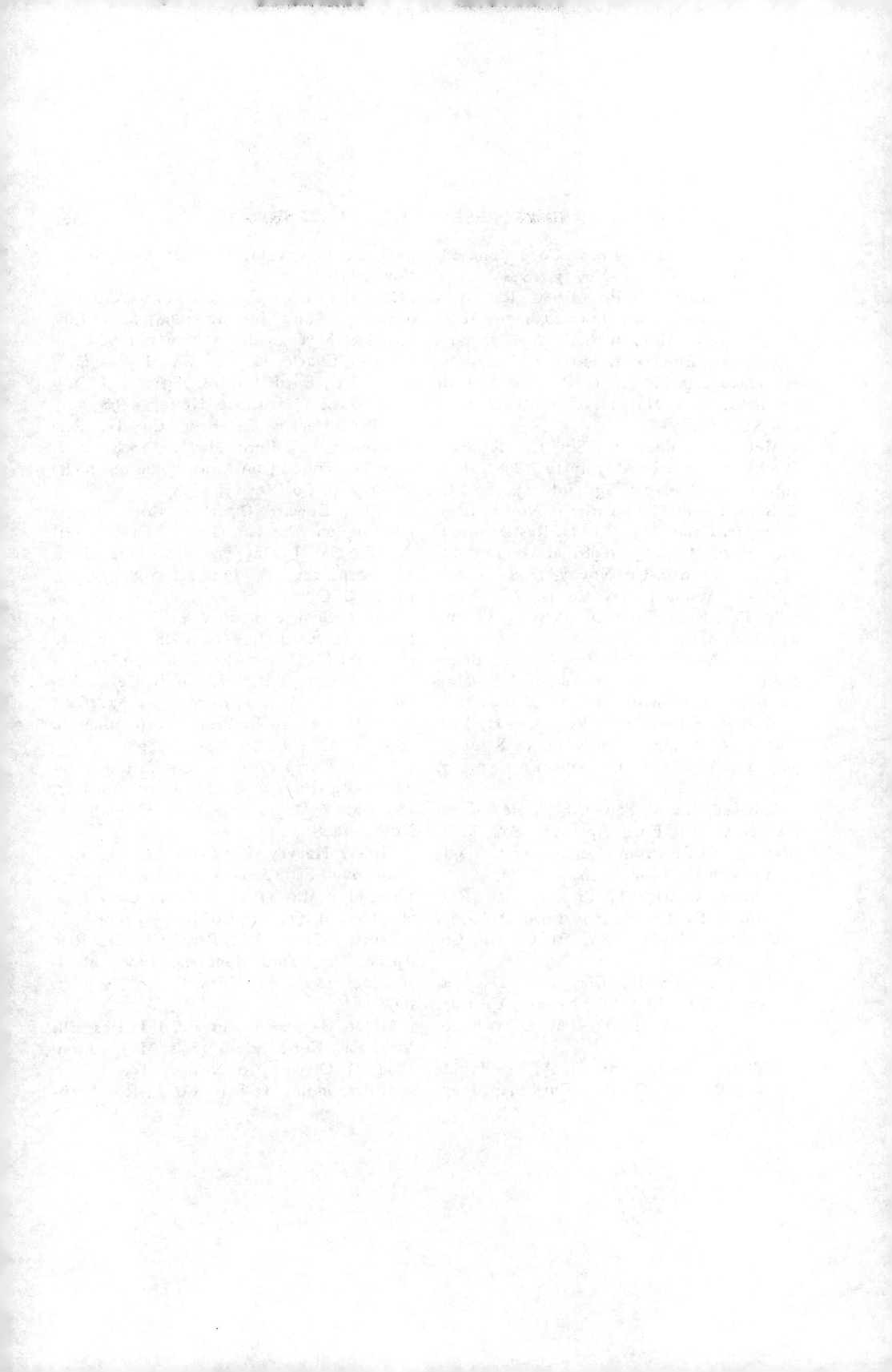

M I May 11, 1898, Prom Corp June 28, 1898, M O with Co Nov 7, 1898

Mench, Homer F, Priv Co C, Res Williamsburg, Pa, Enrd June 20, 1898, M I June 20, 1898, M O with Co Nov 7, 1898

Mentzer, Edward B, Priv Co C, Res Hollidaysburg, Pa (N G P), Enrd April 27, 1898, M I May 11, 1898, M O with Co Nov 7, 1898

Metzger, William C, Sgt Co K, Res Wellsboro, Pa, Enrd July 12, 1898, M I July 14, 1898, Prom Sgt July 23, 1898, G O 8 c s Regt, M O with Co Nov 7, 1898

Meyer, Louis, Priv Co L, Res Munson, Pa, Enrd July 13, 1898, M I July 14, 1898, M O with Co Nov 7, 1898

Meyer, William, Priv Co D, Res Cokeville, Pa, Enrd June 24, 1898, M I June 24, 1898, M O with Co Nov 7, 1898

Miess, Andrew, Priv Co B, Res Bellefonte, Pa, Enrd May 7, 1898, M I May 11, 1898, M O with Co Nov 7, 1898

Mignot, Fernando J, Priv Co L, Res Karthaus, Pa, Enrd July 14, 1898, M I July 14, 1898; M O with Co Nov 7, 1898

Mikesell, Ira B, Priv Co D, Res Kent, Pa (N G P), Enrd April 27, 1898, M I May 11, 1898, Prom Corp June 3, 1898, M O with Co. Nov 7, 1898

Miksitz, Charles J, Priv Co E, Res Clearfield, Pa (N G P), Enrd April 27, 1898, M I May 11, 1898, M O with Co Nov 7, 1898

Miller, Brooks E, Corp Co D, Res Cokeville, Pa (N G P), Enrd April 27, 1898, M I May 11, 1898, M O with Co Nov 7, 1898

Miller, Bruce D, Priv Co A, Res Huntingdon, Pa (N G P), Enrd April 27,

1898, M I May 11, 1898, M O with Co Nov 7, 1898

Miller, Charles, Priv Co K, Res Wellsboro, Pa, Enrd July 12, 1898, M I July 14, 1898, M O with Co Nov 7, 1898

Miller, Charles E, Priv Co M, Res Ottanna, Pa, Enrd July 18, 1898, M I July 20, 1898, M O with Co Nov 7, 1898

Miller, Dorsey G, Priv Co G, Res Lewistown, Pa, Enrd May 10, 1898, M I May 11, 1898, Prom Corp June 28, 1898, M O with Co Nov 7, 1898

Miller, Edward C, Priv Co A, Res Huntingdon, Pa (N G P), Enrd April 27, 1898, M I May 11, 1898, Transfd to Sig Corps, 1st A C June 15, 1898, by S O 140 A G O

Miller, George H, Priv Co L, Res Du-Bois, Pa, Enrd July 13, 1898, M I July 14, 1898, M O with Co Nov 7, 1898

Miller, George P, Priv Co B, Res Bellefonte, Pa (N G P), Enrd April 27, 1898, M I May 11, 1898, Prom Corp June 30, 1898, M O with Co Nov 7, 1898

Miller, Harry L, Corp Co C, Res Hollidaysburg, Pa (N G P), Enrd April 27, 1898, M I May 11, 1898, M O with Co Nov 7, 1898

Miller, Harvey E, Priv Co H, Res Johnstown, Pa (N G P), Enrd April 27, 1898, M I May 11, 1898, Prom Corp June 28, 1898, M O with Co Nov 7, 1898

Miller, Hayes W, Priv Co D, Res Apollo, Pa, Enrd June 24, 1898; M I June 24, 1898, M O with Co Nov 7, 1898

Miller, Herman A, Priv Co I, Res Elk Lick, Pa, Enrd July 6, 1898, M I July 8, 1898, M O with Co Nov 7, 1898

Miller, James B, Priv Co I, Res Stanton Mills, Pa , Enrd July 5, 1898, M I July 8, 1898, M O with Co Nov 7, 1898

Miller, James B , Priv. Co A, Res Lewistown, Pa , Enrd June 24, 1898, M I June 24, 1898, M O with Co Nov 7, 1898

Miller, John V , Priv Co L, Res Clearfield, Pa , Enrd July 13, 1898, M I June 14, 1898, M O with Co as Sgt. Nov 7, 1898

Miller, Lloyd S , Priv Co A, Res Tyrone, Pa , Enrd June 24, 1898, M I June 24, 1898, M O with Co Nov 7, 1898

Miller, Merton R , Priv Co K, Res Liberty, Pa , Enrd July 13, 1898, M I July 14, 1898, M O with Co Nov 7, 1898

Miller, Samuel M , Priv Co H, Res Johnstown, Pa , Enrd June 24, 1898, M I. June 27, 1898, M O with Co Nov 7, 1898

Miller, Thomas B , Priv Co D, Res Kent, Pa (N G P), Enrd April 27, 1898, M I May 11, 1898, Prom Corp June 28, 1898, M O with Co Nov 7, 1898

Million, Ezra L , Priv Co I, Res Elk Lick, Pa , Enrd July 5, 1898, M I July 8, 1898, Prom Sgt July 16, 1898, M O with Co Nov 7, 1898

Minnigh, John H , Mus Co E, Res Altoona, Pa (N G P), Enrd April 27, 1898, M I May 11, 1898, M O with Co Nov 7, 1898

Mitchell, Bruce P , Priv Co I, Res Addison, Pa , Enrd July 5, 1898, M I July 8, 1898, M O with Co Nov 7, 1898

Mitchell, Edsell N , Priv Co K, Res Holiday, Pa , Enrd July 12, 1898, M I July 14, 1898, M O with Co Nov 7, 1898

Mitchell, Harold B , Priv Co E, Res Clearfield, Pa , Enrd June 20, 1898, M I June 20, 1898, M O with Co Nov 7, 1898

Mitchell, John H , Priv Co G, Res Lewistown, Pa., Enrd. June 29, 1898, M I June 29, 1898, M O. with Co Nov 7, 1898.

Mitchell, Merle, Priv Co K, Res Holiday, Pa , Enrd July 12, 1898, M I July 14, 1898, M. O with Co Nov 7, 1898

Monney, Stephen H , Priv Co F, Res Smicksburg, Pa , Enrd June 23, 1898, M I June 23, 1898, M O with Co Nov. 7, 1898.

Monks, Edward K , Priv. Co K, Res Keeneyville, Pa , Enrd July 12, 1898, M I July 14, 1898, M O. with Co Nov 7, 1898

Monroe, Robert J , Priv Co D, Res Blacklick, Pa (N G P), Enrd April 27, 1898, M I May 11, 1898, M O with Co Nov 7, 1898

Moore, Logan R , Priv. Co D, Res. Saltsburg, Pa (N G P), Enrd April 27, 1898, M I May 11, 1898, M O with Co Nov 7, 1898

Moorhead, Alexander R , Corp Co F, Res Indiana, Pa (N G P), Enrd April 27, 1898, M. I May 11, 1898, M O with Co Nov 7, 1898

Moorhead, Hugh M , Priv Co. F; Res. Indiana, Pa (N G P), Enrd April 27, 1898, M I May 11, 1898, M O with Co. Nov 7, 1898

Morrison, James, Corp Co B , Res Bellefonte, Pa , (N G P), Enrd April 27, 1898, M I May 11, 1898, Prom Sgt May 13, 1898, M O with Co Nov 7, 1898

Morrison, John, Priv Co B, Res Bellefonte, Pa ; (N G P), Enrd April 27, 1898, M I May 11, 1898, M O with Co Nov 7, 1898

Morrison, Samuel, Priv Co B, Res Bellefonte, Pa , (N G P), Enrd April 27, 1898, M I May 11, 1898, Apptd Artf May 27, 1898, M O with Co Nov 7, 1898

Moser, Howard, Priv Co M, Res York, Pa , Enrd July 20, 1898, M I July 20, 1898, M O with Co Nov 7, 1898

Mostyn, John E , Priv Co L, Res Osceola Mills, Pa , Enrd July 14, 1898, M I July 14, 1898, M O with Co Nov 7, 1898

Mountain, Joseph C , Priv Co A Res Huntingdon, Pa , Enrd April 27, 1898, M I May 11, 1898, M O with Co Nov 7, 1898

Mountain, Thomas H , Priv Co A, Res Huntingdon, Pa (N G P), Enrd April 27, 1898, M I May 11, 1898, M O with Co Nov 7, 1898

Mourhess, Bert L, Priv Co K, Res Mansfield, Pa , Enrd July 12, 1898, M I July 14, 1898, Prom Corp July 23, 1898, G O 8 c s Regt, M O with Co Nov 7, 1898

Mullen, Walter R, Priv Co L, Res Clearfield, Pa , Enrd July 14, 1898, M I July 14, 1898, M O with Co Nov 7, 1898

Muller, Henry G, Priv Co H, Res Somerset, Pa (N G P), Enrd April 27, 1898, M I May 11, 1898, M O with Co Nov 7, 1898

Mumper, John H, Priv Co M Res Waynesboro, Pa , Enrd July 20, 1898, M I July 20, 1898, M O with Co Nov 7, 1898

Mundorf, Hugh, Priv Co D, Res Cokeville, Pa (N G P), Enrd April 27, 1898, M I May 11, 1898, M O with Co Nov 7, 1898

Murphy, Francis, Chap, Res Pittsburg, Pa , Enrd Aug 8, 1898, M I Aug 8, 1898, Comsd as Chap Aug 1, 1898, M O with Regt Nov 7, 1898

Murphy, John B, Priv Co H, Res Johnstown, Pa , Enrd May 9, 1898, M I May 11, 1898, M O with Co Nov 7, 1898

Murray, Clinton G, Priv Co B, Res Snow Shoe Intersection, Pa , Enrd June 28, 1898, M I June 28, 1898, M O with Co Nov 7, 1898

Murray, James M, Priv Co E, Res Clearfield, Pa (N G P), Enrd April 27, 1898, M I May 11, 1898, Prom Corp June 27, 1898, M O with Co Nov 7, 1898

Murray, William C, Priv Co H, Res Washington, D C, Enrd May 9, 1898, M I May 11, 1898, M O with Co Nov 7, 1898

Musselman, Charles T, Priv Co H, Res Johnstown, Pa , Enrd May 9, 1898, M I May 11, 1898, M O with Co Nov 7, 1898

Musselman, Clarence J, Priv Co M, Res Fairfield, Pa , Enrd July 15, 1898, M I July 20, 1898, M O with Co Nov 7, 1898

Musselman, George W, Priv Co M, Res Fairfield, Pa, Enrd July 15, 1898, M I July 20, 1898, M O with Co Nov 7, 1898

Mutcher, John H, Priv Co I, Res Somerfield, Pa , Enrd July 5, 1898, M I July 8, 1898, M O with Co Nov 7, 1898

Myers, Albertus L, Priv Co F, Res Homer City, Pa (N G P), Enrd April 27, 1898, M I May 11, 1898, M O with Co Nov 7, 1898

Myers, Charles E, Mus Co H, Res Altoona, Pa (N. G P), Enrd April 27, 1898 M I May 11, 1898, M O with Co Nov 7, 1898

Myers, Edward W, Priv Co K, Res Howard, Pa , Enrd July 12, 1898, M I, July 14, 1898, M O with Co Nov 7, 1898

Myers, Harry E, Corp Co C, Res Hollidaysburg, Pa (N G P), Enrd April 27, 1898, M I May 11, 1898, Prom Sgt June 28, 1898, M. O with Co Nov 7, 1898

Myers, John S, Priv Co G, Res McVeytown, Pa, Enrd May 10, 1898, M I May 11, 1898, M O with Co Nov 7, 1898

Naugle, Elmer L, Priv Co I, Res Buckstone, Pa, Enrd July 5, 1898, M I July 8, 1898, M O with Co Nov 7, 1898

Neff, Charles P, Priv Co I, Res Somerset, Pa, Enrd July 6, 1898, M I July 8, 1898, M O with Co Nov 7, 1898

Neff, Harry H, Priv Co B, Res Howard, Pa (N G P), Enrd April 27, 1898, M I May 11, 1898, M O with Co Nov. 7, 1898

Nesbit, Arthur L, Priv Co D, Res Blairsville, Pa, Enrd June 24, 1898, M I June 24, 1898, M O with Co Nov 7, 1898

Newell, Ernest M, Sgt Co A, Res Huntingdon, Pa (N G P), Enrd April 27, 1898, M I May 11, 1898, M O with Co Nov. 7, 1898

Nicholson, Israel R, Priv Co I, Res Somerset, Pa, Enrd July 5, 1898, M I July 8, 1898, M O with Co Nov 7, 1898

Nightsinger, George H, Corp Co G, Res. Lewiston, Pa (N G P), Enrd April 27, 1898, M I May 11, 1898, M O with Co. Nov 7, 1898

Nixon, John, Priv Co G, Res Mifflintown, Pa, Enrd May 10, 1898, M I May 11, 1898; M O with Co Nov 7, 1898

Noel, William J, Priv Co M, Res Gettysburg, Pa, Enrd July 15, 1898, M I July 20, 1898, M O with Co Nov 7, 1898

Noland, Elmer, Mus Co A, Res Altoona, Pa (N G P), Enrd April 27, 1898, M I May 11, 1898, M O with Co Nov 7, 1898

Noll, James O, Priv Co B, Res Milesburg, Pa, Enrd May 7, 1898, M I May 11, 1898, M O with Co. Nov. 7, 1898.

Noll, John S, Priv Co C, Res. Duncansville, Pa (N G P.); Enrd April 27, 1898, M I May 11, 1898, M O with Co Nov 7, 1898

Northcraft, Edward, Priv Co L, Res Clearfield, Pa, Enrd July 13, 1898, M I July 14, 1898, M O. with Co Nov. 7, 1898

Numer, David E, Priv Co A; Res Huntingdon, Pa, Enrd May 7, 1898, M I May 11, 1898, M O with Co Nov 7, 1898

Numer, Jesse H, Priv Co A, Res Huntingdon, Pa, Enrd May 7, 1898; M I May 11, 1898, M O with Co Nov 7, 1898

Nupp, Irvin H, Priv Co F, Res Purchase Line, Pa (N G P), Enrd April 27, 1898, M I May 11, 1898, M O with Co Nov. 7, 1898

Nupp, Orren O, Priv Co F, Res Purchase Line, Pa (N G P), Enrd April 27, 1898, M I May 11, 1898; M O with Co. Nov 7, 1898

O'Dell, Benton, Priv Co E, Res Mahaffey, Pa, Enrd June 21, 1898, M I June 21, 1898, M O with Co Nov. 7, 1898

Odell, Lawrence E., Priv Co G; Res Lewistown, Pa (N G P); Enrd April 27, 1898; M I May 11, 1898, M. O with Co Nov. 7, 1898

Ogden, Jerrad M, Priv Co. E; Res Clearfield, Pa (N G P), Enrd April 27, 1898; M I May 11, 1898, M O with Co. Nov. 7, 1898

O'Hara, Thomas, Priv Co G; Res Lewistown, Pa; Enrd June 29, 1898, M I June 29, 1898, M O with Co. Nov 7, 1898

Olewine, George, Sgt Co C, Res Hollidaysburg, Pa (N G P); Enrd April 27,

1898, M I May 11, 1898, M O with Co Nov 7, 1898

Olmes, Edward, Mus Co C, Res Altoona, Pa (N G P), Enrd April 27, 1898, M I. May 11, 1898, M O with Co Nov 7, 1898.

Onkst, William, Priv Co C, Res Johnstown, Pa (N. G P), Enrd April 27, 1898, M I May 11, 1898, M O with Co Nov 7, 1898

Orner, Harry, Priv Co G, Res Lewiston, Pa. (N. G P), Enrd April 27, 1898, M I May 11, 1898, M O with Co Nov 7, 1898

Osborne, Ray, Priv Co K, Res Draper, Pa, Enrd July 12, 1898, M I July 14, 1898, M O with Co Nov 7, 1898

Osman, Ottis, Priv Co B, Res State College, Pa, Enrd June 27, 1898, M I. June 27, 1898, M O with Co Nov 7, 1898

Osmer, Clarence H, Priv Co B, Res Bellefonte, Pa (N G P), Enrd April 27, 1898, M I May 11, 1898, M O with Co Nov 7, 1898

Oves, Henry B, Priv Co C, Res Altoona, Pa (N G P), Enrd April 27, 1898, M I May 11, 1898, M O with Co Nov 7, 1898

Owens, Alfred, Priv Co H, Res Johnstown, Pa, Enrd June 27, 1898, M I June 27, 1898, M O with Co Nov 7, 1898

Owens, Harry M, Q M Sgt Co G, Res. Lewistown, Pa (N G P), Enrd April 27, 1898, M I May 11, 1898, M O with Co Nov 7, 1898

Oyer, Joseph E, Priv Co K, Res Lamb's Creek, Pa, Enrd July 12, 1898, M I July 14, 1898, M O with Co Nov 7, 1898

Page, George W, Priv Co H, Res Mineral Point, Pa, Enrd June 27, 1898, M I June 27, 1898, M O with Co Nov 7, 1898

Palmer, Alonzo C, Priv Co E. Res Woodland, Pa, Emd May 9, 1898, M I May 11, 1898, M O with Co Nov 7, 1898

Palmer, Mack M, Priv Co F, Res Blacklick, Pa, Enrd June 23, 1898, M I June 23, 1898, M O with Co Nov 7, 1898

Parker, Harry, Priv Co C, Res Altoona, Pa, Enrd May 10, 1898, M I May 11, 1898, M O with Co Nov 7, 1898

Parks, Isaac N, Priv Co H, Res Conemaugh, Pa, Enrd June 27, 1898, M I June 27, 1898, M O with Co Nov 7, 1898

Parks, John K, Priv Co F, Res Indiana, Pa (N G P), Enrd April 27, 1898, M I May 11, 1898, M O with Co Nov 7, 1898

Parr, Charles E, Priv Co E, Res Oliveburg, Pa, Enrd June 20, 1898, M I June 20, 1898, M O with Co Nov. 7, 1898

Parsons, Edgar S, Priv Co K; Res Westfield, Pa, Enrd July 13, 1898, M. I July 14, 1898, M O with Co Nov 7, 1898

Parsons, James H, Priv Co B, Res Fleming, Pa, Enrd May 7, 1898, M I May 11, 1898, M O. with Co Nov 7, 1898

Patrick, William O, Priv Co D, Res Blairsville, Pa, Enrd May 9, 1898, M I May 11, 1898, M O with Co Nov 7, 1898

Patterson, Harry C, Priv Co D, Res Saltsburg, Pa, Enrd May 9, 1898, M I May 11, 1898, M O with Co Nov 7, 1898

Patterson, Howard, Priv Co D, Res New Alexander, Pa, Enrd June 24, 1898, M I June 24, 1898, M O with Co Nov 7, 1898

Paul, David, Priv Co L, Res Philipsburg, Pa, Enrd July 13, 1898, M I July 14, 1898, killed en route to Philadelphia Peace Jubilee Oct 25, 1898, on railroad at Tyrone, Pa

Paul, William J, Priv Co G; Res Lewistown, Pa (N G P), Enrd April 27, 1898, M I May 11, 1898, M O with Co Nov 7, 1898

Pearce, Reese B , Corp Co D, Res Blairs-ville, Pa (N G P), Enrd April 27, 1898, M I May 11, 1898, M O with Co Nov 7, 1898

Pennell, Clarence B , Priv Co G, Res Patterson, Pa , Enrd June 29, 1898, M I June 29, 1898, M O with Co Nov 7, 1898

Peters, Earl J Priv Co K, Res Osceola, Pa , Enrd July 12, 1898, M I July 14, 1898, M O with Co Nov 7, 1898

Peters, Harry A , Priv Co G, Res Lewistown, Pa , Enrd May 10, 1898, M I May 11, 1898, M O with Co Nov 7, 1898

Peters, Rankin D , Priv Co L, Res Curwensville, Pa , Enrd July 13, 1898, M I July 14, 1898, Reduced from rank of Corp at his own request Aug 1, 1898, Detailed as Mus Sept 1, 1898, M O with Co as Mus Nov 7, 1898

Petrikin, Malcolm, Priv Co A, Res Washington, D C , Enrd June 24, 1898, M I June 24, 1898, M O with Co Nov 7, 1898

Pfahler, Frederick P , Priv Co I, Res Meyersdale, Pa , Enrd July 4, 1898, M I July 8, 1898, Prom Q M Sgt July 16, 1898, M O with Co Nov 7, 1898

Pfahler, Herbert H , Priv Co I, Res Meyersdale, Pa , Enrd July 4, 1898, M I July 8, 1898, Prom Corp July 16, 1898, M O with Co Nov 7, 1898

Pier, Clarence E , Priv Co K, Res Corning, N Y , Enrd July 12, 1898, M I July 14, 1898, M O with Co Nov 7, 1898

Pierce, John M , Priv Co F, Res Ambrose, Pa (N G P), Enrd April 27, 1898, M I May 11, 1898, Prom Corp June 28, 1898, M O with Co Nov 7, 1898

Pierce Joseph A , Priv Co D, Res Saltsburg, Pa , Enrd June 24, 1898, M I June 24, 1898, M O with Co Nov 7, 1898

Pitman, William G , Priv. Co G, Res Lewistown, Pa , Enrd May 3, 1898, M. I May 11, 1898, M O with Co Nov 7, 1898

Platt, Morse, Priv Co I, Res Meyersdale, Pa , Enrd July 5, 1898, M I July 8, 1898, M O with Co Nov 7, 1898

Platter, George W , Priv Co I, Res Garrett, Pa , Enrd July 5, 1898, M I July 8, 1898, M O with Co Nov 7, 1898

Pluebell, John A , Priv Co L, Res Osceola Mills, Pa , Enrd July 14, 1898, M I July 14, 1898, M O with Co Nov 7, 1898

Poorman, Lemuel R , Priv Co B, Res Bellefonte, Pa (N G P), Enrd April 27, 1898, May 11, 1898, M. O. with Co Nov 7, 1898

Port, Vance J , Priv Co A, Res Huntingdon, Pa , Enrd May 7, 1898, M I May 11, 1898, M O with Co Nov 7, 1898

Porter, Charles C , Priv Co A, Res Alexandria, Pa , Enrd June 23, 1898, M I June 23, 1898, M O with Co Nov 7, 1898

Portser, William J , Priv. Co D, Res Saltsburg, Pa , Enrd May 9, 1898, M I May 11, 1898, M O with Co Nov 7, 1898

Potter, Henry C , Chief Mus , Res Altoona, Pa (N G P), Enrd April 27, 1898, M I May 11, 1898, M O with Regt Nov 7, 1898

Potter, Ivan C , Priv Co K, Res Mansfield, Pa , Enrd July 12, 1898, M I July 14, 1898, M O with Co Nov 7, 1898

Powers David, Priv Co G, Res Reedsville, Pa , Enrd June 29, 1898, M I June 29, 1898, M O with Co Nov 7, 1898

Pressler, Harris H , Priv Co A, Res Huntingdon, Pa (N G P), Enrd April 27, 1898, M I May 11, 1898, M O with Co Nov 7, 1898

Price, John W , Priv Co G, Res Lewistown, Pa (N G P.), Enrd April 27, 1898, M I May 11, 1898, M O with Co Nov 7, 1898

Price, Walter, Priv Co G, Res Lewistown, Pa, Enrd May 10, 1898, M I May 11, 1898, M O with Co Nov 7, 1898

Printz, Albert E, Priv Co G, Res Lewistown, Pa, Enrd May 10, 1898, M I May 11, 1898, M O with Co Nov 7, 1898

Prothero, Harold N, Priv Co F, Res Indiana, Pa (N G P), Enrd April 27, 1898, M I May 11, 1898, Tranfd to Reserve Amb Corps June 27, 1898, per S O 5.

Prough, Frank, Priv. Co A, Res Huntingdon, Pa (N G P), Enrd April 27, 1898, M I May 11, 1898, Prom Corp June 28, 1898, M O with Co Nov 7, 1898

Pugh, Charles, Priv Co I, Res Somerset, Pa, Enrd July 4, 1898, M I July 8, 1898, M O with Co Nov 7, 1898

Pugh, Robert, Priv Co I, Res Somerset, Pa, Enrd July 4, 1898, M I July 8, 1898, M O with Co Nov 7, 1898

Pugh, Robert G, Priv Co I, Res Somerset, Pa, Enrd July 6, 1898, M I July 8, 1898, M O with Co Nov 7, 1898

Purcell, James F, Priv Co G, Res Newton Hamilton, Pa, Enrd May 10, 1898, M I. May 11, 1898, M O with Co Nov 7, 1898

Quigley, Daniel F, Priv Co G, Res Burnham, Pa, Enrd June 29, 1898, M I June 29, 1898, M O with Co Nov 7, 1898

Quimby, Charles M, Priv Co K, Res Delmar, Pa, Enrd July 1, 1898, M I July 14, 1898, M. O. with Co Nov 7, 1898

Radcliffe, Ralph, Priv Co F, Res Horton, Pa (N G P); Enrd April 27, 1898, M I May 11, 1898, M O with Co Nov 7, 1898

Rambler, Thomas W, Priv Co A, Res McVeytown, Pa, Enrd June 24, 1898, M I June 24, 1898, M O with Co Nov 7, 1898

Randolph, Scott E, Priv Co A, Res Huntingdon, Pa, Enrd June 23, 1898, M I June 23, 1898, M O with Co Nov 7, 1898

Rathbun, Lee, Priv Co K, Res Tioga, Pa, Enrd July 12, 1898, M I July 14, 1898, M O with Co Nov 7, 1898

Read, Amos P, Priv Co E, Res Clearfield, Pa (N G P), Enrd April 27, 1898, M I May 11, 1898, M O with Co Nov 7, 1898

Recknor, William B, Priv Co I, Res Addison, Pa, Enrd July 6, 1898, M I July 8, 1898; M O with Co Nov 7, 1898

Redding, Henry E, Priv Co B, Res Howard, Pa, Enrd May 7, 1898, M I May 11, 1898, M O with Co Nov 7, 1898

Redmond, James, Priv Co H, Res Johnstown, Pa (N G P), Enrd April 27, 1898, M I May 11, 1898, M O with Co Nov 7, 1898

Reed, James C, Priv Co A; Res Huntingdon, Pa, Enrd May 7, 1898, M I May 11, 1898, M O with Co Nov 7, 1898

Reed, Scott B, Priv Co E, Res Clearfield, Pa (N G P), Enrd April 27, 1898, M I May 11, 1898, Det June 13, 1898, by S O 26, 1st Corps Hdqts, dated June 13, 1898

Reed, Walter A, Sgt Co D, Res Kent, Pa (N G P), Enrd April 27, 1898, M I May 1, 1898, M O with Co Nov 7, 1898

Reed, William G, 1st Sgt Co D, Res Blairsville, Pa (N G P), Enrd April 27, 1898, M I May 11, 1898, M O with Co Nov 7, 1898

Rees, William G, Priv Co L, Res Karthaus, Pa, Enrd July 14, 1898, M I July 14, 1898, M O with Co Nov 7, 1898

Reeser, John R, Priv Co M, Res York,

Pa , Enrd July 20, 1898, M I July 20, 1898, M O with Co Nov 7, 1898

Repine, Charles B , Priv Co F, Res Homer City, Pa , Enrd June 23, 1898, M I June 23, 1898 M O with Co Nov 7, 1898

Resinger. Isaac L , Priv Co E, Res DuBois, Pa , Enrd June 21, 1898, M I June 21, 1898, M O with Co Nov 7, 1898

Rhoads. Harry Stoy. Priv Co I, Res Somerset, Pa , Enrd July 4, 1898, M I July 8, 1898, M O with Co Nov 7, 1898

Rhoads. Philip S , Priv Co I, Res Somerset. Pa , Enrd July 5, 1898. M I July 8, 1898, M O with Co Nov 7, 1898

Rhoads, Royal G , Priv Co I, Res Somerset, Pa , Enrd July 5, 1898. M I July 8, 1898, M O with Co Nov 7, 1898

Rhoads, Samuel H , Priv Co B, Res Fleming, Pa (N G P), Enrd April 27, 1898. M I May 11, 1898. M O with Co Nov 7, 1898

Rhodes, Harry H , Priv Co F, Res Homer City, Pa , Enrd June 22, 1898, M I June 22, 1898, M O with Co Nov 7 1898

Rice, Ira N , Priv Co K, Res Draper, Pa , Enrd July 11, 1898. M I July 14, 1898, M O with Co Nov 7, 1898

Richardson, Joseph W , Priv Co A, Res Huntingdon, Pa , Enrd June 23. 1898, M I June 23, 1898, M O with Co Nov 7, 1898

Richardson. William R , Priv Co F Res Rochester Mills. Pa , Enrd May 9, 1898, M I May 11, 1898, M O with Co Nov 7, 1898

Richsten. John, Priv Co M, Res Littlestown Pa , Enrd July 18, 1898, M I July 20, 1898, M O with Co Nov 7, 1898

Riddle, John, Priv Co B, Res Pleasant Gap, Pa , Enrd May 7, 1898, M I May 11, 1898, M O with Co Nov 7, 1898

Rightmire. Charles P , Priv Co K, Res

Tioga, Pa , Enrd July 12, 1898; M. I July 14, 1898; M O with Co Nov 7, 1898

Ringler, Alfred F , Priv Co I, Res Elk Lick, Pa , Enrd July 5, 1898, M I. July 8, 1898, M O with Co Nov 7, 1898

Risbeck, Jacob A , Priv Co I, Res Somerset, Pa , Enrd July 5. 1898, M I July 8, 1898, M O with Co Nov. 7, 1898

Ringler. Theodore O , Priv Co I, Res Elk Lick, Pa , Enrd July 4, 1898, M I. July 8, 1898, M O with Co Nov 7, 1898

Rittenhouse, Lawrence, Priv Co B; Res. Philipsburg, Pa , Enrd May 7, 1898, M I. May 11, 1898, M O with Co Nov 7, 1898

Robb, Milton, Priv Co B, Res Bellefonte, Pa , Enrd June 27, 1898, M I June 27, 1898, M O with Co Nov 7, 1898

Robb, William C , Priv Co A, Res Huntingdon, Pa , May 7, 1898, M I May 11, 1898, M O with Co Nov 7, 1898

Roberts. Edwin M , Priv Co K, Res. Wellsboro Pa , Enrd July 13, 1898, M I July 14, 1898, M O with Co Nov 7, 1898

Roberts, Richard W , Corp Co H, Res. Johnstown, Pa (N G P), Enrd April 27, 1898, M I May 11, 1898, M O with Co. Nov 7, 1898

Robins, George L , Priv Co L, Res. Clearfield, Pa , Enrd July 13, 1898, M I July 14, 1898, M O with Co Nov 7, 1898

Robinson, Joseph C , Priv Co C, Res Altoona, Pa , Enrd June 21, 1898, M I June 21, 1898, died at 3d Div Hosp Aug. 15, 1898

Robinson, William B , Priv Co M, Res Gettysurg, Pa , Enrd July 15, 1898 M I July 20, 1898, M O with Co Nov 7, 1898

Rohrer, Ralph A , Priv Co A Res Altoona, Pa , Enrd May 7, 1898, M I May 11,

1898; Transfd to Reserve Amb Co by S O 26, Hdqts 1st A C

Roller, William C, Priv Co C, Res Hollidaysburg, Pa, Enrd June 20, 1898, M I June 20, 1898, M O with Co Nov 7, 1898

Rook, Frank, Priv Co E, Res Clearfield, Pa (N G P), Enrd April 27, 1898, M I May 11, 1898, Prom Corp May 11, 1898, Prom Sgt June 27, 1898, M O with Co Nov 7, 1898

Rook, William J, Priv Co G, Res Lewistown, Pa (N G P), Enrd April 27, 1898, M I May 11, 1898, M O with Co as Artf Nov. 7, 1898

Roop, Elmer K, Priv Co A, Res Newton Hamilton, Pa (N G P), Enrd April 27, 1898, M I May 11, 1898, Prom Q M Sgt of Regt Aug 16, 1898, by Regtl G O 18, M O with Regt Nov 7, 1898

Rose, William T, Priv Co K, Res Niles Valley, Pa, Enrd July 12, 1898, M I July 14, 1898, M O with Co Nov 7 1898

Ross, James P, Q M Sgt Co A, Res Huntingdon, Pa (N G P), Enrd April 27, 1898, M I May 11, 1898, M O with Co Nov 7, 1898

Ross, Moses R, Priv Co I, Res Addison, Pa, Enrd July 5, 1898, M I July 8, 1898, Prom Sgt July 16, 1898, M O with Co Nov 7, 1898

Roth, George H, Priv Co M, Res New Oxford, Pa, Enrd July 15, 1898, M I July 20, 1898, Prom Sgt Aug 1, 1898, M O with Co Nov 7, 1898

Rothrock, David E, Priv Co B, Res Bellefonte, Pa (N G P), Enrd April 27, 1898, M I May 11, 1898, Prom Corp June 30, 1898, M O with Co Nov 7, 1898

Rothrock, Percy B, Priv Co C, Res Al-

toona, Pa, Enrd June 20, 1898, M I June 20, 1898, M O with Co Nov 7, 1898

Rounsley, Thomas J, Priv Co L, Res Houtzdale, Pa, Enrd July 14, 1898, M I July 14, 1898, M O with Co Nov 7, 1898

Roush, Harry, Priv Co C, Res Roaring Spring, Pa (N G P), Enrd April 27, 1898, M I May 11, 1898, M O with Co Nov 7, 1898

Rowe, Hall S, Priv Co D Res Blansville, Pa, Enrd May 9, 1898, M I May 11, 1898, Tranfd to Reserve Amb Corps July 3, 1898

Rowe, William A, Priv Co G, Res Reedsville, Pa, Enrd June 29, 1898, M I June 29, 1898, M O with Co Nov 7, 1898

Rowles, Lewis C, Priv Co E, Res Clearfield, Pa, Enrd May 9, 1898, M I May 11, 1898, M O with Co Nov 7, 1898

Rowles, Luther, Priv Co E, Res Clearfield, Pa, Enrd June 21, 1898, M I June 21, 1898, M O with Co Nov 7, 1898

Rowles, Perry A, Priv Co L, Res Grampian, Pa, Enrd July 14, 1898 M I July 14, 1898, M O with Co Nov 7, 1898

Ruble, Harry B, Priv Co G, Res Lewistown, Pa (N G P), Enrd April 27, 1898, M I May 11, 1898, M O with Co Nov 7, 1898

Ruffner, Lewis, Priv Co F, Res Tanoma, Pa, Enrd June 23, 1898, M I June 23, 1898, M O with Co Nov 7, 1898

Rummel, John F, Priv Co M, Res Gettysburg, Pa, Enrd July 15, 1898, M I July 20, 1898, M O with Co Nov 7, 1898

Russell, Arthur J, Priv Co F, Res Indiana, Pa, Enrd June 22, 1898, M I June 22, 1898, M O with Co Nov 7, 1898

Russell, Evan, Capt Co M, Res Williamsport, Pa (N G P), Enrd July 21,

1898, M I July 21, 1898, Apptd Capt July 20, 1898, Assumed command of Co July 21, 1898, M O with Co Nov 7, 1898

Russell, James S, Priv Co L, Res Philipsburg, Pa, Enrd July 14, 1898, M I July 14, 1898, M O with Co Nov 7, 1898

Rutty, Wayne E, Priv Co K, Res. Crooked Creek, Pa, Enrd July 11, 1898, M I July 14, 1898, M O with Co Nov 7, 1898

Ryan, Harry H, Corp Co. B, Res Bellefonte, Pa (N G P), April 27, 1898, M I May 11, 1898; M O with Co Nov 7, 1898

Sackett, David R, Sgt Co R, Res Clearfield, Pa (N G. P), Enrd April 27, 1898, M I May 11, 1898, M O with Co Nov 7, 1898

Samuels, William J, Priv Co C, Res Hollidaysburg, Pa (N G P), Enrd April 27, 1898, M I May 11, 1898, Prom Corp June 28, 1898, M O. with Co Nov 7, 1898

Sandoe, James L, Priv Co B, Res Centre Hall, Pa, Enrd May 7, 1898, M I May 11, 1898, M O with Co Nov 7, 1898

Sandoe, Ralph T, Priv Co M, Res Biglerville, Pa, Enrd July 19, 1898, M I. July 20, 1898, M O with Co Nov 7, 1898

Sansom, James B, Priv Co F, Res Indiana, Pa, Enrd May 4, 1898, M I May 11, 1898, M O with Co Nov 7, 1898

Sassaman, Robert F, Priv Co C, Res Altoona, Pa, Enrd May 10, 1898, M I May 11, 1898, M O with Co Nov 7, 1898

Saylor, Frank P, Priv Co I, Res Somerset, Pa, Enrd July 5, 1898 M I July 8, 1898, M O with Co Nov 7, 1898

Saylor, George W, Priv Co H, Res Listie, Pa, Enrd June 27 1898, M I June 27, 1898, M O with Co Nov 7, 1898

Saylor, William A, Priv Co I, Res. Lull, Pa, Enrd July 5, 1898, M. I July 8, 1898, Prom Corp July 16, 1898, M O with Co. Nov 7, 1898

Scanlin, Thomas, Priv Co K, Res Delmar, Pa, Enrd July 12, 1898, M I July 14, 1898, M O with Co Nov. 7, 1898

Schanbacher, Edgar M, Priv Co K, Res Forksville, Pa, Enrd July 12, 1898, M I July 14, 1898, Prom Corp July 23, 1898; G O 8 c s Regt, M. O with Co. Nov. 7, 1898

Schell, Walter S, Priv Co G, Res Harrisburg, Pa., Enrd. June 29, 1898, M I. June 29, 1898, M O with Co Nov. 7, 1898

Schell, William P, 2d Lieut Co G, Res Lewistown, Pa (N G P), Enrd April 27, 1898, M I May 11, 1898, M. O with Co. Nov 7, 1898

Schiefer, Frankland H, Priv Co E; Res Clearfield, Pa. (N G P), Enrd April 27, 1898, M I May 11, 1898, Prom Corp. June 27, 1898, M O with Co Nov 7, 1898

Schluter, Henry L, Priv Co L, Res Philipsburg, Pa, Enrd July 13, 1898, M I July 14, 1898, Died Sept 3, 1898, in Hosp at Pittsburg of typhoid fever

Schreck, Al, Priv Co L, Res Kylertown, Pa, Enrd July 14, 1898, M I July 14, 1898, M O with Co Nov 7, 1898

Schriver, Robert A, Priv Co M, Res. Gettysburg, Pa, Enrd July 15, 1898, M I July 20, 1898, Prom Corp Sept 1, 1898, M O with Co Nov 7, 1898

Schrock, Calvin, Priv Co H, Res Somerset, Pa, Enrd June 27, 1898, M I June 27, 1898, M O with Co Nov 7, 1898

Schuldt, John C, Priv Co A, Res Huntingdon, Pa (N G P); Enrd April 27,

1898, M. I. May 11, 1898, M O with Co Nov 7, 1898

Schultz, George H, Priv Co. C, Res Altoona, Pa (N G P), Enrd April 27, 1898, M I May 11, 1898, M O with Co Nov 7, 1898

Schwab, Fredrick, Priv Co K, Res Ridgway, Pa, Enrd July 12, 1898, M I July 14, 1898, M O with Co Nov 7, 1898

Scott, Charles, Priv Co H, Res Bakersville, Pa, Enrd June 27, 1898, M I June 27, 1898, M O with Co Nov 7, 1898

Sechler, James B, Priv Co I, Res Listie, Pa, Enrd July 6, 1898, M I July 8, 1898, M. O with Co. Nov 7, 1898

Sechrist, John J, Priv Co M, Res York, Pa, Enrd July 19, 1898, M I July 20, 1898, M O with Co Nov 7, 1898

Seibert, William D, Priv Co G, Res McVeytown, Pa, Enrd June 29, 1898, M I June 29, 1898, M O with Co Nov 7, 1898

Sell, Charles H, Priv. Co M, Res Littlestown, Pa, Enrd July 18, 1898, M I July 20, 1898, M O with Co Nov 7, 1898

Sell, Jacob H, Jr, Priv Co M, Res Hanover, Pa, Enrd July 20, 1898, M I July 20, 1898, M O with Co Nov 7, 1898.

Seynor, John M, 2d Lieut Co H, Res. Johnstown, Pa (N G P), Enrd April 27, 1898, M I May 11, 1898, M O with Co Nov 7, 1898

Shadle, John W, Priv Co D, Res Saltsburg, Pa (N. G P), Enrd April 27, 1898, M I May 11, 1898, Prom Corp June 28, 1898, M. O with Co Nov 7, 1898

Shadle, William, Priv. Co M, Res Littlestown, Pa; Enrd July 18, 1898, M I July 20, 1898, M O with Co Nov 7, 1898

Shaffer, Charles S, Priv Co I, Res Jenners, Pa, Enrd July 5, 1898, M I July 8, 1898, M O with Co Nov 7, 1898

Shaffer, Clarence E, Priv Co D, Res Blairsville, Pa (N G P), Enrd April 27, 1898, M I May 11, 1898, Prom Corp June 28, 1898, M O with Co Nov 7, 1898

Shaffer, Frederick L, Priv Co K, Res Forksville, Pa, Enrd July 12, 1898, M I July 14, 1898, M O with Co Nov 7, 1898

Shaffer, John W, Priv Co H, Res Johnstown, Pa, Enrd May 9, 1898, M I May 11, 1898, M O with Co Nov 7, 1898

Shaffer, William, Priv Co F, Res Belsano, Pa, Enrd June 27, 1898, M I June 27, 1898, M O with Co Nov 7, 1898

Shakespeare, Noah, Priv Co D, Res Blairsville, Pa (N G P), Enrd April 27, 1898, M I May 11, 1898, M O with Co Nov 7, 1898

Shannon, Wesley M, Priv Co F, Res Brushvalley, Pa, Enrd June 22, 1898, M I June 22, 1898, M O with Co Nov. 7, 1898

Sharp, William, Priv Co L, Res DuBois, Pa, Enrd July 14, 1898, M I July 14, 1898, M O with Co Nov 7, 1898

Sharp, Wilmer A, Priv Co F, Res West Lebanon, Pa (N G P), Enrd April 27, 1898, M I May 11, 1898, M O with Co Nov 7, 1898

Shaw, Albert J, Priv Co E, Res Clearfield, Pa (N G P), Enrd April 27, 1898, M I May 11, 1898, M O with Co Nov 7, 1898

Sheaffer, Alexander H, Corp Co A, Res Mt Union, Pa (N G P), Enrd April 27, 1898, M I May 11, 1898, Prom Sgt July 28, 1898, M O with Co Nov 7, 1898

Shearer, Clarence S, Priv Co D, Res Blairsville, Pa (N G P), Enrd April 27,

1898, M I May 11, 1898, M. O with Co Nov 7, 1898

Shearer, Michael D, Priv. Co H, Res Johnstown, Pa , Enrd May 9, 1898; M. I. May 11, 1898, M O with Co Nov 7, 1898

Sherbine, Alvin, Priv Co F; Res Wilmore, Pa , Enrd May 9, 1898, M I May 11, 1898, M O with Co Nov 7, 1898

Sheriff, Elmer C, Priv Co. B, Res Philipsburg, Pa , Enrd May 7, 1898, M I May 11, 1898, Tranfd to 3d Div Hosp Corps, 1st A C July 20, 1898.

Sheriff, Thomas M, Priv Co D, Res Cokeville, Pa , Enrd June 24, 1898; M I June 24, 1898, M O with Co Nov 7, 1898

Sheriff, Wallace M, Priv Co B, Res Wigton, Pa , Enrd June 27, 1898, M I June 27, 1898, M O with Co Nov 7, 1898

Sherlock, Thomas M, Priv. Co B, Res Altoona, Pa (N G P), Enrd April 27, 1898, M I May 11, 1898, Tranfd to 5th Regt Hosp Corps June 13, 1898

Shields, George E, Priv Co M, Res Gettysburg, Pa , Enrd July 15, 1898, M I July 20, 1898, M O. with Co Nov 7, 1898

Shields, James A, Priv Co G; Res Burnham, Pa (N G P), Enrd April 27, 1898, M I. May 11, 1898, M O with Co Nov 7, 1898

Shilling, Ralph, Priv Co F, Res Trade City, Pa , Enrd June 23, 1898, M I June 23, 1898, M O with Co Nov 7, 1898

Shimel, Walter, Priv Co L, Res LaJose, Pa . Enrd July 14, 1898, M I July 14, 1898; M O with Co Nov 7, 1898

Shirey, Oscar A, Priv Co B; Res Fleming, Pa (N G P), Enrd April 27, 1898; M I May 11, 1898, M O with Co Nov. 7, 1898

Shirk, Lynn J, Priv Co E; Res Clear-

field, Pa , Enrd May 9, 1898; M. I. May 11, 1898, M O with Co Nov 7, 1898.

Shirley, William J, Priv Co A; Res. Huntingdon, Pa.; Enrd May 7, 1898, M. I. May 11, 1898, M O with Co Nov. 7, 1898.

Shoemaker, John S, Priv Co C, Res. Altoona, Pa , Enrd June 20, 1898, M I June 20, 1898, M. O. with Co. Nov. 7, 1898

Shontz, Edgar, Priv Co L; Res Wigton, Pa , Enrd July 13, 1898; M I. July 14, 1898, M O with Co. as Corp Nov. 7, 1898

Shoup, Samuel E, Mus. Co B; Res Altoona, Pa. (N G P), Enrd April 27, 1898; M I May 11, 1898, M O with Co Nov. 7, 1898

Shove, Herbert D, Priv. Co K, Res Wellsboro, Pa , Enrd July 13, 1898; M. I July 14, 1898, M O with Co Nov 7, 1898

Showers, Ira M, Priv Co E, Res Clearfield, Pa , Enrd May 9, 1898, M I May 11, 1898, Prom Corp June 27, 1898, M O with Co Nov 7, 1898

Shufflebotham, Joseph W, Priv. Co C; Res Hollidaysburg, Pa (N G P), Enrd April 27, 1898, M I May 11, 1898, M O with Co Nov 7, 1898

Shugarts, Fred R, Priv. Co L, Res Luthersburg, Pa , Enrd. July 14, 1898; M I. July 14, 1898 M O. with Co Nov 7, 1898

Shultz, Noah C, Priv Co I; Res Bakersville, Pa , Enrd July 6, 1898, M I July 8, 1898, M O with Co Nov 7, 1898

Simler, Arthur C. Priv Co B, Res Philipsburg, Pa., Enrd June 27, 1898; M. I. June 27, 1898, M O with Co Nov 7, 1898

Simpson, Charles R, Hosp Stew., Res Altoona, Pa (N G P); Enrd April 27, 1898; M I May 11, 1898; M. O with Regt. Nov 7, 1898

Simpson, Warren B, Priv Co A; Res.

Huntingdon, Pa (N G P), Enrd April 27, 1898, M I May 11, 1898, M O with Co Nov 7, 1898

Singer, Chester M, Priv Co H, Res Vinco, Pa, Enrd June 27, 1898, M I June 27, 1898, M O with Co Nov 7, 1898

Sipe, Lawrence E, Priv Co I, Res Somerset, Pa, Enrd July 4, 1898, M I July 8, 1898, Dischd from the Co as Corp Oct 3, 1898, per telegraphic order from W Dept, Washington, D C

Sipes, Charles R, Priv Co M, Res York, Pa, Enrd July 19, 1898, M I July 20, 1898, M O with Co Nov 7, 1898

Sixbee, Jay F, Priv Co K, Res Sylvania, Pa, Enrd July 11, 1898, M I July 14, 1898, M O with Co Nov 7, 1898

Slagle, Louis N, Capt Co G, Res Lewistown, Pa (N G P), Enrd April 27, 1898, M I May 11, 1898, M O with Co Nov 7, 1898.

Slater, John R, Priv Co C, Res Duncansville, Pa (N G P), Enrd April 27, 1898, M I May 11, 1898, M O with Co Nov 7, 1898

Shawley, Robert M, Priv Co C, Res Altoona, Pa, Enrd May 10, 1898, M I May 11, 1898, M O with Co Nov 7, 1898.

Smith, Absalom W, Capt Co D, Res Blairsville, Pa (N G P), Enrd April 27, 1898, M I May 11, 1898, M O with Co Nov. 7, 1898

Smith, Albert M, Priv Co A, Res Latta Grove, Pa, Enrd June 24, 1898, M I June 24, 1898, M O with Co Nov 7, 1898

Smith, Arthur G, Priv Co H, Res Johnstown, Pa, Enrd June 28, 1898, M I June 28, 1898, M O with Co Nov 7, 1898

Smith, Claude E, Priv Co M, Res Em-mitsburg, Md, Enrd July 18, 1898, M I July 20, 1898, M O with Co Nov 7, 1898

Smith, Edward, Priv Co H, Res Johnstown, Pa (N G P), Enrd April 27, 1898, M I May 11, 1898, M O with Co Nov 7, 1898

Smith, Eugene F, Priv Co L, Res Curwensville, Pa, Enrd July 12, 1898, M I July 14, 1898, M O with Co Nov 7, 1898.

Smith, Frank A, Priv Co M Res York, Pa, Enrd July 20, 1898, M I July 20, 1898, M O with Co Nov 7, 1898

Smith, Frank H, Priv Co C, Res Altoona, Pa, Enrd June 20, 1898, M I June 20, 1898, M O with Co Nov 7, 1898

Smith, Frank W, Priv Co E, Res Clearfield, Pa, Enrd May 9, 1898, M I May 11, 1898, M O with Co Nov 7, 1898

Smith, Harry E, Priv Co L, Res Philipsburg, Pa, Enrd July 13, 1898, M I July 14, 1898, M O with Co Nov 7, 1898

Smith, James E, Priv Co C, Res Altoona, Pa, Enrd June 20, 1898, M I June 20, 1898, M O with Co Nov 7, 1898

Smith, James L, Priv Co G, Res Yeagertown, Pa, Enrd June 29, 1898, M I June 29, 1898, M O with Co Nov 7, 1898

Smith, Jonas L, Priv Co A, Res Mapleton, Pa, Enrd June 23, 1898; M I June 23, 1898, M. O with Co Nov 7, 1898

Smith, Victor, Priv Co K, Res Mainsburg, Pa, Enrd July 11, 1898, M I July 14, 1898, M O with Co Nov 7, 1898

Smith, William R, 1st Sgt Co H, Res Johnstown, Pa (N. G P), Enrd April 27, 1898, M I May 11, 1898, M O with Co Nov 7, 1898

Snellings, James A, Priv Co K, Res Cross Fork, Pa, Enrd July 12, 1898, M I

July 14, 1898, Prom Corp July 23, 1898, G O 8 c s Regt , M O with Co Nov 7, 1898

Snoke, Jay, Priv Co L, Res Clearfield, Pa , Enrd July 13, 1898, M I July 14, 1898, M O with Co Nov 7, 1898

Snook, Percy M , Priv Co G, Res Cross Grove, Pa , Enrd June 29, 1898, M I June 29, 1898, M O with Co Nov 7, 1898

Snow, Francis C , Priv Co D, Res Saltsburg, Pa , Enrd May 9, 1898, M I May 11, 1898, M O with Co Nov 7, 1898

Snyder, Aaron, Priv Co E, Res La Jose, Pa (N G P), Enrd May 9, 1898 M I May 11, 1898, M O with Co Nov 7, 1898

Snyder, Carl E , Priv Co C, Res Altoona, Pa (N G P), Enrd April 27, 1898, M I May 11, 1898, M O with Co Nov 7, 1898

Snyder, Charles D , Priv Co C, Res Roaring Spring, Pa , Enrd June 21, 1898, M I June 21, 1898, M O with Co Nov 7, 1898

Snyder, Charles F , Priv Co M, Res York, Pa , Enrd July 20, 1898, M I July 20, 1898, M O with Co Nov 7, 1898

Snyder, Charles W , Corp Co C, Res Hollidaysburg, Pa (N G P), Enrd April 27, 1898, M I May 11, 1898, M O with Co Nov 7, 1898

Snyder, Elmer D , Priv Co E, Res Clearfield, Pa Enrd May 9, 1898, M I May 11, 1898, Prom Corp June 27, 1898; M O with Co Nov 7, 1898

Snyder, George B , Priv Co B, Res State College, Pa , Enrd May 7, 1898, M I May 11, 1898, Prom Corp June 30, 1898, M O with Co Nov 7, 1898

Snyder, John F , Priv Co I, Res Somerset, Pa . Enrd July 4, 1898, M I July 8, 1898, M O with Co Nov 7, 1898

Sollenberger, Samuel B , Priv Co M, Res Baltimore, Md., Enrd. July 19, 1898· M I July 20, 1898, M O with Co Nov 7, 1898

Somerville, Charles H , Priv Co D, Res Blairsville, Pa (N G P), Enrd April 27, 1898, M I May 11, 1898, M O with Co Nov 7, 1898

Sommers, David P , Priv Co A, Res Huntingdon, Pa , Enrd May 7, 1898, M I May 11, 1898, M O with Co Nov 7, 1898

Souders, Frank D , Priv Co E, Res Clearfield, Pa (N G P), Enrd April 27, 1898, M I May 11, 1898, Prom Corp May 11, 1898, M O with Co Nov 7, 1898

Souders, Leo A , Priv Co E, Res Clearfield, Pa (N G P), Enrd April 27, 1898; M I May 11, 1898; Prom Corp May 11, 1898, M O with Co Nov 7, 1898

Southeimer, Harry, Priv Co D. Res Knights, Pa (N G P), Enrd April 27, 1898, M I May 11, 1898, M O with Co Nov 7, 1898

Spangler, Martin E , Priv Co M, Res York, Pa , Enrd July 20, 1898, M I July 20, 1898, M O with Co Nov 7, 1898

Spangler, Newton B , Priv Co B, Res Bellefonte, Pa (N G P), Enrd April 27, 1898, M I May 11, 1898, M O with Co Nov 7, 1898

Speicher, John E , Priv Co H, Res Conemaugh, Pa , Enrd May 9, 1898, M I May 11, 1898, Prom Corp June 28, 1898, M O with Co Nov 7, 1898

Speicher, Pius M , Priv Co I, Res Meyersdale, Pa , Enrd July 5, 1898, M I July 8, 1898, Prom Corp July 16, 1898; M O with Co Nov 7, 1898

Spiglemyer, Milton, Priv Co G, Res Dormantown, Pa , Enrd June 29, 1898, M I June 29, 1898; M O with Co Nov 7, 1898

Spink, Alfred J, Priv Co K, Res Cherry twp, Sullivan Co, Pa, Enrd July 12, 1898, M I July 14, 1898, M O with Co Nov 7, 1898

Spotts, Jacob J, Priv Co B, Res Philipsburg, Pa, Enrd May 7, 1898, M I May 11, 1898, M O with Co Nov 7, 1898

Stackpole, James S, 1st Lieut Co G, Res Lewistown, Pa (N G P), Enrd April 27, 1898, M I. May 11, 1898, M O with Co Nov 7, 1898

Stage, James K, Priv Co E, Res Clearfield, Pa (N G P), Enrd April 27, 1898. M. I May 11, 1898, M O with Co Nov 7, 1898

Stailey, James H, Priv Co A, Res Everett, Pa., Enrd May 7, 1898, M I May 11, 1898, M. O. with Co Nov 7, 1898

Staley, Augustus E, Priv Co M, Res Kingsdale, Pa ; Enrd July 15, 1898, M I July 20, 1898, M O with Co Nov 7, 1898

Staub, Louis R, Priv. Co M, Res McSherrystown, Pa, Enrd July 15, 1898, M I July 20, 1898, M O with Co Nov 7, 1898

Stayer, Andrew S, Surg, Res Altoona, Pa (N. G P), Enrd April 27, 1898, M I May 5, 1898, M O with Regt Nov 7, 1898

Stayer, Edgar S, Battn Adj, Res Altoona, Pa (N G P), Enrd April 27, 1898, M I May 11, 1898, M O with Regt Nov 7, 1898

Stayer, Morrison C, Priv Co H, Res Altoona, Pa, Enrd April 27, 1898, M I May 11, 1898, Tranfd to 3d Div Amb Corps June 16, 1898, per S O 26

Steel, Robert M, Priv Co A, Res Huntingdon, Pa (N G P), Enrd April 27, 1898, M I May 11, 1898, Prom Corp June 28, 1898, M O with Co Nov, 7, 1898

Steffy, William M, Priv Co M, Res Gettysburg, Pa, Enrd July 15, 1898, M I July 20, 1898, Prom Sgt Aug 1, 1898, Died Aug 18, 1898

Stem, George A, Priv Co H, Res Johnstown, Pa (N G P), Enrd April 27, 1898, M I May 11, 1898, M O with Co Nov 7, 1898

Stephens, Harry W, Corp Co H, Res Johnstown, Pa, (N G P), Enrd April 27, 1898, M I May 11, 1898, Prom Sgt Sept 10, 1898, M. O with Co Nov 7, 1898

Stevens, Daniel G, Priv Co K, Res Hammond, Pa, Enrd July 12, 1898, M I July 14, 1898, M O with Co as Mus Nov 7, 1898

Stevens, John R, Priv Co G, Res Lewistown, Pa (N G P), Enrd April 27, 1898, M I May 11, 1898, M O with Co Nov 7, 1898

Stewart, Harry M, Priv Co C, Res Indiana, Pa (N G P), Enrd April 27,. 1898, M I May 11, 1898, Tranfd to Hosp Corps June 23, 1898

Stewart, John E, Priv Co A, Res Huntingdon, Pa (N G P), Enrd April 27, 1898, M I May 11, 1898, M O with Co Nov 7, 1898

Stiers, T E, Priv Co L, Res Plymouth, Pa, Enrd July 14, 1898, M I July 14, 1898, M O with Co Nov 7, 1898

Stiffler, Charles, Sgt Co C, Res Hollidaysburg, Pa (N G P), Enrd April 27, 1898, M I May 11, 1898, M O with Co Nov 7, 1898

Stine, Harry F, Priv Co B, Res Fillmore, Pa , Enrd June 27, 1898; M I June 27, 1898, M O with Co Nov 7, 1898

Stine, James A , Priv Co B, Res Pleasant Gap, Pa , Enrd June 27, 1898, M I June 27, 1898, M O with Co Nov. 7, 1898

Stinson, Herbert E , Priv Co A, Res. Huntingdon. Pa . Enrd June 24, 1898, M I June 24, 1898, M O with Co Nov 7, 1898

Stitzel, John A , Priv Co M. Res Bendersville, Pa , Enrd July 15. 1898. M I July 20, 1898, M O with Co Nov 7, 1898

Stonebraker, William F , Priv Co F; Res Indiana, Pa , Enrd June 23. 1898, M I June 23. 1898, Died at his home, Indiana, Pa of typhoid fever, Sept 29, 1898

Stonesifer, Joseph B , Priv Co M, Res Gettysburg, Pa , Enrd July 16, 1898, M I July 20, 1898, Prom Corp Sept 1, 1898, M O with Co Nov 7, 1898

Stratford, Thomas F , Priv Co G, Res Mt Union, Pa , Enrd June 29, 1898, M I June 29, 1898, M O with Co Nov 7, 1898

Stratton, Charley, Priv Co L; Res Philipsburg, Pa , Enrd July 13, 1898; M I July 14, 1898, M O with Co Nov 7, 1898

Streams, Harry B , Priv Co F, Res Indiana, Pa (N G P), Enrd April 27, 1898, M I. May 11, 1898, M O with Co Nov 7, 1898

Streevy, Walter H , Priv Co K, Res Overton, Pa ; Enrd July 12, 1898, M I July 14, 1898, M O with Co Nov 7, 1898

Strickler, George W , Priv Co M; Res York, Pa ; Enrd July 20. 1898, M I July 20, 1898, Apptd Artf Aug 1, 1898, M O with Co Nov 7, 1898

Strunk, Jesse P , Priv Co A, Res Belle-

ville, Pa , Enrd June 23, 1898, M I June 23, 1898, M O with Co Nov 7, 1898.

Stubbs, William H , Priv Co A , Res Mapleton, Pa , Enrd June 23, 1898, M. I. June 23, 1898, M O with Co Nov. 7, 1898

Stuby, Valentine, Priv Co F, Res Indiana, Pa , Enrd May 9, 1898, M I May 11, 1898; M O. with Co Nov 7, 1898

Stuchell, Harry W , Priv Co D, Res Saltsburg. Pa , Enrd May 9, 1898, M I May 11, 1898. M O with Co Nov 7, 1898

Stull, Elijah W , Priv Co I, Res Stony Creek, Pa , Enrd July 15, 1898, M I July 8, 1898, M O with Co Nov 7, 1898

Stumpf, Harry, Priv. Co D, Res Blairsville, Pa (N G. P); Enrd April 27, 1898, M I. May 11, 1898, M O with Co Nov 7, 1898

Sturrock, Guy, Corp. Co K, Res Wellsboro, Pa ; Enrd July 11, 1898, M I July 14, 1898, Prom Corp July 23, 1898; G O 8 c s Regt , M O with Co Nov 7, 1898

Stutler, Otterbine G , Priv. Co H; Res Jarvesville, Pa , Enrd June 27, 1898, M I June 27, 1898, M O with Co Nov 7, 1898

Stutzman, Otto O , Priv. Co. I, Res Lull, Pa ; Enrd July 6, 1898; M I July 8, 1898, M O with Co Nov. 7, 1898

Sullivan, George A , Priv Co C; Res Roaring Spring, Pa , Enrd. June 20, 1898; M I June 20, 1898, M O. with Co Nov 7, 1898

Sunday, George W , Priv Co B, Res Bellefonte, Pa (N G. P); Enrd April 27, 1898, M I May 11, 1898; M O. with Co Nov 7, 1898

Sutton, James, Jr , Sgt. Co E, Res Clearfield, Pa (N G P), Enrd April 27, 1898, M I May 11, 1898; M O with Co Nov. 7, 1898

Swain, Charles T , Priv. Co G; Res Lewistown, Pa (N G P), Enrd April 27, 1898, M. I May 11, 1898, M. O with Co. Nov. 7, 1898

Swartz, George C, Priv Co G, Res. Lewistown, Pa , Enrd May 10, 1898, M I. May 11, 1898, M O with Co Nov 7, 1898

Swartz, George T., Priv Co I, Res Somerset, Pa , Enrd. July 8, 1898, M I July 8, 1898, M O with Co Nov 7, 1898

Sweeney, Michael F , Priv Co F, Res Indiana, Pa (N. G P), Enrd July 8, 1898, M I July 8, 1898, M O. with Co Nov 7, 1898

Sweet, Wesley, Priv Co K, Res Mansfield, Pa , Enrd July 12, 1898, M I July 14, 1898, M. O with Co Nov 7, 1898

Sweitzer, Samuel H , Priv Co B, Res Bellefonte, Pa , Enrd June 27, 1898; M I June 27, 1898, M O with Co Nov. 7, 1898

Tampsett, William, Priv Co M, Res West York, Pa ; Enrd July 20, 1898, M. I July 20, 1898, M O with Co. Nov 7, 1898

Tampt, William H , Priv Co L, Res Philipsburg, Pa , Enrd July 13, 1898, M I July 14, 1898, M. O with Co Nov 7, 1898

Tate, Frederick M , Priv Co M, Res Gettysburg, Pa , Enrd. July 15, 1898, M I July 20, 1898, Prom Corp Aug 1, 1898, M O with Co Nov 7, 1898

Tate, Rushmore Q , Priv Co K, Res Wellsboro, Pa , Enrd July 13, 1898, M. I July 14, 1898, M O with Co Nov 7, 1898

Taylor, Charles J , 2d Lieut Co B, Res Bellefonte, Pa (N G P), Enrd April 27, 1898, M. I May 11, 1898, M O with Co Nov. 7, 1898

Taylor, Edward R, Priv Co B, Res Bellefonte, Pa (N G P), Enrd April 27, 1898; M I May 11, 1898, Prom Corp May 22, 1898, M O with Co Nov 7, 1898

Taylor, Frank H , Mus Co B, Bellefonte, Pa. (N G P.), Enrd April 27, 1898, M. I May 11, 1898, Died in Div Hosp July 7, 1898

Taylor, Harris L , Priv Co B, Res Philipsburg, Pa , Enrd June 27, 1898, M I June 27, 1898, M. O with Co. Nov 7, 1898

Taylor, Hugh S , Capt Co B , Res Bellefonte, Pa (N G P), Enrd April 27, 1898, M I May 11, 1898, M O with Co Nov 7, 1898

Taylor, Jacob C , Capt Co H, Res Johnstown, Pa (N G P), Enrd April 27, 1898; M I May 11, 1898, M O with Co Nov 7, 1898

Taylor, James W , Priv Co D, Res Saltsburg, Pa , Enrd May 9, 1898, M I May 11, 1898, M O with Co Nov 7, 1898

Taylor, LeRoy, Priv Co D, Res Saltsburg, Pa ; Enrd June 25, 1898, M I June 25, 1898, M O with Co Nov 7, 1898

Taylor, Royden J , Priv Co F, Res Indiana, Pa (N G P), Enrd April 27, 1898, M I May 11, 1898, M O with Co Nov. 7, 1898

Teats, Martin L , 1st Sgt Co G, Res Lewistown, Pa (N G P), Enrd April 27, 1898; M. I May 11, 1898, M O with Co. Nov 7, 1898.

Tebbs, Frederick T , Priv Co B, Res Howard, Pa , Enrd June 27, 1898, M I June 27, 1898; M O with Co Nov 7, 1898

Thomas, Blair A , Priv Co A, Res Huntingdon, Pa ; Enrd April 27, 1898, M I May 11, 1898, M O with Co Nov 7, 1898

Thomas, Charles B , Sgt Co F, Res Indiana, Pa (N G P), Enrd April 27,

1898, M I May 11, 1898, M O with Co Nov 7, 1898

Thomas, Daniel, Priv Co I, Res Elk Lick, Pa , Enrd July 5, 1898, M I July 8, 1898, M O with Co Nov 7, 1898

Thomas, John, Priv Co B, Res Centre Hall, Pa , Enrd June 28, 1898, M I June 28, 1898. Died at Div Hosp Sept 18, 1898

Thomas, Thomas, Priv Co I, Res Elk Lick, Pa , Enrd July 6, 1898, M I July 8, 1898, M O at Fort Thomas, Ky, Dec 21, 1898

Thompson, Benton R, Corp Co F, Res Glen Campbell, Pa (N G P), Enrd April 27, 1898, M I May 11, 1898, M O with Co Nov 7, 1898

Thompson, Earnest D, Corp Co A, Res Huntingdon, Pa (N G P), Enrd April 27, 1898, M I May 11, 1898, M O. with Co Nov 7, 1898

Thompson, Verden R, Priv Co E, Res Clearfield, Pa : Enrd June 21, 1898, M I June 21, 1898, M O with Co Nov 7, 1898

Thomson, Edgar, Priv Co M, Res Frederick, Md , Enrd July 20, 1898, M I July 20, 1898, M O with Co Nov 7, 1898

Threlkeld, James E, Priv Co G, Res Lewistown, Pa (N G P), Enrd April 27, 1898, M I May 11, 1898, M O with Co Nov 7, 1898

Throne, Charles G, Priv Co M, Res East York, Pa ; Enrd July 20, 1898, M I July 20, 1898, M O with Co Nov 7, 1898

Tillburg, William, Priv Co K, Res Mansfield, Pa , Enrd July 13, 1898, M I July 14, 1898, M O with Co Nov 7, 1898

Tipple, Lewis, Priv Co K, Res Wellsboro, Pa , Enrd July 12, 1898, M I July 14, 1898, M O with Co Nov 7, 1898

Tomlinson, Stewart, Priv. Co G, Res Burnham, Pa., Enrd May 10, 1898, M I May 11, 1898, M O with Co Nov 7, 1898

Toner, Samuel E, Priv Co G, Res Lewistown, Pa (N. G. P.); Enrd April 27, 1898, M I May 11, 1898; M O with Co Nov 7, 1898

Townsend, Harry N, Priv Co K, Res Tiadaghton, Pa , Enrd July 12, 1898; M I July 14, 1898, M O with Co Nov 7, 1898

Treese, Elhannan J, Priv Co C; Res Hollidaysburg, Pa (N G P); Enrd. April 27, 1898, M I May 11, 1898, M O with Co Nov 7, 1898

Tressler, Franklin M, Priv Co I, Res Meyersdale, Pa ; Enrd July 7, 1898, M I July 8, 1898, M O with Co Nov. 7, 1898.

Trimmer, Samuel P, Priv. Co M; Res Hanover, Pa , Enrd July 18, 1898. M I. July 20, 1898, Prom Corp Aug 1, 1898, M O with Co Nov. 7, 1898

Trone, Maurice N, Priv Co M; Res. Hanover, Pa , Enrd July 20, 1898, M I July 20, 1898; Prom 1st Sgt Aug 1, 1898, M. O with Co Nov 7, 1898

Trout, Frank W, Priv Co G, Res Lewistown, Pa (N G P.), Enrd. April 27, 1898; M I May 11, 1898, Prom Corp. June 28, 1898, M O with Co Nov 7, 1898

Troxell, Milton E, Priv Co E; Res Clearfield, Pa (N G P); Enrd April 27. 1898, M I May 11, 1898, M O with Co Nov. 7, 1898

Truxal, Albert L, Priv Co L; Res DuBois, Pa , Enrd July 14, 1898; M I July 14, 1898, M. O with Co as Corp Nov 7, 1898

Tully, James, Priv. Co G; Res. Yeagertown, Pa , Enrd May 10, 1898; M I May 11, 1898, M O with Co Nov 7, 1898

Turney, Harry P, Priv Co I, Res.

Marklesburg, Pa , Enrd July 6, 1898, M I July 8, 1898, M O with Co Nov 7, 1898

Twigg, Harry F , Priv Co L, Res Philipsburg, Pa , Enrd July 14, 1898, M I July 14, 1898, M O with Co Nov 7, 1898

Underwood, Jesse, Priv Co B, Res Bellefonte, Pa , Enrd June 28, 1898, M I June 28, 1898, M O with Co Nov 7, 1898

Uphouse, John F , Priv Co H, Res Johnstown, Pa , Enrd May 9, 1898, M I May 11, 1898, M O with Co Nov 7, 1898

Van Allman, William A , 2d Lieut Co C, Res Hollidaysburg, Pa (N G P) Enrd April 27, 1898, M I May 11, 1898, M O with Co Nov 7, 1898

Van Vliet, John A , Priv Co K, Res Delmar, Pa , Enrd July 11, 1898, M I July 14, 1898, M O with Co Nov 7, 1898

Van Zant, James S , Priv Co G, Res Alfarata, Pa , Enrd May 10, 1898, M I May 11, 1898, M O with Co Nov 7, 1898

Varner, Stewart S , Priv Co A, Res Huntingdon, Pa , Enrd June 24, 1898, M I June 24, 1898, M O with Co Nov 7, 1898

Wade, Joseph, Priv Co L, Res Philipsburg, Pa , Enrd July 13, 1898, M I July 14, 1898, Prom Corp , M O with Co Nov 7, 1898

Wagner, George E , Priv Co G, Res Lewistown, Pa (N G P), Enrd April 27, 1898, M I May 11, 1898, M O with Co as Corp Nov 7, 1898

Wagner, Wilber L , Priv Co B, Res Milesburg, Pa , Enrd June 28, 1898, M I June 28, 1898, M O with Co Nov 7, 1898

Wahl, Frederick W , Priv Co C, Res Altoona, Pa Enrd June 21, 1898, M I June 21, 1898, M O with Co Nov 7, 1898

Wakefield, George W , 1st Lieut Co D, Res Blairsville, Pa (N G P), Enrd April 27, 1898, M I May 11, 1898, M O with Co Nov 7, 1898

Waksfield, Louis A , Priv Co H, Res New Florence, Pa , Enrd May 9, 1898, M I. May 11, 1898, M O with Co Nov 7, 1898

Walker, Israel T , Priv Co F, Res Shelocta, Pa (N G P), Enrd April 27, 1898, M I May 11, 1898, M O with Co Nov 7, 1898

Walker, Lewis A , Priv Co B, Res Rebersburg, Pa , Enrd June 27, 1898 M I June 27, 1898, M O with Co Nov 7, 1898

Wallace, Frank, Priv Co B, Res Milesburg, Pa , Enrd June 28, 1898, M I June 28, 1898, M O with Co Nov 7, 1898

Walsh, John, Sgt Co C, Res Hollidaysburg Pa (N G P), Enrd April 27, 1898, M I May 11, 1898, Prom 1st Sgt June 28, 1898, M O with Co Nov 7, 1898

Walters, Lloyd W , Priv Co C, Res Duncansville, Pa (N G P), Enrd April 27, 1898, M I May 11, 1898, M O with Co Nov 7, 1898

Walton, Oliver T , Priv Co D, Res Saltsburg, Pa , Enrd May 9, 1898, M I May 11, 1898, M O with Co Nov 7, 1898

Waple, Charles R , Priv Co E, Res Wallaceton, Pa , Enrd May 9, 1898, M I May 11, 1898, M O with Co Nov 7, 1898

Warfel, George, Priv Co G, Res Greenwood Furnace, Pa , Enrd June 29, 1898, M I June 29, 1898, M O with Co Nov 7, 1898

Warfel, William G , Priv Co A, Res Huntingdon, Pa , Enrd May 7, 1898, M I May 11, 1898, M O with Co Nov 7, 1898

Waring, Charles T , Priv Co B, Res Philipsburg, Pa , Enrd May 7, 1898, M I May 11, 1898, M O with Co Nov 7, 1898

Warner, George N , Priv Co M, Res New Oxford, Pa , Enrd July 15, 1898, M

I. July 20, 1898, Prom Corp Aug 1, 1898, Sgt. Sept 1, 1898; M O with Co Nov 7, 1898

Watson, Harry W, Corp Co F, Res Indiana, Pa (N G P), Enrd April 27, 1898, M I. May 11, 1898, M O with Co. Nov 7, 1898

Watson, John L, 2d Lieut Co E, Res Clearfield, Pa (N G 'P), Enrd April 27, 1898, M I May 11, 1898, M O with Co Nov 7 1898

Watson, Robert W K, Priv Co M, Res Fairfield, Pa., Enrd July 18, 1898, M I July 20, 1898, M O with Co Nov 7, 1898

Waugaman, Milton R, Priv Co D, Res Saltsburg, Pa, Enrd May 9, 1898, M I May 11, 1898, Tranfd to U S Sig Corps July 12, 1898

Way, William C., Priv. Co E, Res Curwensville, Pa (N G P), Enrd April 27, 1898, M. I May 11, 1898, M O with Co Nov 7, 1898

Weatherby, Edmund S J, Priv Co G, Res Millville, N. J; Enrd June 29, 1898; M. I June 29, 1898; M O with Co Nov 7, 1898

Weaver, Calvin, Priv Co E, Res Newtonburg, Pa., Enrd June 21, 1898, M. I June 21, 1898, M. O with Co Nov 7, 1898

Weaver, Edward W, Corp Co D, Res Blairsville, Pa (N G P), Enrd April 27, 1898, M I May 11, 1898, M O. with Co Nov 7, 1898

Weaver, George D, Priv Co M, Res Newry, Pa, Enrd July 15, 1898, M I July 20, 1898, M O with Co Nov 7, 1898

Weaver, Hilarion C, Corp Co H, Res Johnstown, Pa (N G P), Enrd April 27,

1898, M. I May 11, 1898, M O with Co. Nov 7, 1898

Weaver, Howard, Priv Co I, Res Hopewell, Pa, Enrd July 6, 1898, M I. July 8, 1898, M O with Co Nov. 7, 1898

Weaver, John E, Priv. Co F, Res Homer City, Pa, Enrd May 9, 1898, M I May 11, 1898, Apptd Wag June 1, 1898; M O with Co Nov 7, 1898

Weaver, John F, Jr, Priv. Co E; Res Clearfield, Pa (N. G P), Enrd April 27, 1898, M I May 11, 1898; Prom Corp June 27, 1898, M O with Co Nov 7, 1898

Weaver, John J, Priv Co E; Res. Fairbrook, Pa, Enrd June 27, 1898, M I. June 27,1898, M O. with Co Nov 7, 1898

Weaver, Louis S, Priv. Co M, Res Newry, Pa, Enrd. July 18, 1898, M. I. July 20, 1898, Prom Sgt Aug 1, 1898, reduced to Priv. Sept 1, 1898, at his own request, M O with Co Nov 7, 1898

Weaver, Thomas M, Sgt Co. D; Res Blairsville, Pa (N. G. P), Enrd April 27, 1898; M I May 11, 1898; Prom to Q M. Sgt. June 3, 1898; M O with Co Nov 7, 1898

Webb, Charles R, Priv Co K, Res Draper, Pa; Enrd July 12, 1898, M. I July 14, 1898; M O. with Co. Nov 7, 1898

Weber, Carl E, Sgt Co G, Res Lewistown, Pa. (N. G. P.), Enrd April 27, 1898, M I May 11, 1898; M O with Co Nov 7, 1898.

Weber, Clarence, Priv Co L, Res. Clearfield, Pa; Enrd July 13, 1898, M I. July 14, 1898, M O with Co Nov. 7, 1898

Wechtenhiser, Isaiah, Priv Co I, Res Berlin, Pa, Enrd July 5, 1898, M I July 8, 1898; M O with Co. Nov 7, 1898

Weight, David W, Priv. Co C; Res Altoona, Pa.; Enrd. June 20, 1898; M. I. June 20, 1898; M. O. with Co. Nov. 7, 1898.

Weimer, Benton H., Priv. Co. D; Res. Blairsville, Pa.; Enrd. June 24, 1898; M. I. June 24, 1898; M. O. with Co. Nov. 7, 1898.

Weinel, Aldis L., Priv. Co. D; Res. Paulton, Pa.; Enrd. June 24, 1898; M. I. June 24, 1898; M. O. with Co. Nov. 7, 1898.

Weirick, Frank X., Priv. Co. M; Res.. Gettysburg, Pa.; Enrd. July 15, 1898; M. I. July 20, 1898; M. O. with Co. Nov. 7, 1898.

Welch, Leon E., Priv. Co. K; Res. Elk Run, Pa.; Enrd. July 11, 1898; M. I. July 14, 1898; Apptd. Corp. July 23, 1898, G. O. 8 c. s. Regt.; M. O. with Co. Nov 7, 1898.

Welch, Walter, Priv. Co. E; Res. Houtzdale, Pa.; Enrd. May 9, 1898; M. I. May 11, 1898; M. O. with Co. Nov. 7, 1898.

Weld, John H., Priv. Co. E; Res. Glen Hope, Pa.; Enrd. June 21, 1898; M. I. June 21, 1898; M. O. with Co. Nov. 7, 1898.

Welshons, George E., Priv. Co. H; Res. New Florence, Pa. (N. G. P.); Enrd. April 27, 1898; M. I. May 11, 1898; Prom. Corp. June 28, 1898; M. O. with Co. Nov. 7, 1898.

Welty, Charles R., Priv. Co. M; Res. Gettysburg, Pa.; Enrd. July 15, 1898; M. I. July 20, 1898; Prom. Corp. Aug. 1, 1898; M. O. with Co. Nov. 7, 1898.

West, John H., Capt. Co. C; Res. Hollidaysburg, Pa. (N. G. P.); Enrd. April 27, 1898; M. I. May 11, 1898; M. O. with Co. Nov 7, 1898.

West, Vickroy, Priv. Co. H; Res. Johnstown, Pa.; Enrd. May 4, 1898; M. I. May 11, 1898; M. O. with Co. Nov. 7, 1898.

West, William S., Priv. Co. I; Res. Listie, Pa.; Enrd. July 7, 1898; M. I. July 8, 1898; M. O. with Co Nov. 7, 1898.

West, William W., Priv. Co. H; Res. Johnstown, Pa.; Enrd. June 27, 1898; M. I. June 27, 1898; M. O. with Co. Nov. 7, 1898.

Westbrook, Edsal N., Priv. Co. K; Res. Tioga, Pa.; Enrd. July 12, 1898; M. I. July 14, 1898; Prom. Corp July 23, 1898; G. O. 8 c. s. Regt; M. O. with Co. Nov. 7, 1898.

Weston, Forest M., Priv. Co. B; Res. Olivia, Pa.; Enrd. June 27, 1898; M. I. June 27, 1898; M. O. with Co. Nov. 7, 1898.

Wetzel, Lewis G., Priv. Co. F; Res. Marion Centre, Pa.; Enrd. May 9, 1898; M. I. May 11, 1898; M. O. with Co. Nov. 7, 1898.

Wheeler, Lewis A., 1st Sgt. Co. F; Res. Indiana, Pa. (N. G. P.); Enrd. April 27, 1898; M. I. May 11, 1898; M. O. with Co. Nov. 7, 1898.

Whipple, George, Priv Co. L; Res. DuBois, Pa.; Enrd. July 14, 1898; M. I. July 14, 1898; M. O. with Co. Nov. 7, 1898.

White, Joseph C., Priv. Co. F; Res. Crete, Pa. (N. G. P.); Enrd. April 27, 1898; M. I. May 11, 1898; Prom. Corp. June 28, 1898; M. O. with Co. Nov. 7, 1898.

White, Ray D., Priv. Co. A; Res. Pittsburg, Pa. (N. G. P.); Enrd. April 27, 1898; M. I. May 11, 1898; Prom. Corp. June 28, 1898; M. O. with Co. Nov. 7, 1898.

White, William G., Priv. Co. A; Res. Pittsburg, Pa. (N. G. P.); Enrd. April 27, 1898; M. I. May 11, 1898; M. O. with Co. Nov. 7, 1898.

Whittaker, Clarence H., Priv. Co. A; Res. Huningdon, Pa.; Enrd. May 7, 1898; M. I. May 11, 1898; M. O. with Co. Nov. 7, 1898.

Whittaker, Ralph R., Priv. Co. A; Res.

Huntingdon, Pa , Enrd May 7, 1898, M I May 11, 1898, M O with Co Nov 7, 1898

Wiggins, Robert H , 2d Lieut Co D, Res Blairsville, Pa (N G P), Enrd April 27, 1898, M I May 11, 1898 Prom 1st Lieut Co L, 5th Regt, July 31, 1898, M O. with Co L Nov 7, 1898

Wilcox, Charles C , Priv Co D, Res Saltsburg, Pa , Enrd June 24, 1898, M I June 24, 1898, M O with Co Nov 7, 1898

Wildes, Clayton B , Priv Co C, Res Altoona, Pa , Enrd. May 10, 1898, M I May 11, 1898, M O with Co Nov 7 1898

Wiley, Hugh R , Priv Co D, Res Blairsville, Pa (N. G P), Enrd April 27, 1898, M I May 11, 1898, Dischd May 23, 1898, per S O 115 A G O

Wiley, Scott A , Corp Co D, Res Blacklick, Pa (N G P), Enrd April 27, 1898, M I May 11, 1898, M O with Co Nov 7, 1898.

Wilkes, Roy, Priv Co K, Res Landruc, Pa , Enrd July 12, 1898, M I July 14, 1898, M O with Co Nov 7, 1898

Willhelm, William V , Priv Co F, Res Indiana, Pa , Enrd June 22, 1898, M I June 22, 1898, M O with Co Nov 7, 1898

Williams, George W , Priv Co K, Res Forksville, Pa , Enrd July 12, 1898, M. I. July 14, 1898, M O with Co Nov 7, 1898

Williams, Harrison G , Priv Co B, Res Howard, Pa (N G P), Enrd April 27, 1898, M I May 11, 1898, M O with Co Nov 7, 1898

Williams, Henry Clay, Priv Co L, Res DuBois, Pa , Enrd July 13, 1898, M I July 14, 1898, M O with Co Nov 7, 1898

Williams, Lawrence O , Priv Co F, Res Kenwood, Pa , Enrd June 2, 1898, M I June 22, 1898, M O with Co Nov 7, 1898

Williams, Maurice, Priv Co M, Res Gettysburg, Pa , Enrd July 15, 1898, M I. July 20, 1898, Prom Sgt Aug 1, 1898; M O. with Co Nov 7, 1898

Williams, Robert S , Priv Co C, Res Altoona, Pa , Enrd June 21, 1898, M I June 21, 1898, M O with Co. Nov 7, 1898

Williams, Willis, Priv Co B, Res. Bellefonte, Pa (N G P), Enrd. April 27, 1898, M I May 11, 1898, Prom Corp May 16, 1898, M O with Co Nov 7, 1898

Williamson, Richard W , Priv Co A; Res. Huntingdon, Pa (N G P), Enrd April 27, 1898, M I May 11, 1898, Prom Corp June 28, 1898, M O with Co Nov 1898

Willard, George F., Priv Co L, Res DuBois, Pa , Enrd July 13, 1898, M I July 14, 1898, M O with Co Nov 7, 1898

Wilson, George H , Priv Co D, Res Blairsville, Pa (N G P), Enrd April 27, 1898, M I May 11, 1898, M O with Co Nov 7, 1898

Wilson, John D , Priv Co F; Res Indiana, Pa , Enrd June 22, 1898, M I June 22, 1898; M O with Co Nov 7, 1898

Wingert, Samuel T , Priv Co F; Res Marchand, Pa , Enrd June 23, 1898, M I June 23, 1898, M O with Co Nov 7, 1898

Wise, James, Priv Co M, Res Gettysburg, Pa , Enrd July 15, 1898; M I July 20, 1898, Prom Corp Aug 1, 1898, M O with Co Nov 7, 1898

Woleslagle, John A , Priv Co C, Res Altoona, Pa (N G P), Enrd April 27, 1898; M I May 11, 1898, M O with Co Nov 7, 1898

Wolf, Robert F , Priv Co H, Res Johnstown, Pa (N G P), Enrd April 27, 1898; M I May 11, 1898, M. O with Co Nov. 7, 1898

Wolf, William N, Priv Co H, Res Johnstown, Pa (N G P), Enrd April 27, 1898, M I May 11, 1898, M O with Co Nov 7, 1898

Womer, Francis M, Priv Co G, Res Lewistown, Pa (N G P). Enrd April 27, 1898, M I May 11, 1898, Died in Hosp, Chickamauga, Ga. July 22, 1898

Woodend, J W Priv Co D, Res Indiana, Pa, Enrd June 24, 1898, M I June 24, 1898, M O with Co Nov 7, 1898

Woodruff, Lucian D, Jr. Priv Co H, Res Johnstown, Pa (N G P), Enrd April 27, 1898, M I May 11, 1898, Prom Corp June 28, 1898, M O with Co Nov 7, 1898

Woodward, Americus H, Capt Co E, Res Clearfield, Pa (N G P), Enrd April 27, 1898, M I May 11, 1898. M O with Co Nov 7, 1898

Wright, Charles F, Priv Co I, Res Somerset, Pa, Enrd July 4, 1898, M I July 8, 1898, M O with Co Nov 7, 1898

Wright, Nelson A, Priv Co I, Res Addison, Pa, Enrd July 5, 1898, M I July 8, 1898, M O with Co Nov 7, 1898

Wright, Roscoe M, Priv Co A, Res Huntingdon, Pa (N G P), Enrd April 27, 1898, M I May 11, 1898. M O with Co Nov 7, 1898

Wrye, Charles W, Priv Co E, Res Morrisdale Mines, Pa, Enrd June 21, 1898, M I June 21, 1898, M O with Co Nov 7, 1898

Wyland, Daniel D, Priv Co G, Res Burnham, Pa, Enrd June 29, 1898, M I June 29, 1893, M O with Co Nov 7, 1898

Yeagy, William F, Priv Co M, Res Gettysburg, Pa, Enrd July 15. 1898, M I July 20, 1898, Prom Corp Aug 1, 1898, M O with Co Nov 7, 1898

Yocum, George I, Priv Co A, Res Huntingdon, Pa, Enrd May 7, 1898, M I May 11, 1898, M O with Co Nov 7, 1898

Yocum, Samuel F, Priv Co C, Res Altoona, Pa (N G P). Enrd April 27, 1898, M I May 11, 1898, Prom Corp June 28, 1898, M O with Co Nov 7, 1898

Young, Emil, Priv Co H, Res Johnstown, Pa, Enrd April 27, 1898, M I May 11, 1898, M O with Co Nov 7, 1898

Young, Hugh C, Priv Co K, Res. Wellsboro, Pa, Enrd July 13, 1898, M I July 14, 1898, M O with Co Nov 7, 1898

Zeigler, Joseph D E, Priv Co E, Res DuBois, Pa, Enrd June 20, 1898, M I June 20. 1898, M O with Co Nov 7, 1898

Zercher, John W, Priv Co M, Res Littlestown, Pa, Enrd July 15, 1898, M I July 20, 1898, M O with Co Nov 7, 1898

Ziegler, Charles T, Priv Co M, Res Gettysburg, Pa, Enrd July 15, 1898, M I July 20, 1898, Dischd. July 30, 1898, per Par 45, S O W Dept, dated Aug 3, 1898, Dischd to accept commission, Apptd 2d Lieut July 28, 1898, M I July 31, 1898, at Camp Thomas, Ga, M O with Co Nov 7, 1898

Zigler, Foster, Priv C H, Res Johnstown, Pa, Enrd May 4, 1898, M I May 11, 1898, M O with Co Nov 7, 1898

Zimmerman, Edward, Priv Co A, Res Birmingham, Pa, Enrd June 24, 1898, M I June 24, 1898, M O with Co Nov 7, 1898

Zimmerman, Harvey J, Priv Co I, Res Forward, Pa, Enrd July 5, 1898, M I July 8, 1898, Prom Corp July 16, 1898, M O with Co Nov 7, 1898

CHAPTER X

THE PRESS

A Sketch of Journalism in Clearfield County—The First County Paper—A Home-made Press— The "Banner"—Clearfield Republican—Clearfield Whig—Raftsman's Journal—Clearfield Citizen—The Times-Monitor—Evening Herald—Clearfield County Times—Curwensville Herald—County Review—The Mountaineer—DuBois Morning Courier—DuBois Express —The Enterprise—DuBois Morning Journal—Houtzdale Citizen—Osceola Reveille— The Leader-Courier—Coalport Standard—The Hustler, and Other Newspapers

It has been said that "the press is the voice of the people," defending their causes, crying their needs and binding them together So in tracing the development, both material and intellectual, of our county, we find no greater factor than the county press

During the first twenty-three years of our county's history, not one county paper was issued As for other publications, they were often days old before they reached their destination in this part of the country It can be understood, then, with what enthusiasm and interest the establishing of the first county paper was greeted, in the year 1827 Its founders were Christopher Kratzer and George S Irvin, both residents of Philipsburg Mr Kratzer, a cabinet-maker by trade, built the press, while Mr Irvin, who had some experience as a printer, furnished the type

The first issue of this paper was published at Clearfield about 1827, under the name of the "Pennsylvania Banner" It is said that the original "Banner" was not of attractive appearance, indeed being only a slight improvement over the first newspaper of the world, printed four hundred years before! The original partnership was of short duration, Mr Kratzer selling his share to Mr Irvin after a few years. This was the first of a long list of changes in ownership, title and political adherence, for the first county paper In all it has had nineteen owners, five titles and has changed its politics four times This pioneer paper is now in its 83rd year, and is published in Clearfield by John F Short, under the name of the Clearfield "Republican." in spite of the fact that it is radically Democratic

The second county newspaper also made its first appearance in the county seat, about 1834 Ex-Governor Bigler edited this paper for about two years, but soon found that with his many other activities, it was not possible to continue this new undertaking The "Democrat," therefore, was discontinued, after its very brief existence

Next came the "Clearfield Whig,"

174

founded by John R. Edie, who was succeeded by Samuel H Tyson and Samuel T
Williams. This paper, also, was of about
two years duration, being discontinued in
1838

For the next twenty years the "Republican" enjoyed an unrivaled existence, then,
in 1854, "The Raftsman's Journal" was
founded by Hon H Bucher Swoope This
was at the time of the dissolution of the
Whig party, and Mr Swoope was a strong
advocate of the new American party during the two years in which he so ably edited
this paper In 1856, S B Row took charge
of the "Journal," and with the organization
of the Republican party, the "Journal" became a Republican paper Since then it
has changed hands several times, but never
its political complexion and to-day is a Republican paper of wide circulation, under
the management of M L McQuown

The "Clearfield Citizen" was started in
1878 by John R Bixler, a strong advocate
of the Greenback party Later Mr Bixler
saw fit to sever his connection with that
party, and became just as ardent a Democrat Still later the name of the paper was
changed to the "Clearfield Democrat"
Soon after, Matthew Savage acquired its
ownership, and renamed it "The Public
Spirit" Under this name and management
it has been continued, and is to-day one of
the leading papers of the county, published
both daily and weekly

About 1889, S C and J P Watts established a Prohibition paper at Clearfield,
under the name of "The Monitor" In
1905 this paper was purchased by R M
Butler, formerly the local editor of the
Curwensville "Mountaineer" Subsequently, the "Karthaus Times," which had been
started by Dr Neveling a few years before,
was consolidated with the "Monitor," and
these papers are now known as the "Times-
Monitor"

In 1905 Mr Butler started a daily paper
called "The Evening Herald" Both papers
are now published by S V Border and are
independent in politics.

In closing this list of papers published at
the county seat some mention must be
made of the "Multum in Parvo," a most eccentric little paper published by Dr Sweeney about 1883 After a stormy, if brief
career, during which time its editor was
sued for libel, this paper ceased to appear

Previous to 1872 the county seat enjoyed
the honor of publishing the only newspapers in this county But during the summer of that year a stock company, the members of which were W and Z McNaul, E
A Irvin, Samuel Arnold, A H Irvin, W C
Arnold, Faust & Goodwin, John P Irvin,
John Patton, T W Fleming, N E Arnold,
J R Jenkins, Edward Livingston, J F Irwin and L B V Soper, was formed for the
purpose of founding a weekly newspaper,
in Curwensville This paper was called the
"Clearfield County Times," and was published by Tolbert J Robison Daniel Faust,
W C Arnold, J P Irvin, John Patton, Jr,
and Edward Livingston comprised the edi-
torial committee The "Times" proved a
great success as a strong Republican paper
during the Grant-Greeley campaign

The next year R H Brainard bought the
"Times" and became its editor. He continued as such for the next nine years Whittaker and Fee were the next publishers,
and on account of political differences

edited a paper neutral as to party After several changes in its ownership John P Bard purchased the "Times" in 1885, and renamed it "The Curwensville Herald " It now became a successful Republican paper once more, but this success soon failed, for in a year's time the "Herald" passed into other hands and abruptly ceased to be published

Curwensville's second attempt at a paper was a musical publication, called "The Ancilla" established and edited by Professor C C McDonald, in 1881 A year later Professor McDonald changed the "Ancilla" to a sixteen page monthly, under the name of "The County Review " This paper was bought in 1884, by R H Brainard, who became its editor, and continued as such until the time of his death in 1905 The paper was then purchased by V King Pifer, who published it several years, after which it ceased to exist

On April 28, 1903, a four page weekly newspaper under the title of "The Mountaineer" was established in Curwensville by Roland D Swoope, Esq and S Arnold Helmbold Five years later Mr Helmbold sold his interest in this paper to Roland D Swoope, Jr, who has since been its editor and publisher Since its beginning the "Mountaineer" has been devoted to the cause of Republicanism, and is recognized as one of the foremost county papers in the state

"The DuBois Courier" first appeared in 1879, under the management of Butler and Horton Three years later J A Johnston became its manager, enlarging and improving it so that it became one of the leading papers in the county In 1884 E W Gray became a partner of Mr. Johnston, and two years after, the "Courier" was sold to R L Earle, who conducted it as a radical Republican paper Later the paper was again acquired by E S and E W Gray, who have since published it as a Republican daily paper, under the name of "The DuBois Morning Courier" For several years a weekly edition of the "Courier" was published, but this has been discontinued

In 1883, H C Wilson, B S Hoag and Frank McMichael started an independent paper under the name of the "DuBois Express " Later the members of the company were J P Wilson, C A Read, H C. Wilson and Frank McMichael This firm was called the "Express Publishing Company." Still later, David Reams became the proprietor, but in a few years was succeeded by D C Whitehill, who remained its publisher until 1909 Next A E Hasbrook assumed its control, and it is now published as an evening paper, ranking high among the independent papers of the state

Though scarcely a newspaper "The Enterprise" published in DuBois about 1875 by P S Weber, is of interest in discussing the press of the county This unique publication consisted mainly of advertisements, and was issued gratis Needless to say, this experiment did not last long, and was abandoned after three or four issues

The year 1904 marked the birth of another daily paper in the Metropolis of Clearfield county "The DuBois Morning Journal" made its first appearance at that time, under the supervision of W. J and N D Hines They are still its publishers, under the firm name of "The DuBois Printing and Publishing Company" The "Journal" has also a Sunday edition This paper owes its allegiance to the Republican party

In 1881 in the enterprising town of Houtzdale a weekly newspaper was started by the "Observer Publishing Company," under the name of the "Houtzdale Observer" After many changes in its management this paper was absorbed by the "Houtzdale Citizen," which is now owned and published by Hon Harry Boulton and Ralph Richards The "Citizen" is recognized as a loyal Republican weekly

In 1873 a newspaper was started in Osceola by George M Brisbin and his two brothers This paper was called the "Osceola Reveille," and was strictly independent regarding politics After three years the Brisbin brothers retired, and the "Reveille" became "The Independent World," managed by O E McFadden Less than a year later its name was changed to the "Campaign World," and then again to the original title—"Reveille," by J B McFadden, who was manager until 1880, when it was discontinued. In 1888 J B McFadden established the "Leader," and, purchasing the "Courier" three years later, he gave the paper the name of the "Leader-Courier," which it still retains Strictly

neutral in politics this paper under Mr McFadden's editorship has come to fill an indispensable place in the homes of the thrifty and industrious people of the Osceola section

Coalport was the fourth town to attempt a county publication In 1885 G P Penneaker started a small paper, which he called "Coalport Siftings" This proved such a success that Mr Pennebaker enlarged the paper, changed its name to the "Coalport Standard" and started to publish a first-class weekly The present publisher of this independent Republican weekly is Ezra Westover, who issues a clean and newsy four-page sheet

Synonymous with the progressive town of Madera is its recently established weekly publication, known as "The Hustler" This paper was founded in 1909 by B F Rhinehart and promises to advance with the steady growth of that busy region The "Hustler" is classed as a Republican paper

This completes our list of the newspapers of Clearfield county, of which there are now fourteen Five of these are published daily, and the remainder weekly Of the total number, seven are Republican, three Democratic and four Independent

CHAPTER XI

THE BENCH OF CLEARFIELD COUNTY

Clearfield County's Judicial Connection with Centre County Previous to 1822—The Act of 1822 Providing for the Holding of Courts in Clearfield County—Population at That Time—Provision for Keeping Prisoners—Sketch of Hon Charles Huston—Hon Thomas Burnside, Hon W George Woodward, Hon Robert G White, Hon. John C. Knox, Hon James T Hale—The Twenty-fifth District Formed—Sketch of Hon James Burnside—Hon James Gamble—Judge Linn—Hon Joseph B McEnally—Hon Charles A. Mayer—Act of 1874 Providing for an Additional Law Judge—Hon John H Orvis Appointed—Clearfield County Created a Separate Judicial District—Hon David L Krebs—Hon Cyrus Gordon—Hon Allison O Smith

Although Clearfield county was organized by an act of the General Assembly approved March 26th, 1804, it was attached to Centre county for judicial purposes by the provisions of said act, and for all such matters it was practically a part of that county, until 1822, despite the fact that by an act approved April 4th, 1805 (Chapter 2598) the Legislature had appointed Commissioners to fix the seat of justice for the county and the same was established on the lands of Abraham Witmer at Chingleclamouche, and a town laid out and called Clearfield yet it was not until the 29th of January, 1822, that the General Assembly passed a law making the county a part of the Fourth Judicial District and providing that the President Judge of said district should be the President Judge of the Courts of Clearfield county Said act also provided for the holding of Courts in Clearfield county, commencing on the third Mondays of October, December and March and the first Mondays of July in each year, which courts the act wisely provided should each "continue one week if necessary" and that, in case the public business did not in the opinion of the judges of said court require the summoning of a jury to attend all the terms of Court, the Judges might dispense with juries not exceeding two terms in any one year The act further provided that the first term of Court should be held "at the Court House now erected in Clearfield town in said county of Clearfield " At this time the county had, according to the last U. S census, a population of 2342 and a taxable population according to the state census of 1821 of 584 No deaf and dumb persons and no slaves The act of 1822 also made provision for the transfer to Clearfield county of all actions in which both parties were residents of Clearfield county at the time of the passing of said act, and also for the making of copies of

178

all docket entries relating to such actions which with all the pleadings therein were transferred to the Prothonotary of Clearfield county from Centre county It seems there was in 1822 no jail in Clearfield county as the act provides for the keeping of prisoners in the Centre county jail until a jail should be erected in Clearfield

Pursuant to said act of Assembly the first Court was held at Clearfield on the third Monday of October, 1822, and was presided over by Hon Charles Huston

Charles Huston was born in Bucks County, Pa, on the 16th of January, 1771 He received his education at private schools and at Dickinson College, Carlisle, Pa, from which institution he was graduated in the class of 1789 He taught school to maintain himself while he studied law, and was admitted to the bar in August, 1795 He first located at Williamsport, Pa, but removed to Bellefonte, Pa, in 1807 where he resided and practiced law at the time of his appointment as President Judge of the Courts of the Fourth Judicial District Judge Huston served as President Judge of the district until 1826 when he was appointed one of the Justices of the Supreme Court of the state and served as such until 1845, when he retired His death occurred November 10th, 1849 Judge Huston was unusually well equipped to fill the important duties of the judicial office He had the attributes of integrity, legal learning, sound understanding, and that habit of thought that enabled him to view the legal questions before him without bias or prejudice As a judge of the Fourth judicial district he became unusually well versed in the intricacies of the land titles in the state, and after his retirement from the bench he prepared and published a valuable work, entitled "History and Nature of Original Titles to Land in the Province and State of Pennsylvania"

Hon Thomas Burnside was appointed in 1826 to succeed Judge Huston Thomas Burnside was a native of Ireland and was born July 22, 1782 He came to this country in 1782 with his parents and his early youth was spent in Philadelphia He read law with Hon Robert Porter of Philadelphia and was admitted to practice in 1804 and shortly thereafter he located in Bellefonte, Pa He took an active interest in politics and in 1811 was chosen as state senator and in 1815 was elected to Congress In 1816 he was appointed President Judge of Luzerne County, but resigned in 1818 In 1823 he was again elected to the State Senate He presided over the Courts of the Fourth Judicial district until 1841, when he was appointed President Judge of the Seventh Judicial district, where he served until 1845, when he was promoted to the Supreme Court of the state He died March 25th, 1857 Judge Burnside, while an able jurist and a man of more than ordinary ability in many lines, was noted for his eccentricities, and his fondness for a joke regardless of who might suffer

Hon George W Woodward succeeded Judge Burnside and served a full term and was afterwards made Chief Justice of the Supreme Court of the state He was noted for his extreme courtesy and affability as well as for his legal learning and strict impartiality He was firm and final in his decisions upon legal questions, yet because it was always believed that he was strictly just as he recognized justice, he became one of the most popular judges in the state Judge Woodward served on the Supreme

Court Bench until 1867, when he retired by reason of the expiration of his term He died about 1868

Hon Robert G White was the next President Judge Judge White came from Tioga County, Pa, and by reason of a change in the judicial districts that was made by the Legislature, he only served as the Judge of this county for the period of one year

Hon John C Knox was the successor of Judge White He served for a few months, when he was appointed as one of the Judges of the Supreme Court He also served a term as Attorney General of the State In the latter years of his life his mind became impaired and he died in an asylum for the insane

Hon James T Hale succeeded Judge Knox as President Judge in April, 1851 Judge Hale was born in Bradford County, Pa, October 14th, 1810 He was admitted to the Bar in 1832 and located in Bellefonte in 1835 He served as President Judge until April, 1853 After his retirement from the bench he practiced law for a number of years, but devoted most of his attention to business pursuits and to the development of the lumber and coal industries in Clearfield and Centre counties and to the building of the Tyrone and Clearfield railroad He died in April, 1865

By an act of the General Assembly approved April 9th, 1853, P L page 355, the counties of Centre, Clearfield and Clinton were erected into a separate judicial district to be called the Twenty-fifth District and the Governor was empowered to appoint a president judge of said district to serve until the first day of the December follow-

ing the passage of said act Governor William Bigler on the 20th of April, 1853, appointed Hon James Burnside to be the president judge of the new district All of the judges up to this date had been appointed by the Governors, but by reason of an amendment to the Constitution of the state, which had been submitted to and adopted by the people, all judges afterwards commissioned were elected by the voters of the state for terms of ten years in case of Common Pleas judges and fifteen years for judges of the Supreme Court Judge Burnside was elected at the October election of 1853 without opposition and presided over the Courts of the twenty-fifth district until his death on July 1, 1859, by being thrown from a buggy in a runaway Judge James Burnside was generally known as Judge Burnside the younger, to distinguish him from his father, Judge Thomas Burnside

James Burnside was the eldest son of Thomas Burnside and was born at Bellefonte, Pa, on February 22nd, 1807 He studied law in his father's office and was admitted to the Bar in November, 1830 In 1844 he was elected to the state Legislature and served two terms, having been reelected in 1846 He was a man of force and a good legal education and made a fine record as a jurist

During the few months intervening between the death of Judge James Burnside and the election of Judge Linn, Hon James Gamble presided over the Courts of the twenty-fifth district He was an able lawyer and worthily filled the important position, but owing to the brief period of his service in this county, he did not have an opportunity to do much toward becoming acquainted with its people At the October election of 1859 Samuel Linn was elected President Judge of the district and served until 1868, when he resigned

Judge Linn was born in February, 1820, and was twenty-four years of age before he commenced to prepare himself for the legal profession He was admitted to the Bar in 1847 and practiced law in partnership with James T Hale, until 1851, when Mr Hale was appointed to the Bench, and Mr Linn then formed a partnership with W P Wilson which continued until Judge Linn's election as president Judge After his retirement from the bench Judge Linn practiced law until his death Judge Linn tried many important cases in Clearfield county and some of his decisions on the questions of land titles were the foundations of stability that settled disputed lines of boundaries and interfering surveys that had proven a continual source of annoyance and litigation for years prior thereto

Hon Joseph B McEnally was appointed as the successor to Judge Linn in 1868 by the Governor and was the first citizen of Clearfield county to preside over the Courts of the county as president judge Judge McEnally served until December, 1868, when he was succeeded by Charles A Mayer, the latter having defeated Judge McEnally at the October election, at which Judge McEnally was the Republican and Charles A Mayer the Democratic candidate The district at that time being strongly democratic McEnally was defeated, although he polled a large complimentary vote Judge McEnally was born in Lycoming county on January 25th, 1825

He was educated at Dickinson College, Carlisle, Pa , having been graduated in the class of 1845 He was admitted to the Bar in 1849 Shortly after being admitted to practice he came to Clearfield county and resided there until his death which occurred at the ripe old age of eighty-five Judge McEnally was a man of beautiful character, sterling integrity and as a land lawyer he probably had no equal in Pennsylvania

Hon Charles A Mayer, who succeeded Judge McEnally as president Judge, was born in York Co, Pa , December 15th, 1830 At the age of twenty-three he was admitted to the Bar of Clinton County, Pa He served as District Attorney of Clinton county for two terms At the expiration of his term as president judge he was again a candidate and was re-elected in 1878 After Clearfield county became a separate judicial district in 1883 Judge Mayer became by virtue of the rearrangement of judicial districts made by the Legislature, the President Judge of the new twenty-fifth district comprising the counties of Clinton, Cameron and Elk, and held that office up to the time of his death Judge Mayer was one of the best lawyers who ever occupied the bench in this county and his decisions were seldom reversed by the appellate courts

By the act of the General Assembly approved the 9th day of April, 1874, which was passed to carry out the directions of the new state Constitution the Twenty-fifth Judicial District was entitled to an additional law judge to be appointed by the Governor to serve until such additional law judge should be elected at the next general election Pursuant to the authority contained in that act, Governor Hartranft on April 10th, 1874, appointed Hon John H Orvis to be additional law judge of said district, and at the general election following he was elected to said office for the full term of ten years Judge Orvis was born in Sullivan township, Tioga county, Pa, on February 24th, 1835 In February, 1856, he was admitted to the Clinton county Bar, and in December, 1862, he moved to Bellefonte, Pa Judge Orvis resigned in 1868 and resumed the practice of the law in which he was actively and successfully engaged up to the time of his death Judge Orvis was possessed of a fine intellect and a wonderfully retentive memory In the trial of a case he seldom took any notes and yet when he came to charge the jury he could give every important item of testimony with exactness from his memory His ability as a lawyer was very much against his success as a judge He could grasp the very essence of a case, so much more quickly than the ordinary lawyer, and he was so impatient of technicalities and delays, and so anxious that right should prevail, that he sometimes ran afoul of the red tape that hedges in the legal procedure, for the purpose of preventing a too hasty judgment, but his career on the bench and as a lawyer reflected great credit upon the profession which he honored He was particularly kind to young lawyers and it was his delight to aid and assist them wherever he could and as a consequence he made many warm friends among the junior members of the bar

In the year 1883 Clearfield county by virtue of having acquired the necessary population of over 40,000, was in obedience to the Constitution created a separate judicial district, and became entitled to elect its own president judge The first judge to be so elected was Hon David L Krebs, who was the Democratic candidate for the office at the November election of 1883, but was supported by many Republicans who believed that the judicial office should be non-partisan Judge Krebs served a full term of ten years and was a candidate for re-election, but was defeated by Hon Cyrus Gordon, Republican, after a spirited canvass

David Luther Krebs was born in Ferguson township, Centre Co, Pa, on Oct 5th, 1846 In the fall of 1864 he came to Clearfield county and taught school while preparing for the bar with the late Hon William A Wallace About this time his elder brother was drafted to serve in the war of the Rebellion and David offered to take his place, which he did and served in the 98th Pa Vols until mustered out in 1865 In 1867 he returned to Centre County and read law with the late Adam Hoy and was admitted to the Centre County bar in 1869 and in June of the same year located in Clearfield, Pa Upon the appointment by President Grant of the late Hon. H Bucher Swoope as United States Attorney, in 1870, Judge Krebs in connection with John P. Irvin succeeded to his practice In 1873 Judge Krebs became a partner with Hon W. A. Wallace, which partnership continued up to the time of his election to the bench Since the expiration of his judicial term Judge Krebs has been engaged in the practice of law at Clearfield and enjoys a large and lucrative practice and is recognized as one of the leading lawyers of the county

Hon Cyrus Gordon, who succeeded Judge Krebs in January, 1894, served also a full term of ten years and was also a candidate for re-election, but was defeated by the present incumbent of the office, Hon Allison O Smith, after what was probably the most bitter political contest the county has ever known

Judge Gordon was born December 1, 1846, near Hecla Furnace, Centre County, Pa He was educated at Pennsylvania State College in 1866, studied law at the law school of the Michigan University, and in 1869 was admitted to the bar of Centre County, Pa In 1870 he removed to Clearfield and began the practice of law In 1874 he became a partner of Hon Thomas H Murray and this connection continued until Judge Gordon's election to the bench Since 1894 Judge Gordon has been engaged in the practice of law at Clearfield.

and also holds the position of general counsel to the Pure Food Department of Pennsylvania

Hon Allison O Smith, who succeeded Judge Gordon and who is the present presiding judge of the county, assumed the duties of the office in January, 1894 Judge Smith was born October 23rd, 1857, in Montour County, Pa, was educated at the University of Pennsylvania and was admitted to the bar of Philadelphia in June, 1882, and located in Clearfield in September of that year After Judge Gordon was elected to the bench, Judge Smith became a partner of Hon T H Murray and was practicing law in connection with him when elected judge

CHAPTER XII

THE BAR OF CLEARFIELD COUNTY—FORMER MEMBERS

Character of the Clearfield County Bar—First Court—First Resident Member of the Bar— Sketches of the Leading Members of the Bar in Former Days

The Bar of Clearfield County ranks high among similar bodies of the legal profession throughout the state. Many of its members have achieved place and fame by their ability and while it may be that occasionally one failed to realize the dignity and high standard of honor required of those who would acquire the true laurels of a real lawyer, yet such members were fortunately the exceptions and the general tone of the lawyers of the county has always been up to the mark of character and integrity called for by the ethics of the profession

Clearfield county was not organized for judicial purposes until 1822 and the first Court in the county was held in October of that year The first resident of the bar was Josiah W Smith Mr Smith was born in Philadelphia, but when only about 18 years of age came with his brother Lewis to this county and they settled on a farm about two miles below Curwensville, since known as the Benjamin Spackman farm He read law with Judge Thomas Burnside of Bellefonte and was admitted to practice in December, 1826, and at the same time was appointed deputy attorney general for Clearfield county, which office was equivalent to that of district attorney Mr Smith con-

tinued to practice until 1856 when he removed to Philadelphia and resided there until 1862 when he returned to Clearfield and resided there until his death March 22, 1882, at the age of 81 While not distinguished as a trial lawyer Josiah Smith was deeply read in the law and much given to mediation between litigants He was a man of pure character and an upright and respected citizen

Lewis Smith, the brother of Josiah Smith to whom reference has already been made, read law with Josiah and was admitted to practice about 1830 He was a trial lawyer of considerable ability. Mr Smith was engaged in nearly all the cases brought in the courts of the county during his practice, and was generally successful He died in 1847

Joseph M Martin located in Clearfield about 1830 and practiced law until the time of his death, which occurred in 1835 He was a lawyer of ability, but owing to the few years that he was at our bar not much data can be secured regarding him

William Christie located in Curwensville about 1826 He was a man of unusual promise and force, but although he had a fine practice and was very popular, he indulged in ex-

184

cesses which soon ended his career by an untimely death

James B Marr located in Clearfield about 1839, after having read law with James F Linn Esq of Lewisburg, Pa, and being admitted to the bar of Union County He practiced law for several years and was considered as fairly successful He died a few years after coming here, but the exact date of his death has not been ascertained

Daniel G Fenton was admitted to the bar about 1830 He came here from New Jersey and practiced with indifferent success until 1836, when having become involved in financial difficulties, he sold his property and moved to Iowa, after which no further data about him has been obtained

Elmer S Dundy read law in Clearfield and was admitted to the bar here, but shortly afterwards removed to Falls City, Nebraska, where he became judge of the United States Court It is believed that Judge Dundy never practiced law here

Lewis J Crans came from Philadelphia and located at Curwensville He read law with Joseph S Frantz and was admitted to practice here He had a large practice and was quite successful as a lawyer, but after about seven years from his admission to the bar he removed to Philadelphia and from there to Concordia, Kansas

Isaac G Gordon came from Union County where he read law with James F Linn Esq. of Lewisburg, and was admitted to practice in 1843 He first located at Curwensville and subsequently formed a partnership with George R. Barrett, which continued for about three years, when he removed to Brookville, Pa He became a Judge of the Supreme Court of the state and served a full term He died at Brookville a few years ago

James Harvey Larrimer was born in Centre County, Pa, read law with Judge James Burnside and was admitted to the bar of Centre Co about 1853 In 1854 he located in Clearfield and practiced law until 1858, when he became one of the editors and proprietors of the Clearfield Republican, his partner in the enterprise being R F Ward, Jr In 1860 Mr Larrimer retired from the partnership and resumed the practice of the law When the war of the Rebellion broke out he enlisted as a private but was made first lieutenant of Captain Loraine's Company of the Fifth Pa Reserves Subsequently he was promoted to Captain and then to Major and appointed aide on the staff of General Samuel W Crawford Major Larrimer was killed in a skirmish with guerillas near Collett's Station, Va, February 14, 1863 Larrimer Post G A R of Clearfield was named in his honor

Joseph S Frantz came to Clearfield about 1850 from Kittanning, Armstrong Co, Pa. where he had been admitted to the bar He remained in Clearfield about four years and then removed to the west, and was lost track of by his Clearfield friends

George Rodden Barrett was born in Curwensville on the 31st day of March, in the year 1815 In the year 1831 he was apprenticed to Governor John Bigler, to learn the printer's trade In 1833 he became editor of the "Brookville Jeffersonian," published at Brookville, Jefferson county, which he continued for two years He moved to Lewisburg in 1835 and edited the "Lewisburg Democrat" While there he read law with James F Linn, and was admitted to practice in 1836, and in the same year came to Clearfield The next year, 1837, he was made deputy attorney-gentral for Clearfield and Jefferson counties Mr Barrett was elected to the State Legislature in

1840, and re-elected the succeeding year He served as a member of the judiciary committee when the law abolishing imprisonment for debt was passed In 1852 he was chosen as one of the presidential electors On account of his recognized legal ability he was selected by President Pierce for the purpose of codifying the revenue laws He was appointed president judge of the Twenty-second Judicial District, comprising the counties of Wayne, Pike, Monroe and Carbon, in the year 1853 At the general election in the district in 1855, he was elected to the same position and re-elected in 1865 He resigned in 1869, but was appointed to the same office by Governor Geary, and served one year In 1872 Barrett returned to Clearfield and resumed the practice of the law, which practice he continued up to 1884, at which time he retired from the active duties of the profession, content to rest upon the well earned honors of nearly half a century He died, March 9th, 1889

Robert Wallace was a native of Ireland, having been born in Barony Omagh, County Tyrone, March 13, 1792 In the year 1819 he emigrated to America and settled in Mifflin County, Pa , where he taught school He read law with E Banks Esq of Lewistown, Pa and was admitted to the bar in 1824 After practicing a short time in Huntingdon, Pa he came to Clearfield where he remained about one year and then again located in Huntingdon, but made regular trips to Clearfield to attend to the trial of cases In 1836 he removed from Huntingdon to Clearfield where he remained until 1847, when he moved to Hollidaysburgh, Pa In 1854 he again located in Clearfield He died at Wallaceton, Pa , January 2, 1875

Thomas J McCullough was born in Pitts-

burgh, Pa , July 10, 1828 His father was a Methodist minister and in the year 1840 Thomas came with the family to New Washington He read law with Hon G. R. Barrett and was admitted to the bar about 1855. In 1868 and '69 he represented the county in the Legislature and after his services in that capacity he engaged in the oil business Later he opened a law office in Philipsburg, Pa , still residing, however, in Clearfield He died at Philipsburg, Dec 27, 1885

William A Wallace was born in Huntingdon, Pa Nov 27, 1827. He came to Clearfield with his father, Robert Wallace, in 1836 He read law with his father and was admitted to the bar of Clearfield County in September, 1847 In 1862 he was elected to the State Senate and re-elected in 1865, '68, '71 and '74, serving fifteen consecutive years In 1871 he was elected Speaker of the Senate In 1865 he was chairman of the Democratic State Committee and was re-elected in 1866, '67 and '68 and was again chosen in 1871 In 1875 he was chosen by the Legislature as a United States senator from Pennsylvania He was for many years a power in the Democratic party, state and national Mr Wallace was a fine lawyer and until he gave up active practice to engage in politics and the development of the coal interests of Clearfield county, he was one of the leaders of the bar and was recognized as an opponent worthy of battle by those who contested with him in the Courts He died in 1896   .

Joseph Benson McEnally was born January 25th, 1825 and admitted to the bar in 1849 (See sketch of his life in preceding chapter).

John F Weaver was admitted to the bar in 1844 after having read law with James .Burnside of Bellefonte, Pa   He came to Clearfield

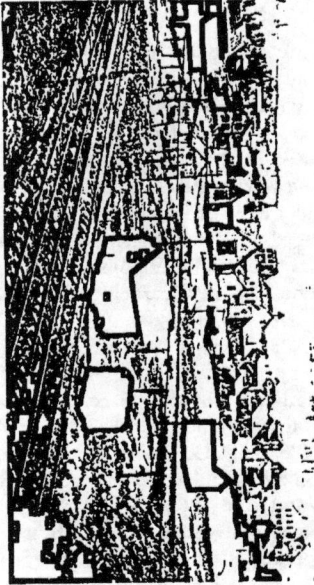

View of Glen Richey

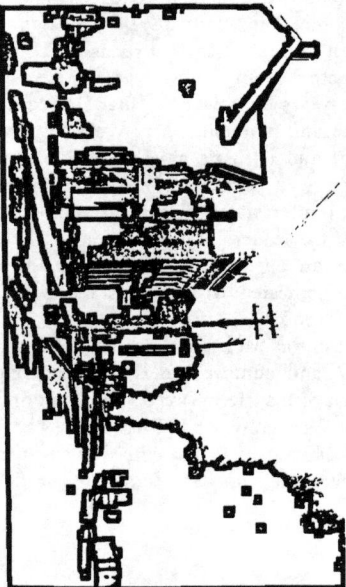

State Street, Looking West from Filbert Street, Curwensville

PIONEERS OF CLEARFIELD COUNTY

in 1845 In 1848 he was made deputy attorney general for the county and served three years, after which he became interested in the lumber business, which absorbed so much of his time that he gave up the practice of the law and devoted himself to business pursuits until his death

J Biddle Gordon was born in Reading, Pa , being a son of Judge Gordon of that city He located in Clearfield in 1853 and practiced law here for a number of years He became involved by reason of his carelessness in business matters and being unable to settle his financial affairs, committed suicide

Henry Bucher Swoope was born in Huntingdon, Pa , in the year 1831 and was a son of the eminent physician, Doctor William Swoope, of that place He was educated at the Academia Academy, read law with the late Hon John Scott of Huntingdon and was admitted to the bar at Huntingdon in 1852 He came to Clearfield in 1853, where he resided and practiced law until 1869, when President Grant appointed him U S district attorney for the district of Western Pennsylvania, when he removed to Pittsburgh He was reappointed by President Grant in 1874, and served until his death in February, 1874 H Bucher Swoope was one of the leading lawyers of Pennsylvania and as an advocate had few equals He was also prominent in politics, having been chairman of the American party when that organization captured the state government and elected Pollock Governor He was after the formation of the Republican party an active leader therein, a strong supporter of President Lincoln and the war to preserve the Union, organizing and commanding a company of soldiers to assist in repelling the rebel invasion of Pennsylvania, and using his voice, pen and

means at all times for the benefit of the Government Mr Swoope was the founder and first editor of the Clearfield "Raftsman's Journal," which under his able editorship assumed an important place in the newspaper field He was also the founder and editor in chief of the "Pittsburgh Evening Telegraph, ' (now the "Chronicle Telegraph") As a prosecuting officer he became celebrated during his incumbency of the office of U S Attorney and his name was a terror to evil doers, as the acquittal of a defendant in a trial in which Mr Swoope represented the Government was an almost unheard of event Yet he was ever willing to aid the repentant criminal and use his influence and efforts to secure him a new chance in life As a political orator he became famous and was one of the most eloquent and brilliant speakers of his time He was also fond of literary pursuits and delivered many lectures and addresses upon such topics

John H Fulford was born in Bedford, Pa , Feby 11, 1838, read law with Frank Gordon Esq of that place and with J B McEnally of Clearfield He was admitted to practice at Clearfield about 1860 While reading law he also taught school He was an active and stanch Republican and took an active part in party affairs He died at Clearfield, June 27, 1877

John Lever Cuttle was born in Lancashire, England, June 22, 1809 He came to America in the year 1823 and located in Clearfield in 1839 He was a machinist and read law in his spare time, with Hon G R Barrett In 1853 he was admitted to practice In 1859 he was elected prothonotary and served one term In 1882 he was elected one of the associate judges of the county and served one term Prior to his admission to the bar, Mr Cuttle served as a justice of the peace and as county surveyor He died at Clearfield a number of years ago

Robert J Wallace, a brother of William A Wallace, was born in Clearfield and read law with his brother He was admitted to practice and served as district attorney of the county He died about 1857

James Hepburn was born in Philadelphia and came to Clearfield in 1822, where he was admitted to the bar and practiced law until his death

James Petrikin was one of the older lawyers but no data is obtainable in regard to him

Samuel M Green came to Clearfield from Centre county in October, 1822, and was admitted to the bar on that date He was appointed deputy attorney-general for the county and remained here a number of years Subsequent to his removal from this county he lived in Bellefonte, Pa, but went west and was lost trace of by his former associates

Frederick O'Leary Buck was born in England Mr Buck practiced law in Clearfield a short time in connection with William McCullough He went west and died a year or two ago

Joseph F McKenrick was born in Adams County, Pa, May 9, 1845 He came to Clearfield in 1865, read law with Hon William A Wallace and was admitted to practice June 24, 1878 In 1879 he was elected district attorney and was re-elected in 1882 Some years ago he removed to Ebensburg, Pa, where he now resides

Israel Test was born in Philipsburg, Centre county, Pa, September 28, 1831 He attended Dickinson Seminary at Williamsport, Pa, studied law with J M Carlisle Esq of Chambersburg, Pa, and was admitted to the bar of Franklin County in June, 1856 He located in Clearfield in 1858 Mr Test was possessed of the peculiar faculty of laughing a case out of court and this sense of humor soon gained him the title of the wag of the bar Although a man of considerale natural ability, he seldom practiced in the civil cases but delighted in the trial of criminal cases, where his ready wit stood him in good stead Father Test was very popular with the people and with the members of the bar He died at Clearfield, Pa., August 12, 1886

William M McCullough, a brother of Thomas J McCullough, was born in Beaver County, Pa, October 1, 1837, and came to Clearfield county in 1840 At an early age he entered the office of Hon H B Swoope, who instructed him in the necessary elements of education as well as in the law. He was admitted to the bar in 1859 was twice chosen district attorney of the county and as a criminal lawyer he stood high Mr. McCullough died at Thomasville, Ga, January 26, 1884

Walter Barrett was born in Clearfield, August 2, 1839, and was educated at the public schools and the University of Pennsylvania In the year 1853 he was appointed a midshipman in the U S Navy He read law with his father, Hon G R Barrett, and was admitted to the bar in 1859 At the breaking out of the war of the Rebellion, Mr Barrett was appointed major of the Eighty-fourth Pennsylvania Volunteers and commanded the regiment after the death of Colonel William G Murray at the battle of

Winchester At the battle of Fort Republic he was made Lieutenant Colonel At Cloud's Mills Colonel Barrett was injured by his horse falling on him at the time of the giving way of a bridge He then resigned from the army and in 1862 he returned home and resumed the practice of law in partnership with his father Colonel Barrett died at Clearfield, Pa, in 1906

William D Bigler was born in Clearfield, Pa, September 17, 1841 He was educated at the West Jersey Academy at Bridgton, N J, and at Princeton College He read law with William A Wallace and was admitted to the bar in 1866 and afterwards entered into partnership with Mr Wallace and Frank Fielding under the firm name of Wallace, Bigler and Fielding, and afterwards was a member of the firm of Fielding, Bigler and Wilson In later years Mr Bigler gave up the active practice of the law and devoted himself to business interests He died at Clearfield, Pa, April 9, 1907

Daniel W McCurdy was born in Charleston township, Chester county, Pa, August 30, 1841 He was educated at Freeland Seminary, Montgomery county, Pa, and at Dickinson College from which latter institution he was graduated in 1862 He then taught school in Luzerne County about two years, when he came to Clearfield and taught in the old Academy for several years In 1865 he entered the office of J B McEnally as a law student He was admitted to the bar in 1868 and in 1872 entered into partnership with Judge McEnally Mr McCurdy died on the 14th of February, 1903

Alonzo A Adams was born in Boggs township, Clearfield county, Pa, December 3, 1847 He read law with Hon H Bucher Swoope and was admitted to the bar in June, 1869 Mr Adams died about 1879

William C Arnold was born in Luthersburg, Clearfield county, Pa, July 15, 1851 He was educated at Millersville State Normale School and at Phillips Academy at Andover, Mass He read law with Hon J B McEnally and was admitted to the bar in May, 1878 He located at Curwensville In 1896 he was the Republican candidate for Congress in the 28th District and was elected and was re-elected for the following term He also served his party as Chairman of the Republican County Committee for several years About the year 1892 Mr Arnold located in DuBois where he resided and practiced law until his death, which occurred in 1906 W C Arnold was a lawyer of ability, and stood well in his profession He was a man of fine presence and agreeable personality As a public speaker he was at his best on the political platform and took an active part in the various campaigns from 1878 to the time of his death

Alonzo P MacLeod was born in Clearfield May 29, 1861 He attended the Lehigh University at Bethlehem, Pa, and the Columbia Law School at New York Mr MacLeod read law with Walter Barrett and was admitted to the bar in May, 1884 He first practiced at Coalport, Pa, and afterwards removed to Altoona, Pa, where he died about 1907

Alfred A Graham was born at Clearfield, February 3, 1845 He read law with William A Wallace and after his admission to practice formed a partnership with William M McCullough A few years prior to his death he removed to DuBois where he died on the 23rd of February, 1880

William Irvin Shaw was born at Clearfield March 20, 1860, was educated at the public schools and at Yale University, read law with Murray & Gordon and was admitted to the bar in June, 1882 After his admission to practice Mr Shaw located at Houtzdale and remained there until his appointment as United States Consul at Barranquilla, South America Mr. Shaw was an active Republican and served as County Chairman for a number of years He died in December, 1900

Joseph W Parker was a native of Mifflin county, Pa, and was admitted to the bar of that county About 1882 he came to Clearfield and practiced law here for a few years, but was more interested in politics After his return to Mifflin county he resumed practice in that county and died there a few years ago

George D. Hamor was born in Freeport, Armstrong county, Pa, June 21, 1855 He was admitted to the bar of Butler county in 1876 and practiced there until 1880 when he came to this county, locating in DuBois He was admitted to the Clearfield county bar in March, 1880 Mr Hamor remained in the county a few years and then moved to New Kensington, Pa

Truman Ames was born in Antioch, Lake county, Ill, June 25, 1851 He read law with Hall & Ames of St Mary's, Elk county, Pa, and with H T Ames Esq of Williamsport, Pa, and was admitted to the bar of Lycoming county in May, 1880, and located in DuBois in February, 1881

George W Easton was born in Clinton county, Pa, May 16, 1860 He read law with Wallace & Krebs and was admitted to the bar in June, 1883 Mr Easton left Clearfield county shortly after his admission to practice

CHAPTER XIII

CLEARFIELD COUNTY BAR—PRESENT MEMBERS

Brief Biographical Notices of the Present Members of the Clearfield County Bar

Frank Fielding was born at Slippery Rock, Butler county, Pa He was educated at Saint Francis College, at Loretto, Pa, and at Saint Vincent's at Latrobe, Pa but was not a graduate from either He received further instruction from Rev W T Hamilton, of Mobile, Ala, while the reverend professor was in the Northern States Mr Fielding studied law with Hon Wm P Hill, at Marshall, Texas, continued his course with John N Thompson, of Butler, Pa, and finished in the office of Hon James Bredin, of Butler, now of Pittsburg, Pa In 1864, Mr Fielding came to Clearfield to practice He became a member of the law firm of Wallace, Bigler & Fielding The firm was afterward changed to Wallace & Fielding, and still later to Fielding, Bigler & Wilson Of late years, however, Mr Fielding has practiced without a partner He was elected to the office of District Attorney and served one term

Thomas Holt Murray was born in Girard township, Clearfield county, on the 5th day of April, 1845 His early education was somewhat limited, being confined to such branches as were taught at the "country schools" In 1862 he entered Dickinson Seminary at Williamsport, but was soon afterward compelled to leave on account of a severe illness From this time until 1864 he remained at home, teaching school and working on the farm, when he returned to the seminary During his course of study at the college Mr Murray read law under the direction of Robert Fleming, Esq He graduated in 1867 In the month of May, 1868, he entered the office of H B Swoope, Esq, at Clearfield, where he completed his course, and was admitted to the bar in May, 1869 The firm of Murray & O'Laughlin of which Thomas H Murray is a member, was formed a few years ago

David S Herron was born in Center township, Indiana county, Pa, April 24, 1844 He received an academic education, and afterward entered the Ohio University, at Athens, O, from which he graduated with the class of 1866, read law with Hugh W Weir, Esq, at Indiana, for two years, and was admitted to practice at the Indiana county bar in June, 1868 He then located in Clarion county and practiced until 1876, at which time he embarked in the mercantile and oil business In 1883 he came to DuBois, Clearfield county, and resumed the practice of his profession In 1874 Mr Herron was admitted to practice in the Su-

193

preme Court of Pennsylvania, and in the year following was admitted to practice in the District and Circuit Courts of the United States Since 1874 Mr Herron has held the office of United States Commissioner for the Western District of Pennsylvania

David Luther Krebs, born October 5, 1846 (See ante, Bench of the county)

Hurxthal W Smith was born in Clearfield county and was a son of Josiah W Smith, one of the pioneer lawyers of the county H W Smith read law in the office of Hon William A Wallace, and was admitted to the bar in 1869

Cyrus Gordon was born December 1, 1846, near Hecla Furnace, Centre County, Pa (See Ante Bench of the County)

Aaron G Kramer was born in Centre county, August 10, 1844 He came to Clearfield in the spring of 1866, and entered the office of Israel Test, Esq, as a student at law, was admitted to the bar of Clearfield county in September, 1871, and has since practiced in the county In the fall of 1886, Mr Kramer was elected member of Assembly to represent Clearfield county

Harry Frank Wallace was born August 8, 1852, in Clearfield borough He was educated at Lawrenceville, N J, entering school there in 1867 and graduated in 1869, entered Princeton College in 1869 and graduated with the class of '73 He then returned home and read law in the office of Wallace & Krebs until 1875, then entered Harvard Law School and attended lectures one year, was admitted to the Clearfield bar in 1876 Mr Wallace then a member of the firm of Wallace & Krebs, and so continued until the election of Mr Krebs to the office

of president judge The firm then became Wallace Bros, Harry F and William E Wallace constituting the firm

William E Wallace was born in Clearfield, February 24, 1855 After attending the common schools at Clearfield he entered Lawrenceville High School, from which he graduated in 1873, attended Harvard Law School two years, read law with Wallace & Krebs three years, and was admitted to the bar in June, 1876 Mr Wallace is now one of the members of the law firm of Wallace Bros, successors to Wallace & Krebs

Oscar Mitchell is a native of Lawrence township, born February 28, 1849 He was educated at the State Normal School at Millersville, Lancaster county, Pa, but did not graduate from there In 1874 he commenced the study of law with Frank Fielding, Esq, and was admitted to the Clearfield bar in June, 1876

Smith Van Valzah Wilson was born in Clearfield, November 21, 1853 He attended the Clearfield school and afterwards took a two years' preparatory course at Lawrenceville High School From there he returned home and read law with Hon William A Wallace nearly a year, when he concluded to attend college In the fall of 1871 he entered Lehigh University for the regular classical course, and graduated in 1874 Mr Wilson then resumed his law studies with Senator Wallace, and was admitted to the bar in March, 1877 Smith V Wilson was elected district attorney in November, 1885, and served one term

Frank Graham Harris was born in Karthaus township, this county, November 6, 1845 In the month of September, 1876, he commenced the study of law in the office of Murray & Gordon, Esqs, and continued until 1879, when on June 14th of that year he was admitted to the Clearfield bar. He was elected Representative in the State Legislature and served two terms. He was elected State Treasurer on the Republican ticket in 1901 and served one term.

William H Patterson was born near Warrior's Mark, Huntingdon county, Pa, November 14, 1851, read law with H M Baldridge, Esq, of Hollidaysburg Blair county, and was admitted to the bar in April, 1878. Mr Patterson came to Houtzdale, Clearfield county, in May, 1878, and has since practiced law at that place. Also at Clearfield and DuBois in connection with James Gleason, under the firm name of Patterson & Gleason.

Roland D Swoope, eldest son of Hon H Bucher Swoope, was born in Curwensville, Pa, August 26, 1856. He was educated at the Clearfield Academy, Hill School, Pottstown, Pa, Phillips Academy, at Andover, Mass, and at the Western University, Pittsburg, Pa, read law in the office of Murray & Gordon, Esqs, at Clearfield, and was admitted to the bar September, 1878. Mr Swoope was chairman of the Republican County Committee for a number of years.

William A Chase was born in Knox township, Clearfield county, July 24, 1847, was educated at the University of Michigan, at Ann Arbor, and graduated with the class of 1877, and admitted to practice in the Supreme Court of Michigan in March, 1877. Mr. Chase was admitted to the bar of Clearfield county in 1879, and commenced practice at Houtzdale, where he re-

mained till 1886. He then moved to Jeffries, this county, and later to Clearfield.

John Franklin Snyder was born in Clearfield borough, June 23, 1855. He was educated at the common schools and at the Leonard Graded School of Clearfield, and when not at school worked with his father, Henry E Snyder, in a blacksmith shop. In 1876 he graduated from school and then resumed his place in the shop. He entered the law office of Hon Augustus Landis, at Hollidaysburg, Blair county, and studied law until 1878, when he was admitted to the bar. Mr Snyder practiced alone until January 1, 1884, when he associated with Hon John H. Orvis, and established an office at Clearfield under the firm name and style of Orvis & Snyder. After the death of Judge Orvis, Mr Snyder removed to New York City where he now resides.

William Alexander Hagerty was born in Glen Hope, this county, January 22, 1857. He attended the Free School at Lumber City, the academy and Leonard Graded School at Clearfield, and the Pennsylvania College at Gettysburg, Pa. He read law in the office of McEnally & McCurdy, and, after a course of study for three years was admitted to the bar in 1879.

Arthur LeRoy Cole was born in Potter county, Pa, December 24, 1857, read law with Olmsted & Larrabee, Esqs, at Coudersport, Potter county, and was admitted to the bar in June, 1881. Mr Cole located at DuBois in October, 1881.

Allison O Smith, born October 23, 1857, in Montour county, Pa. (See Ante Bench of Clearfield county.)

W. Clarence Pentz was born in Brady township, Clearfield county, May 9, 1858,

13

read law with Frank Fielding, Esq, of Clearfield, and was admitted to the bar in September, 1882 Mr Pentz began practice at DuBois, August 15, 1883.

Martin Luther McQuown was born in Indiana county, January 18, 1852, read law in the office of Murray & Gordon, Esqs, of Clearfield, and was admitted to the bar in June, 1883 Mr McQuown was elected county superintendent in 1878, and re-elected in 1881 He was chosen chairman of the Republican County Committee in 1886, and is now editor of the Raftsman's Journal of Clearfield, Pa, and was elected State Senator in 1895 and served four years

James Horton Kelley was born in Bell township, Clearfield county, October 4, 1852 He attended the Dayton Union Academy in Armstrong county, and the Tuscarora Academy in Juniata county, read law in the office of Wallace & Fielding, and afterward with Frank Fielding Esq, and was admitted to the bar in January, 1884 Mr Kelley is the present District Attorney of the County

Singleton Bell, a grandson of the first white male child born in the county, was born in Ferguson township, February 12, 1862, read law in the office of Wallace & Krebs, and was admitted to the bar in January, 1884 Mr Bell is senior member of the firm of Bell & Hartswick

Americus Hodge Woodward, born in Luzerne county, Pa, May 1, 1859, graduated from the State Normal School at Millersburg in July, 1878, entered the University of Michigan in 1881, and graduated in 1882, read law in 1882 in the office of McEnally & McCurdy, and was admitted to the bar in June, 1883 Mr Woodward served two terms as District Attorney

George W Zeigler, was born at Marklesburg, Huntingdon county, Pa, August 23, 1861, read law with George B Orlady, Esq, and B G Zeigler, Esq, and was admitted to the bar of Huntingdon county April, 1883 In 1884 he was admitted to the Clearfield bar After three months at Clearfield he removed to Houtzdale, where he practiced a number of years He is at present located at Philipsburg, Pa

George M Bilger was born at Curwensville, Clearfield county, September 15, 1861, was entered as a law student with William C Arnold, Esq, of Curwensville, in 1883, while attending Dickinson College, Carlisle, Pa, and was admitted to the bar of the county March 22, 1886

William I Swoope was born in Clearfield in 1862 educated at Phillips Academy, Andover, Mass, and at Harvard University, Cambridge, Mass He read law in the office of Roland D Swoope, Esq, and was admitted to the bar at Clearfield in December, 1886 He was twice elected District Attorney of the County

Alexander Patterson was born in Airdire, Scotland, December 19, 1857; came to this country in 1874, entered the office of McEnally & McCurdy in 1884, and was admitted to practice in 1887

Howard B Hartswick was born at Clearfield, Pa, on the 14th day of August, 1865 He read law with Murray & Gordon and was admitted to the bar of Clearfield county September 5, 1887 He is a member of the firm of Bell & Hartswick

William Clark Miller was born in Centre county on September 28th, 1864, was educated at the common schools of Unionville, Centre county, and the Lock Haven State Normal School Read law with McEnally & McCurdy and was admitted to the bar January 14, 1889 Mr Miller served as County solicitor for seven years and is at present Referee in Bankruptcy

George M Fulford was born at Clearfield, Pa, on the 2d day of January, 1870, and was admitted to the bar May 25th, 1891

Benjamin F Chase was born in Woodward township, Clearfield county, February 1, 1869 He was educated at the public schools, Clearfield High School and at the Law School of Michigan University, and was admitted to the bar of Clearfield county September 28, 1891.

George R Bigler was born at Clearfield, Pa He was educated at the public schools, read law with his father, W D Bigler, and was admitted to the bar of Clearfield county, May 24, 1893

Frederick G Betts was born at Clearfield, Pa He was educated at the public schools and at Princeton, and was admitted to the bar of Clearfield county August 27, 1892

Alfred M Liveright was born at Philadelphia, Pa He was admitted to the bar of Clearfield county November 8, 1894 Mr Liveright is at present County Solicitor and a member of the firm of Krebs & Liveright

Harry Byers was born in Bell township on February 21, 1865 He was educated at the public schools and was admitted to the bar of Clearfield county December 8, 1896

John M Urey was born August 27, 1870, in Banks township, Indiana county, Pa He graduated from the State Normal School at Indiana, Pa, in the class of 1891, and was valedictorian of his class He was admitted to the bar of Clearfield county September 7, 1896 1896

Hazard A Murray was born at Clearfield, Pa He was admitted to the bar of Clearfield county on September 5, 1899, and is a member of the firm of Murray & O'Laughlin

James P O'Laughlin was born at Renovo, Pa He was admitted to the bar of Clearfield county on September 20, 1900, and is a member of the firm of Murray & O'Laughlin

Leno W Edwards was born at Smith's Mills, Clearfield county, Pa, and was admitted to the bar of Clearfield county on July 1, 1901.

John W McCracken was born in Ferguson township, Clearfield county, Pa, September 17, 1873 He was educated in the public schools, at Bucknell University from which institution he graduated with the class of 1902, received the Degree of Bachelor of Arts He took a post graduate course and received the Degree of Master of Arts in 1903 After graduation he was a teacher in the University Law Department He read law with E F. Bower, Esq, at Lewisburg, Pa, and was admitted to the bar of Clearfield county on the 14th day of November, 1904

J K Horton was admitted to the bar November 28, 1904, practiced a short time at Clearfield, Pa, and is now located at Philipsburg, Pa

Walter Welch was born at Plymouth, Pa, March 7, 1875 He read law with Murray & O'Laughlin and was admitted to the bar of Clearfield county, April 5, 1907

John C Forsyth was born at Houtzdale, Pa, May 31, 1885 He was educated in the public schools and at Dickinson Law School and was admitted to the bar of Clearfield county, September, 1909 He is at present Republican County chairman

A R Chase was born in Boggs township, Clearfield county, April 2, 1883 He was educated in the common schools and at Dickinson

Law School   He was admitted to the bar of Clearfield county September 14, 1909

Harry Boulton was born in West Hartle Pool, England, October 2, 1872   He was educated at the public schools and was admitted to the bar of Clearfield county September 6, 1894   Mr Boulton served two terms in the Legislature as one of the Representatives of Clearfield county, also as Chairman of the Republican County Committee for several years Mr Boulton resides at Houtzdale, Pa , and is a member of the firm of Gordon & Boulton

John B McGrath was admitted to the bar of Clearfield county on December 4, 1899   Mr McGrath resides at Houtzdale, Pa

Frank Hutton was born in Burnside township, Clearfield county, December 26, 1862 He was admitted to the bar of Clearfield county on February 2, 1891   Mr Hutton resides in DuBois, Pa

George A Lukehart was born in Indiana county, Pa   He was admitted to the bar of Clearfield county in 1890   Mr. Lukehart resides in DuBois, Pa

Herbert A Moore was born at Luthersburg, Pa   He was admitted to the bar of Clearfield county February 23, 1891   Mr Moore resides in DuBois, Pa

Fred R Scofield was born in Huston township, Clearfield county   He was admitted to the bar of Clearfield county on September 3, 1894   Mr Scofield resides at DuBois, Pa. Mr Scofield served two terms in the State Legislature

Louis E Boyer was born at DuBois, Pa. He was admitted to the bar of Clearfield county November 6, 1899   Mr. Boyer resides at DuBois, Pa

W L Calkins was admitted to the bar of Clearfield county September 27, 1904   Mr Calkins resides at DuBois, Pa , and is a member of the firm of Pentz & Calkins

James A Gleason was born at Houtzdale, Pa   He was admitted to the bar of Clearfield county on September 6, 1897 Mr Gleason resides at DuBois, Pa , and is a member of the firm of Patterson & Gleason

Earl G Boose was born in Union township, Clearfield county, March 10, 1878   He was educated in the public schools, and read law with D S Herron and S V Wilson, Esqs ; was admitted to the bar of Clearfield county, February 5, 1908   Mr Boose practices at DuBois, Pa

CHAPTER XIV

THE MEDICAL PROFESSION

Early Physicians of the County—Registration Law of 1881—Alphabetical List of Physicians who have Registered in the County from 1881 to the Present Time, with Biographical Mention

A great deal of mention and romance enshrouds the name of the first physician of Clearfield County, so that it is impossible to obtain any facts concerning his life

This much is known, that Dr Samuel Colman came to this county from Williamsport in 1808, and cleared a farm near that of his friend, Joseph Boone, in what is now Penn Township He did not practice medicine regularly, only giving his services when they were greatly needed

Dr Colman named his farm "Grampian Hills," because of the resemblance his land bore to the far-famed Grampian Hills of Scotland This name has since become associated with that entire neighborhood and the thriving terminus of the Tyrone and Clearfield Railroad is now called Grampian

Although Dr Colman never mentioned his early life, it was generally supposed that he was the son of an English nobleman His superior education and apparent means were the only grounds for this supposition

Dr Colman died in 1819, at the early age of forty He never married and his name and secret died with him

In 1819, Dr John P Hoyt, a native of Troy, N Y, came to Curwensville Five years later a terrible epidemic of dysentery broke out in the county, and Dr Alexander McLeod, of Philipsburg, came to the aid of Dr Hoyt Together these two physicians struggled against the terrible disease, which was wiping out whole families and prostrating hundreds During the time the epidemic raged Dr Hoyt and Dr McLeod were in their saddles night and day travelling over the entire county to give what relief they could

Dr Hoyt died March 1, 1885 In 1843 Dr McLeod resigned from his profession and entered the ministry of the Protestant Episcopal Church He died at Meadville, Pa in 1877

Dr A T Schryver, a native of Oswego county, N Y, was the next physician to come into the county He came to Clearfield in 1826, but did not practice medicine until 1830 He was elected superintendent of the common schools at the first election for that position held in the county Dr Schryver also practiced medicine at Glen Hope

Dr Henry Lorain located as a physician

199

in Philipsburg in 1825 He did not confine his practice to that neighborhood, driving into this county very often In 1835 he came to Clearfield, where he lived until the time of his death, March 3, 1859 Dr Lorain possessed unusual opportunities for the study of his profession and used them to the best advantage He was quick to decide and act and let nothing interfere with the pursuance of his practice

Dr Lewis Iddings came to Curwensville in 1827, but moved away after a few years

Dr Perdue located at Clearfield in 1834, but remained there only a few years

Dr Henry Houty practiced in Curwensville and Clearfield for a short time between 1837-47

Dr Matthew Woods, a native of Penn's Valley, came to Curwensville in 1844 Twelve years later he moved to Clearfield, where he practiced ten years In 1866 he went to Mercer, Pa, where he remained until his death, December 16, 1868

Dr William P. Hills, a native of Prattsburg, practiced medicine in Clearfield from 1846 to 1852, then went West, where he died June, 1885

Dr John C Richards located in Curwensville in 1846, where he practiced five years Later he practiced in Bloomington, Glen Hope and Philipsburg

Dr James Irvin, a native of Centre county, practiced medicine in Curwensville in 1847-8

Dr R V Wilson, a native of Centre county, came to Curwensville in 1850 Soon after he moved to Clearfield where he lived the rest of his life He was very well known as an intelligent and successful physician, and was often called in consul-

tation with eminent doctors He died February 13, 1878

Dr Thomas R Blandy, a native of Delaware, began to practice medicine in Osceola about 1851 He practiced throughout that region until 1881, when he moved to Huntingdon, Pa. He died at that place April 21, 1885 Dr Blandy was held in the highest esteem by all who knew him

Dr Hardman Thompson, a native of Clearfield, came to Curwensville in 1851, here he had a large practice and became a prominent citizen He died September 19, 1866

Dr G. W Caldwell began the practice of medicine at Beccaria Mills in 1851 He afterwards moved to Glen Hope, where he died October 5, 1885 Dr Caldwell's practice extended over a very large area, and he is well remembered in that part of the county

Dr Thomas J Boyer, a native of Bernville, Pa, came to Luthersburg in 1853, where he practiced for fifteen years He then moved to Clearfield where he remained until the time of his death October 23, 1882 Dr Boyer was well known in political circles, and represented this district both in the House of Representatives and in the State Senate.

Dr. D O Crouch, a native of Washington county, Pa, practiced medicine at Luthersburg in 1855-6 He moved to Curwensville, where he practiced until the time of his death, December 26, 1880 During the epidemic of diphtheria, which ravaged the town of Curwensville just before his death, Dr Crouch was untiring in his struggle against the terrible disease, and his own death was the result of his labors

Dr D A Fetzer, a native of Clarion county, Pa, began to practice medicine in Lumber City in 1855 He continued to practice in that town until the time of his death October 20, 1903 Dr Fetzer was a very successful physician, and his opinion at consultations was frequently sought and highly respected Although a man of great culture and considerable wealth, Dr Fetzer chose the hard life of a country doctor At the time of his death he was president of the Curwensville National Bank

In 1864 the Clearfield County Medical Society was organized, in connection with the State Medical Society, and the American Medical Association Its Constitution states that "The objects of this society shall be the advancement of medical knowledge, the elevation of professional character, the protection of the professional interests of its members, the extension of the bounds of medical science, and the promotion of all measures adapted to the relief of suffering, the improvement of the health, and the protection of the lives of the community This society recognizes as binding upon its members the code of medical ethics as established by the American Medical Association "

By a law passed in 1881, physicians wishing to practice their profession in this county must register their name, place of nativity, place of residence, places of practice, and the name of the college or university which conferred their degree

Below is given an alphabetical list of all physicians who were residents of the county, or who practiced in the county, who have registered from 1881 to the present time Owing to the fact that many residents of

the county who registered, never practiced, and that others have retired or are deceased, it is impossible to obtain a correct list of the present practicing physicians of Clearfield county Where information could be obtained it has been added to the data given in the register

Below is also given a copy of an affidavit found in the medical register, which may be of interest

ALPHABETICAL LIST OF DOCTORS

Ackley, B F, a native of Juniata County, Pa, place of residence, DuBois, attended lectures at Pennsylvania College, 1859-60, and Jefferson Medical College 1862-3

Ake, N F K, a native of Reynoldsville, Jefferson County, Pa, place of residence, Curwensville, Pa, place of practice, Curwensville, degree M D, conferred by the Medico Chirurgical College, May 18, 1897

Andrews, Warren W, a native of Lewisburg, Pa, place of residence, Peale, place of practice, Peale, degree M D conferred by the University of Pennsylvania, May 2, 1888

Avery, James W, a native of Delaware, Ohio, place of residence, DuBois, attended Miami Medical College, Cincinnati, Ohio

Bailey, S D, a native of Clearfield County, place of residence and practice, Clearfield, Degree M D conferred by the Jefferson Medical College, March 27, 1884

Baird, J A, a native of Houtzdale, place of residence, Houtzdale, places of practice, Saxton, Bedford County, Pa, and Houtzdale, degree M D conferred by College of Physicians and Surgeons, Baltimore, Md, March 6, 1878

Balliet, L D, a native of Milton, Pa, place of residence, DuBois, degree M D conferred by Hahnemann Medical College, March 10, 1880

Barnfield, J H , a native of Jersey Shore, Pa ; place of residence, Irvona, degree M D , conferred by Jefferson Medical College, April 2, 1886

Bancroft, A A , a native of Poltage, Ohio, place of residence, DuBois, places of practice, Pittsburg, Scranton and DuBois, degree M D and Surgery conferred by Hahnemann Medical College 1869

Belcher, E C , a native of Newark Valley, N Y ; place of residence, Morrisdale Mines, places of practice, Newark Valley, English Centre, Pa , Kylertown, Peale and Morrisdale Mines, degree M D conferred by the Cincinnati College of Medicine, February 26, 1877.

Bell, J Finlay, a native of Aaronsburg, Pa , place of residence, Osceola, places of practice, Glen Hope and Osceola, degree M D conferred by the University of the city of New York March 13, 1873

Bennett, Ash D , a native of Linden, Lycoming county, Pa , place of residence, New Washington, degree M D conferred by the Pennsylvania Medical College, March 20, 1860 Deceased

Bennett, Francis G , a native of New Washington, Pa , place of residence, Clearfield, place of practice, Clearfield, degree M D conferred by Jefferson Medical College, April 3, 1889

Bershad, Leonard, a native of Philadelphia, Pa , place of residence, DuBois, places of practice, Philadelphia and DuBois, degree M D and surgery conferred by the Jefferson Medical College 1904

Blair, H A , a native of Bellefonte, Pa , place of residence, Curwensville, place of practice, Curwensville, degree M D and Surgery

conferred by the University of Pennsylvania June 15, 1906 Degree B S conferred by State College June 15, 1902

Blockwell, Eunock, a native of Pennington, N J , residence, Morrisdale, Pa., degree M. D conferred by the Medico Chisurgical College, June 23, 1903

Bollinger, William E , a native of Huntingdon county, Pa , place of residence, Coalport; places of practice, Cawper, Kansas, Mt Vernon, Pa , and Coalport, degree M D conferred by the Baltimore Medical College, March 8, 1886

Boyer, T J , Jr , a native of Brady Township, place of residence, Jeannette, Pa , places of practice, Madera, Pittsburg and Jeannette; degree M D conferred by the Baltimore Medical College, March 8, 1886

Boyles, Robert M , a native of Clarion county, Pa , place of residence, DuBois, places of practice, Reynoldsville and DuBois; degree M D conferred by Cleveland Medical College, February 4, 1869, and Western Reserve College, March 15, 1882

Brotherlin, H H , a native of Hollidaysburg, Pa , place of residence, Hollidaysburg; places of practice, Curwensville and Hollidaysburg, degree M D conferred by Jefferson Medical College, April 2, 1883

Brockbank, John I , a native of Elk county, Pa , place of residence, Luthersburg, degree M D conferred by the Baltimore University School of Medicine March 4, 1886

Bucke, Hiram A , a native of Vermont, place of residence, Winterberne; degree M D conferred by the Albany Medical College

Bullock, J O , a native of Columbia, Bradford county, Pa , place of residence, Peale; places of practice, Canton, McIntyre and

Peale, degree M D. conferred by University of City of New York March, 1872

Bunn, J McGirk, a native of Shippensburg, Pa , place of residence, Altoona, places of practice, New Washington and Altoona, attended lectures at Jefferson Medical College, 1846 Deceased

Burchfield, James P , a native of Pennsylvania Furnace, Pa , place of residence, Clearfield, places of practice, Philipsburg. U S Army and Clearfield, degree M D conferred by University of Michigan March 26, 1862 Deceased

Burchfield, Samuel E , a native of Allegheny county, Pa , places of practice, Latrobe and Houtzdale, degree M D conferred by Homeopathic Medical Department of University of Michigan June 30, 1881

Burkhard, S P , a native of Blair county, Pa , place of residence, DuBois, places of practice, Altoona, Philipsburg and DuBois, degree M D conferred by Eclectic Medical College 1859, and University of Pa 1872

Burdick, W P , a native of Sirleyburg, Pa , place of residence, DuBois, degree M D conferred by University of Vermont

Buzard, A M , a native of Westmoreland county, Pa , place of residence, Irvona, degree M D conferred by Western Pennsylvania Medical College March 26, 1891

Calhoun, Grier O , a native of Armstrong county, Pa , place of residence, given as Madera, degree M D conferred by Baltimore Medical College

Carlin, Robert G , a native of Petrolia, Pa , place of residence, Houtzdale, degree M D conferred by Jefferson Medical College 1902, and degree Ph B conferred by Grove City College 1898

Chaapel, Victor P , a native of Leroy, Pa ;

place of residence, Irvone, degree M D conferred by College of Physicians and Surgeons, Baltimore, April, 1892

Cherry, Emil T , a native of Altoona, Pa , place of residence, given as Madera, places of practice, Indianapolis, Ind , Ansonville, Madera, degree M D conferred by Medical College of Indiana, February 28, 1884

Clerk, Frank G , a native of Scotland, place of residence, Houtzdale, attended University of Edinborough, Scotland

Coe, B F , a native of Gilleth, Pa , place of residence, Gazzam, place of practice, Gazzam, degree M D conferred by College of Physicians and Surgeons, Baltimore, April 18, 1895

Cohen, Morris S , a native of London, England, place of residence, Karthaus Township, degree M D conferred by the Jefferson Medical College March 12, 1881

Cole, Webster W , a native of Allegheny county, N Y , place of residence, Sabula, place of practice, Sabula

Collins, Howard A , a native of Williamsport, Pa , place of residence, Wallaceton, place of practice, Wallaceton, degree M D conferred by the Jefferson Medical College May 15, 1896

Coltman, Robert J , a native of Washington, D C , place of residence, Houtzdale, degree M D conferred by Jefferson Medical College March 12, 1881

Corey, Horace M , a native of Tioga county, N Y , place of residence, Peale, places of practice, Sayre, Pa , Waverly, N Y , Pine City, N Y and Peale, degree M D conferred by University of Michigan March 27, 1878

Cowdrick, Arthur D , a native of Clearfield, place of residence, Clearfield, place of practice, Clearfield, degree M D conferred by Medico Chi College June 4, 1909

Covert, E Douglass, a native of Jefferson county, Pa, place of residence, Kerrmoor, studied at Homeopathic Hospital, Cleveland, Ohio

Crammer, Carl B, a native of Bradford county, Pa, place of residence, DuBois, place of practice, DuBois, degree M D conferred by Jefferson Medical College May 13, 1898

Cresswell, A E, a native of Missouri; place of residence, near Ansonville, places of practice, Fairview, Cherry Tree and Ansonville, attended lectures at Medical College of Ohio 1871-2, also at Medical Department of University of Michigan 1872

Currier, J, a native of Port Deposit, Md, place of residence, Grampian, places of practice, Troutville and Grampian, degree M D conferred by Kentucky School of Medicine June 28, 1881

Dale, David, a native of Lemont, Pa, place of residence, Bellefonte, Pa, places of practice, Curwensville and Bellefonte, degree M D and Surgery conferred by University of Pennsylvania June, 1904 Degrees B S and M S conferred by Pennsylvania College 1900 and 1903

Dale, W H, a native of Bradford Township, place of residence, Ramey, degree M D conferred by College of Physicians and Surgeons, Baltimore April 18, 1895

Davis, Thomas E, a native of Cambria county, Pa, place of residence, Burnside, degree M D conferred by Jefferson Medical College March 20, 1867

Dyson, W W, a native of Greensburg, Pa, place of residence, Osceola, places of practice, Chambersburg and Osceola, degree M D conferred by Jefferson Medical College March 20, 1882

Edwards, G B, a native of Smith's Mills, Pa, residence, Clearfield, degrees M D and Surgery and B S conferred by Washington and Jefferson College 1905 and 1901

Edwards, W H, a native of Industry, Me, place of residence, Janesville, degree M D conferred by Bowdoin Medical College June 8, 1868

Emigh, G W, a native of Morris Township, place of residence, Woodland, degree M. D conferred by University Medical College of New York March 11, 1884

Elliott, C B, a native of Mt Savage, Md; place of residence, Utahville; places of practice, Osceola, Altoona and Utahville; degree M D conferred by Jefferson Medical College March 14, 1873

Erhard, E S, place of residence, New Millport, place of practice, New Millport, degree M D and Surgery conferred by Western University of Pennsylvania June 12, 1906.

Flegal, Irwin S, place of residence, Lumber City, place of practice, Lumber City; degree M D conferred by Western Pennsylvania Medical College March 22, 1894

Feltwell, John, a native of Chest Township, places of practice, Little Marsh, Pa, and Houtzdale, degree M D conferred by Jefferson Medical College March 12, 1879

Free, Spencer M, a native of New Freedom, Pa, place of residence, DuBois; place of practice, Dagus Mines, Pa, Beechtree, Pa, and Helvetia. degrees A. B and A M conferred by Ohio Wesleyan University 1877, 1880, degree M D conferred by College of Physicians and Surgeons, Baltimore, 1880

Gallagher, John A, a native of Osceola Mills, place of residence, Houtzdale, places of practice, Madera, Loraine and Houtzdale, degree M D conferred by Jefferson Medical College April 2, 1886

George, S F, a native of Perry county, Pa, place of residence, Graham, places of practice, Ebensburg, Pa, Janesville, Graham and Reynoldsville

Gifford, Willis B, a native of Lee, Mass, place of residence, DuBois, places of practice, Attica, Buffalo, N Y, and DuBois, degree M D conferred by University of Buffalo February 23, 1876

Gilliland, W S, a native of Centreville, Pa, place of residence, Central Point, places of practice, Central Point and Congress Hill, attended lectures at Jefferson Medical College 1865-66

Ginter, James E, a native of Troutville, place of residence, DuBois, place of practice, Tyler, degree M D and Surgery conferred by Medico Chi College June 4, 1908

Gold, James A, a native of Frankstown, Pa, place of residence, Brisbin, degree M D conferred by Homeopathic College of Cleveland March 23, 1887

Good, D R, a native of Franklin county, Pa, place of residence, Osceola, places of practice, Altoona and Osceola, degree M D conferred by Jefferson Medical College 1858 Deceased

Gordon, John W, a native of Clearfield, place of residence, Clearfield, places of practice, Philadelphia and Clearfield, degree M D and Surgery conferred by University of Pennsylvania May 14, 1903, degree B S conferred by State College 1900

Gourley, R C, a native of Jefferson county, Pa, place of residence, Troutville, place of practice, Big Run, degree M D conferred by Western University of Pittsburg, Medical Department, March 22, 1894

Graves, William B, a native of Point Peninsula, N Y, place of residence, DuBois,

place of practice, DuBois, degree M D conferred by College of Physicians and Surgeons, Baltimore, April 22, 1901

Gregory, John A, a native of Alexandria, Pa, place of residence, DuBois, places of practice, Luthersburg and DuBois, degree M D conferred by Jefferson Medical College April 2, 1883

Griffith, Matthew M, a native of York, Pa, place of residence, DuBois, places of practice, Parsons, Pa, Irwin, N Y, Bradford and DuBois, degree M D conferred by University of Pennsylvania March 14, 1867

Gurnsey, Charles W, a native of Stuben county, N Y, place of residence, Karthaus

Guthrie, Daniel W, a native of Armstrong county, Pa, place of residence, DuBois, places of practice, DuBois and Beechtree, attended Baltimore University

Haines, Jeremiah, a native of New Cumberland, Pa, place of residence, Woodward Township, time of continuous practice, twelve years

Hancock, Edward C, a native of Philadelphia, place of residence, DuBois, places of practice, Buck county, Montgomery county, Allegheny county, and Clearfield county

Hartswick, John G, a native of Boalsburg, Pa, place of residence, Clearfield, places of practice, Hublersburg, Pa, and Clearfield, degree M D conferred by University of Pennsylvania April 1, 1854 Deceased

Hartswick, Thomas Huston, a native of Clearfield, place of residence, Clearfield, places of practice, Philadelphia and Clearfield, degree M D conferred by University of Pennsylvania May 2, 1887 Deceased

Harper, Francis W, a native of Newberry, Pa , place of residence, Glen Hope, degree M D conferred by College of Physicians and Surgeons, Baltimore, April 15, 1896

Hayes, S E , a native of Luthersburg, Pa , place of residence, Tyler, degree M D conferred by the Medico Chi College May 13, 1896

Heddings, B E , a native of Pennsylvania, place of residence, Morrisdale, degree M D conferred by University of Pennsylvania 1899, degree B S conferred by Dickinson Seminary 1895

Henderson, James L , a native of Lewistown, Pa , place of residence, Osceola, places of practice, Pendleton, Ohio, Karthaus and Osceola, degree M D conferred by Ohio Medical College March 1, 1882

Hennigh, George B , a native of Indiana county, Pa , place of residence, Troutville; degree M D conferred by Baltimore Medical College April 15, 1891

Hepburn, James H , a native of Jersey Shore, Pa , place of residence, Irvona, degree M D conferred by Jefferson Medical College April, 1886

Hern. C D F , a native of Olean, N Y place of residence, DuBois, place of practice, DuBois, degree M D and Surgery conferred by College of Physicians and Surgeons, Baltimore, June 3, 1907

Hilleary, Jesse G , a native of Newark, Ohio, place of residence, DuBois, place of practice, DuBois, degree M D conferred by Ohio Medical College April 9, 1897

Hindman, Charles C , a native of Jefferson county, Pa , place of residence, DuBois, places of practice, Clarion county, Jefferson county and DuBois, degree of M D con-

ferred by Jefferson Medical College March 11, 1876

Hogue, Herbert J , a native of Watsontown, Pa , place of residence, Coalport, places of practice, DuBois and Coalport; degree M D conferred by College of Physicians and Surgeons, Baltimore, March 1, 1885

Hogue, Davis A , a native of Watsontown, Pa , place of residence Houtzdale, places of practice, Glen Hope, Madera and Houtzdale, degree M D conferred by Jefferson Medical College March 11, 1875

Hoover, Percy L , a native of Ferguson township, place of residence, Mahaffey, place of practice, Mahaffey, degree M D. conferred by Jefferson Medical College May 15, 1895

Hotchkin, Gurdon B , a native of Clinton, N Y , place of residence, Morrisdale, degree M D conferred by University of Pennsylvania March 31, 1855

Houck, E E , a native of Indiana county, Pa , place of residence, DuBois, places of practice, Punxsutawney and DuBois, degree M. D and Surgery conferred by Baltimore Medical College May 1, 1906

Hurd, M E , a native of Clearfield county, Pa place of residence, Newburg, degree M D conferred by Jefferson Medical College April 2, 1883

Hunter, Elliott C , a native of Newburg; place of residence, Newburg, place of practice, Newburg, degree M D conferred by Western Pennsylvania Medical College March 22, 1888

Hyskell, W E , a native of Smicksburg, Pa , place of residence, Munson, degree M. D and Surgery conferred by Jefferson Medical College May 28, 1903

Irvin, George R, a native of Clearfield, Pa, place of residence, Clearfield, degree M. D conferred by University of Pennsylvania October, 1897

Jackson, Robert, a native of Philadelphia, Pa., place of residence, Houtzdale, place of practice, Houtzdale, degree M D conferred by Jefferson Medical College of Physicians and Surgeons, Baltimore

Jenkins, George C, a native of Curwensville, place of residence, Curwensville, place of practice, Curwensville, degree M D conferred by University of Pennsylvania June 14, 1878

Johnstone, Charles W, a native of England, place of residence, DuBois, place of practice, DuBois, degree M D and Surgery conferred by College of Physicians and Surgeons, Baltimore, May 21, 1906

Johnson, James M, a native of Huntingdon, Pa, place of residence, Coalport, place of practice, Coalport, degree M D conferred by College of Physicians and Surgeons, Baltimore, April 15, 1896

Jordon, R R, a native of Stewartstown, Pa., place of residence, Tyler, degree M D and Surgery conferred by University of Pennsylvania June 17, 1903

Keffer, Winter, a native of Westmoreland county, Pa, place of residence, Williamsgrove, place of practice, Williamsgrove, degree M. D conferred by Georgia College March 12, 1888

Kelso, John Scott, a native of Jefferson county, Pa, place of residence, Woodland, place of practice, Woodland, degree M D March 26, 1896

King, H O, a native of Jefferson county, Pa; place of residence, Curwensville, place of practice, Curwensville, degree M D

conferred by Jefferson Medical College May 2, 1893

Kline, D D, place of practice, Clearfield, time of continuous practice, 36 years, attended Eclectic College

Kline, John H, a native of Centre county, Pa, place of residence, Grampian, degree M D conferred by Eclectic Medical College January 24, 1867

Kirk, Ellis Irwin, a native of Clearfield, place of residence, Chester Hill, place of practice, Chester Hill, attended Eclectic Medical college, Cincinnati, Ohio

Kirk, George B, a native of Luthersburg, place of residence, Kylertown, degree M D conferred by Baltimore Medical College April 21, 1898

Kirk, Charles H, a native of Luthersburg, Pa, place of residence, New Washington, degree M D conferred by Eclectic Medical Institute, Cincinnati, Ohio

Kirk, Joseph, Jr, a native of Luthersburg, place of residence, Luthersburg, place of practice, Luthersburg, degree M D conferred by Eclectic Medical College, Cincinnati, Ohio, June 3, 1890

Lewis, Edward C, a native of Northumberland, Pa, place of residence, Grampian, degree M. D, conferred by Bellevue Hospital Medical College March 10, 1881

Lewis, Homer H, a native of Vandalia, Missouri, place of residence, Jefferson Line, place of practice, Troutville, degree M D and Surgery conferred by the University of Louisville June 30, 1900

Leipold, B E, a native of Clearfield, place of residence, Clearfield, place of practice, Clearfield, degree M D conferred by Jefferson Medical College May 13, 1896

Litz, Jefferson, a native of Clearfield,

place of residence, DuBois, places of practice, Johnstown, Woodland and DuBois; degree M D conferred by Jefferson Medical College March, 1862

Logan, Samuel G, a native of Jefferson county, Pa, place of residence, DuBois, degree M D conferred by Jefferson Medical College May 15, 1901

Lydic, Joseph M, a native of East Mahoning, Pa; place of residence, Troutville, places of practice, Smithport, Pa, and Troutville, attended Medical Lectures at University of Ann Arbor, 1868-9, 1869-70

Maine, Charles L, a native of Mainesburg, Pa, place of residence, Helvetia; places of practice, Walston, Pa, and Helvetia, degree M D conferred by College of Physicians and Surgeons, Baltimore, April 29, 1892

Maloy, John D, a native of Ireland, place of residence, DuBois, places of practice, Bradford, Emporium and DuBois, degree M D conferred by Medical Department of the University of Buffalo

Mangon, John M, a native of Ireland, place of residence, Houtzdale, places of practice, Kansas and Houtzdale, degree M. D conferred by University of Pennsylvania 1857

Mank, G E, a native of Claysburg, Pa; place of residence, Woodland, degree M D and Surgery conferred by Medico Chi College June 5, 1909

Maxwell, J A, place of residence, Curwensville, place of practice, Curwensville, degree M D conferred by Jefferson Medical College March 10, 1866 Deceased

MacKenzie, A E, a native of Novia Scotia, places of practice, Clearfield and Lock

Haven, degree M D. and Surgery conferred by Hahnemann Medical College May 2, 1898.

McDowell, Samuel I, a native of York county, Pa, place of residence, DuBois; places of practice, DuBois and New Oxford; attended Jefferson Medical College

McKee, Thomas N, a native of Sherrett, Pa, place of residence, DuBois, degree M. D. conferred by Western Pennsylvania Medical College March 27, 1890

McNaul, Caleb G, a native of Pike Township, degree M D conferred by Jefferson Medical College April 2, 1890

Mead, R K, a native of East Brady, Pa; place of residence, DuBois, degree M D and Surgery conferred by University of Pennsylvania

Means, W A, a native of Punxsutawney, place of residence, DuBois, places of practice, Luthersburg and DuBois, degree M D conferred by Cincinnati College of Medicine and Surgery February 3, 1865 Deceased

Miller, S J, a native of Clearfield county, place of residence, Madera, places of practice, Ansonville and Madera, degree M D conferred by University of City of New York 1886

Miller, James A, a native of Clearfield county, place of residence, Grampian, place of practice, Grampian, degree M D conferred by University of Pennsylvania March 25, 1897

Mock, David C, a native of Pavia, Pa, place of residence, DuBois, degree M D and Surgery conferred by the College of Physicians and Surgeons, Baltimore, May 18, 1904

Mortimer, James I, a native of Clarion county, Pa, place of residence, DuBois; places of practice, East Brady, Warren, Ohio;

McKean county, Allegheny City and DuBois, time of continuous practice, fourteen years

Mott, William S, a native of Clearfield county, place of residence, Wallaceton, degree M D conferred by Eclectic Medical Institute, Cincinnati, Ohio, June 2, 1885

Murray, Jno A, a native of Hudson, Pa, place of residence, Mahaffey, places of practice, Ansonville and Mahaffey, degree M D conferred by University of Maryland, March, 1885

Murray, V A, a native of Jefferson county, Pa, place of residence, Mahaffey, place of practice, Mahaffey, degree M D conferred by the Kentucky School of Medicine June 18, 1892

Myers, J G L, a native of Huntingdon county, Pa, place of residence, Osceola, places of practice, Burlington, Indiana, Hill Valley, Pa, Port Matilda, Pa, and Osceola, attended course of lectures at Ann Arbor University 1887-8

Neveling, F S, a native of Brownsville, Ind, place of residence, Clearfield, places of practice, St Lawrence, Pa, Glen Hope, Frenchville, and Clearfield, degree M D conferred by Eclectic Medical College of Pennsylvania January 1, 1870

New, Philip S, a native of Germany, place of residence, DuBois, places of practice, Missouri, Iowa, Indiana, Pa, Punxsutawney and DuBois, time of continuous practice, 28 years

Park, Milo E, a native of Armstrong county, Pa, place of residence, Utahville, degree M D conferred by Medical Department of Western Reserve University March 27, 1884

Park, William C, a native of Whitesburg, Pa; place of practice, Cochran Mills, Pa, and New Millport, degree M D conferred by Western Reserve University March 12, 1882 Deceased

Pettigrew, S H, a native of Kittanning, Pa, place of residence, DuBois; places of practice, Kams City, Pa, and DuBois, degree M D conferred by Jefferson Medical College

Piper, William C, a native of Cypher, Pa, place of residence, Clearfield, place of practice, Clearfield, degree M D and Surgery conferred by Hahnemann Medical College May 21, 1904

Potter, J W, a native of Clarion county, Pa, place of residence, Keewaydin, place of practice, Mulsonburg, attended lectures at National Medical College, Washington, D C Deceased

Prothers, William C, a native of Perry county, Pa, place of residence, Ramey, degree M D conferred by Jefferson Medical College April 27, 1892

Prowell, George F, a native of Lewisburg, Pa, place of residence, Burnside, places of practice, Carlisle, Pa, and Burnside, degree M D conferred by Jefferson Medical College March 10, 1867

Purnell, Howard G, a native of Georgetown, Del, place of residence, Ansonville, degree M D conferred by Jefferson Medical College April 1, 1892

Pussell, Edward W, a native of Fleming, Pa; place of residence, Clearfield, degree M D and Surgery conferred by University of Pennsylvania 1902

Quigley, J M, a native of Wallaceton; place of residence, Winburne, place of practice, Winburne, degree M. D conferred by Baltimore Medical College April 22, 1898

Quinn, L W, a native of DuBois; place of residence and practice, DuBois, degree M

D. conferred by Western Pennsylvania Medical College March 26, 1896

Read, F B, a native of Clearfield; place of residence, Osceola, places of practice, Woodland and Osceola, degree M D conferred by Jefferson Medical College March 10, 1867

Reese, O P, a native of Centre county, place of residence, Kylertown, degree M D conferred by University of Michigan March 9, 1865

Rhoads, J W, a native of Harrisburg, Pa , place of residence, Houtzdale, places of practice, Danville, Tunkhannock and Houtzdale: degree M D conferred by University of Pennsylvania March, 1854

Richards, H Preston, a native of Illinois, place of residence, Karthaus, degree M D conferred by University of Maryland April 8, 1889

Ross J Miller, a native of Morgantown, W Va , place of residence, DuBois, places of practice, Lumber City and DuBois; degree M D conferred by Eclectic Medical College of Pennsylvania May 5, 1857 Deceased

Rowles, J F, a native of Clearfield county, place of residence, Kerrmoor, degree M D conferred by Medico Chi College May 28, 1904

Rowles, L C, a native of Clearfield county, place of residence, Clearfield, degree M D and Surgery conferred by Medico Chi College May 27, 1905

Ruley, W. E, a native of Hanover, Pa , place of residence, Clearfield county, degree M D and Surgery conferred by Southern Homeopathic College May 9, 1907

Russell, Edmund, a native of Brooklyn, N Y , place of residence and practice, Houtzdale, degree M D conferred by University of Pennsylvania June 15, 1904

Rutter, T C, a native of Nottingham, Pa ; place of residence and practice, Tyler; degree M D conferred by University of Pennsylvania June 13, 1900

Scheffer, Julius, a native of Germany, place of residence, Troutville, places of practice, Allegheny, Butler, McKean, Warren and Jefferson counties, and Troutville; degree M D. conferred by Medical College of Herford, Prussia, May, 1865, attended lectures at University of Pennsylvania 1867-68

Scheurer, E M, a native of Hanover, Pa , place of residence, Clearfield; places of practice, Bellefonte and Clearfield, degree M. D conferred by Hahnemann Medical College March, 1871 Deceased

Schneider, Charles, a native of Tyrone, Pa , places of practice, Winterburn, Driftwood and Karthaus, degree M D conferred by College of Physicians and Surgeons, Baltimore, March 1, 1881

Schumacher, F. L, a native of Hazleton, Pa ; place of residence, DuBois, degree M D. and Surgery conferred by University of Pennsylvania June 19, 1908

Senn, W W, a native of Holland, N. Y., place of residence, Munson; degree M D conferred by University of Pennsylvania June 19, 1907, degree B S conferred by Bucknell University June 24, 1903

Sharbaugh, W J, a native of Summitville, Pa ; place of residence and practice, Houtzdale, degree M D conferred by Kentucky School of Medicine June 18, 1891.

Shock, J C, a native of New Washington; place of residence and practice, Ramey; degree M D conferred by Jefferson Medical College 1891

Smathers, W J, a native of Jefferson county, Pa , place of residence, DuBois; degree M. D conferred by Jefferson Medical College March 12, 1873

Smead, J J, a native of Clearfield, place of residence, New Washington, places of practice, Chest Township and New Washington, time of continuous practice, twenty-three years

Smith, Joseph W, a native of York, Pa, place of residence, Osceola, places of practice, New Oxford, Philadelphia and Osceola, degree M D conferred by Bellevue Hospital Medical College March 1, 1870

Smith, Reuben, a native of Tioga county, Pa, place of residence, Grampian, places of practice, Elk county and Grampian, degree M D conferred by American Eclectic College February 18, 1886

Smith, N. W, a native of New Brunswick, Canada, place of residence, DuBois, Pa, degree M D and Surgery conferred by Baltimore College of Physicians and Surgeons June 3, 1907

Spackman, R V, a native of Bellefonte. Pa, place of residence, DuBois, places of practice, Luthersburg and DuBois degree M D conferred by Jefferson Medical College March, 1870 Deceased

Spackman, J P, a native of DuBois. place of residence and practice, DuBois. degree M D conferred by Jefferson Medical College May 15, 1896

Sprankle, P D, place of residence, DuBois, places of practice, Pittsburg. Punxsutawney and DuBois. degree M D and Surgery conferred by Jefferson Medical College May, 1904

Stern, W J, a native of Philadelphia, place of residence, Woodland, Pa, degree M D conferred by Medico Chi College 1902

Stewart, S C, a native of Bradford Town-

ship, place of residence, Clearfield, places of practice, Woodland and Clearfield, degree M D conferred by Jefferson Medical College March 12, 1881.

Stitzel, J W, a native of Ewensville, Pa, place of residence and practice, Houtzdale, degree M D conferred by Hahnemann Medical College May 5, 1896

Strowbridge, H P, place of residence, DuBois, places of practice, Oil City, Rouseville and DuBois, time of continuous practice, twenty-three years

Sullivan, J C, a native of Armstrong county, Pa, place of residence and practice, DuBois, degree M D conferred by Western Pennsylvania College, March 27, 1890

Sweeney. D H, a native of Penn Village, N Y, place of residence, Clearfield; places of practice, New Bloomfield and Clearfield, time of continuous practice forty-four years

Sweeney, Barnabas, a native of Allegheny county, Pa, place of residence, DuBois; places of practice. Brookville and DuBois, time of practice thirty-seven years

Sweeney, G B, a native of Latrobe; place of residence, DuBois, degree M D conferred by Baltimore College of Physicians and Surgeons March 15. 1886

Taylor, J R, a native of Philadelphia, place of residence, Morrisdale, places of practice, Breck, Colorado, Philadelphia and Morrisdale, degree M D conferred by University of Pennsylvania 1875

Thompson. H H, a native of Stormstown, Pa, place of residence and practice, Mahaffey, degree M D conferred by Jefferson Medical College April 3. 1889

Thorn, A I, a native of Clearfield, place of residence, Kylertown, degree M D con-

14

ferred by University of Pennsylvania March 12, 1872

Thorn, Paul, a native of Clearfield, place of residence, Kylertown, degree M D conferred by Baltimore University School of Medicine March 16, 1867

Thorpe, W P, a native of Curry Run, Pa , place of residence, Winburne, places of practice, Winburne and Straight, degree M D and Surgery conferred by Baltimore Medical College May 11, 1905

Thorp, J D, a native of Greenwood township, place of residence, Curry Run, places of practice, Curry Run and McGees Mills, degree M D. conferred by Columbus Medical College March 2, 1892

Tobin, Thomas, a native of Brockwayville, Pa ; place of residence, Bigler, places of practice, Grampian, Wallaceton and Bigler, degree M D conferred by University of Buffalo, February 21, 1882

Todd, Fernandez, a native of Summitville, Pa , place of residence, Houtzdale; degree M D conferred by University of Pennsylvania March 12, 1875

Torbert, J S, a native of Williamsport, Pa , place of residence, Winburne, places of practice, Driftwood and Winburne, degree M D conferred by Jefferson Medical College March 12, 1881

Tracy, E M, a native of Smithport, Pa , place of residence and practice, Houtzdale, degree M D and Surgery conferred by University of Pennsylvania September 28, 1903.

Twitmire, T C, a native of Milesburg, Pa , place of residence. Glen Richie, degree M D conferred by Western Reserve University March 3, 1886

Ulbrich, Seth S, places of practice, Williampsort and Osceola, degree M D conferred by Jefferson Medical College March 14, 1881

Ulmer, Stephen E, a native of Lycoming, Pa., place of residence, Wallaceton; degree M D conferred by Jefferson Medical College June 15, 1896, degree Ph G. conferred by Philadelphia College of Pharmacy

Van Fleet, Walter, a native of Piermont, N Y , place of residence, DuBois, places of practice, Watsontown and DuBois, degree M D conferred by Hahnemann Medical College March 10, 1880

Van Valzah, H B, a native of Millheim, Pa.; place of residence and practice, Clearfield, degree M D conferred by Jefferson Medical College March 12, 1873   Deceased

Vaughn, J E, a native of Madison, Me., place of residence, Houtzdale, degree M D conferred by University of Pennsylvania March 15, 1880

Wagoner, E. F, a native of York, Pa., place of residence, Osceola, places of practice, York, Manchester and Osceola, degree M D conferred by Jefferson Medical College March 29, 1884

Walters, J. L, a native of Loretto, Pa ; place of residence, Houtzdale, degree M D conferred by College of Physicians and Surgeons, Baltimore, March 1, 1881

Waterworth, S J, a native of Baltimore, Md , place of residence and practice, Clearfield, degree M D conferred by College of Physicians and Surgeons, Baltimore, April 8, 1893

Weida, Isadore J, a native of Berks county, Pa , place of residence, Peale, degree M D confered by University of Pennsylvania May 1, 1890

Weidemann, F H , a native of Philadelphia, place of residence and practice, Morrisdale, degree M D conferred by Medico Chi College May 20, 1899

Wesner, W A , a native of Bald Eagle, Pa , place of residence, Houtzdale, places of practice, Loretto, Carlton and Houtzdale, degree M D conferred by Jefferson Medical College March 11, 1876

Whittier, G M , a native of Maine, place of residence, Houtzdale, degree M D conferred by Bellevue Hospital Medical College March 1, 1875

Wilson, Preston, a native of Clearfield, place of residence and practice, Clearfield, degree M D conferred by Jefferson Medical College April 2, 1886 Deceased

Wilson, George, a native of Washington, Pa ; place of residence, Luthersburg, places of practice, Big Run, Grampian, and Luthersburg, time of continuous practice thirty-six years

Wilson, A G , a native of Juniata county, Pa , place of residence, Glen Hope, places of practice, Osceola and Glen Hope, degree M D conferred by University of Pennsylvania May 10, 1876

Wilson, O. W , a native of Clearfield Pa , residence and place of practice, Clearfield, degree M D conferred by Medico Chi College May 24, 1902

Wilson, H Sheridan, a native of Huntingdon county, Pa , place of residence and practice, Smoke Run, degree M D conferred by College of Physicians and Surgeons, Baltimore, April 18, 1895

Winslow, Byron, a native of Elk county, Pa ; place of residence, Curwensville; places of practice, Philadelphia, Clearfield and Curwensville; degree M D conferred by Jefferson Medical College March 12, 1879 Deceased

Wood, Charles D , a native of Elmira, N Y , place of residence, Coalport, degree M D conferred by College of Physicians and Surgeons, Baltimore, 1880

Wood, G W , a native of Wellsville, N Y , place of residence, Houtzdale, places of practice, Glen Hope and Houtzdale, degree M D conferred by College of Physicians and Surgeons March 1890

Woodside, H L , a native of Clearfield county, place of residence, Wallaceton, degree M D and Surgery conferred by Jefferson Medical College June 8, 1908

Woodside, Harry A , a native of Clearfield county, place of residence and practice, Williamsgrove, degree M D conferred by Jefferson Medical College May 14, 1897

Worrell, S W , a native of Newburg, place of residence, Clearfield, degree M D conferred by University of Buffalo May 3, 1892

Wrigley, J Kay, a native of Altoona; places of practice, Tyrone, Altoona and Clearfield, degree M D conferred by Hahnemann Medical College, March 8, 1887 Deceased

Yeaney, G B , a native of New Maysville, Pa , place of residence, Clarion, Pa , places of practice, Clearfield and Clarion, degree M D conferred by Western University May 28, 1903

Yearick, G W , a native of Madisonburg, Pa , place of residence, Woodland, degree M D and Surgery conferred by Medico Chi College 1903

Young, Robert J , a native of England, place of residence, Snow Shoe, degree M D conferred by College of Physicians and Surgeons, Baltimore, March 16, 1889

CHAPTER XV

PUBLIC INSTITUTIONS

The Clearfield Hospital—The DuBois Hospital—The Clearfield County Home

THE CLEARFIELD HOSPITAL

The Clearfield Hospital was incorporated in 1901 The following year, it was consolidated with another hospital, which had been subsequently organized and the charter was amended and the corporation re-organized Through the generosity of the heirs of Frederick Mossop, deceased, and other charitable citizens, about four acres of land and $20,-000 00 in money were donated toward the location and erection of a new hospital, which was completed in July, 1905, at a total cost of $38,358 09, exclusive of the ground The building is 157 x 113 feet The central part known as the "Administration Building," is two stories in height and the wings, in which the public wards are located, are each one story high

The hospital is well equipped and up-to-date in its appearance and appliances It has accommodations for thirty-five patients, twenty-two in the public wards and thirteen in private rooms During the year 1909, 371 patients were treated Of these, 269 were entirely free, or paid but a fractional part of the cost of their care A chartered training school for nurses is maintained under competent management the first class therefrom graduated during 1910

The State Legislature, in 1907, appropriated $23,000 00; $15,000 00 toward paying the indebtedness on the building, and $8,-000 00 to assist in maintaining the Hospital for two years This amount was reduced by the Governor, because of insufficient revenue, to $6,000 00 toward the indebtedness and $4,-000 00 for maintenance for two years The State appropriation for the years of 1909 and 1910 was $8,000 00 for maintenance and $2,-000 00 toward improvements for the two years These appropriations by the State Legislature are insufficient to support the hospital, and the deficiencies have hitherto been provided for by the generosity of the citizens of Clearfield and Curwensville, and other persons interested in the welfare of the institution

Harry M Kurtz of Clearfield has recently donated to the hospital the sum of $5,000 00 for the purpose of erecting a Nurses Home, which will be completed in 1911, and various other improvements are contemplated The demands upon the Hospital are constantly growing and it is one of the most useful institutions in the county.

The following are the officers for 1910
H B Powell, President
Frank Fielding, Vice-President
George R Bigler, Sec and Treas

214

Directors

Geo R Bigler, Attorney at Law
H F Bigler, Pres Clearfield Fire Brick Co
Frank Fielding, Attorney at Law
Frank G Harris, Attorney at Law
Hugh M Irvin, Pres Curwensville National Bank, Curwensville
Fred B Kerr, Treas Clearfield Novelty Works
A W Lee, Pres Central Penna Light and Power Company
Thos H Murray, Attorney at Law
Rembrandt Peale, Pres Peale, Peacock & Kerr, Inc
H B Powell, Pres County National Bank
R A Shillingford, General Manager, Clearfield Bituminous Coal Corp

Ladies Auxiliary

Mrs Frank Fielding, President
Mrs Alexander Ennis Patton, 1st Vice-President
Mrs A R Powell, 2nd Vice-President
Mrs Pascaline Toner, 3rd Vice-President
Mrs Blanche M Biddle, Treasurer
Mrs H J Hartswick, Secretary

Junior Auxiliary

Miss Helen Murray, President
Miss Alice Bigler, 1st Vice-President
Miss Della Savage, 2nd Vice-President
Mrs J Lewis Irwin, Treasurer
Miss Isabel Powell, Secretary

Superintendent

Miss Jessie M Durstine

Nurses Training School

Mrs A H Woodward, President
Mrs Geo R Bigler, Secretary

THE DU BOIS HOSPITAL

The Du Bois Hospital was organized in the year 1897, with a capacity of twenty-three beds, and at the end of the same year it was incorporated under the laws of the Commonwealth of Pennsylvania, by a decree signed by the Hon Cyrus Gordon, President Judge of Clearfield county It is one of the class corporations not organized for profit It is not authorized to accumulate money, if it were possible, excepting for necessary expenditures, nor to use its funds, however obtained, for any other purpose than the proper maintenance and improvement of the Hospital The first members of the board of directors were John E Du Bois, A L Cole, M Lundergan, S Fugate and J C Sullivan These, as well as the Medical Staff, all serve without compensation

The management have constantly aimed to make the institution as nearly self-supporting as possible, and at the same time to be charitably inclined to the poor and needy by not refusing to care for worthy poor, but, as in our community charges must necessarily be moderate, as the vast majority of our patients are really poor, the hospital has never been self-supporting It has, since its organization, been dependent upon the charity of individuals, and the liberally disposed, as well as the State for appropriations

The charity of such individuals, etc, has been such that many poor, without means to help themselves, have been treated free of charge, and those whom poor districts, or in our own county, the county commissioners have met the ordinary expenses of, have had furnished them the advantages of hospital attention and nursing in medical and surgical cases at a rate below the actual cost of board and nursing

In November, 1909, the hospital building was badly damaged by fire All patients were safely removed and provided for

April 15, 1910, the Du Bois Hospital, after undergoing thorough repairs, refurnishing, and the rest, was again opened to the public

Before this was done, a re-organization by the enlarging of the board of directors to its full capacity of fifteen, as provided for in the Constitution of the Du Bois Hospital Association, was effected

The present board of directors are as follows S J Schrecongost, President, James A Gleason, Vice-President, D. E Hibner, Frank Guinzburg, S A Eisenman, George Minns, Jr, James Pifer, A R Van Tassel, E W Webster, H E Ginter, W H Cannon, A L Cole, M Lundergan, Frank Hahne, Hon A S Moulthrop, and J C Sullivan, secretary to the board

At the time of re-organization, the Sisters of Mercy were given the administrative charge of the Du Bois Hospital, and under their supervision, the hospital has prospered as in no other previous period In fact, the work of the institution is limited by its bed capacity only Mother M Camilla is the present superintendent Since the opening of the institution, April 15, 1910, there has been one hundred and thirty-one admissions

THE CLEARFIELD COUNTY HOME

The handsome three-story brick building known as The Clearfield County Home is situated in Lawrence Township on the Pennsylvania railroad, one mile below Clearfield The County Home property comprises 180 acres of what were formerly known as the John F Weaver and Goon farms When the question of organizing the county into a poor district was first submitted to the voters it failed to carry, but the second time it was voted on, at the spring election of February 20, 1894, the project carried, the vote being 4,944 for, and 3,485 against—a majority of only 459 The county commissioners under whose direction the Home was built were James S Read, William T Ross and A E Woolridge Hon. Cyrus Gordon was on the bench at the time, and George E Owens was clerk to the commissioners The contract was let October 1, 1894, to the lowest bidder, W. V. Hughes, of Pittsburgh, the price being $38,650 00. The architect was C M Robinson, of Altoona, who was chosen by the commissioners Jacob Straddler, a skilled mechanic and builder, was the general superintendent of the building and work From the opening day, December 30, 1895, to the present time the tax payers of Clearfield county have looked upon the Home as one of the best investments this county has ever made Indeed, the wonder has always been since its erection, why there could have been so many votes cast against building this splendid institution, which has been a blessing to thousands of the sons of Clearfield county —an asylum for the poor and a home for the needy. There were 143 inmates in the Home in August, 1910. Besides furnishing the county's poor with all the necessities of life and solicitously caring for the sick and aged, the spiritual side of the inmate's nature has not been overlooked as a chaplain in the person of Rev A B Williams, pastor of the United Brethren church of East End Clearfield, every Sunday holds preaching services in the well appointed chapel in the second story which is equipped with all the comforts of a modern church Dining rooms are furnished for both the men and women, while the sleeping quarters on the second floor are similarly arranged A large laundry and kitchen are at the rear of the first floor. Pure wholesome food is sup-

Patton Graded Public School, Cor. State and Walnut Streets, Curwensville

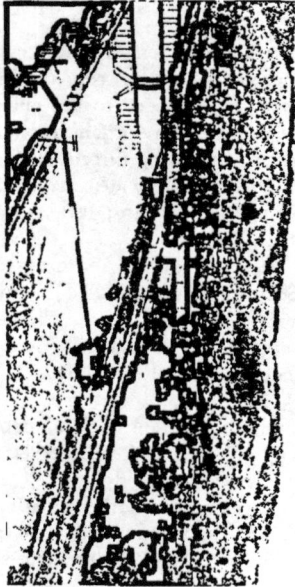

General View of West Clearfield

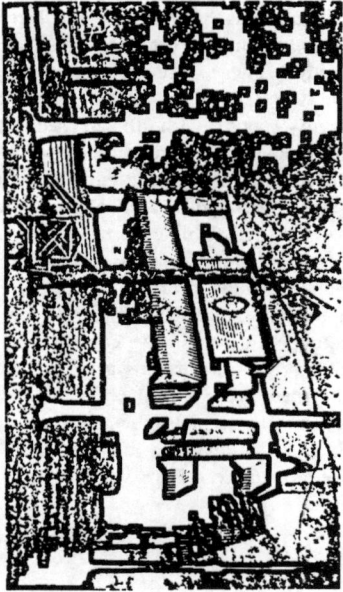

Residence of R. D. Swoope, Curwensville

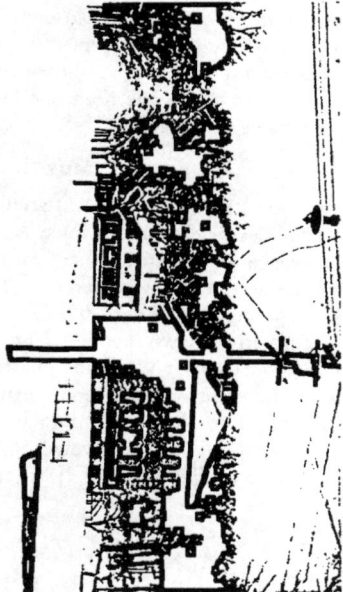

Second Ward School, North Locust Street, Curwensville

plied in abundance. In connection with the Home proper, a fine farm is carefully cultivated under the supervision of the steward Those male inmates who are able to assist in the work are pressed into service,' so there are not many idle men about the premises during the summer and fall months After the larder is stocked with products of the farm and the barns and granary supplied the remainder of the crop is sold by the steward The officials in charge of the Home are as follows Steward, J Sumner Hoyt, Matron, Mrs Hoyt, Physician, Dr J W Gordon, Nurse, C E Wilson The average weekly cost per capita is $2 31 During the year 1909 the number of days' support given inmates, including vagrants, was 63,067 At the present time only 2½ mills are levied for County Home purposes In the year 1909, the total current expenses for maintaining the Home were $19,111 31 Viewed from every standpoint the Clearfield County Home is acknowledged to rank second in the State and no similar institution is more efficiently managed

In addition to maintaining this institution, Clearfield county, in the year 1909, expended $5,265 51 for outdoor relief of its poor, while the sum of $15,469 09 was paid out of its treasury toward the support of its insane in the State hospitals One thousand one hundred and sixty-one dollars and fifty-four cents was also expended by the county for the maintenance of its feeble-minded in the training schools of the commonwealth, and $364 52 was paid for the support of the poor in other institutions Including other outside expenditures, amounting to $1,976 54, Clearfield county, in the year 1909, expended $48,357 12 for the support of the poor, sick and insane within her borders This record for public charity is most commendable and the heart of every true Clearfield countian should rejoice that this worthy benevolence is carried on on such a generous and far reaching scale

CHAPTER XVI

EDUCATION

A History of the Schools from 1834 to the Present Time—School Law of 1834—Compulsory School Law—Early Schools and Schoolhouses—Schools and Academies of Clearfield, Curwensville, DuBois and Other Towns

In the year 1834 a law, a section of which follows, was approved for Pennsylvania by Governor Wolf

Section I "Be it enacted That the city and county of Philadelphia, *and every other county* in this Commonwealth shall each form a school division and that every ward, township and borough within the several school divisions shall form a school district . and each of said districts shall contain a competent number of common schools for the education of every child within the limits thereof who shall apply, either in person, or by his or her parents, guardians or next friend for admission and instruction "

The next year an amendment was made providing that a township or district voting in the negative should not be compelled to accept this system

It was not until many years later, in 1897, that the Compulsory School Law was passed, which requires that every child in the state who is physically able (with certain exceptions), shall attend school regularly between the ages of six and sixteen years

• With the adoption of the law of 1834, be-

gan a new era in the educational history of our State and county The date and location of the first free school held in Clearfield county are not known, but it is probable that it was held in the Clearfield Academy building which had been completed in 1830, or in the Curwensville Academy, opened the following year

School had been held in the Clearfield Academy in 1830-31 by Dr A. T. Schryver, but this was not a free school

The first common school for Pike township was held in the Curwensville Academy about 1835. John Patton, Sr, serving as master at eighteen dollars per month Another common school of early date was that taught by John Carlisle in Brady township about 1836 In 1838 a school-house was erected at public expense on the Penfield Road, and here a free school was held for many years

Having given a general review of the early public and private schools, we will give a brief history of the schools in a few of the larger towns in the county, and some statistics which may be of interest.

Clearfield Schools —From 1830 until

220

1902 schools, both private and public, were held almost continuously in the Clearfield Academy Here, in the early forties, came boys and girls from miles around to receive instruction The Academy was the only source of instruction in French and Latin in the county The girls were taught useful arts, such as needle work, and many grandmothers to-day show with pride, the neat "samplers" which they stitched during their Academy days Later the building was used for various purposes, such as religious meetings, kindergarten and even as a dwelling house In 1902, the old grey walls, so closely associated with the early days of Clearfield county, were torn down, and on their ruins arose a splendid new building, with every modern equipment, typical of the new century, as the other had been of the old

The first building erected for the special use of public schools was the "Town Hall," built in 1851 Here the public schools were held until 1872, when the Leonard Graded School began to be constructed The Leonard Graded School was so named in honor of James T Leonard, a resident of Clearfield, who contributed over $14,000 00 for the erection and furnishing of this school It was completed in 1874, and is a fine building of red brick It is situated at the east end of Market Street, and is still in use as a public school

The High School building was erected on the site of the old Clearfield Academy in 1902 It is a splendid building of yellow brick, and contains every modern convenience, including facilities for instruction in domestic science and manual training

In 1885 a school building known as the "Fourth Ward School," was built This school originally contained seven grades, but additions have since been built, one of two rooms in 1903, and one of four rooms in 1908

Two years ago, in 1908, a brick building containing eight large school rooms was erected in West Clearfield, and is known as the Third Ward High School

Clearfield can also boast a fine Parochial School This splendid structure of yellow brick stands on North Second Street, and is known as the St Francis School It was built in 1904

Curwensville Schools —The educational history of Curwensville dates from the year 1831, at which time John Irvin contributed ground for the erection of the Curwensville Academy This building stood on Filbert Street, on the ground now known as the Samuel Taylor property After a few years the building was turned over to Pike township, and here a public school was held about 1835, by John Patton, Sr The public schools continued to be held there until 1852, when a schoolhouse was built on Walnut street School was also held in the old Methodist church until 1869 Hon John Patton presented two lots, adjoining the one they already owned on Walnut street, to the school board, and additional buildings were erected

In 1854 William Irvin built a brick schoolhouse on State street almost opposite the place where the B R & P station now stands, and for several years it was used as a private school Later it was rented by the borough and used for many years as a "High School"

The Patton Graded School was built in

1885 It was so named in honor of Hon. John Patton, who contributed $16,500 and a lot valued at $3,500 for its erection It is a handsome building of grey sandstone, and originally contained eight schoolrooms A wing has since been built, adding two large rooms to the original number For many years the Patton Graded School was the finest school building in the county, and with its many and continued improvements, still ranks among the best

In 1908 a substantial brick building of four rooms was built in the Second ward and these buildings, together with a school of two grades on the South Side, provide ample accommodations for the six hundred school children of Curwensville

DuBois Schools —Although the borough of DuBois is comparatively new it is the finest equipped of any in the county in regard to public schools. In 1883 the Central School building was erected, and another building, known as the New Central School, was built in 1899

The First Ward School was erected in 1892 An addition to this building became necessary in 1902, and in 1909 an entire new building was constructed

In 1895 a school building was erected in the Third Ward, and an addition built in 1902.

The Fourth Ward School was built in 1892, and two additions have since been built, one in 1895 and one in 1907.

A fine new High School building is now under construction The capacity of the High School will be 400

The total number of ward schools is fifty-eight, with a capacity of 2,500

DuBois has also a fine Parochial school, one of four such schools in the county. The other three are situated at Clearfield, Houtzdale and Frenchville respectively.

Private Girls' Schools —Although a "female school" was taught in connection with the Clearfield Academy as early as 1841, no separate school for girls was held until about 1867, when Miss Belle Welsh started a "select school" in the old Methodist church building in Curwensville This school was continued for several years with great success

About the same year, Miss K S Swan began a school for girls in the Keystone building in Clearfield Miss Swan continued her school until the erection of the Leonard Graded School in 1874

Other Schools —In the larger towns, such as Osceola, Houtzdale, Penfield, Karthaus, Ramey, Madera, Grampian and Mahaffey, large and substantial school buildings have been erected during the past twenty-five years, and to-day there are 538 schools held in this county The number of teachers employed in teaching these schools is 560, and the number of scholars enrolled 20,711.

No words are needed to prove the marvellous growth in public education in our county These figures speak eloquently of the interest and ambition of our citizens concerning education, and insure the intellectual advancement of our coming generation

Following is a list of the county superintendents·

1854-7—Dr A. T. Schryver.

1857-60—L L Still

1860-3—Jesse Broomall

1863-6—C. B Sanford

1866-72—G W Snyder

1872-8—J. A Gregory

1878-84—M L McQuown

1884-90—Matthew Savage

1890-6—G W Weaver

1896-1902—E C Shields

1902—W E Tobias

CHAPTER XVII

TRANSPORTATION FACILITIES

Turnpike Days—Water Transportation—The Tyrone and Clearfield Railroad—The Pennsylvania & Northern—The Buffalo, Rochester & Pittsburg R R —The Karthaus R R —The Beech Creek R R —The Cresson, Clearfield County & New York Short Route R R —The Philipsburg R R —The Clearfield Southern R R —The West Branch R R —The Curwensville & Bower R R —The Buffalo & Susquehanna R R —The Franklin & Clearfield R R —The DuBois Street Railway—The Philipsburg Street Railway Co

In no case does the old proverb, "necessity is the mother of invention," hold more true than in the history of the development of railroads in Clearfield county In the days when the lumbering stage coach traveled the "Erie Turnpike," carrying the government mails and the few travelers who ventured east or west, no better or faster means of locomotion was deemed necessary

Lumbering was the industry followed by the majority of Clearfield county's citizens, and the many streams connecting with the broad Susquehanna afforded ample facilities for lumber transportation Although the vast stores of coal and fire clay were known to exist, there had been no need to develop them as yet This left little need for transportation, and in those peaceful years, before the mania for speed had seized our nation, people were content to live with no other communication with the outside world than that afforded by waterway and turnpike

But soon rumors of a great civil war stirred our country and quickened it to new life No longer were men willing to be cut off from news of affairs which threatened our nation, and it was at this time that the citizens of Clearfield county came to a realization of their need of quicker transportation

The proposed railroad was called the Tyrone and Clearfield, a branch of the Pennsylvania railroad About 1862 the track was built from Vail to Sandy Ridge—the top of the mountain, and a year later was extended to Philipsburg It was not until six years later, and with the financial aid of citizens of Clearfield, that the track was extended to the county seat Here it again rested from its labors, and six years passed before the railroad reached Curwensville, aided financially by citizens of that town For many years Curwensville remained the terminus of the Tyrone and Clearfield railroad, but the coal interests farther west caused the road to be extended as far as Grampian in 1891

Several branches have been added to this road, the most important of which is the Moshannon The Moshannon branch joins the main line of the Tyrone and Clearfield railroad at Osceola, and extends through the coal regions of that section, terminating at McCartney Various branches, leading to the mining towns and coal operations in the vicinity of this line, have been added

The Pennsylvania and Northwestern Railroad, formerly known as the Bell's Gap railroad, extends from Bellwood in Blair county through the northwestern part of Clearfield county by way of Coalport, Irvona and Mahaffey, having its terminus at Punxsutawney This road was begun in 1871 and completed in 1887

The Low Grade division of the Pennsylvania railroad was opened through the west and northwest portion of Clearfield county in 1874 It enters this county at Tyler, running southeast to Du Bois and thence west into Jefferson county

The Buffalo, Rochester and Pittsburg Railroad was built through the northwestern part of Clearfield county in 1883 It originally entered this county from the northwest, running southeast to Du Bois and then south to Stump Creek, below which it again entered Jefferson county In 1893 a branch known as the Clearfield and Mahoning Railroad was constructed from Du Bois Junction, by way of Luthersburg and Curwensville, to Clearfield, being the first and only railroad connecting Du Bois with the county seat The opening of this branch was celebrated by a public meeting in the court house at Clearfield, June 6, 1893, at which representatives were present from various towns along the new railroad, as well as officials of the Buffalo, Rochester and Pittsburg Railroad Company

The Karthaus Railroad, extending from Keating on the Philadelphia and Erie Railroad to Karthaus in Clearfield county was completed in 1883 This road was operated by the Pennsylvania Railroad Company until 1902, when it passed under the control of the New York Central and Hudson River Railroad Company at the time of the completion of their West Branch Valley line, of which it is now a part

The Beech Creek Railroad was constructed in Clearfield county in 1884 It now extends from Jersey Shore, Lycoming county, through Clearfield county to Patton in Cambria county This road has branches connecting with Philipsburg and Clearfield

The Cresson, Clearfield County and New York Short Route Railroad was built in the northern part of the county, between Cresson and Irvona in 1886 It is now operated by the Pennsylvania Railroad Company

The Philipsburg Railroad extends from Philipsburg to Ferndale, by way of Osceola, Houtzdale and Ramey

The Clearfield Southern Railroad completed in 1908, extends from Dimeling station on the Beech Creek Railroad, up Clearfield Creek to Irvona, by way of Madera and Glen Hope It is operated by the New York Central and Hudson River Railroad Company

The West Branch Valley Railroad was completed in 1902 and extends from Clearfield to Keating It is operated by the New York Central and Hudson River Railroad Company and is known as the River Line

The Curwensville and Bower Railroad was constructed in 1903-4 It runs from Curwensville up the West Branch of the Susquehanna river to Bower Station, on the Beech Creek Railroad It is operated by the New York Central and Hudson River Railroad Company as part of the Beech Creek system, the trains using the Buffalo, Rochester & Pittsburg Railroad tracks between Curwensville and Clearfield

The Buffalo and Susquehanna Railroad was built in 1904 and extends from near Tyler through Clearfield county by way of Du Bois and its present terminus is Sagamore, Indiana county

The Franklin and Clearfield Railroad, now under construction, enters Clearfield county near Du Bois It is a branch of the Lake Shore and Michigan Southern Railroad, and the trains now use the tracks of the Buffalo, Rochester and Pittsburg Railroad between Du Bois and Clearfield.

Street Railways—The only town in Clearfield county having a system of street railways is DuBois The lines are operated by overhead trolley The company is known as the Du Bois Street Railway Company, and began business in 1891 It has 21 miles of track

The Philipsburg Street Railway Company has a line extending to Morrisdale, Winburne and several other mining towns in Clearfield county

CHAPTER XVIII

MANUFACTURES

The Lumber Industry—Beginning of the Industry—Its Growth by 1854—Method of Operating—Rafting—Log Drivers and Lumber Arks—Conflict with "Square Timber" Men—Marking the Logs—Small Profits of the Business—Erection of Saw-Mills—Decline of the Business—The Fire Brick Industry—Firms and Companies Engaged in the Business—The Tanning Industry

LUMBERING INTERESTS

The traveler who now journeys over Clearfield county for the first time and sees the coal, fire clay and agricultural development and how little timber remains, can hardly realize that a century ago the whole territory was covered with seemingly boundless forests, the only cleared space at that time being a few acres of land where the town of Clearfield now stands The work of the pioneers in clearing up the wood-land and opening up roads through these great forests, can hardly be realized by the present generation

The first lumbering in the county was not for the purpose of shipping the logs and lumber as a business, but the trees were cut into logs in order that land might be cleared to make room for homes for the early settlers and sufficient fields to cultivate their scanty crops, and the logs used for building Although Daniel Ogden and Frederick Haney had each built saw-mills as early as 1805 and Daniel Turner erected a saw-

mill on Anderson Creek in 1808 and about the same time Robert Maxwell built one near Curwensville and William Kersey one at the Kersey settlement, and James and Samuel Ardary soon afterwards built a saw-mill near the old Clearfield bridge, it was not until the year 1820 that lumbering operations assumed business proportions

When the "Raftman's Journal" was founded in 1854, by the late Hon H B Swoope, lumbering had become such an important business in the county, that the name of the paper was selected on that account, and Mr Swoope, himself, drew the design of the rafting scene, a copy of which is still used as a part of the heading of the "Journal"

For many years lumbering was the chief occupation of nearly every resident of the county. Agriculture was neglected and the magnificent forests were destroyed and the lumber made into "square timber" or logs, was floated down the river, and the proceeds built up the towns of Lock Haven, Marietta and Williamsport where large

227

saw mills were erected to manufacture the lumber and great dams and booms constructed to receive and hold the logs until they could be sawed

This "square timber" was made entirely with an axe, the trees were first chopped down and then squared by the use of a peculiarly shaped axe with which was cut off the branches, bark and sufficient of the tree to square it up These great timber sticks were then hauled during the winter on sleds to the river bank where they were piled, ready to be made into rafts in time for the spring floods These rafts were made by placing the great timber sticks side by side in the water and fastening them together across each end and in the center by long saplings laid across the timber sticks and fastened by hickory hoops held by wooden pins driven into holes bored into the timber sticks The rafts were steered by immense oars, one in front and one at the rear of each raft From two to four men operated each of these oars according to the size of the raft Small cabins or "shanties" were built on the larger rafts in which the crew ate and slept during the trip down the river These "shanties" were usually equipped with a lot of hay or straw, some blankets and a sheet iron stove, using wood as fuel A trip down the river occupied from three to four days, and after delivering the rafts at Lock Haven, Marietta or Williamsport, as the case might be, the sturdy raftsmen footed it back home in time, if possible, to make another trip during the same flood In those days to be a "Pilot" on the river was the great ambition of every boy and young man in nearly every section of the county and, indeed, it required long experience and considerable skill, to successfully navigate the different streams and run the chutes at the dams or steer between the rocks at the "Falls" and at other dangerous points, and many thrilling stories are told of narrow escapes from destruction of both rafts and crews

This method of sending the timber to market continued until about 1857, when a new system was introduced by lumbermen from the New England States, who began floating the timber to market in the form of round saw-logs instead of in "square timber" These saw-logs were not made up into rafts but were turned into the river and allowed to float down with the flood and in the rear of the "drive" of logs there followed the log drivers, who were equipped with "spiked" shoes and what are called "cant hooks" for handling the logs, and also had a number of teams of horses to haul the logs into the water These log drivers lived in "arks," which were great cabins built on rafts and fitted up with bunks for sleeping, dining room and kitchen, and there was usually a separate ark for the horses

These log drivers were usually the men who had been working in the woods all winter, cutting the timber into logs and running them down on the slides to the river bank They were a hardy and picturesque lot of men and when after their winter's work and their log drive was finished, they landed in a town with their pockets full of money, they usually "painted the town red," and at their appearance, the peaceful citizens stayed close at home until the logmen departed When the first attempt was made to float logs down the river, the "square timber" men fought the innovation vigorously, some of them organized a party and attacked the log drivers on Clearfield 'Creek, with such effect as to drive them from the Creek Although some of the attacking parties were arrested, tried and convicted for riot, it was many years before the driving of logs on Clearfield Creek was again engaged in Both the "square timber" and logs were marked on the ends by what was known as the owner's mark or stamp This mark or stamp was put on with a stamping hammer, the metal head of which had the mark cast on it in sharp relief, so that when the head of the hammer was struck against the soft wood of the timber stick or log, it would leave a distinct impression, and thus the timber sticks or logs were easily identified The law provided for the registering of these log marks in the prothonotary's office, and it was a serious offense to use another owner's mark

Many million dollars worth of lumber was floated out of Clearfield county during the period referred to and the results were of comparatively little benefit to the owners of the timber, the hazard and expense of the lumber operations and the uncertainty of the market preventing the Clearfield county lumbermen from realizing the profit that they should have done, and so the mighty forests were sacrificed, and today there is comparatively little merchantable timber standing in Clearfield county

Had this timber been manufactured at home instead of having been floated off to other points, some permanent advantage might have been obtained in the way of building up the various towns along the river in Clearfield county, but lack of railroad facilities, want of capital to secure

them and the necessity of the land owners selling their timber in order to make payments on their lands, combined to prevent the manufacture of the lumber at home, with very few exceptions John E DuBois, who founded the borough of DuBois, was one of the men who saw the advantage of manufacturing the lumber at home and he erected large saw-mills and created an extensive business, as one of the results of which DuBois is the largest town in the county, and Mr DuBois accumulated one of the few fortunes made in the lumber business in this section

The lumber business in Clearfield county is a thing of the past and while it had its proper place in the development of the county, the rapid cutting out of the forests was really a benefit, because with the departure of the timber it became necessary for the inhabitants to engage in some other occupation, and the result was that farming was again taken up, and the people of the county who owned the land, cleared the same up and those who devoted themselves to farming achieved substantial independence The coal and fire clay was opened and the great mineral wealth of the county made available

THE FIRE-BRICK INDUSTRY

From the time that man, in the progress of civilization, discovered the necessity of some material that would withstand the great heat necessary in the use of fire for the purpose of refining metals, many efforts were made to discover a substance suitable for this purpose, but it was not until fire-clay was discovered in Stourbridge, England, in the year 1555, that success crowned the efforts of the experimenters From that date, fire-clay has been extensively mined for the purpose of making a brick to be used as the lining of all receptacles requiring protection from the effects of concentrated heat

In a country like the United States, where such vast capital is invested in the iron, steel and kindred industries, the search for fire-clay commenced at an early date and the first large deposits were found near Morgantown, West Virginia, and have been extensively developed

Fire-clay was known to exist in Clearfield county at an early period in its history, but on account of the lack of railroad facilities, no steps were taken to open it up for commercial use until the extension of the Tyrone & Clearfield Branch of the P R R in 1869, provided means of shipping the clay and its products to market, since which time this has become one of the leading industries of the county As mentioned in the chapter on the geology of the county, large deposits of fire-clay of superior quality have been found The veins vary from two to six feet and over in thickness and the brick made therefrom have a high reputation in the market

The Clearfield Fire Brick Company, organized in 1871, was the first corporation to undertake the development of this business, this company constructed works at Clearfield, which they operated for a number of years until they were taken over by the Harbison-Walker Refractories Company

The Harbison-Walker Fire Brick Company, now the Harbison-Walker Refractories Company, was one of the first concerns to mine the clay and manufacture fire-brick on a large scale and their plant at Woodland was among the earliest erected in the county, and has also been one of the most sucessful. This company, on account of the excellence of its product and the consequent demand therefor, soon enlarged its operations and rapidly secured control of much of the best clay territory, and finally of many of the other plants, so that at the present time, the Harbison-Walker Refractories Company is one of the largest producers of fire-brick in the United States Their headquarters are in Pittsburg, Pa , and their present officers are as follows: President, H W Croft, vice-president, S A Walker, general manager of the works in Clearfield county, Neil McQuillan

The largest independent company is the Bickford Fire Brick Company of Curwensville, Pa This company has what is probably the finest, best equipped and one of the largest fire-brick plants in this country The officers of the Bickford Fire Brick Company are as follows President, Howard Janney, Vice-President and General Manager, J A Bickford, Assistant Manager and Treasurer, S M Bickford

The following are the fire-brick plants in operation in the county at the present time:

HARBISON-WALKER REFRACTORIES COMPANY PLANTS

Clearfield Fire Brick Co at Clearfield
Harbison-Walker Plant at Clearfield
Woodland Fire Brick Works at Woodland
Mineral Springs Works at Mineral Springs
Wallaceton Fire Brick Co at Wallaceton
Stronach Fire Brick Works at Stronach

The following are the plants not controlled by the Harbison-Walker Refractories Company·

Bickford Fire Brick Company at Curwensville
Wynn Brothers & Company at Blue Ball

Osceola Silica Fire Brick Company at Osceola Mills

Karthaus Fire Brick Co at Karthaus

Geo S Good Fire Brick Company at Lumber City.

Irvona Fire Brick Company at Irvona

In addition to the foregoing plants manufacturing fire-brick there are also a number of concerns whose business is the manufacturing of building and paving brick, in which fire-clay is largely used

Clearfield Clay Working Company at Clearfield

Paterson Fire Brick Company at Clearfield

Bigler Fire Brick Company at Bigler

Bigler Reed Fire Brick Company at Krebs

Wrigley Fire Brick and Tile Co, at Riverview

The combined output of the brick plants of Clearfield is over 1,200,000 brick per working day, and their products are shipped to nearly every state in the Union, as well as to foreign countries

THE TANNING INDUSTRY

In the early days of the county's history, on account of the cheapness of bark, by reason of the abundance of timber, several small tanneries were built, two of these were at Curwensville, owned respectively by William McNaul and S B Taylor, the McNaul Tannery was built in 1819, and the Taylor Tannery in 1851, and there was also a tannery at Clearfield, owned by M Shirk   These tanneries were run without steam power and tanned only "Upper Leather," but it was not until the extension of the Tyrone & Clearfield Railroad to the county, thus giving facilities for the shipment of leather to market, that tanneries were constructed on a large scale

In October, 1873, Messrs Wooster & Lull built a tannery in Osceola Mills, which they shortly afterwards sold to W S White & Son, who in turn sold to J B Alley & Company of Boston, Mass, who conducted the tannery for a number of years, until it was finally abandoned

The Summit Tannery was built at Curwensville by W S White & Son and was completed in May, 1877   On April 3, 1878, it was purchased by J B Alley & Co, of Boston, Mass, which firm was succeeded on January 1, 1887, by Alley Brothers & Place, who continued to operate the tannery until it was taken over by the U S Leather Company in 1894

In the year 1879, Hoyt, Fairweather and LaRue erected a large tannery at Clearfield, which they conducted for a number of years, until it passed under control of the U S Leather Co, in the year 1894

In 1881 McKinstry & Clearwater erected a tannery at Penfield in Huston township, which they sold to Thomas E Proctor in 1882   This tannery was operated until bark became scarce, when it was abandoned

In 1886 a large tannery was built in Mahaffey   It is owned by A B Mosser & Company and is still in operation

In 1883 a tannery was built at Irvona by N W Rice & Company   This tannery is now owned by the U S Leather Company and is still running

DuBois and VanTassel Brothers built a large tannery in DuBois in 1884   This tannery is now owned by A R VanTassel and does a large business

Wm F Mosser, now deceased, constructed a large tannery at Westover in the year 1889   This tannery is still in operation and is owned by the Wm F Mosser Company of Boston, Mass

In 1894, after the sale of the tannery of Alley Bros & Place, at Curwensville to the U S Leather Company, that firm in connection with Fred J Dyer, erected a new tannery at that place, which unfortunately was destroyed by fire in the year 1899, but the firm erected a still larger tannery on a new location in Curwensville, which tannery was subsequently sold to the Penna Hide & Leather Company, and is still operated on a large scale

The tanneries controlled by the United States Leather Company manufacture what is known as "Union Crop" sole leather   The tannery of the Pennsylvania Hide & Leather Company manufactures "Upper Leather," which is finished at their plant in Curwensville

Owing to the fact that the supply of bark, within a reasonable distance, has about given out, it is probable that the number of tanneries in Clearfield county will become less, as the years go by

At the present time, a large amount of "Extract," which is made at works in the Southern States, where available timber is still plenty and cheap, is shipped to the tanneries in this county and used in lieu of that much of the bark formerly required, but even advertisement states that the signers to the industry, it has passed its greatest development in this county

CHAPTER XIX

FINANCIAL INSTITUTIONS

Banking in the Early History of the County—Private and State Banks—Special Act of the Legislature Necessary to Incorporation Before 1860—The Act of 1860—Unreliability of the State Banks—Passage of the National Banking Law—Banks of Clearfield County—Officers and Directors

In the early history of the county, the banking was done by the merchants who received the money of their customers for safe keeping and either sent it or took it to the eastern cities, where they kept accounts and where they usually went once or twice each year to purchase goods

About the year 1858 Leonard, Finney & Company conducted a private bank at Clearfield, the partners in this enterprise being James T Leonard, William A Wallace, D A Finney and A C Finney

Prior to 1861, the banking business in Pennsylvania was transacted either by private partnerships or by banks chartered by the State by authority of special Acts of the Legislature, a separate Act of the Legislature being required to authorize the incorporation of each bank

The "Raftsman's Journal," published at Clearfield, Pa, in its issue of August 31, 1859, contains an advertisement of an application for a bank charter for a bank to be called the "Clearfield County Bank," to be located in the Borough of Clearfield, Pa, with a capital of one hundred thousand ($100,000 00) dollars

with the privilege of increasing it to two hundred thousand ($200,000 00) dollars This advertisement states that the signers of the application were J F Weaver, Thomas J McCullough, Isaac Johnson, C D Watson, D F Etzweiler, James Alexander, Jona Boynton, M A Frank, Richard Mossop, A K Wright, W F Irwin and S B Row

The Pamphlet Laws of Pennsylvania do not contain any special Act of the Legislature, incorporating the "Clearfield County Bank" The reason for this probably being because the Legislature, by an Act approved March 31, 1860, to be found in the Pamphlet Laws of that year, at page 459, entitled "An Act to establish a System of Free Banking in Pennsylvania and to secure the public against loss from Insolvent Banks," provided that banks could be incorporated thereunder, without the necessity of having special Acts of the Legislature passed as had before been necessary

Under this Act of 1860 and the supplements and amendments thereto, many state banks were organized, but they were practically without supervision by the State and

233

their notes, except in the localities where the banks were located, could usually only be used at a heavy discount

With the passage of the National Banking Law by the United States Congress and its approval by President Lincoln, in 1863, the banking business of the country was for the first time placed upon a substantial basis and National Banks were soon established at various points in the county The first one being at Clearfield and known as the "First National Bank of Clearfield," and the next at Curwensville, known as the "First National Bank of Curwensville"

With the growth of population and business of the county, various financial institutions have been established and at the present time (1911) the following are in existence, to-wit

County National Bank, Clearfield, Pa

Clearfield National Bank, Clearfield, Pa.

Clearfield Trust Company, Clearfield, Pa

Farmers' & Traders' National Bank, Clearfield, Pa

Curwensville National Bank, Curwensville, Pa

Deposit National Bank, DuBois, Pa

Union Banking and Trust Company, DuBois, Pa

DuBois National Bank, DuBois, Pa

Bituminous National Bank, Winburne, Pa

Mahaffey National Bank, Mahaffey, Pa

Madera National Bank, Madera, Pa

First National Bank, Houtzdale, Pa

First National Bank, Osceola Mills, Pa

First National Bank, Coalport, Pa

These institutions have aggregate deposits of nearly eight millions of dollars

($8,000,000 00) and are conservatively and carefully conducted

The following is a list of the officers and directors of the financial institutions of the county from the latest information furnished to us, and an examination of the same will convince any one who is acquainted with the citizens of Clearfield county that these institutions are under the control of the leading business men of the several communities in which they are located

The County National Bank of Clearfield, Pa.

H B Powell, President, A B Shaw, Vice-President, J L Gilliland, Cashier

Directors—F G. Betts, G W. Jose, W A Porter, A B Shaw, H F Bigler, H A Kratzer, W B Potter, J. P O'Laughlin, H L. Forcey, H. J Patton, H B. Powell, A. K Wright

The Clearfield National Bank, Clearfield, Pa

James Mitchell, President, H. S Whiteman, Vice-President and Cashier

Directors—James Mitchell, H. A Kennedy, John Dimeling, Thos H. Murray, A E Lietzinger, W H Patterson, W I Betts, W P Hopkins

The Clearfield Trust Company, Clearfield, Pa

R A Shillingford, President, A W Lee, Vice-President; P. T Davis, Treasurer.

Directors—G R Bigler, H W Croft, F. G. Harris, F B. Kerr, Chas T Kurtz, A. W Lee, R A Shillingford, Clement W. Smith, S I Snyder, E E Lindemuth

Farmers' & Traders' National Bank, Clearfield, Pa

A E Woolridge, President; G B Pass-

Pennsylvania Hide & Leather Co., Curwensville

The New B. R. & P. R. R. Trestle, Curwensville

Bickford Fire Brick Co. Works, Curwensville

Elk Tanning Co. Tanneries, Curwensville

more, Vice-President, Isaac Straw, Vice-President, E O Hartshorne, Cashier, A K Staver, Assistant Cashier

Directors—A E Woolridge, E C Davis, D R. Woolridge, G B Passmore, Jesse Williams, Dorsey Bailey, W T DeHaas, Isaac Straw, F A Walker, C G McNaul, M. D.

The Curwensville National Bank, Curwensville, Pa

C. S Russell, President, Hugh M Irvin, Vice-President, L W Spencer, Cashier, Anthony Hile, Assistant Cashier

Directors—C S Russell, Sam'l P Arnold, J S Graff, C A Woods, Geo L Benner, H M Irvin, Fred J Dyer, Roland D Swope, I B Norris, C M Porter, M A. Caldwell, Peter Gearhart, H J Patton, Geo F Kittelberger, C E Patton

Deposit National Bank, DuBois, Pa

R H Moore, President, M I McCreight, First Vice-President, D L Corbett, Second Vice-President, B B McCreight, Cashier, J Q Groves, Assistant Cashier, W D I Arnold, Assistant Cashier

Directors—R H Moore, W H Cannon, Walter Hatten, D L Corbett, J H Pifer, C P. Munch, Rembrandt Peale, Austin Blakeslee, R W Beadle, M I McCreight

The Union Banking and Trust Company of DuBois, Pa

A R. Van Tassel, President, A T Sprankle, Vice-President, B M Marlin, Secretary and Treasurer, Jos F Sprankle, Assistant Treasurer

Directors—A R Van Tassel, J E Merris, B M Marlin, Thos W Kennedy, H S Knarr, A T Sprankle, J B Henderson, F W Prothero, C L Hay, William Osborn, F G St Clair.

The DuBois National Bank, DuBois, Pa

John E DuBois, President, J A Gregory, Vice-President, Geo A Lukehart, Vice-President, S C Bond, Cashier, W G Brown, Assistant Cashier

Directors—John E DuBois, J A Gregory, Geo A Lukehart, William Wingert, A S Moulthorp F A Tozier, S C Bond

Bituminous National Bank, Winburne, Pa

James L Sommerville, President, Berten Merritt, Vice-President, J Malcolm Laurie, Cashier

Directors—Jas L Sommerville, A O Sommerville, Jacob Smutzinger, Berten Merritt, R H George, E F Harvey, R H Sommerville, Dr H G Jones

Mahaffey National Bank, Mahaffey, Pa

A B Mosser, President, Thomas Bellis, Vice-President, H N Widdowson, Cashier, W B Clark, Assistant Cashier

Directors—Thomas Bellis, A B Mosser, Geo L Fletcher, B W McCracken, H N Widdowson, W H Thomson

Madera National Bank, Madera, Pa

J E Kirk, President, S J Miller, Vice-President, H B Swoope, Vice-President, E B Mahaffey, Cashier

Directors—S J Miller, W C Park, Joseph Alexander, J H Moore, H B Swoope, J E Kirk, Clark Hileman, J C Root, E B Mahaffey

First National Bank, Houtzdale, Pa

Lewis W. Beyer, President, Julius Viebahn, Vice-President, Geo W Ganoe, Cashier

Directors—John Beyer, Samuel Kirk, John Benson, Julius Viebahn, Jas H Minds, Harry Boulton, Michael Burns, A D Stewart, Lewis W Beyer

First National Bank of Osceola, Osceola Mills, Pa.

John McLarren, President, H W Todd, Vice-President, E C Blandy, Cashier

Directors—John McLarren, Chas R Houtz, E C Blandy, W A Gould, Frank Craig, James S Moore, H W Todd

First National Bank of Coalport, Pa.

Geo D Benn, President, A. L Hegarty, Vice-President, A. P. Silverthorn, Cashier.

Directors—Geo. D. Benn, J. E McDowell, John McNulty, A L Hegarty, C D McMurray, W H. Denlinger, W. W Hegarty, F P McFarland, F V. Perry

CHAPTER XX

AGRICULTURE

The Patrons of Husbandry, "Grange"—Object of the Society—When Founded—The First Grange Founded in Clearfield County—Other Branches of the Society in Clearfield County —The Clearfield County Agricultural Society

THE PATRONS OF HUSBANDRY—GRANGE

At the city of Washington, D C , on the 4th day of December, in the year 1868, O H Kelley and William Sanders, both of whom were then connected with the national department of agriculture, took the initial steps and laid the foundation for this vast organization, and brought into existence the National Grange In each State are societies subordinate to the national order, and which are known as State Granges Auxiliary to the State Grange, are County, Township and District Granges

As the name implies, the aim, object and purpose of the society is to improve the condition and advance the interests of all persons, and their families as well, who may be engaged in agricultural pursuits, not only to improve their condition through a free interchange of opinions in social gatherings where subjects pertaining to agriculture may be discussed, but by thorough organization and honest, open, determined effort to bring about such action on the part of the general government, and also that of each State, as will effectually and permanently overthrow all op-

pression from monopolists, unwise and unfair discrimination on the part of railroad corporations, and the ·exorbitant and needless charges of commission men in every department of trade

So rapid, indeed, has been the growth of membership of the Grange throughout the land that it now numbers among the millions In the year 1875, the movement reached this county, and on the 13th day of April of that year, the enterprising farmers of Penn township met at the residence of Samuel Widemire, where, through the district deputy, O S Cary, of Punxsutawney, the first Grange organization was perfected Although in point of seniority, Penn Grange is entitled to first mention, it is but a district or township Grange, yielding to Pomona Grange the first place, as that although of more recent organization, is a county institution, to which the others are subordinate

Pomona Grange, P of H , No 33, was organized January 1, 1879, with the following charter members J R· Read, Mary W Read, William L Read, O D Kendall, E M Kendall, Catharine Davis, George Emerick, R L Reiter, Hettie Reiter, A Rankin, M C Rankm, J L McPherson, Leander Denning, Eliza Denning, W. P Read, James Spackman, Mary E Spackman, W P Tate, Martha C Tate At the time of its organization the following officers were elected Master, George Emerick, overseer, Elisha M Davis, lecturer, Leander Denning, steward, A Rankin, chaplain, W P. Read, treasurer, James Spackman, secretary, W P Tate, assistant steward, O D Kendall, gate-keeper, R L Reiter, ceres, Catharine Davis, pomona, Sister Spackman, flora, Sister Kendall, lady assistant steward, Mrs L Denning

Penn Grange No 534, P of H, was organized April 13, 1875, by District Deputy O S Cary, with twenty-five charter members The first master was Samuel Widemire, secretary, Miles S Spencer

Lawrence Grange, No 553, P of H, was organized by Deputy O S Cary, on the 12th day of May, 1875, with twenty-one charter members This Grange is located in Lawrence township, from which its name is derived

Goshen Grange, No 623, P of H, was organized November 18, 1875, with a charter membership of eighteen persons Its first master and secretary were H H Morrow and J A Fulton, respectively This Grange is located in Goshen township, on the road leading from Shawsville to Clearfield

Troutdale Grange No 677, P of H, was organized by Deputy J B Shaw, on the 15th day of March, 1876, with twenty-nine charter members This is an organization of Bell township

Greenwood Grange, No —, P of H, was organized by Deputy J B Shaw, May 12, 1876, having a charter membership of twenty-three persons First master, C A Thorp;

secretary, J S McQuown It is located in Greenwood township

Bloomington Grange No 715, P of H was organized by Deputy J S Reed on the 26th of June, 1876, with thirty-three charter members First master, James R Norris; secretary, Mrs Ella M Bloom, located at Bloomington, in Pike township

Sylvan Grove Grange, No 765, P of H, organized by Deputy W P Reed, October 24, 1882 Number of charter members, twenty First officers Master, O P. Reese, secretary, B F Wilhelm, location of Grange, Kylertown, Cooper township

Laurel Run Grange, No 769, P of H, was organized March 10, 1883, by Deputies Davis and Bloom, with a charter membership of fourteen Adam Kephart was elected its first master, and Elijah Reese, Jr, secretary This Grange is located in Decatur township.

Fairview Grange, No 783, P. of H, was organized May 2, 1884, by Deputies Elisha M Davis and James C Bloom, with twenty-three charter members The first officers were: Master, W A Smeal, secretary, W B Barger The Grange is located on the Grahamton and Deer Creek road, two and one-half miles south of Deer Creek bridge

Girard Grange, No 788, P of H., was organized September 16, 1884, by Deputies Elisha M Davis and James C Bloom, with eighteen charter members The first officers elected were Isaac Smith, master, and Louisa Shope, secretary

Mount Foy Grange, No 584, P of H, was organized August 10, 1885, with twenty-five charter members The first officers were Master, J B Shaw, overseer, Matthew Ogden, secretary, J B Ogden This organization is formed mainly of residents of the north part of Lawrence township

Narrows Creek Grange, No 796, P of H, was organized by Deputy Elisha M Davis, January 2, 1886, with fourteen charter members The first master elected was W H Liddle, secretary, Isaac Hess, location of Grange four miles east of DuBois and two miles west of Summit tunnel on A V Railroad

Union Grange, No 802, P of H, was organized by Deputy E M Davis June 3, 1886, with twenty-one charter members, first master, Henry Pentz, secretary, William Welty, location of Grange, thirteen miles west of Clearfield, on turnpike leading to Luthersburg, at the village of Rockton

Du Bois Grange, No —, P of H, was organized October 20, 1886, by Deputy Davis, with a charter membership of sixteen persons Its first master was S C Liddle, secretary, William Woods It is located in the south part of Sandy township, about two miles distant from Du Bois borough

CLEARFIELD COUNTY AGRICULTURAL SOCIETY

The Clearfield County Agricultural Society was incorporated January 14, 1860 The purpose of this society is to encourage the development of agriculture in the county

Notwithstanding the fact that there was very little attention paid to farming in Clearfield county for many years of the county's earlier history, yet this society for a number of years held annual fairs at Clearfield that were well attended and gave indications of the development of this much needed branch of industry For the last few years, however, the society has not been holding fairs but is now offering prizes for the most successful efforts in various lines of agriculture, and in the breeding of fine stock The present officers of the society are T L Way, president, R E Shaw, secretary

CHAPTER XXI

COAL PRODUCTION AND DEVELOPMENT

Early Coal Shipments—Early Coal Mines and Railroad—The Moshannon Branch of the T. & C R R —Coal Companies and Proprietors—Description of the Mines—Statistics

The first shipments of coal from Clearfield county were made during the lumbering days when the coal was loaded in what were called "Arks" and floated down the river to Lock Haven and Williamsport as early as the year 1822 About 1830 a mine was opened on what was known as the Goss farm in Decatur township, and the coal was hauled to Spruce Creek on wagons The coal transported by these crude methods amounted to a very small tonnage, and it was not until the opening of the Tyrone and Clearfield Railroad to Osceola Mills and Philipsburg in 1864, that the real development of the coal industry in the county commenced When we remember that prior to that year not a pound of coal had been shipped by rail from Clearfield county, that the production has grown from a few thousand tons to many million tons per year, that "Clearfield" bituminous coal is known wherever this product is used in this country, and is exported to other countries, we can, in part, realize the great impetus that this industry has given to the progress and growth of the county

The Derby mine, about three-fourths of a mile west of Philipsburg, was opened in 1860 by George Zeigler, and the coal hauled on a tram road to Philipsburg and sold for local use When the railroad reached that point in 1864 this mine was ready to ship Its chutes were located nearly opposite the depot, and it

was the first mine in the county to ship its coal to market by railroad

The Moshannon Branch of the T & C Railroad was commenced in 1864, and completed as far as Moshannon in 1868, with a branch up Coal Run to the old Decatur mine In June, 1866, a mine on the lands of the Moshannon Coal Company, on the south side of the railroad, was opened by the Moshannon Coal Company on the tract formerly known as the "John Anderson," and called "Moshannon" This mine ran until about 1880, when it was abandoned by its owners, a new one having been opened immediately opposite in 1876, and called "New Moshannon" Both of these mines were very successful ventures, and first brought to general notice the Clearfield coals

During the summer of 1868, the Moshannon Branch Railroad was extended about two miles further west, and in the summer of 1869 the rails were laid upon the portion graded, and Sterling No 1 was commenced August 11, 1869, to add to the production This colliery was opened upon the lands of A B Long, formerly the Casper Haines tract, and in a very short time became the largest mine in the region

During the year 1870, the Moshannon Branch Railroad was extended a quarter of a mile further, and the "Eureka" colliery opened

242

and commenced to ship coal March 14, 1870 This colliery was owned by White & Lingle, and was situated on the lands of Dr Houtz, of Alexandria, Huntingdon county The coal in this mine proved to be the purest of any that had been opened up to that time, and the mine itself was without a "fault" from the beginning to the end In 1874 the mine passed into the hands of Berwind, White & Company, and from them to the Berwind-White Coal Mining Company

The Moshannon Branch was extended during the year 1875, three miles, to enable D K Ramey, of Altoona, who owned the lands at the then terminus, to get his lumber to market The extension of this branch also opened the way to a very extensive coal field, and in the fall of 1874 William Kendrick commenced to sink a shaft two miles from Houtzdale, on lands of Mr Ramey, for the purpose of proving the "E Bed," which had dropped below water-level at that point This shaft is seventy feet deep, and was the first in the region, if we except the Sackett shaft at Osceola Mills, sunk in 1866, to reach the "A" Vein, but which was never worked

John Whitehead, Harned Jacobs & Company and other parties opened up a large number of collieries in the Houtzdale region Most of these operations were purchased by Berwind, White & Company, now the Berwind-White Coal Mining Company of Philadelphia, and they became the largest shippers in that region and continued so for a number of years

In the year 1901, Roland D Swoope, Esq, of Curwensville, in connection with other owners of coal lands near Madera in Bigler township, constructed a branch railroad from the Moshannon Branch of the P R R to their lands and opened up the "Bucher" Mine on the "B" Vein of coal This proved to be a very successful operation and developed a new coal territory from which the largest shipments in the district are now made

The Morrisdale Coal Company also opened a mine near Madera, but subsequently sold their interest at that point to the Sylvania Coal Company

The White Oak Coal Company also opened up mines near Madera, and their mines were purchased by the Corona Coal & Coke Company and are now being operated by that company

The coal near Karthaus, in the northeastern corner of the county was first operated by John Whitehead & Company in 1885 This mine was sold to the Berwind-White Coal Mining Company, who also opened the "Cataract" Mine in the same year, about six miles below Karthaus The Beech Creek Railroad was completed as far as Peale in July, 1884, and to Gazzam in July, 1885 At Peale a large coal operation was opened by the Clearfield Bituminous Coal Company, and the same company operates the coal at Gazzam, and also the Grass Flat mines

The Morrisdale Coal Company in 1885 opened up a large colliery on the Hawk Run Branch The Bloomington Coal Mining Company opened up their operations at Bloomington in 1885 and Rembrandt Peale, who was the manager of that company and of Peale, Peacock & Kerr, Inc, pushed their operations on a large scale at Bloomington, and also near DuBois and at other points in the county The Rochester & Pittsburg Coal Company have few operations in Clearfield county, the principal ones being at Helvetia and near Luthersburg

Sommerville & Company opened up mines at Winburne and many other smaller operators developed coal properties along the new railroad

A list of all the coal operations in the county, shipping coal by rail, is given herewith This list is believed to be as complete as it is possible to make it with the data available

In 1862 the tonnage in the county of coal shipped by rail was 7,239 tons Below will be found the report of the mine inspector of District No 18, showing the shipments in this district for the year 1910 There is also a large amount of coal shipped over the Low Grade Division of the P R R, from the vicinity of DuBois and over the Pennsylvania & Northwestern Railroad, that is not reported in this statement, as those sections of the county are included in a different mining district and the counties are not kept separate in the reports of tonnage

REPORT OF THOMAS S LOWTHER, INSPECTOR, EIGHTEENTH BITUMINOUS DISTRICT, PA, FOR THE YEAR 1910

COMPANY	TONS
Corona Coal & Coke Company, H B Swoope & Company, Madera	647,824
Berwind-White Coal Mining Company, Philadelphia	469,835
Rockhill I & C Company, Robertsdale	305,765
Carbon C & C Company, Saxton	255,467
Clearfield C M Company, Clearfield	160,516
Joseph E Thropp, Saxton	155,309
S J Mountz, Morann	144,380
John Langdon, Huntingdon	110,367
Colonial Iron Company, Riddlesburg	88,760
Clark Brothers C M Company, Glen Campbell	87,010
Bulah Coal Company, Ramey	80,828
W A Gould & Brother, Brisbin	80,472
Bulah Shaft Coal Company, Ramey	79,189
Broad Top Coal & Mineral Company, Huntingdon	74,097
Whitney Coal Company, Philadelphia	71,441
Betz Coal Mining Company, Philadelphia	69,248

* Not reported

Madeira-Hill Coal Mining Company, Philipsburg	65,761
James N McIntire & Company, Six Mile Run	64,686
Huntingdon Coal Company, Huntingdon	59,696
Pemberton Coal Company, Altoona	50,602
E Eichelberger & Company, Saxton	42,741
Moshannon Coal Mining Company, Osceola Mills	41,700
Centre C & C Company, Osceola Mills	39,262
A J Black, Broad Top	38,413
Decatur C M Company, Clearfield	37,368
E J Walker & Company, Brisbin	34,678
Leland C M Company, New York	32,836
W R Gallagher & Brother, Smith Mill	30,292
H A Munn and Reed Collieries Co, Dudley	30,250
Atlantic C M Company, Philipsburg	30,224
Miscellaneous Companies	304,254
Total	3,783,271

COAL MINES IN CLEARFIELD COUNTY

Buffalo, Rochester & Pittsburgh Railway Clearfield Colliery Co, Clearfield, operates Bloom mine No 1 at Curwensville Vein "D" Thickness * Drift Pick mine Daily capacity 250 tons Trade name "3C"

Clearfield Steel & Iron Co, Pittsburg, operates mine at Hyde Vein Moshannon Thickness 3½ ft Drift Pick mine Daily capacity 100 tons

Falls Creek Coal Co, Buffalo, N Y, operates Falls Creek mine at Falls Creek (Also P R R) Vein Freeport Thickness 5 to 6 ft Drift Machine mine Daily capacity 1000 tons Trade name "Falls Creek" Analysis on file

Rochester & Pittsburgh Coal & Iron Co, Helvetia, operates Helvetia No 2 Vein "D" Thickness * Compressed air mine Daily capacity 500 tons

Buffalo & Susquehanna Railroad

Buffalo & Susquehanna Coal & Coke Co, Buffalo, N Y, operates DuBois shafts Nos 1 and 2 at DuBois Vein Lower Freeport.

Thickness 6 ft Shafts Machine mines Daily capacity 4000 tons

Cascade Coal & Coke Co, Buffalo, N Y operates Tyler mine at Tyler (Also P R R) Vein. Thickness * Drift Pick mine

Erie Railroad

Northwestern Mining & Exchange Co, New York, N Y, operates Eriton mine at Eriton Vein "D" Lower Freeport Thickness 54 in Shaft Machine mine Daily capacity 2,600 tons

New York Central & Hudson River Railroad

Bellmore Coal Co, Burnside, operates Burnside mine at Burnside Vein "D" Thickness 3½ ft Drift Pick mine Daily capacity 75 tons Analysis on file

Bulah Shaft Coal Co, Ramey, operates Bulah Shaft No 1 at Ramey (Also P R R.) Vein "D" or Moshannon Thickness * Shaft Pick mine Daily capacity 1000 to 1200 tons Analysis on file

Barnes, Harry & Co, Philipsburg, operates the Cater No 15 Vein "D" Drift Pick mine Thickness * Daily capacity 50 tons

Carbon Coal & Mng Co, St Benedict, operates B No 12 Vein Lower Freeport Thickness * Drift Pick mine Daily capacity 100 tons

Clearfield Bit Coal Corporation, Clearfield, operates Gazzam mine at Gazzam Vein "D" Thickness * Drift Pick mine Daily capacity 250 tons

Same company operates Pleasant Hill, Grass Flat and Knox Run mines at Beale Vein "B" Thickness * Drifts Pick mines Daily capacity 1,985 tons

Clearfield Colliery Co, Clearfield, operates Caldwell mine No 2 at Curwensville

Vein "D" Thickness * Drift Pick mine Daily capacity 500 tons Trade name "3C"

Clearfield & Cambria Coal & Coke Co, Port Deposit, Md, operates Lee Hollow mine at La Jose (Also P R R) Vein Upper Freeport or "E" Thickness 3 ft Drift Machine and pick mine Daily capacity 1000 tons

Corona Coal & Coke Co, Madera, operates Shoff mine at Madera Vein "B" Thickness 3 to 5½ ft Drift Pick mine Daily capacity 300 tons Analysis on file

Graham Coal Co, Inc, Philipsburg, operates Hartley mine at Graham Station Vein "B" Thickness 2 ft 10 in Slope Machine and pick mine Daily capacity 200 tons Trade name "Hartley" Analysis on file Same company operates Phoenix mine No 2 at Oak Grove Vein Moshannon "D" Thickness 4 ft 8 in Drift Pick mine Daily capacity 100 tons Trade name 'Phoenix" Analysis on file

Harbison-Walker Refractories Co, Pittsburgh, operates Plane mine at Woodland Vein "C" Thickness 2½ to 3 ft Drift Pick mine Daily capacity 10 tons

Holt, W F, Philipsburg, operates Phoenix mine at Hawk Run Vein "E" Thickness 3 ft Drift Pick mine Daily capacity 100 tons Analysis on file

Irish Bros Coal Co, Philipsburg, operates Colorado mine No 5 at Munson Station Vein "B" Thickness 3 ft 10 in Drift Machine and pick mine

Same company operates Jefferson mines Nos 1 and 2 at Philipsburg (Also P R R) Veins "E" and Moshannon respectively Thickness 3 and 4½ ft respectively Drifts Pick mines

Same company operates Cuba mines Nos

---

* Not reported

1 and 2 at Cuba mines Veins "E" and Moshannon Thickness 3 and 4½ ft respectively Drifts Pick mines

Kelley, M J & Co, Olanta, operates Burnadette mines Vein "B" Thickness * Drift Pick mine Daily capacity 50 tons

Lee, Thos J, Philipsburg, operates Davis at Hawk Run Vein Moshannon Thickness 4½ ft Drift Pick mine Daily capacity 150 tons Trade name "Davis"

Little Creek Coal & Coke Co, Clearfield, operates O'Shanter mine at O'Shanter Veins "D" and "E" Thickness 2½ ft Drift and incline Pick mine Daily capacity 100 tons.

Moshannon Coal Mining Co, Osceola Mills, operates Moshannon mines Nos 7, 8 and 9, Electric Nos 1 and 2, Lenore Nos 1 and 2 and Centre mine at Osceola Mills (Also P R R) Vein "D" Moshannon Thickness 5 to 6 ft Drifts Pick mines Daily capacity 2,700 tons Trade name "Moshannon" Analysis on file

Olanta Coal Mining Co, Hollidaysburg, operates Olanta mines Nos 1 and 2 at Olanta Veins "B" and "C" Thickness 3 ft 8 in Drifts Machine and pick mines Daily capacity 300 tons Trade name "Olanta Steaming"

O'Shanter Coal Co, Philipsburg, operates Manhattan mine at O'Shanter Vein "B" Thickness 3 ft Drift Pick mine

Peale, Peacock & Kerr, Inc, St Benedict, operates Bloomington Nos 3, 4 and 5 at Glenrichey Nos 1, 3, 4, 7 and 8 near Philipsburg No 19 Curwensville, Decatur Ogle Nos 1, 6 and 9 at Winburne Veins Lower Freeport Thickness * Pick mines and compressed air Drifts and shafts Daily capacity 1,000 tons

Peale & Hooten, St Benedict, operates Ogle No 8 at Munson Sta Vein Lower Kittanning Thickness * Drift Pick mine

Penna Coal & Coke Co, operates Nos 45, 46 and 47 Winburne Vein "B" Thickness * Drifts Pick and electric mines Capacity 500 tons

Potter, Bigler & Potter, Inc, Clearfield, operates Horseshoe mine at Karthaus Vein "B" Thickness * Pick mine Daily capacity 150 tons

Potts Run Land Co, Clearfield, operates Potts Run mines Nos 2 and 3 at Boardman Vein "B" or Miller Thickness 38 to 45 in Drifts Pick mines Daily capacity 1,500 tons

Red Jacket Coal Co, Philipsburg, operates Gearhart mine at Gearhartville (Also P R R) Vein "E" Thickness 3 ft 4 in Drift Pick mine

Stage, Isaac, Clearfield, operates Karthaus colliery No 1 at Karthaus Vein "B" Thickness 3½ ft Drift and incline Pick mine Daily capacity 100 tons

Victoria Coal Mining Co, New York, N Y, operates Acme mine at Hawk Run Vein "B" Thickness * Drift and slope Pick mine Daily capacity 1,000 tons Trade name "Acme"

PENNSYLVANIA R R—(PENNA LINES)

Anda Coal Co, Houtzdale, operates the Mountain Branch mine, near Madera Vein "D" Thickness * Drift Pick mine. Daily capacity 50 tons

Atlantic Coal Mining Co, operates Cross Keys mine at West Moshannon Vein "D" Thickness * Drift Pick mine Daily capacity 100 tons

* Not reported

Berwind-White Coal Mining Co , Philadelphia, operates "Eureka" Nos 7, 16, 22, 27 and 28 Vein ' D " Thickness * Drifts and shafts Compressed air and pick mines Daily capacity 1,500 tons

Berwindale Coal & Coke Co , Philadelphia, operates Cheston mine near Irvona Vein Moshannon Thickness 4 ft Drift Pick mine

Betz Coal Mining Co , Philadelphia, operates Betz mine No 2 at Madera Vein "B " Thickness 4½ to 5 ft Drift Pick mine and machine mine Daily capacity 500 tons Analysis on file

Blain Run Coal Co , Coalport, operates mine No 1 at Coalport Vein "B" or Miller Thickness 4 ft 8 in Drift Pick mine Daily capacity 400 tons Analysis on file

Blyth Coal Co , Clearfield, operates Blyth Shaft at Madera Vein "B" Thickness 5½ ft Shaft Machine and pick mine Mine just developing Analysis on file

Brisbin Coal Mining Co , Philadelphia, operates Mascot mine No 1 at Houtzdale Vein "B" Thickness 4 ft Drift Pick mine Daily capacity 50 tons

Bulah Coal Co , Ramey, operates Webster mine No 4 at Bulah Vein "D" or Moshannon Thickness * Drift Pick mine Daily capacity 600 to 800 tons Analysis on file

Bulah Shaft Coal Co , Ramey, operates Bulah Shaft No 1 at Ramey (See N Y C & H R R R)

Burns, M , Brisbin, operates Penn mines Nos 2 and 3 at Grampian Vein Moshannon Thickness 4 ft Drift Pick mine Daily capacity 250 tons

Cascade Coal & Coke Co , Buffalo, N Y , operates Tyler mine at Tyler (See Buffalo & Susquehanna Ry)

* Not reported
16

Clearfield Coal Co , Madera, operates Becarria mine at Becarria Vein "D" or Moshannon Thickness 2½ to 3 ft Drift Pick mine Daily capacity 50 tons Trade name "King Cole " Analysis on file

Clearfield Coal Mining Co , Clearfield, operates Penn mine No 4 at Osceola Mills Vein Miller Thickness 3½ ft Drift Pick mine Daily capacity 200 tons Analysis on file

Clearfield & Cambria Coal & Coke Co , Port Deposit, Maryland, operates Lee Hollow mine at La Jose (See N Y C & H R R R)

Clearmont Coal Mining Co , Philadelphia, operates Clearmont mine at Houtzdale Vein "E" or Cap Thickness 3 ft Drift Pick mine Daily capacity 100 tons Same company operates Clearmont mine at Houtzdale Vein "D" or Moshannon Thickness 5 ft. Drift and slope Pick mine Daily capacity 150 tons Trade name "Clearmont "

Corona Coal & Coke Co , Madera, operates Bucher mine at Madera Vein "B " Thickness 3 to 5½ ft Drift Machine mine Daily capacity 600 tons Analysis on file

Same Company operates Royal mine at Madera Vein "B" Thickness 3 to 5½ ft Slope Pick mine Daily capacity 100 tons Analysis on file

Same Company operates White Oak mine at Madera Vein "B" Thickness 3 to 5½ ft Slope Machine mine Daily capacity 300 tons Analysis on file

Same Company operates Corona, Davis and Hegarty mines at Madera Vein "B " Thickness 3 to 5½ ft Drifts Pick mines Daily capacity 800 tons Analysis on file

Chestnut Hill Coal Co , Ramey. operates Chestnut Hill No 1 Vein "B " Thickness * Drift Pick mine Daily capacity 50 tons

Clark Bros Coal Mining Co , Philadelphia,

operates Falcom Nos 1 and 2 Smoke Run, and 3 and 4 McCartney Vein "D" Thickness * Drifts Pick and electric mines Daily capacity 200 tons

Coaldale Mining Co , St Benedict, operates Coaldale No 12 Munson Sta Vein "A" Thickness * Drift Pick mine Daily capacity 50 tons

Coalport Coal Co , Coalport, operates Superior Nos 1, 2 and 3 Coalport Vein "C & B" Thickness * Drifts Pick mines Daily capacity 100 tons

Dunbar Coal Mining Co , Altoona, operates Fairmont mines Nos 1, 2 and 3 at Osceola Mills Vein "D" or Moshannon Thickness 7 ft Drifts Pick mines Daily capacity 450 tons Analysis on file

Ellsworth-Dunham Coal Co . St Benedict, operates Royal Mine, Munson, Pa Vein "D" Thickness * Slope Pick mine Daily capacity 100 tons

Easton Coal Co , Easton, operates Easton mine at Mahaffey Vein * Thickness 4 ft Drift Pick mine Daily capacity 150 to 300 tons Analysis on file

Falls Creek Coal Co , Buffalo, N Y , operates Falls Creek mine at Falls Creek (See B R & P R R)

Franklin Coal Co , Ltd , Brisbin, operates Sterling mine No 2 at Clearfield Vein Moshannon Thickness 5½ ft Drift Pick mine Daily capacity 100 tons

Gould & Bros W A , Brisbin, operates Midvale mines Nos 1 and 2 at Brisbin and Midvale mine No 1 at McCartney Vein Moshannon Thickness 4½ to 5 ft Drifts Pick mines Daily capacity 400 tons

Same Company operates Henderson mine No 5 at Brisbin Vein "B" Thickness 3½

ft Slope Machine and pick mine Daily capacity 200 tons

Ghem Coal Co , Osceola Mills, operate Ghem mine Vein "B" Thickness * Drift Pick mine Daily capacity 100 tons

Hegartys' Sons, S , Coalport, operate Oakland mines Nos 2 and 3 at Coalport. Vein "B" or Miller Thickness 4 to 5 ft Drifts Pick mines Daily capacity 500 tons Trade names "Black Hawk" and "Oakland " Analysis on file

Henrietta Coal Co , Ltd , Houtzdale, operates Henrietta mines Nos 1, 2 and 4 at Houtzdale Vein Moshannon Thickness 3 to 4 ft. Drifts and slopes Pick mines Daily capacity 200 tons

Industry Coal Mining Co , Philipsburg, operates Industry mine at Industry Vein Moshannon Thickness 4 ft Drift Pick mine Same Company operates Niagara mine at Ashland Vein "B" Thickness 3 ft Drift Pick mine

Irish Bros Coal Co , Philipsburg, operates Jefferson mines No 1 and at Philipsburg (See N Y C & H R R R)

Irvona Coal & Coke Co , Philadelphia, operates Irvona mines Nos 3, 5 and 10 at Blain City Vein "B" Thickness * Drifts Machine mines Daily capacity 1,500 tons Trade name "Irvona" Analysis on file

Kelly & Shadeck, Karthaus, operates Mosquito Creek mine at Clearfield Vein * Thickness 3 ft Drift Pick mine Daily capacity 70 to 100 tons

King Coal Mining Co , Ltd , Madera, operates King mine at Smith Mills Vein "D" Moshannon Thickness 2½ to 3 ft. Drift. Pick mine Daily capacity 100 tons Trade name "King Cole " Analysis on file.

* Not reported

Mosier & Jose, La Jose, operates Wilson Run Mine Vein "C" Thickness * Drift Pick mine Daily capacity 50 tons

Madera Hill Coal Mining Co, Clearfield, operates Clover Run mines Nos 1, 2 and 4 in Bell township Veins "D" and "C" Thickness * Drifts Pick mines Daily capacity 600 tons

Mohawk Coal Co, New York, N Y, operates Beaver mine at Philipsburg Vein "C" and "B" Thickness 3½ ft Drift Pick mine Daily capacity 300 tons Trade name "Mohawk." Analysis on file

Morrisdale Coal Co, The, Philadelphia, operates Morrisdale shafts Nos 1, 2 and 3 at Morrisdale mines Vein "B" Thickness 4 ft 10 in shafts Machine and pick mines Daily capacity 2,500 tons Trade name "Morrisdale Bituminous" Analysis on file

Moshannon Coal Mining Co, Osceola Mills, operates Moshannon mines Nos 1 and 4 at Osceola Mills Vein "D" Moshannon Thickness 5 to 6 ft Drifts Pick mines Daily capacity 600 tons Trade name "Moshannon" Analysis on file

Same Company operates Moshannon mines Nos 7, 8 and 9, electric Nos 1 and 2, Lenore Nos 1 and 2 Centre mine at Osceola Mills (See N Y C & H R R R)

Mountz & Co. S J. Morann, operates Viola mine at Janesville Vein "B" Thickness 5½ ft Slope Pick mine Daily capacity 700 tons Analysis on file

Same Company operates Whiteside mine No 1 at Morann Vein Moshannon Thickness 2 ft 10 in Drift Pick mine Daily capacity 100 tons

Same Company operates Morann and Whiteside mine No 2 at Morann Vein Moshannon Thickness 2 ft 10 in to 4½ ft

Drifts Pick mines Daily capacity 100 tons

Mull, R H, Philipsburg, operates Imperial mine No 1 in Decatur township Vein "D" Moshannon Thickness 5 to 6½ ft Drift Pick mines Daily capacity 200 tons Trade name "Imperial" Analysis on file

North Witmer Coal & Coke Co, Irvona, operates Wister Nos 1, 2 and 3 Veins "B' "D" Drifts Pick mines Daily capacity 100 tons

Pemberton Coal Co, Altoona, operates Pemberton mines Nos 1 and 2 at Osceola Mills Vein "D" or Moshannon Thickness 5½ to 8 ft. Drifts Pick mines Daily capacity 500 tons Trade name "Pemberton" Analysis on file

Penfield Coal Co. South Bethlehem, operates mine at Penfield Vein "B" Thickness 4 ft Drift Pick mine Daily capacity 1,000 tons Analysis on file

Pine Hill Coal Co, Rosebud, operates mine at Rosebud Vein "B" Thickness 4½ ft Drift and incline Pick mine Daily capacity 50 tons

Red Jacket Coal Co, Philipsburg, operates Gearhart mine at Gearhartville (See N Y C & H R R R)

Smith & Co, A, Dysart, operates Superior mines Nos 1, 2 and 3 at Haverly Vein "D" Thickness 3 ft Drift and slope Pick mine Daily capacity 200 tons Analysis on file

Standard Moshannon Coal Co, Williamsport, operates Standard Moshannon mine at Smoke Run Vein Lower Freeport Thickness 3½ ft Drift Pick mine Daily capacity 300 tons

Swoope Coal Co, Madera, operates Eighteen mine at Madera Vein "D" or

Moshannon   Thickness 4 to 5 ft   Drift Pick mine   Daily capacity 225 tons   Trade name "Eighteen"   Analysis on file

Swoope & Co, H B, Madera, operates Morgan Run mine at Madera   Vein "B" Thickness 4 ft   Drift Pick mine   Daily capacity 300 tons   Trade name "Morgan Run" Analysis on file

Sylvania Coal Co, Madera, operates Sylvania mine at Madera   Vein "B"   Thickness 4 to 6 ft   Drift   Machine mine   Daily capacitly 600 tons   Analysis on file

Walker & Co, E J, Brisbin, operates Troy mine No 1 at Brisbin   Vein "B" Thickness 4 ft   Drift Pick mine   Daily capacity 100 tons   Same company operates Stanley Colliery at Moran   Vein "D"   Moshannon   Thickness 5 ft   Slope   Pick mine Daily capacity 200 tons   Analysis on file

Wilkinson, Roy, Philipsburg, operates Girard mine No 3 at West Decatur   Vein "B"   Thickness 3 ft 8 in   Drift   Pick. mine   Daily capacity 50 tons

Whitney Coal Co, Philadelphia, operates the Whitney mine, Ramey, Pa   Vein "B" Thickness.*   Drift   Pick mine   Daily capacity 100 tons

Whitehead Coal Company, Osceola Mills, Operates Peerless 1, 2, 3, 4, 5 and 6   Vein· "B"   Thickness *   Drifts   Pick mines Daily capacity 500 tons

Woolridge Coal Co, Woodland, operates Union No 6   Vein "D"   Thickness * Drift   Pick mine   Daily capacity 50 tons

Yorkshire Coal Mining Co, Madera, operates Yorkshire mine at Banian Junction Vein "B"   Thickness 2½ to 5 ft   Slope Pick mine   Mine just developing

Philipsburg Railroad—(Penna Lines)

Fernwood Coal Co, Ramey, operates Mt Vernon mine No 10 at Fernwood   Vein Moshannon   Thickness 2½ ft   Drift Pick· mine   Daily capacity 150 tons   Analysis on file

---

*Not reported

CHAPTER XXII

RELIGIOUS DEVELOPMENT

Pioneer Clergy of the County — First Services of the Different Denominations — Early Churches and Meeting-houses—Growth of the Various Churches—Y M C A

It is but another proof of the wisdom of the sturdy pioneers of Clearfield county that, hand in hand with the educational, went the religious development

Among the pioneer clergy of the county, in addition to the missionaries of various denominations, whose names are mentioned in the earlier history of the county, the first preachers who held services in the county, of whose names we have been able to find any record, were

Bishop Onderdonk of the Protestant Episcopal church, who held services in 1832, and again in 1838 in the old Court House The Rev Tiffany Lord, rector of the Episcopal church at Philipsburg in 1843, held occasional services in the Old Court House, also Rev George W Natt of Bellefonte made periodical visits to Clearfield, but the first regular Episcopal minister was Rev William Clotworthy, who was sent to Clearfield in 1847

The first Presbyterian ministers were the Revs William Stewart and Henry R Wilson, who preached in Clearfield in 1803 and for several years thereafter

Rev. John Hammond was the first Methodist preacher and he preached in Clear-field in 1822 long before there was any regular church

The first Catholic services were held about 1815 by the Rev Fathers Hayden, Reilly and Leavey, and about 1830 the first Catholic church was built

Rev. G Phillip Geulich, known as Father Geulich, was the first Lutheran preacher, preaching in Luthersburg in 1832

Rev. Samuel Miles was one of the first regular Baptist preachers, preaching in Clearfield about 1842

As is the case with most of these early dates, that of the first church in Clearfield county is a much disputed question One early chronicler states that the first meeting house was built in 1809, on the site of McClure's cemetery in Pike township A later writer just as emphatically declares that the first church in Clearfield county was built in 1822, although he agrees with the earlier writer as to its location

It is impossible to obtain any facts concerning the first house of worship, but as religious meetings were held at homes and in barns before any church building was erected, it is probable that this caused the confusion in dates

251

Such other facts as we have been able to gather concerning the early religious history of our county are set down in the following history of the different denominations

Presbyterian—In the first history of Clearfield county, published in 1878, we find the following lines

"The first meeting house in Clearfield county was built in the year 1809 and was located at the site of McClure's cemetery It was of the Presbyterian faith '

To the members of this denomination, then, must be conceded the honor of having erected the first house of worship in our county

A church building was erected in Clearfield several years later, and one in Curwensville in 1826 These charges were admitted to the Huntingdon Presbytery, which at that time had a total number of 558 communicants

There is now a church membership of 3,111 in this county, and nineteen church buildings

These statistics prove in a most convincing manner the marvelous growth of this denomination, and the powerful and thriving condition of the Presbyterian church in Clearfield county at the present time

Methodist Episcopal — Methodism in Clearfield county had its beginning as early as 1814, in the days of the Huntingdon circuit This circuit covered nearly three hundred miles, and included in its thirty charges those of Clearfield and Centre

The first church building was erected at the latter charge between 1828 and 1834, and Rev John McEnally appointed its pastor.

A "meeting house" was erected at Clearfield about 1839 and one at Curwensville, one in Bradford township and one in the Grampian Hills a few years later

From this time on, the Methodist Episcopal faith grew rapidly in power, and the Clearfield county charges became part of the Altoona District of the Central Pennsylvania Conference

At the present date there are twenty thriving Methodist Episcopal churches in Clearfield county, with a total membership of about 5,000

Baptist Church—An early historian of Clearfield county states that the first sermon preached in this county was preached by Rev Charles Pinnock, a Baptist clergyman

The oldest Baptist church in the county is the one at Curwensville, founded in 1836

The largest Baptist church in the county is the Zion church, which maintains four places of worship—Ansonville, Marion, Bell's Landing and Kerrmoor There are in all fourteen Baptist churches in the county

Clearfield county is not a Baptist stronghold, but commendable progress is being made, and only one church now reports a smaller membership than it did ten years ago The average annual rate of increase is three per cent There are today one-third more Baptists in Clearfield county than there were ten years ago

Evangelical Lutheran Church (English) —In the year 1832, Father Phillip Geulich, called the "Father of Lutheranism," in Clearfield county, began to preach monthly to the people of Luthersburg, in Brady township Ten years later a Union church

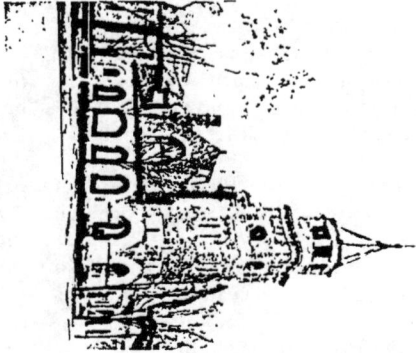

First Methodist Church, Clearfield

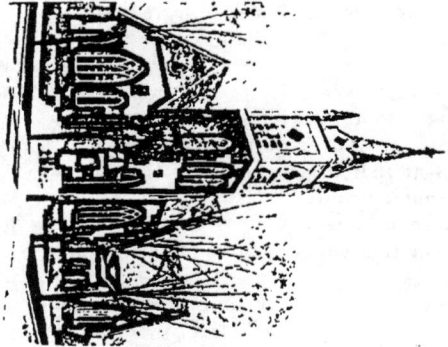

Lutheran Church, Clearfield

Presbyterian Church, Clearfield

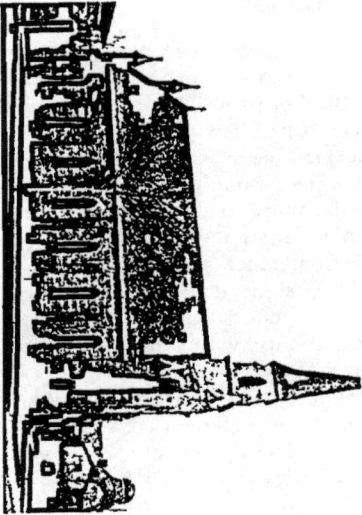

St Francis Church, Clearfield

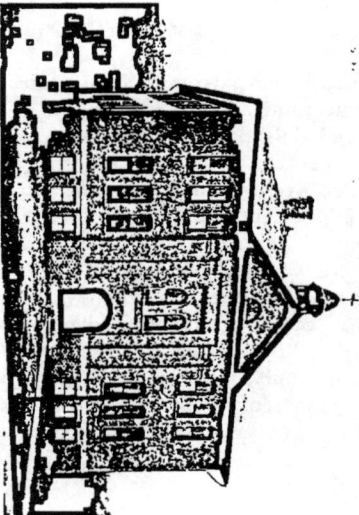

St Francis School, Clearfield

was built by the German Lutherans and Reformers, and services were held there by all branches of the Lutheran faith In 1845 the first English Evangelical Lutheran church in the county was built near Luthersburg

Since that time this denomination has grown greatly in membership, and there are now about twenty-two English Evangelical Lutheran churches in Clearfield county They are united with the Allegheny Synod

The Catholic Church—As early as 1815, priests of the Roman Catholic church visited this county for the purpose of saying mass for the few members of that faith who resided here But it was not until 1830 that a church building was erected at Clearfield Some years later, about 1841, another Catholic church was built at Frenchville These were the only Catholic churches in the county for many years but when the mineral resources of the county began to be mined, a foreign population, largely of the Catholic faith, came into this region, including many Greek Catholics

Since that time the number of the Catholics has steadily increased, until they have a membership of about twenty thousand, and thirty church edifices

Protestant Episcopal Church—Although services were held in this county as early as 1832, no regular organization of the Protestant Episcopal church was made until 1849, when a church of that faith was established at Clearfield

In 1851 a church building was erected, and named St Andrews For many years, this was the only Protestant Episcopal church in the county, but in 1884, two more churches were built—one at DuBois and one at Houtzdale

Although the growth of the denomination has been very gradual its members are noted for their devotion and loyalty to their faith

Society of Friends—The first meeting of this Society in the county was held at the home of James Moore, in Penn township, in 1813 Several years later a school-house was built in the vicinity, and here the Friends met for worship until 1824, when a meeting-house was built on a lot donated by James Moore In 1833 this meeting was regularly established as a monthly meeting by Warrington Monthly Meeting in York county, and the name West Branch was given it

There are now two Friends meeting-houses in the county—one on the original lot near the town of Grampian, and one in Curwensville, built in 1878

African Methodist Episcopal Church— There are but two churches of this denomination in Clearfield county—one at Curwensville and one at Clearfield The total membership of these two churches is thirty-two Although they are few in number they are strong in faith and untiring in their efforts to promote Christianity among their people

United Brethren Church —This church has a large membership in various parts of Clearfield county.

One of the earliest churches of this denomination was the Shiloh church, organized in 1847 The services of this church were held in Shiloh school-house until 1886, when a large church building was erected

There are several other churches of this faith in the eastern townships of the county, and the total membership is very large

German Reformed Church —Brady township, with its large German population, is the stronghold of all branches of the Lutheran faith, and the German Reformed Church in Clearfield county had its beginning in that locality In 1842 the German Lutherans and the members of the Reformed church combined forces, and erected a Union church, three miles from Luthersburg But in 1851 these two congregations could no longer agree, and in 1853, the Reformers erected a church of their own

A Reformed church was built in DuBois in 1883, and another in Huston township in 1884

The membership of the denomination is local, confined almost entirely to the northwestern section of the county

Other Religious Denominations —There are several other religious denominations in Clearfield county, the memberships of which are too small to support regular churches

Among these are the Dunkards, the Methodist Protestants and the Menonites

The Primitive Methodists, though not large in membership, have several churches throughout the county

The Salvation Army supports two barracks in the county—one at DuBois and one at Clearfield

YOUNG MEN'S CHRISTIAN ASSOCIATIONS

There are three Young Men's Christian Associations in the county, one at Clearfield and two at DuBois

The Clearfield Young Men's Christian Association was incorporated February 11th, 1903 The officers at the time of organization were as follows.

President, W. D. Bigler; Vice Presidents, H B. Powell and A B Reed, Secretary, H. E Trout, Treasurer, Andrew Harwick; General Secretary, S W Smith.

The association owns its building, situated on Second street in a fine location, near the center of the business portion of the town The building is well equipped with sleeping rooms, a fine bowling alley, a swimming tank, gymnasium, and assembly room

The association has about one hundred and fifty members and the present officers are as follows·

President, Hon A O. Smith, Vice Presidents, H B Powell, George R. Bigler; General Secretary, H. F. Beck, Recording Secretary, William Bigler, Treasurer, A Harwick, Assistant Treasurer, R I Fulton

Directors—Hon A O Smith, C T Kurtz, A. Harwick, W. I Betts, J B Nevling, W P Sheeder, Geo R Bigler, William Bigler, A B Reed, James Mitchell, J. L Gilliland, A K Wright, H. B Powell, A O Campbell, F B Kerr, R B Thompson, Alfred Graham, Raymond C. Ogden, A J Musser, D B Lucas, C B Porter, Hugh Woodward, Scott McKelvy

Trustees—Thomas H. Murray, C W. Smith, F B Row, H J Flegal, B F Chase, W C Miller

The DuBois Young Men's Christian Association was incorporated November 5th, 1894. Austin Blakslee is the president of the Association and it has a board of directors, composed of prominent business men of DuBois

The Association occupies a desirable building, well equipped for its purposes and it has about two hundred members at the present time

The Buffalo, Rochester and Pittsburg Railway Young Men's Christian Association was organized by the officials of the Buffalo, Rochester & Pittsburg Railway Company in order to furnish a suitable place of recreation and rest for their employees in and about DuBois

The Railway Company has been very liberal in the support of the Institution The Association has a fine building, well equipped with the necessary facilities for carrying on its work

R L Bogardus is the secretary The Association now has several hundred members

CHAPTER XXIII

THE TOWNSHIPS

Sketches of the Different townships—When erected—Boundaries—Population—Occupation of the Inhabitants, etc

BECCARIA TOWNSHIP

This Township is situated in the southern part of the county, having for its southern boundary the dividing line between Clearfield and Cambria counties, and being bounded on the east by Gulich Township, west by Chest and Jordan Townships and north by Bigler Township

This township was one of the earliest settled in the County, but was not created into a township until 1807 It was named in honor of the distinguished Marquis DeBeccaria The township was erected by a decree of the Court of Centre County to which county Clearfield County was attached at that time for judicial purposes

The principal industries of the township are the mining of bituminous coal and agriculture The population, according to the census of 1910 was 3,095

The first settler in this township was undoubtedly Captain Edward Ricketts, an old Revolutionary soldier, who in the latter part of 1798 or the spring of 1799, in company with a party of Indians, came to the place now known as Keaggy's Dead Water, on Clearfield Creek His first stay was brief, but he subsequently returned, bringing with him his wife He died not long after his settlement here, partly from the hardships he had endured and partly from an injury received while hunting It is believed that he was not only the first settler in Beccaria township, but also in Clearfield county In 1801 he was followed into the wilderness by his sons James and Edward, the former of whom afterward moved to what is now the site of Utahville

In 1830 when the township was erected it was so thickly covered with timber—chiefly pine, hemlock and oak—that few pioneers were hardy enough to attempt a settlement Many after a brief stay, allowed their lands to be sold for taxes and moved to other locations The few who remained permanently, however, in time reaped a rich reward, or at least laid the foundation of an abundant prosperity for their descendants Such among the pioneers were John Cree, the Carsons, James Ray, the Turners, John Hegarty, John and James Gill Henry Dillen, Joseph Leonard, James McNeal, Edwin and James Ricketts and Samuel Smiley, all of whom paid taxes on farm land in 1810-12

The first, or one of the first roads in the township was cut across the mountain to Tyrone in 1813 This was for hauling shingles, the first product of the cut timber About this time also the first saw-mills were erected, Samuel Turner putting up a saw-and grist-mill on Turner Run Square timber then sold at five and six cents per cubic foot, and the best pine boards brought but $6 or $7 per thousand

The first church was built at Mt Pleasant, or Utahville, as it is now called, in 1813, though the township then had less than 75 inhabitants It was of the Baptist denomination and Dr John Keaggy was its first pastor This same Dr. Keaggy during the week was engaged in medical practice He was killed by a fall from a horse in 1819

In the next year after the building of the church the first schoolhouse was built, on the site of the building later known as the "Williams schoolhouse" It was of course a log structure and had a clapboard roof

In 1810 John Gill made the first opening of bituminous coal in this township, discovering a vein 14 inches thick, which he used for blacksmith purposes Other veins were soon opened, Samuel Hagerty making the first opening for shipping purposes Other interests of the township—its transportation facilities, its boroughs, etc, will be found treated of under their respective headings, in other chapters of this volume

BELL TOWNSHIP

This township was organized by a decree of Court on May 4th, 1835 It is situated in the extreme western end of the county, having for its western boundary part of the dividing line between Jefferson and Clearfield Counties, and part of the dividing line between Indiana and Clearfield Counties It is bounded on the north by Brady and on the east by Penn and Greenwood Townships and on the south by Burnside and Chest Townships The principal occupation of the inhabitants of this Township is agriculture, although in the last few years some coal operations have been opened up in the township

The population, according to the census of 1910 was 1682

The township is well watered by various streams, chief among which are Chest Creek, which enters the township on the southeast and discharges its waters at or near the borough of Mahaffey, on the south or southeast side of the river, North Run and Deer Run, which discharge their waters therein from the south, and Snyder Run, a small tributary of Chest Creek The streams discharging into the river on the north side are Bear Run, Whiskey Run, Millers Run, and Laurel Run, all of which are small tributaries The northern part of the township is drained by the headwaters of the east branches of the Mahoning, while Curry's Run has its source in the northeast part of the township

Bell township was settled somewhat slowly, as the tide of emigration came from the country down the river, and from the east and northeast, and it was moreover somewhat distant from the county seat When the natural advantages of the location near the mouth of Chest Creek became better known, however, settlers came in abundance and today their labors and those of their descendants are visible in the present thriving borough of Mahaffey

The pioneer of the township was Johannes Ludwig Snyder, a Revolutionary veteran, who came to this country with his father's family about the time of the French and Indian war Coming from Lewisburg about 1820, he settled on lands on Chest Creek He died in 1860 at the remarkable age of 115 years His wife, it is said, lived to the age of 108—a truly, venerable couple

He was followed soon after by John Smith,

who built the first schoolhouse about 1827 or 1828, it being succeeded in 1835 by a more pretentious building

Samuel Sunderlin and family came about 1823, having previously resided in Union county His improvement was made on the river above the site occupied by McGee's He was a sterling citizen and the first class leader of the M E church

The McGees, Wetzels and Johnsons came in 1826, the Rev James McGee coming from Center county He erected a saw-mill and later a grist mill and in course of time made many substantial improvements in the township, in which example he was followed by the younger member of the family He died in 1855 Later settlers were John Weaver, Peter Smith, William Ramsey, Thomas Campbell and Nathaniel Sabins The last mentioned, who came in 1831, was the Nimrod of the settlement and many stories are still extant of his prowess in hunting Mr Campbell was on the first school directors after the organization of the township in 1835, his son, James A Campbell being a successful teacher

Another old settler was Asaph Ellis, who came about 1835, built a saw-mill on the river and engaged in lumbering He was the first justice of the peace elected after the township was formed

The Bell family were the pioneers in the upper part of the county Arthur Bell, Sr, was undoubtedly the second pioneer adventurer up the West Branch, following Daniel Ogden, whom he assisted in the erection of his cabin He was known as Squire Bell, being commissioned a justice of the peace by Gov Thomas McKean The township was named for A Bell, Esq, and his son, Greenwood

There was no church edifice in Bell township

until the year 1860, when the Methodist Episcopal society erected a house of worship Their society had been formed, however, as early as 1830 The Protestant Methodists were also organized about that year, their early services being held in the house of John Weaver

Mention of the borough of Mahaffey will be found in the succeeding chapter of this volume

BIGLER TOWNSHIP

This township is of recent formation, having been erected by a decree of court in 1883. The township was named in honor of Hon William Bigler, a former Governor of Pennsylvania and who was a citizen of Clearfield County The history of its early settlement is contained in the histories of Beccaria, Geulich, Knox and Woodward townships, from which it was formed

The township is bounded on the north by Knox and Woodward Townships, on the east by parts of Woodward and Geulich Townships, on the south by parts of Geulich and Beccaria Townships and on the west by parts of Beccaria and Jordan Townships

The principal business of the township is the mining of bituminous coal, which is carried on on a very large scale, the principal operations being at Madera, in Bigler Township This place, situated on the east side of Clearfield Creek, was originally called Puseyville after Charles Pusey who owned a large part of the lands upon which the town is built

The population, according to the census of 1910 was 4013

BLOOM TOWNSHIP

This township was erected by a decree of

court, dated January 14, 1860 and was formed from parts of Penn, Pike, Brady and Union townships This township is bounded on the north by Union Township, on the east by Pike Township, on the south by Penn Township and on the west by part of Brady Township

The principal occupation of the people of Bloom Township is agriculture The population, according to the census of 1910, was 451

The township was named in honor of one of its pioneer families, and the descendants of William Bloom are now scattered by hundreds all over the county and in various states Its surface is generally hilly and mountainous It is watered by Anderson and Little Anderson Creeks, the former flowing in a generally southeast direction through the eastern and northeastern part of the township, the latter being a tributary stream

The settlement of the township was slow, owing chiefly to its distance from the river, and also because it was heavily wooded, necessitating much labor in the clearing of farms Among its first settlers were Isaac Rodden, who settled on lands along the line of the turnpike in 1815, and who had a numerous family He was a man noted for his ceremonious transaction of business James Bloom, son of William Bloom, the pioneer, was a prominent man in the affairs of the township and was an associate judge of the county He was proprietor of the "Forest House," on the "pike," and also postmaster, his place being a post office station

Jonathan Taylor, a blacksmith, was another pioneer, who lived for a time on the site on which the Forest house was built He had a large family Another man of large family was James McWilliams, who came about the

same time, and lived about a mile south of the hotel He was a great hunter and kept a number of dogs of various kinds

John Ellinger settled in the eastern part of the township, coming from Brady He was still living at an advanced age in 1887 The turnpike to which reference has been made was the Susquehanna and Waterford Turnpike road, incorporated in 1818 It was not long in use, however, being superseded by others Another turnpike company was incorporated in 1828 and was known as the Snow Shoe and Packersville Turnpike Co The town of Packersville, now extinct, was named after Isaac Packer, a person of some prominence in the early days in this region He built and operated a hotel at this place, which was torn down about 1777 by Henry Reams John Neeper was the second proprietor of the hotel Henry Reams was the first class leader of the Methodist Episcopal church, to which belonged also the families of Squire Smith, Joseph Whitmore, William Henry and others

The Methodist Protestants also held early meetings in the "Greenville" schoolhouse, James Cleary, who officiated for a time as a preacher, being a leading member of the society Other members of this society were John Ellinger, John Bilger, Isaac Thompson (a local preacher), George Leech and others The United Brethren, Baptists and Dunkards have also at different times mustered some strength in the township, but in view of the total population of the township, none of these societies have at any time been large or powerful

The township has adequate schools with efficient teachers, being as well provided for in this respect as any other township, in proportion to its size The inhabitants are quiet and orderly and as a whole represent a good class of citizenship

BOGGS TOWNSHIP

This township is situated in the eastern part of the County and is bounded on the north by Bradford and Lawrence Townships, east by Graham and Morris Townships and a part of Decatur Township, south by Decatur and Woodward Townships and a part of Knox Township, and west by Knox and Lawrence Townships The township is about nine and one-half miles from east to west by four and one-half miles from north to south It was erected by a decree of court in 1838, the exact date cannot be given, because the original papers have been lost or mislaid in the prothonotary's office

The principal occupation of the inhabitants of this township is agriculture The population, according to the census of 1910, was 1154

The earlier history of Boggs township belongs to Bradford township, of which it was formerly a part George Shimmel made a settlement on lands about half a mile from the present borough of Wallaceton in the year 1810 In the same year Peter Shimmel began clearing a farm on the old State road, near the point known as Maple Springs Henry Shimmel, another member of the same family, began improvements in the same year

Henry Folk began a clearing in the forest on the present site of Wallaceton in 1813, being the pioneer in this work In the same year Abraham Hess came from York county, settling on the east side of Clearfield creek Another pioneer of 1813 was Nimrod Derrick, who made a clearing on the old State road Abraham Lits also began improvements in the

same year on the banks of Clearfield creek, as also did George Wilson

The following year, 1814, saw the advent of Andrew Kephart and Jacob Haney, who began clearing land on the old State road, George Wilson in the same year building a saw-mill near the mouth of Long Run

The first tavern in the township was built by Alexander Stone in 1820, on the line of the old Erie turnpike, William Lamadue building another on the pike about the same time, which would seem to indicate that there was then a fair amount of travel over the pike.

The Millwood farm was made in 1820 on the road leading from Philipsburg to Clearfield, the road, however, not having yet been built, and in the following year Bresaler's tavern, on the Erie turnpike, was built

In 1815 the Elder saw-mills and carding-machine were erected near the mouth of Little Clearfield Creek, and began operation Abraham Elder's saw-mill, located a short distance from Blue Ball, was built in 1828 The saw-mill of Jerry Smeal, at Blue Ball, was built in 1838 These were the most important settlements and improvements made before the erection of the township

The first election was held in 1838, with the following result Supervisors, William Lamadue and Abraham Hess, constable, Geo. McCord, overseers, Jacob Haney and John Beers, school directors, George Wilson, George Turner, George Goss, George Shimmel, John L Gearhart and Abraham Hess

In 1839 the township had a population of less than 225 persons

In 1840 Warren's saw-mill was built on Laurel Run In 1860 Thompson's grist-mill was built on Morgan Run

The surface of Boggs township is hilly and

rough, though it has less of the mountainous formation than may be found in some other localities in the county The chief stream is Clearfield Creek, which forms the western boundary for a few miles, and which has a number of tributaries, the northern one of these being Long Run Morgan Run is probably the largest tributary of Clearfield Creek lying within the township, and as the lands adjacent have produced fine timber, many sawmills have been erected on it Other streams watering the township are Camp Hope Run, Sanborn Run and Raccoon Run, all of which discharge into Clearfield Creek

Boggs township is amply supplied with good schools and teachers Several church societies are represented, the United Brethren building their first church edifice in 1848, about two miles west of Wallacetown borough from which parent society several others have since grown The borough of Wallaceton will be found treated of in the succeeding chapter

BRADFORD TOWNSHIP

This township was erected by a decree of the court of Centre County made at August Sessions, 1807, Clearfield County being at that time attached to Centre County for judicial purposes

The township was named Bradford in honor of former surveyor-general, William Bradford of Pennsylvania The township is bounded on the north by parts of Goshen Township and Girard Township, east by Graham Township, south by Boggs Township and west by Lawrence Township and part of Goshen Township

Many of the people of Bradford Township are employed in the fire brick works at Woodland and Mineral Spring, and in addition to this industry, the principal business is farming

The population of the township, according to the census of 1910, was 2250

The course of the West Branch of the Susquehanna river, which separates this township on the north from Goshen and Girard townships, is very tortuous and winding Clearfield Creek passes on the west side, just touching the township and dividing it at that point from Lawrence The largest stream having its course within the township is Roaring Run, which drains the whole southern and southwest portion and has several tributaries, namely Fork Valley Run and Forcey's Run, on the north, and Jake's Run on the south The streams discharging their waters directly into the river are Abe's Run, Devil's Run, Millstone Run, Bear Run and Moravian Run, the last mentioned, however, running but a short distance through the township Graffius's Run is a tributary of Moravian Run

The surface of the land generally is very hilly, but not mountainous, some of the best producing lands being classed as "hill farms"

The population of the township, as originally laid out, did not exceed, in all probability, 175 persons There were 34 taxable inhabitants in 1809, besides three single freemen At that time there was neither saw nor grist mill in the entire township The year 1812 showed a slight decrease in the number of taxables Many whose names appeared on the early rolls resided in that part of Bradford, which was subsequently erected into the townships of Decatur, Morris and Boggs, among them being Robert Ross, formerly of Huntingdon county, who settled about 1812 on the river, above the mouth of Trout Run Many of his descendants are still living in this and other townships

Matthew Forcey came to Bradford from old

264 HISTORY OF CLEARFIELD COUNTY

Chincleclamousche township, settling south of Clearfield town in the year 1804, and in Bradford about 1813 or 1814 His descendants have been numerous and some have been very prominent in the business life of the county

Among other early settlers were Robert Graham, who came in 1811 from Lawrence township; Jacob Hoover, who settled in the eastern part of the township, two by the name of Samuel Turner, one coming in 1812 and the other in 1824, the Hurd family, who settled early in the eastern part of the township; John Dale, a hatter, who subsequently lived on the Hurd place, John Kyler, who located on the Susquehanna pike, between Wallaceton and Bigler, Absalom Pierce, who was the assessor of the township in 1812 and who lived in the vicinity of Bigler station, John Woolridge, a native of England, who located on the Clearfield road, about two and a half miles from Woodland, John Shirey, who settled in the Graham neighborhood; Richard Shaw, a pioneer of the Mt Joy Ridges; David Wilson, who owned a farm adjoining Graham's, Archie Campbell, John Stewart, the Graffiusses, Mayhews, the Burges and others

Owing to the numerous streams and the growth of the lumber industry, Bradford township lands were taken up very rapidly about and subsequent to 1820 Numerous saw-mills appeared and the locality of Grahamton became thickly settled and manufactories were built there, largely through the enterprise of the Graham family The construction also of the Tyrone and Clearfield Railroad gave rise to the towns of Woodland and Bigler, in the former of which places the Woodland Fire Brick Company established an extensive plant

The township is well provided with churches and schools, the Methodists, Presbyterians and United Brethren being especially represented among the religious population

BRADY TOWNSHIP.

This township was named in honor of Captain Samuel Brady, a noted Indian fighter and a mighty hunter The township was organized in 1826 and is situated in the northwest corner of the county and about 2000 feet above the sea level

It is bounded on the north by Sandy Township on the east by Union and Bloom Townships, on the south by part of Penn Township and Bell Township and on the West by part of the dividing line between Jefferson and Clearfield Counties The surface is somewhat hilly with a gentle slope to the westward and there are many excellent springs, some of which are mineral There is considerable coal development in the township but the principal business of its inhabitants is agriculture Much valuable timber was destroyed in the process of clearing the farms The population, according to the census of 1910 was 2823 The township is traversed by the B, R & P and the B & S Railroads

The first white settler of this township was James Woodside, a native of Chester county, Pa He located on a tract of land situated on the head waters of Stump Creek, which was surveyed to him in July, 1785, which was known as the "Woodside" and later as the Luther place Here for twenty-two years he had no neighbors but the Red men of the forest He was then cheered by the advent of a new white settler, Joab Ogden, who located a mile further down the creek—this was in 1807, on the spot which afterwards became the site of Carlisle station on the B. R & P Railroad

In 1812 George, Michael and Frederick Scheffer settled on Sandy Lick Creek, George locating on land that is now a part of the site of DuBois Fred and Michael located a few miles further up the creek

James, Benjamin and Thomas Carson came in 1814 In 1820 Lebbeus Luther, a native of Massachusetts, bought and settled on a tract of land located where Luthersburg now stands, the place being named after him He was appointed by Messrs Fox & Co, who owned thousands of acres in this section, as agent to dispose of their lands He made his first sale to Benjamin Bonsall, who came from Perry county in 1824 About this time also Frederick Zeigler, came from Center county and settled on what was later known as the "Thompson" place Mr Bonsall was appointed first justice of the peace after the organization of the township in 1826

John Carlisle, who came from Lebanon county, was another settler on the site of Luthersburgh

In 1830 Jacob Kuntz, a native of Germany, settled near where the Reformed church was later erected The year 1831 saw the advent of the Knarrs, Weisgerbers, Wingerts, Korbs, and Yoases, Jacob Trautwein coming in the following year These settlers were soon followed by many others, whose names we have not space to record Many of these early settlers "squatted" on land—that is, took possession of it, without knowing to whom it belonged, and by keeping undisputed possession of it for 21 years became the lawful owners

The first mill in the township was Ogden's (near Carlisle Station) Two famous hunters among the early settlers were Fred Zeigler and "Uncle Billy" Long Another excellent marksman was Lebbeus Luther All these

men could tell great hunting stories and, as game was exceedingly plentiful, did not have to draw much on their imagination, as modern Nimrods are so often accused of doing

Luthersburgh was the first post office established in Brady township, dating back to the completion of the turnpike about 1820 David Irvin was the first postmaster Troutville post office was established in 1857 to 1858, the first postmaster being Jacob Kuntz The town had been laid out three years previous to this time, and was named, it is said, by Rev John Reams, in honor of Jacob Trautwein, the name as finally adopted being a contraction of Trautweinville, which was found to be inconveniently long

Joab Ogden built the first grist mill in the township, some time previous to 1830, though the exact date is not now known About 1849-50 Jacob Kuntz built a grist mill on East Branch (of Mahoning) a mile and a half south of Troutville, this was later known as Rishel's mill In 1854 Jeremiah built a steam and water-power grist mill on the head waters of Stump creek, two miles west of Luthersburgh It was subsequently operated by his son Samuel, and afterwards passed through various hands

The first saw-mill was built, it is said, by Fred Zeigler between 1824 and 1830, Jesse Line's saw-mill being subsequently erected on the same site The second saw-mill was built by Jeremiah Miles, it being later known as Zeigler's mill

The first minister who preached in Brady township was a Rev Mr Anderson, who came about 1822, and held services in the bar-room of Luther's tavern He was a Presbyterian In 1827 came Rev David Kennison, being sent by the Baltimore conference of the Methodist

17

Episcopal church, he also preached in the tavern at Luthersburgh About the same time came Rev John Althaus, a Reformed minister from Armstrong county, who made occasional visits preaching to the German settlers These early pastors and others who soon followed them were the men who organized the religious element of the township and laid the foundation of the moral and religious development and thriving church societies that exist today in the township, and which in union with good schools, have had so much to do in moulding the character of its inhabitants

BURNSIDE TOWNSHIP

This township was erected by a decree of court May 4th, 1835, and the township was named Burnside in honor of Hon Thomas Burnside, the President Judge of the Courts of this county and the other counties then composing the Fourth Judicial District The township is situated in the extreme southwestern corner of the county It is bounded on the north by Bell Township, on the east by Chest Township, on the south by part of the dividing line between Cambria and Clearfield counties and on the west by part of the dividing line between Indiana and Clearfield counties The principal occupation of the people of this township is agriculture

The population, according to the census of 1910, was 1435

The whole extent of this township was once covered with many varieties of timber—pine and hemlock, together with oak, chestnut, sugar maple, ash, beech and cherry About 1827 the early settlers commenced to hew and run rafts of pine timber to market at Marietta, below Harrisburg In later years it was cut into saw-logs and driven to the booms at Lock Haven and Williamsport, where it was manufactured

The first settler was James Gallaher, who came in 1816, when Burnside was part, of Beccaria township He held the office of justice of the peace and was legal authority for all the neighborhood for many years He was a tall active man and retained his faculties to a great age He died in 1854 aged ninety-five

Caleb Bailey came about 1820 and made a small improvement and patented about 400 acres of land two miles east of Burnside He removed in 1826 to Union township He died about 1886

George Atchison, it is said, settled on the river bank above Burnside, in 1820, when there was no neighbor nearer than New Washington He was born in County Roscommon, Ireland, about 1792, and came to this country to avoid prosecution for poaching under the oppressive game laws of his native land He was a man of strong character, who did much to mould public opinion in the community in which he had cast his lot He was a strong anti-slavery man and one of the conductors of the "Underground Railroad" He left the Methodist church and united with the Wesleyan Methodists, because he would not recognize the fellowship of slave holders He died at Cherry Tree after the Civil war Among later settlers were Samuel McKeehan, John Byers with sons Lemuel, John, Samuel and George, with daughter Helen, who married John Mahaffey; Jacob Lee, who came from Center county in 1822, whose house was an early preaching place for the Methodists, Hugh Riddle, a native of County Down, Ireland, who came to America in 1798, at the time of the Irish Rebellion, and who married Rebecca Lee, David Fulton. from Center county, who settled in 1823 along the river, below the upper Burnside bridge (he was a tailor by trade and died in 1874 aged 87 years), John Westover, John Rorabaugh, David Mitchell, Joseph Hutton (1826), John King, Jacob Neff (1828), Christopher and Henry Neff and others

The first preaching in the township was in Mr Gallaher's cabin, in 1822, by Rev John Bowen, a minister of the Methodist Episcopal church Members of the Evangelical church held meetings at an early day at the home of the Breths—Henry Adam and Peter—who came from Alsace, Germany Camp meetings were held by this society for many years after An account of the boroughs of Burnside and New Washington will be found in the succeeding chapter of this volume

CHEST TOWNSHIP

This township was erected by a decree of court dated October 16th, 1826 It is situated in the southwestern part of the County and is bounded on the north by parts of Greenwood and Bell Townships, on the east by Ferguson and Jordan Townships and part of Beccaria Township, on the south by part of the dividing line between Cambria and Clearfield Counties and on the west by Burnside Township It is one of the oldest townships in the County

The principal occupation of the inhabitants at the present time is farming The population of the township, according to the census of 1910 was 872

Among the early settlers of this township were Daniel Snider and Lewis Snider, Jr, and Sebastian and Jacob Snider, John Rorabaugh, Jr, William Ramsay, John Lees Henry Ross, Jacob P Lingafelter, John Smith, James McGhee, Cyrus Thurston, Elias Hurd, George Smith, Gilbert and Thomas Tozier, B Tozier, David Rorabaugh, William Carson and Salmon T Tozier, Joseph Michael, Nathaniel N Sabin and Christopher Rorabaugh

Valuable timber was found by the early settlers, and upon a market being opened, the greater part of it was cut and floated down to market The settlers in Chest township mainly devoted their attention to farming, the growth of the villages being "slow but sure "

The year 1887 saw the advent of the railroad, in the extension of Bell's Gap Railroad from Irvona, in Clearfield county, to Punxatawney, in Jefferson county, by the Clearfield & Jefferson Railroad Company A branch of the Pennsylvania Railroad now traverses the western part of the township in an almost northerly and southerly direction

From the southern boundary, through the whole length of the township, and to the northwestern corner, flows Chest Creek, which has its source in Cambria county Situated on this creek were some of the oldest lumber camps in the township The creek is usually tortuous, and the difficulties attendant upon the floating of rafts on its waters, resulted in the sudden death of many an old time raftsman

Upon the banks of Chest creek, near the northern boundary of the county, a settlement was made in early days which was first called Hurd's Post office, deriving its name from the Hurd family which lived in the vicinity, and where the first dwelling was erected by Henry Hurd This town was incorporated in 1885 as Newburg borough, and further notice of it may be found in the chapter on Boroughs, which follows the present chapter In the same chapter may also be found a notice of the other flourishing borough of Westover

COVINGTON TOWNSHIP

This township was erected by a decree of the Court of Quarter Sessions of Centre County, to which Clearfield County was at that time attached for judicial purposes, at April Sessions 1817 The Township is situated in the Northeastern part of the County and is bounded on the north by part of the dividing line between the counties of Cambria and Clearfield, east by Karthaus Township, south by Cooper and Graham Townships and west by Girard Township

This township was largely settled by people of French descent, the principal occupation of its people has been agriculture and the township contains some of the finest farms in Clearfield County

Its population, according to the census of 1910 was 649

The surface of Covington township is hilly, broken and irregular The township is well watered and drained,—on the south by the West Branch and its tributaries, Sandy Creek, Mowry's Run and Rock Run Sandy is a stream of considerable size and has Bigleman Run as its main tributary, besides a number of smaller ones Mosquito Run forms the drainage system for the whole northern part of the township, and has been an important factor in the lumbering trade of the upper region Along the banks of Sandy Run are many fine farms This stream has also been utilized for water purposes by many saw-mills

In 1817 Covington township had not over 80 inhabitants The list of its taxable inhabitants in that year shows but seventeen names, and of these two were single freemen They were as follows Jonathan Deckion, Frederick Geisenhamer, John Hanson, Jacob Michael, John Peters, Andrew Peters, Hugh Rider, William Russell, John Rider, Frederick Rider, Michael Rider, George Rider, J. F. W Schnars, John Troutman, Harmon Young, the single freemen being John Neff and Michael Rider Some of the above mentioned were residents of that part of Covington which was set off to the formation of Karthaus township in 1841

While the earliest settlements in the township were made by the above mentioned persons, no active steps were taken towards improvements, and no material growth in population was accomplished until some twelve or fifteen years later, at which time the French settlements were begun

One John Keating owned an extensive tract of land both in Clearfield and Clinton counties, which he offered for sale The first persons to locate on this land, as near as can be ascertained, were Nicholas Roussey and Irene Plubel, who took up lands in the year 1830 They were followed in this vicinity by Francis Courdriet, in 1831, and also by Claude F Renaud in the same year Coudriet became a prominent person in the township and acquired a large estate Soon after came many other French settlers, among them Peter Mulson, Hyacinthe Mignot, Francis Hugueney, Stephen Hugueney, Peter Brenool, Augustus Gaulin, John B Fournier, P Bergey, Alphonso Leconte, and others These French immigrants were, of course, unable to speak English, but were accompanied by an agent, Jacon Weiskopf The central point of settlement was in the neighborhood of Frenchville, by which name the locality has always since been distinguished Since the date of the French settlement many other immigrants have arrived—French, German and American

Among the early lumber men were Bigler & Powell of Clearfield, Leon M Coudriet, Augustus and Alphonso Leconte Francis La-Motte built a saw-mill on the Keating lands on Sandy Creek about 1837, and afterwards erected a grist-mill a short distance further down the creek As help was scarce at that time, his daughters went to work in the mills, and, it is said, turned out both excellent lumber and flour The property afterwards passed into the hands of the Coudriets

Francis Coudriet built a grist-mill on Sandy about the year 1864 It was supplied with two run of French burr stones of fine quality The property was purchased by Leon Coudriet at the time of his father's death Another saw-mill was built on Sandy by Claude Barmont about 1845 and afterwards became the property of F F Coudriet The Picard mill, one of the pioneer industries of the township, was built on Sandy Creek by John J Picard, and was subsequently sold to Leon M Coudriet The firm of L M Coudriet & Co also had another saw-mill built on Sandy, on tract No 1891, and above this stood the saw-mill of Liegley & Beauseigneur In 1839 Alphonso Leconte built a saw-mill on tract 1892, it subsequently becoming the property of Augustus Leconte

Another pioneer industry of the township was the Flood mill, at the mouth of Sandy Creek, which was built when lumbering was in its infancy One Lutz had an early interest in it, but it afterwards passed into the hands of Lawrence Flood

One of the first merchants of Covington was Mr Alexander, who established a store near Frenchville about 1837 He was succeeded by the Maurers, who were in turn succeeded by Levi Lutz and others

A schoolhouse was established near Frenchville about 1838, and it was followed by others at Mulsonburg, Fairmount, Mignot, Union and other places The French settlers have always shown a disposition to educate themselves in English, rather than in their mother tongue, though French has been occasionally taught in the parochial school The Rev Father Leavey was the first priest in the township and said mass at the house of Irene Plubel He was followed by other missionary priests, Father Oriack coming in 1841-42 About this time or soon after a log church was erected, which subsequently gave place to a more commodious structure—a substantial stone edifice, a few rods north of the Clearfield and Karthaus road The Evangelical Lutheran church was built at Keewaydin in 1869, during the pastorate of Rev. Samuel Croft, a substantial parsonage being also built This was an offshoot from the Lutheran Church Society, whose house of worship was erected on Karthaus Hill

Other interests of the township may be found mentioned under their respective headings in other parts of this volume

COOPER TOWNSHIP

This township was erected from Morris township by a decree of the Court of Quarter' Sessions, dated the 18th day of January, 1884 The township was named in honor of the Cooper family, who were among the earliest settlers in the locality. Daniel Cooper having located near Kylertown, in 1828

The township is bounded on the north by Karthaus Township and part of the dividing line between Centre and Clearfield Counties, which line also constitutes its western and southern boundaries, it is bounded on the west by parts of Morris and Graham Townships

Valuable deposits of coal have been found in this township and are being operated at the present time There are also many fine farms in the township The population according to the census of 1910 was 5713

Cooper is one of the youngest townships in the county and its earlier history therefore belongs to Morris township, from which it was taken It has had a considerable increase in population, as in the year 1887 it contained but 375 taxables, the increase having been due to the development of its coal and other mineral resources The village of Kylertown is named from an old and highly respected family that settled in the locality many years ago, substantial representatives of which are still living The other settlements are West Clymer, Winburne and Peale

DECATUR TOWNSHIP

This township was formed in 1828, by dividing Bradford township and was named in honor of Admiral Stephen Decatur The township is bounded on the north by Boggs and Morris townships, on the east by part of the dividing line between Centre and Clearfield counties, on the south by Osceola Borough and Woodward township and on the west by Woodward township

In the territory embraced in this township was one of the earliest settlements made in the county, Abraham Goss having located in the year 1797, at what is now called "Stump Town" There are also a number of coal operations in this township, also some well cultivated farms

The population of the township, according to the census of 1910 was 3,562

This township, covered with magnificent forests of pine and hemlock, early attracted the attention of settlers The greater part of the lands were owned by Hardman Philips, an Englishman, who settled in and gave his name to Philipsburg, a town in Centre county, where he also owned thousands of acres

Mr Goss, above mentioned as the pioneer settler at Stump Town, had a large family of thirteen children, twelve of whom reached maturity and assisted in settling the township His son, Abram, was living in 1887 at Osceola Mills, surrounded by numerous descendants

Valentine Flegel came about 1800, his farm occupying the site subsequently occupied by the Steiner estate He was an M E local preacher, and held services at "Goss's" as early as 1815

A man named Crane bought a tract of land from Mr Philips and established a colony of negroes, but the settlement was a failure, owing to the ravages made among these dusky sons of toil by disease

Elijah Reece, an Englishman, settled on lands subsequently occupied by "Victor No 3 colliery," coming in 1816, accompanied by his young wife They had three sons and two daughters, one of the latter marrying Rev Harvey Shaw, a Presbyterian missionary to Mexico Mrs Reece died in 1873 and her husband in 1883

Other settlers were James Reams, who located at the head of coal run in 1834, Henry Kephart, who located two and a half miles north of Osceola Mills, before 1803, and who had a numerous family, John Crowell, whose farm was absorbed by the Logan and Logan Ridge collieries, and others, some of which settled in that part of Decatur which after-

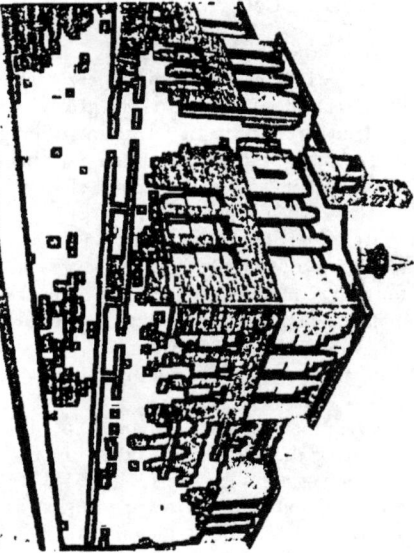

Court of School Building, Du Bois

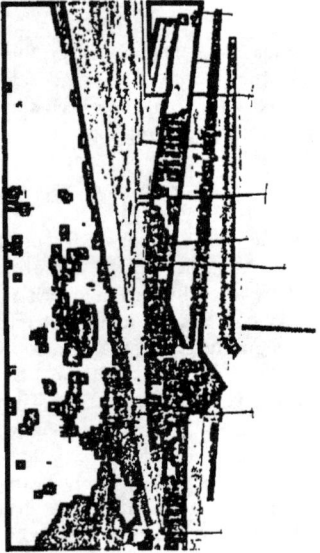

T. E. Du Bois Iron Works, Du Bois

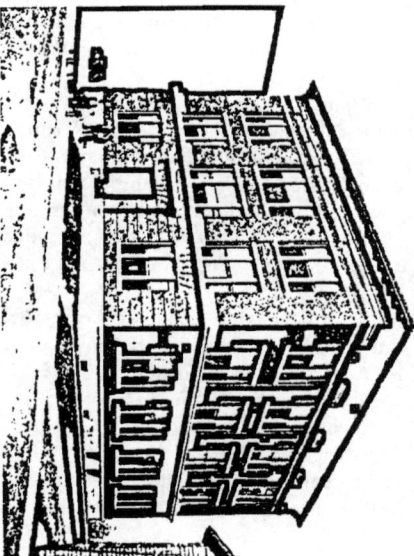

New Division Office Building of the Buffalo, Rochester & Pittsburg Railway, Du Bois

American French Plate and Glass Works, Du Bois

wards became Woodward township, their names being given in the remarks on that township

The religious and educational opportunities of these pioneer settlers were very limited Mention has already been made of the services held by Rev Valentine Flegel The second son of old Henry Kephart (Henry, Jr) was ordained a minister in the United Brethren church, and acted as missionary for that denomination for a number of years His sons all became ministers and one a bishop

For a long time the township had but two schools What was probably the first was built near the spot subsequently occupied by the residence of Andrew Kephart and Abram Goss, Jr, was the teacher Many stories have been told of his prowess with the rod, and the story tellers themselves were not slow to admit that they deserved most of the thrashings they got The other early schoolhouse was built on the Crane farm The Crane and Goss farm houses were about the only houses in the southeast part of the township as late as the year 1860 A sketch of Chester Hill borough may be found in the succeeding chapter of this volume

FERGUSON TOWNSHIP

This township was erected by a decree of court dated February 7, 1839, and named in honor of John Ferguson, one of the earliest settlers in the township The township is bounded on the north by Lumber City borough and Penn township, on the east by part of the line of Pike township and part of the line of Knox township, on the south by Jordan township and part of Chest township, on the west by parts of Greenwood and Bell townships The principal business of its inhabit-

ants is farming The population of the township, according to the census of 1910 was 765

The first settlement within the present bounds of the township was made, in all probability, by Robert McKee, some time previous to 1819, on the farm subsequently owned by W H Smith McKee made but little improvement Some time between 1806 and 1819, James Rea and James Hagarty came with their families to McKee's to a woodchopping In the evening they all returned home except Hagarty, who lingered behind talking to Robert McCracken He did not return and at early dawn Mr Rea went back to see what had become of his neighbor He found him in the woods dead, a short distance below McKee's shanty The surroundings indicated that he had been murdered, but by whom was never clearly proven

John Henry lived on the place a short time, but in 1836 John Miles, Sr, came to the township and purchased 200 acres of land which included the McKee property In 1838 he sold one-half of it to John S Williams and in 1857, a short time before his death, he sold the balance to his son-in-law, William H. Smith, who still occupies it

John Ferguson (for whom the township was named), Thomas McCracken, John Hockenberry William Wiley and John Campbell, all came to the township about 1823

John Ferguson married Elizabeth Wiley, a sister of William Wiley He built a saw-mill on the head waters of Little Clearfield Creek, where he lived several years, subsequently removing to Lumber City, where he engaged in the grocery business He afterwards removed to Lockport, Pa, where his death occurred in 1874

John Hockenberry lived on the farm later

owned by David Read   He had several sons
and daughters   two of whom—David and
Marion—moved to the west, the others remaining in this vicinity

William Wiley moved to Knox township
and later to Wisconsin, where he died some
time in the eighties   Thomas McCracken married Rebecca Bell, of Pike township, in which
township he lived for a few years   He died
in 1847, having had ten children, sons and
daughters, most of whom grew up and married

Among other early settlers of Ferguson
township were John Campbell (born 1797),
who came from Juniata county, and who was
still living on the mountain road between
Janesville and Tyrone in 1887 (had a numerous family), David Ferguson, a brother of
John, who came from the vicinity of Lumber
City in 1839 (he was a civil engineer and
school teacher, and married Rachel McKee, of
Cumberland county, Pa, by whom he had six
children), Grier Bell, son of Arthur Bell, and
said to have been the second white child born
in the county (he married Hettie Roll, of
Armstrong county), Robert McCracken and
George G Williams, the latter coming from
Center county   Most of these pioneers have
numerous descendants now living in the
county, some in this township and others elsewhere   They were a sturdy and energetic
class of people, as were also most of those who
followed them a little later, such as the Straws,
Moores, and Tubbses

The first schoolhouse was built previous to
1841 on the John Ferguson farm, Ross Robison being the first teacher   He was succeeded by Joseph Moore, a prominent citizen
of the township, who has long ago passed
away   David Ferguson was the third teacher

Other schools were later erected, according to
the needs of the community, and the township's present educational facilities will compare favorably with those of almost any rural
community of its size

One of the most terrible events that ever
took place in this township was the burning of
the Nicholas Tubbs residence in the autumn of
1861   Mr and Mrs Tubbs had gone to attend a meeting in the old schoolhouse at Marron, leaving their four children, the eldest of
whom was about twelve, at home   An alarm
of fire was heard and when the congregation
rushed out they found the Tubbs house in
flames   Nothing could be done to save the
children, who were roasted to death in sight
of the frantic parents and neighbors

The village of Gazzam, located on both
sides of the East Branch of Little Clearfield
Creek, in the southern part of the township,
was named in honor of Hon Joseph M Gazzam, of Philadelphia   Mines were opened here
in 1884 by the Clearfield Bituminous Coal Co,
and dwelling houses erected   This is chiefly a
mining community, but there are stores and
other industries, with good church and school
facilities

Kerrmoor—This village was named in
honor of its originators, Moore Bros & Kerr,
and is located at the forks of Little Clearfield
Creek   It sprang into existence as a consequence of the building of the Beech Creek
Railroad   The land was owned by Joseph and
William Moore, two of the early settlers and
prominent citizens of the township, and occupied by Ross McCracken, who lived here alone
for many years in a shanty   In 1884 Robert
and Milton (sons of William) Moore, and
James Kerr, under the firm name of Moore
Bros & Co, purchased the land and immedi-

ately laid it out in town lots The Clearfield Lumber Co built a large steam mill for the manufacture of lumber, while other business enterprises soon followed The community is thriving and has church and school facilities

GULICH TOWNSHIP

This township enjoys the distinction of having as part of its boundaries, portions of the lines of three other counties The township was erected by a decree of court made in 1858 The township was named in honor of Peter Geulich, one of the early settlers in that section of the county, the official spelling having since been changed to "Gulich."

The township is bounded on the north by Bigler and Woodward townships, on the east by part of the dividing line between Centre and Clearfield counties and part of the dividing line between Blair and Clearfield counties, on the south by part of the dividing line between Cambria and Clearfield counties and on the west by Beccaria township

There is considerable coal development in this township, and also many fine farms Its population, according to the census of 1910 was 2,112

The surface of Gulich township shows great inequalities in altitude At the mountain top known as Highland Fling, half a mile from the head waters of Moshannon Creek, it reaches a height of between 900 and 1,000 feet higher than Bellwood or Bell's Mills in Blair county, while the channel of the Muddy Run, near Madera, in the northwest part of the township, the channel is cut deep into gullies and ravines This Run forms the boundary between Gulich and Beccaria townships and originates in a number of beautiful springs but a short distance south of the county line

It was for many years the only means of transporting timber to the eastern market

The first opening for coal in this township was made by George W Davis in 1851 on Muddy Run, blacksmiths and others coming to his bank from long distances for their supplies, since which time the coal industry has grown to considerable proportions

Among the first comers to Gulich township were the Geulichs, with old Peter Geulich before-mentioned, the Glasgows, who were first known by Mr John Glasgow moving in about 1840, the Cresswells, headed by John Cresswell, John Nevling John Hannah (about 1854), Joseph Fry and family; David and Henry Alleman, Harry Hummell, from Dauphin county, the Rameys, the Flynns, the Coonrods, the Ganoes, the Kingstons, the McKiernans, the Davises, the Stevenses and others

Janesville, the first town in Gulich township, was named from Jane Nevling, who afterward became the wife of Dr Caldwell, of Glen Hope When the postoffice was established it was given the name of Smith's Mills In 1851 Abraham Nevling, who had moved to this vicinity, built a house for his own use, and was soon followed in building by Westley and Mrs Nevling This was the origin of the town of Janesville and Smith's Mills The postoffice was established in 1868, Joseph D Ganoe being the first postmaster

Henry Alleman moved into the county and township in 1851, taking possession of a shanty previously occupied by John Potter He afterwards enlarged and rebuilt it It was situated right on the division line between Cambria and Clearfield counties, so that, of a party at table, those sitting on one side were in Cambria and those on the other in Clearfield county Around this place grew up the settlement of Allemansville, where a postoffice was established in 1868 with Henry Alleman as postmaster A Methodist church was built in 1871 and a schoolhouse erected Mr Alleman was for a number of years treasurer of the township

Ramey in the northern part of the township, is a borough and mention of it will be found in the succeeding chapter of this volume

GIRARD TOWNSHIP

The records of the quarter sessions court of Clearfield county do not show when this township was legally erected, but it is believed to have been about the month of September, 1832, because at the term of court held in September 1832, it appears to have been recognized as a township in the returns made by the constables

The township is situated in the northern part of the county, and it is bounded on the north by part of the dividing line between Elk and Clearfield counties, on the east by Covington township, on the south by parts of Graham and Bradford townships and west by Graham township The occupation of the people is mostly agriculture The township had a population, according to the census of 1910, of 606

The surface north of the river is generally rough, hilly, and in some parts quite mountainous In the western part, at what is known as "The Knobs," the hills reach a height of 2,230 to 2,280 feet The township is drained by the waters of Surveyor's Run Bald Hill Run, Deer Creek, Buck Run, Sandy Creek, Mosquito Creek and some smaller streams

Girard township was first settled by Peter and Mordecai Livergood, brothers, who came from Chester county in 1818, Peter making an improvement near the river, a mile east from the mouth of Surveyor's Run, not far from the old Indian path Mordecai Livergood commenced a farm near the mouth of Surveyor's Run, which stream was named from the fact that a party of surveyors encamped at an early date on its banks

John Irwin made the next settlement in 1821, a few miles east from Peter Livergood's clearing Irwin, who was a native of Ireland, afterward moved to Wolf Creek, east of Clearfield

In 1821 came also John Murray from Huntingdon county, accompanied by his family He died in the winter of 1824, leaving his widow with a number of small children to provide for

About 1824 John Spackman and Thomas Leonard, with their families, located in Girard, and about the same time came William Irwin Soon after came Peter Lamm, from Northumberland county He was a millwright and built a mill at the mouth of Deer Creek This mill was afterwards made into a combination saw- and grist-mill It ground no wheat flour, however, but only feed for cattle and a small quantity of corn meal

Other early settlers were Abraham Jury, a potter from Dauphin county, who supplied the residents with earthenware; Zacheus Mead, who started a farm about 1826, and among the French settlers who overflowed into the township from Covington about 1838 were Alphonso and Augustus Leconte, Francis Grossaint, Francis Coudriet and Stephen Hugueny Their lands lay in the vicinity of the Leconte Mills settlement, as it was called Francis Grossaint built a saw mill in 1844, and Francis Coudriet built one in 1846 The first steam mill was erected on the lands of Phelps and Dodge, who were extensive lumbermen, both here in the township and elsewhere The second steam saw mill was built by Irwin & Sons, on Bald Hill Run, about 1867 or 1868 The third, known as the Burgett mill, was built on Deer Creek

Though it was not until nearly 1860 that regular religious services were held in the township, occasional meetings were held as early as 1827, when Rev William McDowell, of the Methodist Society, preached at the house of the widow of John Murray George P Geulich would sometimes hold services at different houses The French residents are principally of the Catholic faith and attend their own church at Frenchville Through the efforts of John McCorkle, a Presbyterian church was erected in 1873

The first school in the township was taught by Cornelia Kincade It was in the locality afterward known as Congress Hill The hamlet of Lecontes Mills owes its origin to the efforts of Augustus and Alphonso Leconte, who built a mill and residence at the confluence of Deer Creek and Buck Run A postoffice was afterward established there of which Augustus Leconte was postmaster until 1872, when he was succeeded by Charles Mignot, who was followed by other incumbents

GRAHAM TOWNSHIP

This township was erected by a decree of court dated August 22, 1856 The township is situated in the eastern part of the county and is bounded on the north by parts of Covington and Girard townships, on the east by Cooper township, on the south by Morris township and on the west by part of Boggs township and by Bradford township

The principal business of the people is farm-ing The population, according to the census of 1910, was 664

Graham township was named after John B Graham, who came to the county with his parents in 1822, but who did not become a resident of this locality until some 14 or 15 years later The town of Grahamton was named for him, he being one of its most enterprising residents He built both saw and grist mills there and also engaged in the lumber business In 1852 he removed to the borough of Clearfield, of which he became a prominent citizen Jacob Hubler and Bassel Crowel, came to this locality about 1827 or 1828 Each reared a large family and cleared up a good farm In 1864 Jacob Hubler was arrested for a political offense and was imprisoned at Fort Mifflin, but was subsequently released He died in 1868

Conrad W Kyler, who came here in 1843 cleared and developed a fine farm He was made county commissioner in 1875 and for ten years was a justice of the peace of Graham township Other early settlers were Samuel Turner, the Monos, the Hitchins, the Kepples, the Smeals, and the Flegels, while among the taxable inhabitants in 1857 (the year following that in which the township was erected) were B F Ackley, M D, Moses Boggs, William Burlingame, William Bennett, William Bagley, William Burge, John Cook, William Cole, M & S Catherman, David Chollar, Henry Colegrove, David Crowell, Israel Crowell, Basil Crowell, Patrick Curley, James Curley, Benjamin Chance, Frederick Conklin, Francis Colegrove, Samuel Davidson, Thomas Duncason, John Dixon, Robert Elder, William English, Thomas H Forcey, Martin French, Francis Graham, Ira Green, William R Green, Amos Hubler,

George Hoover, Jacob Hoover, John Holt, Michael Fink, Jacob Hubler, Simon Hauckenbury, Joseph Ishman, John H Irvin, Edmund Jones, Henry Kyler, Conrad W and Isaac Kyler, Peter Keppler, John M Katon, Samuel Lonsbury, Benjamin and Abraham Lonsbury, Rev J M Mason, Mark McGuire, Gerge Moyer, John Martin, Jacob Mack, George Nearhood, Henry Nearhood, William Phenix, Christian Pace, Jonas Powel Harrison Ross, F W Russell, William Rolston, Alexander Rolston, William P Smeal John Smeal, Samuel Smeal, George Stever, William Shimmel, Jr , John W and David Turner, Joseph Thompson, Samuel Ulrich, John Ummerman, John and Jacob Wilhelm, William Woolridge, James E Watson, George W Wells and others This will serve to show who were the pioneers of Graham township, though some of the above mentioned were the sons or descendants of the original pioneers of this locality

GOSHEN TOWNSHIP

This township was erected by a decree of court of quarter sessions of Clearfield county, dated May 5, 1845 It is situated in the northern part of the county, being bounded on the north by part of the dividing line between Elk and Clearfield counties, on the east by Girard township, on the south by parts of Bradford and Lawrence townships and west by part of Lawrence township

Although a large part of the township is a comparative wilderness, containing only a few scattered inhabitants, the southern part is well cultivated and embraces in its limits some of the finest and most fertile land in the county The people of the township are mostly engaged in farming

The population, according to the census of 1910, was 514

The main streams of Goshen township are Lick Run and Trout Run, in the southern half, both of which discharge into the river, and Laurel Run, which drains the northern half, and which discharges into the Sinnamahoning, and finally into the West Branch

Among the pioneers of the township was the Bomgardner family, who took up lands near the mouth of Trout Run in the year 1820 Joseph Thorndyke, another old settler, located in the same neighborhood two years later He was a trapper and hunter, without family, and made few or no improvements John, Henry and James Irwin were sons of Henry Irwin, Sr , who lived at the mouth of Wolf Run, and afterward in Goshen The sons were natives of the county, but the parents of Irish birth John Irwin early claimed land in Karthaus township

William Ross improved land about a mile below the mouth of Trout Run, the place having been formerly owned by William Leonard, father of Abraham Leonard The latter about 1835 made an improvement on the location subsequently owned by John Sankey

Another pioneer of the township was Jacob Flegel (brother of Valentine), who made a farm about 1842 or '43, not far from the head of Flegel's Run, in the southwest part of the township He afterwards built a saw mill on the Run The Flegels were a numerous family and have many descendants yet living in the township Other settlers were Isaac and Robert Graham, who later emigrated to the West, Matthew Tate, who bought lands on Jerry Run, Robert C Shaw, brother of Judge Richard Shaw, and son of Archie Shaw, the pioneer of Mt Joy Ridges, Joseph Morrison,

William L Shaw, Daniel Lewis, William L Rishel, Merrick Housler, Horatio Hall, Henry Lewis, William Housler, Nathaniel Brittain, Thompson Read, James A Read, John Jenton, Matthew Tate, Q W Graham, John Barr, Isaac Lewis The above, with others, owned land or cattle within the township in 1846, at the time the first enumeration of taxables was made, though possibly some of them may not have been actually residents of the township There was then but one saw mill in the township—that of Bigler, Boynton & Powell, who were residents of Clearfield borough

Ellis Irwin, a former merchant of Clearfield, moved to Lick Run in 1856, having previously purchased property there This was the saw-mill erected on the run by Martin Nichols in 1845 Mr. Irwin completed the mill and began lumbering, which business he followed for many years thereafter In 1847 he bought the uncompleted mill and dam erection below him on the other side of the stream, which had been started by F P Hurxthal and James Irwin, together with adjacent lands, and completed the construction, thus acquiring a valuable water frontage In 1852 he started a general merchandise store, which he managed in connection with his other extensive business interests The Lick Run Mills postoffice was established in 1872 and Mr Irwin appointed postmaster This office took the place of the previous one at Shawsville, further down the river, which was thereafter discontinued The latter place was named in honor of Judge Richard Shaw, who built a grist mill here, at the mouth of Trout Run in 1852, on lands purchased from Stewardson, of Philadelphia At his death the property went to Arnold B Shaw of Clearfield In

1886 the machinery for making roller process flour was placed in the mill A water-power saw-mill was built on Trout Run, above Shawsville, by Morrow and Smith, about 1870, and afterwards became the property of H H Morrow The Shirey saw mill, on the west branch of Trout Run, was built at an early date by William Mapes It was rebuilt by A H Shirey and subsequently became the property of Frederick B Irwin

The first school erected after the formation of the township was on the lands of Isaac Graham, and this was the starting point of the educational interests of the township, which are today well looked after, there being an adequate number of good schools and teachers

GREENWOOD TOWNSHIP

This township was erected from parts of Bell, Ferguson and Penn townships, by a decree of court of quarter sessions of Clearfield county, dated the 19th day of March, 1875 The township is bounded on the north by Penn township, on the east by Ferguson township, and on the south by Chest township, and on the west by Bell township Agriculture is the principal occupation of the people of this township

The population, according to the census of 1910, was 590

The taxables embraced in the new township at the time of its formation were as follows From Bell township, R C Thompson, E B Thompson, Charles Hullihan, John Mills, J N McCracken, D W McCracken, Eli Campbell, Jacob Fryer, J Q A Johnson, G W Dickey, Jacob Uber, John W Bell, Henry Sharp, Marion Sharp, William Bell, James Wiley, Nelson Young, Eli Passmore, J N Kester, William Kester, Frampton Bell,

Samuel Hullihan, James Frampton, G M Passmore, John Cunningham, William D Beck, Thompson McLaughlin, G D Mc-Cracken, Thomas Thompson, C A Rora-baugh, H D Rowles, Frank Sawyer, A T Goldthread, John Robbins, William T Thorpe, Charles Thorpe, David Mitchell, A B Tate, David McCracken, R C McCracken, William Tumblin, John W Haslet, James K Henry, Immanuel Hoover

From Ferguson township Hon John F Hoyt, S H Vanhorn, George Ross, Wesley Ross, John F Wiley, D D Wiley, John A Rowles, William Rowles, Balser Hullihan, Matthias Hullihan, Conrad Hullihan, Thomas Tubbs

From Penn township W C Hoover, Elah Johnson, William Smith, Albert Smith, James Johnson, John L Johnson, David Johnson, Matthew W Johnson, Wesley Horn, James Newcomer, Patrick Rafferty, Aaron Newcomer, Josiah Newcomer, Job Curry, Jesse Kester, Frank Kester

The first election for township officers was directed to be held on the 11th day of May, 1875, at the public house of Samuel Hullihan The first officers elected were as follows Justices of the peace, Isaac Kester and John W Bell, constable, Aaron H Newcomer, assessor, David Bell, supervisors, G D McCracken and Conrad Hullihan, overseers, George M Passmore and Joseph Newcomer, auditors, Frampton Bell, three years, Z L Hoover, two years, Nelson Young, one year, school directors, T J Thompson and John S Johnson, for three years, John A Rowles and John P Hoyt, for two years, James Stevenson and J Q A Johnson, for one year, treasurer, Wilson McCracken, judge of election, David Lee

The Susquehanna River crosses Greenwood township in a general course from southwest to northeast, but its course is exceedingly tortuous and winding The principal streams tributary to the river on the north are Haslet's Run, Curry's Run, and Bell's Run, on the south side are several rivulets of no mentionable size The country generally throughout the township is very hilly and mountainous, but along the valley of the river is much productive farming land

Among the first families to settle in this locality was that of Greenwood Bell, a son of Squire Bell, who was one of the very first settlers of the county. In honor of Squire Bell and his son, Greenwood, Bell township was so named The son, Greenwood, in the erection of this township, comes before the court and public for still further honor, in the formation of this township, it being named in his honor Mr Bell lived on the river near the location of Belleville, one of the small towns of the township Here he cleared a farm and built a saw and grist-mill, they being among the first industries in this part of the county The descendants of Arthur Bell are numerous in this section, and are recognized as being among the substantial men of the county Greenwood Bell married Elizabeth Roll, by whom he had ten children Arthur, Mary, Delilah, John, William, David, Julia Ann, Harvey, Grier, and Frampton He was a man highly respected in the county, and took an active part in every enterprise of public welfare In 1820-1 he held the office of county commissioner In 1822 he was appointed sheriff of the county, being the first incumbent of the office He was again chosen in 1823, and served until 1826

The pioneer worker of Greenwood township, he who took the burden of the labor in its erection, was Dr John P Hoyt In the year 1846, then having had a residence in the county of nearly thirty years, Dr Hoyt moved to a place on the Susquehanna River, about three miles above Lumber City, and in the extreme eastern part of the territory that, in 1875, was erected into Greenwood township Here he lived, and here he died at an advanced age, surrounded by family and friends, and in the enjoyment of the comforts earned by a life of toil and perseverance Dr Hoyt was married, in 1820, to Mary, daughter of Thomas McClure, a pioneer of Pike township, From 1852 until 1857, Dr Hoyt acted with Richard Shaw, as associate judges of Clearfield county

Another of the pioneers of this locality was William Haslet, who came here with his family, from what is now Clinton county, in the year 1828 He settled on lands later owned by William McCracken, the first farm west from the hamlet of Bower He was a substantial resident of Greenwood, or the territory that was formed into that township, for twenty-five years He died in the year 1853

The McClures were represented in pioneer days in this vicinity "Squire" Thomas McClure first came to the county in the year 1799, from Cumberland county, but did not bring his family until the succeeding year

The McCrackens, who are to be numbered among the pioneers of the county, came to the then unsettled river country about the beginning of the present century, soon after the advent of 'Squire Arthur Bell, to whom they were related The pioneer of the McCracken family was James He is remembered as having been a man of great physical strength and activity, a trait that was transmitted to his sons, and of which they made frequent use in

all athletic sports James, Thomas and John McCracken were sons of the pioneer James The descendants of this family are numbered among the substantial residents of Greenwood township

Among the many familiar names of pioneer families, whose descendants now help to make the population of the township, are to be found some representing various localities or sections of the river country There are Thompsons, Johnsons, Young, Passmore, Kester; Hulihan, McLaughlin, Rowles, Robbins, Thorpe, Mitchell, Tate, Henry, Hoover, Ross, Wiley, Smith, Newcomer, Curry, Kester, and perhaps others whose names have been lost

HUSTON TOWNSHIP

This township was organized in 1839 and is bounded on the north by part of the dividing line between Elk and Clearfield counties, on the east by part of Lawrence township, on the south by Pine township and part of Union township, on the west by Sandy township and part of the dividing line between Elk and Clearfield counties

The township has some valuable coal deposits which are now being worked, and also contains a number of well cultivated farms The population of the township, according to the census of 1910, was 2,653

Topographically speaking, Huston township lies in the Bennett's Branch watershed, forming a beautiful and fertile valley, eight hundred feet lower than the towering mountains guarding on either side Bennett's Branch (creek), a tributary of Sinnamahoning, flows through the entire length of the township from west to east

The first settlement was made, according to the best authority, in 1812 Of the original settlers, John S Brockway located where Schofield's Hotel now stands, Jesse Wilson where Franklin Hewitt now lives, and G R. Hoyt where L Bird's house now stands Some time after J S Brockway sold to Jesse Wilson, and moved further north near where Brockwayville (Jefferson county) now stands Other persons then settled above and below Penfield Among these was Ebenezer Hewitt, father of John and Thomas Hewitt

The early settlers depended upon the forest to supply their meat, and johnnycake was the legal tender everywhere Making shingles was about the only means the people had to raise money These were hauled to Clearfield and sold

Religious Services.—Religious services began almost with the settlement Neither were the educational interests neglected, for a schoolhouse was built at an early date near where the iron bridge crosses Bennett s Branch (Penfield) The first blacksmith shop was built in 1842 by E D Patterson There was no important business done until the arrival of Hiram Woodward in 1854, who bought the interest of Wilson & Hoyt and began lumbering Some one had tried to "float" unpeeled logs a few years previous, but utterly failed When Mr Woodward informed them of the number he intended to "drive," to express it in a more modern term, the people were greatly astonished, and, influenced by some "up-and-down" saw-mill proprietors, declared it utterly impossible, and threats were made on all sides against the undertaking, but nothing daunted, Mr Woodward went on The logs were put in and the people were forced to believe the truth From that time forth lumbering has been the principal business of Huston township

Old "Uncle-Billy" Long, the great hunter, lived many years in this township P. P. Bliss, the Gospel singer, was born in this township when it yet belonged to Elk county. L Bird came in 1869, engaged in the real estate business and surveying, prospered, owning considerable real estate in Penfield and vicinity

Penfield is a beautiful little town, having a population at the present writing of over 700 The beginning of the village dates from the settlement of Huston township

Winterburn is next in importance as a town in the township, is situated three miles south-west of Penfield, and ten miles east of Du Bois, it is surrounded on all sides by hills, which afford wild and romantic scenery Prior to 1873 it was a vast wilderness, but in 1873 the railroad was built and with it the high trestle, which was named the "South Fork Trestle," after the small stream running through at this point In the winter of 1873 Mr George Craig named it Winterburn

About this time Craig & Blanchard, who had been in co-partnership, dissolved by mutual consent and divided the timber tract, the small stream (South Fork) forming the boundary In 1874 James Barton, foreman for Craig & Son, commenced clearing the land on the left bank of the stream, and getting it ready for building The mill was built, and in operation by May, 1875

Blanchard's mill, on the opposite bank, was begun in the fall of 1874, and commenced running the following July (1875) His planing-mill was not built until 1879

A schoolhouse was built in 1876, and the first teacher was Alice E Bird, of Penfield, but previous to this Mr A H Rosenkrans had taught a select school

A Methodist Episcopal church was organized in 1878 by Rev A B Hooven, and a Presbyterian church in May, 1882, by Rev J. V Bell

In the fall of 1881 Messrs McKinstry and Clearwater started a tanning plant in Penfield, near the station, but sold to Thomas E Proctor before it was in running order, he completed and stocked it in 1882 Its capacity was three hundred hides per day, between seven thousand and eight thousand cords of bark being consumed annually

Hiram Woodward in 1854 built an old "flutter" saw-mill, which he supplemented in 1870 with a steam saw-mill In the fall of 1882 Hoover, Hughs & Co commenced their large mill on Wilson Run, one mile from Penfield, which they had in running order in April, 1883

In 1856 there were only three schools in Huston township Teachers received from $12 to $15 per month of twenty-four days, and had to "board around" There seems to have been some "crookedness," as a member of the school-board, at about this time, burned the record and vouchers, to prevent investigation as to the disbursement of money received from the county treasurer, on unseated lands But later on the management of schools passed into different hands, and began to prosper, and the educational interests of the township have since been in a healthy condition

JORDAN TOWNSHIP

This township was erected from Beccaria by a decree of the court of quarter sessions of Clearfield county, dated February 5, 1835, and was named in honor of Hugh Jordan, a former associate judge of the county and an ex-soldier of the Revolutionary war The township is bounded on the north by Ferguson and Knox townships, on the east by Bigler township, on the south by Beccaria and Chest townships, and on the west by Chest township

There is considerable coal development in this township and it also has many of the best farms in the county The population of the township, according to the census of 1910, was 1,261

James Rea, the first settler of what is now Knox township, moved in 1819 to the land later owned by his sons, and thus became the first settler of the territory now embraced in Jordan township He was the only son of Samuel Rea, who came from Ireland, and settled in York county, Pa Samuel, his eldest son, married Lydia Ricketts, of Mount Pleasant, and located on a farm in Knox township, of which place he was a citizen until his death, January 5, 1887, Nancy married John Patterson, Thomas married Hannah Bloom, James married Jane, daughter of John Dillen, of Mount Pleasant She died and he then married Mrs Eliza Corrigan, of Columbia, Pa

About 1820 John Swan, Sr, a forgeman by trade, left his home in New York State, where he married Miss Phoebe Tubbs, and started to the State of Ohio He stopped a while near where Tyrone now is, on account of some of his party being sick, but finally concluded to come over into what is now Clearfield county, where land was cheap Accordingly, in company with Truman Vitz, he came into what is now Jordan township, cutting his way through the forest all the way from Tyrone He and Mr Vitz purchased four hundred and thirty-three acres of land, the same land constituting the beautiful farms later owned by his son

18

John, and Major D W Wise   Some time after this Mr Vitz moved to Meadville, Pa Mr Swan commenced the manufacture of lye soon after his arrival   Kettles holding twenty barrels were produced at Pittsburgh, Pa Large quantities of wood were cut and burned, the ashes were leached, and the lye boiled down and shipped in barrels down the river on rafts This made a market for wood ashes, and his neighbors for some distance around hauled their ashes to this immense lye factory   This was soon improved upon by building a large oven, and concentrating the liquid by intense heat into potash, which answered the same purpose, and brought better prices, with a reduced cost of transportation   He also erected machinery for grinding rock oak bark for tanning purposes   This he boxed and shipped to Philadelphia on an ark, receiving sixty dollars per ton for it   He also turned his attention to agriculture, which supplied the family with products of that kind, although in a commercial way it did not pay, for wheat brought only forty-five cents per bushel   Mr Swan died here, and was buried at Zion Cemetery   Anson, the eldest son, for whom Ansonville was named, was never married, but lived with his friends at Ansonville, until his death in 1883, Sophronia married William Hartshorn, who is now dead, Harvey moved to Ohio and married there   He died in 1857   Eliza married a Mr Winslow, of New York State   John married Catherine Williams a sister of David Williams, and they resided on the old homestead about one mile from Ansonville   Henry married Lucinda, daughter of Benjamin Bloom, of Pike township   He kept the only store at Ansonville for many years   He was justice of the peace for many years   Mrs Swan died at her home in Ansonville, in 1883

Harriet, a twin sister of Henry, married Edmund Williams.   They moved to Illinois, where she died in 1867

James McNeel emigrated from County Tyrone, Ireland, when about twenty-one years old, and settled in Sinking Valley, where he married Elizabeth Crawford, of that place. He stayed there a short time, and then came to Jordan township, and purchased three hundred acres of land, the same being later owned by his sons James, Joseph and Isaac, his daughter Mary, his grandson Taylor McNeel and John Mays   The children of the first wife were Nancy, who married James Ramsey, and moved to Illinois; Thomas who married a Miss Russell, died in Illinois   Ann married William Atleman, and moved to Centre county, where she died   Ellen married William Speer, and lived in Johnstown until her death, Marshall, the youngest, died in California in 1883. His second wife was Mary Ricketts, daughter of Isaac Ricketts, of Mount Pleasant, and to them eight children were born   Eliza, the eldest, married John Hunter, and lives on a farm near Ansonville; John married Mary Jane Glasgow, of Blair county   James G married Miss Jane Lynch, of Pike township   Joseph married Mary Jane McCreight   Mary married Frank McCormick, of Ireland   Lydia married Lance Root, both are dead   Isaac married Mary Jane Davis, of Mount Pleasant, Pa   Caroline died when twelve years old The parents lived to a good old age, the mother surviving her husband several years, died at the old homestead about 1883, and was buried by his side in Fruit Hill Cemetery

David Williams came here from Centre county in April of 1833   He purchased the large tract of land which was later owned by his sons, James G, and William, and Martin,

Nolen, and Mrs Green, of Ferguson township, from Shoemaker and Irvin He built a shanty on the Spring Run, below the present residence, in the thick woods He built a grist-mill on the run the same year, which was one of the first mills in this part of the county The millwrights were Joseph, Michael, and Silas Solly The bolting-cloth for this mill was purchased at Lewistown, Pa, and brought here by private conveyance Mr Williams also turned his attention to farming and improved the land mentioned above, but still kept the mill running until it was worn out His widow, who was, previous to her marriage, Mary Glenn, survived him many years, living with her son William, who cultivated the farm James G married Matilda, a daughter of Alfred D Knapp, who improved the farm now owned by James McKeehen, and afterward moved to Iowa, where he now lives Martha married Alexander Henderson, and went to Illinois Lucinda, John, and Austin are dead

Robert Patterson came with his parents from Ireland and settled first in Virginia From there they moved to Maryland, and afterward to Centre county, Pa, where he married Elizabeth McCormick He then came to what is now Clearfield county and lived for some time in Lawrence township From there he moved to Beccaria, afterwards Jordan township, probably about 1823 or '24, and took advantage of the offer made by Morgan Rawles, and Peters, of fifty acres gratis by buying the other fifty acres of a hundred acre tract, at four dollars per acre The land in that vicinity is yet known as "Morgan's Land" Mr Patterson possessed a knowledge of books, as well as of clearing land and cultivating it, and put his talents to use by

farming during the summer season and teaching school in the winter Of his children, Agnes married Thomas Witherow, and lived to an advanced age Jane married Christian Erhard, and died in 1882 at her home in New Millport, leaving several sons and daughters Joseph married Margaret Erhard, a sister of David, and lived on his farm in Ferguson township until his death about 1884 His widow died in 1887, at the home of her daughter, Mrs David Johnston, at the age of eighty-four years Robert married Catherine, daughter of John Thomson, Sr, of this township John married Nancy, daughter of James Rea, mentioned elsewhere She died in the early eighties, and he married Margaret, daughter of John Hunter, of Jordan township She also died, and he then married Mrs Nancy Bright James married Rebecca McCormick, of Armstrong county, and lived on a farm in Beccaria township Jemima married James Wilson and lived in Jordan township

Abram Bloom came from Northampton county, N J, to Northampton county, Pa, and from there moved to Jordan township in 1831 He located on the land now known as the Lafayette Bloom Farm, near Fruit Hill church He lived here a few years and returned to Northampton county Several of his children remained in the township

The Johnstons in this township are descendants of Robert and James, two brothers, who came to this country from Scotland seventy-five or more years ago Robert settled on the tract later owned by his son David Robert M married Priscilla Wise, a sister of ex-Treasurer D W Wise, of this township John C was in the mercantile business in Ansonville for many years His first wife was Christina Curry, who died about 1882 He later married Mrs Martha Witherow, widow of Henry Witherow, and daughter of Frederick Shoff, of Beccaria township He was in partnership with John McQuilkin in a meat market in Ansonville David married Martha Patterson, and lived on the old homestead James married Mary Jane, daughter of John Witherow, of Knox township, and lived on his farm near Ansonville Mary married Reuben Caldwell, and lived in Knox township Belle married Isaac Bloom, and Elizabeth married Samuel Witherow, both well-to-do farmers of this township Mark was killed by a tree while chopping a clearing William was killed by a runaway horse while returning from Charles Lewis's smith shop James Johnston located near Johnston's school-house Some thirty years ago he attended a meeting of the session at the Fruit Hill Presbyterian church He had intended to go home by way of John Thomson's, having some business with Mr Thomson, but for some reason changed his mind and concluded to go over a day or two later He was riding horseback, and just after he passed the residence of R M Johnston, a dead chestnut tree that stood by the road side fell, mashing the horse and his rider to the ground Two sons, James, Jr, and Robert survived him, and one daughter, Mrs John Glasgow, of Glen Hope

John Thomson, Sr, came here from Edinburgh, Scotland, in 1832 He purchased land and made an improvement not far from where Ansonville is now located Soon after settling here he wrote to his only son, John, who had preceded him to this country about two years, and was living at Pottsville, Pa,' that the Carsons wanted to sell their improvement Young John at once packed his effects, came to Jordan and purchased the Carson

place He married Rebecca, daughter of Thomas Lord, and settled down to improve the farm, where he spent the remainder of his life. They had thirteen children

Ansonville is pleasantly located on the elevation or dividing ridge between the headwaters of the South Fork of Little Clearfield Creek and Potts Run The land now occupied by the village was once owned by the Swans, and the place was named in honor of Anson Swan, a deaf and dumb brother of John and Henry Swan The population of the place, including Strawtown or Bretzinville, is over three hundred The first building in the place was built by a Mr Singer, and was at first occupied as a store by John Miles and James Foutz

In 1853 Henry Swan built a large storeroom on the corner opposite the Ansonville Hotel, and occupied it as a general store until 1874 Soon after this it burned down, and the lot remained vacant until 1884 or 1885, when Dr A E Creswell purchased it and built the large store-rooms and dwelling later purchased by C D McMurry, and occupied by him as a general store, and by H Gilliland as a clothing store Other stores and merchants followed and enjoyed a steady trade

As near as we can learn, the Ansonville postoffice was established about 1857 Eliza Chase (later Mrs W T. Bloom) was postmistress Henry Swan had the office from 1864 to 1868, and was succeeded by Joseph Thomson, and he by Arthur B Straw J C Johnston succeeded Mr Straw, and had charge of the office several years until 1886, when C D McMurry was appointed

The first schoolhouse built in the township, was erected in 1820, not far from where the Fruit Hill Presbyterian church was after-

RESIDENCE AND BARN OF E. SCHNARS, LAWRENCE TOWNSHIP

wards built The house was built of logs A square pen-shaped arrangement was built inside to do service as a flue The windows were made by cutting one or two logs off in the side of the building and pasting greased paper over the hole to keep the wind and cold out The writing desks were made by driving pins in the walls of the building and fastening thereto a slab with the flat side up The seats were also made of slabs, with the round side up The first teacher of this school was David Cathcart, who afterward located in Knox township, where he purchased a large tract of land, part of the timber of this land being subsequently sold by his sons for a considerable amount of money He had a large family of children

Robert Patterson, Sr, also taught here, and some say, was the first teacher, but others, that Cathcart was the first We find also that John Watson taught here Some years after a little log schoolhouse was built near the subsequent residence of Major Wise Asil Swan was one of the first teachers The house has long since gone the way of all old houses, and history fails to record any of the exploits of its graduates The old log schoolhouse that stood near the old Zion church is also one of the things of the past Rev S Miles taught school and preached in this house as early as 1843, and the house was built previous to that time The school facilities have been improved as well as the land, and will now compare favorably with those of any similar community Mr A M Buzard taught the first select school in Ansonville during the summer of 1884, with forty students in attendance He also taught the two succeeding years with an increased membership, and was assisted by Harvey Roland Mr Buzard afterwards

went into the drug business here, and the school was subsequently taught by J F Mc-Naul, of Curwensville

KARTHAUS TOWNSHIP

This township was erected from the eastern part of Covington, by a decree of the court of quarter sessions of Clearfield county dated February 3, 1841, and was named in honor of Peter A Karthaus, who was the owner of a large portion of the land in the township

The township is situated in the extreme northwestern corner of the county and is bounded on the north by part of the dividing line between Cambria and Clearfield counties, on the east by part of the dividing line between Clinton and Clearfield counties and part of the dividing line between Centre and Clearfield counties, on the south and west by Covington township

There are a number of coal operations in this township, also some good farms The population, according to the census of 1910, was 1,332

The marked geographical and topographical feature of Karthaus township is the Horseshoe Bend, at which the current tends directly south, then bends around and runs nearly direct north, all within a small area Its greatest length, north and south, is not far short of eleven miles, while its average length is about seven miles From east and west measurement the township extends a distance of about six miles, but the average in this direction is only about four miles The surface of the township, generally, is hilly, broken, and mountainous, the altitude above tide-water averaging something like fourteen hundred feet The township is well watered by the West Branch on the south, and the auxillary streams, Mosquito Creek, Salt Lick and Upper Three Run, the first and last being fair sized mountain streams having several smaller tributaries

The pioneer history of Karthaus township was made many years prior to its separate organization, and while it was still a part of Lawrence township Before Lawrence was erected, the township of Chincleclamousche embraced the territory that subsequently formed Lawrence, Covington and Karthaus, excepting, however, a small tract taken from Lycoming, that was added to the county subsequent to its erection in 1804

One of the earliest settlers in Karthaus or the lands that were afterward embraced by it, was G Philip Geulich, who located there during the month of April, 1814 He first came to the county in 1811, with Charles Loss, as representatives of the Allegheny Coal Company, by whom they were sent to ascertain if the reports concerning an abundant supply of superior coal were true They first came to Clearfield Creek, where they remained during the winter Upon their report the company purchased the land known as the Ringgold tract, on Clearfield Creek, and another tract comprising some three or four thousand acres on the Moshannon After having fulfilled the object of his visit, Geulich was about to return to Huntingdon county, but was finally persuaded to proceed to the lands on the Moshannon, and make an improvement In 1813, in company with Joseph Ritchie, he attempted to ascend the West Branch, but finding the river filled with snow and ice, was compelled to return Another attempt, in company with John Frazer and James Bowman, was made successfully and at the end of a three days' journey the party landed at Karthaus, on the bank

of the Moshannon, on the 8th day of April, 1814 Here they built a cabin, after which several weeks were spent in clearing lands for the future operations of the Allegheny Company at that point Geulich did not remain long in this vicinity, owing to a misunderstanding with one Junge When about ready to leave, the families of Frederick W Geisenhamer, and John Reiter came to the neighborhood, and they urged him to return to the Ringgold tract on Clearfield Creek, which he did Here he lived until 1818, acting as agent for the company, until their lands were all sold, after which he purchased the Kline property, and still later resided at the county-seat In 1829-33 he was treasurer of the county

The early settlement of Karthaus township was materially hastened by the knowledge of her extensive coal and iron deposits Bituminous coal was in great demand at the time, and this demand gave rise to the development of the Karthaus field and shipping therefrom, at a very early day, considerable quantities of coal in arks down the West Branch to Columbia, where it sold readily at thirty-seven and one-half cents per bushel The channel, however, was obstructed with rocks and sunken trees, that proved fatal to many a cargo

In the year 1815, Peter A Karthaus, his son, and J F W Schnars, under the guidance of one Green, a hotel-keeper from Milesburg, Centre county, came to the vicinity Green was on foot, and the others had two horses between them They followed the old Indian path, and, after leaving the Alleghenies, found but two habitations on the route hither, those of Samuel Askey and John Bechtold Worn and tired, they arrived one evening at John Reiter's house There they found David Dunlap, a millwright, engaged in building a saw-mill on the coal company's land, at the mouth of the Little Moshannon Some years later this mill was arranged with country-stones, and the grinding for the settlement was done at this place This proved a great convenience to the people, who had been compelled to convey all flour and feed, either from the Bald Eagle Valley or from Clearfield town, nearly twenty-five miles distant, with no thoroughfare other than the old Indian path

J F W. Schnars, who was the companion and friend of Peter A Karthaus, was a German by birth, born in the year 1785 In the year 1810 he came to Baltimore, and found employment with Karthaus, who was an extensive merchant, engaged in foreign and domestic trade In 1829 Schnars was chosen county commissioner, and still later county auditor He was commissioned postmaster of his township in 1832, and held that office a score and a half of years The family name is still extensive in the county, represented by the descendants of this old pioneer

Peter A Karthaus and his son returned, after a time, to Baltimore, but again came to this vicinity, bringing his family He became the owner of a large tract of land in the township, and by his efforts and enterprise in business, did more toward the settlement and improvement of it than any other person

In the year 1815, Junge and Schnars purchased lands of Karthaus and Geisenhainer, and commenced extensive improvements and settlements thereon About the same time several other families came in, among them, Hugh Riddle, Jacob Michaels, William Russell and others, former residents of Bald Eagle, Centre county They made purchases, and at once began improving the lands

Soon after the first settlements in the town-ship, a deposit of bog ore was discovered near the head of Buttermilk Falls, some four miles down the river from Karthaus The lands were purchased from Judge Bowdinot, of Burlington, N J, who owned them, by Geisenhainer & Schnars The tract comprising three parcels was conveyed to Peter A Karthaus In the year 1817 he, with Geisenhainer, built the old furnace at Moshannon Creek. The ore was conveyed up the river in flat-boats and canoes, and there made into iron Connected with this a foundry was built, and hollow iron wares, stoves, and other articles manufactured The river was cleared of obstructions that had proved fatal to the coal transports, and the manufactured iron wares were shipped to market The people interested in the enterprise lacked experience, the place of manufacture was so far distant from the market, and the expense and danger incident to river traffic was so great that the enterprise was finally abandoned Many of the families induced to settle here on account of the favorable reports concerning locality, became discouraged at the prospect and returned east For a time, instead of an increase there seemed to be a general and sudden decrease in population, but after the excitement had died out and the agricultural advantages of the locality became established, the time of immigration and settlement again set this way, and the increase again became general and healthful.

In the year 1845 Richard Coleburn, the assessor of the township, was directed to make an enumeration of each of the taxable inhabitants then being residents From the roll so made by him, the names of such taxables are made to appear, which will show who were the residents of the township at the time. George Bucher, a tailor, William Bridgens, George

Bearfield, Sr, Reuben Bearfield, laborer, Jacob Cooms, Levi Coffin, farmer, Ann Coleburn, George Conaway, Sr, Dickson Cole, laborer, Richard Coleburn, farmer, Mark Coleburn, laborer, Matthew B Conaway, Benjamin Clark, sawyer, John Gaines, James Gunsaulis, Samuel Gunsaulis, farmer, having, in addition to his two tracts of land, one hundred acres bought of P A Karthaus's "plough deep," Jeremiah Gaines, Robert Gaines, farmer, Lawrence F Hartline, farmer, George Haun, farmer, Levi Harris, laborer, John Harris, laborer, James Hunter, laborer, Andrew Eisenmann, Jacob Eisenman, weaver, John Eisenman, farmer; Michael Eisenman, farmer, John Irvin, "lumberer," having a saw-mill, Peter A Karthaus, no occupation, but having a saw-mill and grist-mill, Robert Lowes, laborer, having one hundred acres of land bought of Keating, Ellis Lowes, farmer, Jacob G Lebs, manager, Benjamin B Lee, carpenter, Francis McCoy, "one saw-mill, burned down," Elizabeth Michaels, John Michaels, farmer, Edward Michaels, laborer; William H Michaels, farmer, Daniel Moore, farmer, James Meny, laborer, Thomas Michaels, farmer, John Price, farmer, Isaac Price, farmer, Joseph Rupley, farmer, J F. W Schnars, saw-mill, Charles Schnars, sawyer, Gottlieb Snyder, farmer, Francis Soultsman, blacksmith, William Teets, laborer, John Vought, farmer, John Wykoff, carpenter; James White, farmer, Washington Watson, laborer, Joseph Yothers, farmer The single freemen then living in the township were Frederick Coffin, William Carson, Thomas Moyers, John Haun, Charles Haun, John Hicks, Jr, Prudence Knyder, John Condly, John Uzzle

From this it appears that there were residing in the township in the year 1845, fifty-four property owners and nine single freemen As further shown by the roll, there were several who had formerly been residents, but who appear to have gone away since the assessment next preceding 1845 Among those are found the names of Sarah Apple, Samuel K Bevan, H O Brittain, Cornelius Conaway, Charles Durow, Henry Harris, Simon Hall, Michael Mays, Jacob Miller, Peter McDonald, John Reiter, Matthew Savage, William Soults, all of whom were regular taxables, owning either real or personal property, besides a few single freemen, as follows William Barefield, Andrew Kiem, and John Summerville. From these facts it can fairly be assumed that the population of Karthaus township, in 1845, did not exceed two hundred inhabitants

The great interest taken by all persons during the lumbering period in that production, materially increased the temporary or floating population, and after the tracts were exhausted and agriculture became the regular avocation of the inhabitants, many who had come with the intention of leaving as soon as the lumber districts were cleared, were induced to remain and permanently reside in the township At that time, if the record is reliable, there were in the township only four saw-mills and one grist-mill, owned as shown above During the period of ten years, from 1850 to 1860, lumbering reached its maximum, after which it began gradually to decline

The original village of Karthaus was laid out on the map of the Keating lands which was made as early as 1827, or perhaps earlier As shown it lay on a sharp bend of the river at the mouth of Mosquito Creek, and on tract No 1901 It contained nineteen hundred and one acres of land The newer Karthaus lies further east, and was built up chiefly through the extensive coal and lumbering interests developed there

The township has adequate school and church facilities

KNOX TOWNSHIP

This township was erected by a decree of the court dated the 19th day of May, 1854, and was named in honor of Judge Knox, one of the first judges, who presided over the courts of Clearfield county The township is bounded on the north by Pike and Lawrence townships, on the east by Woodward and Bigler townships, south by Beccaria township and west by Jordan and Ferguson townships

The principal business of the people of the township is agriculture, although there are some coal deposits that are now being operated The population, according to the census of 1910, was 1,064

The first settlement in Knox township, and one of the first in the county, was made by James Rea, in 1806, who came here from Huntingdon county

The nearest grist-mill at that time was between Tyrone and Birmingham Some time after a mill was erected at Moose Creek, and thither Mr Rea transported his grist on the back of an ox

In a short time James Hegarty, who was murdered soon after, settled what is now the William Witherow farm Thomas McKee improved the land later owned by Robert Witherow's heirs, and Thomas Jordan located where Thomas Witherow subsequently lived John Carson, also one of the first settlers, procured the premises made vacant by the death of James Hegarty

In 1824, Peter Erhard, who lived by the Susquehanna River, near Curwensville, was drowned while crossing the river on horseback About six or eight years previous to this time he had located some land in what is now Knox township By the aid of his four sons this land was improved, and shortly after the death of the father the sons moved to this land, and in connection with it bought the tract upon which grew up the village of New Millport The three eldest sons, Christian, David, and Philip, were interested in the latter purchase, and soon erected a saw-mill, probably the first improvement on Little Clearfield Creek This first mill was built sometime between 1820 and 1825, and after it had served its purpose and time, another was built near the grist-mill

Saw-mills did not pay the operators in that early day, for although surrounded by thousands of acres of immense pine forests, the facilities for transportation were so poor and the demand so limited, that lumber was scarce worth the cutting, and millions of feet that would now be worth forty to sixty dollars per thousand feet, were rolled into heaps and burned

George, a younger son of Peter Erhard, improved a farm, was county commissioner from 1857 to 1860

The first dwelling-house in New Millport village was built by David Erhard, Sr, about 1834, near the mill-race The town was of slow growth, but the building of the Beech Creek Railroad through it in 1885, gave it a new impetus

The first industries being mills, suggested the name—Millport, and the word New, was added when the postoffice was established here, to distinguish it from Millport, in Potter county, Pa The first postmaster was D E Mokel, appointed in 1855 or 1856

The first schoolhouse in Knox township was located across the run from the residence of David Erhard It was built in 1842 The first teacher was Benjamin Roberts, who afterwards became a citizen of the township, and improved the farm later owned by Robert Patterson The township is now well supplied with good schools and teachers, also churches

LAWRENCE TOWNSHIP

This township was erected by a decree of the court of quarter sessions, to which county Clearfield was then attached for judicial purposes, at November sessions, 1813

The township is bounded on the north by part of the dividing line between Elk and Clearfield counties, on the east by Goshen, Bradford and Boggs townships, on the south by Knox township and on the west by Pike, Pine and Huston townships

There are a number of large coal operations in this township, also some fine farms The population of the township, according to the census of 1910, was 4,025

No more accurate record of the early settlers of Lawrence can be made than by a full statement of the taxable inhabitants made by Samuel Fulton, assessor, under and by virtue of an order of the county commissioners, bearing date the 21st day of February, 1814, and signed by Hugh Jordon, Robert Maxwell and William Tate, commissioners

The names of the taxables appearing on the roll are as follows· Elinor Ardery, John Andrews, Arthur Bell, Henry Buck, Samuel Beers, Arthur Bell, Robert Collins George Conoway, Hugh Caldwell, Alexander Dun-

lap, James Dunlap, Hugh Frazier, John Frazier, Thomas Forcey, Samuel Fulton, William Hanna, Jacob Haney, Martin Hoover, Samuel Hoover, George Hunter, Esther Haney, John Hall, John Hoover, Henry Irwin, Hugh Jordon, Samuel Jordon, Thomas Jordon, Thomas Kirk, Thomas Kirk, Jr, John Kline, Nicholas Kline, William Leonard, Rudolph Litch, Lebbeus Luther, David Ligget, Richard Mapes, John Moore, Reuben Mayhew, Adam Myers, Moses Norris, Matthew Ogden, Daniel Ogden, John Owens, William Orr, Joseph Patterson, Robert Patterson, Thomas Reynolds, Alexander Reed, Thomas Reed, Archibald Shaw, Elisha Schofield, John Shaw, Richard Shorter, Mary Shirrey, Robert Shaw, Ignatius Thompson, William Tate, Robert Wrigley, George Welch, Herman Young, Peter Young

The single freemen were Andrew Allison, Samuel Ardery, Benjamin Beers, Benjamin Carson, Jr, Alexander Dunlap, Christian Eveon, Jacob Hoover, Cæsar Potter, John R Reed, Hugh Reynolds, William Shirrey, Hugh McMullen

The settlers living in the Sinnamahoning district were enrolled in a separate list It will be remembered that the settlement down the river was made into an election district, and the voting place was fixed at the mouth of the Sinnamahoning, at Andrew Overdorf's house The taxables of this district were Stephen Barfield, Robert Barr, Daniel Bailey, Jacob Burch, Dwight Cadwell, Thomas Dent, Richard Galat, Joseph Gaugey, Levy Hicks, William T Hardy, Ralph Johnston, Thew Johnston, James Jordon, John Jordon, Henry Lorghbaugh, Jr, Joseph Mason, Amos Mix, James Mix, William Nanny, John Overdorf, Andrew Overdorf, Andrew Overdorf, Jr,

Samuel Smith, Charles Swartz, Curran Sweesey, Benjamin Smith, Jacob Miller, Leonard Morey.

The single freemen in the Sinnamahoning district were as follows James Mix, Joseph Gaugey, James Sweezey, John Ream, John Biss, William Lewis, William Shepherd, George Lorghbaugh, William Calloway, George Derring

The first reduction of the territorial limits of Lawrence township was made by the formation of Covington and Gibson, in the year 1817, by an order of the Centre County Court of Quarter Sessions

In 1845, at a term of court held February 4, Goshen township was erected from Lawrence, Girard, and part of Jay and Gibson townships

The early history of this township antedates, by many years, its civil organization Within its boundaries there was located the old Indian town of Chincleclamousche, the remains of which were discovered by Daniel Ogden, the pioneer, at the time of his settlement, in 1797 Still further back than this we find the country overrun and occupied by a fierce tribe of Indians known to the first white adventurers as the Lenni Lenapes, who made their central station on the river Delaware, and whose descendants occupied this whole region for a hundred years or more Later on came the Shawnees, a supposed branch of the Algonquins, whose language they spoke Then again, during the seventeenth century, the confederated nation of Iroquois, or the Five Nations, as they were commonly known, swept over the entire province of Pennsylvania, as well as the country north and south of it, driving out the occupants or completely subjugating them, and making themselves

conquerors, and their chiefs and sachems rulers and monarchs of the entire country

During the progress of the French and Indian war this vicinity was occupied by the French with view to erecting a fort, but this scheme seems to have failed They did, however, assemble at the village of Chincleclamousche and organize an expedition against Fort Augusta, the key to the whole northwestern part of the province Here it was that Captain Hambright came with orders to destroy the Indian town, and make battle against the inhabitants, but finding the town deserted returned to the fort with his men On a subsequent visit the town was found to be destroyed, and the Indians fled to the protection of the French forts on the western frontier The Indian paths, several of which led through the township, were thoroughfares of travel to and from the points east of the Alleghenies

Daniel Ogden was the first permanent settler in this township, and made the first improvement therein The chief industry at that time was farming and clearing land, and as new residents followed, each in succession was compelled to make a clearing for a cabin and farming purposes

The necessity of lumber and material for building led to the erection of saw-mills at various places, and as the lands became cleared and crops gathered, grist-mills became a like necessity

According to the tax-roll made by Samuel Fulton, assessor for Lawrence and Pike townships, in the year 1814, there were several industries already established in the township of Lawrence, some of which can be located with accuracy Samuel Beers was assessed as having a tan-yard Beers lived on Clearfield

Creek, and had a small tannery near his house
This factory was so small that it was assessed
as nominal only Martin Hoover had a saw-
mill on Montgomery Creek, and was assessed
therefor fifty dollars, which amount would
scarcely buy a cheap saw at the present day
J L McPherson s steam saw-mill was built
near the same locality, which is one of the oldest mill locations in the county

Esther Haney, widow of Frederick Haney,
was assessed this same year for a saw and
grist-mill on Montgomery Creek The saw-
mill was assessed at fifty dollars, and the grist-
mill at thirty dollars Thomas Haney, son of
Frederick, had a saw-mill on Moose Creek

Reuben Mayhew was the local shoemaker,
and his trade assessed at ten dollars

To Matthew Ogden attaches the credit of
having built the first grist-mill in the county,
on Moose Creek, about half a mile above its
mouth Some years later he built a saw-mill
further down and moved his grist-mill to that
point, near the site now occupied by Shaw's
mill In 1821 Ogden built another grist-mill
on Clearfield Creek, which was operated for
many years, but is now entirely destroyed

Thomas Reynolds had a tannery in Clearfield town, that was built about the year 1810,
but no business of account was done there until some five or six years later Another tannery was built by Jacob Irwin about 1820, just
back of the Boyer residence on Second street

In 1814-15, the Elder mills were built on
Little Clearfield Creek by James I Thorn, who
came to the county for that purpose The
building consisted of a saw-mill, a fulling or
woolen-mill, and a tavern The woolen-mill
was the first of its kind in the county, and the
tavern among the first Elder never resided
in the county, but was largely interested in

lands at that place He is remembered as exceedingly kind and generous He had many
cattle at his place, and frequently loaned unbroken cattle to farmers, and allowed them to
break and use them for their keeping

In the Sinnamahoning district a record of
taxables made in the year 1815 showed a total
of forty-one The roll also mentioned two
saw-mills, one assessed to Thomas Dent and
the other to John Jordan.

In 1813, a year after commissioners for the
county were authorized to be elected therein,
the population had increased sufficiently that
a postoffice for the county was found necessary, and this was established at the house of
Alexander Read, better known as "Red Alex "
The neighborhood on the ridge where the
Reads were numerous, was known as Reads-
boro, and the office was designated by that
name It was continued there until about the
year 1819 The old State road passed through
the place, and it was then the most central
point, notwithstanding the fact that the site
for the county seat had already been established at the old Indian town some two or
three miles distant Before this office was established all mail matter came from Philipsburg, on the extreme east line of the county,
once each week

At the time the county seat was fixed there
was no improvement on the lands of Abraham
Witmer, except such as had many years before been made by the Indians The old
cleared fields remained grown up with weeds
and buffalo grass

When Lawrence was made a township
there were but few residents at the county
seat proper, that is, Clearfield town The first
conveyances of town lots were made to Mat-
'hew Ogden, Robert Collins, and William

Tate, in the year 1807 The donation of lands for county building and other purposes was made at the time the county seat was fixed, but the deed was not executed until 1813

The court-house was erected about 1814 by Robert Collins about this time

The township of Lawrence was declared, by an act of the Legislature passed April 2, 1821, to be a separate election district, and the freemen were directed to hold their elections at the court-house in Clearfield town Having from this time a distinct and complete organization, settlement became more rapid, and consequent upon such settlement and growth and the development of its resources, this has become one of the leading townships of the county The surrender of lands for the formation of Covington and other townships, while it reduced its area and population, made it more compact and more readily improved The seat of justice, located in the southern central part of the township, became the natural trading and distributing center for the country roundabout

The chief pursuit followed by the people of the township for many years, outside their regular occupation as farmers, was lumbering Among the early mill erections was that built by Hopkins Boone, John and Maxwell Long and William Porter, on Clearfield Creek, about a quarter of a mile above the old Clearfield bridge, in or about the year 1833 The proprietors were considerably involved and the property was sold to Lewis Passmore about ten or twelve years after its erection The latter sold to John W Miller, who removed the building and machinery for the erection of a saw and grist-mill on the creek opposite the old Elder mills, and were known as the Miller mills They went to decay many years ago

The first erection in the vicinity of ' Porter s Mill," was made about 1836, by Philip Antes and George Leech, with an interest owned by Christopher Kratzer A saw-mill on the east side of the river was first built The property went to James T Leonard on forced sale, but was afterward deeded to the Antes boys, and by them to William Porter and Philip C Heisy Porter bought the Heisy interest The first grist-mill on the place was erected by William Porter in 1877, at a cost of nearly ten thousand dollars It burned in 1882 Another mill was immediately erected in its place, larger and of greater capacity, at a cost of about seventeen thousand dollars Subsequently the roller process machinery was introduced into this mill and was purchased by W R McPherson

On the site of the Ferguson mills in the year 1842, George B Logan and Thomas Read built a saw-mill on the south side of the river, and about 1850, built a grist-mill on the north bank A division of the property was made by which Logan took the grist-mill, and Reed the saw-mill, but subsequently Logan became the owner of the whole property About 1860 he sold to the Farmers' Company, but that was not a successful organization and the property came back to Logan again In the early eighties George E Ferguson became owner and proprietor The dam across the West Branch was constructed at the time the first mill was built

On the site formerly occupied by Matthew Ogden's pioneer mill on Moose Creek, there was built by Alexander Irvin in the year 1830, a substantial grist-mill Irvin sold to Richard Shaw, who operated it until his death, when it went to Richard Shaw, Jr

About the year 1842, William Bigler and

William Powell built a saw mill in the south part of the township, and afterward christened it the "Doniphan Mill," in honor of Colonel Doniphan of Mexican War fame. After Mr Bigler's election to the office of governor of the State, the property went to the firm of G L Reed & Co It has also been owned by Weaver and Betts, William Brown, Daniel Mitchell and again by Weaver and Betts

The Ringgold Mill was built by George R Barrett and Christopher Kratzer, in the year 1847, on Clearfield Creek, about half a mile from the railroad bridge, the cost being about seven thousand dollars During the extremely high water on the creek that year, the mill was carried down stream to the river, and thence down to Karthaus bridge, where all trace of it was lost, no part ever being recovered A new mill was immediately erected on the site of the former structure Both of these were among the very best in the lumber country, the first being an unusually fine mill It was a double mill, having two saws, and manufactured a large amount of lumber for that time The dam built by the owners was very objectionable to raftsmen on account of its height, and many were the rafts and arks that went to pieces in attempting its passage The property was afterward sold to Wilson Hoover, and burned while he owned it

Although Lawrence is one of the pioneer townships of the county, and in all matters of county progress and advancement, she is not entitled to first honor in matters of education so far as the first school erected is concerned, but from the best authority obtainable, the second schoolhouse was built in the township in the year 1806 This was located north and east from Clayville town nearly opposite the mouth of Clearfield Creek Here the redoubt-able Samuel Fulton taught, and was afterward followed by Miss Davis and Miss Goon. An old school was built about twenty rods above the covered bridge at Clearfield town, on the west side of the river within the limits of the present borough of West Clearfield The exact date of its erection is unknown Among the early teachers there can be remembered the names of John Campbell, Miss Brockway and Benjamin Merrell

MORRIS TOWNSHIP

This township was erected by a decree of the Court of Quarter Sessions of Clearfield County, dated April 3rd, 1836, and was named in honor of the Hon Robert Morris. a distinguished patriot of the Revolutionary War

The township is bounded on the north by Graham Township, on the east by Cooper Township, and part of the dividing line between Centre and Clearfield Counties, on the south by Decatur Township and on the west by Boggs Township

The Township contains fine coal deposits and many well cultivated farms The population, according to the census of 1910, was 4994

Morris township as laid out by the viewers was perhaps as irregular in conformation as any in the county, and at the same time it was numbered among the larger in superficial area It extended from a point opposite and west of Philipsburg on the south, to the West Branch on the north, a mean distance of something like thirteen miles, and while it has no parallel sides, its average width was about six or seven miles This, of course, is an estimate of its area before any of its territory was taken for the formation of other townships The West Branch River formed the north, and the Moshannon the east boundary Having such extensive water boundary, of course Morris township was well cut by smaller streams tributary to the larger ones named above Among these tributary to the Susquehanna were Big Run, Wilhelm Run, Alder Run, Rolling Stone Run, and Basin Run Those that discharged their waters into the Moshannon were Crawford Run, Weber Run, Moravian and Little Moravian Runs (neither, however, being the stream that is correctly so named), Grass Flat Run, Brown's Run, Big Run, Hawk Run and Emigh Run It will be seen that some of these names correspond with names of other streams in other townships, which is due to the fact that many of these names were applied at a more recent date by persons not thoroughly acquainted with the county

In the year next succeeding that in which Morris township was erected (1837), James Allport made an enumeration of the taxable inhabitants, the enumeration or assessment roll containing the following names James Allport, Robert Ardery, Henry Beams, Abraham Brown, John Brown, David Cooper, John Coonrod William Dillon George R Dillon, Joseph Denny, Samuel Davison, David Dale, William Everhart, Martin Flegal, Valentine Flegal, David Flegal, Samuel C Hall, George Hoover, Thomas Hancock, Vincent Holt Nicholas Heister, John Hoover, William M Hunter, John W Irvin, Leonard Kyler, Jacob Wise, William Shimmel, George Shimmel, Sr, Philip Shimmel, Jacob F Runk, John Ready Christian Roubly, John Roubly, John Beams Jacob Beams, Jonas Bumbarger, Henry Bumbarger, Jacob Gearhart, Valentine Gearhart, David Gearhart, Peter Gearhart, John L Gearhart, David Gray, Peter Gray, Jeremiah Hoover, Samuel Hoover, Evans Hunter, Reuben Hunt-

er, Abraham Kyler, John B Kyler, Henry Lorain, John Merryman, Joseph Morrison, Jacob Pierce, William Ricord, Joseph Senser, Frederick Senser, Moses Thompson, Samuel C Thompson, Samuel Waring The total amount of the assessment for the year 1837, as shown by the roll made by Mr Allport, was $14,318

In the year 1861, nearly twenty-five years after the above enrollment was made, John Rayhorn became the assessor of the township, and as such made a list of the persons residents of the township, who were subject to militia duty, the names being as follows John Will, George Kehner, Michael Leibatt, Daniel Beams, Joseph Fulmer, Christian Hartle, Robert Rosenhoover, John Miller, John Weaver, Adam Knobb, John Stipple, William McKee, David Wagoner, G L Clapland, George Steincarichner, John Wait, Jacob May, John Steer, John Keen, Vincent Flegal, Miles Pelton, W E Williams, George Wise, John Troy, William Rothrock, David Shimmel, Harry Gleason, Elwood Dehaven, Reuben Wait, Peter Munce, C P Wilder, Leonard Kyler, David Kyler, Zachariah Jones, David Cramer, Jesse Beams, George D Hess, Daniel Zones, John Hoover

It is observed from the foregoing roll that there was a strong element of German settlers that came to the vicinity subsequent to the erection and prior to the year 1861 This locality was, before this growth, largely populated with Germans, or descendants from German parents They were, and always have been a thrifty, energetic and progressive class of people, and make admirable citizens

Amongst the first settlers of the township was Captain Jacob Wise, who located in the southern part, cleared up a farm, and also carried on blacksmithing The "Captain," as he was always called, was endowed with quite a military spirit, and figured conspicuously in military gatherings in his day, and many a good joke that came from him was enjoyed by his many friends He lived to a good old age and his death was much lamented by his many friends and neighbors He reared a large family of children

Another of the old citizens of the township was Samuel C Thompson, who located near to Captain Wise's, and cleared up a fine farm He raised a large family Being a man of good education and fine judgment, he was elected justice of the peace, and served in that capacity for fifteen years His land being underlaid with a vein of excellent bituminous coal, he opened up the bed and supplied the home demand with coal, the only coal that could be used for blacksmithing in the whole neighborhood for many years He was also elected to the office of county commissioner, and filled it with credit to himself and the township He subsequently sold his farm and timber land and removed to near Hublersburg, Centre county The land belonging to Captain Wise was sold to D W Holt & Co, who opened up the coal, commenced and carried on a very successful business for a number of years Then they sold to R B Wigton & Co, who enlarged and increased the business Mr Holt was formerly a citizen of Bradford township, this county, but as an enterprising lumberman, came to this township and purchased a part of the pine timber known as the Allport timber After the second year's operation in square timber, he built a large steam saw-mill and engaged in the manufacturing of sawed lumber for a few years He married Miss Catharine Allport Some time later he purchased the

Captain Wise property, and commenced operating in the coal business, and was the first to ship coal from Morris township Shortly after he purchased a valuable property in Philipsburg, and extended his coal and lumber operations in different parts of the neighborhood very extensively, being one of the foremost among the enterprising men in this vicinity

Another prominent citizen of old Morris township was James Allport, who contributed a great amount to the good of the citizens, and also to the general public William Hunter, likewise, a very good citizen and kind neighbor, was among the pioneers of Morris township, as were also David Dale, George R Dillen, and John W Irvin

We should also mention John Hoover, Sr. a worthy and respected citizen, who came to Morris township from Union county at an early day. He raised a large and industrious family, the sons of whom were, or perhaps still are among the people of Cooper township (a part of Morris), which derived its name from David Cooper, one of the first settlers of that part of Morris township known at Cooper Settlement, and a stalwart pioneer who crossed the Allegheny Mountains to make his home in Clearfield county

The sons of John Hoover, Sr, helped to clear up a farm near to the village of Allport, and then passed on northward in Morris township to what is known as Hickory Bottom Settlement, where they purchased for themselves land in the woods, and by industry and sobriety, and fair dealing became the owners of excellent farms

Among those who settled in that part of the township known as "Cooper Settlement," was Leonard Kyler, Sr, who, with David Cooper, settled at or near Kylertown, where each of them opened for themselves large and productive farms, part of which were later sold off in town lots Leonard Kyler's family consisted of two sons and three daughters The sons were John B and Thomas Kyler, the latter being the founder of the village of Kylertown John B Kyler became the son-in-law of David Cooper, and purchased the Cooper farm He divided a part of it into lots, which form a considerable part of the village site John B Kyler lived on the Cooper homestead, and reared a large family He survived his wife several years, and died about 1883, much lamented by his many friends, as he was a kind and generous neighbor and a consistent member of the Presbyterian Church

Another of the old and worthy citizens of Morris township was Abraham Kyler, familiarly called "Uncle Abraham" He was uncle of John B and Thomas Kyler He located, at an early day, in the southern end of the township He was for many years a successful farmer, an honest and upright man, and died an earnest member of the Presbyterian Church

Among the prominent citizens of Kylertown was James Thompson, eldest son of Samuel C Thompson His parents came from Centre county to Morris township in 1830 He lived with his father until he arrived at manhood, and while at home received a good common school education He taught school for a number of years, then worked at the carpenter's trade After that he was employed as clerk by Joseph C Brenner, at the village of Morrisdale, in this township, where Mr Brenner carried on the mercantile business for a number of years He also started a branch store at Kylertown, and James Thompson took charge of the store and carried on the business for a time Mr Brenner closed his business in Kylertown and moved to Williamsport, where he engaged in the lumber business From there he removed to Philadelphia, where he went into the notion business, and died in 1886

E C Brenner, the eldest son of Joseph C Brenner, was a citizen of Kylertown for over twenty years He removed here to settle the business of his father He was appointed postmaster at Kylertown during the administration of Abraham Lincoln, but, being a Republican in politics, was removed, and succeeded by Peter Moyer, Democrat, under the administration of Grover Cleveland E C Brenner was one of the best and most obliging postmasters that there was in the county, the loss of him as postmaster, and his estimable family, on his removal to Philadelphia, was much regretted He was elected justice of the peace, and served in that office over two years He made an upright and impartial officer, and was much respected by the general public

Another of the old citizens of Morris, now Cooper township, was James Hughes, who lived one half mile east of Kylertown He came to this vicinity in 1841 or '42, and married a daughter of David Cooper, rearing a family of four children After his wife died he married Mrs Sarah J Hall, a widow of Lancaster county, Pa, who, as well as her husband, had a family of children Mr Hughes was one of the early settlers who helped the old and noted surveyor, Joseph Quay, in surveying this and adjoining townships

In the year 1843, Frederick Neabel, a prominent German, came to the Cooper Settlement, bought land and commenced clearing up a farm, lumbering in the winter He made the first timber road to the Susquehanna River, at a point known as the Big Basin, to which place

19

he hauled his square timber to be rafted and run to market He lived and died a prominent member of the Catholic Church, and was greatly lamented by a large circle of friends

Jacob Raymond, Sr, was an old pioneer of the German settlement, who came here in 1844, bought land and settled near the Catholic Church, of which he was a member He raised a large family of sons and daughters

Amongst the other old settlers of the German Settlement may be mentioned the names of Joseph and Michael Steindechner, Michael Rader, Christian Hartle, and Robert Rasenhoover

In 1839 there were but four school-houses in Morris—one in the southern end, which was built on the farm of Abraham Kyler, and was used for a church as well as for school purposes, one at Old Morrisdale, now known as Allport, one on the farm of John Brown, also occasionally used for church or religious meetings, one in the German Settlement, known at that time as Cooper Settlement These houses were built before the common school system came into operation, and could be used in common for school and religious purposes also As the township became more thickly settled, and when the free school system became adopted it became necessary to have more school-houses and at the present time the educational interests of the township are well cared for

PENN TOWNSHIP

This township was erected by a decree of the Court of Quarter Sessions of Clearfield County, dated February 4th, 1834 It is bounded on the north by part of Brady Township and by Bloom Township, on the east by Pike Township, on the south by Ferguson and

Greenwood townships and on the west by Greenwood and Bell Townships

This township has many fine farms well cultivated and also valuable coal deposits. The population of the township, according to the census of 1910, was 936.

The township contains some very high lands, especially in the northern and western part, where the summits rise in places to an altitude of two thousand feet above tide-water. From the river front, on the south, back for a short distance, there is considerable level land, but with a gradual inclination upward as a north or northwest direction is pursued The township is well watered, although not possessed of any streams of note except where the Susquehanna River skirts its south boundary The creeks tributary to the river that have their course through the township are Curry's Run, in the extreme west part; Poplar Run, having its course about two miles east from Curry's Run, Bell's Run, which practically intersects the township, and runs a generally south course just west of the center; Little Anderson Creek, the course of which is opposite to that of the other streams, running a north and east direction, and is tributary to the greater Anderson Creek, into which its waters are discharged in Pike township on the east Besides these, there are other and smaller runs and rivulets incident to a mountainous district

At an early day, and less than ten years after the erection of the county, the lands along the river were nearly all taken up and occupied, so that subsequent pioneers turned to the most available of the hill, or ridge lands, whereon to erect their habitations and make their farms In this locality, as elsewhere, there was but little to attract the notice of settlers, as the entire region was densely wooded, and every

The Reservoir, Clearfield

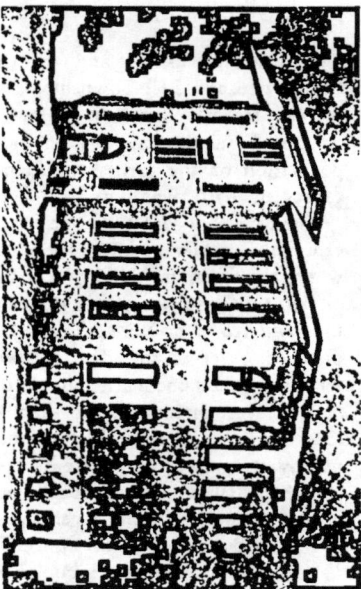

Township High School, Karthaus

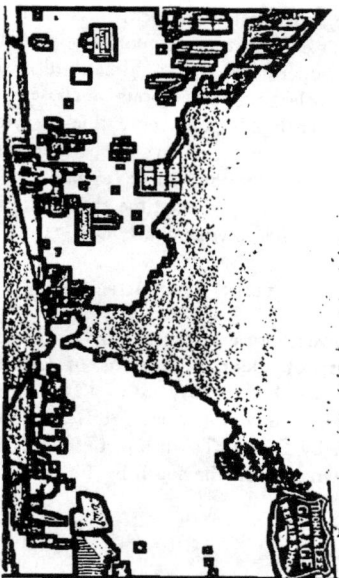

Market Street, Clearfield

Karthaus Fire Brick Plant, Karthaus

effort at improvement or cultivation was attended with great labor and considerable expense, and ready cash was an exceedingly scarce article at that time

The locality known as the "Grampian Hills," was one of the first settled of the upland districts of the county. It may be said to have been divided, so far as settlement was concerned, into two localities, the one toward the river, on the lower lands, near the base of the "Hill," and that more remote from, and back of the bottom lands, or the "Hills" proper. The lowlands were occupied by the Bells, the Fergusons, and the Fentons, and was subsequently taken up by John Bennett, Nun England, William Hepburn, Joseph Spencer, Francis Severns, and Samuel Cochran. From 1805 to 1808, a large tract here was claimed by Charles Smith, but his claim was without foundation, and therefore unsuccessful.

The Bennett improvement was divided among his heirs. The England lands passed to the ownership of other parties, and most of his family left the county many years ago. Job and George England (sons of Nun), left and went to Ohio; Isaac moved to Morris township. William Hepburn, of Scotch descent, was a man possessed of many peculiarities, and yet, withal, a good citizen. He died leaving a family, John and Samuel C., sons, and Catharine, who married James Thompson, being his children

In the year 1808, Joseph Spencer came with his family, and took up lands that had been purchased from Benjamin Fenton, some four hundred and more acres in extent. He divided his farming and wood lands into four parts, of one hundred acres each, and gave one to each of three sons, retaining one tract for his own use. Joseph Spencer, the pioneer, was of the Society of Friends, and a man highly respected in the county. His descendants are numerous in the county

Francis Severns and Samuel Cochran were descendants of African blood. The latter, Cochran, is described as being a light mulatto. His mother, as well as himself, were said to have been born in slavery. Several times Samuel escaped from bondage. Once he was captured, and on the other occasions he voluntarily returned to captivity, but eventually purchased his freedom and came north. Early in the present century he came to Clearfield from Lycoming county, and settled, about the year 1804, on the south side of the river. Later he took up some three hundred acres of land in one of the best localities on the Grampian Hills. He cleared over one hundred acres, built a substantial log house, and a large, double log barn. He kept a number of horses and a large quantity of other live stock, and became one of the most thrifty and successful farmers on the "hills." His house was the popular resort for teamsters on the old Kittanning turnpike. Cochran raised a family of several sons and was anxious that they receive a good education, such that he had not, nor was allowed to acquire during the days of his youth, and in the bonds of slavery

The name of "Grampian Hills" as applied to the locality heretofore mentioned, was not given until the time of the settlement here by Dr. Samuel Coleman, a person of supposed noble birth, who was of Scottish parentage, but who came to this county from the eastern part of the State in the year 1809. From a striking resemblance the locality bore to the Grampian Hills of Bonnie Scotland, the doctor gave it this name in honor of his native country and home

The lands, or a very large body of them, in the townships now included by Bell Pike, and Penn, were surveyed in the name of Hopkins, Griffith, and Boone, and were afterward known as the Nicklin and Griffith lands. This company gave to Dr Coleman a tract of about three hundred acres as an inducement for him to settle thereon, which he accepted. In the year 1809, he commenced clearing, having the assistance of three men, one named Gibson, and one slave (colored), named Otto. They encamped for a time in an open shed, thatched with brush, and slept on pieces of chestnut bark in lieu of beds, and until better quarters could be constructed.

Early in the summer of 1809, Joseph Boone and his family reached the home of Esquire McClure, having come up the West Branch from Williamsport by boat. The party proceeded to Coleman's camp in wagons, upon which they slept on the night of their arrival. The next day a cabin was built of logs, and roofed with bark from the trees in the vicinity. Boone was a man of education and worth, a zealous Catholic, and devoted to his church. He commenced the erection of a grist-mill on Bell's Creek, but through some cause the enterprise was abandoned. He afterward was chosen prothonotary and recorder of the county, and held other positions of public trust, all of which he most satisfactorily filled. He lived for several years at Clearfield town.

James Moore, formerly a resident of Half Moon township, Centre county, came with his family to the "Hills" in the year 1810, and located on the site of the village of Pennville, and near which passed the Glen Hope, and Little Bald Eagle, and also the Punxsutawney turnpikes. This place was distant from the river about four miles. Mr. Moore and his sons Jeremiah, Andrew, and James, built a saw- and grist-mill at an early day. James, Jr, was for a time, agent for the Fox and Roberts land, so called, an exceedingly large tract owned by a wealthy Philadelphia family.

The Moores were a prominent family in the affairs of the locality, always having at heart the interests of all who were around them. They were members of the Society of Friends, and actively participated in the welfare and progress of that society, shows strongly of the efforts of this family, as well as the other resident members of that society. Prior to the settlement of the Moore family there had been no regular religious services held in the vicinity, although, as early as 1806, Rev Daniel Stansbury came and preached occasionally in the neighborhood. Rev Stansbury was a tailor by trade, and his coming was a welcome one on that account, as he could clothe the outer man and provide for his bodily comfort as well as for his spiritual welfare. Rev Linn, of Bellefonte, came to the vicinity and delivered an occasional sermon, but his visits were not frequent. In the year 1822 regular services were begun, and a log edifice was built on Esquire McClure's land. After years of occupancy the old building was abandoned, and a more commodious one was built at Curwensville, in Pike township.

Among the others of the old settlers of Penn township, and who came in about or soon after the year 1810, were the families of Samuel Johnson, David Wall, Caleb Davis, Gideon Widmire, Jonathan Wall, Joseph Giddings, Jonathan Taylor, David Allen and others from time to time, down to the erection of the township, in the year 1835, and later.

PIKE TOWNSHIP

This township was erected by a decree of the Court of Quarter Sessions of Centre County, to which Clearfield County was then attached for judicial purposes, dated November Sessions 1813, and was named in honor of General Zebulon Pike, an officer in the United States Army, during the War of 1812

The township is bounded on the north by Pine Township, on the east by Lawrence township, on the south by Knox Township and west by Bloom, Penn and Ferguson Townships

The township contains many fine and well cultivated farms, also many fine coal and fire clay deposits, which are now being operated on an extensive scale

The population, according to the census of 1910, was 1671

The land of Pike township is mostly of a mountainous character, interspersed with narrow valleys and rolling plateaus varying in elevation from eleven hundred to fifteen hundred feet above the sea level, and presenting many beautiful scenic effects On the high table lands, and along the river valley, are located some of the most productive farms in the county, and despite the extensive lumbering operations of the past many fine bodies of timber still exist

Paul Clover was probably the first settler in the township, having arrived in 1797, and built a house and blacksmith shop where the "corner store," in Curwensville, now stands Thomas McClure, William McNaul, Elisha Fenton, the Blooms, Spencers, Moores, John Smith, Robert Ross, Samuel Caldwell, William Dunlap, the Hartshorns, Robert Maxwell Dr J P Hoyt, James McCracken, the Rolls, Hugh Hall, John and William Irvin, Arthur Bell,

John Patton, Sr, and Daniel Barrett, were among the early pioneers

Dr J P Hoyt came to Clearfield county from Halfmoon Valley, in Centre county, about the year 1814, and located at Curwensville Here he remained for some years, and then removed to a property near Lumber City He was a man of strict integrity, and by a long life of industry and excellent business abilities accumulated considerable property, which he lived many years to enjoy, dying at the ripe age of ninety-one years

John Patton, Sr, was born in Philadelphia, in 1783, moved to Curwensville in 1828, he served as associate judge of the county for five years, was justice of the peace for a number of years, and died in 1848, aged sixty-five years

Jason Kirk, Sr, came to Clearfield county about 1812, settled in what is now Penn township, at that time in Pike, and was one of the most respected citizens, living to an old age, and leaving a large family

Samuel Caldwell was one of the first settlers, arriving about 1804 He was an influential citizen, and left a considerable family

John W McNaul and his wife, Sarah, née Ferguson, emigrated from the northern part of Ireland to this country in about 1793 Mr McNaul was a Scotchman On landing in this country they resided, for a short time, in Chester county, thence removing to Lock Haven, and later living in Nittany Valley Of their eight children, Margaret, James, John and Ann were born in Ireland, William, Alexander, Zachariah, and Mary, were born in this country William McNaul was a tanner and first started business on his own account in Halfmoon, Centre county, where he married Hannah Way In the fall of 1813, he, in compa-

ny with Dr John P Hoyt (then a young physician practicing in Halfmoon), started on horseback, one snowy morning, to cross the mountains and see the famous new town of Curwensville, recently laid out by John F Curwen
Early in the following spring William McNaul,
with his family, moved to Curwensville, occupying a log house located on the lot where the
residence of Mrs Martha Thompson now is
He soon proceeded to erect a house on the site
of the present McNaul residence   He also
built the tannery adjoining   His children
were   Robert, Zachariah, Jane, Urbane,
Lydia, John and Mary   The McNauls belong
to the Society of Friends, and are most highly
respected both at home and abroad

The Hartshorn family is one of the oldest,
and is widely connected, and as a class are
model, respectable citizens   Benjamin Hartshorn, Sr, was born in 1765   He married Isabella McClure, and they emigrated from Maryland to Centre county in the year 1796   In
1806 he moved his family to Clearfield county,
living on the land now known as the Jonathan
Hartshorn farm   This was then nothing but
woods, and the family endured untold hardships before a home could be provided   The
children were   Margaret, Anna, Jonathan,
William, Benjamin, Nancy, Eliza and Mary
Ann, all of whom married, and whose families
reside in or near Curwensville

About the year 1750 the family of Spencers emigrated from England to America   In
1808 Joseph Spencer, Sr, moved from Northumberland county to Clearfield county   His
family consisted of three sons—Samuel, Joseph,
and Jesse—and three daughters   From Benjamin Fenton he purchased four hundred and
forty acres of land, which was in its primitive
state, excepting two acres which was cleared,

and had a small log house upon it   The
tract was situated between the present site of
the village of Pennville and Susquehanna River, about one mile south of Pennville   This
was divided into four farms, the father retaining one and setting apart a farm of corresponding size for each of his three sons   Most
of the family were and are consistent members of the Society of Friends, and are eminently respectable and prosperous citizens

The Blooms, as a class, are worthy citizens,
almost all farmers, and are the largest or one
of the largest families in Clearfield county
William Bloom, Sr., was born in Germany, in
1752 and emigrated to this country at an un-
certain time, reaching Clearfield county in 1801
Previous to this he had been in the State of
New Jersey, also in Centre county, Pa   During the Revolutionary War he served for some
time in the ranks   In 1778 he married Mary
Metter, who was born in 1754   The pioneer
Bloom came to Clearfield county alone, and
settled one mile up the river from Curwensville   Pike township is the stronghold of the
Blooms   Probably two-thirds of the family
are located here

Andrew Moore, Sr, emigrated to America
from Ireland in 1688, and settled in Chester
county, Pa   James, the second son of Andrew
Moore, Jr, was born January 8, 1760, at Sads-
bury, Chester county   He married in 1785,
Lydia, daughter of Abram and Anna Sharpless
In 1795, they removed to Halfmoon, Centre
county, and in 1810, James, with his son Jeremiah and daughter Lydia, started on foot
across the mountains, and in due time arrived
at the site of Pennville, in Penn township,
Clearfield county   He purchased three hundred and seventy-five acres of land, built a
cabin, and commenced clearing, the rest of the

family following He was a consistent member of the Society of Friends, and trained up his family in that religious faith

In 1809 Dr Samuel Coleman settled on a tract of three hundred acres north of the site of Pennville Dr Coleman was a Scotchman, and had no family He gave the name of "Grampian Hills" to his place, remarking that it reminded him of the renowned hills of the same name in Scotland He held office about the time of the organization of the county, being clerk to the county commissioners His grave is on the farm of Colonel Miller, of Penn township At the last meeting of the "County Medical Association" a committee was appointed to solicit subscriptions toward erecting a monument to the memory of the pioneer physician of Clearfield county

The first assessment of the township was made in 1814, and contains the following names Robert Askey, David Allen, George Brown, Alex Caldwell, Sam'l Cochran, Jesse Cookson, Wm Bloom, Jr, Joseph Bloom, Caleb Bailey, Benj Bloom John Brink, Wm Bloom, Peter Bloom, John Bloom, Isaac Bloom, John Bell, Arthur Bell, John Bennett, Benj Carson, Dr Samuel Coleman, Amos Davis, Wm Dunlap, Nimrod Derich, David Dunlap, Caleb Davis, Jonathan Evans, Peter Everhart, Joseph Edding, John Fullerton, David Ferguson, John Ferguson, Jonah Griffith, John Haughenberry, Hugh Hall, Benj, Hartsborn, Wm Hepburn, James Hayes, Saml Johnson, Mark Miller Jordon, John Kyler, Jason Kirk, John Kirk, David Liggit Elijah Meredith, Sam'l Miller, Robert Maxwell, Jos McCracken, Robert McGee, Robert McCracken, John McCracken, Thomas McClure, Thos McCracken, James McCracken, Daniel McCracken, James Moore, Job Ogden, Job Parker, Merchant, Abraham Passmore, James Reed, Alexander Reed, Jr, Alex B Reed, Wm Reed, John Rolls, blacksmith, Geo Shaffer, Geo Shaffer, Jr, Wm Smith, Nicholas Shaw, John Stuggart, Philip Stuggart, Joseph Spencer, Joseph Spencer, Jr, Sam'l Spencer, Francis Severas, Wm Tate, James Woodside, David Walls, John Wrigley, merchant, Geo Williams, weaver, Gideon Widemire, Geo Welsh, Jacob Wilson Town lots in Curwensville were assessed at $12 50, cows, $10, horses, $30, unimproved land, and timber at $1 per acre, farm land at $2 to $3 per acre The early settlers experienced many trials and privation The roads were but little more than trails through the woods Indians frequently visited the locality and usually encamped on the bank of the river An Indian burial-place was located at the mouth of Anderson Creek, and before the floods had made inroads on the lands, stone arrow-heads, and tomahawks were occasionally found

In 1819 Mathew Caldwell cut out the first road from Curwensville to Bloomington The principal towns are Bloomington and Olanta (For Curwensville borough see succeeding chapter)

PINE TOWNSHIP

This township was erected by an act of the Legislature approved the 10th day of April 1873 It has practically no inhabitants and no separate township organization, but for the purpose of taxation, is annexed as a part of Lawrence Township

The township is bounded on the north by Huston Township, on the east by Lawrence Township, on the south by Pike Township and on the west by Union Township It consists mostly of a vast wilderness

The population of the township, according to the census of 1910 was 32

SANDY TOWNSHIP

This township was erected by a decree of the Court of Quarter Sessions of Clearfield County at September Sessions 1878 It is bounded on the north by part of the dividing line between Jefferson and Clearfield counties and part of the dividing line between Elk and Clearfield Counties, on the east by Huston and part of Union Townships, on the south by Brady Township, and on the west by part of the dividing line between Jefferson and Clearfield Counties

The township contains valuable coal deposits, which have been operated for a number of years, also many valuable farms, and is one of the most prosperous townships in the County

The population, according to the census of 1910 was 5695

Prior to 1812 John Casper Stoeber had preempted some land in western Pennsylvania, which came in possession of Mr Stoeber's daughter, who was married to a Mr Scheffer, father of Michael, George, and Frederick Scheffer (now all dead), and ancestor of the present generations of Shafers—as they now write it—in Sandy township

In 1812 the senior Scheffer left Dauphin county, Pennsylvania, with his family, and settled on the pre-empted land of his father-in-law, John Casper Stoeber, which was situated near the present limits of DuBois, then belonging to Centre county They landed on May 12, 1812, and on the next day erected a "bark shanty," beside a cooling spring There was no store nearer than "Old Town"—as Clearfield was then called The merchants at the time "wagoned" their goods from Philadel-

phia The nearest mill was on the Clarion River, forty miles distant In 1814, however, a mill was built at Curwensville, on the Susquehanna River, nineteen miles distant These early settlers subsisted chiefly on deer and bear meat, and other game They lived here for ten long and lonesome years before they had any neighbors Soon after this time some Germans commenced to settle about Troutville, which section was long known by the local name of "Germany"

J P Taylor and W N Prothero were elected the first justices of the peace

After the incorporation of DuBois, 1879, J A Bowersox and J R Keel were elected justices, the latter resigned, and John Lankard was appointed until the next municipal election (February, 1884), when William Liddel was elected to fill the regular term J A. Bowersox at the expiration of his first term was re-elected in February, 1886 Samuel Postlethwait was the first township treasurer, and served four years He was followed in 1883 by Michael Shaffer, who served four years, and was re-elected in February, 1887 The first constable in the township was Henry Raught The population in 1880, estimated (including Du Bois), 3,700 (See borough of DuBois in succeeding chapter)

The first store in Sandy township at "West Liberty," as far as known, was opened by John Hoover, followed by Joseph Cathers, and he by S Lobough "Jerry" Heasly established a foundry about this time, John Heberling opened a general store, which he kept for about twenty years, he also was postmaster during this period at West Liberty—post-office name, "Jefferson Line" The post-office was removed in 1885 to the railroad "cut," at the point where the railroad crosses the "Waterford and Erie" pike, there being a regular station of the same name as the post-office, "Jefferson Line "

The first practical mining in this township was commenced in 1874 or '75 by the "Centennial colliery," opened and operated by Messrs Jones Bros in 1876 This colliery, being located on disputed land, there was more or less litigation from the start, which culminated in the shooting of Montgomery, a representative claimant, by Peter Jones (of the firm of Jones Bros) in self-defense, in May 4, 1878 The mines were shortly after abandoned

In 1876 the Sandy Lick Gas, Coal and Coke Company commenced to ship coal They employed about one hundred men, and shipped about five hundred tons per day Mr Miles B McHugh was superintendent This company operated a few years, when trouble arose between it and Messrs Bell, Lewis & Yates, on the question of royalty due the latter, which resulted in the closing of the "drift," when the Sandy Lick Company opened the "Hildrup" mine on the opposite side of Sandy Lick Creek, but it too was finally closed

The firm of Bell, Lewis & Yates began to develop its property in the year 1876 (consisting of about four thousand acres, lying principally in Sandy township), under the management of A J McHugh They shipped their first coal from Rochester mines on March 27, 1877

The early educational efforts and interests were identical and equally shared with Brady township, from which township the greater portion of Sandy was taken At the time of the organization of the township in 1881, there were nine schools with two hundred and eighty-one pupils, male and female The number of schools had grown to thirteen in 1887, with five

hundred and ninety pupils The educational interests are in a fair stage of development, and the public school fund in a healthy condition

UNION TOWNSHIP

This township was erected by a decree of the Court of Quarter Sessions of Clearfield County, dated December Term 1848 It is bounded on the north by parts of Sandy and Huston Townships, on the east by Pine Township, on the South by Bloom Township and on the west by parts of Brady and Sandy Townships

Although a large part of this township is not suitable for agriculture, yet in the northern part of the township are many farms well cultivated, and very productive The population of the township according to the census of 1910 was 785

The main stream of the township is Anderson Creek Its source is in Huston, on the north, from whence it flows a generally south course, entirely across Union, enters Bloom, then bears to the east by south into Pike, and discharges its waters into the Susquehanna River, at the borough of Curwensville Anderson Creek is a stream of considerable size The runs auxiliary to the creek, and emptying into the same from the east, are Montgomery Run and Blanchard Run, each of which lay almost wholly within the township On the west and having its entire course within the township, is Dressler Run, so named for the Dressler family, who were pioneers in this locality, and one of the most respected of the early settlers The stream known as Sandy Creek also has its head-waters in the western part of Union township, from which it flows a north and west course into Brady, thence across that township and into Jefferson county on the west Sandy, although of less size than Anderson Creek, has been nearly as prominent as the latter, during the period of extensive lumber operations, for which both of these streams have been so noted

The settlers who were possessed of sufficient hardihood and determination to attempt an improvement in this remote locality at an early day, were indeed scarce, and, in fact, no such attempt was made until the river and bottom lands were well-nigh taken up. The only possible inducement, even after the first quarter century of the county's history had been made, was the presence of Anderson's Creek, and its course through the township. This was then parts of Brady and Pike townships. Across the line in Brady there were a few straggling settlers, but generally, the country was a heavily wooded district with hardly sufficient opening for the erection of a cabin.

Caleb Bailey was born in Lycoming county in the year 1797, and came with his father to this county about the year 1809. After having resided in the upper part of the county for about eighteen years, he moved to lands that were, in 1848, erected into Union township, the line being especially run so as to include the Bailey farm within the new township.

Another of the pioneer settlers in this region was John Laborde, a native of Lancaster county. He came to this county in the early part of the year 1828, and located in Brady township, but two years later moved to a point a short distance from Rockton village, where he made an improvement. His brother, David Laborde, lived nearly a mile west of this. They were the first settlers in the vicinity. Both had large families. The children of John Laborde were John, Peter, Jacob, David, Christopher, Polly, who married Henry Lin-

inger, Peggy, Barbara, who married George Doney, and Betsey, who married Lewis Doney. The early life in the township was attended with great privations and dangers, and the Laborde's seem to have had their full share of each. There was no store nearer than Curwensville, and no mill nearer than Pennville. The country at times seemed full of panthers and other dangerous animals, and various members of the family occasionally came in contact with them.

John Hollopeter came soon after and commenced an improvement on the line of the pike leading to Luthersburg and west of Rockton. Matthias Hollopeter, brother of John, came to the county a year later and took up his residence with John. He soon began an improvement, and by hard and steady work made a good farm.

In the year 1839 John Brubaker came to the county and commenced an improvement on lands which he yet occupies about half a mile north of Rockton village. Mr. Brubaker was a native of Mifflin county, now Juniata county, and was born in the year 1810. In his family were nine children, viz. Mary, Fanny, Daniel, Susan, Sarah, John, Joseph, Reuben and Jacob. About the year 1840 Mr. Brubaker built a still-house that the product of his farm might be utilized. This he was compelled to do as grain was then a drug in the market, and the merchants at Clearfield would not receive it in exchange for goods. About 1843 or 1844 he commenced drawing shingles and boards to Clearfield town from a small mill he had built on Sandy Creek. This proceeding was looked upon by his neighbors as a piece of folly, but when they saw the good results of it, numerous other saw-mills were soon afterward erected, and lumbering became a leading pursuit, and agriculture was proportionately neglected

About this time, or possibly a little earlier, Jacob Burns came to the region He built a cabin and commenced an improvement in the Dressler neighborhood He remained here but a short time when he sold out to Dressler, and moved over on Anderson Creek, where he built a cabin and made a clearing, the first in that section This was about a mile above the old mills at Lower Rockton Burns soon found another opportunity to sell to good advantage, which he did, and moved still further east in the township, which was then a part of Pike

John Dressler, who is mentioned as having succeeded Jacob Burns was born in Union county, and came to Clearfield county in the year 1841 The farm he occupied is now reckoned among the best in the county At the time he purchased it there was no settlement nearer than three miles The Dresslers have been among the most thrifty and enterprising people of the township John Dressler died in 1856 He had a large family consisting of twelve children, seven daughters and five sons David Dressler, his son, was the first justice of the peace elected in the township after its organization

Henry Whitehead was a native of England and came to this country nearly a half century ago He took lands on the turnpike leading from Clearfield to Luthersburg, on the east side of Anderson Creek By hard work and energy he made a fine farm, one of the best in the eastern part of the township

The Welty family came into Union township in the year 1855, from Brady, where they settled in 1832, and was among the pioneers in the region north of Luthersburg David Welty was the head of this family He was born in Centre county in 1807 His first purchase in this township comprised about one hundred and sixty-five acres of land, but by subsequent purchases he acquired a tract of about five hundred acres

Incidental mention has been made of the fact that John Brubaker built a small saw and shingle-mill on Sandy Creek about the year 1843, from which he hauled the first lumber and shingles to Clearfield, and there found a market Within the short period of eight or ten years thereafter, other mills were built by David Horn, Joseph Lyons, John Dressler, John Hollopeter and Philip Laborde The other early mills were owned by Samuel Arnold and one Munn, the latter living at the mouth of Little Anderson Creek

At an early day and something like fifty years ago, Jason Kirk and Jeremiah Moore, two substantial residents of Penn township, came to the waters of Anderson Creek at the point now known as Lower Rockton, where they built a mill The land hereabouts, to the extent of fifty acres, was given them for a mill-site, on condition that they make the improvements Here was built a saw-mill, and subsequently a grist-mill A store was established here many years ago

There stood at Lower Rockton an old building that was formerly occupied as a woolen-mill, the property of William F Johnson, of Pennville The saw and grist-mills, and other property at this point were owned by Joseph Seiler and sons, who became proprietors thereof in the year 1877 Upper Rockton was started through the efforts of John Brubaker, and others engaged in lumbering A steam-power feed-mill, owned and operated by Jason E and David W Kirk was built during the year 1885

The first school in the township stood near this place It was built prior to 1839, a log structure with a board roof Some years later it was replaced with a more substantial and modern building

An enrollment of the taxable inhabitants of Union township, made by R W Moore, assessor, in the year 1851, showed the following list of residents and landowners for that year, who were of the age of twenty-one years and upwards Josiah Boomel, Jacob Burns, Peter H Booze, Caleb Bailey, Daniel Brubaker, Robert Britton, Henry Baily, John Brubaker, Joseph Cuttle, John Clowser, George Clowser, John Cunningham, Nicholas Doney, Lewis Doney, George Doney, David Dupler, Franklin Dutry, John Dupler, Sr, John Dupler, Jr, Enos Doney, Isaac Graham, Jacob Gilnett John Haze, David Horn, Jr, Matthias Hollopeter, Elias Horn, Jr, Samuel Horn, Jr, John Hare, John Hollopeter, Jr, Samuel Hare, Frederick Hollopeter, Jr, David Irwin, John Kritzer, John Kiesigle, Hugh Krise, Jacob Laborde, John Laborde, Sr, Luther & Carlisle, Joseph Longacre, Peter Laborde, Philip Laborde, David Laborde, Jr, Henry Lininger, John Laborde, Jr, David Laborde, Sr, Peter Laborde, Jr, Abram Laborde, Christian Laborde, Nathan Lines, John Long, Moore & Whitehead, Samuel Miles, R Moore, Jr, Moore & Kirk, John Nelson, Jr, John Potter, Jr, John Potter, Sr, John Pawley, Daniel Pawley, Henry Shull, William Shull, Alexander Schofield, Shaw & Lines, Joseph Schofield, Henry Whitehead, Jonas Weller, John H Reed and Samuel East

WOODWARD TOWNSHIP

This township was erected by a decree of the court of quarter sessions of Clearfield county dated February 3, 1846, and was named in honor of the late Judge Woodward

The township is bounded on the north by Boggs and Decatur townships, on the east by Decatur township, on the south by Bigler and Gulich townships and on the west by Bigler and Knox townships

This township has some of the finest coal deposits in the county, and these have been operated on a large scale for many years

The population, according to the census of 1910, was 2,535

The major portion of the lands in this township were owned by Hardman Philips, and were settled upon by the same class of people who settled Decatur township, and who bought their lands from Mr Philips

This gentleman sold his lands to these pioneers on credit, and as they were very poor he never expected to get very much out of them in payment, but would take a sack of meal, a bushel of potatoes, or oats, or wheat, or anything they could spare in settlement of what they owed him Or, if they could not pay anything, it was all the same On his return to England he placed his accounts in the hands of Josiah W Smith, Esq, of Clearfield, who was as lenient as the owner

One of the oldest settlers in this township was Henry Cross, an Irishman, who settled on a farm now in sight of Beulah Church, in 1818

Another old settler was the father of Mathew McCully, who settled near Mr Cross, in 1827, on a piece of land now immediately in front of Beulah church, and later owned by T C Heims Mr McCully was but two years old when his father carried him to that farm, or rather that spot in the forest, and he spent a long and happy life in the wilds of Clearfield county.

Robert Stewart moved into the Wheatland Settlement in 1829, having come from Chester county He died during the year 1886, aged nearly one hundred and five years

In 1837 Hugh Henderson moved from Philipsburg to a piece of land he had purchased from James Allport, one hundred and forty-seven acres, near what is now called the Sanborn Settlement Mr Henderson had emigrated ten years before from the parish of Donahachie, County Tyrone, Ireland He was the father of six children—Thomas, Robert, William, Samuel, James and Margaret The boys of this family, being hard workers, soon acquired sufficient means to purchase additional lands, and marrying, they branched out for themselves, buying lands near the parent farm, and thus helping to clear this township As proved afterwards, all the lands in this and Decatur township were underlaid with coal, though these old settlers never dreamt of such a thing, or at least if they knew it, did not suppose it would be of any value to them Coal was opened and worked for smithing, and local consumption as early as 1804, on the Hawkins place, near Philipsburg, but was not accounted of much value to its owner

The farm bought by Samuel Henderson at the head of Goss Run, was sold in 1873 to John Whitehead, and the celebrated Ocean colliery was opened upon it

James Hegarty was another pioneer of this township, emigrating with his father from Ireland when eleven years old, in 1808, and settling on lands later known as the "X Roads" farm, in 1820 He afterwards purchased three hundred acres in what is now known as Geulich township Mr Hegarty died on the 31st of May, 1846, leaving a family of four children

Rev John M Chase is another old settler, having early cleared a farm on Clearfield Creek, in Happy Valley Mr Chase was a minister of the Baptist Church, having been ordained a pastor of the church near his place in 1871

Christian Shoff, of Osceola Mills, was another old settler of this township Mr Shoff's grandfather settled near the village of Puseyville, at the lower ford That his father, Samuel Shoff, settled near Glen Hope in 1811, is known, and Christian was born there in 1830 When five years old his father moved to Wheatland, now called Amesville This, then, may be called the first settlement of the hamlet of Amesville Shoff, the father, moved in company with Benjamin Wright, Billy Myrtle, Abraham Kady, Robert Haggerty, and John Whiteside, the descendants of whom still inhabit the farms in and around this place The Alexander family are later additions to the township, but still can be styled old settlers

Lumbering occupied the time of these old pioneers as much as farming The township being covered with a most magnificent pine and hemlock forest, they, in winter, felled the pine trees, squared them, rafted the timber, and ran it to market by way of Clearfield Creek and the Susquehanna River Wages for hewers in those days was sixty-two and one-half cents per day of twelve hours

Logging, or cutting the trees into logs different lengths, was not commenced for some time after the lumbering, or the making of square timber, and when the first logs were placed in the creek to be run out on the first flood, the anger of the lumbermen was so raised against the loggers that a number of them proceeded to chop the logs to pieces, while others drove nails and spikes into the logs so that they could not be sawed. A lawsuit was the result, which was gained by the loggers, and thereafter logs and rafts had equal rights to the water. William R. Dickinson was the first man to run logs, and his logs were the ones destroyed.

In 1847 a very heavy flood occurred in the waters leading from the county, the river being ten feet higher than has been known since. In 1865 another flood occurred, but not so disastrous as the preceding one.

Mills for the manufacturing of lumber were built as early as the forties, but it was not until 1854 that the first mill was built in the township. This was Houtz, Reed & Co.'s mill at Houtzville (now Brisbin). Another mill was built above Houtzdale, about a mile, by Dull & Kessler, in 1867. The lumber from these two mills was hauled by tram-road to Moshannon mines in 1868, and shipped by rail.

The Reeds built another mill in what is now Houtzdale, in 1869, and from that date on numerous mills were built, notably Heim's mill, in 1871, situated two miles west of Osceola Mills, Kephart & Bailey's "bill mill," in 1873, one mile west of the same place. Isaac Taylor also built a mill on Coal Run in 1869, and S. S. Kephart has a mill there yet. Jesse Diggins built a mill on Goss Run, a little below Houtz, Reed & Co's mill, in 1873, and a man named McOmber had a portable mill at the head of Goss Run as early as 1868, while J. A. G. White built the first shingle mill near Osceola Mills in 1867.

Thomas Henderson also built a mill near his farm in 1877, and a Mr. Allport one at the head of Coal Run the same year. McCaulley & Ramey built a mill at Stirling in 1870, and another one at a point now called Ramey in

1874. The timber of this region was so fine that sticks squared one foot, and seventy-six feet long, were furnished for the Centennial buildings, and seventy-two feet long for the insane asylum at Norristown.

Beyer & Kirk built a mill near Morgan Run in 1882, and another near Madera in 1885. Messrs. Fryberger & Fee had a shingle-mill in operation near Houtzdale in 1881, and Walker Brothers one on Morgan Run, and William Luther one at Madera, while Frederick Ramey had another at Osceola Mills.

There was another saw-mill one mile south of Osceola Mills, and another three miles west of the same place, and though these last two were in Centre county, just over the line, yet they helped to clear the forests of this side of the county line.

Mr. Mays and John Hamerly built a planing-mill one mile west of Houtzdale in 1874. This mill was afterwards sold to Samuel T. Henderson, and by him to Giles Walker in 1885, but Mr. Walker re-sold the mill to Henderson in 1886.

The shipment of lumber from this region from 1867 to 1884 was 1,082,742 tons, averaging two tons per thousand feet, aggregating 541,371,000 feet of lumber. This only represents the amount manufactured in the townships under review. There was a large amount of logs cut and floated to market. Jacob Kepler logged the southern side of the A. B. Long tract as early as 1858, while Howard Matley and John Bordeaux logged the Moshannon Coal Company's tract in 1869.

The Moshannon Branch Railroad was built in 1869, and from that time improvements have followed each other very fast. The population in 1872, when Houtzdale was taken from it, was eighteen hundred, while in 1885 it was over ten thousand by adding the boroughs and townships erected within its borders since the former date

A most sanguinary battle, so tradition has it, was fought between General Anthony Wayne and the Indians, about half a mile south of Houtzdale, and the graves of the slain can be distinctly traced. Many relics, bones, arrow-heads and other relics have been picked up around the spot, and the trees bore many a mark of the conflict. In fact, when these trees were felled and hauled to the mills to be sawed they often destroyed the saws and endangered the life of the sawyer by coming in contact with some stone implement or arrow-head imbedded in the wood.

Before the advent of the railroad, however, Dr Houtz, who had bought large tracts of lands in the township, and on which Houtzdale, Brisbin, and a number of villages stand, determined to make a way to get his lumber to market, and, with this end in view, he deputized his son-in-law, George M Brisbin, to come into the township and see what could be done. Mr Brisbin came here, then, before the advent of railroads, though the Tyrone and Clearfield railway was talked about. He proposed and actually surveyed a route for a plank road from Osceola Mills to Jeansville, and Madera, about ten miles. This was to be supplemented by a tramroad, so as to enable them to haul their lumber to the railroad. This plank and tramroad was never destined to be built, however, for when Mr Brisbin had everything ready to commence, the Messrs Knight, who owned the extensive coal lands at Moshannon, came along and asked Dr Houtz to join with them and build a railroad three miles long. The doctor agreed to this, as it would bring his lands within one mile of an outlet, and the road was built. This was the first of the Moshannon Branch. Mr Brisbin then built a tramroad from the mills at "Houtzville," as it was then called, to Moshannon, one mile long, and hauled his lumber to that point and shipped it.

The cause of the sudden increase of population was the opening the coal beds. It has not been all prosperity, however. The miners did not always work, but created an occasional disturbance by striking. The first general strike occurred in January, 1869, but it did not last very long. Wages were advanced about fifteen per cent. Since then other strikes have taken place with varying success.

Madera is a village situated on the east side of Clearfield Creek, four miles from Houtzdale. It was formerly called Puseyville, after Charles Pusey, who owned the land upon which it was built, and who erected saw-mills and a large grist-mill near the town site. The town is surrounded with hills in which are numerous coal beds. (For Brisbin and Houtzdale boroughs see succeeding chapter.)

CHAPTER XXIV

THE BOROUGHS

Historical Sketches of the Boroughs of Brisbin, Burnside, Chester Hill, Clearfield, Coalport, Curwensville, DuBois, Glen Hope, Grampian, Houtzdale, Irvona, Lumber City, Mahaffey, Newburg, New Washington, Osceola Mills, Ramey, Troutville, Wallaceton and Westover.

BOROUGH OF BRISBIN

The Borough of Brisbin is situated on lands formerly owned by Dr Daniel Houtz of Alexandria, Pa, and was named in honor of George M Brisbin, Esq, of Osceola Mills, a son-in-law of Dr Houtz Mr Brisbin had charge of what are known as the Houtz lands for Dr. Houtz, and located where the town of Brisbin now is in 1854 and erected a saw-mill, which was operated until 1869 In 1874 the Moshannon Branch of the Pennsylvania Railroad was extended to Brisbin and in 1880, Hoover, Hughes & Company having purchased a large quantity of timber in the neighborhood, erected a steam saw-mill at Brisbin and operated it until May 27, 1881, when it was burned and was immediately rebuilt and continued to be operated until the timber was manufactured

The borough was incorporated on January 8, 1883, and on June 20th of the same year, a postoffice was established, John E Vaughn was appointed postmaster

The coal operations in the neighborhood of the town were rapidly developed after the building of the railroad and the population continued to increase and the town prospered and was a thriving place until on the 2nd of May, 1884, it was totally destroyed by fire. The fire first started in the woods, west of the town, and spread so rapidly that the inhabitants were not able to save any of their property or personal belongings, but were forced to flee for their lives One aged lady, who after reaching a place of safety, returned to try to save her cow, lost her life

Although greatly discouraged by the destruction of their town, the people of Brisbin went bravely to work to rebuild their homes and soon a new Brisbin sprang up and prospered until the timber on the adjoining lands was cut and manufactured and the coal underneath exhausted, since which time Brisbin has not increased much in population or business The present population is about five hundred

The town has three churches, good public schools and is supplied with water and electric light from the neighboring town of Houtzdale

BOROUGH OF BURNSIDE

The Borough of Burnside was incorporated October 5, 1874, and is situated in Burnside township, in the southwestern corner of the

318

county, on the West Branch of the Susquehanna River The town is located on high table land and surrounded by a beautiful farming country It is reached by the Cambria & Clearfield division of the Pennsylvania Railroad

In the lumbering days of Clearfield county, Burnside was a thriving and prosperous community, but since the cutting out of the timber in that section of the county, the borough of Burnside has been dependent for its prosperity upon the trade from the surrounding territory

The town has three churches, and a good schoolhouse

The present population of the borough is four hundred and ninety-three (493)

BOROUGH OF CHESTER HILL

The Borough of Chester Hill is situated in Decatur township, on the western bank of the Moshannon Creek, which stream is one of the boundaries between the counties of Clearfield and Centre The town was laid out by the late Jacob F Steiner, who located there in 1849 and engaged in the lumber business The borough was incorporated in the year 1883 Although Chester Hill is in Clearfield county, it is practically a part of the borough of Philipsburg in Centre county, Pa, and many of its citizens are engaged in business in that town

The principal industry upon which the town is dependent, is the Fire Brick Works of the Harbison-Walker Refractories Company, which gives employment to a large number of men There are also several coal operations in the neighborhood

The borough is on the line of the Altoona & Philipsburg Connecting Railroad and it is also reached by the Tyrone Branch of the

20

Pennsylvania Railroad at Steiner's Station and by the New York Central and Hudson River Railroad, which latter company has a branch line from Munson to Chester Hill, but calls its station Philipsburg

The borough has two churches, water and electric lights, good schools, a number of business places and the present population is about five hundred

BOROUGH OF CLEARFIELD

The early history of Clearfield is contained in a former chapter and in this article we will refer only to the history of the town since its incorporation as a borough, by an Act of Assembly approved the 21st day of April, A D 1840, which may be found in the Pamphlet Laws of Pennsylvania for the year 1840, at page 734

The boundaries of the borough, as given in said Act, are as follows

"Beginning at a point on the Susquehanna river about sixty feet south of Walnut street, thence east until it strikes the West line of Hugh Levy's out-lot so as to include the houses and lots now occupied by Dr H Lorain and John Powell, thence north along said lot of Hugh Levy until it again strikes Walnut street, thence east along the southern edge of Walnut street to Fourth street, thence north along the eastern edge of Fourth street to Pine street thence west along the northern edge of Pine street to the Susquehanna river, and along said river by its several courses to the place of beginning, to include the town of Clearfield as at first laid out, according to the plan thereof, and the two lots south of said town now occupied by said Dr H Lorain and John Powell, as above described "

The boundaries of the borough have been enlarged from time to time, and it now contains four wards and includes the former borough of West Clearfield and the borough limits now cover a territory nearly two miles long by one mile wide on both sides of the West

Branch of the Susquehanna River When the town was originally laid out, Abraham Witmer donated certain lands for public buildings, and also two triangular pieces of land bordering on the river to be used as public parks These parks have been beautified by the planting of shade trees and add greatly to the appearance of the town

Having the advantage of being the county seat, Clearfield has rapidly grown in population and wealth, and many fine business blocks and beautiful private residences have been erected

Aside from the public buildings belonging to the county to which reference has been made in a former chapter, the Dimeling Hotel, Clearfield National Bank block, the County National Bank building, the Clearfield Trust Company building, the Keystone block and Leitzinger Brothers store building are the principal business buildings in the town and are all of modern architecture and fully up-to-date in every respect

The town has eight churches, a Young Men's Christian Association building and organization, several fine school buildings, two daily and four weekly newspapers, several miles of brick paved streets, gas and electric light, a public steam heating plant and a splendid supply of pure mountain water

Next to DuBois, Clearfield is the most populous town in the county, it having, according to the census of 1910, 6,851 inhabitants

The railroad facilities are of the very best, the town being reached by three, to-wit —The Tyrone division of the Pennsylvania Railroad, the Beech Creek division of the New York Central & Hudson River Railroad, and the Buffalo, Rochester & Pittsburg Railway, over which latter road, trains of the Lake Shore &

Michigan Southern Railroad are also transported

By means of these railroad connections, Clearfield is within three hundred miles by rail of Philadelphia, Pittsburg, Buffalo, Rochester, Baltimore and Washington

The principal manufacturing establishments are the two large fire brick plants of the Harbison-Walker Refractories Co, the large sole leather tannery of the Elk Tanning Company, the Clearfield Toy Works, the Clearfield Manufacturing Company, the Clearfield Machine Shops, and the Clearfield Clay Working Company.

The social side of life is not neglected by the people of Clearfield The Dimeling Hotel contains a fine ball room and the citizens of Clearfield and Curwensville maintain the Clearfield-Curwensville Country Club, whose grounds, club house, and golf links are situated at Centre, half way between Clearfield and Curwensville

The citizens of the town are progressive and awake to all the interests of their community, and Clearfield is in many respects typical of the results of the best efforts of American citizenship

BOROUGH OF COALPORT

Nearly all of the towns in Clearfield county are situated at points where the natural advantages are such as to draw population or business to the locality The situation of the Borough of Coalport is a good illustration of this fact It is located on Clearfield Creek, in the southern part of the county and near the division line between Clearfield and Cambria counties, twenty-three miles from Altoona, and twenty-five miles from Clearfield It is on the line of the Pennsylvania and Northwestern

Grace Lutheran Church, Curwensville

Presbyterian Church and Parsonage, Curwensville

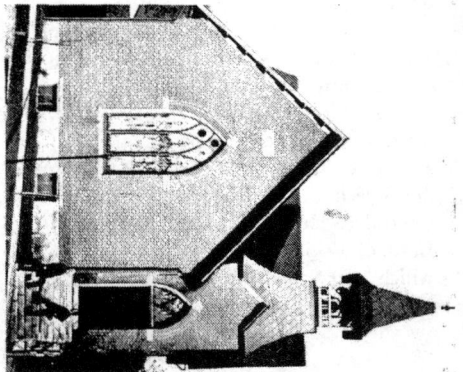

First Baptist Church, Curwensville

M. E. Church, Corner State and Walnut Streets, Curwensville

division of the Pennsylvania Railroad, which connects with the main line at Bellwood, and is also on the Cresson and Coalport division, which connects with the main line at Cresson, Pa, thus giving the town good railroad facilities. Valuable deposits of bituminous coal are found in the neighborhood and the various coal operations make Coalport the center for a large amount of business

The town was originally laid out by James Haines and S M and J D Spangle and was incorporated as a borough in 1883. It has five churches, one weekly newspaper, a National bank, and fine public schools. The present population of the borough is about fifteen hundred.

CURWENSVILLE BOROUGH

On December 10, 1798, John Curwen, Sr, of Montgomery county, Pa, obtained from the Commonwealth a patent for three hundred and fifty-one acres of land on the banks of the Susquehanna River, at the mouth of Anderson Creek, in what was at that time part of Lycoming county. On this property Curwen laid out a town, consisting of forty-eight lots, lying between what are now known as Thompson and Locust streets, which he named Curwensville. John Curwen, Sr. bequeathed this property to his son George Curwen, from whom the greater portion of it was subsequently purchased by John and Wm Irvin. Up to the year 1812, not a single building had been erected on the town plot although from the best information now obtainable, it seems that there were at that time two dwellings on the Curwen lands. One of these was erected by Job England, near where the Patton homestead now stands, and the other by a Mr Weld, near the dwelling now owned by the

Misses Nannie and Alice Irvin. In 1813 Daniel Dale built the first house in the town proper, upon the lot corner of State and Filbert streets, where the Owens block is now located, James Moore, James Young, Mark Jordon and Josiah Evans, Esq, built the next dwellings in about the order named. During the year 1818 William Irvin, Sr, the father of Colonel E A Irvin and John Irvin, Sr, the father of Colonel John Irvin, came to Curwensville. John Irvin erected a saw-mill, and a grist-mill near the present site of the Irvin flouring-mill.

After the completion of the Erie turnpike, in 1824, the progress of the town was rapid, and by an act of the Legislature, approved the 3rd day of February, 1851, it was incorporated as a borough.

The limits of the borough have been enlarged several times, first by an act of the Legislature, approved the 21st day of March, 1856, and again by an act approved the 24th of April, 1869 and the third time, in 1884, on application of the inhabitants of the adjacent territory, the boundaries were extended by the court so as to include what was known as South Curwensville and all the property as far north as Hogback Run, and east as far as the eastern line of the Irvin farm, and west to near Roaring Run.

In 1871, through the efforts of the citizens, subscriptions amounting to over $60 000 were obtained and the extension of the T and C Railroad to the town, was secured. The road was finished and opened for traffic in 1874.

The Clearfield & Mahoning Branch of the Buffalo Rochester & Pittsburg Railroad, which passes through Curwensville, was open for traffic in 1893 and the Curwensville & Bower Railroad, a branch of the New York

Central & Hudson River Railroad was constructed in 1903-4, so that the town is well supplied with railroad facilities

Curwensville has seven churches, a weekly newspaper, a national bank, fine system of graded public schools, good water supply, paved streets and electric lights, and is one of the most thriving and progressive, as well as the most beautiful town in the county

The principal industries are two large tanneries, the largest fire brick plant in the county, two stone quarries, besides other smaller industries

The present population of the borough is about three thousand (3,000)

BOROUGH OF DU BOIS

The Borough of Du Bois is situated in the extreme northwestern part of the county, two miles east from the Jefferson county line It is located on a part of what is known as the "Great Beaver Meadow" This "Beaver Meadow" is from five to six miles long and from one-half to three-fourths of a mile wide and Sandy Lick Creek flows through the center of it The land for a distance of five miles along Sandy Lick Creek, is almost level, there being only a fall of twenty-one feet in the five miles The town has extended far beyond the width of the Meadow and occupies a large portion of the adjacent hills

The site of Du Bois was settled as early as 1812 by the Stoebers, who came from Dauphin county, Pa , but there was no indication of a town being located there until the opening of the low grade division of the Allegheny Valley Railroad in 1872, when John Rumbarger surveyed a plot of lots and called the same Rumbarger About this time John Du Bois appeared upon the scene and proceeded to erect large saw-mills for the purpose of manufacturing into lumber the many thousands of acres of timber in the neighborhood, of which he was the owner He also constructed iron works and laid out a town plot on the opposite side of the creek from Rumbarger and called his town Du Bois The railroad station was also called Du Bois and in 1876 the name of the postoffice was changed to Du Bois

The borough was incorporated in 1881 and has grown very rapidly in population until it is now the largest town in the county, having a population of about 12,000, and being the center of the bituminous coal industry of that section of the county, and, also of the mines in Jefferson county that are tributary to Du Bois

The building of the Buffalo, Rochester & Pittsburg Railroad to Du Bois in 1883 and the opening up of the large coal operations in Jefferson county, belonging to Bell, Lewis and Gates, and now owned by the Rochester & Pittsburg Coal & Iron Company, furnished a large amount of business to the town and more than made up for the loss of business caused by the closing of the Du Bois saw mills on account of the exhaustion of the lumber supply This railroad was extended to Clearfield in 1893, thus giving the first railroad communication with the county seat

The Buffalo & Susquehanna Railroad was constructed to Du Bois in the year 1904

The industries of the town consist of saw mills, large tannery, glass works, iron works, coal mines and many other smaller industrial plants

The town has ten churches, three daily newspapers, two national banks, one trust company, paved streets, electric lights, water supply and an electric street railway system

The business part of the town was almost totally destroyed by fire in the year 1889, but with characteristic pluck, the business men of the town rebuilt on a larger scale than before

Du Bois is the metropolis of the county Its people are energetic and progressive, and the steady growth in population and prosperity are the results of their enterprise

BOROUGH OF GLEN HOPE

The Borough of Glen Hope is situated near the northern end of Beccaria township, on Clearfield Creek

The borough was incorporated in the year of 1878, but the settlement known as Glen Hope had existed for many years before that time, having been one of the earliest improvements in that part of the county The town is well located and it has substantial buildings

The borough has three churches, good public schools and the population at the present time is about four hundred It has no manufacturing industries, but is the centre of good farming country, and its business men are prosperous and progressive

For many years the town had no railroad facilities, but it is now reached by the Clearfield Southern Branch of the New York Central & Hudson River Railroad

BOROUGH OF GRAMPIAN

The Borough of Grampian was originally known as "Pennville" and was incorporated December 6, 1885, but on account of the confusion arising by reason of the similarity of the name with that of Penfield, another town in the county, the name of the borough was changed to Grampian by a decree of the court, dated May 6, 1895

The town lies among what are known as the "Grampian Hills" five miles from Curwensville, and is the present terminus of the Tyrone & Clearfield Branch of the Pennsylvania Railroad

The town has three churches, a fine schoolhouse and an electric light plant, and is a prosperous and progressive community There are several bituminous coal operations near the town, and also a large fire brick plant, located at Stronach, about two miles from Grampian These industries give employment to a large number of men

Grampian has long been known for the attention that its inhabitants have given to educational and literary affairs

The present population of the town is six hundred and sixty-six (666)

HOUTZDALE BOROUGH

The town was named in honor of Dr Daniel Houtz, of Alexandria, Pa , so often named in this history as owning a vast number of acres of land in this vicinity, and upon a portion of whose lands the town was projected, and is situated on the Moshannon Branch Railroad, six miles from Osceola Mills It was made a borough on the 20th day of March, 1872 The borough is surrounded with numerous smaller towns, which join up to her limits, so that a stranger cannot tell where the town begins or ends For three miles along the railroad the traveler is continuously passing through towns and villages— Stirling on the east, West Houtzdale on the west, Loraine joining West Houtzdale further west, and Atlantic joining Loraine still further west, while Brisbin borough's south line is Houtzdale's north line

The town grew very rapidly from the beginning The coal surrounding the borough was proven to be the best then, or now, known, and therefore capital rushed in to secure the prize As the collieries multiplied, the population increased and houses went up as if by magic

A postoffice was granted the borough in 1870, John Brisbin being the first postmaster

The first church building erected was on the corner of Charles and Clara streets, a union church, but it afterwards passed into the hands of the Methodist Episcopal society

At present Houtzdale depends altogether for its business on the mining industry The timber is all cut in and around the town, therefore the saw-mills are abandoned The old mill on the eastern side of the borough, near the Eureka No 1 colliery, and which was built by E N Conn & Co, in 1868, afterwards sold to Frank, Liveright & Co, and which cut the major portion of the timber on Dr Houtz's land, was destroyed by fire in the summer of 1876 The site of the mill pond is now covered by residences, the Presbyterian church, the railroad repot and business places

Houtzdale has seven churches, a national bank, paved streets, a fine water supply, electric plant, a weekly newspaper, and although the hustling town of Madera is pushing it hard as the center of the coal industry of the county, Houtzdale still does a large business in connection with the various coal operations in the neighborhood The people of the town are energetic, and progressive The present population is about fifteen hundred

BOROUGH OF IRVONA

The Borough of Irvona is situated in Beccaria township, about two miles from Coalport It is located on the eastern side of Clearfield Creek

The town was laid out by the Witmer Land & Coal Company and was named in honor of Col E A Irvin, of Curwensville, Pa, who was largely interested in that company

The borough was incorporated September 2, 1890

The town is reached by the Pennsylvania & Northwestern division of the Pennsylvania Railroad, and by the Clearfield Southern Branch of the New York Central & Hudson River Railroad

The borough is well laid out, with wide streets and the buildings are modern and substantial It has three churches, good public schools, and it has a hustling and wide awake population

There are several large coal operations in the neighborhood of the town, and also a large tannery Irvona is also the trading center for a considerable section of Clearfield and Cambria counties

The present population is about five hundred

BOROUGH OF LUMBER CITY

Lumber City is a pleasantly situated borough on the north side of the West Branch River It contains a number of fine residences of brick and frame material On the south side of the river is a steep bluff, or mountain, several hundred feet high, but the beauty of its slope is somewhat marred by the cutting out of its best timber On the north and to the east of the town is a gradual ascent leading back to and approaching the famous Grampian Hills Fine farms surround the borough on all sides, save the south Agricultural pursuits are the leading industry of the vicinity

Lumber City was the third borough to be incorporated in Clearfield county and it was

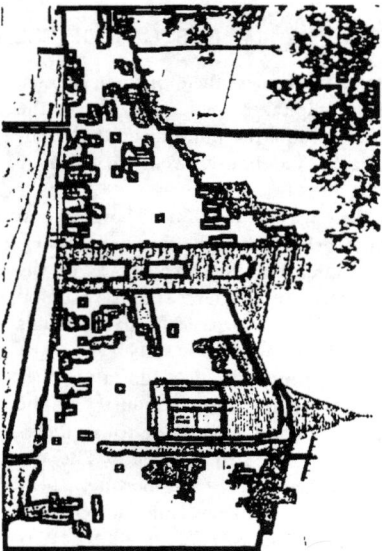

View of First Ward, Du Bois

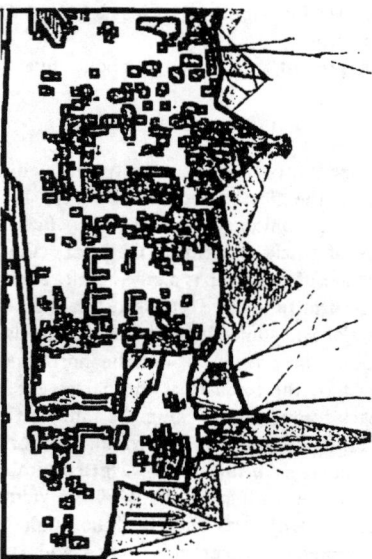

Street Scene in Du Bois

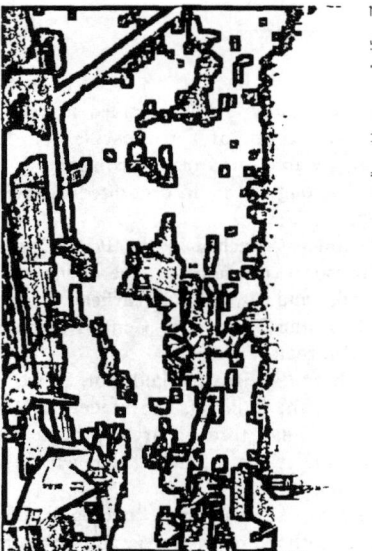

First Presbyterian Church, Du Bois

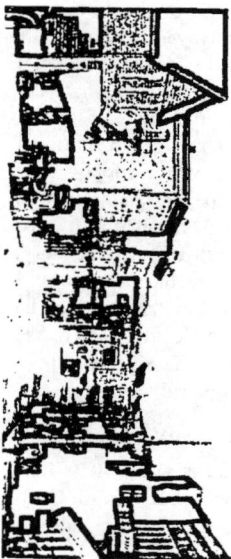

West Long Avenue, Du Bois

erected out of part of Penn township The court records of this incorporation are so incomplete that the date does not appear thereon, but the borough was incorporated in the year 1858 During the lumbering days the town grew rapidly, and on acount of its location was an important point for' the raftsmen

Although comparatively small in point of population, Lumber City is large so far as relates to area When the borough was laid out, the school district from which it was taken was divided, leaving a considerable area without any established school district To remedy this the borough limits were extended so that it is now very large in area, and includes, in whole or in part, several farms in the neighborhood

The borough has two churches, fine school buildings, and is on the Curwensville & Bower Branch of the New York Central & Hudson River Railroad, six miles up the river from Curwensville

The forward movement in education in the borough dates from May, 1873, when the Rev J C Greer established the Academy The first public school building in the borough was, however, erected prior to 1857, and the grammar school building built in 1879 and 1880 A new public school building has recently been erected and was dedicated November 30, 1910, when appropriate exercises were held in the Methodist Episcopal church This is a thoroughly modern, brick-cased building, 63 x 72 feet, single story, four rooms It is steam heated, has ample halls and cloak rooms, and individual seatings, and is well lighted The faculty consists of S LeRoy Bossard, principal, Bessie J Lehman, grammar school, Elizabeth Hile, primary school

The principal industry of Lumber City, in addition to farming, is a large fire brick plant The population of the borough is about three hundred

BOROUGH OF MAHAFFEY

The Borough of Mahaffey is situated on the West Branch of the Susquehanna River, near the mouth of Chest Creek The town was named in honor of the late Robert Mahaffey, who was its founder, having located on the site of the town and made an improvement there in the year 1841 Mr Mahaffey called the place "Franklin," and it was so designated for many years

Mahaffey was incorporated as a borough in the year 1889 It has four churches, fine public schools and its industries consist of a large tannery and a grist-mill

Mahaffey is a junction of the Pennsylvania & Northwestern division of the Pennsylvania Railroad with the Beech Creek division of the New York Central & Hudson River Railroad, both roads having branches leading to the different coal operations in the neighborhood

Mahaffey is a prosperous and growing town and its people are wide awake and progressive The present population of the borough is about five hundred

BOROUGH OF NEWBURG

The Borough of Newburg is situated in the northern end of Chest township and is one of the oldest towns in the county The town is located on the banks of Chest Creek and on the line of the Pennsylvania & Northwestern Railroad, and also on the line of the Clearfield & Cambria Branch of the Pennsylvania Railroad

The village was first called Hurd postoffice, after Henry Hurd, Esq , one of the oldest citizens of the locality, who erected the first dwelling on the site of the present town of Newburg

After the construction of the Pennsylvania & Northwestern Railroad in 1887, the town grew very rapidly and became quite a centre of business for that section of the county

The town was incorporated as a borough in 1885 The name of the postoffice was changed from Hurd to La Jose in honor of George Jose, Esq, who is one of the prominent citizens

Near the town are several coal operations that materially assist its business prosperity The population of the borough at the present time is about three hundred

It has good churches, good public schools, and the people are enterprising and progressive

BOROUGH OF NEW WASHINGTON

The Borough of New Washington was incorporated in the year 1859, and is situated on Chest Creek, one and one-half miles from La Jose

In 1835 the Methodist Protestants built the first church known as the "Mount Zion," this church was built out of hewed logs, and about two years later the Methodist Episcopal denomination built a hewed log church near the location of their present building Both of these old log churches have geen succeeded by handsome new buildings

In the New Washington cemetery are the graves of John Ludwig Snyder and his wife, Anna Maria, believed to have been the oldest people who ever lived in Clearfield county John Ludwig Snyder was born in Ludwig. Germany, March, 1746, and died in November, 1860, at the remarkable age of one hundred and fourteen years, and his wife, Anna Maria, was born in Philadelphia, in May, 1752, and died in August, 1857, aged over one hundred and five years

In the lumbering days of Clearfield county, New Washington was an important point and a large business was transacted there, but it is now principally dependent upon the surrounding farms for business On account of its high altitude, a number of people from other places are in the habit of spending the summer months in this town The present population is about four hundred

BOROUGH OF OSCEOLA MILLS

Osceola Mills was laid out in 1857 and was incorporated as a borough in 1864 It is located on the banks of the Moshannon Creek, four miles south of Philipsburg, and six miles east of Houtzdale The town faces towards the south and is at the foot of the heavy mountain grade on the Tyrone & Clearfield Railroad It is the junction of the Moshannon Branch Railroad with the Tyrone & Clearfield Railroad The Tyrone & Clearfield Railroad was extended to the town in 1863, but was not opened for business until January 1, 1864 The railroad station of the Tyrone & Clearfield Railroad is in Centre county, the Moshannon Creek being the line between the counties of Centre and Clearfield

On May 20, 1875, the town was almost wholly destroyed by fire One and one-half million dollars worth of property was burned up and nearly all of the inhabitants were rendered homeless With the aid of contributions by other communities and their own energy, the people of Osceola Mills soon recovered from the effects of this conflagration and on the ruins left by the fire there sprang a new town more beautiful than the old one

The town has five churches a weekly newspaper, a national bank, paved streets and electric lights The industries consist of two foundries and machine shops, planing-mills and many other smaller industries There are about fifteen coal operations in the vicinity of Osceola Mills and on account of its situation at the junction of the Moshannon Branch with the main line of the Tyrone & Clearfield Railroad a large railroad yard is located near the town, giving employment to many of the inhabitants of the place

The Altoona & Philipsburg Connecting Railroad also passes through the town and connects at Philipsburg with the Beech Creek Railroad

Osceola Mills is a thriving and progressive town and has a population of about two thousand

BOROUGH OF RAMEY

The Borough of Ramey is situated in the northern part of Gulich township and is reached by the Moshannon Branch of the Pennsylvania Railroad, and also by the Philipsburg Railroad

The borough was incorporated in the year 1878 D K Ramey & Company of Altoona, who were the owners of a large amount of timber land in the neighborhood, erected a large mill at this place for the purpose of sawing their lumber, and the town rapidly increased in population and business After the timber was cut away, a number of coal operations were started in the neighborhood and upon these the town is largely dependent for its present business

Ramey has four churches, good public schools, a fine water supply and is a thriving place A few years ago the town suffered a disastrous fire, which wiped out many of its best buildings, but better structures have been erected in their places, and Ramey is now one of the most progressive towns in the county Its present population is about five hundred

BOROUGH OF TROUTVILLE

Troutville was laid out as a town in 1854 It was named after Jacob Troutwein It is situated in Brady township in the northwest corner of the county It was incorporated as a borough in 1890 Jacob Troutwein, after whom the town was named, had located there and built a building used as a hotel about the year 1845 As a sign for this hotel, he had a large painting of a trout and many people called the place "Fish-Town" and it is commonly supposed that the town was named on account of this sign, but as stated above this is an error

The land on which the town is located is nearly two thousand feet above the sea level and the surface gently slopes to the westward There are many fine farms in the neighborhood and large coal operations have been opened up a few miles from the town

Troutville has two churches and good public schools It is principally dependent upon the mining and agricultural interests, as it has no manufacturing industries The present population of the borough is about two hundred

BOROUGH OF WALLACETON

The Borough of Wallaceton is situated in the northeast corner of Boggs township and contains about four hundred and twenty-six square acres of land It was incorporated as a borough in 1873 The town is located on an elevated plateau about fifteen hundred feet above the sea level   The land on either side is rolling, giving the town good drainage

It is on the line of the Tyrone & Clearfield Branch of the Pennsylvania Railroad, and also on the line of the Beech Creek division of the New York Central Railroad

The town has three churches and the principal industry is the large brick manufacturing plant of the Wallaceton Fire Brick Company now owned by the Harbison-Walker Refractories Company

The town was named in honor of the late Senator Wm A Wallace of Clearfield, Pa , and has a population of about five hundred

Although the people of Wallaceton, as a general rule, are law abiding citizens, the little borough has the unfortunate distinction of having been the scene of three homicides, which gave the town a rather unenviable notoriety   The first of these was the killing of Maria Waple, November 3, 1876 Martin V Turner, who was accused of this murder, was arrested and after a hotly contested trial, was convicted in the courts of murder in the first degree, but a new trial was granted by the Supreme Court and the place of trial was changed to Lock Haven, in Clinton county

On the second trial, Turner was acquitted. The second was the death of Ida Douglas, July 1, 1882   For this crime the perpetrator was arrested, tried, convicted and sentenced to five years in the penitentiary   The third tragedy was the murder of Ella Davis, who was shot by James McClain on August 6, 1886, the murderer immediately killed himself in the presence of the victim of his crime

BOROUGH OF WESTOVER

The borough of Westover was incorporated September 6, 1895

The town is situated in Chest township, in the southern part of the county, it is reached by the Cambria and Clearfield division of the Pennsylvania Railroad, and also by trains of the New York Central and Hudson River Railroad, which use the same tracks as the Pennsylvania

The principal industry of Westover is the large tannery of the William F Mosser Company

The town has two churches, a fine schoolhouse and has a large trade from the surrounding territory

The present population is five hundred and sixty-nine (569)

CHAPTER XXV

STATISTICS

Increase in Population Shown by Census Returns by Townships—Wealth of the County—Summary of Assessments for 1910

POPULATION

The population of Clearfield county has increased rapidly since the opening up of its natural resources, in the way of coal, fire clay and other products The population of the county has increased from 875 as shown by the census of 1810, the first census after the county was organized, to 93.766, according to the census of 1910

We give below the detail census returns for 1910, and 1900, showing the difference in population of the various townships and boroughs, according to the census returns

District	1910	1900
Beccaria township	3,095	2,924
Bell township	1,682	1,583
Bigler township	4,013	2 675
Bloom township	451	570
Boggs township	1,154	1,024
Bradford township	2,250	2,075
Brady township	2,823	2,638
Brisbin borough	459	666
Burnside borough	493	647
Burnside township	1,435	1,695
Chest township	872	1,022
Chester Hill borough	648	710
Clearfield borough	6,851	5,081
Coalport borough	876	938
Cooper township	5,713	4,629
Covington township	649	695
Curwensville borough	2,549	1,937
Decatur township	3,562	3,810
DuBois borough	12,623	9,375
Ferguson township	765	914
Girard township	606	570
Glen Hope borough	237	220
Goshen township	514	501
Graham township	664	626
Grampian borough	666	600
Greenwood township	590	806
Gulich township	2,112	1,071
Houtzdale borough	1,434	1,482
Huston township	2,653	1,974
Irvona borough	800	723
Jordan township	1,261	1,284
Karthaus township	1,332	1,066
Knox township	1,064	864
Lawrence township	4,025	3,370
Lumber City borough	363	224
Mahaffey borough	754	741
Morris township	4,994	4,460
New Washington borough	174	213
Newburg borough	274	314
Osceola borough	2,437	2,030
Penn township	936	840

Pike township	1,671	1,575
Pine township	32	
Ramey borough	1,045	866
Sandy township	5,695	3,222
Troutville borough	260	308
Union township	785	944
Wallaceton borough	324	289
Westover borough	569	654
Woodward township	2,535	3,169
Total	93,768	80,614

WEALTH OF THE COUNTY

The statistics given below give but a very imperfect idea of the real wealth of the county, because the assessments for taxation do not average over two-thirds of the actual value of the property They are, however, the most reliable data that we can secure, as they are taken from the official figures of the Triennial Assessment of Clearfield county for the year 1910 The total amount of the valuation of all property in the county as shown by these figures is $26,836,604 75, adding one-third, so as to approximate the real value of the property, would give us a total value of $35,782,-139 66 The figures in detail are as follows.

SUMMARY OF THE TRIENNIAL ASSESSMENT OF CLEARFIELD COUNTY FOR THE YEAR 1910

Number of registered voters	20,835
Value of all real estate . .	$20,557,520 00
Value of all real estate exempt	$2,464,776 00
Value of all real estate taxable	$18,092,744 00
Number horses and mules .	7,146
Value horses and mules	$328,445 00
Number cattle	7,861
Value cattle	$119,655 00
Occupations .	2,095,109 00
Agg value of all property taxable for county purposes .	$20,635,953 00
Total value personal property assessed for State purposes, Money at Interest, Livery Rigs, etc	$3,735,875 75

HON. WILLIAM BIGLER

Representative Citizens

HON WILLIAM BIGLER, deceased, who served the Commonwealth of Pennsylvania as its chief executive from 1851 until 1855, later represented his people with distinction in the United States Senate, and for years responded to the call of public duty, often to the detriment of his private interests, which, from early manhood, were important to himself and to those associated with him His useful life covered the most important years of his country's history and his name is indissolubly connected with its making Where his fellow citizens at times questioned his judgment but never his integrity, the present day conditions have vindicated many of his thwarted plans and shown his wisdom

William Bigler came of sturdy Pennsylvania German stock His parents were Jacob and Susan (Dock) Bigler, types of a class of honest, hard-working people, whose mental outlook is apt to be limited and whose ambitions are negligible One of a large family, William Bigler was born January 13, 1813, at Shermansburg, Cumberland county, Pa , prior to the removal of the family to a pioneer farm in Mercer county The father died there while the children were young The home farm was small and the eldest son soon pushed out into the world beyond, and in 1829 he was ready to offer employment to his young brother William, in his printing office at Bellefonte His name was John Bigler and at that time he was proprietor of the Center Democrat and later attained to gubernatorial honors in California, and left an impress on that state no less indelible than did the younger brother on Pennsylvania

William Bigler was mainly educated in the printing office, his advantages prior to 1829 having been exceedingly limited He remained with his brother until his apprenticeship was completed and then, with characteristic determination, although practically without funds and at that time with absolutely no influential friends, went to Clearfield and there founded the Clearfield Democrat He was thus entirely dependent upon the ability with which he could interest an unknown constituency in his efforts to advance the principles of Jacksonian Democracy At first he was his own complete office force and his initial efforts would have been more or less amusing had they not been tragic However, it was this spirit of persistency and enterprise that first attracted the public, which later read, admired and bestowed confidence and what was then necessary, gave substantial support to the venture This newspaper introduced

337

him into public affairs and his manner of handling the grave questions of the day editorially aroused the political leaders and henceforward until his final retirement, he was more or less in the public eye

Although in 1836, Mr Bigler disposed of his newspaper in order to give his full attention to large lumbering interests with which he became connected in association with his father-in-law, A B Reed, he was not permitted to withdraw from public attention and he was more than once offered the nomination for the state legislature Although he consistently declined these marks of public approval for a time, in 1841 he accepted the nomination to the State Senate and was elected by a very large majority, and in 1844 was re-elected and served two terms and was twice elected speaker This period was one of great moment to the State of Pennsylvania and the speeches and efforts made by Senator Bigler for the passage of a law of taxation to meet the public indebtedness and pay the interest on the state debt, also for the procuring of the passage of a law for abolishing imprisonment for debt, and also for the passage of the laws regulating questions of internal improvement, all testified to the public spirit, ability, and true conception of public duty, that marked him as a statesman and a sincere friend of the people

In 1848 Senator Bigler's name was presented to the Democratic convention as a candidate for governor, but internal conflicts of personal interests resulted in the election of another candidate In 1849 he was appointed revenue commissioner, and in 1851 he was nominated by his party for governor, by acclamation, and was triumphantly elected, and this honor came to him before he had reached

his thirty-eighth year It is an interesting episode to record that his election as governor of Pennsylvania was simultaneous with the election of his brother, John Bigler, to the same high office in California

Governor Bigler's administration was just such as the acts of his public life had indicated prior to this He believed in and advocated the old-time virtues of economy, efficiency, industry and integrity in dealing with public affairs as with private interests and he had the support of all the people with the exception of a class that existed then as now, which sought special privileges and had counted on the executive granting them, and found out their mistake in their estimate of his character. The annals of the state tell how faithfully and fearlessly he faced these private interests and how conscientiously and courageously he carried out the laws according to the constitution In March, 1854, he was again unanimously nominated for governor, but the strain of public cares had told on him and he made no personal canvass and in the contest was defeated by the Know Nothing party In January, 1855, he was elected to the United States Senate, where he served with great credit to himself and his state for six years, and it was during this period, in 1857, that, as a member of the committee on commerce, he made an elaborate report concerning the construction of a ship canal across the Isthmus of Panama, a scheme considered then by the country at large as dangerous and entirely visionary In that, as in many other public projects, Senator Bigler was a man ahead of his times In 1860 he was a member of the Democratic convention that assembled at Charleston where he opposed the nomination of Judge Douglas, and he was temporary chairman of the convention at Chicago, in 1864, which nominated George B McClellan In 1868 he was a delegate to the National Democratic Convention in New York, which nominated Horatio Seymour In 1872, he was nominated a delegate-at-large to the convention for the revision of the constitution, but later he voluntarily withdrew his name, but subsequently, for political reasons consented to fill the vacancy caused by the resignation of S H Raynolds, and took a leading part in the deliberations of that body He was associated closely with party affairs of large importance up to 1875, after which he withdrew more or less in order to give his attention to local matters beneficial to his county and to his individual interests

On March 23, 1836, William Bigler was married to Maria J Reed, who was born in Clearfield county, Pa , a lady well qualified to both advance his public prestige and to adorn his home and rear a happy family Of their children but one survives, a son, Harry F Bigler, who is president of the Clearfield Steam Company and a director in the Center County National Bank

Distinguished as were his public services, William Bigler's memory is tenderly preserved by those who knew him best for the personal qualities which added to their pride in him and also made him generally beloved His death occurred at his home on August 9. 1880

A B SHAW. vice president of the County National Bank and one of its board of directors, is a member of one of Clearfield County's old and honorable families He was born in Clearfield County, Pa , November 12, 1830, and is a son of Richard and Mary (Irwin) Shaw

Richard Shaw was long a prominent citizen of Lawrence Township, Clearfield County, serving with honor in a number of public capacities, at times being a justice of the peace, and also associate judge He was a native of Ireland, born in County Derry in 1792, one of seven children, and his parents were Archibald and Mary Shaw Richard Shaw was young when his parents emigrated to America, settling first in Chester County, Pa , moving later to Mifflin County and in 1810, to Clearfield County In 1816, Richard Shaw was married to Mary Irwin, a native of Philadelphia, and eight of their children reached maturity The mother died in 1874 and the father in 1876

A B Shaw was reared in his native county and was educated in the district schools and the Clearfield Academy He secured a business training under his father's eye. becoming a clerk in the latter's store and later becoming also interested as was his father, in lumbering In 1853 he opened up a general lumber and mercantile business at Shawville, which he continued for twenty-two years, returning to Clearfield in 1875 He became interested also in the coal industry to some extent and owns probably 1,000 acres of rich coal land in Clearfield and Cambria Counties At different times he has accepted stock and served on directing boards of successful commercial enterprises, his name, at all times, being a business asset In 1882, he was elected vice president of the County National Bank of Clearfield, a financial institution then of seventeen years standing and he has continued his association with it up to the present

Mr Shaw was married in 1859, to Miss Agnes Aurand, who was born in Snyder

County, Pa , and eleven children were born to them, namely Clara W , Bertha A , Mary Jane, Edgar, Fannie G , Calvin B , Agnes E , Annie, Charles M , Mattie V and Gussie E , who died in infancy Mr. Shaw and family are members of the Methodist Episcopal church In politics he is a Democrat

CLARK HILEMAN, one of the substantial business men of Madera, Pa , who is largely interested in the lumber industry in Clearfield County, was born in Indiana County, Pa , September 17, 1856, and is a son of William and Elizabeth (Ruffner) Hileman

William Hileman was a son of John and Elizabeth Hileman His business interests throughout life were connected with lumbering He married Elizabeth Ruffner, a daughter of Daniel and Elizabeth Ruffner, and the following children were born to them · Lorenza, who married Oliver Lewis; Ellen, who married Benjamin Tonkin, Joseph S , who is deceased , Jane, who is the wife of Robert Smith, Clark, James S ; Charlotte, who is deceased, was the wife of James Kethcarth, William S , A C , Scott, Isabel, who is the wife of Russell Eaton, and Liberty, who is the wife of William Ruther

Clark Hileman obtained his education in the district schools which he attended through the winter sessions until he was eighteen years of age, after which he went to lumbering and worked in the woods until 1887 He then embarked in the hotel business at Madera in which he continued for twenty-one and one-half years. disposing of his interests in that line in August,

1908 Since then he was given the main part of his attention to the lumber industry, owning a saw mill and lumber yards, and he also owns other property at Madera and additionally is a stockholder in the Madera Water Works and a director of the Madera National Bank

On December 18, 1890, Mr. Hileman was married to Miss Minerva Grove, a daughter of Benjamin and Hannah (Johnston) Grove, and a granddaughter of Andrew and Rebecca Grove and of William and Rebecca Johnston The parents of Mrs Hileman are residents of Huntingdon County. They are members of the Lutheran church Mrs Hileman is the fourth born child of her parents, the others being. Martha, who is the wife of James McElroy; Mary Alice, who is the wife of Jacob Smith, Elmira, who is the wife of Jeremiah Kyles, Laura, who is the wife of Samuel Smith; Maggie, who is the wife of William Blythe, Martin Luther, Ida, who is the wife of Harry Green, Andrew Harvey, Dora E , who is the wife of Clarence Snare, Bessie Rebecca, who is the wife of Bert McCall, Minnie, who is the widow of David Blythe, Lydia, who is the wife of John Worth; Henry Ellsworth, and William Oscar Mr and Mrs Hileman have no children of their own but they reared a little girl, Bertha May, born May 8, 1891. from infancy to young womanhood, and she is now the wife of Albert Rung Mr and Mrs Rung have one son, Harold Albert, who was born February 14, 1910 Mr and Mrs Hileman attend the Presbyterian church In politics he is a Republican as was his father, and for four years he served in the office of township supervisor

ELISHA M. DAVIS, dairyman and farmer, residing one and one-half miles southwest of Grampian, Clearfield County, owns 173 acres of finely cultivated land, lying in Penn Township. He was born on an adjoining farm, in Penn Township, May 26, 1838, and is a son of Joseph Davis, a grandson of Elisha Davis and a great-grandson of Caleb Davis.

Joseph Davis, father of Elisha M., was born at Tyrone, Pa, January 6, 1790, a son of Elisha and Alice Davis, natives of Wales, who emigrated to America and settled at Tyrone. Joseph Davis was married October 16, 1823, to Rebecca Moore, who was born December 5, 1798, a daughter of James and Lydia Moore. To Joseph and Rebecca Davis the following children were born: Lydia, June 13, 1824, Rachel, October 29, 1825, Esther, June 30, 1826 (died July 16, 1866), John, July 26, 1829, Eliza, November 28, 1830 (died May 22, 1877), James, October 6, 1832, Hannah, September 27, 1834; Joseph, June 9, 1836, Elisha, May 26, 1838, and Abraham, born September 10, 1840 (died of fever while serving in the Civil War, October 1, 1862,—the youngest of ten children).

After marriage Joseph Davis, Sr, settled on a tract of 150 acres of wild land in Penn Township, Clearfield County, eighty acres of which he cleared. This farm is now the property of William Pentz. Mr and Mrs Davis were members of the Society of Friends. Joseph Davis was never embroiled in politics, living a quiet, industrious, useful life and passing away May 12, 1868, at the age of seventy-eight years with the respect and esteem of all who had known him. His estimable wife survived but a few years,

21

her death occurring February 23, 1871. They were buried in the Friends' cemetery near Grampian.

Elisha M Davis attended school in Penn Township until he was about eighteen years of age and then went to work as a teamster in the lumber regions in Penn Township. He continued thus engaged more or less for 20 years before and after his marriage, in 1861, when he settled on the home farm for a time and then purchased his present one of Thos Hoover. He has 100 acres of his land cleared and under a fine state of cultivation, being one of the most progressive and one of the successful farmers in this section of the county. Mr Davis also operates a dairy and keeps first class stock. He has made many improvements on his farm and these include the erection of all the substantial buildings now standing, and the arrangement of his attractive surroundings. He is a stockholder and charter member of the Farmers and Traders Bank of Clearfield, Pa.

On September 12, 1861, Mr Davis was married to Katherine Hoover, who was born near Curwensville on the West Branch of the Susquehanna River, January 13, 1840, a daughter of Joseph and Rebecca (Price) Hoover, her parents coming from old pioneer families of this section. It is said that Grandfather Price was killed by the Indians. To Mr and Mrs Davis nine children were born, namely William E, Elias C, Rebecca Ellen, Lydia Jane, Nathan Thomas, Alice, Myrtle May, Vincent Pearl and Elisha Claire. William E Davis was born June 14, 1862, and resides in Brady Township. He was married April 24, 1884, to Susanna Rishell and they have had six children

Vida Hoyt, Oral, Salome, Katherine, Margaret and Leo, the last named dying at the age of eleven months Elias C Davis was born September 11, 1863 He was married October 22, 1890, to Edith Wagoner, a daughter of Edw Wagoner, of Ramey, Pa, and they have two children, Alton C and Elisha W. Rebecca Ellen Davis was born November 10, 1864, and was married June 14, 1888, to George M Rishell and they had the following children O Clifford, Hilda C, Frances Esther, Elisha B, Frederick, Corlus Arden, Joseph D and Lydia Jane The oldest and youngest are deceased and the mother of these children died July 26, 1906, and was buried at Troutville, Pa. Lydia Jane Davis was born October 11, 1867, and was married October 3, 1887, to E B Albert They reside near Woodland, Pa, and have one son, Edwin B Nathan T Davis was born August 12, 1869, was married June 25, 1896, to Mamie Currier and has two children, Twilla Elizabeth and Elma Katherine Alice Davis was born February 1, 1871, and died March 26, 1873 Myrtle May Davis was born May 1, 1874, and was married September 16, 1894, to R P Kester, a lecturer for the department of State Institutes of Pennsylvania They have two children, Elisha Howard and Latricia Mott Vincent Pearl Davis was born May 4, 1878, and was married June 16, 1909, to Vadna Violet Warden, who was born October 8, 1888, a daughter of Clarence and Lottie Warden, of Johnstown, Pa, and they have one son, Edward Laverne Elisha Claire Davis was born April 22, 1881, and was married July 26, 1905, to Gertrude May Slick, of Richmond, Ind They have two children Francis Everett and Alton

Kenneth Mr. Davis is a clerk in the County National Bank

For many years Elisha M Davis has been prominent in the Grange movement, has assisted in the organization of a number of local granges and served two terms in the State Department of Agriculture of Pennsylvania He has also served as president of the Clearfield County Agricultural Society He and his wife are members of the Society of Friends and he is superintendent of the sabbath school at Grampian

JERRY HEGARTY, of Bigler Township, Clearfield County, Pa, a one-half owner of 250 acres of fine farm land, was born in Bigler Township, on the home farm, in July, 1846, and is a son of James and Jane (Boyle) Hegarty The parents were natives of Ireland and came to Clearfield County when young married people and spent their lives here

Jerry Hegarty was the fifth born in his parents' family and with his brothers and sisters attended the district school through boyhood He has followed farming and lumbering during the greatest part of his life and there is a coal mine on the farm, of which he is half owner In 1878 Mr Hegarty was married to Miss Mary Whiteside, who is the youngest daughter of Robert and Nancy (Alexander) Whiteside He was born in Ireland and she in Clearfield County and both were well known people They had six sons and two daughters John D, William A, Isaac, Samuel, Robert, Boaz, Agnes and Mary Mr and Mrs Hegarty have had five children Vida, Vincent, Blaine, Dora and Verna The eldest daughter died at the age of twenty-one years Mr Hegarty and wife attend the Presbyterian Church He votes with the Republican party He is one of the representative men of Bigler Township and commands the respect of his fellow citizens, having always carried on his undertakings according to sound business principles with due regard to the rights of others

MICHAEL HURD, M D , a leading physician and surgeon at Mahaffey, Pa , well known professionally over a wide territory in Clearfield County, was born in this county, at La Jose, in Chester Township, and is a son of Henry and Catherine Hurd

Henry Hurd, father of Dr Hurd, was born in Vermont, and was a son of Elias Hurd In 1842, Henry Hurd came to Clearfield County, where he taught school, after which he purchased a farm in Chester Township and engaged in farming and lumbering They are both living on the homestead in Chester Township

Michael Hurd attended the Chester Township schools and those of La Jose, later spent three years as a student in the graded schools at New Washington and two years in the Curwensville Normal School In 1879 he entered Jefferson Medical College, Philadelphia, and was graduated there in 1883 Dr Hurd located first at Newburg, not far from his birthplace, and continued to practice there until May, 1909, when he moved to Mahaffey, where he has built up a very large practice and has been welcomed as a citizen of enterprise and worth

In 1878, Dr Hurd was married to Miss Orie E Curry, who is a daughter of Austin Curry, a well known farmer and lumberman of Chest Township Dr and Mrs Hurd have had nine children born to them, several of whom died when aged about three years The survivors are Nellie, who is the wife of Frank Markle, of Mahaffey, Lena, who is the wife of James Cardell, of Westover, Pa (they have three children—Vernon, Paul and Cliffton) , Vella, who is a popular and successful teacher in the graded schools at Mahaffey, being a graduate of the Lock Haven Normal School, and Denay, Curry, and Gard Those deceased were Austin, Sue and Zoe Dr Hurd is a member of various medical organizations and belongs also to the P O S A at Newburg

J E GEARHART, a progressive, enterprising and representative business man of Clearfield, Pa , manager of the Gearhart Knitting Machine Company and of the Keystone Vacuum Cleaner, is a member of one of the old settled families of the county

His great grandfather, John Gearhart, emigrated from Germany about the middle of the seventeenth century He served as a soldier in the Revolutionary war, afterward settled at Buffalo Run, Centre Co , Pa He married Miss Catharine Gray, who lived to the age of 97 years To John and Catharine were born ten children, whose names were as follows,—Jacob, John, Adam, Christ, Elias, Peter, Susanna, Eve, Betsey and Catharine These have all died long ago

John Gearhart, the second in order and grandfather of J E Gearhart, was born in 1789 He married Miss Lydia Shivery He served in the War of 1812 and was there when his eldest son David was born He moved to Clearfield County in 1820 He died in 1871 having lived to the age of 82, and his wife Lydia died at the age of 90 within a few days To John and Lydia Gearhart were born eleven children, one dying in infancy, the other ten living to a ripe age, whose names were as follows,— David, Sarah, Catharine, who is yet living at the advanced age of 95, John S the father of J E Gearhart, Susanna, Andrew, Jane, Enoch, Hannah, and Jacob, who is yet living

John S Gearhart was born April 20th, 1818, on his father's farm near Philipsburg, Clearfield Co He also was an agriculturist and spent the greater part of his life on his farm situated in Boggs Township, two miles northwest of Blue Ball, in Clearfield County, where his death occurred Mar 26, 1903, at the age of eighty-four years He was twice married, first to Lydia Showalter, whose death occurred July 3, 1850, when their youngest son, J E Gearhart, was fifteen months old J E Gearhart was born April 22, 1849 There were three other children born to this union, namely William, who was a gallant soldier in the Civil War, a member of Co E, 45th Pa Vol Inf, and who died of starvation in the Confederate prison at Salisbury, N. C, December 10, 1864, Ellis, who died at the age of twenty-one years, and Lloyd, who is a resident of Clearfield The second marriage of John S Gearhart was to Elizabeth Smith, whose death preceded that of her husband by four years, she dying Feb 14, 1898 Eight children were born to this marriage, namely: George S, who lives in Clearfield, John W, who owns the home farm in Boggs Township, A Clark,

who lives in Blair County, Samuel, whose business is carried on at Clearfield, Lydia J, who is the wife of Charles Rickets, of Altoona, James, who is a resident of Braddock, Pa, Charles, who died when seventeen years old, and Lewis, who lives at Pittsburg, Pa

Joseph Emery Gearhart grew to manhood on the home farm and obtained his education in the country schools After he reached manhood he went to work for the lumber firm of Hoover, Hughes & Co, at Bellefonte, Pa, with operations near Philipsburg, and remained with them for nine years, and during that time shipped the most of the lumber that was used in the erection of the buildings for the great Centennial Exposition From youth Mr Gearhart has been more or less interested in mechanics and has invented many devices and utensils of practical use, some of which having been patented, are now manufactured in large numbers He worked on a knitting machine until he perfected every part of it and received a patent and in 1889 opened a small shop at Blue Ball for its manufacture The machine was so well received that by 1890 the business had outgrown his quarters at Blue Ball and he then moved to Clearfield and erected his present plant on Nichols Street, and also a factory in Canada Under the name of the Gearhart Family Knitter, with ribbing attachment which produces seamless hosiery, Mr Gearhart's invention is sold in all countries and with its attachments has been patented in the United States and in thirteen foreign countries In connection with knitting machines, Mr Gearhart manufactures and has on the market, The Keystone Vacuum

Cleaner, and this invention promises to equal his others in popularity Mr Gearhart is a natural mechanic but he attributes a measure of his success to the instruction he received from his father-in-law, the late John Middleton, who was an expert machinist and gunsmith as his father before him had been, the latter manufacturing guns during the Revolutionary War for the Patriot army.

Mr Gearhart was married July 6, 1871, to Miss Mary E Middleton, a daughter of John Middleton, who came to Clearfield from Cambria County Eight children were born to Mr and Mrs Gearhart, namely Sophia, who is the wife of James Gleason, a leading member of the Clearfield bar, residing at Du Bois, and they have one son, James Joseph, Leonard A, Ada B, who married Dr George R Irwin, of Clearfield and they have four children—Robert, Dorothy, George and Joseph, John R, who resides in Clearfield, married Blanche Cardon and they have one son, William, Edna, who married B R Freer of Chicago and they have one child, Marjorie, Jessie P, who is the wife of George A Cardon, of Pittsburg, May, who married J Emmett Harder, of Clearfield and they have one son, John Emmett, and Emery J, who is connected with an advertising house, at Chicago, Ill

Mr and Mrs Gearhart are members of the M E Church in the work of which he has been very active for years

LUTHER H WILLIAMS, who has been a lifelong resident of Clearfield County, Pa, has made his home at Osceola Mills since October, 1891 He was born in Bradford Township, December 16, 1843, and is a son of Edward H. and Elizabeth (Smale) Williams, and a grandson of Edward Williams

Edward Williams was born in Wales and when he came to the United States, located in Lancaster County but subsequently moved to Bradford Township, Clearfield County, where he lived until his death He followed farming and was interested somewhat in lumbering The record preserved of this ancestor shows that he was a man of industry and perseverance and that he reared a family that was creditable in every way.

Edward Hurd Williams, father of Luther H, was probably born in Lancaster County but was quite young when his parents came to Clearfield County He became a farmer, as was his father, and later embarked in storekeeping, being a merchant from 1853 until the close of his life For several terms he served in the office of justice of the peace and was a school director for many years. In all that pertained to public life he was an upright citizen He married Elizabeth Smale, who was born in Graham Township, Clearfield County, a daughter of Benjamin Smale, an old settler To Edward H Williams and wife the following children were born Margaret, deceased, who was the wife of Robert Livengood, of Bradford Township, Elizabeth, deceased, who was the wife of Benjamin Carr, of Pike Township; Catherine, who is the wife of George Washington Graham, of Douglas County, Wash, Henry Ellis, deceased, who was a resident of Bigler, Pa, Isaiah, deceased, who spent almost all of his life in Pike Township, Mary Ellen, deceased, who was twice married, first to Elijah Smale and second to

Frederick Campman, Sylvester, deceased, who lived in Lawrence Township, Clearfield County, Wilson R, deceased, spent his life in Bradford and Graham Townships, Edward Johnson, who lives in Graham Township, Luther H, who resides at Osceola Mills, Henrietta, deceased, who was the wife of William Ogden, of Clearfield County, Martha, who married William Lease, of West Clearfield, and John L, who was a resident of Pittsburg, at the time of his death The parents of this family were members of the Lutheran church

Luther H Williams was reared in Bradford Township and obtained his education in the country schools He followed farming until he came to Osceola Mills, in 1891, since which time he has been connected as an employe with the Car Shops of the Berwind-White Company Mr Williams has witnessed many changes in this section during the twenty years since he came here and he has borne his part, as a good citizen in making Osceola Mills a pleasant, law-abiding town, one in which business enterprises prosper and comfortable living is possible He is not very active in politics, having never been anxious for political office, and casts his vote with the Republican party.

On September 21, 1865, Mr Williams was married to Miss Belinda A Waple, who was born on Chestnut Street, Philadelphia, May 17, 1843, a daughter of Henry and Mary (Wunder) Waple Henry Waple was born in Charles County, Md, December 11, 1816, and for a time engaged in the manufacture of fancy whips, in Philadelphia In June, 1843, he moved to Boggs Township, Clearfield County, and thereafter until April, 1862, conducted the hotel known as the Half-Way House, which was situated between Phillipsburg and Curwensville, after which he moved to Fairfax County, Va, just outside the city of Washington, D C, and resided there until his death on March 18, 1906 Henry Waple married Mary Wunder, who was born at Germantown, Pa, and died when Mrs Williams was six years old The Wunder family is an old one in this country, of Holland ancestry, and it was established in America prior to the Revolutionary War William Wunder, the great-grandfather of Mrs Williams, was an officer in Washington's army and being a butcher by trade he prepared meat for the soldiers and was also a lay reader to them during the fearful winter at Valley Forge His son, William Wunder, was a soldier in the War of 1812 In 1808 he built the first stone house in Germantown, Pa, a picture of which Mrs Williams prizes very highly To Henry and Mary (Wunder) Waple the following children were born Catherine, who is the widow of Henry Shimmel, of Cumberland, Md., Emily, who died at the age of two years, Belinda A, who is the wife of Luther H Williams, Julia, who is deceased, was the wife of Isaac Richardson, and two daughters who died unnamed

Mr and Mrs Williams have had five children, namely Harry Edward, who is a conductor in the railroad service, married Annie Baker, of Phillipsburg, and they have had five children—Oral, Harold, Robert, Marian and Dorothy, Lawrence S, who is a resident of Newton, Centre County, married Mary Thomas, of Phillipsburg, and they have two sons and two daughters—

Violet May, Adaline, Harvey and Leo, Melvin C, who married Edna V Hoyt, and they have had three children—Clayton Hoyt, Luther Sherman and O Blanche, Oral Blanche, who died in October, 1906, aged almost thirty-one years, and Ernest A, who resides at Osceola Mills, adjoining his parents, married Carrie Estep and they have one son, Edward Luther Mr Williams and family are members of the Episcopal church Fraternally he is connected with the Knights of Malta and the Mystic Chain

WALTER H WOODWARD, a prominent citizen of Huston Township, has been identified with public matters for some years, and is the proprietor of Oakmont Farm, a well cultivated tract of 147 acres situated one and one-half miles west of Penfield, Pa. Mr Woodward was born at the present site of Pine Forest, Luzerne County, Pa, February 2, 1855, and is a son of William D and Anna L (Thompson) Woodward

The Woodward family originated in England, and the first of the name came to America in the early part of the seventeenth century Daniel and Nancy (Eike) Woodward, the grandparents of Walter H Woodward, were early settlers of Luzerne County, where the grandfather was a well known lumberman, and they were the parents of seven children Mary, Sarah, Hiram, William D, Martha, Frances and Dennis, all of whom are deceased except Frances, who is the widow of Charles Sutton

William D. Woodward was born in March, 1829, in Luzerne County, Pa, and there spent his boyhood As a young man, with his brother Hiram, he came to Clearfield County with his wife, Ann L (Thompson) Woodward, who was born in New Jersey about 1856 He located at Penfield, where he purchased a hotel property, and operated this hostelry until 1864, when he sold out and removed to Minnesota He remained there but two months, however, at the end of that time returning to Clearfield County, Pa, and engaging in the lumber business In the spring of 1865 he bought eighty-eight acres of the present farm of Walter H Woodward from Jefferson Bundy, and later, in 1868, added to this property by purchase from John Du Bois, and at one time had 316 acres He retired five years previous to his death, which occurred April 3, 1907 His first wife had died in 1884, at the age of fifty-two years, and his second marriage was to a widow, Mrs Clemantine Iddings, who by her first union had six children To Mr Woodward and his first wife there were born the following children Amorvin, who is operating the farm adjoining that of Walter H Woodward, Stanley, also a resident of Huston Township, Walter H, Mattie, who married George Marsden, Americus H, who is a prominent attorney of Clearfield, Anna A, who is the widow of T B Buoy, and Ida E, who is the widow of George R Campbell

Walter H Woodward's early childhood was spent in Luzerne County, where his father was operating a sawmill, and he was still a lad when the family removed to Clearfield County He attended the township schools, and started helping his father in the lumber business when quite young

In 1880 he went West in the interest of the Thompson Consolidated Mining Co, and after his return spent four years as foreman of the factory of P C Thompson & Co, at Philadelphia   He has had charge of his present farm since 1898, and on the settlement of his father's estate he was given possession of it   The residence was erected by Mr Woodward's father in 1875, but the other buildings have been put up by Mr Woodward, who in many ways has improved the farm, making it one of the most valuable in Huston Township   The Bennett's Branch division of the Pennsylvania and B & S Railroads run through this property

Mr Woodward is a Republican in politics, and he has always been an active worker in support of the principles of that organization   He served for some time as township auditor, and is at present acting in the capacities of township assessor and president of the school board

SOLOMON McCULLY. postmaster at Ramey, Clearfield County, Pa, in which office he has officiated since February 13, 1909, is a well known citizen of Gulich Township, where the family has been established for many years   He was born March 23, 1855, in Gulich Township, Clearfield County, and is a son of Matthew and Sarah (Beyer) McCully

Matthew McCully was born in County Derry, Ireland, March 20. 1816 and was the youngest child of George and Isabella McCully   His father died in Ireland and when but 18 months old he came to this country with his mother and seven other children, all of whom have long since passed away

The little band arrived in Philadelphia, remained there a few weeks and then started for Clearfield County on foot with nothing but an Indian path to guide them   They arrived at their destination and made a home near the mouth of Muddy Run. From there Mr. McCully went to Tyrone forges and worked on the canal and about the furnaces where he grew up to manhood, becoming the main support of his mother, whom he cared for until her death in her 84th year; her remains repose in Mt Pleasant Cemetery, this county

Having been born in foreign land and his father being dead, made it necessary for Mr. McCully to take out naturalization papers, which were granted by the court of this country Dec. 6, 1848   Henry Hagerty and Lisle McCully were the witnesses and the prothonotary at that time was Wm C. Welch

On December 30, 1841, Matthew McCully was married to Sarah Beyer, a native of Ohio, Rev M. Betts of Clearfield, being the officiating clergyman   They settled on his farm at Beulah and began life work together   She "sleeps the sleep of the just," preceding him to the grave in August, 1901, he having died April 28, 1902, in his 86th year   They had the following children   Isabel, who is deceased, Christiana, who is the widow of H P R Blandy, David, who is deceased, Caroline, who is the wife of Alvin Frederick, Eliza and George, who is deceased, Solomon, Lavina, who is the wife of J B McFadden, Lewis, deceased, Edith, deceased, who was the wife of H B Brown, and Frank H. The parents were members of the Presbyterian church

Solomon McCully followed farming until

1887 and then came to Ramey and for twenty years followed the carpenter's trade here and was engaged in other lines of business until 1909, but since then has devoted himself to his official duties Although he is an independent voter he is a man of such reliable character that he has been chosen many times for township and borough offices, without reference to party connection For fourteen years he served as constable and also as school director, was a county commissioner for two years and borough treasurer for two years

Mr McCully was married in 1879 to Miss Ella Croyl, a daughter of Henry and Catherine Croyl, residents of Huntingdon County, Pa To the parents of Mrs McCully the following children were born Margaret Victoria, who is the wife of D T Kantner, Martha, who is the wife of Hugh Stoddard, Samuel A , Ella, William, Robert, Henry, Ada, who is the wife of H V Stevens, and June, who is the wife of Frank Johnston Mr and Mrs McCully have five children, namely Bertha, L K , H H , M W , and P S The family attends the Presbyterian church

GEORGE W BOUCH, who is engaged in farming in Bell Township, Clearfield County, Pa , where he is one of the representative citizens, was born December 27, 1840, in Armstrong County, Pa , and is a son of George and Sarah (Daugherty) Bouch

George Bouch was born in Armstrong County, Pa , and moved from there to Clearfield County in 1859, settling at Clover Run Four years later he moved his family to Jefferson County, where his accidental death took place in 1864, at the age of fifty-five years He married Sarah Daugherty, who died in March, 1892, when in her seventy-fifth year The maternal grandfather was of Irish extraction, but the paternal grandparents, Oximas and Rachel (Yont) Bouch, were natives of Germany Seven children were born to George Bouch and his wife, and of these the survivors are George W , Sarah, who is the wife of J Weilick, of Altoona, Pa , Jane, who lives at Sinking Valley, Hannah, who is the wife of John Weilick, Angelina, who lives in Clearfield County, and Florence, who lives at home

George W Bouch had very few early advantages and after boyhood found employment away from home, and after coming to Clearfield County worked at lumbering and in the woods until after his marriage, when he settled on his present farm in Bell Township He is still interested in lumbering to some extent but gives his main attention to agricultural pursuits During the Civil War he served one year as a member of Co K, 105th Pa Vol Inf , under Captain McKnight, in the Army of the Potomac His regiment was encamped near Washington, D C , in the closing months of the war, and he was honorably discharged and mustered out at Pittsburg

In 1862 Mr Bouch was married to Miss Catherine Peace, who was born January 23, 1844, in Center County, Pa , a daughter of Solomon and Mary (Donmire) Peace, and a granddaughter of Adam and Barbara Donmire Mr and Mrs Bouch had the following children born to them William, who lives in Bell Township, married Emma McGinnis, and they have five children,

Joseph, who lives in Bell Township, married Mary Yont, and they have four children, Lizzie, who is the wife of William Weirick, of Altoona, Pa, and they have four children, Ellen, who is the wife of E Henderson, of Bell Township, and they have three children, James, who lives in Bell Township, married Mary Harklerood, and they have two children, Edward, who is in business at Westover, Pa, married Lulu Snyder, and they have three children, Miles, who lives at McGee's Mills, married Lizzie Snyder and they have one child, Clyde, who lives in Bell Township, married Jennie Davis and they have one child, Arthur, who lives with his father, married Elinor Wolf, and they have two children Mr and Mrs Bouch are members of the Methodist Protestant church, with which he united forty-five years ago He is a Democrat in his political views and has served one term as township supervisor He takes a justifiable amount of pride in his large family of vigorous descendants

W I WALL, miller, owner and proprietor of the Grampian Mill, at Grampian, Pa, is a well known business man and respected and representative citizen of this borough He was born June 26, 1861, in Penn Township, Clearfield County, one mile south of Grampian, and is a son of Isaiah and Rosanna (Danver) Wall

Isaiah Wall was born in the eastern part of Pennsylvania and was a small boy when he accompanied his father, Jonathan Ball, to Penn Township, where the larger part of his subsequent life was passed He engaged in farming and lumbering and became a man of ample estate, owning, with his son-in-law, the land on which stands Coalport He was twice married, first to a Miss Widemyer, and second to Rosanna Danver, and seven children were born to the first marriage and one, W I, to the second The following children were born to the first union Eliza, Jennie, Hannah, Mary Ann, T E, Aquilla (a soldier in Civil War who died while serving his country), and an infant son, deceased After his first marriage, Isaiah Wall lived on the Thomas E Wall farm, on which Thos E Wall now lives, and continued there until after the death of his second wife, when he moved to Grampian and later to Tyrone and afterward to Coalport There he operated a coal bank and a saw-mill during his remaining active years and then retired to his farm in Penn Township, on which his death occurred when aged eighty-three years This farm of 125 acres he had cleared and improved, coming to it when it was little but a wilderness In politics he was a Republican and at one time served as constable of Penn Township He was a member of the Society of Friends and his burial was in the Friends' Cemetery. His second wife was a member of the Catholic church and she was buried in the cemetery belonging to that church, at Grampian

W. I Wall was educated in the schools of Penn Township and the Grampian Normal School, after which he engaged in farming in Penn Township, operating on fifty acres of land Later he moved to Grampian and bought his present mill, which is a grist-mill well fitted with modern machinery for producing flour, buckwheat and chop He operates the same with the assistance of one man and does a safe and

ALLISON OPP SMITH

satisfactory business He is an intelligent
and earnest citizen and has served in the
borough council, elected on the Republican
ticket He is a stockholder in the Penn
Township Rural Telephone Company

On June 26, 1884, Mr Wall was married
to Miss Sarah A Davis, who was born in
Penn Township, a daughter of Joseph
Davis, and they have had five children,
namely Earl J, who married Maude E
Bloom, a daughter of Edward Bloom, of
Penn Township, and they have had one
child, Sarah Elizabeth, now deceased Lena
E, who is a school-teacher, Eva Mildred,
who attends the Grampian High School,
Carl W, who is also at school, and Kenzie
Lovelle, who is deceased Mr Wall is a
member of the Society of Friends He belongs to the Penn Grange, to the Odd Fel-
lows and the P O S of A

ALLISON OPP SMITH, president judge
of the Forty-sixth Judicial District of Pennsylvania, comprising Clearfield county, was
born in Limestone township, Montour county,
Pennsylvania, on October 23, 1857, second
child of Simpson and Charlotte Opp Smith
both natives of Lycoming county, of pioneer
stock and of families identified with the early
and successful lumbering and agricultural development of the Susquehanna Valley His
grandfather Jonathan Smith was a native of
Philadelphia county, and his great-grandfather
Col George Smith was a soldier in the Revolutionary war and represented Philadelphia
county in the General Assembly of the State.
His grandmother Ann Simpson, of Bucks
county, Pennsylvania, a great aunt of General
U S Grant, married Jonathan Smith in 1796
and they went direct to Lycoming county,

where they lived the rest of their lives The
parents of Judge Smith moved to Northumberland county in 1867 and settled on a farm
near Watsontown, where they lived until 1879,
when they moved into Watsontown

The subject of our sketch attended the
common district schools of the neighborhood
and also attended academies at Dewart, Mc-
Ewensville and Watsontown, also assisting
on the farm until about sixteen years of age
He then spent one year clerking in a country
store at Dewart, and afterwards went to
Bloomsburg State Normal School and prepared for entrance to State College, Center
county, which he entered in January, 1876,
and graduated with the honors of his class in
1879 During the winter of 1879-80 he was
elected principal of schools and taught the
High School at Watsontown, after which he
began reading law in the office of Oscar
Foust, Esq of that place In September,
1880, he entered the Law Department of the
University of Pennsylvania, at Philadelphia,
as a student at law, from which institution he
graduated two years later in the Law Class of
1882 During said period he was also registered as a law student in the office of William
A Redding, J Levering Jones and Hampton
L Carson, Esquires, of Philadelphia, and
after his graduation, in June, 1882, on motion of J Levering Jones, Esq, one of his
preceptors, he was admitted to practice law in
the several courts of Philadelphia, and later
in the same month was admitted to practice
law in the Northumberland County Court

In September, 1882, he located in Clearfield
and was admitted to practice the law in the
several courts of Clearfield county on the 8th
day of January, 1883 For several years he
successfully practiced his profession alone,

during which time he served as solicitor for Sheriff R. N. Shaw and Sheriff E. L. McCloskey, and later as county solicitor. In 1894, after the elevation of Hon. Cyrus Gordon to the Common Pleas Bench, he formed a partnership with Thomas H. Murray, Esq., under the style of Murray & Smith, and this partnership continued until the junior member was elected to succeed Judge Gordon on the Common Pleas Bench, which honor was won at the November election in 1903 by a majority of 2,016.

In politics Judge Smith has been a Democrat all his life and took an active and earnest interest in party affairs from the time of arriving at man's estate. He served as secretary of the Democratic County Committee for several years beginning in 1886, and in 1890 was elected county chairman and had the distinction of polling the largest majorities for his party candidates that year ever given in the county. In 1896 he was appointed and served as councilman from the First Ward of Clearfield borough, and in 1897 was elected to the office of burgess of Clearfield and served three years in that position. In 1900 he was elected school director and was filling that position when elected to the bench.

As a lawyer Judge Smith soon won his way to the front at the Clearfield bar. He was recognized as possessing a clear, keen, logical mind, which combined with his industry and high character won him the respect and confidence of his clients. While a member of the firm of Murray & Smith he had a wide experience in the practice of corporation law, as that firm represented nearly all the railroads of the county and they also represented a large number of the leading mining corporations. Since going on the bench Judge Smith has gained much prominence in judicial circles all over the State. At his first license court he created a precedent in the conduct and control of the court over the granting of liquor licenses, first, by largely reducing the number of licenses and refusing nearly fifty per cent of the applicants and, second, by establishing what is believed to be wholesome rules for governing the sales of liquor and the maintenance of licensed hotels. Similar rules have since been adopted by a considerable number of the judges of the State and the wisdom of their establishment is apparent to anyone who has occasion to patronize the hotels of Clearfield county. Since he went upon the bench the criminal business has largely decreased, notwithstanding a large increase of population, composed of the people of southern Europe who know little of the laws and customs of this country. This decrease in the criminal business is popularly believed to be largely due to the strict enforcement of the law in both the license and criminal courts as administered by Judge Smith. The general business of the courts under Judge Smith has been conducted with great promptness and dispatch and no one can complain of any delay in the administration of justice. Four times a year all cases at issue, whether in the civil or criminal courts, whether in equity or on the argument list, by order of the court are listed for trial and hearing and a prompt disposal of the same enforced so far as can be done by an early trial and decision.

Judge Smith is a member of the Presbyterian church and has for many years been on the board of trustees. He also belongs to the Masonic fraternity of Clearfield and has gone through all the chairs of the Blue Lodge and is a member of the Chapter. Although always busy with his professional duties, he has at all times been closely identified with movements intended to advance the interests of the community, commercially and morally In 1889 he was an organizer and the first secretary and treasurer, as well as director, of the Electric Light Company at Clearfield, with which he was connected until soon after he went upon the bench He was also an organizer, director and president of the Paterson Clay Products Company, manufacturers of all kinds of paving and building brick He was one of the organizers of the Clearfield Y M C A and on its board of directors ever since its organization and is now president of that body, to the maintenance of which worthy institution he gives largely of his time and means In 1904 he was chairman of the Clearfield County Centennial Association Committee, which conducted to a successful conclusion the celebration of the one hundredth anniversary of the formation of Clearfield county He has been a member of the Pennsylvania Bar Association since its organization in 1894, and is now one of the vice-presidents of that body He is also a non-resident member of the Pennsylvania Society of New York

Judge Smith was married in Clearfield, on October 17, 1888, to Margaret Helen, youngest daughter of the late Senator William A Wallace They have one son, William Wallace, and three daughters, Charlotte, Margaret and Rebecca

WILLIAM M SHAW, deceased, for many years was one of Clearfield's prominent and substantial citizens, and from 1891 until the date of his death, was cashier of the County National Bank He was a member of an old settled family of Clearfield County and was born on the paternal homestead on November 28, 1832 His parents were Richard and Mary Shaw

William M Shaw's boyhood and youth were spent on the home farm and in attendance at the district schools and he continued the home farm for six years following his marriage He then established himself as a merchant in Cedar County, Iowa, but on account of the financial stringency occasioned by the Civil War, he soon closed out his business venture there and returned to Pennsylvania and enlisted as a volunteer in the Federal Army Shortly afterward he was appointed hospital steward, and during his term of service was stationed at Helena, Ark He later engaged tentatively in business at other points prior to entering the office of Dr A M Hills, at Clearfield, where he studied dental surgery and later became skilled in that profession, in which he continued until 1886, when he became identified with the County National Bank, first as teller and later as cashier

Mr Shaw was married in 1853 to Miss Martha Jane Irwin, a daughter of Jacob Irwin, of Clearfield County Mr Shaw's death was preceded by that of his wife

G R McMURRAY, owner and proprietor of a meat market at Beulah, Clearfield County, Pa, was born in Bigler Township, Clearfield County, April 5, 1880, and is a son of J A and Sophia (Young) McMurray, and a grandson of John McMurray

The parents of Mr McMurray are well known residents of Beulah and Bigler Township, where the father formerly was a farmer and lumberman He is still quite active and is janitor of the public school building at this place He married Sophia Young and the following children were born to them Mary, who is the wife of S B Echard, John, William, Emma, who is the wife of John McLaughlin, Margaret, who is the wife of Paul Lindenburg, Bertha, who is the wife of John Forsythe, Sadie, who is the wife of Cloyd Moss, Pearl, Ruth, Orvis, and Sylvester, deceased

G R McMurray attended the common schools and then followed farming until in September, 1910, when he went into the butchering business at Beulah, having purchased his stand in the previous month He is an excellent business man and is prospering

In 1907 Mr McMurray was married to Miss Hannah Beyer, who is a daughter of John and Emma E (Ross) Beyer, and a sister of Lewis W Beyer, who is a merchant and postmaster at Smoke Run Mr and Mrs McMurray live at Smoke Run, where Mrs McMurray owns a fine residence They have had one son, George, who was born May 5, 1910, and died in the following August They attend the Methodist Episcopal church He is a Democrat in his political views but takes no very active part, being much more interested in developing his business

ISAAC KNEPP, owner of a farm of 226 .acres in Bradford township, Clearfield County, Pa, has resided on this farm for 35 years, and comes of one of the early families of the county He was born in 1851 in Bradford township, and is a son of Benjamin and Sarah Knepp His father was born in Juniata County, Pa, and at an early age came with his parents to Clearfield county and settled on the David Dale farm in Bradford township He spent the remainder of his life in this township and died on the John Murray farm

Isaac Knepp was reared in Bradford township and obtained his education in the local schools of the county After his marriage he located on his present farm of 226 acres, which is located about five miles east of Bigler, and has since carried on general farming He has made many improvements on the place during the past 35 years, and has erected a large frame house and a fine barn A prominent citizen of his township, he has served as school director for two terms, as steward of the U B church, and as supervisor of the township

In 1875 Mr Knepp married Jane Hubler, born in 1857, a daughter of Levey Hubler, who during his life was one of the prominent farmers of Graham township, and the following children have been born of their union Otis married Miss Zella Wilson, and they have two children, Esther and Mary Ellen, he resides in Clearfield, and is employed in a furniture store Ashley Knepp, married to Miss Minnie Eshelman, resides at Bigler, employed as a farmer Florence, married to Mr Thomas Luzier, resides at Shiloh Etta died in 1882, aged 2 years Hector is employed as a miner Seymour married to Miss Ruth Lansberry, resides at Caro, Michigan, employed as scientist Ray resides at Pittsburg, employed as a stenographer Merlin is attending college Pearl is employed as teacher in public schools. Verva is attending Normal school

SAMUEL BLAIR ECHARD, owner and proprietor of a blacksmith shop and a dealer also in agricultural machinery and farm implements, at Ramey, Pa, is one of the representative men of the borough which he has served officially on numerous occasions. He was born November 2, 1866, in Freedom Township, Blair County, Pa, and is a son of John and Salome (Stiffler) Echard.

John Echard was born in Blair County and was a son of George Echard. He was a farmer in Blair County and spent his life there. He married Salome Stiffler, who is also deceased, and they had the following children born to them: James F, Catherine, who is the wife of Samuel Stiffler, Henry M, Samuel B, Joseph C, Mary A, who is the wife of David L Semple, Peter W, and Anna B, who is the wife of Calvin Fleming.

Samuel Blair Echard obtained his education in the public schools of Blair County and then worked on the home farm until he was twenty-one years of age, after which he spent one year in the woods. He came to Clearfield County when he was twenty-one and worked for eight years at the carpenter trade and then turned his attention to blacksmithing and dealing in farm implements. Mr Echard is considered an expert mechanic and has proved the justice of this reputation by his successful efforts in both trades. He is an intelligent and active citizen and one who commands the confidence of his fellow citizens. He served in the borough council for two and one-half terms, was borough treasurer for one term and for seven years has been a member of the school board. He is also a member of the board of trustees and treasurer of the Methodist Episcopal church at Ramey.

On November 2, 1894, Mr Echard was married to Miss Mary J McMurray, a daughter of Alexander and Sophia McMurray, and they have three children: John A, Vida May, and William McKinley, all of whom are very satisfactory pupils in the Ramey schools. In politics Mr Echard is a Republican.

CHRISTIAN B HAAG, a lifelong resident of Clearfield County, Pa, who is a representative citizen of Troutville, where he has been in the undertaking business since 1878, also devotes some attention to farming in Brady Township. He was born on the family homestead in Brady Township, September 17, 1853, and is a son of Christian and Catherine (Weise) Haag.

Christian Haag was the eldest of five children born to his parents, the other four being Elizabeth, who was the wife of Jacob Dunmeyer (both deceased), Mary, who is the widow of Moses Ireily, Philip, who lives at Punxatawney, Pa, whose twin brother, Henry, is deceased. His family live in Akron, O. Christian Haag, father of Christian B, was born in Germany, in 1823, and was nine years old when the family set sail for America, a country he almost failed to reach, as one one occasion, he fell from the deck of the vessel and but for the quick action of a sailor, would speedily have been drowned in the Atlantic Ocean. He lived to become a man of large estate and one of Brady Township's most respected citizens. He grew to manhood in Jefferson County, Pa, but later bought fifty acres of land one mile south of Troutville, in Clearfield

County, subsequently adding two more tracts of fifty acres each He devoted himself exclusively to agriculture and remained interested in his crops and stock during all the rest of his active life His death occurred in 1890, in Brady Township He was twice married, first to Charlotte Knarr and they had three children Mary, who is deceased, who was the wife of Henry W Weber, and Henry and Adam The mother of these children died in 1847 Mr Haag was married second to Catherine Weise, who died in 1889, having been the mother of nine children, namely Christian B, John, Catherine, Philip, Frederick, August, William, Jacob and Joseph Catherine is the wife of William McConnell, and Frederick is deceased Christian Haag, the father of Christian B Haag, died in 1890

Christian B Haag spent his boyhood on the home farm but later learned the carpenter's trade and followed the same for many years In 1876 he moved into Troutville, where he lived ten years, afterwards residing ten years on the farm and then returning to Troutville, where he now lives and where he has a fine residence and office adjoining, having resided here for the last fifteen years He went into the undertaking business in 1878, having received his diploma in embalming at the Pittsburg College of Embalming, where he was under the instruction of Prof Sullivan, and where he has returned several times in order to take post graduate work He has since been continuously engaged in this work, a period of 33 years He is well equipped for funeral directing, having a handsome black funeral car and a team of horses that are very generally admired, being well matched blacks, with white star foreheads He has all the appurtenances required for either an elaborate funeral, or for the quieter service that many families prefer

In September, 1876, Mr Haag was married to Miss Sarah M Bonsall, who died April 8, 1911. She was a daughter of Amos Bonsall, a prominent citizen of this section A family of five children has been born to them, namely Amos, who is manager of the railroad company's farms at Helvetia, Clearfield county, married Florence London and they have one child, Arthur, Orpha, married M A Zimmerman, of Troutville, Pa, and they now live in Warren, O (they have two children—Margaret and Donald), Morris, who is a graduate of the dental department of the Baltimore Medical College, is practicing dentistry at Meriden, Conn, and married Belle Hanney, Vina, is the wife of Allen R McHenry, of Sagamore, Pa, who is general manager for the B & O people of that place Miss Huldah resides at home Mr. Haag and family belong to the Lutheran church In his political views he is a Democrat but he has never accepted any public office other than school director, and only that from a sense of duty He has been a very active member of Mingle Lodge, No 753, at Troutville, for many years and belongs also to the auxiliary society, the Rebeccas, and in 1910 he was sent as a representative to the Grand Lodge at Williamsport, which is considered a signal honor

C B ELLIOTT, M D, physician and surgeon, who has been located at Coalport, Clearfield county, Pa, since 1892, was born near Cumberland, Md, April 23, 1854, and is a son of John and Catherine (Miller) Elliott

John Elliott was born near Ligonier, Pa, a son of John Elliott, who came to America from Ireland, in 1792   The history of the Elliotts, or, as originally written—Eliot or Ellis—dates back to the 11th century   William H Eliot was a leader under, and principal adviser of William, Duke of Normandy during the Conquest, 1066   It was a John Eliot who held the fort at Gibraltar, against Spain, at that time being a commander in the British Navy. The family is traced to the north of Britain and the name Eliot perhaps was thus written when the family had estates near Eliot, Dundee, Scotland   The old Eliot stronghold is at Port Eliot, St Germans, Cornwall, England   It was purchased by John Eliot, son of Edward Eliot, of Cutland, Devonshire   The arms of the Eliot family are thus mentioned in heraldy   Argent, a fesse gules, between double coutises wavy azure, Crest an elephant's head, argent, plain collared gules, Supporters two eagles, reguardent wings displayed and inverted proper, each charged on the breast with an ermine spot sable   The motto· "Proedentibus insta" is freely translated as "Press close upon those who take the lead "

Sir John Whitaker Ellis, or Eliot, descended from two chiefs: Charles Ellis, of Abbots Bromley, and George Ellis, who was at the conquest of Jamaica in 1656   The latter's grandson, Charles Rose Ellis, of Claremont, Surrey, was, on July 15, 1826, created Baron Seaford   It was from this branch of the family came Charles Augustus Ellis, the sixth Baron Howard De Walden, while from the Abbot Bromley branch, one of its members, Sir John Whitaker Ellis, represented the City of London as Lord Mayor   The crest of this family is thus described   A female figure ppr vested or, holding in the dexter hand a chaplet of roses gules, and in the senister a palm branch slipped vert (Middlesex)

The progenitors of the American Ellis family can be traced to Wales   Richard Ellis was born in Dublin, Ireland, August 10, 1704   His father, a native of Wales, died when Richard was about thirteen years of age and the next authenticated record is of his appearing at Plymouth, Mass   His descendants are almost without exception people who have achieved importance in some way   Included in these are· O W Ellis, of Chicago, Ill , Rev Charles H Ellis, of Kingston, N Y , Stewart H Elliott, of New York City, C B Elliott, M D , of Coalport, Pa , W Dixon Ellis, of New York City, Marshall Elliott, of Baltimore, Md , born at Wilmington, N C , January 24, 1846, a son of Aaron E Elliott—Harvard, 1868, Ph D , Princeton, 1877, LL D , Wake Forest, N C , 1891 Modern Languages, Associate of the American Philogical Society and the Maryland Historical Society, and John Whittaker Elliott, M D , of Boston Mass , born at Keene, N H , in October, 1852, son of John Henry Elliott, a member of the Maryland University Alumni, the Johns Hopkins and the Rolland Park Country Club

John Elliott, father of Dr Elliott, of Coalport, resided at different places during life, for many years being engaged in lumbering and having his home alternately or successively at Mt Savage, Southampton, Tipton and Tyrone, in 1880 moving from the latter place to Coalport, where he opened the first store in the place, the old building where he conducted it still being in evidence   He died here in 1890 at the age of seventy-four years He married Catherine Miller, who was born at Addison, Somerset county, Pa , and died in

22

1910, aged about eighty years They had three children C B ; Jack M and Laura B Jack M Elliott was active in Republican politics and at one time was the nominee of his party for sheriff, and while the county had a large normal Democratic majority, he came within 200 votes of winning the election He resides at Coalport Laura B Elliott became the wife of J C Weller, county superintendent of schools of Somerset county They reside at Gebhart

C B Elliott was educated at Tipton Academy, where he was a student for five years In 1871 he entered Jefferson Medical College, Philadelphia, where he was graduated in the class of 1874 He located at Osceola Mills and practiced there for one year, when the place was practically destroyed by fire and he then settled at Altoona and four years later moved to Indianapolis, Ind , but one year later came back to Pennsylvania and was established for five years at Utahville, in Clearfield county. He suffered a second loss by fire and in 1884 located again at Altoona, where he was in practice until 1892, when there appeared to be a particularly good professional opening at Coalport, and he has been in active practice here ever since He is one of the county physicians Dr Elliott makes a specialty of diseases of the eye and in treating these delicate organs he has been more than usually successful.

Dr Elliott was married in 1880 to Miss Laura M Cherry, a daughter of John W Cherry, who formerly was an undertaker at Altoona Mrs Elliott died in 1891 Dr Elliott takes a great deal of pride in his ancestral history, although some of the later records are not complete, family annals having been lost with other important documents, in the fire that destroyed his effects while in practice at Altoona

GEORGE MINNS, JR , a representative citizen and prominent business man of DuBois, Pa , a successful coal operator and interested additionally in other enterprises, was born August 4, 1873, at Renovo, Pa , and is a son of George T and Alice (Hunter) Minns

George T Minns was born in England in 1845 and became a miner at an early age, his experience in this direction covering many years He was married in England to Alice Hunter and they remained there until after the birth of two children and then came to America Mr Minns was led to settle at Renovo, Clinton county, Pa , because it was a fine mining district and after working for coal companies there for a time he leased and operated a mine of his own He removed then with his family, to Butler county, Pa , continuing in the coal business and during his period of residence there sold coal to the oil fields at a profit In 1880 he came to DuBois and here entered the employ of John DuBois, for whom he opened up mines and from whom he later bought a farm in the Clear Run neighborhood This land Mr Minns cleared and it is the present place of residence of the family Mr and Mrs Minns had twelve children born to them, namely Bessie, who is now deceased, was the wife of Oscar Long, Sarah, who was the wife of Wm Guntrum, Catherine, who is the wife of Edward Trude, George, John, William, Robert; Alice, who is the wife of George Whipple; Abbie, who is the wife of W B Johnson, Martha, who is the wife of Everett Case, Henry, youngest, at home

George Minns attended school as circumstances permitted, during boyhood, but by the time he was fifteen years of age he had become very useful to his father on the newly purchased farm. Four years later he went to lumbering and continued to farm and to work in the woods until 1896, when, with his father, he leased a tract of coal land from A C Hopkins, of Loch Haven, Pa. There was one mine already on the place and they started then drift on the left of it and began producing coal. In a short time the younger partner bought out the entire interest and ever since has operated this mine alone. It has fulfilled every expectation and has proved a valuable investment. Mr Minns runs three wagons and sells coal to the local trade and supplies the larger number of the factories at DuBois. He has other business interests and owns a large amount of valuable real estate, including a farm in Sandy township and the Hotel Logan, at DuBois, which he leases, having previously remodeled the building. In 1900, Mr Minns erected his handsome brick residence at No 601 First Street.

Mr Minns was married to Miss Ella Bair, a daughter of William Bair, of Falls Creek, Pa, and they have four children Earl, Mary, Alice and Ruth. Mr Minns and family are members of the Episcopal church. In politics he is a Republican and is an active, interested and public-spirited citizen. Since 1905 he has been a member of the borough council of DuBois and has been sincere in his efforts to secure and regulate beneficial measures for the people. He belongs fraternally to the Elks and the Knights of Pythias and socially to the Acorn Club. Mr Minns is a stockholder in the Union Banking and Trust Company of DuBois.

E B MAHAFFEY, cashier of the Madera National Bank of Madera, Pa, is one of the younger business men of this place and his whole business experience has been with banking institutions. He was born in Indiana county, Pa, March 14, 1881, and is a son of John and Mary Jane (Ake) Mahaffey.

John Mahaffey was born in Clearfield county but died in Indiana county, having been engaged for a number of years in the livery business at Hillsdale. He married Mary Jane Ake, who was born in Blair county. She survives and resides at Burnside, Clearfield county. They had three children J L, E B, and Nellie. In politics John Mahaffey was a Republican. His father was Thomas Mahaffey and was born in Snyder county, Pa, and farther back the ancestry can be traced to Ireland. John Mahaffey and wife were members of the Methodist Episcopal church at Hillsdale.

E B Mahaffey was educated in the public schools of his native county and at Purchaseline Academy, after which he entered the First National Bank at Glen Campbell and came from there to the First National at Madera, in 1907. He is interested in property here and is a representative citizen along all lines.

In 1905, in Indiana county, Mr Mahaffey was married to Miss Beulah Long, who is a daughter of Charles and Sarah (Jamison) Long. Mrs Mahaffey has one older sister, Zomie, who is the wife of C C Williams, and a younger sister and brother, Goldie and Newell. Mr and Mrs Mahaffey have one daughter, Sarah Jane. They attend the Presbyterian church. In politics Mr Mahaffey is not very active but casts his vote with the Republican party.

MICHAEL CRAIG, senior member of the firm of M & F Craig, coal operators, at present particularly interested in the Industry mine, at New Castle, Clearfield county, Pa, has been a resident of Brisbin for many years and is one of the prominent men of this borough He was born in Lanarkshire, Scotland, October 11, 1860, and is a son of James and Bridget (Rooney) Craig

Michael Craig accompanied his parents to America and to Brisbin in 1881 and has always since been connected with the coal industry He began operating Sterling mine No 2, October 11, 1888, and leased the property until 1897, when he bought it, and also has a lease on Sterling No 3, and the firm owns extensive coal lands which they lease to Berwind White Co, Kelly Bro Co, and also Blythe Coal Company, and are in the gas and oil business also in West Virginia Mr Craig is a stockholder in the Osceola Bank He has been a very active and public spirited citizen and has frequently served in the borough council and has twice been borough treasurer

Mr Craig was married on June 4, 1907, to Miss Susan McPhilomy, who was born at Snow Shoe, Center county, and was one month old when she was brought to Brisbin by her parents, John McPhilomy and wife Mr and Mrs Craig have one daughter, Catherine They are members of the Roman Catholic church He is identified with the Knights of Columbus at Clearfield He casts his vote with the Democratic party

GEORGE W OAKS, a retired farmer and well known citizen of Burnside township. Clearfield county, Pa, is a native of New England, born October 31, 1831, at Dover, Maine, and is a son of Stephen L. and Sally (Ames) Oaks

Stephen L Oaks was born in Maine, in 1796, a son of Abel and Mehitabel (Jewett) Oaks, and died in Cambria county, Pa, in 1875 He married Sally Ames, who was born in 1799, and died in 1877 In 1838 they moved from New England to Blairsville, Pa, where Mr Oaks followed his trade of millwright, at a later date moving into Cambria county, where he lived until his decease

George W Oaks was seven years old when his parents came to Pennsylvania He had but meagre school opportunities and as soon as old enough worked at farming and provided for himself He continued to follow agricultural pursuits in Pennsylvania until he was twenty-nine years old and then went to Sioux county, Ia, where he entered land and developed a farm He has been retired from active farm work since 1903

Mr. Oaks married Miss Elizabeth Mock, who was born in Bedford county, Pa, June 12, 1833, and died January 26, 1897 They had the following children born to them Phineas, who lives in Iowa, married Alice J Stanton, Amanda, who is deceased, Mary C, who is the wife of Irwin Jones, lives in Iowa, Joseph E, who lives at Hawarden, Ia, John, whose home is also at Hawarden, Charles, who resides at Chatsworth, Ia, and William, who lives at Hawarden Mr Oaks has grandchildren as follows. Walter, Ray and Arthur, sons of Phineas, and of these, Walter has three children and Arthur has two, eight children of his daughter Mary (two sons of this family are married, Orald has two children and Norton has one child), one son of his son Joseph E, one of his son John, one of

ROLAND DAVIS SWOOPE

his son Charles, and five of his son, William Oaks The family is an unusually vigorous one and all its members are prosperous and representative people of the section in which they live

M J KELLY, proprietor of the Aberdeen Hotel, at Grampian, Pa, where he is one of the leading citizens, was born October 27, 1871, at Bellefonte, Center county, Pa, and is a son of Thomas F and Mary (Hehir) Kelly Mr Kelly was educated at Bellefonte and other points and has been a resident of Grampian since 1902, when he succeeded McMillen & Ryan, as proprietor of the Aberdeen Hotel, a modern, hot-water heated building, having twenty bed-rooms and catering to transient trade Mr Kelly makes a specialty of his fine table, the best the market affords being placed before his guests His charges are very moderate, being $1 50 per day His patronage is dependable, travelers making it convenient to return on their trips so that they may enjoy the comforts of Mr Kelly's house at Grampian In addition to his hotel business, Mr Kelly has other interests, being the owner of a coal mine at Fernwood, which is operated under the name of the Fernwood Coal Company He owns sixty acres and leases 100 more, the vein here being two feet and thirty-two inches thick He gives employment to thirty-two or more men

Mr Kelly married Miss Elizabeth Smith, a daughter of Edward Smith, of Snowshoe, Pa, and they have two children, Mary and Katherine Mr Kelly and wife are members of the Catholic church In politics he is a Democrat but has never accepted any office except that of school director of the borough He is identified with the Elks at Clearfield,

and is numbered with the honest, upright and useful men of Grampian

ROLAND DAVIS SWOOPE was born at Curwensville, Clearfield county, Pa, August 26, 1856, and is the eldest son of the late Hon Henry Bucher Swoope and Susanna Patton (Irvin) Swoope On the paternal side he is a lineal descendant of Colonel Jacob Mytinger, who served in the War of the Revolution, as second in command of "VonHeer's Battalion of Light Dragoons" which regiment was the personal escort of General George Washington, between whom and Colonel Mytinger a warm personal friendship existed Colonel Mytinger was also one of the charter members of the "Society of the Cincinnati" On his maternal side, the subject of this sketch is a lineal descendant of Colonel John Patton, who was also actively engaged in the struggle for National Independence, as colonel of the Sixteenth Regiment of Pennsylvania Troops, and for a time had charge of the defenses of Philadelphia Colonel Patton was one of that noble band of patriots in Philadelphia, who raised, on their own personal responsibility, two hundred and sixty thousand pounds to aid the Revolutionary army in the greatest crisis of that memorable struggle He was also a member of the "Society of the Cincinnati"

Hon Henry Bucher Swoope, the father of the subject of our sketch, was one of the most brilliant and distinguished lawyers of Pennsylvania, also famous as a political speaker and as one of the leaders of the Republican party of his State His mother Susanna Patton (Irvin) Swoope was a daughter of William Irvin, one of the pioneer lumbermen and business men of Clearfield county Roland

Davis Swoope spent his boyhood days in Clearfield, where he attended the public schools and the old Clearfield Academy In 1869 his father, having been appointed by President Grant, United States Attorney for the Western District of Pennsylvania, the family removed to Pittsburg, Pa , where they continued to reside until the death of Hon H. B Swoope, in February, 1874, when they returned to Curwensville

In addition to the Clearfield schools, Mr Swoope also attended the High School, Pottstown, Pa , Ayers Latin School at Pittsburg, Pa , Phillips Academy at Andover, Mass , and the Western University of Pennsylvania. While a student at Andover he founded and was the first member of the "K O A " Society, a famous school fraternity, membership in which is the highest ambition of every Phillips Andover student This society numbers among its alumni, many of the most distinguished men in the country

In 1876 he entered the law office of Murray & Gordon, a firm, at that time, composed of Hon Thomas H Murray, who had pursued his legal studies in the office of Hon H Bucher Swoope, and Hon Cyrus Gordon, afterwards president judge of the courts of Clearfield county In order to support himself, while reading law, Mr Swoope engaged in the insurance business, building up a successful business which he disposed of after his admission to the bar, and devoted himself to his profession After passing a successful examination, he was admitted to the bar of Clearfield county in 1878 He is also a' member of the bar of the United States courts, and of the Supreme and Superior Courts of Pennsylvania

He has always taken an interest in public affairs and served as chairman of the Republican County Committee for several years, being first elected chairman in 1888, which was the year of the presidential campaign when Benjamin Harrison was elected president over Grover Cleveland So efficient was the organization and work of the Republican party under Mr Swoope's chairmanship, that he reduced an adverse plurality of 1,501, which the Democratic candidate had received in the previous gubernatorial election, to 869 and in recognition of his efforts he received a medal of honor and a resolution of thanks from the Republican State Committee Mr Swoope has also taken an active part in many political campaigns as a stump speaker for his party, not only in his own county but throughout the state

As a lawyer, Mr Swoope has a large and successful practice and has been engaged in many important and interesting cases He argued the case of Jackson vs the Pennsylvania Railroad Company before the Supreme Court of Pennsylvania and though opposed by John G Johnson, Esq , the leader of the Philadelphia bar, and other eminent counsel, Mr Swoope succeeded in having affirmed a verdict against the railroad company for treble damages for discrimination in failing to furnish coal cars to his client, thus sustaining the constitutionality of the Act of Assembly of 1883, giving the right to recover treble damages in such cases

Among other important cases in which he has been concerned, was that of the Central Trust Company of New York vs the Clearfield Creek Coal Company, an action to foreclose a mortgage by a minority in number and amount of the holders of the bonds secured by said mortgage, although the mortgage contained a provision that it could only be enforced upon the written request of a majority in number and amount, of the holders of the bonds. This case raised a novel legal question in Pennsylvania, but after a vigorous contest, the plaintiffs were successful in obtaining a decree of foreclosure of the mortgage and a judgment for $540,000.00 against the coal company, thus establishing, for the first time in the courts of this state, the right of a minority of the bond-holders secured by a corporation mortgage, to compel a foreclosure. As a lawyer, Mr. Swoope has always refused to represent liquor license applications, and has been active in the cause of temperance, having been one of the officers of the Constitutional Prohibition Amendment Association of Clearfield county, when that question was submitted to the voters of Pennsylvania, and, although the amendment was defeated in the state, it carried Clearfield county by a large majority.

Mr. Swoope is also largely interested in the development of the coal business of Clearfield county. In connection with other owners of coal property near Madera he was active in securing the construction of railroad extensions and he and his associates built part of the necessary railroad branches to reach their lands at their own expense and thus opened up the largest coal territory now being operated in Clearfield county. In the conduct of the numerous coal operations in which he is interested Mr. Swoope has always insisted on recognizing organized labor. Mr. Swoope is a stockholder and one of the directors of the Curwensville National Bank and is also interested in other financial institutions.

Mr. Swoope was one of the founders of the Curwensville "Mountaineer," which is recognized as among the leading Republican country newspapers of the state. He is fond of literary pursuits. He is the owner of a fine library and has prepared and delivered many lectures and patriotic addresses.

Mr. Swoope is an official member of the Methodist Episcopal church of Curwensville, Pa., he is also a member of the Pennsylvania Bar Association, the Union League of Philadelpia, the American Academy of Political and Social Science, the Historical Society of Clearfield county, the Independent Order of Odd Fellows, the Clearfield-Curwensville Country Club and other organizations.

In May, 1880, Mr. Swoope was married to Miss Cora Arnold, daughter of the late Samuel Arnold, of Curwensville, Pa. To this union five children were born, of whom three survive, namely: Henry Bucher Swoope, coal operator, Madera, Pa., Roland Davis Swoope, Jr., editor of the Curwensville "Mountaineer," and also editor of the Clearfield County History, and Miss Mary Swoope of Curwensville, Pa.

REV. JOHN MITCHELL CHASE, deceased, who, for a number of years officiated in various parts of Clearfield county as an ordained minister of the Baptist faith, was long one of the best known citizens of Woodward township and became one of its largest land owners. He was, however, a self-made man, and his accumulations were the result of industry, frugality and sound judgment, while his liberal disbursements came freely, inspired by a kind, charitable and generous nature. He was born in Cuyahoga county, O., March 11, 1820, and was a son of Benjamin and Eliza (Swan) Chase.

In early boyhood John M. Chase was left

fatherless, one of a family of five children bereft of one parent to become burdens on the other The devoted mother had no means either to care for them At that time the family lived in Broome county, N Y, having moved there in 1825, and the mother kept her little ones with her as long as possible The inevitable parting came, however, when John M was seven years old, at which age he left home to earn his own living The mother married again but did not much improve her financial status. It is recorded in the family, as showing the loving, generous and unselfish nature of the youth, that in all his lonely wanderings in search of paying employment, he never forgot to send messages to his mother and as soon as he had secured his first land, a little tract on Little Clearfield Creek, he sent for her and his step-father and gave them filial respect and care as long as they survived

In 1845 Mr Chase was married and in 1852 moved to the northwest part of Woodward township and there engaged in lumbering That was his main business during his active life and he acquired extensive tracts of some of the finest timber land in Clearfield county His home continued to be in Clearfield county

On August 14, 1862, he enlisted for service in the Civil war, entering Company B, 149th Pa Vol Inf, of which he was elected lieutenant, but later, through the intervention of his personal friend, Governor Curtin, he was appointed regimental quartermaster Army exposure brought on a disability which resulted in his honorable discharge, after nineteen months of service He returned to his home and in the course of time resumed his former activities Subsequently he invested in land that was rich in coal deposits From youth

Mr Chase had been serious-minded, probably in part made so by the heavy responsibilities so early placed upon him, and in early manhood had united with the Baptist church, in which he was ordained a minister in 1870 Prior to the Civil war he was an Abolitionist in his political creed and subsequently became a Republican, but late in life he associated himself with the Prohibitionists

On September 18, 1845, Mr. Chase was married to Miss Tabitha Williams and eleven children were born to them Of these, one son, John M. Chase, formerly postmaster of Clearfield but now retired, lives at No 22 S Fourth street, Clearfield. Another son, B F. Chase, now American consul at Leeds, England. For many years he was a very prominent business man of this city

DANIEL RICHARDS, who has devoted the larger part of his business life to farming and lumbering in Clearfield county, Pa, is one of the substantial men of Boggs township and a highly respected resident of Wallaceton He was born in Boggs township, February 8, 1853, and is a son of James and Susan (Dickson) Richards

James Richards was one of the old and representative farmers and lumbermen of Boggs township, coming to this section in his youth He married Susan Dickson, and they had the following children born to them Howard, John, George, James, Sarah and Tamer, twins, Myrtle, Cyrus, Daniel, Kirt, Emma, and Velma Of these, John, James, Sarah and Tamer, are all deceased Sarah was the wife of Alexander Gwynn; Tamer was the wife of Jacob Ulrich, Myrtle was the second wife of Alexander Gwynn; Emma is the wife of Robert White, and Velma is the wife of Mathew

Askey James Richards and wife were members of the Methodist Episcopal church

Daniel Richards obtained the usual amount of schooling that was afforded boys in the section in which he was reared, the most of them, like himself, being needed early to assist on the home farms Mr Richards owns a valuable farm of ninety acres situated in Boggs township, together with two houses and four lots in the village of Wallaceton, all excellent property He has served six years as a member of the Wallaceton School Board, and served also for six years on the borough council He was reared in the Republican party, his father always having given it support after its organization, and he has continued his affiliation with the same

In 1877 Mr Richards was married to Miss Amelia Sloan, who died December 6, 1901 She was a daughter of Charles and Barbara (Stoner) Sloan, who came from Lancaster county to Clearfield county They had two children Amelia and Elizabeth, the latter of whom married Jacob Dimling Mr Richards was married, second, February 24, 1904, to Mrs Mary A (Wetzel) Turner, widow of George Turner, and a daughter of Daniel and Susannah (Cowder) Wetzel The parents of Mrs Richards were born in Lancaster county but their parents moved to Clearfield county when they were children They had three children George, Mary A and Daniel W Mrs Richards owns a farm of fifty acres and also a comfortable house with barn situated in Wallaceton She is an active member of the Methodist Episcopal church, while Mr Richards belongs to the Presbyterian church He is interested in the Grange, at Blue Ball, and is connected with the Odd Fellows at Clearfield

EDGAR WILLIAM TURLEY, a prosperous business man at Irvona, Pa, where he is engaged in the mercantile business, was born at Osceola Mills, Clearfield county, Pa, July 3, 1874, and is a son of George W and Sarah (Potter) Turley

George W Turley was born in 1849, in Center county, Pa He resides with his family at Coalport and for a number of years has been a mine foreman and also a coal operator He married Sarah Potter, who was born in Blair county and is a daughter of Robert Potter, one of the old residents of that section The father of George W Turley was a railroad engineer and met with an accidental death on the line and his burial was at Richmond, Va Six children were born to Mr and Mrs Turley, all of whom survive, namely Jennie, who is the wife of Orville Spencer, of Cape Charles, Va, Estella, who is the wife of Blair Miller, now of Altoona, formerly of Blandsburg, Pa, Minnie, who is the wife of J H Gillman, of Bellwood, formerly of Cambria county, Cora, who is the wife of L B Bland, of Blandsburg, Maud, who resides at home, and Edgar W, of Irvona

Edgar William Turley attended school until he was about sixteen years of age, having advantages in the Normal Schools at New Washington and Mountaindale His first business experience was as a clerk at Altoona and later he became weighmaster and coal mine foreman and subsequently went into the coal business with his father at Mountaindale and other places and has been in business for himself for the last seven years Measured by the success which he has had, it is evident that his capacity is very considerable For a time he was in business at Galitzin, later at Dysart and still later at Osceola, and for the past three years he has been in the mercantile business, operating also the Ent-Turley Coal Company and having other interests. This company employs about sixty men in Clearfield county, working on Vein B, on the South Whitmer branch.

Mr Turley was married in 1900 to Miss Susan Rodgers, of Somerset county, Pa, and they have had five children. Beulah, Ruth, Evaline, George and Edwina, the last two being now deceased. In politics Mr Turley is a Republican. He is identified fraternally with the K M C and the Moose, at Irvona and Coalport. He is a man of frank, pleasant manner and is very popular with his fellow citizens   .

S J MILLER, M D, vice-president of the Madera National Bank, at Madera, Pa, owner and proprietor of a drug store and for the past sixteen years the leading physician and surgeon of this place, is one of the foremost citizens. Dr Miller was born in Pike township, Clearfield county, Pa, in 1859, and is a son of David and Sarah (Welch) Miller.

David Miller was a son of Christian Miller, who was born in Center county, Pa, probably of German parentage. David Miller was a millwright by trade and was considered a good workman. With his wife he attended the Methodist church. In his political affiliation he was a Republican. The children born to David and Sarah Miller were S J; Clara, now deceased, was the wife of John Sarcen, Emory, John, who is a physician in practice at Kansas City; James, who is a practicing physician at Grampian, Pa, and Monroe.

After completing the common school course, S J Miller entered Dickinson Seminary at Williamsport, where he continued his studies for one year, after which he prepared for medical college and became a student in the New York University, where he was graduated in the class of 1886. He entered upon the practice of his profession at Ansonville, Pa, where he remained for ten years and then came to Madera. He is widely known professionally all through this section and for the past twelve years has been the Penn Ry Co's surgeon at Madera. Dr Miller has important business interests at Madera and in addition to those mentioned, he is also president of the Madera Water Company. He is an active and interested citizen and has been a member of the school board for fifteen years and is serving as its president.

In 1873 Dr Miller was married to Miss Emma Klare, a daughter of Andrew and Susan Klare, the former of whom was a shoemaker at Wallacetown, Pa. Mrs Miller is one of the following family. Josephine, who is the wife of John Harkins, May, who is the wife of Ross Wynn, Edna, who is the wife of John Bard, Emma, who is the wife of Dr Miller, and Alfred, Frank, George and Martin.

Dr and Mrs Miller have five children, namely Vera, who is the wife of Fred Byer, of Tyrone, and John Donald, Frank, Lois and Muriel. Dr Miller and family attend the Methodist Episcopal church. He is a prominent Free Mason, belonging to the Blue Lodge at Curwensville, the Chapter at Clearfield; the Commandery at Philipsburg, the Consistory at Williamsport, and the Shrine at Altoona. He is identified also with the P S O of A, at Madera.

PETER BEAUSEIGNEUR, farmer and lumberman of Girard township, Clearfield county, Pa, was born in France and was brought to America by his parents in 1854, and they settled on the homestead now owned by his brother James Beauseigneur In 1875 he purchased a farm of 160 acres, situated two miles west of the old homestead, where he has been living ever since

On October 26, 1875, Peter Beauseigneur was married to Miss Elizabeth McGovern, of Girard township, where she was born and reared Eleven children have been born to them, namely Q E, Blanche, Virginia, Fannie, Vernon A, J B, Cavanaugh, Susie, Monica, Rae and Jane The beloved mother of these children died in 1908 She was a good, Christian woman, a faithful member of St Mary's Catholic church at Frenchville, to which her husband and children also belong Farming and stockraising are carried on by Mr Beauseigneur and his sons and they are numbered with the substantial men of the township They take no very active part in politics but are always ready to perform the duties required of them as good citizens Mr Beauseigneur is well known all through this section and his advice and co-operation are often sought by his fellow citizens

GILLESPIE B YEANEY, M D, who has been successfully engaged in the practice of medicine at Clearfield, Pa, since 1904, was born October 25, 1880 at New Mayville, Clarion county, Pa, and is the only son of Peter M and Nannie (Cummings) Yeaney of Clarion county, Pa His father is vice-president of the Second National Bank of Clarion and has been a resident of Clarion county all his life

Dr G B Yeaney was reared at Clarion, Pa, where he attended the high school, and also took a course at the Clarion Normal He took up the study of medicine at the Western Pennsylvania Medical College, now University of Pittsburg, and after graduating with the class of 1903 He then took a post graduate course in New York City In 1904 he came to Clearfield, Pa, where he has his office at his residence at No 104 South Second street, and has established an extensive practice, and won the confidence and esteem of his fellow citizens

Dr Yeaney was married September 12, 1904, to Ella Olsen, who is a daughter of Larsen Olsen (deceased), and they have one daughter, Catherine Pauline Dr Yeaney is a member of the American, the State and County Medical Societies, and also of several fraternal organizations He is politically a Republican, although inclined to be independent Dr and Mrs Yeaney are members of the Presbyterian church

ISAAC HILLER'S SONS, conducting a general harness store at Houtzdale, established this plant in this borough, in 1883, coming from Luthersburg, Clearfield county, where Isaac Hiller had been in business for fourteen years previously

Isaac Hiller was born September 4, 1832, at Krebstein, Wurtemberg, Germany, and when eighteen years of age accompanied his two brothers to America He learned the harnessmaking trade at Pittsburg and lived there for nine years, and then moved to Glen Hope, in Clearfield county, and eighteen months later to Luthersburg His death occurred at Houtzdale, February 9, 1904, and his burial was in the Brisbin cemetery Isaac Hiller has one brother living, Martin Hiller, residing at Marion, O

On November 4, 1859, Isaac Hiller was married to Miss Charlotte Clara Burket, who was born in 1840, in Doerzbach, Germany, and was seventeen years old when she came to America and lived at Marion, O , and at Pittsburg and also at Tyrone, Pa , where her brother resided One of her brothers, Christian, now lives at Altoona Mr and Mrs Hiller were members of the Lutheran church. They had the following children born to them Mary A , who was born August 21, 1860, died at the age of twenty-nine years. Charles Frederick, who was born January 9, 1862, at Tyrone, died young, Henry William, who was born July 14, 1864, died in infancy Christian Louis, who was born July 26, 1866, died in infancy, William Henry, who was born June 20, 1868, died at the age of fourteen years, Frederick John, who was born February 13, 1872, at Luthersburg, is agent for the Philipsburg and Susquehanna Railroad at Houtzdale, and is also a member of the firm of Isaac Hiller's Sons, married Margaret Conrad, and they have two children—David and Margaret Elizabeth, Edward Herman, who was born October 7, 1875, at Luthersburg, is employed in the First National Bank at Houtzdale, George Albert, who was born March 29, 1879, resides at Ramey, Pa , and Philip Ernest, who was born August 4, 1881, is manager of the business of Isaac Hiller's Sons He is also a member of the Houtzdale Fire Company The Hillers are all Republicans in politics, and Edward H has served several terms as borough auditor They are all representative business men and thoroughly respected citizens They are members and liberal supporters of the Lutheran church

ASHER GURNEY GORMAN GLENN, an enterprising citizen of Burnside township, where he is engaged in agriculture, was born on the old Gorman homestead in this township, June 13, 1872 His father, Daniel Gorman, who was born at Elderton, Armstrong county, Pa , settled at an early date at New Washington, Clearfield county Later he bought land and established the Gorman homestead near Mt Joy church He was engaged during his life in lumbering, farming and rafting His father, the grandfather of our subject, was a tax collector in Indiana county, who, while traveling his rounds during a severe winter storm, lost his way and was subsequently found frozen to death Daniel Gorman died in October, 1885, when he was 60 years old He was three times married, his first wife being Nancy Maria Neff, a daughter of J B and Catherine (Barnhart) Neff, and a granddaughter of John Neff, a former resident of Howardville, Center county, Pa She was a sister of Gideon D Neff, a prominent farmer of Burnside township Of this union were born three children William Gorman, who resides in Kansas, James L , and Maria, who is the wife of William Zimmerman After the death of the mother of these children, Daniel Gorman married Nancy King, a daughter of John and Nancy (McCreary) King Of this marriage there were six children, of whom four are now living—John K , Horace S , Rachel and Asher Gurney Daniel Gorman was a third time married, his third wife being Elizabeth McGarvey, who is still living She was the mother of three children—A. M , residing at LaJose, Pa , David and Daniel Gorman of Connecticut

Asher G Gorman was about twenty months

old when he was deprived of his mother by death and he was then adopted by Daniel and Sarah (King) Glenn of Indiana county, Mrs Glenn being an aunt of his by marriage, or in other words a sister of his father's second wife, Nancy King Gorman On his adoption by them he took the name of Glenn, which he has since retained In his youth he attended school for the usual period, and is also a graduate of Clark's Commercial College of Erie, Pa He was early initiated into habits of industry, following both agriculture and lumbering In 1887 he took up in addition the agricultural implement business, becoming a salesman In 1907 he bought the old Gorman home, the residence being one of the largest and most mansion-like in Burnside township and possessing one of the largest fruit orchards He is also engaged in the breeding of thoroughbred live stock, having shipped to thirteen different States He is a member of the Grange and has served on the township school board Politically he has been a Prohibitionist for many years

Mr Glenn was married in 1894 to Lulu Stephens, a daughter of David and Bella (Dickson) Stephens, and of this union have been born six children, namely Sarah M, now aged thirteen years, Daniel aged eleven, Annabelle, eight, Alice, six, David, three, and Ethel, one year

GEORGE B SHUGART, who owns two valuable farms in Boggs township, Clearfield county, Pa, residing on one which contains seventy-six acres, adjoining the second one, of 107 acres, is one of the leading men of this section, a justice of the peace, township supervisor and treasurer of the school board Mr Shugart was born in Knox township, Clearfield county, in October, 1862, and is a son of Henry B and Elizabeth (Sloppy) Shugart

Henry B Shugart was born in Schuylkill county, Pa, a son of Henry Shugart He followed farming all his life and was a successful business man In his political views he was a Democrat He married Elizabeth Sloppy, who was born in Franklin county, a daughter of Christian Sloppy They were members of the Methodist Episcopal church and reared their children in the same religious faith These were John, Daniel W and Martin, twins, George B, G L, Mary C, wife of Finley Reiter, J Frank, Jennie, wife of Frank Watkins David Milton, and Martha Annetta, wife of Hiram Straw

George B Shugart attended the common schools only but in all the practical things of life is a well informed and broad-minded man Prior to purchasing the farm on which he lives, from William D Bigler, and the second farm from E C Crumrine, he was engaged in lumbering and mining He now carries on a general agricultural line and raises stock for his own use He has been a very active and progressive citizen of his section and his many qualifications that fit him well for office, have been generally recognized In addition to the offices already mentioned, Mr Shugart is fire warden of his district, appointed by Warden Robert S Conklin, and he has served acceptably as township clerk and auditor

Mr Shugart was married June 12, 1881, to Miss Ida Wisor, a daughter of Henry and Mary Ann (Odell) Wisor The father was a native of Clearfield county and the mother of Franklin county They had the following children Ella, who is the wife of David Flegal, Ida, who is the wife of Mr Shugart, Catherine Agnes, who is the wife of Frank

Eberts, Cordelia, who is the wife of P H Flegel, and Fred B Mr and Mrs Shugart have nine children, namely Frank L, Alma A, Foster H, Jacob D, Theresa D, G Fred, Blake B, Emma E and Ellen Alma I is the wife of Thomas Wilsoncroft, and Theresa D is the wife of A H Good Mr Shugart and family attend the United Brethren church He is identified fraternally with the K G E and the I O U A M, both at Clearfield

N F K AKE, M D, physician and surgeon, at Curwensville, Pa, where he has been established in practice since the summer of 1897, is a member of an old Pennsylvania family of high standing He was born August 11, 1873, at Reynoldsville, Jefferson county, Pa, and is the only child of his parents, Samuel V and Frances P (Kelly) Ake His father was a general merchant at Houtzdale, Pa, for a number of years His great-grandfather once owned the land for many miles surrounding the present town of Williamsburg, Blair county, which was then called Akestown, in his honor

N F K Ake was afforded excellent educational advantages and is a graduate of Houtzdale High School and later from the Medico-Chirurgical College at Philadelphia in 1897 On August 3, 1897, he established himself in medical practice at Curwensville, where he has met with more than usual success He is a member of a number of the leading medical societies and has served as medical examiner for numerous insurance organizations Politically he is a Democrat

Dr Ake was married October 21, 1896, to Miss Bertha Biddle Carter, a daughter of William V and Hannah E (Biddle) Carter, of Philadelphia, and they have three children,

Kenneth Whittier, Frances Lenore and Hannah Dorothy Dr Ake is a member of the Masonic fraternity

HON FRANK G HARRIS, formerly a member of the Pennsylvania House of Representatives, state treasurer during a period of national financial stringency, and a representative citizen in business and social life in Clearfield county as well as prominent in public affairs, was born in Karthaus township, Clearfield county, Pa, November 6, 1845 His parents were John and Eleanor (Graham) Harris, and his maternal great-grandfather was Judge James Boggs, once a prominent jurist in Center county

When four years old, Frank G Harris was left motherless and was taken to the home of his uncle and aunt, Clark and Hetty (Graham) Patchin, and he remained with them until he was old enough to begin to provide for himself He was about twelve years of age when he started to work in the lumber regions and he continued lumbering, and rafting on the river, until he was twenty-five years of age This is sturdy man's work and Mr Harris enjoyed its physical difficulties, but he possessed an ambition also that prompted him to prepare for a career in which his intellect would be called into play Thus, while following lumbering during the regular season, he employed himself during the other months of the year in study and made excellent progress, so that in 1873 he was graduated from Dickinson Seminary, at Williamsport, Pa, and in 1876, from Lafayette College, at Easton, Pa.

Mr Harris followed teaching for the next five years, residing during this time at Clearfield, and put in all his spare time studying law, and in 1879 he was admitted to the bar

ROLL B. THOMPSON

of Clearfield county With the broadening and training of his mind came an interest in public affairs and his identification with the Republican party and for many years he has been an important factor in politics in his state From 1881 to 1883 he served as chairman of the Republican County Committee and served seven years as a member of the Clearfield borough council In 1896 he was first elected a member of the House of Representatives and was re-elected in 1898 and again in 1901 In the latter year he was elected state treasurer and served two years in that position In all these and in other public capacities he served with circumspection, honesty and marked ability Since partially retiring from public life, Mr Harris has given attention to his law practice, has traveled extensively and has also been interested in real estate and banking

Mr Harris was married April 15, 1879, at Lock Haven, Pa, to Miss Elizabeth F Baird, of one of the old families of Clinton County, and three children were born to them, all of whom died in infancy Mrs Harris died in Philadelphia, May 1, 1904 Mr Harris later married Miss Glenora Gearhart, of Clearfield, Pa They are members of the Methodist Episcopal church at Clearfield, of which he is an official He is a director in the Clearfield Trust Company and of the Clearfield Hospital In his fraternal relations he is an Odd Fellow and a Mason of high degree, being identified with the advanced branches of the order and is a Shriner

ROLL B THOMPSON, who holds the office of prothonotary of Clearfield county, Pa, in which he is now serving his second term, was born in Curwensville, this county, June 30, 1872 His parents are Alexander I T and Catherine (Lytle) Thompson, the former of whom was born in Clearfield county in 1834 He was formerly interested in the lumber business but is now living retired at the age of seventy-seven years

Roll B Thompson was educated in the public schools of Curwensville and at the Maine Central Institute of Pittsfield, Me, being graduated from the latter institution in 1891 From early manhood Mr Thompson has been an active Republican, and prior to his first term as prothonotary had excellent training in a county office, serving as first deputy under his brother, Grant H Thompson On November 8, 1904, he was elected to his present office, being re-elected in November, 1907 The business of this office is carried on carefully and systematically, and those having business with the courteous officials have generous praise for the present incumbent Mr Thompson is a thirty-second degree Mason of the Williamsport Consistory, belonging to Clearfield Lodge and Chapter and to the Knights Templar Commandery at Philipsburg

On June 9, 1910, Mr Thompson was married to Miss Alma E Dickinson, a daughter of Dr and Mrs Bayard T Dickinson, of Steelton, Pa His residence is at 725 South Second street, Clearfield

DAVID P LOUGHHEAD, one of the substantial citizens of Bigler Township, Clearfield County, Pa, who is the owner of a fine residence at Beulah, Pa, and owner and proprietor of a bakery at this place, has other valuable property including coal lands in different parts of the county   He was born April 17, 1856, in Bradford County, Pa, and is a son of Jefferson and Esther (Palmer) Loughhead

Jefferson Loughhead was of Scotch ancestry but was born in New York   In his earlier years he was a shoemaker but later studied medicine and became a practitioner of the Homeopathic system   He married Esther Palmer, who was a native of Bradford County, Pa, and they had the following children   David P, Charles, John, Clara J, and Frederick J

David P Loughhead had only common school advantages in his youth and is, more or less, a self educated and self made man   He was variously engaged for a number of years and came to Bigler Township in 1879   In 1900 he was appointed constable and subsequently was elected to the office in which he served until 1907   He was elected assessor of Bigler Township, on the Republican ticket, in 1909 and is serving in this office and also is deputy game warden of the State   In August, 1910, Mr Loughhead in association with his son, started the Beulah Baking Company, at Beulah, Pa, and the enterprise has been very successful   The younger partner, David P Loughhead, Jr, is a practical baker, having learned the trade at Cresson, Pa   They have one assistant and run a daily wagon to the surrounding towns, the output being 300 loaves of bread a day together with other bakery goods

In 1887, Mr Loughhead was married to Miss Mary J Miller, a daughter of Solomon and Elizabeth (Shepley) Miller, who had other children, namely Jacob, Caroline, Cyrus, George, Peter, Henry and Emma   Mr and Mrs Loughhead have but the one son David P, Jr, who is a very enterprising young business man   Mr Loughhead and family attend the Methodist Episcopal church   He is identified with Lodge No 669, Odd Fellows, at Glen Hope, Pa

WILLIAM F TOZER, proprietor of the City Hotel at Blain City, Clearfield County, Pa, one of the leading and well patronized hostelries of Beccaria Township, formerly was interested to a considerable extent in farming and lumbering   He was born August 28, 1858, at Newburg, Pa, and is a son of Gilbert S and Margaret (Weaver) Tozer

Gilbert S Tozer was born in New York State and came from there to Clearfield County in the thirties, and became a well known lumberman and raftsman   He met with an accidental death while driving a raft down the Susquehannah River, at Wood Rock, in 1878, when he was aged sixty-eight years   He married in Clearfield County and bought land in Chest Township and built the first house in what was then called Tozertown, now Newburg   He married Margaret Weaver, who was born in Indiana County, Pa, one of seven sisters   Her father was Captain Weaver, who moved subsequently to Clearfield County   In her girlhood, Mrs Tozer assisted her father in his agricultural operations, as there were no sons, and occasionally she would help to cut the grain, using the old fashioned scythe   Mrs Tozer still survives and is now in her eightieth year, although her appearance would indicate that not more than fifty years had passed over her head   She is an active member of the Presbyterian church   To Gilbert S Tozer and wife the following children were born. William F, Isabella, deceased, who was the wife of Alonzo Hurd, Mary, who is the wife of Jefferson Trostle, of New Washington, Pa ; Sarah, who is the wife of Daniel Curry, of Mahaffey,

Pa , Jacob S , who carries on farming on the old homestead in Ferguson Township (married Prudence Jackson, a daughter of Andrew Jackson) , Ashley, who was accidentally killed by a street car, July 4, 1906 (was an employe of the Pennsylvania Railroad Company and had married a daughter of M Reed, of Ferguson Township) , and Hugh, who resides at Tyrone (has been car inspector of piece work in the yards of the Pennsylvania Railroad Company, at Bellwood, for years, married Blanche Hadden)

William F Tozer was the fourth born in the above family In 1871 he accompanied his parents to Ferguson Township, Clearfield County and afterward attended the public schools there for a short time For a number of years he was connected in some way with the lumber industry, being identified at different times with the Clearfield Lumber Company, the Belsena Lumber Company (six years with the former and three with the latter), then four years with the Irvona Lumber Company and for two more years was in the lumber business at Bellwood Then he came to Coalport to educate his children Prior to coming to Blain City he purchased the James Rea farm in Ferguson Township Mr Tozer has been in the hotel business at Blain City for some years and holds his fifth license In politics he is a Democrat and has served in the offices of supervisor and constable He has been a very active citizen in a public spirited way since making Blain City his home and has been particularly interested and useful in advancing the educational interests of the place He took an active part in the erection of the new school building here, contributing time, money and lumber, his activity not ending here, as through his efforts a high standard has been established

23

and a course of four years of thorough training accorded students

Mr Tozer was married in 1883 to Miss Maggie B Johnston, a daughter of James W and Mary Jane Johnston, of Jordan township, Clearfield County, and they have had seven children, namely Roy V , Ory, Alice, Wilson, Sadie, Ira L , and Bessie, the last named being now deceased Four of the above family hold teacher's certificates and all are unusally intellectual The eldest son, Roy V , was principal of the Irvona schools for two years. taught two years at La Jose and four terms in his native township He is a student of law at Valparaiso, Ind , and will be admitted to the bar in June, 1911 Alice has been a teacher in the public schools of Beccaria Township for four years and has four rooms of the Rosebud public school The two younger children are yet in school Mr Tozer and his older sons are identified with several fraternal organizations, he being a member of Lodge No 540, Elks, at Clearfield, the eldest son being a member of the Red Men at Mahaffey, the second son of the Eagles at Bellwood, and the third son, of the Moose at Coalport The family belongs to the Presbyterian church and several of them teach classes in the Sunday-school Mr Tozer placed a beautiful memorial window in this church in memory of his daughter who died in early womanhood

MITCHELL NEWCOMB, who is one of Girard Township's best known and substantial and trustworthy men, lives on the farm of 35 acres in Girard Township, Clearfield County, Pa , on which he was born in 1859, and owns also 235 acres of valuable farm and coal land here He is a son of John and Rebecca (Jury) Newcomb

John Newcomb was born in Ireland He came to Clearfield County on July 4, 1847 and being pleased with the country made up his mind to settle permanently in Girard Township, where he was married in 1851, to Rebecca Jury, who still survives, being now in her seventy-eighth year She is a daughter of Abraham Jury, who was one of the early settlers who died a Catholic in this section John Newcomb was a farmer and died on the farm on which he had lived for half a century, December 14, 1903, aged 89 years, 11 months, 11 days

Mitchell Newcomb obtained his education in the country schools and at Odessa He has always devoted himself to farming and stock-raising and has carried on these industries very successfully His land is very valuable, as a large part is underlaid with coal, which he has never sold Mr Newcomb has never married With his venerable mother he belongs to St Mary's Catholic Church at Frenchville

GEORGE M FULFORD, a representative member of the Clearfield bar, who is also interested in both fire and life insurance here, was born at Clearfield, Pa , January 2, 1870, and is a son of John H and Nannie E (Smith) Fulford

The late John H Fulford was born in Bedford County, Pa , February 11, 1838 He studied law at Bedford and later at Clearfield and after being admitted to the bar, formed a law partnership with his former preceptor, Joseph B Menally, which continued until the latter was elevated to the county bench Mr Fulford continued in the practice of law during the remainder of his life, his death occurring on June 27, 1877 At one time he was principal of the school which held its sessions in an old town hall, which stood on the site of George M Fulford's residence In politics, John H. Fulford was a Republican and during many campaigns worked effectively for his party, being in great demand as an orator. He married Nannie E Smith, who was born at Binghampton, N Y, and is a daughter of Henry Bordman Smith, who came with his family to Clearfield County in her girlhood Henry B Smith was a man of fine business perceptions and for a number of years was largely interested in lumbering, acquiring vast tracts of valuable timber land Mrs Fulford is a member of the Daughters of the American Revolution and is regent of the local body She claims her membership through her great-grandfather, Ichabod Buck, who was a captain in the Revolutionary War, in the Massachusetts line and who lived to the unusual age of 93 years

George M Fulford was the second born in his parents' family of three children, an elder brother, Henry Bordman, being a resident also of Clearfield, and a younger, John H., of DuBois, Pa. After completing the common and high school course at Clearfield, he made preparations to enter college but subsequently decided to immediately become a law student in the office of Menally & McCurdy, at Clearfield, although then but nineteen years of age For a short time prior to this he had served with the engineering force employed in the construction of the Beach Creek Railroad Mr Fulford was admitted to the bar in May, 1891, and after an initial practice of nine months, became a member of the law firm of Orvis & Snyder, continuing this connection until the death of Judge Orvis, since when he has practiced alone. In June, 1904, Mr Fulford, in partnership with his older brother, bought out the insurance business of Ward & Smith Evidences of vigor in the new firm were soon shown and the business has continued to expand until this firm carries fire, life, accident, plate glass, and other risks, having the agency of many old and standard companies. The offices of the firm are located on the third floor of the Trust Building, where Mr Fulford also maintains his law office

In politics Mr Fulford is a Republican but has never tested the sincerity of his friends by permitting the use of his name for office. He was reared in the Presbyterian church and is active in Sunday-school work, being the beloved teacher of a bright class of youths. With his son, John H Fulford, he resides at No 211 Pine Street, Clearfield

JAMES GATEHOUSE, coal-operator, and for the past six years supervisor of Bigler Township, Clearfield County, Pa, was born in South Wales, March 9, 1843, and is a son of John and Mary (Morgan) Gatehouse, both of whom died in Wales. The father was manager of a large farm in Wales belonging to a land company. Both he and wife were members of the Baptist church. They had six children but four died in infancy, James and Thomas being the only survivors. The grandparents, James Gatehouse and John Morgan were both natives of Wales

James Gatehouse remained in his own land until he reached manhood. In 1865 he came to the United States and located at Beaver Meadows, in Carbon County, Pa, but in the next year moved to Center County and from there went to Maryland, and in 1883 came to Clearfield County, where he has lived ever since. For twenty-five years he has been engaged in mining and shipping coal. For six years he was superintendent for a coal mining company at Chesterfield, Pa, in 1908 opening his present mine, under the name of Port No 1, on the New York Central Railroad, and shipped his first coal in 1910. He gives employment to some 65 men and his output is 200 tons daily

On July 31, 1862, Mr Gatehouse was married to Miss Diana Williams, a daughter of Thomas and Anna (Davis) Williams, who also came from Wales. Of their family there are but two surviving daughters. Mrs Gatehouse and Mary, who is the widow of Thomas Parker and lives in Australia. Mr and Mrs Gatehouse have had the following children Mary, who is the wife of John H Steckman, Louisa, who is the wife of Samuel Markley, Thomas W, John, who is deceased, Diana, who is the wife of Frank Havely, Edith, who is deceased, James C, Gomer, and Anna, who was the oldest of the family and died when a beautiful young woman in her eighteenth year. Not connected formally with any political party, Mr Gatehouse casts his vote as his judgment dictates. He is a Knight Templar Mason, belonging to the Blue Lodge at Coalport, the Chapter at Clearfield, and the Commandery at Phillipsburg. He belongs also to the Knights of the Golden Eagles at Brisbin, being a charter member of the lodge there, and also to the B of A, at Chesterfield. With his family he belongs to the Methodist Episcopal church. Mr Gatehouse stands high in the regard of his fellow citizens who recognize in him a man of honesty of purpose, good intentions and strict integrity. He has always been a hard worker and has made his own way in the world, through industry and perseverance gaining long since a sturdy and self respecting independence

GEORGE W WOOD, M D , physician and surgeon at Houtzdale, Pa , and proprietor of a drug store in this borough, has been a resident of the place since May 1, 1891, and during this period has been actively engaged in the practice of his profession   Dr Wood was born January 4, 1860, at Wellsville, N Y , and is a son of Coe Harvey and Adelia (Parrott) Wood

Coe Harvey Wood was born just outside the city of New York, and his wife's people came from the vicinity of Poughkeepsie, N Y   After marriage they moved from New York to Pennsylvania and settled near Shawsville, in Clearfield County, where he purchased a farm and also engaged in lumbering   From there they moved to West Clearfield, in 1904, where Mr Wood died June 28, 1905, and his burial was in the Clearfield Cemetery   He was a son of George W Wood and the family is of Scotch-English descent   The mother of Dr Wood survived until February 27, 1910, her death occurring at Houtzdale   The family consisted of four children, the only survivor being Dr Wood, of this record, who was the third in order of birth   The eldest, Charles, was a physician and died at Coalport, Pa   Alice, who was the wife of T H Litz, died at the old homestead near Shawsville   May, the youngest of the family, was the wife of Dr W H Dale, of Houtzdale, Pa

George W Wood attended school at Shawsville and entered upon his medical studies at the College of Physicians and Surgeons of Baltimore, Md , and later attended the Medico-Chirurgical College of Philadelphia   In the spring of 1890 he began practice at Glen Hope, Clearfield County, and in the following spring came to Houtzdale   In addition to attending to a large practice Dr Wood established his drug store on February 4, 1895, to which he gives careful attention and affords residents of the borough the opportunity to purchase drugs and preparations which are compounded not only by skilled chemists but under the supervision of an experienced physician

In June, 1890, Dr Wood was married to Miss Cora E Barker, who was born at Chest Springs, Pa , and was a baby when the family moved to Grinnell, Ia , and accompanied them in their return in 1889   She is a daughter of Gilbert A and Elizabeth (Allen) Barker, the former of whom died in 1903   Mrs Barker resides at Coalport, Pa   Dr Wood is a Republican in politics   In every sense he is a good citizen, and lending support to every enterprise calculated to advance the public welfare he has won the respect, confidence and esteem of the people with whom he has chosen to make his home

ELMER BRUCE McCARDELL, who is agent at Westover for the New York Central and Pennsylvania Railroads and for the Adams Express Company and American Express Company, was born at New Washington, Clearfield county, Pa , March 7, 1878   He is a son of David Alexander and a grandson of John McCardell, the latter of whom came to this county from Indiana county, locating at Burnside, where he died at the age of 84 years   He married Jane Pilson, a daughter of William Pilson

David A McCardell, father of our subject, was born at Indiana, Pa , December 26, 1841, and was brought up in the farming and lumbering industries   He served three years in the Civil war, in the 105th Pa Volunteers and took part in the battle of Gettysburg and other severe battles, being mustered out in August, 1864   After returning home he resided for a while on the parental homestead in Burnside township, but subsequently bought a farm near the Mt Joy church, not far from New Washington, which he conducted until 1882 He was then engaged in the lumber business at Burnside for several years and afterwards was engaged in the livery business for five years, selling out in 1891 He then carried on a livery business in Westover for several years but sold it in 1895 and was engaged thereafter in the grocery and restaurant business until 1904, when he was appointed postmaster of Westover, an office he now holds He is also proprietor of a general store in Westover He has served as Burgess of the borough and as a member of the school board He is a charter member of the Odd Fellows lodge at Burnside and a member of the Grand Army Post at Cherry Tree He has been twice married, first to Elizabeth Mitchell, who died in 1870 at the age of 28 years, of which union there were three children, all now deceased His second marriage was with Mary P Neff, in 1873, she being a daughter of Joseph L and Eliza M (Gallaher) Neff, and born Oct 27, 1850 The children of this marriage are Emma, wife of V K Rowland, of Westover, Sarah B, wife of George F Westover, Elmer B, subject of this sketch, James B, who married Lena Hurd and resides at Cresson, and Willard D, a resident of Cherry Tree, Pa

After attending school until the age of 18, the subject of this sketch entered the State Normal school at Lock Haven, Pa, where he remained for one term, teaching the following term in Burnside township He then took up the study of telegraphy and in 1899 entered the employ as telegrapher of the Pennsylvania Railroad Co, remaining thus engaged two years He then became joint agent for the New York Central and Pennsylvania Railroads and has thus continued up to the present time, in addition acting as agent for the American and Adams Express companies He is a member and one of the trustees of the Baptist church, also acting as secretary of the board of trustees A Republican politically, he has served on the borough council, and before coming of age acted as the clerk of the council At the age of 23 he was elected burgess of Westover, being at that time the youngest burgess in the county For the past seven years he has served as secretary of the borough school board It will readily be seen that Mr McCardell is a man of good business capacity, enjoying the full confidence of his fellow citizens

Mr McCardell was married, January 17, 1900, to Miss Matilda C Moore, who was born in Westover, February 25, 1876, a daughter of Charles T and Emma (McHenry) Moore Her father, who was a shoemaker by trade, is now deceased, her mother is still living and resides in Westover The latter is the daughter of Levi and Matilda (Shields) McHenry Mr and Mrs McCardell are the parents of three children Emma Belle, aged ten years, Guy Moore, aged six, and Wilbur Ralph, aged two

DORSEY J GINGERY, county commissioner of Clearfield County, Pa, is one of the county's best known and representative citizens and has been identified with public affairs for many years He was born in Center county, Pa, August 6, 1857, and is one of a family of six children born to his parents, who were Samuel and Maria (Dorsey) Gingery, the former of whom died in 1902, the latter having passed from earth in 1897

Dorsey J Gingery obtained his education in

the country schools and until he was nineteen years of age remained on his father's large farm   In 1876 he came to Clearfield County and has continued to reside here   When he reached manhood he identified himself with the Democratic party and is one of its influential factors in the county   His first business experience was as a clerk in a business house, where he made many friends, and in 1892 he was elected county prothonotary and served six years in that office   Shortly afterward he became connected with the clerical force in the sheriff's office, and in November, 1908, he was elected a member of the board of county commissioners

Mr Gingery married Miss Ada Albert, a daughter of George and Sophia Albert   They are members of the Methodist Episcopal church and are interested in its benevolent enterprises He belongs fraternally to L L O M, the order of the Moose, and to the Elks, being the oldest member of the last named organization in the county

MICHAEL REIDY, one of the best known and most respected retired farmers of Boggs Township, Clearfield County, Pa, who has just disposed of a farm of 109 acres but still retains some sixty acres lying just outside of Wallaceton, Pa, was born in Blair County, Pa, March 6, 1842, and is a son of Michael and Margaret (Clossin) Reidy   The father was an educated man and taught school in Blair County   Both he and his wife are now deceased, Michael being their only child

Michael Reidy had but limited school advantages   He entered a mill when he was quite young and learned the milling business and continued in it for fifteen years, in Center, Blair and Clearfield Counties   He then turned his attention more particularly to lumbering and continued nine years in that line   He bought his farm of 109 acres from John Wearning and operated it for many years but quite recently he has sold it to his son, Harry Reidy, who is a very capable and reliable resident of Morris Township   During the Civil War, Mr Reidy enlisted for service in 1861, entering Co H, 7th Pa Vol Inf, and was out for eight months, being fortunate enough to escape all serious injury   He is a member of John W. Geary Post, No 90, G A R, at Phillipsburg

In 1865 Mr Reidy was married to Miss Ella Odell, a daughter of John and Sarah (Ginter) Odell, residents of Clearfield County   Mrs Reidy has the following sisters: Agnes, who is the wife of Banister Benn, Jennie, who is the wife of Hiram Ellis, Cordia, who is the wife of Robert Abanathy, and Emma, who is the wife of John Stone. Mr and Mrs Reidy have three children: Harry, who resides on the home farm as mentioned above, Paul, who lives in California, and Edith, who is the wife of James McGee   Mrs Reidy is a member of the Adventist church   He is a Democrat but has never accepted any township office except that of school director

HARVEY T SMITH, who, for fifteen years has served as high constable of the borough of Curwensville, Pa, and fills other important public offices, was born April 28, 1843, in Pike Township, Clearfield County, Pa, and is a son of John J and Nancy J Smith, both now deceased

Harvey T Smith obtained his education in the old log school house known as the "Oakland"   He afterward helped his father on the home farm until the outbreak of the Civil War, when he enlisted for military service, becoming

JOHN STONE

a member of Co B, 149th Pa Vol Inf, the famous "Bucktail" regiment Mr Smith remained in the Union army until the Rebellion was suppressed and then returned to his home to re-engage in peaceful pursuits He has escaped all the many hazards that attend a soldier's life and came back practically unharmed Finding profitable employment as a lumber man he went into that business and continued until he settled on his present place in Curwensville He has a comfortable and commodious residence on McNaul Street, which he has occupied for twenty-two years

On December 5, 1872, Mr Smith was married to Miss Annie E Gensler, who was born at Sharpsburg, Allegheny County, Pa, June 13, 1855, a daughter of George and Nancy J (Schriver) Gensler George Gensler was born at Newport, Perry County, Pa, and his wife at Sharpsburg Both are now deceased, the father of Mrs Smith passing away at the age of sixty-five years and the mother when aged seventy-two years, his burial being at Curwensville and hers in Tioga County They were members of the Methodist Episcopal and Lutheran Church respectively Mrs Smith is one of a family of nine children, six of whom are living To Mr and Mrs Smith seven children were born, namely Percy E, who married Edith Daugherty, is in the ice and coal business and is constable of the Second Ward, and they have three children—Harold, Lee and Merl W, Clarence B, (who served in the Spanish American war, in Battery B, 4th Artillery) resides at Du Bois, married Mary Jordan, a daughter of Reuben Jordan, of Rockton, Pa, and they have four children—Otto, Ralph, Nellie and Annie, Oliver F, whose residence adjoins his father's at Curwensville, married Tensie Johnson, and they have had

five children—Raymond, Chester, Katie B, Frederick B and Dewey, deceased, Katherine, who died at the age of thirteen years, and is interred in Oak Hill Cemetery, Eugene F, who served in the Spanish-American War, in Co L, 5th Pa Vol Inf, was accidentally killed afterward, when at work, his young life being taken when he was but twenty-one years of age, Alice I, who is the wife of Fred McKenzie, lives across the street from her father, and they have two sons—Eugene and Harvey L, and Harvey, Jr, who is a student at Curwensville Mr and Mrs Smith are members of the Presbyterian church He has been identified with the Republican party ever since he became a voter and has been a very active and useful citizen He is a member of the Board of Health at Curwensville and is serving as a jury commissioner For many years he has been an Odd Fellow and has been through the chairs of the local lodge and belongs to the Encampment at Clearfield, and is a member also of the Red Men He served as street commissioner sixteen years and at present is not employed

JOHN STONE, merchant, farmer and stockraiser, in Boggs Township, Clearfield County, Pa, is also a prominent factor in public affairs in this section and stands as one of the representative men In addition to his store property he owns 325 acres of valuable land He was born in Boggs Township, August 21, 1845, and is a son of Alexander and Mary (Kephart) Stone

Alexander Stone was born in England but spent the larger part of his life in the United States He owned and operated farm land in Boggs Township for many years and was proprietor of a hotel at Stoneville, Pa He married Mary Kephart, who was born in Clearfield County, Pa , a daughter of Andrew Kephart, of German descent   Mr and Mrs Stone were members of the Methodist Episcopal church   They had the following children born to them   Elizabeth, who is deceased, was the wife of Daniel Dugan, Jane, who is the wife of John Blair, Mary Ann, who is now deceased, was the wife of Patrick Gallagher, Charlotte, who is deceased, and John, who was the youngest born of the family

John Stone, the youngest born and the only son of his parents, was given excellent educational advantages, attending the public schools and Clearfield Academy   In his youth and in this neighborhood, the majority of the young men earned their first money through work in the woods and Mr Stone has been interested to some degree in lumbering all his life since, in addition to farming   He inherited 100 acres of the homestead and later purchased 125 acres from Daniel Ross, and subsequently 100 acres more, from Latimer Barger   He engages in general farming and deals quite extensively in stock   His general store is located in the village of Stoneville   He has been an active and useful citizen in his section since early manhood   He was reared in the Democratic party and has continued his identification with the same   For fifteen years Mr Stone has served as school director and has been township assessor two terms and township auditor for the same length of time

Mr Stone was married first to Miss Josephine Lumadue, a daughter of William and Mary Lumadue, natives of Clearfield County   To this marriage four children were born   Alexander, William, Franklin and Harry   He was married second to Miss Emma Odell, a daughter of John and Mary Ann Odell, early settlers in this section and residents of Wallaceton   Three children have been born to this marriage   Sybil, who is the wife of Geo Pearson , Ara, who is the wife of George Stover and John O   Mr Stone and family attend the Methodist Episcopal church   He belongs to the Grange

MRS LAURA N SANKEY, who resides in great comfort on her valuable farm of 180 acres, situated in Goshen township, Clearfield county, Pa , came to this place with her late husband some fifty years ago   Mrs Sankey was born in Lawrence township, Clearfield county, Pa , two miles east of Clearfield, and is a daughter of Henry and Mary (Ogden) Irwin, and the widow of John Sankey

Henry Irwin was of Irish parentage but his birth took place in Lawrence township, Clearfield county, where his life was spent, his death occurring in 1890   For many years he was a representative man in his neighborhood and he and wife were well known and highly regarded people and were leading members of the Presbyterian church   They were parents of three sons and eight daughters and one son and three daughters still survive

Laura N Irwin grew to womanhood on her father's farm and was instructed in all housewifely arts by a careful and capable mother   She obtained her education in the Wolf Run school in Lawrence township   In December, 1854, she was married to John Sankey, who was born in Center county, Pa , and died in 1893, in Goshen township, Clearfield county   His father was William Sankey, an old resident of Center county and John Sankey worked on the home farm and then learned the blacksmith's trade   After marriage, Mr and Mrs Sankey resided at Shawville for six years, where he worked at the

JOHN SANKEY

MRS. LAURA N. SANKEY

blacksmith's trade, and then bought the present farm, of Abraham Leonard Mr Sankey almost completed the clearing of this land and engaged in farming to some degree, but gave the larger part of his time to blacksmith work, erecting his own shop on his farm He was a quiet, reliable, home-loving man and was respected by his neighbors and by all who had business dealings with him At the time of his death he was sixty-one years of age He was a consistent member of the Goshen Methodist Episcopal church and his burial was in the cemetery attached to this church In politics he was a Republican and he took an intelligent interest in the public affairs of his community and at times served efficiently in public office He was a charter member of the Goshen Grange

To Mr and Mrs Sankey the following children were born Mary L, who is the wife of William Lansberry, of Goshen township, William Henry, who died in infancy, John Wesley and Ira B, both of whom also died in infancy, Elva Lucy, who is the wife of Charles Hall, of West Newton, Pa, Lillie Maude, who is the wife of Irwin Passmore, living in California, U S Grant, who lives in Goshen township, married Anna Morrison, Annie L, who is now deceased, was the wife of Harry Shirey, Myron L, who is the wife of John Lynch, of DuBois. Pa, Stella Belle, who resides at Colton, Calif, Burton G, who is a resident of Clearfield, married Estella Read, and Samuel Irwin, in business at Clearfield, who married a Miss Hockenberry Mrs Sankey is a member of the local Bell Telephone Company, belongs to and takes part in the social life of the Goshen Grange and is a charter member of the Goshen Methodist Episcopal church

AARON MURRAY, who, for forty-seven years has been a continuous resident of Guard Township, Clearfield County. Pa, where he is part owner of 204 acres of valuable farm and coal land, was born on this farm and is a son of Anderson and Perninah (Kyler) Murray. the former of whom, a native of Clearfield County, cleared this farm by his own efforts

Aaron Murray attended the district schools in his boyhood when his father could spare him, but from youth has been more or less engaged actively in farming and stockraising, coming into possession of the farm at the death of his parents They were among the best known and most highly respected old settlers of the township Mr Murray takes an active interest in township matters being especially interested at all times in good roads and good schools In politics he is a Republican and on the ticket of that party he was elected township assessor, in February, 1909 He has served acceptably also on the election board and is considered one of the township's representative and trustworthy men

In 1903 Mr Murray was married to Miss Fannie B Graham, of Girard Township, and they have four children Genevieve May, Annabel, Zella Marie, and Hannah Perninah Mr Murray and family belong to the Methodist Episcopal church

JOHN L LIGHTNER, who for more than twenty-three years has served as justice of the peace at Coalport, Pa, has been prominently identified with the progress and development of this section of Clearfield County during a long period Born in Clearfield County. Pa, August 26, 1850, Mr Lightner is a son of John and Annie (Groom) Lightner, and a grandson of John Lightner, a native of Germany and a soldier in the patriot army during the Revolutionary War

John Lightner, the father of John L Lightner, was born near Carlisle, in Cumberland County, Pa, in 1805, and when but thirteen years of age left home to make his own way in the world, securing his first contract in the construction of the old tidewater canal and assisting to build the Columbia bridge which was burned during the Civil War For some time he kept the Oulet lock on the Pennsylvania Canal, but subsequently, in 1847, brought his family by team and wagon to a farm near Blain City, and paid $1,000 in gold for a farm of 150 acres, which he eventually cleared of the pine, hemlock and hardwood timber Here Mr Lightner died May 28, 1890 He married Annie Groom, who was born in Bucks County, Pa, and they became the parents of fourteen children, of whom seven grew to maturity, as follows William, engaged in the lumbering business up to the time of his death in 1909, served during the Civil War as a member of the 105th Pa Vols, and has the distinction of being the only man in Irvona when that town was laid out, Martha, born in Columbia, Lancaster County, married John W Davis, Thomas G, a resident of Blain City, formerly owned 700 acres of coal and timber land on the present site of the town of Coalport, removed to Tyrone in 1867 and there conducted the Clearfield Hotel until his return to Clearfield County about 1886, where he is now living retired, John L, between whom and his elder brothers five children are deceased, Adda married Thomas McQuillen of Tyrone, Alice is the wife of James McClure, of Wilkinsburg, Allegheny County and George, a farmer of Chest Township, Clearfield County, married a daughter of Judge Hockenberry, formerly associate judge of Clearfield County.

John L Lightner attended the local schools and took a four years' course at Tuscarora Academy, in Juniata County, a Presbyterian institution at what was then known as Academia He graduated in 1871, after a four-years course in civil engineering, and immediately engaged in teaching, a profession which he followed for twelve years in Clearfield County and one term in Cambria County About 1883 he identified himself with the firm of Shaw & Dotts, and while with them laid out Blain City and sold the lots, after which, for a time, he was associated with Harry Krotzer. Mr Lightner was instrumental in securing the brick plant for Irvona, which will employ a large number of people, and in many ways has assisted in the building up of this part of Clearfield County He has devoted some time to the insurance business, purchased the Thompson interests after Mr Thompson's death, and since March, 1902, has been actively interested in the land business, as a superintendent of the firm of Whitmer Land Company and others, but he has not let his business activities keep him from what he considers his duties as a citizen and he has always been found doing his full share in this way Mr Lightner has ever been ready to give sound advice and settle disagreements, and his reputation as a peacemaker led his fellow citizens, in 1887, to elect him to the office of justice of the peace, in which capacity he has acted to the present time

In February, 1903, Mr Lightner was married to Miss Zellah McCune, the daughter of Easton McCune, of Irvona In National and state matters the Judge casts his vote with the Democratic party, but in local affairs lets his judgment decide which is the candidate best fitted for the office

WILLIAM J POWELL, superintendent of the plant of the W H Wynn & Co, manufacturers of fire brick, in Boggs Township, Clearfield County, Pa, resides in his attractive residence at Blue Ball, where he is one of the younger business men He was born at Woodland, in Bradford Township, Clearfield County, March 5, 1882, and is a son of George and Rebecca (Bumgarner) Powell

George Powell was born in Clearfield County, a son of William Powell, and resides at Blue Ball His life has been mainly devoted to lumbering He married Rebecca Bumgarner, who died in 1906, a daughter of Joseph and Jane Bumgarner To George Powell and wife the following children were born Cora, who married John Conrad, Lilly, who married John Palmer, William J, Charles, Albert, Margaret, who married Herman Cleaver and Genevieve, Morris, Boyd and Guy

William J Powell obtained his education in the public schools He then became identified with brick manufacturing and has continued in this industry In 1905 he was married to Miss Bertha Snyder, a daughter of Everhart and Margaret (Peters) Snyder Mr and Mrs Snyder reside at Woodland and Mr Snyder is a veteran of the Civil War Mrs Powell is the youngest of their children, the others being Curtin. Charles, Lilly, Marion, Frank and Fred Lilly married Thomas McCullough, and Marion married D E Young

Mr and Mrs Powell have one little daughter, Ethel They attend the United Brethren church He is a member of the P O S of A He is an independent voter but takes no very active interest in politics, devoting himself closely to business and he has become a recognized authority in this section, on brick manufacturing

W S PIPER, M D, one of the leading homeopathic physicians and highly esteemed citizens of Clearfield County, Pa, was born on his father's farm in Bedford County, Pa, January 19, 1882, and is a son of S F and Laura (Trimbath) Piper, old and respected citizens of Bedford County Dr Piper is the only son of a family of five children and spent his boyhood on the farm At the age of 13 years he entered Shirleysburg Academy, where he took a three years' course, and after teaching one year in Bedford County he took up the study of medicine He entered the Hahnemann Medical College of Philadelphia from which he graduated with the class of 1904, and during that same year located in Clearfield in the practice of his profession In 1906 he moved to his present office, which is located at his residence at No 110 Second Ave Dr Piper is a member of the staff of the Clearfield Hospital, and of the Kane Medical Society, the State Homeopathic Society, and the American Institution of Homeopathy He is fraternally a Mason, being a member of the Blue Lodge and Chapter of Clearfield, the Consistory of Williamsport, and the Shrine and Jaffa Temple of Altoona In politics he is a Republican On August 20, 1904, Dr Piper married Lena O Teeter, who is a daughter of A B Teeter, of Bedford County, Pa, and they have one daughter Elda Lenore Dr and Mrs Piper are members of the Presbyterian Church

E J WALKER, who, for the past twenty-five years has conducted a general store at Brisbin, Clearfield County, Pa, operating also in coal, under the firm name of E J Walker & Co , is one of the representative men of Woodward Township and is one of its most substantial citizens He was born January 13, 1856, at Tamaqua, Schuylkill County, Pa , and is a son of James and Mary (Hirsh) Walker

James Walker was a native of England and his wife of Germany Both are now deceased, the father passing away at Snow Shoe, Pa , and the mother at Bellefonte They had the following children Victoria, who is the wife of William W Temple, resides at McKeesport, Pa , Henrietta, who is the wife of Jeremiah Nolan, resides at Bellefonte , Emma, who is the wife of Jacob Rapp, lives at Bellefonte, E J , George W , who resides at Brisbin, Martha, who is the wife of Robert Forsythe, lives at Houtzdale, Snymickson, who is a resident of Bellefonte, and Daniel and John K , both of whom live at Trenton, N J

Edward J Walker was young when his parents moved to Snow Shoe, in Center County, where he was reared After attending school he went into railroad work for a time and during this period made his home at Reading, Pa , and later, for three years, at Trenton, N J From New Jersey he returned to Pennsylvania and lived first at Bellfonte and then spent three more years at Snow Shoe From there he came to Brisbin, a quarter of a century ago, and embarked in a general store business In 1901 the E J Walker & Co began operating in the coal fields, E J Walker being the financial backer, but in 1905 he admitted his sister-in-law, Mrs George W Walker to partnership This firm has high business rating and large operations are carried on

Mr Walker has never been very active politically but has always taken a deep interest in the general welfare of the community and has cast his vote according to his ideas of good citizenship He is a member and liberal supporter of the Baptist church

RAY CHESTER PATCHIN, a prosperous farmer and lumberman, residing at Patchinsville, Burnside township, was born at this place, July 13, 1877, a son of Aaron Wright and Elizabeth (Barrett) Patchin The Patchin family is one of wealth and importance in Clearfield county and is largely connected Samuel Patchin, the great grandfather of our subject, served in the Revolutionary war and being taken prisoner by the British, was sent abroad, but was later exchanged and returned home, passing the rest of his life in the state of New York The grandfather of our subject on the paternal side, was John Patchin, who died in 1863 at the age of 75 years.

Aaron W. Patchin, father of Ray Chester, was a well known and respected resident of Patchinsville, but is now deceased He married Elizabeth Barrett, who was born December 7, 1839, in Nottinghamshire, England, a daughter of George and Frances (Bexson) Barrett Her father came to America with his family in 1850, in a sailing vessel, the voyage taking ten weeks He settled in Indiana county, Pa , where he spent the rest of his life Elizabeth was the eldest of the family of four children, the others being Thomas, now residing in Indiana county, Ann Jane, unmarried, residing at Cherry Tree; and George Jr , a resident of Camden, N J , where he holds the office of sheriff George Barrett, the elder, died April 27, 1902 at the advanced age of 89 years , his wife died in 1892 at the age of eighty-one Before her marriage to Aaron W. Patchin, Elizabeth Barrett was engaged in teaching school in Indiana county She is still residing at Patchinsville, where she holds the office of postmistress, the post office there having been in charge of the Patchin family for the last 75 years, she having held it for the past 33 years She is a member of the Baptist church

Aaron W and Elizabeth Patchin were the parents of seven children, as follows Emma, wife of H P Dowler, who is in the employ of the Pennsylvania Railroad Co as superintendent, Olive, the wife of P Ake, a ship builder at Camden, N J, John H, a dealer in lumber and building supplies at Burnside, and a very prominent business man of that place, who has served in the state legislature, Winnie, who is the wife of J O Clark, president of the national bank at Glenn Campbell, Pa, Flora, wife of W J Dufton, a hardware dealer of Clearfield, Carl E, engaged in the lumber business at Burnside, and Ray Chester, direct subject of this sketch

Ray Chester Patchin attended school for the usual period in his boyhood but began industrial life at a comparatively early age He has been successfully engaged up to the present time in farming and lumbering and is an energetic and enterprising man who knows his business thoroughly and is respected by his fellow citizens In politics he is a Republican and has been quite an active worker for his party He is a member of the lodge of Redmen at Patchinsville, and of the I O O F lodge at Burnside

Mr Patchin was married July 11, 1910, to Miss Jessie Chapman, who was born in April, 1888, a daughter of James A and Anna (Mitchell) Chapman Her father, who was a native of Indiana county, was engaged in farming and lumbering and also in the coal business He died August 26, 1910, at the age

of sixty-one, his wife having previously died in 1906 at the age of 56 years

The latter was the daughter of Joseph and Sarah Ann (Mahaffey) Mitchell Mrs Patchin's brothers and sisters now living are as follows John H, a farmer, Smith S, also engaged in agriculture, Maud, residing at home, Mary, wife of John Hippes, of New Washington, Pa, Nellie, wife of H Young, a farmer, Grace, a teacher residing at home, Wayne, Daisy and Trudell, all teachers, the last mentioned residing at Burnside

JACOB W SCEURMAN, manager of the Grampian Supply Company store, at Grampian, Pa, secretary of the school board and also treasurer of the school funds, is one of the enterprising business men and leading citizens of the place He was born February 1, 1869, at Philipsburg, Center county, Pa, and is a son of Thomas L and Sarah (Williams) Sceurman

Thomas L Sceurman was born at Plainfield, N J He was reared in Monroe county, Pa, and married Sarah Williams, a daughter of Jacob and Elizabeth Williams Sarah Williams was born at Saylorsburg, Monroe county, Pa They became the parents of one son and three daughters Jacob W, Lydia, who died when five years old, Katherine, who is the wife of Samuel K Waring, of East Liberty, Pa, and Mary M, who is the wife of E D Vandling, of Clearfield, Clearfield county, they have two children—Katherine and Robert Thomas L Sceurman was a lumberman and later a carpenter His death occurred February 9, 1889, at the age of fifty-three years His widow died December 12, 1909, aged 77 years They were members of the Methodist Episcopal church at Philipsburg and they were interred in the cemetery belonging to that town

Jacob W Sceurman went to school through boyhood at Philipsburg and his first self-supporting work was done in a brickyard He was sixteen years old when he became a clerk in the general store of Wythes & Huffington, at Philipsburg, where he remained for four years Afterward he was with C Munson & Son, and subsequently with A J Graham, O P Jones and the Onnalinda Supply Company, at Onnalinda, in Cambria county, Pa, going from there to the Valley Supply Company, in Washington county Mr Sceurman was connected with the last named concern for one and one-half years and then came to Grampian His long experience had well qualified him in the line of merchandising and he became a valued employe of M Burns, whose business was later reorganized as the Grampian Supply Company, in which Mr Sceurman is interested as a stockholder, and of which he is general manager

On June 17, 1903, Mr Sceurman was married to Miss Anna R Carr, who was born in Woodland, a daughter of Jacob and Mary Carr, of Karthaus township, and they have one daughter, Sarah Katherine Mrs Sceurman died December 11, 1909, and her burial was at Philipsburg She was a lady of many virtues and was a valued member of the Methodist Episcopal church Mr Sceurman also belongs to this religious body and is liberal in the support he gives to its benevolent enterprises Fraternally he is a member of the Knights of Malta

WILLIAM HILLING, owner and proprietor of the Chesterfield House, a first class hotel at Ventland, Pa, which was started in June, 1906, is a native of Wales, where he was born May 4, 1852, and is a son of George and Eliza (Lewis) Hilling, and a grandson of John Hilling

William Hilling is one of a family of ten children, being the eighth in order of birth, his brothers and sisters bearing the following names James, Mary, Thomas, George, John, Eliza, Margaret, Lewis and Joshua Mr Hilling obtained his education in his native land where he remained until 1881, when he came to the United States He located at Philipsburg, Pa, and worked in the coal mines in that neighborhood for ten years and then conducted a store for six years longer and was also in the coal business there for four years, when he moved to McCartney, Pa, and carried on a coal business there for six years From there he came to Ventland and opened up his present hotel and has been very successful in this enterprise

Mr Hilling was married in 1872 to Miss Margaret Powell, a daughter of William and Margaret (Williams) Powell, who were natives of Wales and had four other children: William, Richard, Sarah and Mary Mr and Mrs Hilling have had three children, Margaret, who died in childhood, and Joshua and Thomas Mr and Mrs Hilling are members of the Episcopal church In politics he is a Democrat and in 1895 he was elected on the Democratic ticket, supervisor in Decatur township, in which he was then living He is a member of the L O O M at Philipsburg

JOSEPH SHAW, deceased, for many years was a representative citizen of Clearfield county, largely identified with the lumber industry and later a leading general merchant at Clearfield He was born March 26, 1817 on his father's farm in Bradford township, Clearfield county, Pa , and was a son of Richard and Mary (Irwin) Shaw

Richard Shaw was born in County Derry, Ireland, February 2, 1792 His parents, Archibald and Mary (Campbell) Shaw, emigrated to the United States when Richard was yet small They settled first in Chester county, from there moved to Mifflin county, and in 1810, to Clearfield county, their first purchased farm being situated in what is now the borough limits of Clearfield Richard Shaw became extensively interested in both farming and lumbering and for many years was active in business and public life In 1816 he married a daughter of Henry Irwin Mrs Shaw was born in Philadelphia and accompanied her parents in childhood to Clearfield county A large family of children were born to Richard Shaw and wife, the eldest of those who reached maturity being the late Joseph Shaw, whose death occurred at Clearfield, in 1907

Joseph Shaw grew to manhood on the family estate in Lawrence township and enjoyed such educational advantages as were obtainable at that day He inherited much of his father's business energy and capacity and very early interested himself in lumbering and conducted a saw-mill on Lick Run Subsequently for many years, he operated other business concerns successfully, conducting a general store at Clearfield until he retired in 1874 He was a Jeffersonian Democrat in his views on public questions, accepted official responsibilities at times and served as treasurer of Clearfield county. While he was noted for his keen business perceptions, he was equally respected for his sterling traits of character

Joseph Shaw married Miss Elizabeth Fulton, who died February 8, 1892, at the age of seventy-two years She was a daughter of Samuel Fulton, who was one of the first, perhaps the very first surveyor of Clearfield county Five children were born to Joseph and Elizabeth Shaw, namely R Newton Cornelia, Thaddeus H , Ella C and Alice The two survivors are Thaddeus H and Ella C , both of whom reside at Clearfield R Newton Shaw, formerly sheriff of Clearfield county, died March 12, 1905, Cornelia died in 1872, and Alice died in 1882 Joseph Shaw and family were members of the Presbyterian church The Shaw family has been so prominently identified with the history of Clearfield county that the prospering town of Shawville appropriately perpetuates the name

ERNEST RENAUD, who has spent his life in Girard township, Clearfield county. Pa , is an enterprising and successful agriculturist and resides on a 10½ acre tract of land adjoining the homestead tract of 84 acres, which is owned by his brother, and which is situated fifteen and one-half miles from Clearfield His parents were Victor and Mary Renaud, natives of France, who settled on this farm prior to his birth in 1870, and spent the remainder of their lives here After his school days were over, Mr. Renaud assisted his father on the home farm and has continued to carry on general farming and stockraising, farming the old homestead for his brother His industry and good judgment have brought him success and he is numbered with the prosperous farmers of this section

In 1898 Mr Renaud was married to Miss Ella Picard, who was born in Covington township, Clearfield county, and is also of French ancestry They have three children, Madeline. Alfonse and Charles Mr Renaud and family are members of St Mary's Catholic church at Frenchville He takes a good citizen's interest in township affairs, favoring good roads and good schools and for four years served as township supervisor

ALVIN U LEONARD, whose valuable farm of 140 acres is situated in Jordan township, Clearfield county, Pa, on the town line of Ansonville, is one of the enterprising and successful young farmers of this section He was born at Ansonville, Pa, March 4, 1886, and is a son of John W and Edith (Swann) Leonard

John W Leonard was born in Clearfield county and spent his entire life here He followed lumbering as his main business He married Edith Swann, who was also born in Clearfield county and now resides at Patton, Pa She is a daughter of Henry and Lucinda Swann John W Leonard was identified with the Republican party but never desired public office although he was a man well qualified to administer in the same He was a member of the Baptist church Of his children, Alvin U is the eldest and the only son, there being four daughters Helen L, Margaret J, Mary E and Harriet C

Alvin U Leonard completed the public school course and then spent one year at Bucknell University, subsequently taking a commercial course at Duff's Business College, at Pittsburg He then returned home and has devoted himself to farming and stock raising ever since This property is known as the Henry Swann farm but John W Leonard bought it about 1885, and at his death, on May 1, 1905, his son purchased it having operated it for three years previously In his success he has demonstrated the value of an educated man in agriculture, his modern methods and his use of improved machinery bringing about very satisfactory returns

Mr Leonard was married in January, 1906, to Miss Delilah Deihl, a daughter of Thomas and Martha (Bell) Deihl, and a granddaughter of Benjamin and Mary Diehl and of Frampton and Matilda Bell The parents of Mrs Leonard were residents of Bell's Landing, in Greenwood township, where Mr Diehl followed the blacksmith trade Mrs Leonard has one brother, Frank Diehl Three sons have been born to Mr and Mrs Leonard to whom have been given the names of John W, Thomas F and Robert H They attend the Baptist church Mr Leonard takes only a good citizen's interest in politics and, like his late father, is identified with the Republican party.

ROLAND DAVIS SWOOPE, Jr, the editor of this History, was born in Curwensville, Pa, on June 4, 1885, and is the second son of Roland D Swoope, Esq, and Cora Arnold Swoope, and a grandson of the late Hon Henry Bucher Swoope, widely known in his life time, as a brilliant orator, noted lawyer and as the founder and first editor of the "Raftsman's Journal," of Clearfield, Pa, and of the "Pittsburg Evening Telegraph," and who at the time of his death, in 1874, was United States Attorney for the Western District of Pennsylvania

Roland Davis Swoope, Jr, was educated at the public schools of his native town and at Mercersburg Academy, at Mercersburg, Franklin county, Pa After leaving school, he entered his father's law office where he remained until October, 1905, when he became editor of the Curwensville "Mountaineer," a

ROLAND DAVIS SWOOPE, JR.

Republican newspaper, in which his father was interested as one of the founders As will be noted by the foregoing, the subject of our sketch inherited his fondness for journalism and "The Mountaineer" under his editorship has become the leading Republican newspaper of Clearfield county and is recognized as a powerful factor in every political campaign

Mr Swoope, like his ancestors, developed a strong likeness for politics and has taken an active part therein Ever since attaining his majority, he has served as a member of the Republican Vigilance Committee of his election district For several years, he has been secretary of the Republican Committee of Clearfield county In April, 1908, he was elected as one of the five delegates to represent Clearfield county in the Republican State Convention, receiving 3,814 votes, the largest vote polled for any candidate

He has also represented the Republicans of his senatorial district at a meeting of the Republican State Committee and was appointed assistant sergeant at arms of the Republican National Convention which met in Chicago in 1908

Mr Swoope is a member of the Methodist Episcopal church of Curwensville, Pa , is a member of the Union League of Philadelphia, the most famous Republican Club in the United States, is also a member of Bethesda Lodge, No 821, Independent Order of Odd Fellows and has served the lodge as Noble Grand

Mr Swoope takes an active interest in all public affairs, and both personally and as editor of "The Mountaineer," he stands for the best interests of the people of the community, State and Nation

24

RICHARD SHAW, deceased, was once a man of high business standing and public station in Clearfield county, Pa He was born in County Derry, Ireland, February 2, 1792, and was a son of Archibald and Mary (Campbell) Shaw

Archibald Shaw was born in County Donegal, Ireland His wife was also of Irish birth but probably of Scotch ancestry Soon after the birth of their second son, Richard, they came to America and found their first home in Chester county, Pa From there they moved to Mifflin county and from there, in 1810, to Clearfield county Archibald Shaw and wife spent the remainder of their lives on the farm on which they then settled, living into the seventies

Richard Shaw was reared on the home farm, which was situated two miles north of the borough of Clearfield When twenty-four years of age he married and then located in Bradford township, Clearfield county, and for four years lived on a tract of 100 acres, locally known as Bid Lands From there he moved into Lawrence township and soon became interested in both farming and lumbering, acquiring in the course of years extensive tracts of land on the west side of the Susquehanna River He was a man of extraordinary enterprise and for years carried on farm industries, operated saw-mills and engaged in merchandising He also led his fellow citizens in public affairs and served continuously as a justice of the peace for years and also served in the office of associate judge He lived to be eighty-four years of age, his death occurring in 1876

Richard Shaw was married in 1816 to Miss Mary Irwin, a daughter of Henry Irwin, who came to Clearfield county as a pioneer from Philadelphia, where Mrs Shaw was born A large family of children were born to them and those who reached mature years were the following Joseph, who resides at Clearfield, Jane, who is now deceased, was the wife of Dr Hills, of Clearfield, Mary E, who is deceased, was the wife of John Patterson, A Henry and Richard, both of whom are deceased, Margaret, who became the wife of William A Wallace, of Clearfield, William (deceased), and A B, who resides at Clearfield Richard Shaw and wife were members of the Presbyterian church The town of Shawville perpetuates their honored name

JOHN A DALE, justice of the peace at Curwensville, Pa, now serving in his third term, is one of the representative citizens of this borough and is identified with numerous important interests He was born in Pike township, Clearfield county, Pa, two miles south of Curwensville, June 13, 1866, and is a son of Joseph L and Christianna (Esau) Dale, the former of whom still resides on the old homestead but the latter is deceased

John A Dale was educated in the Oakland school in Pike township, the High School at Curwensville, and then took a normal course, after which he taught school for some twelve terms, in West Clearfield, Lumber City, and other parts of Clearfield county He was first elected a justice of the peace on the Democratic ticket, in Pike township, and after being elected to the same office at Curwensville, retired from educational work and has given his attention to numerous other interests Following his marriage he continued to reside for a time in Pike township and then came to this borough, establishing his home on River street and his office on the second floor of the Patton Building He is a stockholder in the Curwensville National Bank, a director in the Curwensville Building and Loan Association and is local manager of the State Capital Loan Association, of Harrisburg. He has been a lifelong Democrat and has served on the school board both in Pike township and at Curwensville

On August 31, 1891, Mr. Dale was married to Miss Abbie Hile, a daughter of Warren and Effie Hile, and they have had four children· Joseph Thomas, who is a student in Pierce College, Philadelphia, Christine, who is a student in the Curwensville High School; Evana, who is also a High School pupil, and Frederick, who died when aged three months Mr Dale has been a member of the Curwensville Methodist Episcopal church for twenty-five years, and is now a member of the official board He is connected officially with several fraternal organizations at Curwensville For eight years he has been treasurer of the Bethesda lodge, No 821, I O O F, for fifteen years has been Keeper of Records and Seal of Curwensville Lodge, No 486, Knights of Pythias, and for five years has been Chief of Records of Illini Tribe, No 362, I O. R M

J F KLINE, who is engaged in general farming and stock raising on a farm of 100 acres in Bradford township, Clearfield county, Pa, is one of the prominent and influential citizens of the township, and was born in 1857 in Goshen township, this county, a son of G R and Rebecca (Ogden) Kline G R. Kline was born in Lawrence township, Clearfield county, Pa, a son of Solomon Kline, who was one of the early pioneers of this county. The father of our subject was reared in Lawrence township, and spent his declining years in Union township, where he died in 1889 Our subject's mother died when he was but one week old

J F Kline grew to maturity in Lawrence township and attended the Pine Grove school there After finishing his education he engaged in logging and was engaed in that business continuously until four years ago, when he purchased his present farm of 100 acres in Bradford township Here he carries on general farming and stock raising and is one of the progressive and enterprising farmers of the township Mr Kline is a director and has been treasurer of the Bradford township school board for the past year, and during his residence in Girard township served in almost all the township offices

In 1880 Mr Kline married Ida J Mains of Bradford township, and a daughter of David Mains, who was a well known agriculturist of Bradford township Ten children have been born to Mr and Mrs Kline Blanch, Maud, died in 1884, aged one and a half years Pearl, died at the age of two and a half years Guy, Fanny, married Clem Bellott of Girard township, and is the mother of two children, Christine and Guy, Olive V, married Walter Luzier, and they have one son, Kenneth, Ruth, Walter, Harry, and Jacob

F W SCHMITT, who has been proprietor of a bakery at Clearfield, Pa, for the past sixteen years, was born August 5, 1873, at Philadelphia, Pa, and is a son of Fred and Caroline (Kienzle) Schmitt

F W Schmitt was very young when his parents moved to Troy, Indiana, and he was there reared to man's estate At an early age he began working in his father's bakery, where he learned the trade, and subsequently conducted the business himself In 1894 the family came to Clearfield, Pa, and opened a bakery, locating in their present quarters in 1902 He carries on a wholesale and retail business, the Butternut and Figola being his two leading brands Mr Schmitt is a member of the B P O E, is religiously a member of the Roman Catholic church, and in politics is identified with the Democratic party He has one sister, Catherine, who is the wife of F D Souders

JAMES H CROYL, now a leading business man of Ramey, Pa, senior member of the firm of Croyl & McCully, general merchants, was born January 3, 1862, in Huntingdon county, Pa, and is a son of Henry and Catherine (Gettys) Croyl

Henry Croyl was born in Huntingdon county and was a son of Casper Croyl, who was born in Germany Henry Croyl was a general farmer and was a well known and respected man He married Catherine Gettys, who was a daughter of Patrick Gettys, a native of Ireland To Henry and Catherine Croyl the following children were born Margaret, who is the wife of D T Kantner, Martha, who is the wife of Hugh Stoddard, Samuel Ella who is the wife of Solomon McCully, William, Robert, Marion, who is deceased, James H, Ada, who is the wife of H B Stevens, and June, who is the wife of Frank Johnston

James H Croyl obtained his education in the public schools and afterward worked for ten years at the carpenter trade In 1871 he established his home at Ramey, where he was postmaster for ten years and for three years was a clerk in a store In 1909 he started into a general mercantile business at Ramey, in partnership with his nephew, L K McCully, and they are doing a large business and carry all the assortment of goods usually found in a well managed store of this kind

Mr Croyl was married in June, 1895, to Miss Laura Beyer, a daughter of Thomas and Virginia (Warren) Beyer The parents of Mrs Croyl have lived at Ramey for the past twenty-five years, coming from Tyrone, Pa, when this place was but a village To Mr and Mrs Beyer the following children were born Laura, Myrtle, who is the wife of James Sharer, Florence, who is the wife of Joseph Cassidy, and Clinton and Percival Mr and Mrs Croyl have five children Virginia, Kathleen, Robert, George and Mildred The family attends the Methodist Episcopal church In politics Mr Croyl is a Republican and he has served as a councilman of Ramey borough and has been school director and tax collector

ANTHONY HILE, deceased, whose useful life was prolonged into advanced age, was long a leading citizen of Lumber City, Pa, and was one of the men of ample fortune then living in Clearfield county He was born in Northumberland county, Pa, in 1815, and died in Clearfield county in 1904 His parents were Henry and Mary (Johnson) Hile

Henry Hile was born in New Jersey but he married in Northumberland county, Pa, and all of his children were born there, Anthony being nineteen years of age when the family came to Penn township, Clearfield county At that time this region was a wilderness and was covered with a timber growth that became the foundation of many a fortune Lumber City was appropriately named, for lumbering was the main industry and a part of the town was built on a section of the Hile farm

Anthony Hile followed farming and lumbering for a number of years His qualifications for office were recognized by his fellow citizens and he served carefully and honestly in almost all of the township offices, having been school director, constable, supervisor, assessor, collector and supervisor of the poor He was a member of the Baptist church. In 1839 Anthony Hile married Miss Emily Bloom, a daughter of James and Mary (Passmore) Bloom, early residents of Pike township, and they had the following children born to them, some of whom have passed away but have left descendants James H, D W., John N, Eli B, Martha J, Lewis B, Fanny, Ada M, William B, Mary E and Amanda L Anthony Hile, who perpetuates the name of his grandfather, is the eldest son of James H Hile, and is assistant cashier of the Curwensville National Bank at Curwensville, Pa

FRANK B REED, sole owner and proprietor of the Clearfield Machine Shops and Foundry, is at the head of a large enterprise and is numbered with the representative business men of Clearfield, Pa He was born in this city, April 26, 1853, and is a son of George Lattimer and Sarah (Weaver) Reed

George Lattimer Reed was born in Clearfield county, Pa, in 1823, and died December 23, 1905 He was a son of Alexander Bowman Reed, who came to Clearfield county as a pioneer and became interested in large tracts of timber land and spent the remainder of his life in this county He had the following children Maria, who became the wife of Gov William Bigler, once chief executive of Pennsylvania, Rebecca, who became the wife of John F Weaver, and George Lattimer George L Reed was interested with his father in lumbering and together they owned vast tracts of valuable timber, and later engaged in brick manufacturing, he was also one of the founders and owners of the Clearfield Machine Shops He was a man of fine business capacity and was well known all over this section He married Sarah Weaver, who survived him, her death occurring in 1908 She belonged to a prominent old family of Center county Six children were born to them, as follows Frank B, Alfred B, Elizabeth R, who died in 1910, Virginia, who is the wife of J. W. Chambers, of Williamsport, Pa, Edward B and George B

Frank B Reed enjoyed excellent school advantages, from the public schools of Clearfield entering a preparatory school at Lawrenceville, N J, and going from there to Lafayette College, at Easton, Pa He then entered the machine shops in which his father had an interest, desiring to gain a practical knowledge of the business and continued until he secured the same, the works then being operated by the firm of Bigler, Young & Reed In 1880, Frank B Reed became manager of the plant and through his technical knowledge and energy has done much to place this among the leading industrial plants of the city

A history of the development of this business is interesting The Clearfield Machine Shops were established in 1867, by Al F Boynton and George S Young, on the present site, with accommodations sufficient for the carrying on of a small amount of manufacturing, the product then being machinery for saw mills It was not until the brick industry became of greater importance than the lumber

business in this part of Pennsylvania, that the company started their present line of production-machinery for the manufacture of fire brick In the meanwhile ownership of the works changed, Mr Boynton selling his interest to Hon William Bigler and George L Reed, and in 1880, Mr Young sold his interest to W H Mulhollon and at the same time a part of the George L Reed interest was assigned to Frank B Reed, the firm style then becoming Bigler, Reed & Co In 1901 Frank B Reed bought the entire interests of the other members of the firm, retaining the services of Mr W H Mulhollon as superintendent The Clearfield Machine Shops and Foundry are located on the corner of Fourth and Pine streets, Clearfield, with business office on Fourth street north of Pine From the first the business has had steady growth, its present equipments being perfect of their kind and the railroad facilities being such as to enable rapid shipment in any direction Employment is given to sixty skilled mechanics and other laborers

On October 26, 1876, Mr Reed was married to Miss Rebecca W Shaw, a daughter of Archibald Shaw, and they have had five children, namely Scott B, who died when aged twenty-two years, Alfred B, who was married in 1909, to Miss Edith Dill, and they have one son, Fred Bowman, Robert B, who is a member of the faculty of the Syrian Protestant College, at Beirut, Syria, being professor of Economics, and is a graduate of Princeton College, Harvard College and the Auburn Theological Seminary, Philip, who is a member of the class of 1910, at Princeton College, and one who died young Mr Reed and family are members of the Presbyterian church In his views on public questions he is a Demo-

crat, but has never entered into politics to any
great extent The family residence is situated
at No 724 S Second street, Clearfield, Pa
It is a hospitable home and many pleasant social functions take place there

JOHN T FOULKE, one of the representative business men of Houtzdale, Pa , where
he has been in the hardware business since
1904, under the firm name of J T Foulke &
Company, was born in Clinton county, Pa , in
1877, and is a son of George C and Annie
D (Myers) Foulke

George Foulke was born in Huntingdon
county, Pa , and is now a resident of Indiana
Prior to coming to Houtzdale, in 1880, he
worked as a tinner at Renova and Salona in
Clinton county, and went from there to Lock
Haven and then to Houtzdale He married
Annie D Myers, who was born in Clinton
county, near Millhall She died after the family came to Houtzdale They had seven children, namely Laura, who is the wife of William Dalton, of Bruceville, Ind , Minnie, who
died in childhood, Maude, who is the wife of
W R Gallagher, and they live at Smith Mills,
John T , Carrie H , who lives at Smith Mills,
and Annie and Manning, both of whom died
in childhood

After the close of his school days, John T
Foulke went out on the road for a couple of
years and also was a clerk in a hardware store
and thoroughly learned the business In 1904
he established himself at Houtzdale under the
firm style of J T Foulke & Company, in hardware, plumbing and tinning, and has built up
a good business He is a Republican in his
political views and takes an active interest in
the election of first class men to office, deeming this the duty of a good citizen He be-

longs to the Elks at Phillipsburg, to the Odd
Fellows and Brotherhood of America, at
Houtzdale, and is an advanced Mason, identi-
fied with the Blue Lodge, at Osceola, the
Chapter at Clearfield, the Commandery at
Phillipsburg, the Consistory at Williamsport,
and the Mystic Shrine at Altoona He was
reared in the Methodist Episcopal church.

MICHAEL J COX, owner and proprietor
of the McCartney House, at McCartney, Pa ,
has been in the hotel business at this place for
some ten years and is well known to the traveling public He was born in Knox township,
Clearfield county, Pa , April 16, 1863, and is
a son of William and Mary Cox

The parents of Mr Cox spent their lives in
Clearfield county, where the father engaged in
farming They reared the following children:
Mary, John, Maggie, William, Michael J. and
Elizabeth William and Michael J are twins

Michael J Cox was reared on his father's
farm and attended the country schools. He
then went into the woods and continued a lumberman until 1901 when he came to McCartney and purchased the McCartney House
This is a quiet, well kept hotel, one in which
the comfort of the guests is carefully looked
after while the charges are very moderate

On October 15, 1891, Mr Cox was married
to Miss Sarah McCrossin, who is a member of
one of the substantial old families of Clearfield county They have two children , Luella
and Frances They are members of the Catholic church In politics Mr Cox is a Democrat He belongs to Tyrone Lodge, No 212,
B P O E

J B LYTLE, who carries on general farming on a tract of 100 acres in Lawrence town-

ship, Clearfield county, Pa , is one of the progressive farmers and highly esteemed citizens of the township, and was born December 31, 1839, on the old home farm in Lawrence township, a son of James and Jane (Burchfield) Lytle

James Lytle, father of our subject, was born in 1806 in Center county, Pa , and obtained his education in the district schools of that county In early manhood he left Center county and with his brothers, six in number, worked on the Erie Pike Upon its completion he located at Curwensville, Pa , where he was employed ten years by John Irwin and during that period was married to Jane Burchfield of Juniata county, and to them were born seven daughters and two sons He subsequently located on a farm owned by John Irwin and from there removed to a farm of 100 acres, which is now owned by the subject of this record He cleared the greater part of this land with the aid of his two sons, and placed it in a state of cultivation, although his own time was greatly devoted to lumbering He was politically a Democrat, although in no sense of the word a politician, and his religious connection was with the Presbyterian church James Lytle died on the farm in Lawrence township in 1864 and both he and his wife were buried at Curwensville, Pa

John B Lytle received his educational training in the common schools at Curwensville, Pa and in Lawrence township He has always remained on the home farm, and after the death of his father continued his home there in order to help provide a living for the family He has always followed general farming, and after his marriage made various improvements on the farm, and erected the buildings, which are now on the place About

1890 he sold the coal interests on the land to Kerr and Betts, later known as the O'Shanter Coal Company

Mr Lytle was united in marriage with Celia Leonard, a daughter of Robert Leonard, of Clearfield, Pa , and their union resulted in the following issue Jennie, wife of J W. McDowell, of Butler, Pa , James Leonard, who married a lady of Baltimore, Md , O C , a resident of Lewiston, who married Elizabeth Green, of Scranton, Pa , Josephine, who teaches in the schools of Portland, Oregon, and C C Lytle, who is at home The family attends the Methodist and Presbyterian churches Mr Lytle is, politically, a Democrat, and fraternally a member of the K of P No 383, of Glen Richey

HON JOHNSON W POTTER, M D, deceased, who was widely and favorably known throughout Pennsylvania, having political prominence, large business interests and high professional standing, retired from business activity before his long and unusually busy life came to a close He was born in Clarion township, Clarion county, Pa , March 6, 1835, and died March 31, 1898

Johnson W Potter grew to the age of eighteen years on his father's farm and from there went to Indiana county where he remained one year in a mercantile establishment and then came to Clearfield county as a teacher and as a student of medicine Through the influence of Governor Bigler, the young man received an appointment which made it possible for him to become a student in the National Medical College at Washington, D C , where he continued his medical studies through 1859 and 1860, and then entered upon the practice of medicine in Clearfield county

Eight years of hard country practice broke down his health and for this reason he gave up his profession and then turned his attention to lumbering and merchandising He started a store at Three Runs, in Karthaus township, and increased his interests here by erecting a saw and grist mill, and operated them for a number of years The village of Pottersdale was named in his honor and he was a merchant and postmaster there In 1877 he purchased a farm of fifty acres, situated in Covington township, which he improved with fine buildings, and in 1883 he erected a first class hotel and also went into the mercantile business at Karthaus village

Long before this, however, Dr Potter had become a prominent factor in politics He was an earnest, thoughtful man, with firm convictions of right and wrong irrespective of party ties, and when urged to accept public office consented from a sense of duty In 1868 he was first brought forward as a candidate for the lower house of the state legislature, but in that contest he was defeated by Hon Thomas P McCullough In 1873 he was an independent candidate, being the nominee of the Independent Democrats, but received hearty support also from the ranks of the Republicans His selection practically terminated the oppressive political rings in Clearfield county In 1874 he was again nominated but withdrew during the campaign and from that time took no further active interest in political life

At New Bethlehem, Clarion county, Pa, in 1858, Dr Potter was married to Miss Alamanda Hoffman, and they had eight children born to them Mrs Potter resides in her handsome residence at No 10 N Front street, Clearfield

WILLIAM WINGERT, of Luthersburg, farmer and lumberman, and one of the most substantial residents of Brady township, where he owns much valuable property, including 1,500 acres of both timbered and farm land, is one of the successful and representative men of this section He was born March 9, 1842, near Punxatawney, Jefferson county, Pa, and is a son of Frederick and Mary Margaret (Laudaman) Wingert

Mr Wingert's parents came to this country from Germany, being accompanied by four children—Henry, George H, Frederick and Margaret—which constituted their entire family at that time They settled temporarily in Jefferson county, Pa, until Frederick Wingert, the father, had had the time and opportunity to find a more permanent settlement This after a while he did in Brady township, Clearfield county, where he purchased sixty-two acres of wild land This whole region at that time was practically a wilderness, and in the clearing of a farm Mr Wingert, the elder, found himself confronted by a task that made large demands upon his strength and resolution But the early settlers of this region were, as a rule, men not easily appalled, and Mr Wingert was worthy to rank with the best of them He soon got to work, therefore, made a small clearing for a beginning and built thereon a small cabin of round logs, the cracks being plastered inside and outside with mud or clay, as was the pioneer custom This humble domicile had but one door, which, as it was then impossible to obtain nails without going to great trouble and expense, was hung on wooden hinges otherwise secured and was furnished with a wooden latch Before the door was hung, however, it was necessary to fill the doorway with bundles of straw, to keep

WILLIAM WINGERT

MRS. LOUISA S. WINGERT

out the cold, as it was now getting late in the fall The cabin contained one small window, consisting of nine lights of 6 x 8 glass panes, and in one end was a fireplace The cabin was a story and a half in height and the roof was put on without a nail In place of a stairway to the upper portion, two upright poles, supplied with pegs for steps, led to an opening in the ceiling, by which means the family ascended to the half story above At first they were without even a stove or a time piece, or even chairs, but necessity is the mother of invention, and substitutes for these things, which would nowadays be considered absolutely essential, until Mr Wingert was able to provide them The crowing of the cocks announcing the dawn, told them when it was time to get up, for there was no lying in bed after there was light enough for them to see to work by, and for the rest of the day until evening, the sun was their clock For a long time the only roads were cow paths through the woods

In this cabin home three more children were born—Peter, Jacob and David—the birth of William, our direct subject, having occurred, as we have seen, while the family were sojourning in Jefferson county The family now numbered ten members and as the sons grew up, each had his duties assigned him The little clearing was still further enlarged each year, some of the timber after being felled was burned, as there was no market for it at that time Much of it, however, owing to the difficulty of felling, was simply killed by having a ring cut clear around through the bark, and it was then left to rot on the stump A small quantity was made into shingles, which were sold to store keepers at from $5 50 to $6 00 per thousand These shingles had to be 26

inches long, with a good average width and a five-eighths butt The store keepers would build arks, load them with shingles and float them down the river on the spring floods to Middletown and other markets The shingles were not paid for by the store keepers until after the latter had received their returns from the dealers down the river, and even then they paid only about one-third in cash and the rest in trade Pine, oak and chestnut, of the finest quality, were among the commonest kinds of timber.

For a considerable period the Wingerts had neither horse nor wagon When they first settled here they had a cow from which they raised a calf to be used as an ox, and then, buying another calf, they had a yoke of cattle to do the work of pulling and hauling Instead of a cart or wagon they used a sled, which the father constructed entirely of wood, no iron or nails being used in it, and this was made use of winter and summer

Before long Mr Wingert bought 100 acres more land, paying for it gradually in hand-shaved shingles, which he made in the winter, attending to the farm work, with the help of his elder sons, in the summer time He raised enough grain and produce for the family needs on the land already cleared, continuing to prosecute the work of clearing the rest of his purchase, destroying the timber, except such kinds as would split easily for shingles Such timber, for which there was then no market, would now be worth a large sum

Having now made a fair start in the establishment of a homestead, he began the erection of a new and more commodious dwelling This in itself was a task of some magnitude, as there were then no planing-mills in the vicinity and everything had to be done by hand, the axe and adze being the tools chiefly employed, though the saw and plane were used, the latter in smoothing the lumber for the floors Logs were hewed on four sides for the uprights, which were carried up two stories The joists were also planed by hand, as well as the linings and partitions, which were planed on both sides Nails at that time were very high, $8 00 per hundred By this time, in addition to their oxen, they had a horse team, Mr Wingert having previously bought a cheap mare from which a colt was raised, the two animals forming the team, and proving useful in many ways On the completion of the new house, the family moved into it, the event being a red letter day in the family history It was regarded by all their neighbors as a good house, and cost them quite a little in money, to say nothing of the heavy labor involved Thus, step by step, and year after year they moved forward to an improved condition of life, each member of the family doing his full part as he became old enough The boys all grew to manhood on the homestead, and as the elder ones became of age the father made arrangements with them for their continued stay at home. agreeing to give them each $100 per year in land, besides food and clothing As the land at that time was selling at $4 00 per acre, it took four years of hard work to pay for 100 acres of land This arrangement was continued until most of the sons owned 100 acres—excepting only the three youngest These, on the father's final retirement from active labor, received their portion in cash, which, owing to the increase in the value of land, amounted to about $1,000 apiece, Peter becoming the possessor of the old homestead, on the condition that he should contribute one-third to the support of his

father and mother as long as they lived The mother was the first to pass away, dying March 27, 1885, at the age of seventy-seven years, six months and twenty-five days The father, John Frederick Wingert, died July 13, 1887, aged eighty years, seven months and fifteen days

All the children at this time were still living, and it was ten years before there was another death in the family Then, on October 20, 1897, Peter passed away at the age of fifty-two years, ten months, twenty-eight days George H followed him July 16, 1904, aged seventy years, seven months, eight days Then came Margaret, who died in the year 1908. aged sixty-nine years, seven months, four days, and afterwards Jacob, who died at the age of sixty-four years in January, 1909 Margaret was the wife of David Swope The survivors at this writing are Henry, the eldest brother, who resides in Brady, William, our direct subject, residing in Luthersburg, and Frederick and David, living in or near Bucyrus, Crawford county, Ohio

William Wingert was but an infant when he accompanied his parents and the rest of their family to Clearfield county His educational opportunities were very limited, but he attended a subscription school on his father's farm for a time When but eight or nine years old he had to help to saw the timber for shaved shingles, pulling one end of the saw; and he also made himself useful in supplying wood for the big fireplace that occupied most of one side of the log house About the time that each of the brothers had paid for his own land, he began to work on it, sometimes having the assistance of his sweetheart Thus they grew up and married William in his turn finally got his land paid for and commenced working on it He remained at home. however, another year or more, exchanging his work with his younger brothers he helping at home, and they at times helping him on his land, the account being called square on both sides

In 1864 Mr Wingert enlisted for one year or during the war in the 100th Pa Volunteers, which was assigned to the 5th Brigade, 9th Army Corps The remembrance of these days is still vividly upon him, as he says, "At that time our whole country was sorrow stricken and draped in black, many fathers and mothers weeping for their sons, many a wife weeping for her husband But in June, 1865 the whole country rejoiced over peace and liberty once more restored between the North and the South, and almost the entire North rejoiced that the great battles had been fought and the great and final victory won, that our country was once more a country of freedom and liberty On our way home the women and children of the city of Washington strewed the streets with flowers and roses for the soldiers to walk over—all from joy, and ever since our country has had peace at home May it long continue, so that the generations which come after us may reap the benefit of the hardships we endured while playing a soldier's part in the mighty struggle that almost divided the Nation "

In 1868 Mr Wingert moved onto his own place at Coal Hill, where the Jefferson Coal & Iron Company now have a coal mine in operation He cleaned up a considerable part of that land and then started in the saw-mill and lumbering business, at the same time continuing his farming operations After getting a little money he began investing to some extent in real estate in DuBois, which place was then

enjoying a healthy growth His investments proved successful and after increasing his cash capital he bought some stock in a private bank, called the Bank of DuBois This he did on the positive representations of the president and cashier that it would pay not less than six per cent in dividends, and that he would be put to no trouble in the conducting of the bank, as they would run it This they did, but not to a fortunate or profitable issue, for on March 14, 1895, it closed its doors The bank had a capital of but $50,000, of which our subject owned $10,000 in stock Being a private institution, each stockholder was indirectly liable for its indebtedness This caused Mr Wingert a lot of trouble and expense, but he finally got out of the matter with a loss of over $26,000 00 in cash, besides considerable other property that he had to sacrifice This experience, however, severe as it was, did not discourage Mr Wingert He continued to prosecute his farming and lumbering interests and along these lines his efforts were crowned with success Today he owns five good farms, besides 990 acres of rough or uncultivated lands, amounting altogether to about 1,500 acres To this should be added also several brick buildings in DuBois and some valuable vacant lots in that place He is also a stockholder and director in the DuBois National Bank, and is interested in a timber lot at Oregon, Pa

In 1868 Mr Wingert was married to Louisa Swope, and of this union were born four children, all of whom are now living, namely John J , Mary Emma, Ellis A I , who are married, and Lula Ella, who is single and resides at home Mr Wingert has dealt generously with his children We have seen how he worked for his father until he was of age for $100 per year He on his part, agreed to pay each of his sons $300 per year The younger son, Ellis, worked for awhile on those terms and then married Miss Mary Hartzfield, upon which his father deeded to him a farm and gave him with it all the farming utensils necessary, including a wagon and team of horses Of this marriage have been born five sons, all of whom are living Mr Wingert's elder son, after his brother's marriage, continued to work for his father, and the latter raised his wages from $300 to $600 per year, also deeding to him a farm with all the farming utensils, including wagon and team

The two farms above mentioned as given by Mr Wingert to his sons were underlaid with coal, which they sold—the one in fee simple at $140 per acre, the other (John F) selling the coal only at $100 per acre, and now having his farm rented The latter has built himself a nice brick house in Luthersburg He married Frances Weber and they have two children, a son and a daughter—Roy Sylvester and Lillian Alberta Mary E is the wife of W H Nevil of DuBois Her father bought her a nice lot and built her a substantial brick house thereon, presenting her with the deed Ellis Ai, whose marriage to Mary Hartzfield has been referred to, lives in Brady township, and they have five children—Chester, Lloyd, Edgar, Clifford and Marlin

Much more could be said of Mr Wingert's career did space allow, still a few words more are due to our subject A retrospective glance shows clearly that his main characteristic through life has been that resolute, persevering industry and thoroughness for which the German people are noted His business affairs have been but briefly touched upon In addition to the large sum he lost by the bank failure, he has at different times sustained other losses of no inconsiderable magnitude, as for instance, on a timber tract investment in Wisconsin he lost some $12,000, besides several other losses of from $1,000 to $4,000, yet he never lost courage or determination, but as soon as he realized that he had suffered a misfortune, went to work to repair it, and in this manner has overcome all adverse circumstances He has long been one of the most prominent and useful citizens of the community, he has paid out thousands of dollars to laborers, and during the summer of 1910 he built a telephone line from DuBois to Curwensville, a public improvement that was much needed and which has proved a great boon to the citizens of both places His limited schooling has been briefly referred to Of this period he says himself "During my first years as a boy, I did not know that there was any such thing as a public school After we got the shabby little schoolhouses, we only had two months in a year, and I had to stay at home and help to saw shingle timber I could only go when the weather was too stormy or rainy to work Counting all my days' schooling, I do not think it would reach four months during my life time" Yet he has served on the school board for the last fifteen years, and his communication forming the basis of this article proved that though his education has been self acquired and in the face of very adverse circumstances, amounting almost to an absolute lack of opportunity, he has by self application acquired the ability to express his thoughts in writing in a clear and impressive manner, and the same applies to other branches of knowledge for which the average person has use Such a life is an encouragement to all of limited opportunity Though general conditions are more favorable now than they were in Mr Wingert's boyhood days, there are still some who complain of want of opportunity Let them reflect on reading this brief sketch and they cannot but feel that such a career is an inspiration, and consequently take courage to do their best and win their way to success like the subject of this memoir

ALFRED R HUNTER, a representative citizen of Irvona, Pa, who has been successfully engaged in a general merchandise business for the past ten years, was born near Glen Hope, Clearfield county, Pa, June 18, 1875, and is a son of John M and Martha (Erhard) Hunter, and a grandson of John Hunter

John M Hunter, who was born in Clearfield county, was for some years engaged in hauling timber, but subsequently became a farmer, and still is carrying on operations on his land, although in his sixty-sixth year His wife died about fifteen years ago Of the six children born to Mr and Mrs Hunter, five are now living, namely Elizabeth, who married Lee Roberts of Mahaffey, Alfred R Ira engaged in the butchering business in Irvona, who married Alta Gunsallus of Beach Creek, and Emma and Dora, who are single

Alfred R Hunter attended the public schools of Glen Hope, and on coming to Irvona in 1891 he engaged in the mercantile business, in which he has continued to the present time His fine store was erected by him in 1910, and he resides over his place of business A Prohibitionist in politics, Mr Hunter invariably casts his vote for the candidates of that party, and he is serving as a director and treasurer of the Irvona borough school board His fraternal connections are with the Ancient Order

Knights of the Mystic Chain and the Knights of Pythias

In 1909 Mr Hunter was united in marriage with Miss Cora Fulton, a daughter of Zachariah Fulton of Bigelow, Pa Mr and Mrs Hunter are consistent members of the Presbyterian church

AMOS H RUMBERGER, who is one of the representative business men of Houtzdale, conducting a hardware store and doing a plumbing, gas fitting and heating business in connection with the same, was born January 14, 1862, in Huntingdon county, Pa, and is a son of Balser S and Hannah (Harper) Rumberger

Balser S Rumberger was born in Center county, Pa, but moved to Huntingdon county in early manhood, where he became a man of considerable prominence and served three years as sheriff, being elected on the Republican ticket He met with an accidental death, in September, 1910, while crossing a railroad, and at that time was a resident of the borough of Huntingdon His burial was at Petersburg He married Hannah Harper, who died in 1868, and her burial was at Warrior's Mark

Amos H Rumberger was reared at Warrior's Mark and Petersburg, attending school during the usual period, and at the latter place assisted his father in the mercantile business until 1880, when he came to Houtzdale Here he engaged as shipping clerk and weighmaster at the Van Dusen mines before he entered into the hardware business with R R Fleming In 1902 he became a partner in the business conducted under the firm name of R R Fleming & Co, which continued until January, 1908, when he became sole owner Mr

Rumberger has been quite active in politics and has frequently been the choice of the Republican party for public office and was serving as county auditor when he resigned in order to make a visit to British Columbia He has served as borough auditor and for six years was a member of the council, during three years of which time he was its president He has been a member of the school board for seven years and is its presiding officer at present

Mr Rumberger was married October 28, 1885, to Miss Ida Roushe, who was born in Huntingdon county and is a daughter of William and Helen Roushe, and they have five children, namely Helen, who is the wife of Augustus Gleason, of DuBois, Pa , and they have four children—Andrew, Helen Robert and Ida, Edith, who is bookkeeper for her father, Gertrude, Ida, who is the wife of Mahlon Hagerty, of Philipsburg, and George, who is yet in school

Mr Rumberger has been a member of the Houtzdale Fire Company for twenty years He is identified fraternally with the Masons, at Osceola, and the Odd Fellows and Brotherhood of America, at Houtzdale

R WILLIAM THOMPSON, proprietor of an undertaking establishment located on West Locust street, Clearfield, Pa , was born March 17, 1867, on his father's farm in Lawrence township, Clearfield county, Pa , and is a son of Rufus and Sarah (Daniel) Thompson

Rufus Thompson, father of our subject, was born on the home farm, where he was reared to manhood, and subsequently learned the carpenter's trade, which he followed many years He married Sarah Daniel, a daughter of William and Margaret (Shaw) Daniel, both of whom were natives of Ireland and of their union were born the following children. Reuben H , Martha, the wife of John McCool, Elizabeth, widow of R T Butler, and R William Mrs Thompson died in 1884 at the age of 54 years, and Rufus Thompson died in November, 1908, aged 86 years

R William Thompson was reared on the farm in Lawrence township and attended the local schools At the age of 16 years he took up carpentering with his father, and after his father met with an accident entered the employ of Thorn and Burthfield In 1896 he began learning the undertaking business in the establishment of James Fullerton of Pittsburg, and also took a course at the Champion College of Embalming of Pittsburg After receiving a diploma from that institution he embarked in the business for himself, buying out Gearhart & Sharbough of Clearfield He later built his business block, which is located on West Locust street, near Turn Pike avenue, and since January, 1909, has had his residence in this block, where he also conducts the business and has his office Mr Thompson is fraternally a Mason, a member of the I O O F and Encampment, the P O S of A , the O U A M and Royal Arcanum

A J HUNTER, a well known and popular citizen of Berwinsdale, Pa , where he is connected with the great Pennsylvania Railroad system as agent and telegrapher, was born in Jordan township, Clearfield county, Pa , and is a son of John H and Jennie M. (Van Dyke) Hunter

John H Hunter was born in Scotland, June 8, 1837, and was brought to America when ten years of age He spent sixty years in

Jordan township, and farming was his main occupation. He married Jennie M Van Dyke, of Holland ancestry, who was born September 3, 1841, and the following children were born to them: William B, Mary S, Robert A, A J, Maggie B, and Nelson V. Mary S became the wife of J H Moss, and Maggie B married W F Conley.

A J Hunter is a self-made man. His education was obtained in the public schools and his first work was performed as a clerk in a store at Irvona, where he continued for five years. For one year he was engaged in business for himself at Curwensville, after which he took a course of four months in telegraphy. Proving a very apt pupil, he learned the art quickly and then entered the employ of the Pennsylvania Railroad Company, with which he has been identified ever since, coming to Berwinsdale in his present capacity, on March 1, 1900.

On July 29, 1899, Mr Hunter was married to Miss Edith F Breth, a daughter of William B and Margaret (Montgomery) Breth, and they have two children: Samuel Carl and Sarah Kathryn. Mr and Mrs Hunter are members of the Presbyterian church. He is independent in politics.

ELLIS IRWIN, deceased, for many years one of Goshen township's representative, substantial and esteemed citizens and for several decades postmaster at Lick Run Mills, was born near Bellefonte, Center county, Pa., June 17, 1805. He was of Irish and English ancestry and was reared in the Quaker faith.

Ellis Irwin was educated in the Bellefonte Academy and after his marriage moved on a farm in Penn township. He engaged in agricultural pursuits here for four years and then disposed of his land and moved to Curwensville. In 1835 he was appointed prothonotary, register and recorder and clerk of several counties and acceptably performed these duties for three years. He then entered into the mercantile business at Clearfield and in 1846 was appointed postmaster. He also served three years as sheriff and filled out an unexpired term of county prothonotary of one and one-half years. Ellis Irwin was recognized as a man of such sterling character and as one so well qualified for the responsibilities of public office that the esteem in which he was held by his fellow citizens was unbounded. In 1856 he moved to Lick Run, in Goshen township, and there became associated with his brother, William F Irwin, in a lumbering business in which he continued his active interest even after passing his three score and ten years. In 1827, Mr Irwin was married to Hannah Iddings, who died in February, 1881. She was a member of one of the old and respected Quaker families of this section and her parents were John and Ann Iddings.

John F Irwin, son of Ellis and Hannah Irwin, was born February 20, 1829, and obtained his education in the subscription and district schools. In 1862 he enlisted at Curwensville, Pa, a company of 100 men was enrolled in the U S service as Company B, 149th Regt (Pa), at Harrisburg, Pa. Mustered in as a private, he was made second lieutenant, was afterward promoted to first lieutenant and took part in seventeen battles, including Gettysburg, where he was appointed adjutant on the evening of the first day's battle. He served subsequently until his honorable discharge July 25, 1865.

In November, 1865, he entered into partnership in the drug business with Dr J G Hartswick, but is now associated with his son Ellis in the same business, the son attending to the active part of the business On May 25, 1866, John F Irwin was married to Sarah Rheem, of which union was born the son, Ellis, before mentioned Mr Irwin is a member of the Methodist church, which he joined in 1873 He resides at No 305 Second street, Clearfield

JAMES SPACKMAN, a well known and highly respected citizen of Lawrence township, Clearfield county, Pa , now living retired on his valuable farm of 172 acres, situated five miles from Clearfield and three miles from Curwensville, was born December 10, 1841, on the Richard Spackman farm in this township He is a son of William Spackman and a grandson of Daniel Spackman

Daniel Spackman came to Clearfield county from Chester county, Pa , in 1818, accompanied by his wife and children and his subsequent life was spent on the farm in Lawrence township that was then bought by his sons, Benjamin and Thomas Spackman The children of Daniel Spackman were as follows Benjamin, John, Mary, wife of Thomas Leonard, Elizabeth, wife of William Mitchell, Thomas, William, Jane, Hester, wife of James Mitchell, Sarah, wife of Jerdon Read, and Debbie, wife of David Brown

William Spackman attended the Pine Grove School in Chester county, grew up on the home farm and after marriage settled on an adjoining farm, where he cleared twenty-five acres He married Isabella Read, a daughter of Thomas and Mary (Jerdon) Read, and four children were born to them Thomas, who resides at Detroit, Mich , James, Margaret, who is the wife of Edward Wise, of Knox township, and Alexander, who lives in Lawrence township and married Annie Baker William Spackman was a member of the Friends' church at Curwensville, Pa , his wife was a Presbyterian In early life he was an old-line Whig, but in later years became a Democrat He lived to the venerable age of eighty-four years, and his burial was at Mc-Naul Cemetery in Pike township

James Spackman obtained his schooling in his native township and as soon as age and strength permitted he went to work in the woods and for many years was engaged in lumbering, during that time living with his maternal uncle, Alexander Read In 1867 he bought his present farm but did not locate on it until 1882, from the time of his marriage in 1869 until the above date living along the river Mr Spackman had no clearing to do but has done a large amount of repairing and rebuilding The brick house, which was built in 1833, and the barn, in 1831, were in remarkably good condition considering their age, but each needed modern conveniences This barn is a landmark, having been the first frame barn erected in Clearfield county and in the main the materials in its original construction are still preserved It was put up for Thomas Read by carpenter George Leech Mr Spackman's farm is valuable in many ways In 1903 a 34-inch vein of coal was opened and in that year 5,000 bushels of coal were taken out and since that time the vein has supplied fuel for family use Since Mr Spackman retired from active labor, his sons have had the management of the farm and stock interests and have done well They raise full blood Percheron horses and have high grade mixed cattle and carry on operations according to modern ideas, regarding agriculture as a business and profession

In October, 1869, Mr. Spackman was married to Miss Mary E Read, a daughter of J R and Mary Read, who were both born in Lawrence township and spent all their married life on this farm Three children were born to Mr and Mrs Spackman, two sons and one daughter L. E, L W, and L H Neither son has married The daughter is the wife of Ernest Aughenbaugh, of Curwensville Mr and Mrs Spackman are members of the Methodist Episcopal church at Curwensville In politics, Mr Spackman is an Independent Democrat, keeping faith with the old-time principles of Democracy but reserving the right to vote as his judgment dictates Mr Spackman has served his township as auditor, supervisor and school director and has also been overseer of the poor He is a member of the county agricultural society and belongs also to the Grange, Patrons of Husbandry He is a stockholder in the Farmers and Traders Bank of Clearfield Although his purchase of the old Driftwood schoolhouse and its erection on his farm as a shed was a practical matter, there was also some sentiment in it, for it was in that building that he passed his entire school boy period, and many pleasant memories cluster about it for this reason

MATTHEW KNEPP, owner of 172 acres of very fine land situated in Bradford township, Clearfield county, Pa, was born in this township, one-half mile north of his present farm, in 1866, and Bradford township has been his home all his life His parents were B and Sarah Knepp, the former of whom was born in Juniata county and came to Clearfield

25

county in youth, with his parents, who were pioneers in Bradford township He followed farming and lumbering

Matthew Knepp obtained his education in the public schools of Bradford township He has devoted himself to farm pursuits from boyhood and is numbered with the most successful agriculturists of this section While general farming and stock raising is his rule, he specializes to some extent in wheat and buckwheat He has an easy market for his produce, his land lying on the Gray Hampton road, within five miles of Woodland

In 1876 Mr Knepp was married to Miss Carrie Jury, a daughter of John Jury of Girard township, and seven children were born to them, as follows Blanche Mae, who married first to Roy Lansbury (now deceased) and had one child, Arlema, and secondly to Clyde Wilson, of which union there is one child, Rita Villa, Oma O , Gertie Belle, who died when aged eighteen months, Chester Kale, who died at the age of three years, Jessie Clair, who lived to be nine years old, and Ralph Estil and Thelma Marie Mr Knepp and family belong to the Brethren church of Shiloh, in Bradford township, and he is treasurer of the Sunday school From 1906 until 1908 Mr Knepp served as a school director but has never been willing to accept any other public office He is one of the township's best known and most respected citizens

ABNER B McCARDELL, a prosperous miller and well known citizen of Burnside township, was born in this township, September 8, 1848 His father, John McCardell. who was born September 25, 1816, and who was a blacksmith by trade, was the first of the family to settle in this township, where he subsequently resided all his life, dying March 16, 1900 He married Sarah Johnson Pilson, who was born January 24, 1816, a daughter of Adam Pilson, her mother's family name being Johnson The Pilsons were pioneer settlers of Indiana county Mrs John McCardell died April 16, 1881 She and her husband were members of the Methodist Protestant church The latter was a Republican in politics He came to Clearfield county with his family, settling at Patchinsville The children of John and Jane J McCardell now living, in addition to our subject, were as follows John, living in the west, Edward, a blacksmith residing in Iowa, Charles, engaged in the hotel business in Iowa, D Alexander, postmaster at Westover, Pa , Pilson, who is engaged in farming at Burnside, Pa , James, a physician and surgeon residing in Florida, Sarah, the widow of John C Mitchell of Mahaffey, and Agnes, wife of J L Campbell, of Burnside, this county

Abner B McCardell, after attending school, was variously employed until 1872 He then engaged in the livery business at Burnside, and so continued for eleven years His next five years were spent in making various business trips through the West He then returned and bought the pressed grist mill of John H Patchin, which is one of the oldest mills in this part of the county It is operated both by water and steam power and Mr McCardell has put it in good practical working order, so that the business is now in prosperous condition Mr McCardell is a Republican in politics and served as village treasurer for several terms, and has also been councilman and street commissioner He has long been an active worker for his party and indeed is willing at all times to assist in any feasible project for the good of the community regardless of party ties. For this well known characteristic he is respected by his fellow citizens, who have confidence both in his capacity and integrity.

Mr McCardell was married in 1874 to Harriet Bloom, who was born September 13, 1851, a daughter of J Ross Bloom Her birth took place in Pike township, as did also that of her father, the latter on February 27, 1822 Mrs McCardell's mother was in maidenhood Nancy B McGaughey She was born November 14, 1829, and was a daughter of Thomas and Margaret McPherson McGaughey of Armstrong county Mrs McCardell's paternal grandfather was Benjamin Bloom, born in Center county, August 31, 1790, who married Sally McClurg, born September 20, 1792 The father of Benjamin Bloom came from Germany, settling at an early date in New Jersey, whence in the early part of the nineteenth century, he came to Clearfield county, Pa He fought for American independence in the Revolutionary war He married Mary Metler Mrs McCardell has one sister living, Jane, now the wife of Howard McClosky After her mother's death her father married Matilda R Hoover, of which union there were born two children, Nora R , the wife of P. Pyle; and Reed R , who resides on the old Bloom homestead

Mr and Mrs McCardell are the parents of five children, namely Minnie, residing at home, Horace, at Osceola Mills; Grace, who is the wife of Otis Mitchell, a butcher of Portage, Pa , Beulah, in Clearfield, and Ross, who is employed in the mill at Burnside

FRANK CRAIG, a representative business man of Clearfield county, with interests in different sections, has been a resident of Brisbin, Pa , for twenty-nine years and is a member of the firm of M & F Craig, coal operators He was born March 28, 1864, in Lanarkshire, Scotland, and is a son of James and Bridget (Rooney) Craig, and was, eighteen years of age when he accompanied his parents to America

James Craig was a coal miner all his active life and after coming to Clearfield county, lived at Brisbin until his death, in 1901, his burial being at Houtzdale He married Bridget Rooney, who survived him four years They had seven children born to them, namely. Michael, who resides at Brisbin and is the senior member of the firm of M & F Craig, Frank, Hugh and James, who also live at Brisbin , Robert, who lives at Houtzdale, Patrick, who is a resident of Brisbin, and Margaret, who is the wife of Charles Rodden, and they live at Portage

Frank Craig obtained his education in the schools of his native land He has been continuously in the coal business and has been an active operator for a number of years Since 1882 he has been a resident of Brisbin and has been operating since 1888, at present being extensively interested in the Industry mine at New Castle, Clearfield county He is a director in the First National Bank of Osceola, and has valuable coal lands which he leases in both Geulich and Decatur townships

On February 5, 1902, Mr Craig was married to Mrs Catherine (Coons) Simendinger, who was born at Loretta, Cambria county, Pa , a daughter of William and Anastasia (Byrne) Coons, and the widow of John Simendinger The father of Mrs Craig died in 1895 at Houtzdale, but the mother had died in 1857, when Mrs Craig was a babe of two months Mrs Craig was married first to John Simen-dinger and they had nine children, the three survivors being Raymond L and Albert J , both of whom are students at the Niagara University at Niagara Falls, and Rose, who is a student at Villa Marie Academy, at Erie, Pa Mrs Craig is the youngest of a family of four children She has one brother and two sisters Bernard, who lives at Pittsburg, Mary, who was the wife of Hayden McGuire, of Loretta, and Emma, who is the wife of Charles Kane, of New Kensington, Pa Mr and Mrs. Craig are members of the Catholic church at Houtzdale He is identified with the Knights of Columbus at Clearfield He is an earnest and enterprising citizen, ever ready to work for the betterment of his borough and county and has served thirteen years on the school board In his political views he is nominally a Democrat but is inclined to be more or less independent of party ties

ALBERT SHAFER, proprietor of Albert Shafer's Milk Depot, at Clearfield, Pa , is a representative business man of this city and has been a resident of Clearfield county his entire life He was born on his father's farm in Brady township, Clearfield county, Pa , April 10, 1879, and is a son of Samuel and Lucilla (Porter) Shafer

Samuel Shafer was born on the farm in Clearfield county on which his pioneer parents settled many years ago He still survives, having devoted the greater part of his life to agricultural pursuits, and now lives on a small farm near Luthersburg, entirely retired from hard work He married Lucilla Porter who died about 1880 Six children were born to them, four of whom still survive, as follows Mary, who is the wife of L A Zortman, of DuBois, Pa , Martha, who is the wife of Ellsworth Phillips, of Erie, Pa , William, who lives at Mt Union, Pa , and Albert

Albert Shafer spent his boyhood on the home farm and during six months of the year usually attended the district school, three miles distant from his home, up to the age of ten years He then secured work in the dairy of George Wachob, at Luthersburg, and remained there for several years and later worked for John Watts in the same business, in Ferguson township, and afterward for three years was with the well known dairyman, C F King, at DuBois After then making a trial of the brick business in the yards of Harbison & Walker, he decided to return to the work in which he had become so skilled and re-entered the employ of Mr J. P Watts, opening up a dairy for him at Clearfield Later, Mr J P Watts sold out to Thorp & Kirk, and that firm was succeeded by McPherson & Mitchell, of whom Mr Shafer purchased the plant, January 22, 1909 Mr Shafer has proven himself an excellent business man and through his many years of dealing with the people of this section has won confidence and regard He secures his milk from six large dairy farms near Clearfield and he has a large wagon trade, supplying almost every hotel and many private residences at Clearfield Additionally he supplies the tuberculosis patients and the Clearfield Hospital He has fine sanitary quarters and modern equipments and deals in cream, home milk, skim milk, buttermilk and eggs His private office is at No 213 Reed street

Mr Shafer was married in June, 1902, to Miss Florence Ross, of Huntingdon county, Pa , and they have two children, Esther and Ruth Mr and Mrs Shafer attend the Methodist Episcopal church In politics he is a Republican and his other organization connections are with the Patriotic Sons of America, the Loyal Order of Moose and the Protected Home Circle, all of Clearfield His residence is situated on East Market street, Clearfield

JAMES S HOYT, the efficient superintendent of the Clearfield County Poor Farm, in Clearfield county, Pa , is widely known and has been a lifelong resident of Clearfield county He was born in Lawrence township, October 23, 1860, and is one in a family of three children born to his parents, John S and Maria (Augenbaugh) Hoyt, the former of whom died in 1893 and the latter in 1883

James S Hoyt spent his early years on a farm and obtained his education in the public schools His father was a shoemaker by trade but his choice was different and he became a carpenter and engaged in work as such for a number of years He identified himself with the Republican party when he reached manhood and has been an active factor ever since and his usefulness has been recognized at different times Under the administration of the late President McKinley, he served as postmaster at Glen Richey, eleven years, and resigned to accept the present position of superintendent In January, 1909, he assumed the duties of superintendent of the Clearfield County Poor Farm, which include the care of 155 public charges and the cultivation of 250 acres of land In this position he has acquitted himself with credit

Mr Hoyt married Miss Anna E Kephart, a daughter of the late Abraham Kephart, and they have ten children

FREDERICK MOSSOP

RICHARD MOSSOP, now deceased, to whom this sketch is dedicated, will be remembered as one of the pioneer merchants of Clearfield, Pa He was born in the city of Philadelphia, May 4, 1819, and was a son of John Mossop

In early manhood, Richard Mossop came to Clearfield and engaged in merchandising, conducting a general store until his death, which occurred January 1, 1891 Richard Mossop was married in June, 1845, to Miss Margaret Graham, who was born in Clearfield county, Pa , and died in January, 1894 Her father, Francis Graham, was one of the pioneers of Clearfield county Richard Mossop and wife were members of the Presbyterian church In politics he was a Republican but never consented to have his name brought forward for public office He was a man of ample fortune and a bank director

Frederick Mossop, a son of Richard Mossop, succeeded his father in his mercantile business and successfully continued it until his own death His business methods were, perhaps, more up-to-date than his father's had been, having an ambition to enlarge the scope of the enterprise and to introduce modern appliances He did not confine his public spirited energies to his own business but assisted in developing the commercial interests of Clearfield by erecting many of the substantial structures which are a credit to the business district of the city Suffering frequently from ill health himself, his attention was thus called to the crying need of the city for a well equipped hospital and, following his death, his heirs respected his expressed wish in this relation They donated the hospital site, together with the sum of $20,000, and the Clearfield Hospital stands as a lasting monument to the memory of Frederick Mossop

H L BOWMAN, justice of the peace, is one of the prominent men of Pike township, Clearfield county, Pa , and resides on his well improved farm of seventy acres situated two miles south of Curwensville He was born in Lawrence township, Clearfield county, May 31, 1878, and is a son of Jonathan and a grandson of Daniel Bowman, the latter of whom was one of the pioneers of Knox township, Clearfield county

Jonathan Bowman was born in Union county, Pa , September 14, 1836, and accompanied his father to Clearfield county, when the latter settled in Knox township After he married he continued to operate his father's farm near the Turkey Hill schoolhouse, which he had helped to clear, and also engaged in lumbering Later he purchased what was known as the Powell farm, in Lawrence township, and moved from there into Pike township, buying the A A Long farm, on which he continued to reside until his death, October 13, 1898, when he was aged sixty-three years He was a member and liberal supporter of the Methodist Episcopal church at Mt Zion In politics he was a Democrat but never desired public office, serving however as overseer of the poor when his fellow citizens elected him. He married Eliza Rowles, who still survives, and lives on the old homestead She is a daughter of Tidus H Rowles and a member of a large and substantial family of this section To Jonathan and Eliza Bowman fifteen children were born, as follows Harry, who is a member of the police force at Altoona, married Emma Thompson, of Lawrence township, Elam, who lives in Lawrence township, married Ollie Peoples, Stacy, who resides in Pike township, married Maude Wise, C P, who makes his home in Oregon, Rosa, who is deceased, was the wife of John M Peoples, Julia, who is the wife of A B Owens, of Pike township, John, who lives in Pike township, married Almeda Bloom, Daniel, who lives at Echo, Ore, married Hannah Barnett, Anna, who died at the age of twelve years, Sarah, who is the wife of F T Kyler, of Philipsburg, Pa , H L , Jonathan, who is deceased, married Edna, daughter of Allen Bloom, Lucy, who is the wife of Clarence Withrow, of Pike township, Samuel, who lives in Pike township, married Edna Henderson, and Paul, who lives in Pike township, married Edith Maerfield

H L Bowman attended school in Pike township and later was a student in the Kerrmoor Normal School After marriage he settled at Olanta and subsequently bought his present farm from William Bloom, making a number of improvements and remodeling the buildings He is a prominent Democratic politician in this section and is State fire warden for this district He has been a justice of the peace for ten years and has also been tax collector for the same length of time And is at the present a candidate for county commissioner on the Democratic ticket

On July 23, 1897, Mr Bowman was married to Miss Jessie Ardary, a daughter of James and Martha (Price) Ardary, and they have had two sons one who died in infancy, and Cyrus F , an intelligent and promising youth now attending school Mr Bowman is a member of a number of fraternal organizations, belonging to the Elks, the Eagles, the Moose and the Red Men, and is also identified with the local Grange

GEORGE W GALLAHER, owner of a valuable sixty-acre farm situated in Boggs township, Clearfield county, Pa , was born in White township, Cambria county, Pa , April 6, 1853, and is a son of William and Harriet (Derrick) Gallaher

William Gallaher was born in Cambria county and was reared on a farm and followed farming all his life, passing away in advanced years He married Harriet Derrick, who was born in Clearfield county and is also deceased They were good people, devoted members of the United Brethren church They had the following children born to them Nimrod, who is deceased, Anna, who is the widow of George W Davis, Elizabeth, who is deceased, was the wife of Jacob Mathews, James William, Carrie who is the wife of Israel Wisor, George W , and Victoria, who is deceased, was the wife of Theodore Bloom

George W Gallaher attended the common schools in boyhood but as soon as he was old enough he went into the woods and ever since he has worked more or less every winter at lumbering and has spent his summers on his farm His industry has been rewarded and he is in the enjoyment of a substantial income, and is well and favorably known all through this section in which he has lived for many years

Mr Gallaher was married in April, 1873, to Miss Elizabeth Hammond, a daughter of Joseph and Catherine (Noll) Hammond Mrs Gallaher's mother died and her father was married second to Martha Hoover The children of the first marriage were· Anna Mary, who is deceased, was the wife of George Rickard, Elizabeth, Rebecca, who is deceased, was the wife of Frank Russell; and Simon To the second marriage were born. William,

Frank, Jane, wife of John Ender, David, Edward, Mary, Matilda, who is deceased, and Anna, who married in Iowa

Mr and Mrs Gallaher have had the following children Frank, who is now deceased, Harry, Lala, who is deceased, Fada, who is also deceased, May, who is the wife of Fred Wiser, Pearl, who is the wife of Leonard Smeal, and Leonora, who is the wife of Roland Mease Mr Gallaher and family are members of the United Brethren church In politics he is a Republican and has served two years on the school board He is a leading member of the Grange at Blue Ball

E W HESS, civil engineer, with offices in the Kratzer Building, at Clearfield, Pa, and in the Deposit Bank Building, at DuBois, Pa, has a professional reputation second to few in this section of Pennsylvania Mr Hess was born on a farm in Columbia county, Pa, September 5, 1868

Mr Hess was educated in the public schools and a local academy and taught school for a short time before 1887, when he began work as a surveyor and civil engineer His first important railroad work was for the Louisville & Nashville and after it was satisfactorily completed, he was engaged by the Erie Railroad, the Norfolk & Western Railroad and the Pennsylvania Lines west of Pittsburgh, and later for the New York Central He also assisted in the building of the Lehigh Traction Company line at Hazleton, and from there to Wilkes Barre He opened his Clearfield office in 1900 and his DuBois office five years later and finds it necessary to maintain them both Mr Hess and his associates have done engineering on the construction of many of the street railway systems in the state, nota-

bly the Philipsburg Street Railway, the DuBois Street Railway and the Patton, Pa, Street Railway, and they have also put through a number of railroads in this state and in the Southern States, for lumber and other business firms Mr Hess has done some remarkable work in the line of construction for the water supplies and building of reservoirs in different cities, and the residents of Clearfield, Du Bois and Fall Creek point with justifiable pride to their complete and efficient systems Mr Hess and his firm have charge of the engineering for Clearfield, Curwensville, DuBois, Coalport and Fall Creek, in Clearfield county and for Brockwayville, and Sykesville, in Jefferson county

Mr Hess was married June 10, 1899, to Miss Maude Bouton They enjoy a beautiful home which is situated at No 409 Locust street, Clearfield, and they attend the Presbyterian church In politics Mr Hess is a Republican He is prominent in Masonry, belonging to various branches at Clearfield and to the Consistory at Williamsport

JOHN A GREEN, justice of the peace and engaged in an insurance and real estate business at Irvona, Pa, has been a lifelong resident of Clearfield county and was born at Glen Hope, February 3, 1861 His parents were James H and Sarah (Keagy) Green

The Green and the Keagy families both were early settlers in this section The paternal grandfather was John Green, who established his first home in the county, near what is now Marion postoffice He was a farmer and died on his own land James H Green became a large land owner and a prominent lumberman He bought the logs and paid for the cutting of them and with his brother-in-law, Abraham Beyers, made the first drive of logs down Clearfield Creek The value of these logs was about $16,000, and they were destroyed in what was called the Buckshot war, which was a local trouble between the lumbermen and the raftsmen Mr Green died soon after this misfortune, in 1867, at the age of forty years He married Sarah Keagy, who died in 1883, when aged fifty-one years Her parents were Abraham and Elizabeth Keagy, who came from Delaware and were among the earliest settlers on Clearfield Creek Mrs Elizabeth Keagy was born in 1800 and died in 1881 Five children were born to James H and Sarah Green, one of whom died in infancy, the four survivors being Abraham Keagy, who has been blacksmith at the Pine Run mines for five years, married Emma J, a daughter of G. W Rex, John A, Walter E, who resides on a farm near Marion, adjoining the old Green homestead, married Martha Barrett, and H Irene, who is a trained nurse in Philadelphia, where she has resided for the past seven years

John A Green was educated in the public schools and for twenty-six terms engaged in teaching and also taught in several summer Normal schools He then became manager for the Wister Supply Company and was superintendent for a time, taking charge in the spring of 1906 He was one of the pioneer merchants at Irvona but moved from that place to Glen Hope, where he spent six years and then returned to Irvona where he has been in business for the past eight years In 1909 he was elected a justice of the peace, an office for which he is particularly well qualified In politics he is a Democrat and formerly was very active in party affairs and served as the first treasurer of Irvona borough

'Squire Green was married in 1895 to Miss Margaret Baer, a daughter of David and Mary Baer, of Glen Hope, where Mrs Green was reared, and they have had eight children: Gwendola C, William Russell, Carmen and Dorothy, twins, D Byron, Charles Leroy, and Harry and J Elvin, both of whom are deceased The family belongs to the Methodist Episcopal church at Irvona Mr Green is a member of Glen Hope Lodge, No 669, Odd Fellows, and also of the Encampment at Glen Hope, Pa He is a man of scholarly tastes and during his long period of educational work impressed himself forcibly on his pupils and it is not an unusual occurrence for him to have personal messages from them from either coast, or from Canada to the Gulf of Mexico

FRANK W ESTRICHER, who is engaged in the blacksmith's business at New Washington, Burnside township, was born in this locality, son of Christian and Emily (Orr) Estricher He is a grandson of Adam Estricher, of Hesse-Darmstadt, who came to this country in 1849 at the age of 37 years, but who, being taken sick while on the voyage over, died not long after landing in America

Christian Estricher, father of our subject, was born in Hesse-Darmstadt, June 26, 1840, and was therefore about nine years old when he accompanied his parents to America, they settling in Burnside township, Clearfield county, Pa, where the father died Though this sad event left the family for a time in somewhat straitened circumstances, young Christian found means to attend school until reaching the age of 16 years, after which he was engaged for a short time in agricultural pursuits At the age of 17 he began to learn the blacksmith's trade, and subsequently—

about 1865—opened a blacksmith's shop at New Washington, which he carried on for many years, though now retired   He is a member of the Masonic lodge at Curwensville, and of the Odd Fellows' lodge at New Washington   For many years he has been a member of the Methodist church at New Washington, serving as steward   He is a Democrat politically and has at various times rendered active service to his party   He has frequently held local office and since 1908 has been burgess of the borough

Christian Estricher married Emily Orr, a daughter of John and Elizabeth (Baker) Orr, natives of Cumberland county, who subsequently settled in Clearfield county   She was born in 1837 and died in September, 1898, at the age of 61 years   The children of this marriage were as follows   Ora Matilda, who is the wife of J Day, residing in the state of Washington (has one child), Catherine Elizabeth, wife of Henry Campbell of Braddock, Pa , Edith, wife of J C Harper of Big Run, Pa , who has two children, Alice Maud, wife of Hugh C. Mitchell, of New Washington, and mother of three children, Frank W , whose name appears at the head of this sketch, Charles C , of Braddock, Pa , who is married and has two children, and Adaline, wife of C. King, residing in California, who is also the mother of two children

Frank W Estricher after attending school in his native township, began to learn the blacksmith's trade under his father with whom he was associated until the latter's retirement   Since then he has conducted the shop alone and is doing a thriving business, the shop having an established reputation throughout this section   He married Elizabeth Cummings, whose father, John M Cummings, born in Lycoming county, Pa , came to Clearfield county in 1850, locating at New Washington, where for some years he followed farming   In 1858 he opened a general mercantile store at New Washington, but subsequently sold it and resumed agricultural operations, which he carried on until his death   He married Elizabeth Mahaffey, daughter of Thomas Mahaffey, of the well known Clearfield county family of that name   Our subject and wife are the parents of two children

ANTHONY HILE, who is assistant cashier of the Curwensville National Bank, at Curwensville, Pa , and also treasurer of the borough, was born in what is now Lumber City, Clearfield county. Pa , in 1864, and is a son of James H and Mary H (Henry) Hile

James H Hile was born in August, 1840, in a part of Penn township which has become incorporated with Lumber City, Clearfield county, Pa , a son of Anthony and Emily (Bloom) Hile, and a grandson of Henry and Mary (Johnson) Hile   James H Hile attended school in Penn township as opportunity offered in his youth and spent a number of years working as a stone mason and in making square timber and also as a clerk in a store at Lumber City   For the last twenty-five years of his active life his business was that of scaling logs and was so engaged in Clearfield and Jefferson counties, Pa , and also in West Virginia   This business requires the accuracy and a mathematical sureness of vision and the workers in this field, therefore, are not as numerous as in many others   James H Hile settled at Lumber City after his marriage, where he was elected a justice of the peace, and served one term as auditor of Clearfield county, on the Democratic ticket

He is interested in the Curwensville National Bank In 1861 he was married to Miss Mary H Henry, a daughter of Thomas and Margaret (Moore) Henry, residents then of Ferguson township, Clearfield county Two children were born to this marriage Anthony and Gurney The latter married Edith Hepfer, a daughter of Simon Hepfer, of Fulton county, Pa , and they have two children—Katherine and Hubert

Anthony Hile was educated in the public schools and Lumber City Academy, after which he became a clerk in a store at that place, and at Kerrmoor, covering a period of five years In 1886 Mr Hile came to Curwensville as bookkeeper in the Curwensville Bank At the organization of the Curwensville National Bank in 1904 he was made assistant cashier He is financially interested in this bank and also owns a farm of 100 acres which lies in the north end of Ferguson township, Clearfield county, and was once the homestead of his maternal grandfather This property he has improved and at present is under the management of Mr Hile's brother

On October 22, 1890, Mr Hile was married to Miss Margaret E Mead, a daughter of Henry and Lydia Mead, of Lawrence township Mrs Hile died in 1897, survived by a daughter, Margaret, who attends the public schools The first child, Anthony, who was born in 1894, died in 1895 Mrs Hile was a member of the Presbyterian church Her burial was in Oak Hill Cemetery Mr Hile is an elder in the Presbyterian church, and has been its treasurer since 1887 He is identified with Noble Lodge, F & A M , with Bethesda Lodge, I O O F , at Curwensville, and also with Susquehanna Grange

WILLIAM F LUMADUE, a general farmer in Boggs township, Clearfield county, Pa , who has charge of the Lumadue estate as executor, has occupied this important position since the death of his father, in 1910 He was born December 29, 1886, on this farm of 145 acres, and is a son of Lewis D and Martha (Dixon) Lumadue

Lewis D Lumadue was a well known farmer in Boggs township He married Martha Dixon, who died in 1903, his own death occurring on April 20, 1910 They had the following children John, James, Newton, William Frank, Susie Jane, Anna, Phoebe, Joseph B , Matilda, Jennie, Martha, Frederick and Mary Of the above, Susie Jane is the wife of Walter Williams, Anna is the wife of George Rothrock, and Phoebe is the wife of Foster Woods

William F Lumadue obtained his education in the country schools He carries on general farming on the old homestead and carefully looks after every interest on the place When the youngest child of the family has reached maturity the estate will be divided In 1908 Mr Lumadue was married to Miss Matie A Butler, the youngest child of Robert and Jennie (Ogden) Butler, the others being. Nellie, John, Guard and Fred Mr and Mrs Lumadue have two children Virginia and Lewis G They attend the church of the Brethren In politics Mr Lumadue is a Republican but he takes no very active interest

A G PETERS, who owns and resides on a fine farm of 53 acres in Bradford township, Clearfield county, Pa , is a native of this county, and was born in 1852, a son of J R and Mary (Graffius) Peters The father, born in Lancaster county, was a miller and stone mason by trade, and died in 1895 in Bradford township, Clearfield county, Pa The mother died in 1901 in Bradford township

A G Peters has always lived in Clearfield county, Pa, and has made farming his life occupation After his marriage he located on a farm about a quarter of a mile from his present place, residing there until 1901, when he bought and settled on his farm of fifty-three acres, and is here engaged in general farming and stock raising

In 1875 Mr Peters was united in marriage with Alpharetta Bumgarner, who was reared in Bradford township, and their union has resulted in the following issue Lida May, born in 1876, died June 20th, of that same year Hallie, born in 1877, married William Biesh of Boggs township, and has three children, Earl, Lena, and Ardith. Ashley, married Elva May Thompson of Bradford, Charles W, married Ethel Eshelman of Bradford township, and they have one boy, Marvin Leroy, Mary, born September 13, 1886, died January, 1887, Edith Alma, who has taught four terms in the schools of Bradford township, attended the home normal schools at Houtzdale and at Philipsburg, Pa, and married W R Knepp, formerly of Bradford township

Mr Peters is a citizen of enterprise and public spirit and has served three years as president of the school board, and two years as supervisor of the roads of Bradford township He and his family are members of the U B Church of Woodland, Pa Besides rearing his own family, Mr and Mrs Peters have taken into their home an orphan, Ethel Templeton Clark, and given her their protection and love

JAMES MITCHELL, president of the Clearfield National Bank, at Clearfield, Pa, is one of the representative business men of this section and for many years was prominent in the lumber industry He was born on his father's farm in Lawrence Township, Clearfield County, Pa, May 8, 1842, and is a son of William and Elizabeth (Spackman) Mitchell

William Mitchell was born in Ireland, a son of John and Isabella Mitchell, who were of Scotch-Irish birth When William was six years of age they sailed for St John's, New Brunswick, where they lived for a time before coming to the United States They landed at Philadelphia and went from there to Center County and then settled on 400 acres of land situated in Lawrence Township, Clearfield County This was in 1830 and John Mitchell died on that land in January, 1849 William Mitchell was one of a family of eight children, all now deceased He became a farmer and lumberman, purchasing land of his own adjoining that of his father He married Elizabeth Spackman, who died in 1887, at the age of 74 years, having survived her husband since 1858 She belonged to a prominent old Quaker family of Chester County, Pa The following children were born to William and Elizabeth Mitchell Theodore, John, Eliza, Isabella, James, Sarah, Caroline, Oscar and Alfred, all surviving except Theodore, John and Isabella

James Mitchell remained on the home farm, a tract of 231 acres, which he purchased in 1865, until 1871, following farming and stock raising and being interested also in surveying and lumbering He had country school advantages in his youth, supplemented by three months attendance in the Clearfield schools, the opportunities for securing an education in his youth being very different from those now presented to the boys and girls all over the land   In 1871 Mr Mitchell built and took possession of his comfortable residence at Clearfield and has been identified with the leading interests of the city ever since   He was one of the organizers of the Clearfield National Bank and filled the office of vice president until 1911, when made president   In politics he is a Republican and the confidence of his fellow citizens was shown by his election in 1888 to the responsible office of county treasurer

On May 15, 1883, Mr Mitchell was married to Miss Grace B Row, who is a daughter of the late Samuel B Row, and nine children have been born to them, namely   George, Catherine, John, Elizabeth, James, Theodore, Samuel, Grace and Eugene   Mr Mitchell and family attend the Presbyterian church

JAMES D WALL, assessor of Penn Township, Clearfield County, Pa, of which he is a leading citizen and substantial farmer, resides on his farm of 100 acres, which adjoins the borough line of Grampian, Pa   He was born in this township, one and one-half miles southwest of Grampian, July 15, 1855, and is a son of Thomas and a grandson of Jonathan Wall

Jonathan Wall was born in Chester County, Pa, and later was a resident of York County, moving from there to Center County and in 1820 coming to Clearfield County   He settled on 200 acres of land that was then in Pike Township, but now that section is Penn Township   He improved his property and lived on it until his death, in 1855   This farm is now owned by E M Davis   Jonathan Wall married Jane Thomas, of York County, and they reared a family of children and lived long and

virtuous lives subscribing always to the teachings of the Society of Friends.

Thomas Wall, father of James D, was born after his parents had settled in Penn Township. He was reared on the home farm and remained there for two years following his first marriage and then moved to Pennville, where he was a merchant for two years   After the sale of his store he bought another farm in Penn Township, on which he operated a saw-mill and a grist-mill, together with farming, until 1870, when he bought a tract of 425 acres of timber land, on Bell's Run and continued to be interested in lumbering until his accidental death, at the age of sixty-five years   He was a member of the Society of Friends   In politics he was a Republican and served occasionally in township offices   His first marriage was to Hannah Davis, a daughter of Joseph Davis, Sr, and they had three children ·   James D, Milton, who died in 1888, in California; and Sarah, who is the widow of Clark Norris   The mother of these children died in 1860 and her burial was in the Friends' Cemetery. Thomas Wall married for his second wife, Eliza Nicholson, a daughter of Joseph Nicholson, of Bell Township, and they had six children   Mary, Annie, Leona, Blanche, Charles and Maud

James D Wall obtained his education in the schools of Penn Township and remained at home assisting his father until after his own marriage, in 1879   He spent three years in Colorado and then returned to the old homestead and became manager of the mill and continued until its sale   Mr Wall then purchased his present farm of Isaac B Norris   As the land was already well improved he had little in that direction to do but subsequently built his present commodious and attractive resi-

MRS. MARGARET H. KIRK

GEORGE C. KIRK

dence Mr Wall is a charter director and a stockholder of the Curwensville National Bank

In May, 1879, Mr Wall was married to Miss Clara Miller, who was born in Jefferson County, Pa, October 14, 1860, a daughter of Col James and Louisa (Fainsworth) Miller Politically Mr Wall is a Republican and he has been an active and practical citizen Frequently his fellow citizens have elected him to public office and he has served as school director and auditor, and for nine years was collector of Penn Township, of which he is now assessor

CYRUS ROBISON, who conducts the 111-acre farm in Boggs Township, owned by his wife, Mrs Alice Robison, and carries on general farming and stock raising, is numbered with the substantial citizens of this section He was born July 18, 1872, in Knox Township, Clearfield County, a son of Samuel and Agnes (Sloss) Robison

Samuel Robison was one of the early teachers in this part of Clearfield County and was highly regarded as an instructor He was a son of William and Jane (Vanormer) Robison He married Agnes Sloss, who was a daughter of William and Margaret Sloss They had three children. Cyrus, Eva and Jennie Both daughters are deceased The latter was the wife of Charles Goss Samuel Robison was identified with the Democratic party He and his wife belonged to the Presbyterian church

Cyrus Robison obtained his education in the public schools and had the advantage of fatherly instruction at home, up to the age of eight years, when this parent died The farm came to Mr Robison by inheritance from his father, who purchased it from its former owner who had bought it from a Mr Peters Mr Robison has the deed that proves this farm to have been settled on 104 years ago He has been connected nearly all his business life with sawmill work, formerly quite actively but latterly not to so great an extent

In 1894 Mr Robison was married to Miss Alice Boyd, a daughter of Robert and Matilda (Ralston) Boyd, residents of Clearfield County Mr and Mrs Boyd had the following children Charles, Mary, wife of Samuel Blankley, Alice, Anna, deceased, wife of Ord Shirey, George, Clara, wife of Richard Howell, and William To Mr and Mrs Robison three children have been born Mabel, who died at the age of sixteen months, and William and Leland Mrs Robison is a lady of education and culture and taught school in Boggs Township for three years prior to her marriage Mr and Mrs Robison are members of the United Brethren church He is a Republican in politics, and he is identified with the organization known as the P O S of A

GEORGE C KIRK, civil engineer, surveyor, and for ten years a justice of the peace in Brady township, Clearfield county, Pa, is one of the representative citizens of this section of Clearfield county, all over which he is known in his profession He was born in Brady township, April 3, 1837, and is the oldest of a family of eleven children born to his parents, who were Thomas and Eliza (Brisbin) Kirk, and his grandfather was John Kirk

John Kirk, the grandfather, was the founder of this family in Clearfield county He came of Scotch ancestors and was born May 15, 1777, in York county, Pa From there he moved to Center county and settled in Boggs township, but it is not known that his parents. Thomas and Hannah (Cadwallader) Kirk, accompanied him. He was married in Bald Eagle Valley, Center county, in 1802, to Lydia Fisher, who was a daughter of William and Hannah (Packer) Fisher Ten children were born to them, five sons and five daughters Later John Kirk, about 1832, moved into what was then a wilderness, settling in the deep woods, in Brady township, Clearfield county There his death occurred December 23, 1856, and that of his widow, March 15, 1864

Thomas Kirk, the fifth of his parents' family, was born September 11, 1811, in Boggs township, Center county He accompanied his parents to Brady township, Clearfield county, and four years later, on June 19, 1836, he was married to Eliza Foster Brisbin, who was also born in Center county, November 13, 1817, a daughter of Enos and Jane (Moore) Brisbin They became the parents of eleven children, six of whom still survive Thomas Kirk engaged in farming and cleared off many acres of land which he improved. He was a well known and highly respected resident of Brady township, where he lived until his death, which occurred August 17, 1898, his wife having passed away on April 4, 1892

George Calvin Kirk had to work hard in his youth as the eldest of a large family, but he had unusual ambition although there was little encouragement or even opportunity to stimulate it His educational advantages in the common acceptance of the term, were meager, but he made the most of his chances and later became an acceptable school teacher He learned the carpenter and cabinetmaking trade and worked at it for a time, but whatever occupation or industry he was engaged in he devoted every moment of spare time to acquiring a knowledge of surveying and civil engineering Only those who have been equally persevering can appreciate the hard studying he had to do before he was able to perform satisfactory work along this line, but those who gave him the first contracts soon realized that he thoroughly understood every principle and the method of application, although he was entirely self taught Mr Kirk did a large amount of surveying for John DuBois, when that enterprising man first began his great lumbering operations in the dense woods that still covered the country surrounding DuBois, and has also done professional work of great importance in Clearfield, Jefferson and other counties Mr Kirk continues to work at his profession and each day spends some hours surrounded by his maps and charts, and frequently becomes so interested in his calculations that ordinary bed-time finds him yet busy In addition to his teaching, surveying and engineering, Mr Kirk was a very successful farmer for a number of years, owning several hundred acres of excellent land, purchasing his first 100 acres from James Irvin, paying $800 for the same and clearing it himself He improved his land and erected substantial buildings and still makes his home on the farm, which he sold to his son, Lewis N , on May 7, 1910 Mr Kirk was also one of the organizers of the Luthersburg Pottery, which supplied all this section with earthenware for many years No work has been done in the old building for many years but it still stands as a landmark Mr Kirk was further public spirited, being one of the organizers of the S N B Telephone Company, and has shown interest in and has given encouragement to other enterprises which have proved beneficial to this section

On April 18, 1861, Mr Kirk was married to Miss Margaret Elizabeth Hamilton, who was born in West Buffalo township, Union county, Pa , December 26, 1835, and is a daughter of Joseph and Mary (Michaels) Hamilton Nine children were born to them, as follows Mary E , Lydia J , Ida E , Austin I , Thomas J , Lewis N , Sarah M , William F and Anna M of this family but three survive, namely: Mary E , Lewis N and Anna M Mary E the wife of Charles S Carpenter, and they reside at Ashville, N Y. Lewis N , who now owns the homestead farm in Brady township, married Florence Reams, and they have one child, Marion L In politics Mr Kirk is a Democrat For a number of years he served on the township school board and during a large part of the time was its treasurer He is identified fraternally with Lodge No 753, Odd Fellows, at Troutville, Pa

On April 18, 1911, Mr Kirk celebrated his golden wedding anniversary One hundred and forty-four people ate dinner,—Joseph H Kirk of Tylertown, Pa , Mrs Boyd Kirk and two of our subject's sisters, Mary Ann and Ellen, were at the wedding of our subject, also at the anniversary Mr Kirk was married on what is now known as the Brewery farm in this township, the DuBois Brewing Company being the owners He and his wife were married by Daniel Goodlander, a justice of the peace They received many presents, including gold coins of U S money

WARD O WILSON, M D , whose office is located at No 210 North Second St , Clearfield, Pa , is one of the successful and leading physicians of this borough, and has been a life long resident of Clearfield County He was born December 4, 1875, in the village of Shawsville, Clearfield County, Pa , and is a son of Mark L and Agnes (Shirey) Wilson, and comes of one of the pioneer families of the county The Wilson family originally came to America from Scotland, and first settled in York County, Pa , but subsequently located in Clearfield County John L Wilson, grandfather of our subject, was a brother of Samuel Wilson, who was one of the first men to serve as Justice of the Peace in Bradford township Mark L Wilson, father of our subject, was a life long resident of Clearfield County and was for many years identified with the lumber industry of the county He was for some time associated with A B Shaw, and also Weaver and Betts, who were all well known lumbermen of this section of Pennsylvania, and died January 13, 1884, when a comparatively young man Of this union with Agnes Shirey, who is a daughter of George Shirey of Gillingham, Pa , were born two sons, Walter V , who died aged two years, and Ward O , the subject of this record In 1906 Mrs Wilson formed a second union with Simeon Cross, and they reside on Nichol Street at Clearfield, Pa

Dr Ward O Wilson spent the first ten years of his life on the farm, and then entered the employ of Edward Shaw, who conducted a general store at Shawsville, Pa He continued in the employ of Mr Shaw three years, and during the winter of two years of that time, he attended the local schools of Shawsville, and later took a course at the Central State Normal at Lock Haven, Pa In 1894 Dr Wilson began teaching and followed that profession five years, his schools being at Palestine, Graham township, the Black Oak school of Graham township, the Shawsville school, which he himself had attended, in Goshen township, the Center School in Lawrence township, and his fifth a graded school at Glenn Richey, Law-

rence township, his last assignment   In 1898
Dr Wilson entered a medical college at Philadelphia, from which he graduated with the
class of 1902, and since September 11, of that
year, has been engaged in the practice of his
profession at Clearfield   He first located over
the present Thatcher Drug Store, and in January, 1903, moved temporarily to No. 303 Reed
Street, and subsequently bought and remodeled
his present office and residence, which are located at No 210 No Second Street   On October 29, 1903, Dr Wilson was united in marriage with Lottie I McCoskey, who is a daughter of A E McCoskey of Lock Haven, Pa

JOHN BOAG, postmaster at Boardman,
Pa, and superintendent of Mines No 2 and 3,
for the Potts Run Land Company, in Knox
Township, Clearfield County, is a reliable and
experienced mine man and is well and favorably known all through this section of Pennsylvania   He was born in Scotland, March
14, 1858, and is a son of David C and Margaret (Halbert) Boag

David C. Boag and wife were both born in
Scotland and when they came to America in
December, 1869, their five children accompanied them   They settled first at Arnot, Tioga
County, Pa, and during their years of residence there, eight more children were added
to the family   The mother and ten of the
children still survive   The father died at the
age of sixty-six years, while on a visit at Arnot,
having previously removed to Glen Richey,
where he worked as a miner   He was a Presbyterian in his religious convictions and a Republican in his political views

John Boag was about twelve years old when
the family came to America and he had already
laid the foundation of a good education and

completed his period of school attendance at
Arnot, Pa   Like his father he became a miner
and when he came to Clearfield County, in 1892,
it was as a mine foreman at Glen Richey, where
he remained for four years, after which he
was mine foreman for six years at Burnside.
In 1902 he came to Boardman and accepted
his present position as superintendent, serving
as such ever since   Mr. Boag is not only a
well qualified man in his special line of work
but he is a representative citizen and while
still living in Tioga County served as school
director and as township clerk, being elected on
the Republican ticket   Mr. Boag at present
is identified with the Prohibition party   He
is serving in his second term as postmaster at
Boardman, the mail being received from Olanta or Mitchell by carrier.

Mr Boag married Miss Jennie Patterson,
a daughter of Henry Patterson, of Arnot, Tioga County, and they have seven children,
namely   David C and Harry P, both of
whom are attending college, in preparation for
professional life, John, who is general manager of the Boardman Supply Company store
and assistant postmaster; and Elizabeth, Margaretta, William A, and Park   Mr Boag and
family are members of the Presbyterian church
He is identified fraternally with the Masons,
the Odd Fellows and the Knights of Pythias

JOSIAH S RICHARDS, president of the
board of county commissioners of Clearfield
County, Pa, and a prominent and substantial
citizen of Curwensville, has been identified with
the lumbering interests of this county for a
number of years   He was born in Boggs
Township, Clearfield County, Pa, September
5, 1850, and is a son of James and Susanna
(Dixon) Richards

The Richards family came originally from Wales, the great-grandfather being its founder in America George Richards, the grandfather, established his family in Bald Eagle Valley, in Center County, Pa, and was a farmer and iron worker. Of his eleven children, James, the father of Josiah S, was the eldest

James Richards worked on the home farm and also in the iron furnaces, but his inclinations were in the direction of agricultural pursuits and in 1838 he secured a tract of wild land which he converted into a productive farm and resided on it until 1866, when he moved to Ohio and bought a large farm there He lived only three years longer, his death occurring in 1869 His widow survived until 1876, her death occurring in Clearfield County to which section the family had returned in 1871

Josiah S. Richards was one of the younger members of a large family, eleven of whom reached maturity. When sixteen years of age he started out to make his own way in the world and the best opportunity that presented itself was work in the lumber regions, and, without any material interruption, Mr Richards continued work in the lumber regions for thirty years In 1880 he embarked in business for himself and since then has carried on both farming and lumbering The business of lumbering is carried on in practically the same way in all lumber regions and each section has much to recommend it, not only for the development of manly muscle but also for the good fellowship often established and maintained through years Mr Richards recalls many interesting experiences and occasionally has met with some injuries, one of these, in 1890, necessitating a sojourn in a hospital for a time

26

He has mastered every detail of the work and his advice is frequently solicited concerning lumbering enterprises In 1888 he established a lumber camp on a valuable farm that he had purchased, and later in association with his brother, operated extensively on the estate of the late ex-Governor Bigler

From 1875 until 1887, Mr Richards resided at Houtzdale, in Clearfield County, but since 1895, he has lived on his farm in Greenwood Township He has always been an active and interested citizen and has been elected to numerous township offices, and in 1908 was elected a county commissioner In this important office he is serving with faithfulness and efficiency and since 1909 has been president of the board Mr Richards is well qualified to be entrusted with public responsibilities, and enjoys the confidence and respect of his fellow citizens

In 1875 Mr Richards was married to Miss Rachel Henry, a daughter of Jeremiah and Sarah (Radcliffe) Henry Jeremiah Henry was born in Mifflin County, Pa, later moved to Indiana County, and there married Sarah Radcliffe, a native of Ireland They had the following children Rachel, who is the wife of Josiah S Richards, Emma, who married W Smith, James, Jennie, who is deceased, Mollie, who married J Colmer, William, Sarah, who is deceased, and Samuel and John Henry

To Mr and Mrs Richards seven children were born, namely John D, Edward G, (in U S Army), Naomi Grace, James S (in U S Navy), Earl Daton, Harry L and Elva V Mrs Richards is a member of the Methodist Episcopal church and is interested in its benevolent and missionary work Mr Richards is identified with the Republican party

GEORGE W PIFER, senior member of the firm of George W Pifer and Sons, engaged in a planing mill and contracting business at DuBois, Pa, is also its founder and is one of the leading and representative men of the borough He was born on his father's farm in Allegheny County, Pa, October 24, 1844, about one month after the family settled in America, and is a son of John and Mary Jacobs Pifer

John Pifer was born in Germany and was reared there on a farm and contracted his first marriage there With his wife and one son he came to the United States in 1844 and after landing started for Pittsburg At that time no railroad lines were yet completed across the State of Pennsylvania and the long journey was made partly by wagon and partly on foot Upon their arrival, John Pifer rented a small farm which is the present site of East Liberty, a suburb of Pittsburg, and there he carried on truck gardening for some eight years He then removed with his family to Kittanning, Pa, and went to work in the rolling-mills Later, however, he resumed farming, renting land on the Indiana turnpike road, in Armstrong County In 1859, together with his sons, he bought a farm in Kittanning Township, on which the new owners put up a log house and barn About ten acres of the land had been cleared and put under cultivation when the Civil War broke out and although the old father was left alone on the farm while the brave and sturdy sons were battling for their country's liberties, he received their wages and thus was able to continue the payments on the land John Pifer died on this farm in which he took vast pride and satisfaction, in 1864, at the age of forty-nine years

John Pifer was married three times, first in Germany as noted above, to Mary Jacobs, who died in Allegheny County Five children were born to that union, namely Conrad, who died in Lima, Ohio, (he was a member of Co I, 78th Vol Inf), George W, Henry, who died while serving as a soldier, being a member of Co C, 103rd Pa Vol. Inf, John, who lives in Jefferson County, Pa, and Martha, who is the widow of Rudolph Crooks

George W Pifer was about eight years old when the family moved to Armstrong County and he readily recalls the occasion when he first saw a railroad train that ran to Pittsburg Shortly afterward he went to work on a farm for John Hood, with whom he remained for six and one-half years and then went back to his father and worked on the home farm until September 16, 1861, when he enlisted for service in the Civil War He entered Co C, 103rd Pa Vol Inf, as a private and was promoted to be corporal of his company and remained in the service until the close of the war, being mustered out in July, 1865, in North Carolina and receiving his honorable discharge at Harrisburg, Pa

During this long period, Mr Pifer served under four different captains—Capt S P Townsend, Capt Albert Vanastock, Capt John Coughern and Capt Thomas Coughern Although he participated in twenty-six battles and skirmishes, he was never taken prisoner or wounded, although, on several occasions he had parts of his uniform pierced by bullets At one time a minie ball carried off the number from the front of his cap, and on another occasion, the strap of his haversack was cut in two by a bullet. When the war was over he returned to the old farm, of which he was part owner and remained there until 1877, when he moved to Jefferson, a small town in Clarion County that experienced a boom on account of the discovery of oil in that region, and there conducted the Commercial Hotel for five years When the boom subsided, business died out and Mr Pifer soon looked about for a better business field While living in Clarion County he was more or less interested, like everybody else, in the oil business and after the tide of success had passed on, he found himself with several boilers and engines on his hands for which he had no special use It was in following out a suggestion made by a friend, Delmar Fairchild, that he used this machinery in experimenting in shingle manufacturing and as it seemed a successful venture, in June, 1882, he brought his outfit to Clearfield County and he and Mr Fairchild went into the shingle manufacturing business in the woods near DuBois

This almost accidental experiment was, in fact, the foundation on which Mr Pifer has built up his extensive industry of the present At a later date he sold out to Mr Fairchild and then, in partnership with his brother, John Pifer, set up a portable saw-mill and still later, a second one, with J A Bowersox For many years thereafter, Mr Pifer and Mr Bowersox dealt in lumber At a later date, Mr Pifer, with George Hess as a partner, started into the planing-mill business which has continued until the present time, being developed into a very important business enterprise of DuBois The firm name was Pifer, Hess & Co, until Mr Hess retired As Mr Pifer's sons, James and Charles, reached suitable age, they entered the employ of the firm and subsequently became partners and since then the firm style has been George W Pifer and Sons The work is evenly balanced, the senior member attending to the affairs of the firm on the outside, while the younger partners have charge of the inside work The plant is situated on the corner of S Brady and Tozier Avenue, DuBois, where excellent railroad facilities are enjoyed Employment is given twenty-five men

Mr Pifer has many times demonstrated his business judgment and foresight and never more so than when he bought his first acre of land when he first came to DuBois To this acre, right on the edge of the village he was able to add more acres and, as he foresaw, the time has come when this land has been added to the town and has been built over and is now some of the most valuable real estate in the place He is interested also in real estate at Falls Creek, Pa In 1883 he erected his own comfortable residence at No 715 S Brady Street and his sons, following in his footsteps have also invested in land and have homes in the same neighborhood

On November 2, 1865, Mr Pifer was married first to Miss Hannah Shrumm, who died in 1875 The following children were born to them Bessie, who is now deceased, Sarah E , who is the wife of Samuel Langford and they have two children—Ethel and Bessie, James H , who married Carrie Robinson and they have two children—George Cadmus and Virla Wynona, Charles E , who married Mary Shaw and they have three children—John George, Catherine Eva and Rachel In 1876, Mr Pifer was married secondly to Miss Hannah Malinda Wolfe, a daughter of Isaac and Maria (Ehinger) Wolfe, both deceased Mr and Mrs Pifer have had the following children Elizabeth, who is now deceased, Isabella, George B McClellan, a minister, who is a graduate of Mt Airey Lutheran Seminary; Warren A , who died at the age of nineteen years, Frances Cleveland, Grace May, who is a teacher of music, in Philadelphia, and Florence Leona.

Mr Pifer has always been a strong Democrat and as Sandy Township is strongly of his political way of thinking, he has been called upon to serve in many township offices For many years he has been a member of the township school board and by following his practical advice, the schools are in excellent condition, comparing very favorably with those in other sections He is a member of Easton Post, No 229, G A R, at DuBois, Pa With his family he belongs to the Lutheran church

GEORGE W SMYERS, proprietor of the G W Smyers planing mill and retail lumber yard, situated on Daly Street, DuBois, Pa, has been a resident of this borough since 1900 and is one of the representative business men of the place He was born on a farm in Jefferson County, Pa, November 10, 1863, and is a son of Daniel and Elizabeth (Kerr) Smyers

Daniel Smyers was not a native of Jefferson County but was small when he accompanied his father, also Daniel Smyers, to that section, where he grew to manhood and where he still lives He followed the cabinetmaking trade for forty years and also for many years conducted a planing mill at Big Run, where he makes his home He married Elizabeth Kerr, who died in 1890, and they had eight children, namely: George W.; Benjamin, Anna, who married Clark Brooks, Lucinda, who married Joseph Williams, Lawrence, Haddie, who married B Coleson; and Charles and Janet.

George W Smyers attended the country school near his father's farm in early boyhood but as soon as he was old enough he went to work in the planing mill He discovered that he had a taste and talent for this work and before he was more than a boy he had already become a wood turner with skill equal to that of a more experienced mechanic In his father's factory he had valuable experience and afterward was employed at Pittsburg, Philadelphia and other points, in every shop being made a foreman after a month's work From Punxatawney, Pa, where he was foreman for the Reese and Rodgers Company, he came to DuBois and he and Mr Rodgers built the present planing mill, a small shop being the beginning of the business, and in a few years Mr Rodgers retired Then C A McDonald was admitted as a partner but later he withdrew in order to engage in the hotel business and since then Mr Smyers has been alone From time to time he has enlarged his plant until it is an important one in this line, giving employment to fifteen men while the product is sash, doors, blinds and all kinds of building material Mr Smyers is a practical business man and keeps fully abreast with the times

On December 30, 1886, Mr Smyers was married to Miss Mamie Kelley, a daughter of Robert and Agnes (Barr) Kelley and a granddaughter of John S Barr, once sheriff of Jefferson County Mr and Mrs Smyers have five children· Von, LaRue, Wilda, Vere and Bernard They attend the United Presbyterian church The family home is at No 400 Daly Street, DuBois, and Mr Smyers owns other real estate He is a Republican in politics and is fraternally identified with the Masons, belonging to the Blue Lodge at DuBois and the Chapter at Philadelphia, and with the Knights of the Golden Eagle, at Punxatawney

JAMES J McCAMLEY, a well known and substantial citizen of Madera, Pa, where he owns a comfortable home and has two valuable lots adjoining it, was born in Scotland, February 14. 1855. and is a son of John and Margaret (Clark) McCamley The mother died in Scotland and the father, some years later, died at Madera They had nine children, James J being the eldest of the family

James J McCamley attended school in boyhood in the neighborhood of his home As soon as he was old enough he went to work in blast furnaces and later became a coal miner and has followed mining as his main business ever since He has been a careful, prudent industrious man and has shown his foresight and good judgment in the investments he has made in property He came to the United States in 1883 and lived for four years at Morrisdale, in Clearfield County, but has been a resident of Madera since June, 1887

In November, 1883. Mr McCamley was married in Scotland, to Miss Mary Carroll, who was born July 4, 1861. and is a daughter of Martin and Catherine (Lynch) Carroll They never came to the United States and since leaving her native land, Mrs McCamley has not seen the other members of her family She has one brother, Patrick, but her two younger sisters, Margaret and Elizabeth, are both deceased To Mr and Mrs McCamley ten children have been born, two of whom are deceased—John and Margaret The survivors are Mary, James, Martin, Jane, Agnes, Gertrude, Patrick and Thomas Mary is the wife of Bruce Johnston Mr McCamley and family belong to the Catholic church In politics he is a Democrat

HARRISON STRAW, whose fine farm of 145 acres is situated five and one-half miles north of Clearfield, Pa, carries on large agricultural operations and maintains a large dairy, with Guernsey stock Mr Straw was born April 15. 1861, in Ferguson Township, Clearfield County. Pa, and is a son of John T and Sarah (Young) Straw

John T Straw was born in Ferguson township and attended school in his native county and later taught school, following which he became a farmer and lumberman and spent his life as a resident of Ferguson township He was a man of local prominence and in 1881 was elected on the Democratic ticket, a member of the board of county commissioners and served through one full term He was a member and substantial supporter of the Baptist church His first marriage was to Sarah Young, a daughter of Albert Young, of Ferguson Township She died at the age of twenty-nine years and was buried at Zion Cemetery, in Jordan township She was the mother of six children Jeremiah, Albert Y, Harrison, William, Franklin and Anna Mary His second marriage was to Mary Ellen Barrett, a daughter of Luther Barrett She died when aged thirty years and was survived by three children, Perry, Lottie and Ida His third marriage was to Priscilla Barrett, a daughter of Hiram Barrett, and twelve children were born to this union, namely Rosetta, Cora, Susanna, Blanche, Myrtle, Carrie, John, Peary, Ivy Belle, Jerusha, Nora and Sarah

Harrison Straw was reared in Ferguson township and attended school there and spent one year at the Indiana State Normal School, after which he taught four terms of school, one in Jordan Township, two in

Lawrence Township and one in Ferguson Township After marriage he engaged in farming in Lawrence Township and moved from there to Ferguson Township, where he spent fourteen years and then settled in Goshen township, in January, 1907, purchasing what was known as the Thompson Read farm He has done a large amount of improving in the way of building and rebuilding and has even extended his improvements outside of his own property, practically making a new road to approach it Mr Straw has an income from a coal bank on his land He is a man of commendable enterprise and good citizenship and in all his relations with neighbors and acquaintances, stands well esteemed

On April 9, 1885, Mr Straw was married to Miss Emeline Read, a daughter of D R Read, of Ferguson Township, and eleven children have been born to them, as follows Clara, Russell, Eunice, Bertie, Harriet, David, Howard, Clayton, William, Donald and Sarah Clara is the wife of Harvey Smith and they reside in Goshen township Russell who was a successful school teacher in Goshen and Ferguson townships, is now a resident of Alberta, Canada Eunice, Bertie and Harriet attend the Clearfield High School, while the younger children, with the exception of Sarah, who died when aged two weeks, live at home and attend the Goshen township schools Mr Straw is affording his children every advantage in his power and there is promise of all developing into sensible, capable man and womanhood Mr Straw and family attend the Methodist Episcopal church In his political views he is a Democrat and he has served as school director and also on the election board at different times

LEONARD KYLER, who has been a valued resident of Bradford Township, Clearfield County, Pa, for twenty-six years, resides on his well improved farm of 130 acres, situated two miles south of Woodland, Pa He was born in Boggs Township, Clearfield County, Pa, in 1859, and is a son of John W and Sophia H (Shirey) Kyler.

John W Kyler was also born in Clearfield County and was a son of Jacob Kyler, who came to this section with his parents when young Thus the family naturally is numbered with the early ones of the county John W Kyler bought a farm in Boggs Township upon which he resided until his death, which occurred in 1901, his widow surviving until 1908

Leonard Kyler attended the schools of Boggs Township in his youth and has devoted himself ever since to farm pursuits He has resided on his present place ever since his marriage, with the exception of the first six months, and has developed this farm into one of the best in the township His industries are general farming and stock raising

Mr Kyler was married in 1883, to Miss Edith Smeal, of Bradford Township, Clearfield County, and they have had nine children born to them, namely. Gussie, a successful teacher at Bigler; Rosella, who died at the age of two years, Belva L, who was married in 1910 to Walter B Wagner, they now reside at Blue Ball, Boggs Township, Luella Jane, Catherine, John W, Berton, who died when aged eight months; and Sophia and Robert Leonard Mr Kyler and family are members of the Presbyterian church at Bigler, of which he was treasurer for five years He has been active in local politics. served three years as school director and at present is the efficient assessor of Bradford Township Mr Kyler is widely known and is held in general esteem by his fellow citizens

HON HARRY BOULTON, who has been engaged in the practice of law at Houtzdale, Pa , since 1897 and is a recognized leader of the Clearfield County bar, is also quite prominent in Republican politics in this section He was born in England, in 1872, and came to America in 1886, locating first in Arizona, where he joined his father One year later he came to Houtzdale, Pa , and has resided here ever since

Mr Boulton obtained a public school education, later studied law and was admitted to the bar in 1897 and in 1904 associated with Hon Cyrus Gordon, in the practice of law The death of Judge Gordon in 1911 dissolved this partnership He has taken a large amount of interest in public questions and is considered a leader of his party in Clearfield County He has never sought political honors unduly for himself, however, but is willing to work hard for his friends From 1894 until 1898 he was secretary of the Republican County Committee, and was county chairman from 1899 until 1903 In the latter year his party elected him a member of the state legislature and he served until 1905 and in the special session of 1906 In 1908 he was sent as a delegate to the National Republican Convention at Chicago Quite recently he has been again honored by an appointment as a member of the arbitration board for Central Pennsylvania, representing the coal operators, this being a direct recognition of his fair minded and conservative temperament

Mr Boulton married Miss Emily V Smith, at Houtzdale, who was born in New Jersey, and they have had two children Harold J and Eleanor, the latter of whom died in 1910 Mr Boulton is a Mason, belonging to Osceola Lodge No 515, to the Commandery at Phillipsburg, and to Jaffa Temple, Mystic Shrine, at Altoona He is somewhat interested as a coal operator and is a member of the directing board of the First National Bank of Houtzdale

HENRY E GINTER, president of the Keystone Mercantile Company, at DuBois, Pa , has been a resident of Clearfield County since 1851 and is prominently identified with many of the most important business interests of the county He was born at Harrisburg, Pa , September 17, 1844, and is a son of George and Elizabeth (Miller) Ginter.

George Ginter was born and reared in Bavaria, Germany, where he learned the shoemaking trade, one that he followed all his life After coming to America he located in the city of Philadelphia and there was soon married to Elizabeth Miller In 1835 they moved to Harrisburg and sixteen years later, in 1851, to Clearfield, making a part of the trip in a farm wagon Mr Ginter had come to what was then a very wild region with the intention of securing land for his children and to provide for old age He purchased 120 acres in the woods, in Brady Township and lived as renter until a cabin could be built Fortunately it was the spring of that year, May, and as soon as the other settlers in that region heard of his need of a house, they gathered, as was the friendly custom among pioneers at that time, and soon had a comfortable round log house ready for occupancy, constructing it all in one day. Later a barn was added and before his death, Mr. Ginter had cleared twenty acres of his land. He did not live long enough to be able to really enjoy the results of his enterprise and industry, his death occurring in 1857, when he was fifty-five years of age. His widow survived until 1880, passing away at the age of sixty-seven years. They had six children born to them, three of whom died young. The three who reached maturity were George, Joel A and Henry Edward. George Ginter was killed in the battle of the Wilderness, May 6, 1864, during the Civil War, while serving as a soldier in Co A, 105th Pa Vol Inf. Joel A Ginter was a member of the same regiments as his older brother but lived to return to peaceful pursuits and now resides in Indiana County, Pa.

Henry Edward Ginter was seven years old when his parents came to Clearfield County and he had little chance to go to school as at that time Brady Township's school system was practically unorganized and also, on the pioneer farm there was work for every pair of hands. When thirteen years old, after the death of his father, he was hired by a neighboring farmer to drive the horses on the old-time horse-power threshing machine and for this work he was paid twenty-five cents a day. It was in this way that the present capitalist, manufacturer, man of affairs in which the handling of thousands of dollars is a daily occurrence, earned the money with which to buy his first pair of boots, for which he paid six dollars. Mr Ginter relates as an indication of the caution which probably has had considerable to do with his successful management

of important concerns in later life, that for years he would never enter into any business contract with an employer except on a basis of one day's labor, and by this arrangement was able to terminate any connection which he found undesirable.

When Mr Ginter was seventeen years of age he began rafting, a dangerous and difficult branch of the lumber industry, and from then until he was twenty-one years old his work was taking lumber rafts down Mahoning Creek and the Allegheny River to Pittsburg and frequently as far as Cincinnati, O. In the year that he reached his majority he purchased his first raft, which he safely guided down the river to Pittsburg, selling it there and on this, his first venture, clearing $200. Finding that his undertakings in this line would probably be successful on account of his natural good judgment, Mr Ginter continued his interest in the lumber business, broadening his operations until he found himself the owner of immense timber tracts, operating saw-mills and manufacturing lumber, shingles and square timber, at times having partners in his enterprises and at others being engaged alone. At the present date of writing (1910), he is developing a tract of second growth timber in Brady Township. In 1869, Mr Ginter, in partnership with Samuel Yohe, bought 218 acres of timber land from George Pentz in Brady Township, this being Mr Ginter's first venture in this field. As before he found that his judgment had been correct and in a very short time this tract became so valuable that he was able to sell out his interest at a profit of $3300.

In 1873 Mr Ginter found time to turn his attention to merchandising and in partnership with S G Koontz, embarked in a general mercantile business at Troutville, Pa , engaging also in a lumbering business and this firm continued for nine years, when Mr Ginter sold out his interest in the partnership and again devoted himself more particularly to his lumbering enterprises He has by no means confined his attention, however, to this industry although, as previously mentioned, his interests are large and important in it In 1894 he moved to DuBois and here has identified himself in many ways with leading business interests Among these may be mentioned his presidency of the Keystone Mercantile Company, dealers in wholesale groceries both staple and fancy He is a stockholder in the DuBois National Bank and is also a stockholder in the Punxsutawney National Bank, at Punxsutawney, Pa He was one of the organizers and is vice president of the United Traction Street Railroad Company, and in all these and other enterprises his sound business sense and evenly balanced judgment have proved invaluable, contributing largely to the success which has signally marked them He owns farming as well as timber lands in both Clearfield and Jefferson Counties

Mr Ginter was married in August, 1868, to Miss Louisa Kuntz, who was born in Germany, a daughter of Philip Kuntz Mrs Ginter came to America in 1853 To Mr and Mrs Ginter six children have been born, namely Harry I, who is a resident of DuBois, married Arlene Waterhouse, Elizabeth, who married A S Moulthrop, and they have one son, Henry S , Nora E , who married J W Schoch, and they have one son, Donald, Sallie A , who is the wife of Dr J G Hilleary, James E , who is a practicing physician at Tylor, Pa , married Adria Miles , and Mordacai E , who married Catherine Blakesley, and they have one daughter, Louisa Mr and Mrs Ginter are active members of the Methodist Episcopal church at DuBois and they are liberal in the support they give to the various benevolent organizations conducted and authorized by this religious body Nevertheless they are quiet, home loving people whose bulk of charities are never known by the world They enjoy a pleasant and comfortable home which is situated at No 223 E Long Avenue, DuBois Since 1869, Mr Ginter has been a member of the Odd Fellows, identified with the lodge at Punxsutawney, and he belongs also to the Knights of Pythias His political sentiments have made him a Republican but he has never been a candidate for any public office

W E DERRICK, one of Grampian's enterprising and successful business men who conducts a general store and has frequently held public office, was born in a log cabin, situated four miles northwest of Grampian, Pa , in Bloom Township, Clearfield County, March 6, 1864 He is a son of W G and Eliza (Moore) Derrick

W G Derrick was born in Pike Township, Clearfield County, Pa , on the Thompson farm, on the Erie turnpike road, June 16, 1832, and attended school near Bridgeport He married Eliza Moore, a daughter of James Moore, and they had nine children, of whom James, who is a carpenter, lives at Grampian; Ella. Mrs Dean, lives in Medina County, O , Ellsworth, lives in Stark County, O , W E is the subject of this sketch At the outbreak of the Rebellion, W G Derrick enlisted for service under Col A E Irvin, in the famous "Bucktail" regiment He was wounded in the foot at the battle of the Wilderness and thereby received an injury that troubled him during the remainder of his life When he entered the army his wife and four children moved to Grampian, where he subsequently joined them but in the next year sold out his interests there and moved with his family to Kaoland, Mo Prior to that one more child had been born, Bertha, who is the wife of William Thomas, of Grand Rapids, Mich Mr Derrick resided in Missouri for four years and during that time was a prominent citizen in the community, serving as postmaster and also as mail carrier Before the return of Mr and Mrs Derrick one more child was born, David, who lives in Stark County, O , and after reaching Grampian a daughter, Caroline, was born She is now deceased, having been the wife of Job Spencer The family then moved to a farm in Penn Township, where two more children were born Harry, who died at the age of two years, and Victor, who died aged seven months Mr. Derrick being somewhat incapacitated on account of the injury to his foot, soon sold his farm and returned to Grampian, where he worked as a carpenter He was a Republican after the Civil War and served in several public capacities both in the borough and township His death occurred May 6, 1904, at the age of seventy-three years His wife had passed away July 2, 1894, and both were buried in the Friends' Cemetery at Grampian

W E Derrick attended school at Grampian and when old enough he went to Ohio and worked by the month on farms in Lafayette Township, Medina County, for eight years After his first marriage he engaged as a clerk with M H Lampman, at Lorain, O , afterward going out on the road for W. B Chapman, Jr., a dealer in groceries in Medina County Following the death of his first wife he returned to Grampian and was employed as a clerk by William McDonald for eight years and then for one year was manager for E F Spencer Mr. Derrick then embarked in the meat business with C G Russell, the firm being Russell & Derrick, which continued for three years, when Mr Derrick sold his interest and became a clerk for S T. Orcutt, in the hardware business In 1906 he bought the business of his former employer, William McDonald, and has developed a large and constantly growing enterprise In the winter of 1895, Mr. Derrick worked for Mr. McDonald for fifty cents a day and in 1896, for seventy-five cents a day, and fourteen years later, through his prudence, industry and acquired experience, was able to purchase the business and make it his own He has several valuable pieces of property, two lots being improved with buildings and two lots still vacant. His business capacity has been fully demonstrated

On September 17, 1885, Mr. Derrick was married in Medina county, O , to Miss Macy Kindig, who was born in Wayne County, O , December 13, 1868, a daughter of David Kindig Mrs Derrick died July 21, 1893, and was survived by one daughter, Nora, who is the wife of William L Nolder of Luthersburg, Pa , and they have two children Anna May and Robert Lewis Mr Derrick was married September 21, 1898, to

H. A. WOODSIDE, M. D.

Miss Kittie Shaw, a highly educated lady, who had been a school teacher for eight years previously She is a daughter of G Moody Shaw, of Medina County. They have one son, Charles Edinson, who was born January 6, 1901, who is a bright student in the Grampian graded school On many occasions Mr Derrick has been shown proof of the esteem and confidence of his fellow citizens He has served as assessor and for eight years as borough treasurer and has filled other offices, elected to the same on the Republican ticket He is collector for the Harrison & Industrial Savings and Loan Association, of Grampian, in which he is a stockholder He is also a member of the P O. S of A

H A WOODSIDE, M D, physician and surgeon at Lumber City, Pa, where he is numbered with the public spirited and valuable citizens, was born in Boggs township, Clearfield county, Pa, August 10, 1871, and is a son of T B and Mary Ann (Turner) Woodside

T B Woodside was born in Center county, Pa, in 1842, and was reared and educated in Center and Clearfield counties In early manhood he married Mary Ann Turner, a daughter of John Turner of Boggs township, and they had nine children born to them, as follows H A , J A , who lives at Philipsburg, Pa., W W , who is a clerk in the Bickford store at Curwensville, H L , who is a physician practicing at Clover Run, Clearfield county, Guy, who is an iron worker, at Johnstown, Pa ; Roy, who lives in New Jersey; and Donald, Vada and Letitia, all of whom live at home T B Woodside maintained his home in Boggs township, at Wallacetown and in Gra-

ham township, before he settled permanently as a farmer in Boggs township, where he owns 155 acres of valuable land He has been a lifelong Democrat and has frequently served in township offices Formerly he was identified with the Odd Fellows With his wife he belongs to the Methodist Episcopal church

H A Woodside attended the public schools in Boggs township, then the Mahaffey school under G W L Oster, in the class of 1889, and later the Central State Normal School at Lock Haven, in 1893 He then taught four terms of school, one of these being in the Winburne High School After this he entered Jefferson Medical College, Philadelphia, where he was graduated in 1897, and after a year of experience in the Jefferson Hospital, he came to Lumber City in April, 1898 Dr Woodside is a member of the county and state medical bodies and of the American Medical Association He is a member of the board of health for the borough of Lumber City and also is health officer for Knox and Ferguson townships He is local surgeon for the New York Central Railroad at this point In addition to a large and lucrative practice he has other interests, being a stockholder in two of the leading National Banks of the county, also is concerned in the Bickford store and meat market at Curwensville

In April, 1890, Dr Woodside was married to Miss Belle McClure, who was born in Pike township, a daughter of John R McClure, and they have two children Wendell H and Hobart K In politics Dr Woodside is a Democrat, and a member of Masonic lodge, Noble Lodge No. 480, Curwensville

CHARLES D McMURRAY, who is one of the representative business men of

Jordan Township, Clearfield County, Pa,
where he owns a valuable farm of 180 acres
and has large lumber interests at other
points, was born May 15, 1856, in Knox
Township, Clearfield County, Pa

John McMurray, who was the father of
Charles D McMurray, was a farmer all his
life and was a highly respected man, a leading member of the Methodist Episcopal
church He was a Democrat and was a
man well qualified for public office He
married Jane Alexander Hegarty, and both
are now deceased, the burial of the father
having been at New Washington, Pa, and
that of the mother at Hegarty's Cross
Roads To them were born the following
children John Alexander, Robert Taylor,
Catherine Jane, and Charles D Catherine
Jane is the wife of James D Wiley

Charles D McMurray attended the district schools and afterward went to work in
the woods but later embarked in a mercantile business at Ansonville, to which he
came in 1883, and continued for twenty-
seven years He then resumed lumbering
and at the present time is thus interested in
Beccaria Township and also in Cambria
County

Mr McMurray was married first in 1880,
to Miss Malissa Shoff, a daughter of Samuel
P and Ruth (Ames) Shoff She died in
September, 1881, and her burial was at
Hegarty's Cross Roads They had two
children, Ferman and Mertie Ann, both of
whom are deceased Mr McMurray was
married second, October 5, 1886, to Mary
Lavinia McKeehen, a daughter of James and
Mary Jane McKeehen, and they have had
four children: Georgia Jane, who was born
September 5, 1890, Ruth E, who was born

May 8, 1893; Maud, born November 23,
1896, who is deceased, and Dorcas L, who
was born February 16, 1910 Mr and Mrs
McMurray attend the Methodist Episcopal
church at Ansonville. He is a Democrat in
his political sentiments and has frequently
served in public office, for six years being
township treasurer, for five years auditor,
and also township clerk and school director
He is a member of Curwensville Lodge, F.
& A M, and of the Odd Fellows at Ansonville, and belongs also to the Encampment
at Glen Hope

N R MOORE, funeral director and embalmer, one of the representative business
men of DuBois, Pa, was born August 4,
1873, at Rockdale Mills, Jefferson County,
Pa, and is a son of Thomas and Ellen (Mc-
Morris) Moore

Thomas Moore was one of the pioneer
settlers at Rockdale Mills, Pa He was
born in Ireland, came to America in early
manhood and was married in Philadelphia
to Ellen McMorris, also of Irish birth They
determined to establish a home and as they
had but small capital, they were forced to
seek a still unsettled region, one in which
their thrift and industry would provide for
their future They crossed the mountains
into Jefferson County and reached Tyrone
in Blair County and from there went by ox-
teams to Rockdale Mills, where they started
a general store, Mr. Moore having to haul
all his merchandise from Tyrone, a long
distance He was a cabinetmaker and a
part of his work was the making of coffins
He was a very neat and expert workman
At that time the shape of a coffin was like
that of a kite and Mr. Moore's measure-

ments were very simple, length of body and breadth of shoulders being alone necessary For many years he constructed these temporary receptacles of the dead in his neighborhood He was widely known and lived a busy, useful life, dying at the age of seventy-three years His widow survived until 1903, when aged seventy-four years They had the following children born to them Ella, who is the wife of A U Moore, James, who is deceased, Louisa, who is the wife of A J Riley, John, Bessie, who is the wife of J H Brown, Emma, Matilda M, who is the wife of W F Hay, N Robert, and William

N Robert Moore first attended school at Rockdale Mills and later took a course in the Ohio Normal University, at Ada, O From the age of fourteen years until he was twenty-six years old he followed the carpenter's trade In 1889 he went to Allegheny and there entered the well known undertaking establishment of James Lowery, in order to learn the business in a thorough manner, and later took a course and received his diploma, at the Champion College of Embalming He then engaged in an undertaking business and dealt also in furniture, at Rural Valley, where he continued until 1901, when he came to DuBois Here in 1901 he bought out the business of C N Miller, at his present location, on Long Avenue He purchased the property on September 15, 1910, and on the fifth of the succeeding October, he suffered a loss of his buildings from fire He went into temporary quarters, where he remained until his present complete and commodious buildings were erected His office and show rooms occupy one-half of the ground floor of his building, with a morgue, sanitary in every particular, in the basement His office is handsomely furnished and every convenience is placed at the disposal of those who have business with him Mr Moore has probably the finest general equipments for funerals in all this section He has a number of fine horses, among these being a team of pure white Arabians, which he purchased in Indiana and which are said to be the best matched team in Clearfield County He has a number of vehicles appropriate for his business, including black and white funeral cars, a silver grey ambulance, a call wagon, etc, all of these being given storage in a near-by livery stable Mr Moore's patronage comes from over a wide territory His business is conducted with the dignity that it demands and careful attention is given to every detail

On October 28, 1898, Mr Moore was married to Miss E Pearl Laughery, a daughter of W G Laughery, of Beach Tree, Pa, and they have two children, Harold and Helen Mr and Mrs Moore are members of the Presbyterian church In politics he is a Republican Fraternally he is a member of Garfield Lodge, No 559, F & A M, and Garfield Chapter, No 225, at DuBois, and also of the Odd Fellows and of the Knights of Pythias

PETER BROWN, who, for twenty-six years has been a resident of Girard Township, Clearfield County, Pa, is one of its leading citizens and successfully carries on farming and stockraising on his 118 acres of valuable land Mr Brown was born in Ireland and is a son of James and Grace Brown

When Mr Brown was a child of four years, his parents emigrated to Canada and he was reared and attended school there and helped his father, who was a farmer and stock buyer Both parents died there, some twenty years since They were good people, respected as neighbors and earnest members of the Catholic church

At the age of seventeen years, Peter Brown started out from home to make his own way in the world He crossed the line into New York and then came to Williamsport, Pa , finding plenty of work in the lumber regions and continuing to labor in the woods until 1895, when he bought his present farm and since then has devoted himself mainly to farming and stock-raising, producing wheat, corn and oats, and cattle and hogs His land lies fifteen miles southwest of Clearfield, which is his market It is all underlaid with coal and fireclay and other minerals, and there are 80 acres covered with a fine growth of young timber, such as white oak, red oak, and chestnut, with some pine In the summer time hundreds of people come here from Clearfield to spent the day, driving back in the evening

Mr Brown was married to Miss Hannah Krise, a daughter of Daniel Krise, of Girard township, and they started housekeeping at Laurel Run They had one daughter, Mary, who grew into a beautiful woman She became the wife of Robert Green and the mother of three children Iva, Jennings and C C Her death occurred at the early age of thirty-four years, leaving many to mourn her loss Mr Brown and wife are members of St. Francis' Catholic Church at Frenchville As a man of sterling character, energy and good judgment, Mr Brown has frequently been elected to township offices by his fellow citizens and has served two years as supervisor, seventeen years as tax collector and for fifteen years as school director

ABRAM C SHOFF, owner and proprietor of a general store at Madera, Pa , located on Main Street, was born April 16, 1849, in what was then Beccaria but is now Bigler Township, Clearfield County, Pa His parents were Samuel and Jane (Hegarty) Shoff The father came to Clearfield County from Lancaster, while it is probable that the mother was born on the other side of the Atlantic Ocean, old family records having been lost

Abram C Shoff obtained his education in the country schools and as soon as old enough and strong enough went to work in the woods and continued lumbering until it was no longer profitable in this section, the land being practically all cleared off He owns three acres of land outside of Madera and enjoys looking after its cultivation In 1890 he embarked in the mercantile business at his present stand and has built up an excellent trade and is ably assisted in this enterprise by his capable wife

Mr Shoff was married June 19, 1879, to Miss Cynthia E Lukens, a daughter of J A. and Agnes (Maguigen) Lukens Mrs Abram C (Lukens) Shoff's paternal ancestors can be traced back five generations Gabriel Lukens came to America from Germany, one of two brothers, sons, Charles and John, both surveyors appointed by the Governor under King George The former did much of the early surveying in Centre County John was killed by the Indians near Standing Stone, Huntingdon County

The third in descent was Abraham Lukens, who wedded ———— Brown of Juniata County, he was twice married, his second wife being Miss Maggie Sanderson His son David wedded Elizabeth Sunderland, daughter of David and ——— Hamilton Sunderland of Mifflin County, who were of Scotch descent Four children weer born to this union, James A being the eldest The others were Wm B , Sarah A Jones, and David of Atchison, Kan , all now deceased They were mainly Presbyterians

On the maternal John Maguigen wedded ——— Cross, both of Lancaster County but later came to Mifflin County To this union there were five children Mrs Agnes (Maguigen) Lukens is in her 84th year and is the mother of Cynthia E (Lukens) Shoff Her other children were William A , of Clearfield, Pa ; Clara, Blanche and Jessie W , both of whom are deceased Bertha, who is the wife of W C Smith of Johnstown, Pa , and Emma, who is deceased, was the wife of George C Roland, of Indiana, Pa The grandfathers of Mrs Shoff were David Lukens and John Maguigen Her parents were members of the Baptist church Her father was a Democrat Mr and Mrs Shoff have seven children, namely William A , who lives in Madera, Charles, who is manager of a company store at Beulah, Clearfield County , Edna, who is the wife of E P Hagan, of Osceola Mills, and Benton, V E , Joseph C and Wilhelmina Mr and Mrs Shoff attend the Presbyterian church In politics he is a Republican For a number of years he has belonged to Lodge No 669, Odd Fellows, at Glen Hope, Pa

GEORGE F McMULLEN, owner and proprietor of the Grampian Hotel, at Grampian, Pa , and a member of the borough school board and is one of the representative citizens and enterprising business men

He was born August 2, 1870, in Huntingdon County, Pa , and is a son of John and Katherine McMullen, who never resided in Clearfield County

George F McMullen was reared and educated in Franklin County, Pa In March, 1901, he started in business in the Hotel Aberdeen Selling out he engaged in the mercantile business being in the firm of A McGrath & Co In August, 1904, he again engaged in the Hotel business in Grampian Hotel and in the following year tore down the old building, which had been standing for 40 years, replacing it with a three-story brick hotel, with modern conveniences, heated by a hot water system He has twenty well furnished bed-rooms and six other rooms for hotel purposes Mr McMullen makes the moderate charge of $1 50 per day while he offers his guests a bill of fare that includes both substantials and dainties He is widely known and his house is very popular Mr McMullen carries a license.

In 1901 Mr McMullen was married to Miss Lillie Flynn, who was born at Grampian, a daughter of M M Flynn They have three children, John, Mary and George Mr and Mrs McMullen are members of the Catholic church Politically he is a Democrat and fraternally he belongs to Lodge No 540, B P O E , at Clearfield

ALFRED M LIVERIGHT, county solicitor of the county of Clearfield Pa , and junior member of the well known law firm of Krebs & Liveright, with offices on Locust Street, Clearfield, between First and Second, is a leading member of the Clearfield Bar

He was born at Davenport, Iowa, November

10, 1872, and is one of a family of six children born to his parents, Henry and Henrietta (Fleisher) Liveright, the former of whom was largely interested in the coal industry

Alfred M Liveright was afforded educational opportunities which included collegiate advantages, and in 1891 he was graduated at the University of Pennsylvania In the following year he entered upon the study of law and was admitted to the bar in November, 1894, selecting Clearfield County as the field of his efforts In 1898, during the war with Spain, he was appointed deputy district attorney of the county, and performed the duties of that office until the end of the war In 1900 he entered into a partnership with former Judge David L Krebs, whose death occurred January 25, 1911 The combination of legal talent proved a strong one From early manhood Mr Liveright has been interested in public affairs, and has identified himself with the Republican party In May 1906 he was first elected county solicitor of Clearfield County, and was re-elected in 1909

Mr Liveright was married in 1899 to Miss Margaret Krebs, a daughter of D L Krebs, and they have two children, Mary Krebs and Henry, Jr Mr and Mrs Liveright are prominent in the social and educational life of the borough

PATRICK GRATTAN, mine foreman at Morgan Run mine and the owner of four and one-half acres of land in Bigler Township, Clearfield County, Pa, together with three residence properties at Madera, is a well known and highly respected citizen of this section He was born at Bartley, in Bradford County, March 17, 1871, and is a son of Bernard and Julia (Ague) Grattan

The parents of Mr. Grattan were born and married in Ireland. They came to America in 1862 and the father first found work as a brick-layer and later as a miner and still later was engaged in a mercantile business at Madera, where both he and wife died, the former at Madera Mrs Bernard Grattan died at Centerville, Elk county They were devoted members of the Catholic church They had four children Patrick, Bernard, Thomas and Nora, the last named dying at Madera, Clearfield county, at the age of eleven years.

Patrick Grattan attended the Catholic schools at Centerville, but not satisfied with the opportunities he could command here, he made arrangements with the International Correspondence School of Scranton, and continued a student with that organization for seven years and completed the course in mining In the meanwhile he learned all the practical details by personal experience, having started to work in the mines when he was only twelve years old He has been very enterprising, ambitious and persevering and has won his own way through his own efforts For the past six years he has been mine foreman, working first in this capacity for H B Swoope, afterward for H B Swoope & Co, and at present is with the Arctic Coal Company He took charge of the Betz mine March 16, 1911, as mine foreman for the Arctic Coal Company, H B Swoope, general manager He has worked under H B Swoope for the last nine years He is considered a well informed and thoroughly reliable mine man

Mr Grattan was married December 26, 1893, to Miss Mary Murray, a daughter of Patrick and Bridget (Daugherty) Murray The parents of Mrs Grattan were residents of Brisbin, Clearfield County, and her father was a coal miner They had the following children Mary, who is the wife of Mr Grattan, Daniel and Hugh, both of whom are deceased, James, Rose, who is the wife of Daniel Murphy, Sarah, who is the wife of Bernard Carr, and Catherine, who is the wife of Robert Sturbord Mr and Mrs Grattan have six children Hugh, Leo, Murray, Bernice, May and Sarah The family belongs to the Catholic church Nominally Mr Grattan is a Democrat but he is a man capable of doing his own thinking and frequently votes according to his own judgment He is a member of the A O H at Houtzdale, Pa

JAMES BURTON LUTHER, of the J B Luther Undertaking Co, the oldest established business of its kind at DuBois, Pa, with commodious quarters on the corner of Park Avenue and Brady Street, was born at West Fairfield, Pa, July 19, 1871, and has been a resident of this borough since 1901 His parents are J G and Alice (Peoples) Luther

J G Luther, who is a veteran of the Civil War, was one of a family of fourteen children born to his parents, who were early settlers in Westmoreland County, Pa, and grew to manhood on the pioneer farm In 1861 he enlisted for three years' service in the Civil War, entering an infantry regiment as a private He was once made prisoner and confined for three months at Andersonville but was then exchanged and served out his first term of enlistment He then reenlisted as sergeant in an artillery regiment, and was a second time captured, in the previous fighting barely escaping with his life, his uniform being riddled with bullet holes
27

He was sent to Libby Prison and there endured torture for three months before he escaped After the close of the war he returned to his home and followed the carpenter's trade for a time and also undertaking, making coffins by hand at first He also started a grist mill, but this enterprise he later abandoned He still is engaged in the undertaking business at West Fairfield He married Alice Peoples, who was born in Westmoreland County, and eight children were born to them, namely Margaret, who is the wife of Charles Mabon, James Burton. Cora, who is the wife of L R Hamilton, William P, John M, who is a physician, Harry J, Blanche, who is deceased, and Nan, now deceased, who was the wife of S C Huston

James Burton Luther was educated in the common and High School at West Fairfield and later took a business course at Duff's Commercial College, Pittsburg, Pa In preparation for his future business he then entered the Philadelphia College of Embalming, where he remained until graduation, after which he spent a year in the morgue at Pittsburg, gaining practical experience in his profession For two years Mr Luther was in the furniture and undertaking business at Florence, Pa, and from there came to DuBois Here he entered into the employ of the undertaking firm of Flegel & Weber On September 7, 1909, in partnership with P T Sullivan, he bought out the entire interests of that firm and since then the business has been conducted under the style of the J B Luther Undertaking Co It was established by Mr Flegal who later admitted L E Weber to partnership, by whom he was succeeded in 1907, and in 1909, as stated above, it came into the hands of the present competent business men, both of whom hold state embalmer's licenses The new firm has all necessary equipments for their business, including two fine teams, one white and the other black, four funeral cars, a casket wagon, an ambulance, and cabs to accommodate pall bearers

On July 15, 1899, Mr Luther was married to Miss Anna Brown, who died May 28, 1909 Two children were born to them Francis, in 1903, and Alice, in 1906 Mr Luther was married secondly October 17, 1910, to Mrs Eva C Schwem, widow of Walter Schwem and daughter of S C Christ, of Brookville, Pa Mr Luther and family reside at No 212 E Long Avenue, and they attend the Presbyterian church He belongs to the Royal Arcanum and to the Knights of Pythias

E D BILLOTTE, whose energy and enterprise have made him one of the most prominent men of Girard township, Clearfield county, Pa, not only owns and operates a grist-mill, a saw-mill and a general store, but also owns 550 acres of valuable land Although not a native, Mr Billotte has lived in Clearfield county since he was four years old and all his interests are centered here He was born on Moore's island, in Clinton county, Pa, January 14, 1865, and is a son of Justin and Catherine (Coneway) Billotte, the former of whom was born in France and was brought to America by his parents in the year 1847 when eight years old They settled at Frenchville, Pa

E D Billotte attended school in Girard township, but other duties limited his days at school, and from the age of 12 to 21 he helped his father in lumbering When he reached manhood he married August 22, 1889, Miss Eliza C. Blubell, a daughter of Victor Blubell, a prominent lumberman of Girard township, and seven children have been born to them, namely Ferdinand, Anna, Mabel, Alice, Clare, Levina and Viola They have also an adopted son, Clarence.

In almost all that he has undertaken, Mr. Billotte has been successful, the reason being, perhaps, that he conducts all his business enterprises according to sound business principles He possesses the knowledge and foresight that enables him to carry on store, mills, farming and stockraising where these industries are most needed, and thus, while contributing to his own success, advances the prosperity of his section He has also taken a civil engineering course at Scranton, Pa His mills and large general store are situated at Lecontes Mills, where said postoffice originated Notwithstanding his numerous business interests and his practice in civil engineering, contracting, etc, he has been active for years in public matters. For nine years he has been auditor of Girard township, for seven years has been clerk, and for six years has been assessor of Girard township, in 1901 he was elected justice of the peace and in 1906 was re-elected From 1897 until 1902 he was postmaster at Odessa, Pa, and his wife from 1902 until 1909 Mr Billotte and family are members of the Catholic church at Frenchville, and he belongs to the C M. B A, at Emporium, Pa His large plant is situated at Lecontes Mill, sixteen miles northeast of Clearfield

J L HENDERSON, M D, who has been engaged in the practice of medicine at Osceola Mills, Pa, for more than two decades and is known professionally over a wide territory, is also one of the progressive and representative citizens of the town He was born at Lewistown, Mifflin county, Pa, February 20, 1853, and is a son of Dr Joseph and Margaret (Isenberg) Henderson

Dr Joseph Henderson was born at Carlisle, Pa., in 1792, a son of Matthew Henderson, and a grandson of Daniel Henderson, both of whom were born in Pennsylvania, of Scotch ancestry Daniel Henderson spent his life in Chester county Matthew Henderson, who was the grandfather of Dr J L Henderson, of Osceola Mills, was a civil engineer and surveyor and appears to have been a man of excellent parts He was a collector of excise for the Penn family, prior to the Revolutionary War and was a deputy surveyor in the laying out of Franklin and Cumberland counties He was married in 1796 to Margaret Kearsley, who was living at Valley Forge at the time Washington's army wintered there, and it was her brother Captain Samuel Kearsley and his wife, who gave liberally of their means to provide for the comfort of the starving and freezing soldiers during that terrible winter, and in appreciation of this generosity, General Washington, in the presence of the assembled soldiers, later presented his own sword to Captain Kearsley Margaret Kearsley was a daughter of Jonathan and Jane Kearsley, the former of whom was born in Scotland in 1718, and the latter in 1720 Dr Joseph Henderson located in Mifflin county, Pa, in 1832, where he continued the practice of medicine until

his death, in 1863 He traced his American ancestry back to 1715 He married Margaret Isenberg and they were parents of three sons, two of whom are physicians, William B and James Linn, the former of whom is engaged in practice at Philipsburg, Pa

James Linn Henderson was ten years old when his father died When aged about sixteen years he went west and spent ten years in Kansas and Illinois When he returned to the east he located at Lima, O, where he engaged in medical study under one of the well known old practitioners of that city, and subsequently entered the Ohio Medical College, at Cincinnati, where he was graduated in 1881, receiving his diploma He returned to near Lima and continued to practice among his former friends until failing health caused him to seek another location For three years he was in practice at Karthaus, Pa, and then came to Osceola Mills, where he has continued ever since, building up a fine practice here as the result of professional capacity, and at the same time winning the confidence and esteem of his fellow citizens through personal worth For more than ten years Dr Henderson has been a member of the Board of Health and for fifteen years has served on the school board For ten years he has been also president of the Osceola Mills Building and Loan Association

Dr Henderson was married first to Miss Frances Hughes, of Indiana, who died in 1897, leaving three children William Hughes, who is assistant chief engineer for a steel company at Youngstown, O, Joseph Linn, who is in the U S Government employ, in the Forestry service, in Arizona, and Matthew Francis, who resides at home

Dr Henderson was married second to Miss Annie Allen, of Lewistown, Pa Since its organization, Dr Henderson has been a member of the West Branch Medical Society and belongs also to Clearfield County, Pennsylvania State and the American Medical Associations For twenty years he has been identified with the order of United Workmen

LEWIS W BEYER, postmaster at Smoke Run, owner of a general store, at this point and an extensive lumber dealer, is also president of the First National Bank at Houtzdale, Pa He was born in Bigler township, Clearfield county, Pa , September 25, 1870, and is a son of John and Emma E (Ross) Beyer

John Beyer was born in 1830, near Juniata, in Blair county, and died at Smoke Run October 23, 1910 He settled at what was then called Muddy Run, in 1843 and engaged in lumbering and thus continued during his active years He first married a Miss Keagy of Glen Hope, of which union there were three children. Jennie, who is the wife of Lewis H Irvin, Mary Malissa, who resides at Clearfield, and William V , who was accidentally killed by a railroad train in 1890 Mr Beyer married for his second wife, Emma E Ross, who survives him and resides at Smoke Run They had the following children Sarah, who is the wife of Rev W. J Shaffer, of the Methodist church at Everett, Pa , Christianna, who is the wife of Rev C W Rishell, pastor of the Methodist Episcopal church at Montoursville, Lewis W., and Hannah, who is the wife of G R McMurrey, who conducts a meat market at Beulah, Pa

Lewis W Beyer was educated in the public schools, Williamsport Seminary, and Iron City Commercial College, at Pittsburg, after which he was associated with his father in the lumber business and they continued as long as it was profitable in this section Then Mr. Beyer together with his sister, Miss Mary Malissa Beyer, started a general store under the firm name of L & M. Beyer, and the partnership continued until in November, 1910, when Mr. Beyer purchased his sister's interest He has been postmaster since 1898 He has other important interests, as indicated above, and is one of the representative business men of the county

Mr. Beyer was married December 21, 1892, to Miss Fransena Rumery, a daughter of M D and Martha Rumery. The father of Mrs Beyer was born in New Hampshire and formerly was a lumberman He now owns a general store at Glen Hope, where he is also postmaster In politics Mr Beyer is a stanch Republican With his wife he belongs to the Methodist Episcopal church Fraternally he is identified with the Masonic lodge at Coalport, and the P O S of A , at Madera

MANLEY B GOFF, proprietor of the Brady Street Roller Mills, located at No 340 South Brady street, DuBois, Pa , is one of the representative business men of the place, with which he has been identified since 1900 He was born March 14, 1867, in Jay township, Elk county, Pa , and is a son of Algenorn E and Caroline E. (Pearsall) Goff

Algenorn E Goff was born and reared in Elk county, Pa He was a son of Potter Goff, and was but a boy when his father died

MANLEY B. GOFF

The latter was one of the pioneers of Elk county, a descendant of Lord William Goff, a native of Ireland Great-grandfather Goff was a cooper by trade but became blind in his last years and was taken care of by his children Algenorn E Goff was reared by his half-brothers and followed farming and lumbering in Elk county for many years After retiring from active labor he came to DuBois, where he now resides He married Caroline E Pearsall, a daughter of Alfred Pearsall, formerly of Elk county, and five children were born to them, namely Florence E, who is the wife of W H Weed, of Weedville, Pa ; Manley B , Elvira, who is deceased, was the wife of Edward Henry, of Clearfield county, Mary, who is the wife of R D Hall, of DuBois, and Carrie, who is the wife of U G Green, of DuBois

Manley B Goff grew to manhood on the home farm and attended the district schools of Jay township and the High School at Penfield, Pa After spending twenty-eight years on the farm he determined to engage in other business and moved to Caledonia, Elk county, where he embarked in a general mercantile business, in partnership with Fred A Tozier, which was continued for one year, when Mr Goff removed to Johnsonburg and bought out the grocery, flour and feed business of E C Stanley Mr Goff carried on this enterprise for about eighteen months but not being satisfied with results then spent a short time looking about for a better business field, finding promising prospects at DuBois, to which place he came in April, 1900 Here he purchased the Brady Street Roller Mills, from S J Schrecongost, and conducted the business alone until July, 1909, when he admitted M W Barclay as a partner, the latter of whom

was succeeded in December, 1910, by R L Hunter The capacity of the mill is fifty barrels a day of high grade flour, their chief brand being the Lily White, and buckwheat and other grains are also ground The mill is well equipped and the business is in a very flourishing condition

Mr Goff was married first in September, 1895, to Miss Lulu V Terry, whose death occurred three years later In October, 1900, Mr Goff was married second to Miss Olive May Rexford, a daughter of T E Rexford Their residence is at No 337 S Brady street, opposite the mill

In politics Mr Goff is a Republican and he has always been an active and interested citizen While residing in Elk county he served three years as jury commissioner, was auditor of Jay township and three years served as township treasurer In 1896 he was the Republican candidate for associate judge of Elk county and in the election was defeated by only 200 votes, which was a very close margin, considering that the county is normally Democratic Since becoming a citizen of DuBois he has served three years as a member of the borough council His only fraternal connection is with the Patriotic Order of Sons of America

Algenorn Goff's great-grandfather was Guernsey Goff, who was a blind man and cooper by trade, and worked at his trade although blind

ROBERT V WILSON, M D , deceased In recalling the no longer living professional men who left an impress on the developing agencies of Clearfield, Pa , the name of Dr Robert Van Valzah Wilson readily comes to mind, for he not only possessed the qualities necessary for success as a man of medical science, but also had the broad-minded and enlightened understanding which, combined with a deep respect and love for his felow men, even those most unfortunate, made his influence acknowledged during life and lasting since he passed away

Dr Wilson was born at Spring Mills, Center county, Pa, in October, 1828 He made his preliminary medical preparation with Dr Van Valzah, a relative, at Millheim, in Center county, and in 1849 was graduated from Jefferson Medical College, Philadelphia In 1850 he came to Clearfield county, locating for a short time at Curwensville and then removing to Clearfield Here the remainder of his useful life was spent, his death occurring in the midst of usefulness, February 13, 1878 His reputation as a physician and surgeon extended all over the state, and among his chosen associates were others of like high aims, and his name is linked with theirs when Pennsylvania points with pride to her men of merit He was a member of the State Geological Survey

In 1852 Dr Wilson was married to Miss Carrie Smith, who was a daughter of Josiah W Smith, and a family of seven children was born to them One surviving son, Smith V Wilson, is a leading member of the Clearfield bar, as was his maternal grandfather He married Miss Martha L Thompson, a daughter of Dr Thompson, and they have two children

CHARLES C BAILEY, general farmer and owner of 128 acres of valuable land, situated three miles north of Curwensville, Pa, in Pike township, Clearfield county.

was born on this farm, December 17, 1868, and is a son of Joseph and Elizabeth (Boal) Bailey.

Joseph Bailey was born also in Pike township, where his parents, Daniel and Jane Bailey, were early settlers He attended school in this township and also at Curwensville, after which he assisted his father on the home farm until his own marriage. He then lived for a time on a part of Abraham Bailey's estate, later buying the farm of 128 acres from Isaac Bailey and completing its clearing. He gradually acquired other farms until he owned about 500 acres, only a part of which, however, was put under cultivation He married Elizabeth Boal, a daughter of James Boal, of Center county, Pa, and six children were born to them, as follows Mary Alice, who is the wife of Vincent Spencer, of Curwensville, Martha Jane, who is the wife of Jonathan Ogden, of Lawrence township, James Dorsey, who married Mary Neeper, of Lawrence township; Annie G, who married twice, first Charles Boyd and second William Vangavich, Charles C, and George Boyd, who died when two years of age The father of the above family died in October, 1901, at the age of seventy-eight years, seven months and eleven days, having survived his wife for many years Her death took place in October, 1877, at the age of forty-three years Their burial was in the Center cemetery Both were members of the Center Methodist Episcopal church

Charles C Bailey obtained his education at Curwensville, Pleasant Grove school house and at Clearfield, after which he taught school for some time in the same sections where he had been a pupil Mr.

Bailey remembers this season as a very pleasant part of his life, but farming and stock raising have been of still more importance and after his marriage he settled on his present home in preference to any other He made many improvements here, remodeled the buildings and added modern comforts In addition to his home farm he owns forty acres in another part of Pike township, a one-half interest in another tract of thirty-five acres and a one-fifth interest in one of fifty-seven acres, all these being parts of his father's estate Mr Bailey is a stockholder in the Farmers and Traders Bank, of Clearfield, and a stockholder in the Curwensville Rural Telephone Company

On November 30, 1893, Mr Bailey was married to Miss Myrtle E Leslie, who was born in Clarion county, Pa, September 13, 1868, a daughter of Noah and Mary Elizabeth (Mesner) Leslie, who reside near Home Camp, in Clearfield county Mr and Mrs Bailey have had two children Walter S, born in May, 1895, is a member of the class of 1914 in the Curwensville High School, and Lillian Elizabeth, who was born in 1901 and died in 1902, being laid to rest by the side of her grandparents in the Center cemetery In politics Mr Bailey is a Republican He belongs to Susquehannah Grange at Curwensville He is one of the representative men of this section, is widely known and enjoys the esteem and warm friendship of his fellow citizen

A J POWELL, a prominent and highly esteemed citizen of Woodland, Pa, was born here in 1862, in an old log house which has been standing for more than 100 years, and is a son of William and Hannah (Young) Powell William Powell was a farmer and a miller by trade and in 1859 came to Clearfield County and located at Woodland, where he lived until the time of his death in 1904 His wife died here in 1890

A J Powell grew to man's estate in Woodland, and after obtaining an education in the common schools of Clearfield, worked in the clay mines and in the timbers near Woodland Mr Powell is fraternally a member of the Red Men, No 407, of Clearfield, the Knights of Pythias, the Maccabees, and was a charter member of the order of Golden Eagles

Mr Powell was married in 1904 to Katherine Waite, who was born and reared in Clearfield County, Pa, and whose parents are both now deceased

JOHN T McQUILLEN, who is a member of the borough council of Wallaceton, Pa, is connected with the Harbison & Walker Brick Company at this place as superintendent of their plant He was born at Tyrone, Blair County, Pa, in September, 1856, and is a son of Adam and Mary (Boyle) McQuillen

Adam McQuillen was born in Blair County, a son of Thomas and Jennie (Hunter) McQuillen For many years he was a railroad man and now is postmaster at Woodland, in Clearfield County He married Mary Boyle, a daughter of John and Rebecca (McClure) Boyle, also of Blair County They had the following children born to them John T, Jennie, Cora, William, Nin, Ada, Mary and Walter, the last named being deceased Cora is the wife of John McHail, Ada is the wife of H H Hiles, and Mary is the wife of A I Cowdrick.

John T McQuillen attended the common

schools in boyhood and when he went to work it was in a brick-yard, and he has been connected with the brick industry ever since In 1872 his parents moved to Clearfield County, and in February, 1906, he became superintendent of this brick plant at Wallaceton He has been an active and public spirited citizen of Boggs township ever since residing here and is now serving in the offices of tax collector and school director He owns residence property in Wallaceton and is numbered with the reliable and representative men of the place

In 1880 Mr McQuillen was married to Miss Sarah Swift, a daughter of David and Eliza (Hawthorn) Swift They were born in England The mother of Mrs McQuillen is now deceased but the father resides at Woodland Their children were Samuel, Thomas, Susan, who is the wife of Russell Albert, Willaim, George, Minnie, who is the wife of Roy Gilman, Ella, who is deceased, and Sarah, who is Mrs McQuillen Six children have been born to Mr and Mrs McQuillen, namely Grace, Hayes, Susan, who is the wife of Homer Wilson, Vada, who is the wife of Roy Albert, Edward and Weller Mr McQuillen is a Republican in his political views He is a member of the Knights of Pythias and also of the L O O M, both at Clearfield With his wife he belongs to the Methodist Episcopal church

AUSTIN BLAKESLEE, one of Clearfield county's leading business men, who is identified with important enterprises in different sections, has been a resident of DuBois, Pa, since 1903, and is president of the United Traction and Street Railway Company also president of the DuBois Traction Company

and of the DuBois Electric Company. He was born October 24, 1854, in a lumber camp, at a small place called California, near Bear Creek, Luzerne county, Pa, and is a son of Jacob and Clarissa (Winter) Blakeslee Jacob Blakeslee was largely interested in lumbering in Monroe and Luzerne counties, Pa, and died in the former His family consisted of eleven children, five daughters and six sons, Austin being the only one residing in Clearfield county

Austin Blakeslee spent a large part of his boyhood in the lumber regions and attended country schools in the section where his father's business required that the family should live In 1869 he took a business course in the Wyoming Seminary, in Luzerne county, after which he went to Bradford, Pa, where he secured a position as office boy at the mines and from that humble situation gradually advanced during the thirteen years he remained there, to the position of superintendent In 1885 he moved to Jefferson county, Pa, where he became general manager of the Coal Glenn Mines, which office he still holds, and from there, in 1903, he came to DuBois and established his home in this thriving borough Mr. Blakeslee was not slow in forming an opinion as to the future development of the town and his business sagacity has been shown in the investments he has made and in the public enterprises he has furthered He was one of the organizers of the United Traction & Street Railroad, which line was built in 1905, and he also bought interests in the DuBois Electric Company and the DuBois Traction Company Other capitalists associated with him were Walter Hatten, A L Cole, W. H. Cannon, J H Beadle now deceased, and M. I McCreight Mr Blakeslee succeeded Walter Hatton as president and subsequently the former's four sons also became stockholders Robert B , Irvin, Frank and Albert The Electric Company gives employment to about fifty men in the various departments and give an excellent street car service through DuBois and run an interurban line to Sykesville, Big Run and other points and supplies electric light for DuBois, Sykesville and Big Run Mr Blakeslee was also one of the organizers of the Deposit National Bank at DuBois, of which he is one of the directors

Mr Blakeslee was married in Bradford county, Pa , to Miss Martha Cronk, who was a daughter of James Cronk, a native of New Jersey, who was one of the sturdy old lumbermen of Luzerne county, who operated saw mills for many years and prepared timber for ship building purposes Mr and Mrs Blakeslee have eight children, all of whom have enjoyed exceptional educational and other advantages Robert B , the eldest son, who is general superintendent of the electric concerns in which he and father are interested, is a graduate of Cornell College, of the class of 1899 He married Eliza Osborn and they have two children Frank B , the second son, who is superintendent of the mines at Coal Glenn, is a graduate of Wyoming Seminary He married Blanche Blakeslee and they have three children Robert, Helen and Dorothea Charles Albert, who is a graduate of the civil engineering department of Cornell College, in the class of 1903, resides at Falls Creek, Pa , and is secretary and treasurer of the Crystal Window Glass Company He married Jessie Ormella Coal and they have three children Arthur, Martha and Jean Irvin Blakeslee, the fourth son, who is a graduate of Cornell College, in the class of 1906, is assistant su-

perintendent and purchasing agent for the above electric company Kathryn, the eldest daughter, is the wife of Morde Ginter, of DuBois, and they have one daughter, Louise Colson Edward, who is a graduate of the University of Pennsylvania, Philadelphia, class of 1909, is employed as bookkeeper for the electric company in which he is a stockholder He married Mabel Fry The two youngest children, Lucy and Russell, reside at home The family residence is at No 159 Long Avenue, DuBois Mr and Mrs Blakeslee are members of the First Methodist Episcopal church He is identified with the Masonic fraternity and belongs to the Blue Lodge and Commandery at DuBois

A. W COWDER, a prominent farmer and enterprising citizen of Bradford township, Clearfield county, Pa , has resided on his present farm of 250 acres since 1851, and was born in 1850 in Bradford township, a son of John and Sarah Cowder His parents came from Lancaster county, in 1841, and settled in Bradford township, on a farm near Bigler Ten years later they sold it and bought 400 acres This they farmed a number of years, when they sold all but 250 acres, which is now owned by their son, A W , subject of this record Both parents are now deceased, their deaths having occurred on the farm, one in 1882, the other in 1893

A W Cowder was reared on his present farm and attended the local schools of Bradford township After leaving school he began working on his father's farm and lumbering and has since followed farming on the home place Mr Cowder was married in 1873 to Elmira Wilson, a daughter of John Wilson of Bradford township, and they immediately be-

gan housekeeping on the old homestead Seven
children were born of this union. Ralph, Agnes, Anna, Oscar (died aged seven years),
Wilson (died aged three years), Alvie, and
Fanny   Ralph and Fanny are now deceased
Mrs Cowder died March 9, 1890, aged 38
years, and in the fall of 1892 Mr Cowder
formed a second union with Lizzie A Shirey
of Bradford township The religious connection of the family is with the United Brethren church of Shiloh, of which Mr. Cowder
has been a trustee since the church was built
in 1886 Mr Cowder served ten years as a
school director of Bradford township, and is
a man of public spirit and enterprise, and is
ever ready to give his assistance to those measures which tend toward the advancement of
the community in which he lives

PATRICK THOMAS SULLIVAN, of
the firm of Luther & Sullivan, conducting the
undertaking business under the style of the
J B Luther Undertaking Co , at DuBois, was
born in County Tipperary, Ireland, March
27, 1870, and is a son of Michael and Johanna
(Rooney) Sullivan, the former of whom died
in Ireland in July, 1908, but the latter survives Of their seven children, Patrick
Thomas was the second in order of birth and
with a brother, John, and a sister, Delia, were
the only ones to come to America

Patrick Thomas Sullivan came to the
United States in 1879 with his cousin, Rev
James Brennon, who became the first parish
priest at DuBois Mr Sullivan came to Du-
Bois in 1881 and made his home with Father
Brennon and for twelve years worked in the
mines For ten years more he was employed
as a car inspector for the B R & P. Railroad,
after which he entered the employ of L E

Weber, undertaker. He took a course in embalming under Prof Harry Eckles, at Philadelphia and received his practical knowledge
of the art under his present partner, J B
Luther, and received his state embalmer's license in August, 1910 On September 7,
1909, with Mr. Luther, he established the J
B Luther Undertaking Co

On December 25, 1890, Mr Sullivan was
married to Miss Mary Martin, a daughter of
Charles Martin, who came to Clearfield county
in 1876 Mr. and Mrs Sullivan have six
children. Johanna Loretta, Charles H , Michael F , Thomas J , Susanna and Patrick W
The family residence is No 519, W Washington avenue, DuBois   They are members
of St Catherine's Catholic church He is
identified with the Knights of Columbus and
for the past eighteen years has belonged to the
C T A For ten years he has served as president of Division No 1 of the Clearfield
County A O H , and he belongs also to the
Catholic Order of Foresters

JOHN H McCROSSIN, proprietor of the
Irvona Hotel, one of the leading public houses
at Irvona, Pa , is not only popular as its host
but is also highly esteemed as a citizen He is
one of the younger business men of the borough, born March 1, 1882, at Ramey, Pa , and
is a son of James and Mary (Wilkinson) Mc-
Crossin

James McCrossin was born in Bradford
county, Pa , and came to Clearfield county
when eighteen years of age He settled first
at Osceola and for a number of years was in
the lumber business but in 1892 he went into
the hotel business and conducted hotels at Madera, Houtzdale and Clearfield until 1897 In
1901 he returned to Madera, where he built

the Madera Inn and has conducted it ever since He is well known all over Clearfield county He married Mary Wilkinson, who was born in England and accompanied her parents to America in her girlhood Her father was interested in coal, both as a miner and small shipper, in Clearfield county Seven children were born to James McCrossin and wife, namely Edward G, who is a resident of Madera, John H , Fred, who is with his father at Madera, Thomas, who is a professional base ball player, outfielder with the Memphis Southern League, Frances, who lives at home, a babe that died, and Margaret, who died when about twenty-eight years of age

John H McCrossin attended both the public and parochial schools at Houtzdale and Clearfield His first work was done as an employe of the New York Central Railroad, where he continued for almost a year and then went with the Pittsburg & Lake Erie Railroad In December, 1904, he gave up railroad work and was a clerk in a wholesale business house at Houtzdale, and when he left there it was to come to Irvona, where he bought the Irvona Hotel, in partnership with his brother, Edward McCrossin The partnership continued for two years when John H purchased his brother's interest and has been sole owner and proprietor ever since Mr McCrossin has made many improvements, including the building of a fine new bar in 1910, and the whole house is fitted with modern conveniences It is Mr McCrossin's aim to make his hotel as home-like as possible, and through his care and attention he succeeds and is given generous patronage

In 1905 Mr McCrossin was married to Miss Margaret Meagher, a daughter of John Meagher, of Houtzdale, and they have three children Gilbert Meagher, Margaret and Robert Frederick Mr and Mrs McCrossin are members of St Basil's Roman Catholic church at Blair City He is identified fraternally with a number of organizations, including Tyrone Lodge, No 212, Elks, at Tyrone, Clearfield Aerie, No 812, Eagles, at Clearfield, Canalport Lodge, No 312, Moose, and the Brotherhood of America, at Houtzdale

HARVEY B GROVE, proprietor of the H B Grove general store, dealing in general merchandise, hay, feed and grain, at West Decatur, Boggs township, Clearfield county, Pa , is an enterprising and successful business man of this section He was born March 28, 1883 at Orbisonia, Huntingdon county, Pa , and is a son of James and Margaret (Harris) Grove

James Grove was born in Huntingdon county, a son of Joseph Grove, and is engaged in the contracting business there He has been twice married, first to Margaret Harris, who died when their only child, Harvey B , was eighteen months old Her parents were William and Susan Harris The second marriage was to Lucy Leader, of which there has been no issue James Grove is a member of the Reformed church

Harvey B Grove obtained his education in the common and high school at Orbisonia, graduating from the latter in 1898 He then went into the shops of the Westinghouse Company, at Pittsburg, where he worked until 1905, after which he engaged as clerk in a general store at Orbisonia, where he had charge of a general merchandise and of a hardware store, for two years For one year afterward he was a traveling representative of the International Correspondence School of Scranton, Pa , and then went back to the shops where he had learned his trade, in Pittsburg, and continued there until September 1, 1910, when he came to West Decatur and bought out the firm of Briggs Brothers He has done considerable improving in the way of modernizing his store and is now enjoying a prosperous trade

Mr Grove was married in 1909 to Miss Edna Albert, who is a daughter of John and Mary A Albert, natives of Clearfield county, where Mrs Albert still resides, her husband being deceased Mr and Mrs Albert had three children Roland, who is deceased, Myrtle, who is the wife of J T Guyer, and Edna, Mrs Grove To Mr and Mrs Grove a son was born on March 7, 1911, who bears the name of James B They are members of the Methodist Episcopal church In politics Mr Grove is a Democrat He belongs to Turtle Creek Lodge, No 777, Odd Fellows

JAMES S MOORE, a man of many and varied interests but who devotes a large amount of attention to the livestock industry, has been in this line of business since 1865, and has spent his life in Central Pennsylvania He was born in Frankstown township, Blair county, Pa , December 22, 1840, and is a son of Jesse and Eliza (Smith) Moore

Jesse Moore was born also in Frankstown township and was a son of Samuel and Isabella Moore His death occurred in 1856, when his son, James S , was a youth of sixteen years He married Eliza Smith, who was born in Frankstown township, Blair county, a daughter of James Smith She survived her husband for many years, her death

occurring at Minneapolis Minn , when she had reached her eighty-second year To Jesse and Eliza Moore seven children were born, namely Adie, who is now deceased, was a resident of Frankstown township, James S , Letitia, who died at Minneapolis, Minn , was the wife of Harry Stephens , Charles, who resides at Madera, Clearfield county, Samuel, who is a resident of Los Angeles, Calif , Candace, who is the wife of Angus Confer, of Minneapolis, and Jesse, who lives in California

James S Moore was reared and attended school in Blair county, and resided there until January 3, 1873, when he moved to Center county and for a short time lived just back of Osceola and then settled in Osceola borough where he remained until October, 1875, at which time he came to Houtzdale, which has been his place of residence ever since He is identified with the leading interests of this section and is one of the most substantial and progressive citizens He is a stockholder and director in the First National Bank of Osceola , is interested in the Oak Ridge Coal Company of Hastings, and is also a stockholder and a director in the Water Works Company of Houtzdale Mr Moore owns an excellent farm which lies just outside the borough of Houtzdale, which he supervises He buys his livestock in Pittsburg and other western markets and ships into this section, doing an extensive business

Mr Moore was married in 1868, to Miss Martha Smith, who is now deceased In 1880 Mr Moore was married second to Miss Lulu McClure and they have one daughter, Mabel Mr Moore and family belong to the Presbyterian church In politics he is a Republican and has served frequently in local offices

WILLIAM ELMER PATCHIN is a well known and prominent citizen of Burnside township, where he is engaged in farming, lumbering and is also in the livery business He was born at Patchinville, this county, October 22, 1856, a son of Jackson and Mary (Mahaffey) Patchin The Patchin family is one of the old and representative families of Clearfield county, and was founded here by John W Patchin, who was born in 1789, at Sabbath Day Point, Warren county, N Y, where he married Elizabeth Wright He was early engaged in lumbering and had a slide for logs on the side of Black Mountain, above Lake George In 1835 he came to Clearfield county, purchasing 10,000 acres of timber land along the Susquehanna river He was one of the first to engage in rafting lumber down the Susquehanna river to the distant markets In 1847 he brought his family to this county and they resided first at Curwensville, later removing to the locality now known as Patchinville, which place was named in his honor In 1848 he admitted his sons to partnership in his large lumbering enterprises, and the business was conducted under the firm name of John Patchin & Sons This pioneer and founder of the family here died December 21, 1863, at the age of 74 years His widow died in 1860 They left seven children

Jackson Patchin, son of John and father of the subject of this sketch, was born at Sabbath Day Point N Y, in April, 1830 He came to Clearfield county in 1844, at the age of 14 and was engaged in clerking for his father In 1853 he was admitted as a partner into the firm of John Patchin & Sons, and after his father's death, he and his brother Aaron continued the business Aaron, as his father's chief adviser and assistant, had inherited most

of the latter's estate but he later adjusted all claims satisfactorily with his brothers and sisters The estate now includes 8,000 acres of land.

Jackson Patchin married, January 1, 1856, Mary Mahaffey, a daughter of John and Elen (Byers) Mahaffey, of which union there were two children, namely: William Elmer, our direct subject, and Frank E, who is associated in business with his brother

William Elmer Patchin after attending school in his boyhood went to work at farming and lumbering with his father, with whom he continued until reaching the age of 24 years He then engaged in the livery business at Burnside, in which he has since continued, without, however, relinquishing his other occupations He also deals largely in horses and cattle and other live stock He has been prosperous in his various enterprises and is now one of the substantial citizens of his township He belongs to the Masonic order, being a member of Blue Lodge No 314 at Clearfield In politics he is a Republican and has served two terms on the school board and also two terms as councilman of Burnside

Mr Patchin was married, January 28, 1890, to Emma Conner, a daughter of John C and Emily (McClure) Conner Her father was born in 1831 in Indiana county, Pa, and died at Burnside, February 13, 1909 He was engaged in mercantile business in his native county and afterwards in Clearfield county, coming to Burnside in 1868 He was also a member of the large lumber firm of Hopkins, Irvin & Conner, operating at Rock Haven, whose wealth and commercial interests were practically wiped out by the great Johnstown flood, whereby Mr Conner lost most of his fortune He died on the very day that he had been elected to the office of auditor. His first wife was Emily Widowson and after her death he married Emily V McClure, a daughter of Stansbury McClure. To each marriage three children were born, to the first Nettie (Mrs A K Wray), Jennie (Mrs Elwood Henderson) and John B, who is postmaster at Burnside. The children of the second marriage were William M, Harry C and Emma A (Mrs W E Patchin)

The children of our subject and wife are Don, an electrician, residing at home, Lynn, also at home, Herbert, Joseph, Mary, who died in infancy, and Harry, who also died in infancy. The eldest, Don, is now eighteen years old. Mrs Patchin is a member of the Methodist Protestant church of Burnside

ROBERT EUGENE HUNTER, who is engaged in the hardware and house furnishing business at Irvona and carries on funeral directing at Coalport, Pa, is one of the enterprising young business men of Clearfield county and one whose progress during the past ten years has been almost exceptional. Mr Hunter was born in Wells Valley, Fulton county, Pa, November 26, 1881, a son of Ezekiel and Margaret Jane (McNeal) Hunter

Ezekiel Hunter, who was born in Ireland, came to the United States when eighteen years of age, and here followed his trade, that of tanner. He married Margaret Jane McNeal, the daughter of a paymaster of the Pennsylvania Railroad. Born at Lewistown, Pa, she died December 1, 1899, having been the mother of ten children, namely. Mollie, who is the widow of Harrison Celevenger of Irvona, William, who died at the age of two years, Agnes M, who married Oliver M Des-

Rochers, of Instanter, Elk county, Pa, Jennie, who died in infancy, Mattie, the wife of H T Venatta, of Aroyo, Elk county, Virginia, who married Harry Mays, of Anita, Jefferson county, Carrie Gertrude, who married J A English, of Albion, Mercer county, Margaretta Frances, who is single, Alexander C, who is working for his brother in the store, married Catherine Harrison, and Robert Eugene. After their marriage Mr and Mrs Hunter located for a time near Philadelphia and later went to Fulton county for seven or eight years, but eventually Mr Hunter came to Irvona, before the tannery was built, and worked here until he had made a home for his family, who followed him here in the fall of 1889. Mr Hunter still resides in Irvona, and is now eighty-nine years of age, more than fifty years of his life having been spent at the tanning trade

Robert Eugene Hunter attended the public schools of Irvona until fourteen years of age, at which time he commenced working in the tannery and so continued until the age of twenty years, at which time he entered the employ of J S Gordon, the house furnishing and hardware merchant, for a salary of $20 per month, and so efficient did he prove himself that twenty-three months later, to a day, he was taken into partnership by Mr Gordon, the firm becoming Hunter & Co. For nearly five years this style continued and early in 1908, Mr Hunter purchased Mr Gordon's interest in the business and he has conducted it alone to the present time with great success. Mr Hunter took a post-graduate course in undertaking at Pittsburg, and on January 1, 1910, he took charge of the business of J M Beers, at Coalport, he now being the only funeral director within some distance of Ir-

ROBERT E. HUNTER

vona His residence and the office for his undertaking business are located at Coalport, while his other business interests are in Irvona, and he is known at both places as a self-made, self-reliant business man and as an enterprising and public-spirited citizen He is fraternally connected with Mattawana Castle No 152, A O K of M C, with the Rose Bud and Oconomowak Tribes of the Order of Red Men, and with McKinley Lodge No 181, Knights of Pythias of Irvona

On January 11, 1911, Mr Hunter was united in marriage with Miss Marguerite Williams, daughter of Miles and Susan Williams, who live at Utahville and are old residents of Clearfield county Mr Hunter resided in Irvona until the spring of 1910, since which time he has been living in his comfortable residence at Coalport While making his home in Irvona he took an active interest in political matters and served several terms as judge of election

CHARLES HARVEY NOTTER, proprietor of the DuBois Roller Mills, manufacturer of and wholesale dealer in flour and feed, has been a resident of DuBois, Pa, since 1889 He was born at New Amsterdam, Wis, October 10, 1860, and is a son of David and Mary (Loubshier) Notter

David Notter was born in Germany and came to America when a young man He was married afterward to Mary Loubshier, who was born and reared in Clinton county, Pa, and they made their home in Wisconsin until 1868, when they returned to Clinton county, Pa, where Mrs Notter died shortly afterward David Notter subsequently took up his residence again in Wisconsin and spent the rest of his life there Four children were born to David and Mary Notter, as follows Carrie, who is the wife of J C Dimling, of Renova, Pa, Charles Harvey, David, who lives in New York, and John who is a resident of Allegheny, Pa

Charles H Notter was eight years old when his parents settled in Clinton county, Pa, near Lock Haven, and there he was educated in the public schools At the age of twenty-one years he bought an interest in the Muckelhatten mill at Muckelhatten, which he retained for one year and after disposing of it spent a short time in Ohio and in Western Pennsylvania in search of a promising business location, selecting DuBois in 1889 Here, in association with Sidney Fuller and John McCullough, he built the DuBois Roller mill, the first one erected after the memorable fire that had destroyed so many business houses in the previous year Later, Mr Notter bought Mr Fuller's interest in the plant and still later, Mr McCullough's share The first mill was a rather small affair but after Mr Notter became sole owner he showed a great deal of enterprise in making additions and improvements The present capacity of the mill is fifty barrels of flour and fifty barrels of buckwheat per day, and the feed mill is kept busy all the time, the business being both wholesale and retail The location of the plant, on the corner of Sandy and DuBois streets, affords fine railroad facilities

In June, 1889, Mr. Notter was married to Miss Mary Fugate, a daughter of J J and Elizabeth (Bare) Fugate, both of whom are now deceased Mr and Mrs Notter have four children, namely Mary Irene, who is a graduate of the DuBois High School, of Mrs Meade's Girls' School, of Norwalk, Conn, a student for one year at Wellesley College.

and now in her second year at Oberlin College, John C., who is a graduate of the DuBois High School and is now in his second year in the Pennsylvania State College at Center County, and Charles H and Stephen Fugate Mr Notter believes in higher education and places a value on scholarship, hence he is affording his children superior advantages He is a member of the Masonic fraternity and belongs also to the Modern Woodmen Politically a Democrat, he has been elected by his party to membership on the borough council, where his practical business sense has made him very valuable In 1902 he erected his handsome brown stone residence, at No 42 W Scribner avenue, DuBois

WILLIAM A DEWALT, who is engaged in a mill business at Irvona, Pa, owning saw and grist mills, together with a planing-mill, has other business interests, in the direction of carpenter contracting and is one of the substantial and representative men of the place. He was born November 20, 1858, in Beccaria township, Clearfield county, Pa, and is a son of Joseph J and Sarah Dewalt

The parents of Mr Dewalt were born in Adams county, Pa The father moved with his family to Clearfield county in 1848 and spent his subsequent life in Beccaria township, where he followed the carpenter trade He died in 1896, aged fifty-eight years and was survived two years by his widow They had the following children Jennie, who is the wife of Isaac Smith, of Glen Hope, Ellen, who is the wife of W. K Lull, also of Glen Hope, Catherine, who is the wife of W B Wright, a farmer, living near Glen Hope, George W, who is a carpenter and contractor, residing in Florida, and William A

William A. Dewalt attended the public schools until he was about twelve years of age and then learned the carpenter trade and remained and worked with his father until he was twenty-two years old For the past twenty-two years Mr. Dewalt has been a resident of Irvona, coming here from Glen Hope. He erected his planing-mill in 1895 and added a saw-mill three years later and in 1909 built his grist-mill He has carried on his various business enterprises with prudence and good judgment and has met with satisfactory results in all his undertakings

On November 4, 1880, Mr Dewalt was married to Miss Hattie Lull, a daughter of J W. Lull, residing near Glen Hope, and they have four sons and one daughter, namely: Paul W, who served as a member of the Marine Corps, and was in the Philippine Islands, but who is now assisting his father, Eugene, who is with the Elk Tannery Company, Ralph, who married Martha Bailey, of Irvona, has two children—Catherine and Elsie; Bertha and Lawrence, who are at home Mr Dewalt is a Prohibitionist in politics and is a very consistent man He has served several times in the borough council and for some seven years has been a member of the school board Having always been honest and upright in his dealings with his fellow men, Mr Dewalt has earned and enjoys their friendship and esteem

WALLACE STEELE BRYAN, M. D, physician and surgeon, at Ramey, Pa, has been a resident of this borough for the past three years and has built up a very satisfactory practice and is in the enjoyment of the confidence and esteem of his fellow citizens He was born June 30, 1878, at Indiana, Pa, and is a son of John R and Mary E (Dumm) Bryan

John R. Bryan was also born in Indiana county, a son of John R Bryan The Bryan family is an old one in that section, second only to the Dumm family and both are of Scotch-Irish extraction John R Bryan, father of Dr Bryan, is a contractor and a well known business man He married Mary E Dumm, a daughter of Cyrus M Dumm, and they had two children: Minnie, who is the wife of R M Smith, and Wallace S

Wallace S Bryan enjoyed superior educational advantages and before he started upon the study of medicine secured literary degrees indicative of high scholarship From the public schools of Indiana, Pa, he entered the Normal School there and subsequently became a student at the Washington-Jefferson College, at Washington, Pa, bearing off his degree of A B in 1902, and that of A M in 1905 He then entered Jefferson Medical College Philadelphia, where he was graduated in the class of 1906 Dr Bryan spent one year as an interne at the McKeesport, Pa, Hospital after which he practiced there for two years and then came to Ramey. He is identified with various medical bodies and keeps thoroughly abreast with the times in his profession

Dr Bryan was married June 10, 1907, to Miss Clara V Howell, the only daughter of Josiah and Flora (Mains) Howell, who were natives of Allegheny county, Pa Mr and Mrs Howell had one son, William Howell Dr and Mrs Bryan have one daughter, Mary E They are members of the United Presbyterian church He is not very active politically but casts his vote with the Republican party

28

GEORGE M BILGER, attorney at law and a leading member of the Clearfield bar, was born at Curwensville, Pa, September 15, 1861 His parents were Jacob and Hannah (Gray) Bigler The father for many years was extensively engaged in the lumber industry

George M Bilger was educated at Curwensville and graduated from the High School in 1878 and from Dickinson College in 1883 He then turned his attention to the study of law being accepted as a student by Hon W C Arnold, and in March, 1886, was admitted to the Clearfield county bar and subsequently to the Allegheny county bar His practice has been general in character and his success has been such as to place his name among the foremost attorneys of Clearfield He is in hearty accord with the Democratic party and has done loyal work for the cause

Mr Bilger was married to Miss Annella Furguson, a daughter of William B Furguson, and they have three children Mr Bilger and family reside at No 412 E Market street, Clearfield, Pa For a number of years he has been active in the Masonic fraternity, and has devoted considerable of his time to literary work

E T BIRD, proprietor of the Palace Hotel, a first class hostelry located on the corner of Reed and Third Streets, Clearfield, Pa, is one of the borough's enterprising and wide awake business men He was born at Eaglesville, Center county, Pa, April 4, 1873

Mr Bird was educated in the public schools and the Lock Haven Normal School, receiving a teacher's certificate from the latter institution, but before he made use of this document, he became interested in the saw-mill business at Reynoldsville, Pa, where he continued until 1897 He came then to Clearfield and bought the Palace Restaurant, from J L Heeton, which he has successfully conducted ever since as an all night eating-house Two years later he was granted a license under Judge Gordon and since then has carried on a regular hotel business The Palace Hotel is well arranged for the comfort and convenience of guests, there being forty bed rooms, a dining room, lobby, office and writing room, all well equipped and kept in first class order Mr Bird's moderate charges are $1 50 per day Making a specialty of a good table, in spite of the present high prices of food stuffs, Mr Bird has many patrons and these come from the traveling public and also from settled people who can appreciate comforts

Mr Bird was married in 1908 to Miss Ada S Scott, of Reynoldsville, and they have one son, Carl In politics, Mr Bird is a Republican He is identified with the higher branches of Masonry, belonging to the Consistory at Williamsport and Shrine at Wilkes-Barre, and to the Blue Lodge at Clearfield He belongs also to the B P O E, the F O E, and the Red Men

L W SPENCER, cashier of the Curwensville National Bank, at Curwensville, Pa, has been more or less identified with the business interests of Lumber City and Curwensville, all his mature life He was born at Lumber City, Clearfield county, Pa, and is the only surviving child of H W and Amanda M (Garretson) Spencer

H W Spencer was born at Grampian Hill, Clearfield county, Pa, August 21, 1832 and died at Curwensville at the age of 74 years

He was a man of much business enterprise and was a carpenter and contractor, also a merchant and lumber dealer. He served in numerous public offices, was postmaster of Lumber City and later was burgess of Curwensville He erected many buildings at Lumber City and the Spencer Building in Curwensville, in which the business of L W Spencer & Co, was carried on for a long time, he being the senior partner He married Amanda M Garretson, who died at the age of 67 years She was a woman of many Christian virtues and a consistent member of the Society of Friends H. W Spencer was a member also of the lumber firm of Kirk & Spencer and was a stockholder in the Curwensville National Bank

L W Spencer attended the schools of Lumber City and later took a business course in the Eastman Commercial College at Poughkeepsie, N. Y, and afterward went into the mercantile business with his father at Lumber City In 1877 the family moved to Curwensville and he continued in the mercantile business under the style of L W Spencer & Co, which he subsequently sold He then became cashier of the Citizens National Bank of Curwensville which later consolidated with the Curwensville National Bank, an institution of high financial standing in Clearfield county

In 1902 Mr Spencer was married to Miss Dema England, who is a daughter of John R. and Sarah England, residents of Leroy, O Mr and Mrs Spencer reside on Ridge avenue, Curwensville He is a member of the Society of Friends In politics, like his late father, he is a Republican He served as councilman and on the school board of this borough and on many occasions has served on committees of public importance He is identified fraternally with the Masons, belonging to the Blue Lodge, Chapter and Commandery and to the higher branches at Philadelphia, and also to the Odd Fellows at Curwensville

REUBEN HOLT, one of the leading and best known citizens of Graham township, Clearfield county, Pa, which has been his home for fifty-six years, owns a valuable farm of 115 acres, situated ten miles east of Clearfield and has other public and private interests in this section He was born in Bradford township, Clearfield county, Pa, in 1851, and is a son of John and Drusilla Holt

John Holt was also born in Bradford township, a son of Thomas Holt, a native of England, who was a very early settler there, where his life was subsequently spent as a farmer and lumberman John Holt was reared and educated in Bradford township and became a school teacher He was a man of much public spirit, a natural leader, and he was very frequently elected to public offices of responsibility For fifteen years he was a justice of the peace in Graham township and at different times efficiently served in about all of the other township offices It was through his enterprise that Graham township was organized and he was the first postmaster at Wallaceton After a long, busy and honorable life, he died on the above mentioned farm, in the spring of 1880 His widow survived until 1891

Reuben Holt was three years old when his parents settled in Graham township and here he was reared He attended the public schools and later, preparing for the career of a teacher, became a student in the

Millersville State Normal School Subsequently he taught one term of school at Wolf Run, one at Williamsgrove, one at Wallaceton and one at Stoneville, meeting with excellent results He then embarked in the mercantile business at Osceola, Pa, where he remained for two years and then returned to Graham township, where he has been interested in farming and lumbering ever since Mr Holt, like his late father, has been a very active citizen He was assistant postmaster while his father served as postmaster at Wallaceton, and in 1900 he was appointed postmaster at Sington, the duties being familiar on account of his former training In 1908 he was appointed a justice of the peace, on the Democratic ticket and secretary of the school board Mr Holt also conducts a general store at Sington and is agent for the Graham township Telephone Company

In 1874 Mr Holt was married to Miss Margaret Forcey, of Graham township, and they started to housekeeping at Wallaceton To them were born a large and unusually talented family, all of whom have been given educational advantages and a number of whom have developed into successful teachers The following is the family record H G, who married Miss Jennie Donaldson, of Philadelphia, and has three children—Donald R, Margaret and Graydon, C P, formerly a teacher in Clearfield county, is now district attorney, residing at Shawnee City, Okla, married Miss Mabel Davis, and they have one son, C P, Jr, Anna Edna who taught five terms of school in Clearfield county, is the wife of Walter Harker, of New Jersey, and they have two children—Evelyn and Margaret,

Clyde F, who married Miss Grace McGovern, of Philadelphia, and they had one son, Reuben John, who died in infancy, Mabel M, who taught eight terms of school in Clearfield county, is the wife of Roy Woodside, of Boggs township, and they have one son, Thomas C, Ora B, who taught three terms of school in Clearfield county, married Frank Smith, and they have one son, Leslie C, Minnie, who taught three terms of school in Clearfield county, married Charles Kreder, of New Jersey, and they have three sons—Le Nard, Karl and Kenneth, Grover C, superintendent of gas plant at Shawnee, Okla, who is married and has one daughter, Maurine Estell, Lloyd M, who is a student in Jefferson Medical College, Philadelphia, previously taught school, May C, a teacher who is attending Wilson College, at Chambersburg, Pa, Vida N, who is a student in Perkiomen Seminary, at Pemsburg, Pa, and Carrie V, who is also a student at Perkiomen Seminary   Mr Holt and his family attend the Methodist Episcopal church in Graham township, of which he is a trustee   The first wife of Mr Holt died in 1893   In 1895 he was married to a widow, Mrs Ella M Stillman of Lewistown, Ill, who was born in Columbus, O, but reared and educated in Illinois   Mr Holt has long been identified with the Grange, Patrons of Husbandry, and is a member of Lodge No 885, at Sington, Pa

WILLIAM J JONES, secretary of the school board of Bigler township, Clearfield county, Pa, and a representative business man of Madera, is mine foreman for the Swoope Coal Company, a man of experience in this line, having been more or less connected with coal mining since boyhood   He was born March 24, 1865, at Shafton, Westmoreland county, Pa, and was an only child   His mother subsequently married John Milsom and a large family was born to that union, namely   Alice J, wife of Joseph Knapper, Charles H, John E, Daniel, Elizabeth, wife of Charles E Diehl; Margaret, wife of Thomas Gatehouse, Anna, wife of William Johns, Phebe, wife of A. C Bowser, Sarah J, wife of Charles J Neff, and Edward J

William J Jones was reared by his grandparents, John W. and Elizabeth Jones   He attended school in Trumbull county, O, and in Mercer county, Pa, but was only thirteen years old when he began the hard work of a mine boy.   With the exception of a period of eleven years, during which he conducted a general store at Portage, in Cambria county, he has spent his entire life in connection with coal mines in some capacity   He came to Madera in 1902 to take the place of mine foreman and still fills this important position   He has always been an active and interested citizen since reaching maturity and has accepted public responsibilities on many occasions   During his residence in Cambria county he served three years as county auditor, being elected on the Republican ticket with a plurality of 1,500 votes   He has also served several years as judge of elections and in spite of his many business duties has been willing to serve on the school board on account of his interest in general education   His children are receiving many advantages in the way of schooling that he was never able to enjoy.

On October 2, 1895, Mr Jones was married to Flora A Wilson, a daughter of

George H and Roxanna M (Moreland) Wilson, who had other children as follows Joseph H , Mary, wife of Joel Venable, Clara, wife of O D Thompson, Alice, wife of James H Alexander, Albert M , Edwin D , John W , Laura C , wife of A M Jaxtheimer, and Lanora M , wife of W H McFall The father was a farmer and millwright in Mercer county

Mr and Mrs Jones have two sons—George Raymond and Arthur Leslie—and an adopted daughter, Esther L Wilson, a niece She attends the Madera High School and will graduate with the 1911 class Mr Jones and family are members of the Methodist Episcopal church, of which he is a trustee He is a member of the Masonic fraternity and belongs to the Blue Lodge at Osceola, and is a member of the P O S of A No 593, at Madera Mr Jones has invested in property at Madera and owns a fine residence

CHARLES LIVINGSTON TORRENCE, a marble and granite dealer located on Fourth Street, Clearfield, Pa , has been a resident of this borough since 1900 and was born November 6, 1862, at Punxsutawney, Pa , a son of Silas Fenton and Jennie (McHenry) Torrence

The Hon James Torrence, grandfather of our subject, was born in Westmoreland county, Pa , and was of Irish parentage When a young man Judge Torrence came to Punxsutawney, where he operated a tannery, which is still in existence, and was one of the first to establish a business in this section of the county He was subsequently made associate judge of Jefferson county through the efforts of his Presbyterian and Republican friends He spent the remainder of his life in Punxsutawney and died at the age of 75 years He was the father of the following children Silas F , father of our subject, Dr Monroe Torrence, of Indiana, Pa , William C , who lives at Punxsutawney, Pa , George a resident of Punxsutawney, and two daughters, deceased

Silas F Torrence was born in Punxsutawney, Pa , and died there in 1890, aged 60 years He was a tanner by trade, but also followed lumbering some years He is survived by his widow, Jennie McHenry Torrence (a daughter of James McHenry, now deceased), and the following children. William, Anna, who is the wife of M Kettler, Charles L , Hugh B , Paul F , and Earl M

Charles L Torrence grew to maturity in Punxsutawney, where he attended the local schools, and at the age of fourteen began working at his trade during the summer months with Robinson Brothers He continued in their employ for sixteen years, and in 1900 came to Clearfield and bought out B Koozer, who was located on Third Street. In 1905 he came to his present place on Fourth Street, where he does marble and granite interior work and monumental work.

Mr Torrence was joined in marriage with Savilla C Palmer, a daughter of Philip Palmer, deceased, and their children are: William George, Cecil Miles, Anna Pearl, and Charles L , Jr Mr Torrence is fraternally a Mason and an I O O F, and in politics is a Republican

JULIUS VIEBAHN, vice president of the First National Bank of Houtzdale, Pa , is one of the solid business men and representative citizens of this borough. He was born October 12, 1847, in Germany, and is a son of Frederick William and Anna Marie (Theis) Viebahn

Frederick William Viebahn was a man of much importance and gained so wide a reputation as a mine expert that the German government sent him to America to make a study of anthracite coal. He never had any intention of remaining in the United States. and Julius was the only member of his family who ever settled permanently here

Julius Viebahn was given excellent educational advantages in his own land and later served five years in the Prussian Army, being a lieutenant in his company, and was not yet nineteen years old when he participated in the war of Prussia and Austria, and later the war of 1870-1, taking part in thirty-two battles. He was honorably discharged in March, 1871, and in the following month took passage in the steamer City of New York, and reached the United States in the latter part of April. From May until October he remained at Newark, N J, and then came to Clearfield and in the winter following to Houtzdale. In 1875 he visited Little Horn River, in the Black Hills, where he spent a winter and in the spring reached Springfield, Ill, where he assisted in the construction of the new State House. In 1878 he married and returned permanently to Houtzdale, where, for eighteen years he conducted a wholesale brewing business

On July 18, 1878, Mr Viebahn was married to Miss Margaret Lewis, who was born in Tioga county, Pa. She was a daughter of Owen Lewis, of Welsh birth but who was a resident of Houtzdale at the time of his death. Mrs Viebahn died December 27,

1908, a lady who was beloved in the family circle and esteemed by all her acquaintances. Seven children were born to them: Frederick, John H, Edward Amos, William W, Elizabeth, Anna Mary and Julius, Jr The eldest son, Frederick, who was born February 25, 1879, died at the age of ten years. John H, who was born June 20, 1880, served in the Spanish-American War under Colonel Ray, a member of Co I, U S Vol Inf, and now resides in New York. Edward Amos, who was born June 4, 1882 conducts a hotel at Smoke Run, Pa. He was educated in Germany and while there met the lady who later became his wife, Miss Hedwig Wienhues. William W, who was born March 7, 1884, attended school in Germany for eighteen months and has been a student in Dickinson University and the University of Pennsylvania. He has been much interested in baseball and has contracted to pitch for the season of 1911 for the Nashville, Tenn, baseball team. Elizabeth has been an instructor in the public schools of Clearfield county for some years, a highly cultured young lady. Anna Mary is an accomplished musician. The youngest son, Julius, who was born in December, 1890, died November 9, 1900. He was a musical prodigy, in childhood being able to reproduce on musical instruments at home, operas to which he had listened. His early death no doubt deprived the world of a great musician for the future

Clearfield county is much indebted to Mr Viebahn for its superior school facilities. He has taken a deep personal interest in the advancement of education and it was mainly through his efforts that the township High School was organized and built. For

S. A. NELSON

twenty-five years he has served on the school board and his services have been invaluable

JOHN F GALLAHER, a prosperous farmer and justice of the peace at New Washington, Burnside township, was born in Bell township, Clearfield county, Pa, February 11, 1861, a son of James and Mary L (Horton) Gallaher His paternal grandfather, also named James, settled with his family in Clearfield county in 1806 He was a Revolutionary soldier and took a prominent part in the various Indian troubles of his day, being well known as a sturdy and fearless Indian fighter His wife, whose maiden name was Margaret Ramsey, was probably of Scotch descent His occupation was lumbering and farming

James Gallaher, Jr, father of our subject, was born in Huntingdon county, Pa, in 1801 and accompanied his parents to Clearfield county He followed his father's occupation and was a good example of the hardy type of settlers who developed this region from a wilderness to the rich and well cultivated territory it is today He became a member of the Republican party after its formation and at different times held many local offices His death took place in 1880 He was twice married: first to Sally Lee, of which union there were six children, the only one now living being Margaret, wife of Dr McCune, of Middletown, Va Mrs Sally Gallaher died in 1858, and Mr Gallaher was married secondly to Mary L Horton, who was born at Athens, Ohio, May 13, 1826, a daughter of Isaac and Rose (Funston) Horton Of this second union there were born, in addition to our subject, the following children now living Rose, who

became the wife of W Carlysle, Virginia I., residing at New Washington, Pa ; and George W , a resident of Clearfield A half brother, James H Kelley, residing at Clearfield, holds the office of district attorney

John F Gallaher after his school days were over, was associated with his father in farming and lumbering up to 1895, at which time he retired from active participation in those industries, taking up his residence in the borough of New Washington A Republican in politics, he has held office as commissioner and as a member of the school board, and is now serving in his fourth term as justice of the peace

Mr Gallaher married Cora Mahaffey, who was born December 14, 1867, a daughter of William and Mary M (Estricher) Mahaffey, her grandfather being Thomas Mahaffey, of the prominent Clearfield county family of that name Mrs Gallaher died April 27, 1910 She and her husband were the parents of the following children James Kelley, now aged 21 years, who was a soldier in the war in the Philippines, Frank B , aged 19, who resides in Pittsburg, Rose, 18, who is keeping house for her father, John F , our subject, Eva M , 16, who is attending school, John, 12, who is also attending school, Mary, 11, and Burt, 8, and one that died in infancy

S A NELSON, proprietor of the Nelson House, one of the well kept, comfortable and low priced hotels of DuBois, Pa , which is situated on the corner of DuBois and Main streets, has been a resident of this borough since 1889 He was born at Wermland, Sweden, August 5, 1870, and is a son of Nels and Johanna (Olson) Nelson

In Sweden, the name Nelson is spelled Nilson Both parents of Mr Nelson were natives of Sweden, where the mother still lives His father died in 1880, when in his fortieth year There were six children in the family, namely Carl Emil, Swan August, Gustaf (deceased about four years), Hannah, Julius and Clara The youngest two children were drowned when skating

S A Nelson attended school and gained some knowledge of business, in his own land, for a time being a clerk in a store, before he left home and ventured across the sea to America, the only one of his family He reached Elk county, Pa , in 1887, where he was employed in the Dagus mines for two years and six months After reaching DuBois he continued to work in the coal mines for a time and then worked in a stone quarry, where he became a foreman During all this time he had been careful and prudent, preparing to go into business for himself In 1901 he opened the Nelson House and a few months later bought the building and through good management has made it a paying property The Nelson House offers comfortable accommodations and Mr Nelson still charges the same moderate rate that he asked when the house was first opened, only a dollar a day He has twenty bed-rooms

On February 2, 1892, Mr Nelson was married to Miss Clara Amanda Swanson, who was also born in Sweden They have five children, namely Richard, Carrie, Arthur, Ella and Carl Mr Nelson is a member of the DuBois Business Men's Exchange He belongs to the Elks and the Knights of the Golden Eagle, to the Swedish Brotherhood and to the Swedish-American Club In 1903 Mr Nelson visited his mother in Sweden, also expects to return to his native land to visit his mother, brother and sister, this year

JAMES REDDING, the genial host of the Hotel Leonard, a first class house of public entertainment at Clearfield, Pa , and an experienced man in this line of business, was born at Snow Shoe, Center county, Pa , July 13, 1865, and is a son of James and Catherine (Doyle) Redding The parents of Mr Redding were born in Ireland and were married in Center county, Pa The father operated a hotel at Snow Shoe for many years There were seven children in the family, namely Margaret, Henry, Lawrence, James, Mary, Anna and Michael

James Redding obtained his education in the schools at Snow Shoe but was not very old when he went to work in the mines there and continued until he was twenty-two years old He also worked as a fireman on the Pennsylvania and N Y Central Railroad lines before becoming interested in hotel keeping His first experience in this business was thirteen months in Mrs. Nolen's hotel at Snow Shoe He discovered that he was well fitted to go into this undertaking and from there he went to Mitchels, in Clearfield county, where he bought a licensed public house which he conducted for three years and then sold to James Isenberg From there he came to Clearfield and here purchased the St Charles Hotel, from James Crossman, and nine months later sold it to Edward McLaughlin. Mr Redding then bought the Allegheny House from Leopold Bros , which he sold five years later to James Forshey. About this time he secured a mining contract for eighteen months and after its expiration he opened the Hyde City Hotel and operated it for nine months. For one year he then kept out of business, in the meantime looking out for a desirable opening and when the Hotel Leonard came on the market, he bought this property on August 7, 1905, from B A and E J Smith. Mr Redding offers the public first class quarters with modern improvements, at $1 50 per day and has thirty-two comfortable bed rooms, a sample room and a clean, substantial and satisfying table. He is widely known and enjoys liberal patronage. In his hearty entertainment of guests, no question of either religion or politics comes to the surface.

On February 4, 1891, Mr Redding was married to Miss Sarah Smith, of Center county, Pa, and they have one son, Edward J. Mr Redding and family are members of the Catholic church. He is identified with the order of Elks, at Clearfield.

THOMAS R DAVIS, postmaster at Ventland, Pa, where he is also express agent also conducts a small store in the same building, which he owns together with five other pieces of property. For twenty years Mr Davis has lived at this place but he was born in Schuylkill county, Pa, February 29, 1848, and is the only survivor of a family of eleven children born to his parents who were David and Elizabeth (Reese) Davis, natives of Wales.

Thomas R Davis had very little chance in his boyhood to gain an education as he was sent to work in the mines when he was eleven years of age and mining was his main occupation until 1898 when he was appointed postmaster and later added his other responsibilities. For some time before leaving coal mining, he filled the office of check-weighman at the mines.

Mr Davis was married May 21, 1870, to Miss Margaret Terrell, a daughter of John and Hannah Terrell, the former of whom was born in Ireland and the latter in Huntingdon county. Mr and Mrs Davis have had the following children: David, Richard, who is deceased, T H S, Jennie, who is deceased, Elizabeth, who is deceased, was the wife of J W Withrow, and Edward, Matilda, Blaine, Alfretta, Edith and Clifton M. Mr Davis and family attend the Methodist Episcopal church. In politics he is a Republican and has served as school director in both Bigler and Decatur townships. He is identified with the organization known as the Brotherhood of America. He is a well known and highly respected citizen.

T JEFF BLOOM, contractor, builder and millwright, was born March 31, 1844, on the farm of 160 acres which he owns and occupies and which lies one and one-half miles east of the center of Curwensville, Pike township, Clearfield county, Pa. He is a member of one of the prominent and substantial pioneer families of the county, a great-grandson of William Bloom, a grandson of William Bloom (2), and a son of Isaac Bloom.

Great grandfather William Bloom was born in Hunterdon county, N J, and was of German parentage. He served for six years under General Washington in the Continental Army and continued his military life until the colonies had attained independence. He married a Miss Clover, of New Jersey, and their eldest son was born on the day of the battle of Monmouth, in which the

young father participated Some time prior
to 1798, William Bloom and family traveled
by ox-team to Center county, Pa , and from
there, in 1801, to Clearfield county He
cleared up a small tract of land near the
present borough of Curwensville, in Pike
township, which is now called Peewees'
Nest Owing to some misunderstanding
about the ownership of this land, he waived
his claim and moved to the Col Irvin place,
on the west branch of the Susquehannah
River By that time some of his children
were married, and they established their
own homes on or near the river, although
a large part of the country was nothing but
a wilderness, with Indians numerous and
hostile There were no roads, the county
not yet having been organized, and such
conditions prevailed that only men and
women of courage and endurance could have
been content to make so wild a region their
home William Bloom and wife had eleven
children born to them, namely Isaac, William, John, Abraham, Benjamin, James,
Peter, Annie, Sarah, Nancy, and Mary

William Bloom, son of William, and
grandfather of T Jeff Bloom, was
born in New Jersey, in 1780 He married
Mary Roll, of Clarion county, Pa , and they
had ten children, namely Hannah, Sarah,
Mary, Jane, Mrs Irvin Thayerson, Isaac,
John, David, Harrison and Eli After his
marriage, William Bloom lived in Pike
township, where the farm then included 500
acres, 168 of which he cleared, beginning
with nine acres, which he immediately
started to cultivate He then erected
a large log house, big enough to accommodate his own growing family and
also to offer hospitality to the traveling pub-

lic that was then passing over the Meads
road on the way farther west. He had a
fine trade and was a shrewd business man,
as was evidenced by his moving to a part of
his farm which was adjacent to the newly
constructed Erie turnpike road For years
he conducted a hotel near where Mr. Porter
now resides, in Pike township He was a
very robust, well proportioned man and had
a corresponding strong constitution, living
to be ninety-two years of age, dying in 1872.
He was a Jacksonian Democrat and was
elected to many public offices. He was constable when the township had but sixty-two
voters, later was sheriff of Clearfield county
Having a cash fortune of $30,000 he was
considered the wealthiest man in Clearfield
county His wife lived to be seventy years
old They are both buried in McClure's
cemetery, where the ashes of the pioneers of
the family also repose

Isaac Bloom was born in 1813, on the
present Bloom farm, in Pike township
Three months of school attendance covered
all the educational advantages he ever had,
but nevertheless he became a successful
business man and one whose judgment was
often consulted concerning public matters
He resided on the present farm until within
a few years of his death, when he retired
to Curwensville, where he passed away in
1864, at the age of fifty-two years His
burial was in the Oak Hill cemetery He
was a strong Democrat and probably at that
time the Bloom family held the voting power
in Clearfield county, on account of their
numbers and about all of them being Democrats In 1848 he was elected treasurer of
Clearfield county and for many years he
was a justice of the peace in Pike township

He married Leah Hoover, who was born in 1816, a daughter of George Hoover She died in 1879, at the age of sixty-two years They were most excellent people in every relation of life, setting an admirable example to their thirteen children, whom they reared in the faith of the Presbyterian church Of this family, T Jeff Bloom was the sixth in order of birth, the others being Cortez, Miles, Henrietta, Jane, Hannah, Flora, Belle, Mary, Annie, Blanche, Robert and Walter

T Jeff Bloom was seven years old when he began attending school at Curwensville, and he continued to live there until 1880 For ten years following his marriage he was in the contracting business at Curwensville, combined with building He has done an immense amount of work along this line For three years he did all the contracting at Patton, Cambria county, where he erected all the buildings He estimates that he has done as much as $500,000 worth of contracting since he started into business Among the numerous structures he has contracted for and built, is the handsome Curwensville National Bank

In 1868 Mr Bloom was married to Miss Rosa Thompson, who is a daughter of J W and Annie Eliza (Wilson) Thompson, and they have had nine children, namely Frank P, Ralph, Grace, Charles, Dean, Walter, Henrietta, Seth and Thompson Of the above, Ralph, Charles, Walter and Thompson are all deceased

Mr Bloom retired to his farm in 1880, where he has done a large amount of improving There are still some old landmarks left of his grandfather's time, but his handsome, modern residence he erected himself, and has added other substantial buildings This place is richly underveined with coal and an open mine, which has an output of 200 tons of fine coal daily, exceeding the mines of his neighbors who work their mines with such an output monthly, is a comfortable source of wealth His residence and mine both are on the Ferncliff branch of the B R & P Railroad, making transportation easy This fine mine is leased by the Clearfield-Collier Company, of Clearfield, Pa, Mr Bloom receiving a handsome royalty He is interested also in some 5,000,000 feet of hemlock timber, and has additional interests in financial concerns Like other members of his family, Mr Bloom is a Democrat and is one of the leading factors of the party councils in the county and at times has attended state conventions as a delegate and has also held a number of township offices He attends and contributes to the Baptist church, of which Mrs Bloom is a member Fraternally he is identified with the Order of the Moose and has taken many of the degrees in the Knights of Pythias organization

HON JOSEPH BENSON McENALLY, deceased In the death of Judge McEnally, which occurred at his home in Clearfield, Pa, January 5, 1910, Clearfield lost the Nestor of her bar and the county a citizen of worth and high attainment Judge McEnally was born in Columbia county, Pa, January 25, 1825, and was the youngest son of Rev Peter and Margaret (Bloodhart) McEnally The father was a traveling minister of the Methodist Episcopal church and was well known at Clearfield, having served as pastor here in 1831 and again in 1848-9

Joseph Benson McEnally attended the common schools until he secured a teacher's certificate and after that engaged in teaching until he had accumulated the means to pursue a higher course of study In June, 1845, he was graduated from Dickinson College and then began the reading of law with Judge Jordan, at Sunbury, Pa , and in 1849 was admitted to the Northumberland county bar His legal talent was very soon recognized and he was appointed deputy attorney general of the county, and in this office demonstrated his ability and won a position on the bar which he never lost In 1868 he was appointed president judge of the Twenty-fifth Judicial District, which was made up of the counties of Clearfield, Center and Clinton, and during his term on the bench won an enviable record as a competent judge After his judicial term was over he resumed his private practice and in 1872 formed a partnership with the late Daniel W McCurdy, and after the latter's death was associated with Alexander Patterson At different times in his career public office was tendered him, but his practice was so extensive and engrossing that possible high political position did not particularly attract him Until within the closing years of his life he continued to be actively engaged in professional duties In 1852 Judge McEnally was married to Miss Amelia Wright, whose death occurred June 30, 1895 One son, Wright McEnally, survives

CHARLES G GILL, postmaster of Madera, Pa , taking charge of the office April 1, 1911, is superintendent of the Madera Water Works Company and owner and proprietor of a blacksmith shop at Madera He is one of the enterprising and successful men of Bigler township, Clearfield county, and was born at Madera, December 2, 1871, and is a son of Josiah and Julia (Vedder) Gill

Josiah Gill was born in Clearfield county and for many years operated a blacksmith shop at Madera, and was a well known and respected man In politics he was a Republican He married Julia Vedder, who was born in Tioga county, Pa , and they had the following children born to them Lewis, Charles G , Robert, Emma, Harry and Scott, the three survivors being Lewis, Charles G. and Scott

Charles G Gill attended the public schools of Madera until old enough to learn the blacksmith trade, with his father, and this trade he has followed ever since He has been a very active citizen and has many times been elected to township offices For ten years he served as a justice of the peace, at present is supervisor, has been auditor, and in 1908 was mercantile appraiser for Clearfield county. He was reared in the Presbyterian church but has never united with the same, being liberal minded to all religious bodies and a contributor to benevolent enterprises of which his judgment approves, no matter under what name they are organized

In 1897, Mr Gill was married to Miss Myrtle Johnston, of Huntingdon, Pa , a daughter of David and Hannah (Mencer) Johnston, who were born in Blair county They had four children Elliott, Myrtle, Lydia, wife of F J Shollar, and Vance Mr Gill is a Republican in his political views

BERT EUGENE LEIPOLD, M D, a successful medical practitioner, of Clearfield, Pa , was born August 26, 1874, at Clearfield, Pa., and is a son of George L and Anna (Benn) Leipold

Casper Leipold, grandfather of our subject, was a native of Germany and at an early age came to this country and subsequently purchased a large tract of land, which now forms the site of Allegheny, of greater Pittsburg Some time later he sold the farm and located at Curwensville, Pa , where he was among the early settlers, and there followed his trade as a butcher He subsequently came to Clearfield county and ran a brewery for some time, residing here until the time of his death Casper Leipold was the father of four children Sophia (Mrs Griswald), George L, father of our subject, Mary (Mrs Hamilton), and Daniel George L Leipold was born in 1849 at Curwensville, Pa , and was for many years engaged in the hotel business at Clearfield, Pa , but is now living in retirement at Saxton, Pa

Dr B E Leipold was reared at Clearfield, Pa , where he obtained his education in the local schools After a course of private lessons he entered the Jefferson Medical College in 1893, being graduated with the class of 1896 He immediately thereafter embarked in the practice of medicine at Clearfield and five years later built his office and residence, which are located at No 405 Market street Dr Leipold also makes a specialty of diseases of the eye, ear, nose and throat, and is a member of the medical and surgical staff of the Clearfield Hospital He is also a member of the American, State and county medical societies, and is a stockholder in the County National Bank He is fraternally a member of the local order of B P O E

In December, 1895, Dr Leipold married May Smith, who died August 1, 1906, leaving one son, Hobert F In August, 1908, Dr Leipold married Minnie VanBuskirk, who is a graduated trained nurse, and a daughter of Charles and Mary VanBuskirk, of Penfield, Pa

JOHN DOTTS, one of Pike township's representative citizens and successful farmers, who resides four miles south of Curwensville, Pa , where he owns 116 acres of valuable land, the old Bloom homestead, owns also a farm of forty acres in Ferguson township, two miles east of Lumber City and another tract of 141 acres, rich coal land, situated in Jordan township, one and one-half miles south of McCartney He was born in Beccaria township, Clearfield county, March 31, 1861, and is a son of Philip and Catherine (Stretzel) Dotts

Philip Dotts was born at Germantown, Pa , a suburb of Philadelphia, where he married Catherine Stretzel He was a miller by trade and for some years worked at different places in Clearfield county but later settled on a farm, acquiring 502 acres, which is now owned by his son, William Dotts He cleared about 110 acres of this land himself In politics he was a Democrat and was a man of considerable consequence in Clearfield county and served one term as county treasurer He lived a long and useful life which ended on March 16, 1901, and his burial was in the Fruit Hill Cemetery, attached to the Fruit Hill Presbyterian church of which he was a member and an elder He was identified with the order of Odd Fellows His widow survives, being now in her eighty-ninth year, and is a resident of Glen Hope, Pa Of the ten children born to them there are six survivors, namely Mary, who is the wife of F W Hollenpeter, of Glen Hope; William, who lives on the old homestead in Beccaria township, married Aurilla

Neveling, Ellwood, who lives in Minnesota; Philip, who is a resident of California, Mrs Margaret Hammer, who lives at Germantown, Pa , and John, who is the subject of this record

John Dotts obtained his education in the common schools at Fairview and then followed lumbering and farming on the homestead until his marriage, in 1888, when he settled at Glen Hope and continued work in the woods as a lumberman Later he moved to his coal farm in Jordan township, where he lived for four years and then came to the present home farm, on which his wife was born All the buildings now standing have been remodeled since Mr Dotts came into possession and he has all his land under cultivation, with the exception of thirty-six acres of valuable woodland Mr Dotts is a Democrat in his political views and while living at Glen Hope he served as treasurer and as school director and has also been a school director in Pike township

On January 18, 1888, Mr Dotts was married to Miss Alice S Bloom, who was born on the present home farm on August 27, 1863, and is a daughter of Levi and Susanna (High) Bloom She attended the Curry school in Pike township and grew to womanhood in her own home Her father, Levi Bloom, was born near Curwensville, January 10, 1824, and although he was a very successful business man in after life, he had but two months of schooling He engaged in lumbering and farming and came to this place when only four acres had been yet cleared He was enterprising and industrious and after building a log house and barn began to complete the clearing of his land At the time of his death, June 5, 1896, he owned two other farms in Knox township He was a Democrat in politics He married, in 1845, Susanna High, born January 20, 1825, a daughter of John and Sally High, of Center county Levi Bloom and wife had fourteen children, the six survivors being Jared, who lives near Burnsdale, Alfred, who lives on a farm of seventy-two acres, a part of the old Bloom homestead, married Martha McNeel, Eliza, who is the wife of William Arnold, lives at Curwensville; Wesley, who is a resident of Chicago, Ill , Martin, who resides at Seneca, Kans ; and Alice, who is the wife of John Dotts The mother of the above family died January 7, 1891, and she was buried in the New Millport cemetery, where, five years later her husband was laid by her side They were widely known people and were very highly respected

Mr and Mrs Dotts have had ten children · Levi, Zella, Leon, Carl, Droze, Beryl, Oel, Merrill, Marl and Ethel All survive except the eldest son, who lived to be nineteen years of age His burial was by the side of his grandparents at New Millport Mr Dotts and family are members of the Lutheran church at New Millport

WILLIAM A WALLACE, or Senator Wallace, as he was commonly called, came into public life in January, 1863, when he took his place as state senator from the mountain district, then composed of the counties of Blair, Cambria and Clearfield He occupied a seat in the State Senate continuously from that date until March, 1881 In 1882, as the result of political contention in his senatorial district, he was again chosen state senator, and served as such until January, 1887 Seventeen years as state senator—during one of which he occupied the Speaker's chair—and six years as United States senator, are the sum of the official life of Mr Wallace

He was born at Huntingdon, Pa, November 28, 1827 He comes of Scotch-Irish parentage on both sides The family of both his father and mother trace their ancestry to the north of Ireland, and among Wallaces, Hemphills, McCauleys and Cunninghams who came under Cromwell's orders in the sixteenth century with Sir Richard Wallace from Scotland to occupy the land His father, Robert Wallace, migrated from the County Tyrone in 1819 He was an educated man, taught school in Mifflin county, Pa, read law there with Ephraim Banks, settled at Huntingdon, practiced law and married there, and thence removed to Clearfield county, where he died in January, 1875

When Senator Wallace went to Clearfield he pursued his studies as best he could in the schools of the place, but no opportunity was afforded him to gain more than a fairly good English education and the rudiments of the classics He began the study of law when a little more than sixteen years of age in his father's office and helped to support himself by doing clerical work in the offices of the prothonotary, sheriff, treasurer and commissioners of the county He applied himself with great earnestness to work and study, and his employment in the county offices gave him a knowledge of titles and surveys which was of great value to him after he was admitted to the bar, as the bulk of the cases in that county were ejectment suits and other litigation growing out of disputed titles to land and lines of survey.

During this time, however, he devoted himself to the study of law, and by hard work he gained a foothold He was painstaking, conscientious and untiring, and when he got a case he prepared it with a care that soon attracted attention, and his practice began to increase Many prominent lawyers then practiced at the Clearfield bar, among them Andrew G. Curtin, Judges Hale, Linn and the younger Burnside, and the class of cases he was engaged in were mostly ejectment suits which were of such importance that the parties to the litigation had the means to employ the best talent Attrition with strong minds and the character of the litigation rapidly developed his force as a lawyer and gave him a large practice

The hard work required and his close application told upon his health, so that in 1862 he accepted the nomination of the Democrats for the State Senate as a relief from the drudgery of his practice and in the hope that the change of scene and action might benefit him His opponent was the then speaker of the State Senate, and a recognized leader of his party A sharply-contested fight followed Mr Wallace was successful mainly through the increased majority given him in his own county His election to the State Senate gave the Democrats a majority of one on joint ballot, and his vote made Charles R Buckalew United States Senator For fifteen years after his first election he was returned to the Senate, and, notwithstanding the bitter assaults that were made upon his political action, at each election he ran ahead of his ticket in his own county He went to Harrisburg with merely a local reputation, but he soon made his name known throughout the whole state, and in a very few years it was known throughout the whole country

So rapidly did Mr Wallace develop into a

power in his party that in 1865 he was, without his consent, made chairman of its State Central Committee   He found the Democracy split and demoralized, and at once addressed himself to the work of organization, in which he developed unusual tact and ability   The majority against his party in 1865 and 1866 was under twenty thousand, but in 1867 Judge Sharswood was the candidate for Supreme Court judge and Mr Wallace at the head of the State Committee conducted such an adroit and noiseless canvass that the Republican candidate was defeated   In 1868 the most memorable canvass of his career as a political manager was made   Seymour and Blair were the candidates for the Presidency and Vice-Presidency against Grant and Colfax   The October election in Pennsylvania was the pivotal contest, and the issue was made and fully tested there   He not only gave his party a splendid organization, but good heart, and brought it to the polls in such excellent working condition that the Democratic candidate, C E Boyle, was defeated by less than ten thousand votes in the October election   A change of less than one per cent would have reversed the decision   Even with the prestige of Grant's name and popularity his majority was less than twenty-nine thousand at the Presidential election   The contest that year in Pennsylvania was one of the bitterest ever known in the history of the politics of the state and the Democratic party under the leadership of Mr Wallace was in better condition than for many years before or perhaps since that time

His career in the State Senate was that of a leader   For almost the whole of his term of service he occupied prominent positions upon the important committees of finance, judiciary and apportionment, and his learning as a lawyer and his force as a business man, gave him great opportunities of serving the people in a non-partisan way, and of shaping judicious legislation   His personal record there was above reproach, and his influence was unexcelled by that of any of the body   In 1871, his party having obtained control of the Senate, he was chosen Speaker thereof, and demonstrated in that place his fairness and impartiality, as well as his admirable skill as a parliamentarian   In the winter of 1874, the one prior to that in which Mr Wallace was elected United States Senator, the Legislature was engaged in framing the acts necessary to carry into effect the provisions of the new constitution   To this work Mr Wallace earnestly addressed himself, and much of the important legislation of that session bears the impress of his mind

The general act of incorporation, which is regarded as one of the best of the kind on the statute books of any State in the country, was his work, and the law regulating and classifying cities and providing for their debts also came from his hand   The act of 1883 providing for arbitration of labor disputes, which was first enacted in the United States and was purely tentative in its character, was the work of his hand, and the change in the general railroad law of that session, which gave much more liberality to their construction, was also largely aided by him

In the election of 1874 his party had secured control of the legislature on joint ballot, and by common consent Mr Wallace was turned to by his party as its candidate for the United States Senate   In the few years that had elapsed since he walked into the Senate chamber a pale, delicate and almost unknown young man, he had outstripped many Democratic leaders of less force, but more pretentions Of course, several prominent leaders of his party, were candidates for the nomination for United States Senator, but it did not need the expression of the Democrats in the Legislature to show that Mr Wallace was the choice of two-thirds of them So pronounced was the feeling in his favor that long before the Legislature met the question was practically settled, and when the Democratic caucus met there were only sixteen votes out of 121 cast for all the opposing candidates

Mr Wallace took his seat in the Senate of the United States on the 4th of March, 1875, and almost immediately assumed a leading position in the national councils of his party His reputation as a man of political force, gained by practical service in Pennsylvania, followed him in the broader work at the capital of the Republic, and he had been in the Senate but a very short time before his judgment was sought and his advice taken upon all matters of party management During his term in the Senate he served upon the important committees of finance, appropriations and foreign relations At the time when the Democrats drifted towards division, Mr Wallace was of great service to his party in inducing it to take conservative action upon leading questions and in tempering and controlling the bitterness of opposing factions In all the political events transpiring during his six years at the National Capital, Mr Wallace held a foremost place, and, although antagonized at every step by his rivals for leadership in the State, he maintained his position and almost universally scored a victory over his adversaries

In 1872 he was a delegate to the Democratic National Convention at Baltimore and

chairman of the delegation, and voted against Horace Greeley and for Judge Black, but followed his party in supporting Greeley for the Presidency after his nomination

In 1874 he presided over the convention of his party at Pittsburg, one of the most important of its history It was so impartially controlled and the order maintained was so exemplary that it exerted much influence in winning the Legislature for the Democracy in the then succeeding election In 1876 he was again a delegate to the St Louis National Convention and again was chairman of the delegation In 1880 he was influential at Cincinnati in securing the nomination of General Hancock to the Presidency, although he declined to go upon the delegation In 1884 he was upon the delegation to Chicago, but, declining any of the official places in the delegation he was directed by it to present the name of Mr Randall as the candidate of Pennsylvania He did this in such a spirit of broad-minded fairness, and so forcibly and eloquently, that his brief speech was declared to be the oratorical gem of the occasion

Mr Wallace's career as a lawyer is as eminent as his record as a politician Starting without opportunities or influential friends he rapidly rose to a prominent place among the leaders of the bar of the State While serving in the Senate, he did not neglect his legal work During the labor troubles in the Clearfield region, he took a judicious and equitable part between the coal operators and the striking miners Although counsel for the Commonwealth and the coal operators, he was never violent in his denunciation of the workman In the great trial which took place at Clearfield, when the leaders of the labor strikes were arrested for conspiracy and the question of the organization and conduct of the labor unions was up for judicial investigation, Mr. Wallace was counsel for the coal operators in their actions against the miners The late Senator Matt Carpenter, Judge Hughes, of Pottsville, and other eminent lawyers, defended the action of the labor union Judge Orvis presided and the trial was a long and desperately fought legal battle

John Siney, the head of the labor unions, was acquitted because no overt act could be proved against him, but Xingo Parkes and other prominent labor unionists were convicted and sent to the penitentiary Mr Wallace interposed in behalf of the convicted men and urged upon the court the utmost clemancy He took the ground that the moral effect of the conviction of the leading strikers was greater than a harsh execution of the law. In all the many labor troubles that have occurred in Clearfield county, Mr Wallace has taken a prominent part as assistant counsel to the law officers of the county He has also represented the large coal operators in that region, and by his judicious advice and discreet interposition between contending forces, law and order have been very well preserved, and never have troops been called into the county to preserve the peace, as they have in nearly every other mining district in Pennsylvania In the labor riots in 1877, as in all others that have occurred in the Clearfield region, Mr Wallace's action and advice were effective and all important He took a judicious ground between the workmen and the operators He held that the men had the right to strike, but no right to prevent others working, and the quiet but firm position assumed by the operators and authorities under his advice prevented bloodshed and restored order

in the region. The result of his attitude is best displayed by the fact that since 1877 there has no violence attended any of the strikes in all that region

The qualities of mind that Mr Wallace early exhibited specially fitted him for dealing with the delicate questions which this condition of things imposed He was always noted for great courage, tact and good judgment Untiring energy and tenacity are among his striking characteristics, and his powers of endurance and capacity for work were simply remarkable

The case of Turner vs the Commonwealth, reported in Fifth Norris, gives a fair illustration of the tenacity of purpose with which Mr. Wallace fought his legal battles and followed a trail in spite of all obstacles He was counsel for defense, and feeling ran high against his client, who was convicted of murder in the first degree and sentenced to be hung Mr Wallace took the case to the Supreme Court and his argument for a reversal of the judgment of the lower court is regarded as one of the strongest ever delivered before that tribunal It was also a successful one, for the decision of the court was reversed and a new trial ordered He secured a change of venue from Clearfield to Clinton county and the case was retired The Commonwealth was struck in one of its weakest points, and after one of the most dramatic scenes ever witnessed in a court room in Central Pennsylvania, his client was acquitted Mr Wallace had given three years of hard work to the case and illustrated in a striking manner those qualities of mind and body that brought him fortune and fame

In those branches of the law most useful in the development of an astute and deep legal mind, Senator Wallace was greatly proficient.

The trial of ejectment on original title is one of those branches This field has given to the legal profession, in the last half century, its strongest minds Chief Justices Woodward, Thompson, Black and Agnew graduated in this school and fitted themselves for their high duties by work at the bar and on the local bench The records of the Supreme Court, in many of its cases, show the impress of Mr Wallace's mind upon the creation of a system of law applicable to and resulting from titles, surveys and patents Hagerty vs Mathers, reported in 5th Casey, and again in 1st Wright, is an example of this class of cases One of the most noted of these cases was the celebrated Houtz ejectment, involving the location of the tracts of land upon which Houtzdale is built and perhaps 10,000 people live His position and theories as to the true location were finally vindicated, after three trials in as many different courts, and his clients were successful Governor Beaver and ex-Solicitor General Jenks were his antagonists in the last trial of the case, and it is no reflection on them to say that they were unsuccessful both in the court below and in the Supreme Court

After leaving the Senate Mr Wallace devoted himself to bringing returns from his large landed estate, which had been neglected during his official life In his later years he did more to develop the bituminous coal interests of the Clearfield region than had ever been done before, and he reaped the reward of his industry and enterprise The projection of the Beech Creek Railroad as a branch of the Reading System, and a competitive factor in the transportation of the coal seeking an eastward market, was one of the agencies of this work It is a financial success and has greatly enhanced the value of the coal lands of the section it traverses While not connected with the machinery of its operation, he was its president from the beginning Upon the branches of the Pennsylvania system traversing his county he had also large interests, and constantly aided in developing new fields and giving employment to labor upon new and needed extensions

As years came to him, the asperities that result from the political action of an aggressive man, seemed to grow softer, and broader views and milder thoughts took their place From being somewhat partisan and bitter as a speaker, he became conservative and thoughtful of the future of the people His first appearance at a State convention since 1880 was in 1887, when he was called to preside The views of his party's policy he then presented are well known to have been his own earnest convictions, and those of us who knew him well, know that no prouder trophy could have been his than to have engrafted on the organic law of the State reform looking to the growth of intelligence among her people and elevating the standard of their morals and public purity

It is but natural that a man of his strength of character, habits and disposition and one who bore such a conspicuous part in shaping political controversies, should have been assailed and criticised It is to his credit that he had many bitter enemies, and still more to his honor that he was able to meet them with success and to rise to eminence by sheer force of character, energy and ability

From another source we take the following in regard to this eminent lawyer and citizen·

'August 30, 1847 On reading the certificate of Josiah W Smith, George R Barrett and John F Weaver, board of examiners, and on motion of George R Barrett, William A Wallace, Esq, was admitted to practice as an attorney of Clearfield county and was sworn, etc,

William C Welsh, Prothy (Continuance Docket No 6, page 161)

"He was then 19 years and 9 months old His first case was entered on September 2, 1847, 3 days after his admission, as follows

James Brothers vs Andrew Barnhart

No 33, August Term, 1847 Transcript from Docket of James McMurray, of judgment $14 30 Int 19 Aug 1846 Entered Sept 2, 1847

"He was distinguished from everybody else who has ever practiced law here in these respects He was more aggressive and persistent and industrious To these qualities he added a wonderfully quick apprehension and a comprehensive grasp of his whole case which he never relaxed until he accomplished his purpose Long before I knew him or any of the other men who practiced here I asked my father what there was about him which gave him such a reputation over everybody else He said that he got all the points in his case, that he omitted nothing, when I came to know him afterwards I thought this was a pretty good summary of what distinguished him in the trial of a case.

"No man can practice law to any considerable extent without having occasions which will test the kind of a man he is A lawyer does his work publicly under the direction and supervision of the court and under the glaring criticism of other members of the Bar who may be either arrayed against him in the particular case, or whose sympathies for some reason may be opposed to him In most other employments a man may measurably conceal his action and motives but not so in law. These remarks are suggested by an experience Senator Wallace had in the summer of 1875. A most serious difficulty in protecting property in a conflict between the coal operators and their employes was encountered in this county A large number of men were arrested charged with riot and conspiracy The first trial occurred on the 7th of June and the second trial against the same defendants on the 28th of September, each of them occupying a week or more and each of them resulting in a verdict of guilty The two most noted defendants were known as Siney and Parks. They had a State reputation, if not a National reputation, for their identity with labor organizations Senator Wallace aided only by Judge Krebs, then quite a young man, conducted the prosecutions on the part of the defendants There was perhaps the most noted array of counsel for the defense we have ever had in this county Matt Carpenter, then United States Senator, and with a National reputation as a great lawyer, Frank Hughes, who had been at the head of the Schuylkill county Bar for perhaps 50 years, and Linn Bartholomew, the most noted jury lawyer in that section, appeared with Judge Barrett and Walter Barrett on the part of the defense William M McCullough told me that he had asked Senator Wallace if he realized the effect that his prosecution of these cases would have upon his political future Without a moment's hesitation, the Senator said to him, that he had no fear whatever from any such source, that this was an occasion that required of a lawyer *moral* courage, and that he proposed to assume the responsibility of doing his duty as he understood it

"This generation understands very poorly how much we are indebted to the course taken by Senator Wallace at that time We have never had either before or since such a crisis as occurred at that time—35 years ago W R McPherson was sheriff Wallace prepared his proclamation, which was issued and scattered broadcast throughout the county He repudiated the idea that it was necessary to call for State troops, and acted upon the assumption that the police power of this county was adequate to compel obedience to the laws There was perhaps never an instance when a lawyer of ability and experience, and with a large following in the county, had a better opportunity to perform a great public and professional duty, and no man ever did perform such a duty more courageously and fearlessly than did Senator Wallace It was a service similar to that which Franklin B Gowan performed when he prosecuted to a finish the leaders of the Molly Maguires in Schuylkill county, and similar also to the great public service which was performed by Grover Cleveland on a larger scale in suppressing the labor riots in Chicago and aiding in the conviction of those who with red hands had trampled upon the rights of both liberty and property"

He was married to a daughter of Hon Richard Shaw, of Clearfield, Pa , July 20 1848 He died in New York, May 22, 1896, and was buried in the family plot in Clearfield, Pa Senator Wallace left to survive him a widow, Margaret A Wallace, who died March 18, 1911, at Clearfield, Pa , and the following children who all reside in Clearfield, Pa , Mary W Krebs, widow of David L Krebs, Edgar Shaw Wallace, Harry F Wallace, William E Wallace, Gussie L Wrigley, wife of John W Wrigley, Margaret W Smith, wife of Allison O Smith, President Judge of Clearfield county, Pa

C C SHOFF, general farmer in Bigler township, Clearfield county, Pa , was born on the farm on which he lives, September 6, 1837 He had but few educational advantages when he was young, seven months of schooling, all told, but there are few men in this neighborhood who know more about logging or work in the woods than Mr Shoff

When but thirteen years old Mr Shoff began to work in the timber, and ever since then has given a part of each winter to the lumber business, devoting his summers to farming He has sixty-three acres of land, six acres having formerly been underlaid with fine coal, but it has been about all worked out Mr Shoff is well known and highly regarded in his township and has always, since he reached manhood, so enjoyed public confidence that he has been elected to some office He has served in almost all the township offices and for six years was constable

Mr Shoff was married in 1861 to Miss Elizabeth Stitt, who died December 22, 1906, and is buried at Beulah, Pa She was a daughter of Thomas and Barbara (Glass) Stitt, natives of Cambria county, whose other children were named as follows Ellen, George, Nancy, James and Christopher To Mr and Mrs Shoff the following children were born S T , Emma, who is the wife of Andrew Colwell, and J F , Willis D , Luther, James A , and Lena Mr Shoff and family are members of the Lutheran church

JAMES FRANK McFARLANE, one of the leading citizens of Utahville, Pa., postmaster at this point and ticket, freight and express agent for the Pennsylvania Railroad Company, and also justice of the peace, was born July 18, 1869, at Utahville, and is a son of Simon and Sarah J (Clark) McFarlane

Simon McFarlane was born in Scotland in 1830 His parents remained in Scotland, and some of his brothers went to Australia He came to America when twenty years of age and lived for one year in the State of Maine, living at Bangor, and from there made his way to Williamsport, Pa., where he engaged in cutting square timber and rafting logs He married there in 1858 and then came to Clearfield county and engaged in lumbering and in the mercantile business at Utahville and followed lumbering until his death in 1903 This was accidentally caused by an act of heroism, in an attempt to save a nephew from death from a boiler explosion, both being killed   At Williamsport he married Sarah J Clark, who was a daughter of John Clark, a well known early settler, and she survived until 1895, dying in her fifty-eighth year Four sons and four daughters were born to this marriage, namely   William A , who died in 1879, aged twenty years, Carrie C , who lives at Utahville, Harry C , who also lives at Utahville, May, who is employed in a bank at Coalport, James F , Lillie, who is the wife of Frank Caldwell, of Utahville, Florence, who is the wife of James Edelbute, of Utahville, and John, who died in 1898

James F McFarlane was mainly educated in the local schools, in addition to having a course at the Williamsport Commercial College, after which he followed lumbering with his father, and after the latter's death continued in the same line up to 1909 and still owns a saw-mill. He conducted a store from 1905 until January 1, 1911   For nearly six years he has been agent for the Pennsylvania Railroad Company, and is serving in his second term as justice of the peace, having been first elected in 1905   He is a Republican in politics, and since July, 1905, has been postmaster

Mr McFarlane was married in June, 1902, to Miss Bessie Croyle, who was reared on a farm near Utahville, a daughter of William and Ida Croyle   Mr and Mrs McFarlane have two children, Raymond S and Thelma A   They belong to the Methodist Episcopal church, Mr McFarlane being a trustee of the same   He is identified with Coalport Lodge No 576, F & A M , and with Mt. Pleasant Grange of Utahville   He has spent all his life at this place with the exception of three years in Pittsburg and a short season in Williamsport, and his family and property interests all center here

THE FIRST NATIONAL BANK OF OSCEOLA, Clearfield county, Pa , which occupies a high place among the safe and sound financial institutions of Clearfield county, was incorporated in 1902, with a capital stock of $50,000 The bank opened for business on December 15, 1902, with the officers who have ever since directed its policy and conserved its interests They are the following capitalists and men of high personal standing   John McLaren, president, H W Todd, vice president, and E C Blandy, cashier The following are the

HON. JOHN H. PATCHIN

directors of this bank C R Houtz, of Philipsburg, James S Moore, of Houtsdale, W A Gould, of Brisbin, H W Todd, of Philipsburg, John McLarren, of Osceola Mills, E C Blandy and Frank Craig, of Brisbin, Pa

This bank has always occupied its present site but in 1908 the old building was torn down and in its place was erected the present handsome two-story structure It is finely finished, equipped with all modern conveniences and especially fitted for the banking business This institution has made wonderful strides forward in the comparatively short period of its existence and has paid its twelfth dividend The surplus is $40,000 and the undivided profits total more than $4,000

T C Blandy, cashier of the above bank, was born at Osceola Mills, but when about eight years old was taken by his parents to Lewes, Dela, and from there to Huntingdon, Pa In 1890 he entered the U S Naval Academy at Annapolis, Md, where he continued for four years In 1896 he returned to Osceola Mills where he has been in the banking business practically ever since He was assistant cashier of the Osceola Banking Company, a private enterprise, until 1902, when he was largely instrumental in the organization of the institution of which he now is cashier

HON JOHN H PATCHIN, manufacturer of and dealer in all kinds of lumber and building supplies, at Burnside, Pa, president of the school board of this borough and formerly a member of the state legislature, has been a resident of this place since 1903 and is one of its most active and aggressive public

men He was born at Patchinsville, Clearfield county, Pa, April 9, 1868, and is a son of Aaron W and Elizabeth (Barrett) Patchin The latter survives, being now in her seventy-second year The Patchin family is one of wealth and importance in Clearfield county and is largely connected

John H Patchin is the third oldest in a family of seven children, the others being Emma, who is the wife of H P Dowler, superintendent of the Pennsylvania Steel Company, at Heilwood, Pa, Olive, who is the wife of Jno N Ake, who is a ship builder, at Camden, N J, Winnie, who is the wife of J O Clark, who is president of the National Bank at Glen Campbell, Pa, Flora, who is the wife of W J Dufton, who is in the hardware business at Clearfield, Carl E, who is in the lumber business at Burnside, and Ray C, who is a farmer near Patchinsville

John H Patchin went from the public schools to Bucknell University, where he took a three-year course and then attended Lafayette College, at Easton, Pa Mr Patchin then entered into the lumber business with his father and during a part of this time was engaged in rafting on the Susquehanna river In 1903 he came to Burnside and bought the saw-mill and lumber interests of Horace Patchin and is still managing an estate of 2,000 acres Additionally he is interested in dealing in ship-building supplies, in partnership with his brother-in-law, at Camden, N J, has oil properties in Oklahoma and is a director of the First National Bank at Glen Campbell

In politics, Mr Patchin is a Republican, and he is an active and loyal party worker He served as a member of the Pennsylvania State Legislature for one term, 1894-5 Fraternally he is identified with the leading organizations, belonging to the Blue Lodge and Chapter, Masons, at Clearfield, the Elks, at Clearfield, the Red Men at Glen Campbell, and the Odd Fellows at Burnside, being past master of this lodge Mr Patchin is unmarried

THOMAS GAFFEY, who, as the genial host of the Alpine House, situated on N Brady Street, DuBois, Pa, enjoys a large volume of patronage from the traveling public, has been a resident of this thriving borough since 1883 He was born January 23, 1857, in Staffordshire, England, and is a son of Thomas and Bridget (Meakin) Gaffey

The parents of Mr Gaffey were born in Ireland, where they were reared and married, shortly afterward moving to England In 1867 they came to America and settled in Bradford county, Pa, where Thomas Gaffey died at the age of forty-seven years They became the parents of nine children, namely Michael, Thomas, Patrick, James, John, Luke, Mary, William, and Catherine The last named is the wife of John Norton, and Mary is the wife of Peter Donahue Michael and Patrick are deceased For a number of years, Patrick, John, James, Luke, William, Mary and Catherine, were residents of Osceola Mills, Clearfield county The mother of the above-mentioned family is still living and is in the enjoyment of excellent health She is a devoted member of the Catholic church

Thomas Gaffey may be called a self-made man, for he has worked hard from boyhood and has earned all that he now owns As soon as he had reached a sufficient age, he went to work in an English pottery, where, for a time he had employment every half day, attending school during the other half. He thus laid a foundation for an education and after he came to America he was ambitious enough to attend night school after working hard all the day He grew to manhood in Bradford county, and there became a mine boy, working as a trapper in the Barkley coal mines From there, in 1879, he went to the mining sections of Iowa but remained only a short time, after which he secured a position at Steubenville, O, as a coal weigher From there he went to Reynoldsville, Pa, still being in the coal business, and in 1883 came to DuBois, where he labored for a time in the mines Later he was employed in a hotel here by James H Hine, with whom he was in partnership for one year In 1889 he rented the Alpine House from his father-in-law, William Melvin, and has conducted his business ever since under his own name Mr Gaffey has a centrally located, commodious and well kept house He has twenty-two bedrooms and all the other rooms also well fitted to make his guests comfortable His rates are very reasonable, his charge being but $1 25 per day

In February, 1880, Mr Gaffey was married to Miss Catherine Melvin, a daughter of William and Catherine Melvin They are members of St Catherine's Catholic church In politics he is a Democrat He belongs to the Ancient Order of Hibernians and to the Elks, also is a member of the Hotel Men's Mutual Benefit Association, also chairman of executive committee, Clearfield County Liquor Dealers' Association

JOHN STEVENSON, who is superintendent of twelve mines in the vicinity of Madera, Clearfield county, Pa, and is the owner of a fine residence here, is an experienced mine man, having been identified with mining since he was nine years old He was born March 12, 1865, in Scotland, and is a son of Peter and Margaret (Craney) Stevenson

Peter Stevenson was born in Scotland, a son of Peter Stevenson, and came to America with his family in 1869 He was a coal miner, an honest, industrious man His death occurred at Morrisdale, Clearfield county, where his widow still resides They had the following children John, Elizabeth, Margaret, James, William and Thomas Margaret is the wife of Frank Howe

John Stevenson attended school until he was nine years of age, at which time he was considered old enough to earn his own living and went to work as a mine boy Coal mining has been his business ever since, and his present responsible position proves that he is a well qualified man in this line of work

On September 5, 1892, Mr Stevenson was married to Mrs Catherine (Sullivan) Welsh, the widow of Thomas Welsh, and a daughter of Michael and Catherine (McCarthy) Sullivan The parents of Mrs Stevenson were born and married in Ireland and they had the following children born to them: Mary, who is deceased, Ellen, who is the wife of Daniel Farrel, Michael, who is deceased, Catherine, who is the wife of John Stevenson, Michael (2), Nora, who is the wife of Charles Van Gorder, Johanna, who is the widow of James Purcell, Jeremiah,

who is deceased, Charles, Jeremiah (2), Margaret, who is the wife of James Struthers, Sarah, who is the wife of Anthony Dunlevy, and Elizabeth, who is deceased To Mrs Stevenson's first marriage four daughters were born Mary, Catherine, Nellie and Esther, Mary being the only survivor Mr and Mrs Stevenson have three children Peter, John Lawrence and Margaret They are members of the Catholic church Mr Stevenson gives his political support to the Republican party He is a well known and highly respected citizen

WILLIAM W McQUOWN, who has been a resident of Mahaffey, Pa, for the past quarter of a century, is senior member of the insurance and real estate firm of W W McQuown & Son, of that town, and has also been prominent in local public affairs for many years He was born in February, 1851, in Rayne township, Indiana county, Pa, a son of William and Margaret (Shields) McQuown, and a grandson of Colonel Shields, who held that rank during the War of 1812 and later became one of the leading farmers and lumbermen in Indiana county

William McQuown, the father of William W McQuown, was also a native of Indiana county, Pa, from whence at the age of thirty-six years he enlisted in a Pennsylvania regiment for service during the Civil War, three months of his service being spent as a prisoner in a Southern prison Upon receiving his honorable discharge he returned to Indiana county, but several years later went with his family to a neighboring county, purchased a farm, and there spent the remainder of his life, his death occurring in

1906, when he was eighty years of age His
wife passed away at Mahaffey when she
was seventy-two years old

William W McQuown was reared in Indiana county, and after completing his education took up lumbering in Clearfield
county In 1885 he was elected justice of
the peace on the Republican ticket, an office which he held for twenty years, and in
1907 he was appointed postmaster at Mahaffey He has also acted in the capacity of
clerk of the council for nine years, city auditor and member of the school board For
the past seven years he has been engaged
in the real estate and insurance business,
under the firm name of W W McQuown &
Son Fraternally he is connected with Mahaffey Lodge No 147, Knights of Pythias,
and Clearfield Lodge No 540, of the Elks

In 1875 Mr McQuown was married to
Miss Susan Schaffer, of Indiana county,
Pa , and to this union there have been born
ten children William B , Emma, who prior
to her marriage to J H Bilhart taught
school for three years in Bell township, M
L , who married Miss Louise Buterbaugh,
Esther, who married Joseph Hineman,
Robert, who died at Mahaffey at the age of
six years, Victor, Ulrica, a graduate of the
public schools and the Lockhaven Normal
School, who taught school for three years
and is now assistant principal of the Mahaffey High School, Andrew, Stanley, who
died at the age of one year, and Thomas W

EDWARD H WOOLRIDGE, sheriff of
Clearfield county, Pa , is a member of one
of the substantial old county families and
was born in Bradford township, Clearfield
county, August 12, 1860 He is one of a
family of eight children born to his parents,
John and Jane M (Hitamys) Woolridge,
both of whom are now deceased.

Edward H Woolridge was reared in
Bradford township and obtained his education in the public schools His father was
interested in lumbering, farming and stock
raising and Mr Woolridge engaged in the
same industries and was actively concerned
until he assumed the duties of his present
office. His interests continue in this line
although his personal attention has been
withdrawn to a large degree since he was
elected to the office of sheriff in November,
1909 In the administration of this office
Sheriff Woolridge has displayed the care,
patience, good judgment and intelligence
that has made him successful as a business
man

Mr Woolridge was married to Miss Nettie Wilson, who is a daughter of S B Wilson, formerly county treasurer of Clearfield
county Sheriff and Mrs Woolridge have
three children Ernest, Boyd C and Orvis
He was reared in the Methodist Episcopal
church He has been an important factor
in the ranks of the Republican party in
Clearfield county for a number of years

ISAAC M KESTER, general farmer, operating fifty-six acres of land which is situated in Pike township, Clearfield county, Pa ,
at the edge of the borough of Curwensville,
was born November 1, 1853, at Lumber City,
Pa , and is a son of I M and Mary (Winner)
Kester

I M Kester was born in Columbia county,
Pa , and lived in Greenwood township, where
he owned a farm of sixty-two acres He was
a Democrat and served in township offices at

different times, being a school director and for eleven years a justice of the peace He married Mary Winner, who was born in Lycoming county, Pa , and they had eleven children born to them, eight of whom still live They were good and virtuous people, consistent in their membership in the Society of Friends I M Kester died at the age of seventy-one years and his wife when aged seventy-six they were laid to rest in the Friend's Cemetery at Grampian I M Kester taught school for six years

Isaac M Kester was reared on the home farm and attended school in Greenwood township For six months following his marriage he worked in a grist mill at Grampian, having been taught the milling business, together with farming, and engaged in the former industry for ten years before settling on his present farm, the old Benjamin Bloom place, which had been owned by that pioneer, who was the grandfather of Mr Kester's wife

On August 21, 1879, Isaac M Kester was married to Miss Lydia Lucinda Bloom, a daughter of Thomas and Ruthanna (Walker) Bloom A family of six children has been born to them, namely Walker Bruce, who was born September 11, 1880, resides at Terre Haute, Ind , and married Gertrude Stannert, of Lewisburg, Thomas Vincent, born October 2, 1882, resides at Wilmington, Del , and married Ethel Pierce of Wilmington, Isaac Lynn, who resides at Curwensville, married Lydia Zilhox, of Curwensville, Rutherford Ross, born December 7, 1886, resides at Effingham, Ill ; Benjamin Ellis, born June 13, 1889, lives at Wilmington, Del , Oscar Bloom, who was born October 16, 1892, died October 24, 1892, and his burial was in the Plain View ceme-

tery Mr Kester and family are members of the Society of Friends and he is an elder in this body He gives his political support to the Prohibition party He is a man of substantial standing in his neighborhood and has served his fellow citizens very acceptably in township offices having been a school director for three years, road supervisor for two years and auditor for six years He is secretary of the Plain View Cemetery Association

WILLIAM T DE HAAS, county recorder and clerk of the courts of Clearfield county, Pa , is numbered with the representative men of this section, having been identified with the interests of Clearfield county for almost forty years He was born in Center county, Pa , August 20, 1858, and is one of a family of eight children born to his parents, Joseph M and Sarah (Heckman) De Haas On the paternal side his family originated in Holland and a maternal great-great-grandfather was Edward Shippen, who was the first mayor of Philadelphia The parents of Mr De Haas are both now deceased

William T De Haas obtained his education in the public schools and, like his father, followed agricultural pursuits until he entered official life He came to Clearfield county in 1873 and has been an active and useful citizen In 1904 he was first elected county recorder, on the Republican ticket, and in 1907 was re-elected with an increased majority

Mr De Haas married Miss Virginia Lyles, a daughter of the late James Lyles, of Clearfield, and they have two children, Clara and Lulu B The family attends the Methodist Episcopal church Mr De Haas is identified with the Clearfield Grange and belongs also to the Masonic fraternity

REUBEN HEGARTY, who maintains his home in the pleasant village of Madera, Pa., owns fifty-two acres of valuable land on the outskirts, in Bigler township, from which coal has been taken in large quantities since 1900 He was born in Beccaria township, Clearfield county, Pa., July 22, 1845, and is a son of William and Jemima (Dunlap) Hegarty

William Hegarty was born October 11, 1806, in Ireland, and he was married to Jemima Dunlap, January 26, 1841 They had seven children, namely Eliza, born October 19, 1841, Isaac, born January 15, 1843, Reuben, Susanna, born December 25, 1847, Sarah J, born June 24, 1851, Adaline, born March 4, 1854, and Hannah C, born July 20, 1856

Reuben Hegarty grew to manhood on the old home farm and attended the country schools He learned the principles of farming and also the carpenter trade and also worked in the woods as a jobber He was gifted by Nature with an aptness for mechanics and together with other occupations he has worked as a civil engineer on the Coal Run Branch Railroad, for the Wallace & Reading Railroad Company He has invented a number of useful articles and one of these, patented and on the market, is an improved measuring pole, and another a folding extension table Since his marriage, in 1871, he has mainly followed contracting and building at Madera

Mr Hegarty married Miss Susan Phebe Davis, who was born at Kerrmoor, Clearfield county, May 30, 1852, a daughter of Thomas C and Rebecca (Kooser) Davis, who were married in 1849 Mrs Hegarty had one brother and two sisters William C, deceased, Mary and Laura The father was a native of Clarion county and the mother of Somerset county Mr and Mrs Hegarty attend the Presbyterian church He is identified fraternally with the Odd Fellows and politically with the Republican party

Mr Hegarty was one of the original men to try to make Madera a borough, he devoting both time and money with that end in view.

HARRISON HAYES SWEENEY, postmaster at Houtzdale, Pa., has been a resident of this borough for thirty years and for the past twenty-five years has been associated with his father in the furniture and undertaking business He was born at Powelton, Center county, Pa., June 2, 1872, and is a son of John and Mary (Hayes) Sweeney

John Sweeney was born in Ireland in 1836 and learned the cabinet-making trade in his own land In 1863 he embarked for the United States and safely reached America after a voyage of six weeks and three days He found work at his trade in the city of Philadelphia, where he remained for two years and then moved to Broad Top, Huntingdon county, and in 1873 from there to Houtzdale, where he embarked in the undertaking and furniture business His records show that he has conducted more burials than any other undertaker in the same length of time, in all Clearfield county. He married Mrs Mary (Hayes) Corbin, in 1869, who was the widow of Jesse Corbin, who had been superintendent of schools in Center county She was born in Blair county and was but six years old when she was left an orphan Three children were born to Mr and Mrs Corbin Clara, a Mrs Hayes, who lives at Glen Campbell, B M, who is a conductor on the Middle Division of the Pennsylvania Railroad, at Altoona, and Nettie, who is the wife of Dr D S Rice, a noted physician of Clearfield county.

To Mr and Mrs Sweeney the following children were born Minnie, who is the wife of J R Cornelius, of Patton, Pa , Harrison Hayes, and Nellie, who is assistant postmistress and is associated also in the undertaking business

Harrison Hayes Sweeney was reared at Houtzdale and is a graduate of the Houtzdale High School and also of Duff's Business College, at Pittsburg Prior to settling permanently in the borough, he was on the road for seven years for John Murphy & Co , in undertaking supplies and also taught embalming, being a graduate of an embalming school He is not only a very enterprising and reliable business man but he has been active in public affairs at Houtzdale, where he served for six years as a member of the council, during five years of the period being its president, an unusual honor He has been a member of the school board for the past two years and in February, 1911, was appointed postmaster at Houtzdale He is identified with the Republican party, and is in close touch with party organizers

Mr Sweeney was married in January, 1906, to Miss Alice Gleason, who was born and reared at Houtzdale, and is a daughter of Andrew Gleason, who was one of the old and successful merchants of this place Mr and Mrs Sweeney have had three children, but one of whom survives, John Burke, a sturdy little lad of two years Mr and Mrs Sweeney are active members of the Methodist Episcopal church and Mr Sweeney is an interested and interesting teacher in the Sunday-school He is identified fraternally with a number of organizations, including the Knights of Pythias, the Brotherhood of America, the P O S of A , the Elks at Clearfield, and the I O

R M at Brisbin, together with the United Commercial Travelers, of Clarksburg, W Va He is a charter member of Fire Company No 1, at Houtzdale Personally Mr Sweeney is of frank and engaging manner and as a public official cannot fail to meet with the approbation of his fellow citizens

JOE BENSINGER, proprietor of the Commercial Hotel, at DuBois, Pa , is one of the prominent hotel men of the state and has been interested in this business for many years He was born at Middleport, Schuylkill county, Pa , June 28, 1849, and is a son of Charles and Tena (Kleckner) Bensinger.

Charles Bensinger was born in Schuylkill county, Pa , a son of Jacob Bensinger, who was a pensioner of the Revolutionary war By trade, Charles Bensinger was a tailor His death occurred at the home of his son, Joe Bensinger, in September, 1910 at the age of eighty-eight years He married Tena Kleckner, who was born and died in Schuylkill county Her father, Colonel Kleckner, was also a pensioner of the Revolutionary war Of their children, three died young, the others being as follows Sarah, who is the wife of Theodore Hammer, resides in Philadelphia, Joe, John C , at Stroudsburg, Pa , Emily, who is the wife of Jacob Olhousen, of Philadelphia, Louisa, who is the widow of David Stull, of DuBois, Howard O , who is deceased (was musical director of his regiment in the Spanish-American war, enlisting at DuBois) , and Ida, who is the wife of E Fred Vosburg, of DuBois

Joe Bensinger was educated in the public schools and the State Normal School at Millersburg, after which he taught school for one winter and then went to work in the oil regions, becoming clerk for Mr Miller, manager of the American House, at Titusville That was his introduction to the hotel business and from that time he has been more or less identified with the same until the present From Titusville he went to Bradford and there went into the newspaper business, showing a great deal of enterprise He established and edited a daily paper, the Bradford Evening Times, and also a weekly, the Sunday Mail, for three years, making both first class properties before he sold out in order to come to DuBois, at the earnest solicitation of the late John DuBois He became a resident of DuBois in January, 1886, taking over the management of the DuBois Hotel, on the east side, where he continued until 1887, when he accepted an excellent offer at Pittsburg and took the management of the Colonial Hotel Annex, and remained several years in the hotel business in that city He had retained many pleasant recollections of DuBois and had the business faculty to foresee the subsequent development of the place, therefore, he returned and in 1889 opened the Commercial Hotel, which he conducted until 1896, it then being a two-story brick structure, having forty rooms In 1896 he sold and went then to Kittanning, Pa, where he conducted the Hotel Alexander for three years, after which he built the Lincoln Hotel, at Lancaster, Pa, operating it for two years In 1901 Mr Bensinger again returned to DuBois, bought the Commercial Hotel property and immediately began its enlargement and improvement It is now four stories in height, having 100 rooms and is equipped with all modern conveniences Mr Bensinger's rates are $2, $2 50, and $3 per day Although during the rebuilding a part of the structure was unin-

habitable, Mr Bensinger thoughtfully provided for the comfort of his guests and not a single meal was eliminated Mr Bensinger was one of the organizers of the Pennsylvania State Hotel Men's Association and at different times has served as president of this body. He is chairman of the executive committee, the working body of the organization Mr Bensinger has other claims to popularity He is known far and wide as an orator and after-dinner speaker, and being gifted with a ready wit and overflowing, kindly humor, he is in great demand at many gatherings

On May 28, 1881, Mr Bensinger was married to Louise Lorenz, of Clarion county, Pa, and they have an adopted son, James L In politics, Mr Bensinger is a Republican but his business responsibilities have always been too numerous to permit him to accept office Since 1889 he has been a member of the Elks and for many years has been prominent as a Mason, belonging to the Blue Lodge and Commandery at DuBois, the Chapter at Brackville, Pa, and the Consistory, Shrine and Masonic Veterans' Association, at Pittsburg

PROF HERBERT G MEANS, who is the able and progressive principal of the schools of Madera, Clearfield county, Pa, and a candidate for the office of county superintendent, is well known over Clearfield county as an educator He was born in October, 1879, at DuBois, Pa, and is a son of George and Elizabeth (Stewart) Means

George Means, who is now a retired citizen of Punxatawney, Pa, was born in Pennsylvania and is a son of Foster Means For a number of years he was in the lumber business and was also in the mail service

MR. AND MRS. AMOS BONSALL

He married Elizabeth Stewart, who died in December, 1907 They had the following children born to them Effie, who is the wife of Clayton Sprankle, William N , Herbert G , and Mabel

Herbert G Means was educated in the public schools, Slippery Rock Normal School, and Grove City College, graduating from the first named in the class of 1902 and receiving his degree of Ph B in 1907 Prior to this, however, he had taught school for two years in Jefferson county and after graduation he returned to Jefferson county and taught for one year at Fordham, one year at Rossburg and two years at Eleanor For three years afterward he served as district superintendent of the schools of Sandy township, Clearfield county, and then took charge of the Madera schools During the three years that Prof Means has been at the head of the schools of this borough, he has advanced scholarship and placed these schools on a par with any in the county He is an enthusiastic worker and knows how to inspire others

In June, 1904, Mr Means was married to Miss Ethel Condron, a daughter of William and Catherine (Jewart) Condron, natives of Indiana county, but at present residents of Jefferson county Their family is made up of two daughters Ethel and Mildred, the latter of whom is the wife of David Straitiff Prof Means and wife have two children Fenton, born in January, 1906, and Winnifred, born in March, 1908 They are members of the Lutheran church of Du-Bois In his political views, Prof Means is a Republican He belongs to the P O S of A , an organization that claims a large and representative membership in this section

JAMES H KELLEY, district attorney of Clearfield county, Pa , serving his second term in this office, is a native of Clearfield county and was born October 4, 1852 His parents were James M and Mary (Horton) Kelley, and he is the only survivor of the family

James H Kelley attended the public schools in boyhood and later enjoyed academic advantages After deciding upon the law as a career, he became a student under Senator Wallace, Judge Clark and Frank Fielding and was admitted to the bar on January 14, 1884 He very soon became a recognized force both in his profession and also in political circles In 1906 he was elected district attorney on the Republican ticket and was re-elected in 1909 His administration of the office has distinguished him as a man of more than the ordinary ability, and he is pursuing in his second term the same honorable methods which marked his first and is thereby adding to the esteem in which he is held by his fellow citizens

Mr Kelley married Miss Ida Palmer, a daughter of the late Nathan Palmer, of Washington county, and they have two children William P , who is engaged in the oil business, and Mary, who is the wife of Reuben F Nevling, of Clearfield county Mr Kelley and family are members of the Presbyterian church The pleasant family home is situated at No 312 E Market street, Clearfield

AMOS BONSALL, a retired farmer, residing in Brady township, Clearfield county, Pa , on his valuable farm of 161 acres, near Troutville, is one of the most venerable residents of this section and one of the most highly esteemed   He has spent almost his entire life in Brady township but was born in Perry county, Pa , August 31, 1822, and was brought here when two years, two months and sixteen days old   His parents were Benjamin and Maria (Fowler) Bonsall

Benjamin Bonsall was a tanner in his early manhood, in Perry county, where he also cleared up considerable land and engaged in farming   In 1824 he brought his family to Clearfield county and bought a farm in Brady township, near Luthersburg, where he spent the remainder of his life   Benjamin Bonsall and his wife and youngest son Reuben died within six weeks   They were the parents of eleven children, as follows   Rebecca, John, Jackson, Sarah, Amos, Jane, Emily, Joseph, Anna Maria, Reuben and Louisa, the last named being the wife of Adam Foust of Du-Bois   She and her brother Amos are the only survivors of this large family

Amos Bonsall had but meager school advantages in his youth   The family was a growing one and there was a great deal of necessary work to be done on the farm and very early Mr Bonsall and his older brothers, John and Jackson, were able to be of great assistance to their father   Farming in the summer time and lumbering in the winter seasons in large degree filled up the measure of Mr Bonsall's time prior to his marriage, after which he left the homestead and bought a farm of fifty-two acres at Coal Hill   After clearing one-half of that land he sold it and bought the farm on which he still resides, it having previously been the property of his father-in-law, Jacob Kuntz   Mr Bonsall paid $1,500 for the 161 acres, which was then underlaid with coal which he subsequently sold for $87 50 per acre   He also realized a large

sum from the sale of timber   In 1857 he built his comfortable farm-house   Recently he has disposed of his interests to his son Jackson Bonsall, with whom he now resides

On January 25, 1849, Mr Bonsall was married to Miss Catherine Kuntz, who was born in Germany and came to America with her parents in childhood   She lived to be eighty years of age   Mr and Mrs Bonsall had ten children: three died in infancy; the others were· Jacob L , Susanna (deceased), Sarah (deceased) , Mary, wife of Jonas Peifer, Vina, wife of George H Weber, and Jackson   Mr. Bonsall has a number of grandchildren and even great-grandchildren and takes much pleasure in viewing such a vigorous lot of descendants

For many years Mr Bonsall has not taken much interest in public matters although he never fails to cast his vote for the candidates of the Democratic party   In earlier years, however, he was considered one of the reliable men when it came to appointments to office and it is related that in 1848, against his own wishes, he was made constable of Brady township and while serving in that capacity it became his duty to take Lorrin Solliman to Clearfield, on a charge of murder   It created a great excitement, as that was the first murder case ever tried in the county   Mr. Bonsall is a valued member of the Lutheran church

THADDEUS IRELAND, whose well improved farm of 100 acres is situated seven and three-fourth miles north of Clearfield, Pa , has been a continuous resident of this county since 1885 and is a representative and respected citizen of Goshen township   He was born in Washington county, Me , June 22, 1855, and is a son of Abraham and Mary (Henderson) Ireland

Abraham Ireland and wife were both natives of Maine and he still resides in Washington county, now aged eighty-eight years, but nevertheless hale, hearty and useful He is still interested to some degree in farming and lumbering He married Mary Henderson, who died in 1864, and they had the following children born to them Edward, Amanda, who is now deceased (was the wife of Samuel Rankin), Emma, who is the wife of Alexander Rankin, of North Bend, Clinton county, Pa , Oran, who resides in Montana, Elizabeth, who died at the age of eight years, Nancy, who succumbed to diphtheria at the same age, and Thaddeus, of Clearfield county The mother of the above family was a member of the Baptist church while the father has always attended the Methodist Episcopal body

Thaddeus Ireland knows a great deal about lumbering, having worked in the woods of his native state after his school days were over, and later, after coming to Clearfield county in 1879, in the lumber regions in this section For one year after marriage he lived in Clinton county, Pa , and then bought his present farm, formerly the property of D Cyphers He found about fifteen acres cleared and a barn on the place, and all the subsequent clearing Mr Ireland has done for himself He has erected other substantial buildings and has a very comfortable home as well as valuable land It may be more valuable than he knows, as no tests have yet been made for coal

On July 4, 1883, Mr Ireland was married to Miss Jennie Sankey, a daughter of John and Laura Sankey, well known residents of Goshen township The family of Thaddeus

and Jennie Ireland are as follows · Julia, wife of Ernest Wilson (they have four children— Amanda, Irwin, Margaret and Wayne); Clayton, who died at the age of three months, Bessie, wife of Charles Young (they have two children—Doris and Erma), Gray, Ada, John, Ora, Elon, Leda, Mitchell, Heichhold, A T Theodore, N. L. Neal, Loris, and Omas. Mr Ireland and family attend the Methodist Episcopal church In politics he is a Republican and on the ticket of that party has frequently been elected to important township offices, as supervisor and judge of elections He belongs to the Goshen Grange and takes an interest in agricultural progress

JOHN VEESER, a reliable and prosperous business man of Madera, who is onehalf owner and proprietor of the Veeser Brothers Brewery, which is located on the Houtzdale road, about one and one-half miles from Madera, Pa , was born December 22, 1857, in Germany His parents, Thomas and Julia Veeser never came to America They had the following children: Mary, who is the wife of Charles Mussgung; Cecelia, Elizabeth, and Andrew, who died in August, 1908, survived by his widow, who was formerly Elizabeth Dett, and two children, Julia and John E

John Veeser came to the United States in 1881 He had few educational chances as he went to work in a brewery when only thirteen years of age, but he learned this business very thoroughly, and has engaged in it all his mature life He spent some ten years mainly in Allegheny county, and came to Madera in 1891 and worked at the plant of which he is now half owner, for two years before he and his brother, An-

10

drew, bought it   They conducted it under the name of Veeser Brothers and the name has not been changed since Andrew's death, his widow and children still retaining the half interest   The plant was built in 1887 and became the property of the Veesers in 1894, when they obtained their first license   Three acres of land surround the brewery   The output is 1500 barrels of beer a year and two men are given employment all the time

John Veeser has never married   He was reared in the Catholic faith and belongs to St Lawrence Catholic church at Houtsdale   In politics he is nominally a Democrat, but exercises his own judgment to a large degree when casting his vote

JOHN HARRIS, deceased, spent a quiet, useful, industrious life   For many years he was a respected citizen of Clearfield County, Pa, to which he came when thirty years of age, and faced many difficulties and hardships with Scottish stoicism   He was born at Glasgow, Scotland, in 1810, and like every Scotch youth, was sent regularly to school

In 1840 John Harris settled in Clearfield County, Pa, having been attracted to this region on account of its mining possibilities, and for many years afterward he was engaged in mining for both coal and iron ore in the Karthaus mines   Later in life he moved to Brookville, where he died in 1855   He followed farming also in Clearfield County, but his main business in life, —the one in which he had been trained —was mining

In   Bradford   Township,   Clearfield County, Pa, in 1842, Mr Harris was married to Miss Eleanor Graham, who was born in Center County and was a daughter of Francis and Jane (Boggs) Graham, and a granddaughter of Judge James Boggs, of the Center County Bench   Mrs Harris died at Polk Furnace, Clarion County, Pa, in 1849   She left three sons Joseph, Robert Bruce, and Frank G   Of these sons, Joseph died in April, 1870   Frank G is one of Clearfield County's most prominent citizens, formerly a member of the State Legislature and also state treasurer   Robert Bruce has been identified with the oil industry for many years and in his prospecting trips has visited many lands, and as a representative of an English syndicate, spent some time near the Caspian and Red Seas

In 1851 John Harris was married a second time   This lady was Miss Eliza Scott, of Brookville, Pa, who survived him for some time and died at Brookville.

GEORGE W. WALKER, a well known resident of Brisbin, Clearfield County, Pa, was born at Snow Shoe, Center County, Pa, June 17, 1859, and is a son of James and Mary (Hirsh) Walker

George W Walker was reared at Snow Shoe and accompanied the family from there to Houtzdale and then to Brisbin, where he has resided for a number of years   He was married January 1, 1883, to Miss Mandaine Doherty, who was born at St Johns, New Brunswick, and is a daughter of John and Sarah (Taylor) Doherty

John Doherty was born in Canada and his mother's maiden name was Blackmore   When he was nine years old he was sent to England to live with an aunt, Mrs Kelly, a lady who had large estates there Probably he would have been her heir as she entrusted her affairs to him and treated him well, but he grew homesick and returned to Canada as a stowaway on a vessel He married in Canada and lived there until 1881, when he came to the United States and located at Brisbin He was a filer and saw hammerer by trade and his business was an important one in the days when lumbering was carried on so extensively and tools were yet fashioned by hand He was a man of robust constitution and lived to be eighty years of age. When he was seventy-five years old he was still capable of hard work and could earn as high as $4 50 a day at his trade His death occurred November 3, 1908 He married Sarah Taylor, who was a daughter of Abraham and Matilda (Stover) Taylor, her father being a cousin of Zachery Taylor, who was once President of the United States Although Mrs Doherty was born in Canada her people on both sides were of Pennsylvania Dutch extraction Both of her grandfathers were Revolutionary soldiers, hence she was eligible, as are her daughters, to the Society of the Daughters of the American Revolution She survived her husband for two years, passing away September 4, 1910, at the age of eighty-two years To John and Sarah Doherty, three children were born, namely Mandaine, who is Mrs George W Walker, Willard, who lives at Williamsport, Pa, and Maud, who is the wife of S N Hewlett, civil and mining engineer for the Lackawanna Coal and Coke Company, at Wehr, Ind Mr and Mrs Walker have had six children, as follows: John Doherty, who was born October 7, 1883, and is superintendent for E J Walker & Co, large coal operators, Benjamin F, who was born March 13, 1885, died aged eight years,

Urania, who was born January 1, 1887, married T B Lobb and they have one daughter, Eleanor, Wallace, who was born October 3, 1888, died a babe of two months, Willard, who was born September 15, 1890, is pursuing an electrical engineering course at the Carnegie Technical School at Pittsburg and evidently possesses unusual mechanical skill, and Maud, who was born June 17, 1893, and is a student in the Brisbin High School The family belongs to the Baptist church John D Walker is a member of the Patriotic Order Sons of America

ISAAC STRAW, proprietor of a large general mercantile business at Westover, where he is also largely interested in lumber, was born in Ferguson township, Clearfield county, Pa, Nov 14, 1863 His parents were Enoch I and Mary H (Williams) Straw, and he is a grandson of Joseph Straw, who came here as a pioneer settler from Center county The grandfather, who married M Thompson, was engaged in lumbering as his life occupation

Enoch I Straw was born in Clearfield county and followed farming and lumbering all his life, dying in the year 1900 He was a member of the Baptist church In politics he was a Democrat and at different times held local office, serving as collector and also on the school board His wife Mary was the daughter of George Williams of Center county, her mother's maiden name being Wagoner Of their family, in addition to our subject, there are now living the following children Lydia, who resides with her brother Isaac, Laura Belle, who is the wife of John McKugan of Jordan township, and Hattie, wife of Orlando Williams, residing on the old home farm

Isaac Straw after completing his school attendance as a scholar, taught school for three terms from the age of 20 years, nine months of this time being spent in New Washington   In 1887 he came to Westover, becoming a partner in the firm of Michaels & Straw, general merchandise business   Later Mr Straw bought out his partner and has conducted the business alone up to the present time   His is one of the largest supply stores in this part of the county and in its operation Mr Straw has shown excellent business capacity   Mr Straw is a charter member and is on the advisory board of the Order of Unity of Pittsburg, which was organized in 1906   He was also one of the organizers and directors and for two years vice-president of the Farmers & Travelers National Bank of Clearfield, which was organized in 1907   Of the Reading Life Insurance Company of Reading, which was organized in 1909, Mr Straw was one of the charter stockholders and directors   He is also interested in lumbering to quite an extent and has large farming interests in this vicinity.   He is member of the Grange at Harmony, Pa   A Democrat politically, he has served on the borough school board four terms, and is now auditor, serving his fourth term in this office   He takes an active part in public affairs and is in every way a useful and progressive citizen

Mr Straw married Miss Mary Walls of Cherry Tree, and of this union there is one son, Clay M , born June 17, 1893, who is now a student at Juniata college, Huntingdon, Pa

J A SLAUGHENHOUPT, a leading citizen of DuBois, Pa , formerly president of the DuBois Business Men's Asociation, is proprietor of a large grocery store at DuBois, of which place he has been a resident since 1886   He was born on his father's farm in Clarion County, Pa , September 10, 1861, and is a son of Harrison and Catherine (Wiant) Slaughenhoupt

Harrison Slaughenhoupt and wife were born in Clarion County and were members of old pioneer families that had come to that section from east of the Allegheny Mountains   Harrison Slaughenhoupt was engaged in farming and stock raising during his active years and then retired and he and wife reside in a comfortable home at Rimersburg, Pa   Five children were born to them, namely· James Milton, of Irwin, Pa , Jacob Alvin, of DuBois, Hannah Mary, wife of W T Harley, of Sheffield, Pa , William H , of Oakmont, Pa , and Lawson Merle

Jacob Alvin Slaughenhoupt remained at home until he was seventeen years of age, in the meanwhile assisting his father and attending the district school situated some three miles from the homestead   When he started out for himself he first found employment with neighboring farmers, after which he worked on the grading of the narrow-gauge railroad then being constructed between Foxburg and Kane, Pa   Two years later he went to Brookville and there engaged in teaming and was married there in 1884 and shortly afterward rented a farm in Jefferson County, which he cultivated for one year After a prospecting tour in Florida, he returned to Pennsylvania and in the fall of 1886 settled at DuBois and for the five succeeding years was in the employ of John DuBois in the logging camps in the lumber regions In 1891, he went into railroad work and for two years worked as fireman on the B R & P Railroad Mr Slaughenhoupt then made his first independent business venture, embarking in the dairy business which he conducted until 1895, when he had the opportunity of buying the already established grocery business of M Manthe, of which he took advantage This store is very favorably located for business purposes, at No 42 S Brady Street, almost opposite the post office He carries a large and carefully selected stock of both staple and fancy groceries and enjoys a substantial trade He owns additionally a half interest in the Keesage meat market on S Brady Street and is a stockholder in the Union Banking and Trust Company as well as in the United Electric and Traction Company Starting out with no capital, Mr Slaughenhoupt has acomplished much and now occupies a position of trust and confidence among his fellow citizens which is justifiable He has always taken a thoroughly good citizen's interest in the welfare and advancement of DuBois and has identified himself with those civic bodies which work for such results He was president of the DuBois Business Men's Asociation in 1908 and 1909 In politics he is a Democrat

On February 26, 1884, Mr Slaughenhoupt was married to Miss Anna Parry, a daughter of Henry and Hannah Parry, of Snyder Township, Jefferson County, and they have had five children, namely Clyde, who assists his father in the grocery store, and married Laura McPherson, Bessie E, who married William Newmyer, and Lena May, Hannah C and Anna May The family belong to the Reformed church Mr Slaughenhoupt is a charter member of the order of American Mechanics at DuBois and belongs also to the Odd Fellows and Masons, in the latter fraternity being a member of the Blue Lodge at DuBois, the Chapter at Brookville, the Consistory at Williamsport and the Shrine at Altoona

JOSEPH G HIGGINS, one of the well known citizens of Bigler Township, Clearfield County, Pa, where he owns seventeen and three-fourths acres of well cultivated land and carries on farming and also coopering, was born July 3, 1839, in Oxford County, Me, and is a son of Ivory and Mary (Hunt) Higgins

The parents of Mr Higgins spent their lives in Maine, where the father was a farmer and also a lumberman They were highly respected and well known people To them were born children as follows Ivory, George, Emeline, Caroline, Debora, Joseph G, Sydney, Osburn, Charles, Ellen, Eben and Hannah

Joseph G Higgins attended school in the neighborhood of his home when a boy and then learned the cooper trade which he followed as his main occupation as long as it was profitable In 1903 he purchased his present place from Joseph Kitko

In 1865 Mr Higgins was married to Miss Mary Johnston, a daughter of William and Elizabeth (Shultz) Johnston, who were natives of Huntingdon County, Pa Mrs Higgins was the sixth born in a family of eleven children, the others being James, John, David, Sarah, Hannah, Samuel, Jane, William, Nancy and Ellen To Mr and Mrs Higgins the following children were born. Orlanda, who is deceased, Josephine, who is deceased, was the wife of Joel Cornely, Luella, who is deceased, Stella, Gertrude, who is the wife of George Richards, and Maude, who is the wife of Alfred A Packer

Wherever he has lived, Mr Higgins has been an active and useful citizen and his sterling qualities have been recognized While living in Woodward Township he was frequently elected to office and served as constable there for eleven years, and after coming to Bigler Township he was again elected to office and served two years as supervisor, two terms as school director and two years as road master. With his family he attends the Presbyterian church

MRS MARY C McDONALD, widow of William Henry McDonald, and daughter of David J and Keziah (Wilson) Cathcart, resides on her valuable farm of 116 acres, situated in Knox township, Clearfield County, Pa, in which section she is well and favorably known Her father was born in Ireland and was ten years old when he came to America, landing at New York After his marriage he and his wife lived in Clearfield County, Pa, where all of their children were born

Mary C Cathcart remained with her parents until her marriage She attended the Turkey Hill School near her home three months in the year, during girlhood and later had the advantages of one term in the Jordan Township school and one term at Centerville In January, 1862, she was married to William Henry McDonald He was born in Indiana County, Pa, a son of Robert and Lydia (Potts) McDonald, with whom he moved to Jefferson County, settling on a farm, farming and stock-raising being his business through life On June 27, 1862, he enlisted for service in the Civil War, but returned home in March, 1863, on account of an attack of typhoid fever. Subsequently he was drafted but did not again face the hardships of a soldier's life, hiring a substitute who took his place For sixteen years he resided in Jefferson County, having previously lived in Clearfield County after marriage and there Mr and Mrs McDonald's oldest son was born, John W. He was married first to Elizabeth Dougherty and after her death to Anna Sours Donahue. For some years he engaged in lumbering in Elk and Potter Counties and then located in Tioga County, where he is in the hotel business.

After Mr and Mrs McDonald moved to Jefferson County the first time, four children were born, namely David Aaron, William Henry, Daniel Alfred and David Austin They then moved to Indiana County and while living there two more children were born, namely: Reuben M and Dessa Ellen They returned to Jefferson County, where James Armand, the youngest son was born In April, 1879, Mr McDonald and family came to Knox Township, Clearfield County, where he bought the present homestead and with the help of his sons, cleared almost the whole of it. He made many improvements and built the present substantial barn Mr McDonald was a highly respected citizen of Knox Township, a man of good business capacity, of honorable character and of a kind and friendly nature. He was a Democrat in his political views but never accepted any public office except that of school director, and belonged to no organization except the Grand Army of the Republic His death occurred November 8, 1904, at the age of sixty-four years and his burial was in the Mt Zion Cemetery attached to the Methodist Episcopal church in Knox Township

Since the death of her husband, Mrs McDonald and her son, William Henry McDonald, manage the farm very successfully, carrying on general agriculture Mrs McDonald has a very pleasant home, keeping everything in good repair, and takes pleasure in hospitably entertaining her many friends A coal bank on the farm is profitably worked and there is also a valuable clay deposit Mrs McDonald is a member of Mt Zion Methodist Episcopal Church and is deeply interested in its mission and charitable work

S J WATERWORTH, M D, who occupies a prominent position among the medical practitioners of Clearfield County, Pa, and for the past seventeen years has been a resident of Clearfield, was born at Baltimore, Md, in 1872, and is a son of James Murray and Catherine (Lee) Waterworth Both parents of Dr Waterworth were born at Baltimore, where their lives were spent The father died in 1890, at the age of fifty-five years, the mother is still living There were but two sons, S J. and James Murray, the latter of whom died in childhood

S J Waterworth, in 1890, entered the College of Physicians and Surgeons at Baltimore, where he was graduated in 1893 He immediately entered into practice, selecting Jefferson County and in 1894 came from there to Clearfield Dr Waterworth was married in 1898, to Miss Catherine Cunningham

A R VAN TASSEL, president of the Union Banking and Trust Company, at DuBois, Pa, having also other important business interests at this place, resides on his magnificent stock farm, a tract of 300 acres, situated near DuBois, in Clearfield County, Pa Mr Van Tassel has been a resident of DuBois since 1884 but he was born in the city of New York, March 31, 1853, of Holland ancestry

Mr Van Tassel was educated in the public and in a select school at Brooklyn, N Y, and when he reached manhood he learned the tanning business and served an apprenticeship to it at Woburn, Mass Subsequently he established a small tannery of his own, at Boliver, N Y, which he sold in 1884 and then came to DuBois, where he entered into partnership with a brother and John DuBois, in the tanning business, which was carried on until 1899 under the firm style of DuBois & Van Tassel Bros In the above year A R Van Tassel retired from the firm and erected his own tannery which has become one of the large industrial plants of the town, employment being given to from seventy-five to 100 men This private enterprise, as others in which Mr Van Tassel is interested, has been of public importance to the place, affording remunerative work to a large body of skilled men, serving to solidify capital here and also to exploit DuBois as a favorable point for business investment Mr Van Tassel was one of the organizers of the Union Banking and Trust Company, of which he has been president ever since its founding

In 1879 Mr Van Tassel was married first to Miss Jennie Thomas, who died in New

York She is survived by one son, Stephen T, who is associated with his father in business In 1893 Mr Van Tassel was married second, to Miss Alice Henderson, and they have three children, Blanche, Henderson and Lillian The family home, Hillcrest Farm, is one of the largest and most valuable stock farms in Clearfield County Mr Van Tassel gives special attention here to the breeding of Morgan horses He has exhibited at numerous fairs and stock shows and has won innumerable blue ribbons and cups, the latest triumph in this line being one of his stud, Bob Morgan, won a blue ribbon at the Madison Square Garden exhibition, in 1910 The new residence erected by Mr Van Tassel, on Hillcrest Farm, is beautifully located and is equipped with all modern comforts and conveniences Mr Van Tassel and family attend the Presbyterian church A Republican from principle, he gives his political support to that party but has never consented to permit his name to be used for office He is identified with the Masonic fraternity, and is one of the charter members of the Acorn Club, a social club of DuBois, Pa

A P STEPHENS, a representative business man of Houtzdale, Pa, well known in the retail lumber trade, has been a resident of this borough since 1886 He was born June 6, 1850, at Port Matilda, in Worth Township, Center County, Pa, and is a son of Samuel and Susan (Gill) Stephens

Samuel Stephens was a son of John Stephens, who moved from Center County to Ohio previously to his death Samuel Stephens mainly followed lumbering and spent his entire life in the neighborhood of Port Ma-

tilda He married Susan Gill, a daughter of John and Mary (Rowles) Gill, who at one time lived in Clearfield County She also died at Port Matilda They had a family of six children, namely Annie, who is the wife of H H Osman, of Port Matilda, Abednego Pitman, John, who lives at Port Matilda, Marietta, who is the wife of Bion Williams, of Curtain, Center County, Minnie, who is the wife of Alvin Price, of Port Matilda, and David R, who resides at Altoona

A P Stephens attended school irregularly in his boyhood on account of the long distance he had to walk for his instruction, and was little more than a boy when he started to work in the woods He has been concerned in lumbering ever since For eighteen years he operated a portable saw mill in eighteen different places, partly in Clearfield, Center and Cambria Counties, but for the past six years he has confined himself to retailing lumber at Houtzdale Recently he has associated his son-in-law, John Mills, with him as a partner, and the firm style at present is A P Stephens & Co

Mr Stephens was married first in 1871, to Miss Sarah Woodring, a daughter of Peter Woodring, of Center County, and they had one daughter, Nora M, who is the wife of John Mills Mrs Stephens died in 1878, and her burial was at Port Matilda Mr Stephens was married second to Miss Lizzie Melcher, of West Township, Center County, who died in 1904, and was interred in the Mt Pleasant Cemetery Mr Stephens attends the Presbyterian church He is a Republican in politics but is inclined to be independent He is identified with the Masonic lodge at Osceola Mills

JOHN MILLS, the junior partner in the lumber firm of A P Stephens & Co, was born November 9, 1862, in Yorkshire, England

MRS. AMANDA E. MECKLEY

SAMUEL T. MECKLEY

His father, Edward Mills, came first to America and when seventeen years of age the son joined his father at what is now West Houtzdale, Clearfield County Edward Mills married Eliza Wood, also of an old Staffordshire, England, family, and they had thirteen children, six of whom survived to maturity, namely Stephen H, who lives in Somerset County, Pa, John, Edward. who lives also in Somerset County, Joseph, who resides at Houtzdale, Daniel R, who lives with his brothers at Windber, Somerset County, and William H, who is a resident of Sheridan, Pa

John Mills married Nora M Stephens, and they have six children Abednego Pitman, Nannie E, John L, Fred H, Sarah and Clifford Mr Mills is a Republican and at present is serving in the borough council and also is poor overseer He belongs to the Houtzdale Fire Company, and is identified with the Royal Arcanum and with the Masonic lodge at Osceola Mills

SAMUEL THOMAS MECKLEY, a retired farmer of Bell township, Clearfield county, Pa, and a well known and highly respected citizen, was born in Center county, Pa, February 18, 1836, and is a son of John and Christina (Smith) Meckley

John Meckley was born January 6, 1811, and followed the stone mason trade and also engaged in farming On April 1, 1850, he moved from Center county, Pa, to the old C Neff place, New Washington, Pa, and from there to Bethlehem, Pa, where he resided until his death, December 20, 1883 He married Christina Smith, who was born October 6, 1815, and died March 24, 1896 She was a daughter of Fred and Sally Smith, the former of whom was born in Germany, and came to America and settled with his family at Bellefonte, Pa From there he moved to Penn's Valley and still later to Spring Mills and his death occurred in Center county He was a stone mason by trade Ten children were born to John Meckley and his wife, three daughters and seven sons The daughters are deceased The survivors of the family are Samuel Thomas, George, a farmer residing in Kansas, John J, living in Burnside township, James, living in Bell township, William, residing in Kansas, Henry, a resident of Oregon, and Louis, a carpenter by trade, living at Oakdale, Pa

The early education of Samuel Thomas Meckley was secured in the district schools He learned the stone mason trade with his father and lived at home and followed this trade until his marriage In 1864 he enlisted for service in the Civil war, in answer to the last call, entering Co K, 105th Pa Vol Inf, Army of the Potomac, Captain McKnight, and served one year and was mustered out in July, 1865 After the close of his military service, Mr Meckley returned home and continued to work at his trade, in the same year locating on his present farm He spent many years actively engaged here but is now living retired, being surrounded with all the comforts of life

On October 27, 1867, Mr Meckley was married to Miss Amanda Ellis, who was born in Bell township, Clearfield county, April 11, 1847, a daughter of Richard S and Julia Ann Ellis To Mr and Mrs Meckley the following children were born Warren B, who was born in 1869, married Hattie Sharp and they have five children Millie A, who was born in 1870, is the wife of R Pierce, of Bethlehem, Pa, Margaret J, who was born in 1872, is the wife of D Ganoe, of Bell Township, and they have six children Ollie A , who was born in 1874, is the wife of Charles Beck, of Philipsburg and they have one child, Henderson, who was born in 1878, is the home farmer, Ellis, who was born in 1882, is engaged in farming in Nebraska, and Horace, who was born in 1885, resides at La Jose, Pa He married Nora Gearhart and they have two children

For forty years Mr Meckley has been one of the leading members of the Methodist Protestant church at Mahaffey and was one of its organizers He has never been very active in politics but has voted with the Republican party since he cast his first presidential ballot for Abraham Lincoln He is a valued member of the G A R Post at Curry Run

DAVID ALEXANDER McCARDELL, postmaster at Westover, Chest township, where he also carries on a general merchandise business, was born at Indiana, Pa , Dec 26, 1841 His parents were John and Jane (Pilson) McCardell, and he is a grandson of David McCardell, who came to America from Scotland, settling in Indiana county, Pa

John McCardell, father of our subject, was born in Indiana county, but removed to Clearfield county, locating at Burnside, where he died at the age of 84 years He married Jane Pilson, who was a daughter of William Pilson

David A McCardell, our direct subject, after attending school, engaged in the farming and lumbering industries In 1861, at the age of 20 years, he enlisted for three years' service in Company D, 105th Regt Pa Volunteers, under Col McKnight, his regiment being assigned to the Army of the Potomac He fought under Meade at the great and decisive battle of Gettysburg and was with the army in its subsequent operations under Grant and Meade until he was mustered out August 31, 1864 Although he took part in some hard fighting on various occasions aside from Gettysburg, he was never seriously wounded On his return from the war he took up his residence on the parental homestead in Burnside township, but subsequently bought a farm near the Mt Joy church, not far from New Washington, where he remained engaged in agriculture until 1882. He was then engaged in the lumber business at Burnside for several years, but later entered into the livery business, which he conducted for five years. Selling out in 1891, he came to Westover and engaged in a livery business here, which however he sold out in 1895, and was thereafter engaged in the grocery and restaurant business up to 1904, at which time he was appointed postmaster of Westover He now conducts a general merchandise store, in which the postoffice is located He is a Republican in politics and has served on the school board for 15 years He is also a member of the borough council and has served as burgess, one term in 1905 He has been a member of the Odd Fellows lodge at Burnside for 35 years, being a charter member and having passed all the chairs He also belongs to the Grand Army post at Cherry Tree

Mr McCardell was married in 1865 to Elizabeth Mitchell, who died in 1870 at the age of 28 years Of this union there were three children, all of whom are now deceased Mr McCardell married for his second wife in 1873, Mary P Neff, who was born Oct 27, 1850, a daughter of Joseph L and Eliza M (Gallaher) Neff To this marriage children have been born as follows Emma, wife of V K Rowland, of Westover, Pa, who has five children, Sarah B, wife of George F Westover, who has four children, Elmer B, who married Tillie Moore of Westover and has three children, James, who married Lena Hurd, resides at Cresson, Pa, and has three children, and Willard D, a resident of Cherry Tree Mrs McCardell is a member of the M E church, and also belongs to the Rebecca lodge, I O O F, at Burnside

L WILLIAM ROWLES, whose well cultivated and improved farm of twenty acres lies in Knox Township, three miles east of Olanta, Pa, was born in Lawrence Township, Clearfield County, Pa, May 25, 1866, and is a son of Joseph H and Ruth (Hickok) Rowles

Joseph H Rowles was born March 25, 1835, in Lawrence Township, Clearfield County, and now lives retired on his farm of forty-five acres His father, H F Rowles, came to Clearfield County when he was a boy of eight years and found work at Curwensville when that town had but two houses He there married Susanna Henry and they settled in Pike Township until after the birth of three children, when they moved into Lawrence Township, where three more were born He was one of the old-time pioneers He was a raft pilot and made eight trips on the river between Marietta and Clearfield, and lived to be eighty-six years of age Joseph H Rowles first went to school in a log cabin where slabs were used for seats and desks and later attended other schools, for he was so anxious to obtain an education that he went one term after he was twenty-one years of age He worked hard, sometimes on the farm and at other times in the woods and by cutting in the timber he made enough to enable him to buy his farm, on which he settled after marriage His first house burned down and he thus lost all the old family papers For thirty-five years Mr Rowles served Lawrence Township as a justice of the peace and also was school director. During the Civil War he served seven months in the Federal Army and was fortunate enough to return home entirely unharmed He is a member of Lawrence Post, G A R, Clearfield County

Joseph H Rowles married Ruth Hickok and a family of twelve children was born to them, as follows Melissa, who died when one year old, C L V, William L, Roxie, Susie, Alman and Herman, deceased, and Aaron, James, Lewis, Harriet and Josephine

L William Rowles attended the country schools near his father's house, in boyhood, and afterward went to work in the woods and continued at this hard work for about one year after his marriage and then purchased his twenty-acre farm in Pike Township, of John M Chase At that time it was all woodland and he has completed its clearing and has erected all his substantial buildings The coal is leased to M J Kelly & Co

Mr Rowles was married May 10, 1888, to Melissa M Dunlap, a daughter of John R Dunlap, of Knox Township, and they have ten children, all of whom are yet at home, a large and happy family They are named respectively, Warren, Clem H., Waine A., John R., Clinton K., Crate M., Minerva J., Burley M and Bigler D and Biddle C, who are twins. Mr. Rowles and family are members of Mt Zion Methodist Episcopal Church of which he is a trustee and a steward. He has always been a Democrat since he cast his first vote. For three years he has been a member of the school board of Knox Township. No family in the township is better known than the Rowles.

T LANSING SNYDER, one of Clearfield's representative business men who is prominently identified with many important interests of different kinds, was born in Clearfield County, Pa, December 10, 1860, and is a son of Thomas G and Martha E (Litzenberg) Snyder. On the paternal side his grandfather was David Snyder, once a well known manufacturer and the founder of the Swedenborgian Society in Pennsylvania. On the maternal side his grandfather was John Litzenberg, and one of his great-grandfathers was John Stanley, who came from Derbyshire, England, to Pennsylvania with one of the Penn colonies.

T. Lansing Snyder was but two years old when his father met a soldier's death. He continued with his mother and when he grew to the age of responsibility took charge of her large and important interests, including the management of extensive timber tracts and of coal lands of great value. In 1884 the Bloomington Coal Company leased a large portion of the rich coal property and named their first mining town in honor of T. Lansing Snyder. Mr. Snyder has many individual business in-

terests. He is a director in the Brick and Fire Clay Company, of Clymer, Ind., vice president of the Clearfield Brick Manufacturing Company, of Clearfield, and is officially and otherwise interested in numerous other concerns. He has always been an active and useful citizen but has never been willing to accept city offices. During the legislative session of 1897, he was appointed to the office of sergeant-at-arms, at Harrisburg, by Hon Frank G Harris, and performed the duties of that position acceptably. The Snyders have been generous in their donations of land for public purposes, the mother of Mr Snyder being much interested in the establishing of schools and churches.

On June 28, 1893, Mr Snyder was married to Miss Cora May Ealy, who was born December 25, 1867, in Bedford County, Pa. Her parents were John C and Mary E (Walker) Ealy. Mr and Mrs Snyder have had two sons, Stanley G and Thomas L, the former of whom is deceased. The latter is a sturdy little lad of four years, his birth having taken place March 6, 1907. Mrs Snyder is a member of the Presbyterian church and is active in the work of its various benevolent organizations. The family home is a mansion situated in S Second Street, Clearfield.

JAMES I MEAS, who owns fifty acres of valuable farming land and has, additionally, a one-half interest in 400 acres, all in Boggs Township, Clearfield County, Pa, was born October 30, 1843, in Lycoming County, Pa. His parents, John and Mary (Neice) Meas, were also born in Lycoming County, where the father followed farming and lumbering. James I Meas is one of the following children born to his parents, Thomas, John, Jane, who married Ellis Livergood, Anna, who married Abraham Wisor, James I, David, Sarah, who married James Waple, and Miles

James I Meas had only common school advantages He has been a resident of Clearfield County since he was eight years of age and during the larger part of this time has been engaged in lumbering and farming He has been an active and interested citizen of Boggs Township for many years and has served in public offices, for one year being supervisor and for twenty-seven years a school director

In 1870 Mr Meas was married to Miss Hannah Goss, a daughter of Joseph and Hannah (Milward) Goss Joseph Goss was born in Decatur Township, Clearfield County, while his wife was born in England Mr and Mrs Goss had the following children Adaline, who is the wife of Abraham Pierce, Henrietta, who is the wife of Gideon Smeal, Amelia, who is the wife of David Meas, Amanda, who is the wife of Richard Lang, James, Hannah, who is the wife of James I Meas, Mary Ann, who is the wife of Timothy Pugh, and Bertha, who is the wife of William Meas

Mr and Mrs Meas have had six children, namely Myrtle, who is now deceased, was the wife of William Bush, David, William T, Leonard I, Harvey Wallace, who is deceased, and Dorsey G Mr and Mrs Meas are members of the Brethren church, in which she was reared, while Mr Meas's people were Lutherans They both belong to the Grange and are active in its good work and enjoy its social side as well as its more practical benefits

DELOS EUGENE HIBNER, a representative business man of DuBois, Pa, a member of the Hibner-Hoover Hardware Company of this borough, has resided here since 1873 He was born at Tioga Center, N Y, December 10, 1863, the youngest of a family of fifteen children, eleven of whom grew to maturity His parents were John E and Catherine (Bair) Hibner

John E Hibner was born in Germany, where he learned the shoemaking trade He came to America in early manhood and shortly afterward opened a shoe shop at Williamsport, Pa His trade was largely among the lumber men and they paid well and promptly for the substantial and well made footwear he sold, but in the panic of 1872 he lost his best customers and finally was forced to close out his business there In looking around for a means of livelihood he and his capable wife decided that the opening of a boarding house at Du-Bois, where John DuBois, through his activities was bringing many workmen to that place, would be a wise undertaking, and so it proved They started that business in 1873 and continued it as long as it seemed a satisfactory enterprise John E Hibner lived to be eighty years of age, but his wife died when aged sixty-six years

Delos Eugene Hibner was quite small when his parents came to Pennsylvania and he remembers how small a village was DuBois when they came here The houses were few and scattered, no railroad yet touched the place and the schoolhouse he attended was two miles distant from his home In 1875 he entered the employ of John DuBois, the founder of the place, and in 1877 accepted a position as clerk with the firm of Long & Brady, hardware merchants In 1882 he bought a third interest in the store and has continued in the hardware line until the present   A few years later he became associated with Long & Brady as a partner and subsequent changes came about   Mr Long was succeeded by M W Wise, who, in turn, was succeeded by W S Hollister and about the same time, Mr Brady was succeeded by N L Hoover, Mr Hibner's present partner

In 1890 D E Hibner and N L Hoover sold out their interests to Jesse Dale, but in 1892 they repurchased the store from Mr Dale and have continued to be associated ever since   The store at that time was situated on the present site of the DuBois National Bank, on the corner of Long Avenue and Brady Street   They then bought the building at No 12 N Brady Street, from the Turnbach Hardware Company and after disposing of the Turnbach stock, rented the building to Harry Christman who conducted a furniture store here for a short time   In 1902 the Hibner-Hoover Hardware Company was incorporated, with a capital stock of $100,000   In 1907 they added two more stories to the three-story building on N Brady Street and moved their stock to this location in the latter part of the same year   They occupy five floors and the basement and do a large business, its volume being steadily on the increase   The Hibner-Hoover Hardware Company are jobbers and retailers of heavy and shelf hardware, manufacturing tinners and coppersmiths, dealers in doors, sash and building material, buggies, wagons, surreys and harness, also farm machinery and paints and oils   The business enterprise of the firm was still further demonstrated when, in 1908 they bought out F W Prothero, a hardware merchant at No 321 W Long Ave   This store covers three

floors with a double store room on the first floor   In addition, the firm makes use of five warerooms, affording space for careful storage   This is the largest business of its kind in Clearfield County   Mr. Hibner has additional business interests   He is treasurer and manager of the Vulcan Soot Cleaner Company, which was incorporated under the laws of the State of New Jersey, in 1905, with a capital stock of $500,000, and an issue of $200,000   They do business all over the United States   The main office and factory are located at Du-Bois, Pa , with additional offices at Boston, Mass , and Chicago, Ill   Mr Hibner organized a company and built the first electric light plant at DuBois, in 1889, which was purchased in 1892, by the DuBois Electric Street Railway Company

On December 3, 1890, Mr. Hibner was married to Miss Frances O Ellis, a daughter of J B Ellis, who for many years was a merchant at DuBois   Five children have been born to them   Frances Catherine, Helen Louise (died at age of 6 months) ; Eugene, Mary and Delos   Mr and Mrs Hibner are members of the Methodist Episcopal church   In politics he is a Democrat and has been a useful and loyal party man and was selected as the first candidate for congress after the organization of the Congressional District   He is identified with the Elks and the Masons   The family residence stands at No 525 N. Brady Street, on the same site on which Mr. Hibner's father settled when the present thriving borough was but a little lumber hamlet on the outskirts of the forest

EDWARD LLOYD HUGHES, one of the lifelong residents and highly respected citizens of Decatur Township, Clearfield

County, Pa, lives on the farm of twenty-five acres, a part of the old homestead on which he was born October 24, 1846 He is a son of Richard and Nancy (Kephart) Hughes, and a grandson of William and Mary Hughes, natives of England

William Hughes, the grandfather, brought his family to America, in 1832, landing at the port of Philadelphia after a voyage of seven weeks In 1833 he moved to Huntingdon, Pa, and secured work in the construction of the old Pittsburg Canal and after its completion, moved to Decatur Township, Clearfield County, settling on this place The remainder of his life was passed here, his death occuring at the age of eighty-four years, having survived his wife The children of William and Mary Hughes were five in number, namely. James, who lived at Tylertown, John, who lived in Decatur Township, William, who died on the home farm, Richard, and Adam, who died on the ocean during the voyage from England

Richard Hughes, father of Edward Lloyd Hughes, was born in County Hereford-shire, England, December 23, 1819, and was a youth of fourteen years when he accompanied his parents to the United States When the home farm came into his possession, only five acres of the same had been cleared He followed farming and lumber-ing and during the last ten or twelve years of his life, he was also a coal operator His death occurred June 23, 1898 He married Nancy Kephart, a daughter of Henry Kephart, Sr, an old pioneer in Decatur Township, where Mrs Hughes was born and spent her life She died December 21,

1905, and both she and husband rest in the old cemetery at Center They had eleven children, the family record being as follows William, who has never married, lives on a part of the old homestead, Edward Lloyd, Alice, who is the wife of David Burkett, of Clearfield, John R, who is a farmer in Decatur Township, David, who died in 1890, Benjamin F, who lives on a part of the old home place, Harry M, who also lives on the homestead, Sarah, who is now deceased, was the wife of John W. Ashcroft, Essington, who died in infancy, and two babes that died unnamed The father of the above family was a member of the Episcopal church, while the mother was connected with the United Brethren church

Edward Lloyd Hughes now makes farm-ing his main business but for thirty-two years he worked in the coal mines He built a very attractive and comfortable residence on his farm which occupies a site that gives a pleasant view over the sur-rounding country

Mr Hughes was married May 12, 1872, to Miss Anna R Dunlap, who was born at Williamsburg, Huntingdon County, Pa, a daughter of Benjamin and Catherine (Isen-berg) Dunlap, former residents of Decatur Township and later of Osceola Mills The father of Mrs Hughes was a soldier in the Federal Army during the Civil War To Mr and Mrs Hughes twelve children have been born, the survivors being Charles W, who lives at Osceola Mills, married Maggie Crain, a daughter of Bednego Crain, Richard S, who lives in Decatur Township, married Annie Starline and they

have seven living children—Pearl, Maynard, Willard, Russell, Frederick, Mary
and Richard, Clara May, who is the wife
of W W Boone, of Osceola Mills, and they
have three living children—Mildred, Anna
and William, Edward Lloyd, Jr, who lives
in Decatur Township, married Martha Cad-
man, and they have four children—Ralph,
Lois, Rebecca and Ruth, Carrie Belle, who
married Alexander Davidson, a resident of
Keystone, in Decatur Township, and they
have three children—Lorraine and Lenora,
twins, and Paul, Grace Glen, who married
Daniel Dunn, of Keystone, Pa, and they
have five children—Harold, Wilda, Anna,
Hannah and Carrie, and Anna, Benjamin
F and Olive Pearl, all of whom reside at
home   Three of the children are deceased;
Nancy Ellen, who died at the age of six
years and five months, Rosie Violet, who
lived only two years, and a babe that passed
away unnamed

In politics Mr Hughes is an independent
voter   He belongs to several fraternal organizations, including the Odd Fellows, the
Knights of Pythias and the I O R M

DAVID HEGARTY, who is one-half
owner of a farm of 250 acres situated in
Bigler Township, Clearfield County, Pa,
now lives retired, after a busy life devoted
mainly to farming and lumbering   He was
born on this farm, in September, 1841, and
is a son of James and Jane (Boyle) Hegarty

James Hegarty was born in Ireland, a
son of Samuel and Jane Hegarty   He was
married there to Jane Boyle, a daughter of
James Boyle, and they then came to
America and settled in Bigler Township,
Clearfield County, Pa   James Hegarty was

a farmer and lumberman   Both he and
wife were members of the Presbyterian
church   They had six children born to
them, namely Jane, who is deceased, was
the wife of Robert Alexander, also deceased, Rebecca, who is deceased, was the
wife of John Gordon, David; Mary, who is
the wife of Walker Miles; Jerry, who is one-
half owner of the home farm; and Rachel,
who is deceased, was the wife of James
Luther.

David Hegarty grew up on the home
farm and as soon as old enough worked also
at lumbering   In 1863 he enlisted for a
term of three months in Co E, 30th Pa.
Vol Inf, for service in the Civil War, and
when this enlistment expired, reenlisted in
Battery B, 1st Pa Light Artillery, in which
he served until the close of the war   After
his patriotic duty was done he returned to
peaceful pursuits and continued until he
decided to lay down the responsibilities of
business and take a well earned rest

In 1866 Mr Hegarty was married to
Miss Luella Alexander, who died in 1896
She was a most estimable lady and was a
daughter of William B and Rebecca
(Whiteside) Alexander, he being born in
Clearfield County and she in Ireland   Mrs
Hegarty had one brother, Joseph, older
than herself, and four younger sisters
Rosa, wife of Henry Miles, Agnes, wife of
Edward Miles, Rebecca, wife of Thomas
Askey, and Drusilla, wife of John Jopling
Mr Hegarty has two daughters, Gertrude
and Daisy, both of whom are popular
teachers at Madera   He casts his vote in-
dependently and has never accepted any
public office except membership on the
school board

MELVIN J HURD, a well known merchant conducting a store at La Jose, Chest township, where also he holds the office of postmaster, was born at this place April 4, 1884, son of Alonzo L and Belle (McFadden) Hurd He is a great grandson of Elias Hurd, who settled in Newburg borough in 1832, clearing land on the site of the present village of La Jose He came to Clearfield county from Danville, Vt He died at the age of 75 years, leaving two sons—H H Hurd and L J Hurd, grandfather of our subject The latter, who was born in Vermont, married Rachel Wood, and they became pioneer settlers in Clearfield county, Pa

Alonzo L Hurd was born at La Jose, Clearfield county, Pa, about 1849, and is now living at the age of 62 years In early manhood he was engaged for some time in farming In April, 1892, he opened a general store in La Jose, which he carried on successfully for a number of years, retiring at last from active business life For some time he held the office of Postmaster at La Jose, which postoffice, formerly known as Newburg, in now called Hurd, it having been renamed in his honor He is a member of the Odd Fellows' lodge at Mahaffey, and belongs to the order of P L S of A, at La Jose, of which he is treasurer In politics a Republican, he has served on the school board since coming of age, and has been a member of the borough council since its organization

Alonzo L Hurd was first married to a Miss Tozier, of which union there were two children, namely Bird, a resident of Johnstown, and Louie, wife of C Durwell, of Connelsville, Pa For his second wife, Mr Tozier married Belle McFadden, who was born at La Jose, this county, a daughter of Robert P and Ann McFadden She is still living at the age of 54

years The children of this second union were as follows Melvin J, subject of this sketch, Arthur, who is a partner with our subject in the mercantile business, Oryis, who is agent for the Pennsylvania Railroad Company at Barnesboro, Pa, Joseph, who is attending school at Collinsville, Clair, Herbert and Audrey, all attending school

Melvin J Hurd, after completing his school studies at the age of 15 years, found employment in teaming for his father, with whom he remained until the age of 21 He was then a clerk in the mercantile store of A T Wilson of La Jose for four years He then purchased his present store, being associated at first with both his father and brother, but on the father's retirement has had his brother alone for a partner He has a well equipped store, carrying everything in the line of general merchandise for which there could be any probable demand in this community, and he has met with a gratifying degree of success A Republican in politics, he was appointed postmaster, July 17, 1908 He is also treasurer of the borough and recording secretary He belongs to the Red Men's lodge at Mahaffey Mr Hurd married Miss Edna Markle, who was born in La Jose, a daughter of Isaac and Mary (Williams) Markle, her father being a merchant of this borough Mr and Mrs Hurd have two children—Chetwin, born April 21, 1907, and Mary Belle, born December 8, 1910 Mrs Hurd is a member of the Baptist church

JOHN BERNARD McGRATH was born in a little village on the "Old Portage" Railroad in Washington Township, Blair County, Pa, July 5, 1854, and is the son of John McGrath and Margaret McHugh McGrath

31

His grandfather on his father's side emigrated from Ireland in 1814, and settled in Philadelphia, where John McGrath, Sr, father of John B, was born On his mother's side he is also of Irish descent His mother's father, Dennis McHugh, was prominently connected with the Irish Rebellion of 1798, and was obliged to leave Ireland secretly with his companions, he settled in Lebanon County, Pennsylvania, where his daughter Margaret was born He served a short time in the American Army in the War of 1812.

John B McGrath comes from a family distinguished for its connection with the development of the bituminous coal fields of Pennsylvania His father, John McGrath, Sr, was one of the pioneers in this industry, he it was who first developed the now famous "Miller" vein, as well as the "Lemon" Vein in Cambria County Miles McHugh, an uncle, opened the first coal for railroad shipment in the Clearfield region, and Edward McHugh, an uncle, and M B McGrath, a brother, are largely identified with the development of the Houtzdale or Moshannon coal fields of the county

John B McGrath was less than a year old when his parents moved to Dudley, Huntingdon County, Penna, and he remained there until he was about 14 years of age His father died at Dudley, May 6, 1865, and his mother, with her family, John B included, removed to Osceola, Clearfield County, Penna, on April 1, 1868 and with the exception of one year spent in Jefferson County, the family have resided in Clearfield County since that time

In 1875, shortly before the great fire that destroyed Osceola, Mrs McGrath and her family moved to the Beech Woods Settlement (Jefferson County, Penna), where they resided until early in 1876, when they returned to Clearfield County and settled at Houtzdale, Pa Mrs Margaret McHugh McGrath died at Houtzdale, Dec 1, 1878

John B McGrath has resided in Houtzdale since Feb 15, 1876, he is now practicing law and is a prominent member of the Clearfield County Bar He is also engaged in the fire insurance business, maintaining an office at Houtzdale, Pa, and is the senior member of the firm of McGrath & Moore, insurance brokers of Clearfield, Pa He is also secretary and treasurer of the Anda Coal Company, which conducts a coal operation near Houtzdale, Penna Mr McGrath was educated in the public schools, he attended school at Dudley, Pa, and also at Osceola, Pa He has always taken an active part in politics and all public affairs He is an uncompromising Democrat and has twice served as chairman of the party organization in the county, first in 1902 and was re-elected in 1903 He has held a number of local offices,—school director, justice of the peace, and is at present a member of the Houtzdale Borough Council He takes a great interest in all public affairs and is considered among the progressive citizens of the county

On July 21, 1888, he was united in marriage with Miss Lydia Ingraham Marmion, at Fortress Monroe, Va She was born at Wilmington, S C, and was a daughter of Dr George H. and Elizabeth Coffin (Wood) Marmion. Her father, Dr Marmion, was a native of Harper's Ferry, Va Mrs McGrath was descended from Keziah Coffin, who was a relative of Benjamin Franklin, and her kindred were among the distinguished people of the country At the time of her marriage she was a resident of Hampton, Va Mrs McGrath was a lady of beautiful character and the accident that caused her death threw a shadow over the community where she was much beloved Mr McGrath with his wife and children were driving a spirited team, which ran away when near Ramey, Pa, May 20, 1900, causing injuries from which Mrs McGrath died three days later Mr McGrath was also injured and his little son suffered a broken leg It was a very sad ending to what had promised to be a pleasant recreation

To Mr and Mrs McGrath four children were born, one of whom died in infancy The survivors are Margaret, John J, who is a student in Fordham College, New York, and George H All have been given both educational and social advantages and are being prepared for any position in society Mr McGrath and children are members of the Roman Catholic Church He is identified fraternally with the Knights of Columbus but with no other organization He is one of the valued members of the Clearfield County Historical Society and takes a commendable amount of pride in the preservation of old records and particularly those which tell of the early days in the great mining sections of the state

WILLIAM T FLEGAL, a successful farmer of Boggs Township, Clearfield County, Pa, where he has 200 acres belonging to the Chase estate under cultivation, together with thirty-nine acres of his own, is one of the best known men in this section He was born in Clearfield County in January, 1856, and is a son of Valentine and Charlotte (Bradley) Flegal The father was a farmer, and was a Democrat in politics Both he and wife were members of the Methodist Episcopal church They had a family of eight sons, namely· Gilbert, Samuel, Alexander, Austin, Miles, David, William T and Peter

William T Flegal was occupied until he was seventeen years of age in attending school and working on the home farm He inherited his land from his father and since it came into his possession he has made many improvements, including the erection of a substantial house and barn In addition to farming he has worked more or less in the woods all his life.

In 1891 Mr Flegal was married to Miss Alice Nerhoot, a daughter of Samuel and Anna Nerhoot, of Clearfield County The other members of their family were Ward, Lloyd, Eva, Georgia and Dove Mr and Mrs Flegal have three children Lottie, Furman V and Nettie Abigail They are members of the Methodist Episcopal church In politics Mr Flegal is a Democrat, and he has served on the election board on several occasions.

THOMAS G SNYDER, deceased In remembering the men of worth who once were of Clearfield County and led in her most useful activities and through merit commanded the respect of his fellow citizens, Thomas G Snyder, who sleeps in a soldier's grave, a hero of the Civil War, will not be forgotten He was born in Philadelphia County, Pa, October 24, 1817 His ancestry was German and his parents were David and Mary A (Kelly) Snyder

Thomas G Snyder was the son of a farmer and manufacturer and early associated himself with his parent in the making of shovels, a pioneer enterprise of the kind in Philadelphia Coun-

ty and one which the two Snyders developed
into a large business When he retired from
manufacturing he entered into merchandising
in a suburb of Philadelphia, and in 1851 he
came to Clearfield County He invested
largely and judiciously in land, which is still
held by his family, and from then until the
opening of the Civil War, he gave his entire
attention to lumbering His success in this
industry was marked and a long and prosperous
business career was his reasonable expectation

When Lieutenant Snyder put aside all personal considerations in order to devote himself
to the service of his country, he was already
a man of forty-four years and the act was one
of pure patriotism In October, 1861, he organized a picked body of men which became
Co F, 2nd Pa Cav, which was assigned to the
Army of the Potomac, and he was commissioned its first lieutenant He passed through
several battles safely but in a skirmish at Ac-
quan Creek, Virginia, he received a mortal
wound Through the fraternal act of a
brother Free Mason, no less a person than Gen
Fitz Hugh Lee, the wounded officer was carried to a dwelling and every effort was made
to ease his suffering and prolong his life, but
without avail and within forty-eight hours he
expired, a soldier to the last His aged father
succumbed under the shock The ashes of
both him and his son rest in the old cemetery
belonging to the Swedenborgian church in
Philadelphia County, David Snyder having
been the founder of the Swedenborgian Society
in that county

On November 26, 1840, Thomas G Snyder
was married to Miss Martha E Litzenberg,
who survived him She was of German ances-
ery and was born near Philadelphia, a daughter
of John and Christiana (Stanley) Litzenberg, the former of whom was a prosperous
merchant for many years To Thomas G
Snyder and wife ten children were born, five
of whom survived childhood Horatio, Mary
A, Lucy, Annie E and T Lansing Horatio
left college at the age of eighteen years in order
to enter his father's company, in 1861, survived the hazards of war and after returning
to peaceful pursuits, entered the employ of the
Berwind-White Bituminous Coal Company,
with which he has been identified ever since
Mary A is the wife of E C Brenner Lucy
became the wife of John C Hicklen Annie
E married Lewis M Garrett T Lansing is
one of Clearfield's prominent citizens

E SCHNARS, general farmer and dairyman, having twenty-seven milch cows and owning 121 acres of land in Lawrence Township,
Clearfield County, Pa, was born in Karthaus
Township, March 3, 1847, and is a son of John
and Susan (Solt) Schnars, farming people and
old residents of that section

E Schnars attended the Tinker School not
far distant from his boyhood home and then
went out to Kansas, where he lived for ten
years and during this time had many thrilling
adventures He remembers one season in
which he assisted in killing 500 buffalo After
marriage he came to Clearfield County and
bought a water right at Logan's Dam where
he built a saw mill which was carried away by
the Johnstown flood He next located at Curwensville where he bought a store of John Irvin, which he conducted for eight years and
then traded the store for Sheriff Smith's farm
at Hyde City and subsequently sold the farm
to the steel company After this he operated
a butcher shop for a time and then purchased
his present property which was known as the

MR. AND MRS. E. SCHNARS AND FAMILY

Boyington farm After getting his farm industries well started, in 1904, Mr Schnars started his dairy, having appropriate buildings already on the place and he has greatly prospered in this line He handles 280 quarts of milk daily which he delivers in Clearfield Mr Schnars carries on his business according to modern ideas, has sanitary quarters and running water, and his milk is in great demand and there is more call for cream than he can supply

Mr Schnars was married to Miss Belle Turner of Garden City, Kans, and they have eight children Minnie, who is the wife of William Hoover, Florence, who is the wife of Orvis Ardary, and John Arthur, Glenn, Clara, Mabel, Jane and Charles Mr Schnars and family attend the Methodist Episcopal church of Lawrence Township, the building being on one corner of the home farm He is a Republican in politics and is a member of the Grange at Clearfield For a number of years he owned 160 acres of land in Kansas and subsequently sold his claim for $15,000, which he proposes to invest in Clearfield County He is an intelligent, shrewd business man and there is every indication that this fund will be carefully and sensibly invested

JAMES K TURNER, Esq, a prosperous business man of Wallaceton, Pa, where he is owner and proprietor of a meat market, owns forty-three acres of valuable farming land in Boggs Township, in which he was born January 8, 1847 His parents were James H and Elizabeth (Smeal) Turner

James H Turner was born November 10, 1810, at Philipsburg, Pa, a son of Samuel and Lavina (Simler) Turner His

business through life was farming together with lumbering He was a man of sterling character and occupied positions of trust at different times For some ten years he served as constable and for thirteen years he was a justice of the peace With his wife he was active and interested in the work of the Methodist Episcopal church and was liberal in the support he gave He married Elizabeth Smeal, a daughter of Benjamin and Elizabeth (Wisor) Smeal, old county families To them were born the following children Henry D, M V, Sarah, Benjamin, James K, Jemima, Lavina Jane, Samuel, George, Ella, Emma and Eliza Matilda Sarah, who is now deceased, was the wife of Alexander France Jemima, who is also deceased, was the wife of David Quigley Ella is the wife of Albert Klare, and Emma is the wife of Grant Ross

James K Turner attended school near his father's farm until he was old enough to handle tools, when he learned the carpenter trade and for some years worked in saw mills, subsequently starting to work in brick plants, with which he was connected for twenty-six years, during the last six being foreman In 1909 he embarked in his present business at Wallaceton, where he owns a residence He has been a very prominent and public spirited citizen of this borough, serving as its burgess for one year, for fifteen years as a member of its school board and also as a member of the council For the past sixteen years he has also served continuously in the office of justice of the peace

On February 15, 1870, Mr Turner was married to Miss Henrietta Tomlinson, a daughter of Rev Stephen and Maggie (Hoffman) Tomlinson   The parents of Mrs Turner were residents of Lycoming County and her father was a Methodist minister   Mr and Mrs Tomlinson had the following children Philip, who is deceased, John, William and Frank, Maggie, who is the wife of William Buck, Mercy, who married William Sanders, and Henrietta, who is the wife of Mr Turner

To Mr and Mrs Turner three children were born, namely Benjamin Franklin, who was born November 14, 1870, died at the age of thirty-eight years, Maggie, who is the wife of Samuel Roan, and Mary, who is the wife of Charles I Wolfe Mr Turner and wife are members of the Methodist Episcopal church He is a Democrat

JOHN EUGENE MERRIS, one of the organizers and proprietors of The Merris Beef Company, one of the important business combinations of Clearfield County, Pa, is well known in the great meat industry in this section and is identified with other large interests He has been a valued resident of DuBois, Pa, for twenty-nine years but is a native of New York, born on his father's farm, April 14, 1855 His parents were John E and Caroline (Becker) Merris

John E Merris was both former and merchant and enjoyed a prosperous business career for many years His death occurred at the home of his son, John Eugene, at DuBois, Pa, in 1905, at the age of seventy-two years He married Caroline Becker, who died in 1897, aged seventy-one years They had three sons John Eugene, Howard I, and Anson E, of Buffalo, N Y

John Eugene Merris spent his boyhood on the farm and in his father's store   After attending the district schools he took a course at Griffith Institute, at Springville, N Y, going from there to Aurora Academy, at Aurora, N Y   Beginning when seventeen years of age, he taught school through several winters and then entered the employ of Hon Frank Higgins, who conducted a store at Stanton, Mich, and later was with O T Higgins in the same business at Belfast and at Olean, N Y   In 1881 Mr Merris came to DuBois, with the Bell Lewis & Yates Mining Company and took entire charge of their stores until 1893   At that time he became associated with Armour & Company, at Chicago, Ill   In partnership with Hon I E Long, M W Wise and H I Merris, he organized the Merris Beef Company, consignees for Armour & Company   Later, L B Long took over the interests of I E Long and M W Wise, and since then the membership of the firm has been increased by the admission as partners W H Cawthra, R W Criss and A L Crumpston, all of whom were old employes   The refrigerators are located at DuBois, Ridgway and Punxsutawney, Pa   Additional business interests are indicated by his being a director in the Union Banking and Trust Company, at DuBois, also in the Electric and Traction Company and in the DuBois Land Company. Mr Merris is recognized as one of the able business men of Clearfield County, not only possessing the gift of good judgment which has led him to make wise investments, but also the capacity for hard work that, in these days of competition, is a necessary adjunct to success

On October 8, 1883, Mr Merris was married to Miss Ida B. Grantier, of Canton, Pa, and they have three children: Howard A, who is cashier for Armour & Co, in their Colorado Springs office, married Virginia Macadoo, Helen E , who is a student in the seminary at Birmingham, and J Edward Mr and Mrs Merris attend the Presbyterian church They enjoy the comforts of a beautiful home, their residence standing on the corner of Main Street and Long Avenue, DuBois Mr Merris votes with the Republican party and is an earnest and useful citizen but has never permitted the use of his name for any political office He is prominent in Masonry in Pennsylvania and is past master of Garfield Lodge, F & A M , at DuBois, belongs to the Chapter at Ridgway, to Bethany Commandery at DuBois and to the Zem Zem Shrine at Erie, Pa

H M SHIMEL, who belongs to one of the old and respected families of Clearfield County, one that has been identified for years with the agricultural and lumbering interests of Boggs Township, is the owner of 200 acres of land in Boggs Township He was born in this township, September 20, 1854, and is a son of George W and Mary Jane (Bush) Shimel

George W Shimel was born in Clearfield County, a son of Henry and Sarah Shimel, of German descent He engaged in lumbering and farming, gave political support to the Democratic party, and was liberal in advancing the interests of the United Brethren church, to which both he and wife belonged. He married Mary Jane Bush, a daughter of Joseph and Elizabeth Bush Mrs Bush still survives, being now in her ninety-eighth year and is probably the most venerable resident of Boggs Township To George W Shimel and wife the following children were born Sarah E , wife of Thomas C Kyler, H. M , Laura A , wife of E J Lumadue, and Ardelia, wife of Smith A McNeal

On account of being the only son of his parents, H M Shimel had many responsibilities placed on him very early, his father having need of his assistance He has followed farming and lumbering as did his father and grandfather After his father died he bought the homestead from the other heirs All the buildings were in good condition so that Mr Shimel had but little improving to do In September, 1883, he was married to Miss Clara C Batts, a daughter of William and Hannah (Wisor) Batts, the former of whom was born in Montgomery County and the latter in Clearfield County Mr and Mrs Batts had the following children Henry H , Clara C , Hallie, Hiram, Ella, and Furman, the last named being the wife of Barnard Yasey Clara married H M Shimel, Hallie married John C Cowder, and Ella, now deceased, was the wife of George Stine

Mr and Mrs Shimel have eight children, namely N E , May, who is the wife of John Rothrock, Roxie O , who is the wife of Joseph Fleck, Nellie, Thomas, Hannah, Morris, and Cecil C Mr Shimel and family attend the United Brethren church He is a Democrat in politics and has served in numerous township offices He belongs to the Grange and to the O U A M

JOHN R ARDARY, general farmer and dairyman, in Pike Township, where he owns 131 acres of valuable land, situated three miles south of Curwensville, Pa , was born in Lawrence Township. Clearfield

County, Pa, December 11, 1873 His parents are James M and Martha (Price) Ardary

James M Ardary was born in Lawrence Township, Clearfield County, March 12, 1844, a son of Elisha Ardary, who was born in Center County and came to Clearfield County with his parents, who were James and Eleanor (Coulter) Ardary Elisha Ardary attended school near Clover Hill, on Big Clearfield Creek, in Lawrence Township, and remained at home until he was married to Elizabeth Thompson, who died in 1847 To this marriage the following children were born Eneas, who was a soldier in the Civil War, and being captured by the enemy, died in Andersonville Prison, Samuel, who lives at Clearfield, James M, who resides on Irwin Hill, Curwensville, John, a carpenter, who resides at Curwensville (married Alice Caldwell), and Zenas, a lumberman, who lives at Hawk Run and married a daughter of Henry Hurd Elisha Ardary was married secondly to Mary (Holly) Lanhead and three children were born to that marriage. Love and George, both of whom live on the old farm in Lawrence Township, and Elizabeth, who is the wife of William Gates, of Curwensville After his second marriage, Elisha Ardary moved to Curwensville and lived there at the time of his death

James M Ardary was educated in Lawrence Township and in Iowa After he returned to Curwensville, he was married, in September, 1870, to Martha Price, a daughter of William and Hannah Price, and nine children were born to them, namely· Howard, living in the West, Bertha, who died when aged eight years, John R,

Frank, who lives at Pittsburg, Clark, who is a mine foreman, in California, Emma, who is a trained nurse, at Cleveland, O, Mame, who is a musician, living at Akron, O, William P, who died at the age of fourteen years, and Stanley, who lived but one year For nine years after his marriage, James M Ardary lived in Lawrence Township as a farmer and then moved to Curwensville and from there to Kerrmoor, then to Pike Township, buying a farm near Bloomington, and from there came to Irwin Hill, Curwensville

John R Ardary attended school in Lawrence Township and at Kerrmoor, after which he spent some years as a farmer and for seven years was employed in a dairy at Kerrmoor, after which he bought his present farm from his father In March, 1909, he started his dairy and now operates a house to house morning delivery, through Curwensville, disposing of from twenty-three to twenty-five gallons of milk daily. His cows are of mixed breed but are good producers and his business is in a prosperous condition He keeps hired help and has all his land under cultivation that he can spare from pasturage.

In March, 1900, Mr Ardary was married to Miss Jennie Smith, a daughter of Adam and Elizabeth (Haag) Smith, and they have two children (twins), Martin Watts and Marian Watts, who are bright students in the public school In politics, Mr Ardary is a Republican

ROBERT WALLACE, father of the late ex-United States senator, William A Wallace, of Clearfield, Pa, was born March 13, 1792, in the barony of Omagh, county Tyrone, Ireland He emigrated to America in 1819 and, having received a liberal education, engaged in teaching school in Mifflin county, Pa He subsequently studied law with Hon Ephraim Banks at Lewistown, Pa, and was there admitted to practice in 1824 He then removed to Huntingdon county, Pa, but remained there only a short time, coming to Clearfield county in 1825 and remaining here until the following year Returning again to Huntingdon county, he was there married to Miss Jane Hemphill of Huntingdon He practiced law in Huntingdon, was district attorney of the county, and for a portion of the time edited a newspaper there until 1836 He then removed with his family to Clearfield, where he was engaged in the active practice of the law from 1836 to 1847, when he removed to Hollidaysburg, Blair county He remained there until 1854, at which time he returned to Clearfield county, and he resided in this county subsequently until his death, which took place at Wallaceton, Pa. (a town named after him), January 2, 1875 He was buried in Clearfield, Pa He and his wife were the parents of nine children—William A, Sarah M, Samuel H, Robert J, Thomas L, Francis J, Mary A, Rebecca A, and Jane S—of whom the following is a partial record

William A Wallace, born at Huntingdon, Pa, November 28, 1827, lived in Clearfield, Pa, died May 22, 1896

Sarah M, born April 14, 1829, married George W Saunders, who is now deceased Mrs Saunders died December 12, 1910

Samuel Hemphill Wallace, born October 4, 1830, resides in Philadelphia He was general ticket agent for the Pennsylvania Railroad at Philadelphia until he reached the age limit, when he retired, and is now on the retired list,

having been with the railroad company over 30 years

Robert J Wallace, born in Clearfield, Pa, June 22, 1835, was an attorney He died at Clearfield, Pa, December 23, 1866

Thomas L Wallace, born at Clearfield, Pa, September 8, 1837, resides at Harrisburg, Pa, was general freight agent for the Pennsylvania Railroad at Harrisburg until he reached the age limit, and then retired, having served with the railroad company in that capacity over 30 years He is now on the retired list

Francis J and Mary A Wallace died at Clearfield, Pa, in infancy Rebecca A Wallace, born at Clearfield, Pa, December 21, 1843, resides at Harrisburg On December 21, 1871, she married S J M McCarrell of Claysville, Washington county, Pa Judge McCarrell is one of the present judges of the Dauphin county courts Jane S Wallace, born at Clearfield, August 15, 1846, married C G Cadwallader, of Philadelphia, Pa, November 9, 1870 Mr Cadwallader died April 7, 1909, in Philadelphia, he was general ticket agent of the Pennsylvania Railroad at the time of his death

SIMON KEPHART, who is a member of one of the old families of Decatur Township, Clearfield County, Pa, and a veteran of the Civil War, was born August 26, 1840, in Decatur Township, one mile from Osceola, and has always lived here with the exception of his four years of service in the Civil War and one year's residence in Kansas He is a son of George and Mary Ann (Amy) Kephart, and a grandson of Henry Kephart and a great-grandson of Nicholas Kephart

Nicholas Kephart was born in Switzerland, one of six brothers, and they all came to America in 1750 and settled in Eastern Pennsylvania They were sturdy men and their excellent qualities were perpetuated through large and vigorous families and the name is not an unusual one in Pennsylvania Nicholas Kephart married Mary Frye, who was of Pennsylvania Dutch extraction and possibly was born in Berks County

Henry Kephart, son of Nicholas and Mary Kephart, was probably born in Penn's Valley He often referred to that section and it is known that he came from there in 1804 and settled two miles west of Osceola Mills, where he took up an improved claim, on which he lived until he was seventy-one years of age He was a man of sterling character and of such kind and winning personality that he was much beloved by those who were his neighbors On this account his mysterious death or disappearance, caused wide spread interest and regret At that time wild animals still infested the mountains, but he had spent so many years in these regions that he was well prepared for any attack that could have been made on him by either bears or panthers; but, with his friendly disposition he might not have been equally secure from a murderous assault made by a fellow creature In 1857 he started alone over the mountains to visit two daughters who lived in Bald Eagle Valley, walking to Sandy Ridge, where he met the stage and was taken to his destination His visit over, some two weeks later he was a passenger with one Andy Green, to Sandy Ridge, where they stopped at a hotel for dinner and Mr Green endeavored to have the aged gentleman continue on the stage

as far as Philipsburg, from which place to his home would have been a less tiresome and shorter walk Mr Kephart, however, was too old and seasoned a mountain traveler to consider this proposition, and left his companion, saying "I'll walk over the old mountain road" That was the last ever seen of this old pioneer of Decatur Township, although searchers traced him to a place half way between Sandy Ridge and the old toll gate. He was so well known all through this section and so highly esteemed that the whole country was aroused and hundreds left their farms and ordinary occupations in order to join in the search Suspicious circumstances finally caused a certain man to be suspected of having waylaid Mr. Kephart, possibly for robbery on the supposition that he was carrying money, and that the body may have been placed in the fill that was then being made in the construction of the railroad There were many tragedies in those early days in some sections of the country but none in Decatur Township that ever so disturbed the whole people as the complete disappearance of this kindly, warm-hearted old gentleman

Henry Kephart was married to Catherine Smith, who came also from the Penn's Valley region, and they had twelve children, all of whom have passed off the scene of life David spent his life just beyond Osceola Mills Henry was the father of the eminent Bishop E B Kephart, of the United Brethren church Andrew lived on the farm now occupied by his son, G W. Kephart George resided on a part of the old homestead William lived in what is now New Castle, later moved to Iowa and died in Republic County, Kans Stephen's widow lives at Osceola Mills Mary married Andrew Nearhoof and they lived in Bald Eagle Valley Barbara married Simon Nearhoof, and they also lived in Bald Eagle Valley Charlotte was the wife of John Crain, of Decatur Township Ellen married Daniel Kephart, a second cousin Nancy was the wife of Richard Hughes Peggy married William Harner and died at Freedom Furnace The mother of the above family died in 1856 and at that time had eleven living children, ninety-six grandchildren and sixty-three great-grandchildren

George Kephart, son of Henry and father of Simon Kephart was born on the old home place in 1814 His life was an agricultural one and was spent in Decatur Township where he had seventy acres of the old homestead His death was an accidental one, caused by a falling tree, on March 25, 1865 He had married Mary Ann Amy, who was born in Bald Eagle Valley and survived until 1882 Eleven children were born to them, as follows: Catherine, who was the wife of John M Test, of Phillipsburg, Pa , Simon , Perry C , who lives at Hampton Roads Va , Elizabeth, deceased, who was the wife of Waldron Elliott, of Decatur Township, Alice, who is the wife of John Keller, of Decatur Township, Tamer, deceased, who was the wife of J O Richards Rebecca, who married Nicholas Debuque (they live at Escanaba, Mich), William H , who died in 1910, in Decatur Township, Esther, who is the wife of Allen Britton, of Decatur Township, Mary Ann, who is the widow of Frederick Starline, of Osceola Mills, and Jennie, who is the wife of William Campman, of Tioga County

Simon Kephart grew to manhood on the home farm On September 19, 1861, he enlisted for service in the Union Army for the Civil War, at Camp Crossman, in Huntingdon County, entering Co K, 110th Pa Vol Inf After participating in the battle of Fredericksburg, Co K was consolidated with Co A, and with this organization he remained through all the great events, battles, marches and campaigns until he received his honorable discharge on June 28, 1865 Considering the many battles in which Mr Kephart participated it is remarkable that he escaped without injuries, although on many occasions bullets penetrated his clothing To name the great battles in which this veteran served as a brave, cheerful and obedient soldier, will recall to all lovers of their country the days when its liberties were in the hands of men who daily faced death in its most terrible aspects He was at Winchester, Va , March 23, 1862, at Fort Republic, June 9, 1862, Cedar Mountain, August 9, 1862, Fredericksburg, with the Army of the Potomac, December 13, 1862, Chancellorsville, May 3, 1863, Gettysburg, July 1-3, 1863, Mine Run Heights, November, 1863, Wilderness, under Gen Grant, May 3-5, 1864, Spottsylvania Court House, May 12, 1864, Cold Harbor, June 2, 1864, Deep Bottom, Va , July 27, 1864, and Petersburg, and was in all the skirmishing that immediately preceded the surrender of Gen Lee at Appomattox At Deep Bottom, Va , out of 11 non-commissioned officers and privates that went into the fight, two came out, Mr Kephart and George Traxal

After the close of his military service Mr Kephart returned home and remained with his mother until his marriage In 1870 he came to Osceola and after the town was burned he lived at Moshannon colliery until 1879 He then spent one year in Kansas and then came back to Osceola where he has resided ever since He is a valued member of the Grand Army Post at this place

On June 25, 1868, Mr Kephart was married to Miss Amanda G Peary, who was born in Clarion County but was reared in Center County She is a daughter of John C and Adaline (Lamborn) Peary, the former of whom died in the Union Army during the Civil War, a member of Co E, 45th Pa Vol Inf, and his burial was at Fortress Monroe Mrs Kephart was the second born in a family of seven children To Mr and Mrs Kephart, six children were born, as follows Glencora, who is the wife of Thomas Hobba, and they live at Scalp Level, Cambria County, Pa , Maud, who is the wife of Harry Taylor, of Osceola Mills, Annabel, who is the wife of James Ashworth, of Osceola Mills, Walter Forest, who died when aged three years and 11 months, George C , who lives at home, and Bessie L , who is the wife of Barney Press, of Ashtola, Somerset County, Pa Mr Kephart and wife are members of the Methodist Episcopal church He is a Republican in his political views

FRANK HAHNE, who is identified with many of the leading enterprises of DuBois, Pa , has been a resident of this borough since 1896 He was born in Germany, March 31, 1856, and being left an orphan when quite young, has mainly made his own way in the world and stands today as a telling example of what an honest, right-minded, hard working boy can become

Mr Hahne attended the excellent German schools and at the age of seventeen years started to learn the brewer's trade In 1875 he came to America in search of better industrial conditions, landing in Milwaukee, Wis , where he found employment in a brewery One year later he went to Iowa, where he worked at his trade for three years, when, having accumulated some capital, he took up Government claims in South Dakota, where he engaged in farming for two years In 1881 he became a resident of Chicago, Ill , and there again went into the brewing business and remained until 1887 at which time he went to Allegheny He was there until 1896, and then came to DuBois, where his business interests have been extensively developed

When Mr Hahne decided that this Pennsylvania town offered excellent business opportunities, he organized first the DuBois Brewing Company and was made its president The plant at the beginning was not more than one-half the size of the present one but the growth of the enterprise has been continuous, under Mr Hahne's judicious management and the time will come when the present commodious quarters on South Main Street, on the B R & P Railroad, will have to be enlarged and still better facilities provided It is a growing business The buildings are of brick construction and an average of eighty men are employed The main office is at DuBois, Pa , with branch offices at Buffalo, N Y , and Newark, N J In connection with the brewery proper, the company has a complete ice plant and by contract, the Hygienic Ice Company takes all their over-production of ice In addition to supplying the local trade from the brewery, shipments are made to many points, including Hamilton, Canada The main brands of beer manufactured are DuBois Budweiser, DuBois Wurzburger, Hahne's Export and Hahne's Porter The officers of the DuBois Brewing Company are well known capitalists Frank Hahne is president, J Weil, is vice president, Frank I Schwem is treasurer, and M I McCreight is secretary Mr Hahne is also president of the DuBois Storage and Carting Company, is a director of the DuBois Electric and Traction Company, a director of the United Traction Company, and formerly was president of the J Mahler Glass Company which sold out to the American-French Belgium Glass Company, in 1909

Mr Hahne has also prospered as a farmer and stock raiser He manages a farm of 180 acres of valuable land belonging to the Brewing Company and situated near Luthersburg, in Clearfield County, where he has a large orchard selected by the state as a model demonstrating orchard He is much interested in the breeding of thoroughbred horses and cattle, making a specialty of Percherons and Holsteins His 1800-pound Percheron stallion, DuBois, has taken many blue ribbons when exhibited Improvements of every kind have been made on this farm and Mr Hahne has been heard to express the wish that he may spend his last years in the midst of these beautiful surroundings

On May 30, 1883, Mr Hahne was married first to Miss Carrie A Trom, of Chicago, Ill, who died in 1896 Four children were born to that union, namely Emelia T, Maria A, Frank John and Carolla A In 1900, Mr Hahne was married secondly to Mrs Maria Strey, whose death occurred May 16, 1910 Mr Hahne and children are members of the Roman Catholic church He is identified fraternally with the Elks, at DuBois, and socially with the Acorn Club of DuBois and the German Club, of Pittsburg He belongs also to the Pennsylvania Brewers' Association In 1903 Mr Hahne erected his substantial and comfortable dwelling on South Main Street, DuBois, which has been the family home ever since

E K TURNER, owner and proprietor of a grist mill in Wallaceton Borough, Clearfield County, Pa, and of a farm of 175 acres, situated in Graham Township, and a second farm of 100 acres, in Bradford Township, belongs to one of the old pioneer families of the county He was born in Graham Township, Clearfield County, February 12, 1853, and is a son of John W and Martha (Dixon) Turner

John W Turner was born in Clearfield County, a son of Samuel and Susan (Wisor) Turner He came to Graham Township when few settlers had yet taken up land and settled on what became the homestead farm before any of the timber had yet been cut He cleared this land and developed a fine farm He married Martha Dixon, a daughter of James and Ella Dixon, and to them were born the following children E B, Margaret, who is deceased, was the wife of Martin Taylor, E K, Annabel, who is the wife of Charles Russell, and Martha, who is the wife of William Hambright John W Turner and wife were people of sterling worth and were widely known They were members of the Methodist Episcopal church

E K Turner attended the common schools in Graham Township and spent two terms in the State Normal School at Millersville, Pa His life since then has been devoted to lumbering, farming and milling In 1908 he purchased his grist mill from Harvey Reidy and has operated it continuously ever since and handles grain and flour quite extensively He received 100 acres of the homestead farm from his father and later purchased 175 additional acres For some years he has been a large dealer in stock He is a man of practical knowledge along his various lines of business and has met with much success in his undertakings

Mr Turner was married in August, 1876, to Miss Jane A Graham, a daughter of John and Gwen (Dale) Graham The father of Mrs Turner was a farmer and lumberman in Bradford Township, Clearfield County Of his children, Mrs Turner was the first born, the others being Asbury, Elizabeth, who married Jerome Wilson, Mary, who married Zachariah Hoover, Hettie, and James B Eleven children have been born to Mr and Mrs Turner, as follows J W , Effie, who is the wife of Frederick Fuge, Carrie, who is the wife of Clark Hummel, Ella, who is the wife of Orvis Hubler, and Gwen, Anna, Mabel, William, Ernest, Lynn and Wendell Mr Turner and family attend the Methodist Episcopal church He is a Republican in politics and has served very acceptably and usefully as a member of the school board Mr Turner is one of the leading members of the Grange at Wallaceton

CALEB T BOAL, general farmer residing three miles northeast of Curwensville, Pa , on a farm of ninety acres situated in Pike Township, Clearfield County, was born in this township, April 26, 1868, and is a son of James and Elizabeth (Smeal) Boal

James Boal was born and reared in Center County and remained there until he reached manhood, when he came to Clearfield County and for some years after his marriage to Elizabeth Smeal, lived on the George Smeal farm, afterward going to the West, where he died in 1877 His widow survived until February, 1901, dying at the age of seventy-two years Her burial was in the Center Cemetery She was a daughter of Caleb Bailey and the widow of George Smeal Two sons were born to James and Elizabeth (Smeal) Boal, Charles E and Caleb T The former was born December 25, 1865, and owns a one-half interest in the farm on which Caleb T Boal resides, the latter owning the other one-half interest On August 20, 1891, Charles E Boal married Ella Cleaver, a daughter of Charles Cleaver, of Penn Township, and they have eleven children, namely Lela, Orvis, Curtis, Maude, Elizabeth, Mary, Clark, Ai, Howard, Sarah and Mabel

Caleb T Boal obtained his education in the schools of Pike Township and has devoted himself to farm pursuits, continuing to live on the homestead The substantial buildings on the place he has erected and has made many other excellent improvements Thirty acres of the farm is still in valuable timber Mr Boal raises the grains which do best in this climate, is also to some degree interested in growing stock, has fine orchards, and in fact is surrounded with all that necessarily contributes to a farmer's comfort and independence

On August 27, 1895, Mr Boal was married to Miss Anna B Spencer, a daughter of E Bellman Spencer, of Penn Township, and they have six children Zeula, Pearl, Russell, all three of whom attend the public schools and are bright pupils, and Lester, Willhard and Carrie Mr and Mrs Boal are members of the Methodist Episcopal church, as were their parents In politics Mr Boal is a Republican He is a member of the Curwensville Rural Telephone Company of Pike Township

ANTHONY M GORMAN, who is manager of the Standard Oil Co 's plant at La Jose, and a man of much local prominence, was born on the old Gorman homestead, near Mt Joy church, May 9, 1877 His parents were Daniel and Elizabeth (McGarvey) Gorman His paternal grandfather was a resident of Indiana county, where he held the office of tax collector, and who, while traveling his rounds, lost his way in a severe winter storm and was found frozen to death

Daniel Gorman, who was born at Indiana, Pa , subsequently settled at New Washington, Clearfield county, and was the founder of the homestead near Mt Joy church He died in October, 1885, at the age of 60 years He was thrice married first to Nancy Maria Neff, a daughter of J B and Catherine (Barnhart) Neff, of which union there were three children —William, James L and Maria, secondly to Nancy King, daughter of John and Nancy (McCreary) King, to which marriage there were six children, the four present survivors being John, Horace, Rachel and Arthur G Of Daniel Gorman's third marriage, to Elizabeth McGarvey, there were three children— Anthony M , David, and Daniel Gorman The mother of these children was a daughter

of Anthony McGarvey, who came from Ireland at an early day, settling in Chest township

Anthony M Gorman was but seven years of age when his father died and he was reared until the age of 21 by his grandfather McGarvey He spent a year in the woods, cutting timber, but in 1899 entered the employ of the Atlantic Refining Co , now a plant of the Standard Oil Company, at La Jose, where he has since remained, being now in charge of the works He belongs to Lodge 574, F & A M at Coalport, to the Consistory at Williamsport and the Shrine at Altoona A Democrat politically, he has held the office of tax collector for six years and for the past four years has been constable of the borough He is also a member of the school board

Mr Gorman married Laura Keirn, who was born in Burnside township, this county, in 1877, a daughter of Daniel Keirn, a farmer Our subject and wife have two children Eveline, aged four years , and Kathleen, aged one year

J B SWOOPE, justice of the peace at Blue Ball, Pa , and proprietor of a general store here, is one of the representative citizens of the place He was born March 26, 1872, in Allegheny county, Pa , and is a son of C G and Margaret E (Stuart) Swoope

During the greater part of his life the father of Mr Swoope was connected with the coke and coal business He was never a politician but he was an intelligent citizen and was identified with the Republican party He married Margaret E Stuart and they had the following children born to them Henry, George, J B , Edward,

Ida May and Allen A The one daughter is the wife of Homer Wolfe and they live in the state of Indiana

J B Swoope was educated in the public schools He then entered the U S Army, becoming a member of Co C, 7th Regulars and served five years and fifty-one days, being in the service during the entire period of the Cuban War For several years afterwards he worked in the mines and then came to Blue Ball, where he conducted a barber shop for seven years On January 10, 1909, he started his present general store and is doing a very satisfactory business

On July 2, 1901, Mr Swoope was married to Miss Minnie B Ammerman, a daughter of Alfred G and Laura P (Senser) Ammerman, of Blue Ball Mr and Mrs Ammerman had the following children William A, Minnie B, George, Myrtle, Leroy and Frank Mr and Mrs Swoope have one daughter, Margaret Eveline In politics, Justice Swoope is a Republican and he has served as school director and in 1907 was elected a justice of the peace He belongs to the P O S of A, at Blue Ball, and to the Odd Fellows at Windber, in Somerset County

JOHN I BLOOM, a highly respected retired farmer of Pike Township, Clearfield County, Pa, owns 165 acres of valuable land on which he was born March 22, 1831 His father was John Bloom and his grandfather was William Bloom, the latter of whom was the founder of this large and prominent family in Clearfield County

John Bloom was born in New Jersey, in January, 1786, and accompanied his father to Center County, Pa, and later to Clearfield County He became a farmer in Center County and was there married to Susanna High, who was born in that county, a daughter of John High, June 7, 1788 After marriage, John Bloom bought this farm of 165 acres, in Pike Township, from Matthew Taylor, of Center County, this land then being included in that county It was entirely undeveloped and so dense was the forest that then covered it that John Bloom was forced to join in with other settlers to make a road through this section of country in order that they might reach Curwensville John Bloom was a man of much enterprise and became a citizen upon whom rested public cares to some degree as his neighbors relied upon his judgment and often sought his advice He was a Democrat in his political views and at one time was tax collector for the whole county His death occurred June 30, 1872 He married as stated above and his widow survived but two years afterward, her death taking place May 26, 1874 Their burial was in the McClure Cemetery. They were members of the Presbyterian church Eleven children were born to John and Susanna Bloom, as follows Mary, who was born September 22, 1806, married Thomas Spackman, and died November 7, 1876, Effie, who was born July 17, 1809, was the wife of Peter Mays, of Knox Township, and died in August, 1900, Katherine, who was born February 22, 1811, died December 1, 1859; Abraham, who was born May 20, 1813, married Elizabeth Kyler and died December 1, 1862; Matthew, who was born May 12, 1816, married Sarah Polhamus and died in June, 1900, Margaret, who was born August 22, 1818, was the wife of George W Robins, and died December 26, 1878; George, who was

JOHN I. BLOOM

born March 2, 1821, married first Hannah Carson, and second, Jennie Replow, and died in February, 1905; David, who was born May 18, 1823, married Mary Sloss, and died September 30, 1897; Sophia, who was born April 8, 1826, died in December, 1906, her first husband being Martin Hoover, and her second, James Leech; Abigail, who was born July 12, 1828, married John B Garrison; and John I Bloom, of Pike Township, the youngest of the family and one of the two survivors

In boyhood, John I Bloom first attended the cross roads school which was near the Price farm, a log building with very primitive accommodations Later he attended the Bloomington school for three winter months He then helped his father and brothers to clear off the land and to place it under cultivation Being the youngest, he remained on the homestead and after his brothers settled on farms of their own and his father grew old, he took over the entire management When he came into full possession he erected the present comfortable and substantial farm buildings The land is all cleared with the exception of forty acres of valuable timber A coal bank on the farm is leased to the Bloomington Coal Mining Company and its output is 400 tons daily Until he retired from active labor, Mr Bloom carried on general farming and was always considered a careful and judicious agriculturist He has practically spent his entire life on this farm During the Civil War he was twice drafted for military service but on both occasions was declined on account of physical disability

Mr Bloom was married August 22, 1854, to Miss Mary Frantz, who was born May 5, 1838, in Clarion County, Pa, a daughter of George Frantz and Eliza (Taylor) Frantz

32

Ten children were born to Mr and Mrs Bloom J Showers, Jefferson, Eliza, Alice, Blake, Lucy, Frank, Annie, Howard and Willard J Showers Bloom was born December 11, 1855 He married Elizabeth McHenry and they had four children Lavada (deceased), Winfield, Alverda, who is the wife of John Shaffer, and Lloyd, who married Pearl Bloom Jefferson Bloom was born July 26, 1857 He married Mary Peterman and they had three children Margaret, who is the wife of Abraham Holden, Grover who married Belle Hart, and Lura, who married Calvin Rowles Eliza Bloom was born June 8, 1860, married C M Bloom, and they have three children Thaddeus, who married Ella Byers, Milford, who married Clara Murphy, and Edna, who lives at home Alice Bloom was born November 17, 1864 and married David Crider Blake Bloom was born June 8, 1866, married Sarah Evans and they have one child, Rossie, who is a school-teacher in Clearfield County Lucy Bloom was born March 29, 1870, and died November 9, 1899 Frank Bloom was born March 30, 1872, married Luella Wise and they have three children Roland, Wilfred and Harold Annie Bloom was born March 9, 1876 and married O B Wise Howard Bloom was born August 2, 1879 and married Della Rowles Willard Bloom was born November 21, 1881, married Emma J Bloom and they have one son, Donald Mr and Mrs Bloom are members of the Presbyterian church He is a Democrat in politics and for sixteen years served in the office of constable He is a member of generation When John Bloom moved first the Bloomington Grange

Mr Bloom is a very entertaining conversationalist, having an excellent memory and a wide acquaintance with the other old families of this section which have also assisted in its development He also recalls much that his father told him and many of these tales of early times possess interest for the present to Clearfield County he settled near the river where a tannery now stands One day a stranger came up the river and visited him with a tale of a valuable silver mine that he and some comrades had discovered in this vicinity, when they had made a hunting trip through this region, twenty years before At that time, he represented, that five hunters had each carried off twenty pounds of silver to their distant homes and all intended to return but he was probably the only one who ever came. After showing John Bloom a piece of the ore he said he had picked up, Mr Bloom consented, for hire, to assist him in finding the location of the mine, which the stranger represented as being between Rock Lick and Peewee's Nest They had no ax with which to blaze their path and thus they lost their way Mr Bloom and the stranger worked over two acres of land but without results and if there ever was a silver mine in that locality it probably is still there Among his father's possessions which Mr Bloom has carefully preserved and one that he treasures highly, is a rifle that undoubtedly is 200 years old It was given to John Bloom by an old pioneer Its present owner has used it, in his earlier years being considered a fine shot and has brought down birds from a great distance

HON. DAVID S HERRON, formerly burgess of DuBois, Pa , and at present city solicitor, is one of the representative men of this borough, to which he came in 1883 He was born at Frankfort, Ky , April 24, 1843, and is a son of James Herron, who went from Pennsylvania to Kentucky and then returned to Indiana County, Pa , where his death occurred

David S Herron was quite young when his parents moved to Indiana County, and he was educated in the public schools and the Ohio State University, and was graduated from that institution with the class of 1865 He then read law in the office of Hon H W Wier, of Indiana, Pa , and was admitted to the bar in 1868, after which he located in Beaver County and continued in the practice of his profession there for two years He then went to St Petersburg, Clarion County and remained there until 1883, when he came to DuBois At that time this borough was in its infancy, as it were, but far-thinking men were even then convinced of its future development and certain importance Mr Herron has been an active and valuable citizen ever since coming here, taking a deep interest in all that has has brought about the general welfare On the Democratic ticket he has frequently been elected to office and has always done his duty whether at the head of municipal affairs or in a minor position He has a large and lucrative practice and maintains his office in the Deposit National Bank Building, and he is a stockholder in the Falls Creek National Bank

On October 19, 1876, Mr. Herron was married to Miss Eva C Dunning, of Buffalo, N Y , and three children have been born to them James G , who is in business at DuBois, and married Lucy Burr. they have three children—Homer, Arthur and Theodosha; Charles S , who is in the drug business at St Mary's, Pa ; and Lafayette Mr Herron is well known as a Free Mason, belonging to the Blue Lodge at Petersburg and the Royal Arch at Kittanning, Pa , Pittsburg Commandery, and Jaffa Temple, Mystic Shrine, at Altoona,

Pa He and his family reside at No 28 Park Avenue, DuBois, Pa

CHARLES OLIVER MATTERN, a prosperous farmer and dairyman, residing on his well improved farm of ninety-five acres, situated in Decatur Township, Clearfield County, Pa , was born on the old homestead farm on which his father still resides, in Decatur Township, July 30, 1872, and is a son of George Perry Greene and Angeline (Conrad) Mattern, and a grandson of Samuel Mattern

Samuel Mattern was born and lived out his life on Spruce Creek, Huntingdon County, Pa , where the family can be traced back for 185 years and a farm there has been in the possession of the Mattern family for 125 years The Matterns are of German and Swiss descent Samuel Mattern was a hatter by trade, was also a merchant and, in association with his son, operated woolen mills He married Mary Elizabeth King, who lived to the age of ninety-six years, while his life span was eighty years They had seven children, namely John W , who is now deceased, was a lawyer in Huntingdon County, William, who is deceased, lived for a time in Clearfield County but subsequently returned to Huntingdon County, George Perry Greene, Catherine, who now lives on Coal Run in Decatur Township, was married first to George Tate and second to John R Martin, Eliza Jane who spent her life on the old homestead, one who died young in Spruce Creek, and Mary Ann, who is the wife of Jeremiah Mattern and they live at Gaysport, Blair County, Pa

George Perry Greene Mattern was born August 6, 1826, on the old family homestead in Huntingdon County and when he grew old enough he learned the hatter's trade and the woolen manufacturing business with his father In 1855, with his brother William he came to Clearfield County where they took up land which was valuable on account of its coal deposits, but they were not able to pay for it and William then went back to Huntingdon County and the younger brother moved to a wild tract in Decatur Township, which was then covered with a heavy growth of timber There was an old abandoned church building on the place which Mr Mattern converted into a residence and he set about clearing his two and one-half acres as speedily as possible Through his persevering industry he prospered and as he gradually added to his land from time to time he became possessed of a farm aggregating 200 acres He married Angeline Conrad, who was of German extraction and was born December 2, 1834, in Huntingdon County Her parents were John and Mary Ann (Stonebreaker) Conrad, the former of whom, a shoemaker by trade, made his home at Franklinville

To George Perry Greene Mattern and his wife the following children were born John Asbury, who is a minister in the Methodist Episcopal church, is located at Martinsburg, in Blair County, George Washington, who resides at Osceola, Mary Elizabeth, who is the wife of Jacob Miller, of Decatur Township, Lidie J who resides with her parents, has been a school teacher for fifteen years, Charles Oliver, and William Luman, who died at the age of fourteen years The mother of the above family is a member of the Methodist Episcopal church For some twenty years George P G Mattern was a justice of the peace as well as school director and during a long period was secretary of the school board The family is a long-lived one and both Mr Mattern and wife retain their physical vigor and mental faculties to a remarkable degree

Charles Oliver Mattern obtained his education in the local schools and Stone Valley Academy, in Huntingdon County He then interested himself in farming and dairying and was in the dairy business for three years at Osceola In March, 1901, he bought the Walter B Morgan farm in Decatur Township, a valuable property which he has improved by remodelling the buildings and making changes that have transformed it into a model dairy farm He is a man of practical knowledge along the line of his business and is deeply interested in everything that contributes to the advancement of agricultural conditions He is a charter member of Moshannon Grange, Patrons of Husbandry, at Philipsburg, and the Odd Fellow Lodge at Osceola Mills

Mr Mattern was married February 14, 1895, to Miss Luella Shipton, who was born at McAlevy's Fort, Huntingdon county, Pa, and is a daughter of J Bilger and Clara (Harman) Shipton After the death of Mrs Shipton, Mr Shipton moved to Philipsburg, where he still resides Mr and Mrs Mattern have four children Clara Lucinda, James Lawrence, Angeline Marks and William Luman They are members of the Methodist Episcopal church In politics Mr Mattern is identified with the Republican party and at present he is serving on the township school board He is numbered with Decatur township's representative men

WILLIAM HARRY THOMSON, mining superintendent and manager of a general supply store at Lee Hollow Mines, was born in Greenwood township, Clearfield county, Pa, July 1, 1872 His father was William Thomson, and his mother in maidenhood Eliza Cary Williams, a daughter of David Williams The Thomson family was established in this country by John Thomson, who came from Scotland, at an early day, settling in Clearfield county, Pa This immigrant ancestor was accompanied by his family, or at least, by his son John, the grandfather of our subject, who married a Miss Lord

William Thomson was born on the old Thomson homestead near Ansonville, this county When nineteen years old he enlisted for service in the Civil War, in the 9th Penn Cavalry, his term being for three years After the war he bought a tract of timber land at Cherry Corner and engaged in lumbering His business career was however, short, for he was cut off at the early age of thirty years, in 1872 He was a member of the Baptist church, and was a Mason, belonging to the lodge at New Washington, Pa, of which he was a charter member He was not active in politics His wife, Eliza, survived him and is now living at Bower, in Greenwood township, at the age of 69 years After Mr Thomson's death she married for her second husband John W Bell, a farmer and lumberman of Greenwood township, who is now deceased Of the first marriage there is now living, in addition to the subject of this sketch, a daughter, Martha Margaret, who is the wife of Dr E S

Corson, of Bridgton, N J One child was born of the second marriage, A₁ T Bell, who is engaged in farming at Bower

William Harry Thomson attended school until reaching the age of 17 years His time was then occupied in farming or in working in the woods or in the saw-mill until he was 20 and he also taught school for two terms He then entered the normal school at Lock Haven, Pa , and after a two years' course was graduated therefrom in 1894 Accepting the position of assistant school principal at Cambria, Pa , he remained there for one year, and subsequently entered the State college, from which he was graduated in 1899 In the following year he accepted a position with the Sterling Coal Company of Cambria county and remained with them two years as assistant superintendent He then came to La Jose, in the spring of 1903, becoming engineer for the Clearfield & Cambria Coal & Coke Company, and was later promoted to the position of superintendent of mines He is also general manager of the New Washington Supply Company, and in both positions has proved his capacity as a good practical business man He is a member of the Baptist church at Ansonville, Pa A Republican in politics, he has served on the school board of the borough He belongs to the Masonic lodge at Clearfield

Mr Thomson was married, October 22, 1903, to Emma Delilah Stephenson, whose father, James Stephenson, now deceased, came to America from Ireland when a boy, settling in Bell township He married Elizabeth Bell, who is also now deceased Mr and Mrs Thomson have been the parents of two children Helen Elizabeth, born May 27, 1906, and Glenn Elton, born Dec 30, 1909

GEORGE S COPELIN, who is agent for the Pennsylvania Railroad Company at Mc-Cartney, Pa , has lived at this place for the past seventeen years, has invested in property and is one of the settled and representative citizens He was born November 19, 1864, in Clearfield county, and is a son of David F and Eliza Jane (Spanogle) Copelin

David F Copelin was born in Mifflin county, Pa , and was a veteran of both the Mexican and Civil wars In the latter he was a member of Co K, 110th Pa Vol Inf He followed lumbering during his active years He married Eliza Jane Spanogle, who was born in Center county, and they had the following children born to them Duke, Perry, Electa, Charles, Miriam, George S , Fannie and Willis

George S Copelin obtained his education in the public schools and the State College, spending two terms in that institution He then learned telegraphing with the New York Central Railroad and has been telegraph agent continuously ever since, in the employ of the Pennsylvania Railroad Company, and stands high in the esteem of its officials with whom he is brought into contact

Mr Copelin was married in November, 1896, to Miss Sarah Straw, a daughter of Henry and Emeline Straw, of Clearfield county Mrs Copelin's father was a lumberman She is one of the following family Merritt, Elmer, David, Bruce, Camelia, Sarah, Alta, Margaret, Theresa, and Ruth The last named is the wife of Robert Barnett Camelia is the wife of County Treasurer William Boyce Mr and Mrs Copelin have had three children David, Harold and Maude Little David died when but three years old

They attend the Presbyterian church and own a nice home at McCartney Mr. Copelin belongs to the Masons at Philipsburg

W H LIDDLE, justice of the peace and prominent citizen of Goshen township, Clearfield county, Pa, was born April 11, 1856, in Brady (now Sandy) township, Clearfield county, and is a son of Andrew and Mary A (Fleming) Liddle, and a grandson of James and Elizabeth (Crawford) Liddle

Andrew Liddle, father of Justice Liddle, was born in Ireland in 1820, but was early left an orphan and during boyhood experienced many vicissitudes In March, 1848, he took passage on a sailing vessel for America and landed at Philadelphia He had worked as a farmer and gardener in his native land and secured employment along these lines with men who owned large estates near Wilmington, Del As soon as he had acquired sufficient capital, he bought fifty acres of land for himself, a partially improved tract situated in Brady (now in Sandy) township, Clearfield county, Pa In 1853 he was married to Mary A Fleming, then a resident of Pittsburg, but a native of County Donegal, Ireland, and in her found a beloved companion and a cheerful and willing helpmate With her assistance he greatly prospered and within ten years comfortable buildings were erected on their farm, which had been gradually increased so to acreage, and the time came when hundreds of acres belonged to this worthy couple, all earned through industry and frugality To them the following children were born Fannie J, James A, William H, John T, John T (2d), Fannie A, Eliza Jane, Mary E, Andrew J, Edwin M, and Samuel C Andrew Liddle and wife were members of the Episco-

pal church at DuBois, Pa. In politics, Mr. Liddle was a Democrat and he was one of the first men in his township to be elected to the office of school director

William H Liddle attended the public schools in Brady township and afterward engaged in teaching school and for fourteen years followed this occupation in which line of endeavor he met with success In 1882 he took a commercial course in a business college, at Lebanon, O, and after his graduation returned to Clearfield county On March 7, 1883, he married Miss Josephine Marsh, who died February 6, 1888, three children were born to this union. Celia and Josephine, now living, and John, who died at the age of 10 years Her parents were Zacheus and Mary Marsh, natives of Dutchess county, New York . On September 29, 1891, Mr. Liddle was married to Miss Gertrude M Read, a daughter of John F Read, of Lawrence township, Clearfield county, Pa , four children have been born to this union. Samuel C and James I, living, and Paul and Evelyn, who died in infancy. In 1894 Mr Liddle entered the business of general merchandise at Spangler, Cambria county, Pa , and continued in the business for three years when he sold out. In 1897 Mr. Liddle purchased his valuable farm of 165 acres, which lies in Goshen township, six miles northeast of Clearfield, and additionally owns forty-six acres of land in Sandy township, which was left him by his late father In politics he is a Democrat and on the ticket of that party has frequently been elected to township offices, and has served as school director and road superintendent and for many years has been a justice of the peace and probably one of the most active officials in this relation, in the township He is interested in everything that particularly concerns this section, belongs to the Farmers' Alliance and Industrial Union, being one of the State officers, one of the leading insurance companies of the county, and almost since its organization has given support to the Grange, or Patrons of Husbandry

DAVID McINTOSH, who for forty years has been in the employ of the DuBois Lumber Company, at DuBois, Pa, and enjoys the distinction of being the oldest man in point of service, on the company's payroll, is a well known and highly respected resident of this borough He was born on his father's farm in Nova Scotia, August 10, 1843, and is a son of John and Elizabeth (Kennedy) McIntosh

John McIntosh was born in Scotland, the second of a large family of children born to William and Catherine (Murdock) McIntosh He was eleven years old when he accompanied his parents from Scotland to Nova Scotia In his native land, William McIntosh had been a road builder He acquired large tracts of virgin land in Nova Scotia and became a man of independent means and owned enough land to enable him to leave each of his children a farm Both he and wife lived into advanced age, her death occurring when she was eighty years old and his, in 1878, when he was over ninety years John McIntosh gave his father assistance in youth and later became a prosperous farmer and lumberman and accumulated a modest fortune in selling lumber for ship building He married Elizabeth Kennedy, who was born in Scotland and had accompanied her parents to Canada in childhood They both lived to be about eighty years of age, spending it in peace and good will to each other and to the community in which they were respected and appreciated They were the parents of eleven children, namely William, Agnes, who is the widow of George Brymer, David, James, Mary, deceased, who was the wife of Isaac McClain, John, Peter and Eliza, both of whom are deceased, Jessie, who follows the profession of a trained nurse, residing at Boston, Mass, and Robert and Clarence

David McIntosh grew to manhood in his native land He attended school during the winter seasons, from early boyhood until he reached maturity, his summers being spent in helping his father and working in the woods at lumbering Mr McIntosh was twenty-six years of age when he decided to come to America and as he had so much knowledge of lumbering he naturally sought to establish himself in a lumber region, and thus came to DuBois, Pa Here he entered the employ of John DuBois, on April 5, 1870, and thus became identified with the concern with which he has been continuously connected ever since His first work was teaming, later he was sent by Mr DuBois to Anderson Creek, where he remained two years working in the saw-mill In 1874 he came back to DuBois and was placed in charge of the woods department of the business Mr McIntosh has been a witness of the development of DuBois from the forest into its present borough conditions Forty years ago its site was all woods and one of the first duties to which he was assigned was the cutting down of trees along the newly built railroad to keep them from falling and obstructing the tracks Many acres of now highly cultivated land in the vicinity of DuBois, was cleared by Mr McIntosh, in those early days His business interests have, as mentioned above, always been with the same firm and in the course of years he has accumulated valuable real estate, mainly situated in the Third ward, DuBois His comfortable residence is situated at No 106 Second avenue

Mr McIntosh was married in October, 1875, to Miss Rosa M McGee, a daughter of William McGee, who was an old settler of Beech Woods They have four children, namely Elizabeth, who is the wife of W C Cooper, of Brewster, O, Robert, a resident of DuBois, who married Rosa Johnston, and they have four children—Helen, Alice, David and Warren, Warren, who is in business at DuBois, married Blanche Thompson, and John, who resides at home Mr. McIntosh, with a true Scotchman's respect for learning, gave his children every educational advantage in his power, their opportunities being far better than his own were, in the little log schoolhouse in far off Nova Scotia Mr McIntosh and family are members of the Presbyterian church He has been an active citizen in the building up and governing of DuBois and for three years was a valuable and judicious member of the borough council In his political views he is a Republican

WILLIAM A GOULD, proprietor of a general store at Brisbin, Pa, in partnership with his brother, Thomas V Gould, has been in the mercantile business at this point for the past twenty-two years, under the firm name of W A Gould & Bro, which firm also operates coal mines Mr Gould came here in 1877, but his native land is Wales, where he was born July 29, 1859 His parents were George and Sarah (Davis) Gould

George Gould brought his family to America in 1864 and located in Bradford county,

Pa, where he became a mine superintendent and worked in the same capacity after moving to Huntingdon county, where he remained until 1873, when he came to Clearfield county. He took charge of the old Moshannon mine in Decatur township At the time of his death, in November, 1900, he was living at Brisbin. His widow still survives and resides at Brisbin, being in her seventy-eighth year To George Gould and his wife eight children were born, five living at present, three dead, namely Mary E, who is the widow of William Rosavear, of Parks City, Utah, and John, William A, Thomas V and George, all residing at Brisbin

William A Gould was about fourteen years of age when the family came to Brisbin During 1875-6 he was a student in the State College, near Bellefonte After he returned home he followed mine work for a short time and then became a clerk in a store at Brisbin and later at Houtzdale, and then entered the employ of the firm of Liveright & Co, with which he continued for seven years Mr. Gould then started into business for himself in partnership with L A Flenner, under the style of Gould & Flenner Some five years later Mr Gould bought his partner's interest and conducted the business alone for some time and then admitted his brother, Thomas V, to partnership, about 1900 This firm operates mines at Brisbin, also in Knox township, and also in Cambria county. Mr Gould is a stockholder and a member of the board of directors of the First National Bank of Osceola He is widely known all through this section and has the deserved reputation of being an upright business man and a useful citizen

In 1896 Mr Gould was married to Miss Martha E Greist, who was born in Adams county and was young when she came to Clearfield county with her parents, Nathan and Lucy Greist, who settled at Osceola Mills Mr and Mrs Gould have one daughter, Sara, who is in school. Mr Gould has been secretary of the school board at Brisbin for nine years, having been elected to this office on the Republican ticket He is a member of the order of Odd Fellows at Brisbin and is prominent in Masonry, belonging to the Blue Lodge at Osceola, the Chapter at Clearfield, the Commandery at Philipsburg, the Consistory at Williamsport and Jaffa Temple, Mystic Shrine, at Altoona

WILLIAM HENRY STRICKLAND, burgess of the borough of Burnside and a prominent citizen of this part of Clearfield county, was born in York county, Pa , November 16, 1842, son of Jacob and Mary Jane (Ault) Strickland. The father, who also was a native of York county, first came to this section with his son, our subject, in 1859, walking from Milesburg to Frenchville, Clearfield county After operating a saw mill for about a year he gave that up to take charge of Judge Lamb's water mill at Deer Creek, which he conducted for two years He subsequently resided at Shawsville for two years, finally removed to Clearfield bridge, later moving to Clearfield, following the trade of shoemaker at that place, until his death, which took place in 1896, when he was 76 years old In politics he was a stanch Republican, and very active for his party He married Mary Jane Ault, who died in 1910 at the age of 93 years She was the daughter of Joseph and Sarah Ault, natives of Lancaster county Jacob Strickland and wife had a large family, and their children now living are as follows

George, who is foreman for a manufacturing concern at Curwensville, Jacob, Jr , who is engaged in farming in Maryland, Mary (twin sister of Jacob), who is the wife of Alexander Flegel, of Ashtola, Pa , Joseph, a hotel proprietor in this county, Emma Jane, who is the widow of Albert Walters, and William Henry, the subject of this sketch

William Henry Strickland, who was the second child of his parents, after completing his school studies, was employed in the saw mill industry with his father, until reaching the age of 18 years In February, 1864, he enlisted for service in the Civil war and remained in the army until the close of the great struggle He was in seventeen different engagements, or rather pitched battles, in General Warren's command, and was slightly wounded at the battle of the Wilderness On August 19, 1864, he was captured by the enemy near the Petersburg & Weldon Railway and sent to Belle Isle prison, where he remained 43 days He was then transferred to Salisbury, N C , where he was kept until his release on March 28, 1865, being then in very bad physical condition from his confinement, insufficiency of food and the general treatment he had received as a prisoner After passing through Atlanta and Augusta, he was sent to Washington, and further was stationed for a short time at Fortress Monroe, being finally mustered out at Harrisburg, Pa , June 23, 1865

On his return from the war Mr Strickland re-engaged in the saw mill business in Clearfield county, remaining two years, and then spending three years in the same business at Forest, Pa He was subsequently engaged in lumbering for nine years at Morgan Run, removing later to Lodgeville, Pa , where he resided ten years From there he went to Sidney, Indiana county, where he remained five years He then came to Clearfield county again and engaged in farming, in which occupation he continued seven years, or until 1894 In that year he entered into the hotel business in Arcadia, Indiana county, but after a two years' experience in this line, took up his residence in Burnside, where he now lives retired from active industrial life A Republican politically and an active worker for his party, he was elected burgess of Burnside in 1908, although the honor was unsolicited and even undesired by him He bowed to the will of his fellow citizens, however, and has made a capable official He has also served as a member of the school board

Mr Strickland was married to Mary Rebecca Carr, who was born in Duncansville, Blair county, Pa , January 18, 1844, a daughter of Alexander and Mary Ann (Hoop) Carr Mrs Strickland's father, who was born in Ireland and came to America when a boy, settled in Cambria county, Pa He subsequently went out as a soldier in the war with Mexico and was killed in battle Mr and Mrs Strickland have been the parents of ten children, of whom there are seven now living—four sons and three daughters

LLOYD C. STEVENS, postmaster at McCartney, Pa , is manager of a general store at this point which is owned by his brother, Blair Stevens Mr. Stevens was born May 2, 1856, and is a son of Henry and Susannah (Beck) Stevens, and a grandson of Vincent Stevens and Davis Beck

Henry Stevens and wife were both natives of Huntingdon county, Pa He was a shoemaker by trade and later was also interested in farming During the Civil War he organized and served as captain of Co E, 45th Pa Vol. Inf He married Susannah Beck and both are now deceased, their burial being at Lutheran cemetery, Center Line, Center county They had the following children John, who is deceased; Blair, who is a merchant at Kerrmoor, Martha, who is the wife of Charles Blake; Frank, Lloyd C , George, Anna, who is the wife of Emory Stover, and Vincent, James, Abednego and Charles

Lloyd C Stevens attended the public schools and had two terms of academic training in an institution conducted by the Society of Friends before one term at the Warrior's Mark Academy, after which he taught school for five terms, four in Center county, and one in Blair county. In 1882 with his brother, Frank Stevens, he came to Clearfield, Pa , and they went into the farm implement business there and he remained in that place until 1892 when he came to McCartney where he is one of the leading citizens. He was appointed postmaster during the period when Hon John Wanamaker was postmaster-general

Mr Stevens married Miss Jennie E Confer, of Tyrone, a daughter of David M. and Anna M (Wisegarber) Confer, natives of Bedford county, Pa Mr Confer was a railroad man and met with an accidental death while at the post of duty Mrs Stevens is the third born in a family of seven children, as follows· Anna, who is the widow of J. D Lucas, Leonora, Jennie E, Mrs Stevens, Ella, who is the wife of Garvey Donaldson, Ida R , who is the wife of William Gingery, Samuel Harry Blair, and Margaret,

who is the wife of William H Huss Mr
and Mrs Stevens attend the Presbyterian
church at McCartney, but he is a member
of the Methodist Episcopal church at Ansonville, and she of the United Brethren
church at Tyrone In politics Mr Stevens
is a Republican and formerly served as
auditor of Jordan township and as treasurer for one term, while at present he is a
justice of the peace

IRA F TATE, a representative citizen
and general farmer of Goshen township,
Clearfield county, Pa, where he owns
ninety-six acres of valuable land, was born
in this township, May 23, 1868, and is a son
of Matthew and Jane (Mead) Tate

Matthew Tate was born on Clover Hill,
near Clearfield, and he purchased a part of
the farm now owned by his son Ira F, prior
to his marriage and erected several of the
buildings which now stand He was a
farmer all through his years of strength and
activity, and continued to reside on this
farm until his death, which occurred in his
seventy-ninth year He was a man of sterling character, a member of the Methodist
Episcopal church, a just neighbor and a
broad-minded citizen For a number of
years he was identified with the Goshen
Grange He married Jane Mead, who was
born in Elk county, and who died at about
seventy-six years of age They had the following children; Margaret, who is now deceased, Elizabeth, who is the wife of William Lutz, Rachel, Allen, Emma, Mary,
Samuel J and Ada, all of whom are now deceased, Bertha, who is the wife of George
Fulton, and Edith and Ira F

Ira F Tate grew to manhood on the
home farm and obtained a public school
education in Goshen township. His business interests have been almost entirely
agricultural and he has resided both before
and since his marriage on the farm on which
he was born He has all of his land under
cultivation, with the exception of forty
acres still in woodland He is a wide awake,
progressive farmer, a member of the Goshen Grange, and is numbered with the
township's prosperous agriculturists

Mr Tate married Miss Sarah Morrison, a daughter of George Morrison,
a resident of Goshen township, and they
have one daughter, Elma, who is yet a student Mr Tate and family are members of
the Methodist Episcopal church In politics
he is a Republican, but takes no active part
in public affairs although, when occasion
arises for him to express his opinion, his
fellow citizens never fail to understand his
attitude. He believes in good government,
good schools and good roads

EDWARD FOWLER, proprietor of a
blacksmith shop and owner of a comfortable residence and sixteen acres of cultivated land, on the outskirts of Madera, Pa,
was born in February, 1864, in Clearfield
county, and is a son of Ephraim and Rachel
(Davis) Fowler

Both parents of Mr Fowler were natives
of Pennsylvania, the father of Wayne
county and the mother of Luzerne county
Ephraim Fowler spent his life mainly as a
woodsman He voted with the Democratic
party but never desired to hold any public
office The four children born to Ephraim

Fowler and wife were. Lewis, Edward, Ella, wife of Walter Kipp, and Tabitha, wife of Henry Schuyler

Edward Fowler attended school in his boyhood and afterward was variously employed until the spring of 1886, when he learned the blacksmith trade in a shop at Holly, in Wayne county For the last twenty-one years he has lived at Madera and has built up an excellent business

In 1891 Mr Fowler was married to Miss Edith Hill, a daughter of George W Hill, who was a native of New York Mrs Fowler is the youngest of a family of seven children, namely. Matilda, William, Amanda, Levi, Ashley, Mary and Edith To Mr and Mrs Fowler the following children were born Joseph A and George W, both of whom are manly and industrious young men who assist their father in the shop, and Angie, Kittie, Dewey, Lewis, Agnes and Theodore Roosevelt Perhaps it is unnecessary to state that Mr Fowler is a stanch Republican He is a stockholder in the Madera National Bank

JOSEPH JOHNSON, a well known business man of Clearfield County, who has been a resident of DuBois, Pa, since 1881, is a successful coal operator and one of the proprietors of the Rochester Coal Company, in Sandy Township and has additional interests He was born May 4, 1860, in Huntingdon County, Pa, and is a son of Thomas and Rose (McGlone) Johnson

Thomas Johnson was born in County Meath, Ireland, and when sixteen years old came to America, the only member of his family He stopped for short seasons in New York, Maryland and Virginia before he reached Pennsyl-vania, when he settled in Huntingdon County and from there, in 1882, came to DuBois, which was then a very small place He was a man of considerable enterprise as he opened up a quarry soon after locating here and later purchased another quarry from McCullough & Reed, and also was one of the pioneer coal mine operators He was well known all through this section and had many friends His death occurred in June, 1904, at the age of eighty-two years He was married in Maryland to Rose McGlone, who died in her fifty-fifth year They were the parents of twelve children, the three survivors of the family being Mary, who is the wife of Samuel Witt, Joseph, and Patrick J

Joseph Johnson had but meager educational advantages, as he began to work in the coal mines when he was quite young and mining has been his main business ever since As he grew older he took charge of his father's interests and when the latter died, Mr Johnson and his brother, Patrick J, associated themselves together and continued the business In 1907 Joseph Johnson, Patrick J Johnson and Thomas Kurens leased the old Rochester mines in Sandy Township, which they are developing, they having proved a profitable investment The two Johnsons are also operating the Jack McNamarrow stone quarry, which was opened in 1878 (Johnson Bros now own it), and they, with F P Cummings, are engaged in the sewer and brick pavement contracting business Mr Johnson owns his substantial residence at No 25 N Main Street, DuBois and has other real estate in the borough and also in Sandy Township

In January, 1907, Mr Johnson was married to Miss Ella Kurens and they have one child, Francis Joseph, born April 11, 1910 They

Brady Street Roller Mills, DuBois
Manley B. Goff and R. L. Hunter, proprietors

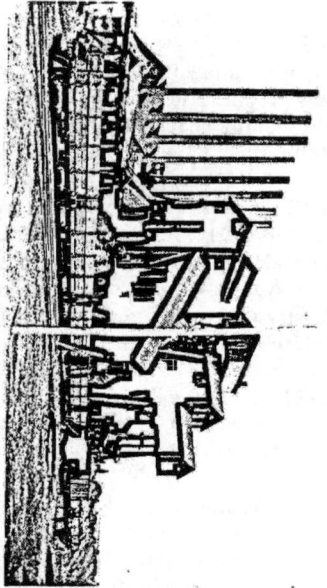

Morrisdale Coal Mining Co.'s Plant

Old Pottery Plant of Joseph Seyler at Luthersburg

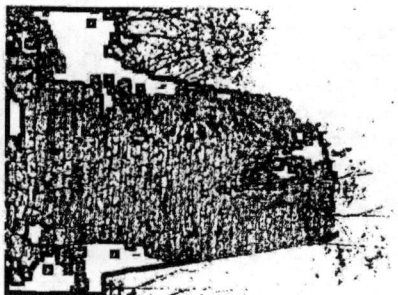

Remains of First Iron Furnace in Central Pennsylvania,
Peter Karthaus, 1817, at Karthaus

are members of St Catherine's Catholic Church Politically he is a Democrat and fraternally he is identified with the A O H

M J GILMARTIN, assistant superintendent of the Buffalo & Susquehanna Railroad, has been a resident of DuBois, Pa , since 1905 and has identified himself with the best interests of the place He was born at Driftwood, Pa , February 6, 1877, and is a son of Thomas and Catherine (Nagle) Gilmartin

Thomas Gilmartin, whose death occurred in 1905, at the age of seventy-eight years, was one of the old and trusted employes of the Pennsylvania Railroad Company, which he had served in various capacities He married Catherine Nagle and they had five children, namely John, Mary, Winnifred, William and Mark James

Mark James Gilmartin attended the public schools of Driftwood and Sterling Run, Pa , and when seventeen years of age became an employe of the Pennsylvania Railroad Company as a section hand He later was made a brakeman and was with the B & S Railroad at Austin, Pa , in 1897 He kept on upward, gaining promotion every few years, becoming freight conductor and then passenger conductor, and came to DuBois in that capacity in 1905 It is the wise policy of the railroad to thoroughly train every employe before advancing him and thus a promotion carries with it an assurance of efficiency In April, 1908, Mr Gilmartin was made assistant superintendent, succeeding G H Crissman He is a well-informed, practical railroad man, and the end of his railroad career is not yet

Mr Gilmartin was married in July, 1902, to Miss Harriet Pouliat and they have one daughter, Alice They are members of the Roman Catholic church of St Catherines, at DuBois, and Mr Gilmartin belongs to the Knights of Columbus Politically he is a Democrat The family residence is No 122 Park Avenue, DuBois

DANIEL W HOOVER, a practical miller, having charge of the A McCardell mill in Burnside township, was born in Bradford township, this county, May 14, 1848 His parents were Abraham and Margaret (Murray) Hoover, and he is a grandson of Jacob Hoover, who settled in Clearfield county early in the 19th century Abraham, who was a farmer, died in 1865 at the age of 64 years, and Jacob died, aged 84 years

Abraham Hoover was born in Clearfield county, March 4, 1881 In early manhood he was engaged in lumbering, but later bought land and cleared a farm, being assisted in this labor by his sons He had lost his mother when ten years old, at which time —in 1831—the father, Jacob, with his family had located in Graham township He married Margaret Murray, who was born in 1825 and who died in 1902 Their family numbered twelve children, of whom ten are now living, as follows Alfred, a wagon maker, residing in Illinois, Melinda, widow of D Houser, Warren, a miner at Morrisdale, Pa , John, who is a coal operator in West Virginia, Jasper, residing in Iowa, Nelson, who is a contracting carpenter in Oregon, Florence, wife of Dr Maines, Louisa, wife of John Baer of Pittsburg, Frank, a veterinary surgeon of Davis, Ill , and Daniel W , the subject of this sketch

Abraham Hoover was a member of the United Brethren church In politics he was a Democrat and held many local offices

Daniel W Hoover, after attending school till the age of fifteen, became connected with the lumber industry, at which he worked during the winters, while he took up the milling trade as a summer occupation, being thus engaged in his native county for four years He then followed the miller's trade in Cambria county for a year and a half, after which, returning to Clearfield county, he was engaged in milling at Cherry Tree for five years He came to Burnside in 1882 and for fifteen years thereafter remained with the H Patchin family as mill operator In 1894 he went to New Jersey, where he was engaged in the milling business for two years Then returning to Pennsylvania, he bought a mill at Garman's Mills, Cambria county, and was located there for three years, being also engaged in the hotel business He also carried on the latter business at Barnesboro, Pa , for two years He then came to Burnside, Clearfield county, to take charge of the A McCardell mill, and has continued thus engaged up to the present time He belongs to the I O O F lodge at Burnside and in politics is a Democrat He has served as borough treasurer two terms and has also been a member of the school board

Mr Hoover was married in 1874 to Mary Ellen Phoenix, who was born in Clearfield county, Pa , April 10, 1854, a daughter of William Phoenix Her mother's maiden name was Armstrong, and both her parents were natives of this county Mr and Mrs Hoover have been the parents of six children. William W , who is a fireman,

married Minnie Barrett and has four children, Fannie is the wife of Henry Plouse of Glen Campbell, and has four children, Anna is the wife of Ed Clark, civil engineer, residing at Greensburg, Pa , Alice is the wife of John Farr, of Greensburg, and the mother of two children, Guy is a telephone operator in West Virginia, Frank C is a resident of Hilewood, Pa

I W COWEN, who is engaged in the livery business at Madera, Pa , where he is a substantial citizen and leading business man, was born, June 4, 1861, in Becarria township, Clearfield county, Pa , and is a son of James and Rachel (Warrick) Cowen

James Cowen was one of the early volunteers from Clearfield county to enter the Federal Army for service in the Civil War, in which he lost his life at the battle of Chancellorsville His widow subsequently married William Riddle To her first marriage but one son, I W Cowen, was born, and to the second was one son, John D Riddle

I W Cowen was a babe of but nine months when his father fell on the battle field He first attended the country schools, but, as a soldier's son, being entitled to the advantages offered at the Soldiers' Orphans' Home in Huntingdon county, he was placed there and remained there until he was thirteen years of age He then went to work to take care of himself, entering the employ of Flynn Brothers, in the lumber business, and remained with that firm for thirteen years, which fact may be recognized as a pretty fair testimonial of the character of this soldier's son He then bought a farm in Bigler township, Clearfield county, and resided on it for three years, when he sold and bought his residence and other real estate at Madera

Mr Cowen was married first to Miss Lydia Kingston, by Rev C A Biddle, a minister of the Methodist Episcopal church She died August 23, 1898, leaving one daughter, Roby Mr Cowen was married second, April 7, 1903, to Miss Matilda Luther, a daughter of William and Eliza Luther, of Clearfield county They attend the Presbyterian church In politics Mr Cowen is a Republican and has frequently been the choice of his party for township offices, serving nine years as auditor of Bigler township, two years as tax collector of Gulich township, two years as judge of elections of Bigler township and at present is a member of the board of supervisors He belongs to the order of Odd Fellows at Houtzdale and is also identified with the Red Men and the P O S of A

S M BICKFORD, one of the leading business citizens of Curwensville, Pa, is secretary, assistant manager and assistant treasurer of the Bickford Fire Brick Company, and is also identified with other large enterprises of this city Mr Bickford was born at Lock Haven, Clinton county, Pa, the third of the twelve children born to J A and Sarah (Bruner) Bickford

Mr Bickford obtained his education in the local schools and early in life started in on a business career He became associated with the Bickford Fire Brick Company, of which his father, J A Bickford, is the general manager and treasurer, and this firm in December, 1907, bought the plant of the Curwensville Fire Brick Company

Since that date the capacity of the plant has been doubled, it now averaging 100,000 brick per day and employing 400 men The plant, which is 560x100 feet in size, is the largest fire brick plant under one roof in the country, and the company receives its raw material from nearby land by the tram-road from its own 1,157 acres of fire clay land and 385 acres of coal land The company uses about 100 tons of coal daily Mr Bickford is also connected with Arch Davidson of Curwensville and Dr Woodside of Lumber City in the Bickford Store Company and the Bickford Meat Market, both of Curwensville

Mr Bickford was married to Estelle Bowes, the daughter of W T Bowes, of Lock Haven, Pa, and to this union there has been born one child, S M Bickford, Jr The pleasant Bickford residence is situated on State Street, opposite the B R & P Ry depot

HON GEORGE A KNARR, who is engaged in a general mercantile business at Troutville, Pa, and is serving in the highest borough office, being chief burgess, is one of the leading men of this section and is a worthy representative of one of the old pioneer families of Clearfield county He was born March 15, 1869, at Troutville, and is a son of George L and Elizabeth (Zilhox) Knarr

The founder of the Knarr family in Clearfield county was George Knoerr, according to the German orthography, and he was born in Bavaria, Germany, and in 1831 came to America, accompanied by his family. He took up 200 acre of government land in Brady township, between Troutville and

Luthersburg, and continued to live there until the close of his life, dying at the advanced age of ninety-two years. His wife, Louisa, died before him. They had six children Henry, Andrew, George, Adam (all long since deceased), Charlotte, who was the wife of Christian Haag (both deceased), and Caroline, who resides at Du-Bois, Pa, and is the widow of Andrew Weaver.

Henry Knarr, the grandfather of George A, was eighteen years of age when the family reached Clearfield county. He bought 100 acres of land near Luthersburg, for three dollars an acre, and to this first purchase later added more land and continued to live there during the rest of his life, his death occurring in 1886, when he was aged seventy-three years. In 1843 he married Catherine Marshall, who was also born in Germany, and she died at Troutville in 1898, at the age of seventy-two years. To Henry and Catherine Knarr seventeen children were born, their names being recorded as follows George L, Caroline, Simon, David, Loraina, Henry S, Reuben, William, Fred, Adam, Mary, Samuel A, Ferdinand, Catherine, Louise, and two who died in infancy.

George L Knarr was born on the old Knarr homestead, May 25, 1846, and was reared there and helped to clear off a large part of the brush and timber, but later learned the shoemaking trade, which he followed at Grampian and later at Troutville. He built up a large shoe business after factories commenced to turn out shoes in such numbers that hand-made shoes were not in such great demand, and gradually added other goods to his stock until he found himself a general merchant and doing well. He conducted this business from 1876 until shortly before his death, December 31, 1910, and was always known as a man of business honor and the strictest personal integrity. He was a Democrat and loyally supported his party's candidates, and was active in the fraternal order of Knights of Pythias. With his wife he belonged to the Lutheran church.

George L Knarr was married first in 1867 to Elizabeth Zilliox, who was born in Brady township and died here leaving three children, George Adam, Mary Emma, who is the wife of J E Rishel, and Sarah Annie, who died at the age of two months, August 22, 1874. The mother of these children died June 27, 1874, aged 24 years, 6 months and 24 days. The second marriage of George L Knarr was to Annis B Johnson, who survives him.

George Adam Knarr attended school at Troutville until his father considered him old enough to be entrusted with duties in the store and he helped his father as a clerk until he was seventeen years old, when he began to carry the mail between Troutville and Luthersburg, this being prior to the construction of the B R & P line from DuBois to Punxsutawney. He is still carrying mail, his route now being from Troutville to Skyesville, and his present term will expire in July, 1913. He has been otherwise interested, for twelve years being secretary of the Troutville branch of the German National Building and Loan Association, of Pittsburg, and for five years secretary of this branch for the Jamestown Building and Loan Association. He is a stockholder in the Citizens' Building and Loan Association at DuBois, and has been interested there since 1889 Mr Knarr is also a stockholder in the Deposit National Bank at DuBois

In December, 1893, Mr Knarr was married to Miss Florence Margaret Weber, a daughter of J F Weber, of Skyesville, and they have one son, Carroll B, who was born July 19, 1896

Shortly before the death of his father, Mr Knarr succeeded to the mercantile business he had founded and the son also bought the homestead farm of eighty-seven acres, which is situated near Troutville He has been a very active citizen and enjoys the confidence of his fellow citizens to such a degree that they have frequently sought him to accept public office For several years he has served as tax collector and in 1910 was made burgess of Troutville borough, and has administered public affairs with the same careful attention that he has ever devoted to his own He is a member of the Knights of Pythias at Troutville, and is a past grand of Mingle Lodge No 753, I O O F, same place In politics he is a stanch Democrat

M. F. SHIMEL, one of the busy and substantial business men of Boggs township, who owns 120 acres of excellent land here, is also the proprietor and operator of a chop and shingle mill at Wallaceton, Pa He was born in Boggs township, May 11, 1861, and is the fourth child of G W and Margaret (Shaw) Shimel

G W Shimel, father of M F, was born in Clearfield county, a son of G W Shimel He was a carpenter by trade and also engaged in farming in Boggs township for

many years He married Margaret Shaw, who was also born in Clearfield county, and their children were Alice (deceased), D D, N J, M F, C W, I G, and L L, all prosperous business men, and Alice (2d), who is the wife of Harry Peters The parents of this family were members of the Church of God

M F Shimel obtained his education in the common schools, after which he learned the carpenter's trade and to some degree he has followed it all his life, together with saw-mill work For ten years before he purchased his mill at Wallacetown he operated it on rental, but in 1907 he bought the mill and with the assistance of his sons he has operated it to great advantage ever since He owns twenty acres in the home farm and 100 acres in a second farm, both tracts lying in Boggs township

Mr Shimel was married in 1884, to Miss Susan Kephart, a daughter of Benjamin F and Jane (Geargart) Kephart, early families in Clearfield county Mrs Shimel was the fifth born in the following family Jessie, William P, Edward, Pauline, deceased, who was the wife of Ellis Smeal, Cornelia, deceased, who was the wife of Samuel Ritchey, Mary, who is the wife of Abraham Wisor, and Susan Mr and Mrs Shimel have the following children Ellsworth, Berva, Homer, Beulah, Eva, Willard, Wesley, Esther and Clyde The eldest daughter is the wife of Henry Willett Mr Shimel and family are members of the Church of God With his sons Mr Shimel casts his vote with the Prohibition party

GRANT CATHCART, a well known citizen and successful agriculturist of Knox

33

township, Clearfield county, Pa, owns a valuable property containing 110 acres, which is situated one mile east of Olanta, Pa, near Turkey Hill He was born February 8, 1868, on this farm which is part of the old homestead, and is a son of James Cathcart

James Cathcart was long a prominent citizen of Knox township He was born near Glen Hope, Clearfield county, in 1829, and died July 27, 1884, at the age of fifty-five years His was the first funeral in Mt Zion cemetery, which tract of land he had donated to the Mt Zion Methodist Episcopal church James Cathcart came to Knox township with his parents and spent his life on this farm, clearing the land and erecting substantial buildings which still stand He acquired a large amount of property, at one time owning 600 acres in Clearfield county, 300 of which are yet owned by his family. He was a loyal supporter of the Union cause during the War of the Rebellion, and broke down his former robust health through three years of army service He was a member of Co F, 100th Pa Vol Inf, the famous "Roundheads" After he returned to Knox township his subsequent life was spent in farming, lumbering and rafting In politics he was a Republican and the only fraternal organization with which he was connected was the Grange

James Cathcart married Rachel Flegal, who was born at Morrisdale, Pa, and whose death occurred March 8, 1911 Nine children were born to them, of whom four survive, namely D W, of Altoona; W W, and Grant, both of Knox township, and Cora, who married a Mr Shelow

Grant Cathcart obtained his education in his native township, mainly at the Turkey Hill school, and afterward became his father's assistant on the home farm, where he has always lived with the exception of two years following his marriage, when he resided at Glen Hope He carries on general farming and stockraising, and is surrounded with all the comforts and conveniences which, in these modern days, make country life the most desirable and independent of all

In 1892 Mr Cathcart was married to Miss Catherine Noel, a daughter of John and Josephine Noel, of Belsena Mills, and they have ten children, namely James W, Vindetta, Hazel, Harry, Della, Helen, Charles, Paul Lewis, Elvin and Evelyn Mr Cathcart and family attend the Methodist Episcopal church In politics he is an Independent Republican, being a man who does his own thinking, and he has never consented to hold any township office He is an interested member of the Grange, Patrons of Husbandry

AARON NELSON WORK, contractor and builder, doing a large business in this line at DuBois, Pa, has been a resident here since 1894 He was born June 26, 1867, in Indiana county, Pa, and is a son of Aaron and Elizabeth (Spencer) Work

Aaron Work was a son of John Work and he came to Indiana county with his parents in his youth He acquired a farm along a water course but preferred to work as a barn builder and it is said that even after he was eighty years of age he might often be found working on a barn roof His death occurred in 1891, when eighty-six years of age His first wife, Nancy (Smith) Work, died in Indiana county, the mother of ten children, two of whom survive, Robert H and Polly. Aaron Work was married secondly to Elizabeth Spencer, a native of Indiana county, and eight children were born to them: Demosthenes, George, Aaron, Nelson, Alexander, Thomas B and three daughters who died young

Aaron Nelson Work spent his boyhood on the home farm in Canoe township, Indiana county, not far from Richmond, Pa, and until he was fourteen years of age attended the little red schoolhouse near his home. He then began to help his father in the latter's saw-mill and in barn building and thus gained much practical knowledge that he put to good use afterward. In 1894 Mr Work left Indiana county and moved with his family to DuBois, where he entered into the employ of John E DuBois as a carpenter, and remained as such for three years, after which he superintended the construction of several of the largest business houses in the place—the D L Corbett dry goods store, working under A Dorner, Hotel DuBois, working for the hotel company. In 1900 he began contracting for himself and has met with more than ordinary success along this line. In fact he has been actively interested in the construction of the leading business structures, schoolhouses and churches, and among the many fine buildings in this borough may be mentioned the following as examples: Commercial Hotel, Central Y M C A, Presbyterian Parsonage, Senor building, Robinson Furniture Company building, Lowe building, Power and Electric plant, B & S Shaft No 2, Friendship Hose House, in the First Ward, and the Cannon and other residences. He built the stately private residence of A Gocellis, at Falls Creek, which cost $35,000, and the Normal School building at Dayton, Pa. He is a large employer of skilled labor and his men work under the best industrial conditions. He furnishes estimates on any department of building and his facilities are such that he is able to suit all tastes and purses. He is vice president of the Falls Creek Planing Mill, which was established in 1904, with Mr McHarl as president. He maintains his office at his residence, No 314 E Webber Street, DuBois

In 1888 Mr Work was married to Miss Zelda Colkitt, a daughter of John and Mary (Hoover) Colkitt, and they have three children: Wilburg, Nora J and Emma D. Mr Work is a member of the United Presbyterian church. He is very active in the cause of temperance and is chairman of the Prohibition party at DuBois. He is a director in the Y M C A and also is a director in the Citizens' Loan Association

JAMES W McGEE, proprietor of the McGee lumber mill in Bell township, was born on the old McGee homestead in this township, May 6, 1846, son of Thomas A and Mary (Holmes) McGee. He is a grandson of the Rev James McGee, who with his wife, whose name in maidenhood was Mary Barnhart, came to this section from Center county in 1826. James McGee was the first postmaster at McGee's Mills, when the first mail route was established between Curwensville and Indiana in 1833 and the postoffice has been conducted by one member of the family or another ever since. The first grist mill in this locality was built by Thomas A McGee, and the McGees were charter members in 1860 of the pioneer M E church in Bell township. When Troutdale Grange, No 677, was organized in 1876, H McGee was its first secretary, all of which shows that the family have taken an active and leading part in local affairs ever since their first settlement here in the first half of the 19th century

Thomas A McGee, father of our subject, was born in Center county, Pa His wife, Mary, was the daughter of John and Mary (Atkinson) Holmes Their family included three other children besides James, namely William, who is engaged in the lumber business in California, Henry H, who is a farmer and lumberman residing in Bell township, and Susannah, who is the wife of W T Mahaffey, of Clearfield, Pa

James W McGee, after his school studies were over, became connected with the lumber industry, working for his father, and he has since continued in the business, operating timber lands in this section For the past fifteen years also he has been interested in timber lands in the South He has enjoyed a gratifying degree of prosperity and is numbered among the prosperous citizens of his township He is well advanced in the Masonic order, belonging to the lodge at Curwensville, the Chapter at Clearfield, Bellfonte Commandery, and the Shrine at Pittsburg

He was married to Esther E McGee, of Indiana county, Pa, who was born February 2, 1850, at Homer City, that county, daughter of Robert McGee Mr and Mrs McGee are the parents of children as follows Isabella, is the wife of Charles Sprenkle of Kane, Pa, and has five children, William is a bookkeeper residing in Philadelphia and is married, Margaret is the wife of Z McFarland, of Clearfield county, and has two children, Roger K, is a civil engineer residing in Pittsburg, Helen S is a school teacher at Hastings, Pa, Ruth is attending the normal school at Indiana, Pa, Walter resides at home

Mr McGee is a Democrat politically and an active worker for his party He has served on the school board and in other offices When a young man he had some experience on the river and on one occasion conducted a raft down the river to Lock Haven without assistance, he being the entire crew He has always shown himself a man of activity and resource and is universally recognized as one of the useful citizens of the township

FRANK SMITH, one of Lawrence township's busy, enterprising and successful men, is in the lumber and saw mill business, owning a portable mill and leasing large tracts of land for his purposes He was born December 20, 1869, in Girard township, Clearfield county, Pa, and is a son of Isaac and Fanny Smith

The father of Mr Smith was a man of considerable prominence in Clearfield county, serving many years as a justice of the peace and as secretary of the township school board, and at the time of his death, in January, 1905, owned 800 acres of land, the timber on which is worth $8,000, many hundred acres also being rich in coal deposits His widow survives and resides on the home farm in Girard township

Frank Smith obtained a public school education in Girard township and then went into the lumbering business, in fact has been interested in this industry from boyhood, having begun by cutting, hauling, and rafting timber to be taken to market via the Susquehanna river He followed this business going down the river each year for eighteen successive years, spending the summers in the bark woods, always working by contract where possible

In 1893 Mr Smith purchased 300 acres of timber land lying along the West Branch of the Susquehanna river and spent several years in profitably clearing same and in 1908 sold the land to Isaac Stage of Clearfield, Pa In 1897 he bought one hundred acres of land in West Keating township, Clinton county When this was cleared he sold, in 1910, to James McGonigal He has some 750 acres of timber land under lease at the present time, keeps three of his own teams at work and gives constant employment to from five to twelve men For two years after his marriage he resided at Clearfield, where he built a residence and a store and engaged in business as a merchant He then sold the store to E L Shirey and resumed his lumbering interests, first in Bradford township, then in Graham township and later in Lawrence township Before coming to this section he had already cut more than 2,500 acres of land Mr Smith is a practical lumber man and his advice is worth taking concerning everything pertaining to this industry In 1909 Mr Smith purchased 124 acres of coal land in Boggs township, which promises to be profitable when developed

Mr Smith married Miss Ora Holt, a daughter of Reuben and Margaret (Forcey) Holt, and they have one son, Leslie Clair In politics he is a Republican He is a member of the Clearfield lodge of Odd Fellows

ISAAC BEISH, who is one of the best known residents of Boggs township, where he has lived since he was three years old, is also one of the most substantial, being the owner of 235 acres of valuable land here He was born in Bradford county, Pa, May 7, 1844, and is a son of John and Rachel (Lyons) Beish

John Beish was a very enterprising business man and was well enough educated to be a successful school teacher for a number of years and to administer in the office of a justice of the peace, in Clearfield county, for thirty years He also was a lumberman, a farmer, and proprietor of a hotel He married Rachel Lyons and they had the following children born to them Orrila, Isaac, J J, Emma, and Mary Emma married Harry Butler, and Mary married John Bumbarger

Isaac Beish obtained his education in the country schools, in reading, and in association with others, and is a well informed man and one whose judgment is relied on by his fellow citizens They have elected him, on the Democratic ticket to numerous township offices and at present he is serving as school director and as tax collector, and has also been township supervisor His business interests have always been along the lines of farming and lumbering

In 1867 Mr Beish was married to Miss Ellen Jane Bennehoof, who died in 1900, her burial being in the Bigler cemetery, in Bradford township To Mr and Mrs Beish the following children were born John, Isaac, Lenora, who is deceased, Emma, who is the wife of Ellsworth Ruffner, Lavina, who is the wife of James Twoey, William Clara, who is the wife of Harvey Knepp, and Howard and Rhoda Mr Beish is interested in several fraternal organizations, belonging to the Knights of Pythias and the Jr O U A M, and is also a member of the Grange

WILLIAM M CATHCART, one of Clearfield County's most highly respected retired farmers and substantial citizens, resides on the line separating Knox and Pike Townships and is one of the largest landowners in this section In addition to 312 acres lying in Knox Township and a one-half interest in 100 acres more in that township, he owns 160 acres lying partly in Knox and partly in Pike Township Mr Cathcart was born at Ansonville, Clearfield County, Pa, February 24, 1827, and is a son of David J and Keziah (Wilson) Cathcart

David J Cathcart was born in Ireland but from the age of twelve years spent his life in Clearfield County, Pa When he reached manhood he married Keziah Wilson, who was born in New Jersey, and nine children were born to them, namely Eliza Ann, William M, James, Martha, Mary, Ellen, Amelia, Sarah and Wilson After marriage David J Cathcart and wife located at Ansonville, where he engaged in farming, shoemaking and teaching school Later he acquired a farm of 312 acres in Knox Township, the same now owned by his son, William M, and lived on this place until his death, at the age of seventy-seven years and his burial was in private grounds on his own place His wife lived only to be fifty-five years of age and her burial was in the same place They were members of the Methodist Episcopal church On account of an injury to his knee, Mr Cathcart did not succeed in clearing more than thirty acres of his land

William M Cathcart remembers his early school days at Glen Hope, when logs roughly hewn served as seats in the primitive cabin where he learned his first lessons He was twelve years old before he ever saw a real school house, at Turkey Hill, where he attended one month His opportunities were meager, as his services were needed on the farm in the summers and in the woods, getting out timber, in the winters After his first marriage he settled on a part of the homestead farm and made use of the buildings then standing, but these were later destroyed by fire and he erected new ones In 1885 he moved to Olanta but continued to partially look after his farm interests, although his son, Edward Cathcart, was the general manager of the farm industries Mr Cathcart sold some land adjacent to Olanta, two acres to a coal company, which has been divided into lots and improved, one acre to John Otter, two acres to Charles Norman and one and three-quarter acres to a company at the mines, contracting in the sale of this land that only reputable people shall be admitted as residents, in this way insuring a first class citizenship Mr Cathcart has leased an open coal bank on his farm to the firm of Brown, Snyder & Co He has had other interests, at one time owning 160 acres of land in California, which he sold, and both he and wife are stockholders in the Curwensville National Bank

Mr Cathcart was married first to Martha Jane Read, in June 1859, a daughter of Ross Read, formerly of Lawrence Township She died in May, 1893, and her burial was at Mt Zion Cemetery in Knox Township She was a member of the Presbyterian church The five children born to this marriage were as follows Edward who is now deceased, married Alice Ferguson, and three of their children survive, Edith Ann, who died at the age of eight years, Mary Alice, who died at the age of four years, Emma Olive, who died aged six-

WILLIAM M. CATHCART

teen years, and Harry Allen, who is now associated with his father, relieving him of many responsibilities, resides in Pike Township He married Rhoda Norris and they have three living children In August, 1897, Mr Cathcart was married to Miss Rebecca Dunlap, a daughter of John and Martha (Read) Dunlap Mr and Mrs Cathcart are members of the Lutheran church at Olanta In politics he is a Republican but has never consented to accept any office of a public nature

JACOB W CORP, who is engaged in the butchering business and also owns eighty acres of farm land situated one mile east of Luthersburg, in Brady township, Clearfield county, Pa , is one of the representative citizens of this township, of which he has been clerk for the past thirty years He was born in Brady township, in 1839, and is a son of Henry and Mary Corp, natives of Germany

In 1837 the parents of Mr Corp came to America and located near Luthersburg, on what is now the Knarr stock farm, having five children at that time, three more being subsequently born to them The family record is as follows Henry W and Frederick, both of whom are deceased, Elizabeth, deceased who was the wife of Henry L Weaver, also deceased, Adam and Lavina, both of whom are deceased, the latter having been the wife of John W Owens, also deceased, Eliza Ann, deceased, who was the wife of William Wilson, also deceased, Jacob Walter, and George, who was born in 1841 and now lives in Missouri

The mother of Jacob W Corp died when he was three years old and his father was accidentally killed by a horse, in 1857 From 1842 until 1855 he grew up in the family of Peter Arnold and learned practical farming and also was given school opportunities In 1859 he attended the Clearfield Academy and afterward taught school in Brady and Union townships for some four years, through the winter seasons In 1870 he started in the butchering business on his farm at Coal Hill, and for twenty years supplied meat to the lumbermen on Anderson Creek, driving his own wagon and frequently covering thirty miles a day He still operates his wagon and deals quite extensively in livestock This farm was a wilderness when he bought it from J M Armagost but Mr Corp has cleared it all with the exception of four acres and has put up all the substantial buildings He is a tireless worker and through his good management and business foresight, has a great deal to show for his industry

On October 3, 1861, Mr Corp was married to Miss Mary Welty, a daughter of David Welty, of Union township, and they have had these children Hannah, who is the wife of Oscar Seyler and they have two children—Felicia and Eugene, David, who died young, Ira M , who died at the age of eighteen years , Nettie, who married David Bonsol, and they have four children—Ivan, Oleeta, Oscar and Walter, Eva, who lives at Grampian, Willis, who died at the age of fourteen years, Mary, who married Edward H Harmon (they have six children—Florence, Raymond, Ralph, Bessie, George and Grace, and live at Helvetia); James N , who married Pearl Neff (they have three children—Walter, Melvin and William, and live at Luthersburg) Mr Corp and family are members of the Methodist Episcopal church and he has been superintendent of the Sunday school for thirty years Formerly he was an active member of the order of American Mechanics and served three years in the office of deputy state councilor He votes as his judgment approves, in local matters and in National affairs gives support to the Prohibition party Mr Corp is also a member of Pomona Grange

MILES R PORTER, who was born in Lawrence township, Clearfield county, Pa, May 12, 1853, is a representative citizen and prosperous farmer of Pike township, where he owns 150 acres of fine land, situated two miles east of Curwensville His parents were Robert and Jemmima (Read) Porter

Robert Porter was born in County Tyrone, Ireland, on November 25, 1815, and came to America in 1835 After a few months spent in Philadelphia, Pa, he came to Lawrence township, Clearfield county, where he found employment as a farmer in the summers and as a lumberman in the winters He was industrious and saving and after his marriage, July 6, 1844, bought 125 acres of land in Lawrence township, three and one-half miles south of Clearfield For five years prior to that he had rented land and when he moved from the farm in Lawrence township he bought and settled on the farm of 150 acres in Pike township, which is now owned by his son, Miles R Porter He came here in 1873 and continued to live on this farm until his death, in May, 1898 He was a Democrat in politics and served as school director and road supervisor As long as he was strong and active he was a hard worker and cleared 100 acres of his first farm The present one was already cleared when he purchased it He married Jemmima Read, who died in January, 1903 They were members of the Presbyterian church The following children were born to them Elizabeth, who

is the widow of W R McPherson, of Clearfield, Emma, who is the widow of R. A Holden, of Clearfield, W A, who married Susan Conly, of Wilmington, Del, Miles R ; Robert F, who is a practicing lawyer of Kansas City, Mo, James M, who is a resident of Clearfield, Helen J, who is the wife of James Conly, of Wilmington, Del

Miles R Porter attended the Pine Grove school in boyhood He then spent two years in the high school at Clearfield and attended Normal School two terms Later he took a commercial course in a business college in Philadelphia, after which he became a school teacher and met with much success in this line of work, having taught in Chest township in Bigler, Woodland and Winterburn He was principal of the school at the latter place for one term Mr Porter then went into the lumber business and for ten years was interested in a saw and shingle mill on Clearfield Creek After his marriage he settled on this farm and for ten years before his father's death was its manager In 1904 his house was destroyed by fire and the present substantial one was erected by him the same year Mr. Porter carries on general farming and also operates a small coal mine on his place

On June 1, 1898, Mr Porter was married to Miss Mary K Bryan, a daughter of Judson and Anna (Longwell) Bryan Mrs Porter was born at Savona, N Y. Mr and Mrs Porter have two children Katharine R, who was born October 8, 1899; and Eleanor A, who was born August 30, 1909 They are members of the Presbyterian church at Curwensville, Mr Porter being an elder and a trustee He is one of the township's substantial men, being a stockholder in the County National Bank, and also of the Farmers and

Traders Bank, both of Clearfield He has been identified with the Democratic party since manhood Mr Porter has been a member of Pittsburg Consistory for many years, and he belongs to the Grange at Curwensville

SAMUEL M JONES, superintendent of Red Jacket Junior mine, of the Lehigh Valley Coal Company, in Boggs township, Clearfield county, Pa , is a thoroughly experienced man in his line of work and is also a representative and substantial citizen of Blue Ball, where he owns considerable real estate He was born in Franklin county, Pa , August 22, 1857, and is a son of John T and Sarah Jane (Neal) Jones

John M Jones was born in Franklin county, Pa , which was his home through life He was a son of Samuel Jones, and a grandson of James and Polly Jones James Jones was a soldier in the Revolutionary war John T Jones was a farmer by occupation He was a loyal and patriotic citizen and served three years in the Civil war He married Sarah Jane Neal, a daughter of Henry Neal Both Mr and Mrs Jones are now deceased They were highly esteemed people in their neighborhood and were consistent members of the Reformed church They had the following children born to them Irene D , who is the wife of Rev Joseph R Jones, who is pastor of a church of the United Brethren faith, at Baltimore, Md , Mary S , who is deceased, was the wife of Henry Wright, Samuel M , Susan E , who is the wife of B F Guyer, Sarah J , who is now deceased, was the wife of Alexander Hoover, J H K , and Ellen C , who is the wife of B A Jones

Samuel M Jones was educated in the public schools in Franklin county and in a Methodist college at Mt Pleasant, Ia He then entered the employ of the McCormick Manufacturing Company and became general agent of the Western District, with headquarters at Chicago, continuing as such for two years Mr Jones returned then to Franklin county for a short time but in 1882 came to Clearfield county He engaged in farming on a tract of sixty-five acres, in Boggs township, which he owns, afterward taking up his present line of work and has been either mine foreman or mine superintendent ever since He still owns his farm of 157 acres, in Franklin county, and has a half dozen pieces of improved real estate at Blue Ball

Mr Jones was married August 19, 1885, to Miss Allie Johnston, a daughter of Charles Johnston, who now is a resident of Wisconsin Mrs Jones has one brother, John Johnston Mr and Mrs Jones have had fourteen children born to them, all of whom survive except the eldest, Maggie E The others are John V , Clara Bertha, Harvey E , Bessie V , Earl McKinley, Sarah, Ida May, Irene, Theodore Roosevelt, Paul W , Nora E , Harry P and Lester The eldest son, John V , is a soldier in the U S Army and at present is stationed at Honolulu Mr Jones and family are members of the Methodist Episcopal church He is a Republican in politics and has served in public office at various times, for a number of years being a member of the school board and twice its president since coming to Blue Ball He is president of the Clearfield Directors Association and has served in the office of justice of the peace For many years he has been identified with the Odd Fellows and belongs to the Encampment as well as the lower branch, and he is a member also of the Elks, the Junior O U A M, and the I O O F

WILLIAM H BROWN, a lifelong resident of Clearfield county and a representative business man of DuBois, engaged in the grocery business in this borough, is located on the corner of Weber and Church streets   He was born on his father's farm in Huston township, Clearfield county, Pa, October 11, 1861, and is a son of Charles and Mary A (Goss) Brown

Charles Brown was born in Armstrong county, Pa   He was a farmer and lumberman for many years and was a well known man in Sandy township, Clearfield county   He married Mary A Goss, who was born in Indiana county, Pa, and they both died in Clearfield county   They had three children   George W, who lives in Sandy township, Samuel I, who lives in Union township, and William H

William H Brown was reared on the home farm and attended the country schools and later the summer sessions of the normal school at Grampian, Pa, after which he taught school for six terms   He then returned to the home farm in Sandy township and later he and his father opened a general store at Sabula, Clearfield county, and afterward, William H Brown conducted a similar business at Homecamp   In 1905 he came to DuBois and started in the grocery business and moved into his present well arranged quarters in 1909   He carries a large stock of both staple and fancy groceries and conducts his business along those lines which have brought him the confidence and patronage of the best people of the borough

Mr Brown was married December 23, 1884, to Miss Hannah Lantz, a daughter of Michael Lantz, of Indiana county, and they have had seven children, namely   Leota, who is the wife of Thomas H Armstrong, of Tacoma, Wash, and Ethel, James, Hazel, Clair, Laviness and Willella   Mr and Mrs Brown are members of the German Reformed church   In politics he is a Republican   His only fraternal connection is with the P O S of A   Mr Brown owns a very attractive residence at No 334 Olive avenue, DuBois

PROF H J BARRETT, principal of the public schools of Curwensville, Pa, and a candidate for the office of county superintendent of Clearfield county, Pa, is well known as an educator in different sections and enjoys the confidence and esteem of the people of this borough to a large degree   He was born at Portsmouth, O, January 7, 1870, and is a son of John H and Ruby G Barrett, both of whom are deceased

H J Barrett was educated at Ironton, O, Wooster University and the University of Chicago, after which he became principal of the schools of Toronto, O, where he remained for three years   In 1902 he was called to Curwensville and has been remarkably successful in raising the public school standards and in increasing efficiency   He has thirteen teachers under his charge and has succeeded in inspiring them with his own ambitions

Prof Barrett was married to Miss Lucinda Lamb, who died in April, 1905, and was buried at Wheelersburg, O, her birthplace   She is survived by two children   Elise May, who is with her father, and Katherine Marcia, who is with her grandfather, Willard Lamb, at

Wheelersburg Prof Barrett is a member of the Methodist Episcopal church In politics he is an independent voter

HOWARD G PURNELL, M D, 'who has been engaged in medical practice at Ansonville, Pa, for the past nineteen years, and is county physician for both Knox and Jordan townships, Clearfield county, also having the largest country practice in Clearfield county He was born at Georgetown, Sussex county, Del, July 1, 1869, and is a son of Hon Charles T and Maggie (Wingate) Purnell

Charles T Purnell, who is now mayor of Georgetown, Del, for many years was engaged in lumbering For ten years he was deputy sheriff of Sussex county and for four years was sheriff The family is one of prominence in that section Dr Purnell is the eldest born of his parents' family, the others being Mattie, who is the wife of Dr George Messick, Mary, now deceased, who was the wife of Eben Townsend, and Anna, who is the wife of George Sharpley

Howard G Purnell was ·educated in the public schools of Georgetown and the Newark Delaware College, and then studied pharmacy and was graduated in the same at the Philadelphia College of Pharmacy For eight years afterward he was in the drug business in Philadelphia, and then turned his attention to medicine, entering Jefferson Medical College, where he was graduated April 1, 1892 For two years prior to locating at Ansonville, he served as resident physician in the Jefferson Hospital, Philadelphia He was one of the founders of the Clearfield Hospital and gave much of his time to the work

Dr Purnell was married in April, 1900, to Miss Cora Straw, a daughter of John T and Priscilla (Barrett) Straw, the former of whom was county commissioner of Clearfield county and a man of public worth Mrs Purnell has one brother and six sisters, namely John, Myrtle, wife of Stewart Williams, Iva Belle, Carrie, wife of Clyde Bollinger, Blanche, wife of Benjamin Gates, Nora and Sarah Dr and Mrs Purnell have three sons Charles, John and Garrett They attend the Baptist church Dr Purnell is a Democrat in his political views and is serving as school director He is a man who stands very high in the esteem of his fellow citizens both personally and professionally He is identified with the Masonic fraternity at Georgetown, Del

R F. KLEINGINNA, a representative business man of long standing and excellent repute, who is engaged in the manufacture of cupboards and wardrobes at DuBois, Pa, came to this borough in its infancy and is identified at present with its best interests He was born in Schuylkill county, Pa, in 1867, and is a son of John and Sarah (Smith) Kleinginna The mother died when her son was four years old and he was reared by a maternal aunt, with whom he came to DuBois in April, 1881

R F Kleinginna is a self made man in every sense of the word He had few opportunities in his youth and that he has developed into a well informed and successful business man and respected and valued citizen, is owing entirely to his own steling traits of character His first work was in the coal mines, 'where he was a trapper Later he was employed for two years in the sash and door factory of Barber & Scully, after which he engaged with John E DuBois for two years and then was employed for a short time by Sidney Fuller but soon returned to Mr DuBois and worked two more years for him He then was employed for one year by the Whirlpool Washing Machine Company All this time he had been hoping that some turn of fortune might give him a little unemployed capital so that he could work out his own practical mechanical ideas for he has a natural gift in that line Securing an old barn as a work-shop, about this time he started to construct musical instruments and later, at the suggestion of John Goodyear, who was a pioneer furniture dealer here, he began the manufacturing of something needed in every house, kitchen cupboards Mr Kleinginna soon had three compact, durable and attractive appearing cupboards finished and these Mr Goodyear immediately took off his hands and paid for them at once This was the beginning of what he has developed into a very large enterprise, one that requires the assistance of seven traveling men to cover the wide territory of his business, his shipments going to New York, Virginia, West Virginia, Maryland and Ohio

There are men who at once would have gone into debt for proper machinery, with this encouragement, but Mr Kleinginna was not of that kind As he had no money and would not borrow, the only way he could solve what was a very important question, was to make his own machinery and his first work was done in the old dilapidated cow-barn, with a foot-power rip saw and with the other machinery that he fashioned for himself, and after his goods became known he installed a four-horse power engine and boiler and built wings on each side of the barn Business grew so rapidly that in a comparatively short time he had to find more commodious quarters and he purchased two acres of land and built his plant, on Hamor street His factory occupies two floors of the building at Nos 14-16 Hamor street, each floor 70 x 48 feet, with sufficient power and modern machinery, although some of this which is best suited to the work, is of his own invention and construction He has large ware-rooms and a dry-house with dimensions of 20 x 38 feet Mr Kleinginna is justified in the pride he takes in the success he has won and DuBois respects him and points to him as an illustration of what an honest, industrious, persevering youth may become if he be willing to strive hard enough

GEORGE H PLANTEN, division foreman for the Pennsylvania Railroad Company at Westover, and a prominent citizen of the borough, was born at Clacton-on-Sea, county Essex, England, October 9, 1860 His parents were William and Susan (Dove) Planten, and he is a grandson of John and Sarah Planten, the former an English farmer who lived to a good old age William Planten, who was born in Suffolk, England, also spent his industrial years in agriculture, and is still living at the age of 83 in London, England His wife, Sarah Dove Planten, died in 1910 at the age of eighty-four The Dove family from which she sprang are well known in English maritime circles as large ship owners Of their children, in addition to the subject of this sketch, there are three sons living and two daughters, namely Anthony, a steamship captain, residing in Scotland, William, a seafaring man residing in England; Charles, a care taker, in London, England, Alice, wife of E Holmes, of London, England; and Elizabeth, wife of J J Easton, also of London

George H Planten, after his school days were over, entered the English army, in which he served five years At the age of 20 years he came to America, settling first in Philadelphia, where at first he did manual labor and afterwards was in the milk business for one year Going then to New York, he became connected with the bridge building industry and worked at it for three years in various states Leaving his employer in New Orleans he went by steamer to Costa Rico, South America, to work for a German-French Railway company and was in their employ fifteen months, engaged chiefly in bridge construction He was next sent to the vicinity of Montreal, Canada, to construct a bridge over the St Lawrence river After this work was done, he returned to New York and soon after entered the employ of a French and Belgium railway company, who sent him to Venezuela as superintendent of bridge and trestle work Returning then to Philadelphia, he married, and soon after entered the employ of the Pennsylvania Railroad Company at Cresson, and has since remained with this company as foreman a period of eighteen years He came to Westover in 1894 He is a member of the United Evangelical church, and belongs to the I O O F lodge at Patton Politically a Republican, he has been active on behalf of his party and served the local committee two terms as president and three years as chairman He was also a delegate one year to the party convention at Harrisburg He was elected justice of the peace in 1906 but resigned the office in 1908 As an instance of his faithful performance of duty, it may be mentioned that on one occasion he received a $50 prize from the Pennsylvania Railroad Company, for services to the company

Mr Planten was married in 1903 to Mrs Grace Zella Lake DeCoursey Stout, who was born in Ireland, March 14, 1860, a daughter of Patrick Sexton and Mary Anne (Burch) DeCoursey Mrs Planten's parents are both deceased, her father dying in 1896 at the age of 72 years, and her mother in 1895 at that of 69 They came to America in 1867, residing first in New York and later removing to Providence R I, where the rest of their lives were spent, Mr DeCoursey being engaged in business as a merchant tailor Their children, in addition to Mrs Planten, were Zella, Ellen, Edward, Johanna, James and Patrick Henry

WILLIAM T WINK, general farmer and dairyman, who owns 105 acres of excellent land situated in Pike township, one and one-quarter miles northwest of Curwensville, was born in Fulton county, Pa, October 24, 1874 His parents were Elias and Florence (Hockinsmith) Wink Elias Wink died September 6, 1878, and his burial was in Fulton county His widow still resides in Fulton county, where she was born July 7, 1849

William T Wink remained with his widowed mother until he was old enough to provide for himself He attended school in Belfast township and lived in Fulton county until he was twenty-one years old and then accepted farm work in Franklin county In 1896 he came to Clearfield county, after which he worked one year at lumbering in Brady township After his marriage, in 1904, he settled on the old Neeper farm and has continued to reside here, having made many improvements including the remodeling of all the buildings He is a member of the Clearfield County Agricultural Association and is one of the model farmers of this section His dairy is maintained with from twenty-five to thirty cows and his milk is disposed of at Curwensville Mr Wink is a stockholder in the Curwensville Rural Telephone Company of Pike township

Mr Wink was married December 1, 1904, to Miss Ruthanna Neeper, who was born on this farm, May 11, 1870, and is a daughter of Robert R and Jane (Hartshorn) Neeper, and a granddaughter of Joseph Neeper, who was a veteran of the War of 1812 and one of the early elders in the Presbyterian church at Curwensville Robert R Neeper was born July 20, 1826, where the opera house now stands in Curwensville, and from there went with his father to Brady township and resided there until his father's death Then he and his widowed mother moved onto the farm on which he lived till his death, which took place March 4, 1902 He was married on April 15, 1863, to Jane Hartshorn, who was born January 19, 1832, and died October 16, 1904 They were well known residents of Pike township and were respected and esteemed Mr and Mrs Wink have four children, namely Robert, born December 19, 1895, Florence Irene, born March 3, 1906, and George Newton and Harold Devere, twins, who were born March 20, 1908 Mr and Mrs Wink attend the Presbyterian church In politics he is an independent Republican but has never consented to hold a township office As mentioned above he is deeply interested in farming in all its branches and is a valued member of Susquehanna Grange, of which he is steward and to which his wife also belongs Mr Wink belongs to the order of Red Men, at Curwensville and to the Order of the Moose, at Clearfield He is one of Pike township's representative men

EDWARD AMOS VIEBAHN, owner and proprietor of the Smoke Run Hotel, at Smoke Run, Clearfield county, Pa , is one of the enterprising and successful young business men of Bigler township He was born in 1882, in Clearfield county, and is a son of Julius Viebahn, a wholesale merchant and prominent citizen of Houtzdale, Pa

Edward A Viebahn was educated in the public schools and graduated from the Woodward High School on June 15, 1900 He then took a commercial course at Poughkeepsie, N Y , where he was graduated April 7, 1903 Mr Viebahn took charge of the Smoke Run Hotel in 1905 and he has conducted it along lines which have made it a credit to the place and which have established his reputation as a host To his guests he offers substantial comforts, an excellent table and attentive service, all at a reasonable price

Mr Viebahn was married in Germany, in April, 1904, to Miss Hedwig Wienhaus, a daughter of Frantz and Ida Wienhaus, who have two other children, Carolina and Frantz Mr and Mrs Wienhaus have never settled in the United States although they spent one pleasant year visiting Mr and Mrs Viebahn Mr and Mrs Viebahn are members of the Lutheran church He is a Republican in his political views He belongs to the Elks at Tyrone and to other organizations

HARRY FRANKLIN KRESGE, who does a large business in meats at DuBois, Pa , having a well arranged shop on South Brady Street, has been a resident of this borough for twelve years and is very generally known He was born on his father's farm in Luzerne county, Pa , April 23, 1870, and is a son of Amos and Julia (Barton)

HON. ALONZO S. MOULTHROP

Kresge, both of whom reside at DuBois Of the four children of the family, Harry Franklin is the eldest He has two brothers and one sister William residing at Tyler, Pa , Charles, living at DuBois, and Ella, wife of C S Nale, whose home is at Niagara Falls

Harry F Kresge was three months old when his parents left the farm and settled in Clarion county, Pa , where his father was a butcher and when the youth was but twelve years old he started to learn the trade with his parent Later he became interested in the oil industry, and established meat markets in the oil fields of Western Pennsylvania, where he spent twenty years In 1889 he came to DuBois and entered the employ of Solomon Spears, who conducted a butcher shop on East Long Avenue, and remained with him for four years Mr Kresge then embarked in the meat business for himself, at his present stand, and has prospered and now handles a large amount of the best trade He requires the assistance of five men in his business

In 1892 Mr Kresge was married to Miss Nellie Hardy, who was born in McKean county, Pa , and they have one child Helen Elizabeth The pleasant and attractive family residence stands at No 21 West Washington Avenue, DuBois In politics Mr Kresge is a Republican but he devotes much more time to his business than he does to public affairs He is a member of the Odd Fellows, belonging to the Encampment, and also is a member of the Modern Woodmen

HON ALONZO SYLVESTER MOULTHROP, a member of the Pennsylvania Legislature, serving in his third term in that august body and ably and usefully representing his constituents, has been a resident of DuBois, Pa, since 1876 He was born at Westport, Clinton County, Pa, April 2, 1863 and is a son of Sylvester and Ellen (Winn) Moulthrop

Sylvester Moulthrop was born in Carbon County Pa From 1863 until 1865 he was a soldier in the Civil War, serving as a member of Co I, 143d Pa Vol Inf and after the close of the war returned to his home practically unharmed In 1876 he moved to DuBois with his family and embarked in a general mercantile business which he continued until his death which occurred April 23, 1883, in his forty-seventh year His widow survived until December 24, 1904, she being sixty-eight years old They had five children, namely Frank, who died at the age of thirteen years, Alonzo S , John Oliver, Isabella, who is the wife of J E Swartz, of DuBois and Francis, who died young

Alonzo S Moulthrop was thirteen years old when his parents came to DuBois and has seen this place grow from a little town of 400 population to the thriving center it now is and he has been connected with its business interests for many years He had the distinction of being the first newsboy and also was employed in the capacity of post boy carrying the mail from the east side to residences in other sections, being in the employ of Postmaster David Throw Mr Moulthrop thinks that about this time also his future political ambitions had their inception and humorously relates how he and a few companions, in a stirring political campaign, in 1876, managed to make a display of banners and bunting on the public thoroughfare that materially aroused enthusiasm where it had been lukewarm and won for the young patriots and politicians the approval of the candidates Mr Moulthrop never changed his political adherence and in the course of time proudly cast his first Presidential vote for Hon James G Blaine

In his boyhood, as indicated, Mr Moulthrop early began to make his own way in the world and hence had no school advantages to boast of except those he provided for himself, night study and the reading of good books filling his mind with useful information that he was naturally quick enough to make use of in his daily life   For about six years he was in the employ of P S Weber, who conducted a general store at DuBois, and in 1882, with D E Hibner, he bought out the general store of John Goodyear Mr Hibner was succeeded by a Mr Miller, and the latter by George McClellen, when the firm style became Moulthrop & McClellen and so continued until the great fire of 1888 burned their stock After this disaster, Mr Moulthrop and partner embarked in the carpet and shoe business, Mr McClellan being succeeded by H E Ginter and the new firm continued until 1892, when Mr Moulthrop sold his interest   He had no idea, however, of retiring and on January 1, 1893, he entered into partnership with his brother, J O Moulthrop, in the hardware business on West Long Avenue, and later, as it expanded and demanded larger quarters the Moulthrops added to their floor space and now occupy Nos 223-225 W Long Avenue They carry a large stock and they also operate four drilling machines and outfits for well drilling, coal testing, etc Enterprise and energy have marked the course of Mr Moulthrop all his business life and the independent position he fills in commercial affairs, he has won for himself He is a director of the DuBois National Bank

and of the Keystone Mercantile Company, vice president of the State Mercantile Insurance Company, at Huntingdon, Pa and also director of the Central Y M. C A In 1907 he was elected a member of the General Assembly, on the Republican ticket and in 1909 was re-elected to this distinguished position, and also in 1911, approval being thus repeatedly shown of his conduct of public affairs Aside from purely personal matters Mr Moulthrop has been an active and useful citizen, earnest in his support of law and order and willing to share in the responsibilities which rest on all good citizens He was one of the organizers of the Sons of Veterans at DuBois and was the first captain of the order and in 1898 was state commander During the Spanish-American War he organized a military company which offered their services to the Government but the war closed before the company was called to the front Since 1885 he has been a member of the volunteer fire department and continues his interest in this organization

Mr Moulthrop was married on December 25, 1890, to Miss Elizabeth Ginter a daughter of H E Ginter, a representative citizen of DuBois, and they have one son Henry Sylvester The family residence is at No 221 W Long Avenue Mr Moulthrop belongs to the Elks and to the Acorn Club Mr and Mrs Moulthrop are members of the Methodist Episcopal church, of which he is a trustee and since 1880 has been an official in the Sunday school

A C WILLIAMS, who resides on his farm of fifty-seven acres, situated in Penn township, Clearfield county, Pa , one and one-half miles from Grampian, on the east, has been in the butchering business for some twenty-three years and is proprietor of a well patronized market at Grampian He was born November 7, 1857, in Jordan township, Clearfield county, and is a son of J G and Matilda (Knapp) Williams

J G Williams was born and died on the same farm, situated in Jordan township, to which his father, David Williams had come, from Center county Grandfather Williams built the first grist mill in Jordan township He bought 500 acres of land and cleared 200 of it He donated the land to the Baptist church on which that edifice was built and the land contained in old Zion cemetery, in which rest all the former members of this family J G Williams lived to be seventy-six years of age He married Matilda Knapp and they had eight children A C, Julia, David, Chauncey, John, Mollie, Harriet and Blair

A C Williams obtained his education in the schools of Jordan township and when old enough to become useful to his father began to assist on the home farm and continued until his marriage Then he moved to Bower, on the John Bell farm, after which he bought the excellent farm on which he lives, purchasing of the Cochran estate He operates a coal mine, having a three-foot vein, and delivers coal in Grampian Mr Williams has always remained in Clearfield county but his next younger brother, David Williams, has ventured far from home and has had a more or less exciting life He left his native place when Goldfield, Colo, came into the lime-light as the center of the gold mining industry, and worked there for a time Seeking further adventures he became one of a crew of forty-two men to start out in a whaling expedition, on the Pacific Ocean He was one

of the five survivors who reached land Then he went to the Klondike region, in Alaska, where he met with considerable success Later he visited his kindred at Grampian and made himself so popular with friends and relatives that they all lamented when he returned to the West

Mr Williams married Miss Mary Ellen Strunk, who was born at New Millport, Pa, a daughter of E L Strunk, and they have had the following children G E, who is a train dispatcher for the New York Central Railroad, at Jersey Shore, Pa, married Edna Arnold and they have two children; Arthur, who resides on his father's farm, married Mabel Freeman, a daughter of Ralph Freeman, Nellie, who is the wife of Ollie Hendrick, who is a machinist in the shops of the New York Central at Williamsport, Dollie, who is the wife of Elmer Beam, an engineer on the Beech Creek branch railroad, and Elby, who is the wife of Orvis Curry, who is a brick molder, employed at Stronach, Pa Mr Williams, like his late father, is a Republican He is a member of the order of Odd Fellows and of the P S of A, at Grampian He is one of the respected citizens and honorable business men of Penn township

CHARLES W MOORE, manager of the meat market for the Madera Trading Company, at Madera, Pa, and the owner of one of the fine residences of this place, was born in Blair county, Pa, in 1845, and is a son of Jesse and Eliza (Smith) Moore

The parents of Mr Moore were farming people in Blair county and spent their lives there, the father dying when Charles W was ten years old Their other children

34

were Ada, Jesse, James, Lucretia, Samuel and Candace

Charles W Moore enjoyed no other educational opportunities than those offered by the common schools of Blair county. For twenty-two years after leaving school he followed farming and then went into the meat business, with which he has been connected ever since

In 1873 Mr Moore was married to Miss Emma Hewitt, of Hollidaysburg, and they have the folowing children, Samuel, Thomas, William, Walter, John, Maude and Helen Maude is the wife of H B Swoope Mr Moore and family attend the Presbyterian church In politics he is a Republican but has accepted no office except membership on the school board, on which he served for several years

ISAAC HOYT, proprietor of Hickory Lane Farm, consisting of 115 acres, situated about eight miles northeast of DuBois, Pa, is one of the enterprising, progressive and successful agriculturists of this section He was born on his father's farm in Huston township, Clearfield county, Pa, June 18, 1861, and is a son of Hiram M and Barbara (Brown) Hoyt, and a grandson of Dr William Hoyt, who came from New England and bought property in Huston township, at Hickory Kingdom, where many of his descendants still reside

Hiram M Hoyt was the youngest of his parents' children and was thirteen years old when his father came to Huston township He was reared here and became a man of local importance and a large land owner, his 160 acres of pine timber being a fortune in itself His death occurred in 1903, when seventy-three years of age. His widow survived until 1909, passing away at the age of seventy-eight years Six children were born to them, namely: William Alexander, who is deceased; Elizabeth, who is the wife of William Bundy, Isaac, Charles E, who is a representative citizen and farmer of Huston township, Ida, who is the wife of Renaldo Bundy, and Ellen, who is the wife of C C Dodd.

Isaac Hoyt attended the district schools and assisted his father on the home farm until his marriage, since when he has followed general farming and dairying on his present place. He has erected first class buildings, maintains a silo and in every way shows that he is a man of progressive ideas concerning agriculture The products, especially butter, from Hickory Lane Farm, command a high price in the market In March, 1882, Mr Hoyt was married to Miss Emma Miller, a daughter of the late Charles Miller, and they have three children· Elva M., Ira D and Blake He is not very active politically but is identified with the Republican party

C. A HILE, owner and proprietor of the Lumber City Supply Company, at Lumber City, Pa, is a leading merchant and one of the representative business men of this place He was born at Lumber City, Clearfield county, Pa, September 20, 1879, and is a son of Allen W and a grandson of Lorenzo D. Hile, an old settler.

Allen W Hile was born also at Lumber City, and spent his life in Clearfield county. He was a plasterer by trade and became a contractor in this line and during his active years he did a large business in this section.

He was a very prominent Odd Fellow and for twenty-five years rented quarters to the fraternity at Lumber City In politics he was a Republican and at times he filled local offices He married Ida V Straw, a daughter of George Straw, of Ferguson township, and six children were born to them, namely C A, Katherine, who is the wife of William Hipwell, George, who is a resident of Lumber City, Elizabeth, who is a teacher at Lumber City, Alice, who is the wife of Joseph Galbraith of Iowa, and Allen, who lives in Franklin county, Pa The father of the above family died at Lumber City at the early age of thirty-five years but the mother survives

C A Hile was afforded educational opportunities and attended the public schools of Lumber City and the summer sessions of Normal School at Lumber City and Kermore, after which he learned the plastering trade and worked at the same for about eight years He then entered the employ of the Harbison-Walker Company as a clerk and in 1908 came to Lumber City as manager of the Lumber City Supply Company and subsequently bought the entire business and has continued the same under the old name He draws trade from miles around Lumber City and, in addition to a full stock in other lines of merchandise, carries a full line of ladies' and gents' furnishings

In June, 1902, Mr Hile was married to Miss Lola Kirk, who was born at Lumber City, a daughter of Samuel Kirk, and died here June 1, 1907, survived by three children Allen Kirk, Lola M and Charles Herbert Mr Hile is a member of the Odd Fellows at Lumber City and of the Moose at Curwensville

CHARLES L CORNELY, postmaster of Madera from June 21, 1901, to April 1, 1911, and proprietor of a general store at Madera, Pa, was born at Madera in 1875, and is a son of James and Christina (Bowers) Cornely The father, who died in December, 1898, was of Irish descent He was a blacksmith by trade and later a merchant He married Christina Bowers, of German extraction, and she survives

Charles L Cornely obtained his education in the Madera schools and afterward assisted his father for several years in his store and has continued the business In politics he is a Republican and for six years served as auditor of Bigler township In 1900 Mr Cornely was married to Miss Rose Stitt, a daughter of James Stitt, of Madera, Clearfield county, and they have four children Vivian, Evelyn, Christian and James Mr and Mrs Cornely attend the Presbyterian church He is identified fraternally with the Masons at Osceola Mills, and the I O R M at Madera

JOHN EARL FAWCETT, manager of the Tyler Mercantile Company, at Tyler, Pa, and one of the enterprising citizens of the place, is a native of England, born at New Castle, May 4, 1874, and is a son of William and Anna (Bolam) Fawcett

The parents of Mr Fawcett were born, reared and married in England They came to America and first lived at McIntire, Pa, then at Morris Run and later at Arnet They returned to England on a visit and while there their second son, John Earl, was born They returned while he was only an infant, and in 1883 settled at DuBois, a small place at that time Six children were born to them, namely David B, residing at Washington, D C , John Earl, Robert M , and Edward, both living at DuBois, Harriet, also a resident of DuBois, and Ralph, a sailor in the U S Navy

John Earl Fawcett attended school until he was eleven years of age and then began doing small jobs around the mines, his responsibilities increasing as he grew older, and for six years he was in the employ of the firm of Bell, Lewis & Yates He then entered the store owned by the same firm, learned to cut meat under J E Merris, and was then sent by the same company to Helvetia as a butcher and continued for four years there Afterward he located at Anita, in Jefferson county, where at first he was meat cutter for the Eureka Supply Company, and later clerk in the company store, then becoming assistant manager at Horatio, Jefferson county, for B T Atwell From there he went to Onondago, Jefferson county, as manager for the Keystone Store Company, then was with G W Imhof, at New Bethlehem, in Clarion county, serving a few months as assistant manager On January 23, 1911, he came to Tyler, succeeding J B Council as manager of the Tyler Mercantile Company, and has made many friends here

Mr Fawcett was married to Miss Sarah M Dick, a daughter of Walter Dick, of Anita, Pa , and they have two children, Mary Elizabeth and Clyde William They attend the Presbyterian church Mr Faw-

cett is a Republican in his political views He is identified fraternally with the Elks at Punxatawney and the Odd Fellows at Anita, Pa

JOHN LEE, a well known and respected citizen of Burnside township, was born on the Lee homestead in this township, November 5, 1836, a son of Isaac and Hannah (Fulton) Lee His paternal grandfather was Jacob Lee, a resident of Center county, who fought for American independence in the Revolutionary war The early progenitors of the Lee family came to this country from Ireland Jacob Lee because of his Revolutionary services received a land grant in Clearfield county, where he settled at an early day, at the locality called Lee Hollow, where he cleared land and carried on farming to the best of his ability, he being a cripple He died in 1847 at the age of 60 years His wife's given name was Margaret

Isaac Lee was born in Center county and accompanied his parents to Clearfield county when young He was engaged in farming and lumbering during his industrial period He was twice married, first to Hannah Fulton, a daughter of David and Mary Fulton, and of this marriage there were ten children, of which there are but two now living—John, the subject of this sketch, and Jacob, who resides at Glenn Campbell, Pa Mrs. Mary Lee died in 1845 and Isaac Lee subsequently married Margaret (Young) Westover, widow of Abner Westover, who bore him three sons, Isaac, who resides at Lee Hollow, James, living on the homestead, and Henry, a farmer

Isaac Lee died in 1880, at the age of 86 years He was a member of the Methodist Protestant church

John Lee, with whom we are more directly concerned, as a boy helped his father on the farm and in clearing off the timber, attending school not more than about three months each winter Until his marriage he lived with his parents on a part of the home farm The house was destroyed by fire, and his father then gave him 50 acres of land to erect the present residence He subsequently purchased the home farm, including the present productive coal field He commenced digging coal in 1870 at Lee Hollow, the coal at that time being free to any one who would take the trouble to dig for it The first mine in the vicinity was opened by Henry Rose and David Plattner Our subject operated his coal field until 1890, when he sold his interests to the company now operating it, and has since confined his activities to the lumber industry He has had a successful business career and is now one of the substantial citizens of Burnside township

Mr Lee married Elizabeth White, who was born in Huntingdon county, November 22, 1831, a daughter of William and Catherine (Holman) White Her father, a wagon maker by trade, resided during his latter years with our subject This marriage, which took place in 1860, resulted in the following offspring Isaac Newton, a farmer residing in Burnside township, married Anna Bonsell, and has five children (and one grandchild through the marriage of a daughter to John Kelly), John W, unmarried, residing at Bethlehem, Pa, Ash Bennett (twin of John), who married a Miss Hutton and has children, William Wallace, residing at home, James Hamilton, who married Emma Lee, and has five children, Edwin Hutton, a farmer, who married Anna Stevens and has seven children, Jesse Hull, living at home, Samuel White, who married Elsie Pennington, and resides at Bethlehem, Pa, and Eva Jane, wife of D Johnson, a farmer, who has eight children The last mentioned, Eva J, is a twin sister of Samuel Mrs Elizabeth Lee, the mother of the above mentioned family, died August 28, 1899 Mr Lee is a Democrat politically and at one time performed much active service for his party He is a member of the Methodist Protestant church

W H MILLER, owner of two fine farms, one of 65 acres and one of 120 acres in Lawrence township, and justice of the peace of Glen Richey, was born April 12, 1853, in Lawrence township, Clearfield county, Pa, and is a son of W H and Mary (Bell) Miller

W H Miller, father of subject, was born in Center county, Pa, and after his marriage resided near Clearfield Bridge until 1871, when he moved to the Ridge in Lawrence township, where he died aged 65 years He was married in Clarion county, Pa, to Mary Bell, a daughter of Alexander Bell, and of their union were born six sons, all of whom but one are living His wife died in her fifty-second year, her death resulting from a broken spine She fell from a wagon shed loft and lived several days after receiving the fall Mr Miller built a large number of the wooden bridges which were erected during his lifetime in Clearfield county He and his estimable wife were members of the Bloomington M E church

W H. Miller was reared in Lawrence township, and with his brother attended the Pine Grove and Clover Hill schools About the time he attained his majority Mr Miller began learning the carpenter trade, and was employed ten consecutive years by the Peale, Peacock & Keir Coal Company, and was later employed by the O'Shanter Company of Glen Richey He resided in Glen Richey since his marriage in 1876 until November 18, 1910, when he moved to his present home Mr Miller is politically a stanch Democrat, and served as tax collector of Lawrence township three years (1894 until 1896) and has been justice of the peace for two years

Mr Miller was married July 4, 1876, to Nevada F Long, a daughter of Philip Long, and they have the following children Ida, Oscar, Ethel, Herman, Stella, May, Ortha, Norman, Meade, Ruth, Clara, and John Mr and Mrs Miller are members of the Primitive M E church

G B CURRY, one of the representative business men of Madera, Pa , and a member of one of the old pioneer families of Clearfield county, was born in Jordan township April 17, 1865, and is a son of John and Elizabeth (Carson) Curry The parents of Mr Curry were born in Center county The father became a substantial farmer in Clearfield county His family consisted of one daughter and two sons, namely Mary H , who is the wife of G W Lamborn, James F , and G B

G B Curry was reared and educated in Jordan township and his life has been mainly spent at Madera. He was one of the organizers and is a stockholder in the Madera Trading Company, of which he is also manager This is one of the large business enterprises of Clearfield county. one that is amply financiered and ably managed In politics Mr Curry is a Democrat and for four years he was postmaster at Madera

HENRY LIXFIELD, general farmer, who is associated with his brother, Fred Lixfield, in operating the two Lixfield farms, one of fifty acres and an adjoining one of 100 acres, situated in Huston township, Clearfield county, Pa , belongs to a well known and highly respected family of this section He was born on his father's farm in Huston township, March 4, 1864, and is a son of Henry and Dorothy (Chaunce) Lixfield

Henry Lixfield, the father, was born in Germany, and in early manhood accompanied his brother, Frederick Lixfield, to America Frederick was a blacksmith by trade, and Henry understood the saw-mill business They worked first in Lehigh county, Pa , and then came to Clearfield county, and Henry Lixfield was for some time in the employ of Hiram Woodward, the pioneer lumberman of Penfield Later the two brothers purchased adjoining farms in Huston township, cleared their land and put up buildings Here Henry Lixfield died His widow (formerly Dorothy Chaunce) and five children survive him, namely Anna; Eliza, wife of C H Hammond; Henry and Fred (twins) and John

Henry Lixfield of the above family went

JAMES L. SMITH

to school in boyhood but as his father died when he was quite young, responsibilities early rested on his and his brother's shoulders He and his twin brother operate in partnership and make their home with their mother and sister They are both members of the Grange and of the Odd Fellows at Penfield They are independent voters neither having any ambition to hold office They are well known and much respected, both being quiet, industrious, practical men, good farmers and excellent citizens

J S SNEDDON, general manager of the Glen Richey Trading Store of Glen Richey, has been postmaster of the borough of O'Shanter since August, 1907, and was born November 16, 1871, in Scotland, a son of William and Hannah (Smiley) Sneddon At the age of fourteen months our subject came to the United States with his parents, who settled in Arnot, Tioga county, Pa, where they resided eighteen years The father retired from business activities in 1908 and is now a resident of O'Shanter He is now 67 years of age, and his wife is 61 years old They are members of the Presbyterian church, and he is politically a Republican

J. S Sneddon received his educational training in the schools at Arnot, Tioga county, Pa In about 1891 he came to Clearfield county and resided for about six years at Glen Richey, where he clerked and delivered for the Peacock & Kerr Mining Company, who operated a general store in that borough He later became general manager and removed to Devlin, where he was located until the mine gave out and the company removed to Glen Richey, where he'

has since been manager of the Glen Richey trading store He has also served as postmaster at O'Shanter since August, 1907, and is assisted in his duties as such by his wife

Mr Sneddon is identified with the Republican party in politics, and is fraternally a member of the Red Men, the Knights of Pythias, of which he has been master of finance for ten years, and is also a member of the Moose lodge of Curwensville

Mr Sneddon was joined in marriage with Jennie Mitchell, a daughter of James Mitchell, of Glen Richey, and of their union have been born the following children Margaret, Hannah, Esther, Myra, and Leslie, who died in February, 1909 The family holds membership with the Congregational church

JAMES L SMITH, furniture dealer and undertaker, whose place of business is on Meadow Street, Curwensville, Pa, was born in Pike Township, Clearfield County, Pa, April 22, 1873 His parents were Adam and Elizabeth (Haag) Smith

Adam Smith was born in Germany and was eighteen years of age when he came to Jefferson County, Pa He had learned the blacksmith trade in his native land and easily secured work at the same, at Whitesville, in Jefferson County Later he moved to Clearfield County and worked at his trade in Pike Township, near Bloomington, and at Curwensville He was an industrious and highly respected man His death occurred at the age of sixty-nine years His burial was in the cemetery belonging to the Methodist Episcopal church at Curwensville, of which religious body he was a member He married Elizabeth Haag, who was also born in Germany and now resides in Pike Township Six of their children survive, three sons and three daughters

James L Smith was given excellent school advantages, attending the public schools at Bloomington and Curwensville and the State Normal School at Lock Haven He began his business career as a clerk, first at Olanta and then at DuBois, Pa, and then learned the undertaking business, securing a diploma from the Pittsburg School of Embalming In 1891, Mr Smith started into business for himself at Curwensville, first purchasing a half interest in a furniture store with Garlock Robinson and later buying the other half interest Mr Smith carries a large stock of furniture and also stoves and does a prosperous business in that line He also is well equipped for funeral directing and undertaking, owning one black and one silver gray hearse and also an automobile truck It is easily within his power to satisfactorily conduct funerals ten or twelve miles distant and his patronage often comes from such points, his reputation for promptness and efficiency having been established He carries all necessary equipments and probably has as large and complete a stock of appropriate and necessary goods as any undertaker in Clearfield County He has one assistant but, being a graduated embalmer, looks after the larger part of the work himself

Mr Smith was married in August, 1906, to Miss Eva McCloskey, a daughter of Howard McCloskey, and they have two children Cecelia J and Katharine Mr Smith and family are members of the Methodist Episcopal church and he is superintendent of the Sunday-school In politics he is a Democrat and he served one term as auditor of Curwensville He is identified fraternally with the Masons, the Odd Fellows, the Order of the Moose and the Red Men He is one of the most reliable business men of Curwensville and commands the respect and confidence of his fellow citizens

CHARLES BOONE, owner and proprietor of the Hileman House, at Madera, Pa, is the very popular host of one of the best conducted public houses of Clearfield county He was born December 1, 1876, at Coalport, Pa, and is a son of William and Amanda (Davis) Boone

William Boone, who is a veteran of the Civil war, resides at Coalport, which has been the family home for many years He married Amanda Davis, who died there and was buried at Utahville She was a woman of many virtues and left a wide circle of friends and the following children Anna, Alice, Mattie, Zillah, William, Charles, Harry and Odis She was a member of the United Brethren church, to which religious body her husband also belongs

Charles Boone obtained his education in the public schools of Coalport Afterward he embarked in a livery business there in which he continued until September 1, 1908, when he purchased the Hileman House from Clark Hileman and has conducted it ever since, enjoying a liberal amount of patronage Mr Boone was married July 11, 1904, to Miss Sadie Anthony, a daughter of Miles Anthony, a resident of Coalport Mrs Boone has an older sister and brother, Cora and John In politics Mr Boone is a Republican He is a member of the L. O O M at Houtzdale, Pa.

GEORGE E TOWNS, who is a representative business man of Penfield, Pa, dealing in hardware, tinware, farm machinery, etc, established his hardware business here in 1896 and moved to his present location in the following year He was born May 11, 1864, at Home Camp, Pa, and is a son of Henry P and Mary (Sarson) Towns

Henry P Towns was born in Maine and reared there and was married to Mary Sarson in New England and they came to Clearfield county in 1860, locating first at Home Camp, where a relative by the name of Philip Blanchard was operating a timber tract From Home Camp Mr Towns moved his family to Curwensville, where he followed his trade of shoemaking Subsequently he spent six months at Sabula, Clearfield county, and moved from there to Penfield, where his death occurred July 30, 1896 His widow survived until December 3, 1903 They had three children Ada, who is the wife of Coston Bartron, George E and Annie, who is the wife of E F Mills

George E Towns was quite young when the family moved to Penfield and he was yet a boy when he began working in the lumber mill In 1881 he entered the store of Robacker & Gray, as a clerk and later worked for other firms and then bought his present business from George R Campbell and has successfully conducted it ever since

In February, 1896, Mr Towns was married to Miss Frances M Scudder, a daughter of the late William Scudder, and they have two children, Henry F and Coston G Mr Towns is a member of Penfield Lodge No 567, Odd Fellows Politically he is a Republican Both he and wife are members of the Presbyterian church

URIAH JAMES IFERT, merchant and justice of the peace at McGees Mills, Bell township, was born in Armstrong county, Pa, March 23. 1856 His father, Conrad Ifert, who was born in Germany, was a manufacturer of organs Coming to America, he settled at Kittanning and followed his trade there all his subsequent life He built the first organ ever manufactured at that place He died at the early age of 24 years in 1856 His wife, who in maidenhood was Mary Remaley, a daughter of John and Christiana (Helfrich) Remaley, married for her second husband James McDonald of Armstrong county and she is still living at the age of 73 years Her children by this second union were Harry, who is engaged in farming in New York state, Milton, an engineer residing in Cambria county, and Agnes, wife of Charles Gress, a farmer of Benton county

Uriah J Ifert was the only child by his mother's first marriage After attending school, he went to work for his maternal grandfather, who reared him and with whom he remained until coming of age He then came to Clearfield county, finding employment in the saw-mill of J W McGee, with whom he remained four years or until about 1881 Subsequently he bought some land in the vicinity, to which he removed, but two years later entered into partnership with his former employer, Mr McGee, in the saw-mill business, they manufacturing lumber, shingles, etc After being thus occupied for five years he sold out his interest and engaged in agriculture, in which occupation he continued for six years In September, 1897, he opened a general store in the village of McGee, which he has since conducted, being also engaged in agriculture He is one of the successful men of his township and is recognized as a good, reliable citizen, an earnest advocate of all measures calculated to improve the moral and material welfare of the community. He is a member of the local Grange, also of the I O O F lodge at Big Run, No 924, to which he has belonged for the past 20 years, and he also belongs to the Red Men's lodge at Mahaffey. In politics he is a Democrat and an active worker for his party. He has been delegate to party conventions, and is now serving his fourth term as justice of the peace. He was for three years a member of the township school board and served one term as constable.

Mr Ifert married Adella P Miller, who was born October 14, 1861, a daughter of E L and Louisa (Beaty) Miller. Her parents were early settlers in Indiana county, subsequently removing to Clearfield county. Mrs Ifert's father is now deceased, but her mother is still living at the age of 85 years. Mr and Mrs Ifert have been the parents of children as follows: Edith, now aged 31 years, is a school teacher, residing at home. Mary, aged 29, is the wife of W B Hall, agent for the Pennsylvania Co at McGee and has two children. Horace, aged 29, married Nettie Myrtle, and resides in Jefferson county, Pa. Erwin, now 25 years old, married Bertha Pennington and lives in Punxatawney, Pa. He has two children. Mildred is the wife of F Guthrie, of Cresson, Pa. William, aged 13, resides at home. Three other children are now deceased. Mr Ifert is a member of the International Bible Students' Association.

PERRY BROWN, an enterprising farmer and highly respected citizen of Lawrence township, Clearfield county, Pa, residing on a farm of 59 acres, was born September 16, 1849, near the Pine Grove school house in this township, and is a son of David and Debora (Spackman) Brown.

David Brown was born in 1818 in Lancaster county, Pa, and when a young man came with his parents to Clearfield county and settled on the Leonard farm in Lawrence township. After his marriage he bought and located on a farm of 160 acres in Lawrence township, later buying a farm in Pike township, where he devoted his energies to general farming. At the time of his death he was the owner of two tracts of farm land, one of 150 acres being divided among three of his heirs, and the other of 100 acres was divided between two heirs. Mr Brown died at the age of seventy years, and of his union with Debora Spackman, who was a daughter of Daniel Spackman, were born six sons, two of whom are deceased, and one daughter. He was politically a Democrat, and he and his wife attended the Presbyterian church, but were both buried at the Lutheran cemetery.

Perry Brown received his early educational training in the Pine Grove school, where his first teacher was Charles Sanford, and remained under the parental roof until the time of his marriage in 1871. He then located on a farm in Lawrence township near his present place, and subsequently came to this farm, known as the John J Reed farm. This place consisting of 59 acres is all cleared with the exception of three acres, and the house has been remodeled by Mr Brown, who has otherwise made improvements.

Mr Brown married Sarah Rachel Owens, a daughter of John Owens of Pike township, and to them were born the following children: J C, living in Oregon, I D, a resident of Clearfield, Pa, who married Della Cleaver;

W T , who married Agnes Kennedy, and is a resident of Alexander, Pa , Dove Stella, who was born in 1876 and died in August, 1887, Viola, born September, 1879, who died in November, 1879, Nona, wife of John Thoughburn, of Clymer, Pa , R J , who is unmarried and lives at Salt Lake City, Utah, Lude, Zoe, and Wayne Mrs Brown, who died February 10, 1895, was buried in the Bloomington cemetery, she was always an active member of the Lutheran church

Mr Brown is politically a Democrat, and is now serving his second term on the Lawrence township school board, of which he is treasurer, he has also served as assessor of the township

D ROSS WYNN, a resident of Philipsburg, Pa , and a representative business man of Blue Bell, Pa , is extensively interested in brick manufacturing here and at other points He was born at Woodland, Clearfield county, Pa , September 5, 1872, and is a son of William H and Margaret G (Ross) Wynn

William H Wynn was born in Westmoreland county, Pa , and was a son of James Ross and Mary Ann (Bitner) Wynn Prior to 1870, when he moved to Woodland, he had been a railroad man In the fall of 1899 he came to Blue Ball and with his son, D Ross, and his son-in-law, James H France, started the building of the brick works here, which have been continuously operated by them since January, 1900 William H Wynn married Margaret G Ross, who was also born in Westmoreland county, a daughter of Daniel Ross, and the following children were born to them Mary and Margaret, twins, the latter of whom is deceased, the former being the wife

of Alexander Patterson, Cora, who is the wife of James H France, D Ross, John and Arthur, both of whom are deceased, Lewis, Ethel, who is deceased, Jessie, who is the wife of P E Ferguson, and Vera, who resides at home

D Ross Wynn was educated in the public schools and at Duff's Commercial College, at Pittsburg He has been connected with the brick industry ever since going into business and in addition to his interests at Blue Ball, is concerned with a brick plant at Sandy Ridge, Center county, and one at Claysburg, in Blair county He is also vice-president of the Moshannon National Bank of Philipsburg He is an enterprising and successful business man and a useful and reputable citizen

In 1896, Mr Wynn was married to Miss May L Klare, a daughter of A J Klare, and they have four children Vivian, Lewis, William and Frank Mr and Mrs Wynn attend the Methodist Episcopal church He is identified fraternally with the Elks and the Masons, both at Philipsburg In politics he is a Republican but is no seeker for office

FRANK S SMITH, manager of the Penfield Supply Company's general store, at Penfield, Pa , has been a resident of Clearfield county since 1892 He was born in County Lincoln, Canada, in September, 1875, on his father's fruit farm, and is a son of Sardis and Sarah (Squires) Smith

Sardis Smith was a native of Canada but his wife was born in Pennsylvania He died on his farm in the Dominion, but she survives They had six children, namely William E , living in Canada, Victor, who is deceased, George, who resides at Warren, Pa , Lena and

Robert, both of whom still live in Canada, and Frank S, who was the fifth born in the family

Frank S Smith attended the public schools in his native county until he was fifteen years of age and then went to Rochester, N Y, where he took a commercial course in a business college From there he went to Warren, Pa, where he became a clerk in a general store at Rice s Tannery, of which his brother George was manager, and from there, in 1892, came to Penfield, first as a clerk for T E Proctor, for the Penfield Store Company, and at present is with the Penfield Supply Company, as manager, succeeding C O Lowstetter He is energetic and progressive and has a fine understanding of business and enjoys the confidence and esteem of the company Mr Smith married Miss Effie Kline, a daughter of Dr J H Kline, of Penfield, Pa, and they have two children, Helen and Victor

JOHN JORDAN BLOOM, whose excellent farm of 150 acres is situated in Pike township, Clearfield county, Pa, three and one-half miles southwest of Curwensville, was born on this place, in 1843, and is a son of John and Mary Ann (Jordan) Bloom, old and substantial families of Clearfield county

John Bloom, father of John Jordan Bloom was a son of Isaac Bloom and a grandson of William Bloom, who founded the family in America He was born in Germany and when he first came to the United States, settled in New Jersey and from there came to Center county, afterward locating near Pee Wee Nest in the vicinity of Curwensville On account of another man laying claim to this land, William Bloom, who was a man of peace, decided to give it up and then moved to a place

two miles south of Curwensville, settling on the very farm which is now owned and occupied by his great-grandson, C Judson Bloom

Isaac Bloom, the eldest son of William Bloom, was born near Bellefonte, in Center county and came with his parents to Clearfield county, where the rest of his life was spent After his marriage he bought 150 acres of land one mile north of Curwensville and later cleared it and developed a valuable farm This land is now owned by Ai and Eli Bloom He married Sarah Apkter and they became the parents of twelve children, namely Katherine, who married Fred Shaffer; Elizabeth, who married Mason Garrison, William, John, Mary, who married Isaac Draucher, Benjamin, who married Nancy Arthurs, Caroline who married Levi Owens; Priscilla, who married John Norris; Nancy, who married John McCracken, James, who married Mary Ann Hile, George, who was married twice, first to Mahala Bloom and second to Rebecca Irwin and Jeniza, who married Samuel B Taylor Isaac Bloom and wife both lived into old age, and their burial was in the McClure cemetery They were members of the Methodist Episcopal church In politics he was a strong Democrat

John Bloom was born on the Hugh Irwin farm where his father lived for a short time In early manhood he married and then went to housekeeping on the farm on which C J Bloom lives and remained there for three years and then moved to the farm now owned by John J Bloom, on which he passed the remainder of his life, dying at the age of seventy-four years He cleared this farm and put it under cultivation and together with farming engaged largely in lumbering He married Mary Ann Jordan, who was born in Perry county, Pa, and was nine years old when her people came to Clearfield county Her parents were John and Eve Jordan, natives of New Jersey and on the maternal side, of German parentage John Jordan was a miller and when he came to Clearfield county he worked where the Bickford fire brick plant stands, going from there to the Rockton mill, which was owned by Jerry Moore, after that accepting the management of a mill at Curwensville, owned by John Irwin He then operated a mill at Stoneville, in Boggs township for a time, after which he went back to Curwensville to take charge of Mr Irwin's second mill, the first one having burned down Afterward he purchased some land which now is partitioned off into town lots, and there he lived until the close of his life, at the age of sixty-nine years, his burial being in Oak Hill cemetery John and Eve Jordan had a family of twelve children, the eldest of these being Mary Ann, the mother of John Jordan, who was named for his maternal grandfather David, the second member of the family, is deceased John Jordan, the third, married Mary Jane McClelland Margaret Jordan, deceased, was twice married, first to Daniel Sweeney and second to Frederick Haney Zeniza Jordan was the wife of David Denmark, both of whom are deceased Rachel Jordan married Frank Sterling and both are deceased Daniel Jordan went to Nebraska and married Sarah Long of Luthersburg Clearfield county Levi Jordan, now deceased, was twice married, first to Sarah Nelis, and second to Ann Cole Susan Jordan, a resident of Lumber City, is the widow of Robert Young William Jordan, who is deceased, married Hannah Winn and they lived in Nebraska Sarah Ann Jordan married Isaac

Haney, of Mehaffey, Pa Samuel Jordan, a resident of Clearfield, married Ellen McClelland, who is deceased

To John and Mary Ann (Jordan) Bloom the following children were born Fred, Mrs Eliza Long, Matilda, Mrs Rachel Long, Isaac, John Jordan, Mrs Mary Jane Bell, Mrs Sarah Ann Bloom, Mrs Susan Moore, Mrs Jehursha Kelly, Mrs Amanda Spackman, and Alfred L, of Knox township The parents of the above family were good, Christian people, active in good works through life and worthy members of the Methodist Episcopal church at Bloomington In politics the father was a Democrat and he served in all the public offices in the township, with the exception of justice of the peace

John Jordan Bloom obtained his education in the Curry school in Pike township, near his father's farm When he was thirteen years of age he was able to do a man's work, both on the farm, which he helped to clear, and in the woods at lumbering He took pride in being able to give such a good account of himself and as an indication of the confidence that was placed in his good judgment, it may be narrated that in the winter of his thirteenth year he was entrusted with the care of four horses and with them hauled lumber He remained with his father until his marriage in the summer of 1868, when he moved to the opposite end of the farm and cultivated land there for ten years In 1893 he moved to his present location, the site of the old homestead He has all his land, with the exception of forty acres in valuable timber, under cultivation, and he owns also some property at Walton, in Pike township, and is a stockholder in the Traders and Farmers Bank of Clearfield, of which he is a charter member Mr Bloom is a representative citizen of this section and his sterling character and excellent business capacity have been many times recognized by his fellow citizens when they have cast about for desirable holders of public office Mr Bloom is a Democrat and in 1910 was chairman of the township committee of his party He is a member of the school board and has been overseer of the poor, road supervisor and tax collector He is a member of Susquehanna Grange, at Curwensville, and formerly was connected with the Bloomington Grange, of which he was a charter member

On June 23, 1868, Mr Bloom was married first to Miss Mary Ellen Peoples, of Center county, who died in 1880 and was interred in the Bloomington cemetery She was a member of the Methodist Episcopal church Two daughters were born to this marriage, namely Ollie, who is deceased, and May, who is the wife of Samuel Askey, of Sharon, Pa Mr Bloom was married, secondly, June 19, 1883, to Miss J Alice Read, who was born in Lawrence township, Clearfield county, Pa, a daughter of William Potter Read Five children have been born to Mr and Mrs Bloom, namely Mary Irene, who died at the age of five months, Cecil R, who is employed in a drug store at Clearfield, Ella and Fred, both of whom are at home, and an infant daughter, who is deceased

Mr Bloom takes considerable interest in the old records of his family, one that has been identified with the settlement and advancement of this section of Clearfield county Elizabeth Bloom, a sister of his grandfather, was married in 1803 to Mathew Ogden, this being the first marriage ceremony recorded in Clearfield county, and it was performed by Samuel Bell, Esq, who was the first justice of the peace in the neighborhood Mathew Ogden had many encounters with the Indians and was known as a successful Indian fighter and Mr Bloom tells several interesting stories of his courage and diplomacy On one occasion, being hard pressed in a running fight with the savages, he jumped into a ditch and as an Indian attempted to also clear the ditch, the opportunity was afforded Mr Ogden of killing his pursuer and thereby saving his own life On another memorable occasion in order to escape capture, he crawled into a hollow log and, strange as it may seem, an industrious spider covered his hiding place with a web and when the Indians caught up with him, he had the satisfaction of overhearing their comments on his escape while they were sitting on the very log in which he was entombed On still another occasion he was at work near his home when two Indians approached him apparently in a friendly way but very soon they informed him that they had come to slay him He had no weapon near but had the presence of mind to invite them into his cabin for refreshment and, there, with the quick movement that had often before saved his life, caught up his gun and killed them both These stories give a true indication of the tragic conditions under which pioneers lived in the early days of 1800, in a section of country that now is noted for its enlightenment and civilization

MATHEW T MORROW, a substantial citizen of Blue Ball, Pa, who has been station agent at this point for the Pennsylvania Railroad for the last fifteen years, was born December 20, 1856, at Clearfield, Pa, and is a son of Henry Hayes and Amelia Jane (Forcey) Morrow

Henry Hayes Morrow was a lumberman during a part of his business life and later owned and conducted a general store at Shawsville, Pa He was a representative citizen of that place and was moderately active in politics, being identified with the Republican party He married Jane Forcey and they had the following children Mathew T , E H , who is engaged in the practice of medicine at Altoona, Margaret E , who is the wife of George W Meyers, Grace S , who is the wife of Dr D E Bottorf, and Ida J , who is the wife of D R Wooldridge

Mathew T Morrow was educated in the common schools and at Williamsport Seminary, spending one year in this well known institution, after which he worked for his father in the lumber business until 1881, when he turned his attention to farming and continued agricultural pursuits until 1894, when he accepted his present position at Blue Ball He has invested in property here and is one of the town's leading citizens

Mr Morrow was married in 1881 to Miss Alice Dimeling, a daughter of Jacob and Elizabeth (Sloan) Dimeling, who were then residents of Blue Ball, members of old county families Mrs Morrow was an only child Mr and Mrs Morrow have one daughter, Amy S , who lives with her parents The family attends the Presbyterian church In politics Mr Morrow is a Democrat He served acceptably as supervisor for one year, but otherwise has accepted no political office

THOMAS J LOWELL, justice of the peace and assistant postmaster at Penfield, Clearfield county, Pa , one of the leading citizens of Huston township, was born at Pen-

field, April 28, 1880, and is a son of Horace H and Anna (Zuber) Lowell

Horace H Lowell is postmaster at Penfield, is a veteran of the Civil war and is one of the best known and most respected citizens of this section He was born on his father's farm in Maine and was reared to the age of eighteen years there, when he enlisted for service in the Civil war, entering Co A, First Maine Vol Cav , as a private and won promotion to the rank of corporal He was a brave soldier in every position in which he found himself, serving three years and enduring thirteen months of imprisonment at Andersonville Later he came to Williamsport, Pa and for twenty years was in the woods as cook in lumber camps Later he operated a general store at North Bend, Pa In 1873 he came to Penfield to make his permanent home engaging in business as a timber contractor and in 1898 was appointed postmaster to succeed L W Lucore His residence is situated on E Woodward street, Penfield, and he also owns a farm in Huston township He is a member of the G A R and the Masonic fraternity At Williamsport, Pa , he married Anna Zuber and they have but one child, Thomas J , of this record

Thomas J Lowell attended the public schools and the Ohio Northern University at Ada, O , after which he spent four years as clerk and bookkeeper in lumber camps in the woods After his father was appointed postmaster in 1898 he was made assistant and in May, 1909, was elected a justice of the peace

Mr Lowell was married in June, 1904, to Miss Ella Overturf, a daughter of L H Overturf, of Penfield, and they have two children Horace H , who was born October 20, 1906, and Kenneth T, who was born February 22, 1908 Mr Lowell and wife attend the Methodist Episcopal church He belongs to the Grange and the Knights of the Maccabees at Penfield and is a member of the Blue Lodge F & A M, at DuBois, and of the Consistory at Williamsport

WILLIAM H RADEBAUGH, proprietor of a truck garden of nine acres and justice of the peace in Lawrence township, was born October 21, 1845, in Clearfield, Pa, and is a son of John S and Mary Ann (Millan) Radebaugh

John S Radebaugh was born in Mifflin, Mifflin county, Pa, and in 1816 came to Clearfield, Pa, there being at that time but thirteen houses in the village He owned several properties here and engaged extensively in the lumber business, buying in partnership with William Powell, a tract of 10,000 acres on Moose Creek in Lawrence township, and in 1852 they built the first road to Moose Creek In 1855 he sold his residence to H B Swope and moved his family to Wayne county, Ohio, where they resided one year He subsequently lived one year in Tyrone, Pa, where he operated a shoe shop and store, in which he employed five men In 1857, while crossing the Allegheny Mountains, he bought the Sandy Ridge Hotel, but after conducting it for one year, he rented and ran the Copeland Hotel on the top of the Allegheny Mountains until 1858, at which time he moved to Philipsburg, where he had charge of the old Runk Hotel until the spring of 1861 Mr Radebaugh then bought a hotel at Blue Ball, Clearfield county, Pa, and erected a large hotel and store, which he operated for seven years He disposed of his goods to R Mossipp, and his real estate to

John Copehaver of Center county, and then moved to Philipsburg, and six months later went to Cory, Erie county, Pa, where he bought and operated a hotel for a time He moved thence to St Mary's, Elk county, Pa, where he worked as a butcher one year and six months, and at that time came to Penfield, Huston township, and after residing here little over two years, operated the Burns Hotel of Reynoldsville one year He purchased seven acres of land where the hospital now stands, then went to Penfield, Pa, where he resided until the time of his wife's death on December 13, 1877 After that Mr Radebaugh made his home with the children, and on his 81st birthday boarded a train to come and see his son, William, the subject of this record He had taken the wrong train, which compelled him to walk one and a half miles, and being extremely deaf, he was run down and killed by a freight train near Fall Creek.

John S Radebaugh was married in 1840 to Mary Ann Millan, who came from Ireland at the age of thirteen years, and their union resulted in the following issue James William Hileand R, a resident of Edinburg, Clarion county, Pa, who served in the Civil war, Sophia E, the wife of Dr J H Kline, of Huston township, Amanda H, deceased, who was the wife of F C Bowman, William H, John H who married a Miss Cress of Ridgway, Ellsworth D, who was accidentally killed on the railroad near Hyde City while driving a team and Bertha, who is the wife of Afton Rodabecker Mr and Mrs Radebaugh were both buried at Penfield, Pa He was politically a strong abolitionist, and attended the Lutheran church, while his wife was a member of the Presbyterian church

William H Radebaugh obtained his education in the public schools of Clearfield, Pa, and in 1856 began working in the hotel operated by Dan Weaver He then went to Sandy Ridge, where he remained until 1858, then took charge of his father's team (in 1862) and hauled merchandise across the Allegheny mountains He also hauled lumber to Alexander, Huntingdon county, where he traded for produce, and in 1865 removed to Huston township and learned the blacksmith trade with Joseph Ruple, in whose employ he remained one and a half years He then worked in a shop at Cursey Run, Elk county, Pa, for William Woodard, and after his marriage in 1868 resided for seven years in Penfield, where he worked as a blacksmith and lumber jobber In 1872 he moved to Glen Hope, where he ran a hotel for eighteen months, when owing to bad luck and the loss of horses, he came to Clearfield, and in March, 1874, purchased a lot and built a house and blacksmith shop He subsequently came to his present place, which is the James Leonard place, and has lived here thirty-three years continuously since that time

On December 24, 1868, Mr Radebaugh married Almeda Brown, a daughter of Austin Brown of Huston township, and of their union were born four children, namely Annie, who is the wife of John Rothrock, a conductor on the B, R & P Railroad, and resides in Bradford City, McKean county, Pa, Gertrude M, a graduate of the Central State Normal School, of Lock Haven, Pa, who taught school successfully for nine terms, and is now the wife of Fred E Rimer, a mail carrier of DuBois, Pa, J L, who is the owner and proprietor of a drug store at Bradford City, and married Myrtle Moore, a daughter of George Moore; and Fred M, who is now deceased

In 1871, Mr Radebaugh joined the Knights of Pythias, which was the first lodge organized in Clearfield county, and in 1872 he joined the United American Mechanics He is also a member of the Grange, and was formerly a member of the I O O F until 1879 Mr Radebaugh is politically a Democrat, and was elected justice of the peace on that ticket in 1909, when he received all the Democratic votes but one He has been a member of the M E Church of Clearfield since 1875

ROBERT K JONES, who is owner and proprietor of the Enterprise Hotel, at Blue Ball, Pa, and has conducted it in a first class manner for seven years, was born in Franklin county, Pa, December 4, 1869, and is a son of J L and Elizabeth (McDonald) Jones The parents of Mr Jones were farming people and were well known and highly respected in Franklin county They had the following children born to them Frank, Louisa, wife of Daniel Reader, Etta, wife of Henry Motter, William, Jennie and Jessie, both deceased, Laura, wife of Lafayette Lindsay, Robert K, and Elmer

Robert K Jones obtained a common school education in his native county and afterward assisted his father on the home farm When he came first to Clearfield county he worked in the clay mines for some fifteen years and then went into the hotel business, conducting a house at Brisbin for two years before coming to Blue Ball and taking charge of the Enterprise Hotel This public house is well patronized as Mr Jones goes to a great deal of trouble in order to insure the comfort of his guests

In 1891, Mr Jones was married to Miss Bertha Meas, a daughter of David and Amelia

(Goss) Meas   David Meas was a farmer in Boggs township   His family consisted of the following children   Joseph, James, Bertha, wife of Mr Jones, Anna, wife of Edward Dixon, Lyda, wife of Martin Woods, Roland, and Rosa, deceased, who was the wife of Theodore Haynes   Mr and Mrs Jones have four children   Albert, Ethel, Ada and Robert   Mr Jones and family attend the Methodist Episcopal church   He is a member of the Grange and belongs to the order of Eagles and also to the Elks, both at Clearfield   He is a Republican in his political views and has served on the election board

HON HENRY S KNARR, formerly burgess of DuBois, Pa , where he is a representative citizen, has large real estate interests here and in Clearfield County and is owner and proprietor of the H S Knarr stock farm, which is situated in Brady Township, one-half mile northwest of Luthersburg, Pa   Mr Knarr was born on his father's farm in Brady Township, Clearfield County, Pa , February 21, 1853, and is a son of Henry and Catherine (Marshall) Knarr and grandson of George Knarr.

George Knarr was born in Germany and emigrated to America with his family in 1826 He took up 200 acres of land near Troutville, in Brady Township, Clearfield County, Pa , the above town now partly being built on his farm Both he and his wife, Louisa (Wisegarber) Knarr, lived into old age, he surviving to be within eight years of the century mark   They had six children, namely   Henry, Andrew, George and Adam, all deceased, Charlotte, who was the wife of Christian Haag, both deceased; and Caroline, who is the only survivor, is the widow of A K Weaver, and now resides at DuBois

Henry Knarr was born in Germany and was about eighteen years of age when he accompanied the family to America and to Clearfield County   At first he assisted his father on the latter's large tract of land but subsequently took up 150 acres for himself, also in Brady Township and to the clearing of this land and its cultivation, he devoted many years of hard work   He also taught school in Brady Township and was one of the first to teach a German school   He died on his place in 1886, at the age of seventy-eight years   He married Catherine Marshall, who was born in Germany and died in her seventy-sixth year, in 1898, having passed her last years at Troutville.   To Henry and Catherine (Marshall) Knarr sixteen children were born, as follows: Louisa, George, Caroline, Simon, David, Lourine, Henry S , Reuben, William Adam, Mary, Samuel A , Ferdinand, and others who died in infancy

Henry S Knarr spent his boyhood on the home farm and attended the country schools   He was a very active and adventurous lad and by accident lost one of his limbs   On this account his father was exceedingly anxious that he should have a college education to enable him to enter one of the professions, but the youth decided otherwise after a trial, and concluded to learn the tailor's trade and served an apprenticeship at Brookville   In 1876 he opened his own establishment at DuBois, which was then but a small place, and conducted a very successful business until 1882, when he became interested in the buying and selling of real estate, in which he has been equally successful   In 1882 he traded a property in DuBois for the John Reed farm of eighty acres, situated near Clearfield, and shortly afterward traded that farm advantageously for the Henry

HON. AND MRS. HENRY S. KNAIR AND FAMILY

Shaffer farm, which is now included in the Fourth Ward, DuBois, although at the time of the above transaction, it was as yet partly covered with timber It is the forethought shown in such affairs that has made Mr Knarr the successful business man he is acknowledged to be He cleared the Shaffer farm and then laid it out in lots and improved them with houses and soon became one of the leading real estate dealers in the place Later he showed still more enterprise, putting up a 66-foot front, two-story brick business block on Brady Street, for the site of which he paid $180, and at present, thirty-five years later, its valuation is $16,000 Still later he erected a second brick business block, locating it on Long Avenue and he retains possession of both properties, which rent high, and owns a number of other lots and dwellings In 1897 his physician advised a rest from the business activities in which he had found so much pleasure and profit, and Mr Knarr bought a farm of 136 acres, in Brady Township, near Luthersburg, not far from the place of his birth, and went back to Nature, as it were, in order to benefit his health He soon became interested here, sparing no expense or trouble to improve the property and make of it a fine stock farm He remodeled the house and has put up barns and other buildings and in the construction of which he has used many barrels of cement He has set out orchards and shade trees and his wife has been equally busy in the tasteful arrangement of flower-beds, so that, added to the natural advantages of considerable elevation, this farm is one of great beauty and exceeding value Although Mr Knarr has been exceedingly successful he has occasionally met with misfortune, the greatest of which, in a financial way, he deems the fire at DuBois, in 1888, when his loss, as a young business man was $46,000 He was one of the organizers of the Union Banking and Trust Company at DuBois and is one of its directors

On June 23, 1879, Mr Knarr was married to Miss Mary A Buchhide, a daughter of Frederick and Elizabeth (Weber) Buchhide, of Jefferson County, Pa, and they have two sons Silas, who is an employe of the Union Banking and Trust Company, married Alice F Nelson, and Burt E Mr and Mrs Knarr are members of the Lutheran church Until May, 1910, Mr Knarr resided in DuBois, driving out to the farm every morning, but the temporary home is maintained there at present, it being his intention to sell the farm as his health is entirely restored, and to reside in the borough as formerly He is a Democrat in politics and served in the borough council and for four years was burgess

CHARLES E HOYT, proprietor of Lone Pine Farm, consisting of ninety acres of excellent land, which lies in Huston township, Clearfield county, Pa, at Hickory Kingdom, was born on this farm, the old home place, July 31, 1863, and is a son of Hiram and Barbara (Brown) Hoyt

The Hoyts came originally from New England, Dr William Hoyt, the grandfather, having been born in Vermont He was married to Ruby Mason in Massachusetts and they came to Clearfield, Pa, in 1819 Here he practiced medicine and also taught school, moving later to Elk county, where he taught the Horton township schools, the first school of the township, and from there to Balltown and taught on the present site of Brockport, Pa From Balltown he moved to Hickory and bought the improved farm of John I Bundy, in Huston township, Clearfield county, later turning it over to his son, William H Hoyt, and then bought another improved farm one and one-half miles southwest ot this He died in Huston township in 1872, aged eighty-four years Dr Hoyt was the father of the following children Cornelia A, who married Benjamin Hulet, Sophia A, who married William F Green, Sarah M, who married Jeremiah Hewett, and William H, Edgar M, Eliza Jane, Seth R and Hiram M Eliza Jane married Norman Write

Hiram M Hoyt, father of Charles E, was born in Elk county, Pa, July 13, 1828 He became a farmer and accompanied his father to Huston township, Clearfield county, and here subsequently bought a farm of about 180 acres on which he spent the rest of his life, following the quiet pursuits of agriculture His death occurred here March 26, 1903 He married Barbara Brown, who survived until December, 1909 Six children were born to Hiram M and Barbara Hoyt, as follows Alexander, who is deceased, Elizabeth, who is the wife of W. H Bundy, Isaac, Charles Edward; Ida, who is the wife of O R Bundy; and Ellen, who is the wife of C C Dodd

Charles E Hoyt attended the country schools and since then has been more or less continuously engaged in farming During ten years of his life he also carried on lumbering He makes a specialty of dairying, keeping twenty-two head of cattle He is a member of the Grange and his practical progressiveness may be seen in the excellent care taken of his land and stock and in his building and maintaining a silo, and in the substantial character of his residence and barns Valuable coal deposits underlie his land and he has coal leases in Sandy township Mr Hoyt is a

stockholder in the Farmers and Traders Bank at Clearfield, of which he was formerly also a director

Mr Hoyt was married February 14, 1889, to Miss Elizabeth Bundy, a daughter of J. G Bundy, of Sandy township, and they have two children, Waneta A and Hiram M In politics he is a Republican and he is now serving on the township school board in his fourth term

GIDEON D NEFF, a prosperous farmer of Burnside township, was born August 26, 1837, in this township, not far from New Washington His parents were J B and Catherine (Barnhart) Neff, and he is a grandson of John Neff, who at one time carried on a distillery at Howardville, Center county, Pa.

J B Neff, father of our subject was born in Lancaster county, Pa, in 1795, and died September 9, 1879 In April, 1829, he came to Clearfield county with his brothers to begin clearing a 400 acre tract of land which had been purchased previously by their father, John Neff He was engaged in farming from 1860 to 1865 He later engaged in distilling, there being convenient springs, known as the "Big Springs" in the vicinity of the homestead The house which he occupied at that time was simply a log shanty J B Neff married Catharine Barnhart, who was born February 17, 1795, and who died May 2, 1879 Her parents were from Center county, Pa Col Jacob Barnhart served in the Revolutionary war. The father of our subject was one of the organizers of the M E church in his locality, the business of a distiller at that time not being thought incompatible with a

Christian life. In 1835 the wives of the Neffs walked to their old home in Center county, where they dried apples and made apple butter, there being no apples then raised in this new settlement. They were obliged to send their grain on horseback to the mill at Tyrone, Pa., and at times it had to be ground in a coffee mill.

Gideon D. Neff is the only one of his parents' children now living. He attended school in his boyhood and remained at home until reaching the age of 25 years, when he removed to his present place, which is known as the Altamont Farm. He has been engaged in farming and lumbering all his life and has been reasonably successful, being now regarded as one of the substantial and prosperous citizens of his township. He is a member of the M. E. church but is not active in politics.

Mr. Neff was married May 14, 1863, to Susannah Troxell, who was born December 24, 1845, at Muncie, Union county, Pa. Her parents were John and Lydia N. (Hessinger) Troxell, natives of Union county. The father, born March 23, 1807, died in 1879. Lydia Hessinger, born October 31, 1813, was a daughter of George and Catherine (Punsins) Hessinger, of Center township, Union county, she died May 2, 1893. Mrs. Neff's grandfather, George Troxell, was born November 30, 1782, at New Caledonia, Pa., his father having come to America from Germany. He married Mary Hoffman, who was born January 19, 1779.

The children of Mr. and Mrs. Neff are as follows. Rose Etta, born June 24, 1864, married Wm. H. McKee, has ten children, (of Huntingdon, Pa.) Carrie Viola, born September 24, 1866, is the wife of I. E. Ricketts of Utahville, Pa. and has four children. Mary, born February 26, 1869, is the wife of L. D. Gardner, of Glen Campbell and has six children. Laura, born June 10, 1871, is the wife of H. S. Gorman of Burnside township and has four children. James D., born 1874, married Mary E. Byers and they have one child. Russel B., born June 21, 1877, is the manager of the home farm. Reuben is deceased. Della Grace born June 15, 1884, is residing at home with her parents.

THOMAS LAURENCE WAY, president of the Clearfield County Agricultural Society, secretary of the Grange at Curwensville, and the owner of a well improved farm of 115 acres, located two miles north of Curwensville, Pa., is one of the representative men of Pike township and belongs to one of the honorable old Quaker families of the county. He was born August 11, 1860, in what is now Greenwood, but formerly was Bell township, Clearfield county, Pa., and is a son of David and Eliza (McGaughy) Way, and a grandson of Job Way.

David Way was born in Center county, Pa., January 12, 1837, came to Clearfield county in 1854, locating on his farm of 106 acres, situated in Pike township, and owns a one-half interest in a second farm of 100 acres, situated also in Pike township. He is a son of Job and Jane (Barlow) Way, the latter of whom was born in Sinking Valley. The children of Job and Jane Way were five in number, namely. Thomas, David, Mary Jane, Robert B. and Adam B. The survivors are. David, Robert B., who married Maria Blackburn, and Adam B., who married Jennie Blackburn. All of these children were born in Center county and from there Job Way moved to Clearfield county in 1854 and settled on a wild tract of 110 acres, in Pike township This land he subsequently cleared and it remained his home until the close of his life, his death occurring at the age of seventy-five years and his burial was at Plain View cemetery His widow survived to be eighty-three years of age They were members of the Society of Friends In his early years he was a Whig in his political views but became identified with the Republican party after its organization

David Way attended the district schools in his youth but his advantages were meager in comparison with those which are now almost thrust upon the present generation Farming and lumbering then claimed his attention and he continued to be interested more or less in both industries during his active years Following his marriage he continued to live in Bell township for one year and then moved to Penn township, remaining there two years, after which he came to Pike township, locating on his farm of 106 acres, situated three miles northwest of Curwensville, as previously stated, where he erected farm buildings He now lives retired on Ridge Avenue, Curwensville, a capable tenant managing the farm Being a consistent member of the Society of Friends, he has never been much of a politician, but has accepted various township offices and performed the duties of the same to the entire satisfaction of his fellow citizens He has served as school director, road supervisor and overseer of the Poor and at one time was also elected township treasurer He is a member of the Clear-field Agricultural Society and belongs to the Grange, taking a deep interest in farming in spite of his years, and anxious to witness the results of modern methods so different from those he made use of for many years Doubtless he has often proved that practice and theory differ widely He is one of Pike township's most esteemed and respected citizens

In November, 1859, David Way was married to Eliza McGaughy, a daughter of Thomas McGaughy, and five children were born to them as follows. Thomas Laurence, Ella J, who married Samuel Smith, of Curwensville, and has seven children—Verna, Maude, Gussie, William, Louella, Ruth and Lester, William E, who resides in the state of Oregon, and who married a Miss Palmer, John A, who lives in Nebraska, who married Ida McMullen, and has four children—David R, Ira L, John C. and Harvey D, and Martha, the wife of E. B Way, residing in Center county, who has the following children —Sarah H, Lydia L, David C, Pauline L, Loraine, E Elsworth and Isabel

Thomas Laurence Way attended the Chestnut Ridge schoolhouse His brother William and sister Ella J, both became school teachers, but he remained at home assisting his father on the farm until his own marriage, in 1882, when he settled on his father's Chestnut Ridge farm for a time, afterward moving to Bridgeport, where he engaged in teaming for L. E. Arnold for a season and then went back to farming In 1887 he moved to the Col E. A Irvin farm and was in the employ of Colonel Irvin for four years, when he bought property near Curwensville and occupied it for two years Mr Way then settled on the farm on which he has lived ever since, which is situated in Pike township and is the old Bloom homestead, formerly owned by the parents of his wife Mr Way has made many substantial improvements here, in 1889 building his fine barn and remodeling his house, which was erected in 1886 The old farm-house is yet standing and is the residence of Mrs Bloom, Mrs Way's mother Mr Way has about 108 acres of cleared land He carries on general farming and stock raising and makes a feature of dairying, selling his milk by wholesale, to the milk depot at Curwensville, keeping about twelve cows and calculating on having twenty-five gallons of milk a day

Mr Way was married November 22, 1882, to Miss S Jennie Bloom, a daughter of Thomas and Ruthanna (Walker) Bloom, and they have had five children, namely. Ruthanna, who married James E Irwin, a son of William T and Sarah Irwin, and has had six children—Wava Lucinda, James Byron, Carl Ellis, deceased, Dorothy Jane, Sarah Chloe and Ruth May, Mabel C, who married Monroe Bloom, a son of Allen and Mary Bloom, and has two children—Ansel Lee and Chester Alvin, Thomas Hugh, who married Olive Annie Moose, and has one son, Hugh Lawrence, Edith Lucinda, who married Earl McFadden, a son of Scott and Fannie McFadden, and has had two children—James Harold and Frances Marie. the latter being deceased, and David Elmer, who died April 11, 1898, aged twenty-two months and is buried in Plain View cemetery

The Bloom family, of which Mrs Way is a member, is one well known through Central Pennsylvania Her grandfather, Benjamin Bloom, was born in Huntingdon county, Pa , December 28, 1790, and died August 13, 1878, and was interred in the McClure cemetery in Pike township He married Sally McClure, who was born October 20, 1792, and died September 14, 1868 She was a daughter of Thomas and Margaret McClure, the former of whom was born in Ireland in 1762 and died in 1832 They had the following children. David, born June 21, 1788, Nancy, born in 1790, Sally, the grandmother of Mrs Way, born in 1792, John, born in 1796, Polly in 1798, Betsey, in 1802 Wilson M , in 1805, Peggy in 1807, and Thomas R , in 1809 Thomas Bloom, father of Mrs Way, was born September 7, 1813, near Curwensville, in Pike township In 1838 he was married first to Hannah Cleaver, who died May 17, 1853 They had nine children Elvina, Phineas, Harris, Alvin, Clark, Mary, Margaret, Susannah and Thaddeus Thomas Bloom was married secondly October 30, 1856, to Ruthanna Walker who still survives and lives on the homestead She was born November 5, 1831, in York county, Pa , a daughter of Azahel and Lydia Walker Two children were born to this marriage, Lydia Lucinda, born November 9, 1859, the wife of Isaac M Kester, and S Jennie, born May 16, 1861, the wife of Thomas L Way Thomas Bloom died November 20, 1892, and his burial was in Plain View cemetery He was a member of the Presbyterian church In politics he was a Democrat

In politics, Thomas L Way has been identified with the Republican party since he reached manhood He has served acceptably as school director, road supervisor, and judge of elections, in Pike township, and at times has served on political committees in his section Since 1888 he has been a member of the order of Odd Fellows and has progressed through the chairs of the local lodge

URIAH H STRAW, one of Boggs township's well known business men who has been engaged in a blacksmith business on his farm of seventy-eight acres of land, in Boggs township, Clearfield county, Pa , for the past sixteen years, was born in Center county, Pa , September 10, 1851, and is a son of John and Frances (Weaver) Straw

John Straw was born in Center county, where he spent his life, his business being farming His parents were Nicholas and Mollie Straw John Straw was a Democrat in politics, and served in some township offices He married Frances Weaver, who was also born in Center county They were members of the United Brethren church, good and worthy people They reared a large family, Uriah H being the eldest The others were Philip, Priscilla, who is deceased, Mary, who is the wife of Michael Murphy, Anna, who is the wife of Benjamin Johnstonbach, Amos, Daniel, William, who is deceased, Andrew, Celia, who is the wife of Calvin Beals, and Jacob and Edward

Uriah H Straw left school early in order to go to work in the woods, where he labored until he was eighteen years of age After that he gave attention to farming and for nine years was also in the blacksmith business in his native county On March 27, 1895, he moved on his present place and has remained here ever since

Mr Straw was married in 1873, to Miss Harriet Fahr, a daughter of Tobias and Mary (Sextman) Fahr, natives of Center county. Mrs Straw is one of the following family Maria, Lydia, Fayette, Aaron, Harriet, Jane, Martha and Elizabeth Mr and Mrs Straw have ten children, namely: Wesley, Lewis, Charles, Blanchard, Allen, Howard, May, Frances, Annabel and Martha The family belongs to the Methodist Episcopal church Mr Straw is a very well informed man and takes an interest in township affairs He casts his political vote with the Democratic party.

FRED CHARLES IMHOF, proprietor of the Hotel Tyler, at Tyler, Pa , is a well known citizen of Clearfield county, in which he has lived for twenty-two years He was born at St Mary's, Pa , in Elk county, January 20, 1869, and is a son of George and Mary (Seabert) Imhof

The parents of Mr Imhof are old and highly respected residents of St Mary's and are well known in Elk county Their family contained six children, as follows Catherine, who married John Keller, of Elk county; George W , who resides at New Bethlehem; Joseph F , who lives in the old home, Fred Charles, who is a resident of Tyler, Mary, who married Philip Kerner, of St. Mary's, and Charles E , his home being also at St Mary's

Fred Charles Imhof attended the public schools at St Mary's until he was fourteen years of age and then went to work in the mines and followed mining there for the following six years From there he came to Tyler in the capacity of a clerk in the store of the Clearfield Coal and Coke Company, remaining until 1893, when he went to DuBois and gained there his first hotel training, as porter

AND REPRESENTATIVE CITIZENS

617

in the National Hotel, later as bar tender Subsequently, in partnership with Lorenzo Bing, he embarked in a saloon and restaurant business on Brady street, securing his license from Judge Gordon Later he and William Schwem bought the Logan House from William Logan and conducted it for four years and then sold to James Chambers In 1904 Mr Imhof came to Tyler and bought the Tyler Hotel from Munch & Hay, and has conducted it ever since He has made many improvements and now has one of the best appointed hotels in this section His house is equipped with electric lights and a hot and cold water system and with steam heat He has fifteen bed rooms fitted with bath and special attention is given to making these comfortable sleeping apartments An elegant lobby leads into a fine dining room, where the best the market affords is provided in the cuisine The location of the Hotel Tyler is conveniently near the railroad station, and the moderate charge for all these accommodations is $1 50 per day

On March 24, 1894, Mr Imhof was married to Miss Clara Shugart a daughter of Joseph Shugart They are members of the Catholic church In politics Mr Imhof is a Democrat and fraternally he is identified with the Elks at DuBois The Hotel Tyler is the only hostelry that has ever been successful at Tyler, and in addition to owning this property, Mr Imhof is interested with a brother in general store at New Bethlehem

ENOCH BELLIS, mine superintendent, merchant, and bank director, of Burnside, is one of the best known business men in this part of Clearfield county He was born at Buckley, North Wales, March 5, 1871, son of Thomas and Ellen (Lamb) Bellis His grandparents on the paternal side were Robert and Elizabeth (Lewis) Bellis, the former a miner and merchant, who died in 1895 at the age of 68 years, his wife dying in 1854 at the age of 35 They were both natives of Wales

Thomas Bellis, father of our subject, was born at Buckley, North Wales, February 2, 1851 After a brief attendance at school, he entered the coal mines at the early age of eight years as a trapper boy, and was subsequently engaged in the mining industry in his native land, in one position or another, until reaching the age of 26 years He then resided for about three years in Lancashire, England By this time he had married and, deciding to better his fortunes by seeking larger opportunities in the New World, he came with his wife and children to this country about 1880, settling at Philipsburg, Pa, where he was engaged in mining until 1890 He subsequently removed to Urey, Indiana county, where he held positions as foreman and superintendent of mines until his death, which occurred November 20, 1910 He was married in 1870 to Miss Ellen Lamb, who was born in his own native town of Buckley, North Wales, May 9, 1848 Her parents were Thomas and Mary (Jones) Lamb, the father being a miner

Thomas Bellis was a man well known in mining circles Either by himself or associated with partners, he was interested financially in various coal companies, including the Urey Ridge Coal Co, the Burnside Coal Co, the Glenwood Coal Co, Cymbria Coal Co, the Springfield Coal Co, of which he was president, the Pioneer Coal Co, and others He was also vice-president of the Mahaffey National Bank, of Mahaffey, Pa, and vice-president of the Clymer Brick and Tile Co, and was interested in the Farmers Bank of Indiana, Pa , and the Eldorado Brick Co , of Altoona, also in the Barnsboro Bank, of Barnsboro, Pa The last three years of his life were spent in retirement from business activity at Altoona In addition to the subject of this sketch, Thomas and Ellen Bellis were the parents of the following children Sarah, who is the wife of Ed Kantz, of Burnside, Mary, who is unmarried and resides at Burnside, Cora, the wife of J N Ake, of Egg Harbor, N J , Maud, wife of John A Plyler, of Brookville, Pa , and Florence, who is single and resides at Mahaffey, Pa As may be seen, Thomas Bellis was a man of great energy and was a highly respected citizen He was a member of the Masonic lodge, No 314, at Clearfield, and the Consistory at Williamsport

Enoch Bellis, like his father, received an early initiation into the mining industry, beginning at the age of ten years, after a brief schooling After coming to this country he found employment as a clerk for the Passmore Burns Co of Urey, Pa , dealers in various supplies Two years later the firm became Passmore & Bellis, with our subject as manager, and he has continued a successful mercantile career, at the present time being in charge of the Burnside Supply Co 's store at Burnside and also of their store at Glen Campbell He is still a member of the firm of Passmore & Bellis at Urey, Pa , and is financially interested in the Springfield Coal Co at Nanty Glo, Pa He is also treasurer of the Springfield Land Co , and director of the Mahaffey National Bank, and is interested in the Farmers Bank of Indiana, Pa , the Eldorado Brick Co , of Altoona, the Bellmore Coal Co , of Burnside, Pa , the Barnesboro (Pa) Bank, and other flourishing business concerns He

has served in public office when it has been the desire of his fellow citizens, having been a member of the school board and being at present a member of the borough council of Burnside and tax collector He is a member, steward and trustee of the Methodist Protestant church, of Burnside He also belongs to the Masonic lodge at Clearfield

Mr Bellis was married June 22, 1907, to Perella Lovelace, who was born in Indiana county, Pa , June 17, 1878, a daughter of Thomas L and Laura (McCullough) Lovelace, the former of whom is still living at the age of 62 years Mrs Bellis's mother died in 1887 at the age of 31 years She was a daughter of Alexander McCullough, born in 1824, who came from Indiana county to Clearfield county, with his parents, John and Margaret (Sharp) McCullough The latter was a daughter of Capt Andrew Sharp of Sharpsburg, who was shot by an Indian on the Ohio river, and died from the effects of his wound Mrs Bellis, who is a graduate of the Burnside high school, belongs like her husband, to the Methodist Protestant church, and is an active member, being president of the Ladies' Aid Society There have been born to our subject and wife four children, namely Helen, April 17, 1899, who is attending school; Catherine Ruth, May 13, 1902, Sarah Jane, November 26, 1905, and Gwendola, who died in infancy

JAMES McCROSSIN, owner and proprietor of the Madera Inn, at Madera, Pa , has had considerable experience in hotel keeping and is a very popular host with the traveling public He was born April 4, 1855, in Bradford county, Pa , and is a son of James and Mary (Donnely) McCrossin

James McCrossin was born in County Ty-

JAMES McCROSSIN

rone, Ireland, and his wife in the city of New York. They were married in Bradford county, where both are buried. They had the following children. Mary, who is deceased, was the wife of Austin Quinlan. Thomas, who is deceased, John, James, Margaret, who is the wife of Daniel Fink, Edward Gilbert, Sarah, who is the wife of Michael Cox, George, William, and Nellie, who is the widow of Edward Moore. Both parents were members of the Catholic church. The father was a farmer.

James McCrossin attended school until he was fifteen years of age and later worked in a saw mill. After that he spent several years at lumbering and for five more years worked in the tannery at Osceola, subsequently becoming a contractor in the woods, in 1884, and continuing until 1890, when he went into the hotel business, operating a public house at Madera for fourteen months. For the following five years he was proprietor of the American House at Houtzdale, afterward, for one year, of the St. Charles Hotel at Clearfield, and three months he directed the affairs of the Woodland Hotel. Mr. McCrossin resumed lumbering and spent two years in the industry in Cambria county, and then again became a hotel man, renting his present property at first and then buying. He demolished the old building and erected a new one which is modern in every equipment and is ornamented with tile blocks, which are very attractive.

On July 3, 1874, Mr. McCrossin was married to Miss Mary Wilkison, a daughter of John H. Wilkison. They have had seven children, namely: Margaret, who is deceased, was the wife of Haskell Read, Rosie, who is deceased, Edward, John, who is proprietor of the Hotel Ben Venue, at Irvona, Pa., and

Fred, Thomas and Frances. Mr. McCrossin and family are members of the Catholic church. In politics he is a Democrat. He belongs to the order of Elks and the L. O. O. M. at Madera.

WILLIAM T. HAY, a member of the firm of Hay Brothers, plumbers, doing business at No. 146 West Long avenue, DuBois, Pa., was born on Lost Creek, Schuylkill county, Pa., August 25, 1871, and is a son of William E. and Anna (Dunsten) Hay.

William E. Hay came to DuBois from Pottsville, Pa., in 1882 and carried on a plumbing business in this borough for many years. He married Anna Dunsten and they had eight children, namely: Millie, who is the wife of Frank Gunsburg, Bertha S., who is the wife of Charles H. Hill, William T., Isaac D., who is a member of the plumbing firm of Hay Brothers, Restore B., Strange P., Anna, who is the wife of Theodore E. Vosburg, and Hazel, who is the wife of Harry S. Hall.

Before coming to DuBois with his parents in 1882, William T. Hay had lived for a short time in Kansas. He began to help his father in the latter's plumbing shop when quite young and thus learned every detail of the business. In 1897, in partnership with his brother, Isaac D. Hay, he embarked in the plumbing business and a very substantial enterprise has resulted, this firm taking the lead in their line at DuBois.

On September 6, 1899, Mr. Hay was married to Miss Matilda M. Moore, and they have three children: Arthur Cole, Howard Robert and Raymond Thomas. Mr. Hay and family reside at No. 16 S. Jared street. In politics he is a Republican.

JOHN NOWRY, a prosperous farmer of Burnside township, was born in Burnside township, October 20, 1862, a son of Robert and Eliza (Smith) Nowry His paternal grandfather, also named Robert, was a soldier in the War of 1812

Robert Nowry, the father of our subject, was born in Pennsylvania in 1835 and came to Clearfield county when a young man He was a machine blacksmith by trade, but on coming to this section he engaged in the lumber business, in which he was reasonably successful His death took place in 1868 His wife, Mrs Eliza Smith Nowry, is still living and resides on the old homestead, being now 82 years of age She is a daughter of John and Rebecca (Dane) Smith, who came to America from County Leitrim, Ireland In addition to John, the subject of this sketch, there are three of her daughters now living, namely Elizabeth, wife of T B Davis of Burnside township, Minnie, wife of Ed Shumway, of Chester City, Pa, and Birdie, who is the wife of John McCormick of Philadelphia

John Nowry, with his sisters, after their father's death, was cared for by an uncle, and he subsequently resided with them until his own death in 1908 He was then quite an elderly man, having taken part in the gold rush to California in 1849, and was familiarly known as "Uncle Ed" He has been engaged since early manhood in farming and lumbering, having followed successfully in his father's footsteps, and is now one of the prosperous citizens of the township He is a member of the Protestant Methodist church, and is a Republican politically He has been supervisor of his township for almost twenty years, and has also served as committeeman He has done active and useful work for his party and believes that it is every citizen's duty to see that good government is maintained

Mr Nowry married Miss Laura Ball, of Big Rapids, Mich She was born in 1868, her parents being John and Rosanna (Baer) Ball Her father, who was born in Ohio, was an officer in the Union army during the Civil war, enlisting with four brothers, in Company D, 35th Illinois Regiment His wife's father was a native of Virginia Mr and Mrs Nowry have one adopted child, Nellie, now aged ten years

H D McKEEHEN, postmaster and general merchant, at Berwinsdale, Clearfield county, Pa, was born in Jordan township, Clearfield county, July 3, 1869, and is a son of James and Mary Jane (Glasgow) McKeehen

James McKeehen was a son of David and Mary Ann McKeehen, of Scotch and Irish descent He engaged in farming and lumbering in Clearfield county and in 1873 embarked in the mercantile business He married Mary Jane Glasgow, a daughter of John and Sarah Glasgow, and they had the following children born to them Mary Lavinia, wife of C D. McMurray, and H D, John and Joel

H D McKeehen was educated in the public schools and the Lock Haven State Normal School, in which institution he was a student for two years Following this he spent two years on the road representing a medical supply house and afterward passed four years on a farm Then he turned his attention to merchandising, buying the stock of L L Hile, at Berwinsdale, and since then has conducted a first class general store, supplying a large surrounding territory On January 24, 1900, he was appointed postmaster at Berwinsdale and

JOHN Y. RAFFERTY

has proved a satisfactory public official In politics he is an independent thinker and voter

On May 23, 1901, Mr McKeehen was married to Miss Josephine Bell, a daughter of Warren and Marian (Snyder) Bell, farming people of Ferguson township Mr and Mrs Bell had four children May, Josephine, Wayne and Lillian, the last named being the wife of R L Williams Mr and Mrs McKeehen are members of the Presbyterian church He is an active and interested citizen of Jordan township and has served for nine years on the school board

CHARLES A McDONALD, one of the enterprising and successful young business men of DuBois, Pa , is proprietor of the Hotel Windsor and also is interested in handling real estate He was born April 8, 1881, and is the only son of Donald and Mary (Harris) McDonald

Donald McDonald was born and reared in Canada and came to Pennsylvania in early manhood, locating in the neighborhood of Mix Run, in Cameron county, where he operated a saw-mill and conducted a general mercantile business He died a comparatively young man He married Mary Harris, who is a daughter of the late James Harris, once a well known man who was connected as a civil engineer with the construction of some of the early railroads in this section Mrs McDonald came to DuBois with her son in 1887 and is associated with him in his numerous business enterprises

Charles A McDonald was educated in the DuBois schools, Pittsburg College and the University of Colorado, being creditably graduated in the latter institution with the class of 1903 For three years afterward he followed his maternal grandfather's profession, civil engineering, on railroads in the West After returning to DuBois he entered into partnership with G W Smyers in the lumber and planing-mill business, on Daily Street, in which he continued until 1909, when he sold his interest to his partner and purchased the Hotel Windsor from H R Burns After taking charge the whole place was remodeled The main building, which contains twenty-six bedrooms, was built by Mr and Mrs McDonald (his mother), and in the annex they have twenty-two comfortable bed-rooms, all fitted up in first class style In connection with the hotel a modern restaurant is conducted, which has quite a local reputation for its excellent cuisine The rates of the Hotel Windsor are very moderate, being $1 50 per day.

Mr McDonald was married April 12, 1905, to Miss Josephine McClure, who is a daughter of the late Dr M L McClure They have an interesting family of four little ones, namely Maime and Josephine, twin daughters, and Donald and Harold, sons The family home is located at No 28 N Main Street, DuBois Mr and Mrs McDonald with Mrs Donald McDonald, are all members of the Roman Catholic church Mr McDonald takes a lively interest in politics and has served as chairman on the Democratic organization in his ward He belongs to the order of Elks at DuBois

JOHN Y RAFFERTY, justice of the peace at Grampian, Pa , auditor of the borough and a general merchant here, is a native of this place, born January 31, 1876, and is a son of John B and Bridget (Casey) Rafferty.

John B Rafferty was born in Penn Township, a son of Thomas and Martha (Young) Rafferty, who were pioneers in Clearfield County, he being a native of Ireland and she of Clearfield County John B Rafferty was an early merchant and was a justice of the peace at Grampian, when the place was still known as Pennsville He was a member of the Catholic church His death occurred April 20, 1877 He married Bridget Casey, who died January 1, 1889, and both were buried in the Catholic cemetery at Grampian

John Y Rafferty is in partnership in the mercantile business, with his brother, James L Rafferty, the firm name being Rafferty Brothers They were educated at Grampian and St Francis College at Loretto John Y Rafferty married Miss Jane McKeown, a daughter of James McKeown, of Penn Township, and they have five children Janetta, John, Francis, Mary and Beatrice They are members of the Catholic church Mr Rafferty was elected a justice of the peace, on the Democratic ticket, to serve from 1910 until 1915 He owns a one-third interest in the John B Rafferty Hunting Club and an estate of 182 acres, situated in Penn township, Clearfield county

James L Rafferty was born at Grampian, Pa, October 11, 1874 He married Miss Ella McKeown, a daughter of James McKeown and a twin sister of the wife of John Y Rafferty Mr and Mrs Rafferty have six children · Ernestine, Inez, Genevieve, Paul Arthur and Leonard Mr and Mrs Rafferty are members of the Catholic church He is a Democrat in politics and is serving as a member of the borough council His business interests are identical with those of his younger brother.

PORTER KINPORTS, a respected resident of Cherry Tree, where he was for many years one of the town's most active business men, but is now retired, was born at Frankstown, Pa, September 6, 1831, son of John and Mary (Rench) Kinports John Kinports, the father, was a native of Pennsylvania, born near Lancaster, and came with his family to Cambria county in 1845, having previously spent some time in Huntingdon and Blair counties In the former he was engaged in farming and lumbering, and later at Hollidaysburg, Blair county, was occupied as a miller and millwright. He was a Free Mason, belonging to the Blue Lodge at Hollidaysburg He died in 1862 at the age of 68 years His wife Mary (Rench) Kinports died at the age of eighty-two She was of Maryland parentage The subject of this sketch is the only one of their family of seven sons and three daughters that is now living

Porter Kinports attended school until reaching the age of 13 years From that time until his father's death in 1862 he was in the latter's employ or was associated with him in business matters, with the exception of two terms that he spent in teaching school during the early part of that period. For one year he was in partnership with a brother, but on the latter's death he conducted the business alone, from 1845 to 1903 being engaged in lumbering, farming and conducting a mercantile business at Cherry Tree Aside from his ordinary business, he is president of the First National

Bank of Cherry Tree, and a director of the Water Company and the Power and Light Company He is however now retired from active business life Mr. Kinports is a Democrat in politics, he served one term as burgess and was for some time a member of the school board and a councilman of the borough He has belonged to the I O O F. lodge at Cherry Tree for the past 57 years He is also a Mason, belonging to the Blue Lodge at Curwensville, the Chapter at Clearfield, the Commandery at Philipsburg, the Consistory at Williamsport, and the Mystic Shrine at Altoona He has also been a member of the A O U W lodge at Cherry Tree for 26 years His connection with the Masonic order dates back to 1867 and he is now the oldest Sir Knight in the southern part of the county He was a charter member of Noble Lodge at New Washington

Mr Kinports was married September 18, 1860, to Margaret B Mahaffey, a daughter of John and Ella (Byers) Mahaffey, born April 1837 Of the ten children born to this marriage, but four are now living, namely Minetta, wife of John Driscoll, residing in West Virginia, who has one child, J Clyde, residing on the old Mahaffey home in this vicinity, who married Mary Belle Lydick, Stella, wife of George Davis of West Virginia, Boyd W, who is engaged in the lumber business at Cherry Tree, and who is unmarried A daughter Gertrude, who is now deceased, was the wife of Joseph Wilson She left one child, who is now living with the subject of this sketch On September 18, 1910, Mr and Mrs Kinport celebrated their Golden Wedding anniversary, some 200 guests being present, and the occasion was a most enjoyable one to all

WILLIAM S MOORE, superintendent for the Corona Coal Company, at Madera, is an experienced man in his line of work and has climbed from a minor clerkship to his present responsible position through absolute merit There is very little sentiment about big business corporations and when they delegate important duties to a man it is very certain that he is deserving of them William S Moore was born February 9, 1878, in Blair County, Pa, and is a son of Charles W and Emma (Hewitt) Moore

Charles W Moore was reared and educated in Blair county, where he followed farming for twenty-two years and then went into the meat business at Madera, with which he is still connected, being manager for the Madera Trading Company He married Emma Hewitt, of Hollidaysburg, and they have seven children William, Samuel, Thomas, Walter, John, Maude and Helen

William S Moore attended the public schools at Brisbin and the High Schools of Madera and Houtzdale All his business life has been connected with the coal industry and for eight years he has been in the employ of the Corona Coal Company

Mr Moore was married in 1898 to Miss Jane E Shoff, a daughter of Robert and Hannah (Dewitt) Shoff, and a granddaughter of Samuel and Jane (Haggerty) Shoff, and of George and Rachel (Bloom) Dewitt Mrs Moore was the eldest of nine children born to her parents Mr and Mrs Moore have four children, namely· Robert, Emma, Henry and Clyde Mr. and Mrs Moore attend the Presbyterian church In politics he is a Republican but takes only the interest of a patriotic and earnest citizen who desires faithful men in public offices as well as in business concerns He is a Knight Templar Mason, belonging to the lower branches at Osceola, Pa , and to the Commandery at Williamsport

WILLIAM MENZIE, president of the borough council of DuBois, Pa , has been continuously in the employ of John E Du-Bois, the largest individual lumber owner of the United States, since 1879, and now has charge of the retail department He came to DuBois from Nova Scotia, where he was born January 12, 1846 His parents were William and Agnes (Donaldson) Menzie, natives of Scotland

William Menzie spent his boyhood on his father's farm and remained there until he reached manhood, when he went to Halifax, N S , where he started a draying and express business on his own account and carried it on for about seven years In 1879 he came to the U S and to DuBois, which was then only a small lumber town He entered the employ of John DuBois and spent the first winter lumbering in the deep woods, afterwards being given charge of the yards, where the labor was not so hard but the responsibilty was greater He has continued, as mentioned above, and now is one of the oldest employes

In 1884 William Menzie was married to Miss Lavina Burns, of Osceola Mills, Clearfield county, and they have two children Mary B and James F Mr Menzie and family are members of the Second Metho-

dist Episcopal church of DuBois and among its most faithful workers Mr Menzie is an ardent Republican and for fifteen years has been a member of the DuBois borough council and has been president of this body since 1905

He has been closely identified with the business interests of the community and his time and means are freely given to anything tending to the betterment of the city and its people He is a past master of Garfield Lodge No 559 Free and Accepted Masons and is the present Eminent Commander of Bethany Commandery No 83, Knights Templar, both bodies being located in DuBois

FRANK G CONLEY, justice of the peace at Westover and a well known agriculturist of Chest township, was born at Cherry Tree, Clearfield county, Pa , January 5, 1861 He is a son of John and a grandson of Bernard Conley The latter, who was a native of Ireland, came to America in 1830, finding employment at Hollidaysburg, Pa , on the construction of the old canal He afterwards followed blacksmithing and farming and died in Cambria county in 1866 at the age of 60 years. The maiden name of his wife was Mary Green.

John Conley, father of our subject, was born at Hollidaysburg, in 1831 He was a blacksmith and farmer by occupation and came to Cherry Tree about 1855 at the time of his marriage In 1864 he removed to Chest township where he continued in the same lines of industry He died December 12, 1892 He was a man of importance in the community, a member of the Methodist Protestant church He also belonged to the Masonic lodge at Curwensville, of which he was a charter member, and to the chapter at Clearfield, also to the I O O. F lodge at Ansonville, Pa , and to the Grange   He was a Democrat in politics and served as justice of the peace for 15 years, also for some time as a member of the school board   Of his children there are three daughters and two sons now living, namely   Etta, wife of Samuel Morrison, Alice, wife of W Billings, of Portage, Pa , Pearl, wife of E M McGarbey, a Christian Alliance minister of Cambria county, Pa , William F , an Evangelical pastor, residing at New Paris, Pa , and Ernest, a Christian Alliance pastor, of Williamsport, Pa

Frank G Conley, after attending school, remained at home with his parents until reaching the age of 29 years   He then came to Westover and entered the employ of the William F Mosser Tanning Company, remaining with them for 20 years, or practically up to the present time   He was also engaged in farming and lumbering before coming to Westover   Mr Conley lived in the county when lumbering and rafting were the principal occupations during the winter and spring, and made several trips down the river   A Democrat politically, he was elected justice of the peace in 1909 and has rendered creditable service in that office   He was assessor of the township three years, has served as burgess of the borough of Westover, and has been ten years a member of the council   He has also served as election officer at various times

Mr. Conley was married in 1879 to Emma Klinger, who was born June 18, 1860, at Newburg, this county, a daughter of Benjamin F and Rebecca (Barto) Klinger   Mr and Mrs Conley have been the parents of five children, as follows   Blanche, wife of Milton Westover, a farmer of Chest township, who has three children, A M Conley of Westover, a barber, who married Verta Westover and has one child, Verda, who is unmarried, and William F and Vincent, who are attending school

JOHN C JOHNSTON, owner and proprietor of a hardware store at Ansonville, Pa , and one of Jordan township's representative and reliable citizens was born in Jordan township, Clearfield county. Pa , September 28, 1833, and is a son of Robert and Mary (Cameron) Johnston

The parents of Mr Johnston were born in Scotland   They came to Clearfield county and settled in Jordan township in 1831 and the father carried on farming here during the whole of his active life   They were quiet, virtuous, hard working people and were consistent members of the Presbyterian church   They had the following children.   Robert M , Mary, wife of Reuben Caldwell, John C ; Isabel, wife of Isaac F Bloom, James W , William, David, Mark L , and Elizabeth, wife of S. H Witherow

John C Johnston had but meager educational opportunities in his boyhood and was thirteen years old before he had a chance to go to school   The country was yet wild and but sparsely settled and few schools had been organized   He then learned the carpenter trade and for twenty-five years worked at the same, spending eighteen years in the West   In 1896 he embarked in his present business at Ansonville and has built up a large trade in all kinds of hardware and argicultural implements

Mr Johnston was married first in 1864, to Miss Christina Curry, who died in 1880 Seven children were born to them but only one of these survives, John J, who now resides in Armstrong county, Pa In 1883 Mr Johnston was married to Mrs Martha M (Shoff) Witherow, a daughter of Frederick Shoff and the widow of Henry Witherow Mrs Witherow had one son, H Lynn Witherow Mr and Mrs Johnston have one son, Cameron S, who resides at Ansonville They are members of the Presbyterian church He is a Republican in politics and at different times has served acceptably in almost all of the township offices, but at present devotes all his attention to his business

ADAM J HAAG, general merchant and a member of the borough council at Du-Bois, Pa, is a representative man of this place, of which he has been a resident since 1889 He was born in Bavaria, Germany, and is a son of Christian and Catherine (Knarr) Haag

Christian Haag and his son Christian served in the German army before coming to the United States in 1867 The family settled in Bell township, Clearfield county, on a wooded tract which they subsequently cleared and converted into a productive farm. The log cabin that was built in the early days of their settlement was burned in 1881 Eleven children were born to Christian and Catherine Haag as follows Christian, Jacob, Henry, Louisa, wife of Jacob Faudie, Elizabeth (Mrs Hartsfelt), Lewis, Frederick, Conrad D, Catherine, wife of Lewis Hartsfelt; Adam J, and Margaret, wife of George Henry

Adam J Haag attended the local schools and later the Normal School at Grampian He began to teach school when but sixteen years of age, spending six years at that work, in Penn, Bloom, Bell and Brady townships, where there are many of his old pupils still living When he came first to DuBois, he entered the employ of A. T. Sprankle, with whom he remained for three years, and then erected a store building on the corner of Olive and Brady Streets where he was engaged in merchandising for five years Mr. Haag then found that his increasing business demanded more commodious quarters, and he erected his present building, on the corner of Jared and Brady Streets, into which he moved in 1897. It is of brick construction and is three stories in height

In March, 1889, Mr Haag was married to Miss Emma J Funk, a daughter of Jacob and Louisa (Sternberger) Funk. Mrs Haag was born in Brady township, Clearfield county, but her parents were natives of Germany. They had four children, namely Louisa, who is the wife of C D. Haag, Rudolph, Emma J, who is the wife of Adam J Haag, and Ella, who is the wife of W O Smiley Mr and Mrs Haag have one daughter, Laura They are members of the German Reformed church Mr. Haag is a prominent Mason, belonging to the Blue Lodge at DuBois, the Chapter at Brookville, and the Scottish Rite at Williamsport In politics a Republican, he has been a faithful party worker and as an active and interested citizen has accepted public responsibilities at times For twelve years he served as a member of the school board, and as a member of the borough council has furthered many public-spirited enterprises designed to benefit the whole community.

SAMUEL MILES KING, a well known and respected citizen, who is engaged in agriculture in Burnside township, was born June 15, 1879, on the old King homestead in this township. He is a descendant and great-grandson of Reeder King, who was the first raftsman on the Susquehanna river. At one time Reeder King built an ark for the transportation of coal, but found that coal was too heavy a substance for river transportation in this manner. As showing the difficulties and privations of pioneer existence, it may be said that at one time the Kings had to dig potatoes before they were half grown in order to keep from starving, as they had no other food.

John King, the grandfather of our subject, came to Clearfield county from Westmoreland county in 1826, settling between the river and Chest creek. His wife in maidenhood was Nancy McCreary.

William King, son of John and father of Samuel Miles King, was born in Burnside township about 1827 and died July 16, 1904, at the age of 77 years. During his active life he was engaged in farming and lumbering. He purchased the present King farm and cleared it of the timber, which he rafted down the river. He also erected a 12x12 log house still standing on the homestead. He was a member of the Baptist church at Westover. In politics he cast his vote for the Democratic ticket, but was not an active politician. He married Mary E. Kinter, a daughter of John and Margaret Kinter, and she is still living at the age of 69 years. Their children were as follows: Lydia, wife of Joseph Brothers, Edward, who resides in Westover, Cynthia, wife of M. Singerman, residing in California, Sabina, wife of John Metzger, of Blandburg, Cambria county; Samuel Miles, the subject of this sketch, and Frank, who is a resident of Spokane, Wash.

Samuel Miles King, after attending school in his boyhood, became actively engaged in farming with his father, with whom he was associated until the latter's death. He has since continued in the same occupation and has been successful, having a valuable and well cultivated farm. He is a member of the Grange at Harmony, and of the order of Red Men. He is a member of the Baptist church. In politics he is a Democrat, and has held local office, having served two terms as supervisor and one term—in 1903 —as township clerk.

He was married January 7, 1902, to Pearl Keim, who was born at Cherry Tree, this county, May 5, 1880, a daughter of John T. and Mary (Kneedler) Keim, the latter a daughter of John Kneedler. Mrs. King's father is still living at Cherry Tree. The Keim family consisted of the following children: Sarah Alma, wife of W. T. Stahl, of Mehaffey; Charles Percy, a carpenter residing in Cambria county, Thomas E., residing at Summer Hill, Cambria county, Mary Ellen, widow of C. C. Davis, Pearl, wife of our subject, Bessie A., wife of J. Diamond, of Summerhill, William P. (twin brother of Bessie), who resides at Summerhill, Steele R., residing at Cherry Tree, and Bernice L., at home.

The children born to our subject and wife are Clarice Esther, born December 27, 1903, Arthur Maxwell, born March 29, 1906, and Thomas Carlton, born August 17, 1910 Mr King is a member of the local Grange and is known as an enterprising and reliable citizen

JOHN F. GROFF, who is owner and proprietor of a commodious and well kept public house at Ramey, Pa , the Hotel Ramey, and is also auditor of the borough, was born in Lancaster county, Pa , November 10, 1866, and is a son of Adam G and Anna (Snyder) Groff

The parents of Mr Groff were born also in Lancaster county, where they spent their lives The father was both merchant and miller and was a well known man Of their family of children, John F. is the eldest, the others being. Fred F ; Hannah, wife of H M Keen, Elizabeth S , wife of Dr. R V. L Raub, and William

John F Groff had excellent educational opportunities afforded him, passing his earlier boyhood in the Lancaster county schools, afterward spending two years in the Millersville State Normal School and later taking a commercial course in the Weidler & Musser Business College, and then learned the milling business and followed the same for eighteen years He is a man of very practical ideas and in order to get better acquainted with modern methods, he spent some time among the great milling plants in Northern Minnesota He subsequently carried on a milling business at Quarryville for five years, and at Houtzdale for two years and then retired from the milling line and purchased his present hotel

Mr Groff was married in May, 1895, to Miss Margaret Neilson Williams, a daughter of W N and Elizabeth (Jacobs) Williams, who were natives of Lancaster county, her father being a railroad man. Other children born to Mr and Mrs Williams were· Elizabeth, wife of Ralph Rapalee, Edward, Margaret, wife of Mr. Groff, as above mentioned, Anna, wife of George M Brientnell, William, Rudolph, and Augusta, wife of W B Hoar Mr and Mrs Groff have the following children Eugene E , Edward D W , Sena R , William A and John J Mr and Mrs Groff attend the Episcopal church, in which she was reared He is identified with a number of fraternal organizations including: Tyrone Lodge, No 212, F. & A M , at Quarryville, the Elks at Tyrone, the Knights of Pythias at Houtzdale, and the Brotherhood of America Politically Mr. Groff is a Republican and is active in public affairs both in borough and county.

Both the Groff and Snyder families as well as the Williams and Jacob families have belonged to Pennsylvania for generations.

JOHN E DUBOIS, a leading business man and representative citizen of DuBois, Pa., was born on his father's farm in the state of New York, May 15, 1861 His ancestors on the paternal side were of French origin, coming to this country in 1634, and settling on the western part of Staten Island, N Y They were members of the Reformed church of France and probably came to America to avoid religious persecution, Staten Island being then numbered among the Dutch colonial possessions Among the posterity of these early immigrants were some whose names are prominent in theology, law, arms and business

The paternal grandfather of the subject of this sketch was John DuBois, a farmer of Tioga county, N Y, who was the owner of considerable tracts of timber land and also built and operated a saw-mill He married Lucy Crocker, daughter of Ezekiel Crocker, one of the first settlers near Binghamton, N Y, who moved there from Connecticut with three of his sons and his daughter Lucy, she being then eleven years of age Lucy became the housekeeper of the family and though so young attended to her multifarious duties with an energy and decision that were later among her most conspicuous characteristics and marked her character throughout her life In those days the Indians constituted almost the entire population of the region John DuBois' family consisted of eight sons and two daughters, the three eldest sons being Ezekiel, John and David Of these Ezekiel was the father of the subject of this sketch

John DuBois, above mentioned, uncle of our subject, was born near Owego, N Y, March 3, 1809 He was educated in the district schools and for a short time attended an academy at Owego He was early trained to habits of industry and received but little schooling after he was fifteen years old Soon after he became engaged in rafting lumber down the north branch of the Susquehanna river to Columbia At the age of twenty his father built a saw-mill about two miles from Tioga Center, and John (with David, a younger brother) stocked the mill with logs in the winter and rafted the lumber when the spring floods served Ezekiel, the elder brother, carried on the business of shoemaking

About the time John was of age his father bought a farm for $6,000 at Tioga Center He asked the three older sons, Ezekiel, John and David, to stay with him until it was paid for, promising to give it to them when the deed was made The father, however, had the deed made to himself, settling with his sons on a different basis, whereby they had a lease of the farm, mill and timberland to work on shares, besides a stipulated salary The three brothers, with one sister to keep house for them, left the old home and took up separate quarters The eldest brother, Ezekiel, soon married Clarissia Badger, they being the parents of the subject of this sketch David died at the age of 33 years, unmarried

Owing to various causes, the brothers (the firm was E DuBois & Bros) were not very successful in their combined enterprise They subsequently engaged in a mercantile business with another brother, Matthias, which connection lasted five years In the winter of 1835 John DuBois took advantage of an opportunity to purchase 1,000 acres of valuable timber land for $3,000, partly on credit This netted the brothers a considerable profit At the end of five years they closed up their business with property and money to the value of $25,000 cash, beside the 1,000 acres from which the pine only had been taken off, it was still well covered with hemlock, also teams, tools, sleds, chains, etc In the division Ezekiel took most of the real estate and personal property for his share, and John and David, constituting a new firm, engaged in a new lumbering enterprise in Lycoming county, Pa, Matthias being subsequently taken into the firm David died in 1848, John and Mathias paying back to the family $4,500 Matthias married and his brother John lived with him in a pleasant residence on the Lycoming.

They were engaged together in various lumber and other enterprises during some ten years, buying large quantities of land in Lycoming and Clearfield counties, including some 32,000 acres in the latter and about 800 acres in the city of Williamsport, besides erecting saw-mills, etc, and a residence in the city of Wil-liamsport. About this time Matthias' health began to fail, and he finally died, and John, after the year 1863, carried on the business alone

After his brother's death John DuBois built a large mill and quite a town situated on the Susquehanna above Williamsport, which was called DuBois town. He supplied this mill with logs from his lands in Clearfield county, floating them down the river. He met with great opposition from men running lumber down the stream in rafts, who sued him in the courts and, when he gained the suits, drove spikes and pieces of iron into his logs, which caused him a great amount of damage. In 1860 the boom built across the river to hold the logs gave way, letting about 50,000,000 feet of logs go adrift, of which about four and a half million feet belonged to Mr DuBois and his partner. Many of these logs floated down to Chesapeake Bay. After considerable con-troversy between the various owners at Lock Haven and Williamsport as to the best way to recover their floating property, Mr DuBois was empowered to go over the ground and see what he could get. He succeeded in sell-ing a large number at a much higher price than any other member of the committee consid-ered them worth, and he and his partner them-selves bought all the logs that were in the Chesapeake Bay, Mr DuBois going to Havre de Grace to make arrangements for securing them. The logs were lying mostly along the

beach and many had been cut up by the own-ers of the land on which they had gone ashore. Some of these owners refused to allow him to take the logs, and in some cases he paid them damages to settle the matter. In other cases he brought suit in the U S courts and in each case recovered their value

In October, 1861, another large lot of logs went adrift, and Mr DuBois being again com-missioned by the lumbermen to recover them, went through many of the same experiences as before, his trouble being chiefly with the owners along the river, the situation being complicated by the war, some of the owners along the Maryland shores refusing to ac-knowledge the jurisdiction of the U S courts. Owing to these troubles and also to another considerable loss due to a flood in March, 1865, a stock company called the "Williamsport Transient Lumber Company" was formed t o better manage such transactions in the future. Mr DuBois made some propositions to the company for the recovery of logs in the bay, but being strongly opposed by a man named Herdic, they were declined and he was left out in the cold. The measures taken by the com-pany proved impracticable and many of the logs were ultimately lost

In the spring of 1861 Mr. DuBois found that his partner was untrustworthy and that the accounts of the concern were in a confused condition, and he consequently found it neces-sary to give his personal attention to the busi-ness in Williamsport. Upon a fuller investi-gation he discovered that his partner had given various notes for large sums, failing to make any record of them, and which now came in for payment. He had also, as was later dis-covered, received large amounts and pocketed the same without making any record of them on the books, and had been guilty of other acts of dishonesty This resulted in a severance of the partnership, after a settlement which left Mr DuBois much poorer than he had thought himself

John DuBois was a man of great inventive genius When the Philadelphia, Wilmington & Baltimore Railroad Company in 1861 decided to build a bridge across the Susquehanna river at Havre de Grace to take the place of the steam ferry boat, Mr DuBois set to work to think of a plan for laying the piers, the water being very deep and a similar attempt having previously failed He finally matured such a plan and sought an interview with the president of the company to lay it before him, but having divulged his plan on the way to a Mr Crossman, who had charge of the bridges who told it to the company's engineer, Mr Parker, the latter laid claim to the invention subsequently, and Mr DuBois having obtained a patent several law suits resulted, whereby Mr DuBois at first lost but subsequently had his prior rights affirmed by the Supreme Court, the railroad company being obliged to pay him damages He subsequently took out many other valuable patents, both in this and foreign countries

Mr DuBois' business enterprises were on a large scale After getting rid of his dishonest partner he sold the mill built by them at Williamsport, together with some other real estate and boom stock for $91,000 and bought a mill near to the one sold for $21,000 and soon after bought a large steam saw-mill, with a number of tenant houses, costing altogether over $120,000 His mills there had a sawing capacity of about 120,000 feet in eleven hours In the spring of 1873 he began to improve his property in Clearfield county, which at that time was mostly a wilderness The site of the now thriving village of DuBois then contained only three houses Here he built several saw-mills of large capacity, with other machinery for cutting shingles, packing-boxes, dressing lumber, framing timber, etc, together with a large brick building for kiln drying lumber He also erected a large brick building for store and hotel, 50 x 100 feet, three stories high besides the basement His lumber yard contained latterly over 15,000,000 feet of sawed lumber, besides an ample stock of logs He also owned a foundry and machine shop, and had a large and well improved farm These various industries gave employment to more than 350 men during the busy season and to a large portion of that number for the whole year Near his land were three collieries working five and a half and two and a half veins of coal of excellent quality

In his younger days Mr DuBois was fond of hunting and often bagged such big game as deer and bears, besides catamounts, wild-cats, etc At different times he lost considerable property by fire, having but partial insurance Had he been fully insured he would have had a considerable amount to pay yearly in premiums

Mention has already been made of his brother Ezekiel, who was for a time associated with him in business matters, and who married Clarissa Badger, they being the parents of John E DuBois, whose name appears at the head of this article John E DuBois spent his boyhood on the farm and received an academic education In 1883 he came to DuBois, Pa, and entered the employ of his uncle John, to whose history we have devoted so much space On the death of his uncle, which took place on May 6, 1886, he was made the latter's executor and continues to carry on the extensive lumber business founded by him. Mr. DuBois is also interested in many other local enterprises, among them the DuBois Iron Works and the DuBois Lumber yard, both important concerns He was one of the organizers of the DuBois National Bank and is now its president In politics he supports the Republican ticket

In 1897 Mr DuBois was married to Miss Willie F Gamble, a daughter of James M Gamble, of Roanoke, Va Mr and Mrs Du-Bois are the parents of five children—John, Lewis, Caroline, David and Sarah

PERRY C STRAW, who owns and operates a 65-acre farm in Greenwood township, two miles southeast of Bell's Landing, was born in Ferguson township, Clearfield county, Pa, March 8, 1870, a son of John T. and Mary H Straw, the latter of whom is now deceased

Our subject received his schooling in his native township and subsequently came to his present farm, which is part of the Martin Watts farm Since coming here Mr Straw has made many improvements in the property, clearing a large portion of the land and erecting the buildings He is an active and progressive citizen and a stockholder in the Farmers and Traders Bank of Clearfield, Pa He also owns and operates a coal bank which is situated on his farm He is a member of Kermoor Grange, serving at the present time as master He is also a member, deacon and trustee of the Baptist church. In politics he is independent and is now holding the office of township auditor

Mr. Straw was married, December 12, 1894, to Miss Isabella Williams, who was born in Ferguson township, this county, March 16, 1873, a daughter of William T and Eliza (Williams) Williams, her parents being residents of that township, well known and widely respected Mr and Mrs Straw have been the parents of seven children: Mervil, Ida May (deceased), Laoma, George, Ruth, Clair, and Beulah, the six living children being well brought up and giving promise of future usefulness Mr Straw is a good type of the industrious and intelligent agriculturist, who thoroughly knows the business of farming and who has achieved a very fair degree of prosperity by his own persevering efforts.

HON GEORGE A HARRIS, burgess of the borough of Ramey, Pa, and proprietor of a general store, is one of the substantial and representative citizens of this place He was born in the State of New York and is a son of George A. and Hannah (Scantlon) Harris. George A Harris was born in New York and his wife came from Ireland They were members of the Methodist Episcopal church Their family consisted of the following children: Isabel, George A, Richard, Lilly May, Charles E, Levi and Maude

George A Harris obtained his boyhood schooling in Canada He was thirteen years of age when he left home in order to go to sea and followed life on the water until he was twenty-one years of age He came to Pennsylvania at that time and worked as a coal miner until 1905, when he embarked in the mercantile business at Ramey In 1907 Mr. Harris was elected to the office of justice of the peace and in 1909 was elected burgess and has two more years to serve. He is giving the borough a good business administration, applying to public matters the same methods by

MR. AND MRS. JACOB L. KUNTZ

which he has been able to advance his personal interests In politics he is a Republican

On December 2, 1885, Mr Harris was married to Miss Sarah Ann James, who was born in Ohio, the eldest daughter of John D and Mary Ann James, natives of Wales They had five other children John D , Hattie, Jennie, Mary Ann and Catherine To Mr and Mrs Harris five children have been born, namely John W , Mary Ann, Sarah, Helen and George J The family attends the Methodist Episcopal church Mr Harris belongs to Lodge No 990, Odd Fellows, at Houtzdale, to the P of H , and to the L O O M , at the same place He has shown himself to be a man of unusual foresight and energy and officially and personally is held in high regard by his fellow citizens He is a member of the volunteer fire department, of which he is a trustee His residence, which is situated on Main street, is one of the finest in the place

JACOB L KUNTZ, whose farm of 173 acres, lying one mile north of Troutville, Pa , is justly considered one of the best in Brady Township, Clearfield County, is one of the representative men of this section and has been a member of the council of the borough of Troutville ever since he moved to the place from the country, some nineteen years since Mr. Kuntz was born May 17, 1844, in Lycoming County, Pa , and is a son of Lewis and Susanna (Boob) Kuntz

Lewis Kuntz was born in 1800, in Bavaria, Germany, where he learned the milling business In 1827 he emigrated to America and settled first at Allentown, Lehigh County, Pa , where he operated a mill From there he moved to Hughesville, in Lycoming County, where he conducted a mill for a Mr Lyon for a time and then bought a farm located within six miles of Hughesville, which he sold six years later and moved to Clearfield county, at which time he bought the present Jacob L Kuntz farm, paying $400 for the place The only improvement was a log cabin and the land was mainly covered with timber Six years later he put up a comfortable frame house which stood until 1903 when it was replaced by a modern ten-room brick structure, which was erected by its present owner Later in life Lewis Kuntz purchased an adjoining farm and there he died in 1884 He was an excellent business man and was ever a highly respected citizen

Lewis Kuntz was twice married, first at Mifflinburg, Union county, to Susanna Boob, who was born in Union county, Pa , and died in Clearfield county in 1871, aged sixty-six years His second marriage was to Margaret Zilliox, who survived him His children were all born to his first marriage and they were seven in number, as follows Sarah, who married Henry Kriner and both are deceased, Elizabeth, who is now deceased, was the wife of David Reems, Henry, who died when three years old, John W , who lives at Troutville; Carolina, who is the wife of Jacob Schwem, of Sagamore, Pa , Jacob L , Catherine, who is deceased, Emanuel, and Franklin P , the last named having left home thirty years ago, and never since communicating with his family

Jacob L Kuntz was three years old when he was brought to Clearfield county, his parents making the trip in a big wagon that conveyed also their household belongings from Lycoming county He grew to manhood in Brady township and at irregular times attended the old fashioned country school but as there was so much work to be done on the farm in those days, all the sons had to give help as soon as their strength permitted Mr Kuntz remained at home and in 1869 bought the homestead from his father and continued to reside on it until 1892, when he moved to Troutville All the pine timber and coal on the place have been sold but there is still a valuable tract of hard-wood timber that commands a high price at the present time Mr Kuntz owns a comfortable residence in this borough and has other property at Troutville which is also improved

Mr Kuntz was married February 3, 1870, to Miss Caroline Knair, who is a daughter of Henry Knarr and a member of one of the old and substantial families of the county They have three children, namely Henry M, who manages his father's farm in Brady township, married Elizabeth Weber and they have had three children—Carrie, Jacob L and George R, Mary Alice, who died aged one year, and Clara, who is the wife of Harry London, of Troutville Mr and Mrs London have two children Carrie Gladys and Freeda Mr Kuntz and family are members of the Reformed church of which he has always been a liberal supporter In politics he is a Democrat and has served six years on the school board He belongs to the Grange and to the Odd Fellows

HENRY HICKMAN, a successful general farmer and respected citizen of Huston township, Clearfield county, Pa, in which is situated his productive farm of 116 acres, situated about three miles from Penfield and known as Sunrise Farm, was born in Prussia-Germany, November 16, 1857 His parents were August and Augusta (Baker) Hickman, both of whom died in Germany, where the

father was a farmer Almost all of the children still reside in Germany

Henry Hickman grew to military age in his native land and then entered the German army and served three years and four months as a member of the second company in the 13th Regiment After that he worked in the rolling mills until 1885, when he came to America and shortly afterward located at Penfield, Clearfield county, Pa For one year he was employed in a tannery and during this time he looked about for a tract of land that would suit his fancy and then purchased sixty-five acres of his present farm in Huston township and has been engaged in farming ever since He cleared his first purchase and gradually added to its acreage and continued to improve the place, in 1907 putting up his present comfortable residence Mr Hickman has shown himself to be a practical, prudent man and through his industry and good judgment has made himself independent

In 1881 Mr Hickman was married in Germany to Miss Augusta Kincher and they have two children, both born in Germany, namely. Henry, who married Blanche Fossler, and has four children—Henry, Jacob, Sophia and Edward, and August, who is also married and has one son, Howard Mr and Mrs Hickman are members of the German Lutheran church He casts his vote with the Democratic party For some years he has been identified with the order of Red Men

J S McQUOWN, a representative citizen of Lumber City, Pa, who has been interested in lumbering for many years and is an expert timber estimator, was born March 2, 1848, in Indiana county, Pa, and is a son of John and Hannah (Wall) McQuown

J S McQuown was early made an orphan, his father dying in Indiana county when the son was but eleven years of age and the mother's death following in the next year He attended school and academy at Covode, Indiana county, and afterward taught one term of school at Richmond in his native county He then came to Grampian, Clearfield county, and worked at making square timber and later began rafting on the river, for thirty years serving as a pilot For several years he operated a saw-mill at Bower, for J W Bell, and then moved to Lumber City, where he resided for five years, afterward buying eighteen acres of land near Lumber City, from Caleb Moore This land he has improved with substantial buildings For twenty years Mr McQuown has followed the difficult calling of timber estimator and in this capacity he has been called to twenty-three States of the Union, and also in the interest of an eastern syndicate, visited the Bahama Islands, as a professional expert He has estimated tracts that have sold for immense sums and is not surprised at a million-dollar proposition

In 1876 Mr McQuown was married to Miss Rebecca Amich, who was born at Big Run, Jefferson county, Pa , a daughter of John and Sophia Amich, and they have five children: Edna, who is the wife of William Hepfer, of DuBois, Pa , Alta, who is the wife of E B Ferguson, of Clearfield; Wayne S , who married Daisy Folks, J Roe, who is a teacher in the schools of Clearfield county, and C R , who is a telegraph operator for the New York Central Railroad Mr and Mrs McQuown are members of the Methodist Episcopal church

ROBERT HENDERSON, deceased, was a successful lumberman for many years in Geulich township, Clearfield county, Pa , where, shortly before his death, he had purchased a farm of 148 acres, to which he retired and on which he died in the following year He was born in 1840, in Center county, Pa , and his death occurred January 12, 1899 His parents were David and Mary (McMonnigal) Henderson His brothers and sisters were Samuel, John, Milton, William, Eva, Mary, Malinda and Anna

Robert Henderson was married January 2, 1873, to Miss Elizabeth Laughlin, who survives and resides at Ramey, Pa Her parents were William and Margaret (Hooper) Laughlin Mr and Mrs Laughlin had the following children Elizabeth, William, Michael, Richard, Mary, Anna, Ellen and Nora. Mr. and Mrs Henderson became parents of the following children William A , Mary G , who is the wife of J R Straw, Anna L , who is a teacher in the Ramey schools, and David R

William A and David R Henderson own and operate a first class livery at Ramey, owning their buildings and stock and are among the representative business men of the place In their political views, like their father, they are Republicans The heirs of Robert Henderson own the well improved farm in Geulich township, 108 acres of which is cleared and under cultivation, and they also have a fine residence at Ramey The family belongs to St Lawrence Catholic church at Houtzdale, Pa

T C HOYT, proprietor of Hillside Farm, which contains seventy-eight acres and is situated in Huston township, Clearfield county, Pa , at Hickory Kingdom, five miles west of Penfield, is one of the leading men and prosperous farmers of this section   He was born on his father's farm at Hickory, Huston township, December 19, 1844, and is a son of William H and Lydia Ann (O'Neill) Hoyt

William H Hoyt was born at Cheshire, Mass , November 7, 1819, a son of Dr William and Roby (Mason) Hoyt, and a grandson of Seth Hoyt, who was a soldier in the Revolutionary war   William H Hoyt was six months old when his parents brought him to Clearfield, which was then a settlement of three houses   He became a farmer, first in Elk county and later moved back to Clearfield county and bought a farm from the English company in Huston township, where he passed the remainder of his life, his death occurring at Hickory, January 2, 1902. He married Lydia Ann O'Neil, who was born in Upper Canada, June 4, 1825, and accompanied her parents to the United States when fifteen years of age   She survived until July 3, 1902, both of her two children surviving her, namely Theodore C and Lydia Maria, the latter being the wife of D Newell, of DuBois, Pa

T C Hoyt grew to manhood according to the manner of country boys, attending school and giving his father help on the farm   In 1870 he bought his farm from his father and has since carried on general agriculture   The larger part of the land he cleared himself and he erected all of the substantial farm buildings   The location of the land is excellent and gives the place its pleasant-sounding name   Mr Hoyt grows excellent crops and raises stock for his own use and has bountiful orchards

Mr Hoyt was married first, June 20, 1867,

to Miss Margaret Beer, who died July 4, 1896. Five children survived her, namely. Edson D , married Agnes Henderson, and they have four children—Emmett G , Margaret I , Theodore C. and Mary Olive, Amanda, married M S Dunlap, and they have one child, Gladys M , George W., married Vida Davis, and they have four children—Ruth, Josephine, John P and Catherine, Mary, married Charles Berkey, and they have six children—Charles E , George R , Margaret D , Agnes M , Harry D and Dorsey W , Raymond E , who is postmaster at Tyler, Pa , married Anna Dodd, and they have one child, Dorsey

Mr Hoyt was married secondly, April 13, 1898, to Mrs Salinda (Beer) Burns, daughter of William Beer and widow of James Burns   Mrs Burns had two children   Mary C , who is the wife of Lewis Sherwood and has three children—James B , Frances Louise and Edna May; and Edith, who married William R Henderson and has three children—James L , Mabel C and Albert

In politics Mr Hoyt is a Republican and he has frequently been selected by his party for important township offices   For seventeen years he served on the school board, for three years was overseer of the poor and for nine years was assessor   He has always been much interested in the Grange, of which he is a member   For forty-six years he has been a class leader in the Methodist Episcopal church and for twenty-seven years was superintendent of the Sunday school

HARRY E WAGNER, owner and proprietor of a general store at Ramey, Clearfield county, Pa , was born in this county in 1868 and is a son of William and Harriet (Wesley) Wagner.

William Wagner has spent his life in Clearfield county and during his active years followed lumbering He has always been identified with the Democratic party He married Harriet Wesley, who was born also in Clearfield county and died about 1880 To William Wagner and wife four children were born: Harry E , Edith, who is the wife of E C Davis , Frank, and Chace

Harry E Wagner attended the public schools and since then has been almost continuously engaged in the mercantile business In 1895 he started for himself, in a small way at first, but has shown much business ability in the development of his enterprise, carrying now a large and well assorted stock and occupying a commodious building which he erected in 1904 In politics he is a Republican Mr Wagner is now serving in the borough council and formerly was auditor and for a number of years was a member of the school board He is well known all over Gulich township and is numbered with the honorable and successful business men of this section

In March, 1893, Mr Wagner was married to Miss Josephine Westover, a daughter of David and Hannah (Baldwin) Westover, residents of Clearfield county Mrs Wagner has the following brothers and sisters. Aaron, Joseph, Cecelia, Elizabeth, Dessie, Anna and Sadie Mr. and Mrs Wagner have four children Edward, Lazeffa, Bernice and Marie Mr Wagner and family attend the Methodist Episcopal church He is identified fraternally with the Masons at Osceola and the P O S of A , at Ramey

JOSEPH A DOLL, owner and proprietor of the South Fork Farm, containing forty-five acres, situated in Huston township, Clearfield county, Pa , two and one-half miles west of Penfield, was born in Alsace Loraine, now Germany, September 4, 1847 He is a son of Jacob and Catherine (Leitzick) Doll, natives of the same place, where they spent their lives, the father being a farmer They had seven children Frank, Jacob, Joseph A , George, Alice, John and Mary

The first twenty years of his life Mr Doll spent on his father's farm, after which he spent five years in the German army, being a member of the 4th Marines During the French and German war he was stationed with his company on an important island near the African border At the close of this war that continued for three years he was honorably discharged and was paid the sum of $1,600, covering the five years of service during which he had proved a brave and obedient soldier After a short visit home, in 1873 he came to America, the journey consuming twenty-four days at that time He located first at Williamsport, Pa , where he worked in a lumber yard for some months and then came to Clearfield county and worked for one year on the grading of the Pennsylvania road-bed Mr Doll then decided to engage in farming and rented land near his present farm in Huston township, from William Woodward, where he remained for five years He then purchased his first five acres of his South Fork farm, from Edward Bunday, and to the original purchase continued to add from time to time, buying from John DuBois He erected all the buildings and otherwise improved the place His land is well watered by Bennetts Branch Creek, that runs through the farm, which is also crossed by the B & S Railroad

Mr Doll was married April 31, 1877, to Miss Margaret Barner, who was born in

Clearfield county, a daughter of Gebhardt Barner. Mr. and Mrs. Doll have three children, Frank, Edward and Arthur, who assist in managing and operating the farm. Politically Mr. Doll is a Democrat and is serving in his ninth year as road supervisor, having been elected and re-elected without solicitation on his part. He is identified with the local Grange. With his family he belongs to the Roman Catholic church. He is one of Huston township's most respected citizens.

WILLIAM ALEXANDER REAMS, who is one of the best known citizens of Decatur township, Clearfield county, Pa., where he has lived since he was nine years old, was born December 25, 1836, at Philipsburg, Center county, Pa., in a building on the present site of the Coal Exchange Hotel. His parents were John and Frances (Karney) Reams.

Both parents of Mr. Reams were born in Penn's Valley, Lycoming county, Pa., where they married. After the birth of two children, they moved to Philipsburg. The present thriving borough was then but a small settlement and there was not enough work in the place to keep an active man, like John Reams, profitably and continuously employed, therefore he accepted work as far away as Warrior's Mark, in Huntingdon county, and walked the distance to and from. In 1845 he moved to Decatur township, Clearfield county, and took up an improved claim, where the old brick plant was located, near Osceola Mills, where he had about fifty acres. This land he soon sold but received only $10 in cash, money being exceedingly scarce at that time in this section. He was quite enterprising,

however, and he next made a line around another fifty-acre claim, at what is now known as Hudsonville, and this land he disposed of for $25 to John Gearhart. The next claim he took was one of ninety acres, it being the same on which his son, Curtis Reams, now lives. This place, with the help of his boys, he cleared off, destroying timber at that time which, if now standing, would represent a fair fortune. One trouble that the early settlers all experienced was the difficulty of protecting their stock from the wild animals that then were numerous in the forest, and even human beings were not always safe in the primitive log cabins. There was a time when a roaring fire was built in the cabin when John Reams and wife and children lay down on their beds of hemlock boughs at night, as the only way of preventing the dangerous visits of wolves and panthers. John Reams and wife died and were buried in the Crain cemetery, half a mile from Osceola, in Deatur township.

Eight children were born to John and Frances Reams, as follows: Samuel, who died in infancy, Frederick, who also died young, Lydia, who died in 1910, aged ninety years (was the wife of William A. Bloom), Sophia, deceased, who was the wife of Andrew Baughman, Curtis, who resided in Decatur township, but died Thursday, April 20, 1911, aged 87 years, and was buried beside his wife at Osceola, John, who also lives in Decatur township, Mary Ann, now deceased (was the wife of Andrew Gardner, of Tyrone), and William Alexander.

William A. Reams, who was the youngest child of his parents, had but few school opportunities in his youth, his education having been mainly acquired through reading and contact with others He went into the woods to work while still young and for many years was in the employ of John M Chase, and was foreman and acted in other capacities He also was a pilot on the Susquehanna River, a position requiring both physical courage and skill, and rafted from Glen Hope to Marietta, Pa, and Peach Bottoms He spent twenty-five years on the water and during four or five seasons was a cook on the log rafts and efficiently performed the duties of this necessary position on log drives that went as far as Williamsport For the last twenty-four years Mr Reams has been opening fire clay and coal mines for the Philipsburg Coal and Land Company, which has its office in New York City, his duties taking him all over Decatur township and into Center county. He was exceedingly active until 1908, since when his duties have not been quite so exacting but still earns a very substantial salary with the company with which he has been so long identified

Mr Reams was married October 28, 1860, to Miss Sarah Miles, who was born one mile from Madera, Pa, in what is now Bigler township, Clearfield county She is a daughter of Lyman and Margaret (Hite) Miles, her father belonging to an old Maine family which came to Clearfield county in pioneer days Her mother was reared in Huntingdon county, Pa To Lyman and Margaret Miles the following children were born Mary, who married Lemuel Alexander (both now deceased), George, who is deceased, Martha, who married John Cathcart (both now deceased), Sarah, who is the wife of William A Reams, and Henry, Edward, Walker and James, all of whom live at Madera, Pa Mrs Reams is a member of the Methodist Episcopal church Mr Reams is nominally a Democrat but is an independent voter in local matters and he has been elected at different times to almost all the township offices He is a member of the order of Golden Eagles

Mr Reams is a very entertaining conversationalist and his recollections of conditions and events which at one time prevailed in this section bring pictures of those days easily to the imagination Reared in a but partially settled neighborhood, his boyhood was spent amid surroundings that belong to a long past time Wild game as well as savage animals abounded in the forest at that time, and in his day of youthful strength, he was a great hunter and probably killed more deer than any other man in either Clearfield or Center counties He remembers that he killed his first deer when he was only eleven years of age and since then more than 400 have fallen before his accurate marksmanship Indeed, in those early days, it was necessary for some member of the family to be more or less of a hunter, as the meat that sustained life had to be found either in the forest or in the streams, which latter, in his day, were full of trout He also excelled as a fisherman and he tells in an amusing way how his good wife, one season, attempted to keep count of the fish he caught, but after her tally reached 1,300 she grew tired and perhaps the total would have doubled the amount Amusements were not wanting, however, in what, to the present generation, seems must have been a life of more or less constant toil, but the friendly feeling that existed among people at that time brought about much sociability and visiting The present day commercialism was not known and people were more considered for their worth than their worldly possessions Hospitality was universal and a stranger was kindly welcomed, his wants attended to and he was sent on his way. It is but natural that Mr. Reams should recall the old days as he looks back so many years and sees the wonderful changes that have taken place in every direction In all the practical development in his immediate neighborhood he has shared and has done his full duty as a citizen

C P CARR, justice of the peace in Pike township, where he owns a valuable farm of 100 acres, situated three and one-half miles northeast of Curwensville, Pa , was born June 6, 1855, in Bradford township, Clearfield county, Pa., and is a son of Benjamin and a grandson of Asil Carr

Asil Carr was probably born in New York, and when he came first to Pennsylvania settled at Red Bank, in Clarion county Possibly he married there, his wife's name being Katherine, and when he moved to Lawrence township, near Center Church, he was accompanied by his wife and four sons and one daughter, bearing the following names. Benjamin, Alexander, Richard, William and Jane He spent the remainder of his life in Lawrence township, mainly engaged in work as a millwright, and built many dams on the river His death occurred at the age of seventy years and his burial was at Center Church

Benjamin Carr and his brothers attended school at Red Bank and was a young man when the family came to Lawrence township. He operated a saw-mill for several years and then purchased the present farm, then containing 165 acres, from J & C. Lenox. With the help of his sons he cleared all but fifteen acres which are now very valuable timber lands He continued in the mill business, hiring help to operate his farm During the Civil War he was in the service, a member of Co. E, 149th Pa. Vol Inf , and toward the end of the war was captured by the Confederates and incarcerated in Libby Prison, where he died from harsh treatment His burial was at Annapolis, Md His marriage was with Elizabeth Williams, a daughter of Edward Williams, of Bradford township, and the following children were born to them Mercy Jane, who is now deceased, was the wife of Austin Trimp, of Bigler; C. P., of Pike township, W. S , who was married first to Mary Thompson, and second to Orie Bloom, a daughter of Zachariah Bloom; Mary, who is the wife of Peter Gearhart, and Richard, who married Alberta King. The mother of the above family died in 1882

C. P. Carr attended school at Pleasant Grove and afterward began the duties of life, naturally becoming a farmer and later engaging in teaming After the death of his mother, the home farm, some ten years later, was divided between W S and C. P. Carr, the former taking the buildings and sixty-five acres of land, and the latter the 100 acres, on which there were no structures Subsequently he erected the solid, substantial buildings now standing and has lived on his land until the present He has a valuable coal bank which produces 200

tons of coal a month which he delivers to
the neighboring tile works He does some
truck farming in addition to his regular
agricultural operations, and a productive
peach orchard gives him some fine fruit to
dispose of each year. He is a member of
the Grange and of the Agricultural Society

On August 31, 1874, Mr Carr was married to Miss Annie Leese, a daughter of
Isaac and Mary (Tomey) Leese, and they
have five children: Harvey, who resides on
the home farm, married Effie Addleman
and they have one child, Helen, Orlo, who
also lives on the farm, married Emma Fullerton, and they have one daughter, Sarah,
Fred, who is also one of the home farmers,
married Pearl Cuppler, and they have two
children, Leonora and Mary, Williard, who
lives at Luthersburg, married Edith Hays,
and Zella, who lives at home Mr Carr and
family are members of the Methodist Episcopal church, of which he is a trustee In
politics he is a Democrat and has frequently
been elected to office on the Democratic
ticket, serving as a useful member of the
school board, as road supervisor and for
the past six years he has been a justice of the
peace, and is serving in his second term
He is a member of the Royal Order of the
Moose and other fraternal organizations

HON CHARLES BIGLER PATRICK,
formerly burgess of Burnside, Pa, and a
member of the borough school board, has
been in the undertaking business here since
1905, and is one of the leading citizens He
was born in Burnside township, Clearfield
county, Pa, August 21 1851, and is a son
of James and Eliza (Rummel) Patrick

James Patrick was born in Lancaster
37

county, Pa From there he moved to Armstrong county, where he married Eliza
Rummel, a daughter of John Rummel He
was a farmer and general laborer and lost
his life while rafting on the Susquehannah
River, when aged seventy-two years He
was a stanch Democrat, but never held office Both he and his wife were members
of the Evangelical church They had the
following children George, who is deceased, Mary Jane, who is the wife of John
Beringer, of Burnside, Chambers, who is
deceased, Margaret, who is the wife of J
Brickley, of Burnside, Libby, who is the
wife of D Redmond, of Falmouth, Ky,
John, who died in infancy, Dallas, who lives
in Bell township, Maria, who is a resident
of Cherry Tree, Mrs Fanny King, who is
deceased, and Charles B

Charles B Patrick obtained his education
in the public schools and afterward, until
twenty-five years of age, was engaged in
teaming and other work He then learned
the carpenter trade at which he was employed until 1905, when he embarked in the
undertaking business He has all necessary
equipments and accommodations and his
trade comes from a wide territory, people
who have known him and his family for
years having the utmost confidence in him

Mr Patrick was married to Miss Mary
Ann Cuningham, who was born February
5, 1850, at Philadelphia, a daughter of William and Margaret (Hannah) Cunningham, natives of Southern Pennsylvania
Seven children have been born to Mr and
Mrs Patrick, namely Margaret, who formerly was treasurer of Burnside borough,
James D, who is deceased, is survived by
four children who live with their grand-

father, Earl R, who is a miner, living at
Burnside, married Etta Stuchel, William
E, who married Floy Tiger, has two children, LeRoy, who is deceased, Murray,
who is a student in the veterinary department of the University of Pennsylvania,
and John A, who is a telephone lineman
living at Pittsburg

Politically Mr Patrick is a Democrat
He is one of the most active members of
the Burnside lodge of Odd Fellows and has
passed through all the chairs, having united
with it in 1882, and he belongs also to the
Encampment and the Daughters of Rebecca Mr Patrick and wife belong to the
Methodist Episcopal church

JAMES O LEONARD,* who is a member of one of the old settled families of
Clearfield county, was born on his present
farm of 110 acres, in Girard township, in
1881, and has always lived here He is a
son of Oliver and Christine (Albright)
Leonard

Oliver Lenoard was born on the farm
mentioned, on which his father had settled
in 1831, and spent his life here engaged in
agricultural pursuits, until his death, in
June, 1905 He married Christine Albright,
who was of German extraction and a native
of Lancaster county She still survives and
is now in her seventieth year

James O Leonard has been engaged in
farming and stock raising ever since his
school days ended and has taken pride in
preserving and improving the estate which
has been continuously in the family for
eighty-nine years His methods are those
of the intelligent, well informed agricultur-

ist of present day, practical ideas In addition to being a successful farmer he is
active in political matters and has satisfactorily served two years as township supervisor and seven years as constable of Girard township He is identified with the
Masonic fraternity, belonging to Lodge No.
341, Clearfield, and belongs also to the Girard Grange The Leonard farm is situated
sixteen miles east of Clearfield

On June 16, 1900, Mr Leonard was married to Miss Fannie Krise, who was born,
reared and educated in Girard township, a
daughter of O D Krise, a well known resident Mr and Mrs Leonard have six children who bear the following names. Irene,
Christine, Alvin, Oliver, Thomas and Mary

WILLIAM L WISE, a foremost citizen of Knox township, who, for the past
fourteen years has held the responsible office of township treasurer, resides on his
well improved farm of 100 acres, which is
situated three miles west of Boardman, Pa
He was born in Ferguson township, Clearfield county, March 28, 1855, and is a son
of William and Jane (Caldwell) Wise.

William Wise was born in Center county,
Pa, a son of Conrad Wise The family
moved to Pike township, Clearfield county,
in his early manhood and he remained with
his parents until his marriage to Jane Caldwell, a daughter of Matthew Caldwell, a
prominent farmer of this section After
marriage, William Wise and his wife settled in Ferguson township, where he acquired a farm of 150 acres, a great part of
which he cleared by his own industry This
farm now belongs to the estate of the late

MR. AND MRS. JOHN H. WILKINSON

Curtis Bell William Wise also engaged in lumbering, and spent all of his life after marriage, in Ferguson township, where his death occurred in December, 1876, at the age of sixty-five years He was a consistent member of the Lutheran church In politics he was a Democrat but never entered into any contest for office His widow lived to be eighty-four years of age and their remains rest side by side at New Millport She was reared in the Presbyterian faith Their children, ten in number, were as follows D A, who is a resident of Altoona, married Ruth McCracken, Susan, who is the wife of James R Cupples and lives at Lumber City, Abbie, who is the widow of William R Curry, of Pike township, Lavina, who is the wife of James Ferguson, lives in Ferguson township, Maggie, who is deceased, was the wife of James R Bloom; George W, who died young, Eliza, who is deceased, was the wife of John N Hile, also deceased, Elmira E, who is the widow of Z L Hoover, resides at Clearfield, an infant son, deceased, and William L

William L Wise, with his brothers and sisters, attended the public schools in Ferguson township and afterward assisted his father on the home farm until his own marriage, ever since which time he has lived on his present farm in Knox township, all of which is under cultivation except ten acres in valuable timber He is not only one of the successful agriculturists of this section but he is also a very prominent and popular citizen Since reaching manhood he has been interested in public matters in his township and on the Democratic ticket has been many times elected to office, serving as treasurer,

collector and auditor He is one of the stockholders of the Farmers' and Traders' National Bank of Clearfield

In January, 1876, Mr Wise was married first to Miss Samantha Glenn, who left one child, Vada He was married second to Miss Olivia Mokel, a daughter of D E Mokel, of New Millport, and two sons were born to them Lester Bryant, who died when aged twenty-three months, and Athol Verne, who, for three years has been in a brokerage office in Philadelphia He is a graduate of Bucknell University, and is married and resides at East Orange, N J

JOHN H WILKINSON, who owns twenty-eight acres of land in Bigler Township, Clearfield County, where he is developing a valuable coal mine, is a well known and highly respected citizen of this section He was born in England, October 8, 1860, and is a son of John and Alice (Limb) Wilkinson

The parents of Mr Wilkinson were born in England and after coming to the United States, located at Osceola, Clearfield County, where the mother still resides, the father being now deceased They had the following children Mary, who is the wife of James McCrossin; Annie, John H, Salina, who is the wife of Thomas Mays, Eliza, who is the wife of John Madison, Florence, wife of Mr Edmunds, and Herbert

John H Wilkinson attended the common schools only and began work in the coal mines when young and coal mining has been his business ever since On his own land he had developed one mine and is opening up a second one and gives employment to six men His prospects are encouraging, his coal being of excellent quality and the vein seemingly inexhaustible

In 1883 Mr Wilkinson was married to Miss Martha Cowfer, a daughter of David Cowfer, of Center County, and she has the following brothers and sisters Mary, Jane, George, Irvin, Rachel, Wall, William and May To Mr and Mrs Wilkinson the following children have been born Rosella, who is the wife of John P. Martin, Florence, who is the wife of Philip Henry, and Frank, Grace, George, Earl, Harry, Martha and Howard In politics Mr Wilkinson is a Republican He is a member of the fraternal order of Odd Fellows and belongs to the lodge at Houtzdale

JOSEPH SEYLER, a representative citizen of Brady township, formerly auditor of the township and member of the school board, resides on his valuable farm of ninety-five acres and carries on general agriculture He was born in Brady township, June 10, 1843, and is a son of John H and Sarah Fisher (Kirk) Seyler

John H Seyler was born in Center county, Pa , a son of Michael Seyler After the death of his mother the father moved to Clearfield county with his two sons, John H and Joseph, locating in Brady township, one and one-half miles north of Luthersburg The father died there and Joseph subsequently died at Rockton, Pa John H Seyler bought the farm and later sold a part of it to H Aurand, but the other part belongs to the estate, John H Seyler dying at Luthersburg, at the age of eighty-two years. He was survived for a short time by his widow, who died at the age of eighty-one years To them ten children had been born, the record being as follows James

H , Joseph, Mary A and Reuben, twins, Ferdinand and Isabella, twins, Austin, Lydia Jane, Elizabeth and Jack

Joseph Seyler assisted on the home farm and attended the country schools until seventeen years of age, when he learned the pottery trade and continued until he became a pottery owner, a member of the firm of Kirk, Porter & Seyler. In 1875 he bought the interests of his partners and conducted the business alone until 1895 when he retired from it and settled then on the farm which he had bought in the meanwhile He has resided here ever since his marriage and has carried on the usual farm industries with satisfactory results A vein of coal is under his farm and it may prove a source of large income

Mr Seyler was married June 26, 1870, to Miss Frances Brockbank, a daughter of Thomas and Isabella (King) Brockbank, natives of England Mr and Mrs Brockbank settled first at Philadelphia and moved from there into Elk county and later came to Clearfield county, where he died in 1900, at the age of seventy-nine years The mother of Mrs Seyler was born in 1824, and resides at DuBois, in the enjoyment of both physical and mental health To Mr. and Mrs Brockbank the following children were born Frances Ann, who was born in England and was two years old when the family crossed the Atlantic Ocean to America, the journey consuming six weeks, Mary, who married Charles Waugh; Margaret, who is the widow of A Pence, once sheriff of Clearfield county, S T and Joseph W , both of whom are deceased, and Isabella, who is deceased, was the wife of Austin Long

Mr. and Mrs Seyler have eight children, namely Mary Emma, who married Jack M Greismer, and they have four children —Frances, Lenora, Alice and Fredericka, all residing at DuBois, Bertha, who married Henry Kirk, residing at Luthersburg, and they have five children—Francis, Phebe, Russell, Fred and Richard, and Bernice, Olive, Eleazer, Lynn, Edgar and Harbison, who is the home farmer In politics Mr Seyler is a Democrat He is a member of the Grange at Luthersburg

JAMES LEWIS WEAVER, who is engaged in the general mercantile business at Burnside, Clearfield county, Pa, a citizen who stands high in public esteem, was born June 10, 1858, in Burnside township, Clearfield county, and is a son of James H and Sarah Ann (Campbell) Weaver

James H Weaver was born in Union county, Pa, December 23, 1816 When he was ten years old he accompanied his parents to Clearfield county and here obtained a district school education, according to opportunities offered at that time, and afterward engaged in farming and lumbering In 1888 he moved to Burnside and resided here until his death, on March 2, 1905 His parents were John and Ruth (Zimmerman) Weaver, the former of whom was born in Northampton county, Pa, and died in Clearfield county, May 10, 1870 When fourteen years of age he started to learn the tailoring trade at Milton, Pa In 1827 he moved into Clearfield county which was largely a wilderness at that time He married Ruth Zimmerman, who was born May 8, 1788, and they had ten children born to them

On May 30, 1843, James H Weaver was married to Sarah Ann Campbell, who was born March 23, 1821, and still survives, residing in the old homestead in Burnside borough Her parents were Thomas and Mary (Wheeland) Campbell, natives of Chester county, the former of whom was born January 12, 1786, and the latter, September 12, 1792 To James H Weaver and wife were born the following children Henrietta, who is the wife of David Mitchell, of Curry Run, Pa, Frances Emma, who is the wife of Thomas Mitchell, of Burnside, Mary K, who is the wife of Alvin Schaeffer, lives in the old homestead, Harriet Ruth, who is the wife of John L Breth, John Thomas, who is deceased, and James Lewis The venerable mother of this family is a member of the Methodist Protestant church, as was the father

James Lewis Weaver attended school at Deer Run and later an academy at New Washington, under Prof G W Innes, after which, like his father, he engaged in lumbering and farming In 1890 he came to Burnside and embarked in the general mercantile business, in which line he has been quite successful and has a place among the foremost business men of the town He has never taken any very active part in politics

On March 21, 1882, Mr Weaver was married to Miss Sarah Edith Black, who was born December 5, 1857, in Indiana county, Pa, a daughter of Samuel P and Nancy (Craig) Black Mr and Mrs Weaver have two daughters, Sarah Inda and Nancy Emma, both of whom are capable young women with modern ideas and both are entirely independent, the older daughter being a milliner and the latter a dressmaker Mrs Weaver set the example, having been a successful and valued school-teacher prior to her marriage   She is a member of the Methodist Protestant church

C E ERHARD, president of the Knox Township School Board, of which he has been a useful member for ten years, carries on general farming on 150 acres of excellent land, which belongs to his father   He was born in Knox township, Clearfield county, Pa , February 10, 1863

Christian Erhard, the paternal grandfather, was born in Center county and before marriage came to Clearfield county and here the father of C E Erhard was born When the latter reached manhood he married Elizabeth Straw, daughter of Christian Straw, of Ferguson township, and ten children were born to them, as follows   Alvin; Maria, who is the wife of George Boyce, Emma, who is deceased, was the wife of David Bright, Edith J., C E , C V , who resides in Oregon, Bigler W , who is deceased, was formerly a teacher in Bedford county, B W , a twin of Bigler W , who is a teacher in Bedford county, J A , who is a resident of Glassport, Allegheny county, married, first, Josephine Shaffer, and second, Clara Cesna, and Maude E , who is the wife of Clarence Bevens, of Jenners, Somerset county After marriage, the parents of Mr Erhard purchased a farm near New Millport and later, after the death of Grandfather Christian Erhard, the father of C E Erhard purchased the interests of the other heirs, in partnership with his brother Enoch. The farm is well improved and under its present management is a very productive property The father still survives, the mother dying May 24, 1901. He is one of the highly respected older residents of the township

C E Erhard was reared in the principles of the Democratic party, by his father, but in late years votes as his judgment directs. At all times, however, he has been a good citizen and is one so well qualified for office and so thoroughly interested in the public schools that his fellow citizens have done themselves credit in retaining his services on the school board He is a member of the Knights of the Golden Eagles

ELWOOD S HENDERSON, a well known citizen of Burnside, whose occupation is the superintendency of planing-mill construction, was born in Burnside township, September 25, 1854, son of John G and Matilda (Trimbell) Henderson. John G Henderson, the father, was born in Armstrong county, Pa and is still living at the age of 82 years At the age of 12 he was bound out to learn the carpenter's trade, and ten years later came to Burnside, where he followed his trade until 1904, when he retired from active industrial life He married Matilda Trimbell, who died October 13, 1903, at the age of 66 Grandfather Henderson was killed by a threshing machine when our subject's father was a boy Mr and Mrs John G Henderson were the parents of the following children · Elwood S , whose name appears at the head of this sketch; Elizabeth, widow of L H Haney; Lilly May, wife of J H Prothero of Punxsutawney, Pa , and Della, wife of Samuel M Wetzel, also of Punxsutawney

Elwood S. Henderson, after his school days were over, took up the carpenter's trade, which he followed up to the age of 21 years He then married, after which he followed his trade in connection with lumbering up to 1890 He was then appointed to a position as superintendent of planing-mill work in portions of West Virginia and Maryland, and Burnside, which occupation he has continued until the present time In 1874 he also became interested indirectly in an undertaking business at Burnside He is a member of the Methodist Protestant church, and belongs to the I O O F lodge at Burnside He votes the Prohibition ticket and has held borough offices, serving one term—in 1900—as burgess of Burnside He also served as councilman for eighteen years, as a member of the school board three years, and as constable two terms Mr. Henderson is the oldest citizen born in the borough of Burnside

Elwood S Henderson married Mary Virginia Conner, who was born February 15, 1856, at Diamondville, Indiana county, Pa , a daughter of John C. Conner Her mother's maiden name was Anne Widdowson Mr and Mrs Henderson are the parents of two children Zulah, a daughter, who was born the 31st of July, 1876, Harry, a son, born September 6, 1878, and died December 26. 1878; Zulah is now the wife of A D Mitchell, a meat market proprietor of Portage, Pa Mr and Mrs Mitchell have four children— Lynn, Torrence, Pauline and Fredrick

W W CATHCART, a prosperous agriculturist of Knox township, who resides on his well improved farm of 100 acres, situated one and one-fourth miles east of Olanta, Pa , was born July 31, 1860, in Knox township, on an adjoining farm His parents were James and Rachel (Flegal) Cathcart, the former of whom died July 27, 1884, and the latter, March 8, 1911 The Cathcart family is one of the old, prominent and substantial ones of this section

W W Cathcart attended the Turkey Hill school in Knox township in his youth and afterward turned his attention to lumbering and farming He lived at home until his marriage and for seven months afterward and then came to his present farm, which is a part of the old homestead, his father at one time having owned 600 acres of land Mr Cathcart has fifty acres of his land cleared and under cultivation and has erected substantial buildings He also has a mill on the place and does his own grinding and custom work for the neighborhood He is a stockholder in the Knox Mutual Telephone Company and is one of the township's enterprising men

In July, 1881, Mr Cathcart was married to Miss Nora A Dunlap, a daughter of John R Dunlap, of Knox township, and they have had nine children, as follows J C , who assists his father on the home farm, Merna, who is in business for herself as a dressmaker, May, who married James Robbins, and Lewis G, Elva, Ralph, Cora and Howard, all at home, and an infant son, deceased Mr Cathcart and family are members of the Methodist Episcopal church at Turkey Hill He is identified with Lawrence Grange, in which he takes much interest and belongs also to the P O S of A and the P O of A , at Olanta, as does his wife and two of their sons, J C and Lewis G In politics he is a prominent Republican and is chairman of the Knox Township Central Committee

WILLIAM CHICK, whose farm of fifty acres is situated in Sandy township, two miles southeast of DuBois, has been a resident of Clearfield county since 1888, but he was born in England His parents, William and Ellen Chick, are both deceased He has one sister, Frances, who is the wife of John Charlton and they also live in Clearfield county

William Chick had but few educational opportunities when he was a boy and started to work in the coal mines in England when he was only eleven years of age He came to America at the age of seventeen years and worked first in the mines in Luzerne county, Pa , later worked for six months in the mines in Carbon county and one year in the Adrian mines at Punxsutawney, Pa In 1888 he came to DuBois and invested his savings in his present farm, purchasing from Harriet Bogle, and for several years afterward kept away from the mines, occupied entirely in cultivating his land and in working in the woods He subsequently turned his attention to the raising of poultry and has made a success of this business, going about it in a very practical way and making suitable preparations, including the building of a large poultry house, constructed of concrete He has excellent water facilities, plenty of running space for his fowls, and his present average of selling is 1,200 Plymouth Rock chickens a year He has improved his place in every way, rebuilding the house and making his surroundings attractive

When Shaft No 1 of the DuBois mines was sunk, Mr Chick entered the employ of the company as sinker and later resumed mining and subsequently was made check weighman. From that position he was promoted to that of fire boss, then was made mine foreman, and in October, 1910, was appointed superintendent of the shaft, succeeding S C Crist. His long experience as a miner makes Mr Chick a valuable official to the company and a popular one with the miners as he has passed through every experience and thus thoroughly understands every condition

Mr Chick was married December 25, 1888,

to Miss Margaret Bogle, a daughter of Robert and Harriet Bogle, and they have had ten children: William R , Harriet, Adeline, Grace, Margaret, Ruth, Joseph, Myrtle, Lillian and Amelia, all of whom survive except little Myrtle, who died when only six years old Mr. and Mrs Chick are members of the Episcopal church He is identified fraternally with the Red Men and the Knights of Pythias, and belongs also to the Grange

A M KIRK & SON, jewelers, with business location on the corner of Filbert and State streets, Curwensville, Pa , is a business name of much importance in this borough and for many years it has been one that is a synonym for business integrity The founder of the business was the late A. M Kirk, who later associated his son, Henry P Kirk, with him and the present firm style was then adopted

A M Kirk was born October 5, 1849, at Lumber City, Pa , and died at Curwensville, September 19, 1904 He was a son of Samuel and Alice (Moore) Kirk, the former of whom was an extensive lumberman at one time and with his father, A M Kirk, was in the same business for some years In 1870 he married and continued to reside at Lumber City for two more years, living on a farm adjoining the town, and then came to Curwensville, where he learned the jeweler trade and opened his first store on the corner opposite to the present building, which he erected in 1882, having lost his first one by fire He became one of the representative citizens of Curwensville, taking his part in public matters as became a good citizen, investing in property and furthering laudable enterprises of different kinds He was one of the charter directors of the Citizens' National Bank of Curwensville In his political views he was a Republican and occasionally he consented to serve in such offices as school director, from a sense of duty He was a birthright member of the Society of Friends, but attended the Presbyterian church with his family and served as a trustee of the same. Fraternally he was identified with the Odd Fellows and the Masons, having attained the thirty-second degree in the latter organization and his funeral, at Oak Hill cemetery, was under the direction of the local Masonic lodge

On March 31, 1870, A M Kirk was married to Miss Rebecca Port, a daughter of Henry and Rebecca (Clover) Port, and six children were born to them, namely· Samuel B, who was born near Lumber City, is a graduate of Swarthmore College and is now in the drug business in Philadelphia, and married Cecelia Morgan of that city, Henry P, who was born near Lumber City, is a graduate of Horological Institute, Philadelphia, is now at the head of the firm of A M Kirk & Son, at Curwensville, and married Laura Haworth; Frank H, who was born at Curwensville, is a graduate of Swarthmore College and is in the drug business at Memphis, Tenn , Alice, who is a graduate of the Women's College, at Frederick, Md , M D, who is a graduate of Lehigh University, resides at Ebensburg, being a mining engineer; and Fred S, who is also a college graduate, is in business at Philadelphia, Pa

W A DENLING* proprietor of a grocery store at Woodland, Pa , has been a resident of this borough for the past twenty-five years, and was born in Indiana county, Pa , a son of William and Nancy (McClain) Denling Both parents were natives of Indiana county, Pa , and the father was a miller by trade

W A Denling was nine years old when his parents died, and he spent his early boyhood days in Indiana county, where he attended the local schools At the age of sixteen years he came to Woodland, Pa , and began working in the Clay mines near here He worked continuously in these mines for twenty years and in 1905 established himself in the grocery business at Woodland He carries a full line of groceries and has met with uninterrupted success

Mr Denling was married in 1882 to Blanche Peters of Woodland and they began housekeeping at Wallaceton, Pa Her father, now deceased, was one of the prominent farmers of this section of the county One child has been born to Mr and Mrs Denling—Mabel They hold membership with the Brethren church of Woodland Mr Denling is a member of the I O O F No 198, of Clearfield, and also in the order of Moose, of Clearfield

HARVEY BLOOM, a leading citizen of Pike township, residing on his well improved farm of 140 acres, which is situated one mile east of Curwensville, was born in this township, September 18, 1841, and is a son of James A and a grandson of Isaac Bloom

James A Bloom was also born in Pike township, the Bloom family being one of the old and substantial ones of this part of Clearfield county He settled on the farm now owned by his son, Harvey Bloom, following a short period on a rented farm north of Curwensville, and this remained his permanent home, his death occurring here at the age of eighty-eight years, four months and eight days   He was a member of the Baptist church   In politics he was identified with the Democratic party and he frequently served in township offices, having been constable, collector and supervisor and also overseer of the poor.   He married Mary Ann Hile, a daughter of Henry Hile, Sr, and they had eleven children born to them, as follows· Naomi, Frampton, Harvey, Jane, Edward, Amos, Harriet, Mary, Daniel, Julia Ann and Lucy The mother of the above family died at the age of seventy-six years and both she and the father were buried in the Bloomington cemetery   They were good people in every sense of the word and enjoyed the respect and esteem of those who knew them

Harvey Bloom attended school at Curwensville   He has devoted himself to agricultural pursuits and has always lived on the old homestead   He has been an active and interested citizen of his community and, like his late father, has frequently been chosen by his fellow citizens for public office in the township and at present is serving as supervisor and as overseer of the poor

Mr Bloom was married to Miss Fannie Leisher, who is a daughter of Daniel Leisher, of Snyder county, Pa , and they have one son, G Gordon, who assists his father   Mr and Mrs Bloom are members of the Baptist church at Curwensville   Formerly he was identified with the order of Knights of Pythias at the same place   He has always given his political support to the Democratic party

PATCHIN   Among the old and representative families of Clearfield county is that of Patchin, one that has been prominently identified with many business interests particularly along the lines of lumbering and merchandising   The family has also been one that has been foremost in good citizenship and through marriage is closely connected also with other leading families of this part of Pennsylvania.

The first of the Patchin family of whom there is record, was John Patchin, who was born in 1789, at Sabbath-Day Point, near Lake George, Warren county, N Y , where he married Elizabeth Wright.   He early engaged in lumbering and had a slide for logs on the side of Black Mountain above the lake. In 1835 he came to Clearfield county and settled among the pines along the Susquehanna river, purchasing 10,000 acres of timber land. He was a man of much enterprise and was one of the first to engage in logging and rafting lumber down the Susquehanna river to supply distant markets   In 1847 he brought his family to Clearfield county and they lived at first at Curwensville but later established a settlement in the county which was named Patchinsville, in his honor, and there he started the first mercantile supply store in this section of the country   In 1848 he admitted his sons to partnership in his large lumbering enterprises and the business was conducted under the firm name of John Patchin & Sons   This pioneer of the family died December 21, 1863, at the age of seventy-four years   His widow survived until 1860   They left seven children

Aaron Patchin, son of John and Elizabeth (Wright) Patchin, was born August 15, 1822, at Hague, Warren county, N Y.   He early engaged in the lumber business on Lake George, N. Y , and in 1847 he followed his father to Clearfield county and became associated with the latter and with his brothers in lumbering on the Upper Susquehanna river, working under the firm name of John Patchin

& Sons When John Patchin died, Aaron, who had been his father's chief advisor, inherited the greater part of John Patchin's real estate, but later settled all claims with his brother and sisters and this estate now covers over 8,000 acres of land Aaron Patchin also became the owner of a general store at Patchinsville, which was founded by and named for his father, at which time it was a supply station for this entire community Aaron Patchin was, like his father, a man of great industry and enterprise In 1887 he acquired large interests at Camden, N J, and established there a saw-mill and also went into the manufacturing of spars, masts, etc, for sailing ships, on an extensive scale On June 26, 1862, Aaron Patchin was married to Elizabeth Barrett, a daughter of George Barrett, of Indiana county, Pa

CONRAD BLOOM, a highly respected citizen and substantial farmer of Pike township, owns 100 acres of excellent land situated six miles south of Curwensville, all but twenty of which is under cultivation, that being in valuable timber He was born in Pike township, December 1, 1839, and is a son of Abraham H and Anna Eliza (Kyler) Bloom

Abraham H Bloom was born also in Pike township, in 1813, and was a son of John Bloom, this family being one of the old and prominent ones of this section Abraham H Bloom married Anna Eliza Kyler, who was born in Morris township, a daughter of Conrad Kyler, of Greencastle, Lancaster county, Pa, and they had nine children, namely Rachel, who is deceased, was the wife of Samuel Snyder, Conrad, Isaac, who is deceased, Katherine, who is the widow of William Withrow, Alexander, who is deceased; Martin,

who first married Theresa Jordan, and second, Mary Kodar, Samuel S, who married Jane Witherow, Mary, deceased, who was the wife of George High, and Abigail, who married Daniel P Bloom After marriage, Mr Bloom resided for a short time in Pike township and then moved to Morris township but returned to Pike township, later removing to Lawrence and then to Knox township, in which section he died at the age of fifty-one years His widow survived to be seventy-six years of age They were members of the Fruit Hill Presbyterian Church and were interred in the cemetery belonging to it Abraham H Bloom was a lifelong Democrat but he never accepted any political position

Conrad Bloom attended school in Pike and Lawrence townships When he was old enough he engaged in lumbering, during the winter seasons, devoting his summers to farming, and continued until he was married, afterward residing upon a farm of 100 acres in Knox township for some years, then sold it and came to his present farm in Pike township, purchasing it from William R Curry He made improvements on the buildings and has everything very comfortable in his surroundings Mr Bloom has been a very successful farmer but the larger burden of responsibility now rests on the shoulders of his son, Allen H Bloom, who is a member of the Pike Township School Board

On March 1, 1866, Mr Bloom was married to Miss Mary Jane Hoover, who was born in Pike township, a daughter of Abraham Hoover Mrs Bloom died December 9, 1893, and her burial was in the Fruit Hill cemetery One son was born to Mr and Mrs Bloom, Allen H, who married Mary C. Tobias, a daughter of Samuel Tobias, and they have five children   Ruth, who teaches at the Oakland school house, Edwin, who is a teacher at Olanta, and Zoe, Oma and Floyd   In politics Mr Bloom is a Democrat   He served as a school director in Knox township and as road supervisor in Pike township   He is an elder in the Fruit Hill Presbyterian church

DAVID TYLER, deceased, for years was one of the leading men of Huston Township, Clearfield County, being identified with its important interests, many of which he founded and encouraged through his progressiveness and public spirit   The prosperous town of Tyler, named in his honor, stands on a part of his 600-acre farm   He was born in Oneida County, N Y , March 19, 1809, and was a son of Martin and Elizabeth (Alfoot) Tyler   The parents were natives of Connecticut and came to Pennsylvania and settled in Bradford County

David Tyler was one of a family of ten children and his boyhood was spent in Oneida County, where he later taught school, and he continued to teach after coming to Lycoming County, Pa   At the time of the building of the West Branch Canal, he went to Northumberland County and worked on its construction for a time   After his marriage, in 1830 he engaged in the lumber business with Dr Reed at Trout Run, in Lycoming County and became a man of public importance there   He was first appointed to the office of justice of the peace by Governor Shultz, second by Governor Ritner, and was elected to his third term   In 1848 he moved to Clearfield County and came to Huston Township, which was then so much of a wilderness that the road had to be cleared in order that his wagons could penetrate the forest, and deer and other wild animals were numerous   The first home was only a log shanty but a substantial frame house soon took its place and later, after he had burned the bricks on his farm, Mr Tyler built the present 16-room brick mansion that continues to be the family homestead

When Mr Tyler came first to Huston Township it was in the interest of John DuBois, the great lumberman of this district, and he was connected with him until he began operating timber tracts for himself   It was while he was yet with Mr DuBois that he took the first load of coal from this section down the creek, in a flat-boat, in order to have it tested   Mr Tyler was a far-seeing, sensible man and his ideas along all lines were far in advance of his fellow citizens   It was he who first saw the wisdom of introducing farm machinery and owned the first threshing machine and other farm implements that before his time had been entirely unknown to even the best informed farmers of the county   He also was the first purchaser of a sewing machine.   He and Mahlon Fisher invented the first log slide   His house was the place of hospitable entertainment for all strangers, there being no inn of any kind in this section at the time, and his kindness, cordiality and good feeling entitled him to the high regard in which he was universally held   He organized the first general store in Huston Township, hauling his goods from Tyrone, Pa   He was the first postmaster at Tyler and remained in office for many years and was succeeded by his daughter, Miss Phebe Tyler, who held the office for thirteen years   He was a generous supporter of schools and churches and not only brought the first M E minister to this section but supported him until the church membership provided a fund   In partnership

DAVID TYLER

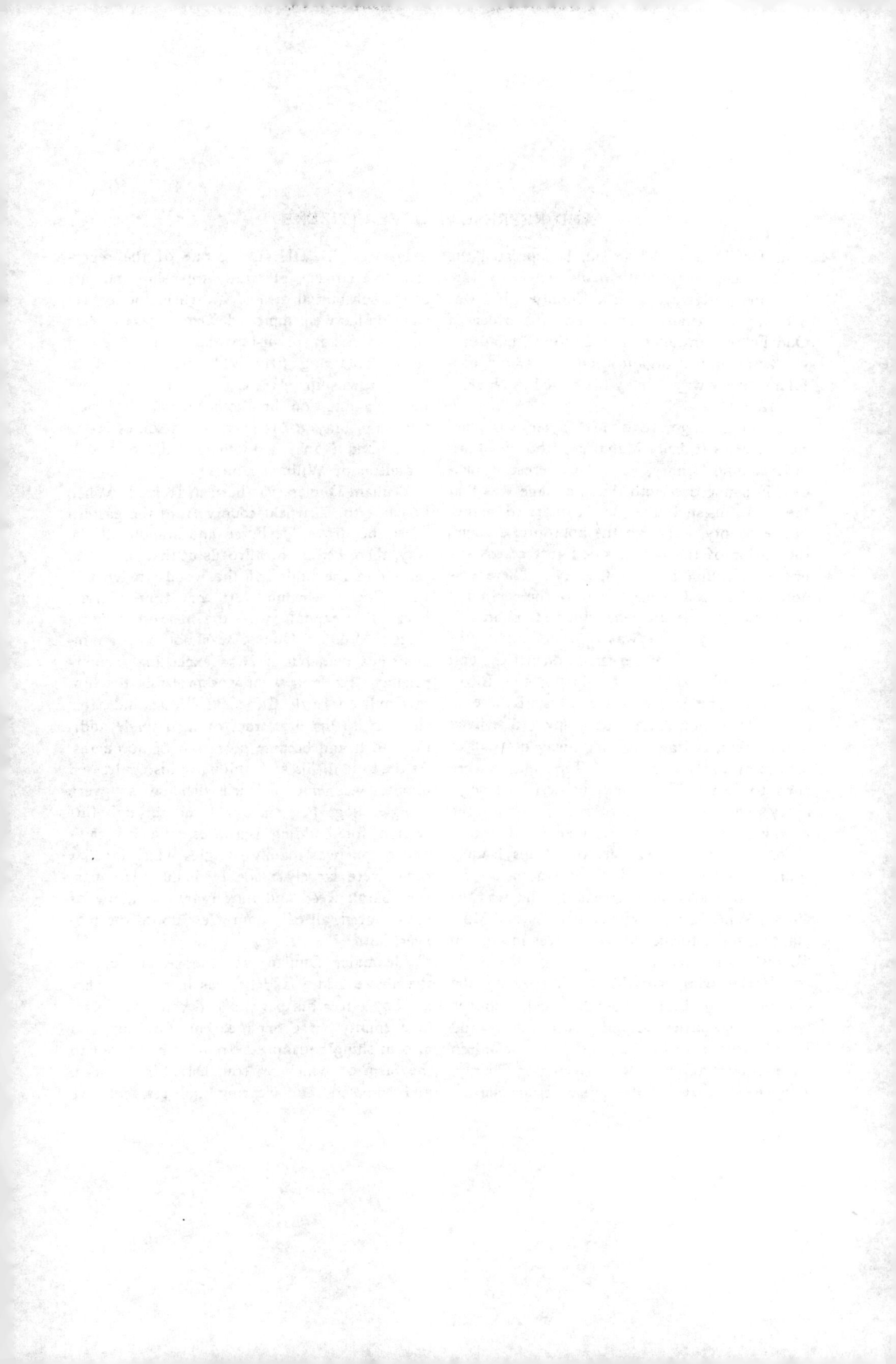

with Dr Hills of Clearfield, he operated the stage coach, carrying the mails between Clearfield and Ridgway, in Elk County He was one of the earliest members of the order of Odd Fellows in this section and until his death was active in that organization His long, useful and every way worthy life closed in November, 1882

On January 30, 1830, Mr Tyler was married to Miss Isabella Mahaffey, who was born in Lycoming County, Pa An interesting incident in connection with this marriage was that the bride insisted that she be married in her native county, although the appropriate room, the parlor of the house, stood just across the line in Northumberland County There was nothing left to do except to have the ceremony performed in the kitchen, which stood in Lycoming county She was a granddaughter of John Clendenen, who served as one of General Washington's bodyguards, during the Revolutionary War, and was a witness of the execution of Major Andre, as a spy She lived into extreme old age, passing away in 1902 at the age of ninety-two years Ten children were born to David Tyler and his wife, namely Mary, who resides at Lock Haven, Pa, is the widow of Robert C Packer, a cousin of former Governor Asa T Packer, of Pennsylvania, John C and Roxanna, both of whom are deceased, Margaret, now deceased, who was the wife of William Schryver, Martin V and Martha, twins, the former of whom lives in Huston Township, the latter dying young, James A and Phebe, who, with Martin V, occupy the old homestead, Emma, now deceased, who was the wife of Charles Coryell, also deceased, and David, who is also deceased The children were all born at Trout Run, Lycoming County They were reared in the Presbyterian church

DAVID T DUNLAP, one of the representative citizens of Brady township and one of the substantial men of Clearfield county, resides on his well improved farm of seventy-five acres in Brady township and owns a second farm containing fifty-five acres, situated in Sandy township He was born in a log house then standing on his home farm, in Brady township, May 30, 1843, and is a son of Alexander and Nancy (Hadden) Dunlap, and a grandson of William Dunlap

William Dunlap was born in Ireland When he came to Clearfield county from the eastern coast, he drove his horse and wagon all the way, there being no railroads at that time, and settled in the midst of the woods in what is now Penn township At that time Harrisburg, the capital, was the nearest trading place William Dunlap was not only an industrious man but he was exceedingly enterprising He built what was probably the first saw mill on Little Clearfield Creek, and after clearing up his first tract of land made additions to it and became possessed of 400 acres At the time of his saw-milling industry dressed lumber was not in such demand as were shingles, logs being available all through this section for building purposes, and his sawmill output was mainly shingles which, at that time, were largely made by hand He married Sarah Reed and they reared a family of ten children, all of whom grew up on the pioneer farm

Alexander Dunlap was the second son in the above family and he was born September 4, 1807, after his parents had come to Clearfield county He engaged in farming and also in shingle making In 1840 he moved to the farm on which his son, David T, resides, and completed its clearing and resided here until his death, which occurred in 1895 He married Nancy Hadden, who was born in Jefferson county, Pa, and died in 1897, an aged woman To Alexander and Nancy Dunlap ten children were born, as follows William, who is deceased, Sarah, who is the wife of Isaac Zartman, Mary J, who is deceased, Archibald H, David Thomas, Isaac Ross, who is deceased, James N, John R, who is deceased, Martha E, who is the widow of David Snyder, and an infant, deceased

David T Dunlap has always lived on his own farm while engaged in agricultural pursuits but spent many winters in the lumber camps and some fourteen years in milling, two of these in Maryland, where some DuBois capitalists were interested, and the rest of the time at Brockwayville, Pa He remained at home with his parents until they died In 1868 he had bought the home farm from his father and for some years has given all his attention to its improvement and development The land is all under cultivation with the exception of twelve acres and there is a valuable six-foot vein of coal which has not been mined The buildings on the place were put up by his father but he has remodeled them and added features which make them more attractive and comfortable

In 1870 Mr Dunlap was married to Miss Sarah Pence, who was born on the old Pence farm in Brady township, and died in March, 1909 Ten children were born to Mr and Mrs Dunlap, as follows Clarence, who lives on the Sandy township farm, married Ella Harman and they have seven children, Cora, who married Sherman Starr, of Jefferson county, Pa, and they have seven children, Jacob, who is deceased, Rose, who is the wife of William Pierson, and they have two children, Pearl, who is the wife of Jesse Barr, of Potter county, Pa ; Thomas, who married Eva Askey, who was born in Sandy, and they live at Beech Creek, Pa, and have two children, Lula, who married James Luther, who assists Mr Dunlap on the farm, and they have three children—Helen, Russell and Jesse, Charles, who is a farmer in Sandy township, married Ruth Carlbaugh, and they have one child; Plumb, who resides with his father; and Firman, who died young

In politics Mr Dunlap is a Democrat and he is serving in his third term as a member of the school board He belongs to the Grange and to the Owl Club at DuBois, and is identified also with the Odd Fellows, the Knights of Pythias and the order of the Moose

THOMAS HUMPHREYS, whose valuable farm of 138 acres is situated in Pike township, two miles southwest of Curwensville, is one of the substantial and useful men of this part of the county He was born in Pike township, July 12, 1840, and is a son of Richard S and Mary Ann (Wright) Humphreys

Richard S Humphreys was born in Huntingdon county, Pa, where he attended school in his early years and then learned the milling business, residing for some years after his marriage at Moose Creek He then moved to Curwensville, where he operated a mill for one year, after which he ran a mill at Clearfield for a year Mr Humphreys then returned to the Curwensville mill and for several years alternated between his farm which adjoined the one now owned by his son, Thomas Humphreys, and Curwensville, finally settling permanently on the farm and there his death occurred March 18, 1891, at the age of eighty-nine years, his birth having taken place on April 2, 1812 From the time of its organization he was a member of the Republican party He married Mary Ann Wright, who was born in Huntingdon county, Pa, a daughter of John Wright, and died December 24, 1888 Her burial was at Oak Hill cemetery and three years later her husband was laid by her side They were members of the Baptist church Ten children were born to them, as follows William, who died in infancy, Louisa, who is the wife of Daniel Fost, Thomas, Mary Ellen, who died in infancy, Annie M, who lives on the old homestead, Judson M, who resides at Reynoldsville, Pa, John W, who lives on the old homestead, Edward, who died when two years old, Emma, who lives with her sister and brother on the old homestead, and Ella, who is deceased

Thomas Humphreys obtained his education in the common schools and the academy at Curwensville, after which he assisted his father on the farm and also worked at lumbering When Civil war was precipitated he, with other loyal young men of his neighborhood, soon gave proof of their patriotism by offering their services to their country He enlisted in Co K, in the famous regiment known as the Bucktail Rifles, and continued in the army until his honorable discharge on December 29, 1862 Mr Humphreys was a brave and efficient soldier but this did not prevent his suffering from many of the dangers of war He participated in many skirmishes and in such terrible battles as the second Bull Run, South Mountain and Antietam He was made a prisoner on one occasion, after having been in a swamp for four days with nothing to eat, and was sent to Belle Isle, where he fared little better but was finally exchanged.

From the Bull Run battle he accompanied his regiment to Frederick City, Md, after which followed South Mountain and Antietam In the latter battle he was wounded in the jaw and also in the neck but it may be noticed that he was never wounded in the back After his discharge he returned to Pike township and here has been engaged in agricultural pursuits ever since With the exception of forty acres still in valuable timber, Mr Humphreys has all his land under a fine state of cultivation

Mr Humphreys was married first to Miss Mary Martha Wilkins, who was born in Jefferson county, Pa Five children were born to this marriage, namely Lida, who lives in Montana, William R, who lives at Grampian, Pa ; John H, who died December 24, 1906, and Edward E and Thomas Roy, both of whom reside at Chicago, Ill Mr Humphreys was married second on May 28, 1879, to Mrs Evanna (Haney) Hile, widow of Warren Hile, who was a son of Henry Hile Mr Hile died December 11, 1874, and was buried in the McClure cemetery He was a member of the Baptist church Two children survive him Henry G, who is a rural mail carrier out of Curwensville, and Abby, who is the wife of John A Dale Mrs Humphreys was born March 19, 1852, a daughter of Frederick and Margaret (Jordan) Haney Mr and Mrs Humphreys have had two children Margaret Irene and James M The former was a highly educated young lady, a graduate of Bucknell University, and a popular and successful teacher Her death occurred January 16, 1909, and her burial was in the Oak Hill cemetery James M is a student in the Patton graded school and will graduate from that branch with the class of 1911 Mr and Mrs Humphreys are members of the Methodist Episcopal church at Curwensville In politics he is a Republican and once consented to serve as treasurer of Pike township He is a stockholder in the Curwensville National Bank and is treasurer of the Oakland Telephone Company of Pike township and Curwensville

T S LUZIER,* who carries on general farming on a tract of thirteen acres, located about four and a half miles west of Bigler in Bradford township, also does considerable carpentering during the off seasons He was born May 15, 1873, in Shawsville, Bradford township, Clearfield county, Pa , and is a son of Thomas and Jane (Hall) Luzier. Thomas Luzier was born and reared in Clearfield county, Pa , and has always resided here, engaged in agricultural pursuits

T S Luzier was reared and has resided all his life in Clearfield county. After his marriage on August 16, 1906, to Florence Knepp, who is a daughter of Isaac Knepp, he began housekeeping on his present farm, which he had purchased the June previous to his marriage Mr Luzier and his wife are both members of the Brethren church of Bradford township, and he has held the office of class leader, and also been superintendent of the Sabbath school Mr Luzier was judge of the election board and also inspector of the election board for a number of years, and is one of the progressive and public spirited citizens of Bradford township

JOHN A JOHNSON, who is a general farmer and stock raiser, in Pike township, owns seventy-five acres of valuable land two and one-half miles southwest of Curwensville He was born February 24, 1869, in Green-

wood township, Clearfield county, Pa , and is a son of Elah and Hannah (Troy) Johnson

Elah Johnson was born in Penn township, Clearfield county He became a millwright and later owned saw mills in different parts of the county, and also a farm of 160 acres He was a lifelong Democrat and served out one term as county commissioner in Clearfield county and a number of terms as school director in Penn township He was a member of the Society of Friends His death occurred June 21, 1888, at the age of seventy-seven years, and his burial was at Grampian He was twice married, first to Elizabeth Horn, a daughter of Samuel Horn She was survived by one daughter, Hannah E McClure His second marriage was to Hannah Troy, who was born December 26, 1832, in Brady township, Clearfield county, a daughter of Samuel and Katherine (Miles) Troy, and eleven children were born to this union, namely: Florence, Elizabeth A , who is the wife of William Hoover, of Bell's Landing, Pa , Manassah, who lives in Michigan, married Lillie Thompson, S Miles, who lives in Bell township, married Henrietta Passmore, A G , who is a resident of British Columbia, married Ida White, who is now deceased, Lewis K , who resides in Greenwood township, married Jennie Bartelbaugh, Ellis I , who moved to British Columbia, Millard F and Mary, both of whom are deceased; John A ; and Lydia Alice, who is now deceased .

John A Johnson attended school in Greenwood township and afterward went to lumbering and still later engaged in mining After he married he lived first at Grampian and then came to his present farm in Pike township, which was known as the Richard Freeman farm, originally belonging to the grandfather of Mrs Johnson At present there is no open coal bank on the place and all the land is under cultivation except about forty acres still in valuable timber

Mr Johnson was married on July 2, 1891, to Miss Alice Freeman, who was born in Pike township, Clearfield county, Pa, March 1, 1876, a daughter of William and Ara Belle (Bloom) Freeman Mr and Mrs Johnson have had three children Hazel, who died at the age of nine years, and Everett and Mildred, both of whom attend the Summit Ridge school where they are bright and attentive pupils The family attends church at Grampian Mr Johnson is a member of the Sons of America and of the Order of the Moose, at Curwensville He is an independent Democrat in his political views and while living in Penn township served on the election board and has been a school director for two years in Pike township

JOHN HEBERLING, whose valuable farm of 125 acres is situated in Sandy Township, about three miles south of DuBois, Pa, is a prominent citizen of the township and has served in numerous public offices with the greatest efficiency He was born on his father's farm in Schuylkill county, Pa, November 23, 1843, and is a son of Abraham and Magdalena (Hand) Heberling, and a grandson of Jacob and Elizabeth Heberling

Jacob Heberling and family came from Schuylkill county to Clearfield county, in 1855, and after reaching here, he bought a large tract of land which is now a part of the First Ward of the borough of DuBois Jacob Heberling sold his land to his son, David Heberling, who later sold it to the

3 8

Rumbargers, all of these transactions taking place before DuBois was laid out Jacob Heberling then bought a farm near West Liberty, which was then in Brady but is now in Sandy township, and spent the rest of his life there, living to be more than eighty years of age When he bought his farm the future prospects for the growth of West Liberty were better than for DuBois The name of his wife was Elizabeth, and they had five children. David, Abraham, Henry, John and Eve, the last named being the wife of John Hand All are now deceased

Abraham Heberling was married before the family left Schuylkill county, to Magdalena Hand, and seven children were born to them, namely Joseph, of Brady township, John, Augustus, of West Liberty, George W and Jefferson T, twins, both residents of West Liberty, Catherine, wife of Henry Utzenger, of Sandy township, and Peter S, also of Sandy township Abraham Heberling accompanied his father to Clearfield county and bought a farm near West Liberty now in Sandy township, and as he had fine water power, built a mill and engaged in the lumber industry He operated the mill at first with water power but later installed machinery and it was one of the first steam mills in the township His first purchase of land was not far from DuBois, the water power above alluded to being on that farm, and from there he moved to the place nearer West Liberty His wife died at the age of sixty years but he lived to be eighty-four years of age

John Heberling was about twelve years old when the family came to Clearfield county and he has spent his life ever since in the same neighborhood His school advantages were rather meager and afterward he worked in his father's mill and helped clear up the farm and later was engaged as a sawyer by his brother, J F. Heberling In 1860 he secured seventy-six acres of land from his father and bought a tract of forty-nine acres which adjoined He partly cleared this second tract and erected buildings which are now used by his son, G E Heberling, who lives there and operates the whole farm When Mr Heberling took possession there was an old log barn on the place, which he subsequently replaced by a bank barn with dimensions of 40 by 40 feet, and made many other improvements

Mr Heberling married Miss Lemontine Kriner, a daughter of David Kriner, who was an old pioneer of Clearfield county, and they have two children Maggie and George E The latter married Venia Askey and they have four children Lloyd E , Grace, Evelyn and Catherine In politics Mr. Heberling is a Democrat and has served as overseer of the Poor, both by appointment and election, and for ten years was a school director, for three years supervisor and one year township treasurer He is a member of the Knights of Pythias at Salem, Pa

JAMES B SMITH, a retired farmer and highly respected citizen of Pike township, who resides on his well improved farm of seventy acres, situated one mile southwest of Curwensville, Pa , was born in Pike township, March 16, 1828, and is a son of John and Nancy (Jordan) Smith

John Smith was born in Germany and remained in his native land until young manhood, when he came to America, landing at Philadelphia From there he came to Clearfield county and settled on a tract of 1,000 acres He cleared up about seventy-eight acres along the river Later he came to the farm which is now owned by his son, James B Smith, where, with the assistance of his children, he cleared forty acres, and he continued to live on this farm until the close of his life, his death occurring at the age of eighty-two years He was a man of sterling character, honest and upright in all his dealings In politics he was a Democrat and on several occasions was elected to township offices He married Nancy Jordan, a daughter of Martin Jordan, and they had fifteen children born to them, all in Pike township· William, David, Sarah, John, Hannah, Susan, Katherine, James B , Mary Jane, Rachel, Nancy, Elizabeth, Emily, Lavina and Harvey The mother of the above family died aged seventy-three years, and both she and husband were buried in the old McClure cemetery They were members of the Presbyterian church

James B Smith attended school in his boyhood at the Oakland school-house. His life has been devoted to agricultural pursuits and he has remained on the home farm. Here he has, at various times, made many improvements, and all the buildings now standing were erected by him For some years past he has lived retired from active farm work but he still enjoys overlooking the industries which he so successfully managed alone for so long a time He has witnessed many changes in methods of farming and has seen the introduction of farm machinery that in his youth was not yet dreamed of

On October 15, 1861, Mr. Smith was

married to Miss Adaline Way, who was born at Curwensville, Pa, a daughter of Samuel and Hannah Way Mrs Smith died October 15, 1905 To Mr and Mrs Smith eight children were born, namely: John L, who died when fifteen months old, Samuel, who married Ella Way, a daughter of David Way, resides on the home farm and they have eight children—Verna, Maude, William, Louella, Gussie, Ruth, Lester and Harry, William, who lives at Grampian, married Mrs Lucy (Bloom) Johnston, widow of Elmer Johnston and daughter of James Bloom, has one daughter, Bertha, Frederick, who married Mary Davis for his first wife and Sarah McDorment for his second wife, resides in New York and has four children—Lizzie, Howard, Lulu and Claire, James B, who married Cora Fritz, a daughter of Daniel Fritz, has had six children—Eva, Daniel, George, Irwin, Jay and Hazel, Charles, who resides at Curwensville, married Alice Norris, a daughter of Clark Norris, and they have had four children—Firman, Raymond, Sarah and Max, Dock, who lives at Curwensville, married Cora Moore, a daughter of Samuel Moore, and they have three children— Samuel, Frances and Lenore, and Minnie, who married James Edmiston, who resides on and assists in operating the home farm, and they have three children—William, Dortha and Lodema Mrs Smith was a member of the Methodist Episcopal church Mr Smith has been a Republican since the formation of the party He has served twice as road supervisor in Pike township He is a member of Susquehannah Grange

HARRY CHARLES CONNER, merchant and assistant postmaster at Burnside,

Clearfield county, Pa, was born at Mitchell Mill, Indiana county, Pa, July 7, 1863, and is a son of John C and Emily V (McClure) Conner

John C Conner was born June 30, 1831, in Indiana county, Pa, and died at Burnside, February 13, 1909 For three years after leaving school he was a clerk in a general store in Indiana county, and then moved to Mitchell Mill, where he carried on a general mercantile business for four years In 1868 he came to Burnside, first as a clerk and later in business for himself, as a member of the firm of Kime & Conner, general merchants, buying his partner's interest two years afterward and continuing under the name of J C Conner in a general mercantile and lumber business In 1885 he admitted his son, Harry Charles Conner, to partnership He was interested also as a partner in the lumber firm of Hopkins, Irvin & Conner, and as his investments were heavy in lumbering, he lost almost the whole of his fortune during the time of the great flood at Johnstown It was lost through the Consolidated Lumber Company on the Susquehannah River He retired then from active life During his earlier years he had been one of the successful as well as most enterprising business men of this section He was a leader also in politics and served first as a justice of the peace in Indiana City and later in the same office at Burnside At the time of his death he was a successful candidate on the Republican ticket for reelection to the office of auditor and many of his friends cast their votes for him on the very day of his decease He was a member of the Baptist church

John C Conner was married first to Emily Widowson, who was survived by three children   Nettie, who is the wife of A K Long, of Burnside, Jennie, who is the wife of Elwood Henderson, of Burnside, and John B, who is postmaster at Burnside   John C Conner was married second to Emily V McClure, a daughter of Stansbury McClure   Her death occurred April 12, 1891, at the age of forty-eight years   Three children were born to this marriage, namely   William M, Harry Charles, and Emma A, the last named being the wife of W E Patchin, of Burnside

Harry Charles Conner attended school at Burnside and as soon as old enough became a clerk for his father and subsequently his partner   After the Johnstown flood caused his father to retire, he then entered his brother's employ and with him is interested in merchandising and serves also as assistant postmaster   While interested in the lumber business, before the flood alluded to, he operated the last raft of lumber that went down the river safely   He has been one of the active and progressive men of the borough and has served two terms as burgess   He served also three years as constable and for nine years as president of the school board and was register of statistics for township and borough   He is a stanch Republican and is chairman of the Vigilance Committee of the party for this district

Mr Conner married Miss Mollie M Mahaffey, who was born May 30, 1863, at New Washington, Pa, a daughter of Robert and Faith Mahaffey, and they have had three children   Emily Gertrude, aged fourteen years, Helen, aged ten years, and a babe that died   Mr and Mrs Conner are members of the Methodist Episcopal church, of which he is a trustee   He belongs to Lodge No 679, Odd Fellows, at Burnside, and to Lodge No 540, Elks, at Clearfield   Mr Conner is one of the representative men of this section, and bears a name that has been held in high esteem for many years here

JOSEPH L DALE, a prominent citizen and progressive agriculturist of Pike township, who resides on his valuable farm of 104 acres, situated two miles southwest of Curwensville, belongs to one of the old county families and was born on this farm on May 8, 1840   He is a son of John P. and Martha (Henry) (Bell) Dale

John P Dale was born in 1799, near Williamsport, Lycoming county, Pa, and died in Clearfield county in October, 1883   He had but few educational privileges in youth, having to walk a distance of three miles through the winter snows, to reach the schoolhouse, but he learned to read, spell and calculate and became a fine penman   When he came first to Clearfield county the present thriving borough of Clearfield was represented by one old cabin on the old Read farm   Mr Dale was accompanied by his mother who built a large stone house on the State road and frequently traded bread she baked to Indians who brought her meat   When he was only ten years old he carried the mail between Bellefonte and Franklin, making the dangerous trip on horseback, and dangerous indeed it was as on one occasion he encountered twenty-one hungry wolves   Frequently he stopped at the Indian camps, in the winter time, and warmed himself by their fires   He treated them all justly and they were kind and friendly to him and his family, and in after years he often told of the real nobility of character the supposed savages showed when they were dealt with justly

John P Dale was thrice married and after his first union he came to the farm now owned by his son, Joseph L After the death of his wife he moved to Bridgeport and lived in a small house on a hillside above the place and while there operated a sawmill From there he moved to Curwensville, where he entered into partnership with a Mr McPherson in the tanning business and while living there his second wife died He was married a third time at Curwensville, and afterward moved to a farm of 100 acres, three miles west of Curwensville, which is now owned by John Woods, afterward purchasing the present farm He was living at Curwensville during the Civil War For fifty years he was a consistent member of the Methodist Episcopal church A lifelong Democrat he was prominent in township politics and served acceptably in township offices. He was a man of whom nothing but good can be recalled, a typical pioneer, and his memory reflects honor on his descendants and on the section in which his industrious and useful life was spent Although thrice married he did not leave very many children His first wife was Margaret McClure, who died with their infant child His second marriage was to a Miss McCracken, and five children were born, only one of whom, the eldest, William Dale, survives His third union was with Mrs Martha (Henry) Bell, widow of William Bell and daughter of James Henry, of Center county, where she was born Four children were born to John P and Martha Dale James, Jennie

C, Joseph L and Martha Of these, Jennie C is now deceased The mother of this family died in 1881 and both she and the father rest in the old McClure cemetery, which is situated near the Dale farm

Joseph L Dale attended school at Locust Ridge schoolhouse, two miles from Curwensville. It was a subscription school, the free school system not yet having been introduced He learned to read in the New Testament, no regular reading books having yet found their way into Pike township Some years later he attended school for one year in New York State When the Civil War broke out, Mr Dale was an enthusiastic supporter of the Union and gave proof of his loyalty by enlisting for service in the army, entering Co B, 149th Pa Vol Inf, the famous Bucktail regiment, and remained until the close of the war During this time he was exposed to all the dangers which war brings in its train and he was ever at the post of duty, but he fortunately escaped both wounds and capture After he returned home he bought the farm from his father and has continued to reside here until the present The pleasant title of Glendale Farm has been given the place and it is known all over this section for its productiveness both as to grain and excellent stock Mr Dale has sixty acres under cultivation

In 1865 Mr Dale was first married, the lady being Miss Christiana Esau, who was born in Germany She died in March, 1895, the mother of ten children, namely: John A, who lives in Curwensville, William L, who married Anna Hagerty, Idella, who died young; Harry and Mary, both of whom are deceased, Frank, who resides at Altoona, married Alice Hagerty and they have four children—Malcolm, Joseph, William and Martha; Walter, who is in business at Altoona, married Mabel Doughman, and they have four children—Lorna, Dortha, Elizabeth and Frederick, Paul, who resides at Curwensville, Annie, who is the wife of John Hudson, of Curwensville, and they have two children—John and Margie. Mr Dale was married second on April 25, 1896, to Mrs Clarissa (Cole) Hoover, widow of Allen Hoover and a daughter of Jacob and Sarah (Welch) Cole. Mrs Dale was born at Center, Pa, April 22, 1845 She, with her husband, is interested actively in the work of the Methodist Episcopal church, of which both are members Mr Dale is identified with Susquehannah Grange, at Curwensville, an organization that claims the majority of the enterprising and successful farmers of this section as members In politics Mr Dale has always been a Democrat and on the Democratic ticket has frequently been elected to township offices and has served as constable, school director, tax collector and overseer of the Poor He is one of the leading members of Kratzer Post, G A R, at Curwensville, and for many years has been a member of the local lodge of Odd Fellows

Q E BEAUSEIGNEUR,* postmaster at Lecontes Mills, in Girard township, where he is engaged in the lumber business, is also engaged in farming and operates a general store, and has spent his whole life in this township and is one of its foremost men His parents, Peter and Elizabeth Beauseigneur, were both born in France, and the latter died in Girard township in 1908 The father was three years old when his father brought him to Clearfield county, settling on 600 acres of land, this being one of the rich old colonizing families of this section that originated in France.

Q E Beauseigneur was reared and educated in Girard township He located on his present farm, which lies thirteen miles northeast of Clearfield, shortly after his marriage He is a man of unusual enterprise and successfully manages numerous interests He was appointed postmaster at Lecontes Mills in 1890, under the administration of President McKinley, and has been retained in office ever since In his general store he carries a well selected stock of goods, mainly groceries, and supplies a large surrounding territory In 1904 he was married to Miss A Daugherty, of Clearfield, and they have one daughter, Rebecca Mr and Mrs Beauseigneur are members of the Roman Catholic church at Frenchville

GEORGE C PASSMORE, a successful farmer and representative citizen of Penn township, where he owns 305 acres of excellent land, which lies two and one-fourth miles southeast of Grampian, Pa, was born in the Bailey settlement, in Pike township, Clearfield county, August 11, 1830, and is a son of Ganer and Mary Elizabeth (McCracken) Passmore

Ganer Passmore was born on the same farm in Pike township which was the birthplace of his son, his father, Abraham Passmore, having been a pioneer settler there Ganer Passmore married Mary Elizabeth McCracken and they continued to live on the old Passmore homestead They were members of the Methodist Episcopal church They had five children, namely: Joseph and Hiram, both of whom are deceased, Eli, Henrietta, who lives near Madera, Pa, and George C, of Penn township

George C Passmore attended school in his youth in Penn, Pike and Ferguson townships, and went to work at lumbering for some years trying his strength in making lumber and his skill in rafting it down the river For a short time following his marriage he lived in Bell township and then settled on his present farm in Penn township, where he carries on farming and stock raising

In 1850 Mr Passmore was married to Miss Elizabeth Rice, who was born in Lycoming county, Pa, July 28, 1834, a daughter of William and Nancy Rice She lost her parents in infancy To Mr and Mrs Passmore five children have been born, namely William, Allen, who is deceased, Viola, who is the wife of George Bowman, of DuBois, and they have two children—William and Lizzie, George McClelland, who married Matilda Happer, a daughter of Simon Happer, and they have four children—Sherman, Berna, Olive and Helen, and Irwin, who married Maude Sankey, lives in California and they have two children

In politics Mr Passmore is a Democrat and being a man of high standing in his neighborhood, has frequently been elected to local offices and has served acceptably as school director, treasurer, assessor and road supervisor

JONATHAN SHAFER, who has lived in Clearfield county since 1848, and owns an excellent farm of forty-nine acres, in Brady township, was born November 22, 1837, in Lebanon county, Pa, and is a son of Jacob and Elizabeth (Heinzerling) Shafer

Jacob Shafer was born in Dauphin county, Pa His ancestors took part in the Revolutionary War He came to Lebanon county as a young man and married a lady who was born in Philadelphia In 1838 they moved to Center county and in 1848 to Clearfield county, making the journey in wagons as at that time there were no railroads through this section Mr Shafer located four miles south of Luthersburg and the first twig ever cut on the land was by Jonathan Shafer, when a boy of eleven years Jacob Shafer cleared this farm with the assistance of his sons and later sold the place to his son Jonathan and moved back to Center county, where he died at the age of seventy-five years His widow survived him, her death taking place at the age of eighty-four years, at the home of her son, Jonathan Eight children were born to Jacob Shafer and his wife, namely Susan, who is deceased, was the wife of D S McCracken, also deceased, Solomon, who is deceased, Jacob, who is deceased, Lydia, who is the widow of Hiram Passmore, Joseph, Jonathan, John H, Samuel, and Rebecca, who is the wife of William Snyder

Jonathan Shafer had but meager school opportunities in his youth, the log schoolhouse being distant from his home When he was twenty-one years old he learned the carpenter trade, with William Fitzpatrick in Illinois, with whom he remained for two and one-half years and later worked for a number of years as carpenter and contractor at DuBois, following the fire at that place After buying his father's farm he kept it for five years and then sold and moved to Salem, where he purchased a house and an acre of land and lived there for five years In 1870 he bought the Johnson farm of 103 acres, near Luthersburg, and put up new buildings and lived there until he bought his present farm in 1897, selling the former one Mr Shafer has always been considered a good and worthy citizen, having ever shown public spirit and commendable interest in all that pertains to his section He has served as school director for the past fifteen years and has held other township offices

Mr Shafer was married August 18, 1864, to Miss Mary E Horn, who was born in Brady township, a daughter of Daniel and Nancy (Michaels) Horn, natives of Chest township They have had eleven children, all of whom survive, a large and united family Elora Jane is the wife of G B Wachob Alva Anson married Inez Brisbain Reuben C married Zoe Clover. Maggie R married Dr Marsh Hay George W. married Ida Swope Ada C married Joseph P Nollen Harvey Q married Mell Clover. David L married Alta Lines. Emma May married Charles Moose Jonathan E married Iva Pence Lena M married Levi Draucker Mr Shafer and family are members of the Methodist Episcopal church. He is a member of the Grange and for ten years has belonged to the order of American Mechanics In his views on public questions he is independent but casts his vote with the Prohibitionists

JOSEPH WILLIAM ROESSNER, proprietor of the Clearfield Brewing Company,

brewers and bottlers of beer and porter, and manufacturers of hygienic ice, is also the owner of a fine farm of 120 acres in Lawrence township, and has been a resident of Clearfield County, Pa , since 1896 He was born October 22, 1857, in Germany and is a son of Frank and Philomena (Gutberled) Roessner, both of whom were born and died in Germany Frank and Philomena Roessner were the parents of nineteen children, six of whom were twins, and but four of whom came to America, Joseph William, our subject was the youngest of the nineteen, Charles, Herman, and Maria, who is the wife of Joseph Och of Pittsburg The three boys all live in Clearfield County, Pa

Joseph William Roessner grew to maturity in Germany, and was educated in the Catholic schools of that country He became a dyer by trade and also engaged in agricultural pursuits until 1882, when he emigrated to America He first located in Red Wing, Minn , where he worked one year on a farm, then came to Pittsburg, Pa , and worked fourteen years for the Adams Express Company, where he worked his way up to assistant agent In 1896, Mr Roessner resigned his position with the Express Company, and came to Clearfield, Pa , where he and his brother Charles rented a brewery from Mrs. Ries They subsequently bought the plant, which at that time was a small one with an output of ten barrels per day, and in 1903 our subject bought his brother's interest in the business, and has since then added a new stock house, cellars, and bottling house He also built an ice plant with a capacity of twenty ton per day, and his son Edward J Roessner is chief engineer of the plant In addition to his brewery Mr Roessner is the owner of a fine farm of 120 acres in Lawrence township, and is a stockholder in the Second National Bank of Clearfield Mr. Roessner is fraternally a

JOSEPH W. ROESSNER

member of the B P O E , F O E , Moose, Red Men, and C M P A

On April 24, 1883, Mr Roessner married Theressa Krug, who crossed to this country on the same boat on which our subject came, and of their union have been born nine children Edward Joseph, married Mary Farrell, and has one son, Edward J , Jr, Theressa (Mrs Gotfred P Johnson) has two children, Earl and Joseph, Frank, is a student at the Carnegie School of Technology, Anna, Catherine, Joseph W , Leo George, and two who died young The religious connection of the family is with the Catholic Church

CHARLES C ADDLEMAN, who carries on general farming in Pike township, where he has 125 acres, 100 of which is under cultivation, belongs to one of the old county families, his grandfather, William Addleman, coming to Clearfield in 1849. He was born on what is known as the Irwin farm, near Curwensville, Clearfield county, January 1, 1872, and is a son of G Lloyd and Annie (Cleaver) Addleman, who are residents of Curwensville, where they have lived since the fall of 1902

Charles C Addleman obtained his education at the Oakland school in Pike township, and in the Curwensville public schools, and then began to assist his father on the home farm, to which his parents had moved in his infancy Since his father retired he has had entire charge About twenty-five acres of the place is still in valuable timber, and four acres are devoted to gardening, Curwensville offering a ready market for all over production on the farm Mr Addleman has no coal bank open, but in all probability a workable vein might be found

as much property in this section has been underlaid with this valuable deposit

Mr Addleman was married May 3, 1893, to Miss Alverta Norris, who was born at Clearfield, Pa , June 8, 1875, and is a daughter of Clark and Sarah (Wall) Norris, of Clearfield Mr and Mrs Addleman have two sons, George L and Charles Wayne, both of whom are bright students in the public schools of Pike township In politics Mr Addleman is a Republican and he has frequently served in township offices, formerly as a school director for three years, also as road master and as supervisor, and has been chosen with other responsible citizens to serve on the election board Both he and his wife are active members of the Union church He is identified with the Odd Fellows lodge at Curwensville

JAMES B STAUFFER, who is prosperously engaged in the lumber business at Burnside, this county, was born in this place, November 26, 1869, a son of John and Anna (Smith) Stauffer His paternal grandfather was John H. Stauffer, who was born at Lancaster, Pa , and subsequently removed to York county, whence he came in 1849 to Clearfield, settling near Burnside He was a broom maker by trade but also followed farming He died in Franklin county, Pa , in 1876, at the age of 65 years His wife, whose maiden name was Susan Troyer, was born in Adams county in 1801; she died in 1892 Of their children there are now living, John, the father of our subject, Susan, who married Andrew Anderson, is now deceased

John Stauffer, who was engaged in farming or farm work up to the age of 18, enlisted in

1864 from Harrisburg, Pa , in an independent company, but later became a member of the First W Va Cavalry and his regiment forming a part of the Army of the Western Potomac, he took part during the 120 days of his service in a number of skirmishes Mustered out March 30th of that year, he took up his residence at Lewisberry, Pa , where he engaged in agriculture, but a year later came to Burnside township, Clearfield county, where he followed teaming and lumbering until 1908 For twelve years he was engaged in conveying merchandise by team from Indiana, Pa to Burnside, and later from Curwensville for ten years He then retired from active industrial life He is a Republican and is now serving his second term as assessor of the borough of Burnside, having also served on the school board and as supervisor He was married July 29, 1867, to Anna Smith, who was born March, 1849, in Burnside township Her father, David F Smith, came from Ireland as a boy with his parents, William and Nellie (Dean) Smith, they settling in Clearfield county Of the fourteen children of John and Anna (Smith) Stauffer, five are now deceased and nine living The latter are James B , whose name appears at the head of this sketch, Gertrude, who is the widow of John Tawzer and resides with our subject, Abram T , who married Emma Bloom and resides in Cambria county (has two children), Beulah, wife of A Null and the mother of four children, Horace, who resides at Heilwood, Pa , is married and has three children, Elizabeth, the wife of A Armstrong, of Jefferson county, who has one child, Mack, who married Effie Strickland and has one child, Paul, who married Rebecca Adams and resides in Clearfield, Pa , Willie, residing at home (and one grandson, Robert)

James B. Stauffer after his school days were over found employment in the woods, cutting timber He also for several years followed the trade of shoemaking and was otherwise variously employed He remained at home until twenty-six years old, when he married and located in Burnside, following teaming here for several years, subsequent to which he was in the employ of John H Patchin for about twelve years About this time he formed a partnership with Carl Patchin in the lumber business, which has since continued Mr Stauffer was bookkeeper and general manager for John H Patchin and has a thorough knowledge of the lumber business both in the inside and outside departments He has been successful in his present connection and is now one of the substantial and prosperous citizens of his township When a boy of sixteen he carried the mail between Burnside and Curwensville and the habits of industry he thus acquired so early have remained with him and have had much to do with his advancement in life He is a member of the I O O F lodge, No 679, at Burnside, and of the Red Men's lodge at Glen Campbell, Pa He also belongs to the Encampment, I O O F A Republican politically, he is at present serving on the school board of the borough and has also served two terms in the council

Mr Stauffer was married June 7, 1895, to Minnie Thompson, who was born in Burnside township, this county, February 19, 1875, daughter of Alexander and Hannah (Fulton) Thompson Her father, who died in 1902 at the age of sixty-one years, was a lumberman and farmer of Burnside township Her grandfather, Ebenezer Thompson, who was a shoemaker, was one of the early settlers at Patchinville He married Julia Crispen Mrs

Stauffer's parents were married in 1862, her mother being then twenty years of age The latter was the daughter of Simon Fulton and a granddaughter of David H Fulton, of Frankstown, Blair county, Pa The latter after learning the tailor's trade in Philadelphia, settled in Burnside borough and later near the Squire Smith home in Clearfield county where he followed his trade and also devoted a part of his time to agriculture He married Elizabeth Rorabaugh Simon Fulton was born in Center county and afterwards followed farming on the parental homestead in Clearfield county He married Elizabeth Young, daughter of Henry and Hannah (Saylor) Young, and she died in 1854 Mrs Stauffer was the sixth born in a family of thirteen children She died February 7, 1911, deeply regretted by her family and a wide circle of friends and acquaintances She was an active member of and worker in the Pentecostal church and an earnest Christian woman Kind and generous of disposition, she was a helpful neighbor and it will be long ere her memory shall pass away To our subject and wife were born the following children Ruth Alice, born July 11, 1896, who is now attending the Burnside high school, Lura Imagene, born April 16, 1898, John A, born December 31, 1899, and George F, born April 13, 1903

JOHN R McCLURE, one of Pike township's most respected citizens, who is a farmer and stock raiser and owns 140 acres of excellent land, situated three miles southwest of Curwensville, Pa, was born in Pike township, Clearfield county, Pa, August 21, 1841, and is a son of Wilson and a grandson of Thomas McClure

Wilson McClure was born in Pike town-ship after his parents had come from Lancaster county and settled in this section At that time there were no public schools and the children obtained their educational training, such as it was, in the subscription schools Wilson McClure remained on the home farm and at one time owned 256 acres of land in Pike township, of which, with the help of his sons, he cleared eighty acres He married Mary Caldwell, a daughter of Matthew Caldwell of Pike township and they had the following children Margaret, who became the wife of Daniel Star, of Curwensville, Porter, who married Maria Tate, lives at Curwensville, Mary Jane, who is the widow of John L Rex, Samuel T, who was killed on the first day of the battle of Gettysburg, in the Civil war, being a member of Co B, 149th Pa Vol Inf, the famous Bucktail regiment, Marian, who resides in Pike township, John R, Sarah Ellen, who is the wife of Foster Williams, of Iowa, Winfield S, who died in Oklahoma, unmarried, and an infant son, deceased The old homestead is owned jointly by John R and Marian McClure The parents died here, the father on December 1, 1851, and the mother on March 18, 1898, and they were buried in the old McClure cemetery They were members of the Presbyterian church In politics, Wilson McClure was a Whig

John R McClure and his brothers and sisters obtained their early education at the old Oakland school-house, since when Mr McClure has been engaged in agricultural pursuits and has also followed lumbering He has always lived on this farm with the exception of a short time spent in Penn township, and has erected all the substantial farm buildings now standing on the place All his land is well cultivated except seventy-five acres still

in woodland and pasturage, Mr McClure having some fine Guernsey cattle of high grade

Mr McClure was married June 10, 1875,
to Miss Hannah E Johnson, who was born in
Union township, Clearfield county, Pa , October 5, 1845, a daughter of Elah and Elizabeth
(Horn) Johnson   Elah Johnson was born in
Penn township, a son of Samuel Johnson, one
of the early pioneers of Clearfield county Elah
Johnson was a millwright by trade and later
became a farmer and owned 160 acres of land
in Greenwood township that is now the prop-
erty of Lewis Johnson   He was a prominent
Democrat and at one time was a county commissioner in Clearfield county   His death occurred in Greenwood township, June 21, 1888,
and his burial was in the Friends' cemetery, at
Grampian, of which church he was a member
He was married first to Elizabeth Horn, who
was born in Chester county, Pa , and died in
December, 1848, and was buried at Grampian
She was a member of the Society of Friends
Of the four children born to that marriage,
Mrs McClure is the only survivor Her father
was married second to Hannah Troy, who was
born in Brady township, a daughter of Samuel and Katherine Troy, and eight of the
eleven children born to the second marriage
are still living

Mr and Mrs McClure have eight children,
as follows. Melissa Belle, who married Dr
Woodside, of Lumber City, and they have two
sons, Wendell and Hobart Keith, Samuel T ,
who resides at Grampian, married Eulala
Fink, a daughter of Elmer Fink, of Clearfield
county, Elah Wilson, who married Mary Murphy, resides at Lumber City and they have
four children—Richard, Paul, Winfield and
John, Clair, who resides at home; Cora Alice,
who is the wife of Roy Caldwell, of Gram-

pian, and they had one child—Merl Blair, who
is now deceased, H. C., who resides at Woodland, Pa , married Clella Iddings, Thomas
Rex, who lives near Blue Ball, on Morgan
Run, married Mabel Kline, and Grace, who
resides at home   Mr McClure and family attend the Friends' church He is identified
with Susquehanna Grange and enjoys meeting
other farmers and discussing questions of interest to agriculturists. Although a stanch
Democrat and at all times intelligently interested in township affairs, he has never consented to accept any public office

PERRY W. DRAUCKER, whose valua-
ble farm of 100 acres is situated in Brady
township, about two and one-half miles east
of Luthersburg, owns also a one-half interest
in 250 acres of timber land, lying in Union
township   He was born on his Brady township farm, April 5, 1849, and is a son of Isaac
and Mary (Bloom) Draucker, the youngest
son and the next youngest child born in a family of fifteen children

Perry W Draucker spent his boyhood on
the home farm and assisted his father to clear
it   In early manhood he learned the harness
making trade, working for two years under
Levi Flegal, at Luthersburg, and later worked
at this trade in Clarion county. After his marriage he bought the home farm and also the
hotel which had been established by his father
on the stage route and had been operated by
his mother after the death of the father. Mr
Draucker conducted the hotel, under license,
until 1894 when he moved to DuBois, where
he took charge of the old DuBois House, on
the east side of the borough, and continued
there for three years, moving then to Clearfield, where he operated what was then known

as the Manton House but has been conducted as the Hotel Dimeling, for six years When he gave up that hostelry he took charge of the Windsor Hotel, at Clearfield, and remained in the hotel business three years more and then returned to the farm This is valuable land both as to productiveness in the way of agriculture and also on account of a vein of coal underlying In 1884 Mr Draucker sustained the loss of his building from fire, but he at once rebuilt and his handsome residence is one of the finest in the township, containing fourteen rooms, heated by a modern furnace and equipped with a cold and hot water system

On August 11, 1870, Mr Draucker was married to Miss Margaret Clark, a daughter of William and Jane (Rafferty) Clark The father and mother of Mrs Draucker were both born in Ireland and he was twenty and she fifteen years of age when they came to America They lived at Grampian, Pa, for many years, where the father died in 1857 aged forty-nine years and the mother in 1893, aged seventy-seven years Margaret Clark was the second born in her parents' family, the others being James B, John, Edward, William, Joseph, Sarah Jane, Mary A and Thomas Augustus John and Edward are deceased Sarah Jane is the wife of George Erick and Mary A is the wife of Harry Yost

Mr and Mrs Draucker have had four children Maude, Mary, Blanche and Frank Maude married Austin Kirk, who is deceased and is survived by five children Vivian, Draucker and Blanche, twins, Joseph and Margaret B Mrs Kirk lives at DuBois Mary, who is now deceased, married Joseph Smiley, also deceased, and they are survived by two children, Helen Dorothy and Lois, both of whom live with their grandparents Blanche lives at

home, and Frank is in a railroad office at DuBois In politics Mr Draucker is a Democrat He is a member of a number of the leading fraternal organizations, including the Odd Fellows, at DuBois, the Elks at DuBois, the Knights of Pythias at New Salem, and the Red Men at Clearfield He is one of the well known representative and substantial men of Brady township

ZACHARIAH M BLOOM, who resides on the farm of seventy-five acres, situated in Pike township, on which he was born, March 16, 1843, is one of the well known and representative men of this section and a member of one of the oldest and most substantial families He is a son of William Bloom and a grandson of Peter Bloom, both of whom were born in Pike township

Peter Bloom was born on a farm two miles south of Curwensville, Pa, and there he carried on farming, and weaving in later years He married Mary King and they had eight children born to them to whom they gave the following names John, William, Rebecca, Martha, Margaret, Matilda, Archer and Joseph

William Bloom, the second born of the above family and the father of Zachariah M Bloom, was born September 18, 1811 He learned the carpenter trade, which he followed until his marriage, when he settled on the farm now owned by his son, Zachariah M, which then included but twenty-five acres, only six acres having yet been cleared He erected a log house with dimensions of 16 x 16 feet, back of the present residence, and devoted his time to farming and lumbering He was a quiet, industrious man and enjoyed the kind friendship of his neighbors, with whom he willingly combined to advance the general interests of the neighborhood For many years he was a member of the Methodist Episcopal church His death occurred March 16, 1865, and his burial was in Center church cemetery, Lawrence township, Clearfield county He married Susanna Passmore, who died September 27, 1878, a daughter of Abraham Passmore, of Pike township A large family was born to this marriage, the eldest and the youngest five dying in infancy The others were Mary Ann, David, Zachariah M , Nancy, John R , Hannah and Bishop Mary Ann, who died in Pike township, was married first to Thomas J Dunlap and they moved into Goshen and later into Lawrence township Four children were born to the first marriage: Frank, Alfred, Elvira and Lumsdon Mary Ann was married second to Andrew N Marks and they had five children. Ada, Lillie, Della, Ella and Jemima David Bloom was a martyr of the Civil war He was a member of Co. B, 149th Pa Vol Inf , under the command of Col John Irwin He was captured by the enemy at the battle of the Wilderness and was incarcerated in Danville prison He was rescued by the Union army but died at Wilmington, N C , April 4, 1865 Nancy and Hannah, of the above family, are both deceased John R Bloom lives in Pike township, while Bishop Bloom resides at Curwensville

Zachariah M Bloom attended the Welsh school when he was a boy but after he was sixteen years of age he worked on the farm during the summers and at lumbering in the winters He was married in 1870 and then settled on a farm in Pike township, near the one he now occupies, moving then to Lawrence township, where he lived for two years, when he returned to the log house on his former

farm and resided there until November, 1881, when he came to the homestead He has added land and has erected a new barn and built an addition to the house His land is all cleared with the exception of six acres in valuable timber During the closing year of the Civil war he enlisted in Co D, 76th Pa Vol Inf , and served until the end, some five months He escaped the misfortunes of his older brother and came home practically unharmed Formerly he belonged to the G A R post at Clearfield Politically he is a Democrat and has frequently been tendered public offices and has served one term on the school board and two terms as road supervisor

Mr. Bloom was married April 3, 1870, to Miss Charlotte Marshall, a daughter of Henry and Mary Ann Marshall Mrs. Bloom was born in Germany, May 19, 1845 To Mr and Mrs Bloom, twelve children have been born, namely. Mary, who is the wife of Archer Dunlap, of Blair county, Orrie, who married W. S Carr, and they have nine children—Winfield, William, Blair, Melvin, Phillip, Elizabeth, Edith, John and Edna, Elva, who married E R Peters, of Woodland, Pa , and they have nine children—Hayes, Lucien, Charlotte, Emma, Carl, Rex, Archie, Theodore and Roy; Emma who is the widow of John H Lewis, resides at Altoona and has three children—Helen, Nora and James; Nellie, who married James Wingert, of Pike township, Charles, who is deceased, Jennie, who married David Hull, and they have six children—Robert, Mabel, Martha, Helen, Trudy and Bruce; Edith, who is the wife of Ernest A Horn, of Pike township; Charlotte, who lives with her parents, Pansy, who is a stenographer with a Pittsburg business house; Thomas J , who is a member of Troop C, First U S Cav , now stationed at Calexico, Calif, and David Lucian, who resides on the homestead, married Elizabeth Bunchko Mr and Mrs Bloom are members of the Methodist Episcopal church The hospitality of their home is known all over Pike township

JOHN A GRAHAM,* a prominent citizen of Girard township, who owns a valuable farm of 170 acres and also operates a general store, being located fourteen miles east of Clearfield, was born in Girard township, in 1875, and is a son of Parley and Jane (Livingston) Graham Parley Graham was also born in Girard township, where he spent his life and for a number of years served in the office of township supervisor

John A Graham was educated in the public schools of Girard township and his business interests have always been centered here He carries on general farming and stockraising, his land being well adapted to both industries He keeps a well assorted stock of seasonable goods and his patronage comes from quite a wide surrounding territory

Mr Graham married Miss Gertrude Farabaugh, who was born, reared and educated in Cambria county, Pa, where her parents yet reside Three children have been born to Mr and Mrs Graham John P, Sarah J and Bertha Irene Mr Graham is an Odd Fellow and is identified with Clearfield Lodge, No 1027, of which he is secretary He is a wide awake business man and a public spirited citizen

FRED J DYER, proprietor of the Fred J. Dyer & Co store, the largest general mercantile establishment in Central Pennsylvania, together with the Fred J Dyer & Co mill, is one of the most enterprising and successful business men of Clearfield county and has been a resident of Curwensville for the past thirty-eight years He is a native of New England, born at Portland, Me, July 2, 1858, and is a son of W N and Caroline (Lovett) Dyer

W. N Dyer was also a native of Portland, where he was reared and educated He came to Pennsylvania and settled in Blair county in 1861 He was a cooper by trade and had plenty of employment as coopering was a very important industry at that time and all sugar and molasses hogsheads as well as all barrels, were made by hand This business he carried on in Hollidaysburg and in 1876 he moved from there to Clearfield county and when the railroad was extended to Curwensville, he came here He was a shrewd and successful business man and owned cooper shops at one time in Cambria, Blair, Center and Clearfield counties, giving employment to many men He was also a man of excellent judgment and of sterling character and served Curwensville in the office of burgess for two years He was married in Maine to Caroline Lovett and two children were born to them in that state Augusta and Fred J Two others were subsequently born in Blair county Lewis C and Carrie G W N Dyer died at Curwensville in June, 1904, his wife surviving until July, 1910 Their burial was at Portland, Me They were members of the Presbyterian church

Fred J Dyer was three years old when he was brought to Clearfield county His parents realizing, however, that their children could have much better educational advantages in New England than in Clearfield county at that time, sent Mr Dyer and his older sister to the home of their grandparents at Portland, and there both remained until they had secured a good education When Fred J Dyer returned to Clearfield county he became a clerk in a store his father was operating in connection with his coopering business, at Lumber City In 1872 he came to Curwensville where, with John B Alley & Co, he learned the tanning business In 1882 he embarked in the general mercantile business on the corner of Filbert and Meadow streets, this location at the time being considered a more or less undesirable one for his undertaking, by his business friends However, the result has shown that Mr Dyer had better foresight than his would be advisers for now his business house stands in the very center of the town Later he became general manager and superintendent of the above tanning firm but in 1892 retired as an active official, his individual business interests having so developed that his time is fully taken up with them In addition to his large store at Curwensville, Mr Dyer conducted branch stores at Curry Run and at Grampian until 1894 In 1900, in partnership with his brother, Lewis Dyer, and E Elms, he organized the Hambleton Leather Company, with tannery in West Virginia, but the buildings were burned in March, 1910 Mr Dyer was also the builder of his up-to-date mill, which draws custom from a distance of fifteen miles, and in both store and mill customers are assured of courteous treatment, honest service and immediate attention Mr Dyer was the main organizer of the Electric Light Company, at Curwensville, was a charter director and formerly vice-president of the Curwensville National Bank, and has been concerned in the founding and fostering of a large number of the town's leading industries, setting an example of public spirit and enterprise that is commendable in any citizen In 1890 he

erected his private residence, on the corner of Locust and State streets, which is one of the most attractive in the borough

In March, 1878, Mr Dyer was married to Miss Henrietta Thompson, a daughter of James and Katherine Thompson, and they have five children: John, Willis, Ellen, Katherine and Marion All reside at Curwensville, with the exception of Willis, who is married and lives in the State of Washington The family attend the Methodist Episcopal church In politics, Mr Dyer is an independent Republican For twelve years he served as a member of the school board, of which he was president for some time, and for twelve years was a member of the borough council Fraternally he is identified with the Masons Undoubtedly Mr. Dyer is a man possessing high qualities of business ability and he impresses a visitor very favorably in the expression of his practical views

FRED KOHLER, one of the best known citizens of Brady township, is probably one of the most venerable, his birth having taken place December 21, 1819, in Wittenburg, Germany, the home of his parents, who were George Frederick and Sophia Kohler

In 1833 the parents of Mr. Kohler decided to leave Germany and find a new home and better opportunities for their children by coming to America After much preparation they embarked on a sailing vessel and after about six weeks on the Atlantic Ocean, were safely landed at the port of New York The father was a dyer by trade and he soon found employment in what was known as the Dressler factory, in New Jersey It was his desire, however, to secure land and give his sons an opportunity to become farmers From New

Jersey he moved to Erie, Pa In the meanwhile one of his daughters had married a Mr Troutwine, quite an important man, for whom the town of Troutville, in Clearfield county, was named, it being built on land that he owned George F Kohler made a visit to his son-in-law and was so pleased with the appearance of the country in Brady township that he made arrangements for the purchase of the farm which his son, Fred Kohler, now owns and shortly afterward moved on the place He did not long survive but his widow lived to the age of ninety-three years Six children were born to them, namely Rosanna, Sophia, Fred, Amiel, Frederica and Wilhelmina, Fred and Amiel, the latter of whom lives in Clarion county, Pa, being the only survivors

Fred Kohler was fourteen years old when he accompanied his parents to America He had attended German schools but had to learn to speak in English after reaching the United States He was about sixteen years old when the family settled on the present farm At that time he saw no immediate way to make any money in this section and decided to follow the suggestion of a relative that he return to New York City, where he could find employment and make excellent wages by engaging in steam-boating Thus he followed the water for some years and then went to California during the first gold excitement, in 1849, not, however, before he had made a payment on the old homestead to the other heirs He remained in California for some years, meeting with many thrilling adventures and being fairly successful at gold mining He then returned to Clearfield county and took charge of his present farm of 200 acres, 100 of which is cleared It is fine land and is sit-

uated between Troutville and the Jefferson county line For a number of years afterward, Mr Kohler devoted much of his time to the lumber industry

Mr Kohler was married first in 1860, to Miss Nancy Crawford, who died two years later, leaving one child, George, who is a resident of DuBois, Pa The latter married Elizabeth Ferris In March, 1867, Mr Kohler was married second to Miss Mary Harwick, a daughter of John and Margaret (Kippler) Harwick, of Huntingdon county, Pa, and five children were born to them, as follows Samuel, who married Catherine Broshes, William, who married Catherine Knarr, Elizabeth, who married Solomon Conrad, Sophia, and Fred A, who married Agnes Wilson Mr and Mrs Kohler are members of the Lutheran church In politics he is a Democrat and is serving as a member of the school board of Brady township In spite of advancing years Mr Kohler still takes an active interest in public affairs and in neighborhood happenings He is held in high regard by all who know him and this circle is very wide

K A SLOPPY, justice of the peace in Knox township, who also conducts a meat business at New Milport, is one of the enterprising and successful business men of this section and is held in respect and neighborly esteem by those who have known him from infancy, for he was born at New Millport, May 13, 1863 His parents were Henry J and Patience (Curry) Sloppy, the former of whom still survives and resides at New Millport

Henry J Sloppy was born in Snyder county, Pa, August 26, 1837, and accompanied his father, Christopher Sloppy, to

Clearfield county, settling in Pike township, where the latter followed the carpenter trade The family is of German extraction Henry J Sloppy was married first to Patience Curry, a daughter of Richard Curry, who died and left one child, K. A. Her burial was in the Lutheran cemetery near New Millport His second marriage was to Nora Bloom, a daughter of George Bloom, and they had five children. James K, Hallie Almeda, Trilby S, Donald and William Byron After marriage, Mr Sloppy located at New Millport, where he lived until after the death of his first wife, when he entered the Union army, becoming a member of a company in the 149th Pa Vol Inf He was wounded in the forehead at the battle of Fort Steadman, but remained in the service until the close of the war, when he returned to New Millport He is a leading citizen and for thirty years has held public office in the township, serving ten years as a justice of the peace, was postmaster, also school director, and at present is township assessor In his political views he is an independent Democrat For some years he has been station agent at New Millport for the N Y Central R R, and also transports the mail He attends the Lutheran church

K A Sloppy obtained his education in the schools of Knox township and afterward became a clerk in a general store and for two years conducted a store of his own and for three years was connected with the store of L C Lanach, at Clearfield He then returned to New Millport He is well established in the butchering business, having a large trade and delivering meat at New Millport, Olanta and Kerrmoor on al-

ternate days In 1907 he was elected a justice of the peace to serve until 1912, having previously served five years as constable of Knox township

Mr Sloppy was married July 2, 1874, to Miss Jennie Lanach, a daughter of Jackson and Ctaherine (Miller) Lanach, natives of Virginia, but residents of Clearfield. Mr and Mrs Sloppy have seven children Orpha M, Oral J, Gussie Almeda, George, Guy, Kelly and Ivan Mr. Sloppy's two elder children are successful and popular teachers, Miss Orpha M having taught for eight terms and now being engaged at the Clover Run school in Clearfield county She is a graduate of the Clearfield County Normal school Oral J, who is teaching the home district school in Knox township has been engaged for five terms. Mr. Sloppy's second son, George, assists him in his meat business. The family belongs to the Methodist Episcopal church at New Millport, of which Mr. Sloppy is a trustee and for three years has been superintendent of the Sunday-school The family is prominent in the pleasant social life of the place.

GEORGE W SMITH, who carries on general farming in Westover borough, was born in Bell township September 12, 1856, and is a son of Charles E and Rebecca (Barnhart) Smith

Charles E Smith was born in Union county, Pa, and died in 1896, aged seventy-six years In his childhood he was brought to Banner Ridge, Chest township, by his parents, who were John and Emma (Snyder) Smith, the latter being a daughter of Jacob Snyder, one of the early settlers in Burnside township The grandfather of

Charles E Smith was one of the earliest settlers in the county and both he and wife were of sturdy, vigorous stock, enduring many hardships in early life but living into extreme old age, the former dying at the age of 108 years, and the latter at that of 112 Charles E Smith was reared near Bethlehem and after his marriage he followed lumbering as his main business He was forty-six years old when he moved to Mercer county, Pa, and nine years later removed to New Washington, where he resided for fifteen years He cast his political vote with the Democratic party but never was willing to accept office He married Rebecca Barnhart, who died in 1886, aged sixty-eight years Their children were as follows Anna, who is the wife of O Kitchen, of Kansas, Kate, who is Mrs Pendergast, living in New York City, John who is in the lumber business in West Virginia, William Smith, who lives in Maryland, is a farmer, Charles, who is deceased, Nancy, who is the wife of D Fettrolf, of Warren county, Louis, who lives in Maryland, Samuel, who resides in York county, Daniel, who is deceased, and George W

George W Smith obtained his education in the public schools and afterward operated the home farm for his father before purchasing the Riddle farm, which he subsequently sold and moved to Westover, still being interested in farming and lumbering, From the age of sixteen to twenty years he was engaged with his brother in digging artesian wells at Baltimore, Md

Mr Smith married Miss Savilla E Roland, who was born January 1, 1861, a daughter of William and Nancy (Brochler) Roland, of Indiana county, Pa, and a granddaughter of Daniel Roland, and they have had three children Orpha, who died at the age of twelve years, and Dora and Melvin, both of whom are at home Mrs Smith is a member of the United Brethren church Mr Smith has been quite active politically and has served in the borough council at Westover and on the school board and has been a delegate on several occasions to conventions of the Republican party He is one of the representative men of Chest township

S C READ, one of Lawrence township's prominent and useful citizens, residing on his farm of eighty acres, was born in Lawrence township, Clearfield county, Pa, June 16, 1858, and is a son of Amos Alexander Read

S C Read grew to manhood on the home place and attended the Goshen Township schools until he was about eighteen years of age, since when he has been engaged in agricultural pursuits He owns eighty acres and has fifty-six of these under cultivation, having systematically cleared his land, not more than four acres at one time In 1878 he cleared the first two acres and two more in 1879 After the great storm of 1880 through this section, much valuable timber was blown down and no more clearing was done in consequence until 1884, when two additional acres were cleared, Mr Read doing all the work thus far under his father's superintendence In March, 1885, he built a part of the present comfortable farm house and in July of this year was married and in the same year he cleared two more acres of his land In 1886 he made further progress in building his house which he completed in 1894, in the former year also erecting his large barn and laying a drain that car-

ries off all waste water The drinking water
is secured from a fine spring on the place Although Mr Read has done almost all the work
on his farm by himself he has his possessions
in fine condition, his fields well fertilized and
cultivated, his orchards healthy and productive
and his stock in the condition that pleases
a careful breeder He carries on general
farming, according to modern methods, for
he is an intelligent and progressive agriculturist, a leading member and an official
of the Clearfield County Grange and for
eight years has been treasurer of the Clearfield County Agricultural Society Among
the interesting exhibits of the office of the
agricultural society is the old fair record
book which was started by James Wrigley
when the first county fair was held, in 1860
Mr Read still uses the same, all transactions of the society since then having been
entered in this volume In politics, Mr
Read is a Democrat and he has frequently
been the choice of his party for office
From 1905 until 1908 he was township assessor and during that time registered more
school children than had any other official
For three years he was also precinct assessor and for one year was committeeman

In July, 1885, Mr Read was married to
Miss Elizabeth Ardrey, a daughter of
James and Hannah (Poorman) Ardrey,
of Center County, Pa, and they have the
following children Leda H, who is a
stenographer with a business firm at Philipsburg, Aaron Shira, who lives in the east
end of Lawrence Township, Thompson
Graham, who lives at Readville, and Mrs
Laura M Sankey, who lives near Goshen
Church Mr Read is a member and is also

secretary of the board of trustees of Goshen
Methodist Episcopal Church. He belongs
to Golden Eagle Lodge No 318 at Clearfield

HENRY BUCHER SWOOPE, who is extensively engaged in the coal business at Madera, Clearfield county, Pa, was born at Curwensville, this county, in 1881, a son of Roland D and Cora (Arnold) Swoope
He is a grandson of the late Hon Henry
Bucher Swoope, who was widely known in
his life time as a lawyer, a brilliant orator,
and the founder and first editor of the
"Raftsman's Journal," of Clearfield Pa, and
of the "Pittsburg Evening Telegraph," and
who at the time of his death in 1874 was
United States Attorney for the Western district of Pennsylvania The father of our subject is a well known lawyer of Curwensville
Henry Bucher Swoope of the present notice
was given a good English education and after
completing his studies entered into industrial
life with a determination to succeed He
soon turned his attention to the coal business
with which he is now connected as manager of
the Corona Coal and Coke Company and also
of the H B Swoope Company—both flourishing concerns He was also connected with
the organization of the Madera Trading
Company in 1903, and with that of the Madera National Bank, of which he is vice-president and the Madera Water Co, of which he
is treasurer In these different enterprises
Mr Swoope has shown good business ability
and is recognized as one of the active and prosperous citizens of the community As he is
still a young man, doubtless the future holds
much in store for him He is a brother of

HENRY B. SWOOPE

Roland D Swoope, Jr, editor of the present volume Mr Swoope was married in January, 1905, to Miss Maude H Moore

WILLIAM H LYONS, whose finely improved and well cultivated farm of forty acres is situated in Sandy township, Clearfield county, Pa, one mile north of West Liberty, was born in this township, November 25, 1860, and is a son of John and Catherine Ann (Hoover) Lyons, and a grandson of Henry Lyons, who settled in Clearfield when the larger part of the land was covered with forest

John Lyons was born in Clearfield county and he devoted his life to farming and lumbering He married Catherine Ann Hoover, whose father, John Hoover, brought his family to Clearfield from Schuylkill County John Lyons and wife reside on a farm that adjoins that of their son, William H, and they are among the most highly respected residents of Sandy Township Ten children were born to them, as follows Mary, who is the wife of George Heberling, Belle, who is the wife of Herman Shaffer, Sarah Jane, who is the wife of Philip Trapper, Emma, who is the wife of Raymond Rensell, Etta Louella, who is the wife of Clark Leach, Nora, who is the wife of William Walbern, William Henry, James, who is deceased, and John D and Norman

William H Lyons has spent his entire life in the section of country in which he was born and is widely known After his school days were over he worked for some time in the woods at lumbering In 1881 he bought his present farm from Ira A Fuller and has made all the improvements, which include the erection of a handsome eight-room frame residence, which is beautifully located and presents a very attractive appearance from the public highway Mr Lyons is a practical and intelligent farmer and has brought his land up to a high producing capacity He has a steady market for all of his produce, at DuBois, and makes a specialty of raising potatoes

Mr Lyons was married in April, 1885, to Miss Clara Kiel, a daughter of John Kiel, and they have five children, namely Charles, who lives at West Liberty, and married Lela Dunlap, Mabel, who married Thomas London (and they live in Jefferson County and have two children—Alfred and Evelyn), Floyd, who lives at DuBois, (married Bertha Kessler and they have one son, Edwin), and Blanche and Sylvester, both of whom live at home Mr Lyons' children have had excellent educational opportunities at DuBois He is a valued member of the Grange

J D BAILEY, who carries on general farming and dairying on a highly improved farm of 132 acres in Lawrence Township, is one of the substantial farmers and representative citizens of Clearfield County He was born July 6, 1860, on the home farm in Pike Township Clearfield County, Pa, and is a son of Joseph and Sarah Elizabeth (Boal) Bailey, and a grandson of Daniel Bailey, who was one of the pioneers of Clearfield County

Daniel Bailey located on a farm in Pike Township after his marriage and died there at the advanced age of eighty years He married Jennie Passmore who died aged eighty-one years, and they reared the following children. Isaac, Abraham, Calvin, Harrison, Levi, Newton, Lewis, Ruth, Ann, Joseph, and George All of the children with the exception of Abraham, Joseph and George, moved west to Iowa, and all are now deceased Daniel Bailey and wife were members of the M E church and were buried at the Center Church Cemetery

Joseph Bailey was born on the home farm in Pike Township, and after his marriage engaged in lumbering and agricultural pursuits He was politically a Republican and served as road supervisor He was an attendant of the M E church At one time he was the owner of 700 acres of land, leaving 250 acres to his heirs, the remaining amount having been sold for a stone quarry, which had not been developed at the time of his death Joseph Bailey married Sarah Elizabeth Boal, and to them were born three sons and three daughters Alice, is the wife of V U Spence of Curwensville, Pa , Boyd, died aged two years, Martha Jane, is the wife of John Ogden, J D , Annie G , is married and resides in the State of Washington; Charles C , resides on the old Bailey farm in Pike Township Joseph Bailey died aged seventy-nine years and his wife died at the age of forty-three years, both being buried at the Center Church Cemetery

J D Bailey was educated in the local schools of Pike Township and at Curwensville, where he attended one term He subsequently remained on the home farm until about two years after his marriage, taking possession of his present farm in 1889 He bought the land from the Welch heirs, remodeled the barn and built all the other buildings on the place, and has one of the best improved and modern farms in the county The house and barn are both equipped with running cold water and electric lights, and there is a fine spring and reservoir on the land Mr Bailey at one time kept a large number of thoroughbred Jersey cows, but now has from twenty-eight to thirty-five head of milch cows and retails about 300 quarts of milk daily at Clearfield, delivering from house to house and to the hotels of the city Mr Bailey also carries on farming extensively in connection with dairying, and is one of the most enterprising and substantial farmers of the county. Mr Bailey is a member of the Grange, of which he is also steward, and was also a member of the executive committee at the time the hall was built He is also identified with the fire insurance company connected with the Pomona Grange, the officers of which are as follows Peter Gearhart, president, E C Davis, vice president, Edward Harmon, secretary, J D Bailey, treasurer, and the twenty-seven directors of the company all reside in Clearfield County Mr Bailey is also a director of the Farmers & Traders Bank, and is a stockholder of the Curwensville Bank Mrs Bailey has an interest in the Fire Clay Company, which is located near Curwensville

Mr Bailey was joined in marriage with Mary E Neaper, of Pike Township, and they have three children Paul, who married Catherine Kelley, resides in Lawrence township, Clarke, and Chester The religious connection of the family is with the M E Center Church, of which Mr Bailey is a trustee

ROBERT H McGARVEY, one of the representative citizens of Chest Township, a general farmer operating 180 acres, was born on this place, the old Anthony McGarvey homestead, June 10, 1855, and is a son of Anthony McGarvey

After he had finished attending school, Mr McGarvey engaged in farming for his father until 1881 and then went to Utahville, where he was in a lumber business for eighteen months He moved from there to Jordan Township, where he followed farming for one and one-half years and in 1884 moved to Ansonville In 1885 he moved to Gazzam, Pa, where he conducted a mercantile business and was postmaster for three years, when he returned to the homestead and conducted operations here until 1893, when he moved to Cambria County, where he resumed merchandising and also was again appointed postmaster In 1894 he was elected a justice of the peace for that borough and served for five years In 1900 he again came back to the farm and has done a large amount of clearing here, cutting timber for the saw mill He has been an active business man for so many years and at different points that he is widely known

Mr McGarvey was married first, in May, 1879, to Miss Emma McQuown, who died February 2, 1888, at the age of thirty-one years, eleven months and three days He was married second, June 25, 1890, to Miss Anna Martha Fowler, a daughter of Robert and Eliza (Fleming) Fowler, and a granddaughter of James and Sarah Fowler and William Fleming and wife, all natives of Ireland in the older generation The parents of Mrs McGarvey settled in Chest Township in 1849, where the father followed farming during all his active years, his death occurring in 1899, at the age of seventy-one years The mother of Mrs McGarvey lives at Ansonville The Fowler family consisted of the following children Sarah, who is the wife of J W Straw, of Jordan Township, Richard James, who is deceased, John Fowler, who lives in Cambria County, married Eva McCully, Emma, who died in infancy, William, who is in the lumber business in West Virginia, and Mrs McGarvey, who is the third in order of birth

To Mr and Mrs McGarvey nine children have been born, namely Minta Ellen, born September 24, 1891, Olin A, born December 6, 1892, Lois Edna, born May 9, 1894, Genevieve Marie, born November 24, 1895, Alvin Delmont, born November 29, 1897, Hazel Eliza, born March 9, 1900, Joel Wilson, born April 22, 1903, Olive Delrose, born November 13, 1904, and Delma Belle, born December 8, 1907 Mrs. McGarvey is a member of the Methodist Protestant church Mr McGarvey has been identified with the Masonic fraternity since 1897, attending lodge at Ebensburg, Pa In politics a Republican, he has frequently been the choice of his party for office

JOHN W YOUNG, who satisfactorily combines general farming and coal operating on a tract of seventy-one acres of exceedingly valuable land, which he owns in Ferguson Township, Clearfield County, Pa, has given his property the pleasant name of Clover Root farm and as such it is known all over the county He was born in Center County, Pa , March 24, 1848, and is a son of Albert and Mary (Wagoner) Young

Albert Young came to Clearfield County with his wife and six of their children, two having previously died in Center County Three of the family survive, namely John W , Mrs Mary Kester, and Mrs Sophia McMurray, all of whom live in Clearfield County Albert Young bought fifty acres of land in Ferguson Township, the same now being owned by his son, which was entirely unimproved He cleared the land and cultivated it according to the old and systematic methods of the Dutch, among whom he had learned farming The land responded to his care and it is now considered some of the most productive soil in the township, Mr Young producing 100 bushels of corn to the acre and other crops with corresponding yields

John W Young attended the country schools in boyhood but as soon as he was old enough to profitably handle a farm implement, there was work for him to do He carries on general farming, occasionally doing a little trucking and giving some attention to raising stock For the past twelve years he has been operating a coal bank which is on the old homestead farm, and has the third opening on the 32-inch vein of coal, taking out some ten thousand bushels of coal annually Mr Young and his son do the most of the mining themselves and also do the delivering They own some fifty acres of this rich coal land Twenty acres of the farm is covered with second growth timber

Mr Young married Miss Mary McCracken, a daughter of Green McCracken, who, with his wife Elizabeth, were old residents of Ferguson Township Mr and Mrs Young have been the parents of thirteen children Elizabeth, Lydia, George, Minta, Albert, Mollie, Sadie, William, Erla, Dove, Leslie, Ruth and Imo Elizabeth was married to Charles Strong, had one child, is now deceased Lydia married Walter Maurer; they have three children George is married to Bertha Witherite, they have seven children Minta married John Lang, have seven children Albert married Alice Williams, have four children Mollie married Clark Witherite, they have four children Sadie married Clark Woods and they have five children William married Lucy Williams, and they have two children Dove has been recently married to Warren Currey Erla, Leslie, Ruth and Imo still reside at home Mr Young and family attend the Baptist church at Kerrmoor, of which they are members In politics he is a Democrat

THOMAS E KEEN, who has earned his present life of ease and now lives in comfortable retirement on his valuable farm of ninety-nine acres, which is situated in Sandy Township, about two miles southwest of DuBois, is an honored veteran of the great Civil War and a member of the Grand Army Post at DuBois, Pa He was born September 11, 1833, at a small lumbering village, known as Union Mills, in the State of Maine, and was the eldest of a large family born to Alby and Nancy (Esterbrooks) Keen, natives of Maine The father was a millwright and lumberman

When Thomas E Keen was fifteen years of age he shipped as cabin boy on a sailing vessel and during his several years on the water, crossed the Atlantic Ocean several times He was still a young man when he came to Pennsylvania and at first was employed at Harrisburg and came from there to Williamsport, where he found summer work in a saw mill and winter employment in the woods Later he spent some time at lumbering but before the outbreak of the Civil War, had returned to Williamsport He was one of the first of the patriotic young men of that place to enlist, on April 23, 1861, becoming a member of Co D, 11th Pa Vol Inf, contracting for three months, and this regiment was the first one sent to the front At the expiration of his first term he reenlisted, entering Co A, 177th Pa Vol Inf, for nine months and during this time he was promoted to be second sergeant and served as such throughout this enlistment The end of the war seeming then to be far away, he enlisted for a third time, entering Co B, 7th Pa Vol Cav, in which he continued until the close of the Rebellion Although he was ever at the post of duty and took part in many battles and long and dangerous marches, he was never wounded, his nearest approach being when his canteen was shot from his side He was captured but once, on August 23, 1865, but was discharged three weeks later according to general orders from the War Department

At the close of his honorable military service, Mr Keen returned to Williamsport and resumed work in the lumber camp He secured employment at the Starkweather & Munson Lath Mill, and later at DuBois in the DuBois Mill, where he had charge of the lath and picket mills Du-

Bois was then a very small place, being given over entirely to lumbermen but they proved to be such a solid and reliable class of men that in a very short time every industry and line of business was represented, schools and churches were built and the village developed the population of a town and soon grew to the importance of a borough Mr Keen has watched all this growth with much interest and can tell of it all in a very entertaining way In 1875 he moved to his present farm, which he had bought from John DuBois, for $20 per acre, being able to pay for the same by selling the timber off the place At first he contentedly lived in a log shanty, which, with a log barn, were the only improvements on the place, but later he built his present comfortable farm-house and substantial barn, both being of modern style of construction He engaged in cultivating his land until recent years, when he shifted his heavier responsibilities to the shoulders of his son, William E Keen

On March 14, 1866, Mr Keen was married to Miss Susan J Pass, who is a daughter of Charles Lloyd and Mary (Kulp) Pass Her grandfather was a soldier in the Revolutionary War and was a member of the Pass family of ironworkers, at Philadelphia, that recast the Liberty Bell Seven children have been born to Mr and Mrs Keen and they also have a goodly number of grandchildren and have also lived to see their name perpetuated into the third generation The family record is as follows Elizabeth May, who is the wife of Frank Carbaugh, residing in Sandy Township, and they have ten children and are grandparents, Alba, who married Della Dickson, lives at DuBois, and they have five children, Charles I, who was accidentally drowned when eight years of age, William E, who married Lottie Skinner, operates the home farm and they have eight children, Winnifred, who resides in Sandy Township, married Grace Spafford and they have two children, Amanda G, who is the wife of Charles F Liddle, of Sandy Township, and they have four children, and Rewel W, who resides at DuBois, married Sadie Thompson, and they have two children Mr and Mrs Keen are well known and at their hospitable home entertain many guests In earlier years Mr Keen was an active member of the order of Knights of Pythias He is a Republican in politics and keeps well posted as to party affairs and prospects as well as to all that is taking place in this great country which his soldierly valor helped to preserve intact

MISS MARGARET HOYT, who is a representative of one of the best known and most substantial families of Clearfield County, Pa, continues to reside on the old Hoyt farm of 400 acres, situated in Greenwood Township, in which she owns a one-third interest Miss Hoyt was born at Curwensville, Pa, December 10, 1836, and is a daughter of Dr and Mary (McClure) Hoyt

Dr Hoyt came of Connecticut stock, of the same family that, as history tells us, ninety days before the signing of the Declaration of Independence, July 4, 1776, had prepared a similar declaration and had issued it This fact indicates that the Hoyts were men of enterprise, patriotism, and courage and the same traits have been manifested in the later generations

The father of Miss Hoyt was born September 12, 1793, at Hudson, N Y, a son of Phineas and Julia Anna (Pennoyer) Hoyt He was afforded excellent educational advantages and appears to have spent his boyhood and youth in study, at one time being a pupil at Dartmouth College He studied medicine with Dr Woodward and Dr White, in Otsego County and received his medical degree in 1818, locating for practice in Half Moon Township, Center County, Pa Shortly afterward he moved to Pike Township, Clearfield County, making the trip on horseback, and carrying his possessions with his medicines in his saddlebags, which have been preserved by his daughter, Miss Hoyt He engaged in medical practice and later engaged also in merchandising at Curwensville In 1842 he moved to Greenwood Township, near Lumber City and Kerrmoor, where he built a mill in 1843, which he later deeded to his son, David Hoyt He acquired about 1000 acres of fine timber land in Clearfield County He lived into honored old age, his death occurring in February, 1885 He was widely known and was universally respected

Dr Hoyt was married in January, 1820, to Miss Mary McClure, a daughter of Thomas McClure, of Pike Township, Clearfield County They lived in Pike Township, near McClure's Cemetery, until after the birth of four children, and then moved to Curwensville, where the six younger children were born The family record is as follows Hiram, who was born in 1821, died in 1824, Julianna, who was born in 1823, died in 1824, Harriet, who was born April 9, 1825, died in February, 1906, David Wilson, who was born April 13, 1828, died in

1889, Elizabeth M, who was born May 29, 1830, is the widow of Martin Watts, to whom she was married January 18, 1854, Mary E, who was born November 2, 1832, married Martin Stirk, and died December 4, 1863, Margaret, who was born December 10, 1836, Christianna, who was born September 21, 1840, died August 21, 1843, and two sons, died in infancy The mother of the above family died in September, 1886 Both she and husband were members of the Methodist Episcopal church For many years their hospitable home was the center of a great deal of the pleasant social life of the time in this section

Miss Margaret Hoyt was the seventh born in her parents' family She remembers attending school in one of the early buildings standing on Filbert Street, Curwensville, where Mr Ross was the teacher, and also a subscription school taught by Miss Goodfellow After her parents moved to the present farm in 1842, she had school opportunities in Ferguson Township and recalls William T Thorp, Sr, as a favorite teacher Her father's house always being one of lavish hospitality, distinguished guests were often entertained and around the generous board or at the fireside she heard all the important questions of the day discussed Miss Hoyt still retains much interest in what is going on in the world and is a very capable business woman In addition to the land interest already mentioned, she is a stockholder in several banks

MRS LAVINA TELFORD, a well known and highly esteemed resident of Westover, Chest Township, was born No-vember 9, 1850, in Indiana County, Pa, and is a member of one of the old and substantial families of that county She is a daughter of John and Sarah (DeArmy) Telford, and the widow of John W Telford, who was one of the most respected citizens of Westover

John Stake, father of Mrs Telford, was born in 1812, in Franklin County, Pa, and in early life accompanied his parents, Frederick and Elizabeth (Read) Stake, to Indiana County John Stake was a farmer and during his entire life from the age of twelve years, he lived in Indiana County He was a member of the Evangelical church He married Sarah De Army, who was born in 1813, in Indiana County, and was a daughter of William and Betsey (Bowers) De Army, early residents of Brush Valley The mother of Mrs Telford died July 16, 1895, the father having passed away March 20, 1886 They had eight children, three of whom survive Lavina, Elizabeth, who is the widow of James Moos, of Groveton, Pa, and Jeremiah, who is a farmer near Cherry Hill The maternal grandfather of Mrs Telford was a transporting agent in the early days before railroads had been built in Indiana County and carried both individuals and merchandise from both east and west

Lavina Stake grew up under the careful and judicious training of a wise and tender mother and from the age of nine years until her marriage, was the mother's main assistant in the duties of the household In 1873 she was married to John W Telford, who was born in Indiana County, Pa, May 3, 1841, and died in 1884 His parents were Alexander and Elizabeth (Wareham) Telford, of Black Lick, Pa One sister and one brother of Mr Telford survive Mary, who is the wife of Joseph Westover, residing at Mahaffey, and James, living in Indiana County

John W Telford was a veteran of the Civil War, in which he served with efficiency and was honorably discharged His burial was the first soldier's interment in the Westover Cemetery He was a successful business man and was engaged both in farming and stock dealing A part of Westover bears the name of Telford, in his honor He was never interested to any great degree in politics, but he was a consistent member of the Baptist church and a liberal supporter of the same Mrs Telford has passed almost all of her married life at Westover and has a wide circle of friends here She is interested in church and social affairs and to some degree is a business woman, very capably taking care of her own interests

ELI L PASSMORE, who has been the owner of the farm on which he was born, September 12, 1849, ever since he was sixteen years of age, is one of the substantial, reliable and representative men of Greenwood Township, Clearfield County, Pa His parents were Joseph A and Caroline (Hoover) Passmore

Joseph A Passmore was born in Bailey Settlement, in Pike Township, Clearfield County, where he had but limited school opportunities After his marriage he lived in Bell, now Greenwood Township, where he was the third settler to begin the clearing of land He lived here until after the birth of all of his children, but died in Mc-

Kean County, November 17, 1908 In politics he was a Democrat He married Caroline Hoover, who was born in Brady Township, Clearfield County, February 27, 1827, a daughter of Peter and Mary Hoover. She died October 5, 1901 They both were members of the Methodist Episcopal church at Lumber City They were united in marriage in 1848 and were permitted to spend sixty years together. Seven children were born to them, namely. Eli L , Allen, who was born June 13, 1851, and died May 1, 1855, Warren, who was born April 2, 1853, is a resident of McKean County; Peter, who was born November 11, 1856, died August 24, 1857, Mary Theresa, who was born June 27, 1858, died August 3, 1907, and was the wife of John Derrick; Frampton B , who was born November 5, 1860, died July 6, 1907, and Lewis H , born July 29, 1863, who died June 23, 1864

In Mr Passmore's boyhood the nearest schoolhouse was a log structure, which he attended irregularly for two years and there laid the foundation of his education In 1859 he had additional advantages in the Bell township school but his assistance was soon required on the home farm and books had to be put aside When he was not more than ten years old he had to walk back and forth to Curwensville to carry merchandise and frequently in those days did not reach home with the heavy load on his back, until after night He was not much more than ten years old when he began lumbering on the river and continued increasing his operations and usefulness as he grew older, until the industry was no longer profitable as a business When sixteen years of age he came into possession of the homestead,

107 acres lying along the west branch of the Susquehannah River, one-half of which is still in valuable timber He has always been a man of industry and even yet, when he can have plenty of assistance, declines to become a mere figurehead, still carrying on his farm work with vigor and according to his own methods All the comfortable buildings on the place he has put here, supplanting the earlier ones erected by his father

Mr Passmore was married January 23, 1870, to Miss Carrie Hall, who was born at Center Corner, Lawrence Township, Clearfield County, February 26, 1843, a daughter of John and Nancy (Passmore) Hall, and a granddaughter of Abraham Passmore Mrs Passmore was educated in the old brick academy at Curwensville and the old academy at Slearfield, and was a successful teacher in the schools for four terms, teaching one term in each of the townships of Bradford, Knox, Huston and Bell To Mr and Mrs Passmore nine children have been born, as follows Charles A, who married Gertrude Hyatt, and resides at Kenshaw, Pa, Walter, who lives in McKean County, married Olive Porter, Alice, who died at the age of four years, Maggie, who is deceased, Alta, who is the wife of Roy McClure, of Curwensville, Lulu, who is the wife of Clarence McCracken, Ellis and Ira, twins, the latter of whom married Sadie Bailey, and George Mr Passmore and family are members of the Baptist church

GEORGE B WACHOB, one of the leading men of Brady Township, master of Pomona Grange, and owner of 100 acres of valuable land which is situated one mile north of Luthersburg, is one of the most successful and enterprising farmers, stock men and dairymen in this section He was born March 22, 1859, in Armstrong County, Pa, and is a son of James C and Mary Ann (Gorley) (Miller) Wachob

James C Wachob was born at what is known as the Stone House, near Ringgold, Jefferson County, Pa, grew to manhood there and was first married to Mrs Mary Ann (Gorley) Miller. She was a widow and had four children William, James, Lewis and David Miller From Jefferson County James C Wachob moved with his family to Armstrong County and from there to Indiana County, where his wife died, in February, 1869 They had four children George Barnard, John, Thomas and Russell, Thomas being now deceased James C Wachob was married second, to Mary Rider, who still lives on the old farm His death occurred in 1901, when he was aged fifty-nine years To James C Wachob's second marriage, three children were born Maggie, wife of John Shaffer, Sarah, wife of William Shaffer, and James In his early manhood, James C Wachob drove a stage covering the distance between Clarion and Bellefonte, and it sometimes happened that he spent twenty-four hours on the top of his conveyance, during periods of bad weather. Later he purchased a farm in North Mahoning Township, Indiana County, Pa, and devoted the remainder of his life to its cultivation

George B Wachob was quite small when the family moved to Indiana County but he recalls that the journey was made in an old four-horse English box-wagon The loss of his mother was deeply felt and he attended

698 HISTORY OF CLEARFIELD COUNTY

school but a short time afterward, deciding to leave home and make his own way in the world He was only fourteen years of age at that time His first employer was his uncle, John Gorley, who was a farmer in Indiana County, and he paid his nephew wages of $9 25 a month This good uncle also gave him a cow, which was the beginning of his business in livestock After leaving his uncle he worked at farming for three years for the late John T Kirkpatrick, at Barnard, in Armstrong County, afterward following rafting and lumbering at Big Run He then went to Luthersburg and engaged for a time in teaming for the pottery, under Joseph Silers and Mr Kirk In 1890 he returned to Armstrong County, where he followed farming for one year, and then worked three years in a saw mill, for D H Waggle, in Clinton County, Pa Prior to this he had kept hard at work but had not been able to lay much money aside, but during his stay in Clinton County, he was able to save $600, and this was his real start

It was just about this time that Mr Wachob bought two small pigs of full blooded stock, from the well known stockman, L B Silver, of Cleveland, had them shipped to Renova and then brought them to his present place He named one of these William Breckenridge and the other Madeline Pollard, taking names that were then prominently before the public The former proved a prize winning animal at the subsequent fair at Grampian, and later dressed 824 pounds

In 1895 Mr Wachob started into the dairy business and has the oldest milk route in DuBois, and supplies the best class of residents as well as the hotels and most exclusive restaurants He does a very large milk business and has shown much enterprise in other directions One of his lines is the manufacture of a certain brand of sausage, which he puts up in a very attractive style, enclosing the edible in a hygienic wrapper This product cannot be supplied fast enough for its market He has about forty head of fine blooded cattle, beginning his herd with Pauline Paul stock, Holsteins, purchased from the Hayes stock farm of Cleveland, O Later he introduced a full blooded Jersey strain In 1910 he went to New York and there bought cattle from Stephenson & Son and from Stephenson Bros, large and well known cattle dealers Later in the same year, Mr Wachob and his son purchased six head of cattle from the Mudget farm, New York In 1897 Mr Wachob built the first silo in Brady Township, to which he has added and this method of preserving green food the year through has kept his cattle in the very finest condition

Mr Wachob's remarkable success in all of his undertakings might give encouragement to other youths situated as he was Starting out a mere boy he had to make his own way with very little help That he has succeeded proves that he combined industry, honesty, courage and good judgment, all with a prudence that his desire to become a man of independence, made him save his money He did not purchase his 100 acres of land all at once His first tract was bought from Jonathan Shaffer. The old way of cultivating the land had been in sections and the entire farm, under such methods, produced no more than one acre does for Mr Wachob, who makes use of entirely different methods He has brought the land to a very high state of cultivation but it has required intelligent study, a great amount of well directed labor and the expenditure of considerable money at first His buildings are suitable and attractive and he has erected two residences, one of which he occupies with his family He was mainly instrumental in having the Farmers' Institute held at DuBois, in March, 1911, and at this time, he and his estimable wife entertained the visiting farmers for two entire days on their farm where the guests were glad to have a chance to view Mr Wachob's admirable plans and his growing crops and valuable herds Without doubt a favorable impression was made and farmers returned to their respective homes with an entirely new set of agricultural ideas For years Mr Wachob has been actively interested in the Grange and, as indicated above, he is serving as the present master of Pomona Grange at Luthersburg

On Christmas Day, 1882, Mr Wachob was married to Miss Laura Shaffer, who is a daughter of Jonathan Shaffer, one of the early settlers in Brady Township Mr and Mrs Wachob have one son, Thomas B, who is associated with his father in the stock business Thomas B Wachob married Miss Hazel Doubles, a daughter of the late Con Doubles, and they have a son, Lynn Ferman, who was born October 17, 1910 Mr Wachob, wife and son are members of the Methodist Episcopal church, in which he is a steward and a trustee He is a charter member of the order of Knights of Pythias, at Salem, Brady Township, where he attends the lodge He is one of

the few Republicans living in Brady Township and recalls many exciting but friendly contested township elections He has never served in any office except as a member of the school board, in which he took a deep interest for some six years

MRS ELIZA C BELL, who was born in Jordan Township, Clearfield County, Pa , February 27, 1842, resides on her valuable farm of ninety acres, which is situated in Greenwood Township She is a daughter of David and Mary (Glenn) Williams, and the widow of the late John W Bell

David and Mary Williams, parents of Mrs Bell, were born and reared in Center County and after their marriage lived there until after the birth of three children They then moved to Jordan Township, near Ansonville, Clearfield County, where David Williams acquired a farm of more than 200 acres His death occurred there when he was but forty-two years of age His widow survived to be eighty years old Their burial was in the old Zion Cemetery in Jordan Township They were consistent members of the Baptist church and were good and worthy people in every relation of life They had six children, namely Martha, Austin C , James G , William G , Eliza C , and John

Eliza C Williams attended the country school and grew to womanhood under the care of a loving and judicious mother She was married in 1868, to William Thompson, who was born in Jordan Township, in 1842, a son of John Thompson, and died September 31, 1872, at the age of thirty years After marriage, Mr and Mrs Thompson lived in Greenwood Township, where he was engaged as a timber marker During the Civil War he served as a soldier in Co M, in a cavalry regiment and for three years was exposed to all the dangers of a soldier's life, but was never either wounded or captured He was a man of excellent standing in his community, an active member of the Republican party and belonged to the local Masonic lodge Two children were born to Mr and Mrs Thompson Martha M and William Harry The former is the wife of the famous missionary, Dr Corson, of Bridgeton, N J, with whom she spent six years in mission work in India. They have one child, Ethera Glenn William Harry Thompson lives with his family at LaJose, Pa He married Emma Stevenson, a daughter of James Stevenson, and they have two children, Helen Elizabeth and Glenn Elton

After the death of her husband, Mrs Thompson returned to her old home in Jordan Township, where she was married a second time, December 28, 1876, to John W Bell To this marriage was born, February, 1878, one child, Ai T, who resides at home John W Bell was born in Greenwood Township, Clearfield County, Pa, July 12, 1838, a son of Arthur and Katherine (Hazlett) Bell He was well educated, having attended the Normal School at Indiana, Pa He became a man of wealth, making a fortune in lumber and acquired 700 acres of land in Greenwood Township He cleared 150 acres of this land and sold much of the timber He was a member of the Baptist church and one of its most liberal supporters In everything pertaining to the advancement and development of Greenwood Township he was progressive

and public spirited. In his early manhood he was a Republican in his political views but later became a supporter of the Prohibitionist party He was a charter member of Greenwood Grange and belonged to both the Masons and Odd Fellows. When his death occurred, February 7, 1904, Greenwood Township lost one of its most worthy men

John W Bell was married first in 1862, to Elizabeth Cook, a daughter of Alexander Cook, and they had five children, namely Ida, who is now deceased; Cora E, who is the wife of Frank Cooper, and lives at Cherry Tree, Pa, Alice C, who is deceased, Arthur A, who is a farmer in Greenwood Township, and Saner C, who resides in New York

Mrs Bell is widely known and is very highly esteemed She is a very active member of the Baptist church at Bells Landing and a liberal contributor to its many benevolent enterprises She is one of the stockholders in the Mahaffey National Bank at Mahaffey, Pa

WILLIAM HELSEL, a highly respected retired citizen of Chest Township, where he engaged in a milling business for a number of years, is also an honored veteran of the great Civil War He was born December 25, 1837, in Cambria County, Pa, and is a son of George and Catherine (Suse) Helsel

George Helsel was born in Cambria County, Pa, and died there in 1867, having reached the great age of ninety-five years. He followed milling and never left the vicinity of his birthplace He married Catherine Suse, who was the daughter of John

J. C. STRICKLAND

Suse and her grandfather and Tobias Helsel, father of her husband, were also natives of Cambria County, among the oldest families The mother of William Helsel died in 1843 He has one surviving sister, Rachel, who is the wife of J King, residing in Bedford County, Pa

William Helsel had but meager educational opportunities when he was a boy and when his school days were over he engaged in farming and learned the milling trade After his mother died he worked away from home until his marriage In October, 1886, he took charge of the old Porter mill, at Center, Pa, which he operated for three years, then conducted a mill at Coalport for one year, then was engaged in milling for four years at Janesville, Pa, and then returned to Cambria County, where he operated the Walters mill for some seven years following which he came to the Hurd grist mill in Chest Township, which he conducted until 1896, since when he has been retired from active work

Mr Helsel has a fine military record On August 6, 1861, he enlisted for service in the Civil War, entering Co A, 54th Pa Vol Inf, under Col J M Campbell, in the Army of the Potomac and served three years and ten months, reenlisting May 15, 1864 He was a brave, cheerful and efficient soldier and was promoted to be corporal of his company, in 1863 He had many narrow escapes from death and capture and was injured quite seriously at one time, from a gunshot wound

In 1858 Mr Helsel was married to Miss Susan C Phenicie, who was born January 31, 1832, in Westmoreland County, Pa, a daughter of Stephen and Susan (Losher)

Phenicie, natives of Germany To Mr and Mrs Helsel the following children were born Stephen, who married Lida Yarlet, and they have five children, Emma J, who is the wife of Arthur Taylor, residing at Middlefield, O, and they have two children, Frances, who is the wife of N Randall, of Providence, R I, Benjamin, who married Emma Wagner, resides near Pittsburg, and they have four children, William, who married Mary Young, and they have three children, and Elizabeth, who is the wife of George M Keck Mr and Mrs Helsel have four great-grandchildren. They are members of the Methodist Episcopal church at New Washington, Pa He casts his vote with the Republican party but has never accepted any public office.

J C STRICKLAND, proprietor of the Park Hotel, a first class hostelry situated at Grass Flat, Pa, has been a resident of Clearfield county for forty-nine years of his life and is well and widely known He was born in Dauphin county, Pa, September 28, 1856, and is a son of Jacob and Mary Jane (Ault) Strickland

Jacob Strickland was born in Dauphin county, Pa, March 28, 1823, and died in May, 1897 He was a shoemaker by trade and followed the same in Dauphin county until 1862, when he moved with his family to Clearfield county, settling at Humphrey's steam mill, which was the first steam mill built in the county At that time the country round about was still covered with timber and it was no unusual thing to see from eight to ten deer in one day Jacob Strickland married Mary Jane Ault, who was born in Lancaster county, Pa, and died July 31, 1910, aged eighty-eight years, eight months and seven days To this marriage there were seventeen children born, J. C being the twelfth in order of birth The other survivors are: W H, who conducts a restaurant at Burnside, Pa (was formerly a lumberman), Emma, residing in West Clearfield, who is the widow of Albert C Walters, who was a veteran of the Civil war, George, who conducts a tannery at Curwensville, Pa, and Jacob and Mary, twins The former went to Maryland in 1872-3 and owns about 500 acres of land in Cumberland county Mary is the wife of A F Flegal.

J C Strickland attended school irregularly until he was about fifteen years old and then went to work in the timber and has followed work in the woods continuously until within the past six years In 1881 he commenced to operate a saw-mill for the firm of Plack & Glunt, in Cambria county and was connected with it until 1905, when he moved to Grass Flat, where he went into the restaurant business, in which he was concerned for two years, five months and ten days, to be exact, when, in August, 1907, he took possession of the Park Hotel, which he had purchased This public house was originally built by a Mr Dunlap and was later improved by Mr Sheffer It contains forty rooms and under Mr. Strickland's management enjoys a large amount of prosperity, he, as host, personally looking after the comfort of his guests and providing a fine table

Mr Strickland was married first to Miss Amanda Turner, on July 10, 1881, who died without issue in 1901 She was a daughter of James H Turner, Esq. of Wallaceton Mr Strickland belongs to the order of the Moose at Philipsburg In his political views he is a Republican

JOHN T STRAW, a retired farmer whose life has been spent in Clearfield County, Pa, and whose large ownership of land and prominence in public affairs have made him well known in different sections, still resides on his farm of 200 acres in Ferguson Township He was born in Pike Township, Clearfield County, Pa, October 7, 1833, and is a son of Joseph and Ann (Thompson) Straw

Joseph Straw was also born in Pike Township and was a son of Christian Straw, who had the distinction of serving on the first jury ever summoned in Clearfield County Joseph Straw obtained his education in what was called the McClure Cemetery schoolhouse After his marriage he continued to live for a short time in Pike Township and then moved on a farm of 100 acres, in Ferguson Township, where he remained until the end of his life, dying in 1877, at the age of seventy-one years and six months He was buried by the side of his first wife After the Civil War he was a Republican He had served as road supervisor and as assessor of Ferguson Township To his 100 acres was joined 100 owned by his wife and this land is all retained in the family

Joseph Straw was married first to Ann Thompson, a daughter of Agnatious Thompson, of Lawrence Township, Clearfield County, and they had the following children Margaret, Maria, who died when small, John T, Isaac and Enoch, twins, the former dying at the age of sixteen years; and Amanda, Mary E, Esther A., Harriet and Joseph N, the last named being accidentally killed while hauling logs The mother of the above mentioned children died at the age of forty-nine years and was buried in the Baptist Cemetery in Jordan Township Joseph Straw's second marriage was to Mrs Elizabeth Templeton, a widow, and they had three children, George, Harvey and Alice, all of whom are now deceased

John T Straw attended schools in Lawrence, Ferguson and Jordan Townships and afterward taught school for some time He was satisfied to become a farmer and after looking over the county found no place that suited him better than his present farm, which he subsequently bought He has about 60 acres cleared and thus still retains some valuable woodland Mr Straw also owns 100 acres of fine coal land in Greenwood Township, has a house and lot at Kerrmoor and an improved lot at Marron, Pa, and is a stockholder in the Ferguson and La Jose Telephone Company, of Ferguson Township, and is a charter stockholder in the Farmers and Traders Bank at Clearfield

Mr Straw was married first to Miss Sarah Young, who was born in 1837, in Center County, Pa, a daughter of Albert Young, and died in July, 1866, her burial being in the old Jordan Township Cemetery. She was a consistent member of the Zion Baptist church To this marriage the following children were born· Albert Y, who lives at Clearfield, married Margret Bailey, a daughter of Abraham Bailey, and they have ten children—Maud, Annie, Earl, Grace, Ruth, John, Abraham, Winfred, Samuel and Albert, Harrison, who married Emmeline Reed, lives in Goshen Township, William E, who married first, Katherine Patterson, has one child, Ethel, and married secondly Mrs Ellison, Anna Mary, who married Amos Reed, lives in Lawrence Township and they have had four children —Edna, Cecil, Ellsworth and Eldon, Jeremiah Franklin is deceased

Mr Straw was married secondly to Miss Mary Ellen Barrett, who was born in 1843, in Ferguson Township, a daughter of Luther Barrett, and died in May, 1874 She was a member of the Baptist church and her burial was in Jordan Township To this marriage the following children were born Perry C, lives in Greenwood Township, Charlotte is the wife of Blake Summers, of Jordan Township, and they have had five children—Cora Luella, Quay and Ray (twins), Mary, and George Melvin, Ida is the wife of James Rowles, lives at Glen Richey, and has one son, Carlton Mr Straw's third marriage was on July 12, 1874, to Miss Priscilla Barrett, who was born in Jordan Township, Clearfield County, August 8, 1856, a daughter of Hiram Barrett They have had the following children Rosetta, whose death occurred January 26, 1911, was the wife of James Lang, of Dixonville, Indiana County, Pa, and three children survive her—Arbutus, Robert and James, Cora is the wife of Dr H G Purnell, of Ansonville, and they have three children—Charles T, John T and H Garrett, Susanna died at the age of fifteen months, Blanche E is the wife of J B Gates, residing in Cambria County; Myrtle is the wife of Stewart Williams, residing at Monmouth, Pa, and they have one daughter, Priscilla, Carrie E, who is the wife of Clyde Bolender, has had two children, George and Mary, the latter now deceased, Perie Z, John T, a teacher at

Millport, Pa , Iva Belle, who is at home, Jerusha, who is deceased, and Nora V and Sarah L

Mr Straw's first purchase of land was of 100 acres and later he bought the second 100 acres, on which he lived for three years and then returned to his first farm He has always been an ardent Democrat and has long been influential in party affairs in this section He was elected county commissioner of Clearfield County in 1882 and served until 1885 With his wife and family he belongs to Zion Baptist church He has always been interested in the Patrons of Husbandry For fourteen years he served as school director in Ferguson township Mr Straw has always been a very robust and vigorous man and has easily attended to his numerous business affairs, never being willing to give himself a needed rest, until some two years ago, when an attack of rheumatism caused him to relieve himself of many of his responsibilities, turning them over to his very capable sons

JOHN R SHAFFER, who is an honored veteran of the great Civil war, resides on his farm of forty-eight acres, which is situated in Sandy township, about one mile southwest of West Liberty, Pa He was born June 3, 1845, on his father's farm which was then situated in Brady township, Clearfield county, but is now included in Sandy township, and is a son of Michael and Polly (Reishall) Shaffer

Michael Shaffer was born in Dauphin county, Pa , one of a family of four sons, the eldest of whom, John, remained in that county The other three, Michael, George and Fred Shaffer, all came to Clearfield county and Michael and Fred bought adjoining tracts of land, on the present site of the B & S. Shaft No 1, and cleared up their property Michael Shaffer sold his land and moved then to West Liberty where he lived during the remainder of his life He married Polly Reishall, who survived him some years, and they had six children Innes, who is deceased, Elias, Emeline, who died when young, John R , Mary, who is the wife of Augustus Heberling, and Caroline, who is now deceased, was the wife of David Lyon

John R Shaffer learned his first lessons in a log schoolhouse where the rough slab benches were arranged around the room, the teacher, with his hickory stick usually in hand ready for any emergency, standing in the center Mr Shaffer was obliged to walk quite a distance through the woods to reach school and frequently saw deer and other wild creatures in the forest When the Civil war broke out he determined to become a soldier, although he was then but a boy of sixteen years He managed to be accepted and on August 31, 1861, was enrolled in Co D, 105th Pa Vol Inf , as a private, but shortly afterward gained promotion and was made corporal In July, 1863, he was detailed as an orderly on hospital duty first at Philadelphia and later at Washington He took part in the battles of Yorktown, Williamsburg, Fredericksburg, Chancellorsville, Kelley's Ford, the Wilderness and the Siege of Petersburg On May 3, 1863, at the battle of Chancellorsville, he was wounded in the arm and was taken to a hospital at Philadelphia, where he remained a patient for five months, after which he returned to his regiment and on May 5, 1864, was wounded by a spent ball, in the shoulder, which injury caused his remaining in a Washington hospital for four months From an attack of lung fever, produced by exposure, he was kept in a hospital at Camp Jamison for two months, this being in the winter of 1861 In June of the following year he was prostrated with typhoid fever and he spent four months recovering from this in a hospital at Brooklyn, N Y In 1863 he was accorded a furlough of thirty days and on July 11, 1865, he was honorably discharged at Washington, D C

Mr Shaffer returned home and as soon as he had sufficiently recuperated, went to work at various things as occasion offered, having his own way to make, and it was not until the summer of 1879 that he was able to invest in farm land as was his desire He then purchased 116 acres of land from Samuel Arnold, paying $800 for the same, and later sold a part, the Mapledale lots having formerly been a part of his farm He cleared off the larger part of his remaining land and put up all the substantial farm buildings He continued to operate his farm until his son, Harvey Le Roy, was old enough to take the responsibility and Mr Shaffer is now somewhat retired

Mr Shaffer has been twice married, his first marriage taking place when he was twenty-one years of age to Miss Mary J Downey, who died shortly afterward He was married second on May 25, 1879, to Miss Penina J Kness, a daughter of Henry and Elizabeth (Morehead) Kness The father of Mrs Shaffer was a soldier in the Civil war, a volunteer from Armstrong county Both of her parents are now deceased She was the second born in a family of six children, the others being John, who is deceased, Nancy, who is deceased, was the wife of Jefferson Labord, William, Isaac, and Amanda, who is the wife of David Lyons Seven children were born to Mr and Mrs Shaffer, namely Mary, who is the wife of Arthur De Lorm, resides in Jefferson county, Pa, and they have two children—Ruby and Myrtle, Harry, who married Grace Marshall, lives in Sandy township, and they have three children—Alice, and Ruth, an infant, unnamed, Veigie, who is the wife of Stacy Lyons, lives in Jefferson county and they have one child, Cecil, Harvey Le Roy, who resides on the homestead and manages the farm, married Martha Horn and they have two children—Robert and Floyd, Olive, who is the wife of James Pierce and they live in Sandy township and have three children—Alto, Calvin and Russell, Myrtle, who is the wife of Dell Askey, and they reside in Montana and have two children—Alberta and Myrtle, and Cora, who lives at home Mr Shaffer and family attend the Baptist church In politics he is a Republican He is a member of the Grange and belongs to Mingle Lodge, No 753, Odd Fellows, at Troutville, while his son belongs to Lodge, No 417, Knights of Pythias, at Salem The family is one that is held in the highest esteem in this section

DAVID R READ, residing on his farm of 103 acres, which is situated in Ferguson township, Clearfield county, Pa, two and one-half miles northwest of Keirmoor, was born August 7, 1837, in this township but on an adjoining farm His parents were William and Jane (Ferguson) Read

William Read was born, reared and educated in Lawrence township, Clearfield county, moving into Ferguson township at the time of his marriage to Jane Ferguson, and he lived there until his death He owned 150 acres of land which had been cleared by his own industry He survived his wife many years, her death taking place when aged forty-three years, while he lived to be seventy-two years They were members of the United Presbyterian church Their family consisted of seven sons and three daughters

David R Read attended what was known as Friendship school, in Ferguson township, when he was a boy, and afterward went into the woods and worked at timbering After his marriage he moved to what was known as the Hockenberry farm, in Ferguson township, after living for a time in Greenwood township Here he found a great deal of improving necessary and has done considerable building, putting up all the substantial structures now standing, except the barn He has carried on general farming and is numbered with the prosperous agriculturists of the township

Mr Read was married on July 7, 1864, to Miss Clara J Owens, who was affectionately known to family and friends as Sis Owens She was born on an adjoining farm, September 16, 1843, and is a daughter of Thomas and Emeline (Hile) Owens Five children have been born to Mr and Mrs Read, namely Emeline, who is the wife of Harrison Straw, of Goshen township, Lyman, who is deceased, B W, who resides in Oregon, and married Nettie McCarty, J Perry, and an infant who died

J. Perry Read assists his father in operating the home farm and owns a tract of forty-three acres adjoining it which is quite valuable He married Miss Stella Hamilton, who is a daughter of Harvey Hamilton, and they have had five children Burl, Curtis, Winnifred, Emeline and Dorothy, Curtis and Dorothy being now deceased

In politics Mr Read and son are strong adherents of the Prohibition party. He has served as school director and also as overseer of the poor, in Ferguson township With his wife and son he belongs to the Grange at Kerrmoor, and there they also are connected with the United Presbyterian church They are all people of high standing, representative of the community's best citizenship

JOHN N WORK, who is interested in general farming in Bell township for the past eighteen years has been identified with the Pennsylvania Railroad Company and is one of the oldest and most trusted employes living in this section He was born April 25, 1865, on the old Weaver farm in Bell township, and is a son of Joseph S and Rolinda (McMasters) Work

Joseph S Work was born in Indiana county, Pa, a son of John Newton Work, and died in Clearfield county, in September, 1900, at the age of sixty-two years He came to this county when a youth of eighteen years, working at McGee's Mills until his marriage, when he bought the old Weaver farm in that neighborhood, and followed farming and lumbering during the remainder of his life He was never very active in politics but was an intelligent and fair-minded citizen and cast his vote in support of good government He married Rolinda McMasters, who was a daughter of Eben and Rebecca McMasters She was born in Burnside township, Clearfield county, and died in 1872 They were members of the Methodist Episcopal church They were parents of the following children. Beatrice, who is the wife of William Croft, of Tyrone, Rebecca, who is the wife of E Sunderland, of McGee's Mills, John N.; Mary, who is the wife of Andrew Gaylor, of Mahaffey, Pa , Margaret, who is the wife of F Cuenley, of McGee's Mills; Eugene, who lives at home, Josephine, who is the wife of Fred Haigh, of Jefferson county, and Robert A , who resides near Lock Haven, Pa

John N Work attended school until he was about fourteen years of age and then went to work in the woods where he continued until he was twenty-one, this hard labor serving to develop him into a strong and vigorous man He then turned his attention to railroading and since May, 1893, has been connected with the great Pennsylvania system He is well known to both employes and officials and stands very high in the estimation of all as to his reliability and efficiency This has been his main business for many years but, with his brother, he also gives some attention to the home farm

Mr Work was married to Miss Ella Irwin, who was born May 16, 1865, at Muddy Run, Cambria county, Pa , a daughter of Alexander and Katherine Irwin, the former of whom is deceased Mr and Mrs Work have had six children Frederick, who lives on the home farm; Max Orville, who died at the age of nineteen years, Mabel Rolinda and Cecil Monroe, both of whom are pursuing higher courses at school, and Joseph S and Martha Catherine Mr Work casts his vote with the Democratic party but has never desired any public office

DAVID S YOUNG, whose valuable farm of 100 acres is situated in Greenwood township, Clearfield county, Pa , was born in this township, on the south side of the west branch of the Susquehanna river, February 18, 1853

and is a son of Samuel and Sarah (Wall) Young

Samuel Young was born in 1821, when Greenwood was still known as Bell township, Clearfield county He was a man of great energy and followed farming in the summer time and lumbering in the winters and thus acquired a good property He was a quiet, home-loving man and was respected and esteemed by all who knew him His death occurred when he was but thirty-two years of age and his burial was in the Bower cemetery He married Sarah Wall, who was born in Penn township, Clearfield county, a daughter of David and Sarah Wall, and she survived her husband until 1892, having all the responsibility of rearing their only child, David S She was a woman of fine character and a member of the Society of Friends Her burial was at Grampian

David S Young obtained his education in the common schools and grew up on the home farm and remained there for some years following his marriage and then bought his present place Here he has made many improvements including the erection of all the substantial buildings on the place, and carries on general farming and stock raising He is one of the representative men of his township in all that pertains to good citizenship

Mr Young was married January 14, 1875, to Miss Lucinda Brooks, who was born in Greenwood township, March 9, 1852, a daughter of Edward and Margaret (Dale) Brooks, the latter of whom is deceased Mr Brooks resides with Mr and Mrs Young Nine children were born to the above marriage as follows Sarah Gertrude, who was born March 25, 1876, married David Patterson, they live at Bell's Landing and have four children—Joseph, Seymour, Truman and Genevieve Anna Margaret, born August 23, 1877, married Frank Daughenbaugh, they live at Mahaffey, Pa, and have children—Lillian, Esther, Etta, Jefferson, Malcolm, Ronald, Chrissie and two deceased Flora Jane, born December 17, 1878, married Ezra Johnson and they live in Greenwood township and the children born to them were Elva, Melvin, Arlean, Nannie, Larue, Enlow, Woodrow and two now deceased Elvira Mae, who was born September 1, 1880, and Truman W, who was born April 1, 1882, are both unmarried Rebecca Lucretia, born December 27, 1883, resides at home Clara Lovena, who was born October 2, 1885, is the wife of William R Potts, of Clearfield, and they have three children—Winnifred, William and Vaulna Elbridge C, born April 28, 1887, and William Edward, born September 21, 1891, are both unmarried Mr and Mrs Young are members of the Zion Baptist church, of which he is a trustee He is a Republican in his political affiliations but has independent tendencies

HARVEY WALLS, who owns seventy-five acres of fine farm land in Sandy township, situated about one-half mile west of West Liberty, on the Clearfield and Jefferson county line, is known to his fellow citizens as a reliable man worthy in every way of their respect and esteem He was born May 24, 1854, on his father's farm south of Luthersburg, Clearfield county, and is a son of James and Sarah (Moore) Walls, and a grandson of David Walls

David Walls was a veteran of the War of 1812 and was one of the pioneers of Clearfield county, having come from the eastern part of the country, and about 1815 he located near Grampian Later he moved into Brady township, where he remained until his death

James Walls was born in 1810 and was quite small when the family came to Clearfield county where his subsequent life was spent. He bought a farm in Brady township, followed farming there and died in 1890 He married Sarah Moore, who survived him three years They had seven children, namely. Margaret, who died at the age of three years; Andrew, who is now deceased, was a soldier in the famous Bucktail regiment, the 149th Pa Vol Inf, during the Civil war, David, Jerry and Harvey, the first named being deceased, Mary Ann, who is the wife of J F. Heberling, and George, who married Maggie De Larme, lives in Sandy township

Harvey Walls attended the country schools until he was twelve years of age, when he was deemed strong enough to go into the woods and work with the lumbermen and he continued until he was twenty-one years old At that time he gave up lumbering and bought his farm from C H Prescott, and has carried on agricultural activities here ever since He sold the timber from thirty acres of his farm, to his brother, George Walls Buildings were standing on the place when Mr Walls bought it but these he took down in 1908 and in place of the old house has built an elegant eight-room brick residence, which is one of the most substantial dwellings in this part of the county. He has made many improvements on the place and thereby has added considerably to its value He is assisted by his brother, Jerry, and they both occupy the residence

Mr Walls has never taken any very active part in politics but has always been ready and willing to assist in the promotion of movements which his judgment convinces him are for the general welfare He casts his vote with the Democratic party He is a member of Red Fern Lodge, Knights of Pythias

BLAIR STEVENS, who has business interests at different points in Clearfield county, Pa , is postmaster at Kerrmoor and proprietor of a general store here which is conducted under the style of Blair Stevens, merchant He was born near Warrior's Mark, Huntingdon county, Pa , February 3, 1851, and is a son of Capt Henry and Susanna (Beck) Stevens

Capt Henry Stevens, who was captain of Co E, 45th Pa Vol Inf , in the Civil war, had been a veteran of the Mexican war and was widely known Both he and wife died in Half Moon township, Center county, Pa They were parents of eleven children

Blair Stevens was educated in the public schools and at a select school in Center county, which was conducted under the supervision of the Society of Friends Before he engaged to any extent in business in his native state, he traveled through the West and visited Kansas and Texas as well as other sections He then followed farming in Center county for a time and then moved to Clearfield county and located at Bigler, where he became postmaster and conducted a store until he came to Kerrmoor Here he bought the Kerrmoor Supply Company and business was at first carried on under the name of F P Stevens & Bro , later as Watts & Company, when the present proprietor became sole owner and since then has operated under his own name He is interested also in the McCartney Supply Company, at McCartney, Pa Mr Stevens is a stockholder in the Lumber City Telephone Company and the Ferguson Township and La Jose Telephone Company In politics he is a Republican and has served as school director and for ten years was tax collector

On August 24, 1882, Mr Stevens was married to Miss Mary Waite, who was born in Center county, Pa , November 5 1858, and is a daughter of Henry and Anna (Eyer) Waite, and they have two children, Lawrence and Anna Lawrence Stevens is a resident of Wilkinsburg, Pa He married Elsie McCreery, a daughter of Robert McCreery, and they have one daughter, Mary Jane Anna is a trained nurse and is connected with the Allegheny General Hospital in North Pittsburg Mr and Mrs Stevens are members of the Presbyterian church

ASH BENNETT LEE, a general farmer and respected citizen of Bell township, was born September 24, 1866, on the old Lee homestead in Burnside township, and is a son of John and Elizabeth (White) Lee, and a grandson of Isaac and Hannah (Fulton) Lee

Isaac Lee was born in Center county, Pa , and when young accompanied his parents, Jacob Lee and wife, to Clearfield county, where he grew to maturity and followed farming and lumbering He was twice married first to Hannah Fulton, a daughter of David and Mary Fulton, and of this marriage there were ten children, of which family there are but two now living John and Jacob The first wife died in 1845 and Mr Lee was married second to Margaret (Young) Westover, widow of Abner Westover, and they had three sons Isaac, James and Henry Isaac Lee died in 1880, at the age of eighty-six years He was a member of the Methodist Protestant church

John Lee, father of Ash B Lee, was born on the Lee homestead above mentioned, November 5, 1836 He assisted his father to clear off the timber and to cultivate the land when prepared for tillage and remained with his parents until his own marriage His father gave him fifty acres of land on which he built his present residence and later he purchased all of the homestead which included a productive coal field He commenced to mine coal at Lee Hollow, in 1870 and operated it until 1890, when he sold his interests to the company now operating it, and has since confined his activities to the lumber industry He is one of the substantial citizens of Burnside township

John Lee married Elizabeth White, who was born in Huntingdon county, Pa , November 22, 1831, a daughter of William and Catherine (Holman) White The following children were born to them Isaac Newton, who resides in Burnside township, John W , who resides at Bethlehem, Pa , Ash Bennett, William Walton, who lives at home, James Hamilton, who married Emma Lee, Edwin Horsey, who married Anna Stephens, Jesse Hall, who resides at home, Samuel White, who lives at Bethlehem, married Elsie Pennington, and Eva Jane, a twin sister of Samuel W , who is the wife of D Johnson The mother of the above family died in August, 1899

Ash Bennett Lee was given the usual country boy school advantages and made the most of his opportunities Until his marriage he resided with his parents and did his share of work on the home farm, but in 1893 he moved to his present place called Old Bethlehem, near Mahaffey, and since then has been engaged in farming, teaming and coaling His many industrial interests have made him

widely known and he is respected both as a business man and as a citizen

Mr Lee was married in 1893 to Miss Bertha Hutton, a daughter of Edward and Sophia (Breth) Hutton, the former of whom was an early settler in Burnside township Mr. and Mrs Lee have eight children Ada, Clair, Ash, Nora, May, Pearl, Bessie and Wilbur. Mr Lee was reared in the Methodist Protestant church. He is actively interested at all times in the success of the Democratic party

HENRY OWENS, deceased, formerly one of the most highly respected residents of Ferguson township, Clearfield county, Pa , for many years was a successful farmer and owned a well improved farm of 187 acres, situated one and one-half miles south of Lumber City. He was born in Ferguson township, March 15, 1847, and spent his long and useful life here, his death occurring April 26, 1910, his burial was at Lumber City

Henry Owens attended what is known as the Friendship school, in Ferguson township, but in his boyhood few educational advantages were afforded in comparison with those which the children of the present day enjoy He was naturally a man of excellent mind and good judgment and in middle life, when his fellow citizens at different times elected him to township offices, he performed the duties of the same with uprightness and efficiency He grew up on a farm and agriculture was his main occupation He was a kind father and good neighbor and there are many who will remember him as a man of sterling worth to his community In his earlier years he was a Democrat but later became identified with the Prohibition party

Mr Owens was married August 18, 1870,

to Miss Elizabeth Moore, who was born in Ferguson township, February 18, 1846 Her parents were Joseph and Mary Moore She died August 13, 1905, and her burial was at Lumber City Both she and husband were members of the Methodist Episcopal church They had six children born to them, as follows the first and second born, both sons, died in infancy, Norman H, born July 7, 1875, resides at Clyde, in Westmoreland county, Pa, Harry M, Clarke E, born September 28, 1882, and Howard W, who was born December 17, 1884, and died at the age of seven years

Harry M Owens, who has charge of the family estate, with power of attorney, was born on this farm October 14, 1877 He was married September 4, 1900, to Miss Stancia Caldwell, who was born in Ferguson township, October 26, 1881, a daughter of James M and Belle F Caldwell, of Lumber City They have two children, Mary Belle and Margaret Elizabeth

SAMUEL A EISENMAN, who is the pioneer merchant of the east side of DuBois, Pa, a busy section of one of the most prosperous and rapidly developing towns of Clearfield county, has been located at his present place of business, on East DuBois avenue, since 1885 He was born on his father's farm in Clarion county, Pa, April 2, 1849, and is a son of Joseph H and Catherine (Hopper) Eisenman

Joseph H Eisenman was born in Germany and was nine years old when his parents came to America The father entered land in Clarion county, and became a farmer and also a distiller, living between Freyburg and Shippensville, Clarion county Joseph H Eisenman secured a farm near the one his father owned and spent his whole subsequent life in Clarion county For twenty-two summers he burned charcoal for the Madison and Lucinda furnaces His death occurred on February 8, 1877, when he was fifty-seven years of age and his burial was in Clarion county He married Catherine Hopper, who was born in Center county, Pa, and died in 1886 Eight children were born to them, namely John, Hiram, Mary Ann, who is the widow of Benjamin Hurley, and Samuel A, Ambrose, Amos, Joseph and James

Samuel A Eisenman spent his early years on the home farm and during this time attended a district school three miles distant for a part of each winter. He was only a boy when he began to earn money for himself by working by the day for neighboring farmers, after that attending school again for a few months He developed considerable business ability even then and secured his capital for entering into the mercantile line by shrewdly purchasing small tracts of timber, mainly in Elk county In 1876 he embarked in the mercantile business at Elk City, Clarion county, which he continued for one year and then sold out and became an oil and gas producer in Clarion county Strangely enough he did not prosper in this line as he had in former undertakings and after five years of experience he gave up working in the oil fields and started all over again in the lumber and rafting business and continued until 1882, when he came to DuBois For three years afterward he worked for John DuBois, in the latter's saw-mills, and then decided to re-enter the mercantile business, his long experience having taught him much of which he had been ignorant before He bought the land on which his buildings stand and cleared off the timber, erecting first a store building of 20 x 40 feet dimensions, in which he opened a general store and prospered from the first As soon as his trade warranted it he put up his present three-story brick and stone block and occupies a store room 30 x 100 feet with his mercantile goods and resides in one of the comfortable apartments fitted up for family use, on the upper floor Through careful attention and honest dealings he has developed a very large business and is now numbered with the substantial men of the place In addition to his other enterprise, Mr Eisenman conducts a flour and feed business, is interested in real estate on the east side, has oil and gas interests in Clarion county and is a stockholder in the Deposit National Bank of DuBois, Pa

On September 21, 1876, Mr Eisenman was married to Miss Eliza Suffolk, a daughter of the late James Suffolk, of Brookville, Pa , and they have two children Edgar, who is a graduate of the DuBois High School and now a student in the University of Pennsylvania at Philadelphia, and Samuel Alvin, his father's namesake In politics, Mr Eisenman is a Democrat and fraternally he is a Mason, belonging to the Blue Lodge at DuBois, the Chapter at Brookville, the Consistory at Williamsport and Jaffa Temple, Mystic Shrine, at Altoona He is a member and liberal supporter of the Baptist church During his long years of residence here he has given support to every movement designed to promote the general welfare and through example and precept has materially aided in the advancement of the town along the best lines of development

S B WELTY, who, for thirty years has filled the office of justice of the peace, in Union township, Clearfield county, Pa , where he is a citizen of prominence and the owner of 580 acres of valuable land, was born in Brady township, Clearfield county, June 19, 1847 His parents were David and Hannah (Best) Welty

David Welty and wife were both born in Center county and both died in Union township, Clearfield county, the former at the age of seventy-four years and nine months, and the latter when aged seventy-one years and seven months They had the following children William, David, John, Simon B , James, Joseph, Mary Ann, Caroline, Harriet, Elizabeth, Sarah, and an infant daughter that died David Welty was a farmer and lumberman and acquired much property through industry and good management He was one of the liberal supporters of the Lutheran church His political convictions made him a Democrat

With his brothers and sisters Simon B Welty attended the Rockton school in his boyhood and afterward gave his father assistance, the latter having moved into Union township when Simon B was a youth The father owned a saw-mill and for a number of years the sons of the family worked there Mr. Welty's land extends to the borough line of Rockton and farming, stock raising and lumbering are all important activities on the place

Mr Welty was married in 1877, to Miss Mary E Brisbin, a practical school teacher, who was born at Troutville, Brady township, Clearfield county, December 17, 1845, and was educated at Luthersburg and Curwensville She is a daughter of William H and Sarah A (Peoples) Brisbin, who were natives of

HON. CYRUS GORDON

Center county Five children were born to Mr and Mrs Welty, namely Sadie E , Everett S , John B , Lillie I J , and Frank D Two of these, Sadie E and Lillie I J , are now deceased Mr Welty and family are members of the Lutheran church Politically Mr Welty is a Democrat and a very influential member of his party He has served in numerous public offices, has been jury commissioner and foreman of the grand jury in Clearfield county, has been school director and has been elected to almost every other township office, while for thirty years he has not only been a justice of the peace but also township clerk He is a stockholder in the S U B Telephone Company of Union township His membership in Susquehanna Grange has been of long standing and he belongs also to the P O S of A , and the Knights of Pythias

HON CYRUS GORDON, senior member of the prominent law firm of Gordon and Boulton, at Clearfield, Pa , has been an honored resident of this city for forty years He is a leading member of the bar and for a number of years was president judge of Clearfield county He is a representative of one of the old pioneer families of Pennsylvania, of Irish extraction, and was born on the old family homestead at Hecla Park, Center county, Pa , December 1, 1846 His parents were James and May (Steel) Gordon, and his grandfather was Robert Gordon

Robert Gordon was born in county Armagh, Ireland He came to America in 1788 and in the following year located in Center county, Pa , acquiring land in the rich Nittany Valley, where, as a farmer, he passed the remainder of his life He had five children, two of them being born after he reached Center county Before leaving Ireland he was married to Elizabeth Leslie

James Gordon, father of Judge Gordon, was born in Center county December 17, 1799 Farming was his occupation. He is recalled as a man possessing many sterling traits of character and which tended to make him an influential citizen in his section His death took place December 17, 1868 He married a daughter of Robert and Rebecca (Dunlop) Steel, the latter being a daughter of James Dunlop, a colonel in the Revolutionary war Mrs Gordon was born in 1825, at Bellefonte, Pa , and died July 20, 1895 To the above marriage ten children were born One son, Robert, who was a soldier in the Civil war, died in 1863 at a hospital in Murfreesboro, Tenn All others of the family are deceased, except I N Gordon, who is connected with the Standard Oil Company of New York as manager of the West India Oil Company, and Cyrus, subject of this sketch, who has remained a Pennsylvanian, not only by birth, but also by preference and since 1870 has lived at Clearfield

Cyrus Gordon was afforded better educational opportunities than were many young men of his time, and in 1866, after several years of study there was graduated from the Pennsylvania State College, with the degree of Bachelor of Science He was a trustee of the college, as a representative of the alumni for a great many years After his graduation from the Pennsylvania State College he entered the University of Michigan and in 1869 was graduated from the law department of that institution with the degree of LL B He then came to Clearfield and this borough has been his home ever since There has been little important litigation in the courts of the county in which his professional services have not been in some way engaged For the term of nineteen years prior to his election to the bench he was associated with Hon Thomas H Murray in the practice of law under the firm name of Murray and Gordon In 1893 he was elected to the office of president judge of Clearfield county and during his term of service on the bench, his decisions demonstrated his learning, his true conception of law and his unusually judicial cast of mind After his term on the bench had expired he was for many years one of the solicitors of the Dairy and Food Division of the Department of Agriculture of Pennsylvania Aside from his profession Judge Gordon has always been a vitally interested citizen in all that relates to the well being of his community He was reared in the Republican party and has never changed his political allegiance

Judge Gordon was married to Miss Mary R Weaver, who was born at Clearfield and is a member of one of the leading families of this section Four children have been born to them, namely Dr John W, Leslie Dunlop, James T, and Rebecca, the last mentioned being now deceased The eldest son, John W, is a practicing physician at Clearfield Judge and Mrs Gordon are members of the Presbyterian church They reside at the corner of First and Market streets, Clearfield, their home being often the scene of pleasant social functions Judge Gordon owns a fine farm of 200 acres at Hecla Park, Center county, where he was born and reared

BALSAR HULLIHEN, one of the highly respected citizens of Bell township, now living retired at McGee's Mills, is probably one of the oldest millers in the county, having op-

erated a grist mill at this place continuously for thirty-four years He was born at New Lisbon, O, August 19, 1838, and is a son of Anthony and Susan Anna (Linderberry) Hullihen

Anthony Hullihen was born in Pennsylvania and accompanied the family to Ohio but later located at Clearfield, Pa, moved from there to Indiana county and from there to Bell township, Clearfield county, at each location following the blacksmith trade His death occurred in Bell township, at the age of seventy-four years He married Susan Anna Linderberry, who was born in Germany but lived at the time of marriage, in Ohio She died in 1868, aged fifty-four years Three of their children survive, namely Balsar, Mathias, who was a soldier in the Civil war, now lives in Greenwood township, and Conrad, who also is a farmer in that township Grandfather Hullihen was a native of Ireland He was drowned in the Susquehanna river, near Williamsport, Pa

Balsar Hullihen worked during early manhood at lumbering, and also learned the milling business In 1864 he enlisted for service in the Civil war, entering Co. F, 58th Pa Vol Inf, 3rd Brig, 3rd Div, 24th Army Corps, under the command of Gen Benjamin F. Butler. He served out his term of enlistment and was honorably discharged at Staunton, Va Mr. Hullihen returned to Pennsylvania and located first at Bower, and then moved to Blair county, where he operated a hotel for two years and moved then to Three Springs, in Huntingdon county and came from there, in 1878, to McGee's Mills Here he was engaged as a miller in the McGee Grist Mills, for more than thirty continuous years He is one of the best known men in Bell township and on numerous occasions has been elected to responsible township offices, in both Bell and Greenwood townships

Mr Hullihen married Miss Mary C Young, who was born in Indiana county, Pa August 30, 1848, a daughter of Jacob and Mary Catherine (Hauck) Young, and they have five children and eight grandchildren, as follows Elmer E, who lives at home and is in the railroad service, Ermine, who is the wife of James Ross, of Colorado, and they have one child· Esther Dora, who is the wife of L J Jones, of Punxatawney, Pa, and they have two children, Frederick N, who lives at Punxatawney, married Mollie Davis and they have five children, and Martha M, who resides with her parents Mr Hullihen is one of the charter members of the G A R Post at McGee's Mills He belongs to the order of Eagles In politics he is a Republican

HARRY J SHOFF, who is one of the representative citizens of Ferguson township, Clearfield county, Pa, owns the farm of 100 acres on which he was born June 3, 1883, and is a son of C J and Annie E (Glasgow) Shoff

C J Shoff, who, for many years has been a well known lumberman was born August 3, 1843, at Hagerty Cross Roads, Clearfield county, and came to the farm above mentioned three years after his marriage He has always been active in the lumber industry and at the present time (1911) he is engaged in cutting timber in Somerset county, Pa He married Annie E Glasgow, who was born February 7, 1847, a daughter of John Glasgow Nine children were born to this marriage, namely Ella V, who married, Herbert Mahaffey, a salesman residing in Boswell, Som-

erset county, Clair J, who married Elizabeth Mott, of Burnside, residing in Olean, N Y, employed in the service of Pennsylvania Railroad Company for many years as electrician, Paul L, married Marie Moler, of Iron Gate, Va, died September 13, 1900, leaving his wife and two boys, who still reside in Iron Gate, G L, who was still single at time of his death on March 26, 1907, was superintendent of the C J Shoff & Sons Lumber Co, in Somerset county, and one of the Union Bargain Store Co, at Boswell, M L, married Effie Whiteside, he is interested in lumbering and mercantile business at Boswell, Somerset county, H C, not married, is also one of the partners in the Union Bargain Store of Boswell, F J, not married, is employed by the Pennsylvania Railroad Company, and is now living in Olean, N Y, Mary J, youngest of the family, is still single and living in Boswell The mother of the above mentioned family died March 8, 1904, and was buried at Glasgow She was a member of the Lutheran church, to which her husband also belongs

Harry J Shoff obtained his education in the public schools of Ferguson township, after which he was in the lumber business with his father and for three years they operated together in Clearfield county Since then he has devoted himself to farming, purchasing 100 acres of the homestead, his father retaining 100 acres, which remains his home and he also owns several tracts of valuable coal land in Clearfield county Mr Shoff, of this sketch, also operates fifty acres of farm land owned by his wife He keeps high grade cattle and carries on dairying on a small scale He is one of the younger agriculturists of Ferguson township but is one of the most enterprising and successful

Mr Shoff was married June 9, 1904, to Miss Ruby Z Rowles, who was born in Greenwood township, Clearfield county, March 28, 1883, and is a daughter of John A and Eleanor Rowles, formerly very prominent people in this section The father of Mrs Shoff died in 1897 and her mother in January, 1904, and their burial was at Lumber City They were members of the United Presbyterian church In politics, John Rowles was a Democrat Mr and Mrs Shoff have two children, Mary Lenore and Anna Glasgow Mr Shoff, as indicated above, is a wide-awake farmer and is an active member of Kerrmoor Grange, in which he holds the office of overseer He is a Democrat in politics but has never accepted any township office except that of school director He is a stockholder in the Ferguson & La Jose Telephone Company

WATSON LOWERY JOHNSTON, of the firm of W L Johnston & Son, real estate dealers, with quarters in the McEwen building, DuBois, Pa , is one of the early residents of this borough and one of its representative men He was born in Indiana county, Pa , September 4, 1851, and is a son of Matthew and Jane (Barclay) Johnston

Matthew Johnston was born in Center county, Pa He married Jane Barclay, who was born in Ireland and was an infant when her parents, Watson Lowery Barclay and wife, came to Center county Eight children were born to Matthew and Jane Johnston, the only survivors of the family being Watson Lowery and an older brother, J A Johnston

Watson Lowery Johnston was reared on the home farm and attended the district schools In 1873 he came to DuBois, or to Rumbarger, which was the early name of what

was then a little lumber settlement. He opened a small grocery and confectionery store, one of the early business houses, and later engaged in building and contracting and by 1895 saw the wisdom of going into the real estate business which he expanded into so important an enterprise that in 1903 he admitted his son, George W Johnston, as a partner The firm subsequently bought the building in which they have ever since maintained their offices As an additional business line, Mr Johnston has been an auctioneer for many years and in this capacity is known all over this part of the state He was one of the organizers of the first fire company at DuBois, in 1881, and served four years as its president In 1889 the company was reorganized as the Union Fire Company and he served two years as president, and when the DuBois Volunteer Fire Department was organized in 1893, he again served one year as its presiding officer. It was through his public spirited efforts that the Firemen's Convention assembled at DuBois, August 21, 1894 Appreciation of his efforts was definitely shown, when, in 1895, he was elected president of the Central District Volunteer Fire Department.

Mr Johnston was married June 9, 1875, to Miss Wilhelmina Wise, a daughter of Michael Wise, and five children were born to them, three of whom survive, namely· George W., Catherine M , who is the wife of Dr. Hugh Morehead, of Erie, Pa , and Nellie B , who married John C Carson, of DuBois, and they have one son, Daniel L

George W Johnston, the junior member of the firm of W L Johnston & Son, was born at DuBois, April 13, 1876, and obtained a common school education When fifteen years of age he became a clerk for J C Merriss, with whom he continued for five years and then learned the carpenter trade, which he followed until 1903, when he entered into partnership with his father. Both members of this firm are able business men and both popular citizens. W L Johnston is a Prohibitionist. He is identified fraternally with the Heptasophs. With his family he belongs to the Methodist Episcopal church, in which, for some years, he was a local preacher.

JOSEPH DAVIS, one of the well known, highly respected and responsible citizens of Penn township, who carries on general farming, owns 147 acres of valuable land which lies in Penn township, one mile northwest of Grampian, Pa. He was born June 9, 1836, on what is now known as the Pentz farm, near Grampian, and is a son of Joseph and Rebecca (Moore) Davis.

Joseph Davis, Sr, was born near Tyrone, Pa, a son of Elisha Davis who came to Pennsylvania from Wales. Joseph Davis spent the early part of his life in Sinking Valley and then came to Penn township and purchased 150 acres, clearing about half of this property by his own industry and residing on it until his death. He married Rebecca Moore, who, like himself, had been reared in the Society of Friends and they belonged to this religious body all their lives. They were among the early members at Grampian, Pa, and their ashes rest in the cemetery connected with the church at that place.

Joseph Davis was the eighth born in a family of ten children. His schooling was in Penn township, where he made the most of his opportunities and even attended one term after he had reached his twenty-first year. Farming and working in the woods at lumbering occupied his time until he purchased his present farm. He is one of the progressive and well informed farmers of Penn township and is a charter member of Penn Grange.

Mr Davis was married in 1862, to Elizabeth Wall, who died May 4, 1909, her burial being in the Friends' cemetery at Grampian. She was a daughter of William and Sarah Wall, of Penn township. Five children were born to Mr and Mrs Davis, namely Truman, who married Jennie Kester, a daughter of Lewis and Alice Kester, and they have six children—Alice, Joseph L, Beulah, Dorsey, Harold and Wilfred; Sarah Ann, who married W. I Wall, of Grampian, and they have four children—Earl, Lena, Eva and Carl; Mary, who is deceased, was the wife of Fred Smith and she is survived by three children—Elizabeth, Lulu and Clair, and Eva and Cora, twins, the former of whom is the wife of Clyde Kendall, and the latter the wife of Bruce Kendall.

Joseph Davis is a prominent member of the Society of Friends and in 1904 was sent as a delegate to a convention of this church held at Toronto, Canada. In politics he is a Republican and has served as auditor, treasurer and school director in Penn township. He is a stockholder in the Curwensville National Bank at Curwensville, Pa.

AUSTIN BEATTY, one of the best known residents of Bell township, where he has lived many years, having settled on his present farm when twenty-one years of age, was born October 19, 1844, in Indiana county, Pa, and is a son of James O and Christianna (Miller) Beatty.

James O Beatty was born in 1819, in the old Beatty homestead in Indiana county, where his parents, Joseph and Catherine (Orr) Beatty, had located when they came from Ireland In 1851 he came to Bell township, settling on the old Samuel McGee farm, which he partly cleared and lived on until 1860, when he moved to Chest Falls, where he resided for seven years From there he moved to the present Beatty farm and during the remainder of his life was engaged in farming and lumbering His death occurred September 25, 1891 He was a member of the Methodist Protestant church In politics he was a Democrat and on numerous occasions was elected to office He married Christianna Miller, who was born in October, 1819, a daughter of John and Catherine (McLaren) Miller Three children of James O Beatty and wife still survive, namely Austin, Foster, who is a farmer in Bell township, and Huston, who lives in Clarion county, Pa

Austin Beatty was not more than twelve years of age when he became his father's chief helper on the homestead and he assisted his parent until he was twenty-one years old, when he came to the farm he has occupied ever since He was one of the first settlers in this section of the township, north of McGee's Mills, and built the first log cabin He has followed general farming and lumbering since twenty-one years of age and has spent almost all his life here, his longest period of absence being when he served in the Civil war He enlisted in 1864 in Co H, 58th Pa Vol Inf, and was mustered out near Richmond, Va, where he had been mainly detailed on picket duty, following the surrender of Gen Lee He then returned home and engaged in saw milling and farming He has long been recognized as one of the representative men of his township and his judgment is consulted

and his opinion is asked in all public matters in his section He is a Democrat in politics and has served many terms as a school director.

On October 5, 1865, Mr Beatty was married to Miss Rachel Young, who was born in Clarion county, Pa, in 1842, a daughter of Joseph and Mary (Hawk) Young, the former of whom died in 1856 and the latter in 1851. They were natives of Butler county, Pa. Mrs Beatty has one brother, Joseph Young, who lives in Indiana county Mr and Mrs Beatty have had the following children Clark, who is a farmer, married Letha Baker, and they have six children; Annis D, who is the wife of C. Flory, who works in the tannery at Mahaffey, and they have six children, Willis, who lives at Newtonburg, Pa, married Elizabeth Stigers, and they have five children; John, who lives near Clearfield, married Myrtle Coleman, and they have five children; and George, Mary and Ward, all three of whom are deceased Mr Beatty is a leading member of the Methodist Protestant church in Bell township and is one of the church trustees

FRANK GUINZBURG, was born at Annapolis, Md, September 2, 1863, and is a son of Adolph and Amelia (Wolf) Guinzburg Adolph Guinzburg came to Clearfield county in 1873 and was engaged in the clothing and gents' furnishing business at Clearfield, for seventeen years, after which he moved to Yonkers, N Y, where he died in 1908 He was twice married, first to Amelia Wolf, who died at Philadelphia, the mother of five children, Frank being the third in order of birth The second marriage was to Leontine Jonawitz, who resides at Yonkers, N. Y. Five children were also born to the second marriage.

Frank Guinzburg was ten years old when his father came with his family to Clearfield and there the boy completed his education in the public school that was then held in the old Methodist Episcopal church building, and in the Clearfield Academy, which was then under the superintendence of Miss Swan. At the age of fifteen years he started to learn the lock and gunsmith trade, under the late John E Harder, with whom he remained for three years. In 1884 the business prospects of Du-Bois attracted him as it did other enterprising young men, and he found a good opening in the line of tobacco and sporting goods. He lost his stock, however, in the great fire which is still talked of by the older residents of Du-Bois, but immediately resumed business with a new stock, temporarily sharing a salesroom with W H Cannon, a shoe merchant. In January, 1904, Mr Guinzburg bought the business of W I Hay, wholesale liquor dealer and continued also his other lines until 1906, when he sold out his tobacco and sporting goods and confined himself more closely to his other interests. His place of business is at No 41 W Long avenue, DuBois. He has other business interests than those mentioned, being a stockholder in the Union Banking and Trust Company, in the Hibner-Hoover Hardware Company, in the D L Corbett Dry Goods Company, all of DuBois, and also is interested in H S Hall & Co, retail shoe dealers, at Brockville, Pa. In all his undertakings he has shown great business foresight and is numbered with the capitalists of Du-Bois.

In May, 1888, Mr Guinzburg was married to Miss Millie A Hay, who is a daughter of W E and Anna (Dunsten) Hay, and they have two children. Roland H and Frances A. They are enjoying as excellent educational advantages as an indulgent father can give them. Roland H graduated with credit from the DuBois High School in 1907 and is a member of the class of 1911 in the University of Pennsylvania. The daughter, Frances A, is a student at Elkins Park, Pa, being a pupil in the exclusive Ogontz Girls' School. Mr Guinzburg is a man of social instincts as may be inferred by his membership in numerous fraternal and social organizations, among which may be mentioned the Elks, the Eagles, the Moose and the Owl Club.

FRED PILKINGTON, coal operator and senior member of the firm of Pilkington & Ellery, operating the Coaldale mines, No 14, at Grampian, Pa, was born November 7, 1866, in England, and the only child living of his father's first marriage. He is a son of Thomas and Elizabeth (Beckett) Pilkington, who came to America from England in 1868, locating at Powelton, Pa, then moved to Philipsburg, where Elizabeth Pilkington died. Thomas Pilkington returned to England in 1873 and while there married Mary Hellowell and before they returned to America, in 1879, two of their seven children had been born. Their family was as follows: William, John, Ernest, Joseph, Thomas, Margaret and Esther, and of these Joseph is deceased.

Thomas Pilkington was an experienced coal miner and for twenty years was mine foreman for Jackman & Ellsworth. He then embarked in the hotel business at Chester Hill, Clearfield county, Pa, and continued until his death, at the age of fifty-nine years, and his burial was at Philipsburg. His widow resides at South Philipsburg. Mr Pilkington became an ardent Democrat and was deeply in-

terested in public questions and public men
During the presidential campaign preceding
his death, he was elected a delegate to receive
Hon William J Bryan and his meeting with
the distinguished politician was a proud moment of his life

Fred Pilkington was educated at Philipsburg and after school he entered the coal
mines In 1896 he became mine foreman for
the Morrisdale Coal Company's shaft No 1,
at Morrisdale, later at the Royal Mines, at
Munson, Pa, for the Jones estate, and later
was with several other mining companies, and
then came to Grampian as superintendent of
the Coaldale Mining Company In 1908, with
a partner, Mr Ellery, Mr Pilkington bought
the interests of this company and is half owner
and superintendent He is also interested in
the Grampian Supply Store at Grampian

On September 1, 1897, Mr Pilkington was
married to Miss Carrie B Shields, a daughter
of Alexander Shields of Morris township, and
they have three children Elizabeth, Ralph
and Dorothy Mr. Pilkington was reared in
the Episcopal church He is not very active
in politics but he takes much interest in the
Masonic fraternity, of which he is a member.

HENRY STAGNER, general farmer and
representative citizen in Bell township, where
he is serving on the school board, was born at
Troutville, in Brady township, Clearfield
county, Pa, November 28, 1850, and is a son
of Jacob and Phillipina (Alleman) Stagner

The parents of Mr Stagner were born in
Germany and they came to America on the
same ship The father died September 1,
1879, at the age of sixty-seven years He
bought wild land in Brady township, Clearfield
county, which he cleared and later cultivated

until the close of his life. He was a man of
honest impulses and was worthy in every way.
He married Phillipina Alleman, a daughter of
Philip Alleman, and the following members of
their family still survive. Henry; Daniel,
who lives at Newtonburg, Jacob, who lives at
Banner Ridge, and Samuel, who lives in Bell
township

Henry Stagner went to school in the neighborhood of his father's farm and afterward
helped in its clearing and cultivating He then
learned the shoemaking trade and worked at
the same until 1877, when he purchased his
present farm He had the land to clear of
timber and for a number of years was obliged
to work early and late, giving attention to the
improving of his property and when farm work
was not possible, continued to follow shoemaking In the panic of 1873 he had lost all
his savings. but through his knowledge of this
excellent trade he was able to again become
independent He sold shingles in order to buy
leather which he made up into substantial
footwear and peddled the same in the lumber
and logging camps, walking with his product
from camp to camp Mr Stagner displayed
the resourcefulness in rebuilding his fortunes
that has characterized him through life and
since 1882 has been able to take things much
easier

Mr Stagner married Miss Theresa Parrish,
who was born in Cambria county, Pa, a
daughter of L J and Martha (Kuntz) Parrish, and a granddaughter of John Parrish and
his wife, Mary McKenzie, who were early
settlers in Cambria county The mother of
Mrs Stagner was born in Germany and was
three years old when her parents settled in
Cambria county. She died August 22, 1901,
aged seventy-five years Mr. Parrish was born

February 13, 1823, and died in October, 1908 Mr and Mrs Stagner have six children living and two dead Martha, who is the wife of J C Withrow and they live at Beaverdale and have five children, Rose, who married I Faust, of Beaverdale, and they have two children, Stella, who is the wife of Robert Nelson, of Beaverdale, and they have two children; Sabina, who is a trained nurse, at Pittsburg, Eva, who is a teacher, Ruth, who is the youngest, lives at home, and Mary Emma and Bessie Ann are deceased Mrs Stagner is a member of the Catholic church In politics he is a Democrat

DAVID BRESSLER, general farmer and representative citizen of Pike township, resides on his farm of sixty-two acres which is situated three and one-half miles southwest of Curwensville, Pa, and he has been a lifelong resident of this part of Pennsylvania He was born in Huntingdon county, April 7, 1830

When twenty-one years old, Mr Bressler came to Clearfield county and was with his brother for four years on a farm and afterward worked one year with him as a blacksmith and then married and during the following year lived on his father-in-law's farm From there he moved to Chestnut Ridge and bought his present farm from Robert Addleman It was known as the old Price farm and the land was not considered in very good condition at that time but under Mr Bressler's excellent methods it has been greatly improved and yields very satisfactory crops of wheat and oats He has a valuable coal bank open, the vein being eighteen inches thick, but he is not selling, merely working for his own use There is also a fine vein of fire clay on the land which has not yet been developed

Mr Bressler was forced to make some improvements in the buildings but the old farm house is still comfortable although it was erected 100 years ago Mr Bressler still has ten acres of woodland on the place

On January 7, 1857, Mr Bressler was married to Miss Jane Elizabeth Passmore, who was born at Curwensville, July 28, 1839, a daughter of George C and Mary Ann (Hartsock) Passmore Mr and Mrs Bressler have had the following children Margaret, who is deceased, was the wife of Robert Bloom, also deceased, George, who lives in Curwensville, married Ida Hammond, Mary Emma, who died when aged five years, Franklin, who lives at Patton, Pa, married Della Turner, who is deceased, Ezekiah, who is a resident of Curwensville, Fannie, who is the wife of Edward Thomas, of Patton, Pa, Jennie, who is the wife of William Walker, of Clearfield county, James E, who is in business at Houtzdale, married Dortha Boaring, Lavinia, who is deceased, was the wife of Samuel Cruikshank, John T, who lives at home and assists his father, Edith, who is the wife of Steward McCollough, of Huntingdon, and Viola, who is the wife of G Welt, of Curwensville Mr Bressler and wife are members of the Primitive Methodist church In his political views he is an independent with strong leanings towards the Prohibition party He has never cared for public office but served acceptably through one term as road supervisor

GEORGE H SLOPPY, proprietor of one of the largest and most modern hostelries of DuBois, Pa, the Hotel Logan, which is centrally located at No 120 N Brady street, is a representative business man of this borough and a member of one of the old Clearfield

county families He was born at DuBois, Pa,
July 26, 1879, and is a son of Milton J and
Mary (Hout) Sloppy

Milton J Sloppy was born in Clearfield
county in 1855, his father having located here
in his early manhood Milton J Sloppy operated the stage line between DuBois and Curwensville before the railroad was completed
and was probably as well known as any man
in this section He also filled out a long service as town constable, for eighteen years being the only officer of that kind at DuBois
His death occurred on New Year's Day, 1906
He married Mary Hout, who still survives,
making her home with her son, George H
She was born in Jefferson county, Pa, of German parentage To Milton J and Mary
Sloppy six children were born, namely Willaim, Harry and George, Baryl, who is the
wife of John Irwin, Grace, who died in infancy, and Lela, who is a student in the Du-
Bois High School

George H Sloppy attended the DuBois public schools and after leaving the High School
entered the employ of John E DuBois, and
worked in the latter's box factory for five
years and while there was given the nickname
of Dudley, by his comrades, by which he is
known to many of his friends From the box
factory, Mr Sloppy went to work in the tannery operated by Mr. DuBois and A R Van
Tassel, where he was employed for nine years,
after which he accepted a position as clerk in
his present place of business, the hotel being
then under the management of James Chambers In 1906 Mr Sloppy became manager
and owner and in 1909 he remodeled the entire building and equipped it with all modern
improvements It is now a beautiful brick
structure, with fifty-five sleeping apartments,

one of the finest lobbies and writing rooms in
any hotel in the place, with a cuisine that is
unexcelled and with close attention paid to the
comfort of every guest Mr Sloppy is very
moderate in his charges, his rates being from
$1 50 to $2 per day He is an active citizen,
being a member of the DuBois Business Men's
Exchange and is interested in everything that
promises to add to the commercial advancement of this prosperous borough Politically
he is a Republican and fraternally he is identified with the Elks and the Eagles

MRS LUELLA BLOOM, a lady who is
well known for her many admirable qualities
as well as her business qualifications, resides
on her very valuable farm of 100 acres, which
is situated three miles south of Clearfield, Pa
She is the widow of the late W. Sloss Bloom,
and a daughter of A A and Jerusha
(Bloom) Kelley.

Mrs Bloom was born near Bloomington,
Pa, and was educated at Lumber City and in
the Pine Grove schoolhouse, in Lawrence
township Her father was a native of Lumber
City, where he was married and he and his
wife lived on a farm near by, on which he
died at the age of sixty-eight years, and was
buried at Bloomington His wife is still living and resides at Curwensville They were
members of the Presbyterian church Five
children were born to them, namely Luella,
who is Mrs Bloom, Lavert, married to Clara
Brooks, of Curwensville, Mary, who conducts
a photographic gallery at Curwensville, Elizabeth, who is the wife of Wesley Milligan, of
Curwensville, and Frank, a resident of Curwensville, who married Mary Daugherty

In February, 1890, Luella Kelley was married to W Sloss Bloom, who died in Decem-

J. M. CORNELY, M. D.

ber, 1906, at the age of fifty-five years His burial was in the Bloomington cemetery, under the direct charge of the order of Eagles and the Grange, of Clearfield, he having been a prominent member of both organizations He was a son of David E and Mary (Sloss) Bloom After marriage, Mr and Mrs Bloom went to housekeeping on the present farm which they bought from John F Read and was known in the neighborhood as the Joseph Tait farm All the attractive and substantial buildings were built by Mr and Mrs Bloom He was an excellent business man and in addition to general agriculture, including some stock raising, opened up a fine coal bank, a 42-inch vein which has been very profitable More recently a new 32-inch vein has been opened Since taking charge of the place Mrs Bloom has shown excellent business capacity and every branch of the farm industries is in a flourishing condition Her residence is a model of comfort and she has recently installed a telephone

Four children were born to Mr and Mrs Bloom, all of whom still live at home Kay, Guy, Wava and Hazel, the two younger ones being students in the Clover Hill School Mrs Bloom and children are members of the Presbyterian church, to which Mr Bloom was also attached He was a stockholder in the Farmers' and Traders' Bank at Clearfield

J M CORNELY, M D, who is engaged in the practice of medicine at Madera, Pa, is a native of this place, born November 12, 1877 He is a son of James and Christina (Bowers) Cornely, the former of whom is now deceased

J M Cornely was educated in the public schools of Madera and the Lock Haven Normal School, spending two years in this institution, after which he became a clerk in a general merchandise store at Madera and continued for eighteen months In the meanwhile he devoted some time to medical study and then entered Jefferson Medical College, Philadelphia, where he was graduated in the class of 1907 For one year he practiced in the Williamsport Hospital, where he had wide experience, and then returned to his native place and established his office He has built up a substantial practice and enjoys the confidence of the people in his professional skill

Dr Cornely was married December 29, 1909, to Miss Blanche Minds, a daughter of James H and Julia Minds residents of Beulah, Clearfield county, and they have one daughter, Margaret Dr and Mrs Cornely attend the Presbyterian church Politically he is a Republican and has served one term as town clerk He is identified fraternally with the Masons at Osceola, the L O O M at Houtzdale, and the I O R M, at Madera

DALLAS PATRICK, general farmer, who has resided on his present home place in Bell township, for the past thirty-three years, is also an honored veteran of the great Civil war, to which he gave three years of his young manhood and suffered from many of its hazards He was born at Cherry Tree, Clearfield county, Pa, in 1846, and is a son of James and Eliza (Rummell) Patrick

James Patrick was a son of James Patrick, and was born in Ireland He was a child when his parents brought him to America He was reared in Lancaster and Cambria counties, Pa, and came from the latter county in 1839, settling near Cherry Tree, where he followed farming and lumbering during all his active life His death occurred April 1, 1879, at the age of seventy-one years He married Eliza Rummell, who died in 1886, aged eighty-four years

Dallas Patrick had but meager school opportunities He gave his father help on the farm and also worked in the woods until the outbreak of the Civil war He was only a stripling of sixteen years when, in September, 1861, he enlisted for service, entering Co A, 11th Pa Reserve Corps, Army of the Potomac, under General Meade Three years of the hardest kind of service followed At Spottsylvania Court House, he was wounded and again at Cold Harbor, in 1864, and on August 18, 1864, he was captured by the Confederates at the Weldon Railroad He was one of the unfortunates who were compelled to spend six months of suffering in Libby Prison and at Belle Isle He was finally released and after his discharge returned home to Cherry Tree It was some time before he regained his strength that prison life had sapped but a good constitution conquered and in the course of time he went back to lumbering in which he has been considerably interested ever since From Indiana county he came to Bell township, Clearfield county, in 1889, and has resided here ever since He is well known all over this section He recalls old times in a very entertaining way and his stories of the early days in the lumber camps are exceedingly interesting He at one time made a record in hauling, while in Jefferson county, transporting at one time 1,100 pounds of hemlock bark It was an unusual feat and created much comment all through the lumber regions

Mr Patrick was married October 29, 1873, to Miss Sarah A Weaver, who was born October 6, 1848, in Jefferson county Pa, a daughter of Jesse and Mary Ann (Magee) Weaver The father of Mrs Patrick died in 1901, aged seventy-one years, and the mother in 1882 Mr. and Mrs Patrick have seven children, namely Harry A, who was born January 29, 1875, resides at home; Mary Ann, who was born August 22, 1877, is the wife of D B Dunlap, of Blairsville, Pa, and they have four children, John Franklin, who was born May 2, 1881, lives at Blairsville, married Elizabeth Connell, and they have one child; Bessie Gertrude, who was born January 24, 1884, is the wife of H N Kerr, of Blairsville, and they have two children; Elsie Maria, who was born June 23, 1886, is the wife of Frank P Beatty, of Blairsville; Elizabeth Nell, who was born July 8, 1889, is a graduate of the Normal School at Burnside, and is a successful teacher, and Frances Jeanette, who was born September 25, 1896, is a student Mrs Patrick taught school nine terms before her marriage She is a member of the M P church at Newtonburg Mr. Patrick is a Democrat at present in his political attitude He recalls the great interest he took during slavery days, being then in close sympathy with the Abolition movement although only a boy at the time He is a valued member of the Grand Army of the Republic, being identified with the post at Altoona, Pa He has served three terms as a member of the Bell township school board and has always taken a good citizen's interest in the welfare of his section

J LEWIS LEIB, who is proprietor of the largest drug store at Curwensville, Pa, is a representative citizen of this borough, interested in its commercial prosperity and its public affairs He was born September 14, 1869, at Sherwood, Md, and is a son of Thomas and Mary H Leib

Thomas Leib for thirty-four years was identified with the Pennsylvania Railroad, in the Baltimore offices He also owned a farm of 212 acres, in York county, Pa, to which he retired and on which he was living at the time of his death, in February, 1905 Following this event the farm was sold, his widow coming then to Curwensville, where she still lives Thomas Leib was a man of sterling character He was identified with the Prohibition party With his wife he belonged to the Methodist Episcopal church Three children were born to Thomas and Mary H Leib, namely Harry L, who resides near Stewartstown, York county, Della, who is the wife of Dr Harry Hooven, of Hartford, Pa, and J Lewis, of Curwensville

J Lewis Leib attended Stewartstown Academy and after he had decided to enter the drug business, he attended Maryland College at Baltimore, where he was graduated in pharmacy From there he came to Curwensville and became a clerk for a Mr Reeser, then in the drug business here, and finally bought an interest and afterward bought his present building on State street, of Mrs Joseph R Irwin, where he has conducted a first class drug store ever since

Mr Leib was married April 20, 1897, to Miss May Dixon Kemp, a daughter of Maj Thomas Kemp, of Baltimore, Md, and they have three children Kemp, Gretchen and Mildred Mr and Mrs Leib are members of the Methodist Episcopal church, of which he is one of the trustees Mr Leib has other business interests aside from his drug store and is interested in a flourishing building and loan association In politics he is a Republican and he has been a member of the borough council for two years Fraternally he is a Mason and an Odd Fellow

MACK DAVIDSON, who carries on general farming in Bell township, owning what is generally agreed to be one of the best tilled and most productive farms in this section, belongs to an old county family and was born on the Davidson homestead, February 22, 1863, a son of Joseph H and Mary Jane (Henderson) Davidson Mr Davidson has three brothers Frank M, residing in Bell township, James M, residing at Bradford, Pa, and Thomas M, living at Mahaffey

Mack Davidson started out to take care of himself when only thirteen years of age and has been successfully engaged in the same way ever since He worked for strangers and by the time he was twenty-four years old not only had secured a fair education but a wide circle of friends and enough capital to make him feel justified in marrying His parents had died when he was only five years old and his older brother, Alexander, took charge of him When only a boy he engaged in hauling lumber and managed a team of horses so that neither they nor the commodities transported were in any way endangered After marriage he bought his present farm and has so improved it and carefully and intelligently cultivated it that it has become one of the most valuable properties in Bell township

Mr Davidson was married to Miss Jenny Reed, who was born September 5, 1869, in Green township, Indiana county, Pa, a daughter of A and Elizabeth (Buterbaugh) Reed, the former of whom died in 1884 and the latter in 1896 Mrs Davidson has six brothers and sisters living Her great-grandfather,

John Buterbaugh, was born in Huntingdon county, Pa, August 3, 1799, and died aged ninety-six years and six months He accompanied his parents to Indiana county in 1831, where he married Elizabeth Learn, a member of an old pioneer family of Clearfield county In 1894, at the age of ninety-five years, Mr Buterbaugh celebrated his anniversary, gathering about him all of his living descendants, and when he died in the following year, was survived by fifty-seven grandchildren and fifty-six great-grandchildren In early days he was a Whig in politics and later a Republican, and he served two terms as a justice of the peace Mr and Mrs Davidson have had the following children Harry M, who married Goldie Staggers and they have one child, Merrill, who is deceased, Howard, who is a general laborer; and Zoe, Neil, Stella, Fay and Reed, the last named being a baby of one year In politics Mr Davidson is a Democrat and is a very loyal party worker He is serving in his third term as township supervisor and has also been overseer of the poor He is one of Bell township's respected and representative citizens

WILLIAM F KRACH, who is associated with his father, Frederick Krach, in a hotel business at DuBois, Pa, under the firm name of Frederick Krach & Son, proprietors of the Keystone Hotel, has been a resident of this borough since he was ten years of age He was born December 5, 1880, in Schuylkill county, Pa, and is a son of Frederick and Minnie (Fredenberger) Krach

Frederick Krach was born in Germany, December 3, 1845, and was reared on a farm. When he reached the legal age for military service, he entered the German army and par-ticipated in the War of 1871, and during his absence, the death of his first wife occurred In 1875 he came to America and located first at Tamaqua, Pa, where he started into the hotel business, opening the Krach House there, which he conducted until he came to DuBois, in 1890, where he bought the Terp House, from Richard Evans It contained twenty-four bed rooms and was situated on Brady street and the regular rate was $1 50 per day. That hotel Mr Krach subsequently sold to Pierson & Logan and then bought the Globe Restaurant, which he conducted for six months Mr Krach then showed his confidence in the business future of DuBois by further investment, becoming the owner of property on which he erected the Keystone Hotel, which stands at Nos 337-339-341 W Long avenue He opened for business in 1894 and has been liberally patronized He has sixteen bed-rooms and all other apartments necessary for the comfort and convenience of guests and his charges are one dollar per day. In 1906 he admitted his son, William F Krach, to partnership, under the firm name as above mentioned Mr Krach was married second, in Schuylkill county, Pa, to Minnie Fredenberger, who died in 1893, aged fifty-three years She also was a native of Germany and was a most estimable woman Seven children were born to this marriage, as follows Gottleib, Millie; Carolina, who is the wife of J R Ferguson, William F, George; Elsie, who is the wife of William Stephenson, of Pittsburg, Pa, and Lulu, who is the wife of Wayde Bloom With the exception of Mrs Vonlear and Mrs Stephenson, Mr Krach has all his children settled near him, at DuBois

William F Krach obtained his education in the public schools of DuBois and then entered the employ of his father, with whom he has ever since continued, in 1906 becoming his partner and gradually relieving the father of the responsibilities of management On September 16, 1901, Mr. Krach was married to Miss Lilly May Shaffer, a daughter of Isaac Shaffer, of DuBois, and they have four children William, Lillian, Helen and Clarence Mr Krach is a member of the Lutheran church He belongs to the DuBois lodges of the Knights of Pythias and the Eagles He is numbered with the borough's able young business men

JOHN C DIEHL, justice of the peace, a general farmer in Chest township, and a leading factor in Democratic politics in this section, was born August 28, 1861, in Greenfield township, Blair county, Pa, and is a son of Samuel and Mary (Mock) Diehl, and a grandson of John Diehl, whose father had founded the family in Blair county

Samuel Diehl was born April 19, 1839, in Greenwood township, Blair county, where he followed farming and lumbering until 1886, when he came to Clearfield county and established a blacksmith shop and to some extent continued to be interested in lumbering in Chest township His death occurred January 2, 1910, while visiting a son at Tyrone He was a member of the Lutheran church He married Mary Mock, who was born in May, 1840, and was a daughter of Joseph and Mary Mock, who were born in Bedford County, Pa, and a granddaughter of Mary Ritchie To Samuel Diehl and wife the following children were born George M, of Cambria County, Joseph, of Tyrone, Pa, Fred, of Chest Township, Frank, of Beccaria Township, Edward, of Irvona, Pa, Blair, of Jordan Township,

Mary Jane, wife of E Kearns, of Cambria County, Catherine, wife of E F Claar, of Bedford County, and Rosanna M, wife of George Arford, of Puritan, Pa

John C Diehl attended school through boyhood in Blair County and for some thirteen years afterward was engaged in work in the woods near Altoona and then engaged in lumbering and farming on the Frank Campbell place in Chest Township He then moved to Wilson Run and built a sawmill there which he subsequently sold and in 1893 built a second mill, near North Camp, which he operated for three years After selling that mill he settled down to farming on his present place in Chest Township, where he has a well improved property and is in the enjoyment of a large degree of comfort

Mr Diehl was married to Miss Margaret Miles, who was born in May, 1866, in Jordan Township, Clearfield County, and is a daughter of George I and Elizabeth (Leonard) Miles, who came from Center County to Clearfield County and settled in Chest Township To Mr and Mrs Diehl eleven children were born, namely Samuel M, who lives in Cambria County, married Cora McGarvey, and they have one child, Jonas who assists his father, Ward, who is a resident of Irvona, Pa, and Dana K, Mary Elizabeth, Evida A, Robert L, Ralph, Laura J, Melvin G and Chester Calvin, all of whom are residing at home

Mr Diehl has been an active and interested citizen ever since coming to Chest Township He has always endeavored to bring about improvement and progress in the public schools and has served on the school board at different times, has also been constable and township supervisor, and in 1907 was elected a justice of the peace in Chest Township

ARCHER DAVIDSON, general merchant, at Curwensville, Pa , where he is interested in some of the borough's most important business enterprises, has been a lifelong resident of Clearfield County

Mr Davidson started in the general store business in March, 1898, as an interested partner with Ross Bros & Davidson, at Curwensville   The business name changed to Thompson & Davidson when John I Thompson became a purchaser, and he in turn sold to Hammond, Berkey & Co , Mr Davidson becoming the manager and continued in that relation until 1907, when he organized the Bickford Store Company and the Bickford Meat Market The Bickford firm controlling this united business, the second largest in the mercantile line at Curwensville, consists of the following men of capital and prominence   Archer Davidson, Dr J A Woodside, and S M Bickford This firm occupies the corner of State and Walnut Streets, Curwensville, in the heart of the business district, and their trade is drawn from a large outside territory, their customers finding it to their advantage to patronize this establishment rather than to send their capital farther away

Mr Davidson was married to Miss Dora F Thompson, a daughter of Watt H Thompson, of Curwensville   Mr and Mrs Davidson are members of the Methodist Episcopal church In politics he is a Republican but is far more of a business man than politician   He has served, however, very acceptably, also, as a member of the borough council, and is identified with the Curwensville Loan Association Fraternally he is both a Mason and Odd Fellow

JOHN J McGARVEY farmer and fruit grower, in Chest Township, where he was born, on the old family homestead, October 16, 1847, is a son of Anthony and Jane McGarvey, and a grandson of William McGarvey

Anthony McGarvey was born in Ireland and accompanied relatives to America when he was a boy of twelve years   His father came from Ireland at a later date and subsequently died at Philadelphia   Anthony McGarvey came from that city and was one of the first settlers in Chest Township, where he followed farming and lumbering during the whole of his active life, surviving into old age   He was married to a lady who had been born in Ireland, who died when their son, John J , was only three years old   Anthony McGarvey was married second to Mrs Ellen Hunter, who was of Scotch descent   John J McGarvey has one sister, Elizabeth, who is the widow of Daniel Gorman, of La Jose, and a half-brother and a half-sister   Robert H , who resides on the old homestead, and Kate, who is the wife of J Sunderland, of Clearfield

John J McGarvey obtained a district school education, although, in his boyhood, school opportunities near his father's farm were meager, and afterward engaged in farming on the old homestead until he secured a farm of his own, where he has resided ever since   In addition to general farming he has also engaged in lumbering, has followed threshing for many seasons and is also largely interested in raising fruit

Mr McGarvey married Miss Martha Ann Robison, who was born in Chest Township, a daughter of John and Mary Ann (Chamberlain) Robison   Mr and Mrs McGarvey have seven children, namely   Thomas, who married Susanne Harrison and they have three children; Mary, who married B Fraıley, and they have four children, Nellie, who lives at home; Robert, who married Blanche McMasters, is a farmer in Chest Township, and they have three children, Elizabeth, who married Hugh Gallaher, of Chest Township, and they have three children, Bradley, who married Elizabeth McMasters, resides at Berwinsdale, Pa, and they have one child, and Martha, who still resides with her parents

Mr McGarvey has always been identified with the Democratic party His standing as a reliable and representative citizen has been frequently recognized by the people with whom he has spent his life, and they have elected him to responsible offices For six years he has been a member of the township school board and for sixteen years served in the office of township auditor He belongs to the Odd Fellows and is identified with the lodge at Clearfield

FRANK R DIETZ, owner and proprietor of one of the leading hostelries of DuBois, Pa, the St James Hotel, a fine structure situated at Nos 136-138-140 W Long Avenue, has had much experience in the hotel business, has a wide acquaintance and is popular as a host He was born at Freyburg, Clarion County, Pa, and is a son of Jacob and a grandson of John Dietz The latter came from Berks to Clarion County as a pioneer in 1816 and hauled merchandise all through this section of Pennsylvania before the railroads were built Jacob Dietz was born in Berks County and accompanied his father to Venango County, where he later became a farmer and passed the remainder of his life

Frank R Dietz was born June 3, 1847, the second eldest in a family of five children He remained at home until he was fourteen years old, attending school in an old log structure not far from his father's farm He then started out for himself, going to the oil fields in Venango County and by the time he was sixteen

years of age became a driller, working as such for four years, and for twenty years continued to be connected with the oil business, the last fifteen years being an operator and was a contractor and producer in Venango, McKean and Clarion Counties For two years he then engaged in the hotel business in the latter county, for two more years was in the livery business at Kane, Pa, and then operated a hotel there for several years This he subsequently sold and for three years afterward was in the hardware business at Kane From there Mr Dietz went to Punxsutawney, where he conducted the National Hotel for six years, afterward moving to Reynoldsville, where he conducted the Hotel Belmont, now the City Hotel, for three years In 1902 he came to DuBois and purchased his present place of business from B K Fisher It is a fine property, well located for all purposes and has forty bed-chambers, together with other rooms, including lobby, office and restaurant, provided for the comfort and accommodation of guests For all the advantages here offered, Mr Dietz makes a moderate charge, his rates being $1 50 and $2 per day He owns other valuable real estate in the borough

Mr Dietz was married in 1883, to Miss Eleanora Hartle, of Clarion, Pa, and they have seven children, as follows Clair, Charles, Helen, Austin, Henry, Walter and Gertrude Mr Dietz is a member of the Roman Catholic church In politics he is a Republican

HENRY J DIEM, farmer and ex-county commissioner, is one of the representative men of Bell Township, where his farm and lumber interests have been important for many years He was born May 7, 1856, in Brady Township, Clearfield County, and is a son of Henry and Louisa (Stegner) Diem

Henry Diem was born January 15, 1815, in

Hessen-Darmstadt, Germany In 1846, with his own family and two older sisters, he came to Pennsylvania and located on wild land in Brady Township, Clearfield County. He cleared and developed his land and resided on the same until 1878, when he moved to the farm his son Henry J Diem had purchased, in Bell Township, where his death occurred July 24, 1885 In every relation of life he was an honest, upright and worthy man In Germany he married Louisa Stegner, who was born September 22, 1813, and died March 28, 1875. Of their seven children there are three survivors Henry J, Louisa, who is the wife of J M Le Barr, a machinist, residing at Clearfield, and David D, who is a farmer residing in Bell Township

Henry J Diem had but indifferent school advantages but he made the most of his opportunities and is a well informed man of excellent judgment, and has served acceptably in numerous important public offices, including those of township assessor, auditor, school director and supervisor and in 1900 was elected county commissioner He is the only ex-county official residing in this section In politics he is a Democrat In his youth, until he was eighteen years of age, he worked for his father assisting him in the clearing of the farm, and when about twenty-one years old he purchased his present farm and subsequently cleared it He has a valuable and well improved property More or less he has devoted his entire mature life to farming and lumbering

Mr Diem was married on October 9, 1879, to Miss Keturah M Long, who was born January 29, 1863, in Pike Township, Clearfield County, Pa, a daughter of Philip A and Elizabeth C (Owens) Long The father of Mrs Diem came to Clearfield County with his parents when five years old and was reared at Pine Grove His death occurred in 1907, at the age of seventy-two years He married Elizabeth C. Owens, a daughter of John and Margery (Caldwell) Owens Mrs Long died January 27, 1875 Mrs Diem has two sisters: Nevada F, who is the wife of William A. Miller, of Glen Richey, Pa, and Sarah Alice, who is the wife of A Snaars, of DuBois, Pa

Mr and Mrs Diem have had five children born to them, namely Stella, who was born July 23, 1880, resides at home, Newton L, who was born January 18, 1882, is now manager of the West Branch Store at Barnesboro, Pa, married Corrie E Haag, and they have one son, Albert E, Vada A, who was born August 12, 1883, married J L Fryer, residing at Jersey Shore, Pa, and they have two children—Alvin L and Alfred D, Nona S, who was born February 11, 1886, is a widow and lives at Jersey Shore and has a son, Theodore M, and Harry M, who was born July 15, 1894, who resides at home Mrs Diem is a member of the Evangelical church and is interested in mission work, being a member of the Ladies Aid Society Both Mr and Mrs Diem are members of the Grange, and he belongs also to Minkel Lodge, No 753, Odd Fellows, at Troutville

CARL EUGENE PATCHIN, one of the substantial business men of Burnside, Pa, and a member of one the old families of this section, was born November 1, 1882, at Patchinsville, Clearfield County, Pa, and is a son of Aaron Wright and Elizabeth (Barrett) Patchin

Carl E Patchin was educated in the local schools and at Lewisburg, where, for three years he had academic advantages After he returned home he engaged in the lumber business and at the present time is associated in the same with J Stauffer, at Burnside He is also interested in extensive farm property, is one of the directors of the Laurel Oil & Gas Company, of Oklahoma, owns property at Camden, N J, and is a director in the First National Bank at Glen Campbell, Pa

Mr Patchin was married on January 31, 1906, to Miss Mayme McKeage, who was born near Cherry Tree, Indiana County, Pa, November 25, 1883 This was the historic spot on which the famous Penn Treaty was signed with the Indians The parents of Mrs Patchin are George and Anabelle (Ake) McKeage, the former of whom is a merchant at Burnside Mrs Patchin has one brother, John A, who lives at home She spent two years in the Indiana County Normal School and prior to her marriage, assisted her father in his store Mr Patchin is a member of the Evangelical church at Patchinsville In politics he is a Republican but has never desired public office Mr and Mrs Patchin take part in the pleasant social life of the town and have a very hospitable home and a wide circle of friends

M V MAPES, one of Lawrence Township's substantial, successful and enterprising business men, whose valuable farm of 120 acres is devoted to general agriculture and the producing of cream, being the only man in the township making a specialty of cream and keeping Jersey and Guernsey cows for this purpose, was born August 3, 1855, in Lawrence Township, Clearfield County, Pa His parents were William and Albina (Irwin) Mapes

William Mapes was born in New Jersey and accompanied his parents from there to Clearfield County He married Albina Irwin, who was a daughter of Joseph Irwin and was born on the farm on which M V Mapes now resides To this marriage seven children were born, four of whom survive William Mapes was a Democrat but he never accepted office, devoting his time to the accumulation of land At one time he owned 580 acres, 280 of which lay in Lawrence Township, and 300 acres of timber was situated in Goshen Township He lived to be eighty-six years of age and his wife to the age of eighty-four years They were charter members and helped to build up the West Clearfield Methodist Episcopal Church

M V Mapes attended the Wolf Run school when he was a boy and as soon as he was old enough to take upon himself such responsibilities, he went into the livestock insurance business and also carried fire risks, and for four years traveled in this line through Ohio and Kentucky After his return and marriage, he settled on his present farm, his maternal grandfather's old property, and among the improvements is the present handsome residence About 100 acres of the farm are tillable Mr Mapes is one of the wide-awake, thinking men of the country and in making the specialty of producing cream for butter purposes, he is following out a theory which has proved of practical value He has been more or less interested in the local creamery for some time and formerly was secretary of the organization and at present is a director He keeps thoroughly informed concerning the modern discoveries in agricultural possibilities and is a valued member of the Grange at Mt Joy

Mr Mapes married Miss Maud L Sheffler, a daughter of John R Sheffler, and they have seven children: Clair F, who is teaching school at Pine Grove, and Charles, Ruth, Gussie, Frances, John E and Dean M Mr Mapes and family attend the Methodist Episcopal church at Clearfield In politics he is a Democrat

WILSON JONES SMATHERS, M D, has been identified with DuBois, Pa , from the time when the present hustling city with its 1910 complement of business houses, schools, churches, cultured homes and thriving industries, was but a little lumber settlement in the green woods, with a population of but twenty-six families On June 20, 1873, the young physician threw in his lot with the other pioneers and during the long and useful life he has since led here, has never regretted his choice of home Dr Smathers was born March 28. 1851, on a farm in Limestone township, Clarion county, Pa , and was just a child when his parents moved to Jefferson county, Pa , where he was reared He is a son of John and Ann (Jones) Smathers

John Smathers, father of Dr Smathers, was born in Clarion county, Pa , January 4, 1828 The Smathers or Smithers family (the latter orthography formerly prevailing) has been in Pennsylvania since 1740, in which year two brothers, Jacob and Robert Smithers, emigrated from England, Robert locating in Delaware, while Jacob selected Luzerne county, Pa , where he subsequently married, and they lived and died in that county

Christian Smathers, one of the sons of Jacob Smathers, lived in Luzerne county until after his marriage and in 1795 moved from there to Butler county, Pa , locating at the village now bearing the suggestive name of Bruin, his wife's people, the Dobinspecks, being very prominent there then as now One year later, Christian Smathers and wife moved to Clarion county and settled on a farm in

Monroe township It was wild land at the time but Mr Smathers cleared it and developed a productive farm and they lived there until death They had eight children

Christian Smathers (2d), son of Christian, was born in Luzerne county, in 1793, and was two years old when the family moved to Clarion county, where he grew to manhood. He became a farmer and also was somewhat noted as a hunter, having a record of no less than fourteen bears killed in one season He married Susanna Hariger, who died in Clarion county, after which he moved to Jefferson county, Pa , where he was married again, to a widow, Mrs. Catherine Rodes They spent the rest of their lives in Jefferson county. Christian Smathers had ten children, all born to his first marriage

John Smathers was the second son of Christian and Susanna (Hariger) Smathers Like his father and grandfather, he became a farmer. He was married in Beaver township, Jefferson county, Pa , to Ann Jones, who was born in Jefferson county, March 9, 1829, and still survives, a venerable lady remarkably well preserved, having reasonable physical health and an unclouded mind that permits her recalling many of the interesting events of early times in Jefferson county. After marriage, John Smathers and wife moved to Jefferson county and in 1853 they settled on a farm in Oliver township, which they sold in 1864, buying one in Ringold township, which remains the family homestead Here the aged mother of Dr. Smathers still resides, his father having died here on August 25, 1895. A large family of children were born to John and Ann Smathers, many of whom died in infancy Five reached mature years, as follows Wilson Jones, Millard Fillmore, who

W. J. Smathers M.D.

lives in Jefferson county, Winfield Scott, who is sheriff of Clarion county, John Curtis, who is a resident of Indiana, Pa, and Charles Emerson, who lives on the old homestead in Ringold township, Jefferson county, and takes care of the venerable mother

Wilson J Smathers recalls the first schoolhouse he ever attended and describes it as a primitive log cabin Later he enjoyed better advantages and spent a short season in an academy at Dayton, Pa He studied hard and prepared himself for teaching and taught the district school near his home, in the winter of 1870-1, and about this time began the study of medicine, with Dr R B Brown, an old practitioner at Summerville, Pa Later in 1871, he entered Jefferson Medical College, at Philadelphia, for a course of lectures and then continued his studies with Dr Brown, subsequently returning to college and was there graduated on March 12, 1873 In looking about for a promising field for practice he decided upon DuBois, where John DuBois was developing his large lumber interests, and four months later the young physician opened an office, being not only one of the first professional men in the place but the very first physician

When Dr Smathers came to the hamlet, which was really a lumber camp only, no organization having as yet been effected, it being in fact but a partially cleared portion of Brady township, there had been no need for any town officials, and as the people were industrious and law abiding, no justice of the peace was required There was one store doing business, mainly in groceries, its site being on the present northeast corner of Main and Long streets, and it was owned and conducted by Thomas P Montgomery The nearest

42

polling place was at Luthersburg and the postoffice was at Jefferson Line, four miles distant

However, no matter how independent a community can be in relation to its luxuries, there are necessities which must be obtainable and among the greatest of these is a physician Dr Smathers found immediate need of his professional services and found that he could very easily qualify for other positions in the neighborhood than physician He being the owner of a horse, was frequently the mail carrier for the entire neighborhood Thomas Jones, an uncle of Dr Smathers, was one of the first settlers and owned the land on which stand the physician's house and office, the same in which he located when he came here, renting the property from his uncle until 1875, when he purchased it He filled the entire professional field for the first year but in the next year another physician came, but the latter remained for only two years and still another year passed before Dr Smathers had the assistance of a co-worker In the destructive fire of 1888 which swept through the town, Dr Smathers suffered severely, losing his office and residence A new office immediately took the place of the burned one and a new residence followed, one which has subsequently been remodeled and modernized These buildings are situated respectively at No 6 and No 8 S Main street, DuBois

On July 22, 1875, Dr Smathers was married to Miss Maggie C Fulton a daughter of S T. and Frances Fulton, of Smicksburg, Indiana county, Pa, and a granddaughter of Dr W N. Simms, who was a pioneer physician there Five children were born to Dr and Mrs Smathers, namely Francis, who is engaged in the practice of medicine at Big

Run, Pa , graduated from the Jefferson Medical College, Philadelphia, in 1905, married Bessie Kearney and they have one child, Marion Elisabeth, Margaretta, John Marion, who is a student in the dental department of the University of Baltimore, Md , in the class of 1913, Bessie Fulton, who is a student in the DuBois High School, a member of the class of 1911, and Dorothy Ruth, who will complete the grammar school course at DuBois, in 1911 Dr Smathers and family attend the Methodist Episcopal church and he was instrumental in the building of the first church edifice at this place In his political views, Dr Smathers is a Republican He has not accepted many public offices, having found his time and strength needed in attending to the claims of his profession, but he served on the school board for a season and since the organization of the DuBois Board of Health, in 1893, has been almost a continuous member and at present is its secretary He is identified with the DuBois Medical Association and belongs to the Heptasophs and the order represented by the R P P A

WILLIAM FENNELL, who, for nineteen years has been proprietor of the New Central Hotel, at Ramey, Pa , of which borough he is a representative citizen, was born in Schuylkill County, Pa , August 17, 1863, and is a son of Michael and Mary (Morgan) Fennell

Michael Fennell was born in England and followed coal mining after coming to Pennsylvania, where he subsequently died He was married in Schuylkill County and his widow now lives in Illinois Six sons were born to them but only one, William, now survives

William Fennell attended school where his parents happened to be living in his boyhood, Illinois and in Huntingdon and Clearfield Counties, Pa Afterward for about sixteen years he worked in the coal mines and then purchased his hotel which he has conducted with great success for almost twenty years As a host he is widely and favorably known and he has retained the patronage of the same traveling guests for many years His house is centrally located and he caters to a first class trade

In 1885 Mr Fennell was married to Miss Anna Westover, a daughter of David and Hannah (Rolley) Westover, the former of whom was born in Canada and the latter in Pennsylvania Mrs Fennell has the following brothers and sisters· Elizabeth, wife of Samuel Tovey, Cecelia, now deceased; Aaron; Dessie, wife of Simon Miller, Joseph, Sadie, wife of Duncan May, and Josephine, wife of H E Wagner

Mr and Mrs Fennell have had two children, Marie and Clay, the latter of whom died when aged nine years Miss Marie Fennell is a teacher of the piano, at Philadelphia, having graduated in music at Combs Conservatory of Music in that city She is a very talented lady Mr Fennell is a Republican in his political views and has been an active and useful citizen of Ramey, serving with capacity on the school board for three years and also in the borough council, of which he was president for three years. He is a member of the Odd Fellows, Knights of Pythias, Red Men, L O O. M and F O E

ADAM S HUTCHINSON, one of Lawrence Township's best known citizens is proprietor of the O'Shanter Hotel, at O'Shanter, Pa He was born at Blossburg, Tioga County,

Pa , September 29, 1866, and is a son of James and Annie (Sampson) Hutchinson, both of whom are deceased

Adam S Hutchinson attended the public schools of Arnot, in Tioga County, and then went to work in the mines at Houtzdale, in Clearfield County, and continued to reside at Houtzdale for six years following his marriage, during this time being general manager in a business house of the place He then came to O'Shanter and for three years rented the O'Shanter Hotel, which was then operated by John Kramer He then bought the property and has been sole owner for eleven years It is a well arranged public house, with twenty-one rooms and seventeen of these are comfortable bed-rooms He has a county license and has the reputation of keeping one of the most orderly and well regulated hotels in this section His charges are exceedingly moderate, not exceeding $1 40 per day In connection with his hotel he also conducts a livery stable, having six horses and also an automobile Travelers who have once enjoyed the comforts afforded by the O'Shanter Hotel under its present management, are very apt to so arrange their connections that they can make a second visit

In 1889, Mr Hutchinson was married at Reynoldsville, Pa , to Miss Nettie Patterson, a daughter of James and Jennetta Patterson, of that place, and twelve children have been born to them, namely James, Anna, Jessie, Florence, Edith, Gordon, Nettie, Mary, Margaret, Ethel, Laura and Adam Jr The only deaths in the family were those of the eldest son, who died at the age of seventeen years, and Ethel, who died in infancy Mr Hutchinson is identified with a number of fraternal organizations and among these are the following

Knights of Pythias, at Houtzdale, Golden Eagles at Glen Richey, Red Men, of Curwensville, and P O S of A , and Royal Order of Moose, at Clearfield In politics he is a Republican and formerly was a very active party man in his section and served several times as chairman of the Republican township committee

REV SAMUEL LEE, who owns two excellent farms in Huston Township, Clearfield County, Pa , comprising forty acres, resides on Cherry Bluff Farm, which lies two and one-half miles north of Penfield He was born July 27, 1846, on his father's farm in Albany Township, Bradford County, Pa , and is a son of Joseph and Hannah (Brewster) Lee

Joseph Lee was born in Bradford County, Pa , and was a son of William Lee, who was a pioneer there from New York William Lee cleared up a large farm and was something of a horticulturist, and his orchard was widely known as the best in Bradford County The children of William Lee were named Polly, Marilla, James, Joseph, William and Betsey, all of whom are deceased Joseph Lee of the above family, became a farmer and also dealt in livestock He lived a long and quietly useful life and died in Bradford County He married Hannah Brewster, who was a descendant in direct line from Colonel Brewster, who came to New England on the Mayflower Her father was Daniel Brewster, who came from Massachusetts to Bradford County and settled at Lime Hill She died in Bradford County She was an admirable woman in every relation of life and was the mother of eleven children, as follows William and Orris, both of whom died in infancy, Solon, who was a member of the 107th Pa Vol Inf , during the Civil War and was killed at the second battle of Bull Run, Rachel, who is now deceased, was the wife of H B Taylor, also deceased, Elizabeth, who is deceased, was the wife of Moses M Carr, a veteran of the Civil War, also deceased, Adrial, who is deceased, served in the Civil War as a member of the 141st Pa Vol Inf, Pamelia, who is the widow of Jacob Schoonover, Edwin, who is deceased, served in the Civil War as a member of Co A, 141st Pa Vol Inf, and was wounded five times, Weston, who died at the age of eighteen years, Samuel, and James W, who is deceased

Samuel Lee grew to manhood on his father's farm and attended the country schools When the Civil War opened he was eager to enter the army and made two attempts before he was accepted, his age and size at first preventing On August 7, 1862, however, he succeeded in enlisting in Co A, 141st Pa Vol Inf, under Capt George W Jackson, and soon proved that a boy of seventeen years could be as brave and patriotic as a more mature individual He participated in the battles of Chancellorsville, Gettysburg, the Wilderness, and Spottsylvania Court House during his service of two years and seven months At the battle of Chancellorsville he was wounded by a shell and at Spottsylvania was carried off the field, May 11, 1864, as one of the dead He revived at the hospital but was retained there until February 25, 1865, when he was honorably discharged He returned to Bradford County, from which he moved to Clearfield County in November, 1867, locating on his present farm, and at first he and F H Brown worked the land together, but later divided Mr Lee cleared up his land and put up all the substantial structures now standing For a number of years Mr Lee has been a minister in the Free Methodist church

He was ordained a minister on October 5, 1891, by Bishop Hart, of New Castle, Pa

Mr Lee was married May 18, 1868, to Miss Avilda A Brown, a daughter of F H and Loiama (Hewett) Brown, of Huston Township They have four children, namely: Minnie is the wife of H D Singer, of Huston Township, and they have the following children—Leonard Ray, George L, Nellie May, Albert B, Hazel, Ralph, Raymond H, Lena M, Alta, Wilmer and Bird, F Burton, who is a resident of Huston Township, married Margaret Davis and they have one child, Crayton W, Emma is the wife of Charles Mitchell, of Potter County, Pa, and they have the following children—Elmer, Jennie E, Eleanor M, Louis S, Arley H, Gertrude E. and Ruby, Louis remains at home to assist his father Mr Lee served three years on the township school board He is a man of temperance and is identified with the Prohibition party

JOHN S HOLDEN, a successful agriculturist and representative citizen of Pike Township, residing on his farm of 120 acres which lies one mile northeast of Curwensville, was born in Clinton County, Pa, July 6, 1835 His parents were William and Ellen (Johnson) Holden

William Holden was born in England, where he secured his education, and although but seventeen years of age when he came to America, had already been employed by a large establishment as a bookkeeper He reached Lock Haven, Pa, in 1786, and was engaged by Judge Fleming as a scrivener, and afterward was a merchant near that town and later engaged in farming He moved from Clinton to Elk County and from there to Clearfield County, settling on the farm now owned by

Charles Addleman, afterward living on the farm now owned by the Thompsons. He had acquired a large amount of land, some 400 acres, and was considered one of the men of fortune in his day. During his last years he was somewhat incapacitated, being accidentally crippled, but he survived to be eighty-two years of age, during the larger portion of his life having been a typical Englishman, stout and hearty. He opened one coal bank in Pike Township and in other ways was very progressive and enterprising. At first a Whig in politics, he later became a Republican. The only offices he would accept were those of school director and membership on the election board. He married Ellen Johnson, who was also a native of England, and they had six children born to them in Clinton County and one in Clearfield County, namely. Algernon, who died in Clearfield County at the age of eighty-three years, married Susanna Bloom, Johnson, who resided near Curwensville at the time of death, William, who died during the Civil War, was a member of the 149th Pa Vol Inf, John S, Catherine, who resides near Curwensville, Margaret, who is deceased, and Alexander, who was a hardware merchant at Coalport at the time of death. The mother died at the age of eighty-eight years and both she and the father were buried at Oak Hill Cemetery. They were members of the Methodist Episcopal church.

John S Holden went to school through boyhood, attending sessions held in what was known as the Holden school-house, his father having donated the building for school purposes, for a period of twenty-one years. Afterward he engaged in farming, his first purchase of land being the old McClure farm of 140 acres, situated in Pike Township. He lived there for some years and then came to his present farm, which is one of great production, averaging 700 bushels of grain a year. He has sold the coal, not wishing to develop it himself, and has some thirty acres of the land in valuable timber.

Mr Holden was married in 1867 to Miss Jane Hile, who was born in Pennsylvania, a daughter of William and Ellen Hile, and died in July, 1903. She was a member of the Presbyterian church, an excellent woman in every relation of life. Six children were born to Mr and Mrs Holden. Horace, who resides at Lewisburg, Pa, married Mary Shaffer and they have four children—Cleo, Alexander, Catherine and Freda, Carrie, who is the widow of David Snyder, resides at Curwensville and has three children—Esther, Cora and Marion, Laurence, who resides in Clearfield, married a Miss Hiles and they have had five children—John, Maria, Catherine, Louisa and Robert, deceased, Ellen, who is the wife of Harry Smeal, of DuBois, has one son, Paul, Mrs Cora Tyce, who lives in Kansas City, Kansas, and Catherine, who is the wife of Donald Hiles, of Illinois. Mr Holden has been a lifelong Republican and has served as school director.

JOSEPH BEAUSEIGNEUR,* whose valuable farm of 112 acres lies fourteen miles northeast of Clearfield, in Girard Township, was born in France and was brought to America by his parents when three years of age. His father possessed capital and soon invested in 500 acres of valuable timbered land in Girard Township, this County.

The parents of Mr Beauseigneur spent the remainder of their lives here and the father cleared almost the whole of his large body of land by himself. He was recognized as a superior man in many ways and served Girard township in public offices, being acceptable as auditor and supervisor and in other capacities

Joseph Beauseigneur was reared and educated in Girard Township and after his school days were over he assisted his father and worked in his lumber camps until his marriage, after which he devoted himself to farming and stockraising He has all of his land under cultivation with the exception of twenty-five acres, on which the timber is very valuable

Mr Beauseigneur was married in 1872 to Miss Margaret Dolin, who was born, reared and educated in Boggs Township, Clearfield County Her parents were John and Anna Dolin, leading farming people of Boggs Township Previous to marriage, Mrs Beauseigneur taught school for a number of terms, both in Boggs and Girard Townships They have one daughter, Maud, who is the wife of Edgar Corbert, of Clarion, Pa Mrs Corbert was given excellent educational advantages, graduating from the Clarion Normal School, and was a popular and successful teacher, in Graham, Norris, Cooper and Girard Townships, in all of which she has a wide circle of friends Mr Beauseigneur and wife are members of St Mary's Catholic church at Frenchville

S J WISE, who resides on his valuable tract of forty-five acres, lying two and one-half miles south of Curwensville, Pa , in Pike Township, was born on this farm, July 8, 1858, and is a son of Michael and Phoebe Ann (Michaels) Wise

Michael Wise was born in Center County, Pa , in 1798, and accompanied his parents, Conrad and Margaret (Rote) Wise, to Clearfield County He remained at home until his mar-

riage and then bought land from William Sloppy, in Pike Township, on which he continued to reside until the time of his death, October 10, 1871 At the time he settled here no improvements had been made and no clearing had been done With the assistance of his neighbors, timber was cut down, logs secured, and a habitable cabin was put up all in one day On many occasions, later in life, he also gave generous help to other settlers, this good feeling being general among the pioneers. Michael Wise was a reliable man, possessed of excellent judgment and frequently he was chosen by his fellow citizens for township offices He was a stanch Democrat Both he and wife were worthy members of the Lutheran church and he was one of those who liberally contributed to the building of the church edifice at Bloomington He married Phoebe Ann Michaels, who was born April 5, 1828, and died July 28, 1908, both she and husband being buried in the Bloomington Cemetery The following children were born to them Elizabeth, who is the wife of Edward Bloom, of Penn township; Lucy, who is deceased, was the wife of L B Hile, also deceased, Sarah Jane, who is the wife of J A Johnston, of DuBois, James C , who married Gertrude Solth; Wilhelmina, who is the wife of W L Johnston, of DuBois, Aby, who is the wife of Thomas Lloyd, of Sykesville, Jefferson County, Pa , S J ; Lydia, who is the wife of Clement W Cardon, of Clearfield, Clara, who is the wife of Frank Robinson, of Curwensville; Margaret, who is the wife of Vernon Bloom, of DuBois; and Lillian, who is the wife of B B McClight, of DuBois, Pa

, S J Wise obtained his education in the old Bloomington school in Pike township and has always lived on the home farm and occupies the house which his father built after leaving the log cabin Mr Wise carries on general farming and stock raising to some extent, and has everything so arranged that he and his family live in great comfort On December 13, 1883, Mr Wise was married to Miss Elizabeth Alice Caldwell, a daughter of Reuben and Mary F Caldwell, and they have had three children, the only survivor being the youngest, Reuben C, who was born November 3, 1889, and at the time of writing (1911) is traveling in the West The eldest, Kitty Marilla, who was born April 25, 1884, died April 19, 1892, and her burial was in the Bloomington Cemetery The second daughter, Mary Priscilla, who was born December 23, 1887, died April 5, 1905 She was a beautiful girl, beloved by all who knew her and one of the brightest students of the DuBois High School Mr Wise casts his vote with the Democratic party but takes no very active part in politics and has never consented to hold any office

SAMUEL T HENDERSON, who has long been one of the prominent men and useful citizens of Houtzdale, Pa, where he started the first electric plant and now does business under the style of the Houtzdale Electric Light, Heat and Power Company, has spent the larger portion of his life in Clearfield County, but was born on the border of Huntingdon County, not far from Tyrone, Pa, August 18, 1844 He is a son of William H and a grandson of John Henderson, the latter of whom spent his life in Huntingdon County

William H Henderson was born in Huntingdon County and after he grew to manhood, operated the Tyrone saw mill for several years which was later known as McDonald's mill, and in 1850 moved to Janesville, where he was in a hotel business until he sold in 1856, when he retired to Tyrone, where he died four years later He married Elizabeth Mays, who was born in Huntingdon County, a daughter of Thomas and Jane (Gardner) Mays The following children were born to them Samuel T, Cynthia J, who is now deceased, was the wife of Charles Custard, of New York, Mary A, who is the widow of John Goss, of Philipsburg, Pa, Amanda, who is now deceased, was the wife of John Adams, Theresa, who is the widow of J Nichols, of Osceola Mills, Pa, William C, who formerly lived at Tyrone, is deceased, and Frank P, who is a resident of Ramey, Pa The mother of the above family died in 1882, at McCauley, Woodward Township, Clearfield County

Samuel T Henderson was reared and attended school in Huntingdon and Clearfield Counties and was engaged in work in the woods and on farms until the opening of the Civil War when he began to consider entering the army and his arrangements were completed by August 18, 1862, when he enlisted as a member of Co H, 110th Pa Vol Inf, contracting for three years This company went out from Tyrone and saw much hard service, participating in all the movements of the regiment and taking an important part at Fredericksburg, Chancellorsville, Gettysburg, Spottsylvania, Cold Harbor, the Wilderness and Petersburg Mr Henderson escaped all serious injury and was honorably discharged May 27, 1865, at Philadelphia, and then returned to Osceola, where he was engaged until 1876, in carpenter work From there he moved then to McCauley, in Woodward Township, where, for thirteen years he was engaged in a planing mill business In 1889 he retired from that and started the electric light plant, which he owns

Mr Henderson was married first in 1862, to Miss Margaret Hare, who was born in Indiana County, Pa, and died December 25, 1869 They had three children, but one of whom, Margaret, survived to be two years old, the others dying younger Mr Henderson was married second to Mrs Sidney C Kephart, who was born in Decatur Township, Clearfield County, and was reared in Woodward Township She died June 18, 1908 Her father was Isaac Goss and she was the widow of Martin V Kephart, who was killed during the Civil War, in front of Petersburg Mrs Kephart had two children Elmer E, who lives at Ashboro, N C, and Robbie J, who resides at Lancaster, Pa Mr and Mrs Henderson had four children, three of whom died in infancy One son, Samuel Ray, grew to manhood and was well educated For his many sterling traits of character he was admired and beloved His health failed and in the hope of restoring it he went to Denver, Col, but even that invigorating climate failed to benefit him and his death occurred there on January 16, 1911, at the early age of twenty-nine years and five months He is survived by his widow, who formerly was Mrs Mary (Birchfield) Hatch He was very popular with all who knew him and the deepest sympathy was felt for his bereaved family

Samuel T Henderson is a member of the Methodist Episcopal church at Houtzdale In his political views he is a Republican He is identified with Post No 293, G A R, at Houtzdale, and with Masonic Lodge No 515, at Osceola Mills

JAMES R CALDWELL, one of the representative men of Pike Township, a former justice of the peace and now a retired farmer, lives on the place on which he was born, July 7, 1835 He has 112 acres of valuable land lying two miles south of Curwensville, Pa His parents were Matthew and Mary (Bloom) Caldwell

Matthew Caldwell was born June 13, 1787, in Lancaster County, Pa, a son of Hugh Caldwell, who married Jane Boyd who was born in Ireland They came to Clearfield County in 1805, settling in Pike Township, near Center Church, on land that is now owned by William Lawhead At this time Matthew Caldwell was a young man and shortly afterward was married to Mary Bloom, who was a daughter of William Bloom, Sr, who had come to Clearfield County as the pioneer of this numerous and prominent family, in 1801 In 1819 Matthew Caldwell moved on the farm in Pike Township which is now the property of his son, James R, having to cut a road through the dense forest in order to reach his property. He was a man of endurance and enterprise and lived into old age on the farm that he had developed out of the wilderness His death occurred April 24, 1869, when he was eighty-one years old and his burial was on his own land, and when his wife passed away she was laid by his side She was born September 25, 1792, and died May 17, 1877, having been the mother of twenty children, as follows· Elizabeth, Annie, Jane, Mary, Margie, Isaac, Samuel, three infants, deceased, Hannah, Nancy, Gary B, Reuben, Lavina, Matthew, Sarah, J R, Harriet and Theresa For forty years Matthew Caldwell was an elder in the Presbyterian church

James R Caldwell attended school at Bloomington until he was old enough to do his share of the farming in the summer time and partake of the hard labors that attended lumbering in the winter season For many years before he retired from active labor he followed farming and stock raising and was known as one of the leading agriculturists of Pike Township, and still is a member of Lawrence Grange Mr Caldwell is a stockholder in the Curwensville National Bank He has traveled a great deal having been east as far as the Atlantic Ocean, west as far as the Pacific Ocean, north as far as the Great Lakes and south as far as the Gulf of Mexico

In January, 1868, Mr Caldwell was married to Hannah Carey, who was born in Jefferson County, Pa, and died August 3, 1872 Her burial was in the Clearfield Cemetery Mr Caldwell has two children Merritt A, who operates one of his father's farms, is in the coal business by lease and a stockholder and a director of the Curwensville National Bank, married Nora Gearhart, of Huntingdon County, and they have one child, Attie, and Merilla, who is the wife of W R McGowen, of Monessen, Pa Mr Caldwell belongs to the Masons and the Odd Fellows He is a Democrat in politics and has filled many township offices, for ten years being a justice of the peace in Pike Township

FRANCIS W HARPER, M D, a well known and public spirited citizen of Irvona, Pa, where for the past fifteen years he has been actively engaged in the practice of medicine, was born September 17, 1865, in Williamsport, Lycoming County, Pa, and is a son of John D and Mary J (Marshall) Harper

The parents of Dr Harper were both natives of Lycoming County, Pa, where the father died about 1890, in his fifty-sixth year, while the mother still survives and makes her home there They were the parents of eight children, namely J M, a resident of Niagara, N Y, H A, an engineer of Williamsport, Cora B, the wife of Rev G L Lovell, of Salem, Ore, Bessie V, the wife of Charles Woods, of Williamsport, Pa, Dr Francis W, and May, Margret and Maud, all three deceased

Francis W Harper received his primary educational training in the public schools of Williamsport and Lycoming County, after leaving which he engaged in teaching school for eight years, and at the end of this time, deciding on the practice of medicine as his life work, he entered the College of Physicians and Surgeons at Baltimore, in 1893, graduating with the class of 1896 He first chose the town of Glen Hope as his field of practice, but after one month there decided to locate in Irvona, where he has since built up a large and lucrative practice For fifteen years he has also conducted a drug store here, and he is known to take a leading part in any movement which has for its object the advancement of his community He is prominently connected fraternally, belonging to McKinley Lodge No 171, Knights of Pythias, Irvona Lodge, No 152, Knights of the Mystic Chain, Tyrone Lodge No 212, Elks, Coalport Conclave No 684, I O H and Coalport Lodge No 350, Loyal Order of Moose He is also a member of the Clearfield County Medical Society His politics are those of the Republican party and he is a school director of Irvona borough

Dr Harper was married to Miss Alice M. Waltz, the daughter of S F Waltz, of Lycoming County, Pa, and to this union there have been born three children, namely Marion C, Gertrude H, and Jennie Evelyn (deceased)

CAPT JOHN H NORRIS, an honored veteran of the Civil War and commander of

the John Kratzer Post, No 184, G A R, at
Curwensville, Pa, was born in Greenwood
Township, Clearfield County, Pa, March 26,
1840, and belongs to a family that was established in Clearfield County in 1812   His father was John Norris and his grandfather was
Moses Norris

Moses Norris was born in Huntingdon
County, Pa, and was twenty-one years old
when he came to Clearfield County, locating
with his father in Lawrence Township, within
three miles of Curwensville   The latter bought
1000 acres of land and of this, Moses, probably, was given 600 acres   Moses Norris married Sarah Read, who was a niece of Col
Read, who was a Revolutionary soldier

John Norris, son of Moses and Sarah Norris, was born in Clearfield County and at the
time of his marriage resided in Pike Township
He was a school teacher for many years and
changed his residence to accommodate his professional engagements, from the Clark Brown
place to Hoyt's Dam, farther up the river, and
then back to the old homestead in Pike Township, where he resided until the close of his
life, at the age of eighty-two years   He was
a Whig in his early political faith and later became a Republican   He was widely known,
his home being one of exceeding hospitality
A man of sterling character, he gave hearty
support to all law abiding movements and was
a liberal contributor to the Methodist Episcopal church, of which religious body the Norris
family have been members for generations
John Norris married Priscilla Bloom, who was
a daughter of Isaac Bloom and a granddaughter of William Bloom, who was a soldier in the
Revolutionary War   There were sixteen children born to John and Priscilla Norris, namely
Sarah, who is deceased, was the wife of Capt

Thomas Moore, and they had two children—
James and Willis, Thomas, who is deceased,
married Mary Jane Askey, and they lived near
New Millport, Mary Janes, who is the wife of
John Star, of Pike Township, and they have
two children—Merritt and Anna, John H,
James, who is a resident of Pike Township,
married Martha A Caldwell, I B, who married Anna, daughter of William Caldwell, has
had three children—Lewis C, J W and
Charles B, M C, who is a resident of Pike
township, married Maria Hockman, Martha,
deceased, was the wife of Jonathan Kirk, who
is also deceased, Clark, who lives in Pike
township, married Sadie Wall, Elizabeth, who
is the wife of James Cassidy, residing at Curwensville, George, who is a resident of West
Clearfield, married a Miss Gulick, Margaret,
who is the wife of Isaac Stage, of West Clearfield, Wesley, who lives in West Clearfield,
married Bertha Brown, Lavina, who is the
wife of T J Wall, of Penn township, William, who is deceased, is survived by his
widow, who lives at Philadelphia, and Ord,
who lives on the old homestead in Pike township, married a Miss Way   The mother of
the above family died at the age of sixty-five
years and both she and her husband were
buried in Oak Hill Cemetery   The old homestead farm contains 250 acres

John H Norris obtained his education in
the district schools of Pike Township, beginning to work in the lumber regions as soon as
old enough   He also learned the carpenter
trade and followed that in the summers and
continued to work through the winters at lumbering until he enlisted for service in the Civil
War   He became a member of Co K, Kane
Rifles, the 13th Pa Reserves, which became famous as the Bucktails, a name which subse-

quently carried dismay into many a Confederate regiment, so great was the fear engendered by the dashing courage of this brave and fearless body of soldiers Mr Norris was made corporal of his company and was promoted to be second sergeant before the expiration of his first term of enlistment He immediately reenlisted, becoming second lieutenant of a company in the 190th Pa Vol Inf, later was made first lieutenant and just at the close of the war received his captain's commission He was twice captured by the enemy, first, in June, 1862, near Richmond, Va, and second, on August 19, 1864, at the Weldon Railroad During both of his terms of imprisonment he became well acquainted with the terrors of Belle Isle and Libby Prison, passing fifty-three days in the first place and sixty days in the second, after which he was paroled His condition was such that he was detailed to light duty only, at Carlisle, Pa, and it was while there that he received his commission as captain, a just recognition of his valor and worth as a soldier He was honorably discharged in 1865 and returned to his home in Pike Township In resuming peaceful pursuits, Captain Norris no doubt, for a long time, felt the results of his years of hardship and exposure Later he accepted an appointment as revenue inspector of York County, Pa, and served in that office with entire efficiency for three years He then returned to Curwensville and subsequently resumed his former activities, engaging in lumbering and carpentering as before

Captain Norris was married March 1, 1864, to Miss Hannah Cecelia McCleary, a daughter of Joseph and Elizabeth (Johnston) McCleary, of Lancaster County, Pa, and they have had four children, namely William, who resides at Grampian, Clearfield County, married Ada

Thurston, and they have one daughter, Myrtle, Aletha, who is a professional nurse at Atlantic City, Nannie, who is a clerk in a store at Albany, N Y, and Franklin, who died when aged six years and seven months and was buried at Oak Hill Cemetery Captain Norris is a steward in the Methodist Episcopal church at Curwensville He belongs to the order of Odd Fellows at Curwensville and has served for two years as commander of the G A R Post mentioned above He was elected a member of the lower house in the State Legislature at Harrisburg on the Democratic ticket on which ticket his father was once elected a county commissioner of Clearfield County

GEORGE J BAUMMER, superintendent of the Cascade Coal and Coke Company, and manager of the Tyler Mercantile Company at Tyler, Pa, who has some timber interests additionally, has been a resident of this place since 1897 He was born September 27, 1872, at Baltimore, Md, and is a son of Sigmund and Geraldine Antoinette (Siebertz) Baum128mer

Sigmund Baummer was born in Bavaria, Germany, and his wife in Maryland By trade Mr Baummer was a cooper and also learned whiskey compounding He accompanied his parents, Christopher Baummer and wife, from Germany to America and was reared at Baltimore, Md, where he spent the remainder of his life, from eight years, his death occurring in 1878, at the age of forty-two years His widow still lives in the city of Baltimore They had four children, namely Elizabeth, who is the wife of F G Michel, lives at Baltimore, John C, who also makes his home in that city, Catherine, who is the wife of H B Schutte, also resides at Baltimore, and George John, of the present record

George John Baummer secured his education in the parochial schools of Baltimore,
after which he began his business career as a
clerk in a grain and feed store, being then thirteen years of age   He proved a reliable, industrious youth and remained with the same
firm for seven years   He then assisted to com-
pile the Baltimore City Directory while still a
resident there   In 1897 he came to Tyler and
accepted a clerkship with the Keystone Store
Company and became its manager, succeeding
Geo W Imhof in 1905. Mr Baummer being
retained with the new firm   In 1910 he was
made superintendent of the Cascade Coal and
Coke Company, succeeding W H Laverack
This is an important enterprise of this section,
doing a large amount of business all over the
country   Mr Baummer is interested in large
tracts of timber lands in Elk and Clearfield
counties which supply this company, and also
has a foreign exchange

On February 18, 1901, Mr Baummer was
married to Miss Elizabeth K Bauer, a daughter of Leonard Bauer, of DuBois, Pa , and
they have six children   Sigismunda G , Ju-
lian L , Theophila M , Virginia I , George J ,
Jr , and Elizabeth K   Mr Baummer and family belong to St Anislaus Roman Catholic
church   In politics he is a Democrat   He is
identified with the Knights of Columbus at
DuBois   He is one of the representative citizens and prosperous business men of Huston
township

D H. BARNETT, general farmer and
well known and highly respected citizen of
Knox township, Clearfield county, Pa , where
he owns 125 acres of valuable land, is also a
survivor of the great Civil war and for five
years has served as commander of Post No

179, G A. R , at Clearfield   Mr Barnett was
born in Jefferson county, Pa , and is a son of
Seneca and Hannah (Snyder) Barnett. They
were lifelong residents of Jefferson county
and the father was accidentally killed in a coal
bank there

D H Barnett attended the country schools
in his boyhood and remained in Jefferson
county until 1860, when he came to Clearfield
county, but returned to Jefferson in the following year and enlisted for service in the
Civil war   He became a member of Co B,
78th Pa Vol Inf , and continued in the army
for thirty-nine months, taking part in many
battles and performing his full duty as a soldier   When he was honorably discharged, on
the day of the second election of President
Lincoln, it was with the rank of corporal   In
the fall of 1865 he came back to Clearfield
county and engaged in lumbering within three
miles of his present farm, on which he settled
after his marriage, in November, 1866   He
now owns 125 acres, as stated above, and has
105 acres cleared, having cleared eighty-five
of them by his own industry   He carries on
general farming and raises some excellent
stock   In politics he is a Republican but holds
no township office   He has preserved his
memories of the Civil war through his association with his military comrades, and not only
has taken a very active part in Grand Army
affairs but belongs also to the order of Patriotic Sons of America

In the fall of 1866, Mr Barnett was married to Miss Cornelia Chase, a daughter of
John M Chase, and the following children
were born to them   Jennie, who is the wife
of Clark Fox, of Knox township; John M ,
who was accidentally killed by a horse, on
Lick Run, at the age of twenty-seven years,

D. H. BARNETT

and was survived by a widow, formerly Miss Mary Dunlap, Maggie, who is the wife of Grant Haines, of Knox township, William A, who was accidentally killed at the Faunce clay mine, July 25, 1901, and was survived by a widow, formerly Miss Susie Rowles, Hannah, who is the wife of D W Bowman, of Echo, Ore , Jesse, who residing in Knox township, who married Jane, a daughter of Jefferson Baughman, of Woodward township, Hattie, who lives at home, Benjamin D, who is a popular and successful county school teacher, now engaged at the Boardman school, Clark, who gives his father assistance at home, Esther C, who is teaching her second term at Stoneville, and Ralph C, who attends school in Knox township Mr Barnett has given his children all educational opportunities within his power and they have developed into intelligent, well informed and earnest young people reflecting credit upon their parents and community Mr Barnett and family are members of the Methodist Episcopal church

G O GOSS, farmer and dairyman, who resides on his valuable farm of 100 acres of land situated three miles north of Curwensville, in Pike township, was born in Center county, Pa , September 5, 1862, and is a son of Adam and Harriet (Keys) Goss

Adam Goss was a general farmer in Half Moon township, Center county, where he died in 1870 His widow survived until 1876 They had four sons G O, James F, Joseph H and William F, all of whom reside in Center county except the eldest Adam Goss and wife were members of the Methodist Episcopal church He never cared for political of-

fice but was a good citizen of his community and a member of the Republican party

G O Goss was reared and educated in Center county After his marriage he moved to Blair county, where he engaged in farming for two years and in 1890 came to his present farm, where he has continued ever since All his land has been cleared with the exception of ten acres He engages in general farming and also delivers about thirty quarts of milk daily to the Curwensville milk depot Mr Goss has done considerable improving since he settled on this farm, including the building of his comfortable residence He is a practical, hard working man, one who takes a deep interest in his business and keeps himself thoroughly posted along agricultural lines through his membership in the local Grange, and the county agricultural society

Mr Goss was married in March, 1888, to Miss Alice Neeper, a daughter of Robert R and Jane Neeper, and they have one son, Lloyd, who resides at home Mr Goss is a Republican in politics and has held various township office He is one of the well known and highly respected citizens of Pike township

WILLIAM TUTTLE MAHAFFEY, a retired banker and lumberman of Cherry Tree, Pa , is one of the best known citizens of this part of Clearfield county, and a man highly thought of wherever known He was born at Locust Villa, the old Mahaffey homestead one mile below Cherry Tree, June 25, 1848, son of John and Ella (Byers) Mahaffey Both the Mahaffey and Byers families are well known and respected ones in Clearfield county A sister of our subject, Margaret B, is the wife of Porter Kinports, of Cherry Tree W T and Margaret B are the only surviving members of John Mahaffey's family that are living at this time in Cherry Tree

William T Mahaffey, after completing his school studies about 1864, took an active part in the war, being drum major of Co D, 78th Regiment. P V He was only thirteen years old at the beginning of the war After the war, in 1869, he engaged in teaching school, which occupation he followed for some seven years, making a great success along this line of work About the time of his marriage in 1876 he entered into the mercantile business, conducting a store for two years at Cherry Tree and during this time was also associated with his father in the lumber business He then engaged in the manufacture of farm, lumber and saw-mill machinery This business which he purchased was the first one of its kind established in northern Pennsylvania, the factory having been built in 1844, and after buying it he continued to operate the concern for twenty-one years He then sold out and was engaged in the lumber business for six years subsequently being one of a company and a director of the company called the St Lawrence Broom & Manufacturing Company, of West Virginia, owning and operating one of the largest and heaviest timber tracts in the state of West Virginia, consisting of 86,000 acres The company called St Lawrence Broom & Manufacturing Company consisted of eight partners, Mr Mahaffey being one of the directors He still owns considerable timber land, besides other real estate In 1902 Mr Mahaffey was also one of the founders of the First National Bank of Cherry Tree, of which he is still a director He was a founder and president of the Cherry Tree Electric

Light Company, and founder and a director of the Cherry Tree Water Company. He has also valuable coal interests in this vicinity As will be seen Mr Mahaffey has been a man of wide and strenuous activities, though now retired from active business life In 1876 he united with the Methodist Protestant church of Cherry Tree but afterward united with the Presbyterian church, and has for many years been active in Sabbath school work, serving now as president of District No 2, of Indiana county Mr Mahaffey was formerly a Republican in politics, but has joined what is known as the Keystone party In 1909 he made a special trip to visit the old home of the Mahaffey family at Dublin, Ireland On this occasion he gathered valuable data in regard to the ancestral history of the Mahaffey's, a subject in which he is much interested, as during a year or more he has been engaged in compiling a history of the family that will be of much interest and value when completed He is president of an organized society that holds annual reunions of the Mahaffey clan each year They meet this year, 1911, in the city of Williamsport, the home of Thomas Mahaffey, who came from Donegal county, Ireland, and settled here in 1723

Mr Mahaffey married Julia Jane, eldest daughter of Col Clark and Hettie (Graham) Patchin, and he and his wife have been the parents of children as follows John C, born September 18, 1877, is cashier in the Cherry Tree Bank He married Mary Beyer, daughter of Dr Beyer of Punxatawney, Pa. Leroy, born October 10, 1879, is a dentist following his profession in Pittsburg Graham Garfield, born July 28, 1881, is deceased Hettie Ellen, born November 2, 1883, is unmarried and resides at home Boyd Tuttle, born April

20, 1886, is superintendent for the Pennsylvania Coal Co, at Amsbry, Cambria county, Pa Crissie C, born January 27, 1888, is residing at home

Mrs Julia J Mahaffey, the mother of the above mentioned children, died October 3. 1894 She was an earnest Christian woman, and an active member of the Methodist church, which she joined at the age of 14 years Mr Mahaffey was again married, December 18, 1902, to Sarah Edmonson, of Glassport, Pa, and she resides with her husband in Cherry Tree She is a lady highly esteemed, and is a very earnest church and Sabbath school worker

JAMES MAHAFFEY, proprietor of the Hotel Windsor, situated on the corner of Market and Third streets, Clearfield, Pa, is a representative citizen of Clearfield county, of which he formerly was sheriff He belongs to one of the old settled county families and was born November 4, 1843, at the village of Mahaffey, which was named in honor of his father, in Clearfield county, Pa His parents were Robert and Mary (McGee) Mahaffey

Robert Mahaffey was born in Lycoming county, Pa, and was a young man when he accompanied his father, William Mahaffey, to Clearfield county The latter was a pioneer of the best class, energetic and enterprising, and made the earliest improvements at what is now Burnside, Clearfield county He was a farmer and lumberman during his active years and lived to be an octogenarian His eight children, bearing the following names, are all deceased· William, Robert, James, John, Thomas, Moses, Hannah and Jane Robert Mahaffey equaled his father in enterprise He engaged also in lumbering and later cleared up

a large farm in Bell township and also conducted a general store and in addition, operated a mill His various enterprises prospered and each one assisted in the developing of the other and ere long many settlers had been attracted to his neighborhood, a village resulted and in his honor was named for the man of energy and progress, who had had the foresight to select this certain section of the wilderness as his place of investment Robert Mahaffey continued to live at Mahaffey until the close of a long and busy life, his death occurring in 1900, at the age of eighty-six years

Robert Mahaffey was married first to Mary McGee, who was survived by three children William, James, and Mary, who became the wife of John Byers Robert Mahaffey was married a second time, to Catherine Johnston, who resides at Mahaffey Seven children were born to the later marriage, namely. Robert F Emery, who is deceased, Elizabeth, who is the widow of George M Ferguson, who formerly was register and recorder in Clearfield county, Nancy Jane, who is the wife of George W Jose, of La Jose, Clearfield county, Alice, who is the wife of Frank K Patterson, of Pittsburgh, Elsie, who is the wife of Bert Galatley, of Pittsburg, and Harry B, who resides with his mother on the old home place The old homestead at the present time is owned by Robert F Mahaffey and Harry B Mahaffey It was one of the first farms in Clearfield county cleared from the forest and is situated at the mouth of Chest Creek, on the Susquehanna river, the town site of Mahaffey Valuable veins of coal and fire clay underlay the homestead and the surrounding property, all of which is very valuable

James Mahaffey attended the public schools of Mahaffey and in 1864 became a student in

the Iron City College, Pittsburg, where he remained one year When he turned his attention to business he found it practicable and
profitable for him to engage in lumbering and
he continued in this industry until 1905 For
many years he also owned a valuable farm in
Bell township, which he improved with handsome buildings, but later disposed of it In
1879 he was elected sheriff of Clearfield
county, on the Democratic ticket and served
with marked efficiency until 1883, retiring
from office with the good will of all his fellow
citizens with the exception of those who, in
his official capacity, he had been forced to treat
as law-breakers He had many experiences in
the line of public duty but discharged his often
troublesome obligations with fidelity and without any flavor of sensationalism In 1884,
Sheriff Mahaffey built the Windsor Hotel, a
brick structure containing forty-five sleeping
apartments and equipped throughout with all
modern conveniences He is a model host and
his friends and patrons are in every part of the
county His table is supplied directly from his
own truck farm, lying on the edge of Clearfield, and the traveling public is very appreciative of these luxuries Mr Mahaffey owns
considerable real estate in the east end of
Clearfield, which he has greatly improved, and
also owns realty at Mahaffey and at Chicago,
Ill, and at Long Island, N Y

Mr Mahaffey was married in 1872, to Miss
Jane Thompson, who died July 3, 1898 Seven
children survived, namely. James Guy, who
married Agnes Hunter, Robert Paul, Malcolm A, who married Lorilla Gaylor, Eugene,
who married Bertha Flood, Charles, who
married Goldie Reed, Daisy, who is the wife
of Chester Heller, and Huston P Albert and
Walter died young Mr Mahaffey is a Thirty-second degree Mason and belongs also to
the Odd Fellows, the Elks and the Moose

C P ROWLES, one of Clearfield county's
representative and substantial citizens, who
resides on his farm of 166 acres, situated in Pike township, two miles from Curwensville, owns also a farm of 200 acres
which lies in Lawrence township He was
born in Lawrence township, Clearfield county,
Pa, September 19, 1846, and is a son of Titus
Harry Rowles and a grandson of John
Rowles, the latter of whom was one of the pioneers in Lawrence township, where all of his
children were born

Titus Harry Rowles had but little schooling
but nevertheless developed into a shrewd business man and a sensible and useful citizen He
engaged in farming and owned fifty acres of
land, which his son, C P, now owns, and
spent his life in its cultivation He was a
Democrat in politics and at different times was
elected to township offices in which he served
honestly and efficiently He was a leading
member of the Baptist church in Lawrence
township His death occurred April 15, 1865,
and his burial was in the Bloomington cemetery He married Susanna Arthur, a daughter of John Arthur, of Jefferson county, Pa
She died April 20, 1885, and her burial was
by the side of her husband They had the following children· Joanna, who is the widow of
James Norris, Lucinda, who is deceased, was
the wife of Reese Trude, Samuel, who resides
in Lawrence township, Eliza, who is the wife
of Jonathan Bowman, of Pike township, Robert, who lives in Pike township, C P., Lewis,
who is deceased, who married Anna Cathcart;
John, who married Lydia Curry, and lives in
Lawrence township, and George W, who

married Mary Harbaugh, and lives in Knox township

C P Rowles was nine years old before he had an opportunity to go to school and then received his first instruction at Crooked Run, where a small building was utilized, one that may be compared to the structure in which he at present houses his winter coal After that he attended the Montcalm school and then the pupils were expected to be on hand six days in the week Afterward he began to work at lumbering and continued it as a side line, until 1902, although farming has been his main business Following his marriage he rented the David Brown farm, near the homestead, and lived on it until he purchased his present home farm from Lewis I Bloom, who erected the buildings on the place

Mr Rowles was married in March, 1868, to Miss Mary Swatsworth, a daughter of Rudolph Swatsworth, of Lawrence township, in which she was born, June 11, 1849 Nine children have been born to Mr and Mrs Rowles, and it is very gratifying to Mr Rowles to know that he has enough land to enable him to give each one a farm The following list includes children and grandchildren. The eldest, Alonzo Rowles, was born July 5, 1868 He married Alice Addleman, a daughter of John Addleman, and they have one daughter, Stella Philip Rowles was born October 26, 1869 He married Myrtle McKee, and they had four children C P, Foster, Mary and Robert Calvin Rowles was born June 24, 1872 He married Laura Bloom and they live in Knox township and have three children Roland, Maude and Guy Winfield S Rowles was born April 6, 1874, married Sadie Lord and they live in Lawrence township They have three children Lloyd,

Grace and Harvey Cynthia Rowles was born November 17, 1875, and married George Aughenbaugh They have had five children: Howard, Curtis, Myrtle, Lettie and Walter Mr Aughenbaugh and family live at Lumber City Alice Rowles was born August 22, 1878, married William Howell and they live at Glen Richey, Pa They have three children Cynthia, Oland and William Arthur Rowles was born March 24, 1882 and lives in Lawrence township He married Lillie Smith and they have had three children: Ethel, Myrtle and Mamie Jesse and Myrtle Rowles, the youngest members of the family, are twins and were born September 12, 1885, and reside at home Mr Rowles and family are members of the Methodist Episcopal church In politics he is a Republican and served as county commissioner from 1903 to 1909, and also two terms as school director He belongs to the Grange at Curwensville

WILLIAM M BOYCE, county treasurer of Clearfield county, Pa, a member of one of the substantial old county families and a well known citizen, was born April 12, 1866, in Clearfield county, one of a family of ten children born to his parents, Samuel and Sarah (Mullin) Boyce

William M Boyce was reared on his father's farm in Clearfield county and was educated in the public schools His father died in 1883 and he then went into the livery business which he successfully conducted for some time and to a degree was also interested in farming and lumbering From early manhood he has been active in politics and has served efficiently in public office, at one time being steward of the Clearfield County Home In 1908 he was elected treasurer of Clearfield

43

county, by a majority of 500 votes, and served one term three years, commanding the respect and confidence of his fellow citizens to the fullest extent.

Mr Boyce was married to a daughter of the late Henry D Straw, who was once an extensive lumberman in this section, and four children have been born to this union Mr Boyce and family are members of the Methodist Episcopal church

JOHN R DUNLAP, who owns the old family homestead in Knox township, a valuable farm of 139 acres, situated one and one-quarter miles east of Olanta, was born here November 1, 1833, in a double log house which his father built when he entered this land from the Government His parents were Isaac and Anna (Jordon) Dunlap

Isaac Dunlap was born in Clearfield county, February 8, 1805, a son of William Dunlap, who was one of the earliest county commissioners Isaac Dunlap cleared a part of this farm, with the help of his sons, and all but thirty-nine acres are now under cultivation He married Anna Jordon, a daughter of Thomas Jordon, of Lawrence township, and they became the parents of six sons and four daughters, eight of the family still surviving Isaac Dunlap was a representative man of his neighborhood during life and both he and wife lived so worthily that the world was better for their having been in it They were valued members of Fruit Hill Presbyterian church and their burial was in the cemetery attached, his death occurring in July, 1868 His widow survived him many years, reaching her eighty-fourth birthday

John R Dunlap obtained his education in the Pleasant Ridge district school, after which he gave his attention to farm work and in 1868, after the death of his father, purchased the homestead For many years he carried on general farming and stockraising with satisfactory results, but has now shifted his responsibilities to the broad shoulders of his sons and lives in comfortable retirement

Mr Dunlap was married August 28, 1856, to Miss Jemima Bloom, a daughter of ex-Judge James Bloom, and a family of thirteen children was born to them, but all of them did not reach mature years Emory Walter, the eldest son, is deceased Nora is the wife of W W Cathcart Twin sons died in infancy. Warren B resides in Knox township Melissa is the wife of William Rowles Lewis C. married Ida Bloom John J lives in Knox township Harry and James B, are both deceased Mary makes her home in St Louis. Clark married Bertha Bloom Luther Y, the youngest of the family, manages the home farm

As far back as the records go, the Dunlap men have given support to the Democratic party Formerly Mr Dunlap acceptably filled numerous township offices but no longer accepts these responsibilities He and wife are members of Mt Zion Methodist Episcopal church

HON JOSEPH ALEXANDER, of Bigler township, Clearfield county, who is now serving as state senator, is a man who has filled many positions of trust to the satisfaction of the public, his abilities having won for him recognition as one of the leaders of the Republican party in this section As a descendant of one of the oldest and most influential families in the country, he has the advantage of an honored name, to which his career has added new distinction

The Alexander family is of Scotch-Irish blood, descendants of James Alexander, who served under Gen Washington during the memorable winter at Valley Forge, Pa , 1777-78, as an officer in the commissary department He settled in Kishacoquillas Valley, in Cumberland county, Pa , part now Mifflin county, Pa Having heard from John Reed, an old hunter and trapper, a favorable report of the lands lying on Clearfield Creek, he in 1784 took out warrants for four tracts of land The first, which he entered in his own name, cornered on the creek at what was then a small ash sapling but grew to be a large tree, which was washed away some time in the seventies Upon it were legible the letters, "J A " and "J R ," which were cut there at that early date as the initials of his own name and that of his friend, John Reed This ash tree was the oldest land mark on the creek, and had an important part in the court trials concerning lands in that region, because the James Alexander warrant, being the oldest, was the starting point to determine other surveys and warrants This land begins at the head of the narrows and lies mostly on the northeast side of the creek On the opposite side he located the John McConnell tract, and farther up the creek he located the John McGill and Cullen tracts His friend, William Brown, located six other tracts still further up the creek, extending to what was called the Crab Orchard

About midsummer of the year 1785, James Alexander returned again to his lands on Clearfield Creek, accompanied by his eldest son, Robert They went by way of Lock Haven, then Great or Big Island on the Sus-

quehanna river, and procured there a flat-boat which they pushed with poles and dragged partly by means of a horse all the way to Muddy Run, a tributary of Clearfield Creek With them they took provisions for a somewhat protracted stay The exposure endured on this trip is said to have had a serious effect on the health of James Alexander, although he did not die until six years later, in 1791 John Reed, the hunter, was in their company during a part of the journey, having crossed the mountains by an Indian path to meet them at a point on the Susquehanna river While ascending the Clearfield Creek at a place now unknown John Reed and Robert Alexander crossed over a hill, while James Alexander kept to the stream with the horse and boat In crossing the hill they discovered a shining ore, some pieces of which John Reed put in his shot pouch He afterward reported that, having sent this ore to Philadelphia, the mint had returned a silver coin, many persons saw this coin, which he alleged had been made from the discovered ore Many a treasure seeker sought diligently for the spot where the ore was found, but in vain

When dividing his lands, James Alexander gave his four younger sons—Hugh, Reed, Joseph, and William B—the four tracts on Clearfield Creek Three of them sold their claims to Sir Henry Philips, a gentleman from England, but William B not only refused to sell what his father had left him, but secreted himself for two days that he might not be solicited to agree to the papers needed to legalize the other sales His brothers finally induced him to agree to their transfer by promising him his choice of the four tracts of land

William B Alexander was born in Kishacoquillas Valley, March 27, 1782 He was named after the lifelong friend of his father, Judge William Brown, who was a very early settler of what is now Mifflin (then a part of Cumberland) county, and a well known and highly respected citizen In the year 1800, when eighteen years of age, William B Alexander visited the lands in Clearfield county (then part of Huntingdon county) and made choice of a tract which his father had entered in his own name It is worth recording that on this journey to Clearfield he took with him a pint of appleseed from Kishacoquillas Valley and gave it for planting to an old man who lived several miles from his lands Nine years later, when he came to settle on his tract, he planted an orchard of trees grown from that seed, now well known as the old Alexander orchard After making his choice and before settling, he made what was then a long journey westward on horseback, visiting West Virginia, Ohio and Kentucky On his return he stated that 200 acres of land, part of the present site of Wheeling, W Va, were offered to him for the horse which he rode, so cheap was the land in that section at that time

On April 23, 1806, soon after his return, William B Alexander married Miss Nancy Davis, daughter of John Davis, of Kishacoquillas. He then rented a farm and remained in that valley three years longer, but in 1809 he moved to Clearfield county, following an Indian path across the Allegheny Mountains, and conveying his wife and two young children and all his effects on pack horses He settled upon the estate, which he continued to occupy until a few months before his death To illustrate the inconveniences and discomforts of that early settlement, we need only state the fact that for many years he was obliged to go forty miles across the mountains on horseback along Indian paths to reach a mill

William B Alexander died at the residence of his son, William B, March 30, 1862, aged eighty years and three days His wife, Nancy D Alexander, died at the old homestead, April 1, 1861, aged seventy-three years and, six months They were the parents of thirteen children, eleven of whom lived until after the death of their father. William B Alexander Jr, the father of our subject, was a resident of Decatur township, later the part erected into Woodward township

Hon Joseph Alexander was born on his father's farm in a log house of the earlier days. He has been extensively engaged in agriculture and lumbering, and as a business man ranks among the best in his locality. He has an honorable war record as a member of Company B, 149th P. V I, of the famous "Bucktail Brigade," in which he enlisted August 14, 1862, and served until the close of the war He took part in many important battles, and was wounded during the first day of the Battle at Gettysburg in the charge by General Stone's brigade at the railroad cut He remained on the field all day and in the evening was carried by colored stretcher-bearers of the Confederate army to a barn on the McPherson farm, where he lay upon some straw until the early morning of July 4th, when Lee abandoned the place In the closing days of the war Mr. Alexander's regiment was sent north to recruit and to guard prisoners at Elmira, N Y Mr Alexander was detailed on detached service, was a member of the guard of honor that escorted the remains of the lamented Lincoln from the White House to the capitol, where the dead President lay in state for some time Mr Alexander served the remaining period of his service as orderly, mostly at the Old Capitol Prison during the trial of the conspirators who plotted the assassination of the president Mr Alexander was discharged from the service June 27, 1865, and in leaving the army was given the following commendation, signed by the officers with whom he had been associated during his detached service

"We, the undersigned, take great pleasure in certifying that 'Orderly' Alexander, late of Company B, 149th Pennsylvania Volunteers, since being in special service, has done his duty as a soldier and conducted himself as becoming a gentleman We can cheerfully recommend him for any position that he is capable of filling, as a trusty and faithful man, strictly temperate and willing to make himself useful"

Very respectfully, etc ,
(Signed) Lieut Walter F Halleck,
Capt J H Bassler,
Maj George Bowers

Mr Alexander has always been an ardent Republican, his first vote having been cast for Lincoln, while he was in the army Until recent years the Democratic party has had a large majority in his locality, but this is now reversed Notwithstanding the odds against him in the earlier days, he was chosen to various positions in Woodward township, serving as town clerk, auditor, supervisor and overseer of the poor, and for two terms as assessor, he was also a school director in the Madera independent district On the formation of Bigler township, he was chosen assessor and held the office three consecutive terms, and one term as school director In 1880 he was appointed census enumerator for his district, and his

work was specially commended by the supervisor of census, J Simpson Africa He also served three years as jury commissioner and with Dr J P Burchfield, his colleague, inaugurated reforms in the selecting of jurors In 1883 he was nominated for the office of prothonotary, unexpectedly and made no canvass , but at the election he led his ticket, although his opponent was no less a personage than the Hon James Kerr His well proven ability and strict integrity won for him the confidence of all classes, his election as representative of his native county three terms in the legislature indicating his hold upon the popular regard He is now senator of the Thirty-fourth Senatorial district of Pennsylvania, comprising the two large central counties of the state—Center and Clearfield

CAPT J ELLIOTT KRATZER, justice of the peace at Curwensville, Pa , and a representative citizen of Pike township, is also an honored veteran of the Civil war, during which stormy period he experienced some of the greatest hardships of a soldier's life but also gained distinction and promotion for unusual bravery Captain Kratzer was born in Pike township, Clearfield county, Pa , January 14, 1837, and is a son of Anthony and Rachel (Hoover) Kratzer

Anthony Kratzer was born in Blair county, Pa , but from early manhood his life was passed in Clearfield county He engaged in lumbering and lived at Curwensville until after his marriage and the birth of six children, when he moved on his farm in Pike township, where he engaged in farming and milling He was a man of more than ordinary business capacity and although he died at the comparatively early age of forty-six years, he had accumulated 600 acres of land in Pike township By trade he was a shoemaker and at one time he also conducted a hotel at Curwensville, on the present site of the Park House He was a Democrat in his political views but never consented to hold office His ashes rest in Oak Grove cemetery Anthony Kratzer married Rachel Hoover, who was born in Clearfield county. She survived her husband for a long period, her death occurring at the age of eighty-five years and her burial being in the State of California The children born to Anthony and Rachel Kratzer were as follows Jane Ann, who died in California, was the wife of James Addleman; J Elliott, James, who is a resident of Wisconsin, married Susan Leech; William, who was killed at the battle of Chancellorsville, during the Civil war, was a member of a Pennsylvania regiment, Louella, who is the wife of John Bacher, of California, Sarah Ann, who is a resident of California; John, who was killed at Bull Run, during the Civil war, was a member of Co K, 42nd Pa Vol Inf, and Edward, who is a resident of Punxsutawney, Pa The parents of the above family were members of the Presbyterian church

J Elliott Kratzer attended school at Clearfield, where he had academic advantages, after which he engaged in business as a clerk in a store at Curwensville and then went west to Iowa where, for two years, he served as bookkeeper in a business house It is probable that homesickness brought him back to Curwensville and after reaching home he took charge of his father's mill and operated it until the outbreak of the Rebellion He was one of the first to offer himself when the famous "Bucktail" Regiment, the 42nd Pa Vol Inf, was organized, becoming sergeant of Co K, of

which he later was made second lieutenant He served one and one-half years with that rank and later was commissioned captain of Co H, 190th P V. It was while serving as second lieutenant of Co K, that he was wounded at Gettysburg, in the right arm, just above the elbow After he was commissioned captain and was inspecting the 3rd Brigade, 3rd Division, 5th Corps, of which he was inspector general, he daringly galloped his horse within the enemy's lines and before he could escape was captured by the Confederate pickets He was sent to Libby Prison and from there was transferred to Salisbury and later to Danville, each bastile being a little worse than the previous one, and in the succeeding February was returned to Libby Prison where he was finally paroled and was given then a leave of absence After the surrender of General Lee, Captain Kratzer was ordered back and was detailed on court martial service and was finally honorably discharged and mustered out in 1865 Capt Kratzer's army record, from the beginning to the close, reflects credit on a brave soldier He is a valued member of the Grand Army Post at Curwensville, of which he has been commander several times

From the army Captain Kratzer returned to Curwensville, where he has resided ever since. In March, 1865, he was first married to Miss Kate Goodwin, of Clarion county, Pa, who died in 1892, aged forty-six years, and her burial was in Oak Grove cemetery Eight children were born to them, namely: May, who is the wife of William Jackson and they reside in California, Joseph, who lives in Wisconsin, Elliott, who is deceased, is survived by his widow, formerly a Miss Blackburn; Alice, who died in infancy, Kate, who is deceased, was the wife of John McDermit; C

Fred and Bessie, who both reside at Spokane, Wash, and John, who is a linotype operator and printer In June, 1906, Capt Kratzer was married to Amanda A Carlisle, of Luthersburg, Clearfield county

In politics, Capt Kratzer is a Republican For five years he has been serving acceptably in the office of justice of the peace and very seldom have any of his decisions been referred to another court He is identified fraternally with the Masonic order and also with the Odd Fellows He is a member of the Methodist Episcopal church

FRANKLIN FINSTHWAIT, a prominent young business man, cashier of the First National Bank at Cherry Tree, Pa, was born at West Newton, Pa, August 28, 1879, son of Franklin B and Caroline (Everhart) Finsthwait He is a descendant on the paternal side of James Finsthwait, born January 14, 1759, of English ancestry, and his wife Mary, who were natives of Kent county, Delaware, where many of their descendants are living today They had five daughters and one son, as follows Sarah C, born February 22, 1806, Ann S, born December 19, 1807, Eliza M, born April 10, 1810, Susan G, born February 3, 1812, Mary S, born June 21, 1814, and James, born March 1, 1816, a few weeks after the death of his father The daughters all married and reared families of children

James Finsthwait, Jr, the date of whose birth is given above, and who is next in the present line of descent, died in 1872 His wife in maidenhood was Lucy Collins Messick, born September 17, 1810, near Georgetown, Sussex county, Del She died in 1890 They had two daughters and four sons as follows

Caroline Collins, born August 11, 1839, Franklin Buchanan, born March 15, 1841, James Purnell, February 28, 1843, Minos Gibson, December 5, 1844, Frederick Marion, January 28, 1847, Sarah Matilda, December 29, 1849 James Purnell Finsthwait was killed at the battle of Gettysburg Caroline married George P Hitch of Laurel, Sussex county, Del They live at Norfolk, Va, and have four children living, having lost two in infancy Gibson married Appia Davis of West Middlesex, where they now live, they have four daughters Frederick married Susan Everhart of West Middlesex, they live in Chicago and have no children Sarah married G W Bement, of Lansing, Mich, she is a widow with two sons, and lives in Lansing

Franklin B Finsthwait, whose nativity has been already given, was connected during his entire industrial period with the oil industry and was formerly a member of the Oil Exchange at Pittsburg He is still living at the age of 66 years and is a resident of Swissvale, Allegheny county, Pa On January 7, 1873, he married Caroline Everhart, of West Middlesex, Mercer county, Pa, and of this union there were four children, namely Ida Harrington, born November 16, 1873, Lloyd E, born June 3, 1877, who is engaged in the wholesale dry goods business at Pittsburg, Franklin, born, as already stated, August 28, 1879, who is the direct subject of this sketch, and Donald E, born January 1, 1882, who is an employee of the American Tobacco Company at Pittsburg Ida is residing at home

Mrs Franklin B Finsthwait is a descendant on the paternal side of Michael Eberhart, who came from Germany in the ship "Friendship," landing at Philadelphia October 16, 1727 He settled in Lehigh county, Pa, and

died in 1788   He had two sons, Henry and
Paul

Paul Eberhart, son of Michael, was born in
1827 on the Atlantic Ocean   He was reared
and lived in Lehigh county, Pa , until he was
46 years old, when in 1773 he moved to Westmoreland county, Pa , where he died at a ripe
old age   He had four sons—Jacob, John,
Christian and Frederick

Abraham F Eberhart (or Everhart, for he
changed the spelling of the family name), son
of Frederick Eberhart, was born in Mercer
county, Pa , October 22, 1810, and was married in 1841 to Susan Haywood of Mercer
county, Pa   He died November 2, 1881, aged
71 years   The following is a record of his
children   Sarah E Everhart, born October
22, 1842, was married May 15, 1866, to Dr.
J W Hillier of Mercer county, Pa   They
have no children   Mary M Everhart, born
October 22, 1843, was married October 22,
1860, to Horatio N Warren of Buffalo, N Y.
They had two sons, Dr Albert E Warren and
Henry D Warren   Caroline Everhart, born
January 21, 1846, married Franklin B Fins-
thwaite, as already noted   William M Everhart, born March 26, 1848, married Rhoda
Long, of Mercer county, Pa , and they have
two sons   Henry Clay Everhart, born August
2, 1850, died March 3, 1854   Susan Everhart was born March 2, 1855, and married F
M Finsthwait

Franklin Finsthwait began his education in
the common schools, subsequently graduating
from the Wilkinsburg (Pa) high school   His
first industrial experience was gained in the
employ of the P Lorillard Tobacco Co , where
he remained for a time   In 1897 he entered
the Second National Bank as a messenger, and
continued there until 1901, at which time he
went to the Mellon National Bank as clearing

house clerk   He was later promoted to the
position of receiving teller, which he held until
he resigned in order to accept his present position as cashier of the First National Bank of
Cherry Tree, Pa , in March, 1903   He is also
treasurer of the Cherry Tree Electric Light
Co and of the Cherry Tree Water Co , in all
these varied positions showing good business
ability and a comprehensive grasp of affairs
He is a member of and an elder in the Presbyterian church of Cherry Tree, and also of the
Masonic order, belonging to the Blue lodge at
Ebensburg, Pa   In politics he is a Republican
and is at present a member of the borough
school board

Franklin Finsthwait was married in October, 1908, to Helen McKeage, who was born
in July, 1887, a daughter of William and
Elizabeth (Harter) McKeage   Her father is
a miller and lumberman residing at Cherry
Tree   Our subject and wife are the parents of
two children, Franklin McKeage, and Ruth
Everhart

ARTHUR A BELL, general farmer and
master of Greenwood township Grange, is a
member of an old Clearfield county family
and was born May 7, 1873, on the old Bell
farm in Greenwood township   He is a son of
John W and Elizabeth (Cook) Bell

John W Bell was born in Greenwood township, Clearfield county, Pa , July 12, 1838, and
died February 7, 1904   For many years he
was a prominent man in this section and one
of the largest landowners   He was married
first in 1862, to Elizabeth Cook, and they had
five children, Arthur A being the fourth born
John W Bell was married secondly on December 28, 1876, to Mrs Eliza C Thompson, who
still survives

Arthur A Bell with his brother and three

LEWIS C. ROWLES, M. D.

sisters, attended the country schools in Green-wood township, besides one term at Lumber City He then became associated with his father in the timber business After his marriage he settled on one part of the homestead farm and lived there until 1906, when he came to his present farm which contains 150 acres, one-half of which is still in woodland He is interested also in 1,200 acres of coal land in Greenwood township Mr Bell has improved his place with the substantial buildings now in evidence and carries on general farming and stock raising

Mr Bell was married September 15, 1892, to Miss Belle Young, who was born November 24, 1870, in Greenwood township, a daughter of Nelson Young, and they have six children John Wade, Alice Dorothy, Bessie Loram, Leslie Glenn, Williard Cook and Ella Elizabeth Mr Bell was reared in the Baptist church of which his father and mother were prominent members In politics he is a Republican but has never been willing to accept public office He is actively interested, however, in all agricultural movements and for a number of years has been a leader in the Grange

ISAIAH JURY,* a representative citizen of Girard township, residing on his well improved farm of fifty-three acres, which lies twelve miles northeast of the borough of Clearfield, was born in this township in 1850 and is a son of John F and Elizabeth (Griffins) Jury John F Jury was also born in Clearfield county and followed an agricultural life until his death in 1906

Isaiah Jury obtained his education in the schools of his native township, after which he turned his attention to farming and stockrais-ing and has carried on these industries ever since, keeping thoroughly abreast with the times in agricultural progress and following methods which he has found eminently successful He is a man with broad and enlightened views and has interested himself very largely in the advancement of the public schools and has served many years on the township school board, of which he has been president since 1908 He has also served in the office of overseer of the poor

Mr Jury was married June 3, 1873, to Miss Mary Shaw, of Wallacetown, Pa She is a lady of education and culture and for thirteen terms was a school teacher Four children have been born to Mr and Mrs Jury, namely Inez, who is teaching school at Shawsville, and has been thus engaged for seven terms, Winnifred, who has taught for four terms, being now engaged at the Congress Hill school, Archie, who assists his father (married Miss A Maines, of Shiloh, Bradford township), and Clemmens I, who died June 13, 1882 Mr Jury and family are members of the U B church at Shiloh

LEWIS C ROWLES, M D, physician and surgeon, at Grampian, Pa, where he is also a representative and useful public spirited citizen, was born near Houtzdale, Clearfield county, Pa, March 1, 1879, and is a son of Matthew and Letitia (Lewis) Rowles

Matthew Rowles was born in Lawrence township, Clearfield county, and he and wife reside at Clearfield They have five living children Mrs C A Crews, of Cumberland, Md, Mrs Frank Stage, of Clearfield, Lewis C, Burton, of Clearfield, and Alice of Cumberland, Md Of the above, Mrs Stage was formerly a successful teacher In politics,

Mr Rowles is a Democrat and at one time was a school director in West Clearfield Mrs Rowles is a member of the Lutheran church

Lewis C Rowles attended school at Clearfield and graduated from West Clearfield High School He later took a course in the summer Normal school and afterward taught school for two years in Bell township He also learned the carpenter's trade before he was twenty years of age In 1898 he enlisted as a private soldier in Co E, 5th Pa Vol Inf , and served through the Spanish-American war. In the meanwhile he had done his preparatory medical reading and in 1905 was graduated from the Philadelphia Chirurgical College and immediately entered into practice, establishing himself at Grampian in September, 1905 Dr Rowles has been very successful in many grave surgical operations and has gained the confidence of his neighbors and fellow citizens in his skill and ability He keeps fully abreast of the times, holding membership in the county and state medical bodies and the American Medical Association

Dr Rowles was married April 24, 1907, to Miss Edna Mill Stetson, a daughter of Lewis Stetson, of Philadelphia, and they have had two children Stetson Dewitt, who died when but three days old, and Eleanor Frances, who was born March 9, 1910 Dr Rowles casts his vote with the Democratic party He retains membership in his college fraternal society but has not identified himself with any other organization He is serving as a member of the Grampian school board

JOSIAH R NEWCOMER, who was born in Somerset county, Pa , July 29, 1848, is one of the representative and respected citizens of Greenwood township, Clearfield county, Pa ,

where he owns and resides on a valuable farm of seventy-three acres, which is situated one and one-half mile northwest of Bell's Landing He is a son of Joseph and Mary (Thomas) Newcomer

Joseph Newcomer was born in Maryland and from there moved to Broad Top, Bedford county, Pa , and later to Somerset county. He married Mary Thomas, who was born in Westmoreland county, Pa , and they lived in Somerset county until after the birth of four children—Frances, Aaron, Nancy and Josiah R —and then moved to Clearfield county and settled in Burnside township, near New Washington While living there their last child, Sarah, was born, who died in 1907, Josiah R being the only survivor of the family. From Burnside township Joseph Newcomer moved to Greenwood township and in May, 1860, settled on the farm above mentioned At that time the land was entirely covered with brush and timber and with the help of his children he cleared his property and developed a farm The only improvement on the place was a small plank house, but there was no barn or other building The family managed to live in the cabin and in 1866 he put up the log barn now standing, which was later enlarged by the present owner In 1880 Joseph Newcomer and wife moved to Cherry Run, where they lived retired, in great comfort, during the rest of their lives He was born January 29, 1822, and died in 1899 She was born October 6, 1821, and died August 4, 1881, and both were laid to rest in the Bower cemetery They were good Christian people, members of the Methodist Episcopal church

Josiah R Newcomer attended school until he was about thirteen years of age, walking a long distance to the Deer Run schoolhouse near New Washington The clearing of the farm had to be accomplished and Mr Newcomer very early became accustomed to heavy work He has always lived on the place and his occupations have been farming, stock raising and lumbering For thirty years he has been a member of Greenwood Grange, taking an interest in the movement when it was first started.

Mr Newcomer was married February 22, 1880, to Miss Margaret Brisbin, who died without issue, November 29, 1881, and was buried at Luthersburg On August 24, 1884, Mr Newcomer was married secondly to Miss Phinella E Newcomer, who was born in Ferguson township, Clearfield county, Pa, a daughter of William and Malissa (Bloom) Newcomer Five children have been born to Mr and Mrs Newcomer Nina A, who was born June 22, 1885, Reese O, who was born December 3, 1887, and is a railroad engineer, in West Virginia, Lulu P, born January 11, 1891, who is the wife of Raymond Bloom (they have one daughter, Fannie) William Joseph, who was born July 10, 1899, and died on the same day, and Eunice, who was born November 7, 1900 Mr and Mrs Newcomer are members of the Methodist Episcopal church at Curry Run He has served three years as a member of the school board In politics he has always been a Democrat

DAVID C HENSAL, who has been a lumberman all his mature life, for a number of years has been a resident of Bigler township, Clearfield county, where he owns forty acres of valuable coal land at Glen Hope, together with a half dozen houses and about thirty lots at Madera He was born March 20, 1833, seven miles west of Gettysburg, Adams county, Pa, and is a son of John and Anna (Coshun) Hensal, and grandson of Jacob Hensal Mrs Anna Coshun Hensal's mother was a Conover, a sister to the wife of the old Commodore Vanderbilt

John Hensal was of French and German ancestry He followed tailoring as his occupation all through life He married Anna Coshun, who was born in Pennsylvania, and they had the following children David C, Hannah Mary, who married Ephraim Bittinger, Jane, who married Reuben Kuhn, and James, Charles, Amos, Emory and John Mrs John Hensal died about twenty-five years ago

David C Hensal never had other than the rather meager educational opportunities offered by the district school He has been more than usually successful as a business man and owns a large amount of property in Pennsylvania and in association with others is interested in the development of other tracts He is in partnership with Allison O Smith and John R Scott, in the ownership of 3,000 acres of coal land in Somerset county, Pa, and with the latter in 2,000 acres in the same county, under lease, and owns also 200 acres also in Somerset county and forty acres of coal and timber land in Clearfield county, also fifty acres in Bigler township, Clearfield county, together with his above mentioned residence properties at Madera, Pa, and two houses at Belsena, Clearfield county

Mr Hensal was married in 1854 to Miss Margaret Mullin, a daughter of George and Sarah Mullin, who came from Ireland to Clearfield county and settled at Glen Hope Mrs Hensal died at Madera, September 20, 1909, and her burial was in the Cross Roads cemetery To Mr and Mrs Hensal the following children were born George, John,

Thomas, Blanche, Cora, Mary (deceased), Sadie (deceased), Sherman, Amos and David (deceased). Of the above family, Cora is the wife of John O Stanley. Mary, who was the wife of Charles Flynn, was a victim of that terrible catastrophe, the Johnstown flood Sadie was accidentally drowned at Madera Mr Hensal is a Republican in his political views He was reared in the Methodist Episcopal church

JAMES T MITCHELL, general farmer, who owns 130 acres of valuable land in Greenwood township, Clearfield county, Pa, all lying along the northwest branch of the Susquehanna river, was born January 24, 1867, in Burnside township, Clearfield county, and is a son of David and Henrietta Mitchell, who reside on an adjoining farm

James T Mitchell was educated in the schools of Greenwood township and attended through one term at Lumber City He then went into the woods and began contracting, cutting by the thousand feet and during several summers had from twenty-five to thirty men in his employ For a time after his marriage, in 1893, he lived near Bell's Landing, in Greenwood township, and then bought his present farm from Alex Patton, but which was the David McCracken farm All of it is cleared except fifty acres still in fine timber All of the substantial and appropriate buildings which in their appearance and surroundings give an idea of thrift and good management, Mr Mitchell erected, or entirely remodeled

On September 21, 1893, Mr Mitchell was married to Miss Nora Rager, who was born in Burnside township, Clearfield county, July 10, 1874, a daughter of Thomas and Agnes (Tibitt) Rager, who still reside in Burnside township Nine children have been born to Mr and Mrs Mitchell, as follows· Daisy, Paul McKinley, Pearl Etta, Bertha June, Lucy May, Margaret, Nan, Pauline Flora, Elizabeth Ann and James David Mr. Mitchell and family are members of the Methodist Protestant church He is a Republican in politics and has occasionally consented to accept township offices He is a leading member of Greenwood Grange and is treasurer of the Curry Run Telephone Company

ALEXANDER MURRAY, deceased For many years Alexander Murray was an honored and respected citizen of Girard township, Clearfield county, where he had acquired a competence through the industry and prudence which had marked his way from early youth He was born in Shaver's Creek Valley, Huntingdon county, Pa, and in youth was brought to Clearfield county by his parents, who were John and Mary Murray, of Scotch ancestry

Alexander Murray was eleven years old when his father died, in January, 1824, leaving the mother with a family of young children to care for, all of them, except himself and the two youngest girls, with no provision made for them, except such as she could secure for herself. She could weave the cloth for her children's clothing, and possibly she may have been able to sell a small portion to others, but their whole living had to be made out of the wild land, very little of which had as yet been cleared or put under cultivation In later years Mr Murray was frequently heard to speak of the industry, patience, fortitude and endurance of this admirable mother She survived to see her son in comfortable circumstances, her death taking place in April, 1871

THOMAS H. MURRAY

Alexander Murray had no educational advantages, but he was naturally apt, and soon acquired enough knowledge to enable him to transact business properly By the time he was fifteen years of age he was busy at different things—farming, lumbering and teaming —and when twenty years old he did the first piece of work for himself, which was the construction of one mile of the old Milesburg and Smithport turnpike road When he received his pay for the latter—fifty dollars in cash and an order for forty-five dollars more—he doubtless felt rich, although the order was never cashed, as the company had become insolvent He engaged in lumbering and cleared and cultivated his land as he was able and finally paid for it He was a typical pioneer, honest and upright, but careful and shrewd in his business transactions He was widely known and was held in honor and esteem by all

Mr Murray was married February 23, 1842, to Miss Isabella Meek Holt, of Bradford township, and they had nine children, six of whom reached maturity The mother of these children died October 1, 1879 On January 19, 1882, Mr Murray married for his second wife Mrs Ermina J Spackman, who died in 1885 Mr Murray survived her for four years, his death taking place April 6, 1889 His mother and her people were Presbyterians, but he united with the Methodist Episcopal church in 1856, and continued a faithful and official member and the principal supporter of that church in his community until his death He was the father of Thomas H Murray, of Clearfield, Pa

EDWARD W FERGUSON, who carries on a general mercantile business at Kerrmoor,

Pa, was born in Ferguson township, Clearfield county, Pa, April 26, 1860, and is a son of J C. Ferguson and a grandson of John Ferguson

John Ferguson with his brother David came to Clearfield county from Northumberland county, Pa, when he was about thirty years of age, and he became one of the prominent and useful men in the early settlement of what is now Ferguson township, which part of the county was named in honor of John and David Ferguson He cleared up a farm of 160 acres here, after which he moved to Lumber City, where he was a merchant for a time, and later to Lock Haven, where he died at the age of seventy-two years He was married after coming to Clearfield county, to Betsey Wiley, and they had five children born to them Mary, who married Dr Ross; Deborah, who married Gibson Jamison, J C, Elizabeth, who married Lewis Hoover, and an infant son, deceased

J C. Ferguson was reared in Ferguson township, and lived on the old homestead, which is now owned by William Thurston He served without injury in the Civil war, and passed his entire life, with the exception of eighteen years, engaged in farming. He was a man of high standing in his neighborhood and of ample fortune, and was a charter member of the Clearfield National Bank at Clearfield, Pa His death occurred at Kerrmoor, when he was aged sixty-two years He married Ann Price, who was born near Bloomington, Pa, and died in her sixty-first year, both she and husband being interred in the McClure cemetery in Pike township They had four children, namely Edward W; Abby, who is now deceased, Harry, who is a member of the business firm of Ferguson & Rossner, at Clearfield, and Robert, who died at the age of eight years

Edward W Ferguson went to school in his boyhood in both Ferguson and Pike township, the old schoolhouse in the latter then standing on the present site of the McClure cemetery, and afterward he taught one term of school in Ferguson township Since marriage Mr Ferguson has lived in Kerrmoor, where he has been engaged in merchandising He has numerous additional interests, being concerned with the milling business of W L Bloom & Co, at Kerrmoor, and is a stockholder in the C & C Telephone Company, the Ferguson & La Jose & Lumber City Telephone Company, being secretary of the same He and his brother, Harry F, conducted a hardware store in Kerrmoor, when the town was first started, in the spring of 1886, they continuing together until April, 1907

Mr Ferguson was married first to Miss Eunice Swan, who was born in Jordan township, a daughter of Henry Swan, of Ansonville, and they had two children, Raymond and Lorraine, the latter surviving Mr Ferguson was married secondly to Miss Bertha Hile, a daughter of John P Hile, of Lumber City, and they have two children, Ellery and Warden Mr Ferguson is a Republican in politics but has accepted no public office

PHINEAS WESLEY RUDOLPH, one of Huston township's successful agriculturists and leading citizens, residing on his farm of twenty-five acres situated two and one-half miles north of Penfield, Clearfield county, Pa, known as Alta Vista Garden, also owns two other farms of fifty acres, also located in Huston township He was born on his father's farm in Henderson township, Jefferson county, Pa, October 20, 1861, and is a son of David Rudolph, who was born in Westmoreland county, Pa

From Westmoreland David Rudolph was taken to Jefferson county by his parents, Jacob Rudolph and wife, who spent the rest of their years in that section, Jacob Rudolph becoming a well known farmer and lumberman David Rudolph moved from Jefferson county to DuBois, Pa, where he was foreman for John DuBois for many years and his death occurred there at the age of seventy-two years During the Civil war he served as a member of the 15th Pa Vol Cav He was married in Jefferson county to Anna Maria Smith, who was a daughter of Peter Smith, an old and respected resident of Punxatawney Nine children were born to David Rudolph and his wife, namely Smith M, Wheeler, George, Lucy, Jane, Phineas W, William, Monroe and Anna Lucy married Peter Hallowell and Jane married Frank Rudolph

Phineas W Rudolph grew to the age of fifteen years in Jefferson county, where he attended the district schools, and grew to manhood at DuBois He learned the carpenter's trade, working at it for three years, after which he worked in the saw mills for John DuBois until 1891, when he came to his present farm, purchasing his residence farm from Abel Gresh and the other land from Stephen Bunday He did not immediately take personal charge of his property, merely overseeing it prior to April, 1911, in the meanwhile working as engineer and electrician in the mines at Tyler, Pa Since the above date he has devoted all his attention to his agricultural affairs

Mr Rudolph was married October 18, 1883.

to Miss Elizabeth Funk, a daughter of Jacob and Louisa Funk Mrs Rudolph was born in Germany and was brought to the United States when two years old To Mr and Mrs Rudolph eleven children have been born, as follows Laura, who died April 12, 1911 (she was the widow of George Paine and had one child, Velma), and Walter, Pearl, Howard, James, Emma and Adam (twins, the latter deceased), Arthur, Vira, and Pauline W and Maxine (twins, the last named being deceased) Mr and Mrs Rudolph are members of the Methodist Episcopal church He belongs to the Grange (as also does Mrs Rudolph) and to the P H C, at DuBois In politics he is a Democrat Mr Rudolph recently turned over twenty-five acres of his land to his eldest son

JOSEPH N. McCRACKEN, who owns the old homestead farm of 100 acres, which was the home of his grandfather, Nicholas McCracken, and which is situated on the north side of the west branch of the Susquehanna river, in Greenwood township, Clearfield county, Pa, was born here December 23, 1871, and is a son of D W and Emma (Nicholson) McCracken

D W McCracken was also born on this farm and spent his life in Greenwood township, his death occurring when he was sixty-three years of age He owned 150 acres of excellent land He was a member of Greenwood Grange and was identified also with the Odd Fellows at Mahaffey D W McCracken married Emma Nicholson, a daughter of Joseph Nicholson They had the following children born to them Edith, who is the wife of Ashey Hill, Belle, deceased, who was the wife of Kirk Richard, Joseph N, and Hannah,

who is the wife of Dell Richards The mother of the above family lived to be seventy-five years of age Her burial was by the side of her husband in the Friends' cemetery at Grampian They were members of the Methodist Protestant church

Joseph N McCracken obtained an education in the schools of Greenwood township and since then has carried on farming and stock raising on the homestead and has all his land under cultivation with the exception of fifty acres in woodland He has substantial and comfortable buildings and assisted in the erection of his residence He has always taken a deep interest in everything pertaining to agricultural matters and is a member of the Greenwood Grange, in which he holds the office of assistant steward Mrs McCracken is ladies' assistant steward in the Grange

Mr McCracken was married June 25, 1902, to Miss Sarah Elizabeth Byers, who was born at Westover, Pa, June 29, 1871 She is a daughter of Samuel and Sarah Jane (Lloyd) Byers, the former of whom was born at New Washington, and the latter in eastern Pennsylvania After Mr and Mrs Byers were married they moved to near Westover and now reside on a farm of 225 acres and the father owns an additional 100 acres in Burnside township They are members of the Baptist church The following children were born to Mr and Mrs Byers, James, who died when two years of age, Barbara, who was married first to Thomas Black and secondly to J L McCracken, John L, who married Ellen Scott, Sarah Elizabeth, William H, who married Ella Westover, Jesse, who lives in West Virginia, Aaron, who lives at Braddock, Pa ; Jane, living at home, and Rose, who is the wife of Ralph Palmer

Mr and Mrs McCracken have two children. Ruth and Earl Wilson Mr McCracken is a stockholder in the Curry Run Telephone Company The family and its connections are all representative people of this section

ADAM BRETH The parentage of this subject is as follows The father's name was Henry Breth, born in 1792, and was the son of Henry Breth, who lived and was born in Germany, not far from the city of Mayance, and lived till he was one hundred and six years old, of the mother nothing is now known Henry, Peter and Adam, three brothers, came to the United States in the year 1819 Henry, was married in Germany, and brought two daughters with him, the mother's maiden name was Mary C Martin This family located at Karthaus in Clearfield county; the father worked for Peter Karthaus as a stone mason when the works at Karthaus were first started. Here at this place the following named children were born to them But first say, that Mary and Margaret were born in Germany, Mary in 1813 and Margaret November 5, 1815, at Karthaus, Elisabeth born February 24, 1820, Susan, February 17, 1822, Samuel, February 14, 1824 The parents then moved to Marsh-Creek, Center county, Pa Here, Henry, the next, was born on April 12, 1826, Jacob, born at the same place, August 3, 1828 The parents then moved to Howard, Center county, Pa, where Joseph Harris, another son, and Adam, the present subject, were born, Joseph Harris on November 30, 1830, and Adam, February 10, 1833 In April of the same year the parents moved to what is Burnside township, near Patchinville Here the family lived and worked at

clearing up land and lumbering In 1843 the family moved onto a farm two miles direct west from New Washington, lived on this farm till April of 1844, and then moved into Bell township and bought a farm in that township Here the father lived till July 4, 1875. The mother died March 22, 1869, in the seventy-sixth year of her age On the 29th of May, 1850, the subject of this sketch left home by the parents' consent to learn the trade of blacksmithing, served till September, 1853, at which time he had served three years, all but two months, for this two months he paid "his boss" $25 00, and went to New Washington, Pa Here he worked in partnership with a brother at the smithing business On the 24th of May, 1854, he was united in marriage with Margaret G Lee, daughter of Isaac and Hannah Fulton Lee, to this union were born ten children, six of these died in infancy, the first born is Lettie Lucretia, born July 18, 1855, and is married to John H Baker; Isaac Henry, born October 5, 1856, and died January 6, 1877, James, born August 31, 1860 He married Alice Fryer; to this union is born two sons, Adam Breth, born October 20, 1884, and Ernest, born January 31, 1885 The parents named were married December 20, 1883 Jane R, born May 8, 1862, she was married to William Thompson, November 11, 1886; to this union were born seven children, as follows Lillian Elisabeth, born May 3, 1887, James Horace, February 4, 1889; Hazel Amanda, February 2, 1894, Margaret Anna, April 14, 1896; John Adam, February 26, 1899; William Herman, January 2, 1902; Helen Maxine, June 4, 1909.

On the 28th day of July, 1869, the mother of the above named children, wife of the subject, died, the oldest girl took charge of the family of younger children On the first day of April, 1872, the subject of this biography was again married, to Maria G Armor, at Smicksburg, Indiana county, Pa She was the daughter of John Armor and Jane Cochran Armor, the father was born in Lancaster county, Pa, and the mother was born in Westmoreland county, Pa (have not the dates of either one's birth) To this union were born two children—a daughter, born September 27, 1873, and died October 3, 1873 Armor Gregg, born May 28, 1875, died September 8, 1876

In 1859 he was first elected justice of the peace for Bell township at the age of twenty-six years, and was elected for that township four terms (twenty years) Followed smithing, farming and lumbering up to February 27, 1877, when he moved to New Washington, Pa Carried on smithing In 1880 was elected justice of the peace, and is still serving out now (May 15, 1911) his eleventh term In 1883 he was employed by a coal company (Clearfield and Cambria Coal and Coke Company) to take options for coal lands, and took up with but a few exceptions nearly 13,000 acres The deeds of nearly all these properties was or were acknowledged before his term as justice of the peace and checks of the company were delivered by him for the payment of the same He continued with this company as bookkeeper-paymaster, and did the general business for the company up to July 5, 1902, when he left the employ of this company

He served as a notary public for two successive terms, of four years each Served a number of terms as school director, one term as burgess, a number of terms on the council, has been borough auditor for years and is now auditor, is under appointment a local registrar of vital statistics of District 390, under the State Department of Health, and is secretary of the Board of Health for this borough

In 1890 he took up the study of surveying and civil engineering, also the study of shorthand and typewriting, and was successful in all these callings Is now, since July 23, 1908, acting postmaster of the New Washington postoffice, Clearfield county, Pa His wife being appointed postmaster, as he could not, under a State law, hold the office of justice of the peace Can now in his seventy-ninth year write four different systems of shorthand, still does surveying, and does the work of the postoffice Has five great-grandchildren

WILLIAM THORP SCHRYVER,* general farmer and representative citizen of Lawrence township, resides on his valuable farm of eighty acres, which lies four miles south of Clearfield, Pa He was born at Coal Range Forge, Center county, Pa, October 8, 1837, and is a son of Abraham Thorp and Rebecca (Wells) Schryver

Abraham Thorp Schryver was born in Osage county, N Y, where he both attended and taught school Later he moved to Westmoreland county, Pa, and there studied medicine with Dr John P Hoyt and became a medical practitioner During the entire subsequent period of life, while interested in many other directions, he kept up a desultory practice and enjoyed public confidence He was a man of inquiring and acquiring mind, not being content with mastering one profession, he enthusiastically investigated and studied others When the old Clearfield Academy was first built, he was one of the earliest teachers and it was Abraham Thorp Schryver who was responsible for the addition of geography and grammar to the public school curriculum in Clearfield county   He was also an advanced mathematician and published a complete arithmetic when he was seventy-eight years of age   After his second marriage he moved to Beccaria Mill, Clearfield county, and in 1854 he was elected county superintendent of schools, with a salary of $300 per year   After this election he settled on the farm on which his son William T resides and lived here during the remaining years of his life   After his first marriage he lived in East Freedom, Blair county, where he practiced medicine and remained there until the death of his first wife   In his earlier years he was a Whig but accepted the principles of the Republican party as his own when that organization came into being   With other leading men of his time, he was a Free Mason   In his religious views he was a Baptist

Abraham Thorp Schryver was married first to Rebecca Wells and subsequently to her sister, Clara Wells   They were daughters of John Wells, who was a justice of the peace in Beccaria township   It was said of Rebecca Wells that she was the sweetest singer in Clearfield county   Mrs Schryver's two children, William and John, were born to his first union   John died at the age of sixty-four years and was buried by the side of his parents in the Clearfield cemetery   For years he had been bookkeeper for a hardware firm at Clearfield

William T Schryver attended school at East Freedom, in Blair county, taught by his father and later continued his studies in Clearfield county, but when fifteen years of age secured the position of teacher of the Plank school, for himself   He found himself well qualified as a teacher and enjoyed the work

and kept on teaching, in Beccaria township, Gordon township, Locust Ridge, in Pike township, four terms in Lawrence township and a term at Lumber City, where he had seventy-eight pupils   He continued to teach, having a school at Penfield, in Huston township, one term in Union township and at the Williams School now in Beccaria township, aggregating eleven winters of teaching, while he had also conducted subscription schools for several terms   In early days the father of Mr. Schryver, with his other interests, owned some 400 acres of timber which it was his purpose to cut and raft down the river   He was unfortunate in his early ventures in this direction and finally abandoned this enterprise   His sons learned rafting and in his early manhood, William T was very skillful and dexterous in this line of work   The New York Central Railroad and Big Clearfield Creek both run through the center of the farm and in old days this was a famous stopping place for raftsmen   The farm is a very productive one and in the present season (1910). Mr Schryver has prospects of a record crop of corn   The farm-house was erected by Mr. Schryver's father, a commodious carefully constructed dwelling   In its building double two-inch pine planks were used, for which Mr Schryver paid $4 per thousand feet   With such excellent accommodations, William T Schryver has found it profitable to open his residence for summer boarders, entertaining guests from June to September.   They come year after year from long distances and he has made it possible to seat forty-eight guests at one dinner table, that number being on hand sometimes at the week end gatherings   It may be mentioned that Mr Schryver has in large measure inherited much of his late father's desire for knowledge and with his other acquirements, is master of the printer's trade

In 1862 Mr Schryver was married to Miss Margaret P Tyler, a daughter of David Tyler, Esq The father of Mrs Schryver, with John Du Bois, was the first man to build slides for rafting on the river Two children were born to Mr and Mrs Schryver. Emma, who is highly accomplished and is a teacher of music, and John, who is a skilled hard wood worker Both reside at home A severe domestic affliction fell on the family in the death of the beloved wife and mother, which occurred at the age of sixty-one years, from paralysis She was a lady of so many endearing qualities and lovable disposition that she was sincerely mourned in the community For years she had been an active member of the Methodist Episcopal church Later, Mr. Schryver was married to the estimable lady now his wife, formerly Miss Arabella P Irwin, a daughter of Lewis Irwin, of Lawrence township Mr and Mrs Schryver are members of the Methodist Episcopal church, with which he united when fourteen years of age and to which he has regularly dedicated a part of his income Mr Schryver is a member of the Rural Telephone Company of Lawrence township, of which his son, John Schryver, is president

SAMUEL ARNOLD, deceased. who had filled a large place in the business life of Clearfield county for many years and had been identified closely with the development of her resources, was not a native of this county but spent the greater part of his life within its lines Samuel Arnold was born in York county, Pa , February 11, 1822, and died May 31, 1899, at his home in Curwensville, Clear-

field county His parents were Peter and Susan (Klugh) Arnold

The Arnold family in America can claim many distinguished members and successful men of affairs Its history, as far as the present branch is concerned, begins with an English colonist who reached New England in 1594 His death is recorded at Hartford, Conn , in 1664 One of his descendants was George Arnold, who was the grandfather of the late Samuel Arnold, and whether he was born in York county, Pa , in 1768, may not have been altogether proved, but it is certain that he died there, in 1827

Peter Arnold, son of George and father of the late Samuel Arnold, was one of many children born to his parents, who then lived in York county and there he remained until 1837, when he came to Clearfield county Here he acquired lands, flocks and herds and in the increasing and managing of these, passed the remainder of his life He married Susan Klugh, who was born in Lancaster county, Pa Her father was a native of Germany and came to the American colonies in time to serve for seven years as a soldier in the Revolutionary war To Peter Arnold and wife were born eight children, five sons and three daughters, namely George, Samuel, Frederick Manassa, Joseph R , Anna, Maria and Clarissa It is worthy of notice that all these five sons developed into men of integrity of character and of more than usual business capacity

Samuel Arnold was fifteen years of age when his parents moved to Clearfield county and he remained under the home roof and continued to help his father until he was twenty-two years of age He then left home for the first time, going to Illinois, which then was a far western state There he accepted farm work, learned different if not better methods, and met with many new experiences At length, satisfied with his glimpse of life beyond his native hills, he returned to Clearfield county He had a district school education and then taught school and engaged in agricultural operations until 1846, when he embarked in the mercantile business at Luthersburg, Pa, where he remained until 1865 In that year he transferred his business to Curwensville, deeming it a better commercial point Until the close of his long and honorable business life, Mr Arnold continued to be identified with Curwensville and many of the enterprises of this town were founded and fostered by his encouragement and financial assistance

Mr Arnold was one of the organizers of the First National Bank and served as its cashier for thirteen years He continued his mercantile business, enlarging its scope until his became the leading general mercantile establishment in this section He also had the foresight to invest in many acres of land covered with timber that was valuable then and in later years became doubly so, and in land containing coal and stone deposits which made mining and quarrying profitable industries, and to his other enterprises he added saw-milling and the handling of lumber on a large scale

The benefit accruing to a community through the enterprise and good judgment of a man like the late Samuel Arnold, can scarcely be adequately computed, including as it does, the opening up of new avenues of income to hundreds, and the distribution of their earnings into other channels While Mr Arnold was thus interested in different parts of the county, he was particularly concerned in the development of Curwensville He set an

example to other capitalists by erecting commodious business blocks and other structures and by so improving his residence and other properties that they added to the attractiveness of the place in which he had chosen to make his home

Mr Arnold was married July 11, 1847, to Miss Mary A Carlisle, who was born at Palmyra, Lebanon county, Pa, January 30, 1825, and died at Curwensville, Pa, January 9, 1911. Her father, John Carlisle, came to Clearfield county with his family in 1832 He was a man of sterling character and left an impress on his community was frequently elected to responsible offices, and served long as a justice of the peace and as a county commissioner. Subsequently he became a general merchant at Troutville, Pa, where he died in honored old age, in 1886. Mrs Arnold was the first born in his family of ten children, four sons and six daughters

To Samuel Arnold and wife the following children were born: N E, William C, Frank L, Samuel P, John, Fannie, Cora and Effie N E Arnold is a resident of Lewisburg, Pa William C, who is now deceased, was a prominent attorney at Du Bois, Pa, and a well known man in public life, having twice been elected to the United States Congress Frank L is a resident of Curwensville Samuel P, who is serving in his second term as postmaster at Curwensville, is engaged in the lumber business here John died when aged eight years Fannie is the wife of William C Hembold, who is the senior member of the well known insurance agency of Hembold & Stewart, a representative business firm of Curwensville Cora is the wife of Roland D Swoope, who is a very prominent attorney at Curwensville Effie is the wife of A Z Wolf, who is one of Curwensville's leading merchants

The late Samuel Arnold was a Republican in his political views and he gave hearty support in promulgating its principles. He never desired public office for himself, however, when called on, in any emergency he was ready to perform every duty that thoroughly honest citizenship demanded. In his church relations he was a member and liberal but unostentatious supporter of the Methodist Episcopal body having connected himself with that church during his residence at Luthersburg. In large measure Samuel Arnold was a self-made man in the true sense of the word. His success in business was a just tribute to his faithfulness, industry, perseverance and integrity. He belonged to that old-time class of men to whom honesty in business was their stepping-stone and who enjoyed its substantial results because they had been legitimately earned. In his personal attitude to family, friends, and to his army of employes, he was noted for the kindness, charity and sympathy which made him beloved and respected by all

JOSEPH J BORST,* one of Lawrence township's respected and substantial citizens, township supervisor and a veteran of the Civil war, resides on his valuable farm of 117 acres, which lies seven miles south of Clearfield, Pa. He was born in Germany, March 19, 1838, and is a son of John and Mary Borst

In 1846 John Borst brought his wife and seven children to America and settled near St Mary's, in Clearfield county, Pa. He moved from there into Lawrence township and then to Pike township, where the father operated a saw-mill for several years. He died on the Holden farm and afterward the mother and

her six sons and one daughter, moved to the Robert Mitchell farm and lived there as tenants for nineteen years. The family then moved to the Hugh Dougherty farm, where the mother died

Joseph J Borst is one of the three survivors of his parents' family of children. He attended school in Pike and in Lawrence townships and thus learned the English language and also speaks the German language. He then went to work as a lumberman in the woods and became a brave and adept rafter and it is still told of him how he took a mighty raft down the river with the help of only two men where six were usually required. He left the woods in order to enlist for service in the Civil war, in May, 1861, entering the army in Captain Lorrain's company recruited at Clearfield, and after serving through his first enlistment, re-entered the service and thus has two honorable discharge papers, the last one bearing the date of August 25, 1865. He then returned to Lawrence township and resumed lumbering. After his marriage, in 1868, he bought his present farm from William W and O Kline, which was formerly known as the Rowles farm. He has cleared about forty acres and has twenty-five in valuable timber and devotes the rest to pasturage. He carries on general farming and stock raising, being assisted by his sons who remain at home and are industrious, capable young men

Mr Borst married Miss Fannie McLaughlin, a daughter of John and Margie (Dougherty) McLaughlin, and the following children have been born to them William, who lives in Lawrence township, married Emma McKee, Charles, who lives at home, Albert, who lives on a farm in Lawrence township, married Lona McCaughey, John, who lives at home, and Paul, Peter, Mary and Carrie, all of whom live under the home roof Mr Borst and family are members of the Roman Catholic church at Clearfield Mr Borst classes himself as an Independent Republican He is a man of standing in his neighborhood and has served acceptably in public office

MRS ELLA MOUNTZ, postmistress at Morann, Clearfield county, Pa, where for the past eighteen years she has also conducted a general store, is associated with her husband, L J Mountz, in coal operating, having six mines in Clearfield county and one in Butler county Mrs Mountz was born at Sharon, Pa, and is a daughter of H B and Elizabeth (Keefe) Dore, and a granddaughter of Abel Dore She was the third born in a family of five children, the others being Joseph, Alfreda, now deceased, who was the wife of Chadwick Stanley, Henry, and Elizabeth, who is the wife of George W Ballard

Mrs Mountz attended school at Sharon and also in Clearfield county, to which she came in 1879. In 1885 she was married to L J Mountz, who was one of a family of eleven children born to his parents, John and Isabel (Amey) Mountz, residents of Vail, Blair county, Pa Mr and Mrs Mountz have one daughter, Viola, a very talented young lady, who is a graduate of the Emerson College of Oratory, at Boston, Mass

Mrs Mountz is widely known and is much admired for her business capacity She enjoys the confidence of the public to a remarkable extent and has done a large amount of business in the line of merchandising and for eighteen years has also held her Government office Mr Mountz is identified with the Democratic party He belongs to the Odd Fellows at Houtzdale and to the Elks at Tyrone

C H HESS,* who is engaged in general farming on a tract of 225 acres, located about two and a half-miles northeast of Woodland, Pa, is one of the largest land owners in Bradford township He was born in 1882 at Philipsburg, Center county, Pa, a son of Charles and Catherine Hess, both of whom are still living. The father is a native of Center county, Pa, and a farmer by occupation

C H Hess grew to maturity on the farm in Center county, Pa, and has always followed farming and stock raising in a general way He bought and located on his present farm of 225 acres in 1906 and has greatly improved it during the four years of his ownership, having brought it to its present standing

Mr Hess was married in 1906 to Jessie Blowers of Center county, Pa, and they have one son, Loye Mr Hess is a member of Grange No 358 of Bradford township, and is one of the representative and progressive agriculturists of the township

JAMES E SOULSBY,* a well known agriculturist of Knox township, Clearfield county, Pa, residing on his valuable farm of seventy-six acres, situated two miles east of Olanta, was born on this farm, February 25, 1861, and is a son of James and Sarah (Bauman) Soulsby

James Soulsby was born at Altoona, Pa, was educated in the public schools and then went to work on the railroad and became a passenger conductor on the Pennsylvania line between Altoona and Pittsburg While in the performance of duty he was taken ill suddenly and was placed in a hospital in Pittsburg

MRS. ELLA MOUNTZ

and died there when aged but twenty-eight years His burial was in Fairmount cemetery, Pittsburg He married Sarah Bauman, a daughter of Daniel Bauman, of Juniata county, and they had one son, James E Some years later Mrs Soulsby married E P Trout, of Schuylkill county, who was a veteran of the Civil war Five children were born to this union, the one survivor being a son, Alonzo Trout, who married Edith Richards, a daughter of H Richards Mr and Mrs Trout live at Juniata, Westmoreland county, the mother of Mr Soulsby being a member of the family She belongs to the Methodist Episcopal church

James E Soulsby obtained his education in the Pleasant Ridge and Turkey Hill schools and later he went to work as a farmer and as a lumberman Following his marriage he bought twenty-five acres of land in Knox township and after selling that place purchased his present farm of seventy-six acres, a part of the old family homestead About fifty acres of his land is under cultivation, four acres having been cleared by himself Mr Soulsby had the misfortune to lose all his buildings and their contents by fire and the substantial structures now standing were all put up by himself at considerable expense He carries on general farming and raises stock for his own use

On June 7, 1879, Mr Soulsby was married to Miss Flora Rowles, a daughter of Price A and Sarah Ann (Rowles) Rowles The father of Mrs Soulsby was born in Clearfield county and spent his life here, owning a farm of 100 acres, on which his death occurred in 1902, at the age of sixty-eight years He married Sarah Ann Rowles, a daughter of Richard Rowles, of Woodward township, Clearfield county, and they had eleven children, Mrs

Soulsby being the second in order of birth The mother of Mrs Soulsby resides in a handsome residence on the corner of Barklay and Hannah streets, West Clearfield In politics, the late Price A Rowles was a Democrat and for fifteen years was a justice of the peace in Knox township He was a leading member of the Lutheran church

To Mr and Mrs Soulsby the following children were born Matilda, who married Frank Soulsby, of Cambria county, resides at Bakertown, Pa , Harry, who married Myrtle Coates, a daughter of John Coates, has three children—Albert, Della and Mary, Frank, who married Verna Bauman, a daughter of Stacy Bauman, resides at Clearfield, Julia, who is the wife of Stanley Taylor, of Akron, O , Bert, who assists his father, McClelland, who lives at Akron, Cora, George and Maude, all of whom are attending school, and Elva May, who died when seven months old Mr and Mrs. Soulsby attend Mt Zion Methodist Episcopal church In politics he is nominally a Democrat but casts his vote independently Both he and wife are interested members of the Grange and the P O S of A, Mrs. Soulsby being ex-ruler of the latter lodge at Olanta They are representative people of Knox township

JOHN CLARK MAHAFFEY, assistant cashier of the First National Bank of Cherry Tree, Pa , was born at Glen Hope, Clearfield county, September 18, 1877, a son of William T. and Julia J (Patchin) Mahaffey His grandparents on the paternal side were John and Ella (Byers) Mahaffey, who resided in the first half of the nineteenth century on the old family homestead near Cherry Tree

Mr Mahaffey's grandparents on the maternal side were Col Clark and Hetty G Patchin Col Clark Patchin was noted in this section as a military officer in the Civil war, having been appointed two terms as brigadier-general under Gov Curtin, of Pennsylvania. He was a fine specimen of military physique He was organizer of almost all companies enlisting in the counties of Indiana, Clearfield and Cambria

William Tuttle Mahaffey, father of the subject of this sketch, is one of the best known men in this part of Clearfield county Born in 1848, his first occupation was teaching school, but he subsequently became associated with his father in the lumber business, and also conducted a general store for a short time at Cherry Tree About 1878 he bought out an old manufacturing business and engaged in the manufacture of farm, lumber and saw-mill machinery, continuing in this business for twenty-one years He then sold out and for some six years following was largely interested in the lumber business, being very successful He finally retired and is now a resident of Cherry Tree He was one of the founders of the First National Bank of this place, in which his son is now assistant cashier, was also a founder and president of the Cherry Tree Electric Light Company, and a founder and director of the Cherry Tree Water Company He was twice married first to Julia Jane, daughter of Col Clark and Hetty (Graham) Patchin, of which union there were six children, including our subject, and secondly, in 1902 (his first wife having died in 1894) to Sarah Edmonson, who is still living

John Clark Mahaffey, after completing the usual school studies at the age of sixteen, entered upon a commercial course at the state normal school, graduating in 1900 He was

then engaged for five years as auditor for the Pennsylvania Railroad on the C & C Division On January 3, 1903, he entered upon his present position as assistant cashier of the First National Bank of Cherry Tree, of which, as already stated, his father was one of the founders, being still a director Our subject is also interested in the coal and lumber business He is a Republican in politics and is now serving as treasurer of the school board He is also a director in the Cherry Tree Water Company He is a member of the Methodist Protestant church of Cherry Tree, and has always been connected with the Christian Endeavor Society, having been president for a number of years He is also a member of the Independent Order of Odd Fellows An energetic, capable business man, he bids fair to prove a worthy successor to his father in advancing the moral and material interests of the town and its vicinity

Mr Mahaffey was married June 17, 1908, to Mary Elinor Beyer, who was born at Punxsutawney, Pa, June 14, 1883, a daughter of Dr William F and Margaret Ann Beyer. Dr. William F Beyer is one of the oldest physicians in Punxsutawney He is also interested in lumber and coal He is president of the Punxsutawney Light Company, a stockholder in the First National Bank and a very influential business man, outside his practice of medicine Mrs Margaret Ann Beyer, mother of Mrs J C Mahaffey and wife of Dr William F Beyer, was a woman of high character, and a very ardent church worker, being president and treasurer of several societies in the M E. church of Punxsutawney Her father, Ralston Mitchell, was a soldier in the Civil war and died in Libby prison

Mrs Mahaffey is a graduate of the Punxsutawney high school, and later of Shelton Hill School, Philadelphia, and was a student at Meadville College, in which latter institution she spent two years She is an active member of the Presbyterian church, belonging to the Ladies' Aid Society and also to the Mission Society

EDGAR T HENRY, an enterprising citizen and substantial farmer of Lawrence township, resides on a fine farm of 125 acres, and was born November 4, 1868, in Lumber City, Pa , a son of Matthew and Mary Elizabeth (Straw) Henry, who were the parents of nine children

Edgar T Henry was educated in the local schools of Lawrence township and at Curwensville, Pa , and then taught school seven terms in Elk county, Pa Mr Henry was then identified with the lumber industry and was employed as superintendent for J H Brennan of St Mary's for five years, and at the end of that time came to his present farm of 125 acres Mr Henry oversees all the work on his farm, but employs help to do the work, and has four tenants' dwellings on the place, besides two summer resort houses There are two general orchards, two large barns, and all of the outbuildings are comparatively new. Locust Grove is located on his farm, as is also the Driftwood schoolhouse of this district, and the Pennsylvania Railroad runs through his farm, stopping directly in front of his doorway, thus making it very convenient in getting to the city

Mr Henry is politically an independent Democrat, and is now serving his fourth year on the Lawrence township school board of which he has been secretary for the past three years While teaching in Elk county Mr

Henry served as auditor of this township for three years He is a member of the Grange, and attends the Presbyterian church of Curwensville

Mr Henry first married Elvira Goff of Elk county, and his second wife is Alice Wood of Clearfield county, Pa They have three children Audrey, Joseph, and Ida May

J A McQUOWN, an enterprising business man of DuBois, Pa , a concrete and paving contractor, at No 502 Piffer street, has been a resident of this borough since 1908 He was born on his father's farm in South Mahoning township, Indiana county, Pa , July 21, 1865, and is a son of John and a grandson of John McQuown

John McQuown, the father, accompanied his father to Indiana county, and they settled near Marion Center He spent the remainder of his life there, engaged in agricultural pursuits, his death occurring in 1894 He married Catherine Wiley, a native of Indiana county, where she still resides Nine children were born to them, as follows Clark, Elizabeth deceased, who was the wife of J E Matthews, Silas, Josiah A , Hannah, deceased, who was the wife of Miles Fisher, Harvey, who is deceased, Archie. Sadie, who is the wife of George Parsons, and Charles, deceased

J A McQuown attended the country schools, helped his father and also worked at the carpenter's trade for some years He was twenty-seven years of age when he left Indiana county and moved to Falls Creek, in Clearfield county, where he resided for eight years and then spent four years at Pittsburg and one year at Indiana, Pa , where he learned the concrete and paving business, with his brother, Archie McQuown Since 1908 he has been doing a large business in this line at Du-Bois, giving employment to four men and having the contracts for the greater part of all the public work Mr McQuown is a thoroughly practical business man and has established himself in the confidence of his fellow citizens by the honest and efficient manner in which his important work has been done He has invested in real estate here and has recently completed a fine modern residence on Piffer street

On September 28, 1892, Mr McQuown was married to Miss Edith M McCall, a daughter of James M and Annie (Ross) McCall, residents of Falls Creek They are members of the Methodist Episcopal church He belongs to the order of Modern Woodmen

ORD L NORRIS, a leading citizen of Pike township, residing on his farm of 340 acres, which is situated two and one-half miles north of Curwensville, was born on this farm, the old homestead, September 29, 1860, and is a son of John Norris and a grandson of Moses Norris

Moses Norris was born and reared in Huntingdon county, Pa , and there was married to Sarah Reed, a native of that county, and they lived there until after the birth of their first child, John Then they moved to Lawrence township, Clearfield county, settling with a brother-in-law, on 500 acres of land near Glen Richey On that place three more children were born, Nancy, Ellen and James Moses Norris subsequently sold his first homestead and bought 160 acres of land near Bloomington and owned that property at the time of death He cleared his land and engaged in lumbering and at the age of sixty years retired, having accumulated a comfortable com-

petency He and wife were charter members of the Center church and their ashes rest in the cemetery adjoining it

John Norris, son of Moses, was born in Huntingdon county in 1811 and was nine months old when his parents moved to Lawrence township, Clearfield county. Although he had few school advantages he was much better educated than the majority of his school mates and became a teacher, first in Lawrence and later in Pike and Penn townships After his marriage he engaged in farming for a time on the homestead and then moved to Hoyt's Mill, in Ferguson township, where he operated a saw-mill for a time, after which he came to Pike township and secured 160 acres of wild and wooded land He erected log buildings and in the course of time cleared 100 acres of his land and subsequently added more to his original holding For many years he was a justice of the peace and almost always held some township office, both because he was better educated than the majority of his fellow citizens and because they had confidence in his honesty and integrity He was a worthy member of the Methodist Episcopal church at Curwensville. In his early manhood he was a Whig and later became a Republican

On September 11, 1834, John Norris married Priscilla E Bloom, who was born in Pike township, Clearfield county, October 9, 1818, a daughter of Isaac Bloom, and sixteen children were born to them, as follows· Sarah, born March 20, 1836, died July 5, 1865; Thomas S , born March 24, 1837, died in 1888, married Mary Jane Askey in 1858: Mary Jane, born May 30, 1838, was married January 29, 1863, to John Star, John H , born March 26, 1840, was married March 1, 1864, to Cecelia McCleary, born June 5, 1847, James

R , born September 10, 1841, was married June 24, 1866, to Martha Ann Caldwell, Isaac B , born July 31, 1843, was married December 20, 1866, to Hannah Ann Caldwell, Moses, born March 22, 1845, was married July 7, 1867, to M Hockman, Martha, born January 14, 1847, was married September 5, 1869, to Jonathan Kirk, Clark B , born September 2, 1848, was married March 10, 1872, to Sarah E Waln, Elizabeth, born May 12, 1850, was married August 15, 1883, to James Cassidy, George L , born April 25, 1851, was married September 14, 1871, to Jane Gulick, Margaret H , born July 31, 1853, was married October 6, 1872, to Isaac M Stage, Wesley, born May 21, 1855, married Bertha Brown, Levina H , born November 28, 1856, was married September 1, 1876, to Truman J Wall, William W , born June 21, 1858, married Electa McNeel, and Ord L The father of this family died September 6, 1894, having survived his wife since February 24, 1882 Their burial was in the Oak Hill Cemetery

Ord L Norris attended the Chestnut Ridge school in his boyhood and afterward assisted in the cultivation of the home farm, on which he has always lived He has also a one-half interest in 100 acres of grazing land in Pike Township Mr Norris carries on large farm industries and is much interested in raising cattle and has done a great deal to raise the standard in Pike Township He was one of the first to introduce Brown Swiss cattle in Clearfield County and now has a fine herd of these valuable animals Agricultural matters along every line have interested him greatly and he has studied the science of farming notably to his benefit He is a member of the Clearfield County Agricultural Society and has been very prominent in the Susquehannah Grange at Cur-

wensville, of which he is the present master, having previously served as gate keeper and steward

Mr. Norris was married on October 5, 1881, to Miss Ella C Way, who was born in Center County, Pa , in Half Moon Township, December 9, 1861, a daughter of Jacob B and Julia M (Downing) Way Jacob B Way was born in Center County July 20, 1836 On March 14, 1860, he married Julia M Downing, who was born January 20, 1842, a daughter of John Downing, who came to Clearfield County with his family of five children Jacob B Way continued to live in Center County for several years after his marriage and then settled in Clearfield town, where he was engaged as freight agent for four and one-half years He then moved to Girard Township and passed four years on a farm and from there came to a farm in Pike Township, where four more years were spent, following which he became freight and ticket agent for the Pennsylvania Railroad and also was postmaster until the time of his death, October 9, 1897, a period of five years His burial was in Oak Hill Cemetery Both he and his wife were members of the Methodist Episcopal church The latter survives and resides with her son, R K Way, at Curwensville Mr Way was a Republican in politics and fraternally was connected with the Masons and Odd Fellows In 1895 Mr Way started the book and stationery business which is continued at Curwensville by the firm of T & R K Way

Jacob B and Julia M Way's children were Ella, who is the wife of Ord L Norris, Ortensie, who was born April 1, 1863, Olive M , who was born December 14, 1864, is the wife of W P Watson, of Clearfield, Pa , W Calder, Howard L , born August 8, 1866, Clara D , who was born September 9, 1867, is the wife of

John N Thompson, Ai Boynton, who was born August 5, 1872, died March 11, 1874, Gertie Belle, who was born April 25, 1875, is the wife of D L Powell, and R K, who was born November 4, 1878

Mr and Mrs Norris have one son, Truman J, who is engaged in the dry cleaning business at Clearfield He was born in Pike Township, July 25, 1883 He married Miss Gussie Johnston, a daughter of Clayton Johnston, and they have one son, E Edward Mr and Mrs Norris are members of the Methodist Episcopal church Politically he is a Republican and has held public office, serving two terms as overseer of the poor in Pike Township He has shown a public spirited and humane attitude in the establishment and proper management of the county home He is a stockholder in the Curwensville National Bank, and the Curwensville Rural Telephone Company of Pike Township He is identified with the lodge of Odd Fellows at Curwensville Mr Norris is thus shown to be a capable business man and a broad minded, well intentioned citizen

JOHN H WEAVER, a well known farmer and dairyman of Burnside township, was born on the old Weaver homestead in this township, June 1, 1868, son of John and Margaret G (McGee) Weaver He is a grandson of John Weaver, a native of Union county, Pa, who died in 1870 at the age of 90 years John's wife, whose maiden name was Ruth Zimmerman, died in 1873 at the age of 90 years

John Weaver, father of our subject, accompanied his parents when young to Burnside township, Clearfield county He was a carpenter by trade, but also followed lumbering and rafting on the Susquehanna river He settled on the present Weaver homestead in 1867, at which time the locality was all timber land, which he cleared for his farm In later years he erected for a residence one of the largest houses in this township His death took place in 1895 He was married in 1853 to Margaret G McGee, who was born March 4 1826, a daughter of Rev James and Mary (Barnhart) McGee, who came from Center county in 1826, settling in Bell township, where they were among the prominent families James McGee was the first postmaster at McGees Mills, when the first mail route was established between Curwensville and Indiana in 1833 and the McGees were charter members of the pioneer M E church in Bell township, this being about 1860 In addition to the subject of this sketch John and Margaret were the parents of two other children, namely J M Weaver, a farmer and dairyman of Burnside township, and Sadie, who is the wife of W B Stevenson, of Mahaffey, Pa

John H Weaver, after attending the local schools, became associated with his father in the lumbering and farming industries He remained on the old homestead and as his parents advanced in years took care of them until their death, and he has since continued agricultural pursuits, establishing also a fine dairy business, in which he has been very successful, and is now regarded as one of the prosperous citizens of his township A man well thought of by his fellow citizens, he has served in public office, having been supervisor for two terms and one term auditor of the township Politically he is a Democrat He belongs to the Odd Fellows' lodge at Burnside and also to the Grange at New Washington

Mr Weaver was married July 6, 1898, to Eva Cummings, who was born at New Washington, Pa, May 13, 1869, a daughter of John

M and Elizabeth (Mahaffey) Cummings Her father who was one of the early merchants of New Washington—a member of the firm of Weaver & Cummings, died in 1892 His wife Elizabeth was the daughter of Thomas and Margaret (Mitchell) Mahaffey, she died in 1888 Mrs Weaver's brothers and sisters now living are—Margaret, who is employed as a teacher at New Washington, Pa , Molly, residing at home, Elizabeth, wife of F W Stricher, of New Washington, and Sarah, who is a teacher in Clearfield

The children of our subject and wife are, Robert, born May 4, 1902, James, born Sept 10, 1906, and Sarah, born April 27, 1907 Mr Weaver is also rearing a nephew of his wife, Ray Cummings, who has resided with them since infancy

LEWIS E BAILEY, who resides on the farm on which he was born, on April 1, 1863, which consists of 240 acres of valuable land, situated in Pike Township, Clearfield County, Pa , two and one-half miles north of Curwensville, belongs to one of the old families of this section and is a substantial and representative citizen He is a son of Abraham and Nancy (Caldwell) Bailey and a grandson of Daniel and Jane (Passmore) Bailey

Daniel Bailey, the grandfather, was born in Lycoming County, Pa , in 1794, and died in 1876 He married Jane Passmore, whose father was Abraham Passmore, and she lived to be seventy-nine years of age After marriage they lived on the Lydia Way farm in Pike Township, which is now owned by Leonard Neeper, and on that place their three oldest children were born, Maria, Isaac and Abraham They then moved to the farm which is now occupied by their grandson, Lewis E

Bailey It was then a tract of 100 acres to which Daniel Bailey added until he owned 400 acres He cleared practically the entire farm and lived on it until his death On this farm nine more children were born, as follows Joseph, Mrs Anna Anspach, who lives in Iowa, Ruth, George, Calvin, Harrison, Levi, Lewis and Newton, all of whom are now deceased Newton Bailey was a veteran of the Civil War and after its close he moved to Iowa for a time but died in Clearfield County

Abraham Bailey was born November 17, 1819 He helped his father to clear the land in Pike Township and passed almost all of his life on the homestead, where his death occurred December 16, 1904 At the time of his decease he was one of the large landowners of the township, having 400 acres His father was probably the first coal operator in this locality, opening a coal bank on his own property, in early days selling down the river but later working the bank only for his own use Abraham Bailey was identified with the Republican party and at times served in township offices He was a well known and highly respected man He married Nancy Caldwell, who was born in Pike Township, in 1814, a daughter of Alexander Caldwell, and died March 16, 1905 Both she and husband were members of the Methodist Episcopal church, of which he was a trustee and steward, and their burial was in the Center Cemetery To Abraham and Nancy Bailey the following children were born Hannah, who is the wife of William Lawhead, of Pike Township, Elizabeth, who was accidentally killed by a falling tree when she was about thirty years of age, Frances Ella, deceased, who was the wife of Harvey Loughrey, of Indiana County, Pa , Samuel D , who is a physician at Clearfield, Lewis E , and Margaret, who is the wife of Albert Straw, of Clearfield

Lewis E Bailey enjoyed excellent school advantages, attending the Pleasant Grove school, the Curwensville public schools and for two years was a student in the University of Pennsylvania Although well qualified for a professional life, Mr Bailey preferred agriculture and returned and engaged in farming and dairying on the homestead   Although his father built the present farm house, Mr Bailey has put up a number of the other substantial farm structures and has made many improvements He carries on agriculture according to modern methods and is one of the active members of the Susquehannah Grange, which is largely made up of the most intelligent and progressive farmers of this section

Mr Bailey was married in 1888, to Miss Jennie M Adams, who was born at Philipsburg, Pa , a daughter of Alexander and Margaret B Adams Mr and Mrs Bailey have had ten children, namely   Norman, who was born October 31, 1889, Margaret, who was born September 4, 1891, and died November 8, 1891, Alexander C, who was born September 5, 1892, Daniel A, who was born June 5, 1894, Helen Marie, who was born September 28, 1895, Abraham S, who was born February 1, 1897, Elizabeth, who was born January 28, 1899, Ellsworth, who was born June 22, 1900, Louise E, who was born November 12, 1902, and Charles G, who was born May 28, 1907 Mr Bailey and family are members of the Pleasant Grove Methodist Episcopal church, in which he is steward, and also is a member of the board of trustees In politics he is a Republican and has served at times on the election board and one term as township clerk but he has never been anxious for political

honors, being more closely interested in agricultural affairs and in public school advancement

JAMES WATSON,* a substantial and representative citizen of Bradford Township, for many years has resided on his well improved farm of 120 acres, which is favorably located six miles north of Woodland Mr Watson was born in Center County, Pa , in 1844, and is a son of William and Catherine (Griffin) Watson

William Watson was born also in Center County, where his father had settled when he came from Ireland He was a shoemaker and followed his trade until his accidental death by drowning in the river, in 1857, in Bradford Township, Clearfield County In 1843 he moved into Lawrence Township, this county, and five years later into Bradford Township, settling on the Thomas Holt property His widow survived a long time, dying at the age of eighty-seven years

James Watson attended the district schools in his youth with as much regularity as did the average country boy and early made farming his choice of occupation After marriage, in 1868, he settled on the farm on which he has lived and has carried on general farming and stock raising for some forty-two years. He follows methods of agriculture which he has proved suitable as to climate and soil and his stock has been remuneratively increased each season through proper feeding and attention His activities have been those of an industrious, common sense, intelligent farmer and he has prospered accordingly He has always taken an interest in public matters, especially those concerning his own county and township, and has served as a county commissioner, school director and township supervisor and road master

In 1868 Mr Watson was married to Miss Amy Graham and six children were born to them, four of whom survive, namely C D, who married T L Livingston, of Bradford Township, and has four children, Arthur, Minnie, who married E P Echiley, and Lamrah The first and second born children, William and Reed, died just one year apart, the former when three years old and the latter when but two years of age Mr Watson's surviving children have all been given public school advantages and are well informed men and women Mr and Mrs Watson are members of the Methodist church

JOSEPH A KUJAWA, who is engaged in the merchant tailoring business at Curwensville, Pa , has been established here since 1891 and is one of the representative business men in his line, at Curwensville He was born in Germany, November 17, 1867, and is a son of Joseph and Agnes Kujawa, who spent their lives in Germany

Joseph A Kujawa was fifteen years old when he came to America, landing at New York and from there coming to Clearfield, Pa He learned his trade with his brother, Anthony Kujawa, at Clearfield, working in the shop there for three and one-half years, after which he traveled as a journeyman and worked at his trade in many of the largest cities of the country, including Pittsburg, Cleveland, Chicago, St Louis, Kansas City, Omaha and Memphis He then went to New York and took a course in the cutting school of the John J Mitchell Company, after which he worked for a time in one of the fashionable establishments on Fifth Avenue Mr Kujawa then

came back to Clearfield and worked for one winter for his brother, in April, 1891, coming from there to Curwensville where he opened up a merchant tailoring establishment for himself, since when he has changed his quarters several times, being now well settled in the Graff Building From long experience he has become a very expert cutter and workman and has secured a large trade from those who are particular as to the quality and fit of their garments He has prospered and now is interested in stores at Curwensville and also at Clearfield

Mr Kujawa was married July 12, 1898, to Amelia Kaminsky, who was also born in Germany and was brought to the United States when she was six years old They have three children Anna, Stanley and Norman They are members of the Roman Catholic church He is a member of the Knights of Columbus and International Custom Cutters' Association of America Mr Kujawa is a self made man, having earned all he possesses through his own steadiness and industry and is one of Curwensville's men of ample means, being a stockholder in the Curwensville National Bank and in the Building and Loan Association His residence stands on Thompson Street

HON FRED LOTT, general merchant and formerly burgess of Troutville, is one of the representative men of this borough, in which he has maintained his home since 1894 He was born July 15, 1841, on his father's farm in Henderson Township, Jefferson County, Pa , and is a son of George H and Catherine (Knarr) Lott

George H Lott was born in Germany and there married Catherine Knarr and after the birth of their first child they emigrated to

America In order to reach Henderson Township, Jefferson County, they were able to travel by railroad as far as Tyrone, Pa , from the place they landed, but the rest of the trip was through a rough country and this they made with horse and wagon   The first wife of George H Lott died in Jefferson County, leaving four children Henry, Adam, Fred and Catherine, Fred being the only one to survive Mr Lott was later married to Catherine Miller, who died without children George H Lott continued to live in Jefferson County and there his death occurred at the age of sixty-one years

Fred Lott grew to manhood on his father's farm and followed farming and lumbering for many years, later purchasing the farm which contained eighty-eight acres Having bought other farm land he sold the old homestead in 1908 In 1894 he moved to Troutville and embarked in a general mercantile business and has continued in the same line, having his son, Joseph H Lott, as his assistant He still owns also a small farm in Brady Township and a timber tract of fifty-five acres located in Bell Township, and in addition to this, a half interest in a lumber tract in Henderson Township and improved real estate at Troutville He is a stockholder in the DuBois National Bank at DuBois, Pa and was one of the organizers of the Citizens National Bank at Big Run, Pa and was one of the organizers of the Citizens National Bank at Big Run, Pa , of which he is still a director In politics he is a Democrat He has been a very active and useful citizen of Troutville and has served in the borough council and as burgess

In 1862 Mr Lott was married to Miss Catherine Walker, of Jefferson County, Pa , and ten children were born to them, as follows Lewis, who married Catherine S Mervine, and they live in Jefferson County and have two children—Mildred and Burnett; William, who is a resident of DuBois, married Millie Stiles; Jesse E , who lives at Troutville, married Josephine Webber, Pauline, who lives at home, Susan C , who is the wife of Dr. F C Willard, of Warren County, Pa , Joseph H , who is with his father in business, married Jennie Schoch, and they have three children—Helen, Brooks Frederick and Louisa, and four who died young   Mr and Mrs Lott are members of the Reformed church Since 1875 Mr Lott has been a member of the Odd Fellows, and belongs to the Rebeccas and also to the Knights of Pythias

JAMES R NORRIS, whose valuable farm of 140 acres lies in Pike township, two miles south of Curwensville, Pa , was born at Hoyt's Mill, in Ferguson township, Clearfield county, Pa , September 10, 1841 He is a grandson of Moses Norris and a son of John Norris

James R Norris attended the Chestnut Ridge school until he was about fifteen years of age, after which he worked in the woods with his older brother, during the winters, and engaged in farming during the summers After marriage he followed lumbering in Lawrence township for one winter and then moved on a farm in Pike township, near Chestnut Ridge, where he remained for one year, moving then to the farm belonging to the John Irwin estate and from there, in October, 1868, to his present farm, where he has continued to reside ever since He found it necessary to do considerable building and improving and had twenty acres of the land to clear   The substantial farm structures now

JAMES R. NORRIS GROUP

standing he put up as they were needed He has a valuable coal bank on his farm, which yields from 200 to 300 tons of coal a month He is a stockholder in the Curwensville National Bank and both he and wife are stockholders in the Farmers' and Traders' Bank, of Clearfield, Pa

On June 24, 1866, Mr Norris was married to Miss Martha A Caldwell, who was born on the Joseph Caldwell farm, at Peewee's Nest, Pike township, Clearfield county, Pa, September 6, 1848 She is a daughter of Joseph A and Mary J (Bloom) Caldwell Joseph A Caldwell was born on the McNaul farm, in this section, September 6, 1820, and died May 19, 1868 He resided with his family on his ninety-acre farm in Pike township, which is now owned by James R Norris and wife He was a leading man in Pike township for many years, on numerous occasions being elected to township offices on the Republican ticket and serving in all with honesty and efficiency He did nearly all the clearing on his farm at Peewee's Nest and during his most active years was engaged mainly in lumbering He was a stockholder in the Curwensville National Bank He married Mary J Bloom, a daughter of Abraham T Bloom, a native of New Jersey Mrs Caldwell died January 9, 1906, and she was laid to rest by the side of her husband in the cemetery of the Methodist Episcopal church at Curwensville. of which they had been members To Joseph A and Mary J Caldwell, five children were born, namely Martha A, who is the wife of James R Norris, Peter A, who resides at Edgar, Neb (married Sarah Bloom, of Bloom township), Mary E, who died young, Nannie J, who is the wife of Joseph Akins, of Kansas, and Emma, who died at the age of five years

45

To James R Norris and wife thirteen children have been born, almost all of whom survive and are comfortably settled near the old home and within easy reach of their parents Annie P married A M Hoover and they have had four children, Austin, Pearl, James and Enna, Pearl being the only survivor Lucy May, who is now deceased, was the wife of F K Flegal Mary J married Henry G Hile, and they have three children, James, Dean and Henry Cora C married John C Rabold and two children have been born to them, Emma and Norris C, the last named being alone surviving Orly C married Alice Drocker, and they have one daughter, Mabel Lavina married Donald C Miller and they have one daughter, Jennett W Atlee J married Ella J Hile and they have two daughters, Thelma and Blanche Mamie V, the eighth in order of birth, is a successful school teacher McVay C, Jean E and Foster G, all reside at home Elizabeth died when six weeks old and Blair C, the youngest, died when four years old Mr and Mrs Norris are active members of the Methodist Episcopal church at Curwensville In politics he is a Republican and at times has accepted township offices, more from a sense of duty than for any other reason He is interested in the educational advancement of his section and served three years on the school board, and as a wide awake and earnest citizen, anxious that his community should be law abiding, he consented to serve on the election board He belongs to the order of Odd Fellows and also to the Grange

LEONARD REED NEEPER, dairyman and farmer and one of Pike Township's best known and most substantial citizens, resides one and one-half miles northwest of Curwensville, Pa , and owns one farm, aggregating 102 acres He was born in Pike Township, Clearfield County, Pa , on a farm that adjoins his own, June 18, 1872, and is a son of Robert R Neeper and a grandson of Joseph Neeper, who was a veteran of the War of 1812 who had fought in the battle of Lake Erie

Robert R Neeper was born near Curwensville, Pa , in 1826 His parents subsequently moved to a farm eight miles from Curwensville, on Ream's turnpike road and he attended school at Luthersburg His life was mainly devoted to farming and lumbering After his marriage he settled on what was known as the Hartshorn farm His death occurred March 4, 1901, at the age of seventy-six years and his burial was in Oak Hill Cemetery He was not very active in politics but was an intelligent citizen and was identified with the Republican party He was also a member of Susquehannah Grange, No 1145, at Curwensville He married Jane Hartshorn, a daughter of Jonathan and Rachel Hartshorn, and they had five children born to them, namely Mary, Rachel, Alice, Ruthanna Leonard R and Howard M The mother of this family died in 1903 She was a member of the Presbyterian church

Leonard R Neeper, with his brother and sisters, attended school at Chestnut Ridge and at Curwensville, after which he engaged in farming on the home place and continued there until the spring of 1903, when he bought his present farm of Lydia A Way He went into the dairy business which he has developed into a large and successful industry He is a practical, wide awake intelligent farmer in all branches and attends closely to his business, not taking any active part in politics or paying much attention to outside concerns He casts his vote with the Republican party He is a stockholder in the Curwensville Telephone Company in Pike Township

On November 25, 1896, Mr Neeper was married to Miss Leota Norris, a daughter of Moses and Maria Norris, of Pike Township, and they have four children. Oscar R , Arthur L , Rufus and James Dorsey Mr and Mrs Neeper are members of the Methodist Episcopal church He belongs to the Grange at Curwensville

MILO E PARK, M D, of Westover, is not only a successful physician and surgeon, but is also a man largely interested in various business and other enterprises, and ranks high among the progressive citizens of Clearfield county He was born at Cochran Mills, Armstrong county, Pa , Feb 13, 1859, a son of James Kelly and Elizabeth (Ludwick) Park The great-grandfather of James Kelly Park was physician for a Queen of the German States While on his second trip to America, he was lost in the Atlantic Ocean, sometime in the 17th century

The father of our subject, James Kelly Park, was born in Westmoreland county, Pa , April 20, 1828, and was graduated from the medical department of the Western Reserve University at Cleveland, Ohio in 1852 He practiced his profession at Murrysville for four years, then removed to Cochran Mills, Armstrong county, where he remained fifteen years From 1871 to 1888 he practiced at Whitesburg Armstrong County, Pa In 1888 he came to Westover, Clearfield county, where he continued in practice until his death in 1889 He was a member of the Methodist church, and belonged also to the Masonic order An active Democrat politically, he was at one time a candidate for the legislature and failed of election only by 102 votes in a strong Republican district His wife Elizabeth, born April 20, 1829, in Westmoreland County Pa, a daughter of John Ludwick She died Sept 28, 1883 Their children now living, in addition to the subject of this sketch, are as follows W C Park, a physician at New Millport, Pa, H L Park, a ginseng farmer residing in Westover, Delmora, wife of Dr J A Kelly of Whitesburg, and Mary Elizabeth, wife of J B McKee of Westover, who is superintendent of a tannery, Hannah Agnes, born in 1866, died in 1886

Milo E. Park, after graduating from the common schools at the age of 18 years, spent three terms at an academy at Elderton, Armstrong county He then taught school in that county for three terms after which he entered the Western Reserve University at Cleveland, his father's alma mater, and was graduated from the medical department there in 1884 He first located for practice in Utahville, Clearfield county, but after a short stay there, removed to Kellys Station, Armstrong county, where he followed his profession for a short time, subsequently returning to Utahville In 1887 he came to Westover, of which place he has since been a resident In addition to practicing medicine, he has considerable business interests in other directions, notably in coal and oil He was one of the promoters of the gas and oil industries near Westover in 1905 and spent considerable money in boring and drilling experiments, both there and elsewhere He has also gold mining interests near Wind river, Wyoming, close to the new Yellowstone Park In 1908 he laid out and opened a deer park near Westover, consisting of 30 acres which now contains seven deer, besides a number of mountain goats He was until recently president of the Clearfield and Cambria Telephone Company, and he is a stockholder in the Mahaffey bank and in various other business enterprises all of which are in a flourishing condition

A Democrat in politics, Dr Park was the first burgess of Westover borough and, in fact, took a leading part in the organization of the borough He held the office of burgess for ten years and is at present serving as councilman

Dr Park was married in 1884 to Emma E Rishel, who was born in Lycoming county, Pa, March 5, 1865, a daughter of P K and Margaret (Miller) Rishel Mrs Park had five brothers, of whom four are now living, namely Henry H, a blacksmith, residing in Westover, John A, who lives in Johnstown, Pa, G C Rishel of Westover, and William Rishel, of Johnstown, Pa The one deceased was Dan C Dr Park and wife have had three children Claud L and Ganelle, who are both deceased, and Margaret Odessa, who is the wife of W B Clark, assistant cashier in the Mahaffey bank Dr and Mrs Park are popular members of the best society in this part of the county The doctor has one of the largest collections of deer and elk mounts that could be found in any private residence anywhere, a source of pleasure to all interested in natural history

Two brothers of the Doctor, who are now deceased, were Kelly Otis, who died in 1895 at the age of 27, while engaged in the practice of medicine in Cambria county, and Robert B, born in 1854, who died in 1893 The latter was an operator on the Pennsylvania Railroad system He married Miss Ollie Neff

The subject of this sketch twice crossed the Rocky Mountains on horseback, in 1905, on a hunting tour, and in 1907, on account of mining interests

FRANKLIN M WOODS, justice of the peace in Chest Township, has resided on his present farm for the past eight years and is engaged with the Clearfield-Cambria Coal Company, as weighing boss He was born in Chest Township, May 2, 1852, and is a son of Israel and Catherine (Fishel) Woods

Israel Woods was born in Tioga County, Pa, and was a son of James and Nancy (Larson) Woods James Woods brought his family from Tioga County to Clearfield County and took up the first homestead in Chest Township and followed farming all his life He was a man of reliable character, as was evidenced by his election to the office of justice of the peace, in which he served continuously for ten years Israel Woods took less interest in politics than either his father or son, devoting himself closely to the clearing of the present farm, in association with his brother, locating here in 1850 His death occurred in 1905, at the age of seventy-two years He married Catherine Fishel, who survives, being now in her seventy-fifth year She is a daughter of Frederick and Nancy Fishel, of Cambria County, Pa The surviving children of this marriage are· Franklin M, Sarah, who is the wife of James Kitchen, of Chest Township, Harriet, who is the wife of Ira Toat, of Clearfield, Nancy, who is the wife of James McCully, of Chest Township, and James F, who resides with his mother on the old homestead

Franklin M Woods attended the district schools in boyhood and afterward made himself useful and self-supporting by his work on the home farm and remained there until after his marriage, when he came to his present place He has been very active in politics for a number of years and is an influential factor in the Democratic party in Chest Township For twenty-seven years he has been a member of the school board and since 1907 has been a justice of the peace

Mr Woods was married to Miss Carrie J Smeed, who was born January 22, 1862, in Burnside Township, Clearfield County, Pa. and is a daughter of Lysander and Sarah (Snyder) Smeed, and a granddaughter of Jonas and Catherine Snyder and Othello and Matilda (King) Smeed Mr and Mrs Woods have five children, namely Emma S, who is the wife of Thomas Lewis, an engineer, residing in Cambria County, and has five children, Mary L, who is a trained nurse residing at DuBois, James Kelly, who resides at home; Sarah Catherine, who is the wife of Benjamin Hurd, a miner, and has two children, and Bessie, who lives with her parents Justice Woods is a member of Lodge No 361, Red Men, at Mahaffey, and Lodge No 561, P O S of A, at La Jose, Pa

JOHN M KINNEY,* who has been manager of the Eureka Stores, at Houtzdale, Pa, since 1907, has been identified with this business enterprise for many years He was born at Houtzdale, June 24, 1880, and is a son of Bernard and Effie (Williams) Kinney

Bernard Kinney was born in Huntingdon County, Pa, came to Houtzdale with his father, Charles Kinney, and has spent the greater part of his life in this borough His father conducted one of the first hotels in this place, subsequently losing his property by fire He married Effie Williams, who was a daughter of Jessie Williams, a well known lumberman of Clearfield County, who died at Beaver Falls, in 1910 To Bernard Kinney and wife six children were born, namely John M , Edward, who has charge of the clothing department in the Eureka Stores, Charles, who is in a business house in Philadelphia, Mary, who resides at home, Margaret, who assists in the above named business, and Rosalie, who is a student at Greensburg, Pa For the past eighteen years, Bernard Kinney has been chief of police at Houtzdale, where he is numbered with the valued and substantial citizens

John M Kinney was educated at Houtzdale and he has had all his business experience in this borough The Eureka Stores were established here some twenty years since and Mr Kinney was connected with the business for eleven years preceding his appointment as manager, and, in fact, may be said to have grown up in it Mr Kinney, with the other members of his family, belongs to the Catholic church

WILLIAM IRWIN YINGLING, a prosperous farmer of Burnside Township, resides on the old family homestead in Burnside Township, on which he was born May 1, 1867, and is a son of Michael M and Elizabeth (Lamer) Yingling

Michael M Yingling was born January 24, 1842, in Burnside Township, and has been interested in lumbering and farming almost all his life, and built a saw-mill which was the oldest in the southern part of the county This he operated until 1870, often working half the night after a laborious day at rafting, but, his health broke down and he sold out his mill interests but continued to follow farming Since 1893 he has been a commercial traveler, representing certain patent medicines in the interest of Dr Burkhart, of Cincinnati, O He mar-

ried Elizabeth Lamer, who died in 1880, at the age thirty-eight years She was a daughter of William Lamer, of Clearfield County Five children of the above marriage survive, three sons and two daughters, namely: William I , A P , who is a salesman residing at Williamsport, Pa , Howard C , who is a farmer, Emma, who is the wife of N Russell, a merchant at Barnesboro, and Maud, who resides at Williamsport

After his school days were over, William I Yingling engaged in lumbering and logging and so continued until 1894, when he bought his present farm on which he has since resided He carries on general farming, adopted practical methods and using improved machinery and meets with very satisfactory results

Mr Yingling married Miss Rosa McKee, who was born February 16, 1873, and is a daughter of Manuel and Jane McKee, who reside at Westover, Pa Mr and Mrs Yingling have five children, their ages ranging from sixteen to one year, namely Blaine, Jane, Birdie, Helen and Mary In politics Mr Yingling is a Democrat He has served as school director and in other offices, being a representative and reliable citizen

G LLOYD ADDLEMAN, a highly respected citizen of Curwensville, residing on the corner of George and Walnut Streets, and a retired farmer still owning 125 acres of fine land in Pike Township, was born in Center County, Pa , April 30, 1843, and is a son of William and Esther Addleman

William Addleman was of German extraction He came to Clearfield County in 1849 and was a farmer and lumberman He reared two families of children four being born to his first marriage and eight to his second, G Lloyd being the third in order of birth in the latter

G Lloyd Addleman attended school in both Lawrence and Pike Townships, the Center and Oakland schools, but when seventeen years of age he went to work in the woods and filled a man's place in the lumber camps   After he married he settled on the Irwin farm in Pike Township, where he lived for three and one-half years, and then purchased the home farm near Curwensville, on which his son, Charles C Addleman now lives   He continued to reside on that place until the fall of 1902, when he retired from active labor and located at Curwensville, where he is very pleasantly established   He is a stockholder in the Curwensville Building and Loan Association   In politics he is a Republican and he served three terms as road supervisor in Pike Township and one term since coming to this borough

Mr Addleman married Miss Annie M Cleaver, who was born in Pike Township, December 15, 1842, a daughter of Nathan and Cynthia (Wrigley) Cleaver, and they have had three children   William H , who died when aged two weeks and three days, Charles C , and Harry B   The latter resides at Curwensville   He was married first to Emma Hipp, who, at death, left three children   Walter, William and Alice   His second marriage was to Mary Grace Hatzenrather   Mr and Mrs Addleman are members of the Methodist Episcopal church   He belongs to and takes an interest in the Susquehannah Grange at Curwensville

FREDERICK J HARRISON, superintendent of the motor power of the B R & P Railroad, has been stationed at DuBois, Pa , since 1901 and since 1910 has filled the important office of superintendent of motive power of the whole system   He was born at Rochester, N Y , February 23, 1865, and is a son of Joseph and Mary (Wilson) Harrison, the former of whom was one of the old and reliable engineers of the New York Central Railroad for many years   Two children of the family survive   Frederick J and Nancy, the latter of whom is the wife of George C Kemp, of Rochester

Frederick J Harrison attended school in his native place until he was fourteen years of age and then started to learn the machinist's trade, which he followed for eleven years, being connected during this time with the Graves Elevator Works   He then became fireman on the New York Central lines and remained for three years and three months, sending in his resignation just one day before he was promoted to be engineer   He then resumed work as a machinist, in October, 1888, entering the shops of the B R & P Railroad, at Rochester, and in 1890 was placed in charge of the shop and in 1894 was made general foreman   Mr. Harrison continued in that responsible position for thirteen years and then came to DuBois, in the same capacity   He had the placing of all the tools and the starting of the new works at this point   Mr Harrison continued to advance in the confidence and esteem of his employers, and in 1904 he was promoted to the position of master mechanic of the DuBois shop and in 1910, as mentioned above, was made superintendent of the whole motive power system   He has been thoroughly and practically educated in his line of work and is considered one of the most competent men in the employ of the company

Mr Harrison was married in August, 1910,

to Miss M Effie Osborn, a daughter of William and Margaret Osborn Mr and Mrs Harrison reside at No 311 E Scribner Avenue They attend the Episcopal church In politics he is a Republican but has never been very active in public matters, his business having very closely absorbed his time and attention He is identified with the Elks at Du-Bois and belongs to all the branches of Masonry and to Damascus Temple, Mystic Shrine, at Rochester, Pa

LEWIS L HILE, postmaster at Ansonville, Pa, where he is also proprietor of a general store, belongs to an old Clearfield County family which was established here by his great-grandfather He was born January 13, 1875, at Curwensville, Pa, and is a son of Rev William P and Laura (Laporte) Hile

Rev William P Hile was born at Curwensville, his father, Henry Hile coming to Clearfield County from Northumberland about 1835 William P Hile was a well educated man and for many years was a minister in the Baptist church His death occurred in December, 1909, in Northumberland County, Pa He married Laura Laporte, who died in 1899, in Indiana County, Pa They were parents of the following children Elizabeth, who is the wife of Walter Norris, Willis, who is deceased, Lewis L, Ada, who is the wife of Dean Rankin, Ella, who is the wife of Atlay Norris, and Henry, George and Ray

After completing the public school course at Curwensville, Lewis L Hile became a student in the South Jersey Institute, at Bridgeton, N J His first business experience was as a clerk in a store at Philipsburg, Pa, where he remained for two years and then served two years in the same capacity in a general store

in Indiana County, after which he was in a store at Berwindale, Pa, where he was postmaster for two years and came from there to Ansonville He erected his present building and carries a large and carefully selected stock of goods He is a Republican in politics and was appointed postmaster in 1909 and is giving general satisfaction as an official

Mr Hile was married in November, 1893, to Miss Margaret Ruffner, who is a daughter of Joseph and Anna (Daugherty) Ruffner, old residents of Indiana County Mrs Hile is the youngest of her parents' family She has two brothers, John and Harry, but her one sister, Emma, who was the wife of Rev Mc-Mann, a Baptist minister, is now deceased Mr and Mrs Hile have one daughter, Kathleen Lucille, who was born May 19, 1905 Mr and Mrs Hile are members of the Baptist church He has served as township clerk and at present is a member of the school board

JAMES PAUL SPACKMAN, M D, who has been successfully engaged in the practice of medicine at Peale, Pa, since 1898, was born February 23, 1871, in Luthersburg, Brady Township, Clearfield County, Pa, and is a son of Dr R V and Frances (Alexander) Spackman

The Spackman family originated in Hankertown, England, and after locating in this country settled in Chester county, Pa, from whence it moved to Center County and eventually to Clearfield County Benjamin and Hannah Spackman, the paternal grandparents of Dr James P Spackman, were for a time residents of Bellfonte, and from that place they removed to Clearfield County where both spent the remainder of their lives Dr R V Spackman, the father of Dr James P, was born in Bellefonte, Pa , March 30, 1838, and was a mere youth when the family removed to Clearfield County In company with Dr Read of Osceola Mills, he read medicine under Dr R V Wilson of Clearfield, and entered Jefferson Medical College in 1864 After a short course there he began the practice of his profession, but deeming a little more study necessary he re-entered the college and was graduated with the class of 1868 Locating in Luthersburg, he was in active practice there for twenty-five years He then changed his field of endeavor to Reynoldsville for about three years, then went to DuBois, where he continued in his profession until his death, which occurred March 20, 1906 Dr Spackman was married to Frances Alexander, who was a daughter of James and Phoebe Alexander, the former a sadler by trade and an early settler of Clearfield County, where he died Mrs Spackman died June 2, 1895, having been the mother of three children James Paul, Olive, who died at the age of eight years, and a child who died in infancy

James Paul Spackman attended the public schools of Luthersburg and the Clarion State Normal school of Clarion, Pa , later becoming a student of Allegheny College at Meadville, Crawford County He entered Jefferson Medical College and was graduated with the class of 1896, after which he practiced for two years at DuBois with his father He located in Peale in November, 1898 as contract physician for the Clearfield Bituminous Coal Company, and here he has remained to the present time A close student, kind-hearted advisor and steady-handed surgeon, Dr Spackman has built up a large and lucrative practice which extends to Grass Flat and Winburne and the surrounding country, and his friends are legion

Dr Spackman was first married in January, 1896, to Miss Helen Wheeler, of Union City, Pa , daughter of James Wheeler, and to this union there was born one son, Francis Wheeler Mrs Spackman died September 2, 1902, and on June 8, 1904, Dr Spackman was married secondly to Mrs Edith (Miller) Sherrard, daughter of W H and Margaret (Stewart) Miller. To this union there has been born one son, James Miller Like his father, Dr Spackman is a Republican in politics and a Presbeterian in his religious views He is a member of DuBois Lodge, F & A M , Williamsport Consistory and Jaffa Temple of the Mystic Shrine of Altoona He is professionally connected with the county and State medical societies and is one of the surgeons on the Pennsylvania Division of the New York Central Railroad In addition to a horse and buggy, Dr Spackman makes use of a large forty horse-power, seven-seated touring car, which he finds valuable when making urgent calls.

HON HENRY RIBLING, formerly burgess of Houtzdale, Pa , where he has resided for forty-one years and for thirty-five of these has been in the undertaking business, is one of the leading and substantial men of this borough He was born in Germany, January 24, 1840, and is a son of Harvey Ribling, who was born and died in Germany and was a soldier under the great Napoleon .

In 1854, when but fourteen years of age, Henry Ribling came to America and found his way to Pittsburg, where he learned fresco painting In 1859 when the old Clearfield County Court House was erected, he was brought to this section to decorate it and he subsequently decorated the new court house and at one time had eighteen men at work under his supervision While he maintained his home at Clearfield he filled contracts at Houtzdale, Harrisburg, and even as far as Gettysburg, churches, opera houses and all kinds of important buildings being beautified by his skill He has long since given up work of that kind, his last contract being the redecorating of the court house at Clearfield, but his reputation was so wide spread that even yet he frequently receives letters asking for his bid on particular decorative work Mr Ribling later embarked in the undertaking business together with dealing in furniture and still continues the latter line He has had much to do with the substantial development of Houtzdale, owns property in the borough and so enjoys the respect and esteem of his fellow citizens that almost any office is within his reach but he has accepted none since he served out his term as burgess

Mr Ribling was married December 1, 1861, to Miss Susanna Harnick, then of Luthersburg, Pa , a native of Germany, a daughter of Daniel Harnick, who had settled in the above borough To Mr and Mrs Ribling, a family of thirteen children was born, namely Elizabeth, Louise, George H , Daniel, Flora, Matilda, Alice, Mary Susie, Harvey Eckert, Nora, Carrie and Harry Victor Elizabeth married R A Strayer and they live at Wilkinsburg, Pa They have four children Mary, who married J H Hoffman and they have a daughter, Elizabeth, Madeline, who married Frank McPherson, and they have a daughter, Madeline Elizabeth, Margaret, who married Paul Jones, and they have two children Madeline and Margaret Elizabeth, and Frank Louise, the second daughter, married Chauncy Saupp, of Houtzdale, and they have the following children James, who has three

sons, Charles, Kenneth and an infant, Frank, who has one son, Frank, Jr , and Blanche, Charles, Catherine, Chauncy and Susan, the two last named dying young George H Ribling, the eldest son, resides at Winber, in Somerset county He married Annie Thomas, and they have eight children Charles, John, Ray, Gladys, Rachel, Susie, George and Harry Daniel, who now resides at home, married Emma Freeman, who is now deceased Flora was married first to John Gillen and they have had three children Mamie, Agatha and John Her second marriage was with Warren E Passmore and they live in Bradford county The next five children all died young, Matilda reaching three years, Alice being eleven years, Mary, being seven years, and Susie dying when three years old, while Harvey Eckert lived but one year Nora became the wife of Joseph Cassidy, of Jersey City, N J , and they have three children Joseph, Marie and Margaret Carrie married Fred Clark, of Freedom, Pa , and they have two children Donald and Frederick Bentley Harry Victor, the youngest of the family still lives with his parents Mr and Mrs Ribling have eight living children, twenty-six grandchildren and eight great-grandchildren When family reunions take place it is a happy occasion for these descendants are, indeed, people to be proud of Family affection is very strong between them and they all unite in showing respect and regard for the heads of the family who, in every way, are worthy of it Mr Ribling is one of the oldest Odd Fellows at Houtzdale and is a charter member of this lodge

C CYRENIUS HOWE, a well known and respected citizen of Cooper township, where he holds the office of justice of the peace, was born in Philipsburg, Pa., June 1, 1860, a son of Robert and Julia (Phillips) Howe His great-grandfather was William Phillips, one of the family for whom Philipsburg was named The latter was born in Herfordshire, England, and was there married to Eleanor Jones They came to Philipsburg in 1820 Jesse Howe removed to Philipsburg in 1844, and died at that place

Robert Howe was twenty-one years of age when he accompanied his parents to Philipsburg He was a millwright by occupation and followed that trade in Philipsburg and vicinity until his death, which took place in 1876 He was a Democrat in politics and both he and his wife were members of the Episcopal church His wife also died in Philipsburg in 1910, at the age of eighty-three years Their children were six in number, as follows Electa, now deceased, as the wife of Charles Leavy of Allport, Clearfield county Lawrence M, who died in February, 1911, was a carpenter He married Emma Beck, of Warrior's Mark, Pa His wife and two sons are also now deceased Eleanor is the wife of Dr G W Emigh, of Philipsburg Linda W is the wife of George R Harris of Parksburg, Chester county, Pa C Cyrenius is the direct subject of this sketch Ira B, who resides in Claiburne county, married Miss Carrie Potter, formerly of Altoona, Pa, but who now resides in Alabama, being engaged in railroad work

C Cyrenius Howe attended the common and high schools of Philipsburg. Pa, until the age of twenty-one years, and after graduating from the high school took a special course He learned the trade of plasterer, but engaged in

the drug business in Kylertown, in which occupation he continued for seven years In 1902 he was elected county clerk, in which capacity he served one term He then associated himself with George E Owens in the purchase of the Clearfield Republican, but after conducting it together for a short time Mr Howe disposed of his interest to John F. Short Returning then to Kylertown, he accepted a position with the Pennsylvania Coal and Coke Company, as electrical machinist, and this position he has held for the past seven years During the last two years of this time he has resided at Winburne He is a charter member of Forest City Lodge, No 176, Kylertown, I O O F In politics a Democrat, he was elected in November, 1908, justice of the peace for Cooper township, assuming the duties of the office in May, 1909 Mr Howe was also the first steward of the County Home, which he furnished and equipped, receiving the first inmates He has been prominent in local politics and received the largest vote that was ever cast for a Democratic candidate for representative

Mr Howe married Miss Alice Stewart, a daughter of James L Stewart, on July 1, 1885 The maiden name of her mother was Elizabeth Kyler Of this union there have been born four children, of whom three are now living, namely Elva E, wife of Hughey Green of Philipsburg, who is the mother of one son, Roland Stewart Green (Mr Green is mine foreman for the Madera Hill Co), Grover S, who died in infancy, Orvis V, unmarried and residing with his parents, who is an employee of Peale, Peacock & Kerr, coal operators, and Ruth Rea, residing at home Mrs Howe died June 2, 1905

MILES WALL

MILES WALL, one of the representative men of Curwensville, Pa., who has long been identified with large business interests here and is prominent in the public affairs of the borough, perhaps is still more widely known as a Faith healer, a name that justly typifies the useful activity in which he has been interested for some time. Mr. Wall was born at Grampian Hill, Clearfield county, Pa., January 10, 1848, and is a son of Reuben and Sidney (Wall) Wall.

Reuben Wall was born October 17, 1811, in Center county, Pa., a son of David and Elizabeth Wall. David Wall secured 160 acres of wild land near Grampian Hills which he cleared with the help of his sons. Reuben Wall attended one of the primitive school houses of the time, which was made of poles, with rough seats inside and with greased paper in place of glass at the windows. It was situated near Moore's Run. He often told of the pranks he assisted his school mates to play on the Irish teacher, none of them being inspired by any ill will but merely the result of overflowing boyish spirits. There were few relaxations in those days for the youths, compared to the present time, for the hardest kind of work awaited almost all as soon as their years and strength permitted. His life was spent as a farmer and his death occurred in February, 1892. He married Sidney Wall, in 1842, who was born in York county, Pa., July 19, 1813. Her parents were Jonathan and Jane Wall, natives also of York county. Three children were born to Reuben and Sidney Wall, namely: an infant that died at birth, Alice, who married S. L. Kester, and resides on the old homestead on which Grandfather Wall first settled, and Miles, of Curwensville. The mother of these children died

July 16, 1885, and her burial was in the Friends' cemetery, where her husband was later laid by her side. They were members of the Friends' church at Grampian Hills.

Miles Wall obtained his education in the district schools of Penn township, Clearfield county, in boyhood walking two miles to attend. Later he assisted his father in carrying on the farm until 1882, when he moved to Curwensville and embarked in the agricultural implement and fertilizer sale business and still later became interested in a planing-mill and general job works and so continued until the spring of 1910, when he retired after a successful business career. This by no means indicates, however, that Mr. Wall is not one of the busiest men in Clearfield county. He was reared in the Society of Friends and has always been a member of this quiet, peaceful religious body, one that has produced men of mighty power in spiritual matters. In 1900 Mr. Wall began to realize that he possessed a spiritual gift that enabled him to lead many of his fellow beings out of what seemed to them the darkest depths of disease and pain. The realization of this gift must have been as a wonderful revelation. Mr. Wall has not hidden his light under a bushel but has devoted himself to helping those who come to him for healing and it is estimated that he now is called on to treat an average of 500 cases monthly. People come from points 100 miles distant and it is not recorded that any patient has ever gone away unhelped both physically and mentally. Mr. Wall modestly denominates himself a Faith Healer. He charges very moderately those who can afford to pay but treats the poor without money and without price and more than that, never permits inclement weather to prevent his attending a patient who solicits his help   He has not placed himself at the head of any cult although his remarkable success indicates that some mighty force is at work that might develop into a vigorous religious movement

Mr Wall was married on October 20, 1871, to Miss Elizabeth Cleaver, a daughter of Charles and Mary Cleaver, and they have had seven children, namely   Dillwyn P, who is deputy postmaster at Curwensville, married Bessie Wright, of Pike township, Mary, who is the wife of W A Thompson, of Curwensville, Charles M, who lives at Curwensville, married Grace, a daughter of Vincent and Alice Spencer, Vernon S, who is superintendent of the electric light plant at Curwensville, married Mae Sharp, of Pittsburg, Wilbur L, who resides at home, and two infants, who died early   Mr Wall is a member of the Royal Arcanum, a beneficiary society   In politics he is a Republican and for five years has been a member of the borough council, of which he has been president for two years

PATRICK GALLAGHER, who, for thirty consecutive years has served in the office of justice of the peace at Osceola Mills, Clearfield county, Pa, came to this borough in 1873 and has been one of the public spirited and successful business men   He was born in North Ireland, March 17, 1834, and is a son of Edward and Mary (O'Donnell) Gallagher

Patrick Gallagher was about fifteen years old when he came to America and in 1849 joined his older brother, Bernard Gallagher, who was already established as a lumberman near Clearfield Bridge, in Boggs township, Clearfield county, Pa   He remained in Boggs township until 1870, when he moved to Wallaceton, and from there, in 1871, to Houtz-

dale, and to Osceola Mills in 1873   He had previously been engaged in both lumbering and merchandising and after settling at Osceola Mills, established a general store which he conducted until 1909, when he retired   He was one of the original stockholders in the Osceola Silica and Fire Brick Company, of which he is vice-president

Mr Gallagher was married first to Miss Mary Ann Stone, a daughter of Alexander Stone, of Stoneville, Clearfield county.   Two children were born to them: Edward, who died when aged one year; and John Alexander, who is a resident of Osceola Mills   The latter married Martha Taber. Mrs Gallagher died in 1863   In 1870 Mr Gallagher married Mary W Cross, who died in August, 1909   Judge Gallagher is nominally a Democrat, but he has independent tendencies   In the capacity of justice of the peace, he has been of incalculable aid to his fellow citizens and business men as the borough has no regularly elected attorney   He has a wide acquaintance and is universally esteemed.   He has been a witness to the remarkable advance made by this borough and has been identified to a considerable extent with much that has added to its material progress

ANDREW LEAFGREN, a well known business man of Winburne, Pa, who is a dealer in grain, hay and all kinds of feed, was born on a farm near the city of Wenners, Sweden, May 13, 1864, and is a son of Erland and Christina (Anderson) Johnson

Erland Johnson was born in Sweden in 1831, and there he devoted his life to agricultural pursuits, his death occurring in January, 1892   His widow, who was born in that country in 1843, survives him and is still a resident of the mother country Eight children were born to Mr and Mrs Johnson, of whom three died in Sweden and five came to America, as follows· John Ellison, who resides in Chicago, Mary, who is the wife of a Mr Thorson of Tacoma, Wash , Edward Ellison, who was formerly a resident of Chicago, but is now engaged in farming in Michigan, Oscar Ellison, who lives in Tacoma, Wash , and Andrew

Andrew Leafgren received his educational training in the schools of his native country, and was reared on the home farm He came to America in 1883 and in the following year located in Peale, Clearfield county, where the operations of the Bituminous Coal Corporation had just been started After a short time he went to Arnett, Tioga county, but in 1888 he came to Winburne, being one of the early settlers of this now thriving city, and entered the employ of the Somerville mines, which had been opened but a short time before In 1898 or 1899 he started to work for his brother-in-law, Gust A Johnson, and in 1906 decided to go into business on his own account, and erected a mill opposite his residence Since that time, through perseverance, well spent efforts and natural ability, Mr Leafgren has become one of the leading business men of Winburne, and he stands high in the estimation of his fellow citizens In addition to his mill, Mr Leafgren is the owner of considerable real estate in Winburne

In 1891 Mr Leafgren was married to Miss Emma Johnson, a sister of Gust A Johnson of Winburne and a native of Sweden Of the four children born to this union, three survive, namely, Ruth, Esther and Reuben Mr Leafgren is a member of the Swedish Free church

of Lanse, and his politics are those of the Republican party

NEWTON BORT YOUNG, a well to do citizen of Burnside township, where he is engaged in agriculture, was born on the old Young homestead in this township, December 22, 1862, a son of Thomas and Mary Ann (Thompson) Young His paternal grandfather was John Young, of Center county

John Young was born in Center county in the year 1797 Hester (Moore) Young, his wife, was born in the same county, July 9, 1803, moved to Clearfield county in the year 1833 To that union were born seven children, namely Archie, Thomas, Hester, John R , Elizabeth, Mary and Robert John Young died in 1860 and Hester, his wife, in 1862 Elizabeth Young and Mary Young are the only surviving members of the family at this date John R Young and Robert were both soldiers in the Civil war

Thomas Young, who was born in Center county, came to Burnside township, Clearfield county, accompanied by his parents He cleared a tract of land here and during the rest of his life was mainly occupied in lumbering. In politics a Democrat, he served in local office His death took place in 1887 when he was fifty-six years of age His wife, Mary Ann, was a daughter of Ebenezer and Jane (Chrispin) Thompson, both natives of Indiana county She died in 1890 at the age of fifty-six Of their children, there are now living in addition to our subject, two sons, namely Matt C , who is engaged in the newspaper business in Chicago, and George M , a farmer residing in Burnside township John died in infancy Joseph Lane was drowned at McGee's on the Susquehanna river in the year 1889, when in his twenty-ninth year, while engaged in rafting

Newton Bort Young, who was the third born of his parents' children, attended school for a while in his boyhood He then began industrial life, working in the woods at lumbering for his father, and afterwards worked out for others until 1889 He then bought the old Young homestead, where he has since resided, engaged in agriculture Owing chiefly to the excellent springs in the vicinity, this place was formerly much used for camp meetings Like his father, Mr Young is a Democrat, and is now serving as township treasurer, which office he has held for five years

Mr Young was married in 1890 to Margaret Weaver Byers, who was born on the old Byers homestead June 16, 1867 Her parents were Samuel and Elizabeth (Davis) Byers, the latter of whom died in 1902 at the age of seventy-six years, and the former in 1873 at the age of seventy-one Mrs Young's grandfather on the paternal side was John Byers His father, also named John, came to Clearfield county from Huntingdon county in 1821, and bought over 400 acres of land near New Washington, this county (Clearfield) He was born at Valley Forge, near Philadelphia, in 1762, a place rendered historic by Washington's winter encampment fifteen years later He died in 1862 having rounded out a full century of existence, and having lived to see the four principal wars in which this country has been engaged, the War of the Revolution, that of 1812, the Mexican war, and the commencement at least of the great Civil war A son of this John Byers, Lemuel Byers, born February 12, 1809, married in 1838, Mrs Stephenson at the home of her uncle George

Atchison In 1841 Lemuel Byers took his first raft of lumber down the river to Harrisburg, Pa, from which place he walked home in four days

John Byers, a brother of Lemuel, married in 1830, Sarah Weaver, a daughter of John and Ruth (Zimmerman) Weaver He was one of the organizers of the Methodist Protestant church in 1829 His death took place in 1881 Sam, another son of John, settled near the old homestead Another member of this family was George, of whom we have no special record Ellen, a sister, married John Mahaffey and resided first at Burnside and later at Cherry Tree During Washington's encampment at Valley Forge in the winter of 1777-78, the Byers homestead was occupied for a time by him John Byers, Mrs Young's grandfather, then a boy of fifteen years, was pressed into the service of the army to haul supplies across the Schuylkill river for the troops

Mr and Mrs Newton B Young are the parents of four children, namely Clifton A, now twenty years of age, who is engaged in teaching school, Lela Elizabeth, aged eighteen, residing at home, Joseph Cloyd, aged nine, and Margaret Byers, aged four years The Young and Byers families have furnished some of the best citizenship to Clearfield county Industrious, law abiding, neighborly, and generally prosperous, they are favorably regarded wherever known

JAMES ADAMSON, who holds the important position of foreman of the Grass Flat mines for the Clearfield County Bituminous Coal Corporation, is a representative citizen of Peale, Pa, and a miner of extended experience, having been identified with coal mining in Pennsylvania for forty-four years in addition to shorter periods in other places Mr Adamson was born March 26, 1846, in Fifeshire, Scotland, and is a son of Campbell and Elizabeth (Hunter) Adamson

Campbell Adamson was a miner in the coal regions of Scotland from boyhood until the end of this active life Both he and wife were born there, married, reared children and finally passed away in the land of their birth They had four children Andrew, John, Thomas and James

James Anderson was only nine years old when he began work in the coal mines, this industry being the main one in the vicinity of his home, and he continued in the mines in Scotland until 1864, when he came to America Mining was his business and he learned facts concerning the main mining sections before he located in Bradford county, Pa where he was employed by the Bartlett Coal Company He remained with that company for one year and then went to the Fallbrook Company, of Tioga county, for a year, later went to Arnett and worked in the mines there for two years In 1870 he went to California and tried gold mining for three years, but in 1873 came back to Pennsylvania Before resuming business relations with any of the mining companies after his return, he made a visit to Scotland, where he renewed old friendships and enjoyed companionship with his kindred

When Mr Adamson came back to Pennsylvania, he entered the employ of the McIntire Coal Company, in Lycoming county, this being in 1874, with which he continued until 1883, when he came to Peale, which place has been his home for twenty-eight years For the past sixteen years he has been mine foreman for the Clearfield County Bituminous Coal Corporation, and for thirteen of these has been foreman at Grass Flat This long continuance with one company proves that Mr Adamson is a reliable and experienced man Personally he is highly thought of both by his employers and by the hundreds of workers who each year are under his supervision

Mr Adamson was married in 1878, to Miss Helen Ramage daughter of William Ramage, of Fifeshire, Scotland Mrs Adamson was born in Scotland but was married in America Mr and Mrs Adamson have had three children, two sons and one daughter Campbell, Elizabeth and James None of these children survived infancy Mr and Mrs Adamson are Presbyterians He is a member of Moshannon Lodge, No 391, F & A M, at Philipsburg, and Peale Lodge of Odd Fellows In politics Mr Adamson is a Republican In 1910 he made a second visit to his native land, remaining two months

JAMES W REESE, one of the representative business men of Karthaus, Pa, who has been engaged in the meat business at this point since 1903, was born in Covington township, Clearfield county, Pa, February 22, 1875, and is a son of John and Mary (Lingle) Reese

John Reese was born in Germany and was a young man when he came to the United States with his brothers and sisters, all of whom located at Baltimore, Md From there he went first to Philadelphia and then came to Covington township, Clearfield county, and resided in that section until his death which occurred in 1899 His burial was at Frenchville He married Mrs Mary (Lingle) Smith, who was born in Germany and was young when her father, Joseph Lingle, came to the United States and settled at St Mary's, Pa She still resides in Covington township Her first marriage was with William Smith and they had six children, as follows John, Solomon, Joseph, William, George and Susan, the last named being the wife of Henry Sinclair To John and Mary Reese the following children were born Winslow, who lived at French-ville, died at the age of thirty-six years, Anna, who is the wife of George Spangler, of Falls Creek, Margaret, who is the wife of Samuel Reiter, of Covington township, George, who lives in Covington township, and James Walter

James Walter Reese grew up and attended school in Covington township and occupied himself in various ways until he went into the meat business, in which he continued and has a fine trade Mr Reese was married June 27, 1906, to Miss Lena V Haley, who was born at Snow Shoe, Center county, a daughter of Martin and Mary (Kelly) Haley, the latter a native of Ireland and both are now deceased Mr and Mrs Reese have three children. Mary Agnes, Margaret Isabel and Joseph Paul In politics Mr Reese is a Democrat and has filled local offices He is identified with the Grange and the order of K O T M, both at Karthaus With his family he belongs to the Roman Catholic church

ROLAND E DALE, a progressive farmer and highly esteemed citizen of Bradford township, Clearfield county, Pa, has resided all his life on his present farm of 312 acres, and was born here in 1870, a son of Elitz and Jane (Hunter) Dale His father was a native of Philipsburg, Pa, and when a child of four years came with his parents to this farm, where he has spent the remainder of his life and is one of the prominent men of Bradford township He taught in this township, and has held various township offices, serving as school director, and was road supervisor a number of years Both parents are still living and reside on the home farm

Roland E Dale obtained his education in the local schools of Bradford township, and since leaving school has lived on the farm with his parents Here he carries on general agriculture, and has one of the finest wheat farms in Clearfield county Mr Dale has served a number of years as road supervisor He is a member and trustee of the M. E church.

GUST ADOLPH JOHNSON, a representative business man of Winburne, Pa, a practical printer, a photographer and a manufacturer of soft drinks, was born November 24, 1864, at Wenersborg, in Sweden, and is a son of John Erickson (son of John) and Sophia Johnson (Erickson) or Johanson, according to the Swedish methods of naming

The father of Mr Johnson was born in Sweden in 1818 and was a farmer in his own land prior to coming to America with his wife in 1887, his death occurring in Cooper township, Clearfield county, in 1897. His wife was born in Sweden in 1825 and died in 1903 They had thirteen children born to them and the survivors are. Erick, who lives at Winburne; Matilda, who is the wife of Lars Danielson, of Lanse, Pa, Carl, who resides at Sugar Grove, Warren county, Pa ; Emma, who is the wife of Andrew Leafgren, a grain dealer and mill owner at Winburne, and Gust Adolph The first of the family to come to America was Mrs. Danielson, who located at McIntire, Lycoming county, Pa Erick followed and still later Gust and Carl came also and all settled at McIntire, in 1882 In 1887 Gust A Johnson returned to Sweden and in the following October came back to Pennsylvania, bringing with him his beloved parents and sister Emma

When Mr Johnson first reached the United States he found that there was no opening for him except at the hardest kind of labor, but he was strong, willing and industrious and from the latter part of 1882 until May, 1883, he worked on the construction of the Pine Creek Railroad, and then went to Landrus, in Tioga county, and secured employment in a shingle mill and saw-mill and later worked again at railroad construction, this time on the Beech Creek Railroad In 1884 he went to New York City and from there to Boston and other points While in New York he was offered a position in a grocery store but the wages promised were too small for him to consider the proposition He then accepted a position on a three-masted schooner running between New York and Boston, in the capacity of an able bodied seaman The duties required of him in this capacity had not been previously explained to him and he very quickly came to the conclusion that life on the sea was not the carer for which Nature had intended him He was so gratified to reach Boston in safety that he was even willing to demand no wages for the trip

After this experience, which, as Mr Johnson relates it, is full of interest and humor, he found work in Boston and at East Long Meadow, Mass In the fall of 1884 he came to Peale, Clearfield county, where coal mines had been opened and he secured employment and worked as a miner until the spring of 1885, when he went to the Allport mines, then

back to Peale and again to Allport and later worked in a slope mine at Munson In 1886 he came to Winburne and built one of the first three houses, Peter A Strand and Nels Olson (both of whom are now deceased), having built the others The first mine was opened in December, 1886, by the Somerville Company, and he was one of the first half-dozen men employed then He continued mining until 1888 Mr Johnson then started a job printing office and also the manufacturing of rubber stamps, which he continues From 1895 until 1902, Mr Johnson was also in the milling business In 1901 he traveled from one end of Sweden to the other, over every railroad, in the meanwhile collecting 3,500 pictures of all the interesting places, public buildings and scenery This collection was prepared as stereoscopic views and was the largest collection of that class of views from Sweden For the past five years he has been a manufacturer of soft drinks, which he wholesales in the surrounding towns He has sustained two serious fire losses, one in July and another in December, 1910, when his plant at Philipsburg was burned He has been a resident of Clearfield county for twenty-seven years and of Winburne for twenty-six of these He was naturalized at Clearfield in 1888 and no native-born American can show better citizenship He is interested vitally in all public questions and as a Republican exerts considerable political influence and has served as precinct chairman for his local party organization He was reared in the Lutheran faith

Mr. Johnson was married to Miss Anna Nelson, in 1891, at which time she was a resident of Chicago, Ill, her parents having died when she was a child Mr and Mrs Johnson have five children Walter, Ruth, Edith, Francis and Theodore

CHRISTIAN MICHAEL HERTLEIN, one of the highly esteemed residents of Karthaus township, Clearfield county, Pa, where he is cultivating an excellent property of 119 acres, was born in this township June 13, 1840, a son of George Lawrence and Johanna (Eisleman) Hertlein

George Lawrence Hertlein, who was a native of Wurtemberg, Germany, came to America in the early thirties, after having completed six years of service in the German army For some time after settling in this country he followed his trade, which was that of a potter, but eventually he decided to take up farming, and settled on the farm on which Tennyson Hertlein now carries on operations in Karthaus township Here he continued to reside until his death, which occurred when he was seventy-four years of age, and he was buried in the cemetery at Keewaydin, where his widow, who survived him some years, was also laid to rest Mr Hertlein was a Democrat in politics and was called upon to fill many township offices In the early days he assisted in building the old Karthaus Furnace George L Hertlein was married to Johanna Eisleman, also a native of Germany who came to this country with her mother, after her father's death in the Fatherland To Mr and Mrs Hertlein there were born the following children Martin, deceased, who lived in Clearfield county, Christian Michael, Lawrence Tennyson, who resides on the old home place; August, who died at the age of fourteen years, John, who died in infancy, Sophia, deceased, who was the wife of John Eberspecher Hannah, deceased, who was the wife of Ed I Gil-

hland, also deceased, Rosanna, who is the wife of James Hunter, of Delaware, and Sarah and another child, who died in infancy The children were reared in the faith of the Lutheran church, to which both parents belonged

Christian Michael Hertlein was reared in Karthaus township, and attended the local schools Later, after he was of age, he took a course in the seminary at Cassville, Huntingdon county Early in life Mr Hertlein engaged in lumbering and farming, and eventually purchased his present property, which then consisted of 103 acres, but did not locate on it until 1869, since which time he has added two pieces of land, of ten and six acres respectively, and he now has one of the highly cultivated, well kept and substantially productive farms of Clearfield county

On November 19, 1867, Mr Hertlein was united in marriage with Miss Annie Reiter, who was born March 20, 1847, at the present site of Keewaydin, a daughter of John Reiter To this union there have been born the following children an infant that died unnamed; Edward Newton, living at Cherrydale, Karthaus township, who married Myrtle Woodling and has two children, Blake and Norman; Eva Sarah, deceased, who married Milton Conaway, by whom she had a daughter, Rhea Eva, who has lived with her grandfather since she was thirteen days old, Blanche Ella, who resides at home, and John Lawrence, who is assisting his father in the duties of the home farm The mother of the foregoing children died March 15, 1891, and was buried in the cemetery at Keewaydin She was a kindly, Christian woman, and a loving and indulgent mother, and was beloved by all who knew her

Mr Hertlein is known as a man of the best

character, as well as one of sound judgment and fair principles, and when his fellow citizens were casting about in search of someone to fill the office of justice of the peace, his name was suggested and he was elected to the position He resigned from the office, however, in order to give his time and attention to the duties of his farm His politics are those of the Democratic party

MATTHIAS SCHWER, who has been a resident of Peale, Pa, since 1884, is now in the employ of the A F Kelley store, the company store of the Bituminous Coal Corporation Mr Schwer was born June 21, 1842, in Somerset county, Pa, a son of John and Lydia (Lininger) Schwer

John Schwer was born in Germany, and when about fifteen or sixteen years of age he came to America and located in Somerset county, residing there until 1855, at which time he removed to Jersey Shore, Lycoming county, and there carried on a jewelry business during the remainder of his active life His death occurred while he was on a visit to Peale, in 1891 Mrs Schwer was born in Indiana county, Pa, and her death occurred in 1883 Six children were born to Mr and Mrs Schwer, namely Matthias. John who was engaged in the hardware business and died in 1884 at Williamsport, Jemima, who was the wife of Charles A Bubb, of Jersey Shore, and died in 1879 Caroline who died single about 1892, William, who for the past thirty years has been engaged in the butchering business at Jersey Shore, and Nancy, who is also a resident of that place John Schwer was a Democrat in his political belief and a stanch member of the Presbyterian church

Matthias Schwer, or Matt, as he is famil-iarly known, attended the common schools of Cambria and Lycoming counties, and at the age of fifteen years gave up his studies to engage in the butchering business at Jersey Shore, continuing there from 1858 until 1880, at which time he removed to McIntire, Pa, and there continued in the same line of business until November, 1884 Just prior to this time the mines had been opened for operation at Peale, and believing this would furnish a larger and more lucrative field for him, he transferred his operations to this point He was engaged in the butchering business until 1890, and since that time he has been connected with the store of the Bituminous Coal Corporation Mr Schwer is one of the most popular men in Peale, being of a sunny, optimistic disposition and having the ability to make friends and keep them During the twenty years that he has been connected with the store here he has displayed much business ability, and he is known to be a man of strict integrity

Mr Schwer was married in 1869 to Miss Sarah McMurray, the daughter of Charles McMurray, and one son was born to that union, McMurray M, a trimmer and finisher of Hackensack, N J The first wife of Mr. Schwer died in 1870, and Mr Schwer married secondly Miss Julia Hillard, the daughter of Owen Hillard of Jersey Shore, by whom he has had the following children Maud, who is the wife of William Lowell of Clymer, Fred O, an electrical engineer of Clymer, who married Miss Annie Hyde, Jessie M, who married J Morris Daily of Reynoldsville, John, who is a chauffeur of Hackensack, N J, and June, who is single and resides at home The mother of these children died in 1905 Mr. Schwer is a member of the Knights of the

Golden Eagle of Peale, and is a Presbyterian in his religious belief He is a Republican in political matters, and served for five years as justice of the peace of Cooper township

BENJAMIN HARTSHORN, one of Pike township's representative and substantial citizens, residing two miles north of Curwensville, Clearfield county, Pa, where he owns 600 acres of valuable land, was born on this farm, November 28, 1833 He is a son of Jonathan and a grandson of Benjamin Hartshorn

Grandfather Benjamin Hartshorn was born in Cecil county, Md He came to Clearfield county, with his family when all this section included in Pike township, then Huntingdon county, was almost a wilderness He was a squatter settler, laying claim to 500 acres of new land, the present farm being a part of that claim He built his log cabin on what is now the McNaul farm, choosing his home near one of the finest springs in the county It is related that bears were frequent visitors to the neighborhood and after they had stolen the milk crocks that had been placed on poles near the spring, as was the early custom, Mr Hartshorn built a bear trap and subsequently had the satisfaction of filling up the larder with bear meat, the animal weighing 600 pounds He was a very enterprising and resourceful man and although he died at the age of fifty-eight years he had accomplished more than many whose life extended much farther He girdled the trees over about forty acres, killing them in this way, and later, with his ox-team, cleared up this land and put it under cultivation He also started a tannery, the first one east of Bellefonte, and after his death his son, William Hartshorn, continued to carry

it on Benjamin Hartshorn was also a man of public importance and was one of the organizers of Clearfield county He had six children, namely Margaret, who married Andrew Caldwell, Anna, who married Robert Ross, Jonathan, William, who married a Swan, Benjamin, who married, and Mary Ann, who married Manning Stephenson With his wife this old pioneer of Pike township rests in the McClure cemetery They attended the Presbyterian church)

Jonathan Hartshorn, father of Benjamin Hartshorn, of Pike township, had few school advantages and by the time a school was established in the neighborhood of his father's farm, he and his older sisters were beyond school age All were inured to pioneer hardships and as they never knew any of the luxuries of life in their youth, did not miss them Jonathan and his brother William assisted their father and sometimes it was necessary to travel a long distance even beyond Center county in order to obtain salt, a commodity necessary to the raising of their cattle as well as for domestic uses. What now costs but a few cents then was one of the extravagant purchases they were obliged to make It is very probable that the youths on these trips carried with them an old flint-lock musket, still in the possession of the family as a relic, and, although it often missed fire, it sometimes killed a bear and on these occasions one-quarter of the carcass would be kept for home consumption and the rest sold at Curwensville Jonathan Hartshorn was as industrious and successful as his father had been He worked on his land during the summer seasons and during the winters was largely engaged in lumbering and was considered a very expert raftsman, frequently taking huge rafts down

JONATHAN HARTSHORN

the river With his brother William he bought a saw-mill and they also conducted the tannery established by their father and continued until the death of Jonathan, after which the saw-mill was sold and the timber on this tract was also disposed of for $47,000 All the timber has been delivered and removed Coal also was found on the land and it took a large amount of work before the stripping of the layer of coal was completed At the time of his death, Jonathan Hartshorn owned 500 acres of land

Jonathan Hartshorn married Miss Rachel Leonard, who was born in Bradford township, Clearfield county, Pa, in 1807, and died in 1894 She was a sister of Judge Leonard, who at one time was an associate judge of Clearfield county Her parents were Abraham and Elizabeth Leonard To Jonathan and Rachel Hartshorn ten children were born, as follows Jane, who married Robert R Neeper, of Pike township, Benjamin, Margaret, who is the widow of Robert Wrigley, of Clearfield, Abraham, who died in infancy, Z L, who is now deceased, Mary Ann, who died unmarried, April 10, 1908, and was buried in the Oak Hill cemetery, at Curwensville, Hannah, who is deceased, was the wife of Martin Braughler, who lives in California, Joshua, who was living on the old homestead at the time of his death, married Nora Lawhead; Jonathan T, who married Josephine Holland, a native of Little Rock, Ark, has one son, Troy K, and they live at Pasadena, Calif; and Lavinia, who died aged thirteen years Both parents of the above family lived to the unusual age of ninety-three years and both were buried at Oak Hill cemetery The father passed away first, his death occurring on February 15, 1882 They were members of the Presbyterian church

In his early years of manhood, Jonathan Hartshorn was a Whig but later became a Republican He never accepted any public office although he was always interested in current events and public affairs He was, however, persuaded to become the mail carrier away back in 1817, between Bellefonte and Kittanning, Pa At that time it took six days to make the round trip, these journeys being two weeks apart He often told his children about the dangers he encountered on these trips and also of the rapid increase in population as evidenced by his having to increase his carrying capacity by 1818 and still more later on The old Indian trail went right through this farm and many Indians journeyed over it east and west Mr Hartshorn treated them well and he never had anything to complain of in the way they met him and his family, friendly relations always existing He maintained an open, hospitable home and his cheerful fireside often had guests beside it whose names were known far and wide One of these was of his own kindred, General Ross Hartshorn, a son of his brother William, the former of whom was the only brigadier-general appointed in Clearfield county among the officers who served in the Civil war

Benjamin Hartshorn obtained his education in the district schools and has always lived on the land that came to him from his father and grandfather, and all of it practically belongs to him About 100 acres have been cleared and are under cultivation, while the remainder is in woodland, the timber being valuable and it is largely used as pasture ground Mr Hartshorn has no coal bank now open but there is an underlay of from four to five feet of fire clay that has never been developed It would seem that the grandfather of Mr Hartshorn had more than ordinary foresight and good judgment when he made his selection of virgin land Mr Hartshorn has lived a quiet, uneventful but busy life and is well known all over Clearfield county He has never taken any active part in political matters He is a stockholder in the Rural Telephone Company of Pike township Mr Hartshorn has never married

GEORGE DALE WOMER, the genial proprietor of the Avondale Park Hotel, which was the first public house erected at Winburne, Pa, was born in Blair county, Pa, January 3, 1868, and is a son of Emanuel and Ellen (Kennedy) Womer

Emanuel Womer was born in Blair county in 1838, a son of George Womer, of German descent He was a forgeman and blacksmith, at which trade he worked for twenty-eight years For thirty-nine years he has been a resident of Morrisdale, where he was one of the first settlers In 1861 he enlisted for service in the Civil war and remained a soldier until its close, when he was honorably discharged in 1865, his whole period of service covering four years and three months. He was fortunate enough to escape serious injury, although he participated in many battles. He is a valued member of the G A R Post at Philipsburg, Pa For three years he has lived retired, his home continuing to be at Morrisdale He married Ellen Kennedy, daughter of Alexander Kennedy, an early settler in Blair county She died in 1903, at the age of sixty-four years They had the following children. Alexander, an engineer, living at

Philipsburg, George Dale, Charles, an engineer, who lives at Morrisdale, Agnes, who is the wife of William Hawkins, of Morrisdale; Myrtle, who died at the age of thirty-one years, Clark, who has charge of a shoe store at St Mary's, for the firm of Hall & Kaul, Margaret, who died unmarried at the age of twenty-eight years, and Ellen, who lives with her father

George Dale Womer was three years old when his parents came to Clearfield county and was reared and educated at Morrisdale He conducted a butchering business as his first independent enterprise and was then elected constable and served eight years as constable in Morris township, and proved a very efficient officer He first embarked in the hotel business in 1899, at Grass Flats, where he remained for two and one-half years, then sold and bought the Morrisdale Hotel, which he conducted for six years After selling that property he went to Wilkesbarre, where he went into a wholesale whiskey business, which he sold eighteen months later and on November 1, 1909, bought the Avondale Park Hotel at Winburne, which he has conducted ever since This hotel is beautifully situated in a park of pine, locust and hemlock trees Mr. Womer had put it in the best of condition and has all modern comforts and appliances, including steam heat, hot and cold water and electric lights He offers to his many satisfied patrons an excellent table, comfortable sleeping rooms and attentive service, all at a reasonable price

In 1895 Mr Womer was married to Miss Janet Mason, a daughter of John and Jane Mason, of Morrisdale, where she was born and reared They have one son, a bright, intelligent school boy of fourteen years Mr

Womer is identified fraternally with the Red Men, the Knights of Pythias, the Jr O A M and the Elks In politics he is a Democrat In addition to his hotel property he owns thirty-eight acres of richly cultivated land, where he raises all his own vegetables and poultry and also keeps cows in order to supply his hotel with fresh cream and butter Mr Womer is a self-made man in the sense that through his own industry and good judgment he has brought about his present prosperity

MATTHEW W JOHNSON, a well known and highly respected citizen of Greenwood township, was born on his present farm September 19, 1849, a son of James and Sarah (Stugarts) Johnson In addition to carrying on agriculture Mr Johnson is interested in the H S Thomas Milling Company, whose plant is located on his farm

Mr Johnson's paternal grandfather, Samuel Johnson, came to Clearfield county from Center county, Pa , settling on a farm near Grampian, in Penn township After clearing and developing this land, he moved to Indiana, where he died in 1868 The farm was sold in 1850 and is now owned by James D Wall Samuel Johnson had seven children, namely James, William, John, Garrison, Thirza, Elizabeth and Nancy

James Johnson, father of Matthew W , was born in 1806 near Milesburg, Center county, Pa , and in 1812 accompanied his parents to Clearfield county He assisted his father in the clearing and development of the pioneer farm, and later, with his brother, Elah Johnson, bought a tract of land and built and operated a saw-mill Subsequently, with the help of his sons, James Johnson established the first woolen mill in this section, erecting it on his farm in Greenwood township He continued to operate it until the spring of 1884, when he sold it to his son, John Johnson He acquired some 700 acres of land and, in association with William Irwin, was the owner of 600 additional acres He was a life-long Democrat, but not a politician A shrewd and careful business man, but honest and upright, he was universally esteemed His death took place when he was in the eighty-first year of his age, on June 28, 1887, and he was buried on one of his own farms

As above indicated, James Johnson married Sarah Stugarts, who was born in Penn township, Clearfield county, Pa , a daughter of John and Elsie Stugarts She died in 1904, in her eighty-eighth year, and was buried in the Friends' cemetery at Grampian, both she and her husband belonging to the Society of Friends To James and Sarah Johnson the following children were born William P , who lives in Ferguson township, Clearfield county, John and David, both of whom met accidental deaths, the former being killed by a kick from a horse, and the latter by a fall of lumber; Hannah, who is the wife of C A Thorp, Matthew W , the subject of this sketch; James A , who resides on a farm in Greenwood township, Frank, who was accidentally killed by a falling tree, and Elizabeth, who is the wife of William Rowles

Matthew W Johnson was educated in the district schools of Penn and Greenwood townships For seventeen years he was financially interested in the woolen mill which his father had established on the home place, but finally finding himself unable to compete with the larger and more heavily capitalized concerns in his line of trade, he was obliged to close the mill and since then has devoted himself to milling and farming. He owns fifty-four acres of valuable land—a part of the old homestead—and carries on general farming He is one of the leading members of Greenwood Grange He started his present mill enterprise on Bell Run, his son-in-law, Sherman Thomas, being interested therein with him The latter is also foreman for a concrete company

Mr Johnson was first married in January, 1872, to Miss Susannah Bloom, a daughter of Thomas Bloom She died in October, 1873, and was buried in the McNaul cemetery One child was born to this marriage, Thomas Bruce Johnson Mr Johnson was married secondly, July 1, 1875, to Miss Martha E Moore, a daughter of Jeremiah Moore, and they have four children Ralph, Harry B , Hannah Lola and Alvin M Ralph is bookkeeper for the Bickford Fire Brick Company He is a graduate of the Williamsport Commercial College and a former school teacher He married Jennie Rafferty, a daughter of John W Rafferty, and they have four children—Burt, Annie, Orvil and Nora Harry B Johnson is a resident of Price county, Wisconsin, where he holds the office of deputy county surveyor He married Amanda Mungason and they have four children—Fred, Nellie, Alvin and Mae Hannah Lola married Sherman Thomas and they have three children—Ansel, Ruby and Georgia Alvin M Johnson is a student of law in the University of Valparaiso, Ind He formerly taught four terms of school in Clearfield county Mr Johnson and family belong to the Society of Friends

THOMAS JEFFERSON SUNDER-LAND, a representative citizen and prosper-ous farmer of Bell township, came to his present place in 1878 and owns one of the well improved properties of this section He was born June 20, 1851, and is a son of Samuel and Harriet A (Ellis) Sunderland

Samuel Sunderland was born February 4, 1822, and died March 30, 1906 His father, David Sunderland, was born in 1792, and his mother, Sarah (McClellan) Sunderland, was born May 14, 1798 and died February 7, 1865 Samuel Sunderland followed farming all his life, in the vicinity of Burnside, Clearfield county, after moving to this section He married Harriet A Ellis, who was born March 5, 1826, and died October 13, 1899 Thomas J Sunderland has three brothers: Samuel, a farmer in Indiana county; Harry and Daniel, residing at Mahaffey, Pa

Thomas J Sunderland has devoted his life since his school days were over, to farming and working in the timber In 1878 he purchased his present farm from his father, a part of the old homestead, and has continued to improve it and develop all its possibilities along the line of careful and practical farming

Mr Sunderland married Miss Mary Alice Baker, who was born March 28, 1851, near Mahaffey, Pa , a daughter of John and Susanna (Smith) Baker. Mrs Sunderland has one brother, Henry, who is a farmer near Banner Ridge To Mr and Mrs Sunderland the following children were born· Henry, now deceased, who married Catherine De Haven (they had five children), John, who is deceased, James, who married Sarah Bendt, lives in Bell township, and has two children; Samuel, who married Charlotte Ling, lives in Bell township and has one child, George, who is deceased, married Minnie Barrett (they live at Mahaffey and have two children), Wilham, who lives at New Washington, married Eva Beam and has one child, Maud, who married F Ruppert, a farmer in Bell township, and has two children, Harriet, who married Ward Smith, residing in Armstrong county, and has one child, Anna, who is now deceased, and Harry, who assists his father In politics Mr Sunderland is a Republican and he has served as roadmaster of the township

JOHN F EDLUND, general merchant, doing a large business at Winburne, Clearfield county, Pa, was born in the Province of Dalsland, near the city of Wennersburg, Sweden, November 7, 1866, and is a son of Jonas and Sophia (Anderson) Edlund.

The parents of Mr. Edlund were natives of Sweden, where the father was born March 21, 1842, and the mother, in 1841 The paternal grandfather of Mr Edlund was a soldier in the Swedish army and died in 1892 His widow still survives and is now in her ninety-seventh year Mr Edlund has the following brothers and sisters Christina, who is the wife of August Levin, of Glen Richey, Clearfield county, Mary, who is the wife of Gustav Carson, of Winburne, Anders Gustav, who lives at Patton, Pa, Anna, who is the wife of Oscar Frid, a railroad man, in Sweden, and Augusta, who is the wife of Otto Thorwaldson, who is a stone-cutter and farmer, living at Prestbacka, Norway

John F Edlund attended school in Sweden until he was fourteen years of age and then engaged in cutting timber and farming On May 28, 1888, he came to Peale Station, Clearfield county, Pa. and worked in the mines at Winburne and Munson, and several months for Jones & Company, and later in a saw-mill at Ford's Run After being in the

United States for four years he returned to Sweden, in March, 1892, where he remained until the following October, when he returned, accompanied by his wife, and resided at Winburne working in the mines for Somerville & Co, until 1901, when he embarked in the mercantile business He was associated with E L Graham for two years but later sold his interest to the Central Trading Company and was employed by the same until 1906, when he re-embarked in the mercantile business in partnership with A G Anderson Subsequently Mr Edlund bought Mr Anderson's interest, the latter returning to Rostock, Sweden Since then Mr Edlund has carried on his business alone and through honest methods and careful attention has prospered and now is numbered with the reliable and substantial business men of the place He stands high in the estimation of every one and in the honorable way in which he has managed the small estate belonging to the three orphan children of a sister, exemplifies his trustworthiness He has reared these children together with his own large family, has cared for and improved their property and has never asked any remuneration

Mr Edlund married a daughter of Anders and Christiana (Hansdotter) Jansen, the latter of whom still lives at Rostock, Sweden Mr and Mrs Edlund have had eight children. Ellen V, who is a student in the Winburne High School, John Albert, who is also in the High School, Arthur Wilhelm, Anna Elizabeth, and four who are deceased Mr Edlund and family belong to the Swedish Lutheran church He is identified with Winburne Lodge, No 164, Odd Fellows, and with the Benefit Association of Boston, belonging to this fraternity Mr Edlund is a sensible, far-seeing man and has provided for the future through a substantial life insurance policy His wife and three children are leaving, May 22, 1911, for a visit to Sweden and other parts of Europe

W. S. GILLILAND, M D, who was been engaged in the practice of medicine at Karthaus, Clearfield county, Pa, for the past twenty years and for a like period has conducted a hardware store, was born at Sprucetown, Center county, Pa, December 9, 1842, and is a son of John and Lydia (Smith) Gilliland, the former of whom was born in Center county in 1806, and died in Karthaus township, Clearfield county, in 1888 He was a well known man The mother of Dr Gilliland was born in Center county in 1808, and died in 1889 Dr Gilliland was the third child and second son born in a family of six children

W S Gilliland was about fifteen years old when his parents came to Karthaus township and he attended the local schools, and secured his professional training in Jefferson Medical College, Philadelphia He commenced to practice at Salt Lick, where his family lived, and went from there to Keewaydin, in Covington township, where he practiced for fifteen years, removing then to Lecontes Mills, where he practiced for ten years and then came to Karthaus, where he has been established ever since He is one of the leading citizens Like his father he is a Democrat but has not been an aspirant for public honors, his professional duties and business affairs demanding his time and attention He is a public spirited citizen, however, and accepted the position of township auditor when elected to the same

Dr Gilliland was married in May, 1870, to Miss Martha A Murray, who was born in Girard township, a daughter of Alexander Murray, and the following of their children survive Blanche, who is the wife of George Spears and they have one son, William Andrew, Alda, who married James McKee Hipple, of Morristown, N J, and they have one daughter, Martha, Harvey T, who resides at Karthaus, married Vida Wooldridge and they have two sons—Lynn and William, and Mabel, Julia, Jennie and Paul Warren

ALEXANDER PATERSON, secretary and treasurer of the Paterson Clay Products Company, a very important business enterprise of Clearfield, Pa, has been identified with the interests of this borough and near-by villages for about thirty-seven years He was born at Airdrie, Scotland, December 19, 1857, and is a son of John and Marion (Dunlop) Paterson, both of whom are deceased. He came from Scotland to this country in 1874, and settled at Woodland, Clearfield county, as an employee of the Woodland Fire Brick Company, his duties being those of bookkeeper and draughtsman In 1882 he went to Dickinson College, Carlisle, Pa, graduating from there in June, 1886 Previous to leaving for Dickinson College and during his stay there he gave attention to the study of the law under the guidance of the Hon J B McEnally of Clearfield, with whom he became registered as a law student in 1884 In January, 1887, he was admitted to the bar of Clearfield county For four years he served as official stenographer in the courts of Clearfield county, and for one year was a member of the law firm of Kelley & Paterson

In 1889 he became president of the Wallaceton Fire Brick Company and in 1899 became the sole proprietor of the works, which he continued to operate until 1902 when they became the property of the Harbison-Walker Refractories Co , he became a director of that company and secretary and treasurer of the Isaac Reese & Sons Co , a group of works also belonging to the Harbison-Walker Refractories Co   In 1904 he concluded to return to the practice of the law, and the firm of Mc-Enally & Paterson was formed, which continued until the organization of the Paterson Clay Products Co , when he withdrew in order to give his sole attention to the brick business   He is at present attending to the business of this company

In 1887 he married Miss Mary Wynn, a daughter of William H and Margaret (Ross) Wynn, and eight children were born to them, three of whom passed away in childhood   The survivors are Richard, Robert Bruce, Alexander, John and Ruth

Richard is in the junior class at Western University, Pittsburg, Bruce is in the sophomore class at Dickinson college, the others are attending the Clearfield schools.

He is a trustee of Dickinson college, he and his wife and two of the children are members of the Presbyterian church of Clearfield, of which church he is an elder.   In politics he is a Republican and has served as chairman and secretary of the Clearfield Republican County Committee   Almost since he became of age he has been a member of the Masonic fraternity, belonging to Clearfield Lodge and Chapter, Moshannon Commandery, Williamsport Consistory, and Jaffa Temple   He is a member of the Clearfield lodge of I O O F , which he joined as soon as he became of age He is a member of the St Andrew's society of Philadelphia, and is an associate member of the Engineers' society of Pennsylvania   He is also treasurer of the Historical Society of Clearfield county

ANTON PETERSON, one of the representative citizens and substantial business men of Clearfield county, Pa , who has been engaged in the mercantile line since 1905 at Lanse, was born September 26, 1864, in Dalsland, near Wenersborg, Sweden, a son of Peter and Anna Eliza (Olsdotter) Anderson

Peter Anderson, or Peterson as it became in this country, was a well-to-do farmer in Sweden, where he died in 1892, aged eighty-three years   He was twice married, and by his first marriage had five children, of whom only one is now surviving, Mrs Lars Olson, who lived for eight years in Arnett, Tioga county, Pa , but who now lives in Dalsland Mr Anderson's second wife, who died in 1910 at the age of seventy-one years, bore him six children, as follows   Alfred, who was an American citizen and died at Arnett, aged forty-two years, Anton, Charlotta, who is the wife of John Johnson of Ramey, Augusta, who is the wife of Adolph Segerlin, of Anita, Jefferson county, Jennie, who married Theodore Fosberg, of Anita, and Catharina, twin of Jennie, who is single and living in Dalsland, Sweden

Anton Peterson attended school in Gerstad, Sweden, and left school at the age of fifteen years to work on his father's farm   In 1883 he came to America, on April 12th of which year he located at Arnett, Pa , and secured employment in the mines and later in the woods   During 1886 he took a trip to Sweden, but on April 24, 1887, he returned to Arnett, and one year later located in Peale, Clearfield county   On April 26, 1888, he entered the employ of the Clearfield County Bituminous Coal Corporation, and during his residence in Peale he was for thirteen and one-half years organist of the Swedish Lutheran church, he having been given a musical education when young On January 11, 1905, Mr Peterson came to Lanse, and on the 19th of the same month, in partnership with John Jacobson, he erected a store room and engaged in the mercantile business Later he bought Mr Jacobson's interest, and he has continued to conduct the enterprise to the present time. Mr Peterson started with little capital, and whatever success he has acquired has been due to his persistent efforts, his natural business ability and his policy of square dealing and honesty towards all He resides in a nice home which he purchased from the Murray Lumber Company of Philipsburg

Mr Peterson was married in 1890, to Miss Mary Larson, the daughter of Andrew Larson, of Peale, and they have had three children, Victoria, Agnes and Herbert Seigfried, all at home and the latter in the eighth grade of the Winburne school Mr Peterson is a member of the Swedish Lutheran church and for twenty-eight years has been a Republican He has done much towards furthering the interests of his adopted country and is a public-spirited and reliable citizen, having been naturalized in Clearfield in 1898, before Judge Cyrus Gordon

AUSTIN H AUGHENBAUGH, car inspector for the Pennsylvania Railroad Company, residing at McGee's Mills, Clearfield county, Pa , was born on the old Philipsburg turnpike road, in Lawrence township, Clearfield county, October 1, 1884, and is a son of A M and Catherine (Rowles) Aughenbaugh

A M Aughenbaugh was born in 1849, in Pike township, Clearfield county, where he lived on his father's farm until his marriage, when he located on the Philipsburg turnpike road, where he still resides He married Catherine Rowles, who is a daughter of Maxwell and Eliza (Litts) Rowles The family ancestry on both sides is German and the paternal grandfather, Jacob Aughenbaugh, came from Germany Austin H Aughenbaugh is the sixth born in a family of eleven children and one of the eight survivors The eldest sister, Anna, is the wife of J F. Isenberg, who conducts a hotel at McGee's Mills, Birdie is the wife of J Green, of Grampian, Pa , Daisy lives at home, Esther is employed as a housekeeper, at McGee's Mills, Warren A is a miner at Woodland, Pa , and married Della Wisor, Alfred lives at Clearfield and married Orressa Peoples, Harry is a miner in Lawrence township and married Etta Spackman The sons are all practical business men and good citizens in every sense of the word

After Austin H Aughenbaugh completed his school attendance he assisted his father, following farming and lumbering and afterward went into railroad work He had been steadily advanced from one position to another and has resided at McGee's Mills as car inspector since 1908 Mr Aughenbaugh married Miss Bessie Schicklang, who was born in Lawrence township in 1886, and is a daughter of Constantine Schicklang and his wife, Rosa Schnars, both of whom were born in Germany Mr and Mrs Aughenbaugh are members of the Presbyterian church In politics he is a Republican but he has never accepted any office He is a member of Tribe No 361, Red Men, at Mahaffey, and of the order of the Moose, at Glen Campbell

LEWIS MELVIN IMPSON, postmaster at Karthaus, Pa , has been a resident of this place since 1884, during a large part of the time being in the mercantile business and also many years postmaster, appointed first by President Harrison in 1891, and secondly in 1899 He was born January 30, 1859, at Geneva, N Y , and is a son of Solomon C and Elizabeth (Scott) Impson

Solomon C Impson was born in Ulster county, N Y , and was a carpenter and builder by trade and after moving to Scranton, Pa , he followed contracting After the panic of 1873 he gave up this business and moved to a farm some twenty-five miles distant from Scranton, on which he lived until after the death of his second wife, when he came to Karthaus and made his home with his son, Lewis M Impson, where his death occurred He was of Scotch-Irish descent He was married first to Elizabeth Scott, who was probably born and reared in Sullivan county, N Y , a daughter of Lewis and Maria (Torrey) Scott Her father and mother moved to New York from Massachusetts and settled in Bethel, Sullivan county, among the pioneers They were people of sturdy character and real worth When their daughter, Mrs Impson, died and left a son of thirteen months, they took the child to their home and hearts and reluctantly gave him up to the father after his second marriage One son, Murray R Impson, survives of this marriage and resides at Elmira, N Y

Lewis Melvin Impson remained with his maternal grandparents until he was ten years old and then joined his father at Scranton, where he attended the High School until 1875, when he accompanied the family to the farm above alluded to, at Boyd's Mills He remained there for one year and then left home and began to look out for himself entirely He worked at the carpenter's trade until 1884, when he came to Karthaus and here followed contracting largely until 1891, the last building in which he was concerned being the schoolhouse at Cataract He then went into a general store business at Karthaus, six years at one place and two years at another, and then built his present store building and devotes himself to the grocery trade in connection with his duties as postmaster Formerly he was very active in Republican politics in the county and in 1908 was a candidate for county commissioner on the Republican ticket, being defeated by a small margin He still is interested and occasionally served in local offices but when importuned to accept the office of justice of the peace, declined

Mr Impson was married January 1, 1881, to Miss Hannah Phillips, who was born in New York but at the time of marriage was living in Wayne county, Pa She is a daughter of Dr Thomas C and Clarissa (Cross) Phillips, both now deceased, her father passing away, January 29, 1906, and her mother prior to that date Mr and Mrs Impson have one daughter, Harriet Adele, who served five years as stenographer in the register's and recorder's office in Clearfield county, and is the wife of Robert Lee Bierly, residing at Renova, they have one son, Robert Lewis Bierly Mr Impson is identified with the Masonic lodge at Renova

DAVID W. JOHNSTON, who is interested in lumber and farming in Jordan township, and owns a beautiful residence at McCartney, was born in Clearfield county, Pa, in October, 1855, and is a son of Robert M and Priscilla (Wise) Johnston

Robert M Johnston was born in Schuylkill county, August 2, 1830, and still lives in Jordan township, one of the venerable citizens For many years he carried on farming there He married Priscilla Wise, who was born in Center county, a daughter of Davis and Mary Wise, and they had the following children David W, Calvin, Emma, Albert and William, all surviving except Calvin

David W Johnston attended school in what was called the Johnston schoolhouse, a log structure that stood on his grandfather's farm Since then his time has been taken up with lumbering and farming, in later years more particularly in dealing in lumber In 1870 he bought a farm of ninety-six acres, which he sold in 1905

Mr Johnston was married in December, 1878, to Miss Lizzie Bright, a daughter of David and Mary (Moore) Bright, who were natives of Canada Mrs Johnston was reared on her father's farm and she had three brothers and one sister William, Jennie, David and Richard, Jennie being deceased Five children were born to Mr and Mrs Johnston, namely Bruce, Lois, who is the wife of James Jones, and Charles Pearl and Alice The family belongs to the Presbyterian church In politics Mr Johnston is a Democrat He has never been willing to accept any public office except that of school director and has served in that capacity for seven years He is one of Jordan township's representative men

ANDREW J PETERSON, a leading citizen of Cooper township, Clearfield county, Pa, of which he is supervisor, is engaged in contract work and custom coal mining He was born January 22, 1869, near the city of Guttenberg, Sweden, a son of Lars and Sophia Peterson

The parents of Mr Peterson are natives of Sweden, where the father was born in 1833 and the mother in 1837 The former came to America in 1881 and the latter in 1883 He engaged first in coal mining but for twenty-three years owned a farm in Tioga county, Pa, which he sold several years ago He still resides in Tioga county Thirteen children were born to Lars and Sophia Peterson, two of whom died in infancy and one at a later age. The survivors are: Charlotta, who is the wife of Andrew Allen, of Antrim, Tioga county; Matilda, who is the wife of Frank Anderson, a farmer of Stony Fork, Tioga county; Charles, who is a farmer in Delmont township, Tioga county, and married Matilda Frisk, Lars, who resides in Oregon; Andrew J, Peter, who lives at Stony Fork, Tioga county, Otto, who is a contractor, living in the West, Jennie, who married Andrew Klang, a miner residing at Antrim, Tioga county, and John and Edward, who live in Colorado, where they own 600 acres of farm land Gustav, who died at the age of thirty-four years, was a resident of Antrim, Tioga county He married Augusta Neilson and his surviving family live in Clearfield county

Andrew J Peterson attended the public schools in his native land and after he was occupied in a self-supporting way in the day time, continued his studies in the night schools When he was eight years old he began to be useful as a cattle herder In 1882 he came to America and was thirteen years of age when he went to work in the mines at Antrim, where he continued until he was eighteen and afterward at odd times, again worked at mining For some years he was engaged in lumbering and during two years of this period followed contract work in the woods After coming to Clearfield county he was with the Sommerville Coal Company, for thirteen months as weighman For some years he has been mainly engaged in contract work and custom coal mining, is a general contractor of bituminous coal, a dealer in fertilizers, and makes a specialty of contracting for water line, concrete work, reservoirs, and other similar constructive work He completed a $5,000 contract for the Winburne water line He is a careful, experienced man in this line of work and the public has confidence both in his ability and business integrity Mr Peterson owns twenty-two and one-half acres of land at Lanse, on which he has lived for thirteen years When he purchased it it was wild and entirely unimproved At that time he was engaged in mine work and frequently after the labor of a hard day was completed, he worked until ten o'clock at night clearing the land He had to clear a space on which to build his house, which he erected in 1899 and later put up his substantial barn Mr Peterson has here a valuable property and a comfortable home and there is every reason for him being proud of it as it is practically all the work of his own hands

On September 22, 1893, Mr Peterson was married to Miss Christiana Erickson, a daughter of Erick Larson According to old Swedish law and custom, the given name and surname are reversed in succeeding generations, thus Erick Larson, in the following generations becomes Lars Erickson The same custom prevails in Wales Eight children have been born to Mr and Mrs Peterson, namely Annie Cecelia, Eric Adolph. Charlotta, Carl Herbert, Hedwig Sophia. Henry Theodore, Agnes and Evaline Elizabeth Mr and Mrs Peterson are members of the Evangelical Lutheran church at Lanse He belongs to the fraternal order known as the Scandanavian Brotherhood In politics he is a Republican and has served two years as school director, one year as auditor of Cooper township, and at present is serving in his second year of a four-year term as township supervisor

BLAIR W DIEHL, who is a trusted employe of the Pennsylvania Railroad Company, being tank keeper for this road at Irvona, Pa, and also a farmer to some extent, was born near Tyrone, Pa, April 25, 1882, and is a son of Samuel and Mary (Mock) Diehl and a grandson of John Diehl, who was in the fourth generation in descent from Samuel Diehl, who was the founder of the family in Pennsylvania There are many representatives of this old family in the state and they have an annual reunion in Clearfield county

When his school days were over, Blair W Diehl went into the woods and worked in the timber for about two years, afterward following saw milling and mining until 1903, when he came to Irvona and was appointed to his present responsible position On December 1, 1903, Mr Diehl was married to Miss Alice McCully who was born December 1, 1885, a daughter of George and Cornelia (Witheright) McCully, old settlers of Chest township Mrs Diehl has one brother and three sisters, namely Dorsey, residing at Bellwood, Bertha, wife of Charles Houser, residing in Chest township, Lena, wife of Harry Dereamer, living at Bellwood, and Lulu, wife of W 'Straw, residing at Vintondale, Pa Mr and Mrs Diehl have three children Guy, Bertha and Gilbert, their ages ranging from seven to one year Mr Diehl is a member of the order of the Mystic Chain, at Irvona

JOHN WHARTON REITER, a well known and influential citizen of Karthaus township, who has resided on his present valuable property for more than forty years, and is now serving as president of the school board, was born in Covington township, Clearfield county, Pa , September 29, 1844, son of John and Amelia (Buck) Reiter

John Reiter, the grandfather of John W Reiter, was a native of Germany, who came to the United States at an early day and settled in Montgomery county, Pa   Later he purchased the old Reiter homestead place in Covington township, and there he resided until his death, his life being spent in agricultural pursuits   He was buried at Keewaydin cemetery   Mr Reiter and his wife had the following children Michael, deceased, who at the time of his death was living at the Reidges, near Milesburg, Pa , Catherine, deceased, who was the wife of F W Schnars of Keewaydin, Betsy, deceased, who was the wife of Joseph Vothers, of Oak Hill, Karthaus township, and John The family have always been members of the Lutheran church

John Reiter, son of John and father of John W Reiter, was born in Montgomery county, Pa , and was fourteen years of age when he accompanied his parents to Clearfield county, the journey being made up-stream from Harrisburg in a flat-bottomed boat The family

first located at Karthaus, where young John drove a team for old Peter Karthaus for a time, and later bought the twenty acres of land from his father in Covington township He next purchased 124 acres of land on the opposite side of the road, and in addition to farming and lumbering to some extent, kept a public inn, which, although not a licensed place, often entertained as high as 100 guests and fed from fifteen to twenty head of horses a night, the inn being located on a road that was extensively used by raftsmen and teams going through to St Mary's, Elk county. Mr. Reiter was a Republican, and held various township offices He died at the age of seventy-five years, and was buried at Keewaydin, where his widow, who survived him for some time, was also laid to rest Mr Reiter was married to Amelia Buck, who was born in Bradford township, Clearfield county, daughter of Henry Buck, a native of Germany and an early settler of Bradford township, and to this union there were born the following children Henry, deceased, who lived on the property adjoining the home farm, Lavina, deceased, who was the wife of George Emerick of Karthaus township, Sarah, deceased, who married William Hoffer, Reuben L , deceased, who was a resident of Keewaydin, Rosaline, who lives at Punxsutawney, Jefferson county, John Wharton, Anna, deceased, who was the wife of Christian M Hertlein of Karthaus township, Mary, who was the wife of Elisha Evans of Oak Hill, and Ella, deceased, who was the wife of Edward Schars of Covington township

John Wharton Reiter attended the school near the old home place and as a young man engaged in farming and lumbering In June, 1871, he came to Karthaus township and settled in the woods, on a tract of five acres which he had purchased He made a clearing, erected a dwelling and started in to improve his property, adding to it from time to time until he now has one of the excellent farms of Karthaus township He also owns some of his father's farm, in addition to some property in Karthaus, and he engages in the coal business to some extent, producing the commodity on his own property

On May 14, 1871, Mr Reiter was married to Miss Mary C Maurer, who was born in Covington township, daughter of Jacob and Lydia (Rigley) Maurer, who came to Clearfield county from Mifflin county To Mr and Mrs Reiter there have been born nine children Harry, living in Karthaus township, who married Clara Heichel and has three children, Claie, Clifford and DeLee, Fred, also living in Karthaus township, who married Emma Brown and has two children, Ruth and Helen, Cameron, living in Tyrone, who married Iva Conaway and has three children, Lauriel, Vida and Burton Taft, Paul, who is living at home, Alma, who is a graduate of Punxsutawney Hospital and is now located at Cleveland, Ohio, Boyd, Frank and Muriel, who are all living at home, and Augusta, who died when three years of age Mr Reiter has served for a number of years as a member of the school board and he is now acting as president of that body

JAMES I POLLUM, M D , coroner of Clearfield county and a skillful and trusted physician and surgeon of DuBois, was born at Foxburg, Clarion county, Pa , December 16, 1876, and is a son of A P and Anna E (Motter) Pollum

A P Pollum resides at Falls Creek, Jef-
47

ferson county, Pa His wife, who was a member of one of the old families of Clarion county, died January 31, 1907 Eight children were born to them, as follows Benjamin, James I , Elizabeth, who is the wife of C E Millieor, of California, Warren, who is a resident of Clearfield, Bert, who is a student in the dental department of the University of Pittsburg, in the class of 1912, Elva, who is the wife of Albert Groves, of Reynoldsville, Pa , Edgar, who lives in Jefferson county, Pa , and Homer, who is also a resident of Jefferson county

James I. Pollum was ten years old when his parents moved to Elk county, Pa . from there going to Jefferson county He was educated in the public schools of Jefferson, and the Clarion State Normal School, where he was graduated in 1896, after which he was engaged in teaching school for ten years, in Washington township, Jefferson county During a part of this time he devoted himself to preparing for medical college and he subsequently entered the University of Pittsburg, where he was graduated in the class of 1906 After a few months of practice in Cambria county, he came to DuBois, where he soon built up a substantial practice and won the confidence and esteem of the public When the county coroner, Dr Ross, was removed by death, Dr Pollum was appointed to serve out the former's unexpired term and in 1909 he was elected to the office of coroner, the duties of which he is still performing

On May 5, 1897, Dr Pollum was married to Miss Mae Hildebrand, a daughter of the late David and Amelia Hildebrand, of DuBois Dr . and Mrs Pollum have one son, Aldridge, who was born in 1900 They reside at No 28 W Scribner avenue, adjoining the DuBois Hospital, Dr Pollum being a member of the staff of this institution. He belongs to the DuBois branch of the Red Bank Protective Association and is identified fraternally with the Masons, the Knights of Pythias, the Eagles and the P H C. Politically he is a Republican

ARCHIE B LANSBERRY was a well known and highly respected resident of Bradford township, Clearfield county, Pa, where his death occurred July 13, 1878 He was a native of Bradford township and a son of James and Elizabeth Lansberry He attended the public schools in boyhood and youth, after which he went to work on his father's farm and continued until his marriage, when he and wife went to housekeeping on a rented farm in Graham township They lived there until 1869, when he bought ninety acres of wild land in Bradford township, all of which he cleared himself and placed under cultivation He continued to improve his property, being a man of great energy and industry, until near the close of his life, when illness made him retire from active work He carried on general farming during the summers and devoted a part of the winter seasons to hauling timber and lumber After his death his eldest son, A B Lansberry, took charge of the farm and his widow in 1890 moved to Clearfield and occupies a residence owned by this son Mr Lansberry was a man of quiet life and domestic virtues He was well known and had a wide circle of personal friends

In 1866 Archie B Lansberry was married to Miss Lavinia Pearce, who was born and reared in Bradford township, a daughter of Absolom and Mary Ann Pearce, and they had three children born to them A B, Walter R and Clarence E A B Lansberry, who now manages the home farm, married Miss Gussie Glaze, of Clearfield county Walter R died at the age of eighteen months Clarence E has been twice married His first union was with Miss Lillie Sherry, of Bradford township, who died at the age of thirty years, survived by two children Cora and Guy His second marriage was to Miss Agnes Couder, of Bradford township, and they had five children Daniel, Doyle, Raymond, Nana and Kenneth, all of whom survive except the eldest

Clarence and A B Lansberry started in the coal business about the year 1895, with one miner and one team, hauling to Woodland and have increased their business from time to time, and finally built tram roads and bought a locomotive, and now are working about fourteen miners and ship about seventy tons per day the greater part of the year.

AUGUSTUS JOHNSON YOUNG, one of the representative business men of Cooper township, Clearfield county, Pa, a member of the general mercantile firm of Young and Lingren, who control the best trade at Grass Flat and in the surrounding territory, was born in Hokantarp, Skaaborgs Lan, Westergotland, Sweden, September 1, 1859 His parents were Jonas and Maja (Stina) Anderson, both natives of Sweden

Jonas Anderson, father of Augustus J, was born in 1828 and died at the age of forty-two years, having been a farmer during all his active life He married Maja Stina, who was born December 13, 1829, and now lives in great comfort in the place where her sons have prospered and made honorable names for themselves She was married a second time,

55

and with her husband, Andrew Mangoson, came to America in 1892 To her first marriage four sons were born and all came to the United States Augustus, John and Charles all reside at Grass Flat, but Frans, the youngest, went to Iowa and is a fireman on the C B & Q Railroad John is a miner and also conducts a small farm Charles was obliged to give up mining on account of failing health and now conducts a bakery

Augustus J Young was the first born of his parents' family He attended school in his native land for a short time but his father was not possessed of large means and the sons were obliged to go to work when yet young It fell to Mr Young's lot to work on a farm and in that way earned enough to pay the rent and if his earnings were more than the rent amounted to, they went to purchase some gift that he could give his mother or to some other laudable purpose. He came to America in 1888 and reached Peale, Clearfield county, on the 18th of May Before long he discovered that in order to compete with native-born Americans, he must learn their language and he began to study at night and to take advantage of every moment when he was not at work He improved rapidly and with his improvement his ambition grew and three years after he had entered the employ of the Clearfield County Bituminous Coal Company, he had enough of his earnings saved to enter college at Rock Island, Ill He continued his studies for five years more During the holidays of 1895, he returned to Grass Flat and while here bought his brother's store, the latter desiring to return to Sweden This store, situated on the Hill, Mr Young continued until, 1900, when he purchased the store, in association with his present partner, which they

conduct, it formerly belonging to Gust Ryberg They are good business men and stand high in the esteem of the public

Mr Young was married to Miss Ida Bloomquist, who was born in Sweden, a daughter of Fritz Bloomquist, on May 16, 1905 She is an educated lady and was a teacher in the parochial schools Mr and Mrs Young have no children of their own but a brother of Mrs Young left two children at death, one of whom, Fritz Egnar, a beautiful fair-haired boy, has been adopted by Mr and Mrs Young They are members of the Lutheran church Mr Young votes with the Republican party but otherwise takes little interest in politics

JAMES DAVISON, one of the leading citizens of Chest township, Clearfield county, Pa, where he owns 200 acres of improved land, was born September 27, 1831, in Albany county, N Y, and is a son of C and Elizabeth (Warner) Davison, and a grandson of a patriot who served through the Revolutionary war The father of Mr Davison died on our subject's farm, in 1891, aged eighty-two years, having survived his wife since 1863 They had seven children, the two survivors being James, of Chest township, and William S, of Indiana county

James Davison obtained his education in the early schools near his parents' home and afterward worked as a blacksmith and in the lumbering industry until 1850, when he came to Clearfield county This land had to be cleared and in the course of years the work was accomplished through Mr Davison's industry and for many years it has been considered one of the best farms of the township Never taking any particular interest in politics, Mr Davison has devoted his attention mainly to the development of his land and in later years has been able to enjoy the comforts his early industry provided for

Mr Davison was married to Miss Ellen Hunter, who was born in Scotland and died in Chest township, at the age of sixty-eight years Four children were born to them Sophia, who lives in California, and Emeline, who is the wife of A Pierce and has had two children, Ellen and Winfield, Elizabeth, who lives at home, and Walter, who is deceased Mr Davison is a member of the Presbyterian church He has been identified with the Grange at Ansonville, for a number of years, and is one of Chest township's most esteemed citizens

SAMUEL T HEPBURN, a representative citizen of Karthaus, Pa, and for the past several years proprietor of the popular Potter House, was born in Penn township, Clearfield county, Pa, September 20, 1853, and is a son of Samuel Coleman and Cynthia (Hoover) Hepburn

When Mr Hepburn was a mere lad his parents moved to Grampian, Pa, and in the schools of that place he secured his education While still a youth he was employed at lumbering, on job work, and he then entered a grist mill, later engaging in that business on his own account with William F Johnson, and, after that gentleman's death, with Dr J Currier, at Grampian He also engaged in rafting to some extent, sometimes going as far as Marietta After disposing of his grist mill interests, he engaged in a meat market business, in conjunction with which he conducted a hotel at New Holland, Lancaster county, but in 1904 became proprietor of the Hyde City

Hotel, at Hyde City, Pa, from whence he came to Karthaus in December, 1908, to become owner of the Potter House He has continued to conduct this hostelry to the present time, and it is one much favored by traveling men as well as the general public

On February 7, 1884, Mr Hepburn was united in marriage with Miss Gertrude Dressler, who was born and reared in Union township, Clearfield county, a daughter of Levi R and Julia (Hall) Dressler Two children were born to this union, Floyd and Grace Floyd Hepburn, who was born July 30, 1885, is a graduate of Lakemont (N Y) Starkey Seminary, attended Rochester University for two years and then completed a business course in Strayer's Business College, of Philadelphia He is now assistant superintendent of Stetcher's Lithograph Company, at Rochester Grace Hepburn was born December 24, 1887, and was married on Thanksgiving Day, November 25, 1910, to Grover C Zimmermann They now reside in Shamokin, Pa

Mr Hepburn is a Democrat in his political belief, and was one of the first councilmen of the borough of Grampian, where he also served on the school board at the time the school was built He is a member of Royal Arcanum, of the Odd Fellows, and the Elks Mrs Hepburn is a member of the Baptist church

REUBEN CALDWELL, a highly respected retired farmer of Knox township, Clearfield county, Pa, residing on his valuable farm of 300 acres, which is situated eight miles south of Curwensville, was born June 1, 1828, in Pike township, Clearfield county, Pa His parents were Matthew and Mary (Bloom) Caldwell

Matthew Caldwell was born and reared in Lancaster county, Pa , where he remained until early manhood, when he came to Clearfield county, where he spent the remainder of his life   He married Mary Bloom who was born in New Jersey, and twenty children were born to them, Reuben being the seventh in order of birth   Matthew Caldwell was the oldest of the sons of Hugh Caldwell and before his marriage resided for a time with his father who then lived near Curwensville   After marriage he settled on a wild tract of ninety acres, in Pike township, to which he subsequently added 100 acres and through hard work cleared one-half of his property   When he died, at the age of eighty-two years, he expressed the wish to be buried on his own land, and his wife was laid by his side   They were members of the Presbyterian church and lived consistent, Christian lives   Matthew Caldwell was an old-time Democrat as were all his sons   The family is one well known in Pennsylvania

Reuben Caldwell learned his first lessons in an old round log schoolhouse but afterward attended what was known as the Arnold school about one mile from his home   The sessions were held but three months in the year but after he was old enough to go into the woods and to help materially on the farm, he had few opportunities for study   It was the object of young men in his early years to work hard and thus acquire land and to find pleasure and profit in developing it   Before he married, Mr Caldwell had become the owner of a part of his present farm and afterward kept adding to it until he now owns 300 acres, land which is valuable both for farming, pasturing and also as coal land, a fine coal bank being on the home place   For some years Mr Caldwell has lived retired from active labor but he keeps in close touch with all that goes on on the farm and gives advice of which he knows the value by experience   Formerly he also followed lumbering

In June, 1857, Mr Caldwell was married to Miss Mary F Johnston, a daughter of Robert and Mary (Cameron) Johnston, both of whom were born in Scotland   To them were born the following children   Mark A , who married Lydia Goon, a daughter of Joseph Goon, Elizabeth Alice, who is the wife of Samuel Wise, of Bloomington, Mary Ellen, who is the widow of Joseph Bechdel, Robert M , who married Amanda Campbell, who lives in Oregon, Priscilla Jane, who is the wife of William McNeal, of Altoona, and Annie Isabella, who is the wife of Frank Moore, residing near Lumber City, Pa

Mr Caldwell and wife are members of the Presbyterian church in Jordan township   During his more active years he served his fellow citizens in many township offices, being a school director, tax collector and road supervisor   Both he and wife are widely known and they are held in much esteem

HERMAN CHARLES KASTEN, manager of the A F Kelley store at Grass Flat, Cooper township, Clearfield county, Pa , has spent a number of years in the mercantile business and possesses not only the business capacity but also the personal gifts that insure success in this line   He was born January 24, 1877, in Germany, and is a son of Frederick C and Catherine (Christopher) Kasten

The parents of Mr Kasten were natives of Germany and came to America in 1882, where the father engaged in the saw-mill business but now lives retired at Williamsport, Pa   The mother is deceased   They had eleven

children and of the family the following sur-
vive Ralph, who is a cabinetmaker, lives at
Williamsport, Augusta, who is the wife of
Joseph Rockel, a merchant of Williamsport,
Frederica, who is the wife of Emil Smaltz,
who is connected with a timber company,
Herman Charles; and Ida, who is the wife of
August Ertle, a merchant at Williamsport.

Herman Charles Kasten came to America
from Baden, Germany, when a child of five
years and was next to the youngest in his parents' family. He obtained his education in the
schools of Williamsport, Pa., where he completed a course in the Williamsport Commercial College, after which he became a grocery
merchant and continued in that line for thirteen years. For nine years he conducted a
general mercantile business at English Center,
Lycoming county, Pa., and in 1906 he moved
from there to Peale, Clearfield county, where
he was engaged until 1908, when he became
manager of his present store at Grass Flat.

In January, 1901, Mr Kasten was married
to Miss Ethel Mary Whitehead, who was born
in Potter county, Pa. Her father was Ezra
Whitehead and both parents died when she
was a child. Mr and Mrs Kasten are members of the Lutheran church. He belongs to
Lodge No 1091, Odd Fellows, at English
Center, Lodge No 233, K O T M, at the
same place, from which he later transferred to
Lodge No 99, Williamsport. He is identified
politically with the Republican party

HENRY HILLIARD, who settled in Bell
township, Clearfield county, Pa, when all this
section was still covered with woods, now
lives retired, after an active life, mainly devoted to agricultural pursuits. He was born
in Clearfield county, March 26, 1836, and is a
son of Adam and Susanna (Musser) Hilliard.

Adam Hilliard was born in Butler county,
Pa, and devoted his entire active life to farming. His death occurred in 1890, in Jefferson
county, at the age of seventy-two years. He
married Susanna Musser, who died in 1893,
aged seventy-five years. Her parents were
Henry and Betsey Musser,· while Mr Hilliard's parents were Jacob and Sarah Hilliard
Henry Hilliard has one sister and three brothers, namely Jacob, who lives at Saxonville,
John and Daniel, both of whom live at Du-
Bois, and Kansas E, who is the widow of J
Jones, and lives at DuBois

Henry Hilliard learned the blacksmith's
trade after his school days were over and followed it more or less for fifty-five years.
After he married he moved to Frostburg and
worked there at his trade for four years moving then to Paradise Settlement, in Jefferson
county, and twenty years afterward came to
his present farm in Bell township. He cleared
this land and now has a valuable and productive farm of 100 acres. During the Civil war
he served as a soldier for six months, enlisting in 1863 in Co C, 2nd Pa Vol Inf, under the command of Gen Lininger. His company was mainly used for picket duty but also
was concerned in considerable light skirmishing. He was mustered out at Pittsburg, in
1864, and returned to peaceful pursuits

Mr Hilliard was married to Lucy Smith,
who was born in Indiana county, Pa, in August, 1839, a daughter of Peter and Lydia
(McPherson) Smith, and a granddaughter of
Peter and Susan Smith and of John McPherson, the last named having served in the Revolutionary war. They were from Center
county. Mr. and Mrs Hilliard have had the
following children: Charles P., who married

Carrie Bloss, has three children and one grandchild, Lydia Ann, who married Henry Filhart, and they have seven children and one grandchild, Malvern, who married Margaret Klein and has five children, John, who married Jane Miller and has eight children, and William, who lives at home Mr Hilliard is a member of the Evangelical church In politics he is a Democrat He is numbered with the representative and substantial men of Bell township

J S BRIEL, one of the representative business men of Karthaus, Pa, of which he has been a resident since 1882, is engaged in the funeral directing business, is a stockholder and director in the Karthaus Fire Brick Company, and a director and formerly treasurer of the Karthaus Rural Telephone Company He was born in Covington township, Clearfield county, Pa, November 27, 1854, and is a son of John and Margaret (McGonigal) Briel

John Briel was born in 1827, in Germany, a son of John and Margaret Briel Grandfather John Briel came to America in 1838, having married a second time, his first wife having died in Switzerland He worked in a foundry at Baltimore, Md, until 1842, when he came to Karthaus and for a time was in the employ of Peter Karthaus but later returned to Baltimore, where his second wife subsequently died. Their youngest child was born on a raft in the Susquehanna river They had six children, namely John, Mary, who is the wife of John Hoyt, of Baltimore; Nancy, who married a Mr Ritz, of Baltimore, George, who was drowned in his fifteenth year, and Margaret and Agnes, all being now deceased

John Briel (2d), father of J S. Briel of Karthaus, was eleven years old when he accompanied his parents to America He was suffering from fever and ague when his people came to Karthaus and was unable to come with them but later also became a resident of Karthaus and learned the blacksmith's trade under Peter Karthaus, on the place where his son lives Some years later he went to Salt Lick and worked as a blacksmith for Edward McGarvey and then started into business for himself at Mulsonburg and continued as a blacksmith and lumberman during the remainder of his active years, his death occurring May 23, 1869 He was an energetic, industrious man and made an honorable name for himself in business although he had many drawbacks to contend with

John Briel was married in Clinton county, Pa, to Margaret McGonigal, who was born at Bellefonte, Pa, and spent the closing years of her life at Frenchville, in Clearfield county, where she died September 8, 1909 Her parents were Hugh and Grace McGonigal, who were natives of Ireland Nine children were born to John and Margaret Briel, as follows. Nancy J, who is the wife of Ernest T Mignot, of Girard township, John Samuel, Grace, who is the wife of Sylvester McGovern, of Baltimore, Anna E, who is the wife of Ferdinand A Mignot, of Covington township; Agnes and Cecelia, both of whom died in childhood, Sarah, who is the wife of John D. Gill, of Cambria county, Pa, George D, who died in Covington township when aged nine years; and Joseph J, who died in Covington township at the age of fourteen years The father of the above family was a Democrat in politics and on several occasions was elected to township offices. He was a leading member of the Catholic church at Frenchville

John Samuel Briel attended the Covington

township schools and then learned the black-smith's trade which he continued to follow there until 1882, when he came to Karthaus, where he opened his own smithy and con-ducted it until 1892 In that year he em-barked in the hardware business with Dr W L Gilliland but at the end of two years with-drew from the firm In the meantime, in 1893, he formed the firm of Mignot & Briel, with Ernest F Mignot as a partner They built a modern mill, a three-story structure, with roller process and conducted a very suc-cessful business until 1905, when they leased the mill and in 1909 sold the property

Mr Briel was one of the enterprising citi-zens who prospected when clay was discovered here and did much to bring the subject to the attention of the public As a wide awake and public spirited citizen he has shown an interest in and has lent his influence in the direction of bringing about various movements that have resulted in benefit to this section As a busi-ness man he has always stood high

Mr Briel was married August 17, 1879, to Miss Lucy A Hugar, who was born in Girard Township, Clearfield County, Pa Her par-ents were James and Rennet (Bigleman) Hu-gar Her maternal grandfather, Christopher Bigleman, served as a soldier under the great Napoleon and took part in the Siege of Mos-cow Her paternal grandfather, Francis Hugar, emigrated from France to America and purchased a tract of timberland in Girard Township, where he developed a farm on which he lived until his death in 1876

James Hugar, father of Mrs Briel, was born January 15, 1837, at Bloomington, Clearfield County, Pa , being a son by his father's first marriage and by his mother's second marriage He married Rennet Bigleman, who was born

at Mulsonburg, Pa , August 15, 1834 She is a daughter of Christopher and Frances (Gross-tat) Bigleman, who spent their last years at Mulsonburg James Hugar and wife now re-side at Karthaus, having moved here from Covington Township Mrs Briel was the first born of her parents' family, the others being: Antied, who lives at Karthaus, John, who died at the age of twenty-one years; Angeline, who is the wife of Victor Renaud, of Karthaus, Caroline, who is the wife of James Murray, of Goshen Township, Ida, who died when aged seven years, Joseph, who is a resident of Renova; Fred, who died when aged eighteen years, and Edmund, who lives at Renova. For many years the father of Mrs Briel en-gaged in teaming and was also a pilot on the river The family and its connections are members of the Roman Catholic church at Frenchville

Mr and Mrs Briel have had fifteen children born to them, not all of whom survive, but those living make up a happy, united family and are well known and respected members of society. The family record reads as follows: Clara, who died at the age of two years, Ce-celia, who resides at Karthaus, is a professional trained nurse, Ida, who lives at Frenchville; James John, who is a resident of Karthaus; a babe that died unnamed and which was a twin with James John, Maude, who married Ferdinand Maines, and has two children— Clare and Gard, Frances, who is a teacher in the public schools at Frenchville; Janet, who lived to the age of seven years, Ferdinand, who met an accidental death on October 21, 1908, from the discharge of a gun (was a prom-ising youth of fourteen years); the tenth in order of birth a babe that died unnamed; Gen-eva, Henrietta, Julia and George, who are all making fine school records, and a babe, the youngest of the family, which passed away before being named The children have all been reared in the Catholic church, and have had school and social advantages In politics he is a Democrat and has served as auditor and on the school board more or less for the past twenty-five years He is identified with the Elks at Clearfield, and the I O R M at Karthaus He is a member of the St John and Paul Roman Catholic Church

JULES DERMINER, one of the foremost men of Girard Township, where he has lived for thirty-nine years, owns 170 acres of valuable land, ninety of which is cleared He was born in France, in 1851, obtaining his education in his native land

In 1871 Mr Derminer came to America and to Clearfield County, Pa , where he went to work for an uncle, who lived in Girard Township One year later he entered the employ of a Mr Leconte, and remained with him until 1873, when his parents came from France, purchasing a farm of 172 acres in Girard Township They spent their remaining years on this farm, where the mother died in 1891 and the father in 1897 Mr Derminer settled on a farm purchased from Mrs Spackman and called the Spackman farm and has made many improvements as the years have passed He carries on general farming and stock raising For many years he has been prominent in the public affairs of the township and in 1892 was elected township auditor and served in that office until 1898 From 1899 until 1910 he served as school director and in 1904 was elected secretary of the school board He was reelected to this office in 1906 and has served to the present time, 1910 Girard Township

is noted for its excellent schools and this is due, in great part, to the interest taken in them by the township's representative men

Mr Derminer was married in Girard Township to Miss Mugnot and they have eight children August, Mary, Arthur, Helen, Kate, Andrew, Lizzie and Clement Mr Derminer and family are members of the Catholic church at Frenchville

IRA E MATTHEWS, superintendent of the fire brick plant of Hiram Swank Sons, which is being completed at Irvona, Clearfield county, Pa , was born in Iowa, September 1, 1881, and is a son of John E and Philena (Rickets) Matthews

Abraham Matthews, his grandfather, was born in Maryland, his parents coming from the north of Ireland, and his great grandfather moved from Maryland to Altoona and thence to Glasgow, Cambria county Abraham Matthews settled in Beccaria township, Clearfield county, in 1838, being a pioneer settler in the county, in which he lived practicaly all his life He cleared the farm now known as the homestead in the early 40's When he began the work of clearing it, he walked from Glasgow, worked all day and walked back at night, and he continued these heavy labors until he had constructed a log house to the square, on which elevation he could sleep without so much danger of the wolves devouring him When he got the house built to the square, he would bring his rations for one week, and squirrels and wood mice were so plentiful that he had to tie his food to a limb with a string, and then at times they would jump to the basket or gnaw off the string which supported it When he got a few acres cleared he would sow it in wheat or other grain, then there was a steady task to keep the deer from eating it up entirely He had a dog, which he trained to chase the deer from the grain and by perseverance and a good backbone he managed to accumulate a goodly portion of this world's goods Many were the hardships of the early settlers at that time All his merchandise was brought on horseback or by wagon from Water street, Huntingdon county, or Tyrone, and at that time wagons had no locks and chains were scarce, so when he came to descend a steep hill with a heavy load, he would stop at the top, cut a tree suited to the size of the load, and attach it to the back of the wagon, but forward, and this would serve as a drag and prevent the load from shoving the oxen, as horses were scarce at that time His wife, Mary (Anderson) Matthews, was born in Maryland They died in Clearfield County, Pa, the former in 1903, at the age of eighty-eight years, six months and two days, and the latter at the age of forty-six years

John E Matthews was born in Beccaria township, Clearfield county, in 1854 Soon after his marriage he moved to Clinton County, Ia, where he worked at farming for three years, living there from 1879 to 1881 He then came to Clearfield County, where he owns 273 acres of land, 120 acres being under cultivation He makes a specialty of stock raising He married Philena Rickets and they have four children Charles A, who is a veterinary surgeon in practice at Cumberland, Md; Ira E; Lottie, who resides at home and Jennie, who is a student in the High School

Ira E Matthews attended the High School at Eutahville for three years and later the summer sessions of the Normal School which were conducted by such well known educators as Silas Frampton, J Frank Rowles and Prof J V. Clark, after which he taught school for one year In 1900 he resumed his studies and passed one term in the State Normal School at Westchester and later, after teaching through a great part of 1901-2, he spent a year at Juniata College, at Huntingdon, Pa In thus thoroughly equipping himself, Mr. Matthews was prepared to fill almost any position where education and careful training might be demanded, and he first accepted a situation with the contracting firm of McAtee, Ache & Reed, as time-keeper, at Clearfield. Four months afterward he became concrete inspector for the N Y. Central Railroad, and resigned there in order to become concrete foreman with the railroad contracting firm of McManman & Simms He continued with that firm and two years later was made superintendent of concrete work and continued to superintend general construction with that company until June, 1910, when he became superintendent of construction and superintendent of the plant for Hiram Swank Sons, at Irvona

The Irvona Fire Brick plant of Hiram Swank Sons, is one of the finest of its kind in the country This plant is being erected by the four sons of Hiram Swank of Johnstown, Pa Hiram Swank is a pioneer in the manufacture of fire brick, he establishing his first plant at Johnstown, in 1856, which is still in operation, conducted by his four sons under the firm name of Hiram Swank Sons. The construction work on the Irvona plant was started in June, 1910, after experts had visited the largest and most modern plants of this kind all over the country, the object being that nothing that would add to the convenience and utility of the new plant should be omitted. The laying out, construction and equipping of the plant has been directly under the supervision of the present superintendent, Ira E Matthews   The main building has dimensions of 306x77 feet, and the boiler-house extension is 70x30 feet   The frame is entirely of steel   The plans are for sixteen kilns, with a contemplated extension of 300 feet additional space to the main building   The product includes the manufacturing of nine-inch brick and all kinds of shapes   If the output was reduced to nine-inch brick exclusively, the capacity provided for would be 80,000 brick daily   At the end of one year if plans are completed employment will be afforded 175 men

The plant is constructed in such a manner that the clay and coal can be conveyed to their respective places without resorting to manual labor, by means of elevator trucks   The concern owns an abundance of the finest grade of clay and has both the New York Central and the Pennsylvania Railroads insuring good rates as well as fine accommodations for shipping both the raw material and the finished product   During the months since this plant has been under construction, real estate in proximity has increased from one hundred to one hundred and fifty percent   The value of the plant is stated to be $100,000

Mr Matthews is a young man to have so thoroughly mastered the details of the business in which he is engaged   He has accomplished much in his thirty years, having taught school for six years before turning his attention into the present channels, and since then has been engaged in construction work in Pennsylvania, Maryland, Virginia and Canada and also passed several months in New Brunswick, 300 miles from civilization   The completion of the present plant and the installation of the machinery, will reflect great credit on him as a careful and accurate business man

In politics Mr Matthews is a Republican He is identified fraternally with the Elks at Tyrone and the order of the Moose at Coalport

NELSON F MOTT, general farmer and mail carrier, in Bell Township, Clearfield County, Pa , was born January 19, 1872, in Jefferson County, Pa , and is a son of David H and Letitia M (Miller) Mott

David H Mott was born in Bell Township, Clearfield County, on the farm now owned by Mrs S S Mott, widow of Sam'l S Mott He has followed farming and lumbering all his life and is still quite active, although now in his sixty-third year   He married Letitia M Miller, who is somewhat younger than her husband   Her parents were Angus and Elizabeth (Ballentine) Miller   Mr and Mrs Mott have had four children Nelson F , Elmer, who is deceased, W Benjamin, who lives in West Virginia, and Angus Miller

Nelson F Mott, when his school days were over, engaged for ten years in the saw-mill business and for the years following his marriage, at Curry Run, and farmed one year at McGee's Mills. In 1906 he erected his present residence adjoining his grandfather's old homestead   It is situated near the old Whiskey Run schoolhouse, which was the first structure used for school purposes in Clearfield County.

Mr Mott married first, Mrs Maggie I Peoples, a daughter of John Peoples, of Rockton, Clearfield County, Pa   Mrs Mott died October 8, 1902, at the age of twenty-five years They had three children, two of whom are now deceased, the one survivor being Arthur, now aged ten years   Mr Mott was married secondly to Mrs Pearl (Bagley) Kring, widow of Jacob Kring   Mrs Kring has one son, Ralph, who is fourteen years old and is attending school   Mr and Mrs Mott are members of Mt Bethel Methodist Protestant Church, in which he is a steward   He has passed all the chairs in the lodge of Odd Fellows at Mahaffey   Mr Mott has carried on general farming with his father but since 1906 his time has been mainly occupied as a Rural Free Delivery mail carrier, distributing from McGee's Mills   In politics he is a Prohibitionist

DAVID FULTON, a well-to-do resident of Burnside township, where he is engaged in agriculture, was born on the old Fulton homestead in this township, August 20, 1840, son of Simon and Elizabeth (Young) Fulton   He is a grandson of David H Fulton, a native of Frankstown, Blair county, Pa , who in 1838 was sent to Philadelphia to learn the tailor's trade, from which place he came to Clearfield county   Settling near the Squire Smith home, he took up farming and also followed his trade in the vicinity   He died in 1867 at the age of ninety-seven years   He married Elizabeth Rorabough, a daughter of David Rorabough

Simon Fulton was born in Center county, Pa , and after coming to Clearfield county was brought up to agriculture on the parental homestead, and he followed that occupation on the homestead all the rest of his life   He was a member of Mt Zion church, and in politics a Democrat   He married Elizabeth Young, a daughter of Henry and Hannah (Saylor) Young   She died in 1854   Of ten children born to Simon and Elizabeth Fulton, but three are now living, namely   David, the

subject of this sketch, Hannah, who is the widow of A Thompson, late of Burnside; and Rebecca, the wife of John Fishel, of Five Points, Clearfield county, Pa

David Fulton had practically no school advantages in his boyhood   He assisted his father in cutting timber until his marriage at the age of twenty-seven years   In 1864 he enlisted for one year in Company F, 5th Regt Pa Heavy Artillery, and served in the army of the Potomac under General Meade, taking part in several battles   He was mustered out June 30, 1865   On his return home he bought land and was engaged in lumbering during the winters   He came to his present home in 1868, and having purchased it, engaged here in general farming and lumbering, in which pursuits he has been quite successful   He is a Republican in politics and has served as overseer of the poor and on the school board

Mr. Fulton married first Elizabeth Ann Smith, who was born in Clearfield county in 1845, a daughter of James and Mary Smith   She died leaving three children, now living, besides two that are deceased   The living are: James, who is associated with his father in farming and lumbering, Harrison, who is married and resides in Alabama, and Simon, unmarried, residing in West Virginia   Mr. Fulton married for his second wife, Nancy Ellen Oaks, born in September, 1865, a daughter of Martin and Nancy (McGarey) Oakes, old settlers in Clearfield county   Of this marriage there were three children   Mabel, now aged seventeen years, who is keeping house for her father, Blair, aged fourteen, and Carrie, aged eight   Mrs Mary E Fulton died in 1903

LESLIE STEWART —One of the leading citizens of Clearfield County, and prominent in

DAVID FULTON

the business and political affairs of the community, is Leslie Stewart, now a resident of the borough of Clearfield Mr Stewart was born in Beccaria Township in Clearfield County on the 22d day of March, 1868, and was the son of Joseph and Rebecca Stewart His father, Joseph Stewart, came to this country from Ireland in 1836, ond in 1845 settled in Clearfield County, which was then an almost unbroken forest He was one of the pioneers who opened the region to settlement and started it on its career of industrial development

The subject of this sketch spent his early life on the paternal farm, and got what schooling he could at the public schools In the meantime he worked at farming and lumbering He early showed his ambition for the best things of life by attending night school, and, after a hard day's labor in the woods, would walk to the little school house, and patiently endeavor to acquire an education

In 1893, when he was twenty-five years old, having saved some capital, he engaged in the mercantile business at West Houtzdale After two years and a half, he started in the insurance business, in which he has been very successful For two years he continued at Houtzdale, but in 1897 moved to Clearfield, and became a partner in the well known firm of Biddle & Helmbold, which afterwards became Helmbold & Stewart, with a very large business in fire, life, accident and liability insurance Mr Stewart has travelled extensively in this business, and has met with great success in writing large lines of insurance He has a wide acquaintance throughout Clearfield County, and is everywhere well and favorably known He enjoys the confidence of the people, and is a man whom all respect and esteem

Mr Stewart has always been interested in public affairs, and for that reason has been an active politician in the best sense of that term He has filled many offices He was elected inspector in 1892 and then judge of election of Bigler township in 1893 He was for years a member of the Republican Vigilance Committee of Bigler township and afterwards of Woodward Township He served as school director of Clearfield Borough for six years In 1905 he was elected treasurer of Clearfield county, an office of great responsibility, and filled it with the commendation of all In 1908 he was chosen chairman of the Republican County Committee, and managed the campaign of that year with signal success

In church affairs Mr Stewart has always been active, and an earnest and liberal supporter of religious institutions He and his family for ten years devotedly labored to build up and support the Eleventh Street M E Church in Clearfield, and is is largely owing to their constant efforts that that church has been able to erect its beautiful buildings and to extend its usefulness

Mr Stewart is an enthusiastic member of a number of fraternal orders, and has taken an active part in them He belongs to Clearfield Lodge, No 314, F and A M, and is a Past Master of the lodge He is a member of Clearfield Chapter, Moshannon Commandery, Knights Templar, No 90, of Philipsburg, Pa, the Consistory of Williamsport, Pa, and of Jaffa Temple at Altoona, Pa Mr Stewart is an Odd Fellow, and a member of Clearfield Lodge No 198, and of Clearfield Encampment He also belongs to Washington Camp, No 591, P O S of A, of Clearfield

Mr Stewart was married on August 28, 1889, to Miss Laura O Patterson, daughter of Peter Patterson, of Jordan township, Clearfield County, and they are the parents of eight children Wade I, born Nov 23, 1890, now a student at the Western College of Pharmacy, J Linn, born April 18, 1892, Blanche R, born February 15, 1894, B Franklin, born December 22, 1895, W Howard, born January 20, 1898, Grace M, born January 23, 1900, Frances M, born October 24, 1902, and Elizabeth E, born January 24, 1906 Mr Stewart and his family occupy a handsome house in Clearfield, which is the centre of a happy, Christian home, in which this large band of children are being reared with the benefit of the best influences, and educated to make the best type of men and women

ROBERT M SHOFF, who owns a valuable farm of 105 acres, richly underlaid with coal and situated in Bigler Township, Clearfield County, Pa, was born on this farm, in an old log house then standing, and is a son of Samuel and Jane (Haggerty) Shoff

Samuel Shoff was born in Clinton County, Pa, a son of Christopher Shoff, who was a native of Germany The former was a farmer all his life He was a Democrat in politics His wife, Jane Haggerty, who was born in Clearfield County, was a member of the Presbyterian church They reared a large family, namely Sarah, who is now deceased (was the wife of George Stitt), Elizabeth, who is deceased, Christopher C, Susanna, who is the wife of Asa Byers, Rebecca, who is the wife of Bigler Dunlap, Isabella, who is the wife of Josiah Lamburn, Robert M, Abraham C, James, and Hannah, who is the widow of James Stitt

Robert M Shoff has devoted himself to farming and looking after his coal interests ever since he left school and went into business For five years coal has been taken out from under the surface of his farm and still the vein has not been exhausted He carries on general farming and raises stock for his own use

On April 4, 1878, Mr Shoff was married to Miss Hannah Dewitt, a daughter of George and Rachel (Bloom) Dewitt, the former of whom was born in the State of New York, and the latter in Clearfield County Mrs Shoff was the first born of their children, the others being William, Amos, Dorsey, Catherine and Fredora (wife of Nelson Raniker), Lewis, Wallace and Edward, and May, who is the wife of George Whitten Nine children have been born to Mr and Mrs Shoff, as follows Jane, who is the wife of William S Moore, May, who is the wife of Milton Shaffer, and Samuel, Clyde, Cam W, Myrtle, Everett, Nellie and Thomas Jefferson Mr Shoff and family attend the Presbyterian church He has been an active citizen in his township and has served very acceptably as school director and road superintendent Since 1873 he has been identified with Glen Hope Lodge, No 669, Odd Fellows

HENRY HOOVER, one of Clearfield County's prominent and successful agriculturists, who is carrying on extensive operations in Cooper (formerly Morris) Township, is a member of an old and honored family, and was born in what was known as Hoover Settlement, Hickory Bottom, February 18, 1845, a son of Jeremiah and Catherine (Beam) Hoover, and a grandson of John Hoover

John Hoover was an early settler at what is now Allport, Pa, and there he spent his life engaged in agricultural pursuits He was the father of seven children, as follows Sarah, who married Joseph Rubly and moved to Kar-thaus Hill, where her death occurred, Hannah, who married William Shippee and for many years lived at Wallaceton where she died, burial being made at Allport (after her death Mr Shippee removed to Illinois), Mrs James Potter, deceased, who for many years lived only one and one-half miles from the home of Henry Hoover, John, who was a lifelong agriculturist of Cooper Township, Samuel, who owned a farm adjoining the old homestead, and George and Jeremiah, who purchased the home farm from their father's estate The maternal grandfather of Henry Hoover, Henry Beam, was one of the early settlers of Clearfield County, whence he came from Dauphin county

Jeremiah Hoover, the father of Henry, spent his life on the old home farm, and was not only successful in agricultural ventures but became a prominent man in public affairs, serving as supervisor and member of the school board for many years He died about 1888, his wife having passed away ten years prior to that time, and they were the parents of the following children William, who was a private in Captain McCullough's company of the famous Bucktails, the 45th Reg, Pa Vols, and he died in 1867 at Lockhaven, of sickness contracted during the war, Wilson, who is engaged in farming one mile from the place of his birth, and who married Miss Harriet Dingie, Gilbert, who married Miss Marjorie Zimmerman, who is now deceased, and is farming one-half mile from the old home, Henry, Margaret, deceased, who was the wife of Aaron Kyler, John, who married Miss Alice Dingie and is now living on the old homestead, Sarah, who married a Mr Murray and resides in the State of Washington, George,

who married a Miss Emerick, now deceased, and lives in Karthaus, Matilda, who married Henry Moyer, of Washington, and two children who died in infancy

Henry Hoover attended school in the Hoover Settlement until he was eighteen years of age and one session in Curwensville under Superintendent George Snyder and during the following year, 1868, he took a normal course at Clearfield He was engaged in farming with his father up to the time he was twenty-seven years of age, at which time he was married and moved to his present property, a tract of 110 acres, of which about seventy acres are under cultivation When he located on this property, all that it boasted in the way of buildings was an old log barn and part of a house, but Mr Hoover soon erected new buildings, completed the house, set out orchards, fenced his property well, and made such improvement on the place that he is now considered to be the model farmer of the township. He has been very successful in his operations and is rated among the solid, substantial citizens of his community This property is underlaid with coal, and it has been leased by Mr Hoover to the Clearfield Bituminous Coal Corporation

In 1872 Mr Hoover was married to Miss Miriem Zimmerman, who was born in Center County, Pa, daughter of William and Sarah (Strausser) Zimmerman, who came from Snyder County Mr Zimmerman, who was a carpenter by trade, had lived for some years in Clearfield County, but his death took place in Center County, while his widow makes her home with Mr Hoover Eight children have been born to Mr and Mrs Hoover William, a fireman and engineer on the New York Central Railway, who married Millie Taylor,

daughter of Latimer Taylor of Kylertown, and
has had two children, Fay and Grace, the latter
being deceased, Ammon, a carpenter by trade,
who recently went to the State of Washington, where he has been located for two years,
Lisle, an employe of the Pennsylvania Railroad shops, who married Birdie Hess, daughter of George Hess of Cooper Township and
has three children, Russell, Eloise and Ethel;
Belle, who married Arthur Brown, a farmer
of Cooper Township and has five children,
Maud, Ruth, Clarence, Foster and Mary,
Clarence, a resident of Youngstown, O, who
married Nellie Ardry, the daughter of Charles
Ardry, Ocie, who married Paul Holt, an employe of the Pennsylvania Railroad shops and
a son of Oscar Holt, and has one child, Grace,
and Frank and Pearl, who are single and reside with their father on the home farm
Mr Hoover is a Democrat in politics and he
has served as school director for several
terms

LUCIUS L DARR, who conducts a sad-
dlery and harness making business at Burnside, Pa, is one of the well known citizens of
this section, where, prior to 1904, he was engaged in farming and lumbering He was
born August 29, 1865, in Indiana County, Pa,
and is a son of Absalom W and Jane (Reed)
Darr

Absalom W Darr was born December 26,
1834, in Indiana County, a son of George
Darr, who was born at Swatara Creek, Dauphin County, Pa In 1822, George Darr, with
his father, also George Darr, took up timber
land at Cherry Tree, Pa, but five years later
returned to Indiana County where he engaged
in milling In 1845 he came to Burnside and
operated what is now known as the Irwin mill

and his death occurred in Burnside Township
in 1868 He married Margaret Bucher, a
daughter of Henry and Jane (Wolf) Bucher,
of Franklin County. Of their children there
are three survivors. Absalom, who is now in
his seventy-sixth year, Henry, who is a farmer
in Burnside Township, and Nancy, who is the
wife of John Kine Absalom W Darr
learned the shoemaker's trade in his youth and
worked at it for seven years, after which he
engaged in farming and lumbering until 1890,
when he retired In 1856 he married Jane E
Reed, who was born March 20, 1833, a daughter of Alexander and Lucy (Henderson) Reed,
who were natives of Indiana County Her
grandparents were John and Jane (Fulton)
Reed, and her great-grandfather was John
Reed, who came to the colonies during the Revolutionary War, being of English birth, and
settled at Baltimore Mrs Darr is now in her
seventy-seventh year To Absalom W Darr
and wife were born the following children:
Vincent, who resides at Dixonville, Pa, Leonard, who lives at Topeka, Kans, Lucius L;
Lucy, a twin sister, who is the wife of L Mahaffey, of La Jose, Pa, Ella, who is deceased;
and Verna, who is the wife of H E. Clark,
who is in the lumber business at Glenn Campbell, Pa

Lucius L Darr was educated in the public
schools In politics he is a Republican and has
served on the election board at Burnside as
judge, clerk and inspector He is identified
with the order of Odd Fellows at this place
and is past grand of the local lodge Mr Darr
is unmarried

WILLIAM SCHULTZ, who came to what
is now Karthaus Township, Clearfield County,
Pa, in the spring of 1868, and has since, ex-

cept for an interval of nine months, lived continuously in this county, was born in Germany, December 25, 1844, and was one year old when his parents, Gangolf and Nancy (Weaver) Schultz came to America

The parents of Mr Schultz came to Clearfield County, Pa, and settled in Covington Township, where they practically spent the remainder of their lives, the father dying at the home of his son-in-law, Lawrence Flood in Cooper Settlement His family consisted of twelve children, as follows William, Elizabeth, who died young, Joseph, who died when aged fifteen years, Andrew, who lived at Karthaus, died at the age of thirty-three years, Paul, who died when aged twenty years, Maggie, who is the widow of James Parker, resides at Philipsburg, Rosa, who is the wife of Washington George Dygert, lives in Maine; Nancy, who is the wife of Harvey Crawford, lives in Philadelphia, Annie, who is the wife of Lawrence Flood, lives at Grass Flat, and three infants who died almost at birth

William Schultz was reared in Covington Township and lived there until 1868, when he came to Karthaus Township, settling first on a farm that adjoins his present one and then coming to this place after passing nine months in Center County, having twenty-seven acres under cultivation He has been a very busy man all his life and has worked at farming and lumbering, also at the blacksmith trade and at mason work He is a natural mechanic and all these trades came easy to him without serving any apprenticeship He is a reliable and efficient worker also in steel and wood

Mr Schultz was married August 31, 1868, to Miss Amelia Mary Shaffer, who was born in Germany and was about seven years old

48

when she accompanied her parents to America They were Nicholas and Margaret Shaffer Mr and Mrs Schultz have children and grandchildren, a large, united and happy family, although death has, at times, invaded the household The eldest, Caroline, married William Bolinger and both are now deceased They have five children, of whom the first and fifth died unnamed, the three others being Honest, Mabel and Earl Mary May, the second daughter, died at the age of five years William Edward, the eldest son, lives on the home place He married Annie Bradford and they have had the following children Guy, who died in infancy, John Irvin, Paul Edward, Violet Amelia, who died at the age of four years, and Charles Raymond, William Earl and James Lea James Andrew, the second son, lives at home Margaret Evelyn is the wife of Edward Bradford and they have one son, Lloyd Adelaide has one son, Harold William Janet and Mary both died young, and a babe died unnamed The youngest two of the family are Charles Gangolf and Gladys Gertrude Mr Schultz and family are members of the Catholic church at Karthaus He belongs to the Odd Fellows and the I O R M, at Karthaus In politics Mr Schultz is a Democrat and is held in high regard by his party which has frequently elected him to township offices He has served three terms as supervisor and has also been overseer of the poor

CHARLES A JOHNSON, a progressive and prosperous citizen of Grass Flat, Clearfield County, Pa, where he is proprietor of a general store, was born near the city of Warberg, Sweden, in the county of Halland, March 28, 1866, and is a son of Johnson Neilson and Johanna (Anderson) Neilson, the family names not being inherited from father to son according to the custom in America

Johnson Neilson and wife were natives of Sweden and the father was a farmer He died in 1889 at the age of sixty-six years and the mother in 1879, at the age of forty-four years They had six children Albertina, now deceased, Josephine, who married M Anton, of Halland, Sweden; Johan Emanuel, who lives on the old home place, Albertina, who married Johan Swan and lives in Sweden, Augusta Louise, who lives in New Jersey, and Charles A

Charles A Johnson wsa educated in his native land which he left in 1885 and came to the United States From New York City he went to Chicago, Ill, where he worked from April 1 to September 10, 1886 He then came to Grass Flat, Clearfield County, Pa, and worked here in the coal mines until 1907, when he gave up mining For the next three years he was engaged in teaming and in the summer of 1902, he conducted an ice cream parlor Mr Johnson proved to be an excellent business man and although he has been dependent entirely upon his own efforts since coming to America, he has accumulated property, has successfully carried out a number of undertakings and has established himself as a reliable, dependable business man and good citizen, having been naturalized at Clearfield In April, 1910, he purchased the general mercantile business of John G Anderson, at Grass Flat and has made it a commercial success He revisited Sweden in 1901

On December 24, 1888, Mr Johnson was married to Miss Julia Anderson, who was born in Sweden, June 5, 1872, a daughter of Andrew K Anderson, and was ten years old when her parents came to America Mr and Mrs Johnson have six children, namely George, who was born April 23, 1891, and died July 18, 1891, Carl Berger, who was born August 2, 1897, Ernest Herbert, who was born June 12, 1900, John Arthur, who was born July 20, 1902, Reinhold Gerhard, who was born November 22, 1905, and died July 1, 1907, and Henry Reinhard, who was born November 30, 1908 Mr Johnson and wife are members of the Swedish Lutheran church In politics he is a Republican

The mother of Mrs Johnson died in 1909, but the father is living at Jersey City, N J, aged sixty-two years He came to America in 1882 and located first at McIntire, Lycoming County, Pa, and moved from there to Peale, Clearfield County, and subsequently to New Jersey

CHARLES F BROTHERS, who is interested in lumbering and farming on the old Brothers homestead, situated in Burnside township, Clearfield County, Pa, was born here July 27, 1857, and is a son of William and Martha Jane (Myers) Brothers

William Brothers followed the lumber business all his life, operating a saw mill as his main business His death occurred on the homestead, October 12, 1887, at the age of sixty years He married Martha Jane Myers, who survives, a daughter of John and Jane (Ruggles) Myers Of their children the following are living: Charles F, John, who lives near the old homestead, Albert, who is a farmer and coal miner in Burnside Township; Joseph, who lives in Burnside Township, Everett, who carries on farming also in Burnside township, Letta, who is the wife of H E Phillips, Minerva, who is the wife of Edward

King, of Westover, Pa , and Jennie, who is the wife of William De Losier, an engineer, at Lilly, Cambria County, Pa

Charles F Brothers obtained his education in the district schools and afterward went into the woods and continued lumbering along the Susquehannah River until 1902, as contractor and jobber and saw mill operator In addition to his farm interests, which, for some years have also been important, he is financially concerned in coal mines He is one of the representative business men of this section, a man of much enterprise and of practical experience As a thoughtful and honest citizen, he has always concerned himself to some degree in public matters, especially in those of local importance His convictions have made him a Republican and on that ticket he has been elected to township offices and has served as judge of elections and also as auditor

Mr Brothers was married to Miss Anna H Westover, who was born April 12, 1859, in Burnside Township, and is a daughter of Oliver J and Cordelia S (Oaks) Westover The mother of Mrs Brothers was born March 22, 1829, in Maine, a daughter of Stephen L and Sally (Ames) Oaks, both of whom were born in Maine Her father died in 1875, aged seventy-nine years and her mother in 1877 Cordelia S Oaks married Oliver J Westover, who was born in August 1825, in Blair County, Pa ; He was twelve years old when his parents came to Cambria County, Pa In March, 1848, he moved to Burnside Township, Clearfield County and settled on the place ever since known as the Westover homestead, which land he cleared His father was John Westover, who was twice married, first to a Ziegler and second to Sally Myers Other members of the Westover family settled in Chest Township Mrs Westover survives and resides near Mr and Mrs Brothers Of the eight children of the Westover family, Mrs Brothers was the fourth in order of birth

Mr and Mrs Brothers have had eight children namely Morie who at the age of twenty-eight years, is foreman of a construction company on Vancouver Island, a successful young business man, Viola, who resides at home, Lilly, who is the wife of Joseph Leamer, and has two children—Evelyn and Harrold, Noel, who is a railroad man in California, Winona, who is the wife of Edward Craver, an engineer in a coal mine and has one child, Burl, Elsie, Hazel and Charlie who reside at home, and three who died in infancy Mr and Mrs Brothers are members of the Evangelical church He is identified with Harmony Lodge, Grange, the Odd Fellows at Cherry Tree and the P S O of A , at Pottsville

MATTHEW SHADEK, who has been prominent in the business affairs of Karthaus, Pa , for the last ten years and is identified with many of the enterprises contributing to its commercial importance, was born January 22, 1863, in Germany, and is a son of Michael and Margaret Shadek The parents of Mr Shadek never came to America, the mother dying when Matthew was nine years old

Matthew Shadek left his native land and came to the United States when he was twenty-one years of age, as have hundreds of others Not all of these, however, have so rapidly secured independence or, within comparatively so short a time, have become useful and important residents of the communities in which they have chosen to live When Mr Shadek reached America in 1884, he located first in

Tioga County, Pa., and went to work at Wellsboro as a railroad section hand, his wages being $1.12 per day, and they were earned. After he married he lived there two years, moving then to Peale, Clearfield County, where he remained six months, from there going to Morrisdale, in Clearfield County. In 1889 he moved onto a farm on which he continued for thirteen years before coming to Karthaus. Mr. Shadek is a man quick to seize business opportunities. He has been operating a saw mill across the river, in Center County, for the past five years, and is a member of the firm of Kelly & Shadek, coal operators, operating the Mt. Carmel and Mosquito Creek mines, having been interested in coal operating ever since coming to Karthaus. He also owns and operates a first class livery, and is still further interested, having a restaurant and a grocery store. All his business undertakings are prospering and he is one of the substantial men of the town.

Mr. Shadek was married in 1880 to Miss Mary Hammes, who was born in Germany, and is a daughter of Nicholas and Susanna (Simon) Hammes, the former of whom is deceased. Mrs. Hammes married secondly Stephen Young, who, now in his eighty-seventh year, is the most venerable resident of Karthaus. Mr. and Mrs. Young reside with Mr. and Mrs. Shadek. They are members of the Catholic church.

To Matthew Shadek and wife eleven children have been born, as follows: Michael, who operates the store and restaurant belonging to his father, married Edna Pecard and they have four daughters—Emma, Helen, Jennie and Agnes; Peter, who died at the age of nineteen years; Matthew, who married Clara Renaud, and they have three sons—Leo, Bernard and Leonard; John, who is a resident of Karthaus, married Mabel Renaud, and they have one son, Earl; Mary, who married Herman Coudreit, of Karthaus, and they have four children—Lawrence, Irene, Paul and Logan; Annie, who married James Renaud, and they have three children—Russell, Francis and Robert, and George August, Agatha, Nicholas, Paul and Joseph. Mr. Shadek and family are members of St. John's and Paul's Catholic church. He is a Democrat in politics.

W. EDGAR REILEY, M.D., a successful homeopathic physician of Clearfield county, Pa., was born December 22, 1882, at Hanover, York County, Pa., and is a son of Rev. William M. and Fanny (Baker) Reiley. Although Dr. Reiley has only been a resident of Clearfield County since 1908, he comes of a family well known for many years in this section of the county. His great grandfather, Rev. James M. Reiley, was one of the early ministers of the Methodist Episcopal church and was well known in this part of Pennsylvania. His circuit extended from Hollidaysburg to Petersburg, Pa., and required a period of six weeks to cover, the entire trip being made on horseback. The four generations following Rev. James M. Reiley have all contributed to the Methodist ministry, two of his sons, Rev. James M., Jr. and Rev. Asbury Reiley, entering it. Rev. William M. Reiley, father of our subject, and son of Rev. James M. Reiley, Jr., followed the ministerial profession for more than forty years. He was a native of West Virginia, and his son, Rev. J. McK. Reiley, had charge of the 11th St. M. E. church, at Clearfield, Pa., seven years, his last assignment being at Newberry, the Fourth ward of Williamsport, Pa., where he died

January 9, 1907 He is still survived by his widow, Fanny Baker Reiley and the following children Harry B , James M , who is a minister, Eleanor, wife of J W Lowther, Ray W , Dr W Edgar, and Alcie

Dr W Edgar Reiley spent his boyhood and obtained his early schooling in the various towns in Pennsylvania, where his father's calling brought the family, and in 1902 was graduated from the Altoona High School In 1903 he entered the Southern Homeopathic Medical College at Baltimore, Md , and was graduated with the class of 1907 On January 20, 1908, he embarked in the practice of medicine at Clearfield, Pa , where he has since been located, having an office with Dr S J Watterworth Dr Reiley is a member of the medical staff of the Clearfield Hospital, and belongs to the Clearfield Medical Society, and also to the Homeopathic Medical Society of Penna He is a member of the I O O F of Clearfield, and of the M E church Politically he is a Republican.

EDGAR A JOHNSON, postmaster and general merchant at Grass Flat, Cooper Township, was born February 1, 1856, in what was then Morris but is now Cooper Township, a son of Abel B and Sarah (Dillon) Johnson

Abel B Johnson was born in Bradford County, Pa , in 1828, and in 1852 came to the farm in Clearfield County on which he has resided for many years He was formerly a lumberman but for thirty-five years devoted himself to agricultural pursuits He married Sarah Dillon who died in 1902, at the age of seventy-one years They had five sons and three daughters born to them, namely Charles, who is now deceased, Edgar A , Mary, who is the wife of William Pelton of Morris Township, Bertha, who is now deceased, was survived by her husband, Helen who is the wife of Edward Hipple who is the home farmer, Miles G , who is a resident of California, Andrew C , who is a resident of Huntingdon County, where he engages in farming, and Guy L , who carries on farming on the homestead, also is a funeral director at Grass Flat.

Edgar A Johnson was reared on the home farm attended the local schools and for a time was in the timber business He then turned his attention to merchandising and in 1892 was appointed postmaster at Grass Flat, the first and only official in this office at this point Both officially and in a business way, Mr Johnson is a popular citizen

In 1879 Mr Johnson was married to Miss Mary J Pelton, a daughter of Ephraim and Elizabeth Pelton, of Cooper Township and their children are as follows Arthur, Allen, who lives at Winburne, married Mary Maggs and has two children, Minnie, who is the wife of Joseph Kondesky, and lives in Cambria County, Bessie, who is her father's assistant in the post office, Warren, who died at the age of nineteen years, Lona, who is a teacher in the public schools, Inez, who is a clerk in Kramer's store, and Floyd, who lives at home The family attend the United Brethren church In politics Mr Johnson is a Republican and by order of the court is serving in the office of township auditor He is a member of the Patrons of Husbandry

HOWARD M FRY, a farmer and prominent citizen of Burnside township, was born at Westover, Clearfield county, Pa , December 15, 1857, a son of John Smith and Julia A (Myers) Fry He is a grandson of Daniel Fry, who settled at Westover with his family in

1849, coming from Lancaster county, Pa , and who died in 1883 at the age of 79 years His wife in maidenhood was Sarah Priestly, a daughter of Jonathan Priestly of Lancaster Daniel Fry was a son of John Fry, who resided in York county, Pa

John Smith Fry, father of our subject, was born February 9, 1832 He followed farming and lumbering at Westover until 1860, and then removed to Burnside township, where he took up land He settled on the present Fry homestead in 1862, and subsequently resided there until his death, which took place June 12, 1881 He was twice married first to Julia Ann Myers, the daughter of John and Jane (Ruggles) Myers, natives of Blair County, who came to Clearfield county about 1840 Of this first marriage there were children as follows Howard M , whose name begins this sketch , Harvey, residing in Texas, Elmer E , also in Texas, John D , a resident of Greensburg, Pa , Ella, wife of Rev B W Lewis, residing in Mississippi, Mrs Julia Ann Fry died in 1876 at the age of 37 years, and Mr Fry subsequently married Jane McEwen, of Burnside township, who was born in 1849, the daughter of James and Elizabeth (Priestly) McEwen She is still living and resides at Westover There were born to this second marriage two children Flora, who is a teacher at Turtle Creek, Allegheny county, Pa , and James S , an engineer, unmarried and living at home John Smith Fry was then a member of the Baptist church He was active in politics as a Republican and served as assessor and treasurer of his township for a number of years up to the time of his death

Howard M Fry after attending school entered upon an agricultural life, being also engaged to some extent in cutting timber He remained at home until reaching the age of twenty-one years, when he took up his residence near Westover and Coalport, successively At his father's death in 1881 he came to his present home, where he has since followed farming successfully A Republican in politics, he is now serving as tax collector, and has served for twenty years as assessor, from 1889 to 1909 He has always taken an interest in good government and has been an active worker for his party He belongs to the Royal Arcanum lodge at Clearfield, and to the lodge of Red Men at Harmony

Mr Fry was married December 25, 1879 to Sarah C McKee, who was born August 27, 1861, a daughter of J R and Susan (Westover) McKee of Burnside township Her father, who was born in 1838, died in 1903, her mother died in 1907 at the age of 69 years Mr and Mrs Fry have been the parents of the following children Olive, who is the wife of E Woods, tax collector of Cambria county, and has four children, Grier R , Venna, Clyde H , Quay and Lois, all living at home Mrs Fry is a member of the Baptist church, and belongs to the Ladies' Aid Society of the same; she is also a member of Grange No 1201 of Harmony

DAVID MITCHELL, who is a prominent and substantial citizen of Clearfield county, Pa , resides on his fine farm of 130 acres which is situated one-half mile west of Curry Run village He also owns a second farm of 218 acres which lies in Greenwood township, and another 110 acres in this township, Clearfield county, and has besides 340 acres in Bell township, and is a representative of a family that was established in this section in the days of his grandfather Mr Mitchell was born in

MR. AND MRS. DAVID MITCHELL

Burnside township, October 14, 1838, and is a son of John and Elizabeth A (McGee) Mitchell

John Mitchell was born also in Burnside township, Clearfield county, and died in Kansas, at the age of seventy years In early years he was a blacksmith but did not work long at that trade, engaging in farming in Burnside township where he reared his family At that time he owned 250 acres of land, which he sold in late middle life and moved to the state of Kansas, where the remainder of his life was spent He married Elizabeth A McGee, who was born in Bell township, Clearfield county, a daughter of Rev James McGee, who was a minister in the Protestant Methodist church Ten of their family of children still survive, namely David, Mary Ellen, James, Thomas M, Ann Elizabeth, Margaret, John, Henry and Virgin and Orlena, twins The mother of these children died in Kansas when aged sixty-five years They were members of the Protestant Methodist church

David Mitchell had but meager school advantages when he was a boy and as soon as old enough he went into the woods and worked at lumbering He has acquired his position of financial independence entirely through his own efforts and when he says that he never loafed a day in his life, it can easily be seen that persevering industry has had much to do with his success He had very practical ideas from the start and began buying timber tracts as soon as he had capital, clearing them off and then selling, and as his foresight and judgment were excellent, by 1869 he had acquired the means to purchase the farm on which he lives, which was formerly the property of Lewis Smith He has about 165 of his 800

acres cleared and under cultivation After his marriage he had settled on a small place in Burnside township near his timber tract, and lived there until he bought his Greenwood township farm Other and later purchases were 130 and 225 acres near Bower, 112 acres of the Hoover farm, and 340 acres in Bell township He is a stockholder in the Farmers and Traders Bank of Clearfield county and a charter member of the Mahaffey National Bank at Mahaffey, Pa He has been a very active citizen and has been foremost in all movements to promote the progress and development of Clearfield county He has served in almost all the township offices and is a man whom his fellow citizens regard with respect and esteem He is proud of the fact that he has never had a law suit in his life and has lived at peace with his neighbors and friendly with all with whom either business or social life has brought him into contact

Mr Mitchell was married December 31, 1863, to Miss Henrietta Weaver, who was born in Burnside township, June 16, 1844, a daughter of James H and Sarah Ann (Campbell) Weaver James H Weaver was born in Union county, Pa, and came to Bell township, Clearfield county, when ten years of age He became a farmer and earlier was a pilot lumberman and took rafts down the river He died at the age of eighty-eight years and three months, leaving an estate of 100 acres He married Sarah Ann Campbell, a daughter of Thomas Campbell, and she accompanied her parents to Clearfield county when eight years old and still survives, residing in Burnside township She is so well preserved both in mind and body that it is difficult to realize that she is in her eighty-ninth year Six children were born to Thomas Campbell and wife, namely   Henrietta, Francis E , Mary Ke-, ziah, John Thomas, Harriet Ruth and James Lewis, the last named being a merchant at Burnside, Pa

To David Mitchell and wife the following children were born   Harry S , who resides in Burnside township, married Ida Thorp, James Thomas, who lives in Greenwood township, married Nora Rager, John Francis, who is a merchant at Bell Landing, married Gertrude Johnson , Robert Clyde, who lives in the state of Washington, Rosetta, who is a teacher of music, David Attley, who is a physician at Pittsburg, married Blanche Dawson, Sarah Elizabeth, who is the wife of Ernest Miller, of Carlisle, Pa , Samuel Orvis, who resides at Seattle, Wash , Della, who lives at home , Mary, who is the wife of Stratton Stevens, of Wilkesbarre, Pa ; Ruth, who is the wife of Henry Hunter, and Cora, who is a teacher in the Clearfield High School   Mr Mitchell is a Republican in his political sentiments   He belongs to the order of Odd Fellows at Mahaffey and for thirty-five years has belonged to Greenwood Grange, of which he is a charter member

WILLIAM J KOPP, one of the leading citizens of Karthaus township, where he is engaged in general farming, was born on his present place, July 6, 1855, and is a son of Martin and Caroline (Heichel) Kopp, who, for years were among the most highly respected people of this section

Both parents of Mr Kopp were born in Germany although in different provinces Martin Kopp came to America with his parents, who settled at Tremont, Schuylkill county, Pa   He had two sisters and four brothers, the latter being   Conrad and Dan-

iel, who lived at Tremont, Philip, who lived in Iowa, and John, who died young   One year after his marriage, Martin Kopp left Schuylkill county and started for Karthaus township, Clearfield county, journeying to Tyrone by way of the canal and from there by wagon   He bought 150 acres of wild land from Peter Karthaus and had to clear a spot before he could erect his first log house   From this little home, in 1864, went out five soldiers to fight the battles of the country, three of these being Heichels, the fourth being Jacob Hertlin, all boarders, and the fifth being Martin Kopp, and all returned alive   Uriah Clark, Mrs Kopp's father, enlisted near the beginning of the Civil war, at Lock Haven, Clinton county, as a private in company D, 7th Regt Pa   Reserve   Volunteer   Infantry, and also served in Co E, 190th Regt Pa Vol Infantry   His period of service was marked with hardship   He took part in many of the most important battles of the war, including Shiloh (where he was wounded in the shoulder), Gettysburg and Roanoke   He was captured by the Confederates at the battle of the Wilderness, and incarcerated in Andersonville prison, nine months and twenty-one days There he was kept until little life remained, his exchange coming just in time to preserve it At Shiloh, where he was wounded, he had a brother killed by his side   His death occurred June 20, 1902, when he was eighty-two years old, and his burial was at Oak Hill

Martin Kopp married Catherine Heichel, a daughter of Christopher and Johanna Catherine (Stein) Heichel   They came to America in 1855 and located in Karthaus township, where Mrs Heichel died in 1869 and her husband in 1879   Mrs Kopp died September 28, 1909, and her burial was also at Oak Hill

Two sons were born to this marriage William J and Daniel, the latter of whom lives at Newburg, Ore

William J Kopp was reared in Karthaus township and attended the local schools With the exception of four years, during which he was in the far West, Mr Kopp has always resided here and is one of the best known men of his township As a citizen he is held in high esteem and is a leader in Democratic politics in this section and has served as assessor, road master and in other offices for a number of years

On May 21, 1885, Mr Kopp was married to Miss Annie Nora Clark, who was born at Beech Creek, Clinton county, Pa, and is a daughter of Uriah and Mary (Liggett) Clark Mr Clark was born in an old stone house where the Potter House now stands, in Karthaus township He died at DuBois, Pa., where the mother of Mrs Kopp still resides Formerly they resided at Winterburne, Clearfield county To Mr and Mrs. Kopp the following children have been born Willard, Margaret, who is a popular teacher in Karthaus township, Edward, who is settled on a ranch in Oregon, Mabel Elizabeth, who is a graduate of the township High School, holds a teacher's certificate, and Theresa, Leona, Gaylord, Beatrice, Genevieve and Harvey, twins, Myra, William and Clark Mr Kopp and family are members of the Lutheran church at Oak Hill He is identified there with the lodge of Odd Fellows With other members of his family, he is a musician of more than usual ability His father was a skilled violinist, while his brother, Daniel, was an instructor in music At one time the brothers had a musical organization of their own which was well known locally as Kopp's Band

REYNOLD LAMONT, owner and proprietor of the Mountain House, a well kept and comfortable hotel at Janesville, Pa, was born in Scotland, October 27, 1860, and is a son of Thomas and Elizabeth (Pollock) Lamont, and a grandson of Daniel Lamont, of Irish descent

The parents of Mr Lamont never left Scotland and only two of their family of six children came across the Atlantic to become residents of America, these being Reynold, of this record, and his sister Rachel, who is the wife of William Rumgey The others are: Catherine, wife of Joseph Reiley, Jennie, wife of Thomas Duffie, Roseann, wife of James Howden, and Elizabeth, wife of John Gorman

Reynold Lamont was educated in the public schools of Scotland and in an academy near his home, which he attended for three years He came to America in his twentieth year and lived first in Lycoming county, Pa, coming from there to Clearfield county, where he has lived for the past twenty-four years During a large part of this time he has worked in the coal mines but since November 14, 1904, when he purchased the Mountain House, at Janesville, he has devoted himself to hotel keeping Travelers through this section find excellent entertainment at his hostelry, where a substantial table is set and clean and comfortable bed-rooms provided Mr Lamont has other property, owning real estate at Beccaria, Pa

In 1882 Mr Lamont was married to Miss Catherine Brogan, who is a daughter of William and Mary (Crawford) Brogan, natives of Ireland William Brogan was a miner and lost his life in the mines when his one little daughter was only six weeks old Mrs Brogan subsequently married James O'Reiley, and they had three children Anna, wife of George E Lambe, Sarah, wife of Burt Brisbine; and Joseph, married to Agnes Hughes To Mr and Mrs Lamont seven children have been born, namely Thomas, Mary, William, Elizabeth, James, Margaret and Reynold Mary is the wife of Frank Callan Mr Lamont and family are members of the Catholic church at Coalport In politics he is a Democrat but has never been willing to serve in office, at all times having plenty of business of his own to engage his attention He is a member of Lodge No 154, L O O M, at Osceola Mills, and of Lodge No 312 Brotherhood of America, at Houtzdale, Pa

ANDREW FRENDBERG, foreman of the Knox Run mine of the Clearfield County Bituminous Coal Corporation, and for more than a quarter of a century a well known resident of Peale, Pa, was born in Dalsland, Sweden, March 18, 1864, and is a son of Lars and Bertha S Frendberg

Lars Frendberg was born in Sweden, in March, 1841, and there he followed the occupation of farmer In 1873 he came to America and located at Fallbrook, Pa, where he was employed in the mines, and was later located at Stockdale, Arnett, Antrim, Houtzdale and Clairmont, also spending a short time in Elk county, Pa, having been employed in and around the mines up to 1880 In that year he went back to Sweden for his family, and on July 22nd of that year they all located in McIntyre Mr Frendberg has charge of the boilers of the Knox Run mine, and is still active and in the best of health in spite of his advanced years Lars and Bertha S Frendberg had seven children, the first four of whom were born in Sweden Andrew,

Charles, who is assistant foreman of the Knox Run mine and resides in Lanse; Lars, who is engineer of the Knox Run mine, Gust, who is a resident of Peale and employed as a miner at Grass Flat, Annie, who is single, Amelia, who married Charles A Carlson, assistant foreman of one of the Winburne mines, and Emanuel, who died in Sweden after the family came to America

Andrew Frendberg was about sixteen years of age when the family came to America, and he went to McIntyre, working there until October 4, 1884, from there coming to Peale, where he dug coal, laid track and acted as assistant foreman under James Adamson and William Creighton, from December, 1884, to February, 1902 At this time he took a course of educational training from the Scranton School of Correspondence, and this enabled him to pass the examination for the position of foreman, which he has held to the present time Since first starting to work at the foot of Big Plain, about one mile east of Ralston, Mr Frendberg has made many acquaintances in the coal fields and he is known by all to be a man of capability, honesty and integrity

On June 7, 1884, Mr Frendberg was married to Miss Christina Peterson (or Pierson) daughter of Peter Peterson, who died in June, 1887, in No 2 drift tunnelside Mr and Mrs Frendberg are the parents of the following children Annie Elizabeth, born January 31, 1886, who is a graduate of Upsala College of Kenilworth, N J, William Robert, born June 21, 1888, who is a student in his sophomore year at that same institution, Victor Conrad, born January 12, 1892, who is a clerk in the A F Kelly store at Grass Flat Mr Frendberg is a member of the Swedish Lutheran church at Peale In politics he is a

Republican, and for four years he served as a member of the school board of Cooper township, it being during his term that the handsome new school building was erected at Winburne Fraternally, Mr Frendberg is connected with Moshannon Lodge, No 391, F. & A M

GEORGE YOUNG HALFPENNEY, who has been connected with the Pennsylvania Railroad Company at McGee, Pa , since the station was first opened in 1887, is a well known railroad official, serving as agent here and in other capacities He was born at Bellwood, Pa , November 29, 1864, and is a son of Col John and Mary Ann (Fisher) Halfpenney

The late Col John Halfpenney was a prominent figure in Blair county politics for a number of years, being appointed in 1856 on the staff of Governor Pollock, with the rank of lieutenant-colonel He was born April 9, 1809, in Columbia county, Pa , and died in his native state in January, 1881 From 1851 until 1875, when his factories were destroyed by fire, he was engaged in manufacturing, and his products, including jeans, woolen cloth and blankets, were known and in wide demand all over the country In 1856 he moved to Bellwood and continued in business there until he retired In his early political life he was a Whig and later became an active worker in the Republican party, in 1875 being elected a county commissioner and serving continuously until 1881 He married Mary Ann Fisher, who was born in 1817 and died in 1891 They had eleven children, George Young being the youngest born There are two other survivors Catherine, who is the

wife of William West, of Olean, N Y , and Benjamin B , an engineer, who lives at Braddock, Pa

George Y Halfpenney attended the Bellwood schools and afterward learned telegraphing and was an operator at Bellwood for three years He was then appointed agent at McGee, or McGee's Mills, and opened the office here In 1908 he engaged with the New York Central Railroad as traveling agent He is an active citizen in a public spirited and political way and has frequently served as a delegate to conventions of the Republican party For years he has served as auditor and on the school board, and has also been chairman of the borough vigilance committee for fifteen years

Mr Halfpenney was married to Miss Anna May Knoll, who was born February 8, 1872, at Howard, Center county, Pa , a daughter of William and Susan O (Mahaffey) Knoll The mother of Mrs Halfpenney is a daughter of James and Elizabeth (Holter) Mahaffey, and she still survives, being in her sixty-third year After the death of her father, Mrs Halfpenney, who was one of four children, was reared in the home of Thomas A McGee Mr and Mrs Halfpenney have one daughter, Mary Elizabeth, who was born September 23, 1900, and is now in school They are members of the Methodist Episcopal church and of the Epworth League Mr Halfpenney is identified with the Elks at Punxsatawney

GEORGE W REESE, who carries on general farming on the old Reese homestead in Covington township, is one of the leading men of this section and at present is serving in the office of township supervisor He was born here in 1873 and is a son of John and Mary (Lingle) Reese

John Reese was born in Germany and was reared there to manhood and then, with his brothers and sisters, came to the United States They lived first at Baltimore, Md , and from there he went to Philadelphia and then came to Clearfield county and settled in Covington township, where he acquired a farm of 300 acres His death occurred here in 1899 and his burial was at Frenchville He was an industrious, prudent man and lived peaceably with his neighbors and had their friendship and esteem He married Mrs Mary (Lingle) Smith, a native also of Germany, who came to America in youth and still resides in Covington township Six children were born to her first marriage, with William Smith, namely John, Solomon, Joseph, William, George and Susan The last named was the wife of Henry Sinclair To John and Mary Reese the following children were born Winslow, who died at the age of thirty-six years, at Frenchville, Anna, who is the wife of George Spangler, of Falls Creek, Pa , Margaret, who is the wife of Samuel Reiter, of Covington township, George, who lives in Covington township on the old homestead, and James Walter, who is in the meat business at Karthaus and is a representative business man of that place

Mr Reese was married in 1899, to Miss Malinda Flood, who was born and reared in Covington township, and is a daughter of Lawrence and Rebecca Flood, of this township Mr and Mrs Reese have three children, Mildred, Ward and Willard In politics Mr Reese is a stanch Democrat and is a man well qualified to serve in township offices as his party may decide He belongs to the Patrons of Husbandry

WILLIAM HELPER*, general farmer and manager of a tract of 194 acres, lying two and one-half miles west of Grampian, in Penn township, Clearfield county, Pa , was born in Penn township, March 11, 1870, and is a son of Charles and Annie (Sharp) Helper.

Charles Helper, who now lives retired on a well improved little farm of twenty acres, at Grampian, Pa , was born May 30, 1844, in Madison county, N. Y He is a son of E and Augusta (Robby) Helper, the former of whom was born in France and the latter in Germany Charles was the fourth born in their family of seven children His father died in 1851 and his mother at about the same age and their burial was in Onondago county, N. Y Charles Helper worked on a farm until the outbreak of the Civil war, when he entered the Union army, becoming a member of the 157th N Y Vol Inf , which was organized and drilled at Hamilton, N Y At the battle of Gettysburg, Mr Helper was wounded below the left knee and this injury became very dangerous on account of blood poisoning, for it must be remembered that at that time the best of surgeons knew little of the preventives in the way of antiseptics as they are in use at the present day After much suffering he recovered and continued with his regiment until the close of the war, when he returned to Madison county, N Y In 1866 he came to Clearfield county, reaching Curwensville, in Pike township, early in March of that year and continued in Pike township for two years after his marriage He then came to Penn township and for seventeen years rented the farm which now is the property of James D Wall Mr Helper then purchased his present place and conducted a license hotel at Grampian until 1895, when his eyesight failed and at the present writing he is blind In politics he is a Democrat On May 3, 1866, Mr Helper was married to Miss Annie Sharp, who was born April 24, 1839, at Bell Landing, a daughter of James and Jane (McCracken) Sharp, of Bell township, Clearfield county, Pa, and four children were born to them, namely Norman, who died at the age of sixteen years, William, Dora, who is the wife of William Woods and is a school teacher at Grampian, resides at home and has three children—Vane A, Inez and Daisy, and Timothy Jerome, who resides at home

William Helper attended school at Pennsville, Pa, until he was fourteen years of age and then went to work in the lumber camps and although but a boy in years, did an amount of hard labor that would have been creditable in a man Since his marriage, in 1897, Mr Helper has been manager of the farm on which he lives and has it well cultivated, thirty acres of the place being yet in timber He also operates a first class dairy and produces fifty pounds of fine butter a week He is a quiet, industrious man, looking carefully after the interests of his business and family and is held in general esteem by the community He votes the Republican ticket and is now serving as a member of the school board of Penn township

On June 30, 1897, Mr Helper was married to Mrs Lovenia (Norris) Wall, widow of Truman J Wall and daughter of John Norris, Sr, of Pike township Mrs Helper was born in Pike township, November 28, 1856, and was married first, in Colorado, September 1, 1876 to Truman J Wall who died January 29, 1891 Seven children were born to Mr and Mrs Wall, namely Sarah, who was born in Colorado, married John Lienell and they live in Maine and have two children—Norris and Frank, Ord, who married Lois Spencer, a daughter of Irwin Spencer, is a clerk in the superintendent's office of the B R P Railroad, at DuBois, Elizabeth, who is the wife of Leslie Merl, resides in Maine, Alice, who married Boyd Crissman, who carries on a blacksmith business at Curwensville, and they have one daughter, Mabel, Cecelia, who is the wife of Charles Stockridge, of Gary, Ind, Truman J, who is a school teacher at Bell Run, Clearfield county, and Irwin Clark, who died at the age of one year and nine days Mr and Mrs Helper have one daughter, Mildred, who now attends school Mrs Helper and her daughter are stockholders in the Curwensville National Bank

JACOB SANCROFT, a leading citizen of Cooper township, Clearfield county, Pa, where he was born on October 5, 1850, is a son of Sebastian and Mary (Schnider) Sancroft

Sebastian Sancroft was born in Crofen, Reinfeldt, Germany, December 12, 1812, and was about thirty-five years of age when he came to America in 1848 He settled at Kylertown, Pa, and there found work at his trade—that of stonemason—and followed it during the greater part of his life He possessed a certain skill in handicraft and was useful to his family and neighborhood in many ways His death occurred November 18, 1875 He married Mary Schnider, who was born March 16, 1816, and died May 7, 1884 They had two children, Jacob and Catherine, the latter of whom lives on the old homestead

For a short time in his youth, Mr Sancroft attended school at Kylertown When seventeen years old he began to work in the timber and followed this occupation for twenty-five years, or up to 1883 In the spring of this year he started in a restaurant business at Kylertown, but subsequently went from there to Munson, in Center county, where, for two years, he was in the hotel business Later he leased a hotel—the Moshannon House—at Munson, which he conducted for eight years and two months, when he sold out his interests there and in 1904 and came to Kylertown, where he purchased a hotel from Wilbur Hoover, which he now rents He is engaged in the real estate business, and owns a farm of fifty-one acres, which he operates and which adjoins Kylertown, in which place he has other property Mr Sancroft is justly proud of the fact that he has made his own way in the world, working hard, saving his money and never having one cent of borrowed money to return

In 1884 Mr Sancroft was married to Miss Catherine Pontcer, a daughter of Joseph and Tressa (Harber) Pontcer, who came from Germany Joseph Pontcer was a lumberman and farmer, owned 150 acres of land and built two lumber mills Of his family of twelve children eleven still survive Three children have been born to Mr and Mrs Sancroft Fred, who was educated at the Lock Haven State Normal School, and Margaretta and Frances, the latter being named for her mother's oldest sister In politics Mr Sancroft is a Democrat and is an active and influential member of his party He has worked hard and has always been accustomed to an active life and even now, when necessity no longer drives, is not contented unless occupied In

every relation of life he has been a good citizen He was devoted to his parents, watched over their declining years and assumed all their indebtedness In times of trouble or disaster, he has been foremost in offering help in the way most appreciated He and family are widely known and highly esteemed and their home is the abode of comfort and hospitality.

JAMES W BYERS, a thriving and well known farmer of Burnside township, was born on the old Byers home near Mt Zion church, in this township, October 12, 1840, son of John and Sarah (Weaver) Byers He is a grandson on the paternal side of John and Mary (Colgan) Byers, early settlers in this region He is a descendant also of John Byers, born at Valley Forge, near Philadelphia, who came to Clearfield county from Huntingdon county in 1821

John Byers, father of our subject, was born about 1798 and died in 1879 at the age of eighty-one He came to the present Byers homestead accompanied by a brother and his death took place at New Washington Of his family, in addition to the subject of this sketch, there are one son and two daughters living, namely Samuel, who resides in Westover, Sarah, wife of H B Darr, a farmer of Burnside township, and Eliza, who is the wife of J C London, of Kane, Pa

James W Byers, after a short period devoted to school studies, became engaged in the lumbering industry Then he and a brother, about 1865, purchased their father's interest in his business, and he has since continued in this line of industry, having met with a gratifying success He has also carried on agriculture, in which he has been equally successful In politics he is a Republican and has served in several of the township offices, proving a capable official Two of his brothers served in the Union army during the Civil war

Mr Byers was married in 1868 to Lucretia McCracken, who died in 1871 at the age of twenty-five years Of this union there is one child living, David Thomas Byers, of Vandergrift, Pa, who married Tallie Kaufman and has two children Mr Byers was again married in 1880 to Elizabeth Kunsman, who was born November 20, 1860, near Bethlehem, Pa Her parents were William and Mary C (Smith) Kunsman Her maternal grandfather, John Smith (born in Lancaster county, 1791, died 1858), settled at Bethlehem and married Mary Snyder, who was born in 1790 and died in 1879 He planted the first orchards in that section of Clearfield county, carrying the young trees and slips all the way from Union county The McGees, Johnsons and Barnharts came to this part soon after William Kunsman was born in 1830 and died in 1899 He and his wife were the parents of nine children, there being three sons and two daughters now living, including Mrs Byers

The children of Mr and Mrs Byers are as follows Ada, is the wife of H M Dinsmore of South Dakota, and has one child, Frank B Lulu, is the wife of Dr J M E Brown, of New Bethlehem, and has one child, Thelma Mary Zella is deceased John Roswell is deceased Lorinda Rose, twin sister of John R, is residing at home Erminnie is teaching school in Dakota, and so also is Margaret Sarah Ruth and Blaine, twins, both unmarried, are residing at home, and so is Anna Catherine, born in 1899, who is attending school Mr and Mrs Byers are both members of the local Grange They are industrious people, good neighbors, and are widely respected

J WILSON RAUCH, who at the expiration of his present term will have served as justice of the peace of Karthaus township for a quarter of a century, has been a resident of Clearfield county since 1857 He was born in Union county, Pa, December 1, 1842, and is a son of James and Caroline (Hartman) Rauch

James Rauch was born in Union county, a son of Henry and Rebecca (Sipe) Rauch, who came to America from Switzerland, although Mr Rauch was of German birth The maternal grandparents of J W Rauch were Simeon and Elizabeth (Bisel) Hartman, early settlers of Union county, having come from Pottsville, Pa The children of James and Caroline (Hartman) Rauch were as follows James Wilson, Emeline, who married Thomas White of Karthaus township, Charles Franklin, who died at the age of nineteen years, Mary Jane, deceased, who was the wife of Charles Welsh, also deceased, William Henry, who lives at DuBois, Simon Peter, who resides in Karthaus township, Rebecca Elizabeth, who married James Michaels of Karthaus township, and Thomas Richard, who lives at Cataract

James Wilson Rauch attended school in Union county until he was fifteen years old, when his parents removed to Clearfield county, and here he spent one winter in school With the exception of one and one-half years spent in West Keating township, Mr Rauch has lived in Karthaus township since that time On his return from West Keating township he had intended to stay one year, or longer if he found conditions satisfactory, and he remained thirty-two years on that property He first bought the Price place, a tract of thirty-two acres, later purchasing the Charles Welsh property of four acres, and here he continued engaged in farming and lumbering until a few years ago In January, 1865, Mr Rauch reported at Ridgeway, Pa, where he became a member of Co M, 100th Pa Vol Inf, known as the "Roundhead" Regiment Third Brigade, 1st Division, 9th Army Corps, and served through the Virginia campaign He was scratched on the hand by a bullet at Petersburg, and in July, 1865, was stricken with typhoid fever, being confined to the hospital at Harrisburg, Pa, for one week He returned to his home in Clearfield county, but recovered sufficiently to participate in the Grand Review at Washington He is a member of Bucktail Post, G A R, at Renovo

On November 25, 1863, Mr Rauch was married to Miss Mary E Conaway, who was born in Clinton county, Pa, and is a daughter of Charles and Catherine (McGonigal) Conaway Mrs Rauch's parents came to Clearfield county from Clinton county, and here spent the remainder of their lives They had four children Gracie Ann, deceased, who was the wife of William White, Hugh, who was killed by a sharpshooter before Petersburg, James Alexander, who was found dead at the tunnel just above Karthaus, and Mary Elizabeth Mr and Mrs Rauch have had the following children James McClellan, deceased, who married Elizabeth Zimmer and had two children, Malvin Earl and Alda May, Charles Henry, living at Barnesville, Clinton county, who married Cynthia Wadsworth and has four children, Raymond, Roy Blanchard, Myrtle May and Arthur Merle; George Thomas, residing in Clearfield, who

married Amanda Rohn and had four children. Alma Elizabeth, Lawrence Herman, Maurice Alonzo and Irvin Dewey, the second named being now deceased, Simon Alexander, who is unmarried, Torrence Hugh, who died aged three months, Alonzo, who is single and lives at home, William Bucher, who married Margaret Conaway and has five children, Labitha Bernice, Lorintha Dorcas, William Charles Wilson, Oliver Samuel and Francis Alexander, the latter being deceased, Mary Ellen, deceased, who was the wife of Herbert Ashley Wadsworth and had seven children, Myrtle Pearl, Leonard Cleo, Bernice May, Albert Wilson, Lottie Elizabeth, Alice Emily and Mary Ellen, Rosanna Caroline, who married James L McGonigal of Karthaus township and had six children, of whom one is now deceased, Francis Lafayette, who is unmarried and living at home; Sarah Milney, who married Roger S Schnars of Karthaus township and has five children, Florence May, Elizabeth Caroline, Rosanna Virginia, James Wilson and David Leslie, Rebecca Emeline, who married James Moore of Karthaus township and has two children, Francis Zell Bucher and Vivian Evelyn, Lucetta B, who died aged one year, Katie Ethel Bell, who married Alpheus S Moore and lives in Karthaus township, and whose only child, Vida Beatrice, died aged one year, and one child which died unnamed In addition to his long service as justice of the peace, Mr Rauch has served as school director and supervisor, was for nine years assessor, and is now serving in his fifth year as collector

AMOS G HAAG, superintendent of the Helvetia Farm, a tract of 600 acres lying in Brady township, which is owned by L W

Robinson, of the B R & P Railroad, is a competent and successful agriculturist He was born at Troutville, Clearfield county, September 22, 1877, and is a son of C B and Sarah (Bonsall) Haag, the former of whom died April 8, 1911

Amos G Haag obtained his education in the public schools and secured the training that has made him successful as an agriculturist, two years with his father and the rest of the time on the Helvetia Farm He first began work on the Helvetia Farm in 1897, where he has continued ever since, with the exception of one year, which he spent in the office of L W Robinson, its owner, at Punxatawney Mr Robinson makes the farm his home Extensive farm industries are carried on and fine stock is raised In August, 1906, Mr Haag was married to Miss Florence London, who is a daughter of Arthur and Pauline London, of Jefferson county, Pa They have one son, Arthur, a sturdy little lad who was aged eleven months on the 24th of April (1911) Mr Haag is a member of the Lutheran church Mrs Haag belongs to the Reformed church

HARRY L JONES, a prominent citizen of Kylertown, Pa, and justice of the peace and president of the school board of Cooper township, was born on the site of the house in which he now resides in Kylertown, Clearfield county, Pa, September 4, 1868, a son of Ferdinand H and Martha (Austin) Jones

Joseph H Jones, the paternal grandfather of Harry L Jones, was of Welsh descent, and was a brickmaker by trade, making the brick for the first brick buildings at Clearfield, where he died On the maternal side Mr Jones is descended from James Austin, who

49

died in Center county aged eighty-five years Joseph H Jones had four children Zacharias, who is living in Missouri aged seventy-five years, Ferdinand H, Alexander, who is deceased, and Lydia, who died at Philipsburg. James Austin was the father of six children, of whom William went to the army during the Civil war and was never again heard from, Nancy married John Straub, a machinist of Bellefonte, Margaret was the wife of Amos Tison and resided near the State College in Center county, Martha became the wife of Ferdinand H Jones, Elizabeth is a widow and resides at Boalsburg, and the youngest died in childhood

Ferdinand H Jones was born in June, 1841, and since 1860 has been a resident of Kylertown, where he has been engaged at the carpenter's trade He married Martha Austin, a native of Center county, and they became the parents of five children, namely James, who died at the age of twenty-three years of typhoid fever, Harry L, Grace, who married Harry Denning of Philipsburg, William Walter, a carpenter near Milesburg, who married Agatha Ammerman of Center county, and Harvey G, a dentist with offices at Kylertown and Winburne, who married Mary Beam

Harry L Jones attended the schools of Kylertown, completing his education at the age of seventeen years, when he took up telegraphy and was employed for eight years by the Beech Creek (now New York Central) Railroad He was first elected justice of the peace in 1896, and he has served for almost fifteen consecutive years, now being in his third term in that office He is serving his second term as president of the school board of Cooper township, and in every way has shown himself efficient and capable and worthy the trust reposed in him by his fellow townsmen His politics are those of the Republican party Fraternally he is connected with Forest City Lodge, No 176, I O O F of Kylertown, and Lodge No 310, O U A M, and he also holds membership in Kylertown Grange No 1406 He is a Presbyterian in his religious belief

Mr Jones was married in June, 1895, to Miss Flora Belle Schreck, a daughter of John A. and Mary Schreck, and to this union there have been born six children, namely Theresa Irene, Harold, Ruel, Malin and Lois and Louise, twins

JOHN A McCLELLAND, justice of the peace at Brisbin, Pa, has been a resident of this borough for thirty-one years and has been identified with many of its leading business interests He was born September 27, 1864, in county Antrim, Ireland, although of Scotch descent, and is a son of Alexander and Ellen McClelland His father died when he was three years old and his mother when he was eleven At that time he was taken to Scotland, living with an aunt until coming to America in 1880 There were three sons Robert, Thomas and John A, all of whom came to America and the two older brothers live in Cambria county, Pa

John A McClelland is a self-made man, having only the opportunities for improvement in his youth that he made for himself He attended night schools in Scotland and this country and started to learn the blacksmith's trade before coming to America when he was fifteen years of age He came to Brisbin, where, through his own industry, he supported himself and soon gained the confidence of those with whom he was associated For fourteen years he successfully represented the Grand Union Tea Company, and then conducted a store for eight years, and later became interested in the coal industry At present Mr McClelland is operating two coal mines at Ashland, in Decatur township He has been quite active politically for a number of years and during the term of office of Representatives Boulton and Scofield, was employed in a state position at Harrisburg For the past fifteen years he has served acceptably as a justice of the peace, his present term expiring in 1914, when he undoubtedly will be re-elected. He has been a Republican since he became a voter and at present is identified with what is termed the insurgent wing of the party, the one that demands progressiveness and stands for purity in politics He was his party's candidate for the General Assembly in 1910 He has served in the borough council and in many local offices and during eleven years as a member of the school board, was its secretary during the larger period

Mr McClelland was married in 1885, to Miss Annie Gertrude Berkstresser, a daughter of Rev Jesse Berkstresser, now of Harrisburg Mrs McClelland died January 26, 1906 Four of the children born to Mr and Mrs McClelland survive, namely: Jesse Valentine, Gertrude, Ellen Beatrice and Ernest, the other two being Catherine and John Ross Since 1885 Mr McClelland has been a member of the Church of God He is identified fraternally with the Red Men and the Brotherhood of the Union, and was for eighteen years superintendent of the Sabbath school

EDWIN E KANTZ, of Burnside, Pa, who is prominently connected with the coal mining industry, as mine superintendent and owner, was born at Patchinsville, this county, in 1877, a son of Reuben and Susannah (Bowder) Kantz His paternal grandfather was John Kantz of Snyder county, who married Sarah Ann Baker, and who came to Patchinsville in 1846

Reuben Kantz was born in Snyder county, Pa, and in addition to lumbering and carpenter work, engaged in agriculture, which occupation he has followed up to the present time, being now sixty-three years old His wife, Susannah, who is living at the age of sixty-one, is the daughter of Jacob and Anna (Bennord) Bowder, the former of whom met an accidental death in 1877 The children of Mr and Mrs Reuben Kantz were as follows Charles E, who is a physician practicing in Philadelphia Howard S, a resident of Burnside, Pa, Milton L, who resides in Oklahoma, Paul S, who is a school superintendent in Idaho, Guy V, Violet Elizabeth, who is a teacher residing at home, Geneva, also at home, Pearl, who died in infancy, and Edwin E, subject of this sketch

Edwin E Kantz after attending school until the age of sixteen years, engaged in farming with his father, and during the winter worked at the stone masons' and carpenters' trades, also learning the creamery business At the age of twenty he entered the mines, in which he worked for three years, for two years subsequently being engineer on the railway for hauling coal He was then engaged in prospecting for coal for two years, locating mines for his company and opening up the Bellwood coal mines In 1895 he passed the state examination for mine foreman and took charge of the Bellmore mines until 1910, when he resigned the position to take that of superintendent for the Bellmore Coal Company, in which he now owns a one-third interest He is also interested in the La Soya Oil Company of Oklahoma Mr Kantz was elected councilman on the Prohibition ticket and is now serving his second term in that office He belongs to the Methodist Protestant church, and is superintendent of the Sunday school He belongs also to the order of Redmen at Patchinsville, Lodge No 522

Mr Kantz was married May 14, 1902, to Sarah Elizabeth Bellis, who was born at Buckley, North Wales, in 1875, daughter of Thomas and Ellen (Lamb) Bellis Her paternal grandparents were Robert and Elizabeth (Lewis) Bellis, both natives of Wales, the former being a merchant and miner, who died in his native land in 1895 Thomas Bellis, father of Mrs Kantz, was also a miner, entering the Welsh mines at the age of eight years as trapper boy Subsequently, after a residence of three years in Lancashire, England, he came at the age of twenty-nine years to America, accompanied by his wife and children, this being about 1880 He settled at Philipsburg, Pa, where he was engaged in mining until 1890 and then removing to Urey, Indiana county, was foreman and superintendent of mines there until his death, which took place in 1910 His wife, to whom he was married in Buckley, N W in 1870, was a daughter of Thomas and Mary (Jones) Lamb, her father being a brick molder To Mr and Mrs Kantz have been born four children, namely—Thomas Bellis, aged eight years; Ellen V, now six, Alice, and Lillian Ruth

I S FLEGAL, M D, who has been a resident of Karthaus Pa, for the past fourteen years, has conducted a drug store at this place since 1901, although it has been his custom to handle and compound his own prescriptions ever since he entered into medical practice He was born at Shawville, Clearfield county, Pa , and is a son of Robert K and Keturah (Irwin) Flegal

The Flegal family is an old one in Pennsylvania and the great-grandparents of Dr Flegal, Valentine and Christina Flegal, lived near Harrisburg, where descendants still are numerous Good citizenship has marked them all

Jacob Flegal, grandfather of Dr Flegal, was born June 3, 1800, and died April 1, 1868 He married Margaret Leonard, born January 23, 1800, who died in June, 1884 She was a daughter of Joseph and Eleanor Leonard They had the following children James L , born March 14, 1823, died February 25, 1857, John A L , born April 19, 1825, died October, 1890, Eleanor, born August 7, 1829, died March 15, 1848, Robert K , born April 11. 1832, died March 20, 1904, Jacob Scott, born August 14, 1834, lives in North Dakota, Mary E , born July 30, 1836, lives in Goshen township, Martin S , born April 27, 1838, died from an accident, February 1, 1869, Sarah Jane, born February 9, 1841, died March 25, 1850

Robert K Flegal, father of Dr. Flegal, was eleven years old when he accompanied his parents to Goshen township, Clearfield county The family had previously lived on the Matthew Read farm in Lawrence township, and prior to that in Bradford township and in the neighborhood of Madera He followed farming and lumbering until 1899, when he sold his effects and moved to Clearfield, where his death followed some six years later He was a Democrat in politics and served in local of-

fices He was a leading member of the Methodist Episcopal church, as his father had been before him The latter was a class leader and was a constant church attendant and on the occasion of his last meeting in the church he left his cane behind him and this relic of a good and worthy man is there preserved as a memorial of him

Robert K Flegal married Marcy Keturah Irwin, who was born in Lawrence township, August 25, 1837 She was a daughter of Henry and Mary (Ogden) Irwin Her death occurred December 29, 1903 The following children were born to them Mertie M , born December 17, 1863, lives in Clearfield; Irwin Scott, Lewis Elmer, born July 22, 1866, lives at Eugene, Ore , married Blanche Read, a daughter of Thompson Read, Forrest K , born October 6, 1867, lives at Altoona, and married Lucy Norris, who is now deceased, Martin Creighton, born November 1, 1871, is a minister of the Methodist Episcopal church, belonging to the Central Presbyterian Conference, and married Dora Smith, of Goshen township, Clark, born February 13, 1876, lives in Clearfield and married Helen Bollinger, and Ruth, born February 3, 1879, died March 2, 1895

I S Flegal was reared in Goshen township and attended the schools there in boyhood and for several years was a student in the summer Normal schools in Clearfield and during one year in the State Normal School at Edinboro He then began to teach school and continued from October, 1883, until 1891, in the meanwhile doing his preparatory medical reading, and in the latter year entered the Western Pennsylvania Medical College at Pittsburg, where he was graduated with his degree in 1894 He chose Lumber City, Pa , as his first field for practice, and remained there for two and one-half years, coming then to Karthaus, where he has been established since January, 1897 He is identified with the leading interests of this section and is recognized as a capable and efficient business man and a skillful and careful physician He was one of the organizers of the Karthaus Rural Telephone Company, of which he is secretary, served as township supervisor for three years and has given time and attention to furthering educational interests He is a member of the American Medical Association together with the county and state organizations

Dr Flegal was married September 20, 1899, to Miss Lulu M Bollinger, who was born in Woodward township, Clinton county, Pa , and was a daughter of Alfred W and Elizabeth (Reed) Bollinger Mrs Flegal died October 3, 1904 Three children were born to this marriage Elizabeth Daphne, July 18, 1900, Helen May, February 19, 1902, and Robert Keith, September 2, 1903, who died September 20th in the same year

R S MAURER, postmaster at West Decatur, Pa , where he is a leading and substantial citizen, was born October 19, 1859, in Clearfield county, Pa , and is a son of Thomas and Jane (Conaway) Maurer

The parents of Mr Maurer were both born in Clearfield county The father was a blacksmith by trade His death occurred some years since but the mother survives and lives at Clearfield Their children were Anna, R S , Alice, William, Henry, Sarah, Dora, Carrie, Arvie and Ralph The paternal grandfather of this family was Solomon Maurer, and the maternal grandfather was George Conaway

R S Maurer was educated in the public schools and the State Normal School at Indiana, and for seven years afterward taught school In April, 1903, he moved to Blue Ball, where he owns a comfortable and attractive residence and also the postoffice building, and has been postmaster at West Decatur ever since He is serving as secretary of the school board and has also served as judge of elections

In 1890 Mr Maurer was married to Miss Alice Thompson, a daughter of William and Mary (Gerhart) Thompson and four children have been born to them, Helen, Florence, William and Louis Mr and Mrs Maurer are members of the Methodist Episcopal church

CHARLES FRENDBERG, assistant foreman of the Knox Run mine of the Bituminous Coal Corporation, has been in the employ of this great company for practically all of the twenty-seven years that he has been a resident of Clearfield county Mr Frendberg was born June 7, 1866, in Dalsland, Sweden, a son of Lars and Bertha Frendberg

Lars Frendberg, who carried on agricultural pursuits in Sweden, came to America in 1873 and entered the mines, working in the coal fields of Tioga, Lycoming, Clearfield and Elk counties for seven years In 1880 he returned to his native country and brought his family back to America, after which he again became employed as a miner, and he now has charge of the boilers of the Knox Run mine Seven children were born to Mr Frendberg and his wife, namely Andrew, who is foreman of the Knox Run mine, Charles, Lars, who is engineer of the Knox run mine, Gust, who is a miner at Grass Flat, Annie, Amelia, who married Charles Carlson; and Emanuel, who is deceased

Charles Frendberg attended a little pay

school in his native country and as a young man came to this country with the family He entered the employ of the Clearfield County Bituminous Coal Corporation, assisting in opening up mines at Grass Flat, and working as a blacksmith and in various other capacities until he was made assistant foreman, a capacity in which he is now serving Mr Frendberg bought a residence in Lanse in 1905, with five acres of land, and here he carries on farming in a small way He is one of the good, reliable citizens of Cooper township, and his acquaintance in the coal fields is extensive

On June 4, 1891, Mr Frendberg was united in marriage with Miss Annie Sophia Larson, who was born in Sweden in 1871, daughter of Peter Larson, and she came to this country when about seven years of age Mr and Mrs Frendberg have had nine children Nellie, who resides in Pittsburg, Ruth, who lives in Williamsport, Abbie, residing at home, Helen, Dora and Mildred, all at home, and Esther, Ellen and an infant, who are deceased Mr Frendberg is a member of Grass Flat Swedish Lutheran church

JOHN M BYERS, a well known resident of Cherry Tree, who is engaged in the monument and tombstone business at that place, was born at Cherry Tree, September 4, 1858, son of Abram and Martha (Conner) Byers The father of our subject came to Cherry Tree with his mother from York county, Pa , while yet a boy, and here followed farming and lumbering for a number of years He died at the age of seventy-one years at Cherry Tree, Pa During the Civil war he enlisted and saw active service in the Union army, serving in Co F, 57th Reg Pa Vol Infantry He married Martha Conner, a daughter of John Conner, and of their children there are four now living, two sons and two daughters, namely John M , the subject of this sketch, A S , who resides at Cherry Tree, Ellen, wife of William H Lutman, of Cookport, Indiana county, Pa , and Carrie M , wife of D Somerville, a justice of the peace, residing in Cambria county, Pa

John M Byers after attending school remained at home with his parents, and worked on the farm until reaching the age of twenty-two years At the end of this period he began to learn the stone mason's trade, which he followed as apprentice and journeyman for eight years In 1889 he engaged in the business of manufacturing tombstones and monuments at Cherry Tree, where he has since continued and is now doing a prosperous business He is a member of Lodge No 417, I. O O F, at Cherry Tree, which he is now serving as recording secretary, and also belongs to the Modern Woodmen of America, Camp No 6924, at Barnesboro, Pa , and several other fraternal organizations In politics a Republican, he has been an active worker for his party and was elected justice of the peace in Burnside township, Clearfield county, Pa , in 1906

In 1882 Mr Byers married Ida M Stiffler, who was born October 7, 1859, in Clearfield county, a daughter of P J and Rebecca (Garman) Stiffler Mrs Byers' parents are both living in Cherry Tree, her father being now eighty-three years of age and her mother eighty-four There have been born to our subject and his wife three children, of whom the only one now living is G Monte, aged twenty-five, a fireman in the Cherry Tree Iron Works, residing at home with his parents

FRANK ROSS, whose excellent farm of seventy-three acres is situated in Greenwood township, one-half mile south of Curry Run, Pa , was born in Greenwood township, March 18, 1873, and is a son of Robert and Sarah (Read) Ross

Robert Ross was also born in Greenwood township, June 2, 1839, his father having been an early settler here Robert Ross followed farming and erected all the substantial buildings now on the property above mentioned About fifty acres of the farm has been cleared and is under an excellent state of cultivation

Robert Ross was married in August, 1861, to Sarah Read, who was born in Ferguson township, Clearfield county, a daughter of William Read They had the following children Alexander, who was born October 12, 1862, married Elizabeth Sharp (now deceased), and had six children—Zoe, Erma, Clell, Maggie, Thomas and Ruth, Clara, who married Robert McMaster, and has five children—John, Merl, Vern, Frank and Stella, Minerva, who married Mert Millen, of Lawrence township, Agnes, Frank and George, all of whom are unmarried, Harry, who married Erma Campbell, and has seven children—Arthur, Pearl, Claire, Minnie, Blair, Ada and Lloyd, Sarah, who is the wife of Harvey Rainey, of Westover, Pa , and has three children—Clara, Robert and Don, and Eli and William, who still live at home The Ross family has always been Democratic in its political faith They all attend the Methodist Episcopal church This family is widely known and its members are held in esteem, father and sons being good farmers, kind neighbors and reliable citizens

ROBERT S MUIRHEAD, one of the representative business men at Winburne, Pa , where he conducts a hardware store, was born in Scotland, ten miles from the historic old city of Glasgow, May 5, 1867, and is a son of John and Martha (Shields) Muirhead

Robert S Muirhead came to Winburne when the mines opened here and began to dig coal in the first mine opened and continued in the mining business until 1905, when he invested his earnings and savings in a hardware store and through honest and upright dealing has built up a fine trade He has spent all of his life since coming to America in this place, with the exception of three months, when he lived first at Snow Shoe, in Center county He is one of a family of eight children, six of whom survive, and he was the fourth in order of birth One brother, John, died in Scotland, when aged seventeen years James lives in Clearfield, Pa , where he has a family. Henry is a coal miner William, who is now employed in a pipe factory at Providence, R I , lived at Winburne for some seven years Archie is a grocery merchant at Winburne and Charles is a mine worker here John the youngest, is deceased

Robert S Muirhead married Miss Margaret Meiklejohn, a daughter of Andrew Meiklejohn She was born in Scotland and came to America when seven years old They have one son, Andrew, who is a bright lad of ten years Mr and Mrs Muirhead are members of the Presbyterian church In politics he is a Democrat

GEORGE A McKEAGE, general merchant and a leading citizen of Burnside, Pa , was born May 11, 1856, at Cherry Tree, Indiana county, Pa , a son of Robert and Jane (Atchison) McKeage

Robert McKeage was born at Egg Harbor, N J When he came to establish himself in business in Pennsylvania, he located at Cherry Tree, where he operated a saw mill, acquired timber lands and rafted lumber and also was interested in a grist mill at this point He married Jane Atchison, a daughter of George and Katie (McClellan) Atchison, the latter of whom belonged to the same family into which Gen George B McClellan, of Civil war fame, was born

George Atchison, the maternal grandfather of George A McKeage, was born in County Roscommon, Ireland, in 1792 In his boyhood while out hunting he rendered himself liable to prosecution for having broken the Tenant law and in order to escape imprisonment, fled to America In Center county, Pa, he was married and with his wife settled in the mountains, far from any settlement and in order to procure the necessities of life had to walk long distances through regions filled with wild and dangerous animals, and carried food back to his family often at the risk of his life He was a radical Abolitionist and was one of the conductors of the so-called Underground Railway, the medium through which many slaves, prior to the Civil war, escaped bondage and found freedom in Canada In 1845 he built a fine mansion by the side of the log cabin in which he had previously lived, but this was subsequently destroyed by fire In this house he had contrived a secret chamber, in which he hid many escaping slaves, but this was never discovered until 1876 Some years before his death he moved to Cherry Tree, Pa The paternal grandfather of Mr McKeage, was Cornelius McKeage who was born in County Latrone, Ireland, and it is said of him that he built the first saw mill in Clearfield county

To Robert and Jane McKeage the follow- ing children were born George A., William, who is a resident of Cherry Tree, Margaret, who is the wife of E B McCormick, a merchant at Cherry Tree, Jennie, who is the wife of D. E Notley, of Cherry Tree, Emily, who is the wife of J M Notley, of Cherry Tree, and John, who lives at Pittsburg

After his school days were over, George A McKeage worked for his father until he was twenty-five years old He then married and for some years followed farming in Indiana county, afterward moving to Hillsdale, Pa, where he was in the mercantile business for ten years In 1900 he came to Burnside and embarked in the mercantile business here and has additional interests

Mr McKeage married Miss Annabelle Ake, who was born August 17, 1863, at Gettysburg, Pa, a daughter of Jacob G and Elizabeth (Nottley) Ake Jacob G Ake was born in 1811 and his wife in 1820 She was a daughter of John Nottley, who was born February 14, 1789, in Ireland, where he married Elizabeth Flanegan, who was born in 1792. John Nottley and wife emigrated to Quebec, Can, in a sailing vessel, in 1829, passing ten weeks on the Atlantic Ocean Later they came to the United States Jacob G Ake was a son of Daniel and Mary (Higgins) Ake. Mr and Mrs McKeage have two children: Mayme, who is the wife of Carl Eugene Patchin, of Burnside, and John A, who is associated with his father in business

JOHN S McCREERY, who has been a justice of the peace in Ferguson township for twenty-seven years, enjoying the distinction of having served continuously in this office longer than any other in this township, is a qualified civil and mining engineer and timber estimator He was born March 4, 1854, at Marion Center, Indiana county, Pa , and is a son of Robert and Nancy McCreery, both of whom are now deceased

John S McCreery was educated in the public schools, Mt Pleasant Institute, and Westminster College, and afterward spent some years teaching school in Westmoreland and Clearfield counties, and in the latter was an instructor in the Lumber City Academy He also had farm interests and engaged also in lumbering to some extent and in a professional way is known all through this section, serving at present as mine engineer for three clay mines and having many contracts on hand for land surveys and timber estimates

Mr McCreery was married to Miss Emma Watts, a daughter of Martin Watts, of Ferguson township They are members of the Presbyterian church, in which he is an elder Mr McCreery is a charter member of Kerrmoor Grange In his views on public questions he is a Prohibitionist He has served several terms as school director in his township and has been a jury commissioner of Clearfield county He is a stockholder in the different telephone companies in this section of the county and is a charter member of the Farmers and Traders Bank of Clearfield

ANDREW J KLARE, who is now living retired, at Wallacetown, Pa , of which he has been a worthy resident for forty years, is a highly respected citizen and is a veteran of the great Civil war He was born in France, April 25, 1831, and is a son of Joseph and Catherine (Fruhhauff) Klare The parents never came to the United States and of their children, Andrew J is the only survivor

Andrew J Klare was twenty-two years of age when he came to America, having previously obtained a good education in his native land He learned the shoemaking trade and for a number of years conducted a shoe store at Wallaceton In 1861 he enlisted for service in the Civil war, entering Co K, 110th Pa. Vol Inf , and served with bravery and courage that won approbation, until his honorable discharge in 1865 He then returned to Wallaceton, resumed business bought a home and has lived here ever since, having made many friends He is a Democrat in politics and has been elected, in the course of years, to every township office except that of assessor, serving acceptably in all

In 1856 Mr Klare was married to Miss Susan Gilman, a daughter of John and Catherine (Kramer) Gilman, of Clearfield county Mrs Klare had one brother, Albert To Mr and Mrs Klare nine children were born, namely Josephine, Alfred, Franklin, Emma, William, George, Martin, May and Edna, all of whom survive except Franklin Mrs Klare and children attend the Methodist Episcopal church Mr Klare was reared in the Catholic faith

EMIL OLSON, who is a very popular citizen of Winburne, Pa , to which place he came early in its settlement, conducts a custom coal mine and is one of the representative business men He was born October 19, 1865, in Warmland, Sweden, and is a son of John and Kate Olson Both parents are now deceased, the mother dying when Emil was only three years old He has one brother and one sister Olof, who is a captain in the Swedish army, and Christiana, who is the wife of John Nordstrom, a baker by trade, and lives in Sweden

Emil Olson was fourteen years old when

he accompanied his father, in 1879, to America They went to McIntyre, Lycoming county, Pa, where both found work in the coal mines In 1883 the father returned to Sweden and he remained in his native land until his death in 1904 In the year in which his father went back to Sweden, Emil Olson left McIntyre and located at Peale. in Cooper township, Clearfield county, where he aided in opening up the coal mines before the railroad had been built that far From Peale, in 1885, he went to Morrisdale, where he secured employment with the Morrisdale Coal Company and worked for them until 1889, when he came to Winburne Here he was employed by the Somerville Coal Company with which he continued until 1907, when he embarked in the wholesale beer business and conducted it at Winburne until June 13, 1910, when he sold it and purchased the custom mine which he has conducted ever since, having a large domestic coal trade He also does general hauling

On September 1. 1887, Mr Olson was married to Miss Ida Watkins, a daughter of B Franklin and Rebecca (McCartney) Watkins Both parents of Mrs Olson were born in Center county, Pa For many years B F Watkins was engaged in the timber business in Center county He came to Morris township. Clearfield county, in December, 1873 For five years he was in the hotel business at Morrisdale He died April 12, 1888, at the age of fifty years and ten months His parents, Alexander and Jane Watkins. were old residents of Center county, and his mother was in her ninety-fifth year at time of death The mother of Mrs Olson was a daughter of Thomas and Rachel McCartney Her death occurred in 1892 at the age of fifty-seven

years and five months. They had ten children, Mrs Olson being the youngest born

To Mr and Mrs Olson eight children have been born, all residing at home, a happy, united family, namely Clara May, Easton, Edward Livingston, Reba, Bertha, Alice, Ross and Richard Gordon In politics, Mr Olson is a Democrat and he has served in the offices of inspector and judge of elections He has seen this place develop from almost a wilderness, heavy timber covering almost the entire country when he first came here, the town having then not more than a half dozen houses, one store and a saw-mill He attended night school which was conducted by John Somerville, who made no charge for his service and is remembered with a great deal of respect by Mr Olson and many others

Mr Olson is a member of the United Mine Workers of America and was the first president of Winburne Local He belongs also to Winburne Lodge, No 61, Odd Fellows, Philipsburg Lodge, No 123, Moose, and belongs additionally to the Scandanavian Brotherhood With his family he is connected with the Presbyterian church

EDWARD A THOMPSON, a leading and representative citizen of Greenwood township, Clearfield county, Pa, was born April 10, 1860, on his present farm which contains 500 acres and is a son of R C and Rebecca (Gressley) Thompson

R C Thompson was born in Indiana county, Pa, where he attended the district schools and when sixteen years of age came to Clearfield county and was in the employ of John Patchen, a well known lumberman, for the next six years He then married and continued to live in the same township for one more year, working still for Mr Patchen, after which he moved to the farm above mentioned which has never left the family It was formerly known as the Jacob Walter place Mr Thompson operated in lumber for William Irwin of Curwensville, and later was engaged on his own account in Bell and Greenwood townships and became associated as a member with the Reed, Irwin & Betts Company He cleared about forty-five acres of this farm, which has now about 100 acres under tillage The larger part of the remaining portion of his life was spent on this farm, although in the meanwhile he made three trips to the far West, visiting Washington, Idaho and California He was a strong Democrat and had been elected to almost all the township offices, as has his son, Edward A, and for years served continuously on the school board He was born in January, 1832, and died April 1, 1901, and was buried at Mahaffey

R C Thompson was married to Rebecca Gressley, who was born March 22, 1840, in York county, Pa, and came to this county when a child Her parents were Henry and Rebecca Gressley, who came to this county from York county To this marriage twelve children were born, as follows Annie L, who is the wife of G A Nelson, of Coeur d'Alene Idaho, Edward A; Joseph B, who resides at Spokane, Wash, Julia M, who is the wife of Harry Hawkins, Thomas J, who resides, with his family, at Park, Idaho, Harry D, who lives at Winchester, Idaho, Sarah E, who is the wife of G F Strausbaugh, of Elk county, Pa, John B, who is a resident of Coeur d'Alene, Idaho, Fannie E, now deceased, who was the wife of William McGee Elmira, Sarah Nevada, who married J A

Allison, and resides at Gillette, Wyo, and J Blair, who is a resident of Coeur d'Alene, Idaho

Edward A Thompson with the other members of the family attended the district schools in Greenwood township, as did many of those who have been his neighbors ever since He early became a timber expert and was only fourteen years of age when he made his first trip down the river, accompanying his father, and when he was seventeen he piloted his first raft as far as Lock Haven, on the river He afterwards worked for Baird & Cassidy and for P & A Flynn, having charge of horse arks After his marriage he settled on a part of the old homestead but later moved to McGee Mills and engaged in scaling lumber for Isett & Ray, of Altoona, for the Bear Run Lumber Company, and for S T Foresman of Williamsport, and had charge of the scaling and purchasing of logs for the firm of Weaver & Betts, Clearfield, Pa When he resigned from that connection he brought his family back to the homestead and afterward, for several years, was engaged in the timber lands and lumber districts of West Virginia, in the interest of Henry McCormick's Sons Co, and ex-Senator J D Cameron, both of Harrisburg, Pa After he returned to Clearfield county he continued to be interested in lumbering He was subsequently appointed administrator of his father's large estate and still fills that office

Mr Thompson was married September 26, 1885, to Miss Rebecca M Newcomer, who was born in Ferguson township, Clearfield county, Pa, December 30, 1864, and is a daughter of W H and Melissa Newcomer They have three children Alfred Reed, unmarried, who is manager of a store for the

P V K Coal Company, now the R M Peil Coal Company, at Emeigh, Cambria county, Vaughn, who is the wife of K Hoyt Thorp, residing in Greenwood township and has one daughter, Josephine, and Genevieve, who resides at home In politics Mr Thompson is a Democrat He is identified with the Odd Fellows at Mahaffey, the Blue Lodge, F & A M, at Clearfield, and the Consistory at Williamsport

SALMON TOZER, a retired farmer living in Chest township, where for many years he also followed the gunsmith s trade was born January 3, 1835, in this township, and is a son of Baurch and Rebecca (Campbell) Tozer

The father of Mr Tozer was born in the state of New York and died in Chest township in 1866, at the age of sixty-five years He came to this section with his brother, Andrew Tozer, in 1830, settling near La Jose, where he spent the remainder of his life His parents were Thomas and Jane (Stevenson) Tozer, natives of Maine, who came very early to Pennsylvania and lived first in Clearfield county and then in Indiana county, where they died The father of Mr Tozer was a gunsmith by trade He married Rebecca Campbell, who died in her seventy-sixth year She was a daughter of John and Jane Campbell, of Campbell town, or Pine Creek, Clearfield county Twelve children were born to this marriage, of which family three survive Salmon, John, who is a clerk in a business house at Brookville, Pa ; and Melissa, who is the wife of John Wherle, a farmer near La Jose

Salmon Tozer attended school in boyhood in Chest township and then learned the gunsmith trade in his father's shop and remained at home, on what was called the Alger place, until he was eighteen years of age He then went into business for himself where he now lives Mr Tozer has a fine record as a soldier He enlisted in August, 1861, and served two years in the Civil war as a member of Co D, 105th Pa Vol Inf, which gained a name for bravery as the "Wildcat" regiment He was in the 3rd Army Corps, Army of the Potomac, under Gen McClellan He participated in many of the great battles of the war but was fortunate enough to escape all serious injury He was honorably discharged in 1863 and then returned to his former home and has been more or less engaged in farming and in working at his trade until the present time, but is now practically retired He is a valued member of the John Telford Post, G A R, at Westover, Pa Mr. Tozer has never married

GEORGE W READ, one of the enterprising and progressive farmers and substantial citizens of Ferguson township, owns the farm of 120 acres on which he was born, October 28, 1875, a son of Emberson and Agnes (Ross) Read

Emberson Read was born also in Ferguson township, but on an adjoining farm, and spent his entire life in Clearfield county After marriage he settled in Greenwood township and lived there until after the birth of his first child, and then moved to Ferguson township, where he acquired the farm now owned by his son, George W, and here he died, at the age of fifty-four years His burial was at Lumber City, he being a member of the Presbyterian church there He was interested in everything that promised to be of substantial benefit to his section and was a charter member of the Grange at Kerrmoor He married Agnes Ross, who survives and resides with her son on the home farm She was born in Greenwood township, a daughter of George Ross, a well known farmer Seven children were born to Mr and Mrs. Read, Ida, Effie, Blanche, George, Frank, Martin and Sadie

George W Read was mainly educated at the Friendship school in Ferguson township, later passing three terms in the Kerrmoor schools He has devoted himself to farming ever since and has kept his buildings repaired and has made improvements as have seemed desirable Like his father he is one of the intelligent agriculturists that follow modern methods understandingly and have satisfactory profits at the close of the season He is an active member of Kerrmoor Grange, being one of its charter members He is a stockholder in the Farmers and Traders Bank at Clearfield, Pa, and belongs to the body of progressive and public spirited men who organized and financed the Ferguson Township and Lumber City Telephone Company

In June, 1906, Mr. Read was married to Miss Julia McCracken, who was born October 27, 1884, in Ferguson township, a daughter of Seth McCracken, and they have two children, Diantha and Blanche Mr Read is a Prohibitionist in his political views, as was his late father, and he has served very acceptably as a member of the township school board for two years

BERTEN MERRITT, a prominent business citizen of Cooper township, was born in Bradford county, Pa, June 23, 1839, son of Elijah and Jane Ann (Yearington) Merritt He is a grandson of Hezekiah Merritt, a native of New Jersey, who with several brothers, settled at an early day on the border of Bedford and Wyoming counties, Pa, where he followed the trades of carpenter and millwright, erecting most of the barns and water-mills in that section In later life he followed farming

Elijah Merritt, father of our subject, was reared in Bradford county, near the Wyoming county line, and was twelve years old when he accompanied his parents to Wyoming county He learned the carpenter's trade, which he followed in his younger days, but became a farmer later in life He died in August, 1874, at the age of eighty-six years He was a Democrat in politics and was always regarded as a worthy, reliable citizen His wife, Jane, was of Scotch ancestry, her parents settling in the Wyoming valley She died in 1844 at the age of forty-four years Elijah Merritt served as a soldier in the War of 1812 He and his wife were the parents of five children—George, Elijah, Nelson, Clarinda and Berten, all being now deceased except the subject of this sketch, George and Nelson came to Clearfield county and died here

Berten Merritt attended the subscription schools for about four months in his boyhood, but devoted many of his leisure hours to private study, by which means he obtained a fair practical education He entered into the lumber business in 1862 on the Morgan Run, he and his brother George purchasing the sawmill of Munson & Hale, which they carried on together for some time Later our subject bought his brother's interest in the mill and business and, taking a new partner, built a new mill and operated it under the firm name of Merritt & Mitchell Of this also after a time he became the sole owner, and he still owns the land, about 700 to 800 acres—which is underlaid with about five feet of fire clay—a valuable holding   About 1887 he entered into a new partnership under the firm name of B Merritt & Co , the firm being composed of himself, John F Weaver, W W Betts, and A B Weaver, and this concern was operated until about 1899, when Mr Merritt, with his son George, purchased the business, operating at Pine Glen, in Center county   The plant was subsequently destroyed by fire, and later Mr Merritt started business on Morgan Run, conducting it until 1909, when he sold out   He rafted square timber down the river to Williamsport   Forty-nine years of his business life have been spent in this county, two years —from 1860 to 1862—were spent at Philipsburg, Center county   During this time he has helped many business friends by indorsements   He is the owner, either entirely or in part, of 125 houses—a substantial result after so many years of effort   He has worked hard all his life and has a thorough practical understanding of the lumber trade, in which he has a wide acquaintance

Mr Merritt was first married, March 4, 1866, to Catherine Coulter, a daughter of John and Mary (Merman) Coulter   Her father was of Irish and her mother of Pennsylvania-German stock, the latter being reared in this county   Her father owned a farm in Woodward township, which he subsequently sold

Of Mr Merritt's first marriage to Catherine Coulter, six children were born—three sons and three daughters, namely   George, John, June, Howard Josephine and Martha, whose records in brief are as follows   George Merritt was educated in the district and high schools of Clearfield and read law under Mc-

Enally and McCurdy, being admitted to practice in Clearfield   Going to Oklahoma, he settled in Pawneetown, Pawnee county, where after a short residence he was nominated for judge of the court, but was defeated by fifty-eight votes, leading his ticket, however, by one hundred votes   He married Miss Stella Bartett, of Erie county, Pa , of which there is one child, Mildred

John Merritt resides at Winburne, Clearfield county, Pa , and is a fireman   He married Miss Etta Wertz, and has three children, Berten, George and Marguerite   June resides at home   Howard M is superintendent of schools at Somerset, Pa , being elected for three years, and served one year as principal   He was educated in the public and normal schools at Lock Haven and in Lafayette college, also taking a special course at Columbia University, N Y   He married Miss Nellie Buzell of Philipsburg, Center county, Pa , and they have three children—one daughter and two sons, namely   Alfretta, Royden, and Donald   Josephine is the wife of A E Hess of Winburne and has two children, Catherine and George Merritt Hess   Martha is the wife of W F Straw of Philipsburg, and has two children, George and Merritt

Mrs Catherine Merritt died January 16, 1885, and Mr Merritt married in December, 1885, Mrs Jane (Dixon) Wiser, a widow, and daughter of James and Sarah Dixon, of this county, both now deceased   Her father died in 1875 and her mother in 1873   Mr Merritt belongs to the Knights of Pythias, having been a member for two years   He is one of the elders of the Presbyterian church and has always been active in church affairs   He served for fourteen years as school director and assessor of the township one year

He came to Winburne from Kylertown in 1898 and erected his present residence At one time he owned all of Winburne and sold part of same to Sommerville He owns an interest in the butcher shops and is vice-president of the Bituminous National Bank of Winburne He erected a saw-mill here and through his instrumentality also the coal bank was opened Mrs Merritt had one daughter by her first marriage, Fannie, who is the wife of Charles Lenig, and she and her husband are the parents of seven children Ruth, Jane, Sallie, Lavina, Berten, Ray and Elizabeth Mr Lenig is a carpenter by occupation

ISAAC J YINGLING, a worthy representative of one of the old and substantial families of Burnside township, Clearfield county, Pa, who is interested in lumbering and farming on the old homestead, on which he was born, October 12, 1845, is a son of Benjamin and Margaret (Hingst) Yingling, and a grandson of Abraham and Mary Yingling

Abraham Yinling, the grandfather, was born July 18, 1770, and died August 9, 1831, probably before his son Benjamin had moved to Clearfield county, in the same year His wife, Mary, was born October 16, 1777, and died April 12, 1853, and she probably was with the family in its exodus to Clearfield county

Benjamin Yingling, the father of Isaac J, was born March 1, 1802, and died July 8, 1862 He married Margaret Hingst or Hengst, who was born February 10, 1804 They were natives of Huntingdon county, Pa They had eight children born to them and three sons and one daughter survive, namely Abraham, Michael, residing in Burnside township, Isaac J, and Mary, wife of Robert McKee, residing in Burnside township Benjamin Yingling was a miller by trade In 1831 he moved with his family to Clearfield county, settling in Burnside township He cleared off the timber from 300 acres of land and showed still more enterprise by erecting a saw mill in 1835, which was the first one built in the southern part of the county In 1852 he erected a larger and more modern mill, near the site of the former one, which he operated for seven years, when it was destroyed by fire He was one of the solid and substantial men of this section in his day, one of the real civilizing factors From the time of the organization of the Republican party he was actively identified with its movements in local affairs and served in many township offices and for fifteen years was a justice of the peace He was one of the leading members of the Lutheran church in Burnside township

Isaac J Yingling obtained his early education in the subscription and district schools He then assisted his father in his farming and lumbering enterprises and after the latter's death, continued the same in association with his brother Michael but has been engaged in business independently since 1869 Like his father, he has been interested in Republican politics, but has never been willing to accept office, his tastes being for a quiet life On March 9, 1872, Mr Yingling was married to Miss Ellen McDermott, who was born in 1850, in Indiana county, Pa She is a daughter of Marshall and Mary (Salsgiver) McDermott, who were born near Punxatawney, Pa Mr and Mrs Yingling attend the Lutheran church

EMORY E OWENS, who is one of Ferguson township's representative and substantial citizens, owns 450 acres of valuable land in Clearfield county and resides on one of his farms which is situated one and one-half miles north of Kerrmoor He was born on an adjoining farm, March 17, 1851, and is a son of Thomas and Emeline (Hile) Owens

Thomas Owens spent his life in Clearfield county, living in Pike township for a short time after his marriage and then moving to Ferguson township, where he died at the early age of forty-two years, his burial being in the cemetery at New Millport In his earlier political days he was a Whig but later identified himself with the Republican party. He was a stanch friend of the public schools and served some years as a school director in Ferguson township He married Emeline Hile, who was a daughter of Henry Hile, Sr She died at the age of forty-five years and her burial was by the side of her husband They were members of the United Brethren church Ten children were born to them, four of whom survive, namely · Clara, Lucy, Nora and Emory E Those deceased are Robert H , Lorenzo, Alfred W , Perry, Liman and Henry

Emory E Owens obtained a common school education and afterward taught school for five years in Greenwood and Ferguson townships, in Clearfield county, and in Jefferson county, and also engaged to some extent in lumbering, this being a leading industry in his early manhood. Since his marriage he has lived on his present farm near Kerrmoor, which he has improved from time to time with substantial and attractive buildings

Mr Owens married Miss Lola Schoning, who was born in Jordan township, Clearfield county, a daughter of Ferdinand and Mary (Moore) Schoning, and they have had the following children Lottie, who is the wife of James Noland, residing in Jordan town-

ship, Alfred and Maude, both of whom are deceased, Chester, who lives in Chester county, Pa , married a Miss Goldthread, Nora, who is a successful teacher in the public schools of Philadelphia, Ralph, who is a member of the class of 1912, in the Ada (Ohio) Normal School, Leonard, Stanley and Ardie, who are students in the State Normal School at Lock Haven, and Edward and Pauline, both of whom are students in the Lumber City High School Mr and Mrs Owens are members of the Methodist Episcopal church. He belongs to the Grange at Kerrmoor and in his political views is identified with the independent branch of the Republican party He has been a member of the school board for eleven years and has also served in the office of constable In all matters relating to the best interests of his neighborhood, he is always concerned, actuated by public spirit, and he is ever ready to do his full share as a man and citizen

WALFRID JOHNSON, who has been engaged in a general mercantile business at Lanse, in Cooper township, Clearfield county, Pa , for the past sixteen years, was born April 28, 1867, at Lidkoping, Sweden, and is a son of John and Eliza Johnson

The parents of Mr. Johnson were born, reared and married in Sweden and there the father died The mother still survives and is now aged seventy-three years She was married second to Carl Sunberg, who is now in his seventy-ninth year and they reside with Mr Johnson The latter has one sister, Mrs. L J Anderson, who is a resident of Allport, Pa

Walfrid Johnson landed at the port of New York, from Sweden, on June 5, 1887, and came thence to Clearfield county, Pa , finding employment in the Morrisdale mines He made his home at Allport and worked four years in the mines but after being sick there for several years, in 1895 he came to Lanse He had very small capital at this time but the place was just started and he was the first merchant and managed his early business affairs so well that he prospered and is now the leading merchant in the town He served ten years as postmaster and then resigned that office in order to give all his attention to his business He erected his business house and carries a large and carefully selected stock His standing is high in business circles and his signature placed at the bottom of a legal paper now possesses value He has every reason to take some pride in his success as it is the result of his own unaided' efforts

In 1891 Mr Johnson was married to Miss Catherine Olson, a daughter of Olaf Olson, of Allport Mrs Johnson died in the summer of 1904, having been the mother of four children, namely Rudolph, Anton, and Ebba and Annie (twins), the last named dying at the age of four months Mr Johnson was married secondly in September, 1906, to Miss Mary Lyon, a daughter of Andrew Lyon, of Cooper township, and they have one son, Iver Walfrid Mr Johnson is a member of the Swedish Evangelical Lutheran church at Lanse In politics he is a Republican and has served as a member of the school board of Cooper township He is actively interested in all that concerns this section and is a well known and influential citizen

JOHN ANDREW MAGEE, a retired farmer and an honored veteran of the Civil war, for many years has been a resident of Burnside township, Clearfield county, Pa He was born in Clarion county, Pa , November 9 1832, and is a son of William and Sarah (Palmer) Magee, and a grandson of John A Magee

William Magee was born in Clarion county, Pa , of Irish parentage His life was one of industry, his business being farming and lumbering He died early, in 1834, when his son, John Andrew, was only two years old He had married Sarah Palmer, who survived him many years, her death occurring in 1890 Her father came from the Isle of Man

John Andrew Magee attended school for a short time in his boyhood, but as soon as his strength permitted, began to take care of himself by his own industry and afterward learned the carpenter's trade In the meanwhile he married and with his wife and family spent some three years in the West, working at his trade in different places When the Civil war broke out, Mr Magee and family were in Iowa, and there he enlisted for three years, entering Co I, 15th Ia Vol Inf He saw much hard service, including many desperate battles and made the memorable march to the sea with General Sherman, and on October 3, 1862, he was seriously wounded, at Corinth, Miss At the expiration of his term of enlistment he was honorably discharged and was mustered out at Davenport, Ia From there Mr Magee came to his present farm, which he not only cleared but has greatly improved Here he carried on farming and stockraising until he passed his responsibilities to younger hands and is now enjoying a period of well earned rest He is a valued member of the G A R, Post No 40, Cherry Tree

Mr Magee married Miss Caroline Brickell, who was born December 6, 1835, in the State

50

of New York, a daughter of John and Ann Maria (Underdunk) Brickell, old New York state people, probably of Holland ancestry. Nine children were born to Mr. and Mrs Magee, namely· Thomas, who married Mary Vasbinder, and has three children and two grandchildren, Mary, who is the wife of S Wilson, of Cherry Tree, and has six children and eight grandchildren, Cordelia, who is the widow of C Lockard, and has five children and six grandchildren, Luella, who married George Lydic, a farmer in Burnside township, and has five children, John, who is the home farmer, married Maud Lydic and has one child, Mona, Cora, who is the wife of Thomas Frank, of Slabtown, Pa, and has three children, and three children who are deceased Mr Magee can take much pride in his fine family of vigorous descendants for they are creditable to their ancestry and community Mr Magee is a leading member of the Methodist Episcopal church in Burnside township In politics he is a Democrat and has served as a member of the school board and also as township supervisor

LEWIS C ROBBINS*, general farmer and well known citizen of Knox township, resides on his finely cultivated and well improved farm of fifty-four acres which is situated two miles southwest of Olanta, Pa His parents were George W and Margaret E (Bloom) Robbins He was born October 16, 1848, in Clearfield county, Pa

George W Robbins was born in Dauphin county, Pa, in 1815, and went to school at Milton, Pa, and from there came to Pike township, Clearfield county in 1840 There he married Margaret E Bloom, a daughter of John and Susanna Bloom, and they lived on a small farm in Pike township until after the birth of all their children, eight in number, namely· Zephaniah, Mary Jane, Lewis C, Annie, Eretta, Sarah, B F, and James H George W Robbins owned two acres of land in Pike township, on which Mrs Isaac Caldwell now resides In 1869 he moved on the farm which is now owned by his son, Lewis C, about twenty acres of which was cleared, and his subsequent life was devoted to farming He was a member of the Presbyterian church at Curwensville In politics he was a stanch Democrat all his life His death occurred at the age of sixty-seven years and his burial was in the McClure cemetery, near Curwensville

Lewis C Robbins attended the Robbins school in Pike township and also the public schools of Curwensville, after which he assisted on the home farm and about 1874 became the owner of his present property He has his land all under cultivation with the exception of ten acres and has erected adequate and substantial buildings

On May 11, 1876, Mr Robbins was married to Mrs Jennie A (Wolfe) Frye, widow of William Frye and daughter of Charles and Margaret (Ambrose) Wolfe Mrs Robbins' father was born in Dauphin county, Pa, and lost his life through accident, at Glen Hope, Clearfield county, at the age of fifty-six years. His wife was born in Center county and died aged thirty-five years Mr and Mrs Wolfe had four children Isaac A, William A, Franklin P and Jennie A They were members of the Presbyterian church By her first marriage, Mrs Robbins had one daughter, Emma F, who is the wife of Thomas Williams of Wilkensburg Mr. and Mrs Williams have children, Mary Margaret, Ethel G,

Mabel, Eugene, Dorothy, William P and Ruth To Mr and Mrs Robbins two children have been born, George W and James W The former married Minta Lord, and they have six children Lewis, Morris, Emma T, Eve Marie, Leata Margaret and Hazel Irene George W Robbins and family reside on the home farm James W Robbins married May Cathcart, a daughter of Wesley and Nora Cathcart, of Knox township, and they have had five children Verda, Howard Leroy, Andrew, Arthur D, and Wesley W, Verda and Wesley W being the only survivors William W Robbins and family live in the state of Washington

In politics Mr Robbins is a Democrat and he has frequently been elected to township offices by his fellow citizens and has served discreetly and honestly and with so much efficiency that on several occasions against his will, he has been elected township collector, declining to serve He has resided on his present farm ever since his marriage He has never sold possible coal deposits Mr Robbins takes an interest in the Grange and attends its sessions at Olanta, having been a member for some years With his family he belongs to the Methodist Episcopal church

JOHN O'CONNOR, one of the efficient and trusted employes of the Pennsylvania Railroad Company, with which he has been identified since he was thirteen years of age, for the past thirty-five years has held the responsible position of express messenger and baggage master He was born June 22, 1848, in Ireland, the eldest of a family of six children born to his parents. Patrick and Anna (Naughton) O'Connor Patrick O'Connor was born in Dublin, Ireland, in 1816 He left

his native land a fugitive, having taken part in the Irish Rebellion and was a leader among the patriots With his wife and infant son, John being then eight months old, he took passage on a sailing vessel that required seven weeks to make the voyage across the Atlantic Ocean He was not only a man of courage and daring but he was capable and energetic in business and had been in the United States but a short time before he was employed by the contracting firm of McAvoy & Purcell, at Pack Saddle, Cambria county, Pa, where he remained and assisted in the grading of the railroad until that contract was finished He moved then into Indiana county, locating five miles north of Blairsville, moving from there to Indiana borough and worked on Black Creek until that branch of the railroad to the county seat was completed Mr O'Connor then went back to Blairsville and went into contracting on his own account and in 1857 moved to Retort, where he had been engaged as contractor to construct four miles of road from Retort to Summit This work being finished he then moved to Tyrone and completed the road from there to Vail and afterward to Powellton Mr O'Connor was so capable and so honest that he gained the respect, confidence and esteem of all those who had business relations with him and there were many outside his immediate family, who mourned him when his death, in 1861, terminated his busy life He had many admirable qualities and among these his strong family affection was a leading one He had had his own way to make but he never forgot those he had left behind in the old country and as soon as fortune had favored him to a sufficient extent, he sent for the old father and later for his three brothers and three sisters, all of whom joined him in Pennsylvania He married Anna Naughton, also a native of Queens county, Ireland She died in 1887, at New Castle, Pa , where her burial took place They had the following children John, Michael, Patrick, Lizzie, Ellen and Mary. Michael followed railroading all his life He was accidentally killed by being blown from a bridge, in 1881, on the low grade division of the Allegheny Valley Railroad Patrick has also followed railroading and is now a passenger conductor on the above mentioned railroad He resides at Driftwood Lizzie, who is the widow of John Ryan, lives at New Castle, Pa Ellen, who also lives at New Castle, is the widow of William Green Mary married William Pitzer and they live at New Wilmington, Mercer county, Pa

John O'Connor obtained his schooling in the various places in which the family lived and immediately after the death of his father went to work, being employed on what is known as the branch road of the Pennsylvania system just before it was completed to Philipsburg He was then promoted to be track-walker, and for three years he walked twenty-four miles each day His next position was at Powellton where he had charge of the coal wharf until the station was completed at Osceola, when he was made baggage man About 1865 he began as a freight brakeman, on a freight train that had one passenger car attached and in 1875, when the regular passenger train was established, he was brakeman on that train until 1876, when he was made baggage master and express messenger In 1881 he moved to Philipsburg and from there in 1889, to Belsena, Clearfield County, and from there in 1892, to Osceola and three years later back to Philipsburg On October 1, 1905, he moved to Lock Haven, where he resided for

two years and then moved to Tyrone for one year In the meanwhile he built his present attractive two-story residence at Osceola Mills, which he has occupied since January 7, 1909

On April 20, 1873, Mr O'Connor was married at the Catholic parsonage, to Miss Isabella J McClellan, who was born at Union ville, Center county, Pa , the eldest daughter of William and Christina Jane (Myer) Mc-Clellan William McClellan was born at Ridgeway, Elk county, Pa , and his wife in Sugar Valley, Center county All their children were born at Unionville, except the youngest They were. Isabella J , who is Mrs. O'Connor, Mary, now deceased, who was the wife of H P Antis, also now deceased, George, who lives in Kentucky, Susan. who is the wife of Albert Lyons, of Lyonsville, Center county, Ellen, who is the wife of Frank Smart, of Keating Summit, Potter county, Pa , John W , who lives in Jefferson county, Pa., Harry B , who is in business at Cleveland, O , Lydia, now deceased, who was the wife of Wallace Woodward, of DuBois, Pa , and Creighton, who died at the age of thirteen years

Mr and Mrs O'Connor have had seven children, namely· William P , who is train dispatcher for the B & O. Railroad at New Castle, Pa. (married Della Lewis, of Youngstown, O), Edward, who lives at Green River, Wyo , Frank, who died of diphtheria, a fine youth of sixteen years, Elsie, who is the wife of Donald Reading, and lives at Philadelphia, Harvey Raymond, who is a resident of Chicago, Ill , Charles Sherwood, who is sergeant of marines, in the United States service, attached to the admiral's flag ship, the Connecticut, and has been in the navy for seven years, and Nell, who is the wife of

Lewis Simler, of Johnstown, Pa   Mr O'Connor is a member of the Catholic church, while Mrs O'Connor was reared a Presbyterian He is a member of the order of Railway Trainmen

The father of Mrs O Connor served in the Civil war and when he entered the army the family moved to a farm near Unionville, Pa He returned from his military service with injuries from which he never recovered and died on the farm eighteen months later   Mrs McClellan then moved with her family to Heckley, in Center county, and later to Osceola Mills, in Clearfield county   Subsequently she married Louis Walkey   Her death was caused by a fall on the ice   She lived for three weeks after the accident, passing away on March 6, 1910, at the home of Mr and Mrs O'Connor   Mrs O'Connor's people all came originally from Ireland and like Mr O'Connor's have been more or less connected with railroading and have filled positions of importance with the trustworthiness that is a characteristic of the Irish people

FRANK W EVANS*, who owns the old homestead farm of 190 acres, which is situated in Graham township, has lived here all the thirty-nine years of his life, his birth having taken place in 1871   His parents were Henry and Catherine Evans   Henry Evans was also born in Clearfield county   His business was farming but a large part of his time was taken up in performing public duties, his fellow citizens electing him many times to township offices, thus showing appreciation of his sterling traits of character   He died on this farm in 1910, having survived his wife for five years

Frank W Evans was educated in the schools of Graham township   He has given his entire attention to farming and stockraising and conducts large agricultural operations according to the best approved methods   He was married in 1900 to Lucia A Maines, a daughter of D A Maines and wife, who are old residents of Bradford township   Mr and Mrs Evans have three interesting children, Ethel, Hazel and Catherine   Mr Evans is a representative citizen, one who takes an interest in township matters, serving occasionally in office, and at all times lending his influence to promote good government, local educational advancement, good roads and all the other movements which are designed to add to the general welfare

C A THORP, justice of the peace and general farmer, resides on his valuable farm of 180 acres, which is situated in Greenwood township   He was born on this farm June 29, 1843, and is a son of William T and Christianna (Bear) Thorp, and was an only child

William T Thorp was a farmer and school teacher and was appointed school examiner for teachers   He erected all the buildings now standing on the above mentioned farm and spent many useful and pleasant years here His death occurred when he was seventy-three years of age

C A Thorp attended school in Greenwood township or Bell township as it was then called, after which he spent many years following farming during the summer seasons and engaging in lumbering in the winter time He is cultivating eighty acres of his farm and has fine pasturage for his stock

In 1864 Mr Thorp was married to Miss Hannah Johnson, a daughter of James John-

son, and they have had the following children
Ida, who married Harry Mitchell, a son of
David Mitchell, William T, who married
Vinnie Kirk, John, who married Eva Rank,
James, who is deceased, Walter, who married
Katherine Cooper, Rentz, who married Mary
Kerr, Lulu, who is the wife of J B Gember-
ling, of Philadelphia, Charles, who married
Julia Bell, daughter of Frampton Bell Hoyt,
who married Vaughn Thompson, and Fran-
ces, who is talented in music of which she
is a teacher In politics Mr Thorp is a
Democrat, as was his father, and he is serving
in his third term as a justice of the peace He
has been an active member of the Grange for
35 years, and is a representative citizen of
Greenwood Township

ELMER B SMITH, who conducts a dairy
business on Scribner avenue, DuBois, Pa, and
is a prosperous merchant and respected citizen, has been a resident of Clearfield county
since 1882 but was born in Clarion county,
Pa, June 1, 1864 His parents were Isaac
and Mary (Fulmer) Smith

Isaac Smith was born in Clarion county, a
son of John Smith, who had early settled near
Reedsburg Isaac Smith owned his farm in
Clarion county and spent his life there, his
death occurring in 1896 He married Mary
Fulmer, who died in 1892 They had eight
children born to them John, Calvin, Elmer
B, Addison, Emma, David, Louetta and Dan-
iel Of the above, Addison is deceased
Emma is the wife of J J Brown

Elmer B Smith obtained his education in
the country schools and remained at home until he was eighteen years of age and then came
to DuBois His first employment here was
with the B R & P Railroad, after which he

engaged in lumbering for John DuBois and
still later he bought a farm of forty-two acres,
in Brady township, which he still owns Subsequently he sold his cattle and returned to
DuBois, purchasing at that time the lot on
which he built and then embarked in the dairy
business

On September 8, 1888, Mr Smith was married to Miss Louella Nolder, a daughter of
the late George Nolder, and they have had
seven children, namely Lon, Fred J, Vernon, Grace, Avenell, Yvone and Aileen Mr
and Mrs Smith attend the Methodist Episcopal church In politics he is a Democrat but
he takes only the interest of a good citizen in
political affairs

FRANK REED COOKER,* a well known
agriculturist of Clearfield County, Pa, who
is carrying on operations on his excellent farm
of seventy acres situated in Huston Township,
near the Elk County line, was born in Philadelphia, Pa, March 4, 1846, a son of Samuel
and Lydia (Reed) Cooker

Samuel Cooker, whose parents were born
in Holland, was born near Philadelphia, and in
that city was for a long period the proprietor
of a store In 1850 he went with a party of
men from the Quaker City overland to California in search of gold, and eventually lost
track of his children, all of whom had been
bound out young to his different relatives His
wife died at Pennsburg, Montgomery County,
at the age of sixty-five years The children of
Samuel and Lydia (Reed) Cooker were Lucinda, who married Noah Grove, both now being deceased, William, a member of Company
C, 51st Pa. Vol Inf, who lost his life in the
battle of Petersburg, Benjamin, a member of
the same company and regiment, who died at

Andersonville Prison, Harry, who was also a soldier in a Pennsylvania regiment, Emma, who married William Hutt of Philadelphia, Hannah, who married William Reed of Philadelphia, Frank R, two who died young, and Samuel, who resides in Huston Township

When he was but a boy, Frank R Cooker was put out on a farm in lower Montgomery County, and he worked thereon until his enlistment, in June, 1862, in Company A, 138th Reg, Pa Vol Inf, under Captain Fisher, and he served three years, being mustered out at the end of the war at Harrisburg He served his country like a brave soldier and in the long marches, skirmishes and battles proved himself a cheerful and reliable comrade After the war had closed he went back to Montgomery County, and in 1867 located in Clearfield County, which was then still heavily timbered He worked for a time for old David Horning, and then for quite a period rented farms, but eventually, in 1878, he purchased his present farm from J B Hewett At that time there was only a house located on this property, but Mr Cooker has made all the necessary improvements, and has his land cleared and well cultivated, making it one of the finest tracts of its size in the township The B & S Railroad runs on the south and east boundaries of Mr Cooker's farm, this being the Bennett's Branch division of that line

On March 14, 1877, Mr Cooker was married to Miss Selinda Hewett, daughter of J B Hewett and granddaughter of Ebenezer Hewett, one of the pioneers of Clearfield County Mrs Cooker died in 1890, having been the mother of two children, namely Harry, who married Nora Reeda and is living with his father, and Irving, who married Gertrude Hadley, by whom he has had a daughter, Beatrice, and is residing at Latrobe, Pa Mr Cooker is a member of the Grange and a popular comrade of the G A R He is a Republican in politics

PETER McDERMOTT, a prominent citizen of Morris township, where he holds the office of road supervisor, is also engaged in business as a representative of the Prudential Life Insurance Company, covering the district lying between Philipsburg and Winburne, including the intermediate points He was born in County Galway, Ireland, October 11, 1865, a son of John and Nora (Tolly) McDermott The father, who is also a native of County Galway, Ireland, is still living in Cambria County, Pa, being now 81 years old His wife, the mother of our subject, died February 13, 1908, at the age of 74 years She was a daughter of John and Cecelia (Mel) Tolly The parents of our subject were married in County Galway, the father being a farmer in his native land He was a son of John McDermott who, with his wife died in Ireland

The children of John and Nora (Tolly) McDermott were nine in number, as follows Thomas, a resident of Nanty Glo, Cambria County, Pa, a miner, Patrick, also engaged in mining at Nanty Glo, Pa, John, who died at the age of thirty years at Hook Run, Morris township, this county, Peter, the subject of this sketch, Cecelia, wife of Thomas Harding, of Hook Run, Pa, foreman for a telephone company at Jersey City, Martin, who for a number of years was a mine foreman at Nanty Glo but who recently moved from Hastings where he was in the hotel business and purchased the Home Hotel at Nanty Glo, Pa, Luke Joseph, a U S railway clerk, residing in Tyrone, Pa, and running between New York City and

Pittsburg, and Ellen, wife of George Myers, of Nanty Glo

The brothers, Thomas, Patrick and Peter, came to America in 1885, and later sent for the other members of the family They located first at Osceola Mills, Pa , where they worked at mining, coming to Hawk Run in 1890

Peter McDermott attended the public schools of his native place in Ireland He was reared on a farm and came to America at the age of twenty years He worked for ten years at mining and during this time held office in the labor organizations of his district In 1896 he accepted a position with the Prudential Life Insurance Company, and has never changed his district since starting with the company He is a member of the order of Red Men, Tribe No 96, I O R M of Morrisdale Mines He is a communicant of St Agnes R C church of that place Since coming to this country he has always been known as a staunch Democrat and has been active in the councils of his party He came within two votes of the popular majority for the nomination on the Democratic ticket for representative of Clearfield county, and is now serving in his fourth year as road supervisor, having been elected in a township of 150 or more Republican majority He numbers some of his strongest friends and supporters among the members of the Republican party, a convincing proof of the fact that he commands the public confidence in high measure and has a record of which he need not be ashamed He has been a township resident since February 18, 1887, and for 26 years a resident of the county, and he has never had a law suit during this entire period Mr McDermott is a ready conversationalist and a man well informed on current events He takes much interest in public affairs, as indeed every good citizen should, but does not always do, and his sterling qualities are widely recognized

GEORGE C ROSS,* who is president of the Ferguson Township School Board, is one of the extensive farmers and representative and substantial citizens of this section of Clearfield County, Pa , where he owns 230 acres of valuable land, which lies three miles south of Kerrmoor He was born at Mountain Dale, Cambria County, Pa , and is a son of Joseph and Margaret (Miller) Ross

Joseph Ross was a farmer in Cambria county when the great Civil War broke out He entered the Union army and it is supposed that he died a soldier's death He married Margaret Miller, who was born in Blair County, Pa , and they had four children Harry, who resides at Falling Timber, Cambria County, Pa , J M , who is deceased, Hannah Belle, who is deceased, and George C After all reasonable doubt of the death of her first husband had been removed, Mrs Ross married Philip Holland and they had one son, James Holland, who now lives in Cambria County Mrs Holland died at the age of sixty-five years and her burial was at Mountain Dale, in Cambria County She was a member of the Brethren church

George C Ross had very few advantages of any kind in his youth and a period of two years covered all the schooling he ever had He was only a boy of twelve years when he came to McGees Mills, Clearfield County and he worked on a farm in that neighborhood for three years, after which he went into the woods and was in the employ of the Clearfield Lumber Company for eight years Having acquired some capital by his hard work he then went into a store business with Milton Braton, at Faunce, Pa , but fire destroyed their stock Mr Ross started up again for himself but subsequently sold out and then came to his present farm in Ferguson Township, which was the old family homestead of his father-in-law, Isaac Moore

Mr Ross was married September 12, 1894, to Miss Roxie Moore, who was born September 27, 1878, on this farm and in the present residence, and has always lived near here Her father, Isaac Moore, was also born in Ferguson Township, where he spent his life, his death occurring at the age of thirty-nine years, in 1884, and his burial was in the Zion Baptist Cemetery in Ferguson Township. He married Esther Straw, who was also born in Ferguson Township and now lives at Marron, Pa They had six children, namely Minnie E and Harriet, both of whom are deceased, Olie, who is the wife of Howard Williams, of Ferguson Township, Daisy, who is the wife of Reuben Summers, of Marron, Pa , Roxie, who is the wife of George C Ross, and Elah, who is now deceased Mr and Mrs Ross have nine children Carrie, Clayton, Harry, Inez, Esther, Mildred, Alta, Wilbur and Ruby Mr and Mrs Ross attend the Baptist church

Mr Ross and family have resided on the present farm since April 5, 1906 He carries on general farming and raises stock for his own use Politically he is a Republican, is a member of Kerrmoor Grange, Ferguson Township, and is a stockholder and a member of the board of directors of the La Jose and Ferguson Telephone Company of Ferguson Township

REUBEN B KANTZ, a prosperous farmer and lumberman of Burnside township, was born in Indiana county, Pa , October 7, 1848, a son of John and Sarah (Baker) Kantz He is a grandson of John Kantz, Sr , a native of Germany, who died in Indiana county, Pa

John Kantz, Jr , was born in Lancaster county, Pa , August, 1818 He removed to Indiana county in 1847, and to Burnside township, Clearfield county in 1851, finding employment at the old Patchin mill, in the locality called Slabtown, and he was subsequently engaged in lumbering and saw-mill work for a part of his time each year, farming during the summer His wife Sarah was a daughter of Philip Baker of that part of Snyder county then known as Union county She survived her husband, dying in 1892, while his death occurred in 1894 Their family consisted of six children, namely Philip, formerly a soldier, but now living retired at Clearfield, Pa , Susanna, who is deceased, Reuben B , the subject of this sketch, Emma, who is the widow of John Irwin, Anna, wife of S Heilman, both living in Tacoma, Wash , and George D , who resides on the old homestead

Reuben B Kantz, after obtaining some elementary schooling, began to make himself useful on the parental homestead, assisting his father by teaming and helping to cut logs, and this work he began when but eight years old Marrying at the age of 20, he bought a piece of wooded land which he cleared, living in his present residence, which he built in 1873, and working in the woods during the winter and spring He spent much time on the river also, in rafting and acting as raft pilot until the decline of that industry In more recent years he has been occupied in building both barns and houses throughout this section He is a Republican politically and has served on the school board and in other offices He is a member of the United Brethren church

Mr Kantz married Sue A Bowder, who was

born in Lancaster county, Pa, in 1850, a daughter of Jacob Bowder, a farmer of that locality, who was a Civil war veteran, serving as wagon master He was killed with three others, near Cresson, by being struck by a train during a snow storm in 1874 His wife in maidenhood was Margaret Jane Bennerd, a native of Ireland Mrs Kantz was reared from the age of nine years by Charles and Elizabeth Eden, going to live with him from the time of her mother's death and father's enlistment in the army Her paternal grandparents were John and Anna (Frankfort) Bowder, the former a shoemaker and farmer by occupation, and the father of seven sons, six of them were in the war at one time, also a grandson

Our subject and wife have been the parents of children as follows Pearl, who is now deceased, Charles, a dentist practicing in Philadelphia, who married Lillian Sparks, Howard, of Burnside, who married Marie Fishel, Edwin E, a prominent coal operator of Burnside, who married Sarah Elizabeth Bellis, daughter of the late Thomas Bellis, Milton Leroy, who married Beyrl Duke, resides in Oklahoma, and has three children; Paul S, who graduated at Valparaiso, Ind, in the classic and scientific course and is now superintendent of schools at Spirit Lake, Ida, Guy V, who is a Valparaiso graduate and engaged in teaching school in the state of Washington, Violet E, who attended school at Valparaiso, Ind, and is now teaching in her native township, and Geneva, who is attending school It will be seen from the above family record that the members of Mr Kantz's family are ambitious and enterprising, and is may be further said that they have a habit of "making good" in whatever position they may find themselves

DANIEL JOSIAH SMEAL,* whose valuable farm of thirty-four acres is situated in Boggs Township, on the town line of Blue Ball, is one of the representative men of this section, in which he has lived for many years He was born in Morris Township, Clearfield County, Pa, July 16, 1853, and is a son of Peter and Mary (Goss) Smeal

Peter Smeal was born in Clearfield County in which he spent his life, engaged in farming and lumbering, his death occurring when his son, Daniel J, was a boy of eleven years He was a Democrat in his political views and his sons have followed in his way of thinking He married Mary Goss, who was a daughter of George Goss, and they had six children Ellis, William, Jessie, Luzetta, Daniel J, and Miles, the last named being deceased Luzetta is the wife of Miles Mease The parents of the above family were members of the United Brethren church

Daniel J Smeal has followed farming ever since he was old enough and strong enough to hold an implement He purchased his farm in 1885, from Ellis Smeal, and carries on general farming and raises just enough stock for home use There is a coal mine on the farm, which Mr Smeal has leased to his son, who operates it and supplies coal to the local trade

In 1876 Mr Smeal was married to Miss Mary Ellen Shaw, a daughter of Robert and Elizabeth (Pierce) Shaw, who were residents of Bradford Township, Clearfield County Mrs Smeal is one of the following family born to her parents Olive, who is the wife of Alexander France, Mary Ellen, who is Mrs Smeal, Hannah, deceased, who was the wife of Edward Albert, Winfield, Henrietta, who is the wife of William McQuillan, Harvey,

Walter, and Viola, who is the wife of James Mallory

Mr and Mrs Smeal have nine children, namely: Frances, who is the wife of James Myers, Sheridan, Mabel, who is the wife of Delbert James, and Foster, Arnold, Grant, Roland, Walter and Raymond Mr Smeal and family attend the United Brethren church He has served his township in the office of roadmaster for two and one-half terms

JOSEPH LAROCK,* who operates a general custom saw mill, cutting timber on State land, by contract, is a resident of Pike township, and owns a valuable farm of fifty acres, situated in Union Township He was born in the Dominion of Canada, April 15, 1842

Mr Larock came to the United States in 1860 and worked for some years in the Maine woods, having been identified with lumber interests ever since He has been a resident of Clearfield County for about forty years and is well and favorably known He was married in this county to Miss Deborah Johnston, and they have nine children, namely Martha, who is the wife of John Rieter, Rebecca, who is the wife of William Durham, Josephine, who moved to Michigan after marriage, and John, Rose, Amanda, Anthony, Andrew and Della all residing at home Mr Larock and family are members of the Catholic church at Rockton, Pa In politics he is a Democrat Although a large part of his time is taken up with his contract timber work, he is interested also in farming and is a member of the Grange

JOSEPH GILLILAND, a leading member of one of the prominent old families of Centre and Clearfield Counties, Pa, who is engaged in a general mercantile business at Karthaus, was born January 6, 1841, at Sprucetown, Centre County, Pa, and is a son of John and Lydia (Smith) Gilliland

John Gilliland was born at Spring Mills, Centre County, July 15, 1806, and his death occurred March 5, 1888 His parents were Joseph and Catherine (Cowden) Gilliland, and his grandfather was James Gilliland, a native of Ireland The Gillilands moved from Chester into Centre County, where Joseph Gilliland settled, acquiring land in Potter Township, which was the old family homestead and was retained as such until 1906, when it was disposed of John Gilliland lost a leg in early youth but nevertheless he became a useful and very active man and although he was forced to use a crutch, became so accustomed to its use that he could walk faster than others who had full use of both limbs For eighteen years he taught school, riding back and forth on horseback He then went into the mercantile business, buying the Penn's Valley Trading Company, under the firm name of Boozer & Gilliland, which later became J & R Gilliland and continued until 1857, when he took up his residence in Karthaus Township, where he had up to this time, conducted a branch store In politics he was a Democrat He married Lydia Smith, who was born March 11, 1808, at Boalsburg, Centre County, Pa, and died in Karthaus Township, Clearfield county, January 22, 1889 She was a daughter of William and Hannah (Lytel) Smith

William Smith, the grandfather of Mrs Gilliland, was an officer in a Pennsylvania regiment in the Revolutionary War and afterward engaged in farming and also operated a mill, in Lancaster County, where his son, William Smith, Jr, was born The latter engaged in teaching during his early manhood and later conducted a store at Warrior's Mark In 1808 he settled at Smithfield, now a part of Bellefonte, where he followed merchandising for a time and later resumed teaching His death occurred before the marriage of his daughter, he and his wife passing away at Boalsburg

Four sons and two daughters were born to William and Lydia Gilliland, namely Hannah Catherine; Joseph; William Smith, Edward I, who was engaged in numerous business enterprises at Pottersdale prior to his death, on July 19th, 1906, Mary Ann, who lives at Karthaus; and Robert Cowden, who resides at Snow Shoe, Centre County

Joseph Gilliland attended school at Centre Hill until he accompanied the family to Karthaus Township, in 1857 After his marriage in 1866, he engaged in farming near Salt Lick and worked at lumbering during the winter seasons He continued to live on that farm until the fall of 1869 and then removed his residence to a hotel at Salt Lick, continuing his farm activities and also operated the hotel from 1869 until 1873, when he sold the same He then became a clerk for Dr J W Potter, at Pottersdale, remaining until 1877, when he disposed of property he still owned in this vicinity and then engaged in operating a mill and general store in partnership with his brother-in-law, Joseph Yothers In the spring of 1882 he bought his partner's interest and continued the mill and store for six years, when he sold to R L Potter and returned to Salt Lick In 1889 he bought store buildings there and with his brother, Edward I Gilliland, conducted a mercantile business until the spring of 1898, when he disposed of the same to James Hunter, and then moved to Lock Haven, where he lived until October 31, 1908, then moving to Karthaus In the following March he bought his

present store from Joseph A. Heckendorn and still continues in the mercantile business at this point During his residence at Lock Haven he was in the cigar manufacturing business and while there he and Aaron Kyler established the second laundry in that city He has always been a man of business enterprise and is widely known through this section of the state

Joseph Gilliland was married May 17, 1866, to Miss Adeline Yothers, who was born in what is now Karthaus Township, and died December 30, 1878, and her burial was at Keewaydin, Covington Township She was a daughter of Joseph and Elizabeth (Reiter) Yothers, people of German extraction, who came to Clearfield from Centre County Two daughters were born to this marriage, Lydia Elizabeth and Clara Bell. The latter is the wife of James Heaney and they live at Vintondale, Cambria County, and they have had four children· Adeline G, born October 24, 1892, who died at the age of one year; Anna Lucetta, born August 1, 1894, Joseph G, born March 12, 1898, and Mabel E, born November 30, 1904

Mr Gilliland was married secondly in October, 1880, to Miss Lucetta B Lucas, of Snow Shoe, Centre County Her father, John Lucas, was in the War of 1812, and was wounded in the battle of Lake Erie, September 10, 1813, and was afterward known at Perry John Lucas He was awarded a medal by Congress as one of Commodore Perry's veterans His death occurred in September, 1858, at the age of sixty-nine years In National politics Mr Gilliland votes with the Democratic party but in local affairs is independent From 1877 until 1881 he was postmaster at Pottersdale He is a member of the Methodist Episcopal church

CHARLES EDWARD ROBACKER,* outside foreman and weigh boss for the Penfield Coal and Coke Company at Penfield, Pa , has lived in Clearfield County all his life   He was born on his father's farm, situated two miles southwest of Penfield, Pa , April 11, 1877, and is a son of Charles and Georgia (Hanes) Robacker

Charles Robacker was born in Luzerne County, Pa , and grew up in the lumber regions there, and was one of the early settlers from Kettle Creek that came to Clearfield County about the time that Hiram Woodward located here   For many years Charles Robacker was foreman for John DuBois in his lumber camps and later he operated a general store at Penfield, in partnership with E S Gray, which was continued for ten years   He then purchased the present C E Robacker farm from a Mr Abbott, an early settler, and finished the clearing of the land and erected buildings and made numerous improvements His death occurred in October, 1894, when he was over sixty years of age   He was a steady, capable man and enjoyed the respect of those with whom he was associated   He was thrice married   His first wife was the mother of two children Lillian, who is the wife of W D Woodward, Jr , and Ella, now deceased, who was the wife of E S Gray   Mr Robacker's second wife was Amelia Thompson, who died without issue   His third marriage was to Georgia Hanes   She was born at Baltimore, Md , and resides with her son, Charles Edward Her second son, Frank O , is foreman of the St Mary's Gazette, at St Mary's

Charles E Robacker has always made his present farm his home   He attended the public schools at Penfield and then engaged in farming in the summers and in teaming in the winters   When his father died he took charge of the farm in Huston Township   On April 14, 1902, he entered the employ of the Penfield Coal and Coke Company, after receiving an injury while at work in the woods   Mr Robacker began with this company as weigh man and in September, 1910, succeeded Alexander Stewart as outside foreman   He has proved reliable, efficient and trustworthy

Mr Robacker married Miss Abigail W Wickett, a daughter of Martin Wickett, who makes his home with Mr and Mrs Robacker They have two children, Mary Helen and Bernice Irene   Mr Robacker is a member of Penfield Lodge No 567, I O O F , and has been through all the chairs, he belongs also to the Grand Lodge at Penfield, of which he has been secretary for the past two years. to the Encampment at Benezette, Pa , and to the Maccabees at Penfield   He usually votes with the Democratic party   For four years he has been a member of the school board and its secretary for three years   Mr Robacker was one of the organizers of the Penfield Band, of twenty-three pieces and is its manager

BLAKE W NORRIS,* one of the prominent citizens and substantial farmers of Ferguson Township, who for the past five years has served continuously as township road supervisor, lives on his valuable farm of 145 acres, which lies one and one-half miles northeast of Kerrmoor, Pa   He was born on Montgomery Creek, in Pike Township, Clearfield County, Pa , October 30, 1871, and is a son of T S and Mary J (Askey) Norris

T. S Norris was born March 24, 1837, in Lawrence Township, Clearfield County, a son of John and Priscilla (Bloom) Norris   He went to school in both Lawrence and Pike

Townships and afterward followed farming
He was a well known and highly respected resident of Ferguson Township for many years,
a member of the Masonic lodge at Curwensville He was a Republican in his political
views In youth he had united with the Methodist Episcopal church He married Mary J
Askey, who was born January 12, 1840, in
Center County, Pa, a daughter of Ellis and
Annie (Wodel) Askey The father of Mrs
Norris was a well known pilot on the Susquehannah River, who lost his life while at the
post of duty, at Lock Haven He was survived by his widow and nine children of whom
three sons and one daughter (Mrs Norris)
still are living To T S Norris and wife the
following children were born Nora, who married Joseph Soul of Clarke County, Mont,
Perry, who married Ella Shoning, and lives on
the old Smith farm near New Millport, Minnie, who died at the age of nineteen years, and
was buried at Curwensville, Laura, wife of
Oscar Ferguson, of Eureka, Calif, Wade, who
married Clara Tobias and lives in Ferguson
Township, Grant, who lives at Braddock, Pa,
and married Katherine Ferguson, Ella, who is
the wife of George M DeHaas Blake W,
who married Lulu Curry, a daughter of William Curry May, who is the wife of George
Thurston, of Clearfield, and Ida, Caleb, Mary
and Thomas, the last twins, all four of whom
are now deceased, their burial being in Williams cemetery, in Ferguson Township

Blake W Norris has spent the larger part
of his life on the home farm His father did
all the remodeling of the buildings, which are
substantial and comfortable Mr Norris has
no open coal bank and has about fifty acres
yet in valuable timber He is a stockholder
in the C & C Telephone Company and is a

member of Kerrmoor Grange He is one of
the active Republicans of Ferguson Township.

JOHN H HORNING, one of the substantial citizens of Clearfield county, Pa, who is
engaged in cultivating Manta Vista Farm, a
tract of 125 acres of excellent land situated
about one mile east of Penfield, in Huston
township, was born on his father's farm in
Montgomery county, Pa, September 22, 1853,
a son of David and Susan D (Hunsicker)
Horning

David Horning was born January 3, 1819,
in Montgomery county, and was there married to Susan D Hunsicker, in March, 1845
Later he came to Clearfield county, locating on
the farm which is now occupied by John H
Horning Here he continued to reside until
his death, which took place in 1905 His wife,
who was born in Montgomery county in 1826,
passed away in 1892 They were the parents
of seven children, as follows William and
Mary, who died when about six years old, David, who died at the age of 27 years, Lewis
H, who resides in Huston township, John
H, subject of this sketch, Sarah Ella, who died
at the age of six years, and Emma, who died
aged three years

John H Horning spent his youth much as
did other farmers' boys of his day, attending
the district schools when he could be spared
from the duties of the farm He accompanied the family to Clearfield county, and on the
settlement of his father's estate received his
present property, which he has been cultivating
successfully ever since Although his agricultural operations have kept him pretty busy,
he has found time to serve his township in several official capacities, having been school director for nine years, and treasurer of the

road fund for three years, an office he now holds In political matters he is a Democrat, and he is also an active worker in behalf of the Grange

On April 28, 1881, Mr Horning was married to Samantha Hevener, a daughter of Nancy Hevener and a granddaughter of Philip Hevener, who at one time owned our subject's present farm, where she spent her childhood She lived for some time in Minnesota and was a resident of Mt Pleasant for 16 years, teaching school and both vocal and instrumental music A member of the Methodist Episcopal church, she played and sang in that church for about 30 years, but is now a member of the Christian Science church Mr and Mrs Horning have been the parents of three children, namely June Bell, who was educated at Clarion Normal School, Grove City College, and the Cincinnati Bible school, and is now an evangelist, John Kline, a graduate of the Penfield High school, who is now at home on the farm, and Willie Hevener (Horning) who died in infancy

GEORGE BREON KIRK, M D, a well known physician and surgeon of Clearfield County, whose field of practice is the thriving town of Kylertown, Pa, has been located here for the past thirteen years, and is a member of one of Clearfield County's old and honored families Dr Kirk was born at Luthersburg, in Brady Township, Clearfield County, Pa, May 10, 1873, and is a son of Joseph H and Anna (Goodlander) Kirk

William Kirk, the grandfather of Dr Kirk, carried on agricultural operations in the vicinity of Luthersburg, where his father had been an early settler On the maternal side, Dr Kirk is descended from another early settler of Luthersburg who was a farmer and hotel keeper and the proprietor of a shoemaking establishment The children of William Kirk were as follows Dr M A Kirk, of Bellefonte, Dr Thomas Kirk, of Burr Oak, Kans, Brady, also of Burr Oak, Kans, Dr Ellis Kirk (deceased), formerly of Cleveland, O, John (deceased), three who died in infancy, Mary, also deceased (Mrs Erastus Luther of Troutville), and Joseph H The mother of Dr Kirk also belonged to a large family, her sisters and brothers being Hon George B deceased, who resided in Clearfield, Daniel, deceased, who lived in Luthersburg, Charles, residing on a farm near DuBois, Sophia, who is the wife of George Nolder of Luthersburg, Mary, who is the widow of the late Joseph Shugarts of Luthersburg; Jane, who is the widow of the late James Schofield, Clara, who is the wife of William Dilley, Mrs Fred Arnold, Reynoldsville, deceased, Sadie, wife of Wm Porter, of Brookville, Pa, Catherine, deceased, Margaret, deceased, and one who died in infancy

Joseph H Kirk was born at Luthersburg, Brady Township, and as a young man learned the trade of wagon and carriage maker, spending his entire life in Luthersburg except the last two years He is of Quaker origin, although his wife's family were all Lutherans Mrs Kirk died in about 1900 Nine children were born to Joseph H and Anna Kirk, namely Alice, who married D A Moyer of Kylertown, Lorana, who is living at home, Nora, also residing at home, Harvey, a bookkeeper of Philadelphia, who married Agnes Clark, George Breon, Dr Charles, who is engaged in practice at Troutville, Elizabeth, who is the wife of the Rev James Heron, of Iowa, a Presbyterian minister, Mary, who is a teacher in the Clearfield public schools and Ralph, who is a student at the State College, taking a course in mining engineering

George Breon Kirk attended the public schools of Brady Township, the Bellfonte High school and the State normal school at Lockhaven, and then taught school for four years in Brady Township At the end of this time he entered the Baltimore Medical College, from which he was graduated with the class of 1898, immediately after which he located in Kylertown, where he has since built up a large and lucrative practice

In the spring of 1899, Dr Kirk was married to Miss Alice Barrett Moore, of Luthersburg, and three sons have been born to this union, namely Robert, Thomas and John Mrs Kirk was educated in the public schools of DuBois, where her parents, R H and Henrietta (Barrett) Moore, resided for some years Dr. Kirk is a member of the Clearfield County Medical Society, of which he is secretary, and also holds membership in the West Branch, State and National associations, and of Moshannon Lodge No 391 of Philipsburg, F. & A M. He is a Democrat in his political views

MARSHALL HUMPHREY LEWIS, for many years a citizen of Clearfield county, Pa, and a veteran of the Civil war, was born at Port Matilda, Center county, Pa, in Bald Eagle Valley, February 13, 1842, and is a son of William and Susan (Neal) Lewis

William Lewis, a son of William Lewis, who came to Center county from near Philadelphia, was born December 31, 1813, at Bellefonte, Center county, Pa, and died January 25, 1909, at Tyrone, Pa, in his ninety-sixth year. In 1840 at Stormstown, in Half Moon Valley, he was married to Susan Neal, then a widow. She was born in Mercer county, in 1813, but was reared in Center county and died in 1854 She was a daughter of John Neal and a cousin of both Judge and Sheriff Neal, both prominent men Three children were born to William and Susan Lewis, namely. Marshall H, Hannah, who is the wife of James B. Williams, of Port Matilda, and Medora, who was married first to James T Marks, and secondly to Henry Bennett, of Port Matilda William Lewis was married secondly to Ann Elizabeth Kelley, who survives and resides at Tyrone There were four children born to this marriage, as follows William M, who lives at Tyrone, Mary, who died in 1908 (was married first to William Ardery and secondly to Rankin Mc-Monigal), Minnie, who is the wife of Charles Trimble, of Tyrone, and Orlando, who lives with his family at Elmira, N Y. William Lewis was an engineer by profession and operated stationary engines during the greater part of his active life

Marshall H. Lewis attended the district school at Port Matilda in his boyhood and for two winters the Buffalo Run School in Center county, Pa When thirteen years of age he went to work for Samuel T Gray and remained with him until July 19, 1861, when he enlisted for service in the Civil war, entering Co I, 5th Pa Reserves After the termination of his first enlistment he re-enlisted, at Catlett Station, Va, entering Co C, 191st Pa. Regt, December 27, 1863, and continued a Federal soldier until he received his final discharge on July 3, 1865, having served four years, less sixteen days He took part in many of the most important battles of the war, including: The seven days' fight under Gen McClelland, the second battle of Bull Run, Antietam, Fredericksburg, Gettysburg and the Wilderness He received a slight wound at Charles City Cross Roads, Va, and was captured in front of what was known as the Yellow House, at Petersburg, Va, and was incarcerated in Libby prison, on Belle Island and at Salisbury, N C He was present at the surrender of General Lee, at Appomattox, and later took part in the Grand Review at Washington, D C He is a member of the John W Geary Post, No 90, G A R, at Philipsburg, Pa, uniting with it in 1878 Mr Lewis still preserves his interest in everything pertaining to that great period, attends reunions and meets frequently the comrades who, like himself had so much to do with preserving the Union He is now in his seventieth year but is as well preserved as a man ten years younger On November 16, 1911, he was present at Salisbury, N C, to witness the unveiling of the monument there in memory of those who died in that prison, during the Civil war, Mr Lewis having been mercifully preserved from the fate that met many of his companions

After the close of his military service, Mr Lewis returned to Port Matilda and worked there in a saw mill until 1867, when he came to what was then Morris but now is Cooper township, Clearfield county, locating on a tract of ten acres, one mile south of Kylertown, where he has carried on general farming

Mr Lewis was married August 3, 1868, in Morris township, Clearfield county, by Andrew Hunter, J P, to Miss Philcy Dillen, a daughter of George R and Catherine (Merritt) Dillen, the latter of whom was a cousin of the late General Merritt, of the U S A Mrs Lewis was born November 18, 1850, in Morris township, to which her father had

moved March 26, 1829, from the Bald Eagle Valley, Center county. He died in Clearfield county in 1875, at the age of seventy-four years, being survived by his widow until 1885, she also being seventy-four years old George R Dillen was a Democrat in politics and filled numerous township offices Mr Lewis now has in his possession the old Morris township record book, which was started in 1836 and is complete as to the affairs of the school board from 1842 until 1870 It is very interesting as it marks the development of the township as to school privileges and incidentally of other matters of progress Mrs Lewis is one of a family of fourteen children, there being seven sons and seven daughters born to her parents

Mr and Mrs Lewis have nine living children, namely Ora Etta, who was born November 18, 1869, married A E Fifield, of New York, and after his death was married secondly to E C Shobert, of Brookville, and now lives in Caledonia, Pa, Ida W, who was born August 12, 1871, married A P Mingle, of Philipsburg, Pa, and they reside at Altoona, Pa, Hannah Gertrude, who was born May 27, 1874, married George Kelley, of Johnstown, Pa, and they live at Altoona, Melville Ralph, who was born June 22, 1876, is an employe of the Whitmer Steel Company, of Hawk Run, Luella Kate, who was born July 14, 1878, married Rufus E Cole, of Philipsburg, and they reside at Clearfield, Rhoda Amber, who was born January 21, 1884, is the wife of Isaac E Lucas, and they live at Winburne, Susan Alta, who was born April 28, 1886, married William McKinney; Edward Thorne, who was born November 5, 1889, lives at home, and Sarah Ruth, who was born March 6, 1894, and resides with her parents Two children died in infancy Jay Clyde and Ark Neal

For forty-four years Mr Lewis has been a citizen of Cooper township and is known practically by every one His comfortable residence he erected in 1888 He has occupied himself with agriculture but for the past twenty-five years he has been a public auctioneer and in this capacity is frequently in different parts of the county He has been a Democratic voter ever since reaching his majority and has always been more or less active in politics and exerts considerable political influence In the fall elections he was elected a jury commissioner on the Democratic ticket but has never been especially anxious for office He enjoys attending political conventions and has to his credit, five Republican gatherings of this kind in the state and eleven Democratic On many occasions he has shown political wisdom that has been of great assistance in furthering the ambition of his friends, while he has refused offices for himself Mr Lewis was reared in the Baptist faith and has always tried to live according to the precepts learned at his mother's knee In peace as well as in war he has lived usefully and uprightly and is worthy of the high esteem in which he is held by his fellow citizens

REV ANTHONY HOUST,* who has been pastor of the Sacred Heart Slavish Roman Catholic Church at Houtzdale Pa , for the past nine years, is a man of scholarly attainments and an authority on many branches of church history Rev Father Houst was born in Bohuslavitz, Austria-Moravia, and was educated in his native land at Munich, at Gaya College, and at Nicholsburg After completing his studies at Munich, he was ordained on September 26, 1882, at Southburg, Austria

Father Houst then came to America landing at New York, on December 8, 1882, where he remained for three months He then went to Louisville, Ky , for six months, after which he spent eleven years at St Louis, Mo His next call was to Long Island City, N. Y , where he labored for one year, going then to Fayetteville, Tex , for nine months, and for two years afterward, had charge of the Bohemian church at Pittsburg, Pa Another year was passed at Yonkers, N Y , and from there he came to Houtzdale, in 1902, becoming pastor of the Sacred Heart church Here he has a congregation of more than 300 and the larger number of these are honest, hard-working people, who own their own homes and willingly contribute to the support of the church in which they desire to rear their children Father Houst takes a personal interest in all his parishioners and encourages them in their prudent acquisition of property The church property has been much improved since Father Houst took charge and its accommodations are modern in character His people are mainly connected with the mining regions and the larger number live outside of Houtzdale, this scattering making the duties of the priest more onerous than they would otherwise be, but through his tender spiritual care and his watchfulness over their daily lives, he has greatly endeared himself and the church is well supported Father Houst has found time to do considerable literary work and in 1890 published a complete history of the Bohemian Catholic Church in the United States He is a member of the Catholic Slavish Union

JOHN WALTER BLOOM,* a prosperous farmer in Ferguson Township, who owns fifty acres of excellent land which is situated three miles west of Kerrmoor, Pa , was born at

Bloomington, in Pike Township, September 19, 1866, and belongs to one of the old county families

Mr Bloom was reared on the home farm and attended the Curry school-house where all his boyhood schooling was obtained He continued to help his father on the home place until his marriage, after which he lived at Bloomington for three years and then bought his present farm, formerly known as the Lewis farm He has it all under cultivation with the exception of fifteen acres still in timber

On April 15, 1896, Mr Bloom was married to Miss Alvina Lewis, who was born on this farm, May 27, 1873, a daughter of T H and Elizabeth (McCracken) Lewis T H Lewis was born in Pike Township, near Curwensville, a son of Washington Lewis, whose last years were spent at Reynoldsville, Jefferson County, where he died at the age of eighty-four years The father of Mrs Bloom was a carpenter by trade and also owned and operated this farm He married Elizabeth McCracken, who died June 8, 1900 They had the following children Ella, Mary, Alvina, Eliza, Margery, Amanda and two that died young Mr and Mrs Bloom are members of the Baptist church In politics he is a Democrat They have four children Lillian, William, Eliza and Harry Mr Bloom is a member of the Grange at Kerrmoor He is a good citizen, law abiding and public spirited, but he has never been willing to accept political office

SAMUEL R MOORE,* whose business is that of a mining engineer, is professionally connected with ten mines at Madera, Pa, and is well known all through this section He was born in Blair County, Pa, and is a son of Charles W and Emma (Hewitt) Moore

Charles W Moore, who is one of Madera's well known business men, was born in 1845 in Blair County, Pa, a son of Jesse Moore, who was an early settler there Charles W Moore was married in 1873 to Emma Hewitt, who was born at Hollidaysburg, Pa, and of their family of six children, Samuel R is the eldest

Samuel R Moore attended the public schools but was more ambitious than many of his schoolmates and made better use of his opportunities Finding that his talents and inclination lay in the direction of his present profession, he applied himself to the study of the same under the superintendence of the International Correspondence School of Scranton, Pa, completed the course and immediately made practical use of his knowledge His present position he has filled for the past two and one-half years

In 1897 Mr Moore was married to Miss May Williamson, who was born in Tioga County but was reared in Jefferson County, Pa, a daughter of Peter and Anna (Bolan) Williamson She is the youngest of a family of six children, the others being Frank, who is deceased, Thomas, John William, Catherine, who is the wife of George Kline, and Anna, who is the wife of Noah Treharne Mr and Mrs Williamson were members of the Catholic church To Mr and Mrs Moore five children have been born, namely Lilly, John, Charles, James and Ellen The political views of Mr Moore make him a Republican With his family he attends the Presbyterian church He belongs to Masonic bodies at Punxsutawney and Williamsport

W S CARR, president of the Curwensville Rural Telephone Company, is one of Pike

Township's substantial citizens and lives on his farm of sixty-five acres, which lies three miles northeast of Curwensville, Pa He was born on this farm, September 17, 1857, and is a son of Benjamin and Elizabeth (Williams) Carr, and a grandson of Asil and Katherine Carr

W S Carr attended the Pleasant Grove school during the winter sessions until he was about eighteen years of age, after which his winters were mainly spent in the lumber regions, while he devoted his summers to farm work As there was no necessity for him to leave the homestead he remained on it and since coming into possession, at the death of his parents, has done a large amount of improving He has cleared about one-third of the farm by himself and now has it all under cultivation with the exception of ten acres in standing timber The buildings erected by his father had became a little dilapidated but he repaired, rebuilt and otherwise improved them Perhaps his farm is underlaid with a vein of coal but he has no open bank nor has he ever leased any land

Mr. Carr was married first in December, 1882, to Miss Mary Thompson, who died in 1893 Her burial was in the cemetery attached to the Center Methodist Episcopal Church, of which she was a member She was survived by a son, Benjamin Frank, who resides at Karthaus, Clearfield County, Pa He married Fannie Shearer and they have one daughter, Florence Mr Carr was married secondly in September, 1896, to Miss Orie Bloom, a daughter of Z M and Charlotte Bloom, and they have eight children, namely William, Blair, Melvin, Phillip, Elizabeth, Edith, John and Edna Mr Carr and family are members of the Methodist Episcopal church He is identified with the Republican party and has frequently served in political positions, having been judge and inspector of elections and several times a delegate to the county conventions of his party He is a member of the local Grange, of which he has been overseer, and he belongs to the Order of the Moose, at Curwensville

FRED B LEAVY,* proprietor of an undertaking establishment, is also engaged in the coal and livery business at Clearfield, Pa , and has been a lifelong resident of Clearfield County He was born December 20, 1877, in Clearfield, Pa , a son of Augustus B and Martha (Merrill) Leavy

Hugh Leavy, grandfather of our subject, was a native of County Donegal, Ireland, and was one of the pioneers of Clearfield County, Pa His cousin, Father Leavy, was a priest, and traveled through this circuit, and it was he who asked Hugh Leavy to come here and build the Roman Catholic Church It was a brick building and the first Catholic Church erected in this section of the country Hugh Leavy married Sarah Wrigley, who was born in Lawrence township, Clearfield County, Pa , and they reared a family of seven boys and two girls, all now deceased

Augustus Leavy was born and reared in Clearfield County, Pa , and was the second eldest of the nine children born to his parents He spent his boyhood on his father's farm and later with his brother James engaged extensively in the lumber business, having been members of the well known firm of Leavy, Mitchell & Company He and his brothers also ran the old stage for a time Mr Leavy married Martha Merrill, who was a daughter of William and Rebecca (Reed) Merrill, and to them were born eight children: Lillian, William J ,

Hugh, deceased, Rebecca, who married Edward Ditmer of Indiana, Pa , Fred Bernard, our subject, Mary Catherine, and Cecil P Mr Leavy died September 9, 1910, and is still survived by his widow, who is the only surviving member of her family

Fred Bernard Leavy was educated in the local schools of Clearfield, and in 1897 formed a partnership with his uncle James L Leavy, with whom he established an undertaking and coal business After the death of his uncle on June 20, 1903, he became sole owner of the business and in 1907 graduated from the Pittsburg School of Embalming, and the following year from the H S Eckles School of Embalming of Philadelphia Mr Leavy has his office and residence on the corner of Second and Cherry streets, and owns his own funeral cars He is fraternally a Mason, and belongs to the B P O E , M O O L , I O O F , K G E , O U A M , and is religiously a member of the Presbyterian church

STACY BOWMAN,* farmer and coal operator and president of the Bloomington Rural Telephone Company, is one of Pike Township's prominent and substantial citizens and resides on his farm of ninety-seven acres, which is situated two and three quarter miles south of Curwensville, Pa Mr Bowman was born April 3, 1865, in Knox Township. Clearfield County, Pa , and is a son of Jonathan and Eliza Bowman

Stacy Bowman attended the McCalm school in Lawrence Township when he was a boy and then accompanied his parents to Pike Township, his father purchasing the A A Long farm, which is now owned by Samuel and Paul Bowman Stacy Bowman remained on the home farm until his marriage, when he moved

to O'Shanter, where he lived for one year, going then to Olanta for a few months, after which he came to the farm he now owns This place remained under his management for three years, when he moved on the George Bowman farm in Knox Township, one year later returning to O'Shanter, where he operated a meat market for one year In 1900, he moved back to this farm, which he purchased Mr Bowman operates a coal bank, having a daily output of from seventy-five to 100 bushels Mr Bowman and family have a very comfortable residence, although it is one of the oldest in the township, having been built in 1822 On June 17, 1903, Mr Bowman was made postmaster of Bloomington and conducted the office in this residence until the introduction of rural mail delivery, in 1907

On April 10, 1890, Mr Bowman was married to Miss Maud E Wise, a daughter of Moses and Elmira J Wise Moses Wise was born in Center County, Pa , October 17, 1817, a son of Conrad and Margaret (Rote) Wise Moses Wise was a boy when he came to Clearfield County, where he spent the remainder of his life He cleared a farm of almost 100 acres and died there On June 22, 1847, he married Elmira Bloom, a daughter of Abraham Bloom Her death occurred in 1870 To this marriage nine children were born, six sons and three daughters. the survivors being John L , Amos Albert, Oliver B , Mrs Thomas Lord and Mrs Stacy Bowman The Wise family has been one of considerable prominence in this section for years The grandfather of Mrs Bowman was born in Germany in 1780 When he moved from Center to Clearfield County, he purchased land that was later locally known as the Lorenzo Price farm Moses Wise, father of Mrs Bowman, on leaving home, purchased the farm formerly owned by Samuel Thomas, who built the old log house still standing, in 1855 Later he sold to David Arnold, from whom Moses Wise bought The latter was a well known lumberman He moved to Altoona some years before his death, which occurred at the home of our subject August 17, 1910, and his burial was in the Bloomington Cemetery He was a member of the Lutheran church and was an example of Christian manhood

To Mr and Mrs Bowman, eleven children have been born, as follows Verna, who is the wife of Frank Soulsby, Clyde, who died September 17, 1893, and Pearl, Lloyd, Goldie, Hazel, Moses Harold, Erla, Lynn, Levada and Stacy Albert Mr Bowman and family are members of the Methodist Episcopal church In his political attitude he is an independent Democrat, and has served four years as a school director in Pike Township He belongs to no fraternal organization except the local Grange Mr Bowman is known as an upright, honorable man in every relation of life and is a worthy representative of Pike Township's best citizenship

GUY L JOHNSON, residing on his farm near Grass Flat, Cooper Township, was born on this farm December 1, 1870, and is a son of Abiah D and Sarah (Dillon) Johnson In addition to farming, Mr Johnson has been a funeral director since 1899

Abiah D Johnson, father of Guy L, was born in Bradford County, Pa, November 9, 1828, and came to Clearfield County in 1852 and purchased the farm on which he still resides It contained 125 acres but a part has been sold in town lots of Grass Flat He bought the land of Samuel Christ, the latter being one of the large landowners of the county It was heavily timbered and wild game was plentiful Guy L Johnson recalls his mother relating that on numerous occasions she saw as many as nine deer leaping over the lane fence near the house, on their way to the deep woods Mr Johnson married Sarah Dillon, who was born in 1831 and died December 7, 1902 To them five sons and three daughters were born, namely Charles, who died at the age of fifty-four years, was survived by his widow, formerly Addie Bryaton, E A, who is postmaster at Grass Flat, Mary, who is the wife of William Pelton, a farmer near Munson Station, Bertha, who is now deceased, was the wife of Willard Marshall, M Grant, who owns property and lived in Cooper Township until the spring of 1910, has been a resident of California since then, married Orpha Ralston, and they have one child, Andrew Curtin, who resides on his farm in Huntingdon county, married Matilda Raymond, Guy L, and Helen, who is the wife of E C Hipple, of Cooper Township

Guy L Johnson attended school in his native locality until he was about eighteen years of age and since then has more or less conducted operations on the home farm As a funeral director he is known all through this section, being well equipped for the business and conducting it on all occasions, with befitting dignity and efficiency.

In 1900 Mr Johnson was married to Miss Zella Hoover, who was reared in Cooper township, a daughter of Gilbert and Margery (Zimmerman) Hoover They have one son and two daughters· Vaughn, Ivy and Vera Mrs Johnson is a member of the Methodist Episcopal church Mr Johnson is deeply interested in the Grange and had much to do with organizing this agricultural order at Grass Flat For three years he has served as a useful member of the school board and is interested in everything pertaining to the welfare and advancement of this section Politically he is a Republican and fraternally he is an Odd Fellow

ROBERT DUDLEY TONKIN,* manager of the Cherry Tree Iron Works, and one of the leading business men of this part of Clearfield county, was born in Burnside township, this county, July 10, 1880, son of Vincent and Margaret J (Hughes) Tonkin His paternal grandparents, John and Mary (Hicks) Tonkin, came to America in 1831 from Cornwall, England, settling first in Baltimore, Md Later they removed to Germantown, Pa, where they remained one year, removing at the end of that time to Hollidaysburg, Blair County, Pa In 1838 they came to Clearfield county, settling in the vicinity of Cherry Tree, where John Tonkin carried on farming and lumbering until about 1861 He died at the age of 84 years and his wife at that of 83 He was a member of the Whig party in politics, and he and his wife belonged to the Episcopal church

Vincent Tonkin, son of the above and father of this sketch, was born in Cornwall, England, January 5, 1830 and was a babe of 18 months when he accompanied his parents to America When old enough he engaged in the lumber business with his father, and he subsequently bought the old homestead of 300 acres, which he conducted until 1899, when he engaged in the mercantile business He also at some time subsequent to 1866 engaged in the manufacture of boots and shoes by hand, purchasing large quantities of leather He was also for some years engaged in the cattle business, operating through Michigan Indiana and Ohio and shipping his cattle to the eastern markets, driving as many as 150 head at a time After 1865 he was engaged in lumbering near Cherry Tree up to 1885 During that time he was superintendent for the large timber firm of Hopkins & Ervin, but later went into business for himself and so continuing until his final retirement In 1903 he built the largest machine foundry in northern Pennsylvania He was one of the charter members and vice president of the First National Bank of Cherry Tree, and was also interested in various tracts of coal and timber land throughout this section In politics a Republican, he was an active worker for his party

Vincent Tonkin was married October 22, 1879, to Margaret J Hughes, who was born March 14, 1853 at Cherry Tree, Pa, a daughter of Robert and Elinor (Douglass) Hughes, natives of Cambria county Robert Hughes, who was a tanner by trade, carried on his business for a number of years at Ebensburg, Pa, and subsequently built the first tannery at Cherry Tree, which he operated until 1878 He died in 1888 at the age of 65 years. Vincent Tonkin's death occurred March 22, 1908, at Cherry Tree By his marriage with Elinor Douglass there were the following children. Robert Dudley, subject of this sketch, Vivian S, residing at home, Maxie E, wife of R McConnell, of Cherry Tree, Vincent Ord, who married Octo O Nottey, Alice D, a teacher living at home, A Worth, attending school

Robert D Tonkin, after attending Mt Union College, at Alliance, Ohio, began industrial life in the foundry and machine business, first at Cresson, Pa, and subsequently in his father's foundry at Cherry Tree In course of time the management of this latter plant devolved upon him and he has since continued to hold this responsible position, having proved his capacity as a thoroughly practical foundryman He is also interested in the First National Bank, and is a director of the Cambria Title, Savings & Trust Co of Ebensburg, Pa

Mr Tonkin was married June 20. 1905 to Birdis Sechler, who was born August 7, 1880. a daughter of Joseph and Emma (Stough) Sechler, of Cherry Tree, where her father holds the office of postmaster Our subject and wife have been the parents of two children One that died in infancy, and Joseph Dudley, born April 5, 1910 Mr and Mrs Tonkin are members of the Presbyterian church, and are people well known and highly esteemed in this part of Clearfield county, Mr Tonkin, indeed, having a wide business acquaintance, both throughout the county and elsewhere

T D SMAIL,* a leading citizen of Curwensville, a member of the borough council and proprietor of a grocery store on Susquehannah Avenue, was born in Monroe County, Pa, January 8, 1862, and is a son of David and Barbara Smail

David Smail was a farmer and also followed the blacksmith's trade He was a worthy Christian man and a member and elder of the German Reformed church To him and his wife Barbara, eleven children were born, three of whom are now deceased, and T D is the only one of the eight survivors to have his home in Clearfield County

T D Smail obtained his education in the public schools of Eldred Township, Monroe County His first work was done on the Lehigh Valley farm, near Wilkesbarre, Pa, and when only eighteen years of age he was made manager of that farm, a position he occupied for two years On November 9, 1888, Mr Smail came to this section and bought three teams of horses and went to work for Robert Bloom in the lumber regions One year later he bought another team for himself, then sold his horses and for a time was in the employ of the Irwin sisters and later worked for the Curwensville Lumber Company In 1891 he began working as a deliveryman for F J Dyer & Co, continuing until 1905, when he embarked in business for himself at his present stand where he has prospered and built up a fine trade He carries a full line of both fancy and staple groceries and deals honestly and fairly with his customers

In 1884 Mr Smail was married to Miss Jessie Parish, who was born in Luzerne county, Pa, a daughter of Isaac Parish She died in 1886 and was buried at Wyoming, Pa, being survived by one son, Thomas Frederick, who lives at Altoona, Pa In 1893 Mr Smail was married a second time, to Miss Mollie Tate, who was born in Snowshoe township, Center county, a daughter of William Tate Mr and Mrs Smail have two children Carl W, a young man of seventeen years who is his father's chief helper in his business, and Chressa, who is a student in the Curwensville High School Mr Smail and family are members of the German Reformed church He is identified with the Odd Fellows at Snowshoe In politics he is a Republican, but as a citizen and member of the council, he devotes his attention, irrespective of party, to those measures that will promote the general welfare Mr Smail is an example of a self-made man and is one of the borough's most respected men

WILLIAM E TOBIAS, superintendent of the public schools of Clearfield county, Pa, is a man especially well qualified for this important office and is widely known in the educational field He was born in Clearfield county, Pa, November 8, 1866, and is a son of Samuel and Eliza (Erhard) Tobias Samuel Tobias was also a native of Clearfield county and was well known He followed the carpenter's trade in this section and was concerned in the erection of many substantial buildings His death occurred in 1909 He married Eliza Erhard and nine children were born to them

William E Tobias attended the common and high schools near his father's residence and later entered the Central Normal School at Lock Haven, where he was graduated in 1889 Later he entered Allegheny College, from which he graduated with honors in 1897 Shortly afterward he entered upon what has since been his life work, beginning to teach in his earlier years as a matter of expediency and continuing from the love of it and because of his marked success as an educator He is well known in various educational organizations in the state and in him Clearfield county evidently has a superintendent whose ideals of scholastic perfection are very high He is always loyal to his profession his main interest being the upbuilding of the county schools, of which he has had charge since 1905 He has been re-elected for the third time, being the only man who has ever served more than two terms as county superintendent of Clearfield county, up to this time Mr Tobias is identified fraternally with the Masons and the Odd Fellows

ALFRED D McCULLY,* general farmer and a representative citizen of Chest town-

ship, who has resided on his present place for the past twenty-five years, was born on the old McCully homestead in Chest township, June 26, 1850, and is a son of George R and Malinda (Wolf) McCully

George R McCully was born in 1820, at what was then called Wheatland, a small village in Clearfield county He was twelve years old when his parents moved to Jordan township, and there he worked through boyhood and until his marriage at digging iron ore and burning charcoal He then bought the old McCully homestead and after that followed farming and lumbering until 1867, when, on account of his father's need of him on the home farm, he moved back to Jordan township and lived there for seven years, giving his aged father filial care during his last days After the death of his parents he returned to his own farm in Chest township, where his death occurred in 1899 He was a man of sterling character, honest and upright in all his business dealings and was respected by every one with whom he was associated in life For twelve years he served acceptably on the township school board He reared his family in the faith of the Baptist church He married Malinda Wolf, who was born in 1825 and was a daughter of Solomon and Martha (Foutz) Wolf Her people were of German extraction, while the McCullys are of Irish descent Joseph McCully, the grandfather of Alfred D McCully was born in Ireland and was eighteen years of age when he came to America In 1837 he bought his farm in Jordan township and lived there until his death at the age of seventy-six years He married Eliza Edmundson The surviving children of George R McCully and wife are Alfred D, the oldest one of the family to be born on the homestead, John, a resident of Irvona, Pa,

George W, a farmer in Chest township, and Levi, a miner, in Jordan township

Alfred D McCully obtained his education up to fourteen years, in an old log schoolhouse near the McGarvey farm Afterward he worked in the woods until he was twenty-one years of age, was married when about twenty-five years old, and since then has been mainly engaged in farming He has made many improvements on his land and has substantial buildings, finely cultivated fields and each year grows some excellent stock He is numbered with the substantial and successful men of this section

Mr. McCully was married in 1875 to Miss Adelia Barrett, who was born June 20, 1854, in Jordan township, Clearfield county, a daughter of Hiram and Susan (Myers) Barrett, who came from Center county Mr and Mrs McCully's family consists of the following children. Minnie Johns, whom they reared from the age of ten years, and who married Wiley Queen, who is in the railroad service and lives at Irvona (they have three children), Katherine, who is a popular teacher in the public schools of Glen Hope, and John T, who assists his father Mr McCully and family are members of the Baptist church at Fairview, in which he has been a deacon for twenty years In politics he is a Democrat and is very active in campaign work In 1905 he was elected township tax collector and has continued to serve in this office until the present

H O KING, M D, the leading physician and surgeon at Curwensville, Pa, a member of the borough board of health, also district medical state inspector of Pike and Bloomfield townships, and physician for the poor, has a private practice that covers many miles in Clearfield county. He was born in Clarion county, Pa, April 8, 1868, and has been a resident of Curwensville, since September, 1893.

Dr. King attended excellent schools in his youth and after leaving the seminary at West Farmington, O, studied medicine and entered Jefferson Medical College at Philadelphia After graduating he located at Curwensville, where he has continued to reside and here has become vitally connected with the best interests of town and people He is a member of the Clearfield county, Pennsylvania state and the American Medical Associations and has been president of the county body In politics he is a Republican but holds his offices through personal worth rather than political patronage

In September, 1889, Dr King was married to Miss Gertrude Carriar, a daughter of Stewart D Carriar, of Jefferson county, Pa, and they have three children Olive, Orville and Elizabeth Dr. and Mrs King attend the Methodist Episcopal church He belongs to the Royal Arcanum and the Royal Order of Moose In addition to his other duties, Dr King officiates as medical examiner for the following life insurance companies· Hartford, Conn, Life and Provident Trust Company, the Travelers, the Equitable; the Penn Mutual, Meridian, Mutual Benefit of New Jersey; Manhattan, and the Aetna, of Hartford, Conn

ALEXANDER H IRWIN
AUTOMATIC MACHINERY
CURWENSVILLE, PA

FREDERICK CAMPMAN, a highly respected and well known resident of Boggs township, Clearfield county, Pa, where he

H. O. KING, M. D.

owns a farm of 100 acres, in addition to a comfortable residence at Wallaceton, has lived retired since 1905, having been very actively engaged in general farming for a number of years previously He was born in January. 1832, in Germany, and was twelve years old when he accompanied his parents, Anthony Campman and wife, to America

Anthony Campman brought his family to the United States in 1844 and settled first in Maryland, moving from there to Pennsylvania, and while living in Mercer county his death occurred His wife had died before leaving Maryland They had the following children Frederick, Henry, who is deceased, David, Timothy who died while serving as a soldier in the Civil war, and Caroline, who was married first to a Mr Mull, and secondly to a Mr Kelly

Frederick Campman attended school before he left Germany and after reaching the United States was variously engaged, being of a very industrious turn In 1864 he enlisted for service in the Civil war, becoming a member of Co F, 88th Pa Vol Inf, 3rd Div, 3rd Brig, Fifth Corps, and was in the army about nine months, fortunately escaping all serious injury In 1870 he came to his present farm in Boggs township and followed agricultural pursuits continuously until he retired

In 1853 Mr Campman was married first to Miss Esther Mange, who died in 1870, the mother of four children, Henry, David, Mary Ellen and Elizabeth In 1871 Mr Campman was married secondly to Miss Mary E Williams Mr and Mrs Campman are members of the Roman Catholic church In politics he is a Democrat and has served as tax collector and also as borough treasurer He is a valued member of the G A R Post No 90 at Philipsburg, Pa Mr Campman had his own way to make in the world and acquired property and gained the confidence and esteem of his fellow citizens through his own efforts He has contributed of his means to schools and churches and when chosen for public office has performed the duties of the same with care and honesty

FRANK A HOWE, hotel proprietor at Winburne, Pa, has been a resident of Clearfield county all his life, his family being among the early settlers He was born at Clearfield, September 2, 1875, and is a son of John W and Maria (Dolan) Howe

John W Howe, who has been engaged in a mercantile business at Morrisdale, Pa for the past eighteen years, was born in Clearfield county in 1849, a son of Sirene Howe, who once was sheriff of Clearfield county Mr Howe resided at Clearfield for some years and moved from there into Girard township and from there to Morrisdale He married Maria Dolan, who was born in county Down, Ireland, in 1852, and was brought to America and to Clearfield county by her parents Five sons and three daughters have been born to them, namely Frank A, Edward C and Harry C. who are in the hotel business together at Morrisdale, Paul, who is associated with his father, Fred, who is a successful physician at Wilkesbarre, Pa, Maggie, who lives at home, Lucy, who is a graduate of the Philadelphia High School, and Annie, who is a student in the Morrisdale High School

Frank A Howe obtained his education in the public schools of Girard township and a Catholic school at Frenchville and later in the Pelton school at Morrisdale Afterward he worked for his father first as a clerk and later at teaming at Shaft No 2, for four years Mr Howe then embarked in the hotel business, first at Blue Ball, in Boggs township, where he conducted the Enterprise Hotel for twenty months He then sold his interest and went to Morrisdale, where he followed teaming for two years In 1905 he came to Winburne and erected the Winburne Hotel making the plans and laying it out himself It is a handsome three-story building, containing forty-six rooms and with probably the finest bar and other equipments of any public house in Clearfield county It is modern in all its appointments and caters to the best trade, offering every comfort and convenience desired by the traveling public Although Mr Howe was obliged to borrow the capital with which to build his house, he had provided for every emergency with business foresight and has made his undertaking a great success

Mr Howe was married, September 28, 1898, by Rev Father Whyner, at St Agnes Roman Catholic church at Morrisdale, to Miss Marguerite Stephenson, a daughter of Peter Stephenson, and they have five children John W, Jr, Thomas Gerome, Cecelia and Irene Mr Howe and family are members of the Catholic church In politics he is a Democrat Mr Howe is a popular citizen, a man of pleasant, genial manner and takes a hearty interest in all that concerns the general welfare of this place

WALDO R FARGO,* dealing in meats and market supplies, is one of the prosperous and enterprising business men of Clearfield and maintains shops on Nichol street, on the West Side, and on the corner of Third and Market streets, both locations being in the busiest trading centers Mr Fargo was born in Berkshire, Mass, August 29, 1863, and is a son of Ezekiel R and Hannah (Daughenbaugh) Fargo

Ezekiel R Fargo was of New England parentage and was born in Massachusetts In early manhood he removed from there to Center county, Pa, where he married and lived until 1869, moving then to Clearfield, Pa, where he followed the carpenter's trade and was active until near the close of his life He died in July, 1895, aged sixty-seven years, his wife having previously passed away They had four children Elizabeth, who became the wife of Joseph Harris, Waldo R, John W, and Alice, who is the widow of Edward Stanton

Waldo R Fargo was one year old when the family returned to Center county from Massachusetts, and in a short time came to Clearfield so that practically all his life has been spent in this county He went to school until he was about twelve years old and then started out independently, relying on his own efforts to provide for his necessities His first employer was Adam Kephart, of Osceola Mills, for whom he did farm work in the summers and had a chance to attend school in winter, receiving no wages except board and clothes, but having a comfortable home for three years He went then to D C Burkett, a merchant at Clearfield, and remained with him for three years, receiving his board and ten dollars a month in wages Finding that a more active life would be better for his health and that he could secure excellent wages by going into the woods, he worked along the river and on the mountains chopping down trees until he was twenty-two years old Mr. Fargo then worked in a tannery at Clearfield for three years and in 1889 he opened up a meat market at Woodland, Pa , buying a half interest in the business of Welcher & Miller, the firm then becoming Miller & Fargo Three years later he sold his interest and in the following year purchased his Nichol street shop from August Brinn Finding himself well qualified for this line of business, Mr Fargo invested more capital, in July, 1909, buying the business of J I Heller, on the corner of Third and Market streets He has his two sons as assistants in his business and has a very capable meat man in charge of his Market street shop and runs a wagon from the same, having in the meantime acquired some of the best trade in the city He has become a man with large interests but these have not been gained through any fortunate combination of circumstances but have been acquired through personal effort and testify to his steadiness as boy and man, to his industry and natural good judgment

In September, 1888, Mr Fargo was married to Miss Wilhelmine Dale, a daughter of the late William Dale, and nine children were born to them Helen, Frank, Blair, Louis, Mary, Martha, Glenn, Genevieve and Isabella Of these, Mary and Martha (twins) are deceased Frank and Blair assist Mr Fargo in his markets He is identified with the Odd Fellows, the Eagles and the Order of the Moose

G M STANLEY, whose excellent farm of sixty acres is situated in Gulich township was born one mile from Tyrone, in Blair county, Pa , March 11, 1835, and is a son of Simon and Susan (Ginter) Stanley

Simon Stanley was a forgeman by trade and worked as such during his earlier years, but later engaged in farming, and after moving to Gulich township, Clearfield county, carried on agricultural operations during the rest of his active life He and his wife Susan had children as follows Wilhelmina, now deceased, who was the wife of John Henderson, Margaret, who is the widow of Edward Fulkerson, who was killed in the Civil war, Elizabeth, who married Boaz Alexander, Sarah, who became the wife of Capt John McKernan, who served in the Mexican and Civil wars, Lucinda, wife of George Curtis, a veteran of the Civil war, Shadrach, Rebecca, who became the wife of Jordan Fox, Dimicious A , and George M , the subject of this sketch

George M Stanley has been interested in farming during the larger part of his life and is numbered among the successful agriculturists of his neighborhood For the past seven years his farm has been leased for its coal deposits

Mr Stanley was married August 21, 1860, to Miss Amelia Cain, who was born in Center county, Pa , a daughter of John and Catherine (Oris) Cain The other members of her parents' family were Mary, who married George Breon, Caroline, who married David Young, Agnes, who was twice married, first to Cornelius Davis, and secondly to James Ginter, both being now deceased , Jacob, John and Calvin, who were all three killed in the Civil war, William H , a surviving veteran of the Civil war Ellen, wife of Ihon Miller, a veteran of the Civil war, and Sarah J , wife of James Kenley, a veteran of the Civil war

Mr and Mrs Stanley have had children as follows May, who was the wife of David Sprankle, now deceased, John Oris, Shadrach, Urelia, who is the wife of Scott Aile ;

Susan, who is the wife of M P Frederick, Calvin, William A, a physician and veteran of the Spanish-American war, Curtis, also a veteran of the Spanish-American war, Charles, and Clarence E Mr. Stanley and wife are members of the Methodist Episcopal church and are among the most highly esteemed residents of Gulich township He and his sons vote the Republican ticket

J T DAVIS,* owner and proprietor of the Grampian Electric Light plant at Grampian, Pa, where he is also interested in other business enterprises, was born July 12, 1863, in Penn township, Clearfield county, Pa, and is a son of Joseph and Elizabeth (Wall) Davis.

J T Davis is a member of one of the old and representative Penn township families He was educated in this township and at Pennville and the Curwensville Normal School, afterward teaching one term in Bloom township and one term in Penn township His family is largely an agricultural one but his talents and inclinations led him in another direction He built the first planing mill at Grampian, Pa, which he operated for three years and then turned his attention more particularly to lumbering and with a portable saw mill, cut over a large tract of timber near Curwensville He then bought a farm of 140 acres in Penn township, but disposed of it and returned to Grampian, where he erected the first electric light plant and still operates it, supplying Grampian with all its electric power Mr Davis also started the first five-cent theater in the place and still owns this property Mr Davis is recognized as an enterprising and forceful business man He takes no very active part in politics, casting his vote independent of any party affiliations

On December 13, 1888, Mr Davis was married to Miss Jennie E Kester, who was born in Penn township, September 23, 1871, a daughter of S Lewis and Alice (Wall) Kester They have six children, namely Alice Elizabeth, who teaches music at Verona, Pa, Joseph L, who is a graduate of the electric department of the Scranton Correspondence School, and Beulah Zelma, Dorsey, Harold and Wilford Mr Davis and family are members of the Society of Friends.

JAMES A REA,* who is interested in the lumber business in Jordan township, and is the efficient manager of a general store at Gazzam, which is owned by A F Kelley, was born September 24, 1867, in Jordan township, and is a son of Robert and Mary (Ames) Rea Both parents were natives also of Jordan township They had two children Isabel, who is the wife of S M Bloom, and James A. They were members of the Presbyterian church

James A Rea obtained his education in the public schools and grew up on the home farm. He early became interested in lumbering' For the past seven years he has been manager of the above store and is one of the best known men in the township He has been quite active in politics, is a leading Democrat of Jordan township, of which he is now treasurer and formerly served as auditor.

In June, 1902, Mr Rea was married to Miss Emma Bloom, who died in September, 1907 She was a daughter of Isaac Bloom, of Jordan township, and she had two sisters and three brothers namely· Elizabeth, now deceased, who was the wife of S K Ames; and Jennie, Herbert, John and W D Mrs Rea is survived by five children· Christopher

C , Belle, Herbert, Blanche and James Mr Rea and children attend the Presbyterian church

MURRAY LYNN BOYCE,* who is successfully engaged in agriculture in Burnside township, was born in the old log house on his present homestead, situated near East Ridge, November 8, 1887, a son of Mordecai and Eliza (Troxall) Boyce His paternal grandfather, Jacob Boyce, was an early settler in this locality, he married Charlotte Davis

Mordecai Boyce was born near Reading, Pa , in 1836, and came to Clearfield county with his parents in 1837, when a mere babe, they settling on the location of the present homestead, which then consisted entirely of timber land As soon as he was old enough he assisted in the work of clearing the farm, but later took up surveying, which occupation he followed all his subsequent life, his death taking place February 4th, in the present year, 1911 He was a member of the United Brethren church He was never actively interested in politics, but in 1861 he was appointed postmaster of what was then known as East Ridge postoffice He married Eliza Troxall, a daughter of John and Lydia (Hessinger) Troxall, both natives of Union county, Pa , and she is still living, being now sixty years of age Her paternal grandfather was George Troxall, born in 1782 at New Caledonia, Pa , his father having come to America from Germany He married Mary Hoffman, who was born in 1779 The children of Mordecai Boyce and wife who are now living are Murray L , the subject of this sketch, and Lydia N , who resides in Eldorado, Pa

Murray L Boyce, after attending school in his boyhood, was trained to the work of the farm By way of securing a practical education, however, he went to Altoona, Pa , where he took a commercial course Returning home later on account of his father's failing health, he resumed agricultural operations, which he has since continued He also follows surveying to some extent, having properly qualified himself for that profession He is regarded as one of the substantial and reliable citizens of his township and is a man who has many friends He is a member of Redwood lodge of Harmony, P S of A , of Plattville, Pa In politics he is a Republican, but so far has not served in public office As he is still quite a young man, energetic and enterprising, the future doubtless holds much in store for him

EDWARD WILLIAM WEBSTER,* plumbing contractor, doing a large business at DuBois, Pa , with quarters at No 14 E Long avenue, has been a resident of this borough since 1889 He was born at Oil City, Pa , February 14, 1871, and is a son of Edward D and Sidney J (Shiner) Webster Edward D Webster was born in Franklin county, Pa , and is now deceased His parents came through this section before any railroads had been built, driving from Philadelphia to Franklin county Edward William Webster is the eldest of his parents' family, the others being Elizabeth, who is the wife of Charles Irvin, Frank R , Rose, who is the wife of Fred Engel, Chester, and Dorothea

Edward W Webster attended school at Oil City and there grew to manhood, in the meanwhile learning his trade with well known firms, Schutter & Bryan and Robinson & Wright He came first to DuBois in the interest of the latter firm and later was connected with the

Hebner-Hoover Company, and in 1900 bought out the last named company He was located on Long avenue until he put up his present building on E Long avenue, in 1904 Mr Webster handles many large contracts yearly and gives employment according to the season to from eighteen to thirty-five men

Mr Webster was married to Miss Emma Polley, a daughter of the late John Polley, of Philadelphia, and they have one daughter, Ruth He has another daughter, Dorothea, of his first marriage, with Emma Smith The family residence is at No 114 E Scribner street In politics he is a Democrat He is identified fraternally with the Elks, the Odd Fellows and the Heptasophs

LAWRENCE M COUDRIET,* the popular host of the Central Hotel, situated at Coalport, was born in Covington township, Clearfield county, Pa, May 23, 1878, and is a son of Leon M and Gonpiere (Guenot) Coudriet

Coincident with the settlement of Covington township, Clearfield county, was the founding here of the Coudriet family, of French extraction This settlement was effected between 1830 and 1840 Francis Coudriet and wife were natives of France and they came to America in 1831 They stopped for a short time at Lebanon, Pa, and it was during this pause that Leon Mitchell Coudriet, father of Lawrence M, was born, May 10, 1831 As soon as mother and babe were able to travel, the family came on to Bellefonte, Center county, where, for a time, Francis Coudriet worked in a furnace He was not quite satisfied, however, and during this time made several trips to what were known as the Keating lands, as Covington township was

then styled, and after careful selection purchased fifty acres in this region, receiving as a bonus, twelve additional acres Shortly afterward he had established his family at Clearfield town, and from that point daily walked to his newly acquired property, ax in hand, and without assistance cleared off sufficient timber to enable him to put up a log house into which the family then moved He was an industrious man and was also one of high character He was a devoted Catholic and contributed the stone from his farm which was used in the erection of St Mary's church at Frenchville He became a man of considerable importance in that village and for eighteen years served in the office of postmaster

Leon Mitchell Coudriet was the second born of eleven children He took charge of his father's business after the death of the latter in 1877 and proved a man of much ability, although he had already been concerned in business for himself He worked in the woods from early years, having but little chance to acquire an education Five of his brothers still survive Prosper, Serdon, Lewis, Frank and Napoleon Coudriet He was married in 1853 and for about one year afterward lived with his parents, working for his father, after which he moved to Girard township, opening a store on Buck Run This business he conducted successfully until 1866, when he succeeded to the business formerly managed by Capt P A Gaulin, at Mulsonburg, and then moved to that place He was also extensively engaged in the lumber business and acquired a great amount of real estate, together with some of the most valuable timber lands in Clearfield county, hundreds of acres being also underlaid with a fine quality of coal

Through the division of his father's estate he became the owner of the greater part of it by purchasing the interests of the other heirs He owned a flour and grist mill at Frenchville, also a saw-mill there and at other points he was interested in mills, at one time having three on Sandy Creek His land possessions reached 10,000 acres In addition he financed many enterprises and owned a large factory for the manufacture of sash, doors and blinds, at Middletown, in Dauphin county

Leon M Coudriet married an orphan, Gonpiere Guenot, who was born January 6, 1833, in France, and came to America after the death of her parents She died November 1, 1908, having survived her husband from April 25, 1888 There were twelve children born to this marriage, namely Francis, who is deceased, lived on the old homestead, Prosper, who lives where his father settled and built the stone house which is still standing, Alpheus, who is also a farmer on the old homestead, Anne J, who lives at Pittsburg, Hillary J, who is manager of the grocery department of a large store at Philipsburg, Felicia, who is the wife of James Gormount, a farmer in Covington township, Jane, who is the wife of A L Picard, lives at Frenchville, Kate A, who is deceased, was the wife of Dr Newling, Celestia, who is the wife of F J Liegey, a justice of the peace in Covington township, Elizabeth and a sister, who both died about nine years of age, and Lawrence M

Leon M Coudriet always took an active interest in public affairs but declined to serve in office, making an exception when he succeeded his father as postmaster at Frenchville, where he served thus for eight years He contributed liberally to the support of St Mary's Catholic church and through advice and money

forwarded many movements which assisted in bringing prosperity to this region

Lawrence M Coudriet was the youngest of his father's family and was given many advantages of every kind He attended school in Covington township, and afterward the Central State Normal School at Lock Haven, Pa His mother built a saw mill on Deer Creek about 1901 and he looked after that and her other interests and remained at home until 1903, when he moved to near the mouth of Deer Creek, where Condley is now situated and there entered into a general mercantile business, soon after applying for the position of postmaster, and receiving the appointment in 1904 He continued to be interested at Condley until 1909, the name of this village having been constructed from the two earliest business men of the place—Lawrence M Coudriet contributing the first part and Albert Stanley the second part of the name In addition to his mercantile interests there, Mr Coudriet was also in the lumber business and operated a saw-mill On October 15, 1909, he purchased the Central Hotel at Coalport and has carried on business here ever since This house is conceded to be one of the best hotels in Central Pennsylvania, having attractions for those who demand real comfort, an excellent table and attentive service at a reasonable price Mr Coudriet has the reputation of having been successful in whatever he has undertaken and his management of the Central Hotel justifies it He makes his guests so comfortable, whether permanent or transient, that he grows in popularity as a host and has a wide circle of warm friends His building is modern in every particular and lighted by electricity and heated by steam

Mr Coudriet has never been very active in

politics nor was his father nor grandfather, but in all matters concerning the best interests of the sections in which they have made their home, they have been foremost in fostering laudable enterprises and have been especially liberal in the cause of religion   Like his ancestors he is a Roman Catholic and is a member of St Basil's church

On May 22, 1901, Mr Coudriet was married to Miss Julia M Donovan, a daughter of John and Rosa Donovan, now of Grampian but formerly of Hawk Run   They have three children   Paul B , Leona M and Earle   The only fraternal organization with which he is connected is the Royal Order of the Moose

ISAIAH NEFF, who has been successfully engaged in farming in Chest township, Clearfield county, Pa , for the past thirty-two years, is also interested in merchandising, in 1889 establishing his general store at Five Points, where he does a large business   He was born September 5, 1856, in Chest township, and is a son of John W and Mary Ann (Barto) Neff

John W Neff is one of Clearfield county's most venerable citizens   He was born ninety-one years ago, in Center county, Pa , and is a son of Christopher and Sophia (Holton) Neff   He was six years old when he accompanied his parents to Burnside township, Clearfield county, and is one of the oldest surviving pioneers   During the entire period of active life he has been engaged in farming and timbering   He has been twice married, his first wife Mary Ann Barto dying in 1860 at the age of thirty-two years, survived by two sons   Isaiah and John, the latter being a farmer in Chest township   The second marriage of John W Neff was to Catherine Wagoner, a daughter

of William and Catherine (Rodebaugh) Wagoner, who is also deceased   To this marriage were born three sons and six daughters

Isaiah Neff obtained his education in the early district schools, and then was associated with his father in farming and lumbering, and remained at home until he was twenty-three years of age   He then became similarly interested on his own account, and later enlarged his business responsibilities as mentioned above   He is numbered with the representative business men of Chest township and is a leading member of Harmony Grange

Mr Neff married into another old family of this section, Miss Susanna Snyder, who was born December 29, 1865, a daughter of Jonas and Mary (Fox) Snyder, who came to Clearfield from Center county

Of the family of children born to Mr and Mrs Neff, the following survive   Irwin L , a thoroughly educated young man, who is at present an instructor in the Penfield High School, married Elma Groh, and they have two children, John C , who is engaged in the lumber business in West Virginia, Belle, who is the wife of Perry Kitchen, and they have two children   Clair, who lives on the home farm, married Carrie Woods, George O , who is a successful school teacher, Foster, who is engaged in farming in the vicinity of Philadelphia; Mazie and Wayne, both of whom attend school, and Myrtle and Quentin   Mr. Neff is identified politically with the Democratic party but has never been willing to assume the duties of any public office

GEORGE D KANTZ, a well known and highly esteemed citizen of Burnside township, where he is engaged in farming on 109 acres of land, and in lumbering, was born on the old

MR. AND MRS. GEO. D. KANTZ

Kantz homestead, at the locality known as Slabtown, this county, August 2, 1856, a son of John and Sarah (Baker) Kantz His paternal grandfather, John Kantz, Sr , was a native of Germany, who came to this country and died in Indiana county, Pa

John Kantz, Jr , father of our subject, was born in Columbia county, Pa , in 1818 He resided for a time in Lancaster county and afterwards in Indiana county, coming to Clearfield county about 1848 Settling in Burnside township, he engaged here in lumbering, rafting his product to market He continued in this line of industry until 1857, at which time he settled on the present Kantz homestead, or rather on the site, which he cleared and developed into a good farm His wife, Sarah Baker Kantz, was born in Snyder, Pa , in February, 1818, a daughter of Philip Baker, who was a pioneer of that county, the section in which he resided, however, being then known as Marion county She survived her husband, dying in 1892, while his death took place in 1884 Their family consisted of six children, namely Philip, now living retired at Clearfield, Pa , Susanna, who is deceased, Reuben B , a farmer residing in Burnside township, Emma, the widow of John Irwin, now residing in Tacoma, Wash , Annie, wife of S Hileman, residing in Tacoma, Wash , and George Daniel, the subject of this sketch

George Daniel Kantz attended school but a short time in his boyhood, as there were but four months of free school a year at that time At the age of eleven years he began to help his father in lumbering, driving a team, making square timber, and cutting logs, and in the spring seasons helping to raft up this square timber and running it down the Susquehanna river to the markets of Lock Haven, Wil-

liamsport and Marietta, and in the summer time being engaged in farming At the age of seventeen he became a pilot on the Susquehanna river He continued to work for his father in this way until he became of age, at the age of twenty-one becoming his father's partner, they working together in this way until 1882 Mr Kantz then bought the homestead of his father, the latter retiring and making his home with our subject, with whom he resided for the rest of his days, as did also our subject's mother George D Kantz continued lumbering until 1903, but which time the virgin pine, hemlock and oak was all cut and run to market Since then he has been heavily interested in mining—timber, such as motor ties, bank ties and props, railroad ties and sawed lumber

Mr Kantz married Marietta Lutz, of Lancaster county, Pa She was born September 20, 1855, a daughter of Samuel Parker and Jane (Scott) Lutz Her father, who was a cabinet maker by trade, later became superintendent of various manufacturing concerns He died January 21, 1910, at the age of eighty-two years His wife died in 1860, at the age of thirty-two She was a daughter of James and Sarah (Leader) Scott, of Lancaster county, the former of whom died in 1858, at the age of seventy-five, and the latter in 1870 at the age of eighty years James Scott for many years was proprietor of an old inn on the Pike road in Lancaster county, known as the Brink Inn, he being also in charge of the toll gate there Grandfather Jacob Lutz died in 1856 at the age of seventy years He was a carpenter by trade

Mrs Kantz at the time of the Civil war, when her father was absent fighting for the Union, was brought with two other members of her parents' family to Clearfield county, and was reared at McGee's Mills by a family named Sunderland, their mother having died, as before mentioned, in 1860 After the father's return from the war he found himself unable to locate his family, and it was not until several years afterwards that he finally found them Mrs Kantz has one brother living, Carson Lutz, who is engaged in mining and truck farming at Glen Campbell

Mr Kantz is an active, enterprising citizen He is a Republican in politics and has performed active service for his party He has held several local offices, having served as township treasurer and as a member of local committees He belongs to the United Brethren church

FRED S McCRACKEN,* whose well kept farm of sixty-seven acres is situated in Ferguson township, two miles northwest of Kerrmoor, was born in this township, April 28, 1850 His parents were John D and Nancy (Bloom) McCracken, of old and substantial families of this section

John D McCracken was born also in Ferguson township He was reared here and spent the larger part of his life in this township, although, after his marriage he lived for a time on the Hoyt farm in Greenwood township He cleared a farm of sixty-five acres subsequently, in Ferguson township and lived on it during the remainder of his life, his death taking place at the age of seventy-seven years He was a worthy member of the Methodist Episcopal church at Lumber City and his burial was in the Methodist cemetery there He always voted the Democratic ticket He married Nancy Bloom a daughter of Isaac Bloom, and she lived to be eighty-one

years of age and her burial was also at Lumber City They had the following children: Eliza Jane, George, Frampton B , Philip, Ann, Phebe, Fred, Harriet, Hannah, William Bigker, John, Caroline, and a son that died in infancy Philip the third son, was a soldier in the Civil war

Fred S McCracken attended school in Ferguson township and afterward helped his father on the farm until his own marriage, after which he lived at Reynoldsville, in Jefferson county, for a time and then came to his present farm, which he purchased from his brother He has erected all the substantial buildings on the place and has made many improvements. Formerly he devoted some attention to sheep raising but not recently There is a valuable twenty-eight-inch vein of coal on the place which Mr McCracken occasionally works

Mr McCracken was married April 20, 1871, to Miss Mary Michael, who was born in Clinton county, Pa , February 17, 1849, a daughter of John and Jane (Lewis) Michael Mr Michael died in Ferguson township when aged sixty years and his burial was at Old Zion cemetery Mr and Mrs McCracken have two children Edward M and Ida, the latter of whom is the wife of Samuel Baer They reside at Glen Hope and have two children, Frederick and Anna Mary Mr and Mrs McCracken attend the Baptist church, of which Mrs McCracken is a member He belongs to the Grange at Kerrmoor In politics, Mr McCracken is a stanch Democrat and he has served in numerous township offices with the utmost efficiency, having been road supervisor, constable, tax collector and assessor He is one of the representative men of Ferguson township

A J JOHNSON,* division superintenden*
of the Buffalo, Rochester & Pittsburg Railroad, who came to DuBois, Pa , in 1905, is a
railroad man whose training in this line began in boyhood   He was born September 4.
1861, at Morefield, O , and is a son of William and Mary Johnson

A J Johnson was ten years old when his
parents moved to Uhrichsville, O , and there
he went to school until old enough to work
in a grocery store, where he remained about
three years   In 1875 he became an employe
of the Panhandle division of the Pennsylvania
Railroad, at Dennison, O , and while working
as a messenger boy had the courage, perseverance and ambition that made him master the
art of telegraphy   He became an expert operator and received promotion in the offices of
that company and continued until 1888, when
he became train dispatcher for the Cincinnati
Southern Railway   One year later he entered
the employ of the Sciota Valley Railroad as
train dispatcher, residing at that time at Columbus, O , and he continued with that road
until it became a part of the Norfolk & Western system   In 1893 he became division superintendent of the Northern division of the
B R & P Railroad, being then located at
Rochester, N Y , and from there was transferred to his present location in 1905, when
he established his home at DuBois

In September, 1882, Mr Johnson was married to Miss Anna Miser, a resident of Columbus, O , and they have three children,
namely   George, an employe of the B R &
P Railroad, at New Castle, Pa , who married
Laura Hicks and has one child, Ruth, Hazel
V , who is the wife of W R Landis, of DuBois, and has one son, Wilbur A , and Ethel
M , who resides with her parents   Mr John-
son is identified fraternally with Lodge No
797, F & A M , at Rochester N Y , and
Lodge No 349, Elks, at DuBois, Pa   He belongs also to the Acorn Club at DuBois

FRANK M CAMPBELL, who has resided on his present farm of 100 acres, situated in Chest township, Clearfield county,
Pa , since 1895, is one of the enterprising
and prominent men of this section   He was
born in Tioga county, Pa , February 23, 1866,
and is a son of Ely and Mary E (Low)
Campbell

Ely Campbell was born also in Tioga
county, a son of Robert and Rhoda (McMasters) Campbell, natives also of Tioga county
but of Scotch extraction   Ely Campbell was
reared on the home farm and worked in the
woods near the old homestead from boyhood
until he was twenty-one years old   In 1870
he came to Clearfield county and located in
Bell township, following rafting and other
work of a woodsman for three years and then
moved to McGee's Mills, where he remained
for three more years   Later he went to Five
Points, in Chest township, and lived there until 1881, when he returned to the old homestead in Tioga county, where he still carries
on farming   He married Mary E Low, who
also survives   Her parents were John and
Ellen Low, natives of Germany   To Ely
Campbell and wife the following children were
born   Frank M , David, who is a farmer in
Tioga county, Edward L and Clayton, both
of whom reside in Tioga county, Ida, who is
the wife of William Robinson, of Mansfield,
Pa , Edith, who is the wife of C Preston, of
Mansfield, Pa , and Della, who is the wife of
F Campman, of Oregon Hill, Pa

When Frank M Campbell was only eleven

years old he accompanied his father to the woods and assisted him until he was twenty-one, after that engaging in farming in Chest township, Clearfield county After marriage he moved to Coalport, Pa, and later to Irvona, where he was in the tannery business for three years, and followed draying and teaming for three years more, after which he settled on his present farm and since then has been interested in farming and lumbering

Mr Campbell was married April 17. 1888, to Miss Isabel McGarvey, who was born October 30, 1866, a daughter of Anthony and Ellen (Hunter) McGarvey, residents of Jordan township for many years, well known and highly respected farming people there Mrs Campbell was accomplished and educated and for some years prior to her marriage taught music, having graduated in music both at Ansonville and Cherry Tree She was a lady of beautiful character and was a devoted member of the Presbyterian church The following children were born to Mr and Mrs Campbell Harry D, who is in the street railway service at Pittsburg, Pa, Vincent A, who is the home farmer, Willis E, although but seventeen years old, has a position in a saw-mill at Pittsburg, Helen Leola, who attends to the domestic affairs for her father and the younger children, Laura Jane, who attends school, and Bennie Charles, Katie, Nettie May and Ruth, the last named being four years old, while three others died in infancy

Mr Campbell is one of the influential Republicans in Chest township and is township supervisor, having been a township official since 1905 He is an active citizen in all that concerns the general welfare of this section and is always ready to do his part in promoting public spirited enterprises of which his judgment approves

LEWIS McCRACKEN,* a retired farmer living on a farm in Ferguson township, adjoining the one on which he was born, February 8, 1838, owns 172 acres, situated one mile northeast of Kerrmoor, Pa His parents were William and Mary (Bell) McCracken

William McCracken was born in Pike township, Clearfield county, March 10, 1807, and died in January, 1891, and his burial was in the Fruit Hill Cemetery He was six years old when his parents moved to the McNaul farm, where he grew to manhood After his marriage he moved to the adjoining farm, in Ferguson township, on which his eleven children were born, and continued to live there until all had grown up Then he sold and moved to Virginia, where he was interested in farming at the time of his death He was an elder in the Fruit Hill Presbyterian church In politics he was a Democrat and he served one term as county commissioner in Clearfield county William McCracken married Mary Bell, who was born in what was then Bell but is now Greenwood township, Clearfield county, a daughter of Greenwood Bell, and died in January, 1886 They had eleven children, namely Hiram, who is deceased· Julia Ann, who is the widow of Christian Straw, Robert, who died in 1907, Lewis, David, who is deceased, Hezekiah, who lives in Lawrence township, Arthur, who died at the age of eight years; Josephine, who died in 1903, Ashley, who lives near Farmville, Va, and Seth and Amanda, the latter of whom is the wife of Emanuel Shaffer, both living in Ferguson township

Lewis McCracken obtained his education in the schools of Ferguson township He worked on the home farm for his father until he was twenty-two years of age and then married and moved to his present farm and here has made many improvements including the erecting of the substantial farm buildings He has his land under excellent cultivation and is utilizing all of it except thirty-five acres on which timber is still standing He has successfully carried on general farming, raising crops, fruit and stock and doing a little dairying Formerly he was very active but in late years has turned his responsibilities to a large degree over to younger workers

Mr McCracken was married first to Miss Dorcas Lewis, who was born in Elk county, Pa, and died in April, 1875 They had four children Ellis, Emily, who is the wife of Joseph Shaw, residing at Marron, William, who lives at Millport, Pa, and Laura, who is the wife of Charles Wiley, of Ferguson township Mr McCracken was married secondly to Miss Elizabeth McGarvey, who was born in Clarion county, Pa, September 17, 1847, a daughter of Hugh and Mary (Boyd) McGarvey, who moved from Clarion to Clearfield county To the second marriage of Mr McCracken, two daughters were born Estella, who is the wife of William Metlack, residing near Kerrmoor, and Delta, who is the wife of Jesse Metlack, residing at New Millport, Pa Mr and Mrs McCracken are members of the Baptist church He has been a Democrat ever since he cast his first vote, and on several occasions has been elected to township offices on the Democratic ticket He is one of the leading members of the Kerrmoor Grange.

ZACHARY TAYLOR PHILLIPS,* general merchant at Irvona, Pa, is one of the enterprising young business men of this place and at present is serving in the office of borough auditor, having been elected to the same on the Republican ticket He was born at Jeffries, Clearfield county, Pa, August 22, 1886 and is a son of John H and Elizabeth (Lowford) Phillips

John H Phillips was born in Clearfield county, Pa, in 1855 His father died when he was young and his mother married Henry Hangham, who lived and died in Clearfield county His widow survives and is now eighty years of age John H Phillips was a farmer for a number of years and then engaged in merchandising at Jeffries, from which place he came to Irvona, where he still lives now retired after twenty years of active business life He married Elizabeth Lowford, a daughter of Joseph and Mary Lowford, who were early settlers near Jeffries Mr and Mrs Phillips have four children Zachary T, Charles E, who is a business man of Clearfield, married Sophia Hampton, Charles E, who is employed in the clay works at Jeffries, married first Edith Hace, and second Mrs Boyer, and Sophronia Sarah, who is the wife of Edwin Newton, of Philadelphia, formerly of Clearfield

Zachary T Phillips was fifteen years of age when he accompanied his father to Irvona and assisted in the latter's store until 1908, when he purchased it and succeeded He does a safe and satisfactory business and as a citizen is interested in all that concerns the development of the place

In December, 1902, Mr Phillips was married to Miss Annie Fitzgerald, a daughter of Joseph and Mary Fitzgerald, and they have four children Mary Elizabeth, Catherine Ellen, Rose Audrey and Geraldine Fitzgerald Mr and Mrs Phillips are members of the

Presbyterian church He is identified with the A O K of M C of Irvona, No 152, Mattawanna Castle

HENRY M COLEMAN, general farmer, residing in Bell township, Clearfield county, Pa , was born October 21, 1852, in Somerset county, Pa , and is a son of Josiah and Ann Maria (Nicodemus) (Coleman) Dull

Josiah Coleman was a farmer in Somerset county, where he died in 1856 He is survived by his widow and two of their four children, Henry M and Ann Eliza, the latter being the wife of Washington Ackuff, of Vinton, Benton county, Ia The mother, who was born April 24, 1826, still survives and resides with her son Her father was John Nicodemus, who was a shoemaker by trade, living in Somerset county

Henry M Coleman had but few educational or other advantages in his youth and as soon as his strength permitted he went to work and until he was eighteen years of age took entire care of his mother He married in Indiana county and there followed farming until 1890, when he came to Bell township, Clearfield county For five years he was engaged in the saw-mill business for Alpha Read, at McGees, afterward was an employe of the New York Central Railroad for four years, having resided at present place for twenty-one years, and is at present working at the tannery

Mr Coleman was married to Miss Maggie Sutter, who was born in Indiana county, Pa , August 8, 1863, a daughter of Philip and Barbara (Piper) Sutter Mr and Mrs Coleman have the following children Myrtle Adella, who is the wife of John Beatty, of Bell township, and they have five children,

Philip, who married Alma Beinhour (he is deceased, and left one child), Manuel, who lives at home, Anna Barbara, who is the widow of Anthony Friedline, and has two children who live with their grandparents, Zetta, a resident of Ohio, and George Arthur, residing in New York state Mr Coleman is a very worthy citizen in every sense of the term but he has never taken any very active interest in politics He is a member of the United Brethren church and formerly was one of its trustees

ALONZO BIGLER MAINES, who is well known to hotel men in Clearfield county as the proprietor of the Eagle Hotel, at Karthaus, Pa , one of the oldest hostelries in this part of the state, was born in Karthaus township, Clearfield county, near the Clinton county line, February 6, 1856, and is a son of John Thomas and Mary Jane (Miller) Maines

The Maines family is an old and honored one in Clearfield county, where the grandfather of Alonzo B Maines settled at an early date; while on his mother's side Mr Maines is descended from a highly respected family of Center county John Thomas Maines was reared in Clinton county, and as a young man gained a wide reputation in that section as a timber hewer, being considered one of the best in the country Later he engaged in lumbering and farming, and he is still hale and hearty in spite of his seventy-eight years and lives at Pottersdale with his wife, who has passed the seventy-two year mark Mr Maines is a Democrat in politics His wife attends the Methodist Episcopal church To Mr and Mrs Maines there were born eight children Alonzo Bigler, Telitha Ellen, who married

John McGarvey of Bellefonte, Alma, who married Frank Condriet of Karthaus township, Libbie, who married Fred Moody of Lock Haven, J Cameron, who resides in Pottersdale, Albert Hamlin, who lives in Grass Flat, Iva, who married George Brown of Clarence, and Lillie, who married Fred Carey and is living at home with her parents at Pottersdale

Alonzo Bigler Maines was reared in Karthaus township, and there attended the local schools As a young man he engaged in lumbering and farming, and for about eight years carried on a butchering business while living on a farm To some extent he also followed rafting down the river to Lock Haven, and for one year after locating in Karthaus he lumbered for George Dimeling Mr Maines owned a farm property at Pottersdale until shortly after buying the old Eagle Hotel stand from Fred Mosebarger in December, 1902, and he has since conducted this well known hostelry as a first-class house

Mr Maines was married to Martha DeHass, who was born in Elk county, Pa, daughter of David DeHass, and to this union there were born nine children Edgar Leslie, born May 10, 1877, who married Miss Lizzie Chatham and lives in Ossining, Ora E, born August 31, 1878, who married Charles Potter of Portage, Pa, Boyd I, born December 30, 1879, who died January 28, 1880, Alfred Leroy, born December 11, 1882, who married Miss Minnie Moses and has a son, A B, Ferdinand, born December 28, 1883, who married Miss Maude Briel and has two children, Clare and Gard, Bessie DeLorence, born March 9, 1887, who married Raymond Meeker of Karthaus, Rhoda Belle, born May 22, 1888, who married Nathan Reese of

Youngstown, Ohio, Ward Lester, born February 9, 1890, who is an operator of Karthaus, and John Guy, who was born April 3, 1894 The mother of the above mentioned children died June 13, 1902, and Mr Maines was again married, February 26, 1903, to Miss Ellen Elizabeth Conway, who was born in Karthaus township, daughter of Hugh and Mary Ellen (Kane) Conway, the former a native of Karthaus township and the latter of Lancaster county Two children have been born to Mr and Mrs Maines June Elzora, born July 5, 1904, and Beulah Fay, born March 15, 1906

Mrs Maines is a member of the Methodist Episcopal church, while her husband is a liberal supporter of all church and charitable movements Fraternally he is connected with the P. O S of A and the Red Men, holding membership in DuBois and Williamsport

JAMES LANG SOMMERVILLE, president of the Bituminous National Bank and a very prominent business man of Winburne, Pa, was born in Scotland, August 16, 1837, and is a son of John S and Elizabeth L (Lang) Sommerville

In 1846 John S Sommerville, after the death of his first wife, came to America with his son, James L, and settled at Snow Shoe, in Center county, Pa He was a coal miner and had a contract on the coal fields of that section His death occurred at the age of sixty-seven years His second marriage was to Sarah Fulmer, who lived but a short time and he was married a third time to a Miss Richards

James Lang Sommerville is the only one of his father's children who survived to maturity He attended Bellefonte Academy and later Lock Haven Academy, both of these being considered excellent schools, and then went into civil engineering He was assistant engineer on the construction of the Snow Shoe Railroad and other lines and was associated with his father in coal mining at Snow Shoe and also with the Bellefonte and Snow Shoe Railroad as engineer, until it was sold to the Pennsylvania Railroad Company Subsequently he engaged in mining on his own account After the building of the Beech Creek Railroad he came to Winburne and leased coal for the firm of Weaver & Betts, operating under the firm name of Sommerville & Buchanan, until the same was merged into the Beech Creek Coal Company The country was nothing but a wilderness in this section at that time and no other coal operating had yet been done

Mr Sommerville came to Winburne in 1888, soon after the railroad had been completed and has been identified ever since with the borough's leading business interests He was one of the organizers and has been the only president of the Bituminous National Bank here He was one of the first to be interested at this point and gave the name to the place, "Win" coming from Winn's Run, a local stream, the last name being the Scotch designation of "burn," the combination making the pleasant sounding name of Winburne. He has been interested in the promotion of all the utilities of the place and is president of the Winburne Water Company, water being piped from Center county, a distance of four miles This company was organized July 30, 1903, Mr. Sommerville's engineering knowledge making him valuable as an advisor as to this improvement He also laid out and built the town of Carnworth, in Knox township,

Clearfield county In 1910 he opened a new coal mine where he employs 100 men He is a wide awake, intelligent, progressive man and his efforts not only benefit himself but add to the general welfare

Mr Sommerville was married in October, 1860, to Miss Jane Harris, a daughter of James D and Mary M Harris, of Bellefonte, where she was reared These children have been born to them, namely: Bond V, who is chief assistant engineer of the southwest system of the Pennsylvania Railroad, residing at Crafton, Bessie L, who resides at home, John S, who is superintendent of the Rock Hill Coal and Iron Company's mines at Robertsdale, Huntingdon county, Pa, Mary H, who lives at home, James H, who was a civil engineer with the West Shore Railroad, and was accidentally killed, Robert H and Allen O, twins, the former of whom has charge of the Sommerville mercantile interests at Winburne, and the latter of whom resides with his family at Arcadia and is superintendent of mines of the Arcadia and Winburne district, D L, who is now assistant superintendent on the Pennsylvania division of the New York Central Railroad, being stationed at Jersey Shore, Pa, and two who died in infancy Robert H Sommerville is also secretary and treasurer of the Carnworth Coal Company, on Potts Run, in Knox township, of which his father is president

Mr. Sommerville is a member of the Winburne Presbyterian church, in which he is an elder, and was instrumental in the establishment of this church and active in its construction He is a member of St Andrew's Society of Philadelphia, and the Pennsylvania Society of New York Winburne owes much to his enterprise and foresight and he is justly considered one of the most prominent citizens of the place

EDWARD M McCRACKEN,* who is one of the representative citizens and substantial business men of Ferguson township, where he is a justice of the peace and the owner of a farm and a saw-mill, has lived in this township since he was four months old He was born January 19, 1872, in Jefferson county, Pa, a son of Frederick S and Mary (Michaels) McCracken

Frederick S McCracken was born also in Jefferson county and moved from there to Ferguson township, Clearfield county, in April, 1872, and has resided on his farm which is situated two and one-half miles west of Kerrmoor, ever since Farming and lumbering have been his occupations together with attending to the duties of the numerous public offices to which he has been elected He is a Democrat and on the Democratic ticket was twice elected assessor of Ferguson township, nine years tax collector and a number of times road supervisor He married Mary Michaels, who also survives, and they have two children Edward M and Ida, the latter of whom is the wife of Samuel Bear, of Glen Hope, Pa They are members of the Baptist church

Edward M McCracken obtained his education in the schools of Ferguson township He went into the woods to work after he left school and through his industry accumulated enough money to purchase twenty-six acres of land, which he subsequently sold and then purchased the Allen W Moore farm, of sixty-five acres, on which he has made many improvements including the building of his farm house He continues to be interested in lumbering and owns a saw-mill and gives employment to ten men in that industry

On May 30, 1890, Mr McCracken was married to Miss Minta Bailor, who was born in Boggs township, September 16, 1876, a daughter of Daniel and Phebe (Thurston) Bailor, and they have had eight children Enloe, David, Margaret, Frederick, John, Levi, Harriet and Ada, all of whom survive except John, who died when only two days old After purchasing his farm, Mr McCracken served eight years as foreman of a gang in the lumber regions At present he is operating on 450 acres of timber land and has just finished cutting the last remaining tract of white pine timber left in Ferguson township He is a charter member and one of the stockholders in the Farmers and Traders Bank of Clearfield

In politics Mr McCracken is a Democrat and in 1908 was elected justice of the peace The first township office he ever held was that of road supervisor, then served two terms as auditor, two terms as township clerk and one term as supervisor under the new law He is a member of Susquehanna Grange, No 1145, at Curwensville, and belongs to the Odd Fellows at Lumber City

EMORY W BELL, farmer and lumberman for many years in Clearfield county, Pa, and the owner of a fine residence at Ansonville, is one of the well known and highly respected men of Jordan township He was born August 25, 1853, in Greenwood township, Clearfield county, Pa, and is a son of William and Martha (Hoover) Bell

William Bell was born also in Greenwood township, and was a son of Greenwood Bell, the Bells being early settlers here as were also the Hoovers He married Martha Hoover, who was a daughter of Joseph and Rebecca (Price) Hoover She died when their son,

Emory W, was three weeks old William Bell was married secondly to Julia Armigust, and they had three children John Henry, Annie Laura and Mary Emma, twins, the former of whom died, the latter married Ernest Shaftner William Bell and wife were members of the Baptist church

Emory W Bell had few educational opportunities in his youth He has always been a hard working man and farming and lumbering have both claimed his attention In 1878 he was married to Miss Mary Deihl, a daughter of Benjamin and Nancy (Smith) Deihl, natives of Pennsylvania Mrs Bell had the following brothers and sisters Urella, wife of William Tate, Thomas, Grant, William, Edward, Gertrude, wife of Harry Chesney, Minnie, wife of Lewis McDarnold, and Lola, wife of Daniel Stitzman Mr and Mrs Bell have one daughter, Nannie, who is the wife of Charles Strong, who is at Ansonville, in the meat business Mr and Mrs Bell attend the Baptist church He gives his political support to the candidates of the Democratic party

JAMES EDWARD McDOWELL, who has been postmaster at Irvona, Clearfield county, Pa, since September, 1897, is a hardware merchant at this place and a representative and reputable citizen He was born December 23, 1853, at Newberry, in Lycoming county, Pa, and is a son of George McClelland and Elizabeth Rosanna (Kyle) McDowell.

George McClelland McDowell was born in Mifflin county, Pa, in 1820, a son of John McDowell, who was born in Ireland but died in Mifflin county In 1854 George M McDowell moved to Millhall, in Clinton county, where he engaged in merchandising, later becoming a farmer He died in 1885, aged sixty-five years He married Elizabeth Hosanna Kyle who was also born in Mifflin county and died in 1872, at the age of forty-nine years. Her father, Joseph Kyle, came from Scotland To George McC McDowell and wife the following children were born Joseph and Samuel, both of whom are deceased, Margaret Jane, who married James Flynn, of Charleton, W Va, James Edward, Mary Catherine, who is the wife of James T Shillingford, of Osceola Mills, John Ralph, who is a hardware and lumber merchant of Pitcairn, Pa, and Rosanna, who is the wife of Dr. Herbert Hogue, of Altoona, Pa

James E McDowell was educated in the public schools at Millhall, to which place his parents moved when he was a babe, and later at the Pennsylvania State College In 1860 he moved to Nittany Valley and carried on farming there until 1885, when he came to Irvona and in 1887 embarked in the hardware business In 1897 he had been so recognized as a prominent citizen that he was appointed postmaster during the first administration of President McKinley and has continued in the office until the present He is the oldest merchant in the place from a business standpoint and is interested in a number of business enterprises that have served to build up the place He was a member of the first borough council

In 1881, Mr McDowell was married to Miss Anna M Heard, a daughter of John P and Mary Jane (McGhee) Heard, the former of whom was a farmer and merchant They have one son, Winfield Heard McDowell, who was born in 1882 and is a resident of Uniontown, Fayette county, Pa, being connected with the engineering department of the H C

Frick Coke Company He was graduated in 1905 at Pennsylvania State College and spent two years in the West with his present company Mr McDowell and son are Republicans He belongs to Coalport Lodge, F & A. M , No 574, Clearfield Chapter, No 228, Moshannon Commandery, No 74, Scottish Rite (Valley) Williamsport, and Jaffa Temple, Mystic Shrine, at Altoona Mr McDowell is a member and liberal supporter of the Methodist Episcopal church at Irvona

GEORGE J WEBER, general merchant at Troutville, Pa , where he is also a justice of the peace, has been a lifelong resident of Clearfield county and was born November 5, 1865, on his father's farm in Bell township His parents were Jacob and Elizabeth (Hoeh) Weber, and his grandfather was John Jacob Weber

Jacob Weber was born in 1833, in Germany, and was thirteen years of age when he accompanied his parents, John Jacob and Susannah (Schoch) Weber, to America John Jacob, or Curly Weber, as he was known to his neighbors in those early days, located one mile south of Troutville, in the dense woods of Brady township, Clearfield county, and there spent the rest of his days, and after his death his son, Jacob Weber, came into possession of the farm He lived on the old homestead until 1900 when he moved to Troutville Jacob Weber was married first to Mrs Elizabeth (Hoeh) Miller, widow of Christian Miller and the daughter of German parents, her birth having taken place in Germany. To her first marriage one child was born, Mary, who is deceased, and three children were born to her marriage with Jacob Weber· George Jacob, our subject, Lewis

Daniel, who is a resident of Troutville, and Susanna, who died at the age of two years. Mrs Weber died in 1870 and in 1872 Mr Weber married her sister, Miss Eva Hoeh Seven children were born to the second marriage, namely Elizabeth, who is the wife of H M Kuntz, of Brady township, Augustus F , who lives in Brady township, Catherine M , of Reynoldsville, Pa , Mary A , who is now deceased, Rosanna, who is the wife of Otto Schoch, of Troutville, Nora, who is the wife of Godfrey Biehl, of Pittsburg, and Freeda

George Jacob Weber was reared on the home farm and obtained a public school education Being the eldest son he was early called on to give his father assistance but he developed more taste for a business career than for an agricultural life and in 1890 became a clerk in the store of a brother-in-law, in York county, and later took charge of a branch store for the same employer, at Philadelphia, where he remained for fifteen months About the time the coal mines started into operation here, Mr Weber returned to Clearfield county and in partnership with his brother, L D Weber, opened up a general store at Troutville, business beginning in April, 1892, and they continued together until June 2, 1902, when George J Weber bought the interest of his brother, who had entered the employ of the Rochester and Pittsburg Coal and Iron Company, and since that time Mr Weber has continued the business alone

In June, 1889, Mr Weber was married to Miss Margaret Rishel, a daughter of Daniel Rishel, late of Troutville, and they have two children: Ruth Golden and Ethel Jeannette Mr Weber and family attend the Reformed church of which he has been a member since he was fifteen years of age In politics he is a Democrat Since 1894 he has been serving on the school board and since 1909 has been a justice of the peace Mr Weber has been one of the stockholders of the DuBois National Bank since its organization

HERMAN SAMUEL MAC MINN, civil engineer, who was one of the pioneer settlers of DuBois, Pa , where he has made his home since 1877, is a descendant of the oldest families of the Colony of Pennsylvania, his forbears on all lines of ancestry having emigrated to Pennsylvania before the Revolution The oldest on the maternal side (of German blood) came over with Pastorius, on invitation of William Penn, and settled at Germantown, near Philadelphia, August 16, 1682 The first on paternal side, was Angus Mac Calman, a boy of fourteen years of age, born in Argyleshire, Scotland, descended through the Calmans from the Buchanans, of Sterlingshire, the clan's possessions were situated on the south and eastern border of Locklomond Angus came to America early in the year 1744, just before the breaking out of the war between England and France The manner of his coming at so early an age, and alone, was peculiar His father and uncle living together with their families, had charge of the Ferry across Lockawe The timber on the mountains in that district was being cut and transported on boats to Belfast Ireland At some act of his uncle, the high spirit of the boy took offence and he resolved to leave home and go to Ireland on one of the boats that was about to leave from the port of Bonawe Here the families had formerly lived, a few miles from Lockawe Once in Ireland, he fell in with the spirit of emigration (at fever heat at that time)

to go to the Plantations, where there was great demand for laborers Crossing Ireland to one of the ports of embarcation he went on board vessel and after a long voyage arrived in Philadelphia, where he had no difficulty in finding an employer, a good home with a countryman from the "Lower Counties," where he was adopted for a number of years for his passage, remaining with his benefactor until grown to manhood, when he went to Chester County, and after a time he married Mary Evans, a daughter of one of the Welsh families settled in those parts His Gaelic name, difficult of pronunciation in English, changed gradually by phonetic spelling until assumed as at present Six children were born to them, three sons and three daughters, namely Samuel, James, John, Ann (married Thomas Edwards), Hannah (married Matthew Doyle), and Mary (married John Anthony Wolf, a sea captain) Angus MacCalman followed farming, his wife died before the Revolution, while his children were yet young Angus, the father, married second, Mary Williams, also Welsh, their issue was two daughters Angus died in Delaware County, in 1804, and was buried in the Middletown township Presbyterian burying ground.

Samuel MacMinn, his eldest son was born in the year 1757, was twenty years of age at the time of the battle of Brandywine, that could be heard plainly from where he lived, he became very expert as a marksman, and served in the Continental army under Washington during the New Jersey campaign On April 19th, 1785, he married Christina Fields, daughter of William Fields, the ceremony was performed in Christ Church, in Philadelphia by the Rev Bishop William White The Fields were of the English family from near Bradford, England, Christiana Field's mother was

Mary Morris They were of the society of Friends, their home was near Coopertown, Delaware County Samuel MacMinn, for a number of years carried on farming for Mr Charles Willing, financier and banker at the time of the Revolutionary war, the farm was located near Sugartown, Willistown township, Chester County Samuel and Christiana Mac-Minn had eight children, namely Albon, was a soldier in the War of 1814, in Captain John G Wersler's company, 2nd Regiment Pennsylvania Volunteers, Light Infantry, he remained a bachelor. Dorothy, married 1st, William Jackson, their descendants reside in Baltimore, 2nd, William Copeland, their descendants reside in Philadelphia John Ross, Samuel, Thomas (his wife was the daughter of Charles McLean, a soldier of the Revolution, was desperately wounded at the storming of Stony Point by General Anthony Wayne, on the night of July 16th, 1779) Lydia married William Johnson, their descendants reside in Chester Valley, Nathan and Edward both died young Mary married George Williams, moved to Solon, Johnson County, Iowa Samuel Mac-Minn died August 8th, 1811, of cancer of the liver, he was buried in the old Revolutionary burying ground at Strafford. Chester County, where his name appears on the monument erected there to mark the burial place of several Revolutionary soldiers, his wife died Oct 4th, 1850, aged eighty-seven years, she was buried in the Goodwill M E churchyard, West Nantmeal, Chester County John Ross MacMinn, their eldest son, grandfather of Herman S MacMinn, was born in Willistown, Chester County, September 20th, 1792, he learned the trade of milling at the Gulf Mills, near Valley Forge, subsequently he operated the flouring and chocolate mills for John Black at Frankford, Philadelphia Here he met and married his employer's niece, Mary Brown, the daughter of Abram Brown, born Oct 1st, 1768, a descendant of Thomas Brown, an emigrant from Barking, Essex County, England He settled in Bucks County as early as 1712, his son Thomas Brown, Jr, became a minister among Friends, his declaration of intention of marriage with Elizabeth Davison, Feb 7th, 1720, was the first made in Buckingham Quarterly Meeting

Rebecca Black, the wife of Abram Brown, born March 13th, 1772, granddaughter of Abraham Black, a Scotch-Irish emigrant from County Antrim, Ireland, who settled on Deep Run, Bucks County, his name appears third on a list of thirty-five petitioners towards the organization of Bedminster township in March, 1741 Abram Brown died Oct 14th, 1799, his wife, Rebecca Brown, died in Chester County, February 5th, 1829, and was buried in the Friends' burying ground at Marshalltown They had five children, two only had issue to survive Abraham, born March 6, 1797, married and settled near Grafton, in southern Illinois, has numerous descendants

Mary Brown, the youngest child of Abram and Rebecca Brown, grandmother of Herman S MacMinn, was born April 11, 1799, in Buckingham, Bucks County John Ross MacMinn and Mary Brown, were married at the home of the bride's uncle, John Black, the 19th of November, 1818, by the Rev John C Murphy Their children were as follows, namely John Matthias, born August 23rd, 1819 Anna Matthias, born July 19th, 1821, died Mar 28, 1824 Reuben Myres, born Nov 8th, 1823, died Oct 14th, 1849 Rebecca Brown, born Oct 24, 1825, married to William Clark of near Brandywine Springs, Delaware, Mar 15, 1855:

she died Feb 9, 1864, issue, four children—
two sons and two daughters—live in Delaware
Samuel MacMinn, born Dec 27, 1827, married, had one son, lives in Honey Brook, Chester County Samuel MacMinn died March 13,
1905 Joseph Brown MacMinn, born April
2, 1830, died Sept 14, 1833 Lydia Ann
MacMinn, born July 22, 1832, died Nov 21,
1843

John Matthias MacMinn, was born at Mill-
town, Philadelphia At the age of eight years—
on the first of April, 1828—his father and family moved to Valley Creek, Chester County,
where he had purchased a grist mill and farm,
here he carried on the business of milling and
farming for thirty-nine years John Matthias
MacMinn was a student of nature, geology and
botany were his favorite studies He attended
the subscription schools of his day, and later
on obtained an advanced education in the
Friends' School in West Chester, taught by
Joshua Hoopes, and at Unionville, Chester
County, taught by Jonathan Gause, renowned
instructors in those days Here he found
companionship, mutual thought and touch with
nature, with Bayard Taylor, afterwards famous traveler, lecturer, and minister of the
United States at the Court of Berlin At the
age of sixteen John Matthias MacMinn began
teaching in his own home school It was at
the beginning of the Public School System, for
five years this was his main occupation
While engaged in teaching in the neighborhood
of Downingtown he became acquainted with
the Pyle family, iron manufacturers Benjamin Pyle, a member of the family, was partner in the firm of Whittaker & Co, of the
Washington Iron Works, Centre County This
was in 1840 Mr MacMinn was offered the
position of bookkeeper for the firm, which he

accepted and continued with them for four
years Mr Pyle died and the firm failed, when
Mr MacMinn became interested in a tannery
with James Hays, who, proving to be dishonest, Mr MacMinn lost all he had saved and
invested in the business. He then went to
Milesburg and engaged in teaching school
which he continued for about four years, when
he went into the lumber business in partnership with Samuel McKean, on the Moshannon,
but by forest fires and a great flood in 1849
he lost all, which caused him great embarrass-
ment for a little time, in 1850, he moved to
Unionville six miles away, and took up civil
engineering and located and constructed the
Bald Eagle and Tyrone Plank Road, in length
thirty-one miles, as engineer and superintendent
until its completion, during this time he paid
off all the claims held against him and acquired
a comfortable home In September, 1853, he
removed with his family to Williamsport As
an engineer, he has claims to be remembered,
as his achievements were of large importance
in this direction At Williamsport he took the
position of first assistant to the chief engineer
in the construction of the Sunbury & Erie Railroad He did much with his pen to promote
the building of this road and that of the Tyrone
& Loch Haven R R, through the Bald Eagle
Valley, being the chief engineer in its location
During sixteen years' residence in Williamsport he was promotor in other large contracts
for the public good When he moved to Virginia, in October, 1869, here he bought a
plantation near Norfolk, proposing to retire
from professional work and spend his remaining years in comparative ease, but at once see-
ing the importance of procuring for the City
of Norfolk one of its most needed utilities, a
system of fresh water supply, he brought the

matter before the people by his public writings and business meetings, its importance was at once seen and acted upon by appointing him chief engineer and general manager He lived to see his plans well under way, but the treacherous miasma in which his work was environed poisoned his system with malaria, fever followed rapidly and after a few days he died, on the eleventh of September, 1870 His remains were taken to Williamsport, Penna , and buried in "Wildwood" that had been his masterpiece as a city of the dead

On October 15th, 1844, Mr MacMinn was married to Miss Caroline Youngman, daughter of Elias P Youngman and Amelia Antes, of Nippenose Amelia Antes was the daughter of Henry Antes, Jr , son of Colonel John Henry Antes, a patriot of the Revolution, and Ann Elizabeth Shoemaker, daughter of Henry Shoemaker of Muncy Her grandmother, the wife of Col Antes, was Mary Paul the daughter of Jonathan Paul, of Philadelphia John Matthias MacMinn and Caroline Youngman had issue, four sons and three daughters, namely Joseph H resides in Williamsport, Pa Charles Von Linnaeus, lives in Newberry, Williamsport, Herman S of DuBois Edwin, pastor of the First Baptist church of Kearney, Nebraska, Mary, married to Isaac M Grier lives in Williamsport, Pa , Caroline widow of Stanley Mackey, resides in Philadelphia, and Benjamin F in the same city

Herman Samuel MacMinn, was nine years old when he went to East Bradford, Chester County, to live with his grandparents, April 16, 1858 He remained there for seven years when he returned to Williamsport He was educated in the common schools, Dickinson Seminary and Williamsport Business College, finding his talents and an inheritance from his

father He worked under the latter supervision for four years, and was his father's assistant in the making of surveys and the first map of Wildwood Cemetery, at Williamsport He also worked from the bottom upward on the surveys, location and construction of the old Winslow Colliery Railroad, a length of 248 miles between Milton and Franklin, of which his father was chief engineer, becoming his assistant In the summer of 1867, he spent three months on preliminary surveys in the Eastern Shore of Maryland, for the Baltimore & Potomac Railroad In March, 1870, going to Philadelphia, to accept a position as principal assistant engineer on the North Pennsylvania Railroad, in which he spent four years, at the end of that time he became assistant to the chief engineer on the Delaware and Bound Brook Railroad from the Delaware River to Bound Brook, a distance of twenty-eight miles, in the state of New Jersey Mr MacMinn then built the Trenton Branch of the same road, being engaged in this engineering enterprise for two and one half years He then came to DuBois and for a year was in the employ of John DuBois, afterward, as division engineer on the construction of the Pittsburg and Lake Erie Railroad in charge of the western division Mr MacMinn was, later, appointed general inspector of masonry and assistant engineer in the construction of the Pittsburg, Youngstown and Toledo Railroad, after the completion of this road he entered the employ of the Andrews Brothers, iron manufacturers of Youngstown, Ohio, and in their interest spent three months in the wilds of the northern Peninsula of Michigan examining some ore lands From there they sent him to the ore ranges in North Hastings County, Canada, where he discovered and opened up a small mining property, which proved to be small pocket of ore and was exhausted after about nine months operation. Mr MacMinn then went east to New York City in the interest of Mr W C Andrews, to secure sites for the location of stations, for his steam plant which he was introducing for heating and power purposes in that city, this being accomplished after a few weeks, Mr MacMinn was sent again to Northern Michigan to explore some lands on the Marquette Range, and again on the Menominee Range, where considerable time was spent with Diamond Drills. In the meantime Mr Andrews had his steam system installed and put into practical operation, he obtained the privilege of laying the pipes on Fifth Avenue, when he sent for Mr MacMinn to take charge of the new work as assistant engineer, this engaged his time for fifteen months, when the Kings County Elevated Railroad in Brooklyn had obtained their charter to construct that road on Fulton Avenue. Mr MacMinn was engaged in the location of the line from Fulton Ferry to East New York, a distance of about five miles. This work required about fifteen months, and construction was commenced only to be delayed by injunction proceedings, this, by the way, only prevented the work from going forward, for about a year, when the injunction was dissolved by the court, however, at the beginning of the delay Mr MacMinn left Brooklyn and returned to DuBois, when in a short time he was engaged by the Andrews Chapin & Co, of Youngstown, Ohio, and Duluth, Minnesota, to examine the iron ore ranges north of Lake Superior, those of Vermillion and Mesaba Ranges, and at the head waters of the Mississippi river. After a year spent in these regions, through a winter when the mercury was as low as fifty-two degrees below

zero, Fahrenheit, and the summer temperature very high, exposed to the tormenting poisonous bites of the insects and miasmic atmosphere of forests and marches, camping out and making long journeys in canoe, and tramping Indian trails after many months, which was making inroads on his hitherto robust constitution, he resolved to make a change. The opportunity came unexpectedly, in the offer of a position as assistant engineer on the Chicago & North Western Railroad with headquarters at Madison, Wisconsin. This appeared, on reflection, as a delightful change, and the offer was accepted. The several roads in Wisconsin making up the division over which Mr MacMinn was placed, included 800 miles; careful semiannual inspections were required, a great deal of new work was carried out, numbers of men employed, and separated at long distances, and being entirely unfamiliar with the road heretofore, it required great exertion and constant work, from sixteen to eighteen hours every day. This was a task endured for nearly a year, when it became no longer endurable and Mr MacMinn resigned his position and returned to DuBois, where he was engaged by Mr John DuBois to make a survey of the DuBois estate, including nearly 20,000 acres in Clearfield County, also by Mr A C of Lock Haven, for the survey of the Osborn Baum and Carrier lands, including several thousand acres in the vicinity of DuBois and Falls Creek. During the time of this work and the years that followed, Mr MacMinn was engaged almost constantly in various lines of work in his calling, in borough work, sewers, water supplies, town plots, and the location of the DuBois Electric Street Railway. In the fall of 1896, Mr MacMinn planned and located a private water supply for Mr DuBois, one of the most complete to be found anywhere The length of the line is about two and one quarter miles, fifteen hundred and forty-two feet of this passes through a ridge of solid rock by a tunnel but four feet high by three feet wide, the work was started in November at both ends and worked continuously for five months (except Sundays) But two men could work together on account of the contracted space The headings came together on Wednesday at noon April 21st, 1897 A short distance below the tunnel a reservoir was constructed in a ravine, covering an area of two and two-thirds acres, containing 4,500,000 gallons, the water of the finest quality is obtained from fifteen springs and small streams flowing from the sandstone formation of Boons Mountain, nearly seventeen hundred feet above sea level, and conveyed through eighteen and twenty-inch vitrified pipe At the tunnel, which is sealed at both ends, the water is allowed to flow freely over the rock bottom which has a fall of but a quarter of an inch in every sixteen feet, at the end of the tunnel the water is again taken up and conveyed to the reservoir in a pipe Each tributary line of six-inch pipe has for its inlet a small reservoir, receiving-box, arranged with settling basin, trap and screens to prevent any floating substance from entering the line, along the main line at several places are sediment basins Each inlet reservoir is carefully fenced with wire to prevent any approach to the water From the main reservoir the water is conveyed to the town a distance of about three miles In May and June of 1896, Mr MacMinn made a survey for a railway line from DuBois to Centreville over Boons Mountain, a distance of eighteen miles, to determine the feasibility of reaching the timber tracts Mr DuBois owned on Hicks Run in Elk and Cameron Counties,

this project was abandoned and it was determined subsequently, to build up that stream from its mouth, Mr MacMinn making the reconnoisance of this Route in April, 1902, from which he followed it up with the location To reach the distant lines of the several timber tracts several switch back tracks have been required, and the removal of the timber has been progressing since that time The almost constant demand for some manner of work has deprived Mr MacMinn of times usually allowed as vacation and recreation has been of rare occurrence with him, the only one of which he can recall with any degree of satisfaction was a trip to the Pacific Coast in the summer of 1891, occupying three months time Mr MacMinn made the study of geology and mineralogy a pastime and his collection is on a large scale, his opportunities for collecting curios appealed to his fancy and these are in great number, along with his interest in Indian relics, compose a museum full of varied interest The gathering together of all this collection was but the passing of many hours in strange lands and in the wilderness, away from home and friends, in an agreeable and contented frame of mind, and with it all his life has been a busy and useful one

H S MacMinn was married first to Miss Mary Louisa Fowler, a niece of John DuBois, in Christ Church Williamsport, Pa, November 23rd, 1875, she died without issue February 28th, 1894 Mr MacMinn married secondly January 1st, 1869, Miss Cora F Fisher, a daughter of William P Fisher, of Unionville, Centre County, Pa They have two children Marjorie and Dorathea Mr MacMinn first united with the Dutch Reformed Church, at Seventh and Spring Garden Streets, Philadelphia, in the year 1870, after coming to DuBois he and his wife united with the Presbyterian Church, his present wife is a member of the Society of Friends, of the Baltimore Yearly Meeting. In politics Mr. MacMinn is a Republican and is now a member of the School Board and of the Building Committee. The family residence is on the corner of DuBois Avenue and Fourth Street, DuBois.

DANIEL MILSOM,* a highly respected citizen of Allport, Pa., who has been foreman of Lane No. 5, of the Todd Brothers Coal Company for the past two years, was born in Brookfield, Trumbull County, Ohio, May 20, 1872, and is a son of John and Elizabeth (Pritchard) Milsom.

John Milsom was born in 1842 in Bristol, England, and when seven years of age started to work in the mines there. In 1865 he came to America, landing here the day of President Lincoln's assassination, and he at once went to Brookfield, Ohio, where he secured work in the mines. After ten or twelve years there he went to Mercer County, Pa., as a miner, and in April, 1887, came to Allport, Pa. He is now mine foreman for the Berwin White Coal Company, at Smoke Run, Clearfield County, with which concern he has been connected for fourteen years. Mrs. Milsom, who was born in Scotland in 1849, preceded her husband to this country. They had a family of eleven children, as follows: W. J., a mine foreman of Madera, Alice, who is the wife of Joseph Napper of Philipsburg, Charles, who is a mine foreman of Osceola, John, who holds a like position in the Pittsburg district, Daniel, Elizabeth, who is the wife of Charles Diehl of Philipsburg, Maggie, who married Thomas Gatehouse of Gates, Pa., Phoebe, who married Adolphus Bowser, a mine foreman of Smoke

Run, Annie, who is the wife of William Johns of Smoke Run, Sarah Jane, who married Charles Smith, an electrician for the Berwin White Coal Company at Janesville, and Eddie, who is a mine foreman near Pittsburg.

Daniel Milsom attended the public schools of Mercer County, and when between twelve and thirteen years of age left school to work in the mine at Hazzard and continued there until coming to Allport, working in both the Allport and Rutherford mines. He was employed for four or five years as a blacksmith in the mines, and for the past eight years has been a foreman. In addition to his comfortable home, Mr. Milsom is the owner of valuable real estate in Allport, and he is considered one of the good, public-spirited men of the town.

On December 22, 1890, Mr. Milsom was united in marriage with Miss Jessie Wilson, whose parents came from Scotland and settled in Tioga County, Pa., later moving to Clearfield County. Seven children have been born to Mr. and Mrs. Milsom, namely: John W., who is deceased, and Nellie, Elizabeth, Jean, Alice, Margaret and Adam. Mr. Milsom is a member of Winburne Lodge No. 931, I. O. O. F., and Clearfield Lodge No. 540, B. P. O. E., also being connected with Moshannon Lodge, F. & A. M., of Philipsburg. He is a Methodist in his religious views and a stanch Republican in politics.

A. H. REED,* an enterprising farmer and highly respected citizen of Lawrence township, Clearfield County, Pa., resides on the old Reed homestead, which consists of 175 acres, and was born here in May, 1866, a son of Alexander and Isabelle (Clyde) Reed.

Amos Alexander Reed was born in 1824 at

Wolfe Run, Lawrence township, Clearfield County, Pa , and obtained his education in the common schools of Lawrence township After his marriage he resided some time in Goshen township, but subsequently removed to Lawrence township, where he followed lumbering and operated a farm of 240 acres During the last five years of his life he lived in retirement at Clearfield, Pa , where he died at the age of 74 years His wife died two years previously at the age of 73 years, and both were buried in the Goshen Cemetery They were members of the Presbyterian Church, and he was politically a stanch Democrat Amos A Reed was united in marriage with Isabelle Clyde, a daughter of Ex-Associate Judge Clyde of Clearfield County, Pa , and their union resulted in the following issue Mrs M J Owens of Lawrence township, J Mansfield, of Lawrence township, Belle, a resident of WilkesBarre, Pa , S C of Lawrence township, Rachel, a physician, now in Japan, A H , the subject of this record, and Amos, who died aged 12 years

A H Reed was reared in Lawrence township, and obtained his education in the common schools of the township and at Clearfield He then engaged in the lumber business and built and operated a saw mill on Lick Run for some time He subsequently sold the saw mill and located at Clearfield, Pa , where he resided about eighteen months, when he removed to the old home farm in Lawrence township The farm consists of 175 acres, of which 25 acres are located in Goshen township, and in 1889 he fitted the house throughout with hot water heat, and also installed a bath Mr Reed is politically a Democrat, and is at present writing candidate for Representative from Clearfield County, and has served as tax collector and several times as Committeeman at the Democratic conventions Mr Reed is a member of the M E Church, of which he has served in all the offices, and was for some time county Deputy of the Grange of this County

In 1891 Mr Reed was joined in marriage with Nettie Price, who is a daughter of Lorenzo Price, formerly a resident of Pike township, but later of Curwensville, Pa , and their union resulted in the following issue Clarke, Bernice, Bruce, Margaret, Bigler and Augusta

SAMUEL E FOWLER,* mine electrician for the Victor Coal Company, at Morrisdale, Clearfield County, Pa , has been a resident of Morris Township for the past twenty-two years and is a member of the township school board He was born at Arnot, Tioga County, Pa , April 6, 1871, and is a son of James and Jeanett (Rumgoy) Fowler

The parents of Mr Fowler were born in Scotland and were married there and came to Tioga County in 1870 and to Clearfield County in 1888 The father resides at Morrisdale and is still an active man although sixty-seven years of age He devoted almost all his life to mining and now performs the duties of janitor in one of the borough's public school buildings The mother died August 2, 1910, at the age of sixty-four years Their nine children all are living as follows Nellie, who is the wife of Oscar Carlson, of Braddock, Pa , Samuel E , Mary, who is the wife of Andrew Campbell, of Morrisdale Mines, James, who lives at Houtzdale, J Walker, who is a resident of Morrisdale, Robert, who is employed at Shaft No 1, Morrisdale, John, who is a coal mine worker at Morrisdale, Margaret, who is the wife of Henry Mansell, of Morrisdale, and William, who is employed as a motorman in the Morrisdale mines

Samuel E Fowler was eighteen years of age

when he came to Clearfield County, having obtained his schooling in Tioga County He worked for the Coaldale Coal Company until 1892 and from then was with the Morrisdale Coal Company until October 15, 1910, for four years being electrician for that company He came then to the Victor Coal Company and has continued with the same and has the reputation of being one of the most efficient men in the employ of the company

On May 28, 1892, Mr Fowler was married to Miss Emma Heane, a daughter of William and Emma (Price) Heane Her parents came to America from England and located first at Philipsburg, Pa, but later moved to Musser, where the father still resides, the mother having died May 28, 1892 Mr and Mrs Fowler have had four children William and Samuel, both of whom are mine workers, James, who is yet in school, and Mary, who is deceased Mr Fowler and wife are members of the Methodist Episcopal church at Morrisdale He belongs to Lodge No 933, Odd Fellows, at Allport, Lodge No 161, Knights of Pythias, at Morrisdale, and to Lodge No 88, Knights of Malta, at Philipsburg In politics he is a Republican

DANIEL MOYER, a successful farmer and citizen of Cooper township, was born in Kylerstown, Pa, Feb 26, 1872, a son of Peter and Mary E (Adams) Moyer His mother, a daughter of Thomas Adams, was born in Montour county, Pa, her marriage to Peter Moyer taking place Feb 11, 1867 Of their three children, two died in infancy, namely Mary Eve and Samuel

Daniel Moyer was the youngest of his parents' children He was educated in the public schools of his native locality and subsequently

learned the butcher's trade, also mercantile business In 1896 he turned his attention to agriculture and now resides on a well cultivated farm of 77 acres, which he managed personally up to Dec 1, 1909 He is a member of Lodge No 161, K of P, of Morrisdale Mines, Allport Lodge No 933, I O O F, Tomoka Lodge Red Men No 96, Morrisdale Mines, Oak Hill Grange at Karthaus, and Royal Order of Moose, No 123 at Philipsburg He was married Oct 9, 1894, to Miss Alice E Kirk, of Luthersburg, this county, a daughter of Joseph H Kirk He and his wife are the parents of three children, namely. Joseph Peter, Anna Mary and Frederick Daniel Mr Moyer is a Democrat in politics but supports the Keystone ticket, and has served as assessor of Cooper township He belongs to the Presbyterian church at Kylertown His paternal grandparents were Adam and Eve Moyer, who came to Clearfield county from Germany with their family

F B READ, M D, physician and surgeon at Osceola Mills, Pa, where he is proprietor of a drug store, is one of the prominent and active citizens of the place, interested vitally in all that concerns the welfare of the community, of which he has been a member for thirty-one years Dr Read was born in Lawrence Township, Clearfield County, Pa, June 7, 1841, and is a son of Ross and Mary (Thompson) Read, and a grandson of Alexander Read The latter was a very early settler in Clearfield County and in 1800 he conducted the first post office between Clearfield and Bellefonte, establishing it on the William Mitchell farm, one mile south of Clearfield He carried the mail between these places on horseback

Ross Read, father of Dr Read, was born

in Lawrence Township and followed farming until past middle age, when he retired with his wife to Clearfield, where both died He married Mary Thompson, a daughter of Ignatius Thompson, who was of Irish birth The mother of Mrs Read was born in England Ross Read and wife became parents of eight children, the four survivors of their family being F B , Margaret Ella McKendrick, residing at Ebensburg, Pa , Alexander Ross, residing at Akron, O , and Rebecca Matilda Spackman, now living at Detroit, Mich

F B Read was reared on a farm and attended the local schools and Clearfield Academy before beginning his medical studies In 1867 he was graduated from Jefferson Medical College, at Philadelphia, having been with Dr Woods, of Clearfield for three years before entering college Dr Read engaged in practice first at Bigler, Pa , where he remained for fifteen years, and in 1880 came from there to Osceola Mills In 1886 he established his drug store, which he has conducted ever since In spite of advancing years, Dr Read still attends to a large practice He preaches the medical value of fresh air and exercise and is himself the best example of these theories, driving out over the country in the roughest kind of weather and seemingly enjoying the stimulation found in battling with the elements

On October 10, 1865, Dr Read was married to Miss Sue A Rider, who was born at Karthaus, Clearfield County, Pa , a daughter of John W Rider, at that time a well known farmer and lumberman Dr and Mrs Read have had eight children, namely Ralph Maynard, who is in a hotel business at Johnstown, Pa , married Winnifred Scollins, and has three children, Paul Shelton, who resides at Osceola, and married Maggie Scollins, Maude, who

is the wife of Frank P O'Brien, who is in the furniture and undertaking business at Osceola Mills, Howard W , who lives at Philadelphia, Mae, who is the wife of S R Hamilton, of Osceola Mills, Haskell, a resident of Philadelphia, who married Bessie Scott Alma, who is a student in her third year at the Women's Medical College, Philadelphia, and Charles, who died in infancy Dr Read and family belong to the Presbyterian church He served some sixteen years as a member of the borough school board and a number of times as burgess, possessing together with his professional qualifications, the natural capacity which has made him ever recognized as a leader in public matters and an example of true citizenship

PETER STOTT, who has been a resident of Munson Station, Clearfield County, Pa , since 1888, where he fills the important position of foreman of the Kyler mine for the Pennsylvania Coal and Coke Company, was born February 16, 1866, at St Helens, Lancashire, England, and is a son of Henry and Jane Stott

Henry Stott was born in England in 1844 and still resides at St Helens where he is well known and much respected His wife was also born in England and died there in 1876, at the age of thirty-four years Three sons and one daughter were born to them, namely James, who is a glass blower by trade, lives at St Helens; Henry, who is in the same business as his older brother, also lives at St Helens, Alice, who is the wife of Thomas Stott, also lives at St Helens, and Peter, the only one of the family in the United States The father is a coal miner

Peter Stott was permitted to attend school at St Helens until he was twelve years of age, when he entered the mines and continued to work as a coal miner in his native land until he was twenty-one years old In his twenty-second year he set sail for America and landed in the port of New York in November, 1888 from which place he came immediately to Munson Station, Clearfield County He has devoted seventeen of the years he has resided here to working in the Kyler mine for R C Fishburn and the rest of the time has worked in nearby mines, always being able to secure remunerative employment, being an industrious and peaceable man For ten years he was assistant foreman of the Kyler mine and since December, 1906, has been foreman

In December, 1890, Mr Stott was married at Houtzdale, Pa, to Miss Edith Woodiwiss, a daughter of Charles and Emma Woodiwiss, of Yorkshire, England, and they have an interesting family of three daughters and one son Jessie, Harry, Jennie Lillian and Frances In politics Mr Stott is a Republican and in 1909 he was elected a school director in Morris Township and has twice served as judge of elections He is a member of Thesbian Lodge, Knights of Pythias, No 293, Munson Station, and has passed all the chairs, and belongs also to Moshannon Lodge No 391, F & A M, Philipsburg and class of 1911 Williamsport Consistory and is a Thirty-second degree Mason He stands high both as a citizen and as a man With his wife he belongs to the Methodist Episcopal church

WILLIAM C LANGSFORD,* county commissioner of Clearfield County, Pa, and a well known and representative citizen, is a native of Great Britain, born in England, Jan 24, 1847 His parents were William and Eliza (Oliver) Langsford, who passed their lives

in England and reared a family of five children

William C Langsford is a self made man He attended school in his native land and then worked in the coal mines until 1869, when he crossed the Atlantic Ocean to America, locating in Pennsylvania coal regions He continued to work in the mines until 1872 and then invested his capital in the barber business and later purchased and conducted a stationery store Still later he went out as a traveling salesman for a tailoring house and also was interested in the same capacity for a piano and organ firm He early identified himself with the Republican party and in 1908, was elected on its ticket, a member of the board of county commissioners Prior to this, however, he served a number of years as a justice of the peace and for seventeen years was a member of the borough council In public as in business life, Mr Langsford has proved efficient and honorable

Mr Langsford married Miss Ellen Charlton and six children were born to them With his family he belongs to the Episcopal church Fraternally he is identified with the Masons and the Knights of Pythias

JOHN F ROWLES, M D,* physician and surgeon at Mahaffey, Pa, was born in Clearfield County, Pa, April 29, 1869, and is a son of John A and Elinor (Wiley) Rowles The father was a native of Lawrence Township and the mother of Greenwood Township, Clearfield County They were the parents of nine children, John F being the youngest born The father was engaged in the lumber business throughout his active life

John F Rowles became an orphan when but five years old He first attended school in

Greenwood Township and later graduated from the Bower graded school, after which he entered the Lock Haven Normal School, graduating from that institution in 1893 For some time afterward he taught school in Clearfield County, in the meanwhile doing preparatory medical reading, and in 1900 he entered the Medico-Chirurgical College, Philadelphia, where he was graduated with credit in 1904 Dr Rowles located immediately at Mahaffey and here has built up an excellent practice and has become one of the representative citizens

In 1906 Dr Rowles was married to Miss Bessie Mahaffey, of Mahaffey, Pa , and they have two children, Elizabeth and John F Dr Rowles is a member of numerous medical organizations and belongs also to Lodge No 574, F. & A M , at Coalport, Pa , and to Anawan Tribe, No 361, I O R M , at Mahaffey, of which latter he has not been a trustee for two years He is not active politically, his professional responsibilities absorbing his time and attention very fully

WESLEY DANIEL LITTLE, mine superintendent for W H Wayne & Co , fire brick manufacturers in Decatur township, Clearfield county, Pa , resides within three miles of the place of his birth, on his farm of thirty acres, which lies in Decatur township He was born in Boggs township, Clearfield county, Pa , January 31, 1873, and is a son of John and Anna (Smeal) Little

John Little was born in Center County, Pa , near Bellefonte He learned the carpenter's trade and followed it until within three years of his death, at the age of fifty-two years, and then engaged in farming His widow survives Their children were born in Boggs Township, namely Jennie, who is the wife of

Matthew Waldron, of Philadelphia , Wesley Daniel, Helen, who is the widow of Harry Pierce, of Philadelphia , Sadie, who also lives in Philadelphia , John, who is engaged in the ice business in Philadelphia, married Mary Thompson, Ethel, who resides in Philadelphia , and Sylvester, who died when aged eight years

Wesley Daniel Little attended school until he was sixteen years of age, after which he engaged in farming in the summers and worked in the mines in the winters until he was twenty-two years old, at which time he accepted the position of engineer for S B Stine, at Osceola Mills He continued there two years and then spent five years with the Clearfield Fire Brick Company In 1902 he moved to Blue Ball, where he was engaged for two years in the boiler room and seven years later became superintendent of the same mine His entire life has been passed in Clearfield County and he is known as a reliable man and well posted on every detail of the manufacture of fire brick He owns property that he has secured through his industry and prudence and has a very comfortable home

Mr Little was married February 19, 1894, to Miss Ella Read, a daughter of John F Read, of Glen Richey Nine children have been born to Mr and Mrs Little, namely Gertrude. William, John Dewey, Maud, Anna, Creighton, a baby, Martha and Charles In politics Mr Little is a Democrat In religious faith he is in sympathy with the views of the United Brethren church

ARTHUR M DRAUCKER, who owns and conducts a blacksmith shop at Luthersburg, Clearfield County, Pa , and has 140 acres of farm land in Brady Township, farming one tract of 80 acres and devoting the other 60 acres to pasture, and renting the buildings, also has a one-half interest in 250 acres of timber land, in partnership with a brother, P W Draucker He has been a lifelong resident of Clearfield County, and is a leading citizen of Brady Township, where he was born on the old home farm, February 5, 1847, a son of Isaac and Mary (Bloom) Draucker

Isaac Draucker was born in Lancaster County, Pa , and came to Clearfield with his brother, John Draucker He located in Brady township, two and one-half miles east of Luthersburg, on the Erie turnpike road, where he conducted a hotel for many years The old Draucker House was well known to travelers along the stage coach line He died there in 1852, at the age of forty-five years His widow continued the business and in turn was succeeded by one of the sons, Perry W , who still lives on the place Isaac Draucker married Mary Bloom, who was born at Curwensville, Clearfield County Her father, William Bloom, was a pioneer in this section, which, at that time was almost a wilderness, the nearest milling point being Bellfonte Mrs Draucker survived until 1888, dying at the age of seventy-seven years, nine months and twenty-six days Fifteen children were born to this marriage The children of this marriage were as follows Sarah, who is now deceased, was the wife of John Scott, also deceased, Levie, who is deceased, Catherine, who is deceased, was the wife of Christian Smith, also deceased, Leah, who is the wife of Daniel Goodlander Ellen, who is the widow of Lever Flegal, Joseph and Porter, twins, both of whom are deceased, Adam, who is also deceased, Hannah, who is the widow of Edward Holley, James, Eliza, who is the wife of Daniel Rodgers, and Arthur M , Perry W and Lucy, the last named being deceased

Arthur M Draucker spent his boyhood on the home farm and in the winter time attended one of the old-fashioned school houses, where slab benches were provided for seats and all other accommodations were primitive. He remained on the farm until his marriage when he purchased his shop at Luthersburg, paying $200 for the business He had learned the trade here with its former owner, Joseph Redding After his mother's death he bought her farm and has since combined farming and blacksmithing In addition to his interests mentioned, for the past thirty-five years he has also been an auctioneer and in this capacity is favorably known all through this section. Mr. Draucker has frequently been elected to important township offices, serving three years as constable, fifteen years as tax collector, six years as assessor and also as a member of the election board

On May 7, 1868, Mr. Draucker was married to Miss Mary E Breon, who was born at Luthersburg, a daughter of Michael Breon, who was born in Lycoming County in 1819, and is the oldest resident of Brady Township The children born to Mr and Mrs Draucker have been as follows Lillian, who is the wife of Wm Gillern, Lucy, who is the wife of Harry C Shay, Lillian and Lucy being twins, Anna, who is the wife of Harry Carlisle, Effie, who was the wife of Jesse Lines and died May 14, 1911, aged 39 years, one month and 25 days; Hattie, who is the wife of Dr T E Farrell, Madge, Ruth, who is the wife of James B Kirk, Jr , Pearl, and Levi, who married Maude Shaffer Mr Draucker and family are members of the Methodist Episcopal church.

In politics he is a Democrat He belongs to the K of P, at New Salem

HON JESSE RICHNER, burgess of Irvona, Pa, is a prominent citizen and representative business man of this flourishing borough, and has spent the greater part of his life connected with coal mining and is now superintendent of a local mine He was born July 7, 1880, near Philipsburg, Pa, and is a son of Jacob and Sarah (Knough) Richner

Jacob Richner and wife were born in Germany and both were brought to the United States when young and grew to maturity and married in Clearfield county, Pa Jacob Richner served as a soldier in the Federal army during the Civil war and was several times wounded He owned a farm and also was interested in lumbering His death occurred when he was about sixty years of age His widow survives and is now in her seventy-sixth year. Their children were as follows Philip, who resides at Clearfield, is a barber by trade, Mary, who is the wife of Frank Westburn, residing in Morrisdale, Maggie, who is the wife of Thomas Haynes, of Decatur township, George, who is a clerk in a store at Osceola, Ida, who is the wife of Fred Baughman, residing on a farm near Turkey Hill, Alice, who is the wife of John Cornell, of Jeffries, David, who is mine foreman at the Burley Clay Works, Jesse, and Amanda, who is the wife of Joseph Kline, of Happy Valley

Jesse Richner attended school more or less regularly until he was seventeen years of age, first at Laurel Run and later at Irvona He then engaged in teaming and afterward went into the mines and for fourteen of the seventeen years of his residence at Irvona, mining

has been his main business and no one better understands mining and the conditions surrounding the lives of miners than does Burgess Richner He is a very level-headed man and when he was elected burgess of Irvona, on the Republican ticket, in February, 1909, he was acceptable to all his fellow citizens and his administration has brought about excellent conditions in the borough

Mr Richner was married May 15, 1901, to Miss Millie Potts, a daughter of Walter and Mittie Potts, residents of Irvona They have two children, Ethel Icie and Flora He owns his comfortable home at Irvona and has acquired property through his industry and prudence He belongs to the Patriotic Sons of America, at Rosebud, and to the Knights of the Mystic Chain

JESSE BUTERBAUGH,* merchant, a representative business man of Burnside Township, who has been established on his present corner, near East Ridge, since 1908, was born August 21, 1865, in Indiana County, Pa His parents were George M and Mary (Zigler) Buterbaugh

George M Buterbaugh was born in Indiana County, where he still lives, being now in his eightieth year His father was William Buterbaugh, of German ancestry, George M Buterbaugh married Mary Zigler, who died at the age of fifty-three years They had the following children Milligan, who is a farmer in Indiana County, Alexander, who is a woodsman in West Virginia, Jesse, Grant, who is a merchant in Somerset County, Daniel, who is in partnership with his next older brother, Rebecca, who is the wife of A Pittman, a farmer in Green Township, Indiana County, Susanna, who is the wife of John

Edmonson, of West Virginia, and Ida, who is the wife of O Hall, of Indiana County

Jesse Buterbaugh attended school more or less regularly until he was fifteen years of age and for three years afterward worked on farms and then worked by the day for about six years, accumulating in this way capital with which he started into a livery business at Cherry Tree, where he continued for three years After selling that business he was interested in lumber for one year, then spent one year in the hotel business in Cambria County and later went into the restaurant business at Cherry Tree Since then Mr Buterbaugh has been in the general mercantile line at his present location

Mr Buterbaugh married Miss Ella Youngling, who was born in 1863, in Burnside Township, a daughter of Jacob and Miranda (King) Youngling, and they have had the following children Mary, who is the wife of William Caldwell, of Indiana County, and they have one chld, Hale, who is employed by the Pennsylvania Railroad Company, and Ethel, Freda, Genevieve, Geraldine and Jesse Mr Buterbaugh is a Republican and always casts his vote as a proof of good citizenship but he has never been willing to accept any office He belongs to several fraternal organizations

MARTIN RUSNAK, proprietor of the Empire Hotel, at Hawk Run, Morris Township, Clearfield County, Pa , was born November 11, 1869, in Austria, and is a son of Steve and Elizabeth Rusnak The mother died in Austria and the father then came to America but subsequently returned to his native land and still survives, being now in his ninetieth year

Martin Rusnak had some educational advantages before coming to the United States when fourteen years of age He first found work in the mines at Snow Shoe, in Center County, Pa , and afterward at the Morrisdale mines in Morris Township, Clearfield County He was then seventeen years of age and he worked in the mines there for seventeen years, and was a miner twenty-six years in all He followed that dangerous calling through all this period without accident but for the past two years has lived a safer and easier life He took charge of the Empire Hotel at Hawk Run, which had been destroyed by fire in 1909 He rebuilt, putting up a modern brick structure, four stories high, and has twenty-three well furnished rooms for the use of the traveling public This house in its management, appearance and equipments would be creditable to a much larger place than Hawk Run and Mr Rusnak is a popular host

Mr Rusnak was married in 1890, to Miss Bertha Striks, of Snow Shoe, and they have a large and happy family of thirteen children, all of whom survive Mary, Martin, John, Steve, Joseph, Mike, Paul, Ludwig, Luke, Elizabeth, Annie, Bertha and Susie The eldest daughter is the wife of George Veras of Hawk Run Mr Rusnak and family are members of the Roman Catholic church In politics he is a Democrat

JOSEPH HULL CHAPMAN,* a well known farmer of Burnside township, a son of James and Sarah Ann (Mitchell) Chapman The father, James Chapman, came to this township at the age of twenty years, or about 1868, settling near the Albright Harmony church, on what is now the old Chapman homestead He followed the occupation of lumbering, and died in 1910 at the age of 62 years He was a son of John and Sarah (Cary) Chapman, of Indiana county, the former of whom died in 1848 Mrs James Chapman died March 6, 1906, at the age of sixty-seven She was the daughter of Joseph and Mary (Fuller) Mitchell She and her husband were the parents of a large family, of whom those now living are as follows Maud, who resides at home, Mary, wife of John Hippe, of New Washington, Joseph H , subject of this sketch, Nellie, wife of S S Young, of New Washington, Grace, a teacher, residing at home, Smith, who resides in Burnside township, Margaret, a teacher residing at home, Jessie, wife of Ray Patchin, Daisy and Trudell, both of whom are engaged in teaching

Joseph Hull Chapman, after the usual period of school attendance, was variously employed until attaining his majority In 1901 he bought the parental homestead and has since carried on farming and lumbering here in this vicinity and further south with gratifying success Mr Chapman is a Democrat politically but is not politically active He is a member of the lodge of Red Men at Patchinville He is recognized by all as a reliable and industrious citizen

Mr Chapman was married June 11, 1899, to Stella Young, who was born June 18, 1881, a daughter of T J and Alsontia (McKee) Young of Burnside township Mrs Chapman's parents are both living, Mr Young being now 54 years of age and his wife forty-eight The children of our subject and wife are as follows James C , now aged twelve, Sylvia, aged nine, Thomas Eugene, eight, and Sarah Belle, eight Mrs Chapman is a member of Harmony church Her brothers and sisters now living, are Stanley, Nora, wife of M Wagoner, of Pittsburg, Aincall, residing in Pittsburg, Sally, wife of Harry Riddle, Wil-

helmina, wife of B Hughes of Jonestown, Pa , Emma, living at home, Edward and Milwood, also residing at home

DE LANCY H WARING, a successful farmer of Morris Township, and formerly a county commissioner, was born in this township, one mile from where he resides, in September, 1850 He is a son of Samuel and Susannah (Shimmell) Waring

Samuel Waring was born in England and came to America and settled in Morris Township, Clearfield County, in March, 1830 He bought a farm from James Allport, who was also a native of England and was the first settler in Morris Township Samuel Waring was an educated man and was not only a farmer but also a teacher and a surgeon His death occurred in 1851, at the age of fifty-seven years His father as well as the father of his wife crossed the Atlantic Ocean, the latter coming from Germany Samuel Waring married Susannah Shimmell, who died in 1879, at the age of sixty-nine years' They had eight children, namely James, who died in infancy, Catherine, who married first Newton Antis, and secondly John Ebbs, and resides at Philipsburg, being now in her seventy-second year, William, who lives near Clearfield, George, who was a lumberman and died in 1899, John, who has lived in Oregon since 1876, Samuel, who lives in the State of Washington, Elizabeth, who was married first to George Wagner and secondly to John Sullivan, is now a widow and lives in Morris Township, and De Lancey H

De Lancey H Waring was the youngest born in his parents' family and he secured his education in the Allport schools and at Pine Grove Academy, in Center County After leaving school he was engaged for a time in the lumber business in Clearfield and Center Counties In 1875 he had bought his farm, originally containing 106 acres, but now having but ninety It was formerly the property of Joseph Rothrock, who built a large barn, but Mr Waring had to move into a log house and it remained the home until 1876, when he put up his present comfortable residence, making many improvements from time to time He found an orchard in bearing condition but he set out the trees that now bear the choice fruit for which the place is noted, while he also made provision for small fruits, and each season brings an abundance of currants, blackberries, strawberries and raspberries He takes pardonable pride in the appearance of his fine estate. From a part of the land he cleared the stumps and with careful methods prepared the soil for the high state of cultivation that it shows

In 1875 Mr Waring was married to Miss Sarah C Hicks, a daughter of William and Elizabeth Hicks, the former of whom was reared in Elk County and the latter in Center County William Hicks was a lumberman and also worked around the mines Both he and wife died near Osceola, Pa Mr and Mrs Waring have had children born to them as follows Millie, who is the wife of Charles Dailey, of Altoona, Elizabeth, who is the wife of Thomas Murphey, and they have five children, Susan, who died unmarried, at the age of twenty-one years, Eliza, who is the wife of John Johnson of Philadelphia who is employed with the Stephen Green Publishing Co (has one child), Marjorie, who is a teacher at Morrisdale, Alfred C, a resident of Altoona, who owns and operates a vacuum cleaner, and Thomas, who assists on the home farm Mr Waring's children have all been well educated

and all the girls have taught school, with the exception of Susan Mr Waring was reared an Episcopalian but the family attend the Methodist Episcopal church He is an interested and useful member of Center Hill Grange, in Graham township, and belongs to Moshannon Lodge No 391, F & A M He is one of the leading Democrats of the township and at different times has held almost every office, serving as school director, treasurer for several terms, auditor for some four terms, filling that important office when this township was united with Cooper township, and at present is township assessor In 1896 he was elected a county commissioner and served out his term with faithful efficiency. Perhaps no man in Morris township stands higher in the personal esteem of his fellow citizens

W O LONG,* who is the operator and half owner of Long's Mill, situated in Pine township, Clearfield county, Pa, a custom mill manufacturing shingles and torpedo caps and doing general contract work, is a well known business man of this section and a substantial and representative citizen He was born in Sandy township, Clearfield county, October 26, 1860

With the exception of some years spent in Jefferson county, Pa, Mr Long has always lived in Clearfield county He resides on his farm of seventy-five acres, which is situated twelve miles from Clearfield and four miles from Penfield, on the Clearfield and Penfield road, ten acres of which is cleared In 1899 he erected his present mill and all of the camp buildings Ever since he has been very closely engaged and at the present time (1910) has just finished cutting 380 acres of timber on the Thompson tract and also has had the contract for cutting and sawing some state timber His mill is an important business adjunct of this section

Mr Long was married the first time to Miss Isabella Rockbach, a daughter of Thomas Rockbach, of Union township She died in Sandy township and her burial was at Grampian, Clearfield county Two children survived her, Thomas J and Belle Mr Long was married a second time, to Miss Bessie Mimm, a daughter of George Mimm, of DuBois, Pa, and four children were born to this union Mayme, Hays, Edward and Viola Mr Long's third marriage was to Miss Fannie Soliday, a daughter of S C Soliday, of Huston township, and they have seven children Mary, Essie, Lottie, George, William, James and Roxie In politics Mr Long is nominally a Democrat but he has independent inclinations He is identified with the fraternal order of Knights of Pythias, at Rockton

JOHN N SMITH, a representative business man of Irvona, Pa, where he conducts a general store, was born in Beccaria township, Clearfield county, Pa, two miles north of Utahville, February 22, 1854, and is a son of Joseph M and Fannie (Shoff) Smith He is a great grandson of Evi Smith, who came to New Jersey from Ludgate Hill, London. England It is known that Evi had three children—two daughters and a son The latter, Samuel M by name, was born in New Jersey in 1796, and died in Clearfield county in 1865, at the age of sixty-nine years He married Ann Monroe, a member of the family from which sprang James Monroe, the fifth president of the United States Of this marriage the following children were born Joseph M,

the father of our subject (deceased), Elizabeth, Mary A and Evi, all three deceased, Samuel, who is living in Virginia, William and David, both of whom are deceased, Salah, who is the widow of Philip Lusher, and Jane, who is the wife of David Persing, of Houtzdale Samuel Smith, father of the above mentioned children, resided in Clearfield county and was an elder in the Hagerty Cross Roads Presbyterian church By a second marriage he had one son, James who lives in Iowa

Joseph M Smith, father of our subject, was born in Clearfield county, Pa, in 1819 and was a farmer by occupation An active and useful citizen, in early days he gave his support to the Whig party, subsequently joined the "Know-Nothing" party, and afterwards became a Republican He served for a number of years as assistant deputy sheriff under Sheriff Perks For sixty-two years he was a member of the church, in earlier life being a Presbyterian, but later joining the Methodists His first marriage was to Fannie Shoff, of Pennsylvania Dutch extraction and lived near Hagerty's Cross Roads, in Clearfield county Seven children were born to this union, those now living being as follows Josiah W, who lives on his grandfather's old homestead near Glen Hope, William M, who is in the employ of the Standard Oil Company, at Sistersville, W Va, Abraham C, who is a farmer at Utahville, Levi, who is with the Prairie Oil and Gas Company at Glen Pool, Okla A half brother, Edward B, is with the Pacific Telephone Company and is also in the real estate business at Seattle, Wash Joseph M Smith died in 1896 at the age of seventy-seven years His second marriage was to Mrs Rebecca (Hunter) Gallagher, who was born in Iowa and is now a resident of Seattle, Wash

John N Smith in his boyhood attended school at Mt Pleasant and at Hagerty's Cross Roads He then began to assist his father on the home farm, and he subsequently followed agriculture until May 7, 1886, with some intervals also devoted to work in the woods On the date last mentioned he came to Irvona, where he erected his present building, and since 1892 he has been prosperously engaged in a general mercantile business His entire life up to date has been spent in Clearfield county, and he belongs to one of its oldest families, dating from 1818, when it took his grandfather two weeks to make the overland trip from Philadelphia Joseph M Smith, our subject's father, spent seven years in that city, but in 1825 was brought to Clearfield county again The old homestead is still owned by his son, Josiah W Smith

In 1875, John N Smith was married to Miss Almira Litz, who died November 2, 1910 She was a daughter of John Litz, a farmer of Beccaria township One son, John Monroe, was born to this marriage, who is a civil engineer, a graduate of the Westchester Normal School, and later of the Massachusetts Institute of Technology at Boston, Mass , and since May, 1909, has been city engineer at McKeesport, Pa He was engineer and superintendent of construction for the new plant of the National Tube Company at McKeesport, the building being the largest of its kind in the world He married Miss Francelia S Huntley, a daughter of Hon George W Huntley, and they have two sons, Conrad Litz and William Huntley

John N Smith is a member of McKeesport Lodge, No 171, K P , at Irvona, and of the I O H at Coalport For the past nineteen years he has been a member of the First Presbyterian church at Irvona

LEWIS P MILLER,* one of the best known residents of Karthaus, Pa , whose name up and down the river is a synonym for bravery, honesty and efficiency, still operates a ferry, which he has conducted since he came here in the spring of 1880, and maintains something of a summer resort for those who enjoy water sports In the old days he has entertained as many as sixty guests a night Mr Miller was born November 13, 1850, at Mulsonburg, Covington township, Clearfield county, Pa , and is a son of William Miller and his wife, Lucy (Mulson) Miller

William Miller was born in Luzerne county, Pa By trade he was a tailor but never followed it very much after coming to Clearfield county, lumbering and rafting being more interesting and profitable to him He won the reputation of being the best pilot on the river in his day, and for forty years he served in the office of justice of the peace He lived to the age of seventy-four years, his death occurring in 1900 William Miller married Lucy Mulson, who was born in France and was but one month old when her parents brought her to America Her father was Peter Mulson, who was a wagonmaker by trade and a man of such pioneering qualities as to have the place where he located called by his name Six children were born to William and Lucy Miller, namely Lewis P , William, who lives at Keewaydin, Minnie, who is the wife of Christopher Rosenhoover, of Johnsonburg, Charles, who died in infancy, Titus, who died at the age of twenty years, and Frederick, who lives at North Bend, Clinton county, Pa

Lewis P Miller was reared and obtained his district school education in Covington township He worked in the oil regions in the vicinity of Tidioute, Warren county, Pa , for some nine years but returned to Clearfield county in 1879 and for one year afterward was engaged in lumbering on Deer Creek On June 4, 1880, he came to his present place, owning 100 acres of land surrounding his residence which is situated one mile distant from any neighbor The place was built in 1869 by Fred Schmarrs About seven years ago, in order to meet with the demands of visitors to this region, Mr Miller fitted his place up for a comfortable summer resort and during the warm season he has as many guests as he can accommodate The residence is situated so near the water that Mr Miller will take good care that in a second disaster like the Johnstown flood, in 1889, none of his family or prized possessions will be left there, as on that memorable occasion there were six inches of water over his floors The river's sudden rise at this point was twenty-seven feet, all told

On October 12, 1880, Mr Miller was married to Miss Clarissa Rosenhoover, who was born in Cooper township, a daughter of Robert and Mary (Dreekle) Rosenhoover, the latter of whom died at the age of eighty-eight years Mr Rosenhoover was born in Germany and was one of the early settlers here, where he still resides Five sons and one daughter were born to Mr and Mrs Miller, as follows Fred C , who is a photographer, John C , who is a student at Williamsport, Paul Eugene, who is a telegraph operator at Rustic, Robert, who was accidentally drowned, falling off the ferry, when a child of thirteen months, Charles, who is a miner at Karthaus, and Grace, who resides with her
54

parents Mr Miller and family attend the Catholic church at Cooper In politics he is a Democrat

From boyhood Mr Miller has been accustomed to the water and his stories of early days on the river, at this point, are intensely interesting He was of great assistance to his father in those days, when the latter piloted immense rafts down the stream, and Mr Miller can remember when this traffic was of enormous proportions, rafts being so close together that one could walk dry shod from shore to shore He has had many exciting adventures in straightening out rafts in troubled waters, and as ferryman, has many times performed heroic deeds that more than entitle him to a Carnegie medal He bears the record of never refusing to carry passengers, no matter what the weather might be or portend, and at least six lives were saved by his timely assistance Frequently he has crossed the flooded stream and with great danger to himself, has tied up rafts which otherwise would have gone to pieces, and thus has saved thousands of dollars to their owners Mr Miller tells of these deeds with a great deal of modesty, notable as they were, and no one can ever assert with truth that he ever hesitated in the face of duty on account of monetary consideration His circle of friends extends over a very wide territory and the mention of his name in this section evokes expressions of high regard

JOHN BALL,* who is superintendent of the Victor Coal Mining Company, Acme Slope, and is a leading resident of Morrisdale Mines, was born October 4, 1863, in Adams county, Pa , and is a son of Patrick and Rachel (Stiner) Ball

Patrick Ball was born in Ireland and in early manhood came to the United States and settled in Adams county, where he engaged in farming He enlisted there for service in the Civil war, and died at the battle of the Wilderness His widow survives and is now aged seventy-five years To Patrick Ball and his wife the following children were born· George, who is a resident of Morrisdale; Mary, who is the widow of Samuel Haywood, a native of England, who was formerly proprietor of a hotel at Hawk Run, Maggie, who is the wife of Jacob Conrad, of Nantiglo, Pa , and John, of the present record

John Ball went to school in boyhood when the sessions were held in an old log structure, but when twelve years of age came to Morrisdale and afterward had no school opportunities He went to work in the Morrisdale Coal Company's mines, for R B Wigton, until twenty-one years old, and then entered the Allport mines and remained for a number of years He has always been connected with the coal industry and for the past fifteen years has been with the Victor Coal Mining Company and has been promoted from the bottom until five years since when he was made superintendent and has filled this responsible position ever since The output of the two mines of this company is about 400 tons daily and employment is given 125 workmen

Mr Ball was married in 1889 to Miss Malettie Hendershot, a daughter of Stephen Hendershot, of Allport, and they have three children I Chauncy, who is a coal miner; and Rosanna and Moncena, who reside with their parents Mr Ball and family are members of the Methodist Episcopal church In politics he is a Republican and is serving in his fifth term as school director He is a member of Morrisdale Lodge, No 161, Knights of Pythias, of the P O S of A , and of the O A M At present Mr Ball is serving as secretary of the Morris township school board

WILLIAM BIGLER POTTER, a merchant and prominent citizen of Karthaus, Pa , has been in the mercantile line here since 1884 He was born at Mulsonburg, Clearfield county, Pa , June 9, 1863, and is a son of Dr Johnson William and Alamanda (Hoffman) Potter

Dr Johnson William Potter was born March 6, 1835, in Clarion county, Pa , and for a period of forty years was one of the leading citizens of Clearfield county He lived with his parents until he was eighteen years of age, then went to Indiana county, Pa , where he was a clerk in a store for one year From there he came to Clearfield county and for two years taught school at Driftwood and then read medicine with Dr Matthew Woods of Clearfield, and through the influence of George Bigler received a government appointment at Washington entitling him to instruction in the National Medical College. where he continued his studies until 1860, when he returned to Clearfield county He practiced first at Lecontes Mills, then at Mulsonburg and later at what is now known as Keewaydin, Covington township He subsequently moved to Three Runs, now known as Pottersdale, where he operated a saw and grist mill, and also conducted a general store. He later returned to Keewaydin, where he had a handsome residence and for a few years was engaged in the lumber business and then retired to Clearfield, where his long and busy life closed March 31, 1898 During his later years he gave up the practice of medicine He was influential in the Clearfield County National Bank and was a director until his death, his son, William Bigler Potter, now serving in the same capacity He was interested in public affairs, was a member of the school board for four years and in 1873 was elected, on the Democratic ticket, a member of the state legislature, in which body he was useful and active

Dr Potter married Miss Alamanda Hoffman, who was born at New Bethlehem, Clarion county, Pa, in 1858, and to this marriage three daughters and six sons were born, three of the latter still surviving, namely. Roger L, who lives at Pittsburg, William Bigler, and Frank, who is a resident of New Jersey Dr Potter was a member of the session of the Presbyterian church

William Bigler Potter attended the local schools regularly through boyhood and youth, and when he reached his majority bought his father's interest in the Karthaus store and conducted it, in partnership with a brother, for one year, when he bought his brother's interest and has since managed the business alone In the fall of 1898 he met with a serious loss in the destruction of his store, house and barn by fire In 1899 he rebuilt the store and resumed business in September of that year He is interested also in coal operating under the firm name of Potter, Bigler & Potter, the company operating the Horse Shoe mine He is otherwise interested in business, being a conservative capitalist, although an energetic and efficient citizen His political preferences are such as to make him a Democrat and he has capably filled many local offices where judgment and foresight were necessary qualifications along with business probity

In February, 1887, Mr Potter was married to Miss Emma B Emerick, who was born and reared in Karthaus township, a daughter of George and Lavina (Reiter) Emerick, both of whom are now deceased They have seven children, namely· Bessie, Grace, Johnson W, Dudley, Mary, George and Harry Bryan Bessie, the eldest daughter, makes her home with her grandmother in Clearfield Mr Potter has been identified with public spirited movements He belongs to the Masonic fraternity, connected with the lodge at Driftwood

ALFRED JAMES HARBER,[*] a successful merchant and representative citizen of Blain City, Pa, was born July 15, 1859, at St Augustine, Cambria county, Pa, and is a son of Henry and Anna Maria (Cramer) Harber.

Henry Harber was a carpenter by trade and in his day was considered an expert and skillful workman He built the first Catholic church at St Augustine, and later engaged there in the hotel business He died in 1869 He married Anna Maria Cramer, who was born in October, 1821, and still survives Of the family of twelve children born to Henry Harber and his wife, Alfred James is the youngest and there are three sons and three daughters living Kate is the wife of F S Burgone, of Ashville, Christiana is the wife of Henry Shepherd, a merchant at Homestead, Peter is a farmer in Dakota; and Robert is a painter at DuBois The parents came from Germany about 1839 and lived in the city of New York for a short time and moved from there to Cambria county, Pa, and later to Williamsport and Altoona The father died at St Louis, Mo, and the mother lives with her youngest son

Alfred James Harber attended the public

schools at Altoona, to which place the family moved after leaving St Augustine, and afterward worked in a blacksmith shop there until 1883, when he came to Blain City Here he embarked in the general mercantile business, on his present site, and in point of time engaged, is the oldest merchant in the place He has devoted himself very closely to the development of this business, has carefully watched markets and has kept closely in touch with the wants and tastes of his customers with the result that he has prospered

Mr Harber was married in 1879 to Miss Edith Grenoder, who was born at Altoona, a daughter of Martin and Eva Grenoder, and five sons and one daughter have been born to them, namely Joseph, who is a telegraph operator, residing at Irvona, Pa , married Mame Clarkson, Leo Martin, who is a telegraph operator, resides at Bellwood, Esther Christina, who is a teacher in the Blain City public schools, Alfred J , who is a student at St Vincent College, Beatty. is captain of the college base ball team, and Clair and Claud, both of whom are in school Mr Harber and family are communicants of St Basil's Catholic church, at Blain City He is a member of the Brotherhood of America and of St George's Society In politics a Democrat, he has been something of a leader in this section in his party, served four years as postmaster, during the first administration of the late President Cleveland and for four years was treasurer of Beccaria township Both as a business man and as a personal factor, Mr Harber stands high in the estimation of his fellow citizens

NATHANIEL H SHEPHERD, a prosperous and well known farmer of Burnside township, residing on the old Shepherd homestead in this township, was born at his present location February 6, 1850 His parents were Frederick and Elizabeth (Breth) Shepherd, and he is a grandson of John Shepherd, a native of England, who came to this country with his parents at the age of five years, they settling in the Shenandoah Valley Here the family were all massacred by the Indians except himself, who was taken prisoner and held for three years by the savages He then found an opportunity of escaping and reached the vicinity of Lock Haven, where he spent the rest of his life It is not known whom he married

Frederick Shepherd, father of our subject, was born at Lock Haven, Pa , in October, 1810 At the age of eighteen he came to Clearfield county, settling at McGee, Burnside township, where he resided for some years with the Young family, being engaged in lumbering In 1835 he removed to Patchinsville, where he lived for five years, at the end of which time he took up his residence on the present homestead, the only building then standing being an old log barn, the land consisting of 100 acres Here the rest of his life was spent in farming and lumbering, his death taking place December 19, 1882 On May 25, 1835, he married Elizabeth Breth, who was born in Germany, February 7, 1820, a daughter of Peter and Margaret Ann (Jenny) Breth, natives of that country Her father came to America in 1819, locating first in Center county, Pa , whence in 1833 he came to Clearfield county, settling in Burnside township, where his death occurred July 4, 1875. his wife, who was born in Germany in 1792, died at Hollidaysburg, Pa , March 22, 1859 They had a family of eleven children

—nine daughters and two sons Mrs Shepherd's paternal grandfather, Henry Breth, died in his native Germany at the remarkable age of 106 years

Immediately after their marriage Mr and Mrs Frederick Shepherd began housekeeping at Patchinsville, where, as already indicated, they lived for five years, afterwards moving to the present homestead, the only building then standing being an old log barn, the land consisting of about 100 acres Mrs Elizabeth Shepherd died July 25, 1875 Her living children, in addition to the subject of this sketch, are Esther, wife of J Mahood, residing in Missouri, Anna, wife of J McKee, a farmer, Crissie E, wife of C Sebring, Benjamin, who is engaged in farming in Burnside township, and McClellan, who is a farmer in Arkansas

After the death of his first wife, Elizabeth, Frederick Shepherd married, May 25, 1876, Mary Irwin (nee McCullough), sister of Nathaniel Shepherd's wife's mother

Nathaniel H Shepherd worked for his father until reaching the age of twenty-one years, at which time he married and bought a farm at Glen Campbell This he sold at the time of his father's death and returned to the homestead, where he has since resided, being engaged in general agriculture A good practical farmer, he has been successful in his operations and is now one of the substantial citizens of his township Mr Shepherd is a Democrat in politics and has served ten years on the local school board, also two terms as auditor He is a member of the Evangelical church

He was married in 1874 to Margaret J McKay, who was born in Indiana county, Pa, August 27, 1852, a daughter of John and Nancy (McCullough) McKay Her father died December 8, 1875 He was a son of Neil McKay, born in county Derry, Ireland, who died in 1840 Neil's wife was in maidenhood Jane Shields Coming to America after his father's death, John McKay resided in New York for two years and later in Philadelphia, finally settling in Clearfield county, in 1845, where the rest of his life was spent The land which he cleared and on which he built a small cabin, is now one of the most valuable coal fields in Pennsylvania

Nancy McCullough, Mrs Shepherd's mother, was born in Indiana county, August 23, 1827, a daughter of John and Margaret (Sharp) McCullough Her father was born in Indiana county, Pa, July 15, 1775, and died at the age of eighty-seven years His wife died May 10, 1863, at the age of seventy-three She was a daughter of Captain Andrew Sharp, who served in the War of 1812, and who was later shot by the Indians in the vicinity of Pittsburg At the same time, by way of amusement, they shot a pipe from his wife's mouth, which they compelled her to hold while they showed their marksmanship Sharpsburg, Pa, was named after Capt Andrew Sharp, he having received by grant for his military service several thousand acres of land near Pittsburg The maiden name of his wife was Ann Wood She was of Scotch descent, her parents settling at an early day in Cumberland county, Pa

Mrs Shepherd's great-great-grandfather Sharp married a Rutherford, and died in 1817, his wife died at the age of 103 years, a truly venerable old lady

Mr and Mrs Shepherd were the parents of four children, namely Edith, residing at home with her father, Pearl, wife of D G Plouse a contractor living in Cambria county, they having five children, Warren E, who married Blanche Rarick, and resides at Westover, having three children, and Clyde, residing at home

JAMES C OWENS, a prosperous farmer of Burnside township, was born on the old Owens homestead in this township, January 11, 1841, son of William and Hannah (Wagner) Owens His paternal grandfather was Robert Owens, who was born May 28, 1787, and who married Margaret Carns Robert Owens came to Burnside township in 1836, settling near Patchin, where he engaged in lumbering and rafting on the Susquehanna river His wife, Margaret, died in 1871

William Owens, father of our subject, was born November 9, 1815, in a Pennsylvania town near the New Jersey line, and he was twenty-one years of age when he accompanied his parents to Clearfield county He was associated industrially with his father and also engaged in farming, buying the present Owens homestead which he cleared Later he purchased an additional farm, and was engaged in lumbering and agriculture for the rest of his life, which closed in January, 1903 He married Hannah Wagner, who was born in Center county, Pa, April 19, 1819, the daughter of well known and respected residents of that county Her mother, Mrs Jane Wagner, who was born in 1784, died October 21, 1853 The subject of this sketch is the only one of their children now surviving

James C Owens, after attending school for a time, was engaged in farming on the parental homestead until reaching the age of twenty-four years He then operated a farm of his own until 1904, subsequently removing

to his present homestead, which he had previously owned He has been successful in his operations and is now one of the substantial citizens of his township He is a member of Harmony Grange, No 1201, and takes an active interest in whatever is calculated to advance the welfare of the community In politics a Republican, he has served as a member of the school board for the last twelve years, being president of the board for one term Mr Owens is a Civil war veteran, having enlisted in Company E, 172d Pa Vol Infantry, for nine months, his regiment forming a part of Gen Howard's command, Army of the Potomac, after the Battle of Gettysburg He is a member of the old G A R post at Westover, Pa

Mr Owens married Sarah Fulton, a daughter of Simon and Elizabeth (Young) Fulton Of this marriage there have been five children, as follows Elizabeth, is the wife of S Brickley of Westover, and the mother of nine children Her daughter, Iva, married Fred Kitchen, and has two children William A married Letta Kitchen and resides in Kansas He has a family of nine children Rosa J is the wife of L Kepler, a machinist residing on the Owens homestead and has three children Rebecca, is the wife of Charles Litchfield and lives in Kansas She has four children Harvey married Ora Jane Fyock, who is associated in the farming industry with our subject He and his wife have three children Thus it will be seen that Mr Owens has no less than twenty-eight grandchildren, besides two great-grandchildren, showing that he and his family have no need of Mr Roosevelt's warning to beware of race suicide Mrs Sarah Owens, the mother of the above mentioned children, died in 1905 at the age of fifty-nine years She was a good wife and mother and highly respected throughout the community

RUSH NORMAN HOSLER, a progressive young business man and representative citizen of Morris township, has been chief engineer for the Morrisdale Coal Company, at the Morrisdale Mines, Clearfield county, Pa, for the past nine years He was born in Fishing Creek, Columbia county, Pa, August 8, 1874, and is a son of White N and Mary Ellen (Dreisbach) Hosler.

The parents of Mr Hosler were both natives of Columbia county, where the father was born April 18, 1843, and the mother, July 6, in the same year White N Hosler served more than three years as a soldier in the Civil war and was a member of the 143rd Pa Vol Inf This regiment lost heavily and Mr Hosler was transferred from one company to another and received his honorable discharge from Company I, after the battle of the Wilderness, in which he lost his good right arm He took part in many notable engagements, including Gettysburg After he left the service he attended a school for wounded soldiers, at Philadelphia, and afterward taught school, both before and after marriage, and later was engaged in the mercantile business for a number of years His death occurred September 8, 1901

In 1867 White N Hosler was married to Ellen Dreisbach, and one daughter and three sons were born to them, namely Annie E, who lives with her mother in Columbia county, William C, who is a chemist, lives at Benton, Columbia county, and married Emma Hartman, Rush Norman, and Frank Kent, the youngest, who is chief inspector for the Standard Steel Car Company, at Hammond, Ind, and married Maud Morton, of Erie, Pa

Rush Norman Hosler was educated in the Jonestown public schools, New Columbus Academy, in Luzerne county, and the State Normal School at Bloomsburg, graduating from this institution in 1896 For about eighteen months he was engaged in Y M C A work and then started with a railroad engineering corps, working on the proposed line of the Independent Anthracite Coal operators and remaining with that body of hard workers through one summer He then became connected with the Lehigh & Wilkesbarre Coal Company in the engineering department, and continued until the spring of 1900 Mr Hosler then went to the West and located as an engineer at Alderson, in what was then Indian Territory, where he was employed by the McAllister Coal Company and remained one year, becoming then chief engineer for the Wilberton Coal Mining Company at Wilberton, Indian Territory, where he remained until July 1, 1902, when he accepted his present responsible position

Mr Hosler was married September 19, 1901, to Miss Margaret McGhee, of Audenried, a daughter of John E and Hannah McGhee John E McGhee was master mechanic for the Lehigh and Wilkesbarre Coal Company Mrs Hosler was reared and educated in Carbon county and for several years prior to her marriage was a successful teacher Mr. and Mrs Hosler have one son, Norman White, who was born April 1, 1905 Mr Hosler is a member of Philipsburg Lodge, No 391, F & A M, Williamsport Consistory, Clearfield Chapter and Jaffa Temple of the Mystic Shrine, at Altoona He belongs also to the Coal Mining Institute of America and to the Western Pennsylvania Engineering Society at Pittsburg In politics he has always been a firm Republican and is serving as supervisor of Morris township, having been elected on a cash tax basis He served as president of the Supervisors Association of Clearfield county   With his wife he belongs to the Presbyterian church at Philipsburg, in which he is an elder

JAMES LAWRENCE McGONIGAL Probably no man in Karthaus township is better or more favorably known than is James Lawrence McGonigal, land owner, coal operator, capitalist and sportsman, who during a residence of about twenty years in Clearfield county has made his influence and personality felt in various lines of endeavor Mr Mc-Gonigal was born in West Keating township, Clinton county, Pa , June 30, 1862, a son of John and Sarah (Conaway) McGonigal

Hugh McGonigal, the grandfather of James L , was born in county Donegal, north of Ireland, and came to America in the early part of the nineteenth century, locating at Center Furnace, in Center county, Pa   At this place John McGonigal was born, and during his schooldays was a playmate of Judge Orvis In early manhood he engaged in lumbering and moved from Center Furnace to Snow Shoe, and thence to West Keating township, Clinton county, owning the present site of the McGonigal Rod and Gun Club He died January 26, 1888, at the age of seventy-one years, and was buried in Ganoe cemetery, in Clinton county, where the mother of James L McGonigal was buried later, her death having occurred October 17, 1892 Mrs McGonigal was the daughter of George Conaway, an early settler of Karthaus township, and a member of an old and honored family Mr. and Mrs McGonigal had the following children Daniel, deceased, who lived in Kar-

thaus township, Hugh G , who is living in West Clearfield; William R , deceased, who lived in Karthaus township, Annie C , who married Daniel T Moore of this township, James Lawrence, Bartley C , who died at Cataract, George B , who resides at Johnsonburg, Elk county, John T , residing in Clearfield, Joseph O , who lives on the Ed McGarvey farm, Permilla Jane, who married A. B Saltsman of Johnsonburg; Miles Alexander, who lives at Erie, Pa , and Sarah Belle, who died when three months old

James Lawrence McGonigal attended the schools of West Keating township, and ever since attaining manhood he has engaged in lumbering, farming and coal operating.   He came to Clearfield county in 1892, and for the past twelve years has been operating at Pottersdale Besides the 100-acre farm on which he has resided since coming to the county, he owns another of 125 acres in Karthaus township, a farm of fifty acres of cleared land in Clinton county, about 450 acres in the New Garden coal basin and 181 acres in Clinton county which are the premises of the McGonigal Rod and Gun Club, a pleasure organization started by Mr McGonigal in 1910, and of which he is the president Mr McGonigal is a stockholder of the County National and Farmers and Traders Banks of Clearfield

On August 27, 1893, Mr McGonigal was married to Annie C Rauch, who was born in Karthaus township, a daughter of J W. Rauch, and to this union there have been born the following children George E , Ira Wilson, Stella Permilla, Jessie Alda, Mary Emaline and E Belle

Mr McGonigal is a Democrat in politics, and for nine years he served Karthaus township as road supervisor Fraternally he is connected with Renova Lodge, No 595, I O O F, of which he has been a member for fifteen years, the Order of Elks, No 540, of Clearfield, the P O S of A Lodge, No 136, of Sinnamahoning, Pa, and the Order of Moose, No 190, at Lock Haven He has always shown himself ready to assist in forwarding those movements which have for their object the betterment of his community and his popularity is shown by his many warm friends and numberless acquaintances

GILBERT JACOBSON, assistant electrician for the Pennsylvania Coal and Coke Company, at Winburne, Pa, was born at Fallbrook, Tioga county, Pa, June 18, 1884, son of Claus and Mary (Alm) Jacobson The parents are now residents of Winburne, the father being aged sixty-six years and his wife, the mother of our subject, being in her sixty-first year They were both born in Sweden and came to America in April 1879, settling at Fallbrook, Tioga county, Pa Claus Jacobson worked in the mines for a short time but after the first year found outside employment They lived for twenty-three years in Fallbrook and one year in Antrim, in the same county, whence they came to Winburne in the fall of 1900 Their children were as follows: Theodore, who married Ellen Strand and has two children, Donald and Oscar, Gustaf, residing at home with his parents, who works for the Pennsylvania Coal and Coke Company (is unmarried), Arthur, unmarried, also an employe of the company above mentioned, Alma, unmarried, residing with her parents, and Gilbert

Gilbert Jacobson attended the public schools of Fallbrook, in which place he resided for fifteen years At the age of thirteen he became a trapper in the mines and was thus employed for one year, after which for a year and a half he held a position as driver. He then moved to Antrim, where he entered the mine as a miner, which he followed for six months He then became a machine helper in the mines, having charge of a machine Coming to Winburne in the fall of 1900, he entered the mines of the Beech Creek Coal and Coke Company (now the Pennsylvania Coal and Coke Company), and spent six years therein occupying various positions In November, 1906, he entered the shops of the same company as electrician's helper, which position he still holds He is a practical man in his line and is a valuable citizen

Mr Jacobson married Miss Jennie Limberg, a daughter of Louis Limberg and Matilda Limberg, of Lanse Mrs Jacobson's father has charge of the Winburne Water Company's repairing Mrs Jacobson was born at Williamsport, Lycoming county, Pa, and removed when young to Lanse, Clearfield county She has two brothers, Albin and Frank Limberg Of the marriage of our subject and his wife, which took place June 5, 1909, one son was born, Lewis Gilbert Mr Jacobson is a member of the Presbyterian church of Winburne He is a Republican in politics and belongs to Lodge No 61, I O O F

WILLIAM BERNARD STEINKERCHNER, proprietor of the hotel at Peale, Cooper township, this county, was born February 12, 1887, on the parental farm at Cooper (P O Drifting), a son of Joseph C and Elizabeth (Ollinger) Steinkerchner His grandparents were George and Cora (Sundaman) Steinkerchner, natives of Germany, the former being a shoemaker by trade, who, however, after coming to America, was engaged in mining at Bellefonte, Pa , for some time   Later he engaged in farming in Cooper township, this being about 1855, when the place was practically wild land, no timber having been cut   Here he developed a good farm, building also a neat residence   He died about 1893 at the age of seventy-four years, and his wife in 1877 at the age of sixty-two   They were Catholics in religion   Of their four children two died in infancy, the living being Joseph C , the father of our subject , and Catherine, wife of William McGowan of Clearfield

Joseph C Steinkerchner aided his father to clear the farm and later became its owner by purchase   He built the present residence in 1894 and about 1898 built a fine barn 45 x 65 feet, besides carrying on agriculture he has been engaged in mercantile business for the last six years, and is postmaster at Drifting   He was married in 1877 to Elizabeth Ollinger, of Pine Glen, Pa , a daughter of John and Mary Ollinger, of which union there were eight children

William B Steinkerchner was educated in the local schools, working in the intervals on the farm of his parents, which also included a fine orchard   He was graduated at Williamsport Commercial College in 1908   He continued agricultural pursuits up to the age of twenty-one years and during the winter of 1906-7 he worked on the Pennsylvania Railroad   In June, 1909, he purchased the Peale Hotel from Wilbur Holt and has conducted it successfully to the present time, making a genial and popular landlord   He is a communicant of St Severine's R C church and in politics is a Democrat   He belongs to the K of C at Bellefonte and to the B P O E of Philipsburg   Mr Steinkerchner married Miss Margaret Gleason, a daughter of Thomas and Mary Gleason of Snow Shoe, Pa , the marriage taking place December 1, 1908   They have one daughter, Genevieve, aged two years.   In addition to carrying on the hotel business, Mr Steinkerchner is a dealer in live stock   He has been all his life a resident of Cooper township and is popular wherever known   He suffered a severe loss by the burning of his hotel, but is not the sort of man to let such an event discourage him, and his energy and perseverance are meeting with due reward

JOSEPH C STEINKERCHNER, one of the most successful farmers in Clearfield county and one of the county's best known citizens, is also postmaster at Drifting, this county, his property being located in this (Cooper) township   He was born January 31, 1849, son of George and Cora (Sundaman) Steinkerchner   The parents of our subject were born in Germany, the father coming to America when a young man, the mother being eight years younger   After coming to America George Steinkerchner was engaged at shoemaking at Bellefonte, Center county, Pa , he was a shoemaker by trade   He and his brother purchased a farm three miles from the present farm of our subject in Cooper township, it being the first one he purchased   The latter was born at Millsburg, Center County, settling on this place in 1855, at which time not a tree or bush had been cut on it   He first built a small shanty, which he afterwards replaced by a neat four-room, two-story residence   This house is still standing   His farm consisted of 114 acres   He had several brothers, one of whom died at Milesburg the year they moved to this place George Steinkerchner died about 1892 in his seventy-fifth year His wife died in 1877 at the age of sixty-two They were the parents of four children, two of whom died in infancy, the subject of this sketch being the oldest survivor The other is Catharine, wife of William McGowan, of Clearfield The father was a Democrat in politics and a communicant of St Severine's R C church Both parents are buried in the Catholic cemetery

Joseph C Steinkerchner in his boyhood days attended a log school house two and a half miles from where he now resides He aided his father in clearing the farm and later became its owner by purchase The present house he erected in 1892, and about 1898 he built a fine barn 45 x 65 feet For the past six years he has been engaged in mercantile business and has been postmaster at Drifting for two years, his daughter Cora, and later his son John, having been previously in charge of the postoffice

Mr Steinkerchner was married in the Catholic church in Cooper township, August 21, 1879, to Miss Elizabeth Ollinger, of Pine Glen, Center county, Pa Her parents were John and Mary Ollinger, the former of whom died about sixteen years ago Of this union there have been children as follows Cora, wife of Clement Coudriet, of St Marys, and the mother of four children, John, of Philipsburg, who worked for three years in the brewery there, and who married Miss Catharine Beezer, of Bellefonte, Center county, and has two children, a son and daughter, Mary residing in Buffalo, N Y, Agnes, residing at home, who looks after the store and postoffice, Austin, who died at the age of six months, William B, who married Margaret Gleason of Snow Shoe, Center, and who conducts a hotel at Peale, Clearfield county, and has one child living, Nora, who is single and resides in Buffalo, N Y, Lucy and Simon, unmarried and residing at home

Mr Steinkerchner has a fine orchard, he himself having set out about one-half of the trees, the others having been planted by his father His farm is in an excellent state of cultivation and is highly productive, being provided also with substantial and commodious buildings. Formerly for a time he was in the lumber business He has seen many changes and improvements since his early days, in the county, since his father used to take hides to the tannery at the old Gillen Mill at Gillentown, Center county, to get leather, of which he made boots and shoes, and carried grain to market to the same place on his shoulders He has kept pace with the times, has availed himself of all modern improvements in the methods of agriculture, and his efforts have been rewarded by a gratifying degree of prosperity He is one of the substantial citizens of his town and a man highly esteemed by his neighbors for his personal characteristics

H B CLARY,* postmaster at Grampian, Pa, and engaged in business as a painter and paperhanger, was born in Bloom township, Clearfield county, Pa, September 29, 1870, and is a son of John and a grandson of Rev James Clary

John Clary was born in 1842, in Mercer county, Pa, and when twenty years of age came to Clearfield county, accompanying his parents His father was Rev James Clary, who came to Penn township to preach the Baptist faith When the Civil war broke out, John Clary enlisted for service in the 105th

Pa Vol Inf , known as the Wildcat regiment, and he was honorably discharged near Petersburg, Va , August 27, 1864 He came home but never fully recovered from the injuries he had received, having been wounded thrice at the battle of Gettysburg and once at the battle of the Wilderness He survived until 1876, Thanksgiving Day in that year being the day of his burial He married Mary Ellen Hepburn, in Bloom township, who was born in Greenwood township, a daughter of John Hepburn, and she resides at Bell Landing, Pa He was a member of the Baptist church In national affairs he was a Republican but in local matters voted with the Democrats He served as a school director and as a justice of the peace in Bloom township While developing a farm and improving it, in Bloom township, he was also interested in lumbering He had four children Edgar Early, H B, Kearney Patton (deceased) and Alice Blanche, who lives at Covington, Ky

Edgar Early Clary, the eldest of the family started to work in a tannery as a laborer and continued until he had worked his way up to the top and is now superintendent of one of the largest tanneries in the country, located at Richwood, W Va He married Jennie Neff, of that place

H B Clary with his brothers and sisters attended school in Penn and Greenwood townships and afterward he learned the painting and paperhanging trade and for some years worked at it in different parts of the state At the outbreak of the Spanish-American war he enlisted for service, entering Co L, 5th Pa Vol Inf , of which he became corporal, and continued until the close of the war, returning home unharmed In 1902 he was appointed postmaster of Grampian and he has shown much public spirit and enterprise both in the manner of conducting the public office as well as in the management of his own affairs He now has two rural mail routes established and the entire business of the office is carried on rapidly and efficiently In politics he is a Republican and he is a member of the borough council and is also borough auditor.

In May, 1900, Mr. Clary was married to Miss Christiana Enzbranner, who was born in Blair county, Pa , December 23, 1876, a daughter of Peter and Margaret Enzbranner, natives of Germany Mr and Mrs Clary have two children, Jean Margaret and Frank Harris The grandmother of Mr Clary, Susan Bigler, was a sister of Hon William D Bigler, once governor of Pennsylvania.

RICHARD HENRY GEORGE, who is an experienced, practical miner, trained in this line of work since boyhood, is superintendent of the mines of Peale, Peacock & Kerr, at Winburne, Pa , and of another mine at Karthaus, is also postmaster at Winburne and is a leading citizen of Cooper township, Clearfield county He was born in Cornwall, England, December 18, 1868, and is a son of Thomas and Mary Ann (Brown) George

The parents of Mr George came to America in 1872 and located at Arnott, in Tioga county, Pa The father was a miner and was employed in mines in Tioga and Clearfield counties His death occurred at Winburne, March 29, 1910, at the age of sixty-four years Two sons and three daughters were born to Thomas George and his wife, namely Thomas, who is with the Westinghouse Company, in East Pittsburg, Minnie, who is the wife of Donald Curry, of East Pittsburg, Susan, who is the wife of William Allen, of the above place, Jane, who is the wife of John Cameron, of Winburne, and Richard Henry, postmaster at Winburne

Eight and one-half years is a very early age to have the burden of self support placed on the shoulders of a child, but Mr George was only that old when he went to work in the mines His education was secured by attendance at night schools He remained in Tioga county until 1886 and then moved to Houtzdale, Clearfield county, and from there in 1890, to Philipsburg, working all this time as a miner In 1892 he entered the employ of Peale, Peacock & Kerr, at the old Victor mine, No 1, at Philipsburg He was first employed as a mule driver and later as a track-man In 1894 he went to Glen Richey and was driver and track-man there until 1895, when he received his certificate as a mine foreman, taking charge of Bloomington No 3 mine For six months he was foreman there, later served in the same capacity for the same length of time at Rathmel, for the same company, and then returned to Glen Richey, where he had charge of Bloomington No 4 mine for two years On February 4, 1898, he came to Winburne as mine foreman under Alexander Dunsmore, taking charge of Mine No 1, and in 1904 being made superintendent Subsequently Mr George opened up Mines Nos 6 and 9, under Mr Dunsmore's supervision The capacity of the mines at Winburne aggregates tonnage 1,300 gross daily The Oak Hill mine at Karthaus gives employment to fifty men

Mr George was married in December 1888, to Miss Marguerite Wilson, a daughter of Robert A and Annie Wilson, and they have seven children· William, James W, Richard E, Adda Grace, Mary, John Lester and Robert Mr and Mrs George attend the Presbyterian church He is a member of Winburne Lodge, Odd Fellows, and Moshannon Lodge, F & A M In politics Mr George is a Republican and in 1902 he was appointed postmaster at Winburne He is a director of the Bituminous National Bank, of Winburne, Pa

JOHN WARREN HURD,* who has been a representative citizen of Chest township for many years, engaging successfully in farming and milling and taking a prominent part in public affairs, was born in this township, on the old Hurd homestead, October 19, 1856, and is a son of Henry Harrison and Catherine (Litzinger) Hurd

Henry Harrison Hurd was born in New Hampshire, September 16, 1817, and in boyhood came to Clearfield county and followed farming and lumbering for many years of his active life, on the L J Hurd farm, in Chest township, near La Jose, and is one of the oldest and most highly respected citizens in this section For thirty-five years he served as justice of the peace and held all other township offices at times, being elected to the same on the Republican ticket He belongs to the Masonic lodge at Edinboro and to the Temple of Honor at La Jose He was married first to Carolina Wilson, a daughter of Thomas Wilson, and two children were born to them and survived her Harrison, who resides at La Jose, and Wilson A, who lives on the old homestead Mr Hurd was married second to Catherine Litzinger, a daughter of Barney Litzinger, of Cambria county She is now in her eighty-third year To the second marriage six children were born, as follows M E, who is a physician at Mahaffey, Frances J, who is the wife of Z L Ardery, Angeline, who died aged four years; Robert E, who lives on the old homestead; Louis Clayton, who is deceased, and John Warren, who is fourth in order of birth Henry G Hurd and wife are members of the Baptist church at La Jose

John Warren Hurd was educated in the schools of Chest township and afterward taught school for six years He had some experience in lumbering in early manhood, but has devoted himself mainly to farming and milling In 1896 he bought the St Lu grist mill and later another mill near La Jose, and still retains the ownership of the latter, operating it in connection with his agricultural activities

Mr Hurd married Mary Caroline Clemson, a daughter of Ely B and Elizabeth Ann (Hancock) Clemson Ely B Clemson came to Clearfield county from Center county, served in the Civil war and later settled at La Jose, where his death occurred The following children were born to Mr and Mrs Hurd Charles Sumner, who resides in Cambria county, married Velma Varner, Dolly, who resides at home, Margaret, who is a school teacher, Harry, who is with his father in business, Daisy, who died when five years old, and William, who survived to the age of two years Mr Hurd and family are members of the Baptist church at La Jose In his political affiliation he is a stanch Republican and has frequently served as a committeeman and as a delegate to important conventions. He served one term as supervisor of Chest township, eleven years as a member of the school board and for seven of these was its secretary, one term as township treasurer, and five years as a justice of the peace

LEWIS ARTHUR PRITCHARD, paymaster for the Morrisdale Coal Company, of the Morrisdale Mines, Clearfield county, Pa, for the past thirteen years, is a leading citizen of Morris township, of which he is serving his fourth term as auditor He was born September 25, 1869, in Trumbull county, O, a son of Daniel W and Sarah (Pickering) Pritchard

Daniel W Pritchard was born in May, 1843, in Victoria, Wales, and came to America in November, 1862, locating first in a village near Pittsburg, Pa He found employment as a clerk in a store and later went to mining which he followed until 1864, when he went into the army and served until the close of the Civil war as a member of Battery E, Knapp's Independent Battery, until he reached the front, when he was transferred to Co H, 147th Pa Vol Inf He participated in many engagements and was with General Sherman in the great march to Atlanta After the end of hostilities and his honorable discharge, he returned to the vicinity of Pittsburg and lived there until 1868, when he moved to Brookfield, Ohio, and there engaged in coal mining He was married there, in that year, to Sarah Pickering, a daughter of Barzilla Eliza Pickering, and they resided at Brookfield until September, 1887, moving then to Warren, Ohio, and from there, in March, 1888, to the Morrisdale Mines, where, for five years, he followed mining, since when he has been chief clerk of supplies for the Morrisdale Coal Company

To Daniel W Pritchard and wife four children were born, namely Daniel, who died at the age of two years, Reuben W, who died when twenty-nine years old (was at that time a clerk in the office of the steel mill at Donora), Albert, who is weighmastetr at the same place, Donora, who married Helen Dutcher of Philipsburg, and Lewis Arthur

Lewis Arthur Pritchard was educated in the public schools of Ohio and the Bryant, Stratton & Smith Commercial School of Meadville, Pa., and was graduated from the above institution in 1889, and from then until 1891, he worked in the mines From 1891 until 1896 he was bookkeeper for the Morrisdale Supply Company and was then transferred to the coal company and was employed on the pay rolls until 1898, when he was made paymaster for the Morrisdale Coal Company and has been connected with this large concern, in some capacity, for the past twenty-one years

Mr Pritchard was married in 1892, to Miss Anna Fuge, a daughter of Thomas and Matilda (Hummel) Fuge, and they have the following children Violet Mae, Velma Anna, Paul Walburton, Clayton Fuge, Virginia Catherine and Lee Arthur Sarah, who died in infancy, was the second child On the maternal side, Mr Pritchard is of English ancestry, his mother having been fifteen years old when brought to America, living first at Sharon, Pa., and later at Brookfield, Ohio, where the Pickering family was well known The father of Mr Pritchard is a member of the G A R Post at Philipsburg

Mr Pritchard is a Republican in politics and has been an active citizen in township matters for a number of years and has served as township clerk in addition to performing his other duties He is identified fraternally with Philipsburg Lodge, No 391, F & A M, Williamsport Consistory, Jaffa Temple of the Mystic Shrine, at Altoona, Center Council, No 803, Royal Arcanum, at Philipsburg, and the O U A M, at Morrisdale With his family he belongs to the Methodist church

CHARLES WRYE, postmaster of Morrisdale Mines, in Morris township, Clearfield county, Pa., is a leading business man of this place, a dealer in groceries, feed, flour and miners' supplies He was born in Half Moon Valley, near Warriors Mark, in Huntingdon county, Pa., February 8, 1875, and is a son of William and Mary (Basser) Wrye

William Wrye was born in Huntingdon county, where he died in 1892 He was twice married, two sons and two daughters being born to his first union Isaac, residing at Grampian, J P D, residing at Winber; Rhoda, wife of George Grazier, of Marengo, and Mary, wife of Dr Myers, of Osceola Mills Two daughters and two sons were born to the second marriage also. Florence and Lettie, living in the old home, Harry, who lives at Marengo, and Charles, who was two years old when his mother died

Until he was seven years old, Charles Wrye lived in the family of Daniel Conrad, in Huntingdon county, following the death of his mother, and then came to Munson and Kylertown and lived three years with Morris Dunlap When he was eleven years of age he went to live with Parker Washburn His boyhood thus was not a very happy one except as he made it so for himself and his school advantages were rather limited He went to work in the Morrisdale mines when twelve years of age and continued until twenty-two years old, then entering the employ of H C Shugert, a merchant, with whom he remained for five years In 1905 he embarked in the mercantile business for himself and has prospered He served in the Spanish-American war as a member of the 5th Pa Inf, for six months In politics he is a Republican and in 1905 he was appointed postmaster and is a popular official, and has served also as township auditor and precinct chairman

Mr Wrye married Miss Melvina Jacobs, a daughter of Robert and Priscilla Jacobs, of Curtin, Center county, Pa, and they have four children Thelma, Layne, Wharton and Rex He belongs to the Jr O A M, the P O S of A, and the order of the Moose Mr Wrye is an example of what an industrious and enterprising boy can do even when left entirely dependent on his own resources at a tender age

PETER MOYER, one of the old and honored residents of Kylertown, Pa, who is now living retired after many years of business activity, is a native of Germany, having been born in Geiselberg, Bavaria, July 29, 1840, a son of Adam and Eva (Adinger) Moyer, natives of the Fatherland

In 1853 Adam Moyer came to America, and made his way from New York City to Clearfield county, settling in Rush township, near the Moshannon Creek, one mile from Winburne Although a stone mason by trade, he worked in the woods and soon earned sufficient money to send to Germany for his family who came to the United States in 1855 Later he purchased a small farm in Center county, but later traded this for his son's interest in a Graham township property He later sold out and spent the remainder of his life in Philipsburg He and his wife had the following children Adam, who came to this country one year after his father and is now a wealthy retired resident of Philipsburg, having for more than thirty years been a specula-

tor, Peter, Henry, who enlisted in the Union army at Bellefonte, Pa, and died during the Civil war, Michael, who is engaged in farming at Knox Run; Jacob, who has mining interests in Montana, Philip, who is a farmer of Clinton county, Gottlieb, who is a successful fruit grower of California, John, who was the only child born in America; Elizabeth, deceased, who was the wife of Jacob May, Catherine, who married Jacob Meisenbach and now resides at LaSalle, Ill, and one daughter who died in infancy The father died at the age of seventy-seven years, his wife having passed away in 1874, when about sixty-two years of age They are buried in Kylertown

Peter Moyer was about sixteen years of age when he accompanied the family to this country, and from New York they traveled over night to Philadelphia and thence to Tyrone, where they arrived about ten o'clock They then walked over the mountain, a distance of about thirty miles, and twelve o'clock at night found them at the little home near Munson As a boy, Mr Moyer had gathered dead wood in the forests of Germany, where the law provided that nothing else could be taken, and here he was delighted to find that there was an abundance of good wood, open and free to whoever cared to take it He worked with his father on the home farm, and spent his spare time in fishing from the banks of the Moshannon Creek, and when but eighteen years of age was considered an expert pilot in the rafting business, which he took up after he had attained his majority, rafting timber to Lock Haven and Middletown In about 1870, Mr Moyer located in Kylertown, where he started a small store, keeping confections at first, and later branching out into the grocery and general store business During the twen-

PETER MOYER AND GRANDSON

ty-five years he was engaged in business in this part of the state he started branch stores at Morrisdale, Stonedale and Mitchell's Mill on Clearfield Creek, owning the latter at the time that the Beech Creek Railroad was under course of construction He was for a time in partnership with William Root, and later with John W Howe, to whom he disposed of his branch stores, and in 1890 he sold his Kylertown establishment to O P Reese Mr Moyer has always been liberal in assisting those who have been less fortunate than he, and more than one successful man of this county can thank him for their start in life During the fifty-six years that he has been a resident of this vicinity he has seen many changes take place, and he has assisted materially in the growth and development of Clearfield county One of his earliest recollections dates back to a Fourth of July during his youth, when his father gave the children permission to do whatever they felt inclined Young Peter took two wooden pails and went to the hills to pick huckleberries, and after filling the buckets he carried them six miles to Philipsburg, where he sold them for two dollars and twenty cents and had to walk eight miles home after his marketing Although advanced in years, Mr Moyer is still hale and hearty, and he can look back over a useful, well-spent life

In 1867 Mr Moyer was united in marriage to Miss Mary E Adams, of Montour county, Pa, and three children have been born to this union Mary E, who died at the age of three years, a son who died in infancy, and Daniel Adams Mrs Moyer died April 12, 1906, and is buried at Kylertown Peter Moyer is a member of Allport Lodge, I O O F, Morrisdale Lodge, Knights of Pythias, and All-

port Lodge of the Golden Eagles In his religious views he is a Presbyterian Politically Mr Moyer is a Democrat, and probably there is no man in Cooper township who is better versed in public matters and conditions He has been active in politics all of his life, serving two years as tax collector when Cooper and Morris townships were known as Morris township, and after the separation serving nine years in Cooper township in the same capacity He was elected on the Democratic ticket, in a township that was strongly Republican He also served as overseer of the poor, and as treasurer, auditor and school director at various times

Daniel Adams Moyer, the son of Peter Moyer, was born in Kylertown, and his educational advantages were secured in the schools at this place As a lad he assisted his father in the duties of the latter's store, and later engaged in agricultural operations, in which he continued for a period covering fifteen years Since December 1, 1909, he has been in the employ of the Bloomington Trading Company, of Winburne, and he also with his father owns a fine farm of eighty-five acres near Kylertown, in Cooper township, which was formerly underlaid with coal, which has been removed

Mr Moyer was married to Miss Alice E Kirk, the daughter of Joseph Kirk, and to this union there have been born three children, namely Joseph Peter, Anna Mary and Frederick, all of whom are attending school Mr Moyer is a member of the Order of Red Men, the Odd Fellows and the Grange Like his father he is a stanch Democrat

Mr Moyer is one of the solid, substantial men of his community, and one who has always had the best interests of his township at heart. Upright and honest in his dealings with his fellow men, capable and earnest as a public official and kind and lenient in his family connections, he is looked up to and respected as a true type of German-American citizenship

ALBERT S. BROWN,* who has long been one of the foremost business men of Osceola Mills, Pa., is secretary and general manager of the Moshannon Coal Company, and has been an operator in the coal fields here for some eighteen years. He is the present head of the well known mercantile firm of Brown, Baird & Reeves. Mr. Brown was born in 1862, at Jersey Shore, Pa., and is a son of William A. and Mary A. (Smith) Brown.

William A. Brown is a member of an old family of Lycoming county, Pa. He came to Osceola Mills, where he still resides, in 1864, in connection with the Moshannon Lumber Company, which concern cleared off the timber through this section. In 1884, with his son, Albert S. Brown, he established the mercantile house of W. A. Brown & Son, with which he is still identified.

Albert S. Brown was two years old when the family moved from Lycoming county to Osceola Mills and here he grew to manhood. After his father retired from the lumber industry, he became associated with him in the general store business under the firm style of W. A. Brown & Son, which continued without change of partners until 1903, when A. S. Brown withdrew, selling his interest to a younger brother. The old firm disposed of their dry goods department to Brown, Baird & Reeves, but retained the meat and grocery departments and still continue in those lines.

The latter firm was organized in 1903 by Albert S. Brown, Lawshe Baird and J. L. Reeves. They have a commodious store, a large stock and do a satisfactory business. Mr. Brown has many additional interests. In 1893 he embarked in the coal business as an operator, in partnership with a Mr. Dyer and the coal firm of Brown & Dyer remained in business for ten years, in 1903 selling out to the Moshannon Coal Company. Of this company, Mr. Brown has been the active manager ever since its incorporation and in the discharge of his duties has given evidence of much business acumen. He is a director of the Osceola Water Company and of the Osceola Building and Loan Association, and was one of the organizers of the Osceola Silica and Brick Company, and served on its directing board until the pressure of other interests resulted in his withdrawal from this official connection.

Albert S. Brown was married to Miss Rosalie Merrill, who was born at Osceola Mills, and they have five children, namely: Herman S., who is engaged in the insurance business at Osceola Mills, married Miss Maud Kline, Fred D., who is in the employ of Brown, Baird & Reeves, and Isabel, Dorothy and Carrie. For many years Mr. Brown has been prominent in Masonic circles and is a member of Osceola Lodge, No. 515, F. & A. M., of which he is past master, Jaffa Temple, A. A. O. N. M. S., at Altoona, and of the Consistory, at Williamsport. Mr. Brown has not only been active and thorough-going in relation to his personal affairs but has watched with interest and assisted by his efforts and influence, the development of public enterprises in the borough. For six years he served usefully as a member of the borough council, where his ripened business judgment was exceedingly valuable, and also for eight years was borough treasurer

CHARLES FOWLER PENEPACKER, one of the progressive young business men connected with the great industries carried on at Morrisdale Mines, Clearfield county, Pa, is manager of the Morrisdale Supply Company's store and has had considerable training along commercial lines He was born December 18, 1878, at Mifflin, Mifflin county, Pa, a son of Rev G D and Nettie (Black) Penepacker

Rev G D Penepacker was born at Lewistown, Pa, and for forty-four years he was actively engaged in the ministry of the Methodist Episcopal church He was a member of the Central Pennsylvania Conference At the time of his death, which occurred on January 7, 1911, in his seventieth year, he was pastor of the Fifteenth Street M E church, at Huntingdon, Pa, and formerly had been stationed at Clearfield He married Nettie Black, who survives him. She was born at Huntingdon, Pa Seven children were born to the above marriage and there are three now living, namely Wilbur F, who is connected with the wholesale dry goods house of J V Farwell & Co, Chicago, Ill, married Martha Bartell, Nettie, who is the wife of James L Curtin, residing at Russelton, where Mr Curtin is manager of the Russelton Store Company, and Charles F

Charles F Penepacker completed the High School course at Clearfield and then entered Dickinson Seminary at Williamsport, where he was graduated in the class of 1898 For a short time he was in the grocery business as manager, at Williamsport and then went to Chicago, where he was engaged as manager of a department in the wholesale dry goods house of John B Farwell From Chicago he came back to Pennsylvania and for five years was manager of the Winburne Trading Company, at Winburne, and in 1908 came to Morrisdale Mines and accepted his present responsible position He has won confidence by his business integrity and has the enviable reputation of being a thorough-going, able man, and a first-class citizen

On November 20, 1907, Mr Penepacker was married to Miss Bessie Maxwell, a daughter of Joseph and Elizabeth (Husted) Maxwell, who were residents of Winburne, Pa, although Mrs Penepacker was reared in Tioga county They have one son, Charles Maxwell In politics Mr Penepacker is a Republican He is a member of Williamsport Lodge, No 106, F & A M, Williamsport Consistory; and the Mystic Shrine at Wilkesbarre They are attendants of the Methodist Episcopal church

JOHN CHARLES SULLIVAN, M D, Physician and surgeon at Du Bois, Pa, and one of the representative citizens, was born in Armstrong County, Pa, October 31, 1866, and is a son of Owen and Bridget (Healey) Sullivan

Owen Sullivan was born August 15, 1814 He was a son of Thomas Sullivan and Catherine (Moore) Sullivan He was the youngest of seven children, four sons and three daughters

He was born on a farm near Tralee, County Kerry, Ireland Came to the United States in 1847 Two brothers, John and Thomas came to America later, but again returned to Ireland

For many years he worked at the Great Western Iron Works, Brady's Bend, Pa His latter years were spent in agricultural pursuits on a farm in the beautiful Mahoning Valley, and there he died in honored old age, having reached the unusual age of ninety-two years and one month His remains are interred in St Charles' Cemetery, New Bethlehem, Pa

Bridget (Healey) Sullivan was the daughter of Michael Healey and Julia (McMahon) Healey She was born February 2 1837 in Ireland, on a farm near Gort, County of Galway She was the eldest of seven children, three sons and four daughters Michael Healey came to America in 1847, Mrs Healey coming with her family two years later, in 1849 Michael Healey settled at Red Bank Furnace, Armstrong Co , Pa , and worked at furnaces in Armstrong and Clarion Counties all his life

Owen Sullivan and Bridget Healey were married at Sligo, Clarion County, Pa June 16, 1859 To this union nine children were born Thomas F , of Pittsburgh, Pa , John Charles, Du Bois, Pa , Owen J , of New Bethlehem, Pa , James P , of Du Bois, Pa , and Bridget E , of New Bethlehem, Pa Michael C , who died November 1, 1895, at that time was resident physician of St Francis Hospital, Pittsburgh, Pa He was a graduate of the University of Pittsburgh in the class of 1894 Three daughters died in early childhood

John Charles Sullivan began the study of medicine in 1887 and entered the Western Pennsylvania Medical College at Pittsburgh, Pa , (now the University of Pittsburgh) from which institution he graduated in 1890 He located at Du Bois, Pa , in April 1890, and at the present time is the third physician in town in respect to years of practice

He is widely known and has taken much interest in medical matters in general in the county and has been particularly interested in the Du Bois Hospital, of which he was one of the organizers and is a member of the staff

Dr Sullivan was married June 7, 1893, to Miss Susan Kane a daughter of Patrick and Mary Kane of Renovo, Pa , and they have had eight children, namely Eugene, Marion, Edward, Loretta, Loyola, John Charles, Susanna, and Jeanne

Eugene lived but a few hours John Charles lived but two years and six months

Dr and Mrs Sullivan and family are members of St Catherine's Roman Catholic Church, Du Bois, Pa Dr Sullivan is identified with the Knights of Columbus In politics he is a Democrat Maintains an office in the Deposit National Bank Building, while his residence is at No 10 S Main Street, Du Bois Pa

WILLIAM HENRY DENSHAM, who conducts a general mercantile business at Oak Grove and Hawk Run, Clearfield county, Pa , is president of the Morris Township School Board and is a representative citizen in every laudable way. He was born in Devonshire, England, March 2, 1872, and is a son of John and Mary Ann (Creber) Densham

John Densham brought his family to Morrisdale, Clearfield county, Pa , in August, 1888. He was a coal miner and his death was occasioned by an injury received in the Morrisdale shaft, March 2, 1899, at the age of fifty-seven years His widow survived, was twice married, and died August 22, 1909 The following children were born to John Densham and his wife Elizabeth Ann, who is the wife of Richard Davy, of Oak Grove, Martha, who is the wife of Harry Barkell, of Plymouth, Eng , John, a farmer, who resides at Oak Grove, Jane, who is the wife of Josiah Jones, of Morrisdale, William H , Samuel, who is foreman for the Morrisdale Coal Company, and married Elizabeth Vinton, and Lena, who is the wife of Henry Vinton, of Clairton, Pa, who is an electrician

William H Densham attended school in his native land and also the night schools of Morrisdale, after the family settled there, and thus secured an excellent education and has always been an active supporter of the cause of education, consenting to serve again and again on the school board of his township He was a mine worker until 1899, and since 1902 has been in business at his present location, at Oak Grove, and in December, 1910, opened a general store also at Hawk Run

Mr Densham was married August 9, 1896. to Miss Agnes Neal, who was born in Tioga county, Pa, February 11, 1872, her parents, Jeremiah and Jane (Tate) Neal, having come from England Mr and Mrs Densham have had eight children Mary, Mildred, Jane, Beatrice, Ruth, Theodore, and two are now deceased Mr Densham is identified fraternally with the Golden Eagles and the Order of Moose In partnership with Mr Shugarts and Charles Wrye, Mr Densham is also interested in a grain and feed business at Morrisdale He is a self made man, having won financial independence entirely through his own efforts As a business man he stands high and his relations with his neighbors socially are kind and friendly Politically he is a Republican

CHARLES E PATTON,* representative in congress from the Twenty-first district of Pennsylvania, composed of the counties of Cameron, Center, Clearfield and McKean, whose total population in 1910 was 192,704, was born in Curwensville, Clearfield county, Pa, July 5, 1859 He still resides in that place He received his early education in the common schools of his native place and later attended Dickinson Seminary at Williamsport, Pa, and was married in 1883 to Mary R Beggs, of Ebensburg, Pa He started in business as a dry goods merchant, but later branched out in various lines of business and won general success in all. He is now identified with many of the most important business ventures of the community in which he resides, being stockholder and director in the Curwensville National Bank, president of the Curwensville Electric Company, interested in lumbering and contracting business, besides owning several fine farms, in which he takes an unusual interest, and his agricultural experiments have been of great benefit to the community He has held nearly every elective office in his own town, in the contest for Republican nomination for congress he defeated Hon Lewis Emery, Jr, of Bradford, Pa, who four years ago was candidate for governor on the independent and Democratic tickets and was defeated by Gov Stuart He carried the district by 1,355 over Emery, was elected to the Sixty-second congress, receiving a plurality over William C Heinle, the Democratic nominee, of 4,953 votes, the largest plurality ever given for congress in the district Like his honored father, the late General John Patton, he is a member of the Methodist Episcopal church of Curwensville, and one of the official board.

Mr Patton is a Mason and an Odd Fellow, as well as a member of the Grange Mr and Mrs Patton have four children, namely Emma Marguerite, wife of William K Ewing, of San Antonio, Tex, John W Patton, and Misses Mary Rebecca Patton and Honora Jane Patton, of Curwensville

EMANUEL S SHAFFER, whose farm of fifty acres lies two and one-half miles north-west of Kerrmoor, in Ferguson township, is one of the leading citizens of this section, in which he has been engaged in general farming for many years He was born November 11, 1846, in York county, Pa, and is a son of William and Katherine (Thoman) Shaffer

William Shaffer was born in 1818, in Mary-land, and moved in early manhood to York county, Pa He was married in 1840 to Kath-erine Thoman and they had seven children Cornelius, Edward, Albert, Mary Ellen, Hen-rietta, Emanuel S and an infant daughter that died at birth The mother of the above fam-ily died in December, 1898 In 1852 William Shaffer moved with his family to Perry county, Pa, and lived there during the re-mainder of his life, his death occurring in Sep-tember, 1897

Emanuel S Shaffer obtained his education in the schools of Perry county He worked as a lumberman there until 1866, when he set-tled along the Susquehanna river and engaged in business as a pilot and as a contractor He lived in Jefferson county for a time and then came to Clearfield county and settled in Ferguson township, this farm then being known as the Barrett farm He cleared about twenty acres of his land and has done all the building and made all the substantial improve-ments

On May 5, 1870, Mr Shaffer was married to Miss Amanda McCracken, who was born in Ferguson township, September 25, 1852, a daughter of William and Mary McCracken

Ten children have been born to Mr and Mrs Shaffer and although some of them have passed away, the family is yet a large and closely united one Ada, the eldest, married Erfford C Holt, and they live in Sweet Val-ley, Potter county, Pa They have had seven children Earl, Louis, Vada, Edith, Gladys, Leslie, and Ruth Emma, the second daugh-ter, survived but eighteen months and her bur-ial was in Jefferson county Elizabeth is the wife of W. D Helsel of Irvona, Pa, and they have five children Lester, Emanuel, Martha, Josephine and John Leslie, the eld-est son, died at the age of six years and his burial was in the Presbyterian cemetery at Fruit Hill Orel M married Cora Mitchell, a daughter of George and Lydia Mitchell, and they have three children, Emanuel, Paul and Lena Norman married Dora Redden, a daughter of James and Emma Redden, and they have one son, James Anderson married Vena Wiley, a daughter of Herbert and Kath-erine Wiley, and they have one son, Pressly. Bertha resides at home Sadie died at the age of eighteen years and her burial was in the Fruit Hill cemetery George S, the youngest, assists his father on the home farm Mr. Shaffer and family are members of the Luth-eran church He belongs to the Grange at Kerrmoor, the Odd Fellows at Ansonville and the Masons at Curwensville In politics, like his late father, Mr Shaffer is a Democrat He has served as school director but has accepted no other township office He is one of the stockholders in the Ferguson-La Jose Tele-phone Company

CHARLES B MAXWELL, who has been a resident of Morrisdale Mines, Clearfield county, Pa, since November 20, 1898, has been identified with the coal industry since he was eleven years of age and has rapidly risen from a humble position, through one office of responsibility to another, until he is now general superintendent of the Morrisdale Coal Company and one of the most representative business men of Clearfield county He was born February 10, 1873, at Morris Run, Tioga county, Pa , a son of George and Margaret (Clement) Maxwell

For many years George Maxwell was connected with coal interests in Tioga county, where both he and wife were born For seventeen years he was superintendent of the Morris Run Coal Company In 1880 he left Tioga county and moved to Houtzdale, Clearfield county, where he had charge of coal operating for a number of years afterward His death occurred in 1902, at Houtzdale, where his widow has lived for the past thirty-one years Of their six children, three grew to maturity, namely Anna M , who lives at Houtzdale, James and Charles B James Maxwell died in 1904, at which time he was bookkeeper for the firm of Harbison & Walker, of Woodland, Pa

Charles B Maxwell went to school at Houtzdale until he was eleven years of age and then went to work in the mines, learning every detail of mine work For fifteen years he was a member of an engineering corps and for four years was engineer of the Morrisdale Coal Company's plant In 1902 he was made superintendent of the Broad Top operations for this company, in 1903 he was made superintendent of the Morrisdale and Broad Top operations, and in 1904 was further promoted, becoming general superintendent of all of the company's operations or mines

The Morrisdale Coal Company was organized in 1895, prior to which, from 1885, its operations were conducted by R B Wigton & Sons, and prior to that, from 1865, by R B Wigton The plant is modern and is equipped with the latest and most approved machinery There are three shafts and two drift mines, and the coal is of a high grade and is well considered in the market The capacity is 22,000 tons daily and employment is given 800 men Few mines have been operated more regularly than the mines of the Morrisdale Coal Company Mr Wigton, the president of the company, is the oldest operator in the Central Pennsylvania field

On June 23, 1898, Mr Maxwell was married to Miss Dollie B Stine, a daughter of S B Stine, a prominent manufacturer of Osceola Mills Mr and Mrs Maxwell have had two children, both of whom are now deceased, neither surviving infancy They are members of the Presbyterian church In politics Mr Maxwell is a Republican His fraternal connections are mainly with the Masonic bodies, he being a member of Philipsburg Lodge, No 391, F & A M , Clearfield Chapter, Philipsburg Commandery, Williamsport Consistory, and Jaffa Temple of the Mystic Shrine at Altoona

THE MOSHANNON COAL COMPANY,* operating extensively in the coal fields surrounding Osceola Mills, Clearfield county, Pa , where the offices of the company are located, had its inception in 1903 In July of that year it took over the interests of Brown & Dyer, T C Heims and C H Rowland The officers of the company are C H Rowland, of Philipsburg, president, John G Anderson, of Tyrone, first vice-president, L Baird, second vice-president, J L Reeves, third vice-president, and A S Brown, secretary, treasurer and general manager The officers serve as the board of directors and are the sole stockholders

The Moshannon Coal Company own ten mines, located on the Pennsylvania and New York Central Railroads, and all of these are in full operation The company is amply financiered and ably officered and the direct result of its successful operations is far reaching and beneficial, bringing plenty and prosperity into many homes

J. J BOYLE, wholesale liquor dealer, with business location at No 237 W Long avenue, DuBois, Pa , is one of the self-made men of this borough, having obtained all he possesses through his own industry He was born in county Donegal, Ireland, June 1, 1869, and is a son of John and Cecely (O'Donald) Boyle, both of whom died in Ireland

J J Boyle is one of a family of eleven children and three of his brothers also live at Du-Bois—Anthony, Niel and Michael He spent his early years on his father's small farm and attended the public school as opportunity offered The family was large and the first one to leave home for America was Anthony, whom our subject followed in 1886 For six years, the boy, for he was little more when he reached Clearfield county, worked in the coal mines for Bell, Lewis & Yates Coal Company In 1889 he was employed by the old Daily House management at DuBois, now the Central Hotel, but in 1891 he left there and accepted a position in what is now the St James Hotel, on Long avenue, after which he was also with the Commercial Hotel In 1903 he entered into partnership with Mr Dempsey and under the firm name of Dempsey & Boyle,

a wholesale license was secured, and three years later removal was made to the present location After the death of Mr. Dempsey, April 8, 1908, Mr Boyle became sole owner, having purchased the Dempsey interest, and has continued in the wholesale trade ever since

Mr Boyle was married in 1898, to Miss Mary Hollihan, who was born at Blairsville, Pa , a daughter of Michael and Mary Hollihan, who were born in Ireland Mr and Mrs Boyle have six children, namely Marcella, John, Lucille, Donald, Mary Josephine and Carl Eugene The family residence is at No 100 N Main street, DuBois Mr and Mrs Boyle are members of St Catherine's Roman Catholic church

HON JAMES W LAING, burgess of Coalport, Pa , one of the leading men of the place in public affairs, is also representative in business and as a dealer in musical instruments and sewing machines, handles a large enterprise He is numbered with the younger element, his birth having taken place August 22, 1881, at Moshannon, Clearfield county, Pa He is a son of Robert and Margaret (Chalmers) Laing

Robert Laing and wife were both born in Scotland and emigrated from that country to America, settling in Tioga county, Pa , in 1873 In 1880 the father moved with his family, to Clearfield county, but in 1885 he returned with his wife to Scotland, where they remained for sixteen years In 1901 they came back to Clearfield county, locating at Coalport, where Robert Laing died in the following year His widow survived until 1909, when she passed away also at Coalport Robert Laing was a coal miner and the greater

HON. JAMES W. LAING

part of his life of fifty-two years was given to work in the coal mines He was a man of sturdy and manly character and his wife was a woman of rare judgment and Christian virtues Their children were as follows John, the oldest, resides in Scotland, where he follows mining Jennie is the wife of Charles Ross, of Fifeshire, Scotland Thomas is a miner in Fifeshire and Robert is a miner at Coalport James W is the fifth of the family in order of birth Alexander is a resident of Coalport Jessie is the wife of John Caynock, who is a coal miner at Portage Peter lives at New Haven, Conn, where he is in the employ of the street railway company Duncan also lives at New Haven, where he is an employe of an automobile company

James W Laing attended school in Scotland and as he early displayed musical talent he was afforded advantages for cultivating it, and holds a certificate for efficiency in music from London College He was about nineteen years of age when he accompanied his parents back to Coalport, after which he went to New Haven, Conn, seeking a business opening, but the serious illness of his father recalled him six weeks later After his father's death he went to New York and then returned to Scotland, at that time determining to remain in the land of his forefathers Within six months, however, he found that America had also a place in his affections and he again crossed the Atlantic Ocean and from the seaboard traveled as far west as Montana, where he remained for a time and then came back to Coalport After his marriage in 1906 he moved to New Haven, Conn, but failed to establish himself there and decided to return once more to Coalport On a borrowed capital of forty-five dollars he started into the

musical instrument business and in the few years since has prospered exceedingly, at the present time carrying a stock valued at $3,000, while his trade relations are such that he enjoys the confidence of the great manufacturing houses with which he deals, in every part of the country

On March 7, 1906, Mr Laing was married to Miss Christina Shanks, a daughter of Richard Shanks, and they have three children Geraldine May, Bessie Marie and Christina Mr Laing was reared in the Presbyterian church and in Scotland was the church organist and filled the same position in St Basil's church, Coalport He has been a very active citizen, a Republican in politics, and was elected burgess in 1909, on the citizens ticket, and is serving in the most efficient and satisfactory manner He is chief and secretary of the local fire department Fraternally he belongs to Lodge No 781, F & A M, Thane of Fife, Scotland, and to the order of Eagles at Bellwood, Pa

PROF HARRY ELMER WARD,* superintendent of the public schools of Clearfield, Pa, is a well known educator and is a member of one of the old and honorable county families He was born May 19, 1876, at Grayhampton, Clearfield county, Pa, and is a son of John Lucine and Henrietta (Forcey) Ward

John Lucine Ward was born in Clearfield county, in 1846, and is a son of Robert F Ward, who was formerly deputy sheriff of Clearfield county Robert F Ward came to this county from Lewisburg, Ky, and later became associated with William Rodebaugh, in the tailoring business at Clearfield, where he died in 1860 John Lucine Ward learned the saddler's trade in early manhood and later was in partnership with F. H Forcey, in the lumber and general mercantile business, at Grayhampton, where he resided until 1898, when he and wife retired to their farm in Graham township, where they still reside She also is a native of Clearfield county and was born in Bradford township To John Lucine and Henrietta Ward five children were born, namely Margaret, William, Harry Elmer, John and Robert F, all of whom live in Clearfield county with the exception of William, who resides at Altoona, in Blair county

Harry E Ward passed from the public schools, where he had been a creditable student, into the Lock Haven State Normal School, from which institution he was graduated in 1900 Shortly afterward he became principal of the Third Ward School at Clearfield and also became a student of law, but finding more satisfaction in educational work than in his law studies, he gave up the latter in order to devote himself more entirely to the former profession He remained at the head of the Third Ward School for four years and then resigned and for a change in occupation, accepted a position with the Hamilton Leather Company, at Hamilton, W Va In August, 1905, Prof Ward returned to Clearfield in order to accept the position of principal of the Market Street School, where he continued until June, 1910, when he was elected superintendent of the city schools More or less continuously Prof Ward has been engaged in school work since 1892 He is widely known throughout Clearfield and adjacent counties and is recognized as an earnest and progressive leader in his profession

Prof Ward was married November 25, 1896, to Miss Margaret Pierce, a daughter of Jacob and Jane (Rigley) Pierce, and they have three daughters, Catherine, Margaret Elizabeth and Helen Lenore Prof Ward and family are members of the Presbyterian church The family residence is situated at No 495 Fifth street, Clearfield In identifying himself with a political party in early manhood, Prof Ward became a Republican and is an interested citizen but by no means a politician He is an educated, cultured man, one who commands the respect and enjoys the esteem of his fellow citizens

HON JOHN E HARDER, long a successful business man and representative citizen of the borough of Clearfield, which, just previous to his death, he was serving as chief burgess, was owner and proprietor of Harder's Gun Works, one of the old and prosperous business concerns of this place, established in 1878 He was born at Lock Haven in 1858, being one of a family of four children born to his parents, who were Jacob and Maud (Fletcher) Harder After graduating from the Lock Haven Seminary, he learned the gunsmith's trade under his father, and when sufficiently skilled, came in 1878 to Clearfield, where he established himself in business Keeping well in touch with the discoveries in mechanical science, Mr Harder was always up to date in the character and quality of his goods, and from time to time found himself obliged to enlarge his plant The Harder's Gun Works manufacture and deal in gas and electric supplies, automobiles, guns, bicycles, fishing tackle, cutlery, base ball supplies and sporting goods, umbrellas, electrical appliances, fireworks and musical instruments They also repair bicycles, automobiles, guns, safes, umbrellas, typewriters sewing-machines, talking machines and skates, and make electric light and bell work a specialty In connection with the factory an automobile garage is also carried on and gasoline, lubricants and supplies handled A wide field is covered and there is a growing demand for the firm s products

Mr Harder was a thirty-second degree Mason and belonged also to other fraternal organizations From early manhood he was politically identified with the Republican party, and whether serving his friends or holding office himself, was always loyal to its principles In 1898 he raised a volunteer company for possible service in the Spanish-American war and was chosen captain In February, 1909, he was elected chief burgess of Clearfield, having a majority of 100 votes over his opponent, although the borough is nominally Democratic, and he was serving in this office at the time of his death, which took place suddenly on the afternoon of October 11, 1910 He had made an excellent record as burgess, and his efforts in the direction of reform and progress were encouraged and supported by the best and most substantial citizens

Mr Harder married Miss Frank L Showers, a daughter of the late David Showers, formerly of Williamsport, Pa , and of this marriage was born a son, J Emmott Harder, who is now the manager of Harder's Gun Works, the business being owned by Mrs J E Harder, the widow of our subject The son. J Emmot Harder, married Miss May Gearhart, of Clearfield Mrs J E Harder. the elder, is a member of the Methodist Episcopal church, as was also her husband The family residence stands at No 319 Locust street, which has been their home for twenty-two years—a place well known to the best society of Clearfield for its cheerful and unostentatious hospitality

HENRY ROUSEY,* who has been a resident of Girard township for thirty years, has spent twenty of them on his valuable farm of 106 acres, which is situated eighteen miles west of the borough of Clearfield He was born in Clearfield county and is a son of Stephen and Amelia Rousey The parents of Mr Rousey were born in France and when they came to Clearfield county settled near Frenchville, where many of their fellow countrymen had located They engaged in farming and passed the remaining years of their lives near or in Frenchville ,

Henry Rousey attended the schools of Covington township and afterward assisted his father on his farm, later going into farming and stockraising for himself When he reached manhood he married Miss Amelia Deminer, who was born in France, a daughter of Peter Deminer, well known in this section Two children were born to them, namely Bertha, who is the wife of Augustus Hughney, of Covington township, and has two children—Dorothy and Gertrude , and Lillie, who married D Bellotte, of Girard township, also of French extraction, and has two children, Boyd and Florence A Mr Rousey and family are members of St Francis' Catholic church, of Frenchville Mr Rousey has always been an active citizen and has been particularly interested in the public schools, serving for some nine years as a school director He has been elected to other offices and has performed the duties in a satisfactory manner He is one of Girard township's most respected citizens

JACOB H MILLER. who has been superintendent for the Clark Brothers Coal Mining Company, having charge of three mines, for the past seven years, is a representative citizen of Bigler township, and resides at Smoke Run   He was born in 1869, in Lehigh county, Pa , and is a son of Phillip and Lydia (Meyer) Miller

Phillip Miller was a millwright and followed his trade in several sections of Pennsylvania   Both he and his wife died at Philadelphia and are buried in Upper Milford township, Lehigh County, Pa   They were members of the Evangelical church   The following children were born to them   Emma, widow of William Bower, Obediah, Catherine, widow of Joseph Kline, Sarah, widow of Manoa Trump, Thomas, Ellen, (Mrs William F Jacoby), Jacob H , and James   Both grandfathers of the above family bore the name of Jacob

Jacob H Miller attended the public schools in Lehigh county and at Philadelphia, after which he learned the art of telegraphy and worked as a telegrapher for fourteen years, during the most of this time for the Western Union Telegraph Company   He then became connected with the electrical repair department of the Metropolitan Street Railway Company, of New York city, and from there went to the Brush Electric Light Company of Philadelphia, having charge of the street lighting there for two years   In 1901 Mr Miller engaged with the Penn Colliery Company, coming then to Smoke Run as their electrician, and in 1904 he accepted his present position, one of large responsibility   Mr Miller has had a large amount of practical experience and has been considered a reliable and efficient man in every company with which he has been connected

In 1897 Mr Miller was married to Miss Minnie G Gillette, a daughter of Thomas and Elmira (Shindler) Gillette, residents of Jersey City, N J   Formerly Mr Gillette was a telegrapher   Mrs Miller has had two sisters and three brothers   Mary, who is the wife of L W Freeman, Grace, who is the wife of H W Heinbach, Robert W , Thomas, and George, who is deceased   Mr and Mrs Miller have one daughter, Edna Hilda, who was born in April, 1904   They attend the Methodist Episcopal church   He is a Republican in politics but has never sought any public office   He is identified with the Masons at Osceola, the Knights of Pythias at Philadelphia, and the P O S of A at Madera, he being president of this organization of District No 3, Clearfield county

ANDREW J MONTGOMERY, A retired farmer and very highly respected citizen of Bell township, Clearfield county, Pa , was born August 25, 1849, in Indiana county, Pa , and is a son of Jehu and Nancy (Spencer) Montgomery

Jehu Montgomery was born in 1803, in Clarion county, Pa , and died in Indiana county when aged sixty-seven years   His business was farming and he was a patriotic and reliable citizen, serving his country all through the Mexican war   He married Nancy Spencer, who was born in Indiana county and died there in 1908, aged eighty-two years   She was a daughter of Andrew and Margaret (Pierce) Spencer, old Indiana county families   To Jehu Montgomery and wife the following children were born   Andrew J ; Thomas, Robert A , residing in Nebraska, Jennie, wife of R B Copp, of Augusta, Me , Samuel G , residing in Bell township, William, living in Indiana county, and Lee, Calvin J , Peter C and Cynthia E , all of whom reside in Indiana county, the last named being the wife of George Lambing

Andrew J Montgomery obtained his education in his native county and afterward followed the carpenter trade for seven years and then went into the woods and was engaged in timber cutting and contracting until 1885, when he became a farmer and continued agricultural pursuits until 1903, when he retired During the Civil war he served as a soldier from April, 1865, until September in the same year, being a member of Co B, 74th Pa Vol Inf, his commanding officers being Col Hobart, of Pittsburg, and Captain P C Spencer, the latter of whom was his uncle His regiment was detailed as guards for the Baltimore & Ohio Railroad

Mr Montgomery was married to Miss Sarah Jane Neal, who was born in Jefferson county, Pa, January 10, 1854, and is a daughter of Thomas and Mary (Graffins) Neal, both of whom were born in Eastern Pennsylvania Mr and Mrs Montgomery have had ten children, as follows Mary, who married R S Miller, of McGee's Mills, and they have ten children and two grandchildren Myrtle B, who married H M Bowers, of Bolivar, Pa, and they have six children, Nancy E, who is the wife of M P Dodson, and they have three children, Theresa, who is the wife of P E Bowers, and they have five children, Irwin, who resides at Fort Woodworth, N Y, May, who is the wife of W F Masters, of Johnstown, Pa, William G who married Cora Johnston, and they have two children, Thomas N, who married Lod Leasur, resides in Indiana county, and Fannie and Pearl, both of whom reside at home Mr and Mrs Montgomery are members of the Methodist Episcopal church In politics he is identified with the Republican party but has never wanted to hold office and when his appreciative fellow citizens elected him a justice of the peace in

Bell township, declined to serve He is a member of the fraternal order of Knights of the Golden Eagles at McGee's Mills, Clearfield county

HOWARD A COLLINS, M D,* of Winburne, Cooper township, Clearfield county, Pa, and a practicing physician in this county for the past sixteen years, was born in Lycoming county, Pa, February 6, 1871, and is a son of William and Mary (Winner) Collins

The Collins family is an old one in Pennsylvania William and Margaret (Brewster) Collins, great-grandparents of Dr Collins, were born in Berks county, Pa, and moved from there as pioneers into Lycoming county, and at the same time several of the Collins brothers settled in New York The first house erected by William Collins was so strongly built that it still stands not far from the present city of Williamsport At that time Philadelphia was the nearest supply station and each fall the long distance had to be covered by wagon in order to provide necessities for the family for the winter

Isaac Collins, son of William and Margaret Collins, was the paternal grandfather of Dr Collins, and he was born in Lycoming county, as was his wife, Margaret Dommy The maternal grandparents of Dr Collins were Jacob and Elizabeth (Tohlman) Winner The Winners and Tohlmans, who were Quakers, settled in Hebron and Eldred townships, in Lycoming county The maternal great-grandfather was Abraham Winner, who moved to Lycoming county from Philadelphia The parents of Dr Collins were both born and reared in Lycoming county and the father was a farmer in Alsop township, where his death occurred in 1909, when he was aged eighty-three years He had survived his wife for eight years, her death occurring in September, 1901, at the age of seventy-six years Of their twelve children, ten grew to maturity and six still survive, namely Howard A, Jennie, who is the wife of George Castleberry, of Williamsport, Irene, who is the wife of Oliver P Stahl, of Williamsport, Cyrus M and Annie M, both of whom live at Williamsport, and William S, who is a resident of Buffalo, N Y Those deceased were Albert, who died in 1877—was a graduate of Dickinson Seminary, Herman M, whose death in 1881 was the result of typhoid fever, Jeffrey A, who died in 1896, from an attack of appendicitis, Sadie L, who was the wife of Ambrose Hyman, of Williamsport, and two who died in infancy

Howard A Collins attended the public schools of Williamsport and the Williamsport Commercial College, leaving his studies at the age of nineteen years in order to take up work as a bookkeeper and stenographer In the meanwhile he had done his preparatory medical reading and in the fall of 1892 entered Jefferson Medical College and was graduated in the class of 1896 His first field of practice was at Wallaceton, where he remained one year and then came to Winburne He is known professionally in many parts of the county, his success as a practitioner having gained for him a large measure of public confidence

In 1892 Dr Collins was married to Miss Delia M Wise, a daughter of James T Wise, of Lycoming County, and they have four children Roy F, Charles, Chalmers Da Costa, and Vivian M Dr and Mrs Collins are members of the Methodist Episcopal church, with which he has been united for thirty years He is an independent in politics but is an interested citizen and has served on the school board of

Morris Township He has been president of the Clearfield County Medical Society and fraternally is identified with the U A M, the Knights of Pythias, the Elks, the Eagles and the P O S of A

WILLIAM A HAGERTY, attorney at law, with offices in the old Masonic Building, at Clearfield, Pa, is a representative citizen and an able member of the Clearfield bar He was born at Glen Hope, Pa, January 22, 1857, and is a son of Joseph and Jane (Alexander) Hagerty

Joseph Hagerty was born and reared in Center County, Pa He was a successful business man and at different times was interested in farming, milling and merchandising, owning a store at Lumber City, Pa, at the time of his death, which occurred in March, 1864 He married Jane Alexander, who was a daughter of William Alexander, the latter of whom died in 1867, at the age of ninety-one years His life had covered a wonderful period of his country's history, extending from the administration of President Washington to that of General Grant He had filled many public positions, was county commissioner, county treasurer and sheriff of Center County Of the large family born to Joseph Hagerty and wife, but three survive. Mary, who is the widow of F C Cromm, Andrew J, who is a prominent merchant of Clearfield, and William Alexander, who preserves his mother's maiden name

William A Hagerty was eight years old when the family came to Clearfield and here he was reared and obtained his education in the public schools and was one of the first three graduates of the Clearfield High School, in 1876 Later he attended a college at Gettys-

ISRAEL TEST

WILLIAM WILSON BETTS

burg for a time, after which he accepted a clerical position in the old Clearfield County Bank When prepared financially to enter upon the study of law, he became a student in the office of J B McEnally, later Judge McEnally, and after four years of training there was admitted to the Clearfield County bar in September, 1879 With the exception of one year spent in the office of Judge McEnally, he has practiced alone and both personally and professionally stands high in Clearfield County

On October 24, 1893, Mr Hagerty was married to Miss Carrie Test, a daughter of Israel Test, who is remembered as one of the most brilliant members of the Clearfield bar, and who died in 1886 His great grandfather, George Test, came to America with William Penn, was the first sheriff of Philadelphia under him and also governor of what was called the Uplands' Mr and Mrs Hagerty have had three children. Julia, William Test and Jane The eldest born died in childhood The attractive family residence is situated at No 213 Pine Street Mr and Mrs Hagerty are members of the Presbyterian church Politically he is a Democrat and for some time has been a member of the State Board of Health In his fraternal relations he is a Knight of Pythias and an Elk, being exalted ruler in the latter organization at Clearfield

HARRY EDMUND DIEHL,* engineer for the Pennsylvania Railroad pumping station in Chest Township, Clearfield County, Pa, belongs to one of the old settled families of the county He was born in Greenfield Township, Clearfield County, Pa, January 24, 1878, and is a son of Samuel and Mary (Mock) Diehl, and a grandson of John Diehl who was in the fourth generation of descent from Samuel

Diehl, who came to Pennsylvania from Loudoun County, Va When Grandfather Diehl died he left ninety direct descendants The Diehls have an annual reunion in Clearfield County

Harry Edmund Diehl attended school until he was thirteen years of age and then learned the saw mill business and worked with his father in a saw mill for six years and afterward worked at mining and lumbering until 1906, when he became tank keeper in the employ of the Pennsylvania Railroad Company, as mentioned above

Mr Diehl married Miss Ella Brink, who was born May 3, 1886, near Smoke Run, and is a daughter of George W and Anna (Shaffer) Brink, who were born in Indiana County and after coming to Clearfield County settled at Irvona Mr Brink, who is now eighty-three years of age, followed lumbering all through his active life Mr and Mrs Diehl have two children Florence, a school girl of nine years, and Gilbert Emmons, who is three years old In politics he is a Republican and he served one term as high constable at Irvona He belongs to the order of the Mystic Chain, also at Irvona

HON WILLIAM WILSON BETTS, deceased, during a long and useful life, was creditably identified with public affairs and business enterprises in the state which became his home when three years old For many years he was one of the leading citizens of Clearfield County, Pa He was born at Newark, N J, May 1, 1838, and was a son of Rev Frederick G and Cornelia (Finley) Betts

Rev Frederick G Betts was born in the city of Philadelphia in 1812 In 1840 he was licensed as a minister by the Huntingdon Presbytery, and in November of the same year he was installed as pastor of the Presbyterian church at Clearfield He served congregations at Clearfield, Curwensville and Forest Hill His death occurred in 1845 He married Cornelia Finley, who survived him, dying in 1853

William Wilson Betts attended school until thirteen years of age and then entered the printing office of the Crawford Journal, at Meadville, with the intention of learning the trade, but impaired eyesight caused him to change his plans At the age of twenty-one years, he was taken into partnership with the firm of Reed, Weaver & Powell, at Clearfield In 1869 G L Reed and William Powell retired from the firm and the business was then conducted under the firm name of Weaver & Betts until he died This firm, during this period, was the most extensive dealer in lumber in this section, and also Mr Betts was largely engaged in other interests, such as coal, fire clay and the industries of Clearfield and the county, and the development of the same, to which he devoted much of his time and influence, always being one of the foremost citizens to labor devotedly for the interests of his town and county

In his business relations, Mr Betts was held in the very highest esteem by those who had dealings with him, and the number was large on account of his extensive operations He was much more, however, than a successful business man, being one who realized at all times, and often accepted, the responsibilities of citizenship While public affairs in his state engaged his attention in a large degree for some years, he never forgot or neglected the claims of his own community, and in the matter of securing public utilities for Clearfield, no citizen was more active or influential In his views on public questions he was a Jacksonian

Democrat and frequently was tendered political office and in 1886 he was unanimously offered by the Democratic Party, the nomination for the State Senate, for the district composed of Clearfield, Centre and Clinton Counties, and having accepted the same, although not having been a candidate, the Republican Party declined to place any candidate in the field in opposition to him ; thereby making his nomination and election practically the unanimous selection by the people of his district He served with characteristic faithfulness in this high office, which he held for four years The Democratic Party again desired him to accept the nomination and return to the Senate, but, not caring for public life, he declined to be a candidate The death of Senator Betts occurred September 24, 1896

On October 28, 1862, Mr Betts was married to Miss Margaret J Irvin, of Curwensville, Pa , who survived him until her death on June 12, 1910 Six children were born to this marriage Two children, John Weaver and Cornelia, died at an early age, the surviving children being Mrs Jennie Betts Hartswick, Mrs Alice Betts Walter, Frederick Gregory Betts and William Irvin Betts

JOHN JOSEPH SCOLLINS, Justice of the Peace, at Houtzdale, Pa , is one of the best known of the younger generation of business men in this Borough He was born at Houtzdale, May 12, 1885, and is a son of Michael and Alicia (Ronan) Scollins

Michael Scollins, his father, was born in England but was reared in Ireland and came from there to America at an early age He lived at Tioga County, prior to coming to Houtzdale in the early 80's He followed mining as an occupation, and for a time conducted a licensed restaurant and the Woodward Hotel at Houtzdale, retiring from this business in 1899 He then went to Pittsburgh and worked for some years in the employ of the Carnegie Steel Company He returned to Houtzdale, where he died in 1905 He married Alicia Ronan, who was born in Huntingdon County Her father, John Ronan, was a miner and a man of considerable prominence at Dudley, where he served on the School Board, and as its secretary, for thirty years Mrs Scollins still survives Seven children were born to Michael Scollins and his wife, namely Nora, who is the wife of Charles W Pie, of Somerset, Pa , Margaret, who died in infancy, John, Agnes. Mary, who died at the age of twelve years , Paul and Catherine

John Scollins received his primary education in the parochial school at Houtzdale and in 1903 graduated from the Houtzdale High School While a student at the High School he was appointed to the office of Town Clerk, which position he held continuously until 1909, when he resigned to assume the duties of his present office Upon graduation, he became connected with the law offices of W H Patterson and J A Gleason, took the necessary examination and secured a teacher's certificate, following which he taught one term at the Beaverton School in Decatur Township, and was then elected to teach the Moshannon School at Osceola He was crippled in infancy and about this time, owing to his active life, his injury developed to an extent that caused the loss of a leg, in 1904 In the meantime he opened a fire insurance agency, which he still conducts in conjunction with his other work He is recognized as a young man of more than the usual amount of ability, while his personality is such that he has hosts of friends He succeeded to

56

the office of Justice of the Peace by appointment of Governor Stuart, and is now serving a full term having been elected to this office on the Democratic ticket He is deeply interested in educational affairs, was one of the organizers of the Alumni Association of the Houtzdale High School, and its secretary since organization, is a member of the Roman Catholic Church, and is identified with the Knights of Columbus

dale, May 12, 1885, and is a son of Michael and Alicia (Ronan) Scollins

Michael Scollins was born in England but was reared in Ireland and came from there to America in early manhood He lived in Tioga County prior to coming to Houtzdale, and in this place conducted a licensed restaurant for some years In 1897 he took charge of the Woodward Hotel, which he conducted for some years, moved then to Pittsburg for a residence of some years and then returned to Houzdale, where he died in 1906 He married Alicia Ronan, who was born in Huntingdon County Her father, John Ronan, was a miner and a man of considerable prominence at Dudley, where he served on the school board for thirty years Mrs Scollins still survives. Seven children were born to Michael Scollins and his wife, namely· Nora, who is the wife of Charles Pie, of Somerset, Pa , Margaret, who died in infancy, John; Agnes, Mary, who died at the age of twelve years, and Paul and Catherine

John Scollins received his primary education in the parochial school at Houtzdale and in 1903 graduated from the Houtzdale High School Later he took the necessary examination and secured a teacher's certificate, following which he taught one term at the Beaverton school in Decatur Township and was then

elected to teach the Moshannon school at Osceola. His health failed however and he grew
worse and an injury developed that caused the
loss of a leg, in 1904   He is recognized as a
young man of more than the usual amount of
ability, while his personality is such that he
has hosts of friends   He is serving in his second term as justice of the peace, elected to this
office on the Democratic ticket   He is a member of the Roman Catholic church, and he is
identified with the Knights of Columbus

JAMES E KIRK,* president of the Madera National Bank and also owner and proprietor of a large hardware business, at Madera,
Pa , is one of the leading men of the borough
and one of the most substantial citizens of the
place   He was born at Utahville, Clearfield
County, Pa , September 27, 1863, and is a son
of Samuel and Rebecca S (Beyer) Kirk, and
a grandson of James E Kirk, who was also
born in Clearfield County   Samuel Kirk survives and resides with his son at Madera   He
was born in Cumberland County and his wife
in Clearfield County, Pa

James E. Kirk enjoyed excellent educational
advantages, after completing the public school
course entering Dickinson Seminary at Williamsport, later taking a course in Birmingham Seminary and finally a course in business
at the Bryant and Stratton Commercial College, Philadelphia   Afterward, for about
eighteen years, Mr Kirk was in the employ of
Beyer & Kirk, lumber men at Madera, and then
became identified with the interests which are
his own   His hardware and house furnishing
establishment is a leading business enterprise
of the town, while the Madera National Bank
enjoys a large amount of patronage   He is
also a stockholder in the Madera Water Com-

pany and is a one-half owner of fifty houses
and 100 building lots at this place

Mr Kirk was married to Miss Della M.
Heck, who was born in Huntingdon County,
Pa , and they have the following children.
Samuel R S , who is attending school at Clearfield, and James E , David John and Ninevah
Viana   Mr Kirk and family attend the Methodist Episcopal church   In politics both he
and his father are Republicans and he has
served two terms as treasurer of Bigler Township   He is identified with the Masonic lodge
at Tyrone

ROBERT JACKSON, M D , who has
been engaged in the practice of his profession
at Osceola Mills, Pa , since January 1, 1898,
has been a resident of this borough since 1880
He was born March 11, 1871, at Philadelphia,
Pa , and is a son of Robert A and Anna M
(McFeeters) Jackson

Robert Aiken Jackson, father of Dr Jackson, was born in the city of Philadelphia, December 7, 1847, and was a son of Robert and
Jane (Knox) Jackson. The elder Robert
Jackson and wife came from Ireland to America and he was engaged in a retail grocery business at Philadelphia until the close of his life
Of their children, Robert Aiken is the only survivor   He moved from Philadelphia to Warrior's Mark, in Huntingdon County, in 1873,
and from there to near Petersburg, Va , and
from there in 1880, to Osceola Mills   He married Anna M McFeeters, who was born in
Philadelphia, a daughter of Andrew and Martha McFeeters, who were natives of Ireland and
later residents of Philadelphia   Of the children of Andrew McFeeters and wife the following survive Jennie, who resides in Philadelphia, Martha, who is the wife of Smiley

Orr, of Philadelphia, Abbie, who is the wife of Joseph Houston, of Philadelphia, James, who is also a resident of Philadelphia; and Anna M, who is the wife of Robert A Jackson

Seven children were born to Robert A Jackson and his wife, the eldest being an infant that died when a few days old William, the second born, died at the age of four years, Robert was the third in order of birth Andrew Charles, born December 20, 1873, at Warrior's Mark, lives in Philadelphia Clifford Lowry and Howard Knox both reside at Philipsburg The youngest, Russell A, was born in 1889 For almost thirty years Mr Jackson has been a coal operator He has served as a member of the borough council and of the school board and Osceola Mills, and belongs to the Masonic lodge at the same place

Robert Jackson attended school at Osceola Mills from nine to fifteen years of age, after which he spent several years in Philadelphia He then returned to Osceola and remained until his preparatory medical reading had been done, in 1892 entering Jefferson Medical College, where he was graduated in 1896 Dr Jackson spent the three months of his initial practice in Houtzdale In 1898 he established himself permanently at Osceola Mills where he is in the enjoyment of a substantial practice

Dr Jackson was married June 21, 1899, to Miss Susan Jane Brown, who was born April 3, 1873, a daughter of J R and Louise Brown, residents of Osceola Mills Dr and Mrs Jackson have two children George Clifford, born August 7, 1903, and Louise Brown, born August 22, 1908 Dr and Mrs Jackson are members of the Presbyterian church in which they were reared In politics he is a Republican but is not an active politician He

is a member of the order of Odd Fellows at Osceola Mills

T F CASEY is owner and proprietor of the Central Hotel, a comfortable and well patronized hostelry at Curwensville, Pa, and also owner of a valuable farm on the borough line This farm is in a high state of cultivation but is more valuable on account of being underlaid with fire brick clay and coal Mr Casey was born near Corsica, Jefferson County, Pa, on August 5, 1861, eldest son of John L and Margaret (Daly) Casey

John L Casey was a native of Ireland, emigrating to New York City at the age of nineteen He was a graduate of Dublin University and was well fitted for the occupation of contracting builder, which he followed the remainder of his life The family moved to DuBois in the early 80's, where Mr Casey died after a lingering illness of several years and was buried in the Catholic cemetery at DuBois He was married to Margaret Daly at Grampion Hills in 1856 To this union were born ten children, seven of whom are living Mrs Casey still lives at her pleasant home at 519 South Main Street, DuBois One daughter, Mrs Reyburg and family also live in DuBois Two daughters, Mrs James Marshall (the eldest) and Mrs Rosco Zimmers, reside in Nebraska and Mrs James Gaffey in Olean, N Y J D and F A, both in the U S mail service, reside respectively in Buffalo, N Y, and Harrisburg, Pa

T F Casey obtained what education he got in the public schools of Jefferson and Clearfield Counties before the age of fourteen, when he started to battle with the world for a living for the large family left to his care by the father, who did not regain his health after about this time His first work was on farms, he afterward working in the pine woods where he learned to be an expert camp cook He remained in the woods in this capacity several years This was an excellent preparation for operating a restaurant, which he established in DuBois in 1889 After building up what was then said to be the best restaurant business in that section of the state, he sold in 1893, at a good price, buying the Central Hotel, DuBois, Pa , which place he conducted successfully for ten years

Before leaving the hotel he became interested in life insurance and took up a special agency with the New York Life Insurance Company Mr Casey proved very successful in this line, to which he was well adapted He stuck to this business for two years after he sold the hotel, or until the big Hughs shakeup Business becoming slack, he started to look for work and found it at the Central Hotel, Curwensville, buying the property from L C Bloom and the hotel business from E C Lewis, he took possession on Thanksgiving Day, 1905, two years after buying the farm from the Vorice Clark Estate. Mr Casey is known as one of the town's hard workers and a representative citizen, he says he likes the place, is going to build a country home and live his days out here.

The Central Hotel under Mr and Mrs Caseys' management is a well kept, orderly, up-to-date hotel and is patronized by the best of the traveling public Mrs Casey, herself, being a high class cook, looks after the culinary department of the house at all times and sees that everything going to the tables is first class Mr Casey was married to Mary, daughter of Philip and Margaret Reitzel (now) of Winterburn, Pa , in Williamsport, on October 7,

1885, theirs being the first license recorded in Clearfield County under the marriage license law of 1885. The Caseys were residents of DuBois sixteen years, Mr Casey having been watchman on the big mill one year, and connected with restaurant three years, hotel ten years, and insurance two years

In politics Mr Casey was known as an aggressive democrat, always ready to fight for what he thought was right His standing in DuBois was shown when in 1892 he ran for chief burgess against James P Rosco, a well known prominent Republican and came within fifty-three votes of winning, although the normal Republican majority was over 500 He was one of the organizers of the Volunteer Fire Department, served two years as its treasurer and two years as assistant chief He was three years a member of Council, being chairman of the Fire Apparatus Committee, also serving on the Water Committee at the critical time that had much to do with the building up and making one of the best country towns in the United States He was a charter member of the Elks, being one of its first officers, also a charter member of the Royal Order of Moose, Curwensville, being its first ruler This was the youngest Moose lodge in the state to buy and own their own home Mr Casey is probably one of the best known sportsmen in the county, taking an active interest in everything pertaining to the propagation and protection of game and fish He is a director of the McGonigal Rod and Gun Club of Karthaus, Pa , one of the best equipped and most prominent clubs in western Pennsylvania

S DORSEY GRIFFITH, owner and proprietor of the Park House, a commodious hotel which is conveniently situated on the corner of Filbert and State Streets, Curwensville, Pa , is an experienced hotel man and has been a resident of this pleasant borough since January, 1904 He was born at Johnstown, Pa , February 12, 1873, and is a son of David D. and Mary Malinda (Parson) Griffith

S Dorsey Griffith attended school in Somerset County and after completing the Normal School course, went west and enjoyed one term in the Nebraska State Normal School He subsequently became interested in farming and stockraising in Nebraska and remained in the West for seven years After he returned to Johnstown he spent six years in electrical work and for one year after his marriage resided at Somerset as superintendent of a telephone company He has previously succeeded more than the average in all his business undertakings and when he moved to Vintondale and purchased a hotel there, he was so well satisfied that he conducted it for four years lacking one month He then sold that property and purchased his present one at Curwensville, from John Langan, in January, 1904 The hotel has a fine business situation and since Mr Griffith has repaired and remodeled it, is one of the handsomest buildings in the borough It is finely equipped, having modern improvements, baths, etc , and Mr Griffith conducts it in first class style In contains forty-five rooms, thirty-four of which are bed chambers, and all have been so equipped that the comfort and convenience of guests are assured His moderate charges of $2 a day are appreciated by the public and he has a large amount of patronage He is considered an ideal host and his wife presides over the excellent table

On November 7, 1899, Mr Griffith was married to Miss Catherine Glock, a daughter of Christian Glock, a well known German resident of Johnstown, and they have three children, Samuel Dorsey, Charles Creston and Frederika Mr Griffith has never taken any very active interest in politics but votes with the Democratic party He is a member of Lodge No 175, Elks, at Johnstown, Pa

JOHN BEXTON CONNER, postmaster of Burnside borough, and a prosperous business man of this place, where he also keeps a drug store and job printing establishment, was born in Indiana county, Pa , March 5, 1859, a son of John Chapman and Anna (Widowson) Conner His father, John C Conner, was born in Indiana county, in 1831, and died at Burnside, Clearfield county, February 13, 1909 When a young man he was engaged in mercantile business in Indiana county and subsequently carried on a store of his own at Mitchells Mills, that county, for about four years He came to Burnside in 1868, and was at first employed here as a clerk, but later opened a store of his own, being a member of the firm of Kine & Conner, general merchants. Two years after he bought out his partner's interest and continued the business under the name of J C Conner, adding thereto a lumber business His son, Harry Charles Conner, was admitted as a partner in 1885

John C Conner was also a partner in the lumber firm of Hopkins, Irvin & Conner, having heavy investments in this concern Their business was wiped out at the time of the great Johnstown flood, May 31, 1889, which destroyed the town, causing great loss of life In this, one of the memorable disasters in the world's history, he lost nearly all his fortune, and retired from active business life During his earlier years he had been one of the most enterprising and successful business men of this locality, and his misfortunes were due to no fault of his He was active in politics and served as a justice of the peace in Indiana county and later at Burnside He was elected on the Republican ticket for the office of county auditor He was reelected justice of the peace, dying on the very day of his election He was a member of the Baptist church Mr Conner married first Anna .Widowson, who died, leaving three children Nettie, who is the wife of A K Long, of Burnside, Jennie, wife of Elwood Henderson, of Burnside, and John B , the subject of this sketch Mr J C Conner married for his second wife, Emily V. McClure, a daughter of Stansburg McClure She died at the age of 48 years, April 12, 1891 Three children were born of this marriage, William M , Harry Charles, and Emma A , the last mentioned being the wife of W E Patchin, of Burnside

John Bexton Conner, after his school days were over, acted as clerk for his father until reaching the age of 25 years He then entered into partnership with Dr Prowell of Burnside, taking up the study of pharmacy, and subsequently buying out his partner, engaged in the drug business for himself at Burnside He later opened a drug store at Glen Campbells He later established a bottling works for soft drinks at Glen Campbell in 1899, and also established a branch of the same at Burnside In the latter place, in 1908, he opened a printing office for job work, which he has conducted successfully In 1897 Mr Conner was appointed postmaster for the borough of Burnside, and has so continued up to the present time He also served a previous appointment to this office under the Harrison administration A staunch Republican in politics,

he has also held office as councilman and treasurer of the borough, as well as burgess

J B Conner was married, October 25, 1892, to Lura J. Weaver, a native of Burnside township, born April 2, 1877. Her parents were Charles C and Agnes (McCardell) Weaver, and she is a great-great-granddaughter of John Weaver, who was born in Switzerland and a granddaughter of John Weaver, who was born in Northampton county, Pa , and who died May 18, 1870, at the advanced age of 90 years and three days His wife, whose name in maidenhood was Ruth Zimmerman, died November 20, 1873, at the age of 86 years, six months and thirteen days

Samuel B Weaver, Mrs. Conner's grandfather, was born February 2, 1815, and when a young man followed the carpenter's trade in New York state Coming subsequently to Clearfield county, Pa , he settled in Burnside township and in 1835 built the old log edifice of the Mt Zion church, then one of the very few church buildings to be found in this section Its site is now marked by an old hemlock tree He also built many of the large barns in this locality He married Keziah Logan, who was born January 1, 1817, a daughter of David and Charlotte (Feree) Logan, the former born March 29, 1789 and the latter June 4, 1788

Charles C Weaver, Mrs Conner's father, was born in Burnside township December 25, 1841, and was occupied as a farmer and lumberman during all his industrial period His death took place in 1889 when he was 47 years old He was a Civil war veteran, enlisting October 25, 1861, for three years, in Company C, 105th Regt. Pa Inf , Col A McKnight. He served in the Army of the Potomac under Generals McClellan and Burnside, was pro-

FREDERICK GREGORY BETTS

WILLIAM IRVIN BETTS

moted to corporal April 1, 1864, and to sergeant August 28, 1864 At the end of the three years' service he re-enlisted and served to the close of the war, being mustered out July 11, with an honorable record as a soldier His wife Agnes, who was born April 7, 1852, was a daughter of John and Jane (Pilson) McCardell, pioneer settlers of this region

Mr and Mrs John B Conner have been the parents of seven children, whose names with dates of birth are as follows· John B, Jr, born 1894, Charles, who died in infancy, Samuel Arthur, 1899, Mark, 1902, Percy, 1904, Mary Agnes, 1906, and Lura Elizabeth, 1908.

FREDERICK GREGORY BETTS was born at Clearfield, Pa, April 11, 1869, son of Hon William W Betts and Margaret J (Irvin) Betts He was graduated at Princeton College in 1892 and admitted to the Bar in 1894 He was married in Clearfield, November 9, 1897, to Bessie Bridge, of which union three children were born, namely Margaret Catherine, Frederick Gregory and William W Besides practicing law Mr Betts is engaged in other business, principally in the mining of coal He is president and director of the Goshen Coal Company, president and director of the Clearfield Cemetery Company and director of the County National Bank He is a member of the Cottage Club of Princeton, N J, and of the Princeton and Racquet Club, Philadelphia He is interested in many of the enterprises of Clearfield and vicinity

WILLIAM IRVIN BETTS was born in Clearfield, Pa, June 3, 1870, son of William W Betts and Margaret Irvin Betts After receiving his education in the schools of Clearfield and at Greenwich, Conn, and Peekskill, N Y, he entered his father's office in 1889, becoming interested with him in his many business enterprises He was married in Clearfield, Pa, December 28, 1904, to Isabel Holt Murray, and has four children,—Thomas Murray, Dorothy, William Irvin, Jr, and Donald Betts He is president and director of the Clearfield Colliery Company, director in the Clearfield National Bank, vice president and member of the Board of Governors of Clearfield-Curwensville Country Club, director in the Y. M C A of Clearfield, trustee of the Presbyterian church of Clearfield, and has served one term as burgess of Clearfield He is a member of the American National Red Cross, member of the Racquet Club, of Philadelphia, and a member of the Board of Governors of the Clearfield Chamber of Commerce

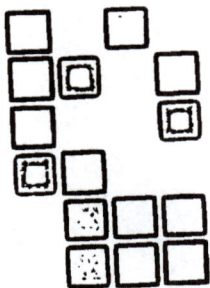

CPSIA information can be obtained
at www.ICGtesting.com
Printed in the USA
LVHW022343061222
734662LV00006B/125